FIFTH EDITION

Strategic Management

Competitiveness and Globalization

FIFTH EDITION

Strategic Management

Competitiveness and Globalization

Michael A. Hitt
Arizona State University

R. Duane Ireland
University of Richmond

Robert E. Hoskisson
The University of Oklahoma

THOMSON
™
SOUTH-WESTERN

Australia · Canada · Mexico · Singapore · Spain · United Kingdom · United States

THOMSON

SOUTH-WESTERN

Strategic Management: Competitiveness and Globalization (Concepts and Cases) 5e

Michael A. Hitt, R. Duane Ireland & Robert E. Hoskisson

Editor in Chief:
Jack W. Calhoun

Vice President/Team Director:
Michael P. Roche

Executive Editor:
John Szilagyi

Developmental Editor:
Michele Heinz, Elm Street Publishing Services, Inc.

Senior Marketing Manager:
Rob Bloom

Senior Production Editor:
Kara ZumBahlen

Manufacturing Coordinator:
Rhonda Utley

Compositor:
Parkwood Composition

Production House:
Elm Street Publishing Services, Inc.

Printer:
QuebecorWorld, Versailles

Internal Design:
Christy Carr

Cover Designer:
Christy Carr

Cover Images:
© Cartesia Software and © PhotoDisc

Photography Manager:
Deanna Ettinger

Photo Researcher:
Terri Miller

Library of Congress Control Number:
2002108280

ISBN: 0-324-11479-6

To my young grandson, Mason. Pa Pa loves
you
—Michael A. Hitt

To Mary Ann and to Rebecca and Scott,
our children. I love each of you deeply.
Always remember that "When you need
me, call my name; because without you, my
life just wouldn't be the same."
—R. Duane Ireland

To my loving and supportive wife, Kathy
Hall Hoskisson, with whom life is much
more special, and to my wonderful
children, who are uniquely wonderful
examples to me.
—Robert E. Hoskisson

Brief Contents

Contents

Part Two   *Strategic Actions: Strategy Formulation*   *107*

Chapter 4   Business-Level Strategy   108

Chapter 7 Acquisition and Restructuring Strategies 212

Chapter 8 International Strategy 240

Part Three   *Strategic Actions: Strategy Implementation* 305

Part Four   *Cases*

Contents

Case Title	Industrial Manufacturing	Service	Consumer Goods	International Perspective	High Technology
Acer	X			X	X
Affymetrix					X
Air Power				X	
AmBev			X	X	
Bang & Olufsen	X		X	X	
Beijing Jeep	X			X	
Boeing	X				X
British Broadcasting		X		X	
Caterpillar	X			X	
Chicagotribune.com		X			X
Cisco	X	X			X
Dell	X		X	X	X
eBay.com		X		X	X
Embraer	X				X
FedEx Corp.		X		X	X
Halterm		X		X	
home_improvement.com		X	X		X
Hopewell Holdings	X	X		X	
Interpost Prague		X		X	
Kacey Fine Furniture		X			
Kentucky Fried Chicken		X	X	X	
Luby's Cafeteria		X			
Lufthansa		X		X	X
MetaSolv Software		X			X
Monsanto	X			X	
Newell Company	X		X		
Nike	X		X	X	
Otis Elevator	X			X	
Palm Economy	X		X		X
Paradise Farm			X		
Perdue Farms Inc.			X	X	
Priceline.com		X			X
PricewaterhouseCoopers		X		X	
Sony	X		X		X
Virgin Group		X		X	

Media/Entertainment	Food/Retail	Social/Ethical Issues	Entrepreneurial	Industry Perspective	Chapters
				X	1, 2, 4, 5
		X	X		9, 13
			X		8, 13
	X				7, 8
					2, 3, 4, 9
				X	1, 2, 8, 9
				X	2, 3, 4, 6
X				X	1, 3, 8
				X	1, 6, 11, 12
X			X		3, 4, 6, 11, 13
					6, 7, 9, 11, 12
					1, 2, 4, 8
					3, 4, 5, 7
					4, 9, 11
					5, 6, 7
					1, 2, 4, 5, 10
	X				3, 4, 5, 11
					2, 3, 6, 8
X					2, 4, 7, 8
	X		X		1, 2, 3, 5
	X			X	2, 5, 8
	X			X	2, 3, 5, 10
					7, 9, 11,12
				X	2, 3, 4, 12
	X	X	X		6, 12, 13
					5, 6, 7
		X			2, 3, 12
					2, 8, 9, 10
			X	X	2, 3, 4, 13
	X	X	X		4, 5, 13
	X	X			4, 5,11, 12
			X		3, 4, 5, 13
					1, 4, 5, 8, 11
			X		2, 5, 13
					3, 6, 8, 12

About This Book

As with the earlier editions of *Strategic Management: Competitiveness and Globalization*, we have carefully integrated "cutting edge" research with practical applications of companies competing in global markets to develop this Fifth Edition. We continue to use this approach because we strongly believe that melding research findings with managerial practices provides you, our readers, with a comprehensive, timely, and accurate explanation of how companies use the strategic management process to successfully compete in the 21st century's dynamic and challenging competitive landscape. Our goals in preparing this edition remain as they were with the first four editions, which are to (1) introduce the strategic management process in a way that illustrates both traditional approaches and the dynamics of strategic change; (2) describe the full set of strategic management tools, techniques, and concepts as well as how firms use them to develop competitive advantages; and (3) present contemporary strategic thinking and issues affecting 21st century firms and the strategic decisions made in those companies. Thus, our major goal in preparing this fifth edition has been to present you, our readers, with a concise, complete, accurate, up-to-date, and interesting explanation of the strategic management process as it is used by firms competing in the global economy.

Using an engaging, action-oriented writing style, we have taken great care to sharpen our presentation of strategic management tools and concepts. We relied on valued feedback from adopters, students, and colleagues to carefully rewrite the chapters to make them clear and concise. Although we fully describe all relevant parts of the strategic management process, the chapters in this edition are more succinct. However, the noticeable reduction in chapter length has not come at the expense of informative practical examples. In fact, while reading the chapters, you'll find descriptions of many different types of firms as we explore the strategic management process. These examples are current and show how firms are competing in today's constantly changing global environment.

Supporting our commitment to provide you with a comprehensive and current exposure to strategic management in a global context are 35 new cases. Concerned with firms competing in global markets across the world, this collection of totally new cases deals with all parts of the strategic management process. The companies in the cases represent a variety of strategic management challenges and issues. A matrix on pages xx–xxi clearly illustrates for each case the type of organization, the topics discussed, and the relevant text chapters that are appropriate for its discussion.

New Features and Updates

Many new features and updates to this edition enhance the book's value.

- All new chapter *Opening Cases* (13 in total).
- All new *Strategic Focus* segments (three per chapter for a total of 39).
- New *company-specific examples* illustrating each chapter's central themes.
- *Full coverage of strategic issues that are prominent in the 21st century competitive landscape*. Chapter 13, for example, has been rewritten to focus on *Strategic Entrepreneurship*. Important in established firms as well as start-up ventures, strategic

entrepreneurship is concerned with combining opportunity seeking behavior with advantage seeking behavior. As we describe in the all-new Chapter 13, firms that learn how to use a strategic perspective to identify and exploit entrepreneurial opportunities increase their ability to outperform their rivals. In Chapter 5, we've sharpened the discussion of patterns of competition that occurs between firms as they try to outperform each other.

- *Discussion of new topics.* In this edition, we discuss the use of profit pools (see Chapter 2), activity mapping (see Chapter 4), and the use of the balanced scorecard as a means of measurement and control (see Chapter 12). These new tools are gaining importance as parts of an effective strategic management process.
- *Thirty-five full-length all-new cases* representing highly current examples of strategy in action.
- A continued emphasis on *global coverage* with more emphasis on the international context and issues, both in the chapters and the cases.
- Updated *Review Questions* at the end of each chapter.
- *Experiential exercises* at the end of each chapter. New to this edition, these exercises present real-life strategic management issues and are followed by questions. The exercises can be individual or group-based and are sophisticated, yet simple to use.
- *New full four-color design* with enhanced readability and pedagogical treatment.

These new features and updates provide a unique competitive advantage for this book. With 13 new *Opening Cases and* 39 new *Strategic Focus* segments, we offer 52 major case examples in the chapters. In addition, virtually all of the shorter examples used throughout each chapter are completely new. The 35 new full-length cases comprehensively cover an interesting mix of industries and company sizes. In addition, many strategic issues such as mergers and acquisitions, competitive rivalry and competitive dynamics, strategic entrepreneurship, cooperative strategies, especially in the form of strategic alliances, and expansion into global markets are covered in the cases.

This new edition also emphasizes a global advantage with comprehensive coverage of international concepts and issues. In addition to comprehensive coverage of international strategies in Chapter 8, references to and discussions of the international context and issues are included in every chapter. The Opening Cases, Strategic Focus segments, and individual examples in each chapter cover numerous global issues. In addition, 60 percent of the 35 full-length cases focus on international contexts and markets (e.g., Acer in Canada, Beijing Jeep Co., InterPost Prague, s.r.o., and Otis Elevator in Vietnam).

Importantly, this new edition solidifies a research advantage for our book. For example, each chapter has more than 100 references. On average, at least 60 percent of these references are new to this edition. Drawn from the business literature and academic research, the materials in these references are vital to our explanations of how firms use the strategic management process.

The Book's Focus

The strategic management process is our book's focus. Organizations use the strategic management process to understand competitive forces and to develop competitive advantages. The magnitude of this challenge is greater today than it has been in the past. A new competitive landscape exists in the 21st century as a result of the technological revolution (especially in e-commerce) and increasing globalization. The technological revolution has placed greater importance on innovation and the ability to rapidly introduce new goods and services to the marketplace. The global economy, one in which goods and services flow relatively freely among nations, continuously pressures firms to become more competitive. By offering either valued goods or services to customers, competitive firms increase the probability of earning above-average returns. Thus, the strategic management process helps organizations identify *what* they want to achieve as well as *how* they will do it.

The Strategic Management Process

Our discussion of the strategic management process is both traditional and contemporary. In maintaining tradition, we examine important materials that have historically been a part of understanding strategic management. For example, we thoroughly examine how to analyze a firm's external environment (see Chapter 2) and internal environment (see Chapter 3).

Contemporary Treatment

To explain the aforementioned important activities, we try to keep our treatments contemporary. In Chapter 3, for example, we emphasize the importance of identifying and determining the value-creating potential of a firm's resources, capabilities, and core competencies. The strategic actions taken as a result of understanding a firm's resources, capabilities, and core competencies have a direct link with the company's ability to establish a competitive advantage, achieve strategic competitiveness, and earn above-average returns.

Our contemporary treatment is also shown in the chapters on the dynamics of strategic change in the complex global economy. In Chapter 5, for example, we discuss the competitive rivalry between firms and the outcomes of their competitive actions and responses. Chapter 5's discussion suggests that a firm's strategic actions are influenced by its competitors' actions and reactions. Thus, competition in the global economy is fluid, dynamic, and fast-paced. Similarly, in Chapter 7, we explain the dynamics of strategic change at the corporate level, specifically addressing the motivation and consequences of mergers, acquisitions, and restructuring (e.g., divestitures) in the global economy.

We also emphasize that the set of strategic actions known as strategy formulation and strategy implementation (see Figure 1.1) must be carefully integrated for the firm to be successful.

Contemporary Concepts

Contemporary topics and concepts are the foundation for our in-depth analysis of strategic actions firms take to implement strategies. In Chapter 10, for example, we describe how different corporate governance mechanisms (e.g., boards of directors, institutional owners, executive compensation, etc.) affect strategy implementation. Chapter 11 explains how firms gain a competitive advantage by effectively using organizational structures that are properly matched to different strategies. The vital contributions of strategic leaders are examined in Chapter 12. In the all-new Chapter 13, we describe the important relationship between the ability to find and exploit entrepreneurial opportunities through competitive advantages.

Key Features

Several features are included in this book to increase its value for you.

Knowledge Objectives

Each chapter begins with clearly stated Knowledge Objectives. Their purpose is to emphasize key strategic management issues you will be able to learn about while studying each chapter. To both facilitate and verify learning, you can revisit the Knowledge Objectives while preparing answers to the Review Questions that are presented at the end of each chapter.

Opening Cases

An Opening Case follows the Knowledge Objectives in each chapter. The Opening Cases describe current strategic issues in modern companies such as Federal Express, Southwest Airlines, eBay, and Dell Computer Corporation, among many others. The purpose of the Opening Cases is to demonstrate how specific firms apply an individual chapter's strategic management concepts. Thus, the Opening Cases serve as a direct and often distinctive link between the theory and application of strategic management in different organizations and industries.

Key Terms

Key Terms that are critical to understanding the strategic management process are bold-faced throughout the chapters. Definitions of the Key Terms appear in chapter margins as well as in the text. Other terms and concepts throughout the text are italicized, signifying their importance.

Strategic Focus Segments

Three all-new Strategic Focus segments are presented in each chapter. As with the Opening Cases, the Strategic Focus segments highlight a variety of high-profile organizations, situations, and concepts. Each segment describes issues that can be addressed by applying a chapter's strategy-related concepts.

End-of-Chapter Summaries

Closing each chapter is a Summary that revisits the concepts outlined in the Knowledge Objectives. The Summaries are presented in a bulleted format to highlight a chapter's concepts, tools, and techniques.

Review Questions

Review Questions are directly tied to each chapter's Knowledge Objectives, prompting readers to reexamine the most important concepts in each chapter.

Experiential Exercises

Developed by Luis Flores, Northern Illinois University, and presented at the end of the chapters, each Experiential Exercise provides an action-oriented opportunity for readers to enhance their understanding of strategic management. Materials come to life as readers use a chapter's materials to answer questions concerned with strategic management issues.

Examples

In addition to the Opening Cases and Strategic Focus segments, each chapter is filled with real-world examples of companies in action. These examples illustrate key strategic management concepts and provide realistic applications of strategic management.

Indices

Besides the traditional end-of-book *Subject Index* and *Name Index*, we offer a *Company Index* as well. The Company Index includes the names of the hundreds of organizations discussed in the text. The three indices help to find where subjects are discussed, a person's name is used, and a company's actions are described.

Full Four-Color Format

Our presentation and discussion of the strategic management process is facilitated by the use of a full four-color format. This format provides the foundation for an interesting and visually appealing treatment of all parts of the strategic management process. Exhibits and photos further enhance the presentation by giving visual insight into the workings of companies competing in the global business environment.

Cases

Included in this fifth edition are 35 all-new case studies that involve many different strategic issues. As shown by the cases, strategic issues surface for firms competing in high technology, manufacturing, service, consumer goods, and industrial goods industries. Importantly, given the 21st-century competitive landscape and the global economy, many of these cases represent international business concerns (e.g., Air Power in Mexico, Bang & Olufsen, British Broadcasting, Lufthansa, Beijing Jeep, PricewaterhouseCoopers, and Virgin Group). Also, we offer cases dealing with high technology firms (e.g., eBay, Dell, MetaSolv Software, Palm Economy, and Priceline.com), media/entertainment (e.g., Chicagotribune.com, Interpost Prague), and service firms (e.g., FedEx Corporation, www.Home_Improvement.com, and Luby's Cafeterias). Some cases focus specifically on the wave of merger and acquisition activity (AmBev, Cisco, Newell Company), while others emphasize strategic issues of entrepreneurial or small- and medium-sized firms (e.g., Affymetrix, Kacey Fine Furniture, and Paradise Farm Organics). Finally, a large number of the cases include detailed perspectives and information about the characteristics of the industry in which a particular focal firm or organization competes (e.g., Boeing, Caterpillar, and Kentucky Fried Chicken).

Selected personally by the text authors, this unique case selection has been reviewed carefully. Consistent with the nature of strategic issues, the cases included in this book are multidimensional in nature. Because of this, and for readers' convenience, a matrix listing all cases and the dimensions/characteristics of each one is provided following the table of contents. Furthermore, the matrix lists each text chapter that provides the best fit for teaching that particular case. While most of the cases are concerned with well-known national and international companies, several examine the strategic challenges experienced in smaller and entrepreneurial firms.

Support Material*

With this edition, we continue our commitment to present you with one of the most comprehensive and quality learning packages available for teaching strategic management. Talented and dedicated people—people who are recognized for their academic achievements and their skill as excellent strategic management teachers—prepared the supplements for this fifth edition. We worked jointly with each person to make certain that all parts of the supplement package are effectively integrated with the text's materials.

For the Instructor

Instructor's Resource Manual with Video Guide and Transparency Masters

(ISBN: 0-324-11483-4) Les Palich, Baylor University, prepared a comprehensive *Instructor's Resource Manual.* The Manual provides instructors with a wealth of additional material and presentations that effectively complement the text. Using each chapter's Knowledge Objectives as an organizing principle, the Manual has been completely revised to integrate the best knowledge on teaching strategic management to maximize student learning. The Manual includes ideas about how to approach each chapter and how to emphasize essential principles with additional examples that can be used to explain points and to stimulate active discussions in your classrooms. Lecture outlines, detailed answers to the Review Questions at the end of each chapter, guides to the videos, additional assignments, and transparency masters are also included, along with instructions for using each chapter's Experiential Exercise. Flexible in nature, these exercises can be used in class or in other ways, such as homework or as an out-of-the-classroom assignment. The video guide provides information on length, alternative points of usage within the text, subjects to address, and discussion questions to stimulate classroom discussion. Suggested answers to these questions are also provided. The transparency masters are printed from the PowerPoint presentation files and include figures from the text and innovative adaptations.

Test Bank

(ISBN: 0-324-11482-6) The *Test Bank* has been thoroughly revised and enhanced for this edition by Janelle B. Dozier, Ph.D., S.P.H.R., who has also added new questions for each Opening Case and Strategic Focus segment. In addition, Mason Carpenter, Nasgovitz Fellow, University of Wisconsin–Madison, has contributed a unique new set of scenario-based questions to each chapter to add an innovative problem-solving dimension to exams. All objective questions are linked to chapter Knowledge Objectives and are ranked by difficulty level, among other measures.

ExamView™ Testing Software

(ISBN: 0-324-11487-7) All of the test questions in the printed *Test Bank* are also available in *ExamView,* a computerized format available in Windows and Macintosh versions. *ExamView* is easy-to-use test-creation software that makes it possible for instructors to easily and efficiently create, edit, store, and print exams.

PowerPoint

(ISBN: 0-324-11485-0) R. Dennis Middlemist, Colorado State University, has prepared attractive all-new sets of *PowerPoint* slides that can be downloaded from the Web site designed to be used with this text at http://hitt.swcollege.com. The easily followed presentations include clear figures based on the text and innovative adaptatiions to illustrate the text concepts. The PowerPoint slides, available both with and without animation, are provided in two versions to allow instructors to choose the most appropriate presentation for their teaching method, whether lecture or discussion.

Transparency Acetates

(ISBN: 0-324-17151-X) For those unable to access PowerPoint, a concise set of transparency acetates adapted from the PowerPoint presentation files is available on request. The transparency acetates include clear figures based on the text.

Instructor's Case Notes

(ISBN: 0-324-11484-2) C. Bradley Shrader, Iowa State University, prepared all-new *Instructor's Case Notes* for this edition. The all-new case notes provide details about the cases within the framework of case analysis. The structure allows instructors to organize case discussions along common themes and concepts and also feature aspects of the cases that make them unique. The format includes a summary of the case, teaching objectives, discussion questions and answers, and case analysis, and incorporates information from teaching notes prepared by the individual case writers as well. The cases are directly related to appropriate chapters of the text, thus allowing the instructor the opportunity to use and re-use the case for discussion and to make each case an integrative exercise.

Videos

(ISBN: 0-324-17170-6) *Management and Strategy* is a 45-minute video of short clips providing news and information about firms and current strategic management issues that are of particular relevance to students of strategic management, using the resources of Turner Learning/CNN, the world's first 24-hour all-news network. A separate multimedia integration guide, developed by Ross Stapleton-Gray, Ph.D., CISSP, chief university spokesperson on IT security issues for the University of California, accompanies the videotape and provides video descriptions, topical guides, and discussion questions for each clip.

(ISBN:0-324-26131-4) *Entrepreneurship and Strategy* is a 45-minute video based on the remarkable resources of "Small Business School," the series on PBS stations, Worldnet, and the Web. It looks at seven firms that capitalized on their beginnings and used strategic management to grow market share and create competitive advantage. A resource guide within the *Instructor's Resource Manual* describes each segment and provides discussion questions.

(ISBN: 0-324-11488-5) *Corporate Strategy* is a 45-minute video featuring corporate strategy situations for classroom viewing. A resource guide within the *Instructor's Resource Manual* describes each segment and provides discussion questions.

Instructor's Resource CD-ROM

(ISBN: 0-324-17686-4) Key ancillaries (Instructor's Resource Manual, Instructor's Case Notes, Test Bank, ExamView, and PowerPoint) are provided on CD-ROM, giving instructors the ultimate tool for customizing lectures and presentations.

Simulations

(ISBN: 0-324-16867-5) *Strategic Management in the Marketplace* is a unique and adaptable Web-based simulation that has been tailored to use with our text for the strategic management course. We worked closely with Ernest Cadotte of the University of Tennessee and his colleagues at Innovative Learning Solutions, Inc. to develop this product. Designed around important strategic management tools, techniques, and concepts, the simulation is easy to administer. Visit http://hitt.swcollege.com to learn more.

(ISBN: 0-324-16183-2) *The Global Business Game* simulation challenges students to deal with a host of strategic issues in a global context and make decisions that will lead to the firm's success. We worked with author Joseph Wolfe to prepare the second edition of this simulation, which includes clear operational instructions that closely match topics in the text.

For the Student

Infotrac College Edition

 The *Infotrac College Edition* gives students access—anytime, anywhere—to an online database of full-text articles from hundreds of scholarly and popular periodicals, including *Newsweek* and *Fortune*. Fast and easy search tools help you find just what you're looking for from among tens of thousands of articles, updated daily, all at a single site. For more information or to log on, please visit http://www. swcollege. com/infotrac/infotrac.html. Just enter your passcode as provided on the subscription card packaged free with new copies of *Strategic Management*.

Web Tutor™ on WebCT and WebTutor™ on Blackboard

 (ISBN: 0-324-15084-9) WebTutor, developed by Craig V. VanSandt of Augustana College to complement *Strategic Management: Competitiveness and Globalization*, provides interactive reinforcement that helps you master complex concepts. Questions and answers for self-study, Internet exercises, useful links to sites relevant to your study of strategic management, InfoTrac resources, and more are included. *WebTutor's* online teaching and learning environment brings together content management, assessment, communication, and collaboration capabilities for enhancing in-class instruction or for delivering distance learning. For more information, including a demonstration, go to http://swcollege.webtutor.com.

For the Student and Instructor

Strategic Management: Competitiveness and Globalization Website

(http://hitt.swcollege.com) This edition's website offers students and instructors access to a wealth of helpful material, including Instructor Resources, Student Resources, Interactive Study Center, and Interactive Quizzes, and links to Strategy Suite, eCoursepacks, and Careers in Management. Resources available on the website include continually updated case information, an Internet index with important strategy URLs, and a section on how to write a case analysis. Additional Experiential Exercises, an online glossary, and the new PowerPoint presentations are also available, as are additional Strategic Focus Applications, Discussion Questions, Ethics Questions, Internet Exercises, and Global Resources. In addition, all Strategic Focus segments from the fourth edition are offered for students and instructors to use as strategy examples, including discussion questions. These are indexed by broad subject categories. The *Strategic Management* website provides information about the authors and allows you to contact the authors and publisher.

The Wall Street Journal

 Bring the most up-to-date real-world events into your classroom through *The Wall Street Journal. The Wall Street Journal* is synonymous with the latest word on business, and *Strategic Management*, Fifth Edition, makes it easy for students to apply strategic management concepts to this authoritative publication through a special subscription offer. For a nominal additional cost, *Strategic Management*, Fifth Edition, can be packaged with a card entitling students to a 15-week subscription to both the print and interactive versions of *The Wall Street Journal*. Contact your South-Western/Thomson Learning sales representative for package pricing and ordering information.

e-Coursepack

(ISBN: 0-324-25244-7) Current, interesting, and relevant articles are available to supplement each chapter of *Strategic Management* in an e-Coursepack—the result of a joint effort between the Gale Group, a world leader in e-information publishing for libraries, schools, and businesses, and South-Western. Full-length articles to complement *Strategic Management* are available 24-hours a day, over the Web, from sources such as *Fortune, Across the Board, Management Today,* and the *Sloan Management Review.* Students can also access up-to-date information of key individuals, companies, and textbook cases through predefined searches of Gale databases. For more information, contact your South-Western/Thomson Learning sales representative or call Thomson Custom Publishing at 1-800-355-9983.

Acknowledgments

We want to thank those who helped us prepare the fifth edition. The professionalism, guidance, and support provided by the South-Western editorial and marketing teams of John Szilagyi, Mike Roche, Rob Bloom, and Kara ZumBahlen, and Michele Heinz and Becky Dodson of Elm Street Publishing Services are gratefully acknowledged. We appreciate the excellent work of our supplement author team: Mason Carpenter, Janelle Dozier, Dennis Middlemist, Les Palich, C. Brad Shrader, Ross Stapleton-Gray, and Craig VanSandt. In addition, we owe a debt of gratitude to our colleagues at Arizona State University, University of Richmond, and the University of Oklahoma. Finally, we are sincerely grateful to those who took time to read and provide feedback on drafts of either this fifth edition and previous editions of our book. Their insights and evaluations have enhanced this text, and we list them below with our thanks.

Barbara R. Bartkus, *Old Dominion University*

Tim Blumentritt, *Marquette University*

Denis Collins, *University of Bridgeport*

Anthony F. Chelte, *Western New England College*

Wade Dennis, *Marquette University*

Sam DeMarie, *Iowa State University*

Kimberly M. Ellis, *Michigan State University*

Howard Feldman, *University of Portland*

Walter J. Ferrier, *University of Kentucky*

Luis G. Flores, *Northern Illinois University*

R. Bruce Garrison, *Houston Baptist University*

Jeffrey S. Harrison, *University of Central Florida*

Richard C. Johnson, *University of Missouri*

Alfred L. Kahl, *University of Ottawa*

Vincent P. Luchsinger, *University of Baltimore*

Luis Marino, *University of Alabama*

Catherine A. Maritan, *State University of New York, Buffalo*

David Olson, *California State University, Bakersfield*

Annette L. Ranft, *Wake Forest University*

Wm. Gerard (Gerry) Sanders, *Brigham Young University*

Laszlo Tihanyi, *University of Oklahoma*

Arieh A. Ullman, *Binghamton University*

John J. Villarreal, *California State University, Hayward*

Greg Young, *North Carolina State University*

Final Comments

Organizations face exciting and dynamic competitive challenges in the 21st century. These challenges, and effective responses to them, are explored in this fifth edition of *Strategic Management: Competitiveness and Globalization*. The strategic management process conceptualized and described in this text offers valuable insights and knowledge to those committed to successfully meeting the challenge of dynamic competition. Thinking strategically, as this book challenges you to do, increases the likelihood that you will help your company achieve strategic success. In addition, continuous practice with strategic thinking and the use of the strategic management process gives you skills and knowledge that will contribute to career advancement and success. Finally, we want to wish you all the best and nothing other than complete success in all of your endeavors.

Michael A. Hitt

R. Duane Ireland

Robert E. Hoskisson

FIFTH EDITION

Strategic Management

Competitiveness
and Globalization

Strategic Management Inputs

1

1

Chapter One

Strategic Management and Strategic Competitiveness

Knowledge Objectives

Studying this chapter should provide you with the strategic management knowledge needed to:

1. Define strategic competitiveness, competitive advantage, and above-average returns.

2. Describe the 21st-century competitive landscape and explain how globalization and technological changes shape it.

3. Use the industrial organization (I/O) model to explain how firms can earn above-average returns.

4. Use the resource-based model to explain how firms can earn above-average returns.

5. Describe strategic intent and strategic mission and discuss their value.

6. Define stakeholders and describe their ability to influence organizations.

7. Describe strategists' work.

8. Explain the strategic management process.

In Bad Times, Good Companies Stand Out

In poor economic times, many firms struggle, as evidenced on a recent cover of *The Economist* titled, "2001 Things to Do in a Recession: 1. Get a Parachute." The accompanying cover photo featured a person on the ledge outside a window of a multistory building. However, some businesses do better in a recession. For example, the weak economic conditions in the United States during 2001 seemed to provide a boost to coffee sales. But, the growth in coffee sales largely occurred in institutional sales to offices. The president of Aramark Corporation suggested that providing coffee is a relatively inexpensive way to keep employees in the office and stimulated. Having this outcome with employees does not necessarily suggest that firms selling coffee are well managed strategically. Rather, they simply benefit from conditions in their external environment.

Other firms perform well even when many of their competitors are suffering from the poor economic conditions. These firms are more likely to have effectively managed strategies. Brinker International, eBay, and the perennially successful Southwest Airlines are three examples of such firms. Why are these firms profitable when many in their industries are not? To paraphrase an old and often-used saying, "It's the strategy and its implementation, stupid!" For example, Brinker, which owns nine restaurant chains, including Chili's, uses a decentralized approach allowing each of its restaurant chains to operate entrepreneurially in local markets. The approach pays off—sales per restaurant have increased by approximately 3.7 percent per year while sales for its competitors, Bennigan's and Houlihan's, have declined. Brinker has also developed new dining concepts such as the popular Eatzi's, a meal-to-go operation that provides gourmet foods for take-out dining.

eBay, one of the few Internet-based firms still profitable in 2000–2001, has enjoyed strong performance when many Internet-based firms are performing poorly and a number of them have ceased operations. eBay provides an online auction service where people can buy and sell personal goods. During the weak economic conditions of 2001, the firm actually forecasted an increase in revenues and earnings, a dream for many Internet firms, such as Amazon.com. eBay's business model is effective, and the firm is the best at what it does. It provides strong consumer value with a brand known for quality and safe transactions on the Internet.

Shown here is the corporate headquarters of Dallas-based Brinker International, which owns and operates restaurants in 48 states and 22 countries. In addition to Chili's and Romano's Macaroni Grill, its largest brands, Brinker has also developed such successful new dining concepts as Maggiano's Little Italy, the Corner Bakery Cafe, and Big Bowl, a new Asian concept.

Because Southwest Airlines has been discussed so much in the past, it may seem passé to comment on its continuing success. Southwest's success is particularly noteworthy in poor economic times and following the retirement of legendary founder and CEO Herb Kelleher. In the first quarter of 2001, when all other major airlines but one suffered net losses, Southwest announced a 65 percent increase in net profits with a 15 percent increase in revenue. Additionally, it also was the only major airline to make a profit in the third quarter of 2001 after the tragic events of September 11.

What accounts for Southwest's success? Southwest is positioned well for poor economic conditions because of its integrated cost leadership/differentiation strategy that results in low fares, but other airlines offer low fares as well. Southwest also has the fewest customer complaints of all major airlines; in contrast, another airline with relatively competitive fares, America West, was rated as the worst airline in the United States. Southwest's well-known positive culture helps it attract the best employees and they treat the customers positively. It also has a high on-time performance. Thus, its cost leadership is not the primary reason for its success. The competitive advantage enjoyed by Southwest results from its highly successful strategy implementation that differentiates the services provided to the customers relative to competitors. Additional comments about Southwest and its successful use of the integrated cost leadership/differentiation strategy appear in Chapter 4.

SOURCES: K. Stewart & K. Hussey, 2001, eBay weathers the dot.com storm, posting solid profits, growth, *Wall Street Journal Interactive*, http://interactive.wsj.com/articles, January 20; 2001, Southwest's net income rises 65%, amid a 15% increase in revenue, *Wall Street Journal Interactive*, http://interactive.wsj.com/articles, April 19; A. Edgecliffe-Johnson, 2001, Bean counters stay smiling, *Financial Times*, http://www.ft.com, April 27; A. Farnham, 2001, America's worst airline? *Forbes*, June 11, 105–115; 2001, Brinker International: Red-hot Chili's, *Forbes*, http://www.forbes.com, June 14.

Although Brinker International, eBay, and Southwest Airlines are highly successful, the reasons for their effective performances differ. Their strategy formulation and implementation actions helped them gain an advantage over their competitors. Brinker International's restaurants offer innovative and quality foods, and Brinker's several restaurant chains are more entrepreneurial than their competitors. eBay provides a high quality unique service allowing access to products through online auctions that others have been unable to imitate. Southwest provides much higher quality customer service for a lower price than its competitors can offer.

The actions taken by these firms are intended to achieve strategic competitiveness and earn above-average returns. **Strategic competitiveness** is achieved when a firm successfully formulates and implements a value-creating strategy. When a firm implements such a strategy and other companies are unable to duplicate it or find it too costly to imitate,[1] this firm has a **sustained (or sustainable) competitive advantage** (hereafter called simply *competitive advantage*). An organization is assured of a competitive advantage only after others' efforts to duplicate its strategy have ceased or failed. In addition, when a firm achieves a competitive advantage, it normally can sustain it only for a certain period.[2] The speed with which competitors are able to acquire the skills needed

Strategic competitiveness is achieved when a firm successfully formulates and implements a value-creating strategy.

A **sustained** or **sustainable competitive advantage** occurs when a firm implements a value-creating strategy and other companies are unable to duplicate it or find it too costly to imitate.

PART 1 / Strategic Management Inputs

to duplicate the benefits of a firm's value-creating strategy determines how long the competitive advantage will last.[3]

Understanding how to exploit a competitive advantage is important for firms to earn above-average returns.[4] **Above-average returns** are returns in excess of what an investor expects to earn from other investments with a similar amount of risk. **Risk** is an investor's uncertainty about the economic gains or losses that will result from a particular investment.[5] Returns are often measured in terms of accounting figures, such as return on assets, return on equity, or return on sales. Alternatively, returns can be measured on the basis of stock market returns, such as monthly returns (the end-of-the-period stock price minus the beginning stock price, divided by the beginning stock price, yielding a percentage return).

Firms without a competitive advantage or that are not competing in an attractive industry earn, at best, average returns. **Average returns** are returns equal to those an investor expects to earn from other investments with a similar amount of risk. In the long run, an inability to earn at least average returns results in failure. Failure occurs because investors withdraw their investments from those firms earning less-than-average returns.

Dynamic in nature, the **strategic management process** (see Figure 1.1) is the full set of commitments, decisions, and actions required for a firm to achieve strategic competitiveness and earn above-average returns.[6] Relevant strategic inputs derived from analyses of the internal and external environments are necessary for effective strategy formulation and implementation. In turn, effective strategic actions are a prerequisite to achieving the desired outcomes of strategic competitiveness and above-average returns. Thus, the strategic management process is used to match the conditions of an ever-changing market and competitive structure with a firm's continuously evolving resources, capabilities, and competencies (the sources of strategic inputs). Effective strategic actions that take place in the context of carefully integrated strategy formulation and implementation actions result in desired strategic outcomes.[7]

In the remaining chapters of this book, we use the strategic management process to explain what firms should do to achieve strategic competitiveness and earn above-average returns. These explanations demonstrate why some firms consistently achieve competitive success while others fail to do so.[8] As you will see, the reality of global competition is a critical part of the strategic management process.[9]

Several topics are discussed in this chapter. First, we examine the challenge of strategic management. This brief discussion highlights the fact that strategic actions taken to achieve and then maintain strategic competitiveness demand the best efforts of managers, employees, and their organizations on a continuous basis.[10] Second, we describe the 21st-century competitive landscape, created primarily by the emergence of a global economy and rapid technological changes. This landscape provides the context of opportunities and threats within which firms strive to meet the competitive challenge.

We next examine two models that suggest the strategic inputs needed to select strategic actions necessary to achieve strategic competitiveness. The first model (industrial organization) suggests that the external environment is the primary determinant of a firm's strategic actions. The key to this model is identifying and competing successfully in an attractive (i.e., profitable) industry.[11] The second model (resource based) suggests that a firm's unique resources and capabilities are the critical link to strategic competitiveness.[12] Comprehensive explanations in this chapter and the next two chapters show that through the combined use of these models, firms obtain the strategic inputs needed to formulate and implement strategies successfully. Analyses of its external and internal environments provide a firm with the information required to develop its strategic intent and strategic mission (defined later in this chapter). As shown in Figure 1.1, strategic intent and strategic mission influence

---

Above-average returns are returns in excess of what an investor expects to earn from other investments with a similar amount of risk.

Risk is an investor's uncertainty about the economic gains or losses that will result from a particular investment.

Average returns are returns equal to those an investor expects to earn from other investments with a similar amount of risk.

The **strategic management process** is the full set of commitments, decisions, and actions required for a firm to achieve strategic competitiveness and earn above-average returns.

Figure 1.1   The Strategic Management Process

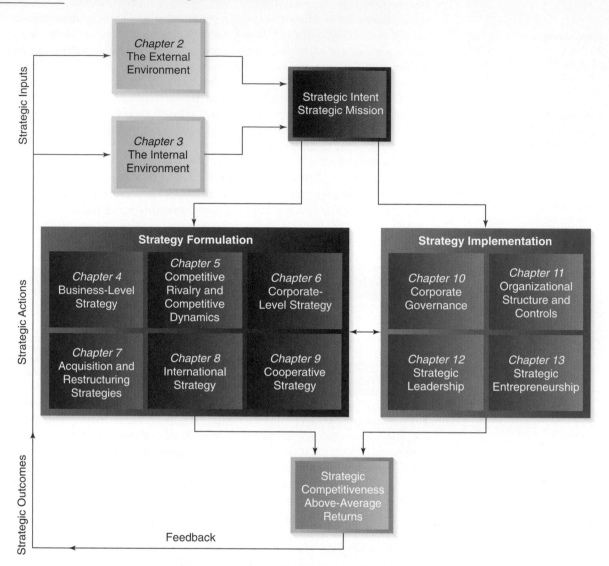

strategy formulation and implementation actions. The chapter's discussion then turns to the stakeholders that organizations serve. The degree to which stakeholders' needs can be met increases directly with enhancements in a firm's strategic competitiveness and its ability to earn above-average returns. Closing the chapter are introductions to organizational strategists and the elements of the strategic management process.

The Challenge of Strategic Management

The goals of achieving strategic competitiveness and earning above-average returns are challenging—not only for large firms such as IBM, but also for those as small as a local computer retail outlet or dry cleaner. As suggested in the Opening Case, the performances of some companies, such as Brinker International, eBay, and Southwest Airlines, have more than met strategic management's challenge to date.

For other firms, the challenges are substantial in the dynamic competitive landscape. Evidence the rapid changes experienced by Cisco Systems. During the 1990s,

Cisco's overall performance was among the best—it was among the top ten firms whose stock price increased over 10,000 percent in that decade. However, in 2001, the firm experienced significant reductions in its stock price. One writer referred to Cisco as a fractured fairy tale.[13] Analysts claim that Cisco managers did not know how to operate in poor economic conditions and did not react effectively or rapidly as conditions changed. Alternatively, Cisco's top management argued that their new strategic actions would, over time, regain the high performance once enjoyed by the firm.[14]

Business failure is rather common. In 2000, for example, 35,325 U.S. businesses filed for bankruptcy, with over 40,000 filing in 2001. Because data about business start-ups and failures are incomplete, the actual number of companies closing their doors exceeds the official count.[15] These statistics suggest that competitive success is transient.[16] Thomas J. Watson, Jr., formerly IBM's chairman, once cautioned people to remember that "corporations are expendable and that success—at best—is an impermanent achievement which can always slip out of hand."[17]

Successful performance may be transient and impermanent, as Levi Strauss found. It was once a highly successful company, with a strong global brand and good financial performance. In the middle of a robust economy in 1997, however, Levi Strauss announced that it was closing 29 plants and laying off over 16,000 employees—the first formal layoff in its history. The firm had made a number of strategic mistakes, but the most serious blunder was that it did not keep up with the changes in the marketplace. As a result, it allowed competitors Gap and Tommy Hilfiger to take away prominent market share. These competitors sold a broader variety of clothing in line with consumer tastes through their new concept retail stores. As shown by this example, a weak or ineffective strategy is a major reason for the impermanence of firm success.

Interestingly, Levi Strauss's major competitor, Gap, has also recently experienced problems after enjoying robust success. Its growth has been driven by new store openings, but sales per store decreased in 2000 and 2001. In 2001, Gap announced that it was laying off up to 7 percent of its workforce and significantly reducing its new store openings.[18]

This same problem of a weak or ineffective strategy is reflected in the substantial decline in performance experienced by such companies as Xerox and eToys. These two companies' difficulties are described in the Strategic Focus on page 10.

It is interesting to note that a survey showed CEOs did not place "strong and consistent profits" as their top priority; in fact, it was ranked fifth. A "strong and well-thought-out strategy" was regarded as the most important factor to make a firm the most respected in the future. Maximizing customer satisfaction and loyalty, business leadership and quality products and services, and concern for consistent profits followed this factor.[19] These rankings are consistent with the view that no matter how good a product or service is, the firm must select the "right" strategy and then implement it effectively.[20]

CEOs' concern for strategy is well founded, as shown by the case of Xerox described in the Strategic Focus. Some firms create their own problems by formulating the wrong strategy or by poorly implementing an effective strategy. Although Xerox clearly had the opportunity to be a dominant corporation with the new technologies it developed, it did not take advantage of them. Furthermore, it squandered its market leadership in copying machines.

In recognition of strategic management's challenge, Andrew Grove, Intel's former CEO, observed that only paranoid companies survive and succeed. Firms must continuously evaluate their environments and decide on the appropriate strategy. **Strategy** is an integrated and coordinated set of commitments and actions designed to exploit core competencies and gain a competitive advantage. By choosing a strategy,

Strategy is an integrated and coordinated set of commitments and actions designed to exploit core competencies and gain a competitive advantage.

The Impermanence of Success

There are no guarantees of success. Old, well-established companies such as Xerox can experience problems, as can young but highly successful firms such as eToys, as shown by recent performance outcomes for each.

Xerox is a well-known company with a brand name that is virtually synonymous with copying. Many people may be unaware that the Palo Alto Research Center developed by Xerox in the 1970s was also the birthplace of the personal computer, the laser printer, and the Ethernet, all technologies subsequently exploited by others. Xerox executives did not foresee the potential value of these important new technologies developed in its laboratory. The effects of this lack of foresight are shown by the fact that the Hewlett-Packard division that manufactures and sells laser printers has more total revenue than all of Xerox.

Even with these strategic blunders, Xerox has enjoyed significant success in some areas. For example, in the 1990s, it developed digital presses and copiers, creating lucrative new markets. Digital copiers became a $3 billion-a-year business for Xerox. Unlike its digital copier business, Xerox's diversification into financial services, beginning with its 1983 acquisition of Crum & Forster, was highly unsuccessful. Xerox began exiting the financial services business in 1993. In 1998, it sold Crum & Forster at a major loss and took a $1 billion write-off.

Originally hired from IBM in 1997 to become Xerox's chief operating officer (COO), Rick Thoman was appointed CEO in 1999. Former CEO Paul Allaire remained as chairman of the board. During this time, Thoman and Allaire had conflicting views about the appropriate strategy and changes for the company. As a result, Xerox made more strategic mistakes and began to lose market share in the copier market, its primary business. Although Xerox's stock price reached a high of $64 shortly after Thoman became CEO, he was fired in late 2000 following a bleak financial forecast.

Allaire took the helm again for a short time, but the firm's performance continued to decline. In 2001, the stock price fell as low as $7 per share, eliminating $38 billion in shareholder wealth, and Allaire was replaced by Anne Mulcahy. She immediately announced plans to reduce Xerox's expenses by $1 billion and spoke positively about the company's future, even though it seems unclear to many observers.

eToys was once a highly successful Internet-based retailer of toys. It began operation in 1997 and grew rapidly, soon challenging the market leader, Toys "R" Us. In fact, eToys captured significant market share before Toys "R" Us was able to respond with its own Internet sales operation. Although eToys sales reached a high of $182 million, it accumulated net losses of almost $500 million. Its stock price declined from a high of over $76 to less than 10 cents. In 2001, the firm filed for bankruptcy when analysts described its stock as worthless. Its inventory and other assets were bought at auction by KB Toys, which relaunched the eToys website in the fall of 2001.

SOURCES: 2001, Xerox CEO Mulcahy says company still seeks profitability in 4th period, *The Wall Street Journal Interactive,* http://interactive.wsj.com/articles, August 21; D. Ackman, 2001, For Ford, a Ford; for Xerox, an original, *Forbes,* http://www.forbes.com, July 27; W. Bulkeley & J. S. Lublin, 2001, Xerox names president Mulcahy to succeed Allaire in CEO post, *The Wall Street Journal Interactive,* http://interactive.wsj.com/articles, July 27; M. Sanchanta, 2001, Xerox names Anne Mulcahy as chief executive, *Financial Times,* http://www.ft.com, July 27; A. Bianco & P. L. Moore, 2001, Downfall: The inside story of the management fiasco at Xerox, *Business Week,* March 5, 82–92; http://www.kbtoys.com.

a firm decides to pursue one course of action over others. The firm's executives are thus setting priorities for the firm's competitive actions.

Firms can select effective or ineffective strategies. For example, the choice by Xerox to pursue a strategy other than the development and marketing of the personal computer and laser printers was likely an ineffective one. The purpose of this book is to explain how firms develop and implement effective strategies. Partly because of Grove's approach described above, Intel continuously strives to improve in order to remain competitive. For Intel and others that compete in the 21st century's competitive landscape, Grove believes that a key challenge is to try to do the impossible—namely, to anticipate the unexpected.[21]

The 21st-Century Competitive Landscape[22]

The fundamental nature of competition in many of the world's industries is changing.[23] The pace of this change is relentless and is increasing. Even determining the boundaries of an industry has become challenging. Consider, for example, how advances in interactive computer networks and telecommunications have blurred the definition of the television industry. The near future may find companies such as ABC, CBS, NBC, and HBO competing not only among themselves, but also with AT&T, Microsoft, Sony, and others.

Other characteristics of the 21st-century competitive landscape are noteworthy as well. Conventional sources of competitive advantage, such as economies of scale and huge advertising budgets, are not as effective as they once were. Moreover, the traditional managerial mind-set is unlikely to lead a firm to strategic competitiveness. Managers must adopt a new mind-set that values flexibility, speed, innovation, integration, and the challenges that evolve from constantly changing conditions. The conditions of the competitive landscape result in a perilous business world, one where the investments required to compete on a global scale are enormous and the consequences of failure are severe.[24]

Hypercompetition is a term often used to capture the realities of the 21st-century competitive landscape. Hypercompetition results from the dynamics of strategic maneuvering among global and innovative combatants. It is a condition of rapidly escalating competition based on price-quality positioning, competition to create new know-how and establish first-mover advantage, and competition to protect or invade established product or geographic markets.[25] In a hypercompetitive market, firms often aggressively challenge their competitors in the hopes of improving their competitive position and ultimately their performance.[26]

Several factors create hypercompetitive environments and the 21st-century competitive landscape. The two primary drivers are the emergence of a global economy and technology, specifically rapid technological change.

The Global Economy

A **global economy** is one in which goods, services, people, skills, and ideas move freely across geographic borders.

A **global economy** is one in which goods, services, people, skills, and ideas move freely across geographic borders. Relatively unfettered by artificial constraints, such as tariffs, the global economy significantly expands and complicates a firm's competitive environment.[27] Interesting opportunities and challenges are associated with the emergence of the global economy. For example, Europe, instead of the United States, is now the world's largest single market with 700 million potential customers. The European market also has a gross domestic product (GDP) of $8 trillion, which is comparable to that of the United States.[28] In addition, by 2015, China's total GDP will be greater than Japan's, although its per capita output will likely be lower.[29] In recent years, as the competitiveness rankings in Table 1.1 indicate, the Japanese economy has lagged behind that of the United States and a number of European countries. A few Asian countries, in particular Singapore and Hong Kong (now part of China), have maintained their rankings, which is commendable considering the Asian financial crisis of the latter part of the 1990s.[30] Unfortunately, Japan's economic

Table 1.1	Country Competitiveness Rankings		
Country	2001	2000	1999
U.S.	1	1	1
Singapore	2	2	2
Finland	3	4	5
Luxembourg	4	6	3
Netherlands	5	3	4
Hong Kong	6	12	6
Ireland	7	5	8
Sweden	8	14	14
Canada	9	8	10
Switzerland	10	7	7
Australia	11	10	11
Germany	12	11	12
Iceland	13	9	13
Austria	14	15	18
Denmark	15	13	9
Israel	16	21	22
Belgium	17	19	21
Taiwan	18	20	15
U.K.	19	16	19
Norway	20	17	16
New Zealand	21	18	17
Estonia	22	–	–
Spain	23	23	20
Chile	24	25	25
France	25	22	23
Japan	26	24	24
Hungary	27	26	26
Korea	28	28	41
Malaysia	29	27	28
Greece	30	34	32

SOURCE: From *World Competitiveness Yearbook 2001*, IMD, Switzerland. http://www.imd.ch.wcy.esummary, April. Reprinted by permission.

problems have persisted into the 21st century, and these problems continue to affect the economic health of Southeast Asia.[31]

Achieving improved competitiveness allows a country's citizens to have a higher standard of living. Some believe that entrepreneurial activity will continue to influence living standards during the 21st century. For example, a report describing European competitiveness concluded that, "it is only through the creation of more new businesses and more fast-growing businesses that Europe will create more new jobs and achieve higher levels of economic well-being for all of its citizens."[32] The role of entrepreneurship is discussed further in Chapter 13. A country's competitiveness is achieved through the accumulation of individual firms' strategic competitiveness in the global economy. To be competitive, a firm must view the world as its marketplace. For example, Procter & Gamble believes that it still has tremendous potential to grow internationally because the global market for household products is not as mature as it is in the United States.

Although a commitment to viewing the world as a company's marketplace creates a sense of direction, it is not without risks. For example, firms operating in Asian and Latin American countries experienced sales declines at the time the financial crisis began in Asia and spread to Latin America. In 1998, Whirlpool's sales decreased by about 25 percent in Brazil.[33] Large firms such as Whirlpool often commit to competition in the global economy more quickly than do midsize and small firms. Recently, however, U.S. midsize and small firms are demonstrating a strong commitment to competing in the global economy. For example, 60 percent of U.S. firms now exporting goods are defined as small businesses.

The March of Globalization

Globalization is the increasing economic interdependence among countries as reflected in the flow of goods and services, financial capital, and knowledge across country borders.[34] In globalized markets and industries, financial capital might be obtained in one national market and used to buy raw materials in another one. Manufacturing equipment bought from a third national market can then be used to produce products that are sold in yet a fourth market. Thus, globalization increases the range of opportunities for companies competing in the 21st-century competitive landscape.

Wal-Mart, for instance, is trying to achieve boundaryless retailing with global pricing, sourcing, and logistics. Most of Wal-Mart's original international investments were in Canada and Mexico, in close proximity to the United States. However, the company has now moved into several other countries including Argentina, Brazil, Indonesia, and China. By the end of 2000, Wal-Mart was the largest retailer in the world. It changes the structure of business in many countries it enters. For example, in Mexico, it has reduced the prominence of distributors and middlemen with its 520 stores, including Supercenters and Sam's Clubs. By 2001, 25 percent of Wal-Mart's stores were in international locations.[35]

A new German BMW luxury convertible at an outlet in downtown Shanghai draws shoppers. Luxury cars are shattering sales records in China, sharpening the appetite of automobile manufacturers to develop their local production capacity and increase their imports to the country

The internationalization of markets and industries makes it increasingly difficult to think of some firms as domestic companies. For example, Daimler Benz, the parent company of Mercedes-Benz, merged with Chrysler Corporation to create DaimlerChrysler. DaimlerChrysler has focused on integrating the formerly independent companies' operations around the world. In a similar move, Ford acquired Volvo's car division. Ford now has six global brands: Ford, Lincoln, Mercury, Jaguar, Mazda, and Aston Martin. It uses these brands to build economies of scale in the purchase and sourcing of components that make up 60 percent of the value of a car.[36]

Unlike the 1980s, when imports increased their sales significantly, today foreign competitors have a 30 percent share of the U.S. auto market. Competition is especially tough for luxury brands, with BMW, Mercedes (DaimlerChrysler), and Lexus (Toyota) increasing their market share against Ford and GM brands. U.S. auto companies are also challenged to be more aware of other nations' cultures, including the languages. Ford, for example, launched a car that it had built in Europe in Japan. Called the Ka, this car's name translated into the word "mosquito" in the Japanese language.[37] These automobile firms should not be thought of as European, Japanese, or American. Instead, they can be more accurately classified as global companies striving to achieve strategic competitiveness in the 21st-century competitive landscape. Some believe that because of the enormous economic benefits it can generate, globalization will not be stopped. It has been predicted that genuine free trade in manufactured goods among the United States, Europe, and Japan would add 5 to 10 percent to the three regions' annual economic output, and free trade in their service sectors would boost aggregate output by another 15 to 20 percent. Realizing these potential gains in economic output requires a commitment from the industrialized nations to cooperatively stimulate the higher levels of trade necessary for global growth. In 2001, global trade in goods and services accounted for approximately 25 percent of the world's GDP.[38]

Evidence suggests that the globalization of some U.S. firms lags behind that of companies in other industrialized countries. Although most large U.S. firms compete in international markets to some degree, not all of them are aggressively responding to global market opportunities.[39] Global competition has increased performance standards in many dimensions, including quality, cost, productivity, product introduction time, and operational efficiency. Moreover, these standards are not static; they are exacting, requiring continuous improvement from a firm and its employees. As they accept the challenges posed by these increasing standards, companies improve their capabilities and individual workers sharpen their skills. Thus, in the 21st-century competitive landscape, only firms capable of meeting, if not exceeding, global standards typically earn strategic competitiveness.[40]

The development of emerging and transitional economies also is changing the global competitive landscape and significantly increasing competition in global markets.[41] The economic development of Asian countries—outside of Japan—is increasing the significance of Asian markets. Firms in the emerging economies of Asia, such as South Korea, however, are becoming major competitors in global industries. Companies such as Cemex are moving more boldly into international markets and are making important investments in Asia. Cemex, a cement producer headquartered in Mexico, also has significant investments in North America and Latin America. Thus, international investments come from many directions and are targeted for multiple regions of the world.

There are risks with these investments (a number of them are discussed in Chapter 8). Some people refer to these risks as the "liability of foreignness."[42] Research suggests that firms are challenged in their early ventures into international markets and can encounter difficulties by entering too many different or challenging international markets. First, performance may suffer in early efforts to globalize until a firm develops the skills required to manage international operations.[43] Additionally, the firm's performance may suffer with substantial amounts of globalization. In this instance, firms may overdiversify internationally beyond their ability to manage these diversified operations.[44] The outcome can sometimes be quite painful to these firms.[45] Thus, entry into international markets, even for firms with substantial experience in them, first requires careful planning and selection of the appropriate markets to enter followed by developing the most effective strategies to successfully operate in those markets.

Global markets are attractive strategic options for some companies, but they are not the only source of strategic competitiveness. In fact, for most companies, even for those capable of competing successfully in global markets, it is critical to remain committed to the domestic market.[46] In the 21st-century competitive landscape, firms are challenged to develop the optimal level of globalization that results in appropriate concentrations on a company's domestic and global operations.

In many instances, strategically competitive companies are those that have learned how to apply competitive insights gained locally (or domestically) on a global scale.[47] These companies do not impose homogeneous solutions in a pluralistic world. Instead, they nourish local insights so that they can modify and apply them appropriately in different regions of the world. Moreover, they are sensitive to globalization's potential effects. Firms with strong commitments to global success evaluate these possible outcomes in making their strategic choices.

New technology such as handheld computers can create a competitive advantage for firms, but once accepted, the technology is subject to almost immediate imitation by competitors.

PHOTODISC, INC.

Technology and Technological Changes

There are three categories of trends and conditions through which technology is significantly altering the nature of competition.

Increasing Rate of Technological Change and Diffusion

Both the rate of change of technology and the speed at which new technologies become available and are used have increased substantially over the last 15 to 20 years. Consider the following rates of technology diffusion:

> It took the telephone 35 years to get into 25 percent of all homes in the United States. It took TV 26 years. It took radio 22 years. It took PCs 16 years. It took the Internet 7 years.[48]

Perpetual innovation is a term used to describe how rapidly and consistently new, information-intensive technologies replace older ones. The shorter product life cycles resulting from these rapid diffusions of new technologies place a competitive premium on being able to quickly introduce new goods and services into the marketplace. In fact, when products become somewhat indistinguishable because of the widespread and rapid diffusion of technologies, speed to market may be the primary source of competitive advantage (see Chapter 5).[49]

There are other indicators of rapid technology diffusion. Some evidence suggests that it takes only 12 to 18 months for firms to gather information about their competitors' research and development and product decisions.[50] In the global economy, competitors can sometimes imitate a firm's successful competitive actions within a few days. Consider, for example, that approximately 75 percent of the product-life gross margins for a typical personal computer are earned within the first 90 days of sales.[51] Once a source of competitive advantage, the protection firms possessed previously through their patents has been stifled by the current rate of technological diffusion. Today, patents are thought by many to be an effective way of protecting proprietary technology only for the pharmaceutical and chemical industries. Indeed, many firms competing in the electronics industry often do not apply for patents to prevent competitors from gaining access to the technological knowledge included in the patent application.

The other factor in technological change is the development of disruptive technologies that destroy the value of existing technology and create new markets.[52] Some have referred to this concept as Schumpeterian innovation, from the work by the famous economist Joseph A. Schumpeter, who suggested that such innovation emerged from a process of creative destruction, in which existing technologies are replaced by new ones. Others refer to this outcome as radical or breakthrough innovation.[53] The development and use of the Internet for commerce is an example of a disruptive technology.

The Information Age

Dramatic changes in information technology have occurred in recent years. Personal computers, cellular phones, artificial intelligence, virtual reality, and massive databases (e.g., Lexis/Nexis) are a few examples of how information is used differently as a result of technological developments. An important outcome of these changes is that the ability to effectively and efficiently access and use information has become an important source of competitive advantage in virtually all industries.

Companies are building electronic networks that link them to customers, employees, vendors, and suppliers. These networks, designed to conduct business over the Internet, are referred to as e-business.[54] e-business is big business. For example, Internet trade in the U. S. reached $251 billion in 2000, up from only $7.8 billion in 1997. It is predicted that e-business will eventually represent 75 to 80 percent of the U.S. gross domestic product. By 2002, 93 percent of firms were expected to conduct some portion of their business on the Internet. While e-business in Europe has taken longer to develop, it is predicted to increase over 300 percent by 2002, up to $67.6 billion.[55]

Both the pace of change in information technology and its diffusion will continue to increase. For instance, the number of personal computers in use is expected to reach 278 million by 2010. The declining costs of information technologies and the increased accessibility to them are also evident in the 21st-century competitive landscape. The global proliferation of relatively inexpensive computing power and its linkage on a global scale via computer networks combine to increase the speed and diffusion of information technologies. Thus, the competitive potential of information technologies is now available to companies of all sizes throughout the world, not only to large firms in Europe, Japan, and North America.

The Internet provides an infrastructure that allows the delivery of information to computers in any location. Access to significant quantities of relatively inexpensive information yields strategic opportunities for a range of industries and companies. Retailers, for example, use the Internet to provide abundant shopping privileges to customers in multiple locations. The pervasive influence of electronic commerce or e-business is creating a new culture, referred to as e-culture, that affects the way managers lead, organize, think, and develop and implement strategies.[56]

Increasing Knowledge Intensity

Knowledge (information, intelligence, and expertise) is the basis of technology and its application. In the 21st-century competitive landscape, knowledge is a critical organizational resource and is increasingly a valuable source of competitive advantage.[57] As a result, many companies now strive to transmute the accumulated knowledge of individual employees into a corporate asset. Some argue that the value of intangible assets, including knowledge, is growing as a proportion of total shareholder value.[58] The probability of achieving strategic competitiveness in the 21st-century competitive landscape is enhanced for the firm that realizes that its survival depends on the ability to capture intelligence, transform it into usable knowledge, and diffuse it rapidly throughout the company.[59] Firms accepting this challenge shift their focus from merely obtaining information to exploiting that information to gain a competitive advantage over rival firms.[60]

To earn above-average returns, firms must be able to adapt quickly to changes in their competitive landscape. Such adaptation requires that the firm develop strategic flexibility. **Strategic flexibility** is a set of capabilities used to respond to various demands and opportunities existing in a dynamic and uncertain competitive environment. Thus, it involves coping with uncertainty and the accompanying risks.[61]

Firms should develop strategic flexibility in all areas of their operations. To achieve strategic flexibility, many firms have to develop organizational slack—slack resources that allow the firm some flexibility to respond to environmental changes.[62] When larger changes are required, firms may have to undergo strategic reorientations. Such reorientations can drastically change a firm's competitive strategy.[63] Strategic

Strategic flexibility is a set of capabilities used to respond to various demands and opportunities existing in a dynamic and uncertain competitive environment.

reorientations often result from a firm's poor performance. For example, when a firm earns negative returns, its stakeholders (discussed later in this chapter) are likely to pressure top executives to make major changes.[64]

To be strategically flexible on a continuing basis, a firm has to develop the capacity to learn. Continuous learning provides the firm with new and up-to-date sets of skills, which allow the firm to adapt to its environment as it encounters changes.[65] As illustrated in the Strategic Focus on pages 18–19, new economy firms Excite@Home and PSINet were not able to adapt effectively to their environments. They followed flawed strategies too long and failed. Hewlett-Packard tried to make needed changes but experienced considerable problems with internal resistance and external criticism. As these firms learned, being flexible, learning, and making the necessary changes are difficult, but they are necessary for continued survival.

Next, we describe two models used by firms to generate the strategic inputs needed to successfully formulate and implement strategies and to maintain strategic flexibility in the process of doing so.

The I/O Model of Above-Average Returns

From the 1960s through the 1980s, the external environment was thought to be the primary determinant of strategies that firms selected to be successful.[66] The industrial organization (I/O) model of above-average returns explains the dominant influence of the external environment on a firm's strategic actions. The model specifies that the industry in which a firm chooses to compete has a stronger influence on the firm's performance than do the choices managers make inside their organizations.[67] The firm's performance is believed to be determined primarily by a range of industry properties, including economies of scale, barriers to market entry, diversification, product differentiation, and the degree of concentration of firms in the industry.[68] These industry characteristics are examined in Chapter 2.

Grounded in economics, the I/O model has four underlying assumptions. First, the external environment is assumed to impose pressures and constraints that determine the strategies that would result in above-average returns. Second, most firms competing within a particular industry or within a certain segment of it are assumed to control similar strategically relevant resources and to pursue similar strategies in light of those resources. The I/O model's third assumption is that resources used to implement strategies are highly mobile across firms. Because of resource mobility, any resource differences that might develop between firms will be short lived. Fourth, organizational decision makers are assumed to be rational and committed to acting in the firm's best interests, as shown by their profit-maximizing behaviors.[69] The I/O model challenges firms to locate the most attractive industry in which to compete. Because most firms are assumed to have similar strategically relevant resources that are mobile across companies, competitiveness generally can be increased only when firms find the industry with the highest profit potential and learn how to use their resources to implement the strategy required by the industry's structural characteristics.

The five forces model of competition is an analytical tool used to help firms with this task. The model (explained in Chapter 2) encompasses many variables and tries to capture the complexity of competition. The five forces model suggests that an industry's profitability (i.e., its rate of return on invested capital relative to its cost of capital) is a function of interactions among five forces: suppliers, buyers, competitive rivalry among firms currently in the industry, product substitutes, and potential entrants to the industry.[70] Using this tool, a firm is challenged to understand an industry's profit potential and the strategy necessary to establish a defensible competitive position, given the industry's structural characteristics. Typically, the model

Flawed Strategies, Hubris, and Entrenchment

Excite@Home was formed in November 1999 by the $6.7 billion merger of broadband Internet service provider At Home and Excite.com, an Internet portal that competed with Yahoo! The deal combined Excite's content with At Home's high-speed Internet access. Two months later, its stock was trading at almost $60. However, Excite@Home has struggled since that time. A questionable business plan had been implemented without much analysis. The firm was saddled with high debt and substantial competition on the content side from Yahoo! and others. It had service delivery problems, disagreements among its board members, multiple executive departures, and morale problems among its employees. AT&T bought controlling interest in the firm, but its backing provided little help with the major problems.

In April 2001, a new Excite@Home CEO, Patti Hart, was named. She promptly negotiated new debt financing of $100 million, but the debt was short term. By August 2001, the stock price had fallen to 47 cents; one of its lenders demanded repayment of $50 million by the end of the month, claiming that Excite@Home had misrepresented its financial condition at the time of the original loan. Auditor Ernst & Young questioned Excite@Home's viability following its analysis of the firm, which spread bankruptcy fears. Two of its largest distributors, Cox Communications and Comcast, announced they would end their relationship with Excite@Home at the end of their contract. The strategic mistakes of the firm's former managers resulted in a highly uncertain future which culminated in the firm's filing for bankruptcy in the later part of 2001. Subject to the bankruptcy court's approvals, the close of 2001 found Excite@Home selling portions of its assets in order to focus on its core broadband products and services.

Analysts believe that PSINet also used a flawed strategy. At its peak, PSINet provided Internet services to approximately 100,000 companies in 27 countries. Founder and CEO William Schrader's strategy sought growth through acquisitions and building fiber optic networks to serve customers in multiple countries. PSINet financed this growth with substantial debt, often resorting to junk bonds. In four years, the debt increased 3600 percent to $4 billion and annual debt payments reached $400 million. One reporter referred to PSINet's strategy as "half-cocked and fully hocked." A number of the ill-planned acquisitions proved to be overpriced; some were virtually worthless and had to be written off as bad investments. In 2001, the firm defaulted on its debt payments and Schrader was asked to resign.

A third firm trying to implement needed changes to adapt to its new environment but encountering substantial internal retrenchment and external impatience is Hewlett-Packard. In 1999, the firm appointed Carly Fiorina as CEO to make changes that were necessary for it to regain the competitive position it had lost in recent years. Fiorina's planned strategic and structural changes are substantial, and internal managers and professional employees have been highly critical and resistant to them. Not only have they been slow to implement the changes, some have implemented them ineffectively, according to a survey of employees.

While many observers feel that the proposed changes are needed, Hewlett-Packard's financial performance has substantially decreased since Fiorina became CEO. Undoubtedly, some of the downturn in performance is due to the process of changes being made, but the poor strategies and ineffective operational approaches of Fiorina's predecessor are also to blame. Even though the firm's performance is down, Hewlett-Packard's board has provided strong and vocal support for Fiorina's actions. The board publicly stated that she was making the changes it requested and that performance was better than expected. Still, some analysts have been critical, and it is unclear how patient major investors will be for the changes to improve performance. The firm's market capitalization was $40 billion when Fiorina was hired in 1999. By 2001, it had fallen to $31 billion.

Carly Fiorina, Hewlett-Packard CEO, faced internal resistance in her efforts to improve the firm's flexibility and timely response to market demands.

AFP/CORBIS

Hewlett-Packard's latest effort to reverse its decline was to agree to acquire Compaq Computer Corp. The proposed acquisition represents another attempt to change the firm and its culture. As of mid-April 2002, it appeared that HP shareholders approved the decision to acquire Compaq, although the final outcome of the vote hadn't been determined.

SOURCES: M. Richtel, 2001, Excite@Home executive in crisis control at warp speed, *The New York Times*, http://www.nytimes.com, September 2; M. Roman, 2001, More money woes for Excite@Home, *Business Week*, September 10, 56; L. Kehoe, 2001, Hewlett-Packard directors 100% behind Fiorina, *Financial Times*, http://www.ft.com, August 21; M. Noer, 2001, Lights out for Excite@Home? *Forbes*, http://www.forbes.com, August 21; Q. Hardy, 2001, Backstabbing Carly, *Forbes*, June 11, 54–64; S. Woolley, 2001, Digital hubris, *Forbes*, May 28, 66–70; 2001, Why Disney and AT&T went astray, *Knowledge@Wharton*, http://www.knowledge.wharton.upenn.edu, May 14; M. Mangalindan & D. Solomon, 2001, Excite at home is expected to name Patti Hart as its new CEO, *The Wall Street Journal Interactive*, http://interactive.wsj.com/articles, April 17.

suggests that firms can earn above-average returns by manufacturing standardized products or producing standardized services at costs below those of competitors (a cost-leadership strategy) or by manufacturing differentiated products for which customers are willing to pay a price premium (a differentiation strategy, described in depth in Chapter 4).

As shown in Figure 1.2, the I/O model suggests that above-average returns are earned when firms implement the strategy dictated by the characteristics of the general, industry, and competitor environments. Companies that develop or acquire the internal skills needed to implement strategies required by the external environment are likely to succeed, while those that do not are likely to fail. Hence, this model suggests that external characteristics rather than the firm's unique internal resources and capabilities primarily determine returns.

Research findings support the I/O model. They show that approximately 20 percent of a firm's profitability can be explained by the industry. In other words, 20 percent of a firm's profitability is determined by the industry or industries in which it chooses to operate. This research also showed, however, that 36 percent of the variance in profitability could be attributed to the firm's characteristics and actions.[71] The results of the research suggest that both the environment and the firm's characteristics play a role in determining the firm's specific level of profitability. Thus, there is likely a reciprocal relationship between the environment and the firm's strategy, thereby affecting the firm's performance.[72] As the research suggests, successful competition mandates that a firm build a unique set of resources and capabilities. This development should be done within the dynamics of the environment in which a firm operates.

A firm is viewed as a bundle of market activities and a bundle of resources. Market activities are understood through the application of the I/O model. The

Figure 1.2   The I/O Model of Above-Average Returns

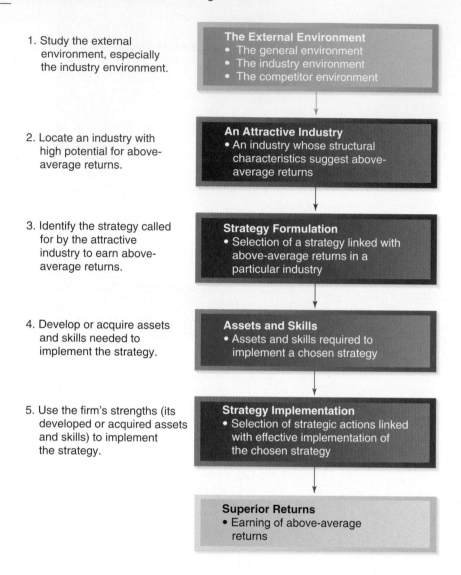

1. Study the external environment, especially the industry environment.

The External Environment
- The general environment
- The industry environment
- The competitor environment

2. Locate an industry with high potential for above-average returns.

An Attractive Industry
- An industry whose structural characteristics suggest above-average returns

3. Identify the strategy called for by the attractive industry to earn above-average returns.

Strategy Formulation
- Selection of a strategy linked with above-average returns in a particular industry

4. Develop or acquire assets and skills needed to implement the strategy.

Assets and Skills
- Assets and skills required to implement a chosen strategy

5. Use the firm's strengths (its developed or acquired assets and skills) to implement the strategy.

Strategy Implementation
- Selection of strategic actions linked with effective implementation of the chosen strategy

Superior Returns
- Earning of above-average returns

development and effective use of a firm's resources, capabilities, and competencies are understood through the application of the resource-based model. As a result, executives must integrate the two models to develop the most effective strategy.

The Resource-Based Model of Above-Average Returns

The resource-based model assumes that each organization is a collection of unique resources and capabilities that provides the basis for its strategy and that is the primary source of its returns. This model suggests that capabilities evolve and must be managed dynamically in pursuit of above-average returns.[73] According to the model, differences in firms' performances across time are due primarily to their unique resources and capabilities rather than the industry's structural characteristics. This model also assumes that firms acquire different resources and develop unique capa-

    PART 1 / Strategic Management Inputs

bilities. Therefore, not all firms competing within a particular industry possess the same resources and capabilities. Additionally, the model assumes that resources may not be highly mobile across firms and that the differences in resources are the basis of competitive advantage.

Resources are inputs into a firm's production process, such as capital equipment, the skills of individual employees, patents, finances, and talented managers. In general, a firm's resources can be classified into three categories: physical, human, and organizational capital. Described fully in Chapter 3, resources are either tangible or intangible in nature.

Individual resources alone may not yield a competitive advantage.[74] In general, competitive advantages are formed through the combination and integration of sets of resources. A **capability** is the capacity for a set of resources to perform a task or an activity in an integrative manner. Through the firm's continued use, capabilities become stronger and more difficult for competitors to understand and imitate. As a source of competitive advantage, a capability "should be neither so simple that it is highly imitable, nor so complex that it defies internal steering and control."[75]

The resource-based model of superior returns is shown in Figure 3. Instead of focusing on the accumulation of resources necessary to implement the strategy dictated by conditions and constraints in the external environment (I/O model), the resource-based view suggests that a firm's unique resources and capabilities provide the basis for a strategy. The strategy chosen should allow the firm to best exploit its core competencies relative to opportunities in the external environment.

Not all of a firm's resources and capabilities have the potential to be the basis for competitive advantage. This potential is realized when resources and capabilities are valuable, rare, costly to imitate, and nonsubstitutable.[76] Resources are *valuable* when they allow a firm to take advantage of opportunities or neutralize threats in its external environment. They are *rare* when possessed by few, if any, current and potential competitors. Resources are *costly to imitate* when other firms either cannot obtain them or are at a cost disadvantage in obtaining them compared with the firm that already possesses them. And, they are *nonsubstitutable* when they have no structural equivalents.

When these four criteria are met, resources and capabilities become core competencies. **Core competencies** are resources and capabilities that serve as a source of competitive advantage for a firm over its rivals. Often related to a firm's functional skills (e.g., the marketing function is a core competence at Philip Morris), core competencies, when developed, nurtured, and applied throughout a firm, may result in strategic competitiveness.

Managerial competencies are important in most firms. For example, they have been shown to be critically important to successful entry into foreign markets.[77] Such competencies may include the capability to effectively organize and govern complex and diverse operations and the capability to create and communicate a strategic vision.[78] Managerial capabilities are important in a firm's ability to take advantage of its resources. For example, as described in the Strategic Focus on page 10, Xerox created the technology for the personal computer and the laser printer. Yet, its management did not have the foresight to develop these technologies and take them to the marketplace. Worse, Xerox essentially gave these technologies to other firms who then successfully exploited them. As shown in the Strategic Focus on page 18, management at Excite@Home and PSINet mismanaged their resources as well.

Another set of important competencies is product related. Included among these competencies is the capability to develop innovative new products and to reengineer existing products to satisfy changing consumer tastes.[79] Firms must also continuously develop their competencies to keep them up to date. This development requires a systematic program for updating old skills and introducing new ones.

Resources are inputs into a firm's production process, such as capital equipment, the skills of individual employees, patents, finances, and talented managers.

A capability is the capacity for a set of resources to perform a task or an activity in an integrative manner.

Core competencies are resources and capabilities that serve as a source of competitive advantage for a firm over its rivals.

Figure 1.3 The Resource-Based Model of Above-Average Returns

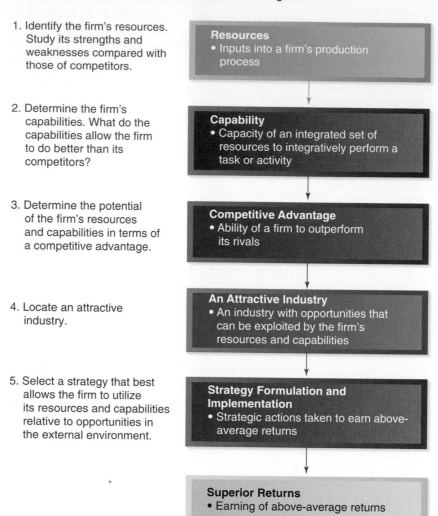

1. Identify the firm's resources. Study its strengths and weaknesses compared with those of competitors.

2. Determine the firm's capabilities. What do the capabilities allow the firm to do better than its competitors?

3. Determine the potential of the firm's resources and capabilities in terms of a competitive advantage.

4. Locate an attractive industry.

5. Select a strategy that best allows the firm to utilize its resources and capabilities relative to opportunities in the external environment.

Resources
• Inputs into a firm's production process

Capability
• Capacity of an integrated set of resources to integratively perform a task or activity

Competitive Advantage
• Ability of a firm to outperform its rivals

An Attractive Industry
• An industry with opportunities that can be exploited by the firm's resources and capabilities

Strategy Formulation and Implementation
• Strategic actions taken to earn above-average returns

Superior Returns
• Earning of above-average returns

Dynamic core competencies are especially important in rapidly changing environments, such as those that exist in high-technology industries. Thus, the resource-based model suggests that core competencies are the basis for a firm's competitive advantage, its strategic competitiveness, and its ability to earn above-average returns.

Strategic Intent and Strategic Mission

Resulting from analyses of a firm's internal and external environments is the information required to form a strategic intent and develop a strategic mission (see Figure 1.1). Both intent and mission are linked with strategic competitiveness.

Strategic Intent

Strategic intent is the leveraging of a firm's resources, capabilities, and core competencies to accomplish the firm's goals in the competitive environment.[80] Strategic

Strategic intent is the leveraging of a firm's resources, capabilities, and core competencies to accomplish the firm's goals in the competitive environment.

Unilever's Dove brand is the top-selling bar soap in the world. The firm capitalized on the brand's popularity by offering personal cleansing products in more than a dozen forms, from facial cleansing cloths to four types of body wash.

intent exists when all employees and levels of a firm are committed to the pursuit of a specific (and significant) performance criterion. Some argue that strategic intent provides employees with the only goal worthy of personal effort and commitment: to unseat the best or remain the best, worldwide.[81] Strategic intent has been effectively formed when employees believe fervently in their company's product and when they are focused totally on their firm's ability to outperform its competitors.

For example, Unilever has stated its strategic intent to make Dove a megabrand—to make Dove to personal care products what Coke is to soft drinks. For 40 years, Dove signified a bar of soap. However, in recent years, Unilever has been developing other personal care products under the Dove brand, including deodorant, vitamins, body wash, facial tissues, and bar soap. Dove helped propel Unilever to become the largest producer of bar soap with more than $330 million in annual sales and a 24 percent share of the U.S. market, and more than $1 billion in sales worldwide.[82]

It is not enough for a firm to know its own strategic intent. Performing well demands that the firm also identify its competitors' strategic intent. Only when these intentions are understood can a firm become aware of the resolve, stamina, and inventiveness (traits linked with effective strategic intents) of those competitors.[83] For example, Unilever must identify and understand Procter & Gamble's strategic intent with its Olay brand. A company's success may be also grounded in a keen and deep understanding of the strategic intent of customers, suppliers, partners, and competitors.[84]

Strategic Mission

As the preceding discussion shows, strategic intent is internally focused. It is concerned with identifying the resources, capabilities, and core competencies on which a firm can base its strategic actions. Strategic intent reflects what a firm is capable of doing with its core competencies and the unique ways they can be used to exploit a competitive advantage.

Strategic mission is a statement of a firm's unique purpose and the scope of its operations in product and market terms.

Strategic mission flows from strategic intent. Externally focused, **strategic mission** is a statement of a firm's unique purpose and the scope of its operations in product and market terms.[85] A strategic mission provides general descriptions of the products a firm intends to produce and the markets it will serve using its core competencies. An effective strategic mission establishes a firm's individuality and is inspiring and relevant to all stakeholders.[86] Together, strategic intent and strategic mission yield the insights required to formulate and implement strategies.

The strategic mission of Johnson & Johnson has a focus on customers, stating that the organization's primary responsibility is to "the doctors, nurses, and patients, mothers and fathers and all others who use our products and services."[87] An effective strategic mission is formed when the firm has a strong sense of what it wants to do and of the ethical standards that will guide behaviors in the pursuit of its goals.[88] Because Johnson & Johnson specifies the products it will offer in particular markets and presents a framework within which the firm operates, its strategic mission is an application of strategic intent.[89]

Research has shown that having an effective intent and mission and properly implementing it has a positive effect on performance as measured by growth in sales, profits, employment, and net worth.[90] When a firm is strategically competitive and earning above-average returns, it has the capacity to satisfy stakeholders' interests.

Stakeholders

Stakeholders are the individuals and groups who can affect, and are affected by, the strategic outcomes achieved and who have enforceable claims on a firm's performance.

Every organization involves a system of primary stakeholder groups with whom it establishes and manages relationships.[91] **Stakeholders** are the individuals and groups who can affect, and are affected by, the strategic outcomes achieved and who have enforceable claims on a firm's performance.[92] Claims on a firm's performance are enforced through the stakeholder's ability to withhold participation essential to the organization's survival, competitiveness, and profitability.[93] Stakeholders continue to support an organization when its performance meets or exceeds their expectations. Also, recent research suggests that firms effectively managing stakeholder relationships outperform those that do not. Stakeholder relationships can therefore be managed to be a source of competitive advantage.[94]

Although organizations have dependency relationships with their stakeholders, they are not equally dependent on all stakeholders at all times; as a consequence, not every stakeholder has the same level of influence. The more critical and valued a stakeholder's participation is, the greater a firm's dependency on it. Greater dependence, in turn, gives the stakeholder more potential influence over a firm's commitments, decisions, and actions. As shown in the Strategic Focus on page 25, managers must find ways to either accommodate or insulate the organization from the demands of stakeholders controlling critical resources.[95]

Cisco changed from being a star to most of its stakeholders to displeasing many of them. In particular, its substantial reduction in stock price concerned shareholders. Its employee layoffs created concern and displeasure among Cisco's workforce, particularly because the need to cut costs was caused by poor strategic decisions that produced large inventories. There seems to be hope but much uncertainty at present among Cisco's stakeholders.

Classification of Stakeholders

The parties involved with a firm's operations can be separated into at least three groups.[96] As shown in Figure 1.4, these groups are the capital market stakeholders (shareholders and the major suppliers of a firm's capital), the product market stakeholders (the firm's primary customers, suppliers, host communities, and unions representing the workforce), and the organizational stakeholders (all of a firm's employees, including both nonmanagerial and managerial personnel).

Each stakeholder group expects those making strategic decisions in a firm to provide the leadership through which its valued objectives will be accomplished.[97] The objectives of the various stakeholder groups often differ from one another, sometimes placing managers in situations where trade-offs have to be made. The most obvious stakeholders, at least in U.S. organizations, are shareholders—those who have invested capital in a firm in the expectation of earning a positive return on their investments. These stakeholders' rights are grounded in laws governing private property and private enterprise.

Shareholders want the return on their investment (and, hence, their wealth) to be maximized. Maximization of returns sometimes is accomplished at the expense of investing in a firm's future. Gains achieved by reducing investment in research and development, for example, could be returned to shareholders, thereby increasing the short-term return on their investments. However, this short-term enhancement of shareholders' wealth can negatively affect the firm's future competitive ability, and

PART 1 / Strategic Management Inputs

Can Cisco Satisfy All of Its Stakeholders?

In the decade of the 1990s, Cisco Systems created more wealth for its shareholders than any other firm. Its stock price increased by 124,825 percent—a $100 investment in Cisco stock in 1990 was worth $1,248,250 by the end of the decade. Cisco was able to satisfy many of its stakeholders during the decade, but with the downturn in the U.S. economy and the poor performance of Internet-based and telecommunications firms (Cisco's major customers), its fortunes turned sour. Its stock price declined by almost 78 percent, from a high of over $71 in 2000 to below $16 in 2001, and Cisco had to lay off employees.

During the earlier strong economy, Cisco experienced delays in obtaining supplies and was unable to meet customers' orders for its systems. As a result, it signed long-term contracts with suppliers to ensure supply. When sales declined significantly, Cisco was faced with large inventories. One analyst suggested that Cisco managers did not know what to do when the economy slowed. Neither shareholders nor employees were pleased with the results.

During this slowdown, CEO John Chambers remained optimistic and vowed to stay the course. He compared the Internet slump to a 100-year flood that had not been anticipated by his team. Such a flood causes considerable destruction, so his analogy was appropriate. Chambers suggested that the firm's focus had changed from revenue growth to profitability, earnings contribution, and growth through internal development rather than acquisitions. He noted that he had learned always to be concerned about profit contribution when entering new markets.

Chambers predicted that brand would become especially important and promised to protect the good brand of Cisco. Chambers also believes that there is a period of consolidation where the strong get stronger and that Cisco is one of the strong. Later in 2001, Chambers announced that Cisco had stabilized and was on track to meet its projections. If so, Cisco should again please many of its stakeholders.

SOURCES: S. Day, 2001, Shares surge after Cisco says its business has stabilized, *The New York Times,* http://www.nytimes.com, August 25; B. Elgin, 2001, A do-it-yourself plan at Cisco, *Business Week,* September 10, 52; G. Anders, 2001, John Chambers after the deluge, *Fast Company,* July, 100–111; S. N. Mehta, 2001, Cisco fractures its own tale, *Fortune,* May 14, 105–112; P. Abrahams, 2001, Cisco chief must sink or swim, *Financial Times,* http://www.ft.com, April 19.

sophisticated shareholders with diversified portfolios may sell their interests if a firm fails to invest in its future. Those making strategic decisions are responsible for a firm's survival in both the short and the long term. Accordingly, it is not in the interests of any stakeholders for investments in the company to be unduly minimized.

In contrast to shareholders, another group of stakeholders—the firm's customers—prefers that investors receive a minimum return on their investments. Customers could have their interests maximized when the quality and reliability of a firm's products are improved, but without a price increase. High returns to customers might come at the expense of lower returns negotiated with capital market shareholders.

Because of potential conflicts, each firm is challenged to manage its stakeholders. First, a firm must carefully identify all important stakeholders. Second, it must prioritize them, in case it cannot satisfy all of them. Power is the most critical criterion in prioritizing stakeholders. Other criteria might include the urgency of satisfying each particular stakeholder group and the degree of importance of each to the firm.[98]

When the firm earns above-average returns, this challenge is lessened substantially. With the capability and flexibility provided by above-average returns, a firm can more easily satisfy multiple stakeholders simultaneously. When the firm is earning only average returns, however, the management of its stakeholders may be more difficult. With average returns, the firm is unable to maximize the interests of all stakeholders. The objective then becomes one of at least minimally satisfying each stakeholder. Trade-off decisions are made in light of how dependent the firm is on the support of its stakeholder groups. A firm earning below-average returns does not have the capacity to minimally satisfy all stakeholders. The managerial challenge in this case is to make trade-offs that minimize the amount of support lost from stakeholders.

Societal values also influence the general weightings allocated among the three stakeholder groups shown in Figure 1.4. Although all three groups are served by firms in the major industrialized nations, the priorities in their service vary because of cultural differences. It is important that those responsible for managing stakeholder relationships in a country outside their native land use a global mind-set. A **global mind-set** is the "capacity to appreciate the beliefs, values, behaviors, and business practices of individuals and organizations from a variety of regions and cultures."[99] Employing a global mind-set allows managers to better understand the realities and preferences existing in the world region and culture in which they are working. Thus, thinking globally means "taking the best [that] other cultures have to offer and blending that into a third culture."[100]

A **global mind-set** is the "capacity to appreciate the beliefs, values, behaviors, and business practices of individuals and organizations from a variety of regions and cultures."

Capital Market Stakeholders

Shareholders and lenders both expect a firm to preserve and enhance the wealth they have entrusted to it. The returns they expect are commensurate with the degree of risk accepted with those investments (that is, lower returns are expected with low-risk investments, and higher returns are expected with high-risk investments). Dissatisfied

| Figure 1.4 | The Three Stakeholder Groups |

Stakeholders → People who are affected by a firm's performance and who have claims on its performance

Capital Market Stakeholders
• Shareholders
• Major suppliers of capital (e.g., banks)

Product Market Stakeholders
• Primary customers
• Suppliers
• Host communities
• Unions

Organizational Stakeholders
• Employees
• Managers
• Nonmanagers

REUTERS NEWMEDIA INC./CORBIS

DaimlerChrysler CEO Juergen Schrempp is shown here addressing shareholders about the firm's three-year plan to increase profitability. The shareholder group of stakeholders expects the firm to preserve and enhance the financial investment the shareholders have made in the firm.

lenders may impose stricter covenants on subsequent borrowing of capital. Dissatisfied shareholders can reflect their dissatisfaction through several means, including selling their stock.

When a firm is aware of potential or actual dissatisfactions among capital market stakeholders, it may respond to their concerns. The firm's response to dissatisfied stakeholders is affected by the nature of its dependency relationship with them (which, as noted earlier, is also influenced by a society's values). The greater and more significant the dependency relationship is, the more direct and significant the firm's response becomes.

As discussed in the Strategic Focus on page 18, capital market stakeholders were displeased with Excite@Home's performance. Questions arose as to the firm's continued viability. Although the company was able to delay a debt payment to one major lender, it had to find the cash to continue, especially while operating under the guidelines associated with its filing for bankruptcy. Likewise, AOL Time Warner invested $100 million in Amazon.com's stock. The cash injection allowed Amazon to continue its plan to expand from retailing to be a services company (supplying services to other firms). The investment by AOL also suggests confidence in the firm's future potential and may encourage other shareholders and potential investors to invest in Amazon.[101]

Product Market Stakeholders

Some might think that there is little commonality among the interests of customers, suppliers, host communities, and unions (product market stakeholders). However, all four groups can benefit as firms engage in competitive battles. For example, depending on product and industry characteristics, marketplace competition may result in lower product prices being charged to a firm's customers and higher prices paid to its suppliers (the firm might be willing to pay higher supplier prices to ensure delivery of the types of goods and services that are linked with its competitive success).

As is noted in Chapter 4, customers, as stakeholders, demand reliable products at the lowest possible prices. Suppliers seek loyal customers who are willing to pay the highest sustainable prices for the goods and services they receive. Host communities want companies willing to be long-term employers and providers of tax revenues without placing excessive demands on public support services. Union officials are interested in secure jobs, under highly desirable working conditions, for employees they represent. Thus, product market stakeholders are generally satisfied when a firm's profit margin yields the lowest acceptable return to capital market stakeholders (i.e., the lowest return lenders and shareholders will accept and still retain their interests in the firm).

All product market stakeholders are important in a competitive business environment, but many firms emphasize the importance of the customer. As the Strategic Focus on page 25 suggests, Cisco experienced problems with consumer demand even before the poor economic conditions at the end of the decade. Some of Cisco's major telecommunications customers were displeased with the firm's practice of allowing them access to its other customers in return for their business. The problem was that Cisco had made the same promise to all telecommunications customers, who are competitors. Thus, low consumer satisfaction was also harmful to Cisco's current sales efforts. The relationship between satisfaction of customers' needs and strategic competitiveness is examined in Chapter 4.

Organizational Stakeholders

Employees—the firm's organizational stakeholders—expect the firm to provide a dynamic, stimulating, and rewarding work environment. They are usually satisfied working for a company that is growing and actively developing their skills, especially those needed to be effective team members and to meet or exceed global work standards. Workers who learn how to use new knowledge productively are critical to organizational success. In a collective sense, the education and skills of a firm's workforce are competitive weapons affecting strategy implementation and firm performance.[102]

Organizational Strategists

Organizational strategists are the people responsible for the design and execution of strategic management processes. These individuals may also be called top-level managers, executives, the top management team, and general managers. Throughout this book, these names are used interchangeably. As discussed in Chapter 12, top-level managers can be a source of competitive advantage as a result of the value created by their strategic decisions.

Small organizations may have a single strategist; in many cases, this person owns the firm and is deeply involved with its daily operations. At the other extreme, large, diversified firms have many top-level managers. In addition to the CEO and other top-level officials (e.g., the chief operating officer and chief financial officer), other managers of these companies are responsible for the performance of individual business units.

Top-level managers play critical roles in a firm's efforts to achieve desired strategic outcomes. In fact, some believe that every organizational failure is actually a failure of those who hold the final responsibility for the quality and effectiveness of a firm's decisions and actions. Failure can stem from changing strategic assumptions, which can cause the strategic mission to become a strategic blunder. This appears to have been a problem at Excite@Home, as described earlier in the Strategic Focus on page 18. Additionally, a firm's method of operating may entail routines that create strategic inertia, where established relationships create shackles that prevent change. Finally, a shared set of beliefs may become dogma that prevents a change in corporate culture.[103] Strategic managers need to ask the right questions to overcome the inertia that success often creates.

Decisions that strategists make include how resources will be developed or acquired, at what price they will be obtained, and how they will be used. Managerial decisions also influence how information flows in a company, the strategies a firm chooses to implement, and the scope of its operations. In making these decisions, managers must assess the risk involved in taking the actions being considered. The level of risk is then factored into the decision.[104] The firm's strategic intent and managers' strategic orientations both affect their decisions. Additionally, how strategists complete their work and their patterns of interactions with others significantly influence the way a firm does business and affect its ability to develop a competitive advantage.

Critical to strategic leadership practices and the implementation of strategies, **organizational culture** refers to the complex set of ideologies, symbols, and core values that are shared throughout the firm and that influence how the firm conducts business. Thus, culture is the social energy that drives—or fails to drive—the organization. For example, Southwest Airlines, one of the successful firms discussed in this chapter's Opening Case, is known for having a unique and valuable culture. Its culture encourages employees to work hard but also to have fun while doing so. Moreover, its culture entails respect for others—employees and customers alike. The

Organizational culture refers to the complex set of ideologies, symbols, and core values that are shared throughout the firm and that influence how the firm conducts business.

firm also places a premium on service, as suggested by its commitment to provide POS (Positively Outrageous Service) to each customer. These core values at Southwest Airlines provide a particular type of social energy that drives the firm's efforts. Organizational culture thus becomes a potential source of competitive advantage.

After evaluating available information and alternatives, top-level managers must frequently choose among similarly attractive alternatives. The most effective strategists have the self-confidence necessary to select the best alternatives, allocate the required level of resources to them, and effectively explain to interested parties why certain alternatives were selected.[105] When choosing among alternatives, strategists are accountable for treating employees, suppliers, customers, and others with fairness and respect. Evidence suggests that trust can be a source of competitive advantage, thereby supporting an organizational commitment to treat stakeholders fairly and with respect.[106]

The Work of Effective Strategists

Perhaps not surprisingly, hard work, thorough analyses, a willingness to be brutally honest, a penchant for always wanting the firm and its people to accomplish more, and common sense are prerequisites to an individual's success as a strategist.[107] In addition to possessing these characteristics, effective strategists must be able to think clearly and ask many questions. But, in particular, top-level managers are challenged to "think seriously and deeply . . . about the purposes of the organizations they head or functions they perform, about the strategies, tactics, technologies, systems, and people necessary to attain these purposes and about the important questions that always need to be asked."[108]

Just as the Internet has changed the nature of competition, it is also changing strategic decision making. Speed has become a much more prominent competitive factor, and it makes strategic thinking even more critical. Most high-tech firms operate in hypercompetitive industry environments. As a result of the intense competition in these industries, some product life cycles have decreased from a period of one to two years to a period of six to nine months, leaving less time for a company's products to generate revenue. Speed and flexibility have become key sources of competitive advantage for companies competing in these industries. Thinking strategically, in concert with others, increases the probability of identifying bold, innovative ideas.[109] When these ideas lead to the development of core competencies, they become the foundation for taking advantage of environmental opportunities.

Our discussion highlights the nature of a strategist's work. The work is filled with ambiguous decision situations for which the most effective solutions are not always easily determined. However, the opportunities afforded by this type of work are appealing and offer exciting chances to dream and to act. The following words, given as advice to the late Time Warner chairman and co-CEO Steven J. Ross by his father, describe the opportunities in a strategist's work:

> There are three categories of people—the person who goes into the office, puts his feet up on his desk, and dreams for 12 hours; the person who arrives at 5 A.M. and works for 16 hours, never once stopping to dream; and the person who puts his feet up, dreams for one hour, then does something about those dreams.[110]

The organizational term used for a dream that challenges and energizes a company is strategic intent (discussed earlier in this chapter).[111] Strategists have opportunities to dream and to act, and the most effective ones provide a vision (the strategic intent) to effectively elicit the help of others in creating a firm's competitive advantage.

Predicting Outcomes of Strategic Decisions

Top-level managers attempt to predict the outcomes of strategic decisions they make before they are implemented. In most cases, managers determine the outcomes only after the decisions have been implemented. For example, executives at Montana Power decided to change the firm from a utility company to a high-tech company focusing on broadband services. The firm announced in March 2000 that it would invest $1.6 billion to build a coast-to-coast fiber optic network. Unfortunately for Montana Power, the utility industry began to grow and the broadband industry declined substantially in 2001. As such, the firm's stock price declined from $65 per share in 2000 to less than $8 per share in 2001.

While it may have been difficult for Montana Power to predict the rapid decline in the high-tech businesses, it should have been much easier to predict the growth in the utility business.[112] One means of helping managers understand the potential outcomes of their strategic decisions is to map their industry's profit pools. There are four steps to doing this: (1) define the pool's boundaries, (2) estimate the pool's overall size, (3) estimate the size of the value-chain activity in the pool, and (4) reconcile the calculations.[113]

A **profit pool** entails the total profits earned in an industry at all points along the value chain.

A **profit pool** entails the total profits earned in an industry at all points along the value chain.[114] Analyzing the profit pool in the industry may help a firm see something others are unable to see by helping the firm understand the primary sources of profits in an industry. After these sources have been identified, managers must link the profit potential identified to specific strategies. In a sense, they map the profit potential of their departmental units by linking to the firm's overall profits. They can then better link the strategic actions considered to potential profits.[115]

Mapping profit pools and linking potential profits to strategic actions before they are implemented should be a regular part of the strategic management process. General Motors managers would have done well to take these actions when they decided to continue investing resources in the Oldsmobile brand instead of investing them in their Saturn brand. The firm's investments in Oldsmobile in essence starved Saturn for resources, even though Oldsmobile was no longer a successful product in the market. Finally, after making a decision to stop marketing Oldsmobile, GM decided to invest $1.5 billion in developing a full line of Saturn products.[116]

The Strategic Management Process

As suggested by Figure 1.1, the strategic management process is intended to be a rational approach to help a firm effectively respond to the challenges of the 21st-century competitive landscape. Figure 1.1 also outlines the topics examined in this book to study the strategic management process. Part 1 of this book shows how this process requires a firm to study its external environment (Chapter 2) and internal environment (Chapter 3) to identify marketplace opportunities and threats and determine how to use its core competencies in the pursuit of desired strategic outcomes. With this knowledge, the firm forms its strategic intent to leverage its resources, capabilities, and core competencies and to win competitive battles. Flowing from its strategic intent, the firm's strategic mission specifies, in writing, the products the firm intends to produce and the markets it will serve when leveraging those resources, capabilities, and competencies.

The firm's strategic inputs provide the foundation for its strategic actions to formulate and implement strategies. Both formulating and implementing strategies are critical to achieving strategic competitiveness and earning above-average returns. As suggested in Figure 1.1 by the horizontal arrow linking the two types of strategic actions, formulation and implementation must be simultaneously integrated. In formulating strategies, thought should be given to implementing them. During implementation, effective strategists also seek feedback to improve selected strategies. Only when these two sets of actions are carefully integrated can the firm achieve its desired strategic outcomes.

In Part 2 of this book, the formulation of strategies is explained. First, we examine the formulation of strategies at the business-unit level (Chapter 4). A diversified firm competing in multiple product markets and businesses has a business-level strategy for each distinct product market area. A company competing in a single product market has but one business-level strategy. In all instances, a business-level strategy describes a firm's actions designed to exploit its competitive advantage over rivals. On the other hand, business-level strategies are not formulated and implemented in isolation (Chapter 5). Competitors respond to and try to anticipate each other's actions. Thus, the dynamics of competition are an important input when selecting and implementing strategies.

For the diversified firm, corporate-level strategy (Chapter 6) is concerned with determining the businesses in which the company intends to compete as well as how resources are to be allocated among those businesses. Other topics vital to strategy formulation, particularly in the diversified firm, include the acquisition of other companies and, as appropriate, the restructuring of the firm's portfolio of businesses (Chapter 7) and the selection of an international strategy (Chapter 8). Increasingly important in a global economy, cooperative strategies are used by a firm to gain competitive advantage by forming advantageous relationships with other firms (Chapter 9).

To examine actions taken to implement strategies, we consider several topics in Part 3 of the book. First, the different mechanisms used to govern firms are explained (Chapter 10). With demands for improved corporate governance voiced by various stakeholders, organizations are challenged to satisfy stakeholders' interests and the attainment of desired strategic outcomes. Finally, the organizational structure and actions needed to control a firm's operations (Chapter 11), the patterns of strategic leadership appropriate for today's firms and competitive environments (Chapter 12), and strategic entrepreneurship (Chapter 13) are addressed.

As noted earlier, competition requires firms to make choices to survive and succeed. Some of these choices are strategic in nature, including those of selecting a strategic intent and strategic mission, determining which strategies to implement, choosing an appropriate level of corporate scope, designing governance and organization structures to properly coordinate a firm's work, and, through strategic leadership, encouraging and nurturing organizational innovation.[117] The goal is to achieve and maintain a competitive advantage over rivals.

Primarily because they are related to how a firm interacts with its stakeholders, almost all strategic decisions have ethical dimensions.[118] Organizational ethics are revealed by an organization's culture; that is to say, a firm's strategic decisions are a product of the core values that are shared by most or all of a company's managers and employees. Especially in the turbulent and often ambiguous 21st-century competitive landscape, those making strategic decisions are challenged to recognize that their decisions do affect capital market, product market, and organizational stakeholders differently and to evaluate the ethical implications of their decisions.

As you will discover, the strategic management process examined in this book calls for disciplined approaches to the development of competitive advantage. These approaches provide the pathway through which firms will be able to achieve strategic competitiveness and earn above-average returns in the 21st century. Mastery of this strategic management process will effectively serve readers and the organizations for which they choose to work.

- Through their actions, firms seek strategic competitiveness and above-average returns. Strategic competitiveness is achieved when a firm has developed and learned how to implement a value-creating strategy. Above-average returns (in excess of what investors expect to earn from other investments with similar levels of risk) allow a firm to simultaneously satisfy all of its stakeholders.

- In the 21st-century competitive landscape, the fundamental nature of competition has changed. As a result, managers making strategic decisions must adopt a new mind-set that is global in nature. Firms must learn how to compete in highly turbulent and chaotic environments that produce disorder and a great deal of uncertainty. The globalization of industries and their markets and rapid and significant technological changes are the two primary factors contributing to the 21st-century competitive landscape.

- There are two major models of what a firm should do to earn above-average returns. The I/O model suggests that the external environment is the primary determinant of the firm's strategies. Above-average returns are earned when the firm locates an attractive industry and successfully implements the strategy dictated by that industry's characteristics.

- The resource-based model assumes that each firm is a collection of unique resources and capabilities that determine its strategy. Above-average returns are earned when the firm uses its valuable, rare, costly-to-imitate, and nonsubstitutable resources and capabilities (i.e., core competencies) as the source of its competitive advantage(s).

- Strategic intent and strategic mission are formed in light of the information and insights gained from studying a firm's internal and external environments. Strategic intent suggests how resources, capabilities, and core competencies will be leveraged to achieve desired outcomes. The strategic mission is an application of strategic intent. The mission is used to specify the product markets and customers a firm intends to serve through the leveraging of its resources, capabilities, and competencies.

- Stakeholders are those who can affect, and are affected by, a firm's strategic outcomes. Because a firm is dependent on the continuing support of stakeholders (shareholders, customers, suppliers, employees, host communities, etc.), they have enforceable claims on the company's performance. When earning above-average returns, a firm can adequately satisfy all stakeholders' interests. However, when earning only average returns, a firm's strategists must carefully manage all stakeholder groups in order to retain their support. A firm earning below-average returns must minimize the amount of support it loses from dissatisfied stakeholders.

- Organizational strategists are responsible for the design and execution of an effective strategic management process. Today, the most effective of these processes are grounded in ethical intentions and conduct. Strategists can be a source of competitive advantage. The strategist's work demands decision trade-offs, often among attractive alternatives. Successful top-level managers work hard, conduct thorough analyses of situations, are brutally and consistently honest, and ask the right questions, of the right people, at the right time.

- Managers must predict the potential outcomes of their strategic decisions. To do so, they must first calculate profit pools in their industry that are linked to the value chain activities. In so doing, they are less likely to formulate and implement an ineffective strategy.

1. What are strategic competitiveness, competitive advantage, and above-average returns?

2. What are the characteristics of the 21st-century landscape? What two factors are the primary drivers of this landscape?

3. According to the I/O model, what should a firm do to earn above-average returns?

4. What does the resource-based model suggest a firm should do to earn above-average returns?

5. What are strategic intent and strategic mission? What is their value for the strategic management process?

6. What are stakeholders? How do the three primary stakeholder groups influence organizations?

7. How would you describe the work of organizational strategists?

8. What are the elements of the strategic management process? How are they interrelated?

Strategic Mission Statements

Strategic intent and strategic mission influence strategy formulation and implementation actions. Following are brief mission statements of some of the firms mentioned in this chapter as they appear on the firms' websites (the firms are identified later in the exercise). Refer to the mission statements to complete this exercise.

a. To leverage the strengths of each member of the . . . team to create a strong, committed, and unified . . . team focused on people, quality and profits.

b. The achievements of an organization are the result of the combined efforts of each individual in the organization working toward common objectives. These objectives should be realistic, should be clearly understood by everyone in the organization and should reflect the organization's basic character and personality.

c. . . . is dedicated to the living spirit of the American dream. We believe the spirit of youth is our greatest inspiration. Resourcefulness is the key to value and excellence. In making quality a priority of our lives and products. By respecting one another we can reach all cultures. By being bold in our vision we continually expand our boundaries.

d. Our mission: To become the world's most respected and valued company by connecting, informing and entertaining people everywhere in innovative ways that will enrich their lives.

e. Our purpose in . . . is to meet the everyday needs of people everywhere—to anticipate the aspirations of our consumers and customers and to respond creatively and competitively with branded products and services which raise the quality of life.

f. Our strategic intent is to be the leader in the global . . . market, providing . . . solutions (hardware, software and services) that enhance business productivity and knowledge sharing.

Break into small groups of three to five students for this exercise.

1. The firm's strategic mission, as defined in the chapter, is a statement of a firm's unique purpose and the scope of its operations in product and market terms. Do the above statements serve as strategic mission statements? As a group, choose a statement you feel best achieves this purpose and one that does not. Be ready to defend your choices to the other groups.

2. As a group, identify an industry for which each statement seems to apply. Do any of the statements seem to apply to several industries? Discuss whether you feel the statements should be broader or narrower across industries to be effective strategic mission statements.

Statement	Industry
a.	
b.	
c.	
d.	
e.	
f.	

3. Now refer to the list below to identify the firms. Based on the material in the text and your everyday knowledge of the firms and their products or services, which statement does your group feel most effectively reflects the firm's strategic intent and mission? Which statement is most closely tied to an individual firm and which to an individual industry?

a. To leverage the strengths of each member of the Brinker team to create a strong, committed, and unified Brinker team focused on people, quality and profits. *(Brinkers International);* b. The achievements of an organization are the result of the combined efforts of each individual in the organization working toward common objectives. These objectives should be realistic, should be clearly understood by everyone in the organization and should reflect the organization's basic character and personality. *(Hewlett-Packard);* c. The Tommy Hilfiger Corporation is dedicated to the living spirit of the American dream. We believe the spirit of youth is our greatest inspiration. Resourcefulness is the key to value and excellence. In making quality a priority of our lives and products. By respecting one another we can reach all cultures. By being bold in our vision we continually expand our boundaries. *(Tommy Hilfiger);* d. Our mission: To become the world's most respected and valued company by connecting, informing and entertaining people everywhere in innovative ways that will enrich their lives. *(AOL Time Warner);* e. Our purpose in Unilever is to meet the everyday needs of people everywhere - to anticipate the aspirations of our consumers and customers and to respond creatively and competitively with branded products and services which raise the quality of life. *(Unilever);* f. Our strategic intent is to be the leader in the global document market, providing document solutions (hardware, software and services) that enhance business productivity and knowledge sharing. *(Xerox)*

1. C. A. Maritan, 2001, Capital investment as investing in organizational capabilities: An empirically grounded process model, *Academy of Management Journal*, 44: 513–531; C. E. Helfat, 2000, The evolution of firm capabilities, *Strategic Management Journal*, 21(special issue): 955–959; J. B. Barney, 1999, How firms' capabilities affect boundary decisions, *Sloan Management Review*, 40 (3): 137–145.

2. W. Mitchell, 2000, Path-dependent and path-breaking change: Reconfiguring business resources following acquisitions in the U.S. medical sector, 1978–1995, *Strategic Management Journal*, 21(special issue): 1061–1081; K. M. Eisenhardt & S. L. Brown, 1999, Patching: Restitching business portfolios in dynamic markets, *Harvard Business Review*, 77(3): 72–84.

3. E. Bonabeau & C. Meyer, 2001, Swarm intelligence, *Harvard Business Review*, 79(5): 107–114; D. Abell, 1999, Competing today while preparing for tomorrow, *Sloan Management Review*, 40(3): 73–81; D. J. Teece, G. Pisano, & A. Shuen, 1997, Dynamic capabilities and strategic management, *Strategic Management Journal*, 18: 509–533.

4. T. C. Powell, 2001, Competitive advantage: Logical and philosophical considerations, *Strategic Management Journal*, 22: 875–888; R. Coff, 1999, When competitive advantage doesn't lead to performance: The resource-based view and stakeholder bargaining power, *Organization Science*, 10: 119–133.

5. P. Shrivastava, 1995, Ecocentric management for a risk society, *Academy of Management Review*, 20: 119.

6. R. P. Rumelt, D. E. Schendel, & D. J. Teece (eds.), 1994, *Fundamental Issues in Strategy*, Boston: Harvard Business School Press, 527–530.

7. M. J. Epstein & R. A. Westbrook, 2001, Linking actions to profits in strategic decision making, *Sloan Management Review*, 42(3): 39–49.

8. Rumelt, Schendel, & Teece, *Fundamental Issues in Strategy*, 543–547.

9. M. A. Hitt, R. D. Ireland, S. M. Camp, & D. L. Sexton, 2001, Strategic entrepreneurship: Entrepreneurial strategies for wealth creation, *Strategic Management Journal* 22(special issue): 479–491; S. A. Zahra, R. D. Ireland, & M. A. Hitt, 2000, International expansion by new venture firms: International diversity, mode of market entry technological learning and performance, *Academy of Management Journal*, 43: 925–950.

10. M. A. Hitt, L. Bierman, K. Shimizu, & R. Kochhar, 2001, Direct and moderating effects of human capital on strategy and performance in professional service firms, *Academy of Management Journal*, 44: 13–28.

11. A. Nair & S. Kotha, 2001, Does group membership matter? Evidence from the Japanese steel industry, *Strategic Management Journal*, 22: 221–235; A. M. McGahan & M. E. Porter, 1997, How much does industry matter, really? *Strategic Management Journal*, 18(summer special issue): 15–30.

12. J. B. Barney, 2001, Is the resource based "view" a useful perspective for strategic management research? Yes, *Academy of Management Review*, 26: 41–56.

13. S. N. Mehta, 2001, Cisco fractures its own fairy tale, *Fortune*, 105–112.

14. S. Day, 2001, Shares surge after Cisco says its business has stabilized, *The New York Times*, http://www.nytimes.com, August 25.

15. 2001, ABI World, Filing statistics, abiworld.org/stats/newstatsfront.

16. Rumelt, Schendel, & Teece, *Fundamental Issues in Strategy*, 530.

17. C. J. Loomis, 1993, Dinosaurs, *Fortune*, May 3, 36–46.

18. A. Edgecliffe-Johnson, 2001, Gap reins in plans to expand number of stores, *Financial Times*, http://www.ft.com, June 22; N. Munk, 1999, How Levi's trashed a great American brand, *Fortune*, April 12, 83–90.

19. V. Marsh, 1998, Attributes: Strong strategy tops the list, *Financial Times*, http://www.ft.com, November 30.

20. J. Nocera, 1999, Five lessons from Iomega, *Fortune*, August 2, 251–254.

21. A. Reinhardt, 1997, Paranoia, aggression, and other strengths, *Business Week*, October 13, 14; A. S. Grove, 1995, A high-tech CEO updates his views on managing and careers, *Fortune*, September 18, 229–230.

22. This section is based largely on information featured in two sources: M. A. Hitt, B. W. Keats, & S. M. DeMarie, 1998, Navigating in the new competitive landscape: Building competitive advantage and strategic flexibility in the 21st century, *Academy of Management Executive*, 12(4): 22–42; R. A. Bettis & M. A. Hitt, 1995, The new competitive landscape, *Strategic Management Journal*, 16(special summer issue): 7–19.

23. D. Tapscott, 2001, Rethinking strategy in a networked world, *Strategy & Business*, 24 (third quarter), 34–41.

24. R. D. Ireland & M. A. Hitt, 1999, Achieving and maintaining strategic competitiveness in the 21st century: The role of strategic leadership, *Academy of Management Executive*, 13(1): 43–57.

25. R. A. D'Aveni, 1995, Coping with hypercompetition: Utilizing the new 7S's framework, *Academy of Management Executive*, 9(3): 46.

26. W. J. Ferrier, 2001, Navigating the competitive landscape: The drivers and consequences of competitive aggressiveness, *Academy of Management Journal*, 44: 858–877.

27. D. G. McKendrick, 2001, Global strategy and population level learning: The case of hard disk drives, *Strategic Management Journal*, 22: 307–334; T. P. Murtha, S. A. Lenway, & R. Bagozzi, 1998, Global mind-sets and cognitive shifts in a complex multinational corporation, *Strategic Management Journal*, 19: 97–114.

28. S. Koudsi & L. A. Costa, 1998, America vs. the new Europe: By the numbers, *Fortune*, December 21, 149–156.

29. T. A. Stewart, 1993, The new face of American power, *Fortune*, July 26, 70–86.

30. S. Garelli, 2001, Executive summary, *The World Competitiveness Yearbook*, http://www.imd.ch.wcy.esummary.

31. W. Arnold, 2001, Japan's electronics slump takes a toll on Southeast Asia, *The New York Times*, http://www.nytimes.com, September 1.

32. E. Tucker, 1999, More entrepreneurship urged, *Financial Times*, June 22, 2.

33. S. Thurm & M. Tatge, 2000, Whirlpool to launch Internet-ready refrigerator, *The Wall Street Journal*, January 7, B6; I. Katz, 1998, Whirlpool: In the wringer, *Business Week*, December 14, 83–87.

34. V. Govindarajan & A. K. Gupta, 2001, *The Quest for Global Dominance*, San Francisco: Jossey-Bass.

35. D. Luhnow, 2001, Lower tariffs, retail muscle translate into big sales for Wal-Mart in Mexico, *The Wall Street Journal Interactive*, http://www.interactive.wsj.com/articles, September 1; Govindarajan & Gupta, *The Quest for Global Dominance*.

36. 1999, Business: Ford swallows Volvo, *Economist*, January 30, 58.

37. R. McNast, 1999, Tora, tora, taurus, *Business Week*, April 12, 6.

38. Govindarajan & Gupta. *The Quest for Global Dominance;* R. Ruggiero, 1997, The high stakes of world trade, *The Wall Street Journal*, April 28, A18.

39. M. A. Carpenter & J. W. Fredrickson, 2001, Top management teams, global strategic posture, and the moderating role of uncertainty, *Academy of Management Journal*, 44: 533–545.

40. M. Subramaniam & N. Venkataraman, 2001, Determinants of transnational new product development capability: Testing the influence of transferring and deploying tacit overseas knowledge, *Strategic Management Journal*, 22: 359–378; S. A. Zahra, 1999, The changing rules of global competitiveness in the 21st century, *Academy of Management Executive*, 13(1): 36–42; R. M. Kanter, 1995, Thriving locally in the global economy, *Harvard Business Review* 73(5): 151–160.

41. Zahra, Ireland, Gutierrez, & Hitt, 2000, Privatization and entrepreneurial transformation: Emerging issues and a future research agenda, 25: 509–524.

42. S. Zaheer & E. Mosakowski, 1997, The dynamics of the liability of foreignness: A global study of survival in financial services, *Strategic Management Journal*, 18: 439–464.

43. D. Arnold, 2000, Seven rules of international distribution, *Harvard Business Review*, 78(6): 131–137; J. S. Black & H. B. Gregersen, 1999, The right way to manage expats, *Harvard Business Review*, 77(2): 52–63.

44. M. A. Hitt, R. E. Hoskisson, & H. Kim, 1997, International diversification: Effects on innovation and firm performance in product-diversified firms, *Academy of Management Journal*, 40: 767–798.

45. D'Aveni, *Coping with Hypercompetition*, 46.

46. G. Hamel, 2001, Revolution vs. evolution: You need both, *Harvard Business Review*, 79(5): 150–156; T. Nakahara, 1997, Innovation in a borderless world economy, *Research-Technology Management*, May/June, 7–9.

47. J. Birkinshaw & N. Hood, 2001, Unleash innovation in foreign subsidiaries, *Harvard Business Review*, 79(3): 131–137; N. Dawar & T. Frost, 1999, Competing with giants: Survival strategies for local companies in emerging markets, *Harvard Business Review*, 77(2): 119–129.

48. K. H. Hammonds, 2001, What is the state of the new economy? *Fast Company*, September, 101–104.

49. K. H. Hammonds, 2001, How do fast companies work now? *Fast Company*, September, 134–142; K. M. Eisenhardt, 1999, Strategy as strategic decision making, *Sloan Management Review*, 40(3): 65–72.

50. C. W. L. Hill, 1997, Establishing a standard: Competitive strategy and technological standards in winner-take-all industries, *Academy of Management Executive*, 11(2): 7–25.

51. R. Karlgaard, 1999, Digital rules, *Forbes*, July 5, 43.

52. C. M. Christiansen, 1997, *The Innovator's Dilemma,* Boston: Harvard Business School Press.

53. G. Ahuja & C. M. Lampert, 2001, Entrepreneurship in the large corporation: A longitudinal study of how established firms create breakthrough inventions, *Strategic Management Journal,* 22(special issue): 521–543.

54. R. Amit & C. Zott, 2001, Value creation in e-business, *Strategic Management Journal,* 22(special summer issue): 493–520.

55. Ibid.

56. R. M. Kanter, 2001, *e-volve: Succeeding in the Digital Culture of Tomorrow,* Boston: Harvard Business School Press.

57. Hitt, Ireland, Camp, & Sexton, Strategic entrepreneurship, 479–491.

58. F. Warner, 2001, The drills for knowledge, *Fast Company,* September, 186–191; B. L. Simonin, 1999, Ambiguity and the process of knowledge transfer in strategic alliances, *Strategic Management Journal,* 20: 595–624.

59. L. Rosenkopf & A. Nerkar, 2001, Beyond local search: Boundary-spanning, exploration, and impact on the optical disk industry, *Strategic Management Journal,* 22: 287–306; T. H. Davenport & L. Prusak, 1998, *Working Knowledge: How Organizations Manage What They Know,* Boston: Harvard Business School Press.

60. D. F. Kuratko, R. D. Ireland, & J. S. Hornsby, 2001, Improving firm performance through entrepreneurial actions: Insights from Acordia Inc.'s corporate entrepreneurship strategy, *Academy of Management Executive,* 15(4): 60–71; T. K. Kayworth & R. D. Ireland, 1998, The use of corporate IT standards as a means of implementing the cost leadership strategy, *Journal of Information Technology Management,* IX(4): 13–42.

61. K. R. Harrigan, 2001, Strategic flexibility in old and new economies, in M. A. Hitt, R. E. Freeman & J. R. Harrison (eds.), *Handbook of Strategic Management,* Oxford, U.K.: Blackwell Publishers, 97–123.

62. J. L. C. Cheng & I. F. Kesner, 1997, Organizational slack and response to environmental shifts: The impact of resource allocation patterns, *Journal of Management,* 23: 1–18.

63. C. Markides, 1998, Strategic innovation in established companies, *Sloan Management Review,* 39(3): 31–42; V. L. Barker III & I. M. Duhaime, 1997, Strategic change in the turnaround process: Theory and empirical evidence, *Strategic Management Journal,* 18: 13–38.

64. M. A. Hitt, R. D. Ireland, & J. S. Harrison, 2001, Mergers and acquisitions: A value creating or value destroying strategy? In M. A. Hitt, R. E. Freeman, & J. S. Harrison (eds.), *Handbook of Strategic Management,* Oxford, U.K.: Blackwell Publishers, 384–408; W. Boeker, 1997, Strategic change: The influence of managerial characteristics and organizational growth, *Academy of Management Journal,* 40: 152–170.

65. R. T. Pascale, 1999, Surviving the edge of chaos, *Sloan Management Review,* 40(3): 83–94; E. D. Beinhocker, 1999, Robust adaptive strategies, *Sloan Management Review,* 40(3): 95–106; N. Rajagopalan & G. M. Spreitzer, 1997, Toward a theory of strategic change: A multi-lens perspective and integrative framework, *Academy of Management Review,* 22: 48–79.

66. R. E. Hoskisson, M. A. Hitt, W. P. Wan, & D. Yiu, 1999, Swings of a pendulum: Theory and research in strategic management, *Journal of Management,* 25: 417–456.

67. E. H. Bowman & C. E. Helfat, 2001, Does corporate strategy matter? *Strategic Management Journal,* 22: 1–23.

68. A. Seth & H. Thomas, 1994, Theories of the firm: Implications for strategy research, *Journal of Management Studies,* 31: 165–191.

69. Ibid., 169–173.

70. M. E. Porter, 1985, *Competitive Advantage,* New York: Free Press; M. E. Porter, 1980, *Competitive Strategy,* New York: Free Press.

71. A. M. McGahan, 1999, Competition, strategy and business performance, *California Management Review,* 41(3): 74–101; A. M. McGahan & M. E. Porter, 1997, How much does industry matter, really? *Strategic Management Journal,* 18(special summer issue): 15–30.

72. R. Henderson & W. Mitchell, 1997, The interactions of organizational and competitive influences on strategy and performance, *Strategic Management Journal* 18:(special summer issue), 5–14; C. Oliver, 1997, Sustainable competitive advantage: Combining institutional and resource-based views, *Strategic Management Journal,* 18: 697–713; J. L. Stimpert & I. M. Duhaime, 1997, Seeing the big picture: The influence of industry, diversification, and business strategy on performance, *Academy of Management Journal,* 40: 560–583.

73. C. Lee, K. Lee, & J. M. Pennings, 2001, Internal capabilities, external networks, and performance: A study on technology-based ventures, *Strategic Management Journal* 22 (special issue): 615–640; C. C. Markides, 1999, A dynamic view of strategy, *Sloan Management Review,* 40(3): 55–72; Abell, Competing today while preparing for tomorrow.

74. R. L. Priem & J. E. Butler, 2001, Is the resource-based "view" a useful perspective for strategic management research? *Academy of Management Review,* 26: 22–40.

75. P. J. H. Schoemaker & R. Amit, 1994, Investment in strategic assets: Industry and firm-level perspectives, in P. Shrivastava, A. Huff, & J. Dutton (eds.), *Advances in Strategic Management,* Greenwich, Conn.: JAI Press, 9.

76. Barney, Is the resource-based "view" a useful perspective for strategic management research? Yes; J. B. Barney, 1995, Looking inside for competitive advantage, *Academy of Management Executive,* 9(4): 56.

77. A. Madhok, 1997, Cost, value and foreign market entry mode: The transaction and the firm, *Strategic Management Journal,* 18: 39–61.

78. W. Kuemmerle, 2001, Go global-or not? *Harvard Business Review,* 79(6): 37–49.

79. Ahuja & Lambert, Entrepreneurship in the large corporation; A. Arora & A. Gambardella, 1997, Domestic markets and international competitiveness: Generic and product specific competencies in the engineering sector, *Strategic Management Journal* 18(special summer issue): 53–74.

80. G. Hamel & C. K. Prahalad, 1989, Strategic intent, *Harvard Business Review,* 67(3): 63–76.

81. Hamel & Prahalad, Strategic intent, 66.

82. J. E. Barnes, 2001, The making (or possible breaking) of a megabrand, *The New York Times,* http://www.nytimes.com, July 22.

83. Hamel & Prahalad, Strategic intent, 64.

84. M. A. Hitt, D. Park, C. Hardee, & B. B. Tyler, 1995, Understanding strategic intent in the global marketplace, *Academy of Management Executive,* 9(2): 12–19.

85. R. D. Ireland & M. A. Hitt, 1992, Mission statements: Importance, challenge, and recommendations for development, *Business Horizons,* 35(3): 34–42.

86. W. J. Duncan, 1999, *Management: Ideas and Actions,* New York: Oxford University Press, 122–125.

87. R. M. Fulmer, 2001, Johnson & Johnson: Frameworks for leadership, *Organizational Dynamics,* 29(3): 211–220.

88. P. Martin, 1999, Lessons in humility, *Financial Times,* June 22, 18.

89. I. M. Levin, 2000, Vision revisited, *Journal of Applied Behavioral Science,* 36: 91–107.

90. I. R. Baum, E. A. Locke, & S. A. Kirkpatrick, 1998, A longitudinal study of the relation of vision and vision communication to venture growth in entrepreneurial firms, *Journal of Applied Psychology,* 83: 43–54.

91. J. Frooman, 1999, Stakeholder influence strategies, *Academy of Management Review,* 24: 191–205.

92. T. M. Jones & A. C. Wicks, 1999, Convergent stakeholder theory, *Academy of Management Review,* 24: 206–221; R. E. Freeman, 1984, *Strategic Management: A Stakeholder Approach,* Boston: Pitman, 53–54.

93. G. Donaldson & J. W. Lorsch, 1983, *Decision Making at the Top: The Shaping of Strategic Direction,* New York: Basic Books, 37–40.

94. A. J. Hillman & G. D. Keim, 2001, Shareholder value, stakeholder management, and social issues: What's the bottom line? *Strategic Management Journal,* 22: 125–139.

95. R. E. Freeman & J. McVea, 2001, A stakeholder approach to strategic management, in M. A. Hitt, R. E. Freeman, & J. S. Harrison (eds.), *Handbook of Strategic Management,* Oxford, U.K.: Blackwell Publishers, 189–207.

96. Ibid.

97. A. McWilliams & D. Siegel, 2001, Corporate social responsibility: A theory of the firm perspective, *Academy of Management Review,* 26: 117–127; D. A. Gioia, 1999, Practicality, paradigms, and problems in stakeholder theorizing, *Academy of Management Review,* 24: 228–232.

98. Freeman & McVea, A stakeholder approach to strategic management; R. K. Mitchell, B. R. Agle, & D. J. Wood, 1997, Toward a theory of stakeholder identification and salience: Defining the principle of who and what really count, *Academy of Management Review,* 22: 853–886.

99. 1995, Don't be an ugly-American manager, *Fortune,* October 16, 225.

100. G. Dutton, 1999, Building a global brain, *Management Review,* May, 23–30.

101. A. Edgecliffe-Johnson, 2001, AOL Time Warner to invest $100m in Amazon stock, *Financial Times,* http://www.ft.com, July 27.

102. Hitt, Bierman, Shimizu, & Kochhar, Direct and moderating effects of human capital.

103. D. N. Sull, 1999, Why good companies go bad, *Harvard Business Review,* 77(4): 42–52.

104. P. Bromiley, K. D. Miller, & D. Rau, 2001, Risk in strategic management research, in M. A. Hitt, R. E. Freeman, & J. S. Harrison (eds.), *Handbook of Strategic Management,* Oxford, U.K.: Blackwell Publishers, 259–288.

105. R. McGrath & I. MacMillan, 2000, *The Entrepreneurial Mindset,* Boston: Harvard Business School Press.

106. J. H. Davis, F. D. Schoorman, R. C. Mayer, & H. H. Tau, 2000, The trusted general manager and business unit performance: Empirical evidence of a competitive advantage, *Strategic Management Journal,* 21: 563–576.

107. W. C. Taylor, 1999, Whatever happened to globalization? *Fast Company,* September, 288–294.

108. T. Leavitt, 1991, *Thinking about Management,* New York: Free Press, 9.

109. K. Lovelace, D. L. Shapiro, & L. R. Weingart, 2001, Maximizing cross-functional new product teams' innovativeness and constraint adherence: A conflict communications perspective, *Academy of Management Journal,* 44: 779–793.

110. M. Loeb, 1993, Steven J. Ross, 1927–1992, *Fortune,* January 25, 4.

111. Hamel & Prahalad, Competing for the Future, 129.

112. B. Richards, 2001, For Montana Power, a broadband dream may turn out to be more of a nightmare, *The Wall Street Journal Interactive,* http://www.interactive.wsj.com/ articles, August 22.

113. O. Gadiesh & J. L. Gilbert, 1998, How to map your industry's profit pool, *Harvard Business Review,* 76(3): 149–162.

114. O. Gadiesh & J. L. Gilbert, 1998, Profit pools: A fresh look at strategy, *Harvard Business Review,* 76(3): 139–147.

115. M. J. Epstein & R. A. Westbrook, 2001, Linking actions to profits in strategic decision making, *Sloan Management Review,* 42(3): 39–49.

116. 2001, Trading places, *Forbes,* http://www.forbes.com, June 14.

117. R. D. Ireland, M. A. Hitt, S. M. Camp, & D. L. Sexton, 2001, Integrating entrepreneurship and strategic management actions to create firm wealth, *Academy of Management Executive,* 15(1): 49–63; Rumelt, Schendel, & Teece, *Fundamental Issues in Strategy,* 9–10.

118. D. R. Gilbert, 2001, Corporate strategy and ethics as corporate strategy comes of age, in M. A. Hitt, R. E. Freeman, & J. S. Harrison (eds.), *Handbook of Strategic Management,* Oxford, U.K.: Blackwell Publishers, 564–582.

2

Chapter Two

The External Environment: Opportunities, Threats, Industry Competition, and Competitor Analysis

Knowledge Objectives

Studying this chapter should provide you with the strategic management knowledge needed to:

1. Explain the importance of analyzing and understanding the firm's external environment.

2. Define and describe the general environment and the industry environment.

3. Discuss the four activities of the external environmental analysis process.

4. Name and describe the general environment's six segments.

5. Identify the five competitive forces and explain how they determine an industry's profit potential.

6. Define strategic groups and describe their influence on the firm.

7. Describe what firms need to know about their competitors and different methods used to collect intelligence about them.

September 11, 2001: The Economic Aftermath

When terrorists flew airplanes into the twin towers of the World Trade Center and the Pentagon and crashed a third plane in Pennsylvania, the world of business was changed forever. However, certain industries were affected more than others. Indeed, firms in the insurance, air travel, financial services, and tourism industries took much of the initial brunt of the economic fallout from the attacks. For example, air travel in the United States was halted for several days after the attacks, and demand was lower for some time following its resumption. Many scheduled conventions were either cancelled or conducted with fewer participants than planned. In the short term, demand for other means of travel, such as trains and buses, increased significantly. In fact, demand for train service was so great that Amtrak applied for emergency federal funding to expand its service.

Firms in the above industries were not the only ones immediately affected—suppliers serving these industries were affected as well. Some airlines cancelled or substantially reduced their contracts with food service providers, partly because of lower demand but also to reduce costs in order to survive. Another supplier to the airlines, Boeing, was also affected when many airlines postponed existing contracts for new aircraft. Boeing executives predicted that their firm might lay off as many as 30,000 employees by the end of 2002 as a direct result of the terrorist attacks. A number of firms have changed their policies on meetings between company personnel who work at different geographical locations. For example, Masimo, a medical-technology company, installed a major videoconferencing system to facilitate meetings without travel.

Firms with manufacturing plants or suppliers located outside their home countries are also experiencing transportation delays in obtaining goods needed for normal operations. As a result, these firms have to maintain more inventory and cannot take advantage of just-in-time systems, thereby increasing costs. Express mail packages between Europe and the United States now require as many as four days for delivery, up from an average of two days before September 11, and have also been slowed as a result of concerns about anthrax attacks by terrorists.

While the U.S. government has tried to reduce September 11's negative effects on the economy in several ways, such as direct payments and

In the wake of the 9/11 terrorism attacks, Amtrak accepted all airline tickets and added capacity to its trains for both passengers and emergency supplies to New York and Washington. Combined ridership on the passenger railway's high-speed Acela Express and Metroliner was about 40 percent higher for the months of October and November 2001 compared to the same period in 2000, and continues slightly over projections in spite of a general travel slowdown in the United States.

JOHNATHAN NOUROK/PHOTOEDIT

loan guarantees to the airlines totaling $15 billion, it cannot buffer most businesses from these effects. For example, it cannot buffer businesses from significant increases in security and insurance costs they are likely to experience for many years.

Few—if any—businesses were prepared for such attacks on the United States and the many changes they brought. They provide a dramatic illustration of the dynamic environment within which firms must operate and to which they must respond. The many significant effects of the external environment suggest the substantial importance both of the strategies firms employ and of their ability to adapt or change those strategies when required to survive and compete in a rapidly changing landscape.

SOURCES: A. Michaels, 2001, Hope for an early deal on WTC insurance, *Financial Times*, http://www.ft.com, December 14; T. Weber, 2001, Companies rethink role of face-to-face, *The Wall Street Journal Interactive*, http://interactive.wsj.com, September 24; J. Fuerbringer, 2001, As the economic ground zero shudders, ripples spread, *The New York Times*, http://www.nytimes.com, September 24; L. Alvarez, 2001, Congress allocates $15 billion to help the airline industry, *The New York Times*, http://www.nytimes.com, September 22; A. Brady & T. Locke, 2001, Cancellation of meetings and conferences deal a heavy blow to convention cities, *The Wall Street Journal*, September 21, A8; J. Lunsford & A. Pasztor, 2001, Boeing Co.'s course in terror's wake seen as a wider U.S. test, *The Wall Street Journal*, September 21, A1, A8; D. Machalaba & C. Tejada, 2001, As demand for train service jumps, Amtrak seeks emergency funding, *The Wall Street Journal Interactive*, http://interactive.wsj.com, September 21.

Companies' experiences and research suggest that the external environment affects firm growth and profitability.[1] Major political events such as the terrorist attacks on September 11, 2001, the strength of different nations' economies at different times, and the emergence of new technologies are a few examples of conditions in the external environment that affect firms in the United States and throughout the world. External environmental conditions such as these create threats to and opportunities for firms that, in turn, have major effects on firms' strategic actions.[2]

Airlines changed their strategies due to the threats in their external environment. They took a number of actions to reduce their costs while simultaneously enticing customers to return to air travel. All airlines but Southwest reduced the number of flights and personnel, and some eliminated routes as well. Southwest Airlines had substantial cash on hand, based on a conscious strategy to have cash available to operate during an emergency or crisis situation. Southwest Airlines' financial resources and human capital, described in Chapter 1 and discussed further in Chapter 4, afforded it strategic flexibility.[3]

This chapter focuses on what firms do to analyze and understand the external environment. As the discussion of September 11, 2001 vividly shows, the external environment influences the firm's strategic options, as well as the decisions made in light of them. The firm's understanding of the external environment is matched with knowledge about its internal environment (discussed in the next chapter) to form its strategic intent, to develop its strategic mission, and to take strategic actions that result in strategic competitiveness and above-average returns (see Figure 1.1).

As noted in Chapter 1, the environmental conditions in the current global economy differ from those previously faced by firms. Technological changes and the continuing growth of information gathering and processing capabilities demand more timely and effective competitive actions and responses.[4] The rapid sociological changes occurring in many countries affect labor practices and the nature of products demanded by increasingly diverse consumers. Governmental policies and laws also affect where and how firms may choose to compete.[5] Deregulation and local government changes, such as those in the global electric utilities industry, affect not only the general competitive environment, but also the strategic decisions made by companies competing globally. To achieve strategic competitiveness, firms must be aware of and understand the different dimensions of the external environment.

Firms understand the external environment by acquiring information about competitors, customers, and other stakeholders to build their own base of knowledge and capabilities.[6] Firms may use this base to imitate the capabilities of their able competitors (and even may imitate successful firms in other industries) and they may use it to build new knowledge and capabilities to achieve a competitive advantage. On the basis of the new information, knowledge, and capabilities, firms may take actions to buffer themselves against environmental effects or to build relationships with stakeholders in their environment.[7] To build their knowledge and capabilities and to take actions that buffer or build bridges to external stakeholders, organizations must effectively analyze the external environment.

The General, Industry, and Competitor Environments

An integrated understanding of the external and internal environments is essential for firms to understand the present and predict the future.[8] As shown in Figure 2.1, a firm's external environment is divided into three major areas: the general, industry, and competitor environments.

The **general environment** is composed of dimensions in the broader society that influence an industry and the firms within it.[9] We group these dimensions into six environmental *segments:* demographic, economic, political/legal, sociocultural, technological, and global. Examples of *elements* analyzed in each of these segments are shown in Table 2.1.

> The **general environment** is composed of dimensions in the broader society that influence an industry and the firms within it.

| **Figure 2.1** | The External Environment |

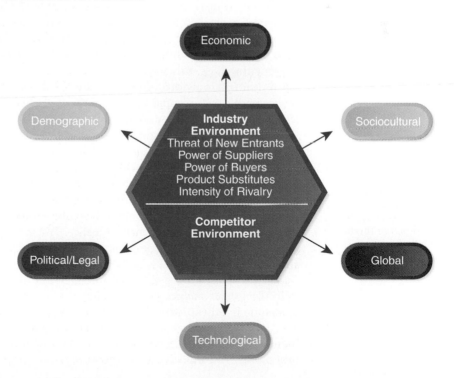

Demographic Segment	• Population size • Age structure • Geographic distribution	• Ethnic mix • Income distribution
Economic Segment	• Inflation rates • Interest rates • Trade deficits or surpluses • Budget deficits or surpluses	• Personal savings rate • Business savings rates • Gross domestic product
Political/Legal Segment	• Antitrust laws • Taxation laws • Deregulation philosophies	• Labor training laws • Educational philosophies and policies
Sociocultural Segment	• Women in the workforce • Workforce diversity • Attitudes about the quality of work life	• Concerns about the environment • Shifts in work and career preferences • Shifts in preferences regarding product and service characteristics
Technological Segment	• Product innovations • Applications of knowledge	• Focus of private and government-supported R&D expenditures • New communication technologies
Global Segment	• Important political events • Critical global markets	• Newly industrialized countries • Different cultural and institutional attributes

Firms cannot directly control the general environment's segments and elements. Accordingly, successful companies gather the information required to understand each segment and its implications for the selection and implementation of the appropriate strategies. For example, the terrorist attacks in the United States on September 11, 2001 surprised most businesses throughout the world. As explained in the Opening Case, this single set of events had substantial effects on the U.S. economy. Although individual firms were affected differently, none could control the U.S. economy. Instead, companies around the globe were challenged to understand the effects of this economy's decline on their current and future strategies.

The **industry environment** is the set of factors that directly influences a firm and its competitive actions and competitive responses: the threat of new entrants, the power of suppliers, the power of buyers, the threat of product substitutes, and the intensity of rivalry among competitors. In total, the interactions among these five factors determine an industry's profit potential. The challenge is to locate a position within an industry where a firm can favorably influence those factors or where it can successfully defend against their influence. The greater a firm's capacity to favorably influence its industry environment, the greater is the likelihood that the firm will earn above-average returns.

How companies gather and interpret information about their competitors is called *competitor analysis*. Understanding the firm's competitor environment complements the insights provided by studying the general and industry environments.

Analysis of the general environment is focused on the future; analysis of the industry environment is focused on the factors and conditions influencing a firm's profitability within its industry; and analysis of competitors is focused on predicting

The **industry environment** is the set of factors that directly influences a firm and its competitive actions and competitive responses: the threat of new entrants, the power of suppliers, the power of buyers, the threat of product substitutes, and the intensity of rivalry among competitors.

the dynamics of competitors' actions, responses, and intentions. In combination, the results of the three analyses the firm uses to understand its external environment influence its strategic intent, strategic mission, and strategic actions. Although we discuss each analysis separately, performance improves when the firm integrates the insights provided by analyses of the general environment, the industry environment, and the competitor environment.

External Environmental Analysis

Most firms face external environments that are highly turbulent, complex, and global—conditions that make interpreting them increasingly difficult.[10] To cope with what are often ambiguous and incomplete environmental data and to increase their understanding of the general environment, firms engage in a process called external environmental analysis. The continuous process includes four activities: scanning, monitoring, forecasting, and assessing (see Table 2.2). Those analyzing the external environment should understand that completing this analysis is a difficult, yet significant, activity.[11]

An important objective of studying the general environment is identifying opportunities and threats. An **opportunity** is a condition in the general environment that if exploited, helps a company achieve strategic competitiveness. The fact that 1 billion of the world's total population of 6 billion has cheap access to a telephone is a huge opportunity for global telecommunications companies.[12] And General Electric believes that "e-business represents a revolution that may be the greatest opportunity for growth that [the] Company has ever seen."[13]

A **threat** is a condition in the general environment that may hinder a company's efforts to achieve strategic competitiveness.[14] The once revered firm Polaroid can attest to the seriousness of external threats. Polaroid was a leader in its industry and considered one of the top 50 firms in the United States, but filed for bankruptcy in 2001. When its competitors developed photographic equipment using digital technology, Polaroid was unprepared and never responded effectively. Mired in substantial debt, Polaroid was unable to reduce its costs to acceptable levels (and unable to repay its debt) and eventually had to declare bankruptcy.

Likewise, executives of Enron openly displayed contempt for regulators and consumer groups in its quest for fully deregulated energy markets. Jeffrey Skilling, former CEO of Enron stated, "We are on the side of angels. People want to have open, competitive markets." Unfortunately, Enron's shareholders and employees have been big losers in its meltdown when Enron filed for bankruptcy in 2001, the victim of the economy and reportedly questionable financing practices. Enron executives seemed

An **opportunity** is a condition in the general environment that if exploited, helps a company achieve strategic competitiveness.

A **threat** is a condition in the general environment that may hinder a company's efforts to achieve strategic competitiveness.

Table 2.2	Components of the External Environmental Analysis
Scanning	• Identifying early signals of environmental changes and trends
Monitoring	• Detecting meaning through ongoing observations of environmental changes and trends
Forecasting	• Developing projections of anticipated outcomes based on monitored changes and trends
Assessing	• Determining the timing and importance of environmental changes and trends for firms' strategies and their management

to overlook the reporting of significant losses in the firm's energy trading business and were subject to SEC and Congressional investigations.[15] As these examples indicate, opportunities suggest competitive *possibilities*, while threats are potential *constraints*.

Several sources can be used to analyze the general environment, including a wide variety of printed materials (such as trade publications, newspapers, business publications, and the results of academic research and public polls), trade shows, and suppliers, customers, and employees of public-sector organizations.[16] External network contacts can be particularly rich sources of information on the environment.[17] Much information can be obtained by people in the firm's "boundary-spanning" positions. Salespersons, purchasing managers, public relations directors, and customer service representatives, each of whom interacts with external constituents, are examples of individuals in boundary-spanning positions.[18]

Scanning

Scanning entails the study of all segments in the general environment. Through scanning, firms identify early signals of potential changes in the general environment and detect changes that are already under way.[19] When scanning, the firm often deals with ambiguous, incomplete, or unconnected data and information. Environmental scanning is critically important for firms competing in highly volatile environments.[20] In addition, scanning activities must be aligned with the organizational context; a scanning system designed for a volatile environment is inappropriate for a firm in a stable environment.[21]

Enron became the subject of an SEC investigation at the end of October 2001 after reporting that its third quarter earnings fell by $618 million. In December 2001 Enron entered bankruptcy proceedings, laid off 4000 employees in its Houston headquarters, and saw its share price, once as high as $83, fall to less than $1, and by spring 2002 was also being investigated by the U.S. Justice Department and the FBI.

Some analysts expect the pressure brought to bear by the early retirement trend on countries such as the United States, France, Germany, and Japan to be quite significant and challenging. Governments in these countries appear to be offering state-funded pensions to their future elderly populations—but the costs of those pensions cannot be met with the present taxes and social security contribution rates.[22] Firms selling financial planning services and options should analyze this trend to determine if it represents an opportunity for them to help governments find ways to meet their responsibilities.

The Internet provides multiple opportunities for scanning. For example, Amazon.com records significant information about individuals visiting its website, particularly if a purchase is made. Amazon then welcomes them by name when they visit the website again. The firm even sends messages to them about specials and new products similar to those purchased in previous visits. Additionally, many websites and advertisers on the Internet obtain information from those who visit their sites using files called "cookies." These files are saved to the visitors' hard drives, allowing customers to connect more quickly to the website, but also allowing the firm to solicit a variety of information about them. Because cookies are often placed without customers' knowledge, their use can be a questionable practice. A new privacy standard, Platform for Privacy Preferences, has been developed that provides more control over these "digital messengers" and allows users to block the cookies from their hard drives if desired.[23]

Monitoring

When *monitoring*, analysts observe environmental changes to see if an important trend is emerging from among those spotted by scanning.[24] Critical to successful monitoring is the firm's ability to detect meaning in different environmental events and trends. For example, the size of the middle class of African Americans continues to grow in the United States. With increasing wealth, this group of citizens is beginning to more aggressively pursue investment options.[25] Companies in the financial planning sector could monitor this change in the economic segment to determine the degree to which a competitively important trend and a business opportunity are emerging. By monitoring trends, firms can be prepared to introduce new goods and services at the appropriate time to take advantage of the opportunities these trends provide.[26]

Effective monitoring requires the firm to identify important stakeholders. Because the importance of different stakeholders can vary over a firm's life cycle, careful attention must be given to the firm's needs and its stakeholder groups over time.[27] Scanning and monitoring are particularly important when a firm competes in an industry with high technological uncertainty.[28] Scanning and monitoring not only can provide the firm with information, they also serve as a means of importing new knowledge about markets and how to successfully commercialize new technologies that the firm has developed.[29]

Forecasting

Scanning and monitoring are concerned with events and trends in the general environment at a point in time. When *forecasting*, analysts develop feasible projections of what might happen, and how quickly, as a result of the changes and trends detected through scanning and monitoring.[30] For example, analysts might forecast the time that will be required for a new technology to reach the marketplace, the length of time before different corporate training procedures are required to deal with anticipated changes in the composition of the workforce, or how much time will elapse before changes in governmental taxation policies affect consumers' purchasing patterns.

For example, Dow Chemical experienced performance declines between 1999 and 2001. The chemical industry in general has suffered, with the S&P Index down 20 percent during this time. However, Dow forecasted earnings to increase from $2.26 in 2001 to $5.00 in 2004. The positive forecast is partially based on completing its long awaited merger with Union Carbide (announced in 1999), although the U.S. Federal Trade Commission has not yet approved the merger. Part of Dow's forecast is based on increased business it anticipates because of better customer service (the online system it implemented in 2002 includes all customer information, allowing a sales representative to review a customer's account from anywhere in the world).[31]

Assessing

The objective of *assessing* is to determine the timing and significance of the effects of environmental changes and trends on the strategic management of the firm.[32] Through scanning, monitoring, and forecasting, analysts are able to understand the general environment. Going a step further, the intent of assessment is to specify the implications of that understanding for the organization. Without assessment, the firm is left with data that may be interesting but are of unknown competitive relevance.

For example, Ford, General Motors, and DaimlerChrysler sold an increased number of vehicles in the U.S. automobile market in 2001. However, in past years, all three firms lost market share in vehicles to competitors such as Honda, Toyota, Volkswagen, Audi, and BMW. The primary reason for the U.S. firms' increase in sales levels in 2001 was their offers to sell the vehicles at zero percent interest on loans. Without these generous loans, high volume sales are unlikely to persist. Thus, firms must assess the reasons for sales relative to competitors to be able to accurately forecast future sales.

Segments of the General Environment

The general environment is composed of segments (and their individual elements) that are external to the firm (see Table 2.1). Although the degree of impact varies, these environmental segments affect each industry and its firms. The challenge to the firm is to scan, monitor, forecast, and assess those elements in each segment that are of the greatest importance. Resulting from these efforts should be a recognition of environmental changes, trends, opportunities, and threats. Opportunities are then matched with a firm's core competencies (the matching process is discussed further in Chapter 3).

The Demographic Segment

The **demographic segment** is concerned with a population's size, age structure, geographic distribution, ethnic mix, and income distribution.[33] Demographic segments are analyzed on a global basis because of their potential effects across countries' borders and because many firms compete in global markets.

The **demographic segment** is concerned with a population's size, age structure, geographic distribution, ethnic mix, and income distribution.

Population Size

Before the end of 1999, the world's population grew to 6 billion, from 5 billion in 1987. Combined, China and India accounted for one-third of the 6 billion. Experts speculate that the population might stabilize at 10 billion after 2200 if the deceleration in the rate of increase in the world's head count continues. By 2050, India (with over 1.5 billion people projected) and China (with just under 1.5 billion people projected) are expected to be the most populous countries.[34]

Observing demographic changes in populations highlights the importance of this environmental segment. For example, some advanced nations have a negative population growth, after discounting the effects of immigration. In some countries, including the United States and several European nations, couples are averaging fewer than two children. This birthrate will produce a loss of population over time (even with the population living longer on average).[35] However, some believe that a baby boom will occur in the United States during the first 12 years of the 21st century and that by 2012, the annual number of births could exceed 4.3 million. Such a birthrate in the United States would equal the all-time high that was set in 1957.[36] These projections suggest major 21st-century challenges and business opportunities.

Age Structure

In some countries, the population's average age is increasing. In the United States, for example, the percentage of the population aged 65 and older increased less in the 1990s than the population less than 65 years of age. However, in the period 2010–2020, the population of 65 and older is projected to grow by 35.3 percent.[37] Contributing to this growth are increasing life expectancies. This trend may suggest numerous opportunities for firms to develop goods and services to meet the needs of an increasingly older population. For example, GlaxoSmithKline has created a program for low-income elderly people without prescription drug coverage. The program provides drugs to these individuals at a 25 percent reduction in price. In so doing, the firm is able to increase its sales and provide an important service to a population who might not be able to afford the drugs otherwise.[38]

It has been projected that up to one-half of the females and one-third of the males born at the end of the 1990s in developed countries could live to be 100 years old, with some of them possibly living to be 200 or more.[39] Also, the odds that a U.S. baby boomer (a person born between the years 1946 and 1964) will reach age 90 are now one in nine.[40] If these life spans become a reality, a host of interesting business opportunities and societal issues will emerge. For example, the effect on individuals' pension plans will be significant and will create potential opportunities for financial institutions, as well as possible threats to government-sponsored retirement and health plans.[41]

Geographic Distribution

For decades, the U.S. population has been shifting from the north and east to the west and south. Similarly, the trend of relocating from metropolitan to non-metropolitan areas continues and may well accelerate with the terrorist attacks in New York City and Washington, D.C. These trends are changing local and state governments' tax bases. In turn, business firms' decisions regarding location are influenced by the degree of support different taxing agencies offer.

The geographic distribution of populations throughout the world is also affected by the capabilities resulting from advances in communications technology. Through computer technologies, for example, people can remain in their homes, communicating with others in remote locations to complete their work.

Ethnic Mix

The ethnic mix of countries' populations continues to change. Within the United States, the ethnicity of states and their cities varies significantly. For firms, the challenge is to be sensitive to these changes. Through careful study, companies can develop and market products that satisfy the unique needs of different ethnic groups.

Changes in the ethnic mix also affect a workforce's composition. In the United States, for example, the population and labor force will continue to diversify, as immigration accounts for a sizable part of growth. Projections are that the Hispanic and Asian population shares will increase from 14 percent in 1995 to 19 percent in 2020. By 2006, it is expected that (1) 72.7 percent of the U.S. labor force will be white non-Hispanic (down from 75.3 percent in 1996), (2) 11.7 percent will be Hispanic (compared with 9.5 percent in 1996), (3) 11.6 percent will be African-American (up from 11.3 percent in 1996), and (4) 5.4 percent will be Asian (up from 4.3 percent in 1996). By 2020, white non-Hispanic workers will make up only 68 percent of the work force.[42]

As with the U.S. labor force, other countries also are witnessing a trend toward an older workforce. By 2030, the proportion of the total labor force of 45- to 59-year-olds of countries in the Organisation for Economic Co-Operation and Development (industrialized countries) is projected to increase from 25.6 to 31.8 percent; the share of workers aged 60 and over is expected to increase from 4.7 to 7.8 percent. Because a labor force can be critical to competitive success, firms across the globe, including those competing in OECD countries, must learn to work effectively with labor forces that are becoming more diverse and older.[43]

Workforce diversity is also a sociocultural issue. Effective management of a culturally diverse workforce can produce a competitive advantage. For example, heterogeneous work teams have been shown to produce more effective strategic analyses, more creativity and innovation, and higher quality decisions than homogeneous work teams.[44] However, evidence also suggests that diverse work teams are difficult to manage to achieve these outcomes.[45]

Income Distribution

Understanding how income is distributed within and across populations informs firms of different groups' purchasing power

Hispanic Americans are part of an increasingly diverse workforce in the United States. According to a Census Bureau official, "The nation is much more diverse in the year 2000 than it was in 1990, and that diversity is much more complex than we've ever measured before." Hispanic Americans are the fastest growing population group in the United States, with a 58 percent increase from 1990 to 2000, and constitute 12.5 percent of the U.S. population. The group is a significant presence in almost every state, often drawn by employment opportunities.

MICHAEL NEWMAN/PHOTOEDIT

and discretionary income. Studies of income distributions suggest that although living standards have improved over time, variations exist within and between nations.[46] Of interest to firms are the average incomes of households and individuals. For instance, the increase in dual-career couples has had a notable effect on average incomes. Although real income has been declining in general, the income of dual-career couples has increased. These figures yield strategically relevant information for firms.

The Economic Segment

The health of a nation's economy affects individual firms and industries. Because of this, companies study the economic environment to identify changes, trends, and their strategic implications.

The **economic environment** refers to the nature and direction of the economy in which a firm competes or may compete.[47] Because nations are interconnected as a result of the global economy, firms must scan, monitor, forecast, and assess the health of economies outside their host nation. For example, many nations throughout the world are affected by the U.S. economy.

The U.S. economy declined into a recession in 2001 that extended into 2002 despite efforts to revive it by the U.S. government. In the summer of 2001, Alan Greenspan, Chairman of the U.S. Federal Reserve, observed that the asset quality of U.S. banks was eroding. Bank loans were becoming riskier because of the economic recession. But, Greenspan cautioned banks not to tighten loan requirements, fearing it would worsen the economy. In the same time period, it was announced that advertising revenue had fallen for most publishers. For example, advertising pages fell by 47.2 percent at *Fast Company* and by 44.3 percent at *Inc* in the first six months of 2001.[48] The economy looked to be on the mend by mid-2002.

DaimlerChrysler's CEO Jurgen E. Schrempp is a strong proponent of completing a transatlantic integration between Europe and North America. Schrempp supports largely unrestricted trade and believes that economic integration between Europe and North America is logical in that "Europe and the United States each account for close to 20 percent of the other's trade in goods while services account for more than 38 percent of bilateral trade." Principles developed by the Transatlantic Business Dialogue (a group of businesspersons and politicians) could support an integration effort. The principles include the removal of all trade barriers and differing regulatory controls and the acceptance of a product in all parts of the transatlantic marketplace once it has been approved.[49] Creating truly "borderless commerce" permitting free trade among nations is a significant challenge, however, because of differing regulations for trade between separate countries.

While bilateral trade can enrich the economies of the countries involved, it also makes each country more vulnerable to negative events. For example, the September 11, 2001 terrorist attacks in the United States have had more than a $100 billion negative effect on the U.S. economy. As a result, the European Union (E.U.) also suffered negative economic effects because of the reduction in bilateral trade between the U.S. and the E.U.[50]

As our discussion of the economic segment suggests, economic issues are intertwined closely with the realities of the external environment's political/legal segment.

The Political/Legal Segment

The **political/legal segment** is the arena in which organizations and interest groups compete for attention, resources, and a voice of overseeing the body of laws and regulations guiding the interactions among nations.[51] Essentially, this segment repre-

The **economic environment** refers to the nature and direction of the economy in which a firm competes or may compete.

The **political/legal segment** is the arena in which organizations and interest groups compete for attention, resources, and a voice of overseeing the body of laws and regulations guiding the interactions among nations.

sents how organizations try to influence government and how governments influence them. Constantly changing, the segment influences the nature of competition (see Table 2.1).

Firms must carefully analyze a new political administration's business-related policies and philosophies. Antitrust laws, taxation laws, industries chosen for deregulation, labor training laws, and the degree of commitment to educational institutions are areas in which an administration's policies can affect the operations and profitability of industries and individual firms. Often, firms develop a political strategy to influence governmental policies and actions that might affect them. The effects of global governmental policies on a firm's competitive position increase the importance of forming an effective political strategy.[52]

Business firms across the globe today confront an interesting array of political/legal questions and issues. For example, the debate continues over trade policies. Some believe that a nation should erect trade barriers to protect products manufactured by its companies. Others argue that free trade across nations serves the best interests of individual countries and their citizens. The International Monetary Fund (IMF) classifies trade barriers as restrictive when tariffs total at least 25 percent of a product's price. At the other extreme, the IMF stipulates that a nation has open trade when its tariffs are between 0 and 9 percent. To foster trade, New Zealand initially cut its tariffs from 16 to 8.5 percent and then to 3 percent in 2000. Colombia reduced its tariffs to less than 12 percent. The IMF classifies this percentage as "relatively open."[53] While controversial, a number of countries (including the United States, nations in the European Union, Japan, Australia, Canada, Chile, Singapore, and Mexico) are working together to reduce or eventually eliminate trade barriers.

An interesting debate occurring in the United States concerns the regulation of e-commerce. In part, laws regulating e-commerce attempt to prevent fraud, violations of privacy, and poor service. Some think that governmental policies should also be developed to regulate Internet gambling.[54] Another challenging Internet issue being debated by U.S. government officials is taxation on sales made using Internet sites. A concern of all parties is to develop government policies that will not stifle the legitimate growth of e-commerce.[55] In 2001, the U.S. federal government passed legislation extending the tax-free status of sales over the Internet for several more years. How government agencies can affect business is discussed in the Strategic Focus on page 50.

The Strategic Focus explains some of the effects that governments have on how business is conducted. The regulations related to pharmaceuticals and telecommunications, along with the approval or disapproval of major acquisitions, shows the power of government entities. This power also suggests how important it is for firms to have a political strategy.

The Sociocultural Segment

The **sociocultural segment** is concerned with a society's attitudes and cultural values.

The **sociocultural segment** is concerned with a society's attitudes and cultural values. Because attitudes and values form the cornerstone of a society, they often drive demographic, economic, political/legal, and technological conditions and changes.

Sociocultural segments differ across countries. For example, in the United States, 14 percent of the nation's GDP is spent on health care. This is the highest percentage of any OECD country. Germany allocates 10.4 percent of GDP to health care, while in Switzerland the percentage is 10.2.[56] Countries' citizens have different attitudes about retirement savings as well. In Italy, just 9 percent of the citizenry say that they are saving primarily for retirement, while the percentages are 18 percent in Germany and 48 percent in the United States.[57] Attitudes regarding saving for retirement affect a nation's economic and political/legal segments.

Government Can Have a Large Effect on Businesses

Governmental entities can have major effects on businesses. Essentially, government establishes the rules by which business is conducted within the country's boundaries or geographic region it governs. Federal government regulations generally have the most profound effects on business.

Government regulations usually cover many industries and areas of conducting business. For example, the U.S. Food and Drug Administration (FDA) must approve all new drugs sold in the United States. In 2001 the FDA disapproved a new injectable pain relief medicine developed by Pharmacia, asking for additional data before it would consider approving the drug. Similarly, Pfizer received an unfavorable ruling on a new diabetes drug it developed. Likewise, the U.S. Federal Communications Commission must license all telecommunications operators; the Federal Trade Commission and the Justice Department oversee potential mergers and acquisitions.

Regulations are a global phenomenon affecting firms doing business in a country even though their home base may be located in another country. As an example, the European Union's antitrust officials from several different Commissions disapproved the acquisition of Honeywell by GE. Even though the home bases of both firms are in the United States, they have significant operations in Europe. Alternatively, the U.S. Justice Department argued that the proposed alliance between American Airlines (a U.S.-based firm) and British Airways (a U.K.-based firm), be rejected unless they agreed to sell some of their landing and takeoff slots at specific airports to enhance competition on routes between London and the United States.

Firms may also be subject to regulations by more than one government group within a country. For example, Enron had developed a major political strategy designed to encourage deregulation of energy markets. However, the firm's financial problems that became public in 2001 have invited substantial scrutiny and investigations by several government entities to determine if Enron's executives were involved in any wrongdoing. For example, the U.S. Justice Department, the Securities and Exchange Commission, and the U.S. Congress all initiated investigations of Enron activities. The Justice Department's pursuit of the antitrust suit against Microsoft represents another example of the effects government can have on business.

Not all government activity involves controls and regulations. For example, the U.S. Congress passed legislation providing $15 billion of aid for the airlines to reduce the negative effects of the events of September 11, 2001. This package includes $5 billion of direct cash payments and $10 billion of loan guarantees. In some cases, these actions may have allowed some airlines to survive. Governments may take other positive actions, such as reducing taxes, providing advice and support for firms to enter international markets, and promoting tourism, among others.

SOURCES: 2001, Pfizer gets unfavorable ruling in case related to complication of diabetes drug, *The Wall Street Journal Interactive*, http://interactive.wsj.com, December 21; S. Labaton, 2001, U.S. criticizes trans-Atlantic air alliance, *The New York Times*, http://www.nytimes.com, December 18; D. Ackman, 2001, Enron on the Hill, *Forbes*, http://www.forbes.com, December 14; S. Kirchgaessner, 2001, FCC and wireless carriers settle over licences, *Financial Times*, http://www.ft.com, October, 27; D. MacGregor, 2001, Governments act to avert airline industry crisis, *Financial Times*, http://www.ft.com, September, 22; S. Lohr, 2001, States press U.S. to take tough stand on Microsoft, *The New York Times*, http://www.nytimes.com, September 8; B. M. Mantz, 2001, FDA deems Pharmacia pain medication 'not approvable,' seeks additional data, *The Wall Street Journal Interactive*, http://interactive.wsj.com, July 15; P. Shishkin & L. Cohen, 2001, EU antitrust officials recommend blocking GE's Honeywell acquisition, *The Wall Street Journal Interactive*, http://interactive.wsj.com, June 19.

In the United States, boundaries between work and home are becoming blurred, as employees' workweeks continue to be stretched, perhaps because a strong Protestant work ethic is a part of the U.S. culture. Describing a culture's effect on a society, columnist George Will suggested that it is vital for people to understand that a nation's culture has a primary effect on its social character and health.[58] Thus, companies must understand the implications of a society's attitudes and its cultural values to offer products that meet consumers' needs.

A significant trend in many countries is increased workforce diversity. The number of female workers is an important indicator of this, and women are a valuable source of highly productive employees. Some argue, for example, that "educated hardworking women double the talent pool in the U.S. and give the nation a big competitive advantage over countries that deny women full participation in their economies."[59] However, women also comprise an increasing percentage of employees across multiple global workforces. In the United States, women now account for approximately 47 percent of the workforce. In Sweden, they account for roughly 52 percent; in Japan, 44 percent; in France, 40 percent; in Germany, 41 percent; and in Mexico, 37 percent. In the United States, women hold 43 percent of the managerial jobs. In Sweden, women hold 17 percent of managerial positions, while in Japan, the figure is only 9.4 percent.[60]

Because of equal pay and equal opportunity legislation in many countries, relative pay for women is increasing. However, pay differentials between men and women still exist. Among Western European countries, the pay gap between men and women is greatest in the United Kingdom, where men earn 34 percent more than women do, and lowest in Sweden, where a 17 percent gap exists.[61]

An increasing number of women are also starting and managing their own businesses. For example, the U.S. Census Bureau reports that approximately 5.4 million businesses, with $819 billion in annual sales, are owned by women. The National Foundation for Women Business Owners suggests that these figures substantially understate the number of women-owned businesses. The foundation claims that over 9 million businesses were started by women in 2000. Approximately 55 percent of women-owned businesses are in services, with the second largest group (about 18 percent) in some form of retailing. The number of new businesses started by women continues to increase, and thus women own a larger percentage of the total number of businesses.[62]

The growing gender, ethnic, and cultural diversity in the workforce creates challenges and opportunities,[63] including those related to combining the best of both men's and women's traditional leadership styles for a firm's benefit and identifying ways to facilitate all employees' contributions to their firms. Some companies provide training to nurture women's and ethnic minorities' leadership potential. Changes in organizational structure and management practices often are required to eliminate subtle barriers that may exist. Learning to manage diversity in the domestic workforce can increase a firm's effectiveness in managing a globally diverse workforce, as the firm acquires more international operations.

Another manifestation of changing attitudes toward work is the continuing growth of contingency workers (part-time, temporary, and contract employees) throughout the global economy. This trend is significant in several parts of the world, including Canada, Japan, Latin America, Western Europe, and the United States. The fastest growing group of contingency workers is in the technical and professional area. Contributing to this growth are corporate restructurings and a breakdown of lifetime employment practices. Because of tight labor markets for technical and professional workers, agencies providing these contingency workers to companies are offering multiple inducements to those they hire.

Another major sociocultural trend is the continued growth of suburban communities in the United States and abroad. The increasing number of people living in the suburbs has a number of effects. For example, because of the resulting often-longer commute times to urban businesses, there is pressure for better transportation systems and super highway systems (e.g., outer beltways to serve the suburban communities). On the other hand, some businesses are locating in the suburbs closer to their employees. Suburban growth also has an effect on the number of electronic telecommuters, which is expected to increase rapidly in the 21st century. This work-style option is feasible because of changes in the technological segment, including the Internet's rapid growth and evolution.[64]

The Technological Segment

Pervasive and diversified in scope, technological changes affect many parts of societies. These effects occur primarily through new products, processes, and materials. The **technological segment** includes the institutions and activities involved with creating new knowledge and translating that knowledge into new outputs, products, processes, and materials.

The **technological segment** includes the institutions and activities involved with creating new knowledge and translating that knowledge into new outputs, products, processes, and materials.

Given the rapid pace of technological change, it is vital for firms to thoroughly study the technological segment. The importance of these efforts is suggested by the finding that early adopters of new technology often achieve higher market shares and earn higher returns. Thus, executives must verify that their firm is continuously scanning the external environment to identify potential substitutes for technologies that are in current use, as well as to spot newly emerging technologies from which their firm could derive competitive advantage.[65]

Numerous surveys suggest that executives are aware of the potential of a major technological development—the Internet. A survey completed by Booz Allen & Hamilton in partnership with *The Economist* revealed that (1) 92 percent of executives who participated in the survey believed that the Internet would continue to reshape their companies' markets, (2) 61 percent thought that effective use of the Internet would facilitate efforts to achieve their firms' strategic goals, and (3) 30 percent noted that their competitive strategies had already been altered because of the Internet's influence.[66]

The value of the Internet is shown in its use by Staples Inc., the office supply superstores. Staples invested $250 million to create Staples.com to continue its market share leadership in the industry. The firm's online sales reached approximately $1 billion by 2001, up from $99 million in 1999. This accounts for 10 percent of the company's total annual sales. Thomas Steinberg, founder and CEO of Staples, forecasted that sales on the Internet would reach $50 billion annually and represent 25 percent of the office supply industry's total sales in the next few years.[67]

Among its other valuable uses, the Internet is an excellent source of data and information for a firm to use to understand its external environment. Access to experts on topics from chemical engineering to semiconductor manufacturing, to the Library of Congress, and even to satellite photographs is available through the Internet. Other information available through this technology includes Security and Exchange Commission (SEC) filings, Commerce Department data, information from the Bureau of the Census, new patent filings, and stock market updates.

Another use of Internet technology is conducting business transactions between companies, as well as between a company and its customers. According to Dell Computer Corporation's CEO Michael Dell, the Internet also has great potential as a business-organization system. Dell uses this technology to reduce its paperwork flow, to more efficiently schedule its payments, and to coordinate its inventories. Dell accomplishes these tasks by linking personal computers with network servers, which the firm's CEO believes have the potential to revolutionize business processes "in a

Staples Inc., the second-largest office supply firm after Office Depot, showed a profit for 2001 and expects to improve upon it with plans to reduce its prototype to 20,000 square feet, decrease square footage growth without sacrificing convenience, and benefit from smaller investment in fixtures and inventory. The firm is also offering software tools to their customers to integrate their e-procurement systems with Staples for office supplies purchases and will add 200 people to its special sales force to increase catalog and Internet orders at Staples.com.

way that blurs traditional boundaries between supplier and manufacturer, and manufacturer and customer. This will eliminate paper-based functions, flatten organization hierarchies, and shrink time and distance to a degree not possible before."[68] Thus, a competitive advantage may accrue to the company that derives full value from the Internet in terms of both e-commerce activities and transactions taken to process the firm's workflow.

While the Internet was a significant technological advance providing substantial power to companies utilizing its potential, wireless communication technology is predicted to be the next critical technological opportunity. By 2003, handheld devices and other wireless communications equipment will be used to access a variety of network-based services. The use of handheld computers with wireless network connectivity, web-enabled mobile phone handsets, and other emerging platforms (i.e., consumer Internet access devices) is expected to increase substantially, soon becoming the dominant form of communication and commerce.[69]

Clearly, the Internet and wireless forms of communications are important technological developments for many reasons. One reason for their importance, however, is that they facilitate the diffusion of other technology and knowledge critical for achieving and maintaining a competitive advantage.[70] Technological knowledge is particularly important. Certainly on a global scale, the technological opportunities and threats in the general environment have an effect on whether firms obtain new technology from external sources (such as licensing and acquisition) or develop it internally.

The Global Segment

The **global segment** includes relevant new global markets, existing markets that are changing, important international political events, and critical cultural and institutional characteristics of global markets.

The **global segment** includes relevant new global markets, existing markets that are changing, important international political events, and critical cultural and institutional characteristics of global markets.[71] Globalization of business markets creates both opportunities and challenges for firms. For example, firms can identify and enter valuable new global markets. Many global markets (such as those in some South American nations and in South Korea and Taiwan) are becoming borderless and integrated.[72] In addition to contemplating opportunities, firms should recognize potential threats in these markets as well. For instance, companies with home bases in Europe and North America may be subject to terrorist threats in certain parts of the world (such as Middle Eastern regions and parts of Asia).

China presents many opportunities and some threats for international firms. Creating additional opportunities is China's recent admission to the World Trade Organization (WTO). A Geneva-based organization, the WTO establishes rules for global trade. China's membership in this organization suggests the possibility of increasing and less-restricted participation by the country in the global economy.[73] In return for gaining entry to the WTO, China agreed to reduce trade barriers in multiple industries, including telecommunications, banking, automobiles, movies, and professional

ANDREW WONG/AFP/CORBIS

Star TV chairman and CEO James Murdoch (left), China Central Television chairman Zhao Huayong (center), and Guangdong Cable TV Networks chairman Wang Changli (right) toast their December 2001 agreement for a new 24-hour Mandarin language entertainment channel in southern China.

services (for example, the services of lawyers, physicians, and accountants). These reduced barriers are likely part of the reason that Rupert Murdoch realized a major goal of entering the Chinese market. In 2001, Star TV (Murdoch's company), News Corporation, and Chinese television authorities announced an agreement to launch a 24-hour entertainment channel for the wealthy Guangzhou and Zhaoqing cities. The purpose of the channel is to establish a relationship and a track record with the hope of expanding it to other cities and regions of China, a huge potential market.[74]

Moving into international markets extends a firm's reach and potential. Toyota receives almost 50 percent of its total sales revenue from outside Japan, its home country. Over 60 percent of McDonald's sales revenues and almost 98 percent of Nokia's sales revenues are from outside their home countries.[75] Because the opportunity is coupled with uncertainty, some view entering new international markets to be entrepreneurial.[76] Firms can increase the opportunity to sell innovations by entering international markets. The larger total market increases the probability that the firm will earn a return on its innovations. Certainly, firms entering new markets can diffuse new knowledge they have created and learn from the new markets as well.[77]

Firms should recognize the different sociocultural and institutional attributes of global markets. Companies competing in South Korea, for example, must understand the value placed on hierarchical order, formality, and self-control, as well as on duty rather than rights. Furthermore, Korean ideology emphasizes communitarianism, a characteristic of many Asian countries. Korea's approach differs from those of Japan and China, however, in that it focuses on *Inhwa*, or harmony. Inhwa is based on a respect of hierarchical relationships and obedience to authority. Alternatively, the approach in China stresses *Guanxi*—personal relationships or good connections, while in Japan, the focus is on *Wa*, or group harmony and social cohesion.[78] The institutional context of Korea suggests a major emphasis on centralized planning by the government. Indeed, the emphasis placed on growth by many South Korean firms is the result of a government policy to promote economic growth.[79]

Firms based in other countries that compete in these markets can learn from them. For example, the cultural characteristics above suggest the value of relationships. In particular, Guanxi communicates social capital's importance when doing business in China.[80] But, social capital is important for success in most markets around the world.[81]

Global markets offer firms more opportunities to obtain the resources needed for success. For example, the Kuwait Investment Authority is the second largest shareholder of DaimlerChrysler. Additionally, Global Crossing sought financial assistance from potential investors in Europe and Asia. But, it was to no avail as Global Crossing, citing overcapacity in the telecommunications network market as the primary cause of its problems, filed for bankruptcy in 2001.[82] Alternatively, globalization can be threatening. In particular, companies in emerging market countries may be vulnerable to larger, more resource-rich, and more effective competitors from developed markets.

Additionally, there are risks in global markets. A few years ago, Argentina's market was full of promise, but in 2001, Argentina experienced a financial crisis that placed it on the brink of bankruptcy.[83] Thus, the global segment of the general environment is quite important for most firms. As a result, it is necessary to have a top management team with the experience, knowledge, and sensitivity that are necessary to effectively analyze this segment of the environment.[84]

A key objective of analyzing the general environment is identifying anticipated changes and trends among external elements. With a focus on the future, the analysis of the general environment allows firms to identify opportunities and threats. Also critical to a firm's future operations is an understanding of its industry environment and its competitors; these issues are considered next.

Industry Environment Analysis

An **industry** is a group of firms producing products that are close substitutes. In the course of competition, these firms influence one another. Typically, industries include a rich mix of competitive strategies that companies use in pursuing strategic competitiveness and above-average returns. In part, these strategies are chosen because of the influence of an industry's characteristics.[85] Some believed that technology-based industries in which e-commerce is a dominant means of competing differ from their more traditional predecessors and that free exchange of information improved the competitiveness of the industries. However, while there were features of the e-commerce and information technology industries that differed from more traditional industries, the economic recession of 2001 and early 2002 showed the vulnerability of these industries as discussed in the Strategic Focus on page 56.

Compared to the general environment, the industry environment has a more direct effect on the firm's strategic competitiveness and above-average returns, as exemplified in the following Strategic Focus. The intensity of industry competition and an industry's profit potential (as measured by the long-run return on invested capital) are a function of five forces of competition: the threats posed by new entrants, the power of suppliers, the power of buyers, product substitutes, and the intensity of rivalry among competitors (see Figure 2.2).

The five forces model of competition expands the arena for competitive analysis. Historically when studying the competitive environment, firms concentrated on companies with which they competed directly. However, firms must search more broadly to identify current and potential competitors by identifying potential customers as well as the firms serving them. Competing for the same customers and thus being influenced by how customers value location and firm capabilities in their decisions is referred to as the market microstructure.[86] Understanding this area is particularly important, because in recent years industry boundaries have become blurred. For example, in the electrical utilities industry, cogenerators (firms that also produce power) are competing with regional utility companies. Moreover, telecommunications companies now compete with broadcasters, software manufacturers provide personal financial services, airlines sell mutual funds, and automakers sell insurance and provide financing.[87] In addition to focusing on customers rather than specific industry boundaries to define markets, geographic boundaries are also relevant. Research suggests that different geographic markets for the same product can have considerably different competitive conditions.[88]

The five forces model recognizes that suppliers can become a firm's competitors (by integrating forward), as can buyers (by integrating backward). Several firms have integrated forward in the pharmaceutical industry by acquiring distributors or wholesalers. In addition, firms choosing to enter a new market and those producing products that are adequate substitutes for existing products can become competitors of a company.

An **industry** is a group of firms producing products that are close substitutes.

Three Industries with Different Experiences in Economic Recession

Firms in the steel industry have experienced substantial rivalry in recent years, even during good economic times. Thus, the steel industry grappled with significant problems in the 2001–2002 economic recession. In this global industry, firms from Asia, Europe, and North America compete against one another. Since 1998, 12 companies have closed their doors and 17 more filed for bankruptcy. LTV, one of the largest steel manufacturers in the United States operated in bankruptcy during 2000–2001. It ceased operations in 2002 and sold its remaining assets. The firm had suffered from more efficient foreign competitors and competition from U.S. mini-mills and could not survive. In an attempt to save large steel manufacturing firms in several countries, the economically most powerful countries agreed to incrementally reduce by 10 percent the output of steel worldwide by 2010. This decision was too late to save LTV but may affect others competing in this struggling industry.

The information technology (IT) industry also has suffered with the economic recession. Actually, the IT industry has multiple segments. While many companies in the IT industry have ceased to operate and others have filed for bankruptcy with hopes of surviving, this industry is quite different than the steel industry. As with others in recent years, the IT industry is consolidating. However, it also has a bright future. Oracle's CEO, Larry Ellison, argues that the industry is maturing but others disagree. Former stars Cisco and Sun Microsystems have retreated but are preparing for improved markets. In fact, GE continued to spend heavily on its IT infrastructure when its competitors were severely reducing their IT spending. GE's intent was to be ahead of its competition as the economy improved. In particular, the firms investing in wireless communications technology may be the future winners. For example, 80 percent of the cell phones sold in 2001 contained Texas Instruments' DSP or analog chip.

For reasons beyond the U.S. or world economy, the U.S. defense industry is again thriving. The industry has many fewer firms than a decade ago. Following a long period of consolidation after the Cold War ended with the crumbling of the Berlin Wall, a few mostly large firms remain active in the industry. Its economic health is due partly to the Bush administration's renewed emphasis on military preparedness, partly to major world events such as September 11, 2001, and partly to unrest in the Middle East. Lockheed Martin, a leader in the industry, won a major $200 billion contract for a new jet fighter plane. Boeing and Lockheed each received $660 million to design and build prototypes of the plane, and Lockheed won the competition for the contract.

SOURCES: R. D. Atlas, 2001, LTV seems on the verge of a shutdown, *The New York Times*, http://www.nytimes.com, December 19; R. G. Matthews, 2001, World steelmakers agree to cut levels, but amount is less than U.S.'s request, *The Wall Street Journal Interactive*, http://interactive.wsj.com, December 19; R. Waters, 2001, Oracle Chief dispels fantasy of young IT sector, *Financial Times*, http://www.ft.com, December 14; 2001, Lockheed wins $200 billion contract from Pentagon to build strike fighters, *The Wall Street Journal Interactive*, http://interactive.wsj.com, October 26; E. Alden, 2001, Lockheed-Martin wins $200 billion fighter contract, *Financial Times*, http://www.ft.com, October 26; S. Lohr, 2001, After the fall, a tech star stays scrappy, *The New York Times*, http://www.nytimes.com, September 30; E. Williams, 2001, Mixed signals, *Forbes*, May 28, 80–89; D. Lyons, 2001, Lion in winter, *Forbes*, April 30, 68–70.

Threat of New Entrants

Evidence suggests that companies often find it difficult to identify new competitors.[89] Identifying new entrants is important because they can threaten the market share of existing competitors. One reason new entrants pose such a threat is that they bring additional production capacity. Unless the demand for a good or service is increasing, additional capacity holds consumers' costs down, resulting in less revenue and lower returns for competing firms. Often, new entrants have a keen interest in gaining a large market share. As a result, new competitors may force existing firms to be more effective and efficient and to learn how to compete on new dimensions (for example, using an Internet-based distribution channel).

The likelihood that firms will enter an industry is a function of two factors: barriers to entry and the retaliation expected from current industry participants. Entry barriers make it difficult for new firms to enter an industry and often place them at a competitive disadvantage even when they are able to enter. As such, high entry barriers increase the returns for existing firms in the industry.[90]

Barriers to Entry

Existing competitors try to develop barriers to entry. In contrast, potential entrants seek markets in which the entry barriers are relatively insignificant. The absence of entry barriers increases the probability that a new entrant can operate profitably. There are several kinds of potentially significant entry barriers.

Economies of Scale. *Economies of scale* are "the marginal improvements in efficiency that a firm experiences as it incrementally increases its size."[91] Therefore, as the quantity of a product produced during a given period increases, the cost of manufacturing each unit declines. Economies of scale can be developed in most business functions, such as marketing, manufacturing, research and development, and purchasing. Increasing economies of scale enhances a firm's flexibility. For example, a firm may choose to reduce its price and capture a greater share of the market. Alternatively, it may keep its price constant to increase profits. In so doing, it likely will increase its free cash flow that is helpful in times of recession, as Radio Shack was able to do in 2001.[92]

New entrants face a dilemma when confronting current competitors' scale economies. Small-scale entry places them at a cost disadvantage. Alternatively, large-scale entry, in which the new entrant manufactures large volumes of a product to gain economies of scale, risks strong competitive retaliation.

Figure 2.2　　The Five Forces of Competition Model

Also important for the firm to understand are instances of current competitive realities that reduce the ability of economies of scale to create an entry barrier. Many companies now customize their products for large numbers of small customer groups. Customized products are not manufactured in the volumes necessary to achieve economies of scale. Customization is made possible by new flexible manufacturing systems (this point is discussed further in Chapter 4). In fact, the new manufacturing technology facilitated by advanced computerization has allowed the development of mass customization in some industries. Mass customized products can be individualized to the customer in a very short time, often within a day. Mass customization is becoming increasingly common in manufacturing products.[93] Companies manufacturing customized products learn how to respond quickly to customers' desires rather than developing scale economies.

Product Differentiation. Over time, customers may come to believe that a firm's product is unique. This belief can result from the firm's service to the customer, effective advertising campaigns, or being the first to market a good or service. Companies such as Coca-Cola, PepsiCo, and the world's automobile manufacturers spend a great deal of money on advertising to convince potential customers of their products' distinctiveness. Customers valuing a product's uniqueness tend to become loyal to both the product and the company producing it. Typically, new entrants must allocate many resources over time to overcome existing customer loyalties. To combat the perception of uniqueness, new entrants frequently offer products at lower prices. This decision, however, may result in lower profits or even losses.

Capital Requirements. Competing in a new industry requires the firm to have resources to invest. In addition to physical facilities, capital is needed for inventories, marketing activities, and other critical business functions. Even when competing in a new industry is attractive, the capital required for successful market entry may not be available to pursue an apparent market opportunity. For example, entering the steel and defense industries would be very difficult because of the substantial resource investments required to be competitive. One way a firm could enter the steel industry, however, is with a highly efficient mini-mill. Alternatively, a firm might enter the defense industry through the acquisition of an existing firm, because of the knowledge requirements.

Switching Costs. Switching costs are the one-time costs customers incur when they buy from a different supplier. The costs of buying new ancillary equipment and of retraining employees, and even the psychic costs of ending a relationship, may be incurred in switching to a new supplier. In some cases, switching costs are low, such as when the consumer switches to a different soft drink. Switching costs can vary as a function of time. For example, in terms of hours toward graduation, the cost to a student to transfer from one university to another as a freshman is much lower than it is when the student is entering the senior year. Occasionally, a decision made by manufacturers to produce a new, innovative product creates high switching costs for the final consumer. Customer loyalty programs, such as airlines awarding frequent flier miles, are intended to increase the customer's switching costs.

If switching costs are high, a new entrant must offer either a substantially lower price or a much better product to attract buyers. Usually, the more established the relationship between parties, the greater is the cost incurred to switch to an alternative offering.

Access to Distribution Channels. Over time, industry participants typically develop effective means of distributing products. Once a relationship with its distributors has been developed, a firm will nurture it to create switching costs for the distributors.

Access to distribution channels can be a strong entry barrier for new entrants, particularly in consumer nondurable goods industries (for example, in grocery stores where shelf space is limited) and in international markets. Thus, new entrants have to persuade distributors to carry their products, either in addition to or in place of those currently distributed. Price breaks and cooperative advertising allowances may be used for this purpose; however, those practices reduce the new entrant's profit potential.

Cost Disadvantages Independent of Scale. Sometimes, established competitors have cost advantages that new entrants cannot duplicate. Proprietary product technology, favorable access to raw materials, desirable locations, and government subsidies are examples. Successful competition requires new entrants to reduce the strategic relevance of these factors. Delivering purchases directly to the buyer can counter the advantage of a desirable location; new food establishments in an undesirable location often follow this practice. Similarly, automobile dealerships located in unattractive areas (perhaps in a city's downtown area) can provide superior service (such as picking up the car to be serviced and then delivering it to the customer) to overcome a competitor's location advantage.

Government Policy. Through licensing and permit requirements, governments can also control entry into an industry. Liquor retailing, banking, and trucking are examples of industries in which government decisions and actions affect entry possibilities. Also, governments often restrict entry into some utility industries because of the need to provide quality service to all and the capital requirements necessary to do so. The European Competition Commission's blocking of GE's acquisition of Honeywell is a prime example of government actions controlling entry to a market.[94] Also, the agreement among governments to restrict the output of steel (as discussed in the Strategic Focus on page 56) places substantial restrictions on new entrants to that industry.

Expected Retaliation

Firms seeking to enter an industry also anticipate the reactions of firms in the industry. An expectation of swift and vigorous competitive responses reduces the likelihood of entry. Vigorous retaliation can be expected when the existing firm has a major stake in the industry (for example, it has fixed assets with few, if any, alternative uses), when it has substantial resources, and when industry growth is slow or constrained. For example, any firms that attempt to enter the steel or IT industries at the current time can expect significant retaliation from existing competitors.

Locating market niches not being served by incumbents allows the new entrant to avoid entry barriers. Small entrepreneurial firms are generally best suited for identifying and serving neglected market segments. When Honda first entered the U.S. market, it concentrated on small-engine motorcycles, a market that firms such as Harley-Davidson ignored. By targeting this neglected niche, Honda avoided competition. After consolidating its position, Honda used its strength to attack rivals by introducing larger motorcycles and competing in the broader market. Competitive actions and competitive responses between firms such as Honda and Harley-Davidson are discussed fully in Chapter 5.

Bargaining Power of Suppliers

Increasing prices and reducing the quality of its products are potential means used by suppliers to exert power over firms competing within an industry. If a firm is unable to recover cost increases by its suppliers through its pricing structure, its profitability is reduced by its suppliers' actions. A supplier group is powerful when

- It is dominated by a few large companies and is more concentrated than the industry to which it sells.
- Satisfactory substitute products are not available to industry firms.
- Industry firms are not a significant customer for the supplier group.

- Suppliers' goods are critical to buyers' marketplace success.
- The effectiveness of suppliers' products has created high switching costs for industry firms.
- It poses a credible threat to integrate forward into the buyers' industry. Credibility is enhanced when suppliers have substantial resources and provide a highly differentiated product.

The automobile manufacturing industry is an example of an industry in which suppliers' bargaining power is relatively low. Actions taken by Nissan and Toyota demonstrate this. Recently these two firms placed significant pressure on their suppliers to provide parts at reduced prices. Toyota, for example, requested price reductions of up to 30 percent. As a result of the success of its requests, Nissan reduced its purchasing costs by $2.25 billion annually. Because they sell their products to a small number of large firms and because they aren't credible threats to integrate forward, auto parts suppliers have little power relative to automobile manufacturers such as Toyota and Nissan.[95]

Bargaining Power of Buyers

Firms seek to maximize the return on their invested capital. Alternatively, buyers (customers of an industry or firm) want to buy products at the lowest possible price—the point at which the industry earns the lowest acceptable rate of return on its invested capital. To reduce their costs, buyers bargain for higher quality, greater levels of service, and lower prices. These outcomes are achieved by encouraging competitive battles among the industry's firms. Customers (buyer groups) are powerful when

- They purchase a large portion of an industry's total output.
- The sales of the product being purchased account for a significant portion of the seller's annual revenues.
- They could switch to another product at little, if any, cost.
- The industry's products are undifferentiated or standardized, and the buyers pose a credible threat if they were to integrate backward into the sellers' industry.

Armed with greater amounts of information about the manufacturer's costs and the power of the Internet as a shopping and distribution alternative, consumers appear to be increasing their bargaining power in the automobile industry. One reason for this shift is that individual buyers incur virtually zero switching costs when they decide to purchase from one manufacturer rather than another or from one dealer as opposed to a second or third one. These realities are forcing companies in the automobile industry to become more focused on the needs and desires of the people actually buying cars, trucks, minivans, and sport utility vehicles. These conditions of the market combined with the recession in 2001 and early 2002 are part of the reasons that Nissan and Toyota are pressuring their suppliers to reduce costs. In so doing, they can better serve and satisfy their customers who have considerable power.

Threat of Substitute Products

Substitute products are goods or services from outside a given industry that perform similar or the same functions as a product that the industry produces. For example, as a sugar substitute, Nutrasweet places an upper limit on sugar manufacturers' prices—Nutrasweet and sugar perform the same function, but with different characteristics. Other product substitutes include fax machines instead of overnight deliveries, plastic containers rather than glass jars, and tea substituted for coffee. Recently firms have introduced to the market several low-alcohol fruit-flavored drinks that many customers substitute for beer. For example, Smirnoff's Ice was introduced with substantial advertising of the type often used for beer. Other firms have introduced lemonade with 5 percent alcohol (e.g., Doc Otis Hard Lemon) and tea and lemon combinations with alcohol (e.g., Bodean's Twisted Tea). These products are increasing in popularity especially among younger people and as product substitutes, have the potential to reduce overall sales of beer.[96]

In general, product substitutes present a strong threat to a firm when customers face few, if any, switching costs and when the substitute product's price is lower or its quality and performance capabilities are equal to or greater than those of the competing product. Differentiating a product along dimensions that customers value (such as price, quality, service after the sale, and location) reduces a substitute's attractiveness.

Intensity of Rivalry among Competitors

Because an industry's firms are mutually dependent, actions taken by one company usually invite competitive responses. Thus, in many industries, firms actively compete against one another. Competitive rivalry intensifies when a firm is challenged by a competitor's actions or when an opportunity to improve its market position is recognized.

Firms within industries are rarely homogeneous; they differ in resources and capabilities and seek to differentiate themselves from competitors.[97] Typically, firms seek to differentiate their products from competitors' offerings in ways that customers value and in which the firms have a competitive advantage. Visible dimensions on which rivalry is based include price, quality, and innovation.

As explained in the Strategic Focus, the rivalry between competitors, such as Fuji and Kodak, Airbus and Boeing, and Sun Microsystems and Microsoft, is intense.

The firms described in the Strategic Focus on page 62 are taking different competitive actions and competitive responses in efforts to be successful. Airbus is using a first mover strategy (explained in Chapter 5), Fuji is buying equity in a local competitor and infusing it with resources, Sun must improve the effectiveness of its Web service to achieve even competitive parity, and Samsung is taking advantage of a major shift in technology to differentiate its products from those of its rivals.

As suggested by the Strategic Focus on page 62, various factors influence the intensity of rivalry between or among competitors. Next, we discuss the most prominent factors that experience shows to affect the intensity of firms' rivalries.

Numerous or Equally Balanced Competitors

Intense rivalries are common in industries with many companies. With multiple competitors, it is common for a few firms to believe that they can act without eliciting a response. However, evidence suggests that other firms generally are aware of competitors' actions, often choosing to respond to them. At the other extreme, industries with only a few firms of equivalent size and power also tend to have strong rivalries. The large and often similar-sized resource bases of these firms permit vigorous actions and responses. The Fuji and Kodak and Airbus and Boeing competitive battles exemplify intense rivalries between pairs of relatively equivalent competitors.

Slow Industry Growth

When a market is growing, firms try to effectively use resources to serve an expanding customer base. Growing markets reduce the pressure to take customers from competitors. However, rivalry in nongrowth or slow-growth markets becomes more intense as firms battle to increase their market shares by attracting competitors' customers.

Typically, battles to protect market shares are fierce. Certainly, this has been the case with Fuji and Kodak. The instability in the market that results from these competitive engagements reduces profitability for firms throughout the industry, as is

The High Stakes of Competitive Rivalry

While most industries produce situations where multiple firms compete against each other, there are some industries in which two major competitors compete "head to head" in multiple markets. Among these competitors are Fuji and Kodak, Airbus and Boeing, and Sun Microsystems and Microsoft. Fuji and Kodak have had an almost storied rivalry over the last decade. For example, Kodak invested heavily in developing digital products. Fuji was aware that Kodak was ahead in serving the digital market, so it decided to capture market share in the traditional film market in hopes of changing Kodak's strategy. Fuji engaged in severe price competition in the U.S. market capturing major gains in market share from Kodak. Eventually, Kodak shareholders became dissatisfied, and Kodak had to respond. It reduced its prices and investment in R&D, slowing its move into digital products. Recently, however, Kodak has made major strides in capturing the high potential Chinese film market with approximately 50 percent of the market. To combat Kodak, Fuji, with 30 percent of the Chinese market, is negotiating to acquire equity in Lucky Film, China's only film manufacturer, which has 20 percent of the market. If the acquisition is finalized, Fuji will contribute financial capital, technology, and management while Lucky will provide the manufacturing and distribution.

For a number of years, Airbus and Boeing have competed directly to serve the large airline market. During most of that time, Boeing was the clear winner with a majority of the market with its 700 (including the 727, 737, 747, 757, and 767) series of aircraft. In recent years, Airbus has begun to capture a greater share of this market. Boeing didn't react quickly to these changes, but when Airbus announced that it would produce a new super jumbo jet aircraft, Boeing responded with an announcement that it would develop a larger version of its 747. However, Airbus was the clear winner here, taking all of the contracts in "head to head" competition. Boeing gave up and dropped its plans to develop the larger aircraft. Instead, it announced the development of a smaller and much faster aircraft, but it must invest much time and money to do so. Boeing was not prepared well for the future and seemed to be resting on its laurels. As a result, Airbus has captured leadership of the global large aircraft market.

Scott McNealy, CEO of Sun Microsystems, is wealthy with approximately $668 million in Sun equity and became a success at a relatively young age. Given the economic travails of 2001 and 2002, he considered retiring to a less stressful life, but he still has a major goal. He believes that he must stop Sun's rival Microsoft from dominating the Internet and has stated, "It is mankind against Microsoft." The rivalry between Microsoft and Sun seems to be almost personal between McNealy and Microsoft's Bill Gates. McNealy faces a tough challenge—Microsoft leads Sun in four of six markets in which they compete and executed its Web strategy effectively. Additionally, Sun was not profitable in 2001, while Microsoft was. As a result, Sun's stock price faltered while Microsoft's increased. For Sun to reverse its performance and to successfully challenge Microsoft, it must be effective in providing Web services. While Sun is unlikely to beat Microsoft, it needs to slow down Microsoft's advance to keep it from dominating the Web.

These three competitions are unique, in that in each instance, only two major rivals are involved. In contrast, Samsung faces many competitors in the consumer electronics market, including five with higher market shares (and three of those rivals have more than twice Samsung's annual sales in this market). Nevertheless, Samsung established a goal to become the leader in this market by 2005. Just as Sony became a major player in the consumer electronics market with analog technology and the Trinitron color TV, Samsung is attempting to take the market with digital technology. Samsung executives believe that the change from analog to digital technology leveled the competitive playing field. The current battle is for "mind share" to be followed by the battle for market share.

SOURCES: P. Burrows, 2001, Face-off, *Business Week*, November 19, 104–110; H. Brown, 2001, Look out, Sony, *Forbes*, June 11, 96–101; D. Michaels, Airbus's 'Honest Abe' attitude adds fuel to rivalry with Boeing, *The Wall Street Journal Interactive*, http://interactive.wsj.com, April 3; J. Kynge, 2001, Fuji considers Chinese tie-up to rival Kodak, *Financial Times*, http://www.ft.com, February 27.

demonstrated by the commercial aircraft industry. The market for large aircraft is expected to decline or grow only slightly over the next few years. To expand market share, Boeing and Airbus will compete aggressively in terms of the introduction of new products, and product and service differentiation. Both firms are likely to win some and lose other battles. In early 2002, Airbus seemed to have an edge over Boeing in this market segment.

High Fixed Costs or High Storage Costs

When fixed costs account for a large part of total costs, companies try to maximize the use of their productive capacity. Doing so allows the firm to spread costs across a larger volume of output. However, when many firms attempt to maximize their productive capacity, excess capacity is created on an industry-wide basis. To then reduce inventories, individual companies typically cut the price of their product and offer rebates and other special discounts to customers. These practices, however, often intensify competition. The pattern of excess capacity at the industry level followed by intense rivalry at the firm level is observed frequently in industries with high storage costs. Perishable products, for example, lose their value rapidly with the passage of time. As their inventories grow, producers of perishable goods often use pricing strategies to sell products quickly.

Lack of Differentiation or Low Switching Costs

When buyers find a differentiated product that satisfies their needs, they frequently purchase the product loyally over time. Industries with many companies that have successfully differentiated their products have less rivalry, resulting in lower competition for individual firms.[98] However, when buyers view products as commodities (as products with few differentiated features or capabilities), rivalry intensifies. In these instances, buyers' purchasing decisions are based primarily on price and, to a lesser degree, service. Film for cameras is an example of a commodity. Thus, the competition between Fuji and Kodak is expected to be strong.

The effect of switching costs is identical to that described for differentiated products. The lower the buyers' switching costs, the easier it is for competitors to attract buyers through pricing and service offerings. High switching costs, however, at least partially insulate the firm from rivals' efforts to attract customers. Interestingly, the switching costs—such as pilot and mechanic training—are high in aircraft purchases, yet, the rivalry between Boeing and Airbus remains intense because the stakes for both are extremely high.

High Strategic Stakes

Competitive rivalry is likely to be high when it is important for several of the competitors to perform well in the market. For example, although it is diversified and is a market leader in other businesses, Samsung has targeted market leadership in the consumer electronics market. This market is quite important to Sony and other major competitors such as Hitachi, Matsushita, NEC, and Mitsubishi. Thus, we can expect substantial rivalry in this market over the next few years.

High strategic stakes can also exist in terms of geographic locations. For example, Japanese automobile manufacturers are committed to a significant presence in the U.S. marketplace. A key reason for this is that the United States is the world's single largest market for auto manufacturers' products. Because of the stakes involved in this country for Japanese and U.S. manufacturers, rivalry among firms in the U.S. and the global automobile industry is highly intense. It should be noted that while close proximity tends to promote greater rivalry, physically proximate competition has potentially positive benefits as well. For example, when competitors are located near each other, it is easier for suppliers to serve them and they can develop economies of scale that lead to lower production costs. Additionally, communications with key industry stakeholders such as suppliers are facilitated and more efficient when they are close to the firm.[99]

High Exit Barriers

Sometimes companies continue competing in an industry even though the returns on their invested capital are low or negative. Firms making this choice likely face high exit barriers, which include economic, strategic, and emotional factors causing companies to remain in an industry when the profitability of doing so is questionable. Common exit barriers are

- Specialized assets (assets with values linked to a particular business or location).
- Fixed costs of exit (such as labor agreements).
- Strategic interrelationships (relationships of mutual dependence, such as those between one business and other parts of a company's operations including shared facilities and access to financial markets).
- Emotional barriers (aversion to economically justified business decisions because of fear for one's own career, loyalty to employees, and so forth).
- Government and social restrictions (more common outside the United States, these restrictions often are based on government concerns for job losses and regional economic effects).

Interpreting Industry Analyses

Effective industry analyses are products of careful study and interpretation of data and information from multiple sources. A wealth of industry-specific data is available to be analyzed. Because of globalization, international markets and rivalries must be included in the firm's analyses. In fact, research shows that in some industries, international variables are more important than domestic ones as determinants of strategic competitiveness. Furthermore, because of the development of global markets, a country's borders no longer restrict industry structures. In fact, movement into international markets enhances the chances of success for new ventures as well as more established firms.[100]

Following study of the five forces of competition, the firm can develop the insights required to determine an industry's attractiveness in terms of its potential to earn adequate or superior returns on its invested capital. In general, the stronger competitive forces are, the lower the profit potential for an industry's firms. An unattractive industry has low entry barriers, suppliers and buyers with strong bargaining positions, strong competitive threats from product substitutes, and intense rivalry among competitors. These industry characteristics make it very difficult for firms to achieve

Samsung is competing with many other firms for the cell phone market, even as worldwide sales of new cell phones fell by 3.2 percent, from 412.7 million handsets in 2000 to 399.6 million in 2001—a steep decline from the annual 60 percent growth rate between 1996 and 2000. Sales were up in North America despite a mild recession in the United States. Finland's Nokia led all cell phone makers with a 35 percent market share, followed by Motorola Inc., Siemens AG, Ericcson, and Samsung.

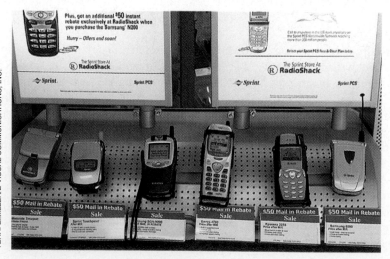

TERRI L.MILLER/E-VISUAL COMMUNICATIONS, INC.

strategic competitiveness and earn above-average returns. Alternatively, an attractive industry has high entry barriers, suppliers and buyers with little bargaining power, few competitive threats from product substitutes, and relatively moderate rivalry.[101]

Strategic Groups

A **strategic group** is a set of firms emphasizing similar strategic dimensions to use a similar strategy.

A set of firms emphasizing similar strategic dimensions to use a similar strategy is called a **strategic group**.[102] The competition between firms within a strategic group is greater than the competition between a member of a strategic group and companies outside that strategic group. Another way of saying this is that intra-strategic group competition is more intense than is inter-strategic group competition.

The extent of technological leadership, product quality, pricing policies, distribution channels, and customer service are examples of strategic dimensions that firms in a strategic group treat similarly. Describing patterns of competition within strategic groups is evidence suggesting that "organizations in a strategic group occupy similar positions in the market, offer similar goods to similar customers, and may also make similar choices about production technology and other organizational features."[103] Thus, membership in a particular strategic group defines the essential characteristics of the firm's strategy.[104]

The notion of strategic groups can be useful for analyzing an industry's competitive structure. Such analyses can be helpful in diagnosing competition, positioning, and the profitability of firms within an industry.[105] Research has found that strategic groups differ in performance, suggesting their importance.[106] Interestingly, research also suggests that strategic group membership remains relatively stable over time, making analysis easier and more useful.[107]

Using strategic groups to understand an industry's competitive structure requires the firm to plot companies' competitive actions and competitive responses along strategic dimensions such as pricing decisions, product quality, distribution channels, and so forth. Doing this shows the firm how certain companies are competing similarly in terms of how they use similar strategic dimensions. For example, there are unique radio markets because consumers prefer different music formats and programming (news radio, talk radio, and so forth). Typically, a radio format is created through choices made regarding music or nonmusic style, scheduling, and announcer style.[108] It is estimated that approximately 30 different radio formats exist, suggesting that there are 30 strategic groups in this industry. The strategies within each of the 30 groups are similar, while the strategies across the total set of strategic groups are dissimilar. Thus, firms could increase their understanding of competition in the commercial radio industry by plotting companies' actions and responses in terms of important strategic dimensions such as those we have mentioned.

Strategic groups have several implications. First, because firms within a group offer similar products to the same customers, the competitive rivalry among them can be intense. The more intense the rivalry, the greater is the threat to each firm's profitability. Second, the strengths of the five industry forces (the threats posed by new entrants, the power of suppliers, the power of buyers, product substitutes, and the intensity of rivalry among competitors) differ across strategic groups. Third, the closer the strategic groups are in terms of their strategies, the greater is the likelihood of rivalry between the groups.

Competitor Analysis

The competitor environment is the final part of the external environment requiring study. Competitor analysis focuses on each company against whom a firm directly competes. For example, Fuji and Kodak, Airbus and Boeing, and Sun Microsystems and Microsoft should be keenly interested in understanding each other's objectives, strategies, assumptions, and capabilities. Furthermore, intense rivalry creates a strong need to understand competitors. In a competitor analysis, the firm seeks to understand

- What drives the competitor, as shown by its *future objectives.*
- What the competitor is doing and can do, as revealed by its *current strategy.*
- What the competitor believes about the industry, as shown by its *assumptions.*
- What the competitor's capabilities are, as shown by its *capabilities* (its strengths and weaknesses).[109]

Information about these four dimensions helps the firm prepare an anticipated response profile for each competitor (see Figure 2.3). Thus, the results of an effective competitor analysis help a firm understand, interpret, and predict its competitors' actions and responses.

Critical to an effective competitor analysis is gathering data and information that can help the firm understand its competitors' intentions and the strategic implications resulting from them.[110] Useful data and information combine to form **competitor intelligence:** the set of data and information the firm gathers to better understand and better anticipate competitors' objectives, strategies, assumptions, and capabilities. In competitor analysis, the firm should gather intelligence not only about its competitors, but also regarding public policies in countries across the world. Intelligence about public policies "provides an early warning of threats and opportunities emerging from the global public policy environment, and analyzes how they will affect the achievement of the company's strategy."[111]

Competitor intelligence is the set of data and information the firm gathers to better understand and better anticipate competitors' objectives, strategies, assumptions, and capabilities.

Figure 2.3   Competitor Analysis Components

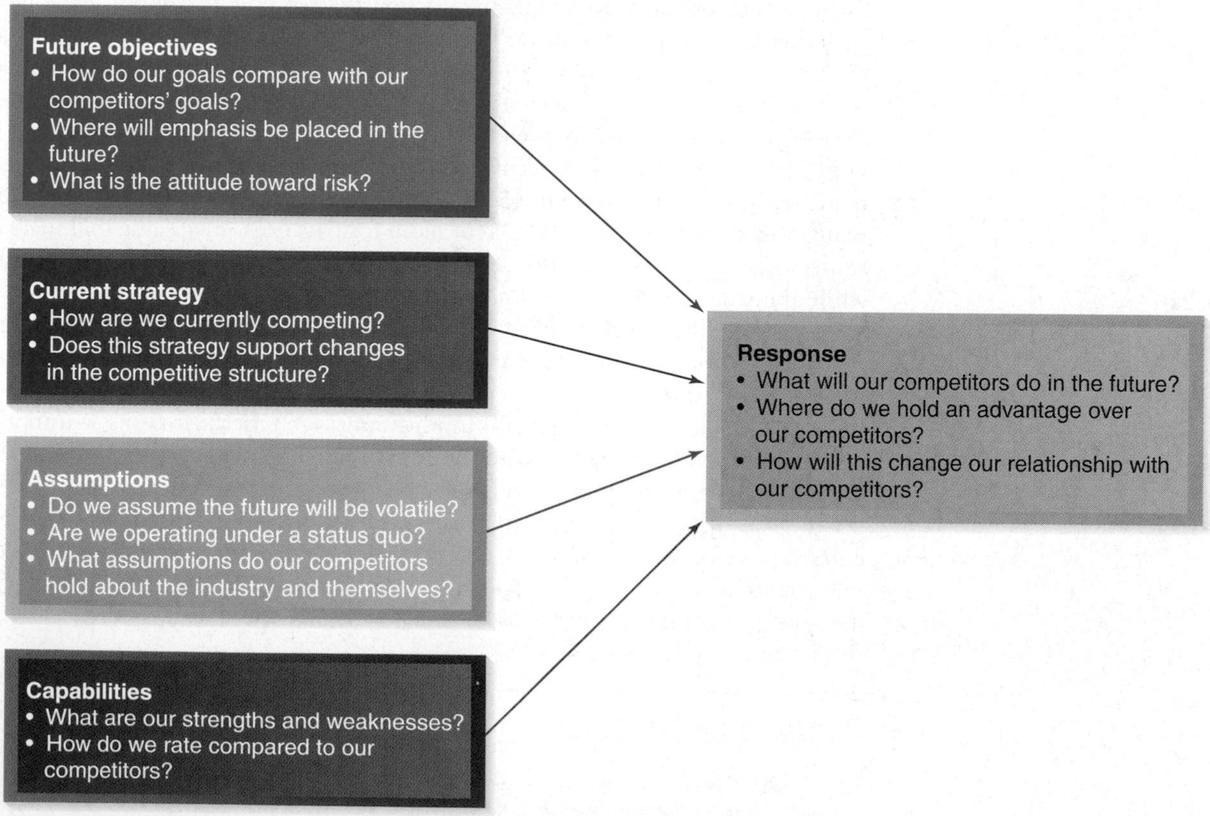

Future objectives
- How do our goals compare with our competitors' goals?
- Where will emphasis be placed in the future?
- What is the attitude toward risk?

Current strategy
- How are we currently competing?
- Does this strategy support changes in the competitive structure?

Assumptions
- Do we assume the future will be volatile?
- Are we operating under a status quo?
- What assumptions do our competitors hold about the industry and themselves?

Capabilities
- What are our strengths and weaknesses?
- How do we rate compared to our competitors?

Response
- What will our competitors do in the future?
- Where do we hold an advantage over our competitors?
- How will this change our relationship with our competitors?

Through effective competitive and public policy intelligence, the firm gains the insights needed to create a competitive advantage and to increase the quality of the strategic decisions it makes when deciding how to compete against its rivals. Claire Hart, CEO of Factiva, a news and information service, believes that competitor intelligence helped her firm to move from the number three to the number two position in her industry. Additionally, she states that competitor intelligence will play an important role in her firm's efforts to reach its objective of becoming the top firm in the industry.[112]

Firms should follow generally accepted ethical practices in gathering competitor intelligence. Industry associations often develop lists of these practices that firms can adopt. Practices considered both legal and ethical include (1) obtaining publicly available information (such as court records, competitors' help-wanted advertisements, annual reports, financial reports of publicly held corporations, and Uniform Commercial Code filings), and (2) attending trade fairs and shows to obtain competitors' brochures, view their exhibits, and listen to discussions about their products.

In contrast, certain practices (including blackmail, trespassing, eavesdropping, and stealing drawings, samples, or documents) are widely viewed as unethical and often are illegal. To protect themselves from digital fraud or theft that occurs through competitors breaking into their employees' PCs, some companies buy insurance to protect against PC hacking. Chubb's new ForeFront plan, for example, offers up to $10 million coverage against digital fraud, theft, and extortion. Cigna's information asset protection division sells anti-hacker policies that cover up to 10 percent of a firm's revenues. The number of clients making claims seems to suggest the value of having one of these policies.[113]

Some competitor intelligence practices may be legal, but a firm must decide whether they are also ethical, given the image it desires as a corporate citizen. Especially with electronic transmissions, the line between legal and ethical practices can be difficult to determine. For example, a firm may develop website addresses that are very similar to those of its competitors and thus occasionally receive e-mail transmissions that were intended for its competitors. According to legal experts, the legality of this "e-mail snagging" remains unclear.[114] Nonetheless, the practice is an example of the challenges companies face when deciding how to gather intelligence about competitors while simultaneously determining what to do to prevent competitors from learning too much about them.

In 2001, Procter & Gamble (P&G) notified Unilever that its own rules regarding gathering intelligence on competitors were violated when obtaining information on Unilever practices. Thus, P&G returned over 80 documents that were taken from Unilever's trash bins. The two firms then negotiated a potential settlement. Unilever wanted P&G to delay several of its planned new product launches, but P&G resisted. Moreover, both firms had to take special care in the negotiations not to violate antitrust laws thereby spurring regulators to take actions. Therefore, for several reasons, competitive intelligence must be handled with sensitivity.[115]

Open discussions of intelligence-gathering techniques can help a firm to ensure that people understand its convictions to follow ethical practices for gathering competitor intelligence. An appropriate guideline for competitor intelligence practices is to respect the principles of common morality and the right of competitors not to reveal certain information about their products, operations, and strategic intentions.[116]

Despite the importance of studying competitors, evidence suggests that only a relatively small percentage of firms use formal processes to collect and disseminate competitive intelligence. Beyond this, some firms forget to analyze competitors' future objectives as they try to understand their current strategies, assumptions, and capabilities, which will yield incomplete insights about those competitors.[117]

- The firm's external environment is challenging and complex. Because of the external environment's effect on performance, the firm must develop the skills required to identify opportunities and threats existing in that environment.

- The external environment has three major parts: (1) the general environment (elements in the broader society that affect industries and their firms), (2) the industry environment (factors that influence a firm, its competitive actions and responses, and the industry's profit potential, and (3) the competitor environment (in which the firm analyzes each major competitor's future objectives, current strategies, assumptions, and capabilities).

- The external environmental analysis process has four steps: scanning, monitoring, forecasting, and assessing. Through environmental analyses, the firm identifies opportunities and threats.

- The general environment has six segments: demographic, economic, political/legal, sociocultural, technological, and global. For each segment, the firm wants to determine the strategic relevance of environmental changes and trends.

- Compared to the general environment, the industry environment has a more direct effect on the firm's strategic actions.

The five forces model of competition includes the threat of entry, the power of suppliers, the power of buyers, product substitutes, and the intensity of rivalry among competitors. By studying these forces, the firm finds a position in an industry where it can influence the forces in its favor or where it can buffer itself from the power of the forces in order to increase its ability to earn above-average returns.

- Industries are populated with different strategic groups. A strategic group is a collection of firms that follow similar strategies along similar dimensions. Competitive rivalry is greater within a strategic group than it is between strategic groups.

- Competitor analysis informs the firm about the future objectives, current strategies, assumptions, and capabilities of the companies with whom it competes directly.

- Different techniques are used to create competitor intelligence: the set of data, information, and knowledge that allows the firm to better understand its competitors and thereby predict their likely strategic and tactical actions. Firms should use only legal and ethical practices to gather intelligence. The Internet enhances firms' capabilities to gather insights about competitors and their strategic intentions.

Review Questions

1. Why is it important for a firm to study and understand the external environment?

2. What are the differences between the general environment and the industry environment? Why are these differences important?

3. What is the external environmental analysis process? What does the firm want to learn as it scans, monitors, forecasts, and assesses its external environment?

4. What are the six segments of the general environment? Explain the differences among them.

5. How do the five forces of competition in an industry affect its profit potential? Explain.

6. What is a strategic group? Of what value is knowledge of the firm's strategic group in formulating that firm's strategy?

7. What is the importance of collecting and interpreting data and information about competitors? What practices should a firm use to gather competitor intelligence and why?

Environmental Analysis

The results of an environmental analysis provide crucial knowledge for the firm's strategic decisions. The following activities can be worked in small groups or individually and then discussed in class.

General Environment Activity. As the manager of environmental analysis for an up-and-coming competitor to Wal-Mart, you've been asked to identify two trends for each of the segments of the general environment and to evaluate the potential impact of those trends on the firm's future strategy. Provide your findings in the table below.

Segment	Trend	Impact on Strategy
Demographic	1.	
	2.	
Economic	1.	
	2.	
Political/legal	1.	
	2.	
Sociocultural	1.	
	2.	
Technological	1.	
	2.	
Global	1.	
	2.	

Industry environment activity. You've also been asked to provide a brief analysis of the industrial environment and the five forces model of competition. Indicate in the following table the strength (high, medium, low) of each force on your industry and its impact on your firm's strategy.

Five Forces Model	Strength	Impact on Strategy
Bargaining power of suppliers		
Bargaining power of buyers		
Threats of substitute products		
Rivalry of competing firms		
Threat of new entrants		

Notes

1. J. Song, 2002, Firm capabilities and technology ladders: Sequential foreign direct investments of Japanese electronics firms in East Asia, *Strategic Management Journal*, 23: 191–210; D. J. Ketchen, Jr. & T. B. Palmer, 1999, Strategic responses to poor organizational performance: A test of competing perspectives, *Journal of Management*, 25: 683–706; V. P. Rindova & C. J. Fombrun, 1999, Constructing competitive advantage: The role of firm-constituent interactions, *Strategic Management Journal*, 20: 691–710.

2. P. Chattopadhyay, W. H. Glick, & G. P. Huber, 2001, Organizational actions in response to threats and opportunities, *Academy of Management Journal*, 44: 937–955.

3. H. Lee & M. A. Hitt, 2002, Top management team composition and characteristics as predictors of strategic flexibility, working paper, University of Connecticut; A. Edgecliffe-Johnson, 2001, Southwest braced to weather trouble, *Financial Times*, http://www.ft.com, October 2; L. Zuckerman, 2001, With seats empty, airlines cut fares to bargain levels, *The New York Times*, http://www.nytimes.com, December 18.

4. R. J. Herbold, 2002, Inside Microsoft: Balancing creativity and discipline, *Harvard Business Review*, 80(1): 73–79; C. M. Grimm & K. G. Smith, 1997, *Strategy As Action: Industry Rivalry and Coordination*, Cincinnati: South-Western; C. J. Fombrun, 1992, *Turning Point: Creating Strategic Change in Organizations*, New York: McGraw-Hill, 13.

5. J. M. Mezias, 2002, Identifying liabilities of foreignness and strategies to minimize their effects: The case of labor lawsuit judgments in the United States, *Strategic Management Journal*, 23: 229–244.

6. R. M. Kanter, 2002, Strategy as improvisational theater, *MIT Sloan Management Review*, 43(2): 76–81; S. A. Zahra, A. P. Nielsen, & W. C. Bogner, 1999, Corporate entrepreneurship, knowledge, and competence development, *Entrepreneurship: Theory and Practice*, 23 (3): 169–189.

7. M. A. Hitt, J. E. Ricart I Costa, & R. D. Nixon, 1998, The new frontier, in M. A. Hitt, J. E. Ricart I Costa, & R. D. Nixon (eds.), *Managing Strategically in an Interconnected World*, Chichester: John Wiley & Sons, 1–12.

8. S. A. Zahra & G. George, 2002, International entrepreneurship: The current status of the field and future research agenda, in M. A. Hitt, R. D. Ireland, S. M. Camp, & D. L. Sexton (eds.), *Strategic Entrepreneurship: Creating a New Mindset*, Oxford, U.K.: Blackwell Publishers, 255–288; W. C. Bogner & P. Bansal, 1998, Controlling unique knowledge development as the basis of sustained high performance, in M. A. Hitt, J. E. Ricart I Costa, & R. D. Nixon (eds.), *Managing Strategically in an Interconnected World*, Chichester: John Wiley & Sons, 167–184.

9. L. Fahey, 1999, *Competitors,* New York: John Wiley & Sons; B. A. Walters & R. L. Priem, 1999, Business strategy and CEO intelligence acquisition, *Competitive Intelligence Review*, 10(2): 15–22.

10. R. D. Ireland & M. A. Hitt, 1999, Achieving and maintaining strategic competitiveness in the 21st century: The role of strategic leadership, *Academy of Management Executive*, 13(1): 43–57; M. A. Hitt, B. W. Keats, & S. M. DeMarie, 1998, Navigating in the new competitive landscape: Building strategic flexibility and competitive advantage in the 21st century, *Academy of Management Executive*, 12(4): 22–42.

11. J. K. Sebenius, 2002, The hidden challenge of cross-border negotiations, *Harvard Business Review*, 80(3): 76–85; J. Kay, 1999, Strategy and the delusion of grand designs, Mastering Strategy (Part One), *Financial Times*, September 27, 2.

12. R. Karlgaard, 1999, Digital rules: Technology and the new economy, *Forbes*, May 17, 43.

13. 2000, GE Overview, General Electric home page, http://www.ge.com, January 12.

14. V. Prior, 1999, The language of competitive intelligence: Part four, *Competitive Intelligence Review*, 10(1): 84–87.

15. A. Berenson & R. A. Oppel, Jr., 2001, Once mighty Enron strains under scrutiny, *The New York Times*, http://www.nytimes.com, October 28; C. H. Deutsch, 2001, Polaroid, deep in debt since 1988, files for bankruptcy, *The New York Times*, http://www.nytimes.com, October 13.

16. G. Young, 1999, "Strategic value analysis" for competitive advantage, *Competitive Intelligence Review*, 10(2): 52–64.

17. M. A. Hitt, R. D. Ireland, S. M. Camp, & D. L. Sexton, 2001, Strategic entrepreneurship: Entrepreneurial strategies for wealth creation, *Strategic Management Journal*, 22(Special Summer Issue): 479–491.

18. L. Rosenkopf & A. Nerkar, 2001, Beyond local search: Boundary-spanning exploration, and impact in the optical disk industry, *Strategic Management Journal*, 22: 287–306.

19. D. F. Kuratko, R. D. Ireland, & J. S. Hornsby, 2001, Improving firm performance through entrepreneurial actions: Acordia's corporate entrepreneurship strategy, *Academy of Management Executive*, 15(4): 60–71; D. S. Elenkov, 1997, Strategic uncertainty and environmental scanning: The case for institutional influences on scanning behavior, *Strategic Management Journal*, 18: 287–302.

20. K. M. Eisenhardt, 2002, Has strategy changed? *MIT Sloan Management Review*, 43 (2): 88–91; I. Goll & A. M. A. Rasheed, 1997, Rational decision-making and firm performance: The moderating role of environment, *Strategic Management Journal*, 18: 583–591.

21. R. Aggarwal, 1999, Technology and globalization as mutual reinforcers in business: Reorienting strategic thinking for the new millennium, *Management International Review*, 39(2): 83–104; M. Yasai-Ardekani & P. C. Nystrom, 1996, Designs for environmental scanning systems: Tests of contingency theory, *Management Science*, 42: 187–204.

22. R. Donkin, 1999, Too young to retire, *Financial Times*, July 2, 9.

23. B. Richards, 2001, Following the crumbs, *The Wall Street Journal*, http://interactive.wsj.com, October 29.

24. Fahey, *Competitors*, 71–73.

25. P. Yip, 1999, The road to wealth, *Dallas Morning News*, August 2, D1, D3.

26. Y. Luo & S. H. Park, 2001, Strategic alignment and performance of market-seeking MNCs in China, *Strategic Management Journal*, 22: 141–155.

27. I. M. Jawahar & G. L. McLaughlin, 2001, Toward a prescriptive stakeholder theory: An organizational life cycle approach, *Academy of Management Review*, 26: 397–414.

28. M. Song & M. M. Montoya-Weiss, 2001, The effect of perceived technological uncertainty on Japanese new product development, *Academy of Management Journal*, 44: 61–80.

29. H. Yli-Renko, E. Autio, & H. J. Sapienza, 2001, Social capital, knowledge acquisition, and knowledge exploitation in young technologically-based firms, *Strategic Management Journal*, 22(special Summer Issue): 587–613.

30. Fahey, *Competitors*.

31. 2001, Weathering the storm: Dow Chemical, *Forbes*, http://www.forbes.com, June 14.

32. Fahey, *Competitors*, 75–77.

33. L. Fahey & V. K. Narayanan, 1986, *Macroenvironmental Analysis for Strategic Management*, St. Paul, MN: West Publishing Company, 58.

34. D. Fishburn, 1999, *The World in 1999, The Economist* Publications, 9; Six billion . . . and counting, 1999, *Time*, October 4, 16.

35. J. F. Coates, J. B. Mahaffie, & A. Hines, 1997, *2025: Scenarios of US and Global Society Reshaped by Science and Technology*, Greensboro, NC: Oakhill Press.

36. R. Poe & C. L. Courter, 1999, The next baby boom, *Across the Board*, May, 1; 1999, Trends and forecasts for the next 25 years, World Future Society, 3.

37. 2001, Fewer seniors in the 1990s, *Business Week*, May 28, 30.

38. M. Peterson & M. Freudenheim, 2001, Drug giant to introduce discount drug plan for the elderly, *The New York Times*, http://www.nytimes.com, October 3.

39. D. Stipp, 1999, Hell no, we won't go! *Fortune*, July 19, 102–108; G. Colvin, 1997, How to beat the boomer rush, *Fortune*, August 18, 59–63.

40. J. MacIntyre, 1999, Figuratively speaking, *Across the Board*, November/December, 15.

41. Colvin, How to beat the boomer rush, 60.

42. 1999, U.S. Department of Labor, Demographic change and the future workforce, *Futurework*, November 8, http://www.dol.gov.

43. P. R. Drucker, 2002, They're not employees, they're people, *Harvard Business Review*, 80(2): 70–77.

44. G. Dessler, 1999, How to earn your employees' commitment, *Academy of Management Executive*, 13(2): 58–67; S. Finkelstein & D. C. Hambrick, 1996, *Strategic Leadership: Top Executives and Their Effect on Organizations*, Minneapolis: West.

45. L. H. Pelled, K. M. Eisenhardt, & K. R. Xin, 1999, Exploring the black box: An analysis of work group diversity, conflict, and performance, *Administrative Science Quarterly*, 44: 1–28.

46. E. S. Rubenstein, 1999, Inequality, *Forbes*, November 1, 158-160.

47. Fahey & Narayanan, *Macroenvironmental Analysis*, 105.

48. A. Kutczynski, 2001, Chief abruptly quits magazine group, *The New York Times*, http://www.nytimes.com, August 1; 2001, Update 1-Greenspan says U.S. banks asset quality eroding, *Forbes*, http://www.forbes.com, June 20.

49. J. E. Schrempp, 1999, The world in 1999, Neighbours across the pond, *The Economist*, 28.

50. J. L. Hilsenrath, 2001, Shock waves keep spreading, changing the outlook for cars, hotels—even for cola, *The Wall Street Journal*, http://interactive.wsj.com, October 9.

51. G. Keim, 2001, Business and public policy: Competing in the political marketplace, in M. A. Hitt, R. E. Freeman, J. S. Harrison (Eds.), *Handbook of Strategic Management*, Oxford, U.K.: Blackwell Publishers, 583–601.

52. A. J. Hillman & M. A. Hitt, 1999, Corporate political strategy formulation: A model of approach, participation, and strategy decisions, *Academy of Management Review*, 24: 825–842.

53. M. Carson, 1998, *Global Competitiveness Quarterly*, March 9, 1.

54. R. L. Riley, 1999, Will Uncle Sam trump Internet gamblers? *The Wall Street Journal*, May 14, A14.

55. 1999, Cyberspace: Who will make the rules? *Business Week*, March 22, 30D–30F.

56. J. MacIntyre, 1999, Figuratively speaking, *Across the Board*, May, 11.

57. A. R. Varey & G. Lynn, 1999, Americans save for retirement, *USA Today*, November 16, B1.

58. G. F. Will, 1999, The primacy of culture, *Newsweek*, January 18, 64.

59. 1999, Woman power, *Worth Magazine*, September, 100–101.

60. B. Beck, 1999, The world in 1999, Executive, thy name is woman, *The Economist*, 89; P. Thomas, 1995, Success at a huge personal cost: Comparing women around the world, *The Wall Street Journal*, July 26, B1.

61. R. Taylor, 1999, Pay gap between the sexes widest in W. Europe, *Financial Times*, June 29, 9.

62. J. Raymond, 2001, Defining women: Does the Census Bureau undercount female entrepreneurs? *Business Week Small Biz*, May 21, 12.

63. C. A. Bartlett & S. Ghoshal, 2002, Building competitive advantage through people, *MIT Sloan Management Review*, 43(2): 33–41.

64. 2001,The American metropolis at century's end: Past and future influences, *The Fannie Mae Foundation Survey*.

65. A. Afuah, 2002, Mapping technological capabilities into product markets and competitive advantage: The case of cholesterol drugs, *Strategic Management Journal*, 23: 171–179; X. M. Song, C. A. Di Benedetto, & Y. L. Zhao, 1999, Pioneering advantages in manufacturing and service industries, *Strategic Management Journal*, 20: 811–836.

66. 1999, Business ready for Internet revolution, *Financial Times*, May 21, 17.

67. G. Rifkin, 2001, New economy: Re-evaluating online strategies, *The New York Times*, http://www.nytimes.com, June 25.

68. M. Dell, 1999, The world in 1999, The virtual firm, *The Economist*, 99.

69. 2001, Technology forecast: 2001–2003, PricewaterhouseCoopers, Menlo Park, CA.

70. M. A. Hitt, R. D. Ireland, & H. Lee, 2000, Technological learning, knowledge management, firm growth and performance, *Journal of Technology and Engineering Management*, 17: 231–246.

71. S. Zahra, R. D. Ireland, I. Gutierrez, & M. A. Hitt, 2000, Privatization and entrepreneurial transformation: Emerging issues and a future research agenda, *Academy of Management Review*, 25: 509–524.

72. A. K. Gupta, V. Govindarajan, & A. Malhotra, 1999, Feedback-seeking behavior within multinational corporations, *Strategic Management Journal*, 20: 205–222.

73. 1999, China and the U.S. sign trade deal, clearing hurdle for WTO entry, *The Wall Street Journal*, www.interactive.wsj.com, November 15.

74. J. Kynge, 2001, Murdoch achieves Chinese goal with Star TV deal, *Financial Times*, http://www.ft.com, December 19.

75. R. D. Ireland, M. A. Hitt, S. M. Camp, & D. L. Sexton, 2001, Integrating entrepreneurship and strategic management actions to create firm wealth, *Academy of Management Executive*, 15(1): 49–63.

76. J. W. Lu & P. W. Beamish, 2001, The internationalization and performance of SMEs, *Strategic Management Journal*, 22(special Summer Issue): 565–586.

77. M. Subramaniam & N. Venkatraman, 2001, Determinants of transnational new product development capability: Testing the influence of transferring and deploying tacit overseas knowledge, *Strategic Management Journal*, 22: 359–378; P. J. Lane, J. E. Salk, & M. A. Lyles, 2001, Absorptive capacity, learning and performance in international joint ventures, *Strategic Management Journal*, 22: 1139–1161.

78. S. H. Park & Y. Luo, 2001, Guanxi and organizational dynamics: Organizational networking in Chinese firms, *Strategic Management Journal*, 22: 455–477; M. A. Hitt, M. T. Dacin, B. B. Tyler, & D. Park, 1997, Understanding the differences in Korean and U.S. executives' strategic orientations, *Strategic Management Journal*, 18: 159–167.

79. T. Khanna & K. Palepu, 1999, The right way to restructure conglomerates in emerging markets, *Harvard Business Review*, 77(4): 125–134; Hitt, Dacin, Tyler, & Park, Understanding the differences.

80. Park & Y. Luo, Guanxi and organizational dynamics.

81. M. A. Hitt, H. Lee, & E. Yucel, 2002, The importance of social capital to the management of multinational enterprises: Relational capital among Asian and Western firms, *Asia Pacific Journal of Management*, in press.

82. 2002, Global Crossing denies resemblance to Enron, *Richmond Times Dispatch*, March 22, B15; S. Romero, 2001, Global crossing looks overseas for financing, *The New York Times*, http://www.nytimes.com, December 20; T. Burt, 2001, DaimlerChrysler in talks with Kuwaiti investors, *Financial Times*, http://www.ft.com, February 11.

83. J. Fuerbringer & R. W. Stevenson, 2001, No bailout is planned for Argentina, *The New York Times*, http://www.nytimes.com, July 14; K. L. Newman, 2000, Organizational transformation during institutional upheaval, *Academy of Management Review*, 25: 602–619.

84. M. A. Carpenter & J. W. Fredrickson, 2001, Top management teams, global strategic posture and the moderating role of uncertainty, *Academy of Management Journal*, 44: 533–545.

85. Y. E. Spanos & S. Lioukas, 2001, An examination into the causal logic of rent generation: Contrasting Porter's competitive strategy framework and the resource based perspective, *Strategic Management Journal*, 22: 907–934.

86. S. Zaheer & A. Zaheer, 2001, Market microstructure in a global b2b network, *Strategic Management Journal*, 22: 859–873.

87. Hitt, Ricart, Costa, & Nixon, The new frontier.

88. Y. Pan & P. S. K. Chi, 1999, Financial performance and survival of multinational corporations in China, *Strategic Management Journal*, 20: 359–374; G. R. Brooks, 1995, Defining market boundaries, *Strategic Management Journal*, 16: 535–549.

89. P. A. Geroski, 1999, Early warning of new rivals, *Sloan Management Review*, 40(3): 107–116.

90. K. C. Robinson & P. P. McDougall, 2001, Entry barriers and new venture performance: A comparison of universal and contingency approaches, *Strategic Management Journal*, 22(special Summer Issue): 659–685.

91. R. Makadok, 1999, Interfirm differences in scale economies and the evolution of market shares, *Strategic Management Journal*, 20: 935–952.

92. T. McGinnis, 2001, Improving free cash flow, *Forbes*, http://www.forbes.com, December 21.

93. R. Wise & P. Baumgartner, 1999, Go downstream: The new profit imperative in manufacturing, *Harvard Business Review*, 77(5): 133–141; J. H. Gilmore & B. J. Pine, II, 1997, The four faces of mass customization, *Harvard Business Review*, 75(1): 91–101.

94. P. Spiegel, 2001, Senator attacks 'protectionist' EU over GE deal, *Financial Times*, http://www.ft.com, June 21.

95. C. Dawson, 2001, Machete time: In a cost-cutting war with Nissan, Toyota leans on suppliers, *Business Week*, April 9, 42–43.

96. G. Khermouch, 2001, Grown-up drinks for tender taste buds, *Business Week*, March 5, 96.

97. T. Noda & D. J. Collies, 2001, The evolution of intraindustry firm heterogeneity: Insights from a process study, *Academy of Management Journal*, 44: 897–925.

98. D. L. Deephouse, 1999, To be different, or to be the same? It's a question (and theory) of strategic balance, *Strategic Management Journal*, 20: 147–166.

99. W. Chung & A. Kalnins, 2001, Agglomeration effects and performance: Test of the Texas lodging industry, *Strategic Management Journal*, 22: 969–988.

100. W. Kuemmerle, 2001, Home base and knowledge management in international ventures, *Journal of Business Venturing*, 17: 99–122; G. Lorenzoni & A. Lipparini, 1999, The leveraging of interfirm relationships as a distinctive organizational capability: A longitudinal study, *Strategic Management Journal*, 20: 317–338.

101. M. E. Porter, 1980, *Competitive Strategy*, New York: Free Press.

102. M. S. Hunt, 1972, Competition in the major home appliance industry, 1960–1970 (doctoral dissertation, Harvard University); Porter, *Competitive Strategy*, 129.

103. H. R. Greve, 1999, Managerial cognition and the mimetic adoption of market positions: What you see is what you do, *Strategic Management Journal*, 19: 967–988.

104. R. K. Reger & A. S. Huff, 1993, Strategic groups: A cognitive perspective, *Strategic Management Journal*, 14: 103–123.

105. M. Peteraf & M. Shanely, 1997, Getting to know you: A theory of strategic group identity, *Strategic Management Journal*, 18(Special Issue):165–186.

106. A. Nair & S. Kotha, 2001, Does group membership matter? Evidence from the Japanese steel industry, *Strategic Management Journal*, 22: 221–235.

107. J. D. Osborne, C. I. Stubbart, & A. Ramaprasad, 2001, Strategic groups and competitive enactment: A study of dynamic relationships between mental models and performance, *Strategic Management Journal*, 22: 435–454.

108. Greve, Managerial cognition, 972–973.

109. Porter, *Competitive Strategy*, 49.

110. P. M. Norman, R. D. Ireland, K. W. Artz, & M. A. Hitt, 2000, Acquiring and using competitive intelligence in entrepreneurial teams. Paper presented at the Academy of Management, Toronto, Canada.

111. C. S. Fleisher, 1999, Public policy competitive intelligence, *Competitive Intelligence Review*, 10(2): 24.

112. 2001, Fuld & Co., CEO Interview: Claire Hart, President and CEO, Factiva, http://www.dowjones.com, April 4.

113. V. Drucker, 1999, Is your computer a sitting duck during a deal? *Mergers & Acquisitions*, July/August, 25–28; J. Hodges, 1999, Insuring your PC against hackers, *Fortune*, May 24, 280.

114. M. Moss, 1999, Inside the game of e-mail hijacking, *The Wall Street Journal*, November 9, B1, B4.

115. A. Jones, 2001, P&G to seek new resolution of spy dispute, *Financial Times*, http://www.ft.com, September 4.

116. J. H. Hallaq & K. Steinhorst, 1994, Business intelligence methods: How ethical? *Journal of Business Ethics*, 13: 787–794.

117. L. Fahey, 1999, Competitor scenarios: Projecting a rival's marketplace strategy, *Competitive Intelligence Review*, 10(2): 65–85.

Chapter Three

The Internal Environment: Resources, Capabilities, and Core Competencies

Knowledge Objectives

Studying this chapter should provide you with the strategic management knowledge needed to:

1. Explain the need for firms to study and understand their internal environment.

2. Define value and discuss its importance.

3. Describe the differences between tangible and intangible resources.

4. Define capabilities and discuss how they are developed.

5. Describe four criteria used to determine whether resources and capabilities are core competencies.

6. Explain how value chain analysis is used to identify and evaluate resources and capabilities.

7. Define outsourcing and discuss the reasons for its use.

8. Discuss the importance of preventing core competencies from becoming core rigidities.

Reputation as a Source of Competitive Advantage

Reputation is defined as the evaluation of a firm by its stakeholders in terms of respect, knowledge or awareness, and emotional or affective regard. A firm's reputation is an intangible resource upon which the company can build capabilities and ultimately core competencies. A company's reputation is also very important in regard to the valuation of the company. The reputation of Coca-Cola, for example, has been valued at $52 billion. Similarly, the reputations of Gillette, Eastman Kodak, Campbell Soup, and Wrigley's Gum have been valued at $12 billion, $11 billion, $9 billion, and $4 billion, respectively.

Because reputation has been such a distinguishing intangible resource, many firms have tried to build perceptual measures of this asset that provide a signal to rivals and stakeholders of the competitive value of their reputations. Each year several periodicals publish rankings of firms based on reputation. For instance, *Fortune* surveys 10,000 executives, directors, and securities analysts to develop its America's Most Admired Companies list (see Table 3.1). The *Financial Times* World's Most Respected Companies survey has an exclusive emphasis on peer evaluation—its ratings are based on evaluations by peer CEOs. Other services, including those provided by Burson-Marsteller, Delahaye Medialink, the Reputation Institute, and Corporate Branding LLC, use various approaches to rank their clients' reputations. Each ranking service maintains that its ranking provides a unique and valuable perspective.

During his two decades as GE's CEO, Jack Welch (left) guided the firm to consistent growth and had a legendary reputation for his leadership style. Jeff Immelt (right) took over from Welch on September 10, 2001, and faced the toughest economy in 20 years, skepticism about financial reporting, and uncertainty. He quickly responded by tightening costs, providing full disclosure in reporting, and reaching out to the customer. "This is not just a job," Immelt says. "This is a passion. This is my life."

Charles Fombrun and colleagues have argued that many ranking services are in the business of public relations rather than academic measurement. In their research, Fombrun and his colleagues use 20 attributes to develop a "reputational quotient." These attributes are divided into six reputation categories: emotional appeal, social responsibility, financial performance, vision and leadership, workplace environment, and products and services.

A firm can develop intangible distinctions between itself from its rivals within each reputational category. These value-creating distinctions help the firm develop the type of reputation that can become a core competence.

Southwest Airlines (further discussed in Chapter 4) has an *emotional appeal* based on its reputation for being a maverick in the rather commodity-like airlines industry. Since cofounder and now retired CEO Herb Kelleher took over in 1978, the company has not lost money in any year. While fare wars, recessions, oil crises, and other disasters have plagued the industry at large and created massive losses for larger airlines such as Delta, United, and American, Southwest's reputation has helped it to sustain its competitive advantage during difficult industry cycles.

Many firms have built their reputations by emphasizing *social responsibility*. The Body Shop, 3M, and DuPont are all firms whose environmental expenditures created an environmentally based competitive advantage. On the other hand, a firm's reputation and image can both suffer when it is involved in a disaster. Exxon lost its reputation in the area of social responsibility following the Valdez oil tanker disaster, for example, and it faced a long road back to regain it. Firestone tire failures on Ford's Explorers hurt the reputations of both Ford and Firestone.

Under former CEO Jack Welch, General Electric (GE) enjoyed consistently high *financial performance* over a number of years and, in the process, built a reputation for steady value creation for its shareholders. It will be interesting to see if GE retains its reputation as a competitive advantage under the leadership of new CEO, Jeffrey Immelt.

Welch also helped GE's reputation for its financial performance with his *vision* and *leadership*. Many of the corporations mentioned above also attribute their success to leaders who produced and communicated a strategic mission (see Chapter 1) to employees, fostering the implementation of the firm's strategic intent. Apple has risen, fallen, and risen again through various leaders, but Steven Jobs, in particular, has had a significant influence on Apple's fortunes over the years, as cofounder and CEO.

If a company can hire better-skilled people because of its reputation for building human capital, it will likely increase its "intellectual capital" (the sum of everything that everybody in the company knows) relative to other firms and enhance its reputation for its *workplace environment*.[1] Intellectual capital can provide competitive advantage for the firm as it competes against its rivals. Merck & Company has been voted as one of America's most admired companies in *Fortune*'s annual survey every year since the list's 1982 inception. Its employees have invented more new medicines than any other American pharmaceutical company. Merck's reputation for supporting the people who bring value-creating intellectual capital to the firm enables it to hire productive researchers, whose work contributes to Merck's success. But without a strong reputation for treating its employees fairly and professionally, it's unlikely that a firm will attract and retain the people required for it to be a leader in intellectual capital.

The most recognized reputational attribute is a firm's brand or trademark. Coca-Cola Company has one of the world's most famous—and some think most valuable—brands. Microsoft also has a strong brand. However, the brands for both companies have recently suffered damage to their reputations. Poor product quality in Europe undermined Coca-Cola's brand; for Microsoft, it's a continuing antitrust case. A strong reputation for a *product* or *service* takes years to develop, but this intangible asset can lose value quickly if the firm does not take care to address reputation threats that might reduce its value. Thus, firms must manage their reputations to build a strong base of value for this important intangible asset. Without appropriate attention to managing this resource, its value can dissipate rapidly.

SOURCES: M. Boyle, 2002, The shiniest reputations in tarnished times, *Fortune*, March 4, 70–72; G. Khermouch, 2002, What makes a boffo brand, *Business Week* (Special Issue), Spring, 20; A. Diba & L. Munoz, 2001, How long can they stay? *Fortune*, February 19, http://www.fortune.com; T. A. Stewart, 2001, Intellectual capital, *Fortune*, May 28, http://www.fortune.com; C. J. Fombrun, N. A. Gardberg, & M. J. Barnett, 2000, Opportunity platforms and safety nets: Corporate citizenship and reputational risk, *Business and Society Review*, 105(1): 85–106; D.L. Deephouse, 2000, Media reputation as a strategic resource: An integration of mass communication and resource-based theories, *Journal of Management*, 26: 1091–1112; C. Eidson & M. Master, 2000, Top ten . . . Most admired . . . Most respected; Who makes the call? *Across the Board*, 37(3): 16–22; P. M. Morgan & J. G. Covin, 2000, Environmental marketing: A source of reputational, competitive and financial advantage, *Journal of Business Ethics*, 23(3): 299–311; J. A. Petrick, R. F. Scherer, J. D. Brodzinski, J. F. Quinn, & M. F. Ainina, 1999, Global leadership skills and reputational capital: Intangible resources of sustainable competitive advantage, *Academy of Management Executive*, 13(1): 58–69.

The firms mentioned in the Opening Case have used their resources and capabilities (see Chapter 1) to create reputation as a source of competitive advantage. Organizations that rely on reputation as a competitive advantage want that advantage to be *sustainable*. Table 3.1 lists several firms that have sustained their reputations and the advantages associated with being rated as America's Most Admired Corporations by *Fortune* magazine. However, as discussed in the first two chapters, several factors in the global economy, including the rapid development of the Internet's capabilities, have made it increasingly difficult for firms to develop a competitive advantage that can be sustained for any period of time.[2] In these instances, firms try to create advantages that can be sustained longer than can others. Regardless of its sustainability, however, a sustainable competitive advantage is developed when firms use the strategic management process to implement strategies that uniquely use a firm's resources, capabilities, and core competencies.

The fact that "competitive advantage continues to provide the central agenda in strategy research"[3] highlights its importance. Competitive advantage research is critical because "resources are the foundation for strategy and (the) unique bundles of resources (that) generate competitive advantages leading to wealth creation."[4] To identify and successfully use their competitive advantages over time, firms think constantly about their strategic management process and how to increase the value it creates.[5] As this chapter's discussion indicates, firms achieve strategic competitiveness and earn above-average returns when their unique core competencies are effectively leveraged to take advantage of opportunities in the external environment.

Increasingly, people are a key source of competitive advantage as organizations compete in the global economy.[6] At Walt Disney Company, for example, the importance of intellectual capital has become increasingly apparent. Walt Disney Studios,

Table 3.1	*Fortune*'s Most Admired Corporate Rankings in 2001, 2000, and 1999

2001 The Top Ten	2000 The Top Ten	1999 The Top Ten
1. General Electric	1. General Electric	1. General Electric
2. Southwest Airlines	2. Cisco Systems	2. Microsoft
3. Wal-Mart Stores	3. Wal-Mart Stores	3. Dell Computer
4. Microsoft	4. Southwest Airlines	4. Cisco Systems
5. Berkshire Hathaway	5. Microsoft	5. Wal-Mart Stores
6. Home Depot	6. Home Depot	6. Southwest Airlines
7. Johnson & Johnson	7. Berkshire Hathaway	7. Berkshire Hathaway
8. FedEx	8. Charles Schwab	8. Intel
9. Citigroup	9. Intel	9. Home Depot
10. Intel	10. Dell Computer	10. Lucent Technologies

SOURCES: M. Boyle, 2002, The shiniest reputations in tarnished times, *Fortune,* March 4, 70–72; A. Diba & L. Munoz, 2001, America's most admired companies, *Fortune,* February 19, 64–66; G. Colvin, 2000, America's most admired companies, *Fortune,* February 21, 108–116.

which in recent years has led the movie industry in market share, is experiencing competitive difficulties. The company's top strategic leaders, Chairman Michael D. Eisner and President Peter Schneider, are focusing on greater financial discipline in the studio at a time when Disney is producing fewer movies and generating less impact on the market. This focus on cost cutting has lead to corporate downsizing and, many believe, the loss of some of the "creative fire" in Disney's animation division. The firm "has become . . . famous in recent years for the people who have left [the studio]." One of the firm's newer animated productions, "Atlantis: The Lost Empire," did not generate as much excitement in the marketplace as past Disney releases, which suggests that Disney's cost cutting and loss of important employees have seriously decreased the quality and quantity of that all-important resource, intellectual capital, and especially the creativity aspect of intellectual capital.[7]

Over time, the benefits of any firm's value-creating strategy can be duplicated by its competitors. In other words, all competitive advantages have a limited life.[8] The question of duplication is not *if* it will happen, but *when.* In general, the sustainability of a competitive advantage is a function of three factors: (1) the rate of core competence obsolescence because of environmental changes, (2) the availability of substitutes for the core competence, and (3) the imitability of the core competence.[9]

The challenge in all firms is to effectively manage current core competencies while simultaneously developing new ones.[10] In the words of Michael Dell, CEO of Dell Computer Corporation, "No [competitive] advantage and no success is ever permanent. The winners are those who keep moving. The only constant in our business is that everything is changing. We have to be ahead of the game."[11] Only when firms develop a continuous stream of competitive advantages do they achieve strategic competitiveness, earn above-average returns, and remain ahead of competitors (see Chapter 5).

In Chapter 2, we examined general, industry, and competitor environments. Armed with this type of knowledge about the realities and conditions of their environments, firms have a better understanding of marketplace opportunities and the goods or services through which they can be pursued. In this chapter, we focus on the firm itself. Through an analysis of its internal environment, a firm determines what it *can do*—that is, the actions permitted by its unique resources, capabilities, and core competencies. As discussed in Chapter 1, core competencies are a firm's source of competitive advantage. The magnitude of that competitive advantage is a function primarily of the uniqueness of the firm's core competencies compared to those of its competitors.[12] Matching what a firm *can do* with what it *might do* (a function of opportunities and threats in the external environment) allows the firm to develop strategic intent, pursue its strategic mission, and select and implement its strategies. Outcomes resulting from internal and external environmental analyses are shown in Figure 3.1.

We examine several topics in this chapter, beginning with the importance and challenge of studying the firm's internal environment. We then discuss the roles of resources, capabilities, and core competencies in developing sustainable competitive advantage. Included in this discussion are the techniques firms can use to identify and evaluate resources and capabilities and the criteria for selecting core competencies from among them. Resources, capabilities, and core competencies are not inherently valuable, but they create value when the firm can use them to perform certain activities that result in a competitive advantage. Accordingly, we also discuss in this chapter the value chain concept and examine four criteria to evaluate core competences that establish competitive advantage.[13]

The Importance of Internal Analysis

In the global economy, traditional factors—such as labor costs, access to financial resources and raw materials, and protected or regulated markets—continue to be sources of competitive advantage, but to a lesser degree than before.[14] One important reason for this decline is that the advantages created by these sources can be overcome through an international strategy (discussed in Chapter 8) and by the relatively free flow of resources throughout the global economy.

Few firms can consistently make the most effective strategic decisions unless they can change rapidly. A key challenge to developing the ability to change rapidly is fostering an organizational setting in which experimentation and learning are expected and promoted.[15] The demands of 21st-century competition require top-level managers to rethink earlier concepts of the firm and competition. For example, Polaroid Corporation sought to accommodate a significant technological shift by changing from analog to digital imaging. Polaroid's managers needed to gain a different understanding of their competitive world and the firm's existing capabilities as well as the new capabilities that were needed. The firm had to overcome the trajectory of its analog imaging capabilities so it could focus on developing and using capabilities required by digital imaging.[16] While the Polaroid story clearly illustrates the importance of managers seeking to direct the firm through a completely new competitive environment, Polaroid's management was not successful and the firm was facing bankruptcy by the end of 2001[17] and preparing to sell major portions of its assets in mid-2002.

Figure 3.1   Outcomes from External and Internal Environmental Analyses

By studying the external environment, firms identify
- what they *might* choose to *do*

By studying the internal environment, firms determine
- what they *can do*

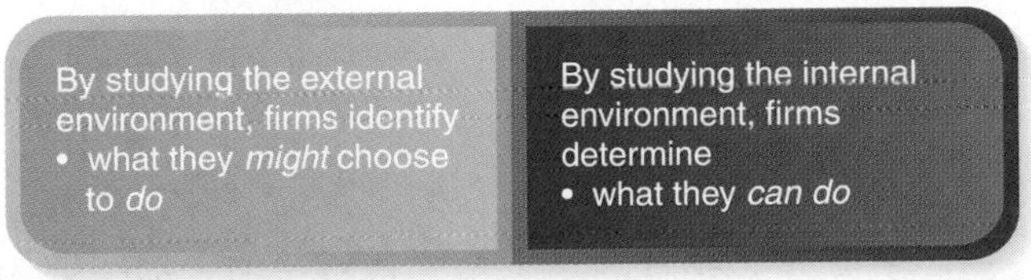

In addition to the firm's ability to change rapidly, a different managerial mind-set is required for firms to be successful in the global economy. Most top-level managers recognize the need to change their mind-sets, but many hesitate to do so. In the words of the European CEO of a major U.S. company, "It is more reassuring for all of us to stay as we are, even though we know the result will be certain failure . . . than to jump into a new way of working when we cannot be sure it will succeed."[18] Jacques Nasser, Ford Motor Company's former CEO, was quite outspoken in his belief that all employees—especially senior-level executives—had to change their mind-set from concentrating on their own area of operation to encompassing a view of the company in its entirety. Nasser felt this change was key to generating the type of rapid decision making required for Ford to be successful in a fast-changing world.[19] Ultimately, however, Nasser may have forced too much change too quickly on Ford employees. One analyst suggested, "I think Ford management is really stretched. There are just too many initiatives going on. Now, they're paying the price for taking their eye off the ball."[20]

Also critical is that managers view the firm as a *bundle* of heterogeneous resources, capabilities, and core competencies that can be used to create an exclusive market position.[21] This perspective suggests that individual firms possess at least some resources and capabilities that other companies do not—at least not in the same combination. Resources are the source of capabilities, some of which lead to the development of a firm's core competencies.[22] Figure 3.2 illustrates the relationships among resources, capabilities, and core competencies and shows how firms use them to create strategic competitiveness. Essentially, the mind-set needed in the global economy requires decision makers to define their firm's strategy in terms of a *unique competitive position*, rather than strictly in terms of operational effectiveness. For instance, Michael Porter argues that quests for productivity, quality, and speed from using a number of management techniques—total quality management (TQM),

Figure 3.2 Components of Internal Analysis Leading to Competitive Advantage and Strategic Competitiveness

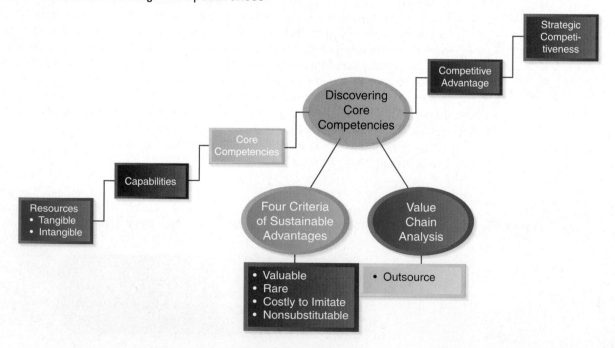

benchmarking, time-based competition, and re-engineering—have resulted in operational efficiency, but have not resulted in strong sustainable strategies.[73] As we discussed in Chapter 1, strategic competitiveness results when the firm satisfies the operational efficiency demands of its external environment while simultaneously using its own unique capabilities to establish a viable strategic position. Because of its importance to business-level strategies, strategic positioning is discussed in greater detail in Chapter 4.

Creating Value

Value is measured by a product's performance characteristics and by its attributes for which customers are willing to pay.

By exploiting core competencies and meeting the demanding standards of global competition, firms create value for customers.[24] **Value** is measured by a product's performance characteristics and by its attributes for which customers are willing to pay.[25]

Sometimes consistency and predictability provide value to customers, such as the type of value Walgreens provides. As noted by a business writer, "Do you realize that from 1975 to today, Walgreens beat Intel? It beat Intel nearly two to one, GE almost five to one. It beat 3M, Coke, Boeing, Motorola."[26] Walgreens was able to do this by using its competencies to offer value desired by its target customer group. Instead of responding to the trends of the day, "During the Internet scare of 1998 and 1999, when slogans of 'Change or Die!' were all but graffitied on the subway, Walgreens obstinately stuck to its corporate credo of 'Crawl, walk, run.' Its refusal to act until it thoroughly understood the implications of e-commerce was deeply unfashionable, but . . . Walgreens is the epitome of the inner-directed company."[27] Thus, Walgreens creates value by focusing on the unique capabilities it has built, nurtured, and continues to improve across time.

Ultimately, creating customer value is the source of a firm's potential to earn above-average returns. What the firm intends regarding value creation affects its choice of business-level strategy (see Chapter 4) and its organizational structure (see Chapter 11).[28] In Chapter 4's discussion of business-level strategies, we note that value is created by a product's low cost, by its highly differentiated features, or by a combination of low cost and high differentiation, compared to competitors' offerings. A business-level strategy is effective only when its use is grounded in exploiting the firm's current core competencies while actions are being taken to develop the core competencies that will be needed to effectively use "tomorrow's" business-level strategy. Thus, successful firms continuously examine the effectiveness of current and future core competencies.[29]

During the last several decades, the strategic management process was concerned largely with understanding the characteristics of the industry in which the firm competed and, in light of those characteristics, determining how the firm should position itself relative to competitors. This emphasis on industry characteristics and competitive strategy may have understated the role of the firm's resources and capabilities in developing competitive advantage. In the current competitive landscape, core competencies, in combination with product-market positions, are the firm's most important sources of competitive advantage.[30] The core competencies of a firm, in addition to its analysis of its general, industry, and competitor environments, should drive its selection of strategies. As Clayton Christensen noted: "Successful strategists need to cultivate a deep understanding of the processes of competition and progress and of the factors that undergird each advantage. Only thus will they be able to see when old advantages are poised to disappear and how new advantages can be built in their stead."[31] By emphasizing core competencies when formulating strategies, companies learn to compete primarily on the basis of firm-specific differences, but they must be very aware of how things are changing as well.

The Challenge of Internal Analysis

The decisions managers make in terms of the firm's resources, capabilities, and core competencies have a significant influence on the firm's ability to earn above-average returns.[32] Making these decisions—identifying, developing, deploying, and protecting resources, capabilities, and core competencies—may appear to be relatively easy. In fact, however, this task is as challenging and difficult as any other with which managers are involved; moreover, it is increasingly internationalized and linked with the firm's success.[33] Managers also face great pressure to pursue only those decisions that help the firm to meet the quarterly earning numbers expected by market analysts.[34] Recognizing the firm's core competencies is essential before the firm can make important strategic decisions, including those related to entering or exiting markets, investing in new technologies, building new or additional manufacturing capacity, or forming strategic partnerships.[35] Patterns of interactions between individuals and groups that occur as strategic decisions affect decision quality as well as how effectively and quickly these decisions are implemented.[36]

The challenge and difficulty of making effective decisions is implied by preliminary evidence suggesting that one-half of organizational decisions fail.[37] Sometimes, mistakes are made as the firm analyzes its internal environment. Managers might, for example, select resources and capabilities as the firm's core competencies that do not create a competitive advantage. When a mistake occurs, decision makers must have the confidence to admit it and take corrective actions.[38] A firm can still grow through well-intended errors—the learning generated by making and correcting mistakes can be important to the creation of new competitive advantages.[39] Moreover, firms can learn from the failure resulting from a mistake; that is, what *not* to do when seeking competitive advantage.[40]

To facilitate the development and use of core competencies, managers must have courage, self-confidence, integrity, the capacity to deal with uncertainty and complexity, and a willingness to hold people accountable for their work and to be held accountable themselves. Thus, difficult managerial decisions concerning resources, capabilities, and core competencies are characterized by three conditions: uncertainty, complexity, and intraorganizational conflicts (see Figure 3.3).[41]

Figure 3.3   Conditions Affecting Managerial Decisions about Resources, Capabilities, and Core Competencies

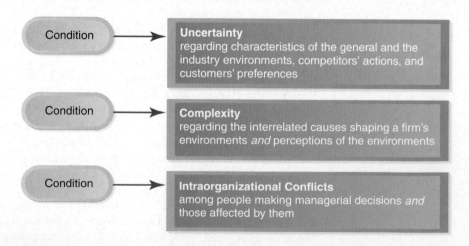

SOURCE: Adapted from R. Amit & P. J. H. Schoemaker, 1993, Strategic assets and organizational rent, *Strategic Management Journal*, 14: 33.

Managers face *uncertainty* in terms of new proprietary technologies, rapidly changing economic and political trends, transformations in societal values, and shifts in customer demands.[42] Environmental uncertainty increases the *complexity* and range of issues to examine when studying the internal environment. Biases about how to cope with uncertainty affect decisions about the resources and capabilities that will become the foundation of the firm's competitive advantage. Finally, *intraorganizational conflict* surfaces when decisions are made about the core competencies to nurture as well as how to nurture them.

In making decisions affected by these three conditions, judgment should be used. *Judgment* is the capability of making successful decisions when no obviously correct model or rule is available or when relevant data are unreliable or incomplete. In this type of situation, decision makers must be aware of possible cognitive biases. Overconfidence, for example, can often lower value when a correct decision is not obvious, such as making a judgment as to whether an internal resource is a strength or a weakness.[43]

When exercising judgment, decision makers demonstrate a willingness to take intelligent risks in a timely manner. In the current competitive landscape, executive judgment can be a particularly important source of competitive advantage. One reason for this is that, over time, effective judgment allows a firm to build a strong reputation and retain the loyalty of stakeholders whose support is linked to above-average returns.[44]

Significant changes in the value-creating potential of a firm's resources and capabilities can occur in a rapidly changing global economy.[45] Because these changes affect a company's power and social structure, inertia or resistance to change may surface. Even though these reactions may happen, decision makers should not deny the changes needed to assure the firm's strategic competitiveness. *Denial* is an unconscious coping mechanism used to block out and not initiate painful changes.[46] For example, Opel was once Germany's number one "everyman's car." Of late, however, the GM-owned European carmaker has suffered operating losses ($429 million in 2000 alone) and poor brand image. Concentrating on making changes in how the firm performs its primary and support activities, Carl-Peter Forster, head of Opel, candidly faced the problem and developed a restructuring plan that should reduce purchasing costs, streamline and modernize the firm's ineffective sales unit, and define new areas of potential growth beyond car sales. These actions, some of which could be painful, may improve the image of the firm's brand and subsequently, its competitive ability.[47]

Because some people have a strong tendency to resist the changes needed to cope with intensely competitive environments, involving a range of individuals and groups is important when making changes in a firm's value-creating abilities.[48]

Resources, Capabilities, and Core Competencies

Resources, capabilities, and core competencies are the characteristics that make up the foundation of competitive advantage. Resources are the source of a firm's capabilities. Capabilities in turn are the source of a firm's core competencies, which are the basis of competitive advantages.[49] As shown in Figure 3.2, combinations of resources and capabilities are managed to create core competencies. In this section we define and provide examples of these building blocks of competitive advantage.

Resources

Broad in scope, resources cover a spectrum of individual, social, and organizational phenomena.[50] Typically, resources alone do not yield a competitive advantage.[51] In

Amazon.com showed a profit for the first time ever in the last quarter of 2001, helped by lucrative fees it earned by selling other firms' products. The world's largest online seller of books, CDs, and DVDs has huge revenues but slender profit margins. It hopes to become the top online resource for electronics, toys, and housewares through partnerships with traditional retailers Target, Toys 'R' Us, Circuit City, and Borders.

fact, a competitive advantage is created through the *unique bundling of several resources*.[52] For example, Amazon.com has combined service and distribution resources to develop its competitive advantages. The firm started as an online bookseller, directly shipping orders to customers. It quickly grew large and established a distribution network through which it could ship "millions of different items to millions of different customers." Compared to Amazon's use of combined resources, traditional bricks-and-mortar companies, such as Toys 'R' Us and Borders, found it hard to establish an effective online presence. These difficulties led them to develop partnerships with Amazon. Through these arrangements, Amazon now handles online presence and the shipping of goods for several firms, including Toys 'R' Us and Borders—which now can focus on sales in their stores. Arrangements such as these are useful to the bricks-and-mortar companies because they are not accustomed to shipping so much diverse merchandise directly to individuals.[53]

Tangible resources are assets that can be seen and quantified.

Intangible resources include assets that typically are rooted deeply in the firm's history and have accumulated over time.

Some of a firm's resources are tangible while others are intangible. **Tangible resources** are assets that can be seen and quantified. Production equipment, manufacturing plants, and formal reporting structures are examples of tangible resources. **Intangible resources** include assets that typically are rooted deeply in the firm's history and have accumulated over time. Because they are embedded in unique patterns of routines, intangible resources are relatively difficult for competitors to analyze and imitate. Knowledge, trust between managers and employees, ideas, the capacity for innovation, managerial capabilities, organizational routines (the unique ways people work together), scientific capabilities, and the firm's reputation for its goods or services and how it interacts with people (such as employees, customers, and suppliers) are all examples of intangible resources.[54]

The four types of tangible resources are financial, organizational, physical, and technological (see Table 3.2). The three types of intangible resources are human, innovation, and reputational (see Table 3.3).

Tangible Resources

As tangible resources, a firm's borrowing capacity and the status of its plant and equipment are visible. The value of many tangible resources can be established through financial statements, but these statements do not account for the value of all of a firm's assets, because they disregard some intangible resources.[55] As such, each of the firm's sources of competitive advantage typically are not be reflected fully on corporate financial statements. The value of tangible resources is also constrained because they are difficult to leverage—it is hard to derive additional business or value from a tangible resource. For example, an airplane is a tangible resource or asset, but: "You can't use the same airplane on five different routes at the same time. You can't put the same crew on five different routes at the same time. And the same goes for the financial investment you've made in the airplane."[56]

Although manufacturing assets are tangible, many of the processes to use these assets are intangible. Thus, the learning and potential proprietary processes associated

Table 3.2	Tangible Resources	
Financial Resources	• The firm's borrowing capacity	
	• The firm's ability to generate internal funds	
Organizational Resources	• The firm's formal reporting structure and its formal planning, controlling, and coordinating systems	
Physical Resources	• Sophistication and location of a firm's plant and equipment	
	• Access to raw materials	
Technological Resources	• Stock of technology, such as patents, trademarks, copyrights, and trade secrets	

SOURCES: Adapted from J. B. Barney, 1991, Firm resources and sustained competitive advantage, *Journal of Management,* 17: 101; R. M. Grant, 1991, *Contemporary Strategy Analysis,* Cambridge, U.K.: Blackwell Business, 100–102.

with a tangible resource, such as manufacturing equipment, can have unique intangible attributes such as quality, just-in-time management practices, and unique manufacturing processes that develop over time and create competitive advantage.[57]

Intangible Resources

As suggested above, compared to tangible resources, intangible resources are a superior and more potent source of core competencies.[58] In fact, in the global economy, "the success of a corporation lies more in its intellectual and systems capabilities than in its physical assets. [Moreover], the capacity to manage human intellect—and to convert it into useful products and services—is fast becoming the critical executive skill of the age."[59]

There is some evidence that the value of intangible assets is growing relative to that of tangible assets. John Kendrick, a well-known economist studying the main

Table 3.3	Intangible Resources	
Human Resources	• Knowledge	
	• Trust	
	• Managerial capabilities	
	• Organizational routines	
Innovation Resources	• Ideas	
	• Scientific capabilities	
	• Capacity to innovate	
Reputational Resources	• Reputation with customers	
	• Brand name	
	• Perceptions of product quality, durability, and reliability	
	• Reputation with suppliers	
	• For efficient, effective, supportive, and mutually beneficial interactions and relationships	

SOURCES: Adapted from R. Hall, 1992, The strategic analysis of intangible resources, *Strategic Management Journal,* 13: 136–139; R. M. Grant, 1991, *Contemporary Strategy Analysis,* Cambridge, U.K.: Blackwell Business, 101–104.

Microsoft's Resources and Capabilities

All companies need financial resources to grow and be successful, and there is really no such thing as a firm having too many financial resources, especially if they are used wisely. The firm with excellent access to external and internal funds is in the enviable position of being able to develop in ways that allow it to use its strategies effectively. Microsoft, the world's leading software company, has $30 billion in cash—a figure made even more amazing by the fact that its average growth rate is $1 billion every month. What could Microsoft do with this tangible resource, and what does it actually do with it?

Microsoft is best known for its two main products, Microsoft Windows and Microsoft Office, which generate the bulk of its income. Among numerous other product and market development projects, the company is establishing a presence in the small business market; it is developing an online position through MSN.com, and it is entering the console-game market with a new brand, the Xbox. Many of the markets Microsoft is pursuing are already well established with market leaders and entrenched products. For instance, Xbox competes against Sony's PlayStation 2 and Nintendo's GameCube. Even though it has no competitive advantage in this market, Microsoft has the resources and capabilities to enter it.

Microsoft's cash hoard also allows it to rapidly enter new markets and literally acquire market share by purchasing companies that already have a market presence. For example, in December 2000, Microsoft purchased Great Plains Software Inc. for $1.1 billion. Great Plains is a leader in finance and accounting software for smaller businesses, a market in which Microsoft had not been a serious contender.

Because Microsoft earns above-average returns, it has the financial resources to stimulate continued growth. When MSN.com was first introduced, initial customer reaction wasn't supportive. The brand languished for years. However, through perseverance and Microsoft's purchases of other Internet service providers, MSN.com has emerged as the second-most popular portal on the Web behind AOL. The venture's success was also helped by Microsoft investments of $100 million in Radio Shack Corp. and $200 million in

drivers of economic growth, found a general increase in the contribution of intangible assets to U.S. economic growth since the early 1900s: "In 1929, the ratio of intangible business capital to tangible business capital was 30 percent to 70 percent. In 1990, that ratio was 63 percent to 37 percent."[60]

Because intangible resources are less visible and more difficult for competitors to understand, purchase, imitate, or substitute for, firms prefer to rely on them rather than tangible resources as the foundation for their capabilities and core competencies. In fact, the more unobservable (that is, intangible) a resource is, the more sustainable will be the competitive advantage that is based on it. Another benefit of intangible resources is that, unlike most tangible resources, their use can be leveraged. With intangible resources, the larger the network of users, the greater is the benefit to each party.[61] For instance, sharing knowledge among employees does not diminish its value for any one person. To the contrary, two people sharing their individualized knowledge sets often can be leveraged to create additional knowledge that although new to each of them, contributes to performance improvements for the firm.[62]

As illustrated in the Opening Case, the intangible resource of reputation is an important source of competitive advantage for companies such as Coca-Cola, General Electric, and Southwest Airlines. Earned through the firm's actions as well as its words, a value-creating reputation is a product of years of superior marketplace competence as perceived by stakeholders.[63] A well-known and highly valued brand name is an application

Best Buy Co. in exchange for their promotion of MSN's access service. Microsoft's investments were possible only because of Microsoft's tremendous cash flow.

Microsoft's significant financial resources also supported its introduction of the Xbox to an established home video-game market. In addition to the cost of designing and developing the Xbox, Microsoft spent $500 million to market it—an amount of money that few other companies could afford.

A strong financial resource also makes possible Microsoft's competitively superior research and development (R&D) skills. As part of an innovation intangible resource (see Table 3.4), R&D contributes significantly to Microsoft's historic ability to earn above-average returns. In 2000, for example, Microsoft allocated $3.7 billion to R&D, and $4.2 billion in 2001—more than the combined R&D allocations for Microsoft rivals America Online, Sun Microsystems, and Oracle. The integration of a strong tangible resource (financial capacity) with an effective intangible resource (R&D) creates an important competitive advantage for Microsoft.

An old adage says: "You must spend money to make money." Microsoft's robust financial resource allows it to support its intangible resources in ways that can create new competitive advantages or that can support the continuing development of existing advantages. Furthermore, Microsoft uses its resources well. For instance, its purchasing capabilities allowed the firm to recently reduce its annual purchasing costs by $46 million. As discussed later in this chapter, a reduction in a firm's purchasing costs is an example of how value can be created through support activities.

Thus, Microsoft expertly uses a key tangible resource—cash—to foster its intangible resources, including R&D and marketing activities, as well as to build Microsoft's brand name. The result is a powerful capability to develop new products and enter new markets.

SOURCES: S. Avery, 2001, Microsoft cuts buying costs by $46 million, *Purchasing*, January 25, 48–57; 2001, Case vs. Gates: Playing for the web jackpot, *Businessweek Online*, http://www.businessweek.com, June 18; P. Burrows, J. Greene, & A. Park, 2001, SOS: Microsoft to the rescue? *Businessweek Online*, http://www.businessweek.com, June 25; N. Croal, 2001, Game wars 5.0, *Newsweek*, May 28, 65–66; J. DiSabatino, 2001, Microsoft officially launches Office XP, *Computerworld*, June 4, 10; J. Green, 2001, Microsoft: How it became stronger than ever, *Business Week*, June 4, 74–85; A. Hamilton, 2001, Office whizbang, *Time*, June 4, 82; P. Rooney, 2001, Microsoft pushes ahead with Office XP, http://www.CRN.com, June 4; B. Schlender, 2001, Microsoft: The beast is back, *Fortune*, June 11, 75–86.

of reputation as a source of competitive advantage. The Harley-Davidson brand name, for example, has such cachet that it adorns a limited edition Barbie doll, a popular restaurant in New York City, and a line of L'Oreal cologne. Moreover, Harley-Davidson MotorClothes annually generates over $100 million in revenue for the firm and offers a broad range of clothing items, from black leather jackets to fashions for tots.[64]

Decision makers are challenged to understand fully the strategic value of their firm's tangible and intangible resources. The *strategic value of resources* is indicated by the degree to which they can contribute to the development of capabilities, core competencies, and, ultimately, competitive advantage. For example, as a tangible resource, a distribution facility is assigned a monetary value on the firm's balance sheet. The real value of the facility, however, is grounded in a variety of factors, such as its proximity to raw materials and customers, but also in intangible factors such as the manner in which workers integrate their actions internally and with other stakeholders, such as suppliers and customers.[65]

Capabilities

As a source of capabilities, tangible and intangible resources are a critical part of the pathway to the development of competitive advantage (as shown earlier in Figure 3.2). This is illustrated well in the Strategic Focus on Microsoft on page 84.

Capabilities are the firm's capacity to deploy resources that have been purposely integrated to achieve a desired end state.[66] The glue binding an organization together, capabilities emerge over time through complex interactions among tangible and intangible resources. The discussion of Microsoft in the Strategic Focus demonstrates these complex interactions. Critical to the forming of competitive advantages, capabilities are often based on developing, carrying, and exchanging information and knowledge through the firm's human capital.[67] Because a knowledge base is grounded in organizational actions that may not be explicitly understood by all employees, repetition and practice increase the value of a firm's capabilities.

The foundation of many capabilities lies in the skills and knowledge of a firm's employees and, often, their functional expertise. Hence, the value of human capital in developing and using capabilities and, ultimately, core competencies cannot be overstated. Firms committed to continuously developing their people's capabilities seem to accept the adage that "the person who knows how will always have a job. The person who knows why will always be his boss."[68]

Global business leaders increasingly support the view that the knowledge possessed by human capital is among the most significant of an organization's capabilities and may ultimately be at the root of all competitive advantages. But firms must also be able to utilize the knowledge that they have and transfer it among their operating businesses.[69] For example, researchers have suggested that "in the information age, things are ancillary, knowledge is central. A company's value derives not from things, but from knowledge, know-how, intellectual assets, competencies—all of it embedded in people."[70] Given this reality, the firm's challenge is to create an environment that allows people to fit their individual pieces of knowledge together so that, collectively, employees possess as much organizational knowledge as possible.[71]

To help them develop an environment in which knowledge is widely spread across all employees, some organizations have created the new upper-level managerial position of chief learning officer (CLO). Establishing a CLO position highlights a firm's belief that "future success will depend on competencies that traditionally have not been actively managed or measured—including creativity and the speed with which new ideas are learned and shared."[72] In general, the firm should manage knowledge in ways that will support its efforts to create value for customers.[73]

As illustrated in Table 3.4, capabilities are often developed in specific functional areas (such as manufacturing, R&D, and marketing) or in a part of a functional area (for example, advertising). Research suggests a relationship between capabilities developed in particular functional areas and the firm's financial performance at both the corporate and business-unit levels,[74] suggesting the need to develop capabilities at both levels. Table 3.4 shows a grouping of organizational functions and the capabilities that some companies are thought to possess in terms of all or parts of those functions.

Core Competencies

Defined in Chapter 1, *core competencies* are resources and capabilities that serve as a source of a firm's competitive advantage over rivals. Core competencies distinguish a company competitively and reflect its personality. Core competencies emerge over time through an organizational process of accumulating and learning how to deploy different resources and capabilities. As the capacity to take action, core competencies are "crown jewels of a company," the activities the company performs especially well compared to competitors and through which the firm adds unique value to its goods or services over a long period of time.[75]

Not all of a firm's resources and capabilities are *strategic assets*—that is, assets that have competitive value and the potential to serve as a source of competitive advantage.[76] Some resources and capabilities may result in incompetence, because they represent competitive areas in which the firm is weak compared to competitors. Thus, some resources or capabilities may stifle or prevent the development of a core

Table 3.4	Examples of Firms' Capabilities

Functional Areas	Capabilities	Examples of Firms
Distribution	Effective use of logistics management techniques	Wal-Mart
Human resources	Motivating, empowering, and retaining employees	AEROJET
Management information systems	Effective and efficient control of inventories through point-of-purchase data collection methods	Wal-Mart
Marketing	Effective promotion of brand-name products	Gillette
		Ralph Lauren Clothing
		McKinsey & Co.
	Effective customer service	Nordstrom
		Norwest
		Solectron Corporation
		Norrell Corporation
	Innovative merchandising	Crate & Barrel
Management	Ability to envision the future of clothing	Gap, Inc.
	Effective organizational structure	PepsiCo
Manufacturing	Design and production skills yielding reliable products	Komatsu
	Product and design quality	Gap, Inc.
	Production of technologically sophisticated automobile engines	Mazda
	Miniaturization of components and products	Sony
Research & development	Exceptional technological capability	Corning
	Development of sophisticated elevator control solutions	Motion Control
	Rapid transformation of technology into new products and processes	Engineering Inc. Chaparral Steel
	Deep knowledge of silver-halide materials	Kodak
	Digital technology	Thomson Consumer Electronics

competence. Firms with the tangible resource of financial capital, such as Microsoft (see Strategic Focus on page 84), may be able to purchase facilities or hire the skilled workers required to manufacture products that yield customer value. However, firms without financial capital would have a weakness in regard to being able to buy or build new capabilities. To be successful, firms must locate external environmental opportunities that can be exploited through their capabilities, while avoiding competition in areas of weakness.[77]

An important question is "How many core competencies are required for the firm to have a sustained competitive advantage?" Responses to this question vary. McKinsey & Co. recommends that its clients identify three or four competencies around which their strategic actions can be framed.[78] Supporting and nurturing more than four core competencies may prevent a firm from developing the focus it needs to fully exploit its competencies in the marketplace.

Firms should take actions that are based on their core competencies. Recent actions by Starbucks demonstrate this point. Growing rapidly, Starbucks decided that it could use the Internet as a distribution channel to bring about still additional growth. The firm quickly realized that it lacks the capabilities required to successfully

distribute its products through this channel and that its unique coffee, not the delivery of that product, is its competitive advantage. In part, this recognition caused Starbucks to renew its emphasis on existing capabilities to create more value through its supply chain. Trimming the number of its milk suppliers from 65 to fewer than 25 and negotiating long-term contracts with coffee-bean growers are actions Starbucks has taken to do this. The firm also decided to place automated espresso machines in its busy units. These machines reduce Starbucks' cost while providing improved service to its customers, who can now move through the line much faster. Using its supply chain and service capabilities in these manners allows Starbucks to strengthen its competitive advantages of coffee and the unique venue in which on-site customers experience it.[79]

Of course, not all resources and capabilities are core competencies. The next section discusses two approaches for identifying core competencies.

Forbes named Starbucks the world's best food and beverage company for 2002. Pictured here is the firm's original store in Seattle, Washington, opened in 1971.

Building Core Competencies

Two tools help the firm identify and build its core competencies.[80] The first consists of four specific criteria of sustainable advantage that firms can use to determine those resources and capabilities that are core competencies. Because the capabilities shown in Table 3.4 have satisfied these four criteria, they are core competencies. The second tool is the value chain analysis. Firms use this tool to select the value-creating competencies that should be maintained, upgraded, or developed and those that should be outsourced.

Four Criteria of Sustainable Competitive Advantage

As shown in Table 3.5, capabilities that are valuable, rare, costly to imitate, and non-substitutable are strategic capabilities. Also called core competencies, strategic capabilities are a source of competitive advantage for the firm over its rivals. Capabilities failing to satisfy the four criteria of sustainable competitive advantage are not core competencies. Thus, as shown in Figure 3.4, every core competence is a capability, but not every capability is a core competence. Operationally, for a capability to be a core competence, it must be "valuable and nonsubstitutable, from a customer's point of view, and unique and inimitable, from a competitor's point of view."[81]

A sustained competitive advantage is achieved only when competitors have failed in efforts to duplicate the benefits of a firm's strategy or when they lack the confidence to attempt imitation. For some period of time, the firm may earn a competitive advantage by using capabilities that are, for example, valuable and rare, but that are imitable.[82] In this instance, the length of time a firm can expect to retain its competitive advantage is a function of how quickly competitors can successfully imitate a good, service, or process. Sustainable competitive advantage results only when all four criteria are satisfied.

Valuable capabilities allow the firm to exploit opportunities or neutralize threats in its external environment.

Valuable

Valuable capabilities allow the firm to exploit opportunities or neutralize threats in its external environment. By effectively using capabilities to exploit opportunities, a firm is able to create value for customers.

Table 3.5	Four Criteria for Determining Strategic Capabilities
Valuable Capabilities	• Help a firm neutralize threats or exploit opportunities
Rare Capabilities	• Are not possessed by many others
Costly-to-Imitate Capabilities	• Historical: A unique and a valuable organizational culture or brand name
	• Ambiguous cause: The causes and uses of a competence are unclear
	• Social complexity: Interpersonal relationships, trust, and friendship among managers, suppliers, and customers
Nonsubstitutable Capabilities	• No strategic equivalent

Sometimes, firms' capabilities become valuable only through modifications that improve their ability to satisfy customers' needs. As individuals browse the Web for information, for example, many feel that an insufficient amount of value is created online to make a purchase. About 3 percent of website visitors actually make a purchase, while 97 percent only browse. However, firms are learning to modify their websites to create more value for visitors, thereby turning them into buyers. The results from a recent study suggested that the order-conversion rate increased from 1.8 percent to 3.2 percent in 1999.[83] In this case, a valuable capability converts visitors into buyers. Over time, computer models that analyze website visits of consumers will play an important role in helping firms turn visitors into buyers. Interestingly, the models' real value may be that they make the website more like a human salesperson. "Think of the old-time shoe-store salesman who knew his customers, knew what they had bought for years, and knew who had to try on 11 pairs before one pair would feel right."[84]

Figure 3.4	Core Competence as a Strategic Capability

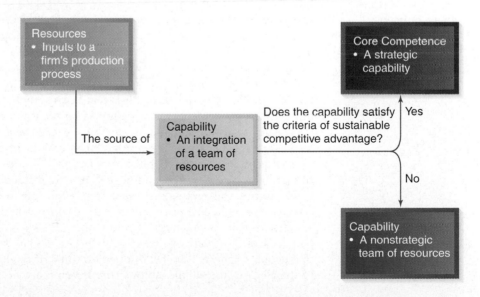

In regard to value creation, e-commerce has a long way to go before a meaningful portion of it behaves like a human salesperson. However, this capability is what most Web businesses such as Amazon.com seek to achieve. In fact, Amazon has amazingly high satisfaction levels among its website visitors as well as buyers. "Customers love Amazon not because it offers the lowest prices—it doesn't—but because the experience has been crafted so carefully that most of us actually enjoy it."[85] Similarly, relying initially on its distribution capabilities to pursue an opportunity, Wal-Mart started its business by offering startlingly low prices on a vast selection of brand-name goods. Analysts believe that Wal-Mart changed the way consumers thought about value, letting them know that they did not have to pay the prices charged by most retailers.[86]

Rare

Rare capabilities are possessed by few, if any, current or potential competitors. A key question managers answer when evaluating this criterion is, "How many rival firms possess these valuable capabilities?" Capabilities possessed by many rivals are unlikely to be a source of competitive advantage for any one of them. Instead, valuable but common (i.e., not rare) resources and capabilities are sources of competitive parity.[87] Competitive advantage results only when firms develop and exploit capabilities that differ from those shared with competitors.

For example, when Palm Computing was established, it had an operating system that was different from its competitors in the PC sector. Palm's software was designed to run on a small handheld device. The first product using the software, Apple's Newton, did not create enough value for consumers and failed. However, funding from US Robotics allowed the founders to create better software and design the hardware as well and incorporate them into the Palm Pilot, and the product was successful. The Palm Pilot sold 350,000 units in 1994, 750,000 in 1995, and one million in 1996. In 1998, 3Com purchased Palm Computing and spun it into a separate corporation in 2000. However, its software is still a rare product and is licensed by 3Com's competitors, such as Handspring. Although Microsoft has a competing operating system, to this point it has not been as successful as the Palm operating system and application software.[88] Thus, Palm's operating system and associated software are still rare.

Costly to Imitate

Costly-to-imitate capabilities are capabilities that other firms cannot easily develop. Capabilities that are costly to imitate are created because of one or a combination of three reasons (see Table 3.5). First, a firm sometimes is able to develop capabilities because of *unique historical conditions*. "As firms evolve, they pick up skills, abilities and resources that are unique to them, reflecting their particular path through history."[89] Another way of saying this is that firms sometimes are able to develop capabilities because they were in the right place at the right time.[90]

A firm with a unique and valuable *organizational culture* that emerged in the early stages of the company's history "may have an imperfectly imitable advantage over firms founded in another historical period"[91]—one in which less valuable or less competitively useful values and beliefs strongly influenced the development of the firm's culture. This may be the case for the consulting firm McKinsey & Co. "It is that culture, unique to McKinsey and eccentric, which sets the firm apart from virtually any other business organization and which often mystifies even those who engage [its] services."[92] Briefly discussed in Chapter 1, organizational culture is "something that people connect with, feel inspired by, think of as a normal way of operating. It's in their hearts and minds, and its core is voluntary behavior."[93] An organizational culture is a source of advantage when employees are held together tightly by their belief in it.[94]

UPS has been the prototype in many areas of the parcel delivery business because of its excellence in products, systems, marketing, and other operational business capabilities. "Its fundamental competitive strength, however, derives from the organization's unique culture, which has spanned almost a century, growing deeper all along. This culture provides solid, consistent roots for everything the company does, from skills training to technological innovation."[95]

A second condition of being costly to imitate occurs when the link between the firm's capabilities and its competitive advantage is *causally ambiguous*.[96] In these instances, competitors can't clearly understand how a firm uses its capabilities as the foundation for competitive advantage. As a result, firms are uncertain about the capabilities they should develop to duplicate the benefits of a competitor's value-creating strategy. Gordon Forward, CEO of Chaparral Steel, allows competitors to tour his firm's facilities. In Forward's words, competitors can be shown almost "everything and we will be giving away nothing because they can't take it home with them."[97] Contributing to Chaparral Steel's causally ambiguous operations is the fact that workers use the concept of *mentefacturing*, by which manufacturing steel is done by using their minds instead of their hands. "In mentefacturing, workers use computers to monitor operations and don't need to be on the shop floor during production."[98]

Social complexity is the third reason that capabilities can be costly to imitate. Social complexity means that at least some, and frequently many, of the firm's capabilities are the product of complex social phenomena. Interpersonal relationships, trust, and friendships among managers and between managers and employees and a firm's reputation with suppliers and customers are examples of socially complex capabilities. Nucor Steel has been able to create "a hunger for new knowledge through a high-powered incentive system for every employee." This socially complex process has allowed Nucor "to push the boundaries of manufacturing process know-how."[99]

Nonsubstitutable

Nonsubstitutable capabilities are capabilities that do not have strategic equivalents. This final criterion for a capability to be a source of competitive advantage "is that there must be no strategically equivalent valuable resources that are themselves either not rare or imitable. Two valuable firm resources (or two bundles of firm resources) are strategically equivalent when they each can be separately exploited to implement the same strategies."[100] In general, the strategic value of capabilities increases as they become more difficult to substitute.[101] The more invisible capabilities are, the more difficult it is for firms to find substitutes and the greater the challenge is to competitors trying to imitate a firm's value-creating strategy. Firm-specific knowledge and trust-based working relationships between managers and nonmanagerial personnel are examples of capabilities that are difficult to identify and for which finding a substitute is challenging. However, causal ambiguity may make it difficult for the firm to learn as well and thus may stifle progress because the firm may not know how to improve processes that are not easily codified and thus ambiguous.[102]

For example, competitors are deeply familiar with Dell Computer's successful direct sales model. However, to date, no competitor has been able to imitate Dell's capabilities as suggested by the following comment: "There's no better way to make, sell, and deliver PCs than the way Dell does it, and nobody executes that model better than Dell."[103] Moreover, no competitor has been able to develop and use substitute capabilities that can duplicate the value Dell creates by using its capabilities. Thus, experience suggests that Dell's direct sales model capabilities are nonsubstitutable.

Nonsubstitutable capabilities are capabilities that do not have strategic equivalents.

In summary, sustainable competitive advantage is created only by using valuable, rare, costly-to-imitate, and nonsubstitutable capabilities. Table 3.6 shows the competitive consequences and performance implications resulting from combinations of the four criteria of sustainability. The analysis suggested by the table helps managers determine the strategic value of a firm's capabilities. Resources and capabilities falling into the first row in the table (that is, resources and capabilities that are neither valuable nor rare and that are imitable and for which strategic substitutes exist) should not be emphasized by the firm to formulate and implement strategies. Capabilities yielding competitive parity and either temporary or sustainable competitive advantage, however, will be supported. Large competitors such as Coca-Cola and PepsiCo may have capabilities that can yield only competitive parity. In such cases, the firms will nurture these capabilities while simultaneously trying to develop capabilities that can yield either a temporary or sustainable competitive advantage.

Value Chain Analysis

Value chain analysis allows the firm to understand the parts of its operations that create value and those that do not. Understanding these issues is important because the firm earns above-average returns only when the value it creates is greater than the costs incurred to create that value.[104]

Primary activities are involved with a product's physical creation, its sale and distribution to buyers, and its service after the sale.

Support activities provide the support necessary for the primary activities to take place.

The value chain is a template that firms use to understand their cost position and to identify the multiple means that might be used to facilitate implementation of a chosen business-level strategy.[105] As shown in Figure 3.5, a firm's value chain is segmented into primary and support activities. **Primary activities** are involved with a product's physical creation, its sale and distribution to buyers, and its service after the sale. **Support activities** provide the support necessary for the primary activities to take place.

| Table 3.6 | Outcomes from Combinations of the Criteria for Sustainable Competitive Advantage |

Is the Resource or Capability Valuable?	Is the Resource or Capability Rare?	Is the Resource or Capability Costly to Imitate?	Is the Resource or Capability Nonsubstitutable?	Competitive Consequences	Performance Implications
No	No	No	No	Competitive disadvantage	Below-average returns
Yes	No	No	Yes/no	Competitive parity	Average returns
Yes	Yes	No	Yes/no	Temporary competitive advantage	Above-average returns to average returns
Yes	Yes	Yes	Yes	Sustainable competitive advantage	Above-average returns

The value chain shows how a product moves from the raw-material stage to the final customer. For individual firms, the essential idea of the value chain "is to add as much value as possible as cheaply as possible, and, most important, to capture that value." In a globally competitive economy, the most valuable links on the chain tend to belong to people who have knowledge about customers.[106] This locus of value-creating possibilities applies just as strongly to retail and service firms as to manufacturers. Moreover, for organizations in all sectors, the effects of e-commerce make it increasingly necessary for companies to develop value-adding knowledge processes to compensate for the value and margin that the Internet strips from physical processes.[107]

Table 3.7 lists the items to be studied to assess the value-creating potential of primary activities. In Table 3.8, the items to consider when studying support activities are shown. As with the analysis of primary activities, the intent in examining these items is to determine areas where the firm has the potential to create and capture value. All items in both tables should be evaluated relative to competitors' capabilities. To be a source of competitive advantage, a resource or capability must allow the firm (1) to perform an activity in a manner that is superior to the way competitors perform it, or (2) to perform a value-creating activity that competitors cannot complete. Only under these conditions does a firm create value for customers and have opportunities to capture that value.

Sometimes start-up firms create value by uniquely reconfiguring or recombining parts of the value chain. Federal Express (FedEx) changed the nature of the delivery business by reconfiguring outbound logistics (a primary activity) and human

---

Figure 3.5   The Basic Value Chain

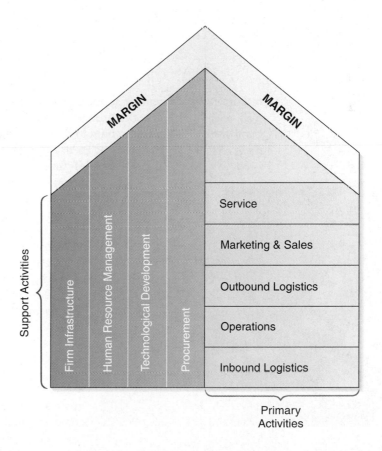

Table 3.7 | Examining the Value-Creating Potential of Primary Activities

Inbound Logistics

Activities, such as materials handling, warehousing, and inventory control, used to receive, store, and disseminate inputs to a product.

Operations

Activities necessary to convert the inputs provided by inbound logistics into final product form. Machining, packaging, assembly, and equipment maintenance are examples of operations activities.

Outbound Logistics

Activities involved with collecting, storing, and physically distributing the final product to customers. Examples of these activities include finished-goods warehousing, materials handling, and order processing.

Marketing and Sales

Activities completed to provide means through which customers can purchase products and to induce them to do so. To effectively market and sell products, firms develop advertising and promotional campaigns, select appropriate distribution channels, and select, develop, and support their sales force.

Service

Activities designed to enhance or maintain a product's value. Firms engage in a range of service-related activities, including installation, repair, training, and adjustment.

Each activity should be examined relative to competitors' abilities. Accordingly, firms rate each activity as *superior*, *equivalent*, or *inferior*.

SOURCE: Adapted with the permission of The Free Press, an imprint of Simon & Schuster Adult Publishing Group, from *Competitive Advantage: Creating and Sustaining Superior Performance*, by Michael E. Porter, pp. 39–40, Copyright © 1985, 1988 by Michael E. Porter.

Celera Labs, pictured here, started the biotech rally and expects to map the entire human genome by 2003. In 2001 Celera acquired Axys Pharmaceuticals, which specializes in drug chemistry and early-stage drug testing, to identify and eventually develop new drugs based on genetic research. Until it can develop and market new drugs, however, Celera's database subscriptions and licensing are its main source of revenue.

© Mari Tama/AFP/CORBIS

resource management (a support activity) to originate the overnight delivery business, creating value in the process. As shown in Figure 3.6, the Internet is changing many aspects of the value chain for a broad range of firms. As an example of many of these changes, see the Strategic Focus on page 96 on the upheaval in the value chains of firms in the pharmaceutical industry, creating many entry opportunities for new participants.

Rating a firm's capability to execute its primary and support activities is challenging. Earlier in the chapter, we noted that identifying and assessing the value of a firm's resources and capabilities requires judgment. Judgment is equally necessary when using value chain analysis. The reason is that there is no obviously correct model or rule available to help in the process.

As discussed in the Strategic Focus on page 96, the pharmaceutical industry is undergoing a significant change in its value chain. Millennium Pharmaceuticals has exploited an opportunity to reduce costs in the research and exploration upstream stage in the value chain and has thereby created significant opportunity for itself.

Table 3.8	Examining the Value-Creating Potential of Support Activities

Procurement

Activities completed to purchase the inputs needed to produce a firm's products. Purchased inputs include items fully consumed during the manufacture of products (e.g., raw materials and supplies, as well as fixed assets—machinery, laboratory equipment, office equipment, and buildings).

Technological Development

Activities completed to improve a firm's product and the processes used to manufacture it. Technological development takes many forms, such as process equipment, basic research and product design, and servicing procedures.

Human Resource Management

Activities involved with recruiting, hiring, training, developing, and compensating all personnel.

Firm Infrastructure

Firm infrastructure includes activities such as general management, planning, finance, accounting, legal support, and governmental relations that are required to support the work of the entire value chain. Through its infrastructure, the firm strives to effectively and consistently identify external opportunities and threats, identify resources and capabilities, and support core competencies.

Each activity should be examined relative to competitors' abilities. Accordingly, firms rate each activity as *superior, equivalent,* or *inferior.*

SOURCE: Adapted with the permission of The Free Press, an imprint of Simon & Schuster Adult Publishing Group., from *Competitive Advantage: Creating and Sustaining Superior Performance,* by Michael E. Porter, pp. 40–43, Copyright © 1985, 1998 by Michael E. Porter.

Furthermore, because larger more established pharmaceutical firms have recognized Millennium's capabilities they have sought partnerships with Millennium to accelerate identifying genetic leads to foster cures using Millennium's platform for genetic exploration. Through partnering with firms such as Eli Lilly and Abbott Laboratories, Millennium has raised $1.8 billion, which, in turn, has helped the firm solidify its R&D platform even further.[108]

What should a firm do about primary and support activities in which its resources and capabilities are not a source of competence and competitive advantage? One solution these firms should consider is outsourcing.

Outsourcing

Outsourcing is the purchase of a value-creating activity from an external supplier.

Concerned with how components, finished goods, or services will be obtained, **outsourcing** is the purchase of a value-creating activity from an external supplier.[109] In multiple global industries, the trend toward outsourcing continues at a rapid pace.[110]

In some industries virtually all firms seek the value that can be captured through effective outsourcing. The automobile manufacturing and more recently the electronics industry are examples of these situations.[111] A number of examples of outsourcing are provided in the Strategic Focus on page 99.

Outsourcing is effective because few, if any, organizations possess the resources and capabilities required to achieve competitive superiority in all primary and support activities. With respect to technologies, for example, research suggests that few companies can afford to develop internally all the technologies that might lead to competitive advantage. By nurturing a smaller number of capabilities, a firm increases

Significant Changes in the Value Chains of Pharmaceutical Firms

Over the last few years, significant changes have taken place in the value chains of many pharmaceutical firms. The first medical remedies dated back to herbs and potions that people took to treat illnesses. In the pharmaceutical industry's early history, medical remedies began to be created through chemistry. Companies, especially in Germany, began to systematically isolate ingredients, test them for efficacy, and sell them as pills and serums. Firms such as Pfizer and Eli Lilly began during this phase and used a vertical integration strategy (defined in Chapter 6) along the value chain stages of research, testing, and delivery to the consumer.

In the 1960s, following Crick and Watson's discovery of DNA, biology and genetics became major sources of inputs to pharmaceutical firms. The genetic revolution brought two new *upstream*—or early stage—steps to the industry's value chain: research into genes that cause disease and identification of proteins that those genes produce. Highly specialized biotech firms such as AmGen and Genentech were started through these developments in the upstream research part of the value chain. For the most part, small rather than large companies dominated this new segment of the value chain. With no small firm having market power, this segment was highly fragmented (that is, the segment had a relatively large number of small firms competing against each other but with no firm able to significantly influence the competition among them).

More recently, the mapping of the human genome has further expanded the industry. Firms such as Millennium Pharmaceuticals have been involved in human genome research and mapping. Many of these upstream biopharmaceutical companies are now seeking to move downstream (later stages in the value chain) where larger, more established pharmaceutical companies are positioned with expertise in testing (pre-clinical trials and clinical trials) and delivery (manufacturing and marketing).

To expand downstream, many smaller biopharmaceutical firms have structured partnerships with the larger pharmaceutical firms, who invest in the smaller biotech firms. Biotech firms such as Celera, the major developer of the genome mapping project, and Millennium Pharmaceuticals have research platforms that are attractive to larger downstream pharmaceutical firms because they allow the smaller biotech firms to accelerate the process of identifying genetic leads to develop cures. For example, scientists can now study dozens of experiments in the space of a week, rather than just one experiment, by leveraging information technology in association with gene finding technologies to improve productivity in the discovery stage, one of the early segments of the value chain. Once a lead looks promising, a move to the testing stage is possible.

Because the early testing stages take considerable time, many information and Web-based strategies are employed. In the United States, 15 years and approximately $500 million are needed to develop a drug and bring it to market through both the pre-clinical trials and clinical trials' stages. Any time that can be pared from the 15-year period leads to reduced testing and staging costs. Small specialty online firms using a focus strategy (see Chapter 4) have sought to develop Web-based approaches to help speed up the trial testing phases of the value chain. For instance, Schering-Plough has contracted with Phase Forward Inc., whose system allows clinical investigators (doctors and researchers) to enter patient data directly to a website. This step eliminates error-checking of paper records and "can shave one to two years off getting a drug to market," says Phase Forward CEO Shiv Tasker. Datatrak, another trial contractor, offers online software that is estimated to cut the total trial time by 30 percent. Although these technologies are promising, they account for only a tiny fraction of all trials underway. One consultant suggests that "Everyone is waiting for a Quicken for clinical trials."

Not only does the Internet offer reduced error checking and time during the testing period, a Web-based approach can cost $35 per patient, compared with $350 per person now spent on advertising for patients, phone calls, and other means for the trial period. It also reduces error because the software automatically checks information as it is entered and catches most mistakes. The Web cannot speed up all pharmaceutical research. To determine how many cancer patients survived after two years of treatment, a two-year study is still required.

In regard to the value chain areas of manufacturing and marketing, although Web technologies offer alternative methods of delivery of prescription medicines, 90 percent of customers placing orders on the Web prefer to pick up their orders at a nearby store rather than have them shipped to their homes. A firm like Walgreens with its extensive network of stores has a potent advantage, even as ordering has shifted to the Internet. Accordingly, although online operations such as drugstore.com were forecasted to make brick-and-mortar pharmacies such as Walgreens obsolete and provide cheaper medicines for the consumer more directly from the producer, this has not turned out to be the case.

In summary, the value chain of pharmaceutical firms is changing drastically. In the upstream research stage, computer technologies speed the discovery of useful compounds, and the mapping of human genome project has fostered significant progress. Furthermore, testing has the potential to be shortened through Web-based strategies. Finally, significant changes have occurred in the downstream marketing and delivery of drugs. These changes in the value chain have created significant opportunities for new entrants as well as established producers.

SOURCES: D. Champion, 2001, Mastering the value chain: An interview with Mark Levin of Millennium Pharmaceuticals, *Harvard Business Review,* 79(6): 108–115; E. Licking, J. Carey, & J. Kerstetter, 2001, Bioinformatics, *Business Week,* Spring (Industrial/Technology Edition), 166–170; B. O'Keefe, 2001, Post-genome, Celera now shoots for profits, *Fortune,* February 19, 226; M. E. Porter, 2001, Strategy and the Internet, *Harvard Business Review,* 79(3): 62–78; R. Burcham, 2000, New pharma business model: Can we survive it? *Pharmaceutical Executive,* November, 94–100; J. Carey & E. Licking, 2000, An Rx for drug trials, *Business Week,* December 11, EB66–EB68.

the probability of developing a competitive advantage because it does not become overextended. In addition, by outsourcing activities in which it lacks competence, the firm can fully concentrate on those areas in which it can create value.[112]

Other research suggests that outsourcing does not work effectively without extensive internal capabilities to effectively coordinate external sourcing as well as internal coordination of core competencies.[113] Dell Computer, for example, outsources most of its manufacturing and customer service activities, allowing the firm to concentrate on creating value through its service and online distribution capabilities. However, as the Strategic Focus indicates, a company should exercise caution when most firms in the industry are engaged in outsourcing. Although many firms in the athletic shoe industry (for example, Nike and Reebok) outsource their manufacturing to lower average wage countries, some companies, such as New Balance, have decided not to ship the bulk of their manufacturing overseas. Although the Strategic Focus segment suggests that low-skilled labor and codified technologies logically should be outsourced to countries with lower cost structures and comparative advantage, New Balance has successfully challenged this assumption. Instead of outsourcing all of its production, like most other shoe companies, 20 percent of New Balance's production is kept within the company by upgrading low-skill jobs to improve efficiency. While shoes are still cheaper to produce in China ($1.30 per shoe compared to $4.00 per shoe in the United States), New Balance's domestically produced shoes are made more efficiently (24 minutes per shoe compared with three hours per shoe in China). New Balance believes that the ability to produce domestically, with the advantages of design and quality control that come with it, is worth the extra cost of only 4 percent

Figure 3.6 Prominent Applications of the Internet in the Value Chain

Firm Infrastructure
- Web-based, distributed financial and ERP systems
- On-line investor relations (e.g., information dissemination, broadcast conference calls)

Human Resource Management
- Self-service personnel and benefits administration
- Web-based training
- Internet-based sharing and dissemination of company information
- Electronic time and expense reporting

Technology Development
- Collaborative product design across locations and among multiple value-system participants
- Knowledge directories accessible from all parts of the organization
- Real-time access by R&D to on-line sales and service information

Procurement
- Internet-enabled demand planning; real-time available-to-promise/capable-to-promise and fulfillment
- Other linkage of purchase, inventory, and forecasting systems with suppliers
- Automated "requisition to pay"
- Direct and indirect procurement via marketplaces, exchanges, auctions, and buyer-seller matching

Inbound Logistics	**Operations**	**Outbound Logistics**	**Marketing and Sales**	**After-Sales Service**
• Real-time integrated scheduling, shipping, warehouse management, demand management, and planning, and advanced planning and scheduling across the company and its suppliers • Dissemination throughout the company of real-time inbound and in-progress inventory data	• Integrated information exchange, scheduling and decision making in in-house plants, contract assemblers, and components suppliers • Real-time available-to-promise and capable-to-promise information available to the sales force and channels	• Real-time transaction of orders whether initiated by an end consumer, a sales person, or a channel partner • Automated customer-specific agreements and contract terms • Customer and channel access to product development and delivery status • Collaborative integration with customer forecasting systems • Integrated channel management including information exchange, warranty claims, and contract management (versioning, process control)	• On-line sales channels including websites and marketplaces • Real-time inside and outside access to customer information, product catalogs, dynamic pricing, inventory availability, on-line submission of quotes, and order entry • On-line product configurators • Customer-tailored marketing via customer profiling • Push advertising • Tailored on-line access • Real-time customer feedback through Web surveys, opt-in/opt-out marketing, and promotion response tracking	• On-line support of customer service representatives through e-mail response management, billing integration, co-browse, chat, "call me now," voice-over-IP, and other uses of video streaming • Customer self-service via websites and intelligent service request processing including updates to billing and shipping profiles • Real-time field service access to customer account review, schematic review, parts availability and ordering, work-order update, and service parts management

← • Web-distributed supply chain management →

of the typical $70 shoe. While not all low-skill jobs could be made more efficient, New Balance raises the question as to which capabilities should be outsourced, even if they seem logical candidates for it.[114] We further study New Balance in Chapter 4 when we describe its use of the focused differentiation business-level strategy to compete against its rivals.

To verify that the appropriate primary and support activities are outsourced, four skills are essential for managers involved in outsourcing programs: strategic thinking; deal making; partnership governance; and managing change.[115] Managers should understand whether and how outsourcing creates competitive advantage within their company—they need to be able to think strategically.[116] To complete effective outsourcing transactions, these managers must also be deal makers, to be

Outsourcing Is an International Trend

Because of the significant economic downturn in Japan, many Japanese electronics firms are giving up the cherished dream of keeping everything in a vertically integrated family, where the firms manufacture most of the component parts of the products they ultimately produce. They can no longer ignore the global outsourcing trend. Many of the contract electronic manufacturers (CEMs) are buying Japanese-owned plants in the United States as well as in other countries. Hewlett-Packard, Cisco, IBM, Lucent, EMC, Ericsson, Motorola, and Nortel Networks all outsource to contract electronic manufacturers. One forecast estimated that 9.5 percent of the electronic goods sold throughout the world by original equipment manufacturers (OEMs) are now assembled in CEM plants. This percentage is expected to grow to 17 percent by 2003.

The largest CEMs are Solectron, SCI Systems, Celestica, Flextronics International, and Jabil Circuit. Most provide services besides manufacturing, ranging from product design and testing to supply chain management and even repair of brand-name equipment in the field. OEMs maintain control over critical parts and inbound logistics in regard to design and sourcing. For instance, Nortel uses Solectron and has asked the firm to assume much of the sourcing and procurement responsibilities in the manufacturing processes. Critical and customized components are excluded in order to maintain control over strategic capabilities, as Nortel wants to maintain negotiating power over its "crown jewel components."

Japanese firms are now turning to outsourcing more than in the past. Retailing has been a difficult area for outsourcing because of an archaic distribution system. However, entrepreneur Tadashi Yanaihas pursued a new type of distribution system based on outsourcing, which has allowed significant discounts. His firm, Fast Retailing, sells clothes at a 70 percent discount at its GAP-like Uniqlo stores in Japan. Fast Retailing's business model includes sending craftsmen from Japan to China to teach the latest production technology and styles. The firm contracts with factories in China that operate at 5 percent of the cost of those in Japan and ultra-cheap goods are sent directly to Fast Retailing's retail outlets, completely bypassing Japan's tangled distribution system.

Toys 'R' Us Japan is Japan's largest toy retailer. Since its first store opened in 1989, it is one of the few foreign retailers to have effectively made the transition to the Japanese market. The firm offers low-price toys at 120 stores and reports record profits for fiscal year 2002, outperforming other retailers weakened by the economic slump in Japan.

© Erioko Sugita/Reuters NewMedia Inc./CORBIS

Although Fast Retailing's approach is unique in Japan, the firm plans to roll out 50 apparel stores in the United Kingdom in late 2001. Firms such as Gap already get 80 percent of their apparel from overseas, with a large portion of these goods coming from China. Fast Retailing may find it difficult to compete with firms that already outsource where cheap labor is available.

Besides electronic and fashion goods, services are also being outsourced. Evalueserve is a firm in New Delhi, India that performs various business processes for clients in Europe and North America. This company offers not only cheaper but also better and faster service than its clients can deliver through their own networks. Firms such as Evalueserve do a lot of back-office work. Their clients electronically send data to them, which is processed in India and then returned to the client in a new, value-added form. A number of services are offered, including medical transcription; rule-set processing, such as whether an airlines' rules allow a passenger to upgrade to business class; problem solving, in which, for instance, the teleworker decides if an insurance claim should be paid; direct customer interaction, in which teleworkers handle transactions with client-customers, such as collecting delinquent payments from credit card customers; and expert knowledge services, where teleworkers predict how credit card users' behavior will change if their credit rating improves.

As broadband capability increases, other services, such as high-level media production for American filmmakers, are expected to grow. These higher end services have already been offered in India's software houses, which have built an $8 billion-dollar business on the quality and the price of Indian programming talent. Similarly, much R&D work is done in India because of India's ability to produce large numbers of hard scientists with PhDs. Much work is now shifting to India in regard to R&D on plastics and other areas of highly skilled manufacturing.

The automobile industry also uses outsourcing. For many years, the large auto manufacturers built vertically integrated systems that included wholly owned auto part suppliers. Recently in the United States, these firms have been spun off into independent parts suppliers, and the auto manufacturers now focus on outsourced supplier networks.

Outsourcing has produced significant savings across many industries, such as autos, electronics, apparel and back-office services. However, it can be carried too far, for instance, if a firm outsources its central areas of core competence. Dell successfully uses outsourcing because the personal computer industry uses standardized modules. Cisco exploited the modular architecture of its routers to compete in the telecommunications switching business from the low end. The firm efficiently outsourced much of its manufacturing to suppliers and much of its new product development to the startups it acquires.

However, once Cisco moved towards optical networks, it was forced to do more integration and perform product design and manufacturing activities internally. Once a firm moves into higher levels of technology where the technology is not solidified, internal sourcing (or vertical integration, as discussed in Chapter 6) constitutes a competitive advantage versus outsourcing. Over time, firms shift back and forth between vertical integration and outsourcing, and managers need to make sure that outsourcing fits their particular situation.

SOURCES: A. Bernstein, 2001, Low-skilled jobs: Do they have to move? *Business Week,* February 26, 94; C. M. Christensen, 2001, The past and future of competitive advantage, *Sloan Management Review* 42(2): 105–109; 2001, Business Special: Back office to the world, *The Economist,* May 5, 59–62; B. Fulford, 2001, One-man restructuring act, *Forbes,* July 9, 106; C. Serant & R. Lamb, 2001, Mega outsourcing deals stall as OEMs re-evaluate demand, *Electronic Business News,* June 18, 12–3; G. Bylinsky, 2000, For sale: Japanese plants in the U.S., *Fortune,* February 21, 240B–240D.

able to secure rights from external providers that can be fully used by internal managers. They must be able to oversee and govern appropriately the relationship with the company to which the services were outsourced. Because outsourcing can significantly change how an organization operates, managers administering these programs must also be able to manage that change, including resolving employee resistance that accompanies any significant change effort.[117]

Core Competencies: Cautions and Reminders

Tools such as outsourcing can help the firm focus on its core competencies. However, evidence shows that the value-creating ability of core competencies should never be taken for granted. Moreover, the ability of a core competence to be a permanent competitive advantage can't be assumed. The reason for these cautions is that all core competencies have the potential to become *core rigidities.* As Leslie Wexner, CEO of The Limited, Inc., says: "Success doesn't beget success. Success begets failure because the more that you know a thing works, the less likely you are to think that it won't work. When you've had a long string of victories, it's harder to foresee your own vulnerabilities."[118] Thus, each competence is a strength and a weakness—a strength because it is the source of competitive advantage and, hence, strategic competitiveness, and a weakness because, if emphasized when it is no longer competitively relevant, it can be a seed of organizational inertia.[119]

Events occurring in the firm's external environment create conditions through which core competencies can become core rigidities, generate inertia, and stifle innovation. "Often the flip side, the dark side, of core capabilities is revealed due to external events when new competitors figure out a better way to serve the firm's customers, when new technologies emerge, or when political or social events shift the ground underneath."[120] However, in the final analysis, changes in the external environment do not cause core capabilities or core competencies to become core rigidities; rather, strategic myopia and inflexibility on the part of managers are the cause.[121]

These shortcomings may be the case at Bavarian Motor Works (BMW). Historically, BMW's unique internal process for designing automobiles has been a competitive advantage that other firms have not been able to duplicate. The firm's design process has required extensive and complex cooperative interactions among a large group of engineers. Recently, to reduce costs, BMW created a system that enables its engineers to use computer simulations to crash-test the cars they have designed and thereby improve them. This technology codifies into a set of algorithms what formerly had been achieved only through complex social interaction among BMW engineers. As such, the firm has codified what had been a complex intangible resource (interactions among design engineers), jeopardizing what had been a competitive advantage. It is much easier for BMW's rivals to imitate a computer simulation than to understand the complex, often unobservable interactions among the firm's engineers. Thus, at least in part, this competitive advantage may not be as valuable as it once was. However, continuous learning by BMW design engineers may allow the firm to maintain its competitive advantage in the long run.[122]

Summary

- In the global landscape, traditional factors (e.g., labor costs and superior access to financial resources and raw materials) can still create a competitive advantage. However, this happens in a declining number of instances. In the new landscape, the resources, capabilities, and core competencies in the firm's internal environment may have a relatively stronger influence on its performance than do conditions in the external environment. The most effective firms recognize that strategic competitiveness and above-average returns result only when core competencies (identified through the study of the firm's internal environment) are matched with opportunities (determined through the study of the firm's external environment).

- No competitive advantage lasts forever. Over time, rivals use their own unique resources, capabilities, and core competencies to form different value-creating propositions that duplicate the value-creating ability of the firm's competitive advantages. In general, the Internet's capabilities are reducing the sustainability of many competitive advantages. Thus, because competitive advantages are not sustainable on a permanent basis, firms must exploit their current advantages while simultaneously using their resources and capabilities to form new advantages that can lead to competitive success in the future.

- Effective management of core competencies requires careful analysis of the firm's resources (inputs to the production process) and capabilities (capacities for teams of resources to perform a task or activity in an integrative manner). To successfully manage core competencies, decision makers must be self-confident, courageous, and willing both to hold others accountable for their work and to be held accountable for the outcomes of their own efforts.

- Individual resources are usually not a source of competitive advantage. Capabilities, which are groupings of tangible and intangible resources, are a more likely source of competitive advantages, especially relatively sustainable ones. A key reason for this is that the firm's nurturing and support of core competencies that are based on capabilities is less visible to rivals and, as such, is harder to understand and imitate.

- Increasingly, employees' knowledge is viewed as perhaps the most relevant source of competitive advantage. To gain maximum benefit from knowledge, efforts are taken to find ways for individuals' unique knowledge sets to be shared throughout the firm. The Internet's capabilities affect both the development and the sharing of knowledge.

- Only when a capability is valuable, rare, costly to imitate, and nonsubstitutable is it a core competence and a source of competitive advantage. Over time, core competencies must be supported, but they cannot be allowed to become core rigidities. Core competencies are a source of competitive advantage only when they allow the firm to create value by exploiting opportunities in the external environment. When this is no longer the case, attention shifts to selecting or forming other capabilities that do satisfy the four criteria of sustainable competitive advantage.

- Value chain analysis is used to identify and evaluate the competitive potential of resources and capabilities. By studying their skills relative to those associated with primary and support activities, firms can understand their cost structure and identify the activities through which they can create value.

- When the firm cannot create value in either a primary or support activity, outsourcing is considered. Used commonly in the global economy, outsourcing is the purchase of a value-creating activity from an external supplier. The firm must outsource only to companies possessing a competitive advantage in terms of the particular primary or support activity under consideration. In addition, the firm must continuously verify that it is not outsourcing activities from which it could create value.

Review Questions

1. Why is it important for a firm to study and understand its internal environment?

2. What is value? Why is it critical for the firm to create value? How does it do so?

3. What are the differences between tangible and intangible resources? Why is it important for decision makers to understand these differences? Are tangible resources linked more closely to the creation of competitive advantages than intangible resources, or is the reverse true? Why?

4. What are capabilities? What must firms do to create capabilities?

5. What are the four criteria used to determine which of a firm's capabilities are core competencies? Why is it important for these criteria to be used?

6. What is value chain analysis? What does the firm gain when it successfully uses this tool?

7. What is outsourcing? Why do firms outsource? Will outsourcing's importance grow in the 21st century? If so, why?

8. What are core rigidities? Why is it vital that firms prevent core competencies from becoming core rigidities?

Organizational Resources

The organizations listed in the table below have different capabilities, core competencies, and competitive advantages.

Part One. In small groups, consider each firm and use logic and consensus to complete the table. Alternatively, complete the table on an individual basis.

Organization	Capabilities	Core Competencies	Competitive Advantage
McDonald's			
NBC			
Post Office			
Microsoft			

Part Two. Based on your responses to the table, now compare each type of firm in terms of its resources and suggest some reasons for the differences.

	Is the Resource or Capability				Competitive consequences: • Competitive disadvantage • Competitive parity • Temporary competitive advantage • Sustainable competitive advantage	Performance implications: • Below-average returns • Average returns • Above-average returns
	Valuable?	Rare?	Costly to Imitate?	Nonsub-stitutable?		
McDonald's						
NBC						
Post Office						
Microsoft						

Notes

1. C. A. Bartlett & S. Ghoshal, 2002, Building competitive advantage through people, *MIT Sloan Management Review*, 43(2): 34–41.
2. R. R. Wiggins & T. W. Ruefli, 2002, Sustained competitive advantage: Temporal dynamics and the incidence of persistence of superior economic performance, *Organization Science*, 13: 82–105.
3. M. J. Rouse & U. S. Daellenbach, 1999, Rethinking research methods for the resource-based perspective: Isolating sources of sustainable competitive advantage, *Strategic Management Journal*, 20: 487–494.
4. C. G. Brush, P. G. Greene, & M. M. Hart, 2001, From initial idea to unique advantage: The entrepreneurial challenge of constructing a resource base, *Academy of Management Executive*, 15(1): 64–78.
5. R. Makadok, 2001, Toward a synthesis of the resource-based and dynamic-capability views of rent creation, *Strategic Management Journal*, 22: 387–401; K. M. Eisenhardt & J. A. Martin, 2000, Dynamic capabilities: What are they? *Strategic Management Journal*, 21: 1105–1121.
6. M. A. Hitt, L. Bierman, K. Shimizu, & R. Kochhar, 2001, Direct and moderating effects of human capital on strategy and performance in professional service firms: A resource-based perspective, *Academy of Management Journal*, 44: 13–28; J. Lee & D. Miller, 1999, People matter: Commitment to employees, strategy and performance in Korean firms, *Strategic Management Journal*, 20: 579–593.
7. R. Lyman & G. Fabrikant, 2001, Suddenly, high stakes for Disney's film and TV businesses, *The New York Times Interactive*, http://www.nytimes.com, May 21.
8. E. Autio, H. J. Sapienza, & J. G. Almeida, 2000, Effects of age at entry, knowledge intensity, and imitability on international growth, *Academy of Management Journal*, 43: 909–924.
9. P. L. Yeoh & K. Roth, 1999, An empirical analysis of sustained advantage in the U.S. pharmaceutical industry: Impact of firm resources and capabilities, *Strategic Management Journal*, 20: 637–653.
10. D. F. Abell, 1999, Competing today while preparing for tomorrow, *Sloan Management Review*, 40(3): 73–81; D. Leonard-Barton, 1995, *Wellsprings of Knowledge: Building and Sustaining the Sources of Innovation* (Boston: Harvard Business School Press); R. A. McGrath, J. C. MacMillan, & S. Venkataraman, 1995, Defining and developing competence: A strategic process paradigm, *Strategic Management Journal*, 16: 251–275.
11. K. M. Eisenhardt, 1999, Strategy as strategic decision making, *Sloan Management Review*, 40(3): 65–72.
12. H. K. Steensma & K. G. Corley, 2000, On the performance of technology-sourcing partnerships: The interaction between partner interdependence and technology attributes, *Academy of Management Journal*, 43: 1045–1067.
13. J. B. Barney, 2001, Is the resource-based "view" a useful perspective for strategic management research? Yes, *Academy of Management Review*, 26: 41–56.

14. J. K. Sebenius, 2002, The hidden challenge of cross-border negotiations, *Harvard Business Review*, 80(3): 76–85; P. W. Liu & X. Yang, 2000, The theory of irrelevance of the size of the firm, *Journal of Economic Behavior & Organization*, 42: 145–165.

15. P. F. Drucker, 2002, They're not employees, they're people, *Harvard Business Review*, 80(2): 70–77; G. Verona, 1999, A resource-based view of product development, *Academy of Management Review*, 24: 132–142.

16. M. Tripsas & G. Gavetti, 2000, Capabilities, cognition, and inertia: Evidence from digital imaging, *Strategic Management Journal*, 21: 1147–1161.

17. D. Whitford, 2001, Polaroid, R.I.P. *Fortune*, November 12, 44.

18. S. Ghoshal & C. A. Bartlett, 1995, Changing the role of top management: Beyond structure to processes, *Harvard Business Review*, 73(1): 96.

19. L. Greenhalgh, 2000, Ford Motor Company's CEO Jac Nasser on transformational change, e-business, and environmental responsibility, *Academy of Management Executive*, 14(3): 46–51.

20. J. Muller, 2001, Ford: Why it's worse than you think, *Business Week*, http://www.businessweek.com, June 25.

21. Barney, Is the resource-based "view" a useful perspective for strategic management research? Yes; V. P. Rindova & C. J. Fombrun, 1999, Constructing competitive advantage: The role of firm-constituent interactions, *Strategic Management Journal*, 20: 691–710; M. A. Peteraf, 1993, The cornerstones of competitive strategy: A resource-based view, *Strategic Management Journal*, 14: 179–191.

22. Barney, Is the resource-based "view" a useful perspective for strategic management research? Yes; T. H. Brush & K. W. Artz, 1999, Toward a contingent resource-based theory: The impact of information asymmetry on the value of capabilities in veterinary medicine, *Strategic Management Journal*, 20: 223–250.

23. M. E. Porter, 1996, What is strategy? *Harvard Business Review*, 74(6): 61–78.

24. S. K. McEvily & B. Chakravarthy, 2002, The persistence of knowledge-based advantage: An empirical test for product performance and technological knowledge, *Strategic Management Journal*, 23: 285–305; P. J. Buckley & M. J. Carter, 2000, Knowledge management in global technology markets: Applying theory to practice, *Long Range Planning*, 33(1): 55–71.

25. 1998, Pocket Strategy, *Value*, The Economist Books, 165.

26. J. Useem, 2001, Most admired: Conquering vertical limits, *Fortune,* February 19, 84–96.

27. Ibid.

28. J. Wolf & W. G. Egelhoff, 2002, A reexamination and extension of international strategy-structure theory, *Strategic Management Journal*, 23: 181–189; R. Ramirez, 1999, Value co-production: Intellectual origins and implications for practice and research, *Strategic Management Journal*, 20: 49–65.

29. S. W. Floyd & B. Wooldridge, 1999, Knowledge creation and social networks in corporate entrepreneurship: The renewal of organizational capability, *Entrepreneurship: Theory and Practice*, 23(3): 123–143; A. Campbell & M. Alexander, 1997, What's wrong with strategy? *Harvard Business Review*, 75(6): 42–51.

30. M. A. Hitt, R. D. Nixon, P. G. Clifford, & K. P. Coyne, 1999, The development and use of strategic resources, in M. A. Hitt, P. G. Clifford, R. D. Nixon, & K. P. Coyne (eds.), *Dynamic Strategic Resources*, Chichester: John Wiley & Sons, 1–14.

31. C. M. Christensen, 2001, The past and future of competitive advantage, *Sloan Management Review*, 42(2): 105–109.

32. T. H. Davenport, 2001, Data to knowledge to results: Building an analytic capability, *California Management Review*, 43(2): 117–138; J. B. Barney, 1999, How a firm's capabilities affect boundary decisions, *Sloan Management Review*, 40(3): 137–145.

33. P. Westhead, M. Wright, & D. Ucbasaran, 2001, The internationalization of new and small firms: A resource-based view, *Journal of Business Venturing* 16(4): 333–358; A. McWilliams, D. D. Van Fleet, & P. M. Wright, 2001, Strategic management of human resources for global competitive advantage, *Journal of Business Strategies* 18(1): 1–24; N. Athanassiou & D. Nigh, 1999, The impact of U.S. company internationalization on top management team advice networks: A tacit knowledge perspective, *Strategic Management Journal*, 20: 83–92.

34. H. Collingwood, 2001, The earnings game: Everyone plays, nobody wins, *Harvard Business Review*, 79(6): 65–74.

35. Eisenhardt, Strategy as strategic decision making.

36. R. S. Dooley & G. E. Fryxell, 1999, Attaining decision quality and commitment from dissent: The moderating effects of loyalty and competence in strategic decision-making teams, *Academy of Management Journal*, 42: 389–402.

37. P. C. Nutt, 1999, Surprising but true: Half the decisions in organizations fail, *Academy of Management Executive*, 13(4): 75–90.

38. M. Keil, 2000, Cutting your losses: Extricating your organization when a big project goes awry, *Sloan Management Review*, 41(3): 55–68.

39. P. G. Audia, E. Locke, & K. G. Smith, 2000, The paradox of success: An archival and a laboratory study of strategic persistence following radical environmental change. *Academy of Management Journal*, 43:837–853; D. A. Aaker & E. Joachimsthaler, 1999, The lure of global branding, *Harvard Business Review*, 77(6): 137–144; R. G. McGrath, 1999, Falling forward: Real options reasoning and entrepreneurial failure, *Academy of Management Review*, 24: 13–30.

40. G. P. West III & J. DeCastro, 2001, The Achilles heel of firm strategy: Resource weaknesses and distinctive inadequacies, *Journal of Management Studies*, 38: 417–442; G. Gavetti & D. Levinthal, 2000, Looking forward and looking backward: Cognitive and experimental search, *Administrative Science Quarterly*, 45: 113–137.

41. R. Amit & P. J. H. Schoemaker, 1993, Strategic assets and organizational rent, *Strategic Management Journal*, 14: 33–46.

42. R. E. Hoskisson & L. W. Busenitz, 2001, Market uncertainty and learning distance in corporate entrepreneurship entry mode choice. In M. A. Hitt, R. D. Ireland, S. M. Camp, & D. L. Sexton (eds.), *Strategic Entrepreneurship: Creating a New Integrated Mindset*, Oxford, U.K.: Blackwell Publishers, 151–172.

43. A. L. Zacharakis & D. L. Shepherd, 2001, The nature of information and overconfidence on venture capitalist's decision making, *Journal of Business Venturing*, 16: 311–332.

44. P. Burrows & A. Park, 2002, What price victory at Hewlett-Packard? *Business Week*, April 1, 36–37.

45. H. Thomas, T. Pollock, & P. Gorman, 1999, Global strategic analyses: Frameworks and approaches, *Academy of Management Executive*, 13(1): 70–82.

46. J. M. Mezias, P. Grinyer, & W. D. Guth, 2001, Changing collective cognition: A process model for strategic change, *Long Range Planning*, 34(1): 71–95.

47. U. Harnischfeger, 2001, Opel limits its ambitions in a grim market, *Financial Times*, http://www.ft.com, June 21.

48. N. Tichy, 1999, The teachable point of view, *Harvard Business Review*, 77(2): 82–83.

49. Brush, Greene, & Hart, From initial idea to unique advantage.

50. Eisenhardt & Martin, Dynamic capabilities: What are they?; M. D. Michalisin, D. M. Kline, & R. D. Smith, 2000, Intangible strategic assets and firm performance: A multi-industry study of the resource-based view, *Journal of Business Strategies*, 17(2): 91–117.

51. West & DeCastro, The Achilles heel of firm strategy: Resource weaknesses and distinctive inadequacies; D. L. Deeds, D. DeCarolis, & J. Coombs, 2000, Dynamic capabilities and new product development in high technology ventures: An empirical analysis of new biotechnology firms, *Journal of Business Venturing*, 15: 211–229; T. Chi, 1994, Trading in strategic resources: Necessary conditions, transaction cost problems, and choice of exchange structure, *Strategic Management Journal*, 15: 271–290.

52. S. Berman, J. Down, & C. Hill, 2002, Tacit knowledge as a source of competitive advantage in the National Basketball Association, *Academy of Management Journal*, 45: 13–31.

53. S. Shepard, 2001, Interview: 'The company is not in the stock', *Business Week*, April 30, 94–96.

54. M. S. Feldman, 2000, Organizational routines as a source of continuous change, *Organization Science*, 11: 611–629; A. M. Knott & B. McKelvey, 1999, Nirvana efficiency: A comparative test of residual claims and routines, *Journal of Economic Behavior & Organization*, 38: 365–383.

55. R. Lubit, 2001, Tacit knowledge and knowledge management: The keys to sustainable competitive advantage, *Organizational Dynamics*, 29(3): 164–178; S. A. Zahra, A. P. Nielsen, & W. C. Bogner, 1999, Corporate entrepreneurship, knowledge, and competence development, *Entrepreneurship: Theory and Practice*, 23(3): 169–189.

56. A. M. Webber, 2000, New math for a new economy, *Fast Company*, January/February, 214–224.

57. R. G. Schroeder, K. A. Bates, & M. A. Junttila, 2002, A resource-based view of manufacturing strategy and the relationship to manufacturing performance, *Strategic Management Journal*, 23: 105–117.

58. Brush & Artz, Toward a contingent resource-based theory.

59. J. B. Quinn, P. Anderson, & S. Finkelstein, 1996, Making the most of the best, *Harvard Business Review*, 74(2): 71–80.

60. Webber, New math, 217.

61. Ibid., 218.

62. R. D. Ireland, M. A. Hitt, & D. Vaidyanath, 2002, Managing strategic alliances to achieve a competitive advantage, *Journal of Management* (in press).

63. D. L. Deephouse, 2000, Media reputation as a strategic resource: An integration of mass communication and resource-based theories, *Journal of Management*, 26: 1091–1112.

64. M. Kleinman, 2001, Harley pushes brand prestige, *Marketing*, May 17, 16; G. Rifkin, 1998, How Harley-Davidson revs its brand, *Strategy & Business*, 9: 31–40.

65. G. Gavetti & D. Levinthal 2000, Looking forward and looking backward: Cognitive and experimental search. *Administrative Science Quarterly*, 45: 113–137; R. W. Coff, 1999, How buyers cope with uncertainty when acquiring firms in knowledge-intensive industries: Caveat emptor, *Organization Science*, 10: 144–161; S. J. Marsh & A. L. Ranft, 1999, Why resources matter: An empirical study of knowledge-based resources on new market entry, in M. A. Hitt, P. G. Clifford, R. D. Nixon, & K. P. Coyne (eds.), *Dynamic Strategic Resources* (Chichester: John Wiley & Sons), 43–66.

66. C. E. Helfat & R. S. Raubitschek, 2000, Product sequencing: Co-evolution of knowledge, capabilities and products, *Strategic Management Journal*, 21: 961–979.

67. Hitt, Bierman, Shimizu, & Kochhar, Direct and moderating effects of human capital on strategy and performance in professional service firms: A resource-based perspective; M. A. Hitt, R. D. Ireland, & H. Lee, 2000, Technological learning, knowledge management, firm growth and performance: An introductory essay, *Journal of Engineering and Technology Management*, 17: 231–246; D. G. Hoopes & S. Postrel, 1999, Shared knowledge: "Glitches," and product development performance, *Strategic Management Journal*, 20: 837–865; J. B. Quinn, 1994, *The Intelligent Enterprise*, New York: Free Press.

68. 1999, Thoughts on the business of life, *Forbes*, May 17, 352.

69. L. Argote & P. Ingram, 2000, Knowledge transfer: A basis for competitive advantage in firms, *Organizational Behavior and Human Decision Processes*, 82: 150–169.

70. G. G. Dess & J. C. Picken, 1999, *Beyond Productivity*, New York: AMACOM.

71. P. Coy, 2002, High turnover, high risk, *Business Week* (Special Issue), Spring, 24.

72. T. T. Baldwin & C. C. Danielson, 2000, Building a learning strategy at the top: Interviews with ten of America's CLOs, *Business Horizons*, 43(6): 5–14.

73. D. F. Kuratko, R. D. Ireland, & J. S. Hornsby, 2001, Improving firm performance through entrepreneurial actions: Acordia's corporate entrepreneurship strategy, *Academy of Management Executive*, 15(4): 60–71; M. T. Hansen, N. Nhoria, & T. Tierney, 1999, What's your strategy for managing knowledge? *Harvard Business Review*, 77(2): 106–116.

74. M. A. Hitt & R. D. Ireland, 1986, Relationships among corporate level distinctive competencies, diversification strategy, corporate structure, and performance, *Journal of Management Studies*, 23: 401–416; M. A. Hitt & R. D. Ireland, 1985, Corporate distinctive competence, strategy, industry, and performance, *Strategic Management Journal*, 6: 273–293; M. A. Hitt, R. D. Ireland, & K. A. Palia, 1982, Industrial firms' grand strategy and functional importance, *Academy of Management Journal*, 25: 265–298; M. A. Hitt, R. D. Ireland, & G. Stadter, 1982, Functional importance and company performance: Moderating effects of grand strategy and industry type, *Strategic Management Journal*, 3: 315–330; C. C. Snow & E. G. Hrebiniak, 1980, Strategy, distinctive competence, and organizational performance, *Administrative Science Quarterly*, 25: 317–336.

75. K. Hafeez, Y. B. Zhang, & N. Malak, 2002, Core competence for sustainable competitive advantage: A structured methodology for identifying core competence, *IEEE Transactions on Engineering Management*, 49(1): 28–35; C. K. Prahalad & G. Hamel, 1990, The core competence of the corporation, *Harvard Business Review*, 68(3): 79–93.

76. C. Bowman & V. Ambrosini, 2000, Value creation versus value capture: Towards a coherent definition of value in strategy, *British Journal of Management*, 11: 1–15; T. Chi, 1994, Trading in strategic resources: Necessary conditions, transaction cost problems, and choice of exchange structure, *Strategic Management Journal*, 15: 271–290.

77. C. Bowman, 2001, "Value" in the resource-based view of the firm: A contribution to the debate, *Academy of Management Review*, 26: 501–502.

78. C. Ames, 1995, Sales soft? Profits flat? It's time to rethink your business, *Fortune*, June 25, 142–146.

79. N. D. Schwartz, 2001, Remedies for an economic hangover, *Fortune*, June 25, 130–138.

80. Barney, How a firm's capabilities; J. B. Barney, 1995, Looking inside for competitive advantage, *Academy of Management Executive*, 9(4): 59–60; J. B. Barney, 1991, Firm resources and sustained competitive advantage, *Journal of Management*, 17: 99–120.

81. C. H. St. John & J. S. Harrison, 1999, Manufacturing-based relatedness, synergy, and coordination, *Strategic Management Journal*, 20: 129–145.

82. Barney, Looking inside for competitive advantage.

83. M. Betts, 2001, Turning browsers into buyers, *Sloan Management Review*, 42(2): 8–9.

84. Ibid.

85. G. Colvin, 2001, Shaking hands on the Web, *Fortune*, May 14, 54.

86. R. Tomkins, 1999, Marketing value for money, *Financial Times*, May 14, 18.

87. Barney, Looking inside for competitive advantage, 52.

88. Brush, Greene, & Hart, From initial idea to unique advantage, 65–67.

89. Barney, Looking inside for competitive advantage, 53.

90. Barney, How a firm's capabilities, 141.

91. Barney, Firm resources, 108.

92. J. Huey, 1993, How McKinsey does it, *Fortune*, November 1, 56–81.

93. J. Kurtzman, 1997, An interview with Rosabeth Moss Kanter, *Strategy & Business*, 16: 85–94.

94. R. Burt, 1999, When is corporate culture a competitive asset? Mastering Strategy (Part Six), *Financial Times*, November 1, 14–15.

95. L. Soupata, 2001, Managing culture for competitive advantage at United Parcel Service, *Journal of Organizational Excellence*, 20(3): 19–26.

96. A. W. King & C. P. Zeithaml, 2001, Competencies and firm performance: Examining the causal ambiguity paradox, *Strategic Management Journal*, 22: 75–99; R. Reed & R. DeFillippi, 1990, Causal ambiguity, barriers to imitation, and sustainable competitive advantage, *Academy of Management Review*, 15: 88–102.

97. Leonard-Barton, *Wellsprings of Knowledge*, 7.

98. A. Ritt, 2000, Reaching for maximum flexibility, *Iron Age New Steel*, January, 20–26.

99. A. K. Gupta & V. Govindarajan, 2000, Knowledge management's social dimension: Lessons from Nucor steel, *Sloan Management Review*, 42(1): 71–80.

100. Barney, Firm resources, 111.

101. Amit & Schoemaker, Strategic assets, 39.

102. S. K. McEvily, S. Das, & K. McCabe, 2000, Avoiding competence substitution through knowledge sharing, *Academy of Management Review*, 25: 294–311.

103. A. Serwer, 2002, Dell does domination, *Fortune*, January 21, 70–75.

104. M. E. Porter, 1985, *Competitive Advantage*, New York: Free Press, 33–61.

105. G. G. Dess, A. Gupta, J.-F. Hennart, & C. W. L. Hill, 1995, Conducting and integrating strategy research at the international corporate and business levels: Issues and directions, *Journal of Management*, 21: 376; Porter, What is strategy?

106. J. Webb & C. Gile, 2001, Reversing the value chain, *Journal of Business Strategy*, 22(2): 13–17; T. A. Stewart, 1999, Customer learning is a two-way street, *Fortune*, May 10, 158–160.

107. R. Amit & C. Zott, 2001, Value creation in E-business, *Strategic Management Journal*, 22(Special Issue): 493–520; M. E. Porter, 2001, Strategy and the Internet, *Harvard Business Review*, 79(3): 62–78.

108. D. Champion, 2001, Mastering the value chain: An interview with Mark Levin of Millennium Pharmaceuticals, *Harvard Business Review*, 79(6): 108–115.

109. J. Y. Murray & M. Kotabe, 1999, Sourcing strategies of U.S. service companies: A modified transaction-cost analysis, *Strategic Management Journal*, 20: 791–809.

110. S. Jones, 1999, Growth process in global market, *Financial Times*, June 22, 17.

111. A. Takeishi, 2001, Bridging inter- and intra-firm boundaries: Management of supplier involvement in automobile product development, *Strategic Management Journal*, 22: 403–433; H. Y. Park, C. S. Reddy, & S. Sarkar, 2000, Make or buy strategy of firms in the U.S., *Multinational Business Review*, 8(2): 89–97.

112. Hafeez, Zhang, & Malak, Core competence for sustainable competitive advantage; B. H. Jevnaker & M. Bruce, 1999, Design as a strategic alliance: Expanding the creative capability of the firm, in M. A. Hitt, P. G. Clifford, R. D. Nixon, & K. P. Coyne (eds.). *Dynamic Strategic Resources*, Chichester: John Wiley & Sons, 266–298.

113. A. Takeishi, Bridging inter- and intra-firm boundaries: Management of supplier involvement in automobile product development, 403–433.

114. A Bernstein, 2001, Low-skilled jobs: do they have to move? *Business Week*, February 26, 94.

115. M. Useem & J. Harder, 2000, Leading laterally in company outsourcing, *Sloan Management Review*, 41(2): 25–36.

116. R. C. Insinga & M. J. Werle, 2000, Linking outsourcing to business strategy, *Academy of Management Executive*, 14(4): 58–70.

117. M. Katz, 2001, Planning ahead for manufacturing facility changes: A case study in outsourcing, *Pharmaceutical Technology*, March: 160–164.

118. G. G. Dess & J. C. Picken, 1999, Creating competitive (dis)advantage: Learning from Food Lion's freefall, *Academy of Management Executive*, 13(3): 97–111.

119. M. Hannan & J. Freeman, 1977, The population ecology of organizations, *American Journal of Sociology*, 82: 929–964.

120. Leonard-Barton, *Wellsprings of Knowledge*, 30–31.

121. West & DeCastro, The Achilles heel of firm strategy; Keil, Cutting your losses.

122. Christensen, The past and future of competitive advantage.

Strategic Actions: S̶t̶r̶a̶t̶e̶g̶y̶ ̶F̶o̶r̶m̶u̶l̶a̶t̶i̶o̶n̶

4

Chapter Four

Business-Level Strategy

Knowledge Objectives

Studying this chapter should provide you with the strategic management knowledge needed to:

1. Define business-level strategies.

2. Discuss the relationship between customers and business-level strategies in terms of *who*, *what*, and *how*.

3. Explain the differences among business-level strategies.

4. Use the five forces of competition model to explain how above-average returns can be earned through each business-level strategy.

5. Describe the risks of using each of the business-level strategies.

Developing and Using Carefully Designed Strategies: The Key to Corporate Success

Internet technology has a tremendous effect on how firms compete in the 21st century. In Chapter 2, we noted how the Internet affects both industry structures and the potential to operate profitably within them. Internet technology itself, however, is rarely a competitive advantage. It actually makes it more essential for a firm to develop well-designed business-level strategies in order to detail how Internet technology can enable the success of the firm's other strategic actions. According to Michael Porter, many of the companies that succeed in the 21st century ". . . will be ones that use the Internet as a complement to traditional ways of competing, not those that set their Internet initiatives apart from their established operations."

Whatever business-level strategy the firm chooses, it should be carefully developed. Moreover, because of the importance of human capital to a company's competitive success (as discussed in Chapter 3), the ultimate effectiveness of a business-level strategy is strongly influenced by the quality of the people the organization employs. In light of environmental changes and the capabilities of Internet technology, companies across most industries are changing their business-level strategies. For example, an analysis of a number of property-casualty insurers shows that many of these companies have not effectively integrated the Internet into their business-level strategies. However, the competitive pressures within this industry to have an effective on-line presence are influencing the actions many of these firms are taking to establish a competitive advantage while using their business-level strategy.

In mid-2001, networking firms such as Cisco Systems, Nortel Networks, and Lucent Technologies refocused their optical technology strategies in response to dramatically altered conditions in their environments. Cisco decided to place less emphasis on the enterprise market so it could concentrate more on lucrative sales to service providers. Cisco also decided that part of its optical technology business-level strategy of focused differentiation would be to pursue opportunities for fiber-optic related products in metropolitan area networks (MANs). These decisions allowed Cisco to continue its growth-oriented strategies during its mid-2001 decline in sales revenue.

Senior vice president for Cisco Systems' Internet Switching and Services Group and former chief strategy officer Mike Volpi is responsible for developing products, including Cisco's Catalyst 4000, which allows broadband access over fiber-optic networks.

CISCO SYSTEMS, INC.

Lucent's strategy in the core optical technology market is to offer cheaper alternatives, while maintaining at least acceptable levels of differentiation such as quality with each alternative. These actions demonstrate Lucent's use of the cost leadership business-level strategy in this particular product line. Some of Lucent's recent customers are located in nations outside the United States. The firm's strategy appears to have been successful. Belgacom of Belgium and P&T Luxembourg recently chose Lucent to expand the capacity of the two parallel optical network connections between their networks in Belgium and Luxembourg. Lucent has also signed a contract with GNG Networks, one of the leading broadband Internet infrastructure providers in Korea, to provide a high-speed optical networking system for GNG's backbone network.

According to an analyst, Nortel's optical technology strategy is to ". . . compete in key segments of the industry, such as Internet data centers and broadband, and to dominate the optical market and grow related businesses off that." Nortel's concentration on serving only key segments of an industry demonstrates the use of the focused differentiation business-level strategy. With 75 percent of all North American Internet traffic riding across Nortel's optical network equipment, and more than 750 optical Internet customers worldwide, the firm is now working on making networks that are 20 times faster and capable of handling even more traffic.

Smaller, nimbler companies, such as RedBack Networks, Sycamore Networks, and Ciena, are also creating new optical technology strategies. For the most part, these entrepreneurial ventures competing against Cisco, Lucent, and Nortel are using focused differentiation business-level strategies to serve the needs of particular market segments more effectively than companies with strategies aimed at serving all of a market. However, as will be discussed in the next chapter, one firm's strategies are met with responses from its competitors.

SOURCES: G. Anders, 2001, John Chambers after the deluge, *Fast Company*, July, 100–111; G. Biehn, 2001, Yes, you can profit from e-commerce, *Financial Executive*, May, 26–27; A. P. Burger, 2001, Getting your program back on track. *American Agent & Broker*, May, 69; S. Lee, 2001, Optical titans refocus, *InfoWorld*, April 2, 1, 29; M. E. Porter, 2001, Strategy and the Internet, *Harvard Business Review*, 79(3): 63–78; A. C. Trembly, 2001, Most P-C insurers lack web strategy, *National Underwriter*, February 26, 1, 23; E. Zimmerman, 2001, What are employees worth? *Workforce*, February, 32–36; http://www.lucent.com; http://www.nortel.com.

Strategy is concerned with making choices among two or more alternatives. When choosing a strategy, the firm decides to pursue one course of action instead of others. Indeed, the main point of strategy is to help decision makers choose among the competing priorities and alternatives facing their firm.[1] Business-level strategy is the choice a firm makes when deciding how to compete in individual product markets. The choices are important, as there is an established link between a firm's strategies and its long-term performance.[2] Thus, the choices Cisco, Lucent, and Nortel have made to develop their optical technology strategies will affect the degree to which the firms will be able to earn above-average returns while competing against companies such as RedBack Networks, Sycamore Networks, and Ciena.

Determining the businesses in which the firm will compete is a question of corporate-level strategy and is discussed in Chapter 6. Competition in individual product markets is a question of business-level strategy, which is this chapter's focus. For all types of strategies, companies acquire the information and knowledge needed to make choices as they study external environmental opportunities and threats as well as identify and evaluate their internal resources, capabilities, and core competencies.

In Chapter 1, we defined a *strategy* as an integrated and coordinated set of commitments and actions designed to exploit core competencies and gain a competitive advantage. The different strategies that firms use to gain competitive advantages are shown in Figure 1.1 in Chapter 1. As described in the individual chapters outlined in the figure, the firm tries to establish and exploit a competitive advantage when using each type of strategy. As explained in the Opening Case, Lucent is using a cost leadership strategy while Cisco and Nortel are using the focused differentiation business-level strategy in the optical technology market. Each firm hopes to develop a competitive advantage and exploit it for marketplace success by using the strategy it has chosen.

Every firm needs a business-level strategy.[3] However, every firm may not use all the strategies—corporate-level, acquisition and restructuring, international, and cooperative—that are examined in Chapters 6 through 9. For example, the firm competing in a single-product market area in a single geographic location does not need a corporate-level strategy to deal with product diversity or an international strategy to deal with geographic diversity. Think of a local dry-cleaner with only one location offering a single service (the cleaning and laundering of clothes) in a single storefront. In contrast, a diversified firm will use one of the several types of corporate-level strategies as well as choosing a separate business-level strategy for each product market area in which the company competes (the relationship between corporate-level and business-level strategies is further examined in Chapter 6).

Not only large corporations rely on strategies to guide their actions. Even a one-person operation, such as this vegetable stand vendor, uses a business-level strategy.

Thus, every firm—from the local drycleaner to the multinational corporation—chooses at least one business-level strategy. Business-level strategy can be thought of as the firm's *core* strategy—the strategy that must be formed to describe how the firm will compete.[4]

Each strategy the firm uses specifies desired outcomes and how they are to be achieved.[5] Integrating external and internal foci, strategies reflect the firm's theory about how it intends to compete.[6] The fundamental objective of using each strategy is to create value for stakeholders. Strategies are purposeful, precede the taking of actions to which they apply, and demonstrate a shared understanding of the firm's strategic intent and strategic mission.[7] An effectively formulated strategy marshals, integrates, and allocates the firm's resources, capabilities, and competencies so that it will be properly aligned with its external environment.[8] A properly developed strategy also rationalizes the firm's strategic intent and strategic mission along with the actions taken to achieve them.[9]

Information about a host of variables, including markets, customers, technology, worldwide finance, and the changing world economy must be collected and analyzed to properly form and use strategies.[10] As noted in the Opening Case, Internet technology affects how organizations gather and examine information that must be carefully studied when choosing strategies.

A **business-level strategy** is an integrated and coordinated set of commitments and actions the firm uses to gain a competitive advantage by exploiting core competencies in specific product markets.

Business-level strategy, this chapter's focus, is an integrated and coordinated set of commitments and actions the firm uses to gain a competitive advantage by exploiting core competencies in specific product markets.[11] Only firms that continuously upgrade their competitive advantages over time are able to achieve long-term success with their business-level strategy.[12] Key issues the firm must address when choosing a business-level strategy are the good or service to offer customers, how to manufacture or create it, and how to distribute it to the marketplace.[13] Once formed, the business-level strategy reflects where and how the firm has an advantage over its rivals.[14] The essence of a firm's business-level strategy is "choosing to perform activities differently or to perform different activities than rivals."[15]

Customers are the foundation of successful business-level strategies. In fact, some believe that an effective business-level strategy demonstrates the firm's ability to "... build and maintain relationships to the best people for maximum value creation, both 'internally' (to firm members) and 'externally' (to customers)."[16] Thus, successful organizations think of their employees as internal customers who produce value-creating products for which customers are willing to pay.

Because of their strategic importance, this chapter opens with a discussion of customers. Three issues are considered in this analysis. In selecting a business-level strategy, the firm determines (1) *who* will be served, (2) *what* needs those target customers have that it will satisfy, and (3) *how* those needs will be satisfied.

Descriptions of five business-level strategies follow the discussion of customers. These five strategies are sometimes called *generic* because they can be used in any business and in any industry.[17] Our analysis of these strategies describes how effective use of each strategy allows the firm to favorably position itself relative to the five competitive forces in the industry (see Chapter 2). In addition, we use the value chain (see Chapter 3) to show examples of the primary and support activities that are necessary to implement each business-level strategy. We also describe the different risks the firm may encounter when using one of these strategies.

Organizational structures and controls that are linked with successful use of each business-level strategy are explained in Chapter 11.

Customers: Who, What, and How

Strategic competitiveness results only when the firm is able to satisfy a group of customers by using its competitive advantages to compete in individual product markets. The most successful companies constantly seek to chart new competitive space in order to serve new customers as they simultaneously try to find ways to better serve existing customers.

Flexibility is important to the firm that emphasizes customers as a vital component of its strategies. For example, Compaq Computer Corp. recently moved away from its "Everything to the Internet" approach, which it had undertaken to compete more successfully against Dell Computer Corp's highly successful direct-manufacturing model. However, Compaq did not have the competencies required to maintain pace with Dell's pricing agility. As a result, Compaq changed that approach and recently decided to portray itself as "the leading information technology solutions provider." The firm is targeting large markets such as health care and media as it moves into the lucrative technology services competitive arena.[18] As this example shows, Compaq is flexible enough to change its focus to corporate customers' software needs rather than the personal computer hardware needs of primarily individuals and small businesses. According to Compaq's CEO, service customers' "demand for simplification" is the core need his firm will address as an information technology services provider.[19] However, the degree to which Compaq will be able to satisfy this customer need could be influenced by the transaction between Hewlett-Packard and Compaq. The interest in merging demonstrates flexibility on the part of both of these firms as they seek to become large enough to develop the economies of scale that are necessary to successfully compete against Dell.

A key reason that the firm must satisfy customers with its business-level strategy is that returns earned from relationships with customers are the lifeblood of all organizations.[20] Executives at Motley Fool capture this reality crisply by noting that, "the customer is the person who pays us."[21] The quality of these returns for Internet ventures is dictated by the conversion rate. The conversion rate measures returns by dividing the number of people who visit a site within a particular period by the number of visitors who take action (e.g., purchasing or registering) while visiting.[22]

The Importance of Effectively Managing Relationships with Customers

The firm's relationships with its customers are strengthened when it is committed to offering them superior value. In business-to-business transactions, superior value is often created when the firm's product helps its customers to develop a new competitive advantage or to enhance the value of its existing competitive advantages.[23] Receiving superior value enhances customers' loyalty to the firm that provides it. Evidence suggests that loyalty has a positive relationship with profitability. Ford Motor Company, for example, estimates that each percentage-point increase in customer loyalty—defined as how many Ford owners purchase a Ford product the next time—creates at least $100 million in additional profits annually. MBNA, a credit-card issuer, determined that reducing customer defection rates by 5 percent increases the lifetime profitability of the average customer by 125 percent.[24]

Selecting customers and deciding which of their needs the firm will try to satisfy, as well as how it will do so, are challenging. One reason is competition at the global level, which has created many attractive choices for customers. As discussed in Chapter 2, a large set of what appear to be equally attractive choices increases customers' power and influence relative to companies offering products to them. Some even argue that increased choice and easily accessible information about the functionality of firms' products are creating increasingly sophisticated and knowledgeable customers, making it difficult to earn their loyalty.[25]

Several products are available to firms to help them better understand customers and manage relationships with them. For example, firms can use customer relationship management (CRM) software programs to develop Web-based profiles of their customers and to fully integrate customer communications with back-office activities, such as billing and accounting.[26] Salesforce.com's popular CRM program helps a firm's sales and marketing staffs communicate with customers: "A salesperson can, for instance, quickly check on the status of a customer account, while marketing people can collaborate to plan and execute promotional e-mail campaigns."[27] The unique attribute of Salesforce.com's program is that it is hosted and maintained entirely via the Web. A successful CRM program can be a source of competitive advantage as the firm uses knowledge gained from it to improve strategy implementation processes.

A number of companies have become skilled at the art of *managing* all aspects of their relationship with their customers.[28] In the fast-paced, technologically sophisticated global economy, firms that participate in e-commerce (Internet-based ventures and firms that provide a strong Internet presence along with their storefront operations) can understand their customers as well as manage their relationships with them more effectively than can companies without an Internet presence. As noted in the Opening Case, the probability of successful competition increases even more when the firm carefully integrates Internet technology with its strategy, rather than using Internet technology on a "stand-alone basis."[29]

For example, Amazon.com is an Internet-based venture widely recognized for the quality of information it maintains about its customers and the services it renders. Cemex SA, a major global cement company based in Mexico, uses the Internet to link its customers, cement plants, and main control room, allowing the firm to automate orders and optimize truck deliveries in highly congested Mexico City. Analysts believe that Cemex's integration of Web technology with its cost leadership strategy is helping to differentiate it from competitors.[30] GE's prominent e-commerce position is integrated into its strategies. In fact, this old-economy icon buys and sells more through its private online marketplaces—approximately $20 billion in 2001 alone—than is traded in all the independent business-to-business (B2B) marketplaces combined. GE is using Internet technology to save money and to enhance relationships with its customers by reaching them faster with products of ever-increasing quality.[31]

Reach, Richness, and Affiliation

As the foundation on which e-commerce is linked with the firm's business-level strategy, Internet technology can help the firm establish a competitive advantage through its relationship with customers along the dimensions of *reach, richness,* and *affiliation.*

The *reach* dimension is about the firm's access and connection to customers. For instance, the largest physical retailer in bookstores, Barnes & Noble, carries about 200,000 titles in 900 stores. By contrast, Amazon.com offers some 4.5 million titles and is located on roughly 25 million computer screens, with additional customer connections expected in the future. Thus, Amazon.com's reach is significantly magnified relative to that associated with Barnes & Noble's physical bookstores.[32]

Richness, the second dimension, is concerned with the depth and detail of the two-way flow of information between the firm and the customer. The potential of the richness dimension to help the firm establish a competitive advantage in its relationship with customers led traditional financial services brokers, such as Merrill Lynch, to offer online services in order to better manage information exchanges with their customers. Broader and deeper information-based exchanges allow the firm to better understand its customers and their needs. They also enable customers to become more knowledgeable of how the firm can satisfy them. Internet technology and e-commerce transactions have substantially reduced the costs of meaningful information exchanges with current and possible future customers.

Affiliation, the third dimension, is concerned with facilitating useful interactions with customers. Internet navigators such as Microsoft CarPoint help online clients find and sort information. CarPoint provides data and software to prospective car buyers that enables them to compare car models along 80 objective specifications. The program can supply this information because Internet technology allows a great deal of information to be collected from a variety of sources at a low cost. A prospective buyer who has selected a specific car based on comparisons of different models can then be linked to dealers that meet the customer's needs and purchasing requirements. A company, such as GM, Ford, and DaimlerChrysler, represents its own products, creating a situation in which its financial interests differ substantially from those of consumers. Because its revenues come from sources other than the final customer or end user (such as advertisements on its website, hyperlinks, and associated products and services), CarPoint represents the customer's interests, a service that fosters affiliation.[33]

As we discuss next, effective management of customer relationships, especially in an e-commerce era, helps the firm answer questions related to the issues of *who, what,* and *how* to serve.

Microsoft president Steve Ballmer (right) listens to fomer Ford CEO Jacques Nasser (left) speak at the launch of Microsoft's CarPoint. The Carpoint website increases customer affiliation by allowing users to compare automotive data across all brands and models, to create a profile for their autos, and to choose to be alerted of scheduled maintenance.

© MARK RICHARDS/PHOTOEDIT

Market segmentation is a process used to cluster people with similar needs into individual and identifiable groups.

Who: Determining the Customers to Serve

A crucial decision at any company related to a business-level strategy is the one made about the target customers for the firm's goods or services *(who)*.[34] To make this decision, companies divide customers into groups based on differences in the customers' needs (needs are defined and further discussed in the next section). Called **market segmentation**, this process clusters people with similar needs into individual and identifiable groups.[35] As part of its business-level strategy, the firm develops a marketing program to effectively sell products to its target customer groups.

Almost any identifiable human or organizational characteristic can be used to subdivide a market into segments that differ from one another on a given characteristic. Common characteristics on which customers' needs vary are illustrated in Table 4.1. Based on their core competencies and opportunities in the external environment, companies choose a business-level strategy to deliver value to target customers and satisfy their specific needs. For example, Rolls-Royce Motor Cars, Ltd. uses a focused differentiation strategy (defined and explained later in this chapter) to manufacture and sell Bentleys and Rolls-Royces. The firm considered both demographic characteristics (e.g., age and income) and socioeconomic characteristics (e.g., social class) (see Table 4.1) to identify its target customers. Customer feedback as well as additional analyses identified psychological factors (e.g., lifestyle choices) that allowed additional

---

Table 4.1	Basis for Customer Segmentation

Consumer Markets
1. Demographic factors (age, income, sex, etc.)
2. Socioeconomic factors (social class, stage in the family life cycle)
3. Geographic factors (cultural, regional, and national differences)
4. Psychological factors (lifestyle, personality traits)
5. Consumption patterns (heavy, moderate, and light users)
6. Perceptual factors (benefit segmentation, perceptual mapping)

Industrial Markets
1. End-use segments (identified by SIC code)
2. Product segments (based on technological differences or production economics)
3. Geographic segments (defined by boundaries between countries or by regional differences within them)
4. Common buying factor segments (cut across product market and geographic segments)
5. Customer size segments

SOURCE: Adapted from S. C. Jain, 2000, *Marketing Planning and Strategy*, Cincinnati: South-Western College Publishing, 120.

segmentation of the firm's core target customer group. Based on this information, the firm further segmented its target customer group into those *who want to drive* an ultra-luxury car themselves and those *who want to be driven* by a chauffeur in their ultra-luxury automobile. The Bentley targets the first individual, while the Rolls Royce satisfies the interests of the chauffeur-driven owner.[36]

Characteristics are often combined to segment a large market into specific groups that have unique needs. For example, McDonald's dominates the fast-food market. However, for college students interested in healthy eating, surveys suggest that Subway is the dominant fast-food choice.[37] This more specific breakdown of the fast-food market for college students is a product of jointly studying demographic, psychological, and consumption-pattern characteristics (see Table 4.1). This knowledge suggests that on a relative basis, Subway's business-level strategy should target college students with a desire for healthier foods more aggressively than should McDonald's.

Demographic characteristics (see the discussion in Chapter 2 and Table 4.1) can also be used to segment markets into generations with unique interests and needs. Evidence suggests, for example, that direct mail is an effective communication medium for the World War II generation (those born before 1932). The Swing generation (those born between 1933 and 1945) values taking cruises and purchasing second homes. Once financially conservative but now willing to spend money, members of this generation seek product information from knowledgeable sources. The Baby Boom generation (born between 1946 and 1964) desires products that reduce the stress generated by juggling career demands and the needs of older parents with those of their own children. Ellen Tracy clothes, known for their consistency of fit and color, are targeted to Baby Boomer women. More conscious of hype, people in Generation X (born between 1965 and 1976) want products that deliver as promised. The Xers use the Internet as a primary shopping tool and expect visually compelling marketing. Members of this group are the fastest growing segment of mutual-fund shareholders, with their holdings overwhelmingly invested in stock funds.[38] Different marketing campaigns and distribution channels (e.g., Internet for Generation X customers as compared to direct mail for the World War II generation) affect the implementation of strategies for those companies interested in serving the needs of different generations.

The Generation X (top left), Swing Generation (top right), Baby Boomer (left in lower photo), and Generation Y (right in lower photo) market segments each have unique needs and interests that firms target.

© BILL VARIE/CORBIS

© WALTER HODGES/CORBIS

© DAVE BARTRUFF/CORBIS

Increasing Segmentation of Markets

Companies frequently use sophisticated systems and programs to gather and interpret information about customers. Using these tools allows firms to gain the insights that are needed to further segment customers into specific groups that have unique needs. For example, many companies segment markets on a global basis. Indeed, because of increasing globalization of the world's economies, global market segmentation has become important to many firms' success. *Global market segmentation* is the process of identifying specific segments—consumer groups across countries—of potential customers with homogeneous attributes who are likely to exhibit similar buying behavior.[39] As discussed later in the chapter, McDonald's understands that customers in different regions in the world prefer slightly different versions of its core food products.

Part of our discussion in the previous section suggests that companies are segmenting markets into increasingly specialized niches of customers with unique needs and interests. Generation Y (born between 1977 and 1984) is a market segment with specific characteristics that affect how firms use business-level strategies to serve these customers' needs. Analysis of purchasing patterns for this customer group shows that this segment prefers to buy in stores rather than online, but that they may use the Internet to study products online prior to visiting a store to make a purchase. This preference suggests that companies targeting this segment might want to combine their storefront operations with a robust and active website.[40] Other examples of targeting specific market segments include New Balance's marketing its shoes to members of the Baby Boom generation (see the Strategic Focus on page 133), Christopher & Banks's focus on working women over the age of 40, and Abercrombie & Fitch's targeting the subgroup of teenagers who demand stylish clothing seen on television shows such as *Dawson's Creek* as well as in music videos.[41]

Once their customer groups have been carefully segmented, companies are also improving their ability to provide individual goods and services with specific functionalities that can satisfy the unique needs of those groups. Sometimes, the needs of domestic and global customers are virtually identical. When customer needs and interests are homogeneous or relatively so across global markets, the firm has a single or only a few target customer groups rather than many.

What: Determining Which Customer Needs to Satisfy

Needs (what) are related to the benefits and features of a good or service.[42] A basic need of all customers is to buy products that create value for them. The generalized forms of value products provide are either low cost with acceptable features or highly differentiated features with acceptable cost.

Successful firms constantly seek new customers as well as new ways to serve existing ones. As a firm decides *who* it will serve, it must simultaneously identify the targeted customer group's needs that its goods or services can satisfy. Top-level managers play a critical role in recognizing and understanding these needs. The valuable insights they gain from listening to and studying customers influence product, technology, distribution, and service decisions. For example, Volkswagen AG planned to base several Volkswagen and Audi models on the same chassis and to use the same transmissions. Upper-level executives at the firm listened to concerns from customers about this decision, who asked why they should pay for the premiere Audi brand when they could obtain much of its technology at a lower cost by purchasing a Volkswagen product. As a result, Volkswagen AG "intends to invest six billion marks ($3.32 billion) during the next few years to ensure that each of its brands retains a separate identity."[43]

Creating separate brand identities, such as Audi and Volkswagen, helps a firm's products convey benefits and features that customers want to purchase. Another way of saying this is that brands can satisfy needs. In late 2000, General Motors (GM) executives concluded that the Oldsmobile brand was no longer crisply differentiated from the company's other major automobile groups (Chevrolet, Pontiac, Buick, and Cadillac). Because it no longer conveyed specific benefits and features that satisfied target customers' needs, GM dropped the Oldsmobile brand from its product lines.[44]

How: Determining Core Competencies Necessary to Satisfy Customer Needs

As explained in Chapters 1 and 3, *core competencies* are resources and capabilities that serve as a source of competitive advantage for the firm over its rivals. Firms use core competencies to implement value-creating strategies and thereby satisfy customers' needs *(how)*. Only those firms with the capacity to continuously improve, innovate, and upgrade their competencies can expect to meet and hopefully exceed customers' expectations across time.[45]

Companies use different core competencies in efforts to produce goods or services that can satisfy customers' needs. IBM, for example, emphasizes its core competence in technology to rapidly develop new service-related products. Beginning in 1993, then newly appointed CEO Lou Gerstner changed IBM by leveraging its ". . . strength in network integration and consulting to transform (the firm) from a moribund maker of mainframe computers to a sexy services company that can basically design, build, and manage a corporation's entire data system."[46]

SAS Institute is the world's largest privately owned software company. Based on over 6.5 million lines of code, SAS programs are used for data warehousing, data mining, and decision support. Allocating over 30 percent of revenues to research and development (R&D), the firm relies on its core competence in R&D to satisfy the data-related needs of such customers as U.S. Census Bureau and a host of consumer goods firms (e.g., hotels, banks, and catalog companies).[47] Vans Inc. relies on its core competencies in innovation and marketing to design and sell skateboards. The firm also pioneered thick-soled, slip-on sneakers that can absorb the shock of five-foot leaps on wheels. Vans uses what is recognized as an offbeat marketing mix to capitalize on its pioneering products. In lieu of mass media ads, the firm sponsors skateboarding events, supported the making of a documentary film that celebrates the "outlaw nature" of the skateboarding culture, and is building skateboard parks at malls around the country.[48]

All organizations, including IBM, SAS and Vans Inc. must be able to use their core competencies (the *how*) to satisfy the needs (the *what*) of the target group of customers (the *who*) the firm has chosen to serve by using its business-level strategy. Next, we discuss the business-level strategies firms use when pursuing strategic competitiveness and above-average returns.

Types of Business-Level Strategy

Business-level strategies are intended to create differences between the firm's position relative to those of its rivals.[49] To position itself, the firm must decide whether it intends to *perform activities differently* or to *perform different activities* as compared to its rivals.[50] Thus, the firm's business-level strategy is a deliberate choice about how it will perform the value chain's primary and support activities in ways that create unique value.

Successful use of a chosen strategy results only when the firm integrates its primary and support activities to provide the unique value it intends to deliver. Value is delivered to customers when the firm is able to use competitive advantages resulting from the integration of activities. Superior fit among primary and support activities forms an activity system. In turn, an effective activity system helps the firm establish and exploit its strategic position. In the Strategic Focus on pages 120–121, we use Southwest Airlines to examine these issues in greater detail.

Favorably positioned firms such as Southwest Airlines have a competitive advantage over their industry rivals and are better able to cope with the five forces of competition (see Chapter 2). Favorable positioning is important in that the universal objective of all companies is to develop and sustain competitive advantages.[51] Improperly positioned firms encounter competitive difficulties and likely will fail to sustain competitive advantages. For example, its ineffective responses to competitors such as Wal-Mart left Sears Roebuck Co. in a weak competitive position for years. These ineffective responses resulted from the inability of Sears to properly implement strategies that were appropriate in light of its external opportunities and threats and its internal competencies. Two researchers describe this situation: "Once a towering force in retailing, Sears spent 10 years vacillating between an emphasis on hard goods and soft goods, venturing in and out of ill-chosen arenas, failing to differentiate itself in any of them, and never building a compelling economic logic."[52] Firms choose from among five business-level strategies to establish and defend their desired strategic position against rivals: *cost leadership, differentiation, focused cost leadership, focused differentiation,* and *integrated cost leadership/differentiation* (see Figure 4.1). Each business-level strategy helps the firm to establish and exploit a competitive advantage within a particular competitive scope.

When selecting a business-level strategy, firms evaluate two types of potential competitive advantage: "lower cost than rivals, or the ability to differentiate and command a premium price that exceeds the extra cost of doing so."[53] Having lower cost derives from the firm's ability to perform activities differently than rivals; being able to differentiate indicates the firm's capacity to perform different (and valuable) activities.[54] Competitive advantage is thus achieved within some scope.

Scope has several dimensions, including the group of product and customer segments served and the array of geographic markets in which the firm competes.

Figure 4.1 Five Business-Level Strategies

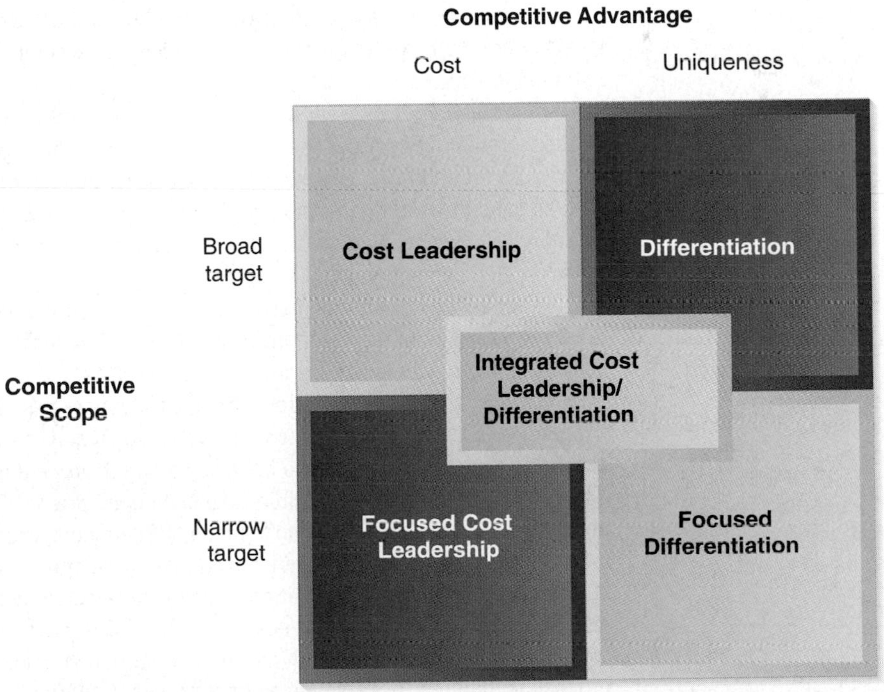

SOURCE: Adapted with the permission of The Free Press, an imprint of Simon & Schuster Adult Publishing Group, from *Competitive Advantage: Creating and Sustaining Superior Performance,* by Michael E. Porter, 12. Copyright © 1985, 1998 by Michael E. Porter.

Southwest Airlines' Activity System: Is It Imitable?

Launched in 1971 with service among three Texas cities—Dallas, Houston, and San Antonio—Southwest Airlines has followed its mission of "dedication to the highest quality of customer service delivered with a sense of warmth, friendliness, individual pride, and company spirit." Southwest has become the fifth-largest U.S. carrier and eighth-largest carrier in the world.

Relying on its mission to direct its activities, the company offers short-haul, low-cost, point-to-point service between midsize cities and secondary airports in large cities. It performs its activities in ways that drive the firm's costs lower and lower. According to company officials, Southwest is ". . . always looking for an opportunity to make the lowest even lower." Meals, assigned seating, interline baggage transfers, and premium classes of service are not available on Southwest flights—not offering these services helps the firm keep its costs lower than rivals. What Southwest does offer its customers are low cost, frequent departures to its destinations, and an often entertaining experience while in the air (a form of differentiation).

Because Southwest charges fares as low as 20 percent of those charged by mainstream carriers, the firm's effect on pricing in the markets it serves can be dramatic. Government officials in one city expected many fares to drop by at least half once Southwest's decision to serve their community was implemented. Moreover, because Southwest's low fares tend to attract people who might have driven to their destinations, officials also anticipated that total passenger traffic from the local airport would double within two years of Southwest's entry into their community's market.

According to Southwest, the secrets of its success are simple:

- *Keep costs down.* Throughout its operations, Southwest has maintained a constant focus on keeping costs down. Turning planes around quickly at the gate results in planes being able to log more hours in the air. Using a standardized fleet of Boeing 737 jets reduces maintenance costs and pilot training expenses. Southwest's operating costs are from 25 percent to 80 percent lower than most major carriers.
- *Focus on customers.* Southwest's commitment to customer service and satisfaction is legendary. Some gate agents have even invited stranded passengers to spend the night in their homes.
- *Keep employees happy.* Southwest's culture and benefits create a positive work atmosphere, and its employees are more productive than their counterparts at other airlines, even though their pay is similar. Looking for people who want to serve a cause rather than fill a job, the airline invests significantly in its recruiting and training procedures. Founder Kelleher believes that corporate culture is the most important difference between his and other airline companies.
- *Keep it simple.* Although some longer-haul flights have been added over the years, Southwest is still primarily a point-to-point, short-hop airline. Its destinations are often smaller airports with less air traffic.

The careful fit or integration among Southwest's primary and support activities allows it to keep costs down, focus on customers, keep employees happy, and keep its work simple. This fit is instrumental to the development and use of the firm's two major competitive advantages—organizational culture and customer service. The importance of fit between primary and support activities isn't unique to Southwest, in that fit among activities is a key to the sustainability of competitive advantage for all firms. As Michael Porter comments, "Strategic fit among many activities is fundamental not only to competitive advantage but also to the sustainability of that advantage. It is harder for a rival to match an array of interlocked activities than it is merely to imitate a particular sales-force approach, match a process technology, or replicate a set of product features. Positions built on systems of activities are far more sustainable than those built on individual activities."

An activity system can be mapped to show how individual activities are integrated to achieve fit, as the accompanying map for Southwest's activities shows. Higher-order strategic themes are critical to successful use of the firm's strategy. For Southwest Airlines, these strategic themes are limited passenger service, frequent, reliable departures, lean, highly productive ground and gate crews, high aircraft utilization, very low ticket prices, and short-haul, point-to-point routes between midsize cities and secondary airports. Individual clusters of tightly linked activities make it possible for the outcome of a strategic theme to be achieved. For example, no meals, no seat assignments, and no baggage transfers form a cluster of individual activities that support the strategic theme of limited passenger service.

Southwest Airlines' Activity System

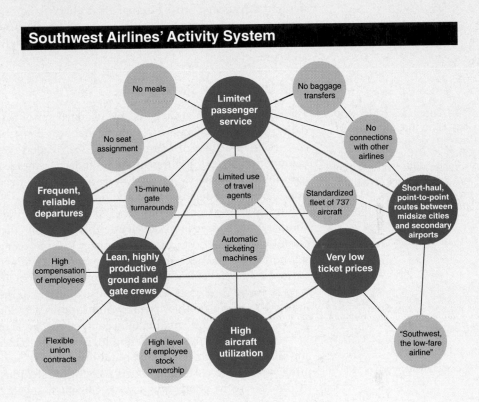

Southwest's tightly integrated primary and support activities make it difficult for competitors to imitate the firm's strategy. The firm's culture influences these activities and their integration. In fact, the firm's unique culture has become a competitive advantage that rivals have not been able to imitate. The firm's executives believe that motivated and dedicated employees and how they work together are the inimitable source of how Southwest develops effective linkages among its activities. This careful integration of *how* Southwest Airlines' employees perform the activities that support the firm's strategic themes reduces the probability that competitors will be able to successfully imitate its activity system.

SOURCES: M. Arndt, 2001, A simple and elegant flight pattern, *Business Week*, June 11, 118; T. Bolden, 2001, Southwest Airlines' philosophy keeping it in front of pack now, *Richmond Times-Dispatch*, November 12, D29; J. H. Gittell, 2001, Investing in relationships, *Harvard Business Review*, 79(6): 28–30; C. Jones, 2001, Coming . . . soon? *Richmond Times-Dispatch*, June 22, A1, A9; W. Zellner, 2001, Southwest: After Kelleher, more blue skies, *Business Week*, April 2, 45; 2001, The squeeze on Europe's air fares, *The Economist*, May 26, 57–58; M. E. Porter, 1996, What is strategy? *Harvard Business Review*, 74(6): 61–78; http://www.southwestairlines.com.

Competitive advantage is sought by competing in many customer segments when implementing either the cost leadership or the differentiation strategy. In contrast, when using focus strategies, firms seek a cost competitive advantage or a differentiation competitive advantage in a *narrow competitive scope, segment,* or *niche.* With focus strategies, the firm "selects a segment or group of segments in the industry and tailors its strategy to serving them to the exclusion of others."[55]

None of the five business-level strategies is inherently or universally superior to the others.[56] The effectiveness of each strategy is contingent both on the opportunities and threats in a firm's external environment and on the possibilities provided by the firm's unique resources, capabilities, and core competencies. It is critical, therefore, for the firm to select an appropriate strategy in light of its opportunities, threats, and competencies.

Cost Leadership Strategy

The **cost leadership strategy** is an integrated set of actions designed to produce or deliver goods or services with features that are acceptable to customers at the lowest cost, relative to that of competitors.

The **cost leadership strategy** is an integrated set of actions designed to produce or deliver goods or services with features that are acceptable to customers at the lowest cost, relative to that of competitors.[57] Cost leaders' goods and services must have competitive levels of differentiation. Indeed, emphasizing cost reductions while ignoring competitive levels of differentiation is ineffective. At the extreme, concentrating only on reducing costs could find the firm very efficiently producing products that no customer wants to purchase. When the firm designs, produces, and markets a comparable product more efficiently that its rivals, there is evidence that it is successfully using the cost leadership strategy.[58] Firms using the cost leadership strategy sell no-frills, standardized goods or services (but with competitive levels of differentiation) to the industry's most typical customers. Cost leaders concentrate on finding ways to lower their costs relative to those of their competitors by constantly rethinking how to complete their primary and support activities (see Chapter 2) to reduce costs still further while maintaining competitive levels of differentiation.[59]

As primary activities, inbound logistics (e.g., materials handling, warehousing, and inventory control) and outbound logistics (e.g., collecting, storing, and distributing products to customers) often account for significant portions of the total cost to produce some goods and services. Research suggests that having a competitive advantage in terms of logistics creates more value when using the cost leadership strategy than when using the differentiation strategy.[60] Thus, cost leaders seeking competitively valuable ways to reduce costs may want to concentrate on the primary activities of inbound logistics and outbound logistics.

Cost leaders also carefully examine all support activities to find additional sources of potential cost reductions. Developing new systems for finding the optimal combination of low cost and acceptable quality in the raw materials required to produce the firm's goods or services is an example of how the procurement support activity can facilitate successful use of the cost leadership strategy.

The Vanguard Group, the large mutual-fund company, uses a cost leadership strategy. Facilitating the success of Vanguard's strategy is the tight, effective integration of the activities comprising its activity system.[61] Portraying fees and costs as evil and extolling efficiency, the corporate culture encourages employees' commitment to controlling costs while designing and completing their work. Vanguard's performance outcomes demonstrate the firm's low-cost position. In 1999, for example, the firm incurred average operating costs of 0.27 percent of its assets—less than one-fourth of the estimated average operating costs of 1.31 percent for the mutual fund industry.[62] Vanguard's pioneering index funds, introduced in 1976, help keep the costs down as do its low-cost bond funds with specific maturity ranges (i.e., short, intermediate, and long term). Other cost saving activities include Vanguard's low trading levels and its policy of discouraging "... customers from rapid buying and selling because doing so drives up costs and can force a fund manager to trade in order to deploy new capital and raise cash for redemptions."[63] The firm also searches for the least costly, yet still effective, means of providing customer service and of marketing its products.

Vanguard's low cost position for many investment products suggests the quality of its cost control efforts. However, the firm is also committed to providing high quality services (such as the firm's effective and easily navigable website) to its customers. Thus, the firm's products are offered with at least competitive levels of differentiation. Vanguard describes the effectiveness of having the low-cost position with at least competitive levels of differentiation by suggesting that it uses a "lowest reasonable cost" strategy to serve the needs of individual and institutional investors.

Consolidated Stores, Inc., which recently changed its name to Big Lots, Inc., also uses the cost leadership strategy. Committed to the strategic intent of being "The World's Best Bargain Place," Big Lots has become the largest U.S. retailer of closeout merchandise. The company sells goods in over 1,300 locations with positions in 46 states. The firm's stores sell name-brand products at prices that are 15 to 35 percent below those of discount retailers and roughly 70 percent below those of traditional retailers.[64] Big Lots' buyers travel the country looking through manufacturer overruns and discontinued styles, finding goods priced at well below wholesale prices. The firm thinks of itself as the undertaker of the retailing business, purchasing merchandise that others can't sell or don't want.

Having products available to customers at what the firm calls "extreme value" demonstrates the firm's commitment to being the low cost leader. By offering name-brand products in multiple locations and states rather than in only major metropolitan area, Big Lots also provides its target customers (the budget-conscious consumer) with competitive levels of differentiation (e.g., location, convenience). Big Lots captures the essence of the low cost and competitive (but not the most) differentiation position by operating as a "low-cost, value retailer."

As described in Chapter 3, firms use value-chain analysis to determine the parts of the company's operations that create value and those that do not. Figure 4.2 demonstrates the primary and support activities that allow a firm to create value through the cost leadership strategy. Companies unable to link the activities shown in this figure typically lack the resources, capabilities, and core competencies needed to successfully use the cost leadership strategy.

Effective use of the cost leadership strategy allows a firm to earn above-average returns in spite of the presence of strong competitive forces (see Chapter 2). The next sections (one for each of the five forces) explain how firms are able to do this.

Rivalry with Existing Competitors

Having the low-cost position is a valuable defense against rivals. Because of the cost leader's advantageous position, rivals hesitate to compete on the basis of price. Wal-Mart is known for its ability to both control and reduce costs, making it difficult for firms to compete against it on the basis of the price variable. The discount retailer achieves strict cost control in several ways: "Wal-Mart's 660,000-square foot main headquarters, with its drab gray interiors and frayed carpets, looks more like a government building than the home of one of the world's largest corporations. Business often is done in the no-frills cafeteria, and suppliers meet

Big Lots, Inc. used the cost leadership strategy to become the nation's largest broadline closeout retailer with stores in 46 states. The firm is converting and renaming its Odd Lots, Pic 'N' Save, and MacFrugal's stores to share the Big Lots identity.

© TERRI L. MILLER/E-VISUAL COMMUNICATIONS

A value chain diagram (house-shaped) showing primary activities across the bottom (Inbound Logistics, Operations, Outbound Logistics, Marketing and Sales, Service) and support activities down the left side (Firm Infrastructure, Human Resource Management, Technology Development, Procurement), with MARGIN on the roof.

Firm Infrastructure: Cost-effective management information systems; Relatively few managerial layers in order to reduce overhead costs; Simplified planning practices to reduce planning costs

Human Resource Management: Consistent policies to reduce turnover costs; Intense and effective training programs to improve worker efficiency and effectiveness

Technology Development: Easy-to-use manufacturing technologies; Investments in technologies in order to reduce costs associated with a firm's manufacturing processes

Procurement: Systems and procedures to find the lowest cost (with acceptable quality) products to purchase as raw materials; Frequent evaluation processes to monitor suppliers' performances

Inbound Logistics: Highly efficient systems to link suppliers' products with the firm's production processes

Operations: Use of economies of scale to reduce production costs; Construction of efficient-scale production facilities

Outbound Logistics: A delivery schedule that reduces costs; Selection of low-cost transportation carriers

Marketing and Sales: A small, highly trained sales force; Products priced so as to generate significant sales volume

Service: Efficient and proper product installations in order to reduce the frequency and severity of recalls

SOURCE: Adapted with the permission of The Free Press, an imprint of Simon & Schuster Adult Publishing Group, from *Competitive Advantage: Creating and Sustaining Superior Performance,* by Michael E. Porter, p. 47. Copyright © 1985, 1998 by Michael E. Porter.

with managers in stark, cramped rooms. Employees have to throw out their own garbage at the end of the day and double up in hotel rooms on business trips."[65] Saying that it wasn't competitive, Kmart recently initiated a price-cutting initiative. Wal-Mart followed with immediate price reductions. Because of Kmart's higher cost structure and less efficient distribution system, some believed that it was poorly positioned to compete against Wal-Mart on the basis of price even as Kmart attempted to become more efficient by overhauling its product delivery software system and closing at least two aging distribution centers, and restructuring its operations after filing for bankruptcy in 2002.[66]

As noted earlier, research suggests that having a competitive advantage in terms of logistics significantly contributes to the cost leader's ability to earn above-average returns.[67] Because Wal-Mart developed a logistics competitive advantage that has become the world standard, it is unlikely that Kmart can successfully compete against it by engaging in pricing battles.

Bargaining Power of Buyers (Customers)

Powerful customers can force a cost leader to reduce its prices, but not below the level at which the cost leader's next-most-efficient industry competitor can earn average returns. Although powerful customers might be able to force the cost leader to reduce prices even below this level, they probably would not choose to do so. Prices that are low enough to prevent the next-most-efficient competitor from earning average returns would force that firm to exit the market, leaving the cost leader with less competition and in an even stronger position. Customers would thus lose their power and pay higher prices when they are forced to purchase from a single firm operating in an industry without competitive rivals.

Bargaining Power of Suppliers

The cost leader operates with margins greater than those of competitors. Among other benefits, higher margins relative to those of competitors make it possible for the cost leader to absorb its suppliers' price increases. When an industry faces substantial increases in the cost of its supplies, only the cost leader may be able to pay the higher prices and continue to earn either average or above-average returns. Alternatively, a powerful cost leader may be able to force its suppliers to hold down their prices, which would reduce the suppliers' margins in the process.

Potential Entrants

Through continuous efforts to reduce costs to levels that are lower than those of its competitors, a cost leader becomes highly efficient. Because ever-improving levels of efficiency enhance profit margins, they serve as a significant entry barrier to potential competitors. New entrants must be willing and able to accept no better-than-average returns until they gain the experience required to approach the cost leader's efficiency. To earn even average returns, new entrants must have the competencies required to match the cost levels of competitors other than the cost leader. The low profit margins (relative to margins earned by firms implementing the differentiation strategy) make it necessary for the cost leader to sell large volumes of its product to earn above-average returns. However, firms striving to be the cost leader must avoid pricing their products so low that their ability to operate profitability is reduced, even though volume increases.

Product Substitutes

Compared to its industry rivals, the cost leader also holds an attractive position in terms of product substitutes. A product substitute becomes an issue for the cost leader when its features and characteristics, in terms of cost and differentiated features, are potentially attractive to the firm's customers. When faced with possible substitutes, the cost leader has more flexibility than its competitors. To retain customers, it can reduce the price of its good or service. With still lower prices and competitive levels of differentiation, the cost leader increases the probability that customers will prefer its product rather than a substitute.

Competitive Risks of the Cost Leadership Strategy

The cost leadership strategy is not risk free. One risk is that the processes used by the cost leader to produce and distribute its good or service could become obsolete because of innovations by its competitors. These innovations may allow rivals to produce at costs lower than those of the original cost leader, or to provide additional differentiated features without increasing the product's price to customers.

A second risk is that too much focus by the cost leader on cost reductions may occur at the expense of trying to understand customers' perceptions of "competitive levels of differentiation." As noted earlier, Wal-Mart is well known for constantly and aggressively reducing its costs. However, the firm must simultaneously remain focused on understanding when a cost-reducing decision to eliminate differentiated features that can create value in a low-cost environment (e.g., extended shopping hours, increases in the number of check-out counters to reduce waits) in order to reduce costs to still lower levels would create an unattractive value proposition for customers.

A final risk of the cost leadership strategy concerns imitation. Using their own core competencies (see Chapter 3), competitors sometimes learn how to successfully imitate the cost leader's strategy. When this occurs, the cost leader must increase the value that its good or service provides to customers. Commonly, value is increased by selling the current product at an even lower price or by adding differentiated features that customers value while maintaining price.

Even cost leaders must be careful when reducing prices to a still lower level. If the firm prices its good or service at an unrealistically low level (a level at which it will be difficult to retain satisfactory margins), customers' expectations about a reasonable price become difficult to reverse.

Differentiation Strategy

The **differentiation strategy** is an integrated set of actions designed by a firm to produce or deliver goods or services (at an acceptable cost) that customers perceive as being different in ways that are important to them.

The **differentiation strategy** is an integrated set of actions designed by a firm to produce or deliver goods or services (at an acceptable cost) that customers perceive as being different in ways that are important to them.[68] While cost leaders serve an industry's typical customer, differentiators target customers who perceive that value is added by the manner in which the firm's products are differentiated.

Firms must be able to produce differentiated products at competitive costs to reduce upward pressure on the price customers pay for them. When a product's differentiated features are produced through non-competitive costs, the price for the product can exceed what the firm's target customers are willing to pay. When the firm has a thorough understanding of what its target customers value, the relative importance they attach to the satisfaction of different needs, and for what they are willing to pay a premium, the differentiation strategy can be successfully used.[69]

Through the differentiation strategy, the firm produces nonstandardized products for customers who value differentiated features more than they value low cost. For example, superior product reliability and durability and high-performance sound systems are among the differentiated features of Toyota Motor Corporation's Lexus products. The often-used Lexus promotional statement—"The Relentless Pursuit of Perfection"—suggests a strong commitment to overall product quality as a source of differentiation. However, Lexus offers its vehicles to customers at a competitive purchase price. As with Lexus products, a good or service's unique attributes, rather than its purchase price, provide the value for which customers are willing to pay.

Continuous success with the differentiation strategy results when the firm consistently upgrades differentiated features that customers value, without significant cost increases. Because a differentiated product satisfies customers' unique needs, firms following the differentiation strategy are able to charge premium prices. For cus-

© TERRI L. MILLER/E-VISUAL COMMUNICATIONS

The differentiation strategy used by Robert Talbott Inc. to provide high quality dress shirts at a premium price is reflected in founder Robert Talbott's philosophy in 1950—"If you want to be number one in your industry, . . . you must create the finest product, and you must be number one in serving your customers. . . ."

tomers to be willing to pay a premium price, a "firm must truly be unique at something or be perceived as unique."[70] The ability to sell a good or service at a price that substantially exceeds the cost of creating its differentiated features allows the firm to outperform rivals and earn above-average returns.

For example, clothing manufacturer Robert Talbott follows stringent standards of craftsmanship and pays meticulous attention to every detail of production. The firm imports exclusive fabrics from the world's finest mills to make men's dress shirts. Single-needle tailoring is used, and precise collar cuts are made. According to the company, customers purchasing one of its shirts can be assured that they are being provided with the finest quality available.[71] Thus, Robert Talbott's success in shirt making rests on the firm's ability to produce and sell its differentiated shirts at a price significantly higher than the costs of imported fabrics and its unique manufacturing processes.

Rather than costs, a firm using the differentiation strategy always concentrates on investing in and developing features that differentiate a good or service in ways that customers value. Overall, a firm using the differentiation strategy seeks to be different from its competitors on as many dimensions as possible. The less similarity between a firm's goods or services and those of competitors, the more buffered it is from rivals' actions. Commonly recognized differentiated goods include Toyota's Lexus, Ralph Lauren's clothing lines, and Caterpillar's heavy-duty earth-moving equipment. Thought by some to be the world's most expensive and prestigious consulting firm, McKinsey & Co. is a well-known example of a firm that offers differentiated services.

A product can be differentiated in many ways. Unusual features, responsive customer service, rapid product innovations and technological leadership, perceived prestige and status, different tastes, and engineering design and performance are examples of approaches to differentiation. There may be a limited number of ways to reduce costs (as demanded by successful use of the cost leadership strategy). However, virtually anything a firm can do to create real or perceived value is a basis for differentiation. The challenge is to identity features that create value for the customers the firm has chosen to serve.

Firms sometimes introduce a new source of differentiation to test consumer reaction before extending it. H.J. Heinz, for example, recently added color as a source of differentiation for its highly successful ketchup. Green instead of the traditional red, the new color does not change the product's taste. Initial customer reaction was quite favorable, suggesting that color creates perceived value. In response, the company has also introduced purple ketchup and is evaluating orange, yellow, and hot pink as potential new colors.[72]

A firm's value chain can be analyzed to determine whether the firm is able to link the activities required to create value by using the differentiation strategy. Examples of primary and support activities that are commonly used to differentiate a good or service are shown in Figure 4.3. Companies without the core competencies needed to link these activities cannot expect to successfully use the differentiation strategy. Next, we explain how firms using the differentiation strategy can successfully position themselves in terms of the five forces of competition (see Chapter 2) to earn above-average returns.

Figure 4.3   Examples of Value-Creating Activities Associated with the Differentiation Strategy

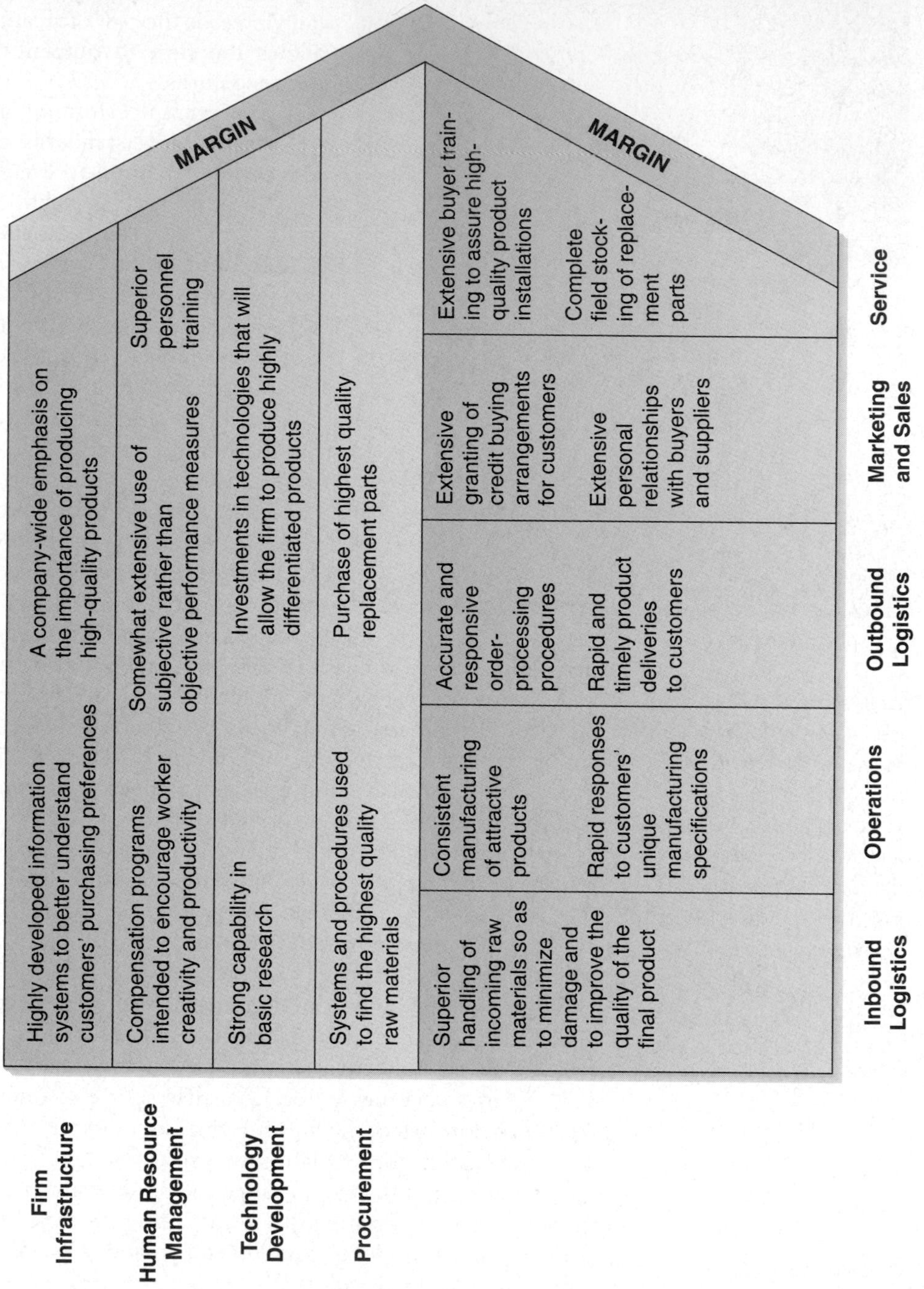

Support Activities (MARGIN):

Firm Infrastructure
- Highly developed information systems to better understand customers' purchasing preferences
- A company-wide emphasis on the importance of producing high-quality products

Human Resource Management
- Compensation programs intended to encourage worker creativity and productivity
- Somewhat extensive use of subjective rather than objective performance measures
- Superior personnel training

Technology Development
- Strong capability in basic research
- Investments in technologies that will allow the firm to produce highly differentiated products

Procurement
- Systems and procedures used to find the highest quality raw materials
- Purchase of highest quality replacement parts

Primary Activities:

Inbound Logistics	Operations	Outbound Logistics	Marketing and Sales	Service
Superior handling of incoming raw materials so as to minimize damage and to improve the quality of the final product	Consistent manufacturing of attractive products	Accurate and responsive order-processing procedures	Extensive granting of credit buying arrangements for customers	Extensive buyer training to assure high-quality product installations
	Rapid responses to customers' unique manufacturing specifications	Rapid and timely product deliveries to customers	Extensive personal relationships with buyers and suppliers	Complete field stocking of replacement parts

SOURCE: Adapted with the permission of The Free Press, an imprint of Simon & Schuster Adult Publishing Group, from *Competitive Advantage: Creating and Sustaining Superior Performance,* by Michael E. Porter, p. 47. Copyright © 1985, 1998 by Michael E. Porter.

Rivalry with Existing Competitors

Customers tend to be loyal purchasers of products that are differentiated in ways that are meaningful to them. As their loyalty to a brand increases, customers' sensitivity to price increases is reduced. This is especially true of those purchasing high-end, big-

Heinz's EZ Squirt Blasting Green ketchup, which tastes just like Heinz's traditional ketchup, illustrates the company's effort to be innovative by offering a differentiated product when the firm's research found kids would like to see ketchup in some color other than red. "We wanted to create something where that bottle is pulled out of the fridge more often," a Heinz spokesperson said.

ticket items (e.g., luxury automobiles and custom interior design services for the home and office).[73] The relationship between brand loyalty and price sensitivity insulates a firm from competitive rivalry. Thus, McKinsey & Co. is insulated from its competitors, even on the basis of price, as long as it continues to satisfy the differentiated needs of its customer group. Bose is insulated from intense rivalry as long as customers continue to perceive that its stereo equipment offers superior sound quality at a competitive cost.

Bargaining Power of Buyers (Customers)

The uniqueness of differentiated goods or services reduces customers' sensitivity to price increases. On the basis of a combination of unique materials and brand image, "L'Oreal has developed a winning formula: a growing portfolio of international brands that has transformed the French company into the United Nations of beauty. Blink an eye, and L'Oreal has just sold 85 products around the world, from Maybelline eye makeup, Redken hair care, and Ralph Lauren perfumes to Helena Rubinstein cosmetics and Vichy skin care." L'Oreal is finding success in markets stretching from China to Mexico as some other consumer product companies falter. L'Oreal's differentiation strategy seeks to convey the allure of different cultures through its many products: "Whether it's selling Italian elegance, New York street smarts, or French beauty through its brands, L'Oreal is reaching out to more people across a bigger range of incomes and cultures than just about any other beauty-products company in the world."[74]

L'Oreal seeks to satisfy customers' unique needs better than its competitors can. One reason that some buyers are willing to pay a premium price for the firm's cosmetic items is that, for these buyers, other products do not offer a comparable combination of features and cost. The lack of perceived acceptable alternatives increases the firm's power relative to that of its customers.

Bargaining Power of Suppliers

Because the firm using the differentiation strategy charges a premium price for its products, suppliers must provide high-quality components, driving up the firm's costs. However, the high margins the firm earns in these cases partially insulate it from the influence of suppliers in that higher supplier costs can be paid through these margins. Alternatively, because of buyers' relative insensitivity to price increases, the differentiated firm might choose to pass the additional cost of supplies on to the customer by increasing the price of its unique product.

Potential Entrants

Customer loyalty and the need to overcome the uniqueness of a differentiated product present substantial entry barriers to potential entrants. Entering an industry under these conditions typically demands significant investments of resources and patience while seeking customers' loyalty.

Product Substitutes

Firms selling brand-name goods and services to loyal customers are positioned effectively against product substitutes. In contrast, companies without brand loyalty face a higher probability of their customers switching either to products that offer differentiated features that serve the same function (particularly if the substitute has a lower price) or to products that offer more features and perform more attractive functions.

© FELICIA MARTINEZ/PHOTOEDIT

Competitive Risks of the Differentiation Strategy

As with the other business-level strategies, the differentiation strategy is not risk free. One risk is that customers might decide that the price differential between the differentiator's product and the cost leader's product is too large. In this instance, a firm may be offering differentiated features that exceed target customers' needs. The firm then becomes vulnerable to competitors that are able to offer customers a combination of features and price that is more consistent with their needs.

Another risk of the differentiation strategy is that a firm's means of differentiation may cease to provide value for which customers are willing to pay. A differentiated product becomes less valuable if imitation by rivals causes customers to perceive that competitors offer essentially the same good or service, but at a lower price. For example, Walt Disney Company operates different theme parks, including The Magic Kingdom, Epcot Center, and the newly developed Animal Kingdom. Each park offers entertainment and educational opportunities. However, Disney's competitors, such as Six Flags Corporation, also offer entertainment and educational experiences similar to those available at Disney's locations. To ensure that its facilities create value for which customers will be willing to pay, Disney continuously reinvests in its operations to more crisply differentiate them from those of its rivals.[75]

A third risk of the differentiation strategy is that experience can narrow customers' perceptions of the value of a product's differentiated features. For example, the value of the IBM name provided a differentiated feature for the firm's personal computers for which some users were willing to pay a premium price in the early life cycle of the product. However, as customers familiarized themselves with the product's standard features, and as a host of other firms' personal computers entered the market, IBM brand loyalty ceased to create value for which some customers were willing to pay. The substitutes offered features similar to those found in the IBM product at a substantially lower price, reducing the attractiveness of IBM's product.

Responding to the effects of this reality, IBM now emphasizes service to drive product sales as a source of differentiation. Through IBM Global Services Inc., the firm is becoming product-service centered rather than remaining true to its origins, when it was product centered.[76] The firm's objective is to sell services to customers, especially when they purchase IBM hardware products.[77] IBM's actions are an example of what a firm can do to offer new, value-creating differentiated features for its current customers as well as to serve new customers.

Counterfeiting is the differentiation strategy's fourth risk. Makers of counterfeit goods—products that attempt to convey differentiated features to customers at significantly reduced prices—are a concern for many firms using the differentiation strategy. For example, Callaway Golf Company's success at producing differentiated products that create value, coupled with golf's increasing global popularity, has created great demand for counterfeited Callaway equipment. Through the U.S. Customs Service's "Project Teed Off" program, agents seized over 110 shipments with a total of more than 100,000 counterfeit Callaway golf club components over a three-year period.[78] Companies such as Callaway also work with government officials in other nations to influence the formation of tighter import regulations to curb the flow of counterfeit products.

Focus Strategies

The focus strategy is an integrated set of actions designed to produce or deliver goods or services that serve the needs of a particular competitive segment.

Firms choose a focus strategy when they want their core competencies to serve the needs of a particular industry segment or niche at the exclusion of others. Examples of specific market segments that can be targeted by a focus strategy include a (1) particular buyer group (e.g., youths or senior citizens), (2) different segment of a product line (e.g., products for professional painters or those for "do-it-yourselfers"), or

Callaway Golf Company uses the differentiation strategy for its golf equipment, using top quality materials and incurring considerable research and development costs to create its high-cost clubs. Counterfeiters offer lower-priced imitations, as shown in the photo. The genuine Callaway Big Bertha club is at left, while the club at the right resembles the Big Bertha but is poorly made of low quality materials.

(3) different geographic market (e.g., the east or the west in the United States).[79] Thus, the **focus strategy** is an integrated set of actions designed to produce or deliver goods or services that serve the needs of a particular competitive segment.

Although the breadth of a target is clearly a matter of degree, the essence of the focus strategy "is the exploitation of a narrow target's differences from the balance of the industry."[80] Firms using the focus strategy intend to serve a particular segment of an industry more effectively than can industry-wide competitors. They succeed when they effectively serve a segment whose unique needs are so specialized that broad-based competitors choose not to serve that segment or when they satisfy the needs of a segment being served poorly by industry-wide competitors.[81]

To satisfy the needs of a certain size of company competing in a particular geographic market, Los Angeles-based investment banking firm Greif & Company positions itself as "The Entrepreneur's Investment Bank." Greif & Company is a "leading purveyor of merger and acquisition advisory services to medium-sized businesses based in the Western United States."[82] American Services Group Inc. (ASG) specializes in providing contract health care for prisons and jails. Partly because of costs and liability, governments are outsourcing health care to private companies. Recently, ASG, which has earned the nickname "HMO behind bars," was awarded a three-year contract to care for 13,000 prisoners at New York's Rikers Island facility.[83] Through successful use of the focus strategy, firms such as Greif & Company and ASG gain a competitive advantage in specific market niches or segments, even though they do not possess an industry-wide competitive advantage.[84]

Firms can create value for customers in specific and unique market segments by using the focused cost leadership strategy or the focused differentiation strategy.

Focused Cost Leadership Strategy

Based in Sweden, Ikea, a global furniture retailer, follows the focused cost leadership strategy.[85] Young buyers desiring style at a low cost are Ikea's market segment. For these customers, the firm offers home furnishings that combine good design, function, and acceptable quality with low prices. According to the firm, "low cost is always in focus. This applies to every phase of our activities. The foundation is our range that shall offer good design and function at a low price."[86]

Ikea emphasizes several activities to keep its costs low. For example, instead of relying primarily on third-party manufacturers, the firm's engineers design low-cost, modular furniture ready for assembly by customers. Ikea also positions its products in room-like settings. Typically, competitors' furniture stores display multiple varieties of a single item in separate rooms, and their customers examine living room sofas in one room, tables in another room, chairs in yet another location, and accessories in still another area. In contrast, Ikea's customers can view different living combinations (complete with sofas, chairs, tables, and so forth) in a single setting, which eliminates the need for sales associates or decorators to help the customer imagine how a batch of furniture will look when placed in the customer's home. This approach requires fewer sales personnel, allowing Ikea to keep its costs low. A third practice that helps keep Ikea's costs low is expecting customers to transport their own purchases rather than providing delivery service.

Although a cost leader, Ikea also offers some differentiated features that appeal to its target customers, including in-store playrooms for children, wheelchairs for customer use, and extended hours. Stores outside those in the home country have "Sweden Shops" that sell Swedish specialties such as herring, crisp bread, Swedish caviar, and gingerbread biscuits. Ikea believes that these services and products "are uniquely aligned with the needs of (its) customers, who are young, are not wealthy, are likely to have children (but no nanny), and, because they work for a living, have a need to shop at odd hours."[87] Thus, Ikea's focused cost leadership strategy finds the firm offering some differentiated features with its low cost products.

Focused Differentiation Strategy

Other firms implement the focused differentiation strategy in the pursuit of above-average returns. As noted earlier, firms can differentiate their products in many ways. Consider the following examples of firms using a focused differentiation strategy: The Internet venture Casketfurniture.com targets Generation X people who are interested in using the Internet as a shopping vehicle and who want to buy items with multiple purposes. The firm offers a collection of products including display cabinets, coffee tables, and entertainment centers that can be easily converted into coffins. The $1,975 display cabinet is the company's best selling item. With 16 units on the East Coast, hair salon Cartoon Cuts serves children between the ages of 8 to 14. This age group is a profitable and growing niche in the $50 billion U.S. hair salon industry. Get Well Network Inc. provides products to augment the cable-connected television set found in most hospital rooms. With charges posted to the hospital room bills, patients use the firm's interactive systems to watch pay-per-view movies and to connect to the Internet. StilicForce, a French firm, designed and sells the Trottibasket, a durable plastic basket that slides onto the vertical bar of a Razor scooter. Shaped like a cone, the Trottibasket is used to carry relatively small items the scooter rider needs to transport.[88]

In the Strategic Focus on page 133, we discuss individual sources of differentiation that two firms—New Balance and Maserati (part of Fiat Group)—have created to use the focused differentiation strategy. As described in the Strategic Focus, both New Balance and Maserati use the focused differentiation strategy to target a narrow customer segment. However, the competitive advantages on which the companies rely to serve their unique market segments differ. Technology, R&D capability, managerial creativity, and an empowered and talented workforce are the advantages New Balance uses to offer customers a shoe with an ideal "fit." Relying on its reputation, design skills, and manufacturing expertise, the Maserati Spider appeals to the *emotions* of its target customer group. In both instances, perceived value is created for a narrow segment of broader markets (for athletic shoes and automobiles, respectively).

Firms must be able to complete various primary and support activities in a competitively superior manner to achieve and sustain a competitive advantage and earn above-average returns with a focus strategy. The activities required to use the focused cost leadership strategy are virtually identical to the activities shown in Figure 4.2, and activities required to use the focused differentiation strategy are virtually identical to those shown in Figure 4.3. Similarly, the manner in which each of the two focus strategies allows a firm to deal successfully with the five competitive forces parallel those described with respect to the cost leadership strategy and the differentiation strategy. The only difference is that the competitive scope changes from an industry-wide market to a narrow industry segment. Thus, a review of Figures 4.2 and 4.3 and the text regarding the five competitive forces yields a description of the relationship between each of the two focus strategies and competitive advantage.

Satisfying Unique Needs: Of Shoes and Cars

As mentioned earlier, New Balance concentrates on the athletic shoe needs of the Baby Boom generation (born between 1946 and 1964). The high quality "fit" that its shoes provide is the primary source of differentiation, for which the firm's target customer group is willing to pay a premium price.

Early research by New Balance suggested that active Baby Boomers want shoes that fit extremely well rather than shoes that are recognized for their style. A key indicator of the company's commitment to fit is that it is the only shoe manufacturer producing a complete line in a variety of widths—from AA to EEEE. New Balance's philosophy about fit is straightforward: "The better your shoes fit, the more comfortable you will be, the better you will enjoy yourself."

To support the design and manufacture of products with the "best possible fit," New Balance invests significantly in technological research and development (R&D) activities. Several patented technologies resulting from the firm's R&D efforts have been instrumental in the development of some shoes' suspension systems. Well-trained workers use highly sophisticated manufacturing equipment to produce the firm's differentiated products. The differentiation of New Balance's shoes in terms of fit is suggested by the fact that several models have received special recognition by the American Podiatric Medical Association.

Surveys also show that a commitment to provide jobs to U.S. workers is important to Baby Boomers. As mentioned in Chapter 3, New Balance manufactures more of its goods in the United States than do competitors such as Nike Inc. and Reebok International. Company officials observe that, "While most of the footwear industry has moved its production overseas to take advantage of low labor costs and generally cheaper production costs, we have continued to make many of our shoes in the United States and have expanded production substantially." This commitment results in an hourly wage cost disadvantage to the firm. New Balance production employees earn approximately $14 per hour as compared to the 20 cents to 40 cents per hour earned by shoe factory workers in China, Indonesia, and Vietnam—three countries where many U.S. apparel manufacturers, including shoe companies, outsource production of their goods. To counter this cost disadvantage, New Balance cross-trains its employees, allowing them to gain multiple skills that are used in largely self-managed work teams.

In addition, the firm's managers are known for their creative ability to adapt new technologies to shoemaking processes. Self-managed workers, technologically innovative managers, and an award-winning R&D capability are the competitive advantages that allow New Balance to overcome the negative effects of labor cost differentials. Currently, for example, New Balance workers produce a pair of shoes in 24 minutes versus the three hours it takes to make a pair of shoes in China.

Fiat Group, the Italian manufacturer of mass-market cars, owns 90 percent of Ferrari SpA, the famous sports car company with the well-recognized Prancing Horse emblem on its products. Ferrari claims that its highly specialized design and production processes allow it to produce cars that are "unique and unrepeatable." Ferrari's sports car range from $143,000 to $230,000 in price.

In the late 1990s, Ferrari bought Maserati. After a ten-year absence from the U.S. market, a Maserati product was reintroduced in early 2002 after being successfully relaunched earlier in France, Italy, Switzerland, and Germany. Demonstrating precise segmentation of the market for expensive sports cars, Ferrari determined that the Maserati would appeal to wealthy sports car enthusiasts lacking either the resources or the desire to purchase a Ferrari. The target customer was the person with "good taste who is looking for a unique emotion from driving." The narrowness of the competitive scope associated with this target customer is suggested by Ferrari's decision to introduce only 1,200 Maserati cars into the U.S. market in 2002. Priced at approximately $80,000, the two-seater Maserati Spider (the product offered in the United States) competes against the Porsche

911 and the Jaguar XKR. Like its rivals, the Spider travels from zero to 60 miles per hour in roughly 5.3 seconds. Thus, speed is not a dimension on which the Spider is differentiated. Instead, product customization and racing lessons are the intended sources of differentiation of the Maserati.

To emphasize the exclusivity and service that come with the brand, Maserati customers receive a car they helped design, down to the color of the leather stitching in the upholstery, if they so desire. Describing the extent to which Maserati is willing to customize the Spider, the firm's CEO commented that, "If you come to me with denim and want that in the interior, I will do it for you." For customers wanting to sharpen their "race car driving skills," the Master GT driving course is an option. Run by former Formula One driver Ivan Capelli, the course is available to Spider owners to zip around the Varano de Melegari circuit near Parma. Professional instructors guide the learning experience for customers, who leave the experience with a taste of what it is like to drive on a race course and with an improved knowledge of the Spider's performance capabilities.

SOURCES: A. Bernstein, 2001, Low-skilled jobs: Do they have to move? *Business Week*, February 26, 94–95; A. Kirkman, 2001, Zoom! Zoom! *Forbes*, May 14, 208; http://www.ferrari.com; http://www.newbalance.com.

Competitive Risks of Focus Strategies

With either focus strategy, the firm faces the same general risks as does the company using the cost leadership or the differentiation strategy respectively on an industry-wide basis. However, focus strategies have three additional risks.

First, a competitor may be able to focus on a more narrowly defined competitive segment and "outfocus" the focuser. For example, Big Dog Motorcycles is trying to outfocus Harley-Davidson, which is pursuing a broader-focus differentiation strategy. While Harley focuses solely on producing heavyweight motorcycles, Big Dog builds motorcycles that target only the very high end of the heavyweight market—the high-end premium cruiser market—with names such as Pitbull, Wolf, Mastiff, and Bulldog. Big Dog is careful to differentiate its products from those of Harley Davidson, citing its larger motors, fat rear tires, unique state-of-the-art electronics, and 4-piston caliber brakes as examples of value-creating features. With additional value-creating differentiated features (e.g., performance capabilities made possible by larger engines), Big Dog may be able to better serve the unique needs of a narrow customer group.[89]

Second, a company competing on an industry-wide basis may decide that the market segment served by the focus strategy firm is attractive and worthy of competitive pursuit. No longer content with only its traditional customer group, Home Depot now has plans to concentrate on more narrow segments that it has not previously served, such as people who are involved in large-ticket home renovations. In addition, the firm acquired Maintenance Warehouse America Corp. Now called Maintenance Warehouse, this separate Home Depot company is the leading supplier of over 13,000 maintenance repair and replacement products. The owners and managers of multi-housing, lodging, and commercial properties form Maintenance Warehouse's target customer group.[90] Because of its size and capabilities, firms competing in focused market segments (e.g., multi-housing properties only) may be threatened by Home Depot's market segment entrance.

The third risk involved with a focus strategy is that the needs of customers within a narrow competitive segment may become more similar to those of industry-wide customers as a whole. As a result, the advantages of a focus strategy are either reduced or eliminated. At some point, for example, the needs of Ikea's customers for stylish furniture may dissipate, although their desire to buy relatively inexpensive furnishings may not. If this change in needs were to happen, Ikea's customers might buy from large chain stores that sell somewhat standardized furniture at low costs.

Integrated Cost Leadership/Differentiation Strategy

Particularly in global markets, the firm's ability to integrate the means of competition necessary to implement the cost leadership and differentiation strategies may be critical to developing competitive advantages. Compared to firms implementing one dominant business-level strategy, the company that successfully uses an integrated cost leadership/differentiation strategy should be in a better position to (1) adapt quickly to environmental changes, (2) learn new skills and technologies more quickly, and (3) effectively leverage its core competencies while competing against its rivals.

In this chapter's first Strategic Focus (see page 121), the Southwest Airlines activity map demonstrates how a firm gains a competitive advantage by tightly integrating its primary and support activities. Southwest successfully uses the integrated cost leadership/differentiation strategy, allowing the firm to adapt quickly, learn rapidly, and meaningfully leverage its core competencies while competing against its rivals in the airline industry.

Concentrating on the needs of its core customer group (higher-income, fashion-conscious discount shoppers), Target Stores also uses an integrated strategy. Target relies on its relationships with Michael Graves in home, garden, and electronics products, Sonia Kashuk in cosmetics, Mossimo in apparel, and Eddie Bauer in camping and outdoor gear, among others, to offer differentiated products at discounted prices. Committed to presenting a consistent upscale image to its core customer group, the firm carefully studies trends to find new branded items that it believes can satisfy its customers' needs.[91]

Evidence suggests a relationship between successful use of the integrated strategy and above-average returns.[92] Thus, firms able to produce relatively differentiated products at relatively low costs can expect to perform well.[93] Indeed, a researcher found that the most successful firms competing in low-profit-potential industries were integrating the attributes of the cost leadership and differentiation strategies.[94] Other researchers have discovered that "businesses which combined multiple forms of competitive advantage outperformed businesses that only were identified with a single form."[95] The results of another study showed that the highest-performing companies in the Korean electronics industry combined the value-creating aspects of the cost leadership and differentiation strategies.[96] This finding suggests the usefulness of integrated strategy in settings outside the United States.

McDonald's is a global corporation with a strong global brand, offering products at a relatively low cost but with some differentiated features. Its global scale, relationships with franchisees, and rigorous standardization of processes allow McDonald's to lower its costs, while its brand recognition and product consistency are sources of differentiation allowing the restaurant chain to charge slightly higher prices.[97] Thus, the firm uses the integrated cost leadership/differentiation strategy.[98]

The future success of McDonald's has been questioned. One analyst suggests that, "Already in the U.S., competition is eroding its dominance; its great days are probably over. It must now manage a decline which will be bumpy, even violent."[99] Does this comment accurately describe McDonald's future as it uses the integrated strategy? Are the firm's great days "over" as the analyst foresees? We consider these matters in the Strategic Focus on the next page.

Global Burgers: Will McDonald's Future Be as Good as Its Past?

McDonald's has a strong and growing global presence, earning more than $9 billion in sales revenue in European countries alone. The firm has over 28,000 restaurants operating in 120 countries. It serves more than 45 million people daily and opens a new store every five hours somewhere in the world.

Committed to stringent standards of product quality, service, and cleanliness, McDonald's uses value pricing (the source of relatively low costs to customers) while offering menu and storefront variety and relying on the power of its brand name (sources of differentiation). Globally, the company seeks to provide its combination of relatively low costs and some levels of differentiation in a culturally sensitive manner. In India, for example, the Maharaja Mac, which is made from lamb, substitutes for the beef-based Big Mac. Popular corn soup is offered on the chain's menu in its Japanese units.

Marketing penetration and expansion plans are based on local customer preferences and cultural practices. In China, for example, early competitive actions concentrated on children as a target market. With a decline in the nation's birth rate and other social and economic changes, some young parents have more money to spend on what is often an only child. McDonald's promotes children's birthdays by aiming advertising at them. Parties with cakes, candles, hats, and gifts are emphasized to young consumers. The party can be hosted in a children's enclosure, sometimes called the Ronald Room. These parties have become popular with upwardly mobile children in Hong Kong, Beijing, and Shanghai. An indicator of the success of this approach is that some parents in Hong Kong take their children to the local McDonald's as a reward for good behavior and academic achievement.

In 1999, McDonald's launched its "Made for You" system. Replacing its historic practice of producing food and storing it in a large tray until purchased, the new system was designed to increase product quality, variety, and delivery speed (sources of differentiation). To do this, new computer equipment and cooking and food preparation machinery were installed in each unit. Crewmembers and managers received extensive training to learn how to maximize efficiency by using the new system. However, after two years and a $1 billion investment, McDonald's moved from "Made for You" to a more simplified system. A primary reason for this change was that the cost of using the "Made for You" system to increase sources of differentiation exceeded acceptable levels for successful use of the integrated cost leadership/differentiation strategy.

To control costs through simplification, McDonald's decided to trim its 36-item core menu, jettisoning various items such as the McFlurry. Simultaneously, the firm intended to introduce new concepts (e.g., "McDonald's with a Diner Inside" and McCafe) as sources of differentiation from competitors. With 300 units already established in 17 countries, the first U.S. McCafe unit opened in Chicago in April, 2001. The U.S. McCafe uses separately trained staff and specialized equipment and features comfortable furniture, including couches. Competition from Starbucks (with 3,300 existing units and 15 new stores opening each week) could affect McCafe's success. McDonald's ruled out the possibility of testing a deli concept because of high labor costs—costs that would exceed those in line with a successful integrated strategy.

Coin changers, double drive-throughs, self-order kiosks, electronic menu boards, and cashless drive-throughs are relatively inexpensive services (and further sources of differentiation) that McDonald's is evaluating for introduction by mid-year 2005. To improve customer frequency and track purchasing behavior, the firm has established the McRewards program. Each purchase earns points that can be used to obtain prizes from several partner firms, including Mattel and Walt Disney Co.

SOURCES: M. Arndt, 2001, McLatte and croissant? *Business Week*, April 2, 14; R. Dzinkowski, 2001, McDonald's Europe, *Strategic Finance*, May, 24–27; K. MacArthur, 2001, McDonald's sees 100%, *Advertising Age*, May/June, 12–134; J. Ettlie, 1999, What the auto industry can learn from McDonald's, *Automotive Manufacturing & Production*, 111(10), 42–43; C. Murphy, 1999, How McDonald's conquered the UK, *Marketing*, February 18, 30–31.

The imitability of many of its newly designed sources of differentiation will affect the degree of success McDonald's can achieve with the integrated cost leadership/differentiation strategy. Major competitors such as Burger King and Wendy's may be able to imitate the value created through McDonald's new products and services, such as double drive-throughs, electronic menu boards, and the McRewards program. Additionally, both competitors have the resources to purchase technologies and equipment that reduce production costs. As a result, McDonald's must simultaneously seek new ways to differentiate its product offerings and storefront concepts and reduce its cost structure to successfully use the integrated strategy. Supporting McDonald's efforts is its commitment to serve the unique needs of customers in different countries. Being able to satisfy country heterogeneity in terms of customers' desires can lead to a competitive advantage.[100]

Will McDonald's efforts to reduce costs through a more simplified menu while offering some additional differentiated features in new storefront formats be sufficient to assure success in the years to come? Time will tell, but history suggests that the firm has the potential to perform well. The rivalry among firms in the fast-food industry is quite intense. As discussed in Chapter 2, this intensity reduces the profitability potential for all companies. However, McDonald's recent actions to enable it to more successfully use a strategy that integrates relatively low costs with some differentiated features may have the potential to contribute to the firm's strategic competitiveness as it competes vigorously with its rivals.

Unlike McDonald's, which uses the integrated cost leadership/differentiation strategy on an industry-wide basis, air-conditioning and heating-systems maker Aaon concentrates on a particular competitive scope. Thus, Aaon is implementing a focused integrated strategy. Aaon manufactures semi-customized rooftop air conditioning systems for large retailers, including Wal-Mart, Target, and Home Depot. Aaon positions its rooftop systems between low-priced commodity equipment and high-end customized systems. The firm's innovative manufacturing capabilities allow it to tailor a production line for units with special heat-recovery options unavailable on low-end systems. Combining custom features with assembly line-production methods results in significant cost savings. Aaon's prices are approximately 5 percent higher than low-end products but are only one-third the price of comparable customized systems.[101] Thus, the firm's narrowly defined target customers receive some differentiated features (e.g., special heat-recovery options) at a low, but not the lowest cost.

A commitment to strategic flexibility (see Chapter 1) is necessary for firms such as McDonald's and Aaon to effectively use the integrated cost leadership/differentiation strategy. Strategic flexibility results from developing systems, procedures, and methods that enable a firm to quickly and effectively respond to opportunities that reduce costs or increase differentiation. Flexible manufacturing systems, information networks, and total quality management systems are three sources of strategic flexibility that facilitate use of the integrated strategy. Valuable to the successful use of each business-level strategy, the strategic flexibility provided by these three tools is especially important to firms trying to balance the objectives of continuous cost reductions and continuous enhancements to sources of differentiation.

Flexible Manufacturing Systems

Modern information technologies have helped make flexible manufacturing systems (FMS) possible. These systems increase the "flexibilities of human, physical, and information resources"[102] that the firm integrates to create differentiated products at low costs. A *flexible manufacturing system* is a computer-controlled process used to produce a variety of products in moderate, flexible quantities with a minimum of manual intervention.[103] Particularly in situations where parts are too heavy for people to handle or when other methods are less effective in creating manufacturing and assembly flexibility, robots are integral to use of an FMS.[104] In spite of their promise, only one in five *Fortune* 1000 companies are using the productive capabilities of an FMS.[105]

The goal of an FMS is to eliminate the "low-cost-versus-product-variety" trade-off that is inherent in traditional manufacturing technologies. Firms use an FMS to change quickly and easily from making one product to making another.[106] Used properly, an FMS allows the firm to respond more effectively to changes in its customers' needs, while retaining low-cost advantages and consistent product quality.[107] Because an FMS also enables the firm to reduce the lot size needed to manufacture a product efficiently, the firm increases its capacity to serve the unique needs of a narrow competitive scope. Thus, FMS technology is a significant technological advance that allows firms to produce a large variety of products at a relatively low cost. Levi Strauss, for example, uses an FMS to make jeans for women that fit their exact measurements. Customers of Andersen Windows can design their own windows using proprietary software the firm has developed. Tire manufacturers Pirelli and Goodyear are turning to robots and other advanced technologies as part of their quest to transform the traditional time-consuming, complex, and costly method of making tires into a more flexible and responsive system.[108]

The effective use of an FMS is linked with a firm's ability to understand the constraints these systems may create (in terms of materials handling and the flow of supporting resources in scheduling, for example) and to design an effective mix of machines, computer systems, and people.[109] In service industries, the processes used must be flexible enough to increase delivery speed and to satisfy changing customer needs. McDonald's, for example, is testing three "vision" stores in three stages to learn how to reduce service times. In addition to installing more automated equipment, the company is experimenting with splitting counter service between two employees—one person taking the order and payment while the other assembles the order.[110] In industries of all types, effective mixes of the firm's tangible assets (e.g., machines) and intangible assets (e.g., people's skills) facilitate implementation of complex competitive strategies, especially the integrated cost leadership/differentiation strategy.[111]

An FMS is a complex engineering project. Some companies use a differentiation strategy to develop and implement flexible manufacturing systems for end users. Generating over $2 billion in annual sales, UNOVA, Inc. follows a differentiation strategy to supply manufacturing technologies and integrated production systems to automotive, aerospace, and heavy equipment producers. In markets throughout the world, the firm provides customers with the most technologically advanced, high-quality systems. To enhance the flexibility its systems provide to end users, UNOVA continuously evaluates its own manufacturing processes to find ways to enhance the sources of value its differentiated features create for customers.[112]

Information Networks

By linking companies with their suppliers, distributors, and customers, information networks provide another source of strategic flexibility. Among other outcomes, these networks facilitate the firm's efforts to satisfy customer expectations in terms of product quality and delivery speed.

As noted earlier, customer relationship management (CRM) is one form of an information-based network process that firms use to better understand customers and their needs. The effective CRM system provides a 360-degree view of the company's relationship with customers, encompassing all contact points, involving all business processes, and incorporating all communication media and sales channels.[113] The firm can then use this information to determine the trade-offs its customers are willing to make between differentiated features and low cost, which is vital for companies using the integrated cost leadership/differentiation strategy.

Information networks are also critical to the establishment and successful use of an enterprise resource planning (ERP) system. ERP is an information system used to identify and plan the resources required across the firm to receive, record, produce, and ship customer orders.[114] For example, salespeople for aircraft parts distributor Aviall use handheld equipment to scan bar-code labels on bins in customers' facilities to determine when parts need to be restocked. Data gathered through this procedure are uploaded via the Web to the Aviall back-end replenishment and ERP system, allowing the order fulfillment process to begin within minutes of scanning.[115] Growth in ERP applications such as the one used at Aviall has been significant.[116] Projections are that the annual sales of ERP software and service will exceed $84 billion before 2003.[117] Full installations of an ERP system are expensive, running into the tens of millions of dollars for large-scale applications.

Improving efficiency on a company-wide basis is a primary objective of using an ERP system. Efficiency improvements result from the use of systems through which financial and operational data are moved rapidly from one department to another. The transfer of sales data from Aviall salespeople to the order entry point at the firm's manufacturing facility demonstrates the rapid movement of information from one function to another. Integrating data across parties that are involved with detailing product specifications and then manufacturing those products and distributing them in ways that are consistent with customers' unique needs enable the firm to respond with flexibility to customer preferences relative to cost and differentiation.

Total Quality Management Systems

In the 1970s and 1980s, executives in Western nations, including the United States, recognized that their firms' success and even survival in some industries (e.g., automobile manufacturing) depended on developing an ability to dramatically improve the quality of their goods and services while simultaneously reducing their cost structures. The relatively low costs of relatively high-quality products from a host of Japanese companies emphasized this message with resounding clarity.[118]

Focused on *doing things right* through efficiency increases, total quality management (TQM) systems are used in firms across multiple nations and economic regions to increase their competitiveness.[119] TQM systems incorporate customer definitions of quality instead of those derived by the firm, and demand that the firm focus on the root causes of a problem rather than its symptoms.[120] Accepted widely as a viable means of improving the firm's competitiveness, TQM systems have been a worldwide movement since the early 1980s.[121]

A key assumption underlying the use of a TQM system is that "the costs of poor quality (such as inspection, rework, lost customers, and so on) are far greater than the costs of developing processes that produce high-quality products and services."[122] This relationship may partially account for financial difficulties Ford Motor Company experienced in mid-2001, when poor product quality and related production delays in the previous year were estimated to have cost Ford over $1 billion in lost profits. A comparison of the estimated warranty costs for Ford and for two of its competitors also demonstrates the competitive disadvantage resulting from poor quality. Deutsche Bank estimated Ford's average warranty cost per vehicle at $650, GM's at $550, and Toyota's at $400.[123] Cost disadvantages such as these make it difficult to compete successfully against rivals (see Chapter 5) and to earn returns that satisfy investors' expectations.

Firms use TQM systems to achieve several specific objectives, including (1) at least meeting customers' expectations while striving to exceed them, especially in terms of quality, (2) focusing on work activities to drive out inefficiencies and waste in all business processes, and (3) incorporating improvements in all parts of the firm while continuously striving for additional improvement opportunities.[124] Achieving these objectives improves a firm's flexibility and facilitates use of all business-level strategies. However, the outcomes suggested by these objectives are particularly important to firms implementing the integrated cost leadership/differentiation strategy. At least meeting (and perhaps exceeding) customers' expectations regarding quality is a differentiating feature, and eliminating process inefficiencies allows the firm to offer that quality at a relatively low cost. Thus, an effective TQM system helps the firm develop the flexibility needed to spot opportunities to simultaneously increase differentiation and/or reduce costs.

Competitive Risks of the Integrated Cost Leadership/ Differentiation Strategy

The potential to earn above-average returns by successfully using the integrated cost leadership/differentiation strategy is appealing. However, experience shows that substantial risk accompanies this potential. Selecting a business-level strategy requires the firm to make choices about how it intends to compete.[125] Achieving the low-cost position in an industry or a segment of an industry by using a focus strategy demands that the firm reduce its costs consistently relative to the costs of its competitors. The use of the differentiation strategy, with either an industry-wide or a focused competitive scope (see Figure 4.1), requires the firm to provide its customers with differentiated goods or services they value and for which they are willing to pay a premium price.

The firm that uses the integrated strategy yet fails to establish a leadership position risks becoming "stuck in the middle."[126] Being in this position prevents the firm from dealing successfully with the competitive forces in its industry and from having a distinguishable competitive advantage. Not only will the firm not be able to earn above-average returns, earning even average returns will be possible only when the structure of the industry in which it competes is highly favorable or if its competitors are also in the same position.[127] Without these conditions, the firm will earn below-average returns. Thus, companies implementing the integrated cost leadership/differentiation strategy, such as McDonald's and Aaon, must be certain that their competitive actions allow them both to offer some differentiated features that their customers value and to provide them with products at a relatively low cost.

There is very little if any research evidence showing that the attributes of the cost leadership and differentiation strategies *cannot* be effectively integrated.[128] The integrated strategy therefore is an appropriate strategic choice for firms with the core competencies required to produce somewhat differentiated products at relatively low costs.

- A business-level strategy is an integrated and coordinated set of commitments and actions the firm uses to gain a competitive advantage by exploiting core competencies in specific product markets. Five business-level strategies (cost leadership, differentiation, focused cost leadership, focused differentiation, and integrated cost leadership/differentiation) are examined in the chapter. A firm's strategic competitiveness is enhanced when it is able to develop and exploit new core competencies faster than competitors can mimic the competitive advantages yielded by the firm's current competencies.

- Customers are the foundation of successful business-level strategies. When considering customers, a firm simultaneously examines three issues: *who, what,* and *how.* These issues respectively refer to the customer groups to be served, the needs those customers have that the firm seeks to satisfy, and the core competencies the firm will use to satisfy customers' needs. Increasing segmentation of markets throughout the global economy creates opportunities for firms to identify unique customer needs.

- Firms seeking competitive advantage through the cost leadership strategy produce no-frills, standardized products for an industry's typical customer. However, these low cost products must be offered with competitive levels of differentiation. Above-average returns are earned when firms continuously drive their costs lower than those of their competitors, while providing customers with products that have low prices and acceptable levels of differentiated features.

- Competitive risks associated with the cost leadership strategy include (1) a loss of competitive advantage to newer technologies, (2) a failure to detect changes in customers' needs, and (3) the ability of competitors to imitate the cost leader's competitive advantage through their own unique strategic actions.

- The differentiation strategy enables firms to provide customers with products that have different (and valued) features. Differentiated products must be sold at a cost that customers believe is competitive given the product's features as compared to the cost/feature combination available through competitors' offerings. Because of their uniqueness, differentiated goods or services are sold at a premium price. Products can be differentiated along any dimension that

some customer group values. Firms using this strategy seek to differentiate their products from competitors' goods or services along as many dimensions as possible. The less similarity with competitors' products, the more buffered a firm is from competition with its rivals.

- Risks associated with the differentiation strategy include (1) a customer group's decision that the differences between the differentiated product and the cost leader's good or service are no longer worth a premium price, (2) the inability of a differentiated product to create the type of value for which customers are willing to pay a premium price, (3) the ability of competitors to provide customers with products that have features similar to those associated with the differentiated product, but at a lower cost, and (4) the threat of counterfeiting, whereby firms produce a cheap "knock-off" of a differentiated good or service.

- Through the cost leadership and the differentiated focus strategies, firms serve the needs of a narrow competitive segment (e.g., a buyer group, product segment, or geographic area). This strategy is successful when firms have the core competencies required to provide value to a narrow competitive segment that exceeds the value available from firms serving customers on an industry-wide basis.

- The competitive risks of focus strategies include (1) a competitor's ability to use its core competencies to "outfocus" the focuser by serving an even more narrowly defined competitive segment, (2) decisions by industry-wide competitors to serve a customer group's specialized needs that the focuser has been serving, and (3) a reduction in differences of the needs between customers in a narrow competitive segment and the industry-wide market.

- Firms using the integrated cost leadership/differentiation strategy strive to provide customers with relatively low-cost products that have some valued differentiated features. The primary risk of this strategy is that a firm might produce products that do not offer sufficient value in terms of either low cost or differentiation. When this occurs, the company is "stuck in the middle." Firms stuck in the middle compete at a disadvantage and are unable to earn more than average returns.

1. What is a business-level strategy?

2. What is the relationship between a firm's customers and its business-level strategy in terms of *who, what,* and *how*? Why is this relationship important?

3. What are the differences among the cost leadership, differentiation, focused cost leadership, focused differentiation, and integrated cost leadership/differentiation business-level strategies?

4. How can each one of the business-level strategies be used to position the firm relative to the five forces of competition in a way that permits the earning of above-average returns?

5. What are the specific risks associated with using each business-level strategy?

Business-Level Strategy

Natural and organic foods are the fastest growing segment of food retailing, and almost every supermarket in America has begun offering at least a limited selection of these products. According to chairman and CEO John Mackey, "Whole Foods is the 'category killer' for natural and organic products, offering the largest selection at competitive prices and the most informed customer service."

The first Whole Foods Markets opened in 1980, in Austin, Texas, and realized $4 million in sales. By 2001 the firm had become the world's largest retailer of natural and organic foods, with 126 stores across the country and the District of Columbia. A strong performer for several years with consistently high same-store sales, cash flow, gross margins, and controlled expansion, the firm's sales grew to $2.27 billion and earnings per share to $1.03 for fiscal 2001, ended in September. Shares are up more than 50 percent over the previous year, and analysts expect the performance to continue, anticipating 18 percent earnings growth in fiscal 2002 and 20 percent growth in 2003.

Whole Foods purchases its products both locally and from all over the world, supporting organic farming on a global level, and prides itself on providing its customer with the highest quality, least processed, most flavorful and naturally preserved foods. While the firm concedes that organic foods generally cost more than conventional foods, it notes that organic farming is not government subsidized and that organic products must meet stricter regulations governing growing, harvesting, transportation, and storage. All of these steps make the process more labor and management intensive.

Whole Foods staff members are encouraged to make their own decisions and play a critical role in helping build the store into a profitable and beneficial part of its community.

Answer the following questions and be prepared to make a short presentation or to discuss your findings with the rest of the class.

1. What type of business-level strategy does Whole Foods appear to follow, based on the above information?

2. What are some of the risks Whole Foods faces with this strategy?

3. Use the following table and show how Whole Foods might apply each strategy to its business activities, based on the information given above (also see Figures 4.2 and 4.3).

Activities	Cost Leadership Strategy	Differentiation Strategy
Inbound Logistics		
Operations		
Outbound Logistics		
Marketing and Sales		
Service		

SOURCES: L. DiCarlo, 2001, The overachievers, *Forbes.com*, http://www.forbes.com, December 5; 2000, Whole Foods Annual Report, Chairman's Letter, http://www.wholefoodsmarket.com/ investor/AR00letter.html.

1. J. Stopford, 2001, Should strategy makers become dream weavers? *Harvard Business Review*, 79(1): 165–169.

2. C. A. De Kluyver, 2000, *Strategic Thinking*, Upper Saddle River, NJ: Prentice-Hall, 3.

3. E. H. Bowman & C. E. Helfat, 2001, Does corporate strategy matter? *Strategic Management Journal*, 22: 1–23.

4. G. Hamel, 2000, *Leading the Revolution*, Boston: Harvard Business School Press, 71.

5. R. S. Kaplan & D. P. Norton, 2001, *The Strategy-Focused Organization*, Boston: Harvard Business School Press, 90.

6. J. B. Barney, 2002, *Gaining and Sustaining Competitive Advantage*, 2nd ed., Upper Saddle River, NJ.: Prentice-Hall, 6; D. C. Hambrick & J. W. Fredrickson, 2001, Are you sure you have a strategy? *Academy of Management Executive*, 15(4): 48–59.

7. R. D. Ireland, M. A. Hitt, S. M. Camp, & D. L. Sexton, 2001, Integrating entrepreneurship and strategic management actions to create firm wealth, *Academy of Management Executive*, 15(1): 49–63.

8. M. A. Geletkanycez & S .S. Black, 2001, Bound by the past? Experience-based effects on commitment to the strategic status quo, *Journal of Management*, 27: 3–21; C. E. Helfat, 1997, Know-how and asset complementarity and dynamic capability accumulation: The case of R&D, *Strategic Management Journal*, 18: 339–360.

9. D. F. Kuratko, R. D. Ireland, & J. S. Hornsby, 2001, The power of entrepreneurial actions: Insights from Acordia, Inc., *Academy of Management Executive*, 15(4): 60–71; T. J. Dean, R. L. Brown, & C. E. Bamford, 1998, Differences in large and small firm responses to environmental context: Strategic implications from a comparative analysis of business formations, *Strategic Management Journal*, 19: 709–728.

10. L. Tihanyi, A. E. Ellstrand, C. M. Daily, & D. R. Dalton, 2000, Composition of top management team and firm international diversification, *Journal of Management*, 26: 1157–1177; P. F. Drucker, 1999, *Management in the 21st Century*, New York: Harper Business.

11. P. Rindova & C. J. Fombrun, 1999, Constructing competitive advantage: The role of firm-constitute interactions, *Strategic Management Journal*, 20: 691–710; G. G. Dess, A. Gupta, J. F. Hennart, & C. W. L. Hill, 1995, Conducting and integrating strategy research at the international, corporate, and business levels: Issues and directions, *Journal of Management*, 21: 357–393.

12. Hamel, *Leading the Revolution*.

13. De Kluyver, *Strategic Thinking*, 7.

14. S. F. Slater & E. M. Olsen, 2000, Strategy type and performance: The influence of sales force management, *Strategic Management Journal*, 21: 813–829; M. E. Porter, 1998, *On Competition*, Boston: Harvard Business School Press.

15. M. E. Porter, 1996, What is strategy? *Harvard Business Review*, 74(6): 61–78.

16. B. Lowendahl & O. Revang, 1998, Challenges to existing strategy theory in a postindustrial society, *Strategic Management Journal*, 19: 755–773.

17. M. E. Porter, 1980, *Competitive Strategy*, New York: Free Press.

18. P. Burrows & A. Park, 2001, Can Compaq escape from hardware hell? *Business Week*, July 9, 38–39.

19. L. B. Ward, 2001, Compaq changes direction, *Dallas Morning News*, June 26, D1, D12.

20. L. L. Berry, 2001, The old pillars of new retailing, *Harvard Business Review*, 79(4): 131–137; A. Afuah, 1999, Technology approaches for the information age, in *Mastering Strategy (Part One)*, *Financial Times*, September 27, 8.

21. N. Irwin, 2001, Motley Fool branches out, *The Washington Post*, May 22, B5.

22. 2001, Clicking with customers: New challenges in online conversion, *Knowledge@Wharton*, http://www.knowledge.wharton.upenn.edu, May 26.

23. M. Schrage, 2001, Don't scorn your salespeople—you will soon be one, *Fortune*, May 14, 256; D. Peppers, M. Rogers, & B. Dorf, 1999, Is your company ready for one-to-one marketing? *Harvard Business Review*, 77(5): 59–72.

24. T. A. Stewart, 1999, *Intellectual Capital*, New York: Currency Doubleday, 144.

25. K. Ferguson, 2001, Closer than ever, *Business Week Small Biz*, May 21, 14–15; R. S. Winer, 2001, A framework for customer relationship management, *California Management Review*, 43(4): 89–105.

26. Ferguson, Closer than ever, 15.

27. M. Warner, 2001, Salesforce.com, *Fortune*, June 25, 164.

28. P. B. Seybold, 2001, Get inside the lives of your customers, *Harvard Business Review*, 79(5): 81–89.

29. M. E. Porter, 2001, Strategy and the Internet, *Harvard Business Review*, 79(3): 62–78.

30. L. Walker, 2001, Plugged in for maximum efficiency, *The Washington Post*, June 20, G1, G4.

31. 2001, While Welch waited, *The Economist*, May 19, 75–76.

32. 2002, http://www.bn.com, March 15.

33. P. Evans & T. S. Wurster, 1999, Getting real about virtual commerce, *Harvard Business Review*, 77(6): 84–94; S. F. Slater & J. C. Narver, 1999, Market-oriented is more than being customer-led, *Strategic Management Journal*, 20: 1165–1168.

34. 2001, How good, or bad, marketing decisions can make, or break, a company, *Knowledge@Wharton*, http://www.knowledge.wharton.upenn.edu, May 14.

35. W. D. Neal & J. Wurst, 2001, Advances in market segmentation, *Marketing Research*, 13(1): 14–18; S. C. Jain, 2000, *Marketing Planning and Strategy*, Cincinnati: South-Western College Publishing, 104–125.

36. 1999, Associated Press, Rolls Bentley targets U.S. drivers, *Dallas Morning News*, May 2, H5.

37. B. J. Knutson, 2000, College students and fast food-how students perceive restaurant brands, *Cornell Hotel and Restaurant Administration Quarterly*, 41(3): 68–74.

38. C. Burritt, 2001, Aging boomers reshape resort segment, *Lodging Hospitality*, 57(3): 31–32; J. D. Zbar, On a segmented dial, digital cuts wire finer, *Advertising Age*, 72(16): S12; Gen-er-a-tion, *Richmond Times-Dispatch*, April 2, E1–E2; 2001, The America Funds Group, *The American Funds Investor*, Spring/Summer, 24.

39. V. Kumar & A. Nagpal, 2001, Segmenting global markets: Look before you leap, *Marketing Research*, 13(1): 8–13.

40. 2001, Is Gen Y shopping online? *Business Week*, June 11, 16.

41. D. Little, 2001, Hot growth companies, *Business Week*, June 11, 107–110; 2001, http://www.newbalance.com, May 10.

42. D. A. Aaker, 1998, *Strategic Marketing Management*, 5th ed., New York: John Wiley & Sons, 20.

43. S. Miller, 1999, VW sows confusion with common platforms for models, *The Wall Street Journal*, October 25, A25, A38.

44. D. Welch, 2000, GM: 'Out with the Olds' is just the start, *Business Week*, December 25, 57.

45. A. W. King, S. W. Fowler, & C. P. Zeithaml, 2001, Managing organizational competencies for competitive advantage: The middle-management edge, *Academy of Management Executive*, 15(2): 95–106; Porter, Strategy and the Internet, 72.

46. S. N. Mehta, 2001, What Lucent can learn from IBM, *Fortune*, June 25, 40–44.

47. C. A. O'Reilly III & J. Pfeffer, 2000, *Hidden Value: How Great Companies Achieve Extraordinary Results with Ordinary People*, Boston: Harvard Business School Press, 102.

48. A. Weintraub & G. Khermouch, 2001, Chairman of the board, *Business Week*, May 28, 94.

49. M. E. Porter, *Competitive Advantage*, New York: Free Press, 26.

50. Porter, What is strategy?

51. Bowman & Helfat, Does corporate strategy matter?, 1–4; B. McEvily & A. Zaheer, 1999, Bridging ties: A source of firm heterogeneity in competitive capabilities, *Strategic Management Journal*, 20: 133–156.

52. Hambrick & Fredrickson, Are you sure you have a strategy?

53. M. E. Porter, 1994, Toward a dynamic theory of strategy, in R. P. Rumelt, D. E. Schendel, & D. J. Teece (eds.), *Fundamental Issues in Strategy*, Boston: Harvard Business School Press, 423–461.

54. Porter, What is strategy?, 62.

55. Porter, *Competitive Advantage*, 15.

56. G. G. Dess, G. T. Lumpkin, & J. E. McGee, 1999, Linking corporate entrepreneurship to strategy, structure, and process: Suggested research directions, *Entrepreneurship: Theory & Practice*, 23(3): 85–102; P. M. Wright, D. L. Smart, & G. C. McMahan, 1995, Matches between human resources and strategy among NCAA basketball teams, *Academy of Management Journal*, 38: 1052–1074.

57. Porter, *Competitive Strategy*, 35–40.

58. J. A. Parnell, 2000, Reframing the combination strategy debate: Defining forms of combination, *Journal of Management Studies*, 9(1): 33–54.

59. C. Malburg, 2000, Competing on costs, *Industry Week*, October 16, 31.

60. D. F. Lynch, S. B. Keller, & J. Ozment, 2000, The effects of logistics capabilities and strategy on firm performance, *Journal of Business Logistics*, 21(2): 47–68.

61. Porter, What is strategy?, 67.

62. http://www.vanguard.com

63. Porter, What is strategy?, 66.

64. http://www.cnstores.com

65. A. D'Innocenzio, 2001, We are paranoid, *Richmond Times-Dispatch*, June 10, E1, E2.

66. L. Grant, 2001, Kmart, Wal-Mart face off in price-cutting fight, *USA Today*, June 8, B1; A. R. Moses, 2001, Kmart's long road back, *Richmond Times-Dispatch*, November 24, C1, C10.

67. Lynch, Keller, & Ozment, The effects of logistics capabilities.
68. Porter, *Competitive Strategy*, 35–40.
69. Ibid., 65.
70. Porter, *Competitive Advantage*, 14.
71. http://www.roberttalbott.com
72. 2001, Business in Brief, *The Washington Post*, June 20, E2.
73. Joyce, Luxury sales, E1.
74. G. Edmonsdson, E. Neuborne, A. L. Kazmin, E. Thornton, & K. N. Anhalt, 1999, L'Oreal: The beauty of global branding, *Business Week e-biz*, June 28.
75. Barney, *Gaining and Sustaining Competitive Advantage*, 268.
76. Ward, Compaq changes direction.
77. R. More, 2001, Creating profits from integrated product-service strategies, *Ivey Business Journal*, 65(5): 75–81.
78. H. R. Goldstein, A. E. Roth, T. Young, & J. D. Lawrence, 2001, US manufacturers take a swing at counterfeit golf clubs, *Intellectual Property & Technology Law Journal*, May, 23.
79. Porter, *Competitive Strategy*, 98.
80. Porter, *Competitive Advantage*, 15.
81. Ibid., 15–16.
82. 1999, Lloyd Greif Center for Entrepreneurial Studies, Discussion of the Greif Center's founder http://www.marshall.usc.edu.
83. D. Foust & B. Grow, 2001, This company likes it in jail, *Business Week*, June 11, 112.
84. Porter, *Competitive Advantage*, 15.
85. Porter, What is strategy?, 67.
86. http://www.ikea.com
87. Porter, What is strategy?, 65.
88. O. Kharif, 2001, You can take this furniture with you, *Business Week*, April 16, 16; S. Jones, 2001, Cutting a swath in hair care, *The Washington Post*, May 5, E1, E8; F. McCarthy, 2001, Get Well Network enlivens patients' stay at hospital, *The Washington Post*, May 7, E5; A. Overholt, 2001, Basket case, *Fast Company*, July, 60.
89. http://www.bigdog.com
90. http://www.homedepot.com; J. R. Hagerty, 2000, Home Depot strikes at Sears in tool duel, *The Wall Street Journal*, January 10, B1, B4.
91. 2001, The engine that drives differentiation, *DSN Retailing Today*, April 2, 52.
92. Dess, Lumpkin, & McGee, Linking corporate entrepreneurship to strategy, 89.
93. P. Ghemawat, 2001, *Strategy and the Business Landscape*, Upper Saddle River, NJ: Prentice Hall, 56.
94. W. K. Hall, 1980, Survival strategies in a hostile environment, *Harvard Business Review* 58, 5: 75–87.
95. Dess, Gupta, Hennart, & Hill, Conducting and integrating strategy research, 377.
96. L. Kim & Y. Lim, 1988, Environment, generic strategies, and performance in a rapidly developing country: A taxonomic approach, *Academy of Management Journal*, 31: 802–827.
97. Ghemawat, *Strategy and the Business Landscape*, 56.
98. Ibid., 56.
99. M. Naim, 2001, McAtlas shrugged, *Foreign Policy*, May/June, 26–37.
100. A. K. Gupta & V. Govindarajan, 2001, Converting global presence into global competitive advantage, *Academy of Management Executive*, 15(2): 45–56.
101. S. A. Forest, 2001, When cool heads prevail, *Business Week*, June 11, 114.
102. R. Sanchez, 1995, Strategic flexibility in product competition, *Strategic Management Journal*, 16(Summer Special Issue): 140.
103. Ibid., 105.
104. R. Olexa, 2001, Flexible parts feeding boosts productivity, *Manufacturing Engineering*, 126(4): 106–114.
105. I. Mount & B. Caulfield, 2001, The missing link, *Ecompany Now*, May, 82–88.
106. Ibid., 82.
107. 2001, ABB: Integrated drives and process control, *Textile World*, April, G0–G1.
108. M. Maynard, 2001, Tiremaking technology is on a roll, *Fortune*, May 28, 148B–148L; J. Martin, 1997, Give 'em exactly what they want, *Fortune*, November 10, 283–285.
109. R. S. Russell & B. W. Taylor III, 2000, *Operations Management*, 3rd ed., Upper Saddle River, NJ: Prentice-Hall, 262–264.
110. K. MacArthur, 2001, McDonald's sees 100% increase in U.S. sales, *AdAge.com*, http://www.adage.com, April 2.
111. J. B. Dilworth, 2000, *Operations Management: Providing Value in Goods and Services*, 3rd ed. (Fort Worth, TX.: The Dryden Press), 286–289; D. Lei, M. A. Hitt, & J. D. Goldhar, 1996, Advanced manufacturing technology, organization design and strategic flexibility, *Organization Studies*, 17: 501–523.
112. R. E. Chalmers, 2001, Assembly systems maximize efficiency, *Manufacturing Engineering*, May, 130–138.
113. S. Isaac & R. N. Tooker, 2001, The many faces of CRM, *LIMRA's MarketFacts Quarterly*, Spring, 20 (1): 84–89.
114. P. J. Rondeau & L. A. Litteral, 2001, The evolution of manufacturing planning and control systems: From reorder point to enterprise resource planning, *Production and Inventory Management*, 42(2): 1–7.
115. M. L. Songini, 2001, Companies test their wireless supply chain wings, *Computerworld*, May 21, 35.
116. N. Checker, 2001, An integrated approach, *Chemical Market Reporter*, June 4, S8–S10.
117. V. A. Mabert, A. Soni, & M. A. Venkataramanan, 2000, Enterprise resource planning survey of U.S. manufacturing firms, *Production and Inventory Management Journal*, Second Quarter, 52–58.
118. D. Chatterji & J. M. Davidson, 2001, Examining TQM's legacies for R&D, *Research Technology Management*, 44(1): 10–12.
119. Kaplan & Norton, *The Strategy-Focused Organization*, 361; M. A. Mische, 2001, *Strategic Renewal: Becoming a High-Performance Organization*, Upper Saddle River, NJ: Prentice-Hall, 15.
120. J. Pfeffer, 1998, *The Human Equation: Building Profits by Putting People First*, Boston: Harvard Business School Press, 156.
121. W. M. Mak, 2000, The Tao of people-based management, *Total Quality Management*, July, 4–6.
122. J. R. Hackman & R. Wageman, 1995, Total quality management: Empirical, conceptual, and practical issues, *Administrative Science Quarterly*, 40: 310.
123. J. Muller, 2001, Ford: Why it's worse than you think, *Business Week*, June 25,
124. Chatterji & Davidson, Examining TQM's legacies, 11.
125. De Kluyver, *Strategic Thinking*, 3; C. H. St. John & J. S. Harrison, 1999, Manufacturing-based relatedness, synergy, and coordination, *Strategic Management Journal*, 20: 129–145.
126. Porter, *Competitive Advantage*, 16.
127. Ibid., 17.
128. Parnell, Reframing the combination strategy debate, 33.

5

Chapter Five
Competitive Rivalry and Competitive Dynamics

Knowledge Objectives

Studying this chapter should provide you with the strategic management knowledge needed to:

1. Define competitors, competitive rivalry, competitive behavior, and competitive dynamics.

2. Describe market commonality and resource similarity as the building blocks of a competitor analysis.

3. Explain awareness, motivation, and ability as drivers of competitive behavior.

4. Discuss factors affecting the likelihood a competitor will take competitive actions.

5. Discuss factors affecting the likelihood a competitor will respond to actions taken against it.

6. Explain competitive dynamics in slow-cycle, fast-cycle, and standard-cycle markets.

Of Trucks and E-commerce:
Competitive Rivalry between FedEx and UPS

FedEx and UPS compete directly against each other in several product markets. These competitors are locked in fierce battles to dominate not only package delivery but emerging e-commerce and logistics markets as well. Across time, the rivalry between these firms has resulted in a great deal of competitive behavior (competitive actions and competitive responses taken to build or defend a firm's competitive advantages and improve its market performance).

In 1907, 19-year-old Jim Casey started UPS as a local delivery service. From its founding, strict operational guidelines have been in place at UPS. Even today, drivers are taught 340 steps that are to be precisely followed to successfully deliver a package the "UPS way."

Historically, UPS's rigid culture tended to discourage risk taking and innovation. Nonetheless, in the 1950s, UPS became the first company to use airplanes to deliver packages overnight. However, because of the higher cost compared to package delivery via trucks, UPS decided not to further pursue its innovation of overnight delivery.

In the 1970s, the shipping industry was substantially changed when Frederick Smith founded Federal Express (now called FedEx). Convinced that customers would value not only overnight deliveries but also the ability to electronically track them, FedEx developed a proprietary computerized tracking system called Cosmos. This system introduced computer technology to the shipping industry in previously unheard-of ways and permanently altered the nature of competition within it.

Study of its new competitor convinced UPS that overnight delivery was a market that it couldn't ignore. Thinking of Cosmos as a competitive advantage for FedEx, UPS set out to understand and imitate the system's capabilities. UPS employees even followed FedEx's trucks, partly to understand how Cosmos worked. In 1988, roughly 17 years after FedEx's entry into the overnight market, UPS introduced its rival service. However, it wasn't until 1995 that UPS was able to develop its own electronic tracking system comparable to

Although known for its overnight service, FedEx expected its ground unit to grow by 20 percent in the first quarter of 2002 as companies cutting costs choose this less expensive delivery option. Not only are the firm's gross margins for this service double those of overnight delivery, FedEx hasn't had to cut prices to compete in these markets. The firm's delivery arrangement with the U.S. Postal Service is expected to help both organizations. UPS, the traditional ground service carrier, continues to move in the other direction—its deliveries to and from China have more than doubled its revenue since the firm launched direct flights there. It is opening a new hub in the Philippines to cut transit time and to increase its position against Asia's strongest shipper, DHL.

© BONNIE KAMIN/PHOTO EDIT

Cosmos. At that time, many analysts concluded that UPS's slow market entry and inability to duplicate Cosmos's value-creating ability had permanently disadvantaged the firm. This conclusion hasn't proven to be the case. Although FedEx remains dominant in the overnight market, UPS's overnight business grew 8 percent in 2000, compared to 3.6 percent growth for FedEx.

Beyond this, though, UPS decided in the mid-1990s that some of the technological capabilities it had developed to match the sophistication of FedEx's Cosmos system also had commercial applications for Internet-based businesses. This decision was based on experience gained from efforts the firm started in the 1980s to study FedEx's operations methods. During that time period, UPS started applying technology such as tracking software, electronic clipboards, bar codes, and scanners to streamline its operations and cut costs. Efficiencies gained from its technology investments enabled UPS to almost double its operating margins from 8 percent to 15 percent. Study of e-commerce transactions convinced UPS that what it had learned from internal uses of technology could also benefit e-commerce retailers (e-tailers). In short, UPS caught FedEx off guard when it used its internally generated technology skills to offer e-tailers a multitude of shipping options and prices. Additionally, UPS began programming software tools, such as package tracking and returns management, directly into its customers' websites. These tools made it possible for shoppers to track orders with one click of a button and for e-tailers to more efficiently handle returns. Although FedEx and UPS compete for e-tailers' business, UPS remains the shipping partner of choice, as shown by recent market shares for the delivery of online purchases (55 percent for UPS; 10 percent for FedEx).

Encouraged by its success in e-commerce, UPS has initiated other competitive actions to evolve beyond its traditional capital-intensive transportation business. For example, the firm again relied on its technology skills to establish a logistics group in 1994. This unit helps firms such as National Semiconductor and Ford Motor Company learn how to use logistics technology to streamline their supply chains. FedEx competes against UPS in logistics; although both firms help customers better utilize information to track and ship inventory, UPS is pulling ahead of its competitor. Accounting for this success could be UPS's decision to offer warehouse management services. A customer choosing this service outsources its product logistics to UPS, allowing it to then concentrate on its own core competencies. UPS has built a sophisticated central warehouse in Louisville, KY to store, pack, and deliver such products as Samsung cell phones and Nike.com apparel. UPS is even going beyond the handling of physical goods, operating customer service call centers and offering financial products to facilitate e-commerce, such as trade credit and electronic invoicing. The diversity of its logistics business is resulting in an annual growth rate of 40 percent while FedEx tries to reverse a decline in this area.

UPS's competitive actions in logistics seemingly have created an advantageous market position for the firm over its major rival. However, FedEx is responding to UPS's actions. For example, it quietly spent approximately $4 billion to acquire trucking companies and build hubs. In 2000, FedEx directly attacked UPS when it started offering home package delivery by ground. Although UPS still dominates that market with a 77 percent share, FedEx is making strides as its ground shipping business grows by 8 percent to 10 percent annually. Furthermore, FedEx believes that UPS's capital-intensive approach to its logistics business is flawed. According to the head of FedEx's worldwide e-solutions, "the benefit (to customers) is in moving things quickly and coordinating those moves, not in having parts sitting somewhere." This comment reflects FedEx's decision not to warehouse customers' goods, citing the high costs of building warehouses.

SOURCES: 2002, Intrigue on the orient express, *The Economist*, January 19, 55; C. Haddad & J. Ewing, 2001, Ground wars, UPS' rapid ascent leaves FedEx scrambling, *Business Week*, May 21, 64–68; J. Kirby, 2001, An interview with Jim Kelly of UPS, *Harvard Business Review*, 79(10): 116–123; B. Schiffman, 2001, FedEx has guts, *Forbes*, http://www.forbes.com, November 20; E. Schonfeld, 2001, The total package, *eCompany Now*, http://business2.com/articles, June 1; K. G. Smith, W. J. Ferrier, & H. Ndofor, 2001, Competitive dynamics research: Critique and future directions, in M. A. Hitt, R. E. Freeman, & J. S. Harrison (eds.), *Handbook of Strategic Management*, Oxford, U.K.: Blackwell Publishers, 315–361; M. Tagte, 2001, Start the ground war, *Forbes*, http://www.forbes.com, October 26; K. Barron, 2000, Logistics in brown, *Forbes*, http://www.forbes.com, January 10; B. O'Reilly, 2000, They've got mail! The growth of Internet commerce has raised the stakes in the boxing match between UPS and FedEx, *Fortune*, http://www.forbes.com, February 7; M.-J. Chen, 1996, Competitor analysis and interfirm rivalry: Toward a theoretical integration, *Academy of Management Review*, 21: 100–134.

Firms operating in the same market, offering similar products and targeting similar cutomers are **competitors.**

Competitive rivalry is the ongoing set of competitive actions and competitive responses occurring between competitors as they compete against each other for an advantageous market position.

Competitive behavior is the set of competitive actions and competitive responses the firm takes to build or defend its competitive advantages and to improve its market position.

Firms operating in the same market, offering similar products and targeting similar customers are **competitors**.[1] Obviously, FedEx and UPS are competitors. **Competitive rivalry** is the ongoing set of competitive actions and competitive responses occurring between competitors as they compete against each other for an advantageous market position. Competitive rivalry influences an individual firm's ability to gain and sustain competitive advantages.[2] A sequence of firm-level moves, rivalry results from firms initiating their own competitive actions and then responding to actions taken by their competitors.[3] As noted in the Opening Case, **competitive behavior** is the set of competitive actions and competitive responses the firm takes to build or defend its competitive advantages and to improve its market position.[4] Through competitive behavior, the firm tries to successfully position itself relative to the five forces of competition (see Chapter 2) and to defend and use current competitive advantages while building advantages for the future (see Chapter 3). Increasingly, as with FedEx and UPS, competitors engage in competitive actions and responses in more than one market.[5]

All competitive behavior—that is, the total set of actions and responses taken by all firms competing within a market—is called **competitive dynamics**. The relationships among these key concepts are shown in Figure 5.1.

This chapter focuses on competitive rivalry and competitive dynamics. The essence of these important topics is that a firm's strategies are dynamic in nature. Actions taken by one firm elicit responses from competitors that, in turn, typically

Figure 5.1 From Competitors to Competitive Dynamics

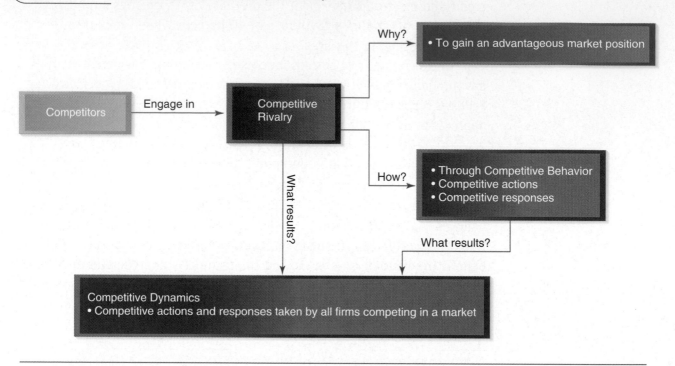

SOURCE: Adapted from M.-J. Chen, 1996, Competitor analysis and interfirm rivalry: Toward a theoretical integration, *Academy of Management Review,* 21: 100–134.

All competitive behavior—that is, the total set of actions and responses taken by all firms competing within a market—is called **competitive dynamics.**

Firms competing against each other in several product or geographic markets are engaged in **multimarket competition.**

result in responses from the firm that took the initial action.[6] This chain of events is illustrated in the Opening Case that describes FedEx and UPS's competitive rivalry as they compete against each other in several markets (e.g., package delivery and logistics services). Firms competing against each other in several product or geographic markets are engaged in **multimarket competition.**[7]

Another way of highlighting competitive rivalry's effect on the firm's strategies is to say that a strategy's success is determined not only by the firm's initial competitive actions but also by how well it anticipates competitors' responses to them *and* by how well the firm anticipates and responds to its competitors' initial actions (also called attacks).[8] Although competitive rivalry affects all types of strategies (for example, corporate-level, acquisition, and international), its most dominant influence is on the firm's business-level strategy or strategies. Recall from Chapter 4 that business-level strategy is concerned with what the firm does to successfully use its competitive advantages in specific product markets.

In the global economy, competitive rivalry is intensifying,[9] meaning that the significance of its effect on firms' business-level strategies is increasing. In the automobile industry, for example, Ford Motor Company CEO William Ford Jr. believes that firms engage in "cutthroat" competition. Companies with strong brand names (such as Coca-Cola, Microsoft, GE, Intel, and IBM) increasingly rely on them as ambassadors to enter new markets or offer new products.[10] This reliance is especially noticeable for firms using a differentiation business-level strategy. Strong brands affect competitive rivalry, in that companies without them must find ways (such as price reductions) to reduce their appeal to customers.[11] A competitor's decision to reduce prices likely will elicit a response from the firm with a strong brand, increasing competitive rivalry as a result.

An expanding geographic scope contributes to the increasing intensity in the competitive rivalry between firms. Some believe, for example, that an aptitude for cross-border management practices and a facility with cultural diversity find European Union firms emerging as formidable global competitors.[12] Similarly, former GE CEO Jack Welch believes that GE's most significant future competitive threats may be from companies not currently in prominent positions on the firm's radar screen, such as those in emerging countries.[13] Thus, the firm trying to predict competitive rivalry should anticipate that in the future it will encounter a larger number of increasingly diverse competitors. This trend also suggests that firms should expect competitive rivalry to have a stronger effect on their strategies' success than historically has been the case.[14]

We offer a model (see Figure 5.2 to show what is involved with competitive rivalry at the firm level).[15] We study rivalry at the firm level because the competitive actions and responses the firm takes are the foundation for successfully building and using its competitive advantages to gain an advantageous market position.[16] Thus, we use the model in Figure 5.2 to help us explain competition between a particular firm and each of its competitors as they compete for the most advantageous market position. Successful use of the model in Figure 5.2 finds companies able to predict competitors' behavior (actions and responses), which, in turn, has a positive effect on the firm's market position and its subsequent financial performance.[17] The sum of all the individual rivalries modeled in Figure 5.2 that are occurring in a particular market reflects the competitive dynamics in that market.

The remainder of the chapter discusses the model shown in Figure 5.2. We first describe market commonality and resource similarity as the building blocks of a competitor analysis. Next, we discuss the effects of three organizational characteristics—awareness, motivation, and ability—on the firm's competitive behavior. We then examine competitive rivalry in detail by describing the factors that affect the likelihood a firm will take a competitive action and the factors that affect the likelihood a firm will respond to a competitor's action. In the chapter's final section, we turn our

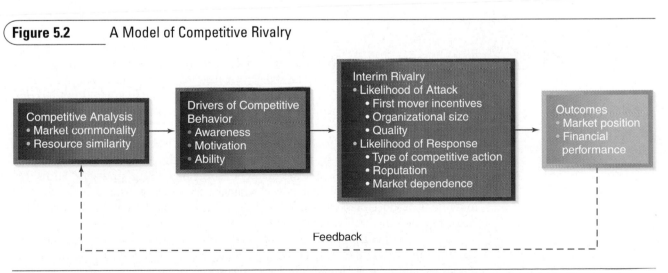

Figure 5.2   A Model of Competitive Rivalry

SOURCE: Adapted from M.-J. Chen, 1996, Competitor analysis and interfirm rivalry: Toward a theoretical integration, *Academy of Management Review*, 21: 100–134.

attention to competitive dynamics to describe how market characteristics affect competitive rivalry in slow-cycle, fast-cycle, and standard-cycle markets.

A Model of Competitive Rivalry

Over time, the firm takes many competitive actions and responses.[18] As noted earlier, competitive rivalry evolves from this pattern of actions and responses as one firm's competitive actions have noticeable effects on competitors, eliciting competitive responses from them.[19] This pattern shows that firms are mutually interdependent, that they feel each other's actions and responses, and that marketplace success is a function of both individual strategies and the consequences of their use.[20]

Increasingly too, executives recognize that competitive rivalry can have a major and direct effect on the firm's financial performance.[21] Research findings showing that intensified rivalry within an industry results in decreased average profitability for firms competing in it supports the importance of understanding these effects.[22] Rivalry in the PC market demonstrates these points.

In 2001, Dell Computer Corporation launched an intense price war in the PC business, causing prices for PCs as well as servers to drop by as much as 50 percent. Profit margins declined for all firms, including Dell, as noted by analysts who suggested that Dell's action was draining gross profit dollars out of the PC segment for all companies.[23] CEO Michael Dell, however, believed that the direct sales model on which his firm's cost leadership strategy is based would enable it to better survive reduced profitability than its competitors could, in that nimble execution of strategy, which means selling machines directly to consumers, is more important than economies of scale in the PC business.[24]

At the core of the intensified rivalry created by Dell's pricing action was the firm's intention of increasing its share of the PC market. Competitors responded to Dell's competitive action, intensifying rivalry in the process. The most dramatic response was Hewlett-Packard's merger with Compaq Computer Corporation.[25] Initially, negative reaction from Walter Hewlett and David Packard, sons of the company's founders, as well as other shareholders, jeopardized the transaction's approval.[26] Although opinions vary, a number of analysts suggest that the new company's competitive position is unattractive compared to Dell's.[27] Further showing the complexity of the merger is the suggestion that Compaq's future would have been shaky had the merger collapsed.[28] Because of its unattractive competitive position, analysts propose that had Compaq remained an independent firm, its competitive position would have been stronger if it were to exit the PC business to concentrate on technology services and the server market.[29]

The intensity of rivalry within a particular market, such as what we described in the PC market, is affected by many factors, including the total number of competitors, market characteristics, and the quality of individual firms' strategies. Firms that develop and use effective business-level strategies tend to outperform competitors in individual product markets, even when experiencing intense competitive rivalry.[30] According to some, Dell's use of an effective business-level strategy may contribute to its ability to frequently outperform its competitors. Indeed, it has been suggested that "Dell sets the standard for the industry, reflecting the strength of its direct sales model (strategy), and its superior cash flow management."[31]

Financial analysts feel that Dell Computer Corp., under founder and CEO Michael Dell (pictured here), has done a great job of exceeding the overall trends in the industry. Dell's policy of direct sales has positioned it well as the low-cost provider, especially when customers want to maximize their computer expenditures both for business computers and home equipment.

We now turn directly to Figure 5.2 as our foundation for further discussion of competitive rivalry such as that experienced in the PC market.

Competitor Analysis

As noted above, a competitor analysis is the first step the firm takes to be able to predict the extent and nature of its rivalry with each competitor. Recall that a competitor is a firm operating in the same market, offering similar products and targeting similar customers. The number of markets in which firms compete against each other (called market commonality, defined below) and the similarity in their resources (called resource similarity, also defined below) determine the extent to which the firms are competitors. Firms with high market commonality and highly similar resources are ". . . clearly direct and mutually acknowledged competitors."[32] However, being direct competitors does not necessarily mean that the rivalry between the firms will be intense. The drivers of competitive behavior—as well as factors influencing the likelihood that a competitor will initiate competitive actions and will respond to its competitor's competitive actions—influence the intensity of rivalry, even for direct competitors.[33]

In Chapter 2, we discussed competitor analysis as a technique firms use to understand their competitive environment. Along with the general and industry environments, the competitive environment comprises the firm's external environment. In the earlier chapter we described how competitor analysis is used to help the firm *understand* its competitors. This understanding results from studying competitors' future objectives, current strategies, assumptions, and capabilities (see Figure 2.3). In this chapter, the discussion of competitor analysis is extended to describe what firms study as the first step to being able to *predict* competitors' behavior in the form of its competitive actions and responses. The discussions of competitor analysis in Chapter 2 and Chapter 5 are complementary in that firms must first *understand* competitors (Chapter 2) before their competitive actions and competitive responses can be *predicted* (Chapter 5).

Market Commonality

Each industry is composed of various markets. The financial services industry has markets for insurance, brokerage services, banks, and so forth. Denoting an interest to concentrate on the needs of different, unique customer groups, markets can be further subdivided. The insurance market, for example, could be broken into market segments (such as commercial and consumer), product segments (such as health insurance and life insurance), and geographic markets (such as Western Europe and Southeast Asia).

In general, competitors agree about the different characteristics of individual markets that form an industry.[34] For example, in the transportation industry, there is an understanding that the commercial air travel market differs from the ground transportation market that is served by firms such as Yellow Freight System. Although differences exist, most industries' markets are somewhat related in terms of technologies used or core competencies needed to develop a competitive advantage.[35] For example, different types of transportation companies need to provide reliable and timely service. Commercial airline carriers such as Southwest Airlines and Singapore Airlines must therefore develop service competencies to satisfy its passengers, while Yellow Freight System must develop such competencies to serve the needs of those using its fleet to ship their goods.

Firms competing in several or even many markets, some of which may be in different industries, are likely to come into contact with a particular competitor several

times,[36] a situation bringing forth the issue of market commonality. **Market commonality** is concerned with the number of markets with which the firm and a competitor are jointly involved and the degree of importance of the individual markets to each.[37] Firms competing against one another in several or many markets engage in multimarket competition.[38] For ex-ample, McDonald's and Burger King compete against each other in multiple geographic markets across the world,[39] while Prudential and Cigna compete against each other in several market segments (institutional and retail) as well as product markets (such as life insurance and health insurance).[40] Airlines, chemicals, pharmaceuticals, and consumer foods are other industries in which firms often simultaneously engage each other in multiple market competitions.

While cutting back on expansion in Latin America to boost sales and profitability in existing restaurants in the region, McDonald's plans more stores in China in 2002. Operating in more than 57 countries, Burger King competes with McDonald's in several markets, such as in Israel.

Firms competing in several markets have the potential to respond to a competitor's actions not only within the market in which the actions are taken, but also in other markets where they compete with the rival. This potential complicates the rivalry between competitors. In fact, recent research suggests that ". . . a firm with greater multimarket contact is less likely to initiate an attack, but more likely to move (respond) aggressively when attacked."[41] Thus, in general, multimarket competition reduces competitive rivalry.[42]

Market commonality is concerned with the number of markets with which the firm and a competitor are jointly involved and the degree of importance of the individual markets to each.

Other research suggests that market commonality and multimarket competition sometimes occur almost by chance.[43] However, once it begins, the rivalry between the unexpected competitors becomes intentional and oftentimes intense. This appears to be the case for AOL and Microsoft. In the Strategic Focus on page 155, we describe the multimarket competition with which these firms are involved as well as some of the competitive actions and responses occurring between them.

As described in the Strategic Focus, the competition between AOL and Microsoft is complex and intense as each firm initiates competitive actions and responds to those of its competitor. The fact that they compete against each other in several markets has the potential to increase the scope and intensity of their rivalry. For example, actions taken by either AOL or Microsoft to improve its market position in instant messaging could result in a competitive response in the online music subscription service market. When predicting their competitor's actions and responses, AOL and Microsoft must consider the strong likelihood that some competitive responses will take place in a market other than the one in which a competitive action was taken.

Resource Similarity

Resource similarity is the extent to which the firm's tangible and intangible resources are comparable to a competitor's in terms of both type and amount.

Resource similarity is the extent to which the firm's tangible and intangible resources are comparable to a competitor's in terms of both type and amount.[44] Firms with similar types and amounts of resources are likely to have similar strengths and weaknesses and use similar strategies.[45] The competition between competitors CVS Corp. and Walgreens to be the largest drugstore chain in the United States demonstrates

Internet Wars—A Competition for Dominance between AOL and Microsoft

Companies are sometimes driven to compete in the same markets because of changing conditions. For example, AOL Time Warner and Microsoft traditionally have competed in different markets of the broadly defined technology industry. Microsoft's strength is in software development and sales. Windows, its desktop operating system, runs on 9 out of 10 computers and accounts for approximately 95 percent of Microsoft's operating income. In addition to its thriving online services business, AOL is primarily a media company with HBO, Time Warner, Netscape, and CNN as some of its recognized brands.

With reduced growth in their core businesses, however, AOL and Microsoft find themselves competing to gain dominance of the Internet. Both firms appear to believe that the same set of anywhere, anytime Web services is the key to future success. The desired Web services range from stock quotes to online music to interactive television with delivery being to the office, a customer's living room, or any wireless device. With the common strategic intent of gaining the prominent Web services delivery position via the Internet, the companies increasingly find themselves competing against each other in multiple markets. As an Internet analyst for CIBS World Markets observed, the companies are saying, "I'm keeping my fingers in all of your pies, and you're keeping a finger in all mine."

The key to Internet dominance is gaining online subscribers and then selling products and services to them. With over 31 million subscribers, AOL has a significant size advantage over Microsoft's MSN Online, which has 7 million subscribers. However, the rivalry for customers is becoming more intense. When AOL took the competitive action of increasing its rates for online access by $1.95 per month to $23.90 in July 2001, Microsoft responded by holding its monthly price at $21.95. MSN Online then launched its own competitive action, which was an offer of free service for three months. MSN Online claims that 40 percent of new subscribers in the first few months following this action were former AOL customers. Rivalry for subscribers likely will intensify further as a result of AOL's decision (action) to directly negotiate with PC manufacturers to install AOL on PC desktops.

The scope of competition between AOL and Microsoft is broad, as the firms' multimarket competition finds them competing against each other in online services for entertainment, communication, and information. Commonly free today, many of these services will eventually generate fees for providers. The firms are introducing competing online music subscription services, for example. AOL is partnering with Bertelsmann and EMI to offer its service while Microsoft is offering PressPlay though its partnership with Vivendi Universal and Sony.

Instant messaging is another online market in which both firms compete. AOL pioneered this concept, which allows users to send and receive messages using the Internet when they are simultaneously connected. Instant messaging is vital to customer retention because subscribers are less likely to switch services once they establish a screen name that their friends know and use. AOL currently dominates instant messaging with several million customers using the service during peak times. In an effort to take market share from AOL, Microsoft has bundled MSN Messenger, its instant messaging service, with its newest Windows version. This competitive action is intended to entice all Windows XP purchasers, including AOL subscribers, to switch to MSN Messenger.

SOURCES: 2002, Who's afraid of AOL Time Warner? *The Economist*, January 26, 54–55; 2001, From friends to foes, *The Economist*, June 23, 56–57; J. Angwin & R. Buckman, 2001, AOL, MSN unveil Web-service changes, *The Wall Street Journal*, October 16, B6; A. Borrus, 2001, AOL's point man in the Web war: How CEO Barry Schuler plans to leave Microsoft in the dust, *Business Week*, July 2, 56–57; P. Garcia, 2001, The big fight, *Money*, August 1, 29–33; J. Greene, 2001, Why AOL nixed a Microsoft deal, *Business Week*, July 2, 58; P. Lewis, 2001, AOL vs. Microsoft: Now it's war, *Fortune*, July 23, 88–89; J. Green & A. Borrus, 2001, Case vs. Gates: Playing for the Web jackpot, *Business Week*, June 18, 42; C. Yang, J. Greene & A. Park, 2001, AOL vs. Microsoft: With core operations slowing, both see future growth in the same places, *Business Week*, August 13, 28–30.

these expectations. These firms are using the integrated cost leadership/differentiation strategy to offer relatively low-cost goods with some differentiated features, such as services. Resource similarity, as shown by the firms' recent net income amounts ($746 million for CVS; $776.9 million for Walgreens), suggests that the firms might use similar strategies.[46]

As our discussion shows, in a competitor analysis, the firm analyzes each of its competitors in terms of market commonality and resource similarity. Determining market commonality isn't difficult. CVS and Walgreens, for example, are quite aware of the total number of markets in which they compete against each other as well as the number of storefronts each operates. Recent statistics show that there are 4,133 CVS stores in 34 states and 3,165 Walgreens stores in 43 states. Thus, these firms compete against each other in many markets.

In contrast to market commonality, assessing resource similarity can be difficult, particularly when critical resources are intangible (such as brand name, knowledge, trust, and the capacity to innovate) rather than tangible (for example, access to raw materials and a competitor's ability to borrow capital). As discussed in Chapter 3, a competitor's intangible resources are difficult to identify and understand, making an assessment of their value challenging. CVS and Walgreens know the amount of each other's annual net income (a tangible resource). However, it is difficult for CVS and Walgreens to determine if any intangible resources (such as knowledge and trust among employees) its competitor possesses can lead to a competitive advantage.

The results of the firm's competitor analyses can be mapped for visual comparisons. In Figure 5.3, we show different hypothetical intersections between the firm and individual competitors in terms of market commonality and resource similarity. These intersections indicate the extent to which the firm and those to which it has compared itself are competitors.[47] For example, the firm and its competitor displayed in quadrant I of Figure 5.3 have similar types and amounts of resources and use them to compete against each other in many markets that are important to each. These conditions lead to the conclusion that the firms modeled in quadrant I are direct and mutually acknowledged competitors. In contrast, the firm and its competitor shown in quadrant III share few markets and have little similarity in their resources, indicat-

---

Figure 5.3   A Framework of Competitor Analysis

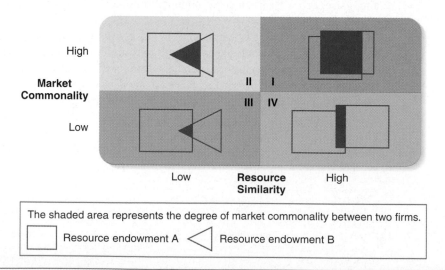

SOURCE: Adapted from M.-J. Chen, 1996, Competitor analysis and interfirm rivalry: Toward a theoretical integration, *Academy of Management Review*, 21: 100–134.

PART 2 /Strategic Actions: Strategy Formulation

ing that they aren't direct and mutually acknowledged competitors. The firm's mapping of its competitive relationship with rivals is fluid as firms enter and exit markets and as companies' resources change in type and amount. Thus, the companies with whom the firm is a direct competitor change across time.

Drivers of Competitive Actions and Responses

As shown in Figure 5.2, market commonality and resource similarity influence the drivers (awareness, motivation, and ability) of competitive behavior. In turn, the drivers influence the firm's competitive behavior, as shown by the actions and responses it takes while engaged in competitive rivalry.[48]

Awareness, which is a prerequisite to any competitive action or response being taken by the firm or its competitor, refers to the extent to which competitors recognize the degree of their mutual interdependence that results from market commonality and resource similarity.[49] A lack of awareness can lead to excessive competition, resulting in a negative effect on all competitors' performance.[50] Awareness tends to be greatest when firms have highly similar resources (in terms of types and amounts) to use while competing against each other in multiple markets. CVS and Walgreens are fully aware of each other, as are FedEx and UPS, and Wal-Mart and France's Carrefour. The last two firms' joint awareness has increased as they use similar resources to compete against each other for dominant positions in multiple European markets.[51] Awareness affects the extent to which the firm understands the consequences of its competitive actions and responses.

Motivation, which concerns the firm's incentive to take action or to respond to a competitor's attack, relates to perceived gains and losses. Thus, a firm may be aware of competitors but may not be motivated to engage in rivalry with them if it perceives that its position will not improve as a result of doing so or that its market position won't be damaged if it doesn't respond.[52]

Market commonality affects the firm's perceptions and resulting motivation. For example, all else being equal, the firm is more likely to attack the rival with whom it has low market commonality than the one with whom it competes in multiple markets. The primary reason is that there are high stakes involved in trying to gain a more advantageous position over a rival with whom the firm shares many markets. As we mentioned earlier, multimarket competition can find a competitor responding to the firm's action in a market different from the one in which the initial action was taken. Actions and responses of this type can cause both firms to lose focus on core markets and to battle each other with resources that had been allocated for other purposes. Because of the high stakes of competition under the condition of market commonality, there is a high probability that the attacked firm will respond to its competitor's action in an effort to protect its position in one or more markets.[53]

In some instances, the firm may be aware of the large number of markets it shares with a competitor and may be motivated to respond to an attack by that competitor, but it lacks the ability to do so. *Ability* relates to each firm's resources and the flexibility they provide. Without available resources (such as financial capital and people), the firm lacks the ability to attack a competitor or respond to its actions. However, similar resources suggest similar abilities to attack and respond. When a firm faces a competitor with similar resources, careful study of a possible attack before initiating it is essential because the similarly resourced competitor is likely to respond to that action.

Resource *dissimilarity* also influences competitive actions and responses between firms, in that "the greater is the resource imbalance between the acting firm and competitors or potential responders, the greater will be the delay in response"[54] by the firm with a resource disadvantage. For example, Wal-Mart initially used its cost leadership strategy to compete only in small communities (those with a population of 25,000 or less). Using sophisticated logistics systems and extremely efficient purchasing practices as advantages, among others, Wal-Mart created what was at that time a new type of value (primarily in the form of wide selections of products at the lowest competitive prices) for customers in small retail markets. Local stores, facing resource deficiencies relative to Wal-Mart, lacked the ability to marshal resources at the pace required to respond quickly and effectively. However, even when facing competitors with greater resources (greater ability) or more attractive market positions, firms should eventually respond, no matter how daunting doing so seems.[55] Choosing not to respond can ultimately result in failure, as happened with at least some local retailers who didn't respond to Wal-Mart's competitive actions.

Competitive Rivalry

As defined earlier in the chapter, *competitive rivalry* is the ongoing set of competitive actions and competitive responses occurring between competing firms for an advantageous market position. Because the ongoing competitive action/response sequence between a firm and a competitor affects the performance of both firms,[56] it is important for companies to carefully study competitive rivalry to successfully use their strategies. Understanding a competitor's awareness, motivation, and ability helps the firm to predict the likelihood of an attack by that competitor and how likely it is that a competitor will respond to the actions taken against it.

As we described above, the predictions drawn from study of competitors in terms of awareness, motivation, and ability are grounded in market commonality and resource similarity. These predictions are fairly general. The value of the final set of predictions the firm develops about each of its competitor's competitive actions and responses is enhanced by studying the "Likelihood of Attack" factors (such as firstmover incentives and organizational size) and the "Likelihood of Response" factors (such as the actor's reputation) that are shown in Figure 5.2. Studying these factors allows the firm to develop a deeper understanding in order to refine the predictions it makes about its competitors' actions and responses.

Strategic and Tactical Actions

Firms use both strategic and tactical actions when forming their competitive actions and competitive responses in the course of engaging in competitive rivalry.[57] A **competitive action** is a strategic or tactical action the firm takes to build or defend its competitive advantages or improve its market position. A **competitive response** is a strategic or tactical action the firm takes to counter the effects of a competitor's competitive action. A **strategic action or a strategic response** is a market-based move that involves a significant commitment of organizational resources and is difficult to implement and reverse. A **tactical action or a tactical response** is a market-based move that is taken to fine-tune a strategy; it involves fewer resources and is relatively easy to implement and reverse. UPS's 1994 decision to establish a logistics group (see the Opening Case) is an example of a strategic action. Hyundai Motor Co.'s expenditures on research and development and plant expansion to support the firm's desire to be one of the world's largest carmakers by 2010[58] also are strategic actions. The Strategic Focus on page 159 describes strategic actions taken by competitors Airbus Industrie and Boeing.

A competitor's strategic action signals that significant amounts of resources are being committed to a project and that once underway, it will be difficult for the action to be reversed. As explained in the Strategic Focus, Boeing and Airbus Industrie are initiating strategic actions that differ based on the companies' interpretations of the future of air travel.

A **competitive action** is a strategic or tactical action the firm takes to build or defend its competitive advantages or improve its market position.

A **competitive response** is a strategic or tactical action the firm takes to counter the effects of a competitor's competitive action.

A **strategic action or a strategic response** is a market-based move that involves a significant commitment of organizational resources and is difficult to implement and reverse.

A **tactical action or a tactical response** is a market-based move that is taken to fine-tune a strategy; it involves fewer resources and is relatively easy to implement and reverse.

Airplane Wars—Airbus and Boeing's Use of Different Strategic Actions

As competitors, Boeing and Airbus Industrie share multiple markets, have relatively similar resources in terms of what is available for the commercial aircraft market, and have pursued similar strategies. However, based on their predictions of the air transport industry's future, they are taking different strategic actions regarding the manufacture of tomorrow's large commercial airliners.

The differences in the firm's strategic actions started to become visible in December 2000 when Airbus launched efforts to build the A380, the world's largest commercial aircraft. The 550-650 seat double-decker superjumbo jet is designed to compete directly against the high end of Boeing's lucrative 747 series. The A380 is a primary challenger to the more than three-decade dominance of the 350-plus seat commercial airliner market Boeing has enjoyed with its 747 series. Airbus has committed $12 billion to the A380's design and development, which is scheduled to make its commercial debut with Singapore Airlines in 2006. Airbus is touting the need for the A380 based on its belief that airline traffic will continue to grow, intensifying problems in already congested airport hubs.

In response to Airbus's A380, Boeing announced plans to build a 520-seat version of the 747 as a competing superjumbo aircraft. In March 2001, after failing to win orders for the 747X, Boeing changed direction and scrapped the project. As part of an evolving strategic action, Boeing made this decision before it committed significant levels of resources to design and build the 747X. Boeing's announcement effectively ceded the superjumbo jet market to Airbus.

Reflecting a radical change, Boeing also indicated that it believed that speed, not size, will be the most important consideration in the future regarding air travel. Rather than the continued dominance of the hub system, Boeing concluded after further analyses that passenger demand for increased point-to-point travel options will result in market fragmentation and a reduction in the importance of hub systems. In fragmented markets, Boeing believes that carriers will need speedy, long-range mid-size planes to bypass major hubs for nonstop service from more remote destinations. In Boeing CEO Alan Mulally's words: "We decided point-to-point routes are the heart of the market. There was a lot of talk on large aircraft, but at the end of the day, after working with airlines, we decided to focus on longer range and increasing speed." Based on these beliefs, Boeing started design development of its futuristic Sonic Cruiser, a 250-passenger jet designed to travel at 95 percent of the speed of sound and to fly above 40,000 feet. The Sonic Cruiser is expected to reduce air travel time by 20 percent as a result of a radical new design, featuring a dramatically swept wing and two wing-mounted jet engines in the rear.

Some analysts believe that the A380 may have a ready market. In the words of one, "There will always be huge amounts of tourist traffic." Boeing's Sonic Cruiser may be a riskier project in terms of consumer acceptance and design feasibility. Indeed, industry experts estimate that because of fuel burn, the Sonic Cruiser's operating costs will be 12 percent to 15 percent higher than the 250-seat 767 that it would replace. Making an airplane travel faster requires using bigger engines, which weigh more and consume additional fuel. In turn, the aircraft body must be made larger to support the bigger engines, which creates more drag and ultimately burns more fuel. To obtain revenues that exceed this higher operating cost would require the Sonic Cruiser to fly mostly business class passengers, who are willing to pay a 20 percent premium over today's fares. Airbus is skeptical of the Sonic Cruiser's viability, as shown by a company official's claim that airline companies' "... expectations are economics and environment-friendly aircraft—the Sonic Cruiser is more public relations than engineering."

The reality of September 11, 2001 challenges the viability of Airbus and Boeing's evolving competitive actions regarding next generation commercial jets. Previous predictions that airline traffic will continue to grow 5 percent annually over the next 20 years are being tested. Not only have airlines reduced flights and employees in response to lower passenger levels, they also decreased or are canceling orders for new aircraft. These actions are affecting both Boeing and Airbus. Boeing has laid off 30,000 employees and cut production by 20 percent. Airbus recently received cancellation notices for 73 planes in a single month and halted plans for increasing capacity. This climate of severe uncertainty could potentially derail plans for development of the A380 and the Sonic Cruiser. Airbus requires 250 orders for the A380 project to be profitable. Even before September 11, the company had only 62 firm orders and 40 options to purchase. Boeing may now be less willing to commit substantial resources to the design and potential development of an aircraft that differs radically from current commercial jets. Thus, both firms must think carefully about the viability of their strategic actions in light of a highly uncertain and unpredictable external environment.

SOURCES: C. Matlack, 2002, Earth to Airbus: What's the flight plan? *Business Week*, January 21, 48; 2001, Place your bets, *The Economist*, June 23, 60–61; H. Banks, 2001, Paper plane, *Forbes*, May 28, 52–53; G. Cramb & M. Odell, 2001, Companies and finance Europe: Airbus plans for expansion on hold, *Financial Times*, September 21, 33; S. Holmes, 2001, Boeing's sonic bruiser, *Business Week*, July 2, 64–68; S. Holmes, C. Dawson, & C. Matlack, 2001, Rumble over Tokyo, *Business Week*, April 2, 80–81; C. Matlack & S. Holmes, 2001, Why Airbus could go into a dive, *Business Week*, October 1, 83; S. McClenahen, 2001, Planely different, *Industry Week*, June 11, 68–72; A. Sequeo, 2001, Boeing plans to build smaller, faster jet, *The Wall Street Journal*, March 20, A3; P. Sparaco, 2001, Airbus and Boeing snipe over speed versus size, *Aviation Week & Space Technology*, June 25, 26–27; P. Sparaco, 2001, Airbus thinks bigger, not faster, *Aviation Week & Space Technology*, June 18, 106–112; P. Sparaco, 2001, Airbus' production schedule riding out times, *Aviation Week & Space Technology*, September 24, 33; B. Sweetman, 2001, Three was a crowd, *Air Transport World*, September, 76–80.

© TOSHIFUMI KITAMURA/AFP/CORBIS

Hyundai has become a popular brand in Montgomery, Alabama. The city provided more than $234 million in public incentives to Hyundai to open a plant there (about $117,317 for each of the anticipated 2,000 jobs). The $1 billion plant may help the firm achieve its goal to become one of the world's largest automakers, as Hyundai expects it to produce 300,000 vehicles a year by 2005.

As the discussion in the Strategic Focus indicates, Airbus and Boeing have committed significant amounts of organizational resources to develop the A380 and the Sonic Cruiser, respectively. These actions will be difficult to reverse in that start-up development costs have been incurred and expectations have been established for two customer groups—airline companies and travelers. Disappointing these groups could damage either firm's reputation for being an innovator as well as each company's objective to gain dominance over its major rival. On the other hand, even strategic actions should be reversed when dramatic external environmental changes (such as those caused by September 11) call their viability into serious question.

As we noted earlier, a tactical action or a tactical response is a market-based move that a firm makes to fine-tune a strategy. It involves fewer and more general organizational resources and is relatively easy to implement and reverse, compared to a strategic action or a strategic response. Price changes in particular markets such as those made by airline companies are tactical actions. While reversing their strategic decisions to develop the A380 and Sonic Cruiser is difficult, deciding to reverse a tactical action or response, such as a minor modification to an existing aircraft, is relatively easy for both Airbus and Boeing.

Likelihood of Attack

In addition to market commonality, resource similarity, and the drivers of awareness, motivation, and ability, other factors also affect the likelihood a competitor will use strategic actions and tactical actions to attack its competitors. Three of these factors—first mover incentives, organizational size, and quality—are discussed next.

First-mover Incentives

A **first mover** is a firm that takes an initial competitive action in order to build or defend its competitive advantages or to improve its market position.

A **first mover** is a firm that takes an initial competitive action in order to build or defend its competitive advantages or to improve its market position. The first mover concept has been influenced by the work of the famous economist Joseph Schumpeter, who argued that firms achieve competitive advantage by taking innovative actions[59] (innovation is defined and described in detail in Chapter 13). In general, first movers "allocate funds for product innovation and development, aggressive advertising, and advanced research and development."[60]

The benefits of being a successful first mover can be substantial. Especially in fast-cycle markets (discussed later in the chapter) where changes occur rapidly and where it is virtually impossible to sustain a competitive advantage for any period of time, ". . . a first mover may experience five to ten times the valuation and revenue of a second mover."[61] This evidence suggests that although first mover benefits are never absolute, they are often critical to firm success in industries experiencing rapid technological developments and relatively short product life cycles.[62]

In addition to earning above-average returns until its competitors respond to its successful competitive action, the first mover can gain (1) the loyalty of customers who may become committed to the goods or services of the firm that first made them available and (2) market share that can be difficult for competitors to take during future competitive rivalry. For example, Yahoo! Japan moved first to establish an online auction market service in Japan. Rival eBay entered the market five months later. eBay's delayed response in an industry rife with rapid technological change was a critical mistake, as shown by the fact that first mover Yahoo! Japan recently held 95 percent of the online auction market in Japan while rival eBay's share was only 3 percent. A company official commented about why Yahoo! Japan moved first to establish an online auction market in Japan. The firm wanted to do so because, "We knew catching up with a front-runner is hard, because in auctions, more buyers bring more sellers."[63]

The firm trying to predict its competitors' competitive actions might rightly conclude that the benefits we described above could serve as incentives for many of them to act as first movers. However, while a firm's competitors might be motivated to be first movers, they may lack the ability to do so. First movers tend to be aggressive and willing to experiment with innovation and take higher, yet reasonable levels of risk.[64] To be a first mover, the firm must have readily available the amount of resources that is required to significantly invest in R&D as well as to rapidly and successfully produce and market a stream of innovative products.

Organizational slack makes it possible for firms to have the ability (as measured by available resources) to be first movers. *Slack* is the buffer or cushion provided by actual or obtainable resources that aren't currently in use.[65] Thus, slack is liquid resources that the firm can quickly allocate to support the actions such as R&D investments and aggressive marketing campaigns that lead to first mover benefits. This relationship between slack and the ability to be a first mover allows the firm to predict that a competitor who is a first mover likely has available slack and will probably take aggressive competitive actions to continuously introduce innovative products. Furthermore, the firm can predict that as a first mover, a competitor will try to rapidly gain market share and customer loyalty in order to earn above-average returns until its competitors are able to effectively respond to its first move.

Firms studying competitors should realize that being a first mover carries risk. For example, it is difficult to accurately estimate the returns that will be earned from introducing product innovations to the marketplace.[66] Additionally, the first mover's cost to develop a product innovation can be substantial, reducing the slack available to it to support further innovation. Thus, the firm should carefully study the results a competitor achieves as a first mover. Continuous success by the competitor suggests additional product innovations, while lack of product acceptance over the course of the competitor's innovations may indicate less willingness in the future to accept the risks of being a first mover.

A **second mover** is a firm that responds to the first mover's competitive action, typically through imitation. More cautious than the first mover, the second mover studies customers' reactions to product innovations. In the course of doing so, the second mover also tries to find any mistakes the first mover made so that it can avoid the problems resulting from them. Often, successful imitation of the first mover's innovations allows the second mover ". . . to avoid both the mistakes and the huge spending of the pioneers (first movers)."[67] Second movers also have the time to develop processes and technologies that are more efficient than those used by the first mover.[68] Greater efficiencies could result in lower costs for the second mover. Overall, the outcomes of the first mover's competitive actions may provide an effective blueprint for second and even late movers (as described below) as they determine the nature and timing of their competitive responses.[69]

Determining that a competitor thinks of itself as an effective second mover allows the firm to predict that that competitor will tend to respond quickly to first movers' successful, innovation-based market entries. If the firm itself is a first mover, then it can expect a successful second mover competitor to study its market entries and to respond to them quickly. As a second mover, the competitor will try to respond with a product that creates customer value exceeding the value provided by the product that the firm introduced initially as a first mover. The most successful second movers are able to rapidly and meaningfully interpret market feedback to respond quickly, yet successfully to the first mover's successful innovations.[70]

A **late mover** is a firm that responds to a competitive action, but only after considerable time has elapsed after the first mover's action and the second mover's response. Typically, a late response is better than no response at all, although any success achieved from the late competitive response tends to be slow in coming and considerably less than that achieved by first and second movers. Thus, the firm competing against a late mover can predict that that competitor will likely enter a particular market only after both the first and second movers have achieved success by doing so. Moreover, on a relative basis, the firm can predict that the late mover's competitive action will allow it to earn even average returns only when enough time has elapsed for it to understand how to create value that is more attractive to customers than is the value offered by the first and second movers' products. Although exceptions do exist, the firm can predict that as a competitor, the late mover's competitive actions will be relatively ineffective, certainly as compared to those initiated by first movers and second movers.

> A **second mover** is a firm that responds to the first mover's competitive action, typically through imitation.

> A **late mover** is a firm that responds to a competitive action, but only after considerable time has elapsed after the first mover's action and the second mover's response.

Organizational Size

An organization's size affects the likelihood that it will take competitive actions as well as the types of actions it will take and their timing.[71] In general, compared to large companies, small firms are more likely to launch competitive actions and tend to be quicker in doing so. Smaller firms are thus perceived as nimble and flexible competitors who rely on speed and surprise to defend their competitive advantages or develop new ones while engaged in competitive rivalry, especially with large companies, to gain an advantageous market position.[72] Small firms' flexibility and nimbleness allow them to develop greater variety in their competitive actions as compared to large firms, which tend to limit the types of competitive actions used when competing with rivals.[73]

Compared to small firms, large ones are likely to initiate more competitive actions as well as strategic actions during a given time period.[74] Thus, when studying its competitors in terms of organizational size, the firm should use a measurement of size such as total sales revenue or total number of employees to compare itself with each competitor. The competitive actions the firm likely will encounter from competitors larger than it is will be different than the competitive actions it will encounter from competitors who are smaller.

The organizational size factor has an additional layer of complexity associated with it. When engaging in competitive rivalry, the firm usually wants to take a large number of competitive actions against its competitors. As we have described, large organizations commonly have the slack resources required to launch a larger number of total competitive actions. On the other hand, smaller firms have the flexibility needed to launch a greater variety of competitive actions. Ideally, the firm would like to have the ability to launch a large number of unique competitive actions. A statement made by Herb Kelleher, former CEO of Southwest Airlines, addresses this matter: "Think and act big and we'll get smaller. Think and act small and we'll get bigger."[75]

In the context of competitive rivalry, Kelleher's statement can be interpreted to mean that relying on a limited number of type of competitive actions (which is the large firm's tendency) can lead to reduced competitive success across time, partly because competitors learn how to effectively respond to what is a limited set of competitive actions taken by a given firm. In contrast, remaining flexible and nimble (which is the small firm's tendency) in order to develop and use a wide variety of competitive actions contributes to success against rivals.

Wal-Mart appears to be an example of a large firm that has the flexibility required to take many types of competitive actions. With $216 billion in sales and a $252 billion market capitalization, Wal-Mart is one of the world's two largest companies in terms of sales revenue along with ExxonMobil. In only six years following its entry into the grocery market, Wal-Mart has become one of the largest grocery retailers in the United States. This accomplishment demonstrates Wal-Mart's ability to successfully compete against its various rivals, even long-established grocers. In spite of its size, the firm remains highly flexible as it takes both strategic actions (such as rapid global expansion) and tactical actions.

Analysts believe that Wal-Mart's tactical actions are critical to its success and show a great deal of flexibility. For example, "every humble store worker has the power to lower the price on any Wal-Mart product if he spots it cheaper elsewhere."[76] Decision-making responsibility and authority have been delegated to the level of the individual worker to make certain that the firm's cost leadership strategy always results in the lowest prices for customers. Managers and employees both spend a good deal of time thinking about additional strategic and tactical actions, respectively, that might enhance the firm's performance. Thus, it is possible that Wal-Mart has met the expectation suggested by Kelleher's statement, in that it is a large firm that ". . . remains stuck to its small-town roots" in order to think and act like the small firm capable of using a wide variety of competitive actions.[77] Wal-Mart's competitors might feel confident in predicting that the firm's competitive actions will be a combination of the tendencies shown by small and large companies.

In the Strategic Focus on page 164, we describe Lehman Brothers' ability to outperform its larger rivals. Although smaller than its primary competitors, its success is resulting in growth, partly at the expense of competitors. The competitive challenge for Lehman will be to continue thinking and acting as a small firm as it becomes a larger organization.

Investment Banking Competition: How Lehman Brothers Outperformed Its Larger Rivals

Competing in an industry known for high profile mergers and acquisitions, Lehman Brothers is proving that size is not the most important determinant of competitive success. Its $19 billion market capitalization is relatively small compared to capitalizations of $50 billion for Merrill Lynch and $71 billion for Morgan Stanley. However, Lehman's recent return on equity performances exceed those earned by its peers. Lehman has strong positions in fixed income, equities, and investment banking.

To remain successful, the firm is taking a number of competitive actions, including diversifying into different product markets such as equity issuance and mergers and acquisitions (M&A) advisory work. In 2001, Lehman more than doubled its share of the equity underwriting market from 3 percent to 7 percent. Lehman also is diversifying geographically, with 30 percent of earnings now being generated in Europe. Possibly contributing to Lehman's competitive success is its ability to avoid problems (such as frequent top-level managerial changes) that have affected its competitors.

Lehman's past hasn't been trouble free. The early 1980s saw the company's investment bankers and debt traders in the midst of a bitter battle over compensation and firm strategy. Undercapitalized and demoralized as a result of its internal struggles, Lehman sold itself to American Express in 1984. The two companies' cultures never meshed, resulting in the weakened Lehman's spinoff in 1994.

Making Lehman's current success somewhat impressive is that roughly five years ago, industry analysts were speculating that the firm would either be acquired or be forced to file for bankruptcy. Wall Street's growing belief that smaller, independent investment banks couldn't compete against larger rivals accounted for the dire predictions about Lehman's independence and performance ability. Industry characteristics seem to provide partial support for the predictions, in that investment banks in recent years have faced increasing pressure to offer credit to their corporate customers in addition to traditional advisory services. Most investment banks lack the sizable balance sheets required to lend significant sums of money to support their customers' intended merger or acquisition plans or other business expansions. These pressures resulted in investment banks becoming vulnerable to well-capitalized commercial banks, which succeeded in attracting the investment banks' most lucrative corporate relationships and infringed on their advisory business. In response, boutique investment banks merged with commercial banks and each other, creating industry giants such as J. P. Morgan Chase and Saloman Smith Barney.

Determined to find innovative competitive actions his firm could take to successfully compete against larger rivals, Lehman's current CEO, Richard Fuld, has worked diligently to foster cooperation within the firm. The focus is on being cost efficient and nimble as it competes against its rivals. The company's compensation structure creates incentives for employees to work together to achieve these goals. At the managerial level, for example, division heads are compensated identically based on overall firm performance. "When we line up with a customer, it's about how we approach them as a team," states Fuld, "It's not about the lone rangers. Lone rangers do not live long." Many of Lehman's larger competitors use compensation systems that reward primarily on the basis of individuals' performance.

Additionally, Fuld has fostered an organizational culture that is more open than traditionally is the case with Wall Street companies. He has shunned the executive suite in favor of a centrally located glass office and routinely invites employees to breakfast. As a member of the team, each employee is expected to contribute ideas about competitive actions Lehman can take to continue outperforming its competitors. Employee turnover is lower at Lehman than is the case at many of its competitors. In fact, Lehman's top management team has been together since 1996, and the average tenure of the firm's senior executives is 22 years.

The success attained through some of Lehman's strategic actions (for example, entering and exiting product markets on the basis of strict guidelines) and tactical actions (such as making changes to how services are delivered to customers) is eliciting responses from competitors. For example, Merrill Lynch's new CEO recently noted that his firm will ". . . double up in areas that are high-profit and chop unflinchingly where making money is harder." Merrill Lynch executives believe that actions such as these should improve their firm's ability to successfully compete against Lehman Brothers and its other competitors as well.

SOURCES: 2001, Surviving Wall Street's blues, *The Economist*, September 8, 69; S. Brady, J. Brown, C. Cockerill, A. Currie, A. Helk, P. Lee, J. Marshall, J. Morris, & F. Salmon, 2001, A new global bulge bracket, *Euromoney*, July, 55–68; R. Frank & A. Raghaven, 2001, Rebuilding Wall Street, *The Wall Street Journal*, November 7, C1; C. Gasparino, 2001, Bear Stearns and Lehman push their way past big guns, *The Wall Street Journal*, July 6, C1; G. Silverman & C. Pretzlik, 2001, Interview—Lehman Brothers' Richard Fuld, *Financial Times*, August 16, 16–18; E. Thornton, 2001, Lehman Brothers: So who needs to be big? *BusinessWeek Online*, http://www.businessweek.com, July 16; E. Thornton, A. Tergesen, & D. Welch, 2001, Shaking up Merrill, *Business Week*, November 12, 96–102.

As described in the Strategic Focus, Lehman Brothers has taken a number of competitive actions, such as changing its compensation system and entering new markets, since being spun off in 1994. Moreover, its compensation system contributes to the firm's flexibility and the variety of competitive actions it can take. An outcome of the compensation is the expectation that all employees will offer ideas about what the firm can do to improve its performance. This flexibility should serve Lehman well as some of its competitors (for example, Merrill Lynch) attempt to respond with actions similar to Lehman's.

Quality

Quality has many definitions, including well-established ones relating it to the production of goods or services with zero defects[78] and seeing it as a never-ending cycle of continuous improvement.[79] From a strategic perspective, we consider quality to be an outcome of how the firm completes primary and support activities (see Chapter 2). Thus, **quality** exists when the firm's goods or services meet or exceed customers' expectations.

In addition to the more traditional manufacturing and service sectors, quality is also important in business-to-business (B2B) transactions.[80] Customers may be interested in measuring the quality of a firm's products against a broad range of dimensions. Sample quality dimensions for goods and services in which customers commonly express an interest are shown in Table 5.1. Thus, in the eyes of customers, quality is about doing the right things relative to performance measures that are important to them.[81] Quality is possible only when top-level managers support it and when its importance is institutionalized throughout the entire organization.[82] When quality is institutionalized and valued by all, employees and managers alike become vigilant about continuously finding ways to improve quality.[83]

Quality is a universal theme in the global economy and is a necessary but not sufficient condition for competitive success. Another way of saying this is that "Quality used to be a competitive issue out there, but now it's just the basic denominator to being in the market."[84] Without quality, a firm's products lack credibility, meaning that customers don't think of them as viable options. Indeed, customers won't consider buying a product until they believe that it can satisfy at least their base level expectations in terms of quality dimensions that are important to them. For years, quality was an issue for Jaguar automobiles as the carmaker endured frequent

Quality exists when the firm's goods or services meet or exceed customers' expectations.

Table 5.1	Quality Dimensions of Goods and Services

Product Quality Dimensions

1. *Performance*—Operating characteristics
2. *Features*—Important special characteristics
3. *Flexibility*—Meeting operating specifications over some period of time
4. *Durability*—Amount of use before performance deteriorates
5. *Conformance*—Match with preestablished standards
6. *Serviceability*—Ease and speed of repair
7. *Aesthetics*—How a product looks and feels
8. *Perceived quality*—Subjective assessment of characteristics (product image)

Service Quality Dimensions

1. *Timeliness*—Performed in the promised period of time
2. *Courtesy*—Performed cheerfully
3. *Consistency*—Giving all customers similar experiences each time
4. *Convenience*—Accessibility to customers
5. *Completeness*—Fully serviced, as required
6. *Accuracy*—Performed correctly each time

SOURCES: Adapted from J. W. Dean, Jr., & J. R. Evans, 1994, *Total Quality: Management, Organization and Society*, St. Paul, MN: West Publishing Company; H. V. Roberts & B. F. Sergesketter, 1993, *Quality Is Personal*, New York: The Free Press; D. Garvin, 1988, *Managed Quality: The Strategic and Competitive Edge*, New York: The Free Press.

complaints from drivers about poor quality. As a result of recent actions addressing this issue, quality has improved to the point where customers now view the cars as credible products.[85]

Poor quality also increases costs, which damages the firm's profitability. For example, Ford Motor Company recently ranked worst of the top seven global auto companies in quality. According to former Ford CEO Jacques Nasser, quality problems (which led to higher warranty expenses) and related production delays cost the firm more than $1 billion in lost profits in 2000 alone.[86]

Total quality management (TQM) is a "managerial innovation that emphasizes an organization's total commitment to the customer and to continuous improvement of every process through the use of data-driven, problem-solving approaches based on empowerment of employee groups and teams."

To improve quality or to maintain a focus on it, firms often become involved with total quality management. **Total quality management (TQM)** is a "managerial innovation that emphasizes an organization's total commitment to the customer and to continuous improvement of every process through the use of data-driven, problem-solving approaches based on empowerment of employee groups and teams."[87] Through TQM, firms seek to (1) increase customer satisfaction, (2) cut costs, and (3) reduce the amount of time required to introduce innovative products to the marketplace.[88] Ford is relying on TQM to help "root out" its quality flaws[89] while competitor General Motors is ". . . scrambling to narrow the quality gap that its executives say is the main reason consumers shy away from GM."[90]

Quality affects competitive rivalry. The firm studying a competitor whose products suffer from poor quality can predict that the competitor's costs are high and that its sales revenue will likely decline until the quality issues are resolved. In addition, the firm can predict that the competitor likely won't be aggressive in terms of taking competitive actions, given that its quality problems must be corrected in order to gain credibility with customers. However, once corrected, that competitor is likely to take competitive actions emphasizing significant product quality improvements. Hyundai

PART 2 /Strategic Actions: Strategy Formulation

Motor Co.'s experiences illustrate these expectations.

Immediately upon becoming CEO of Hyundai Motor Co. in March 1999, Chung Mong Koo started touring the firm's manufacturing facilities. Appalled at what he saw, he told workers and managers alike that, "The only way we can survive is to raise our quality to Toyota's level."[91] To dramatically improve quality, a quality-control unit was established and significant resources (over $1 billion annually) were allocated to research and development (R&D) in order to build cars that could compete on price and deliver on quality. Essentially, Koo introduced Hyundai to TQM through the decisions he made to improve the firm's performance.

Outcomes from Hyundai's focus on quality improvements are impressive. Survey results indicate that Hyundai's quality has improved 28 percent in the last few years as compared to an average 14 percent improvement in the industry. Another indicator of dramatic quality improvements is *Car & Driver*'s rating of Hyundai behind only Nissan, Honda, and Toyota, but ahead of Dodge, Chevrolet, Ford, and Buick in the magazine's recent tests of eight mid-size sedans. Quality was an important criterion used in the tests.[92]

While concentrating on quality improvements, Hyundai didn't launch aggressive competitive actions, as competitors could predict would likely be the case. However, as could also be predicted by firms studying Hyundai as a competitor, improvements to the quality of Hyundai's products has helped the firm to become a more aggressive competitor. Signaling a strong belief in its products' quality, Hyundai now offers a 10-year drive-train warranty in the United States, which the firm has selected as a key market. As a result of improved quality and the innovative outcomes from its R&D investments, Hyundai also introduced the Santa Fe in 2000. A well-conceived sport-utility vehicle (SUV), the Santa Fe was designed and built to outperform Toyota's RAV4 and Honda's CR-V. The Santa Fe's introduction indicates that Hyundai is willing to aggressively attack its competitors in the SUV market with what has turned out to be an innovatively designed and quality-built product.[93]

Likelihood of Response

The success of a firm's competitive action is affected both by the likelihood that a competitor will respond to it as well as by the type (strategic or tactical) and effectiveness of that response. As noted earlier, a competitive response is a strategic or tactical action the firm takes to counter the effects of a competitor's competitive action. FedEx's decision to offer home package delivery by ground is a strategic response to at least one strategic action (establishing a logistics business) taken by UPS (see the Opening Case). In general, a firm is likely to respond to a competitor's action when the consequences of that action are better use of the competitor's competitive advantages or improvement in its market position, or when the action damages the firm's ability to use its advantages or when its market position becomes less defensible.[94]

In addition to market commonality and resource similarity and awareness, motivation, and ability, firms study three other factors—type of competitive action, reputation, and market dependence—to predict how a competitor is likely to respond to competitive actions.

Type of Competitive Action

Competitive responses to strategic actions differ from responses to tactical actions. These differences allow the firm to predict a competitor's likely response to a competitive action that has been launched against it. Of course, a general prediction is that strategic actions receive strategic responses while tactical responses are taken to counter the effects of tactical actions.

In general, strategic actions elicit fewer total competitive responses.[95] The reason is that as with strategic actions, strategic responses, such as market-based moves, involve a significant commitment of resources and are difficult to implement and reverse. Moreover, the time needed for a strategic action to be implemented and its effectiveness assessed delays the competitor's response to that action.[96] The almost 17-year delay for UPS to respond to FedEx's strategic action of establishing the overnight delivery market shows how long it can take for a competitor to launch a response (see the Opening Case). In contrast, a competitor likely will respond quickly to a tactical action, such as when an airline company almost immediately matches a competitor's tactical action of reducing prices in certain markets. And, either strategic actions or tactical actions that target a large number of a rival's customers are likely to be targeted with strong responses.[97]

Actor's Reputation

In the context of competitive rivalry, an actor is the firm taking an action or response while *reputation* is ". . . the positive or negative attribute ascribed by one rival to another based on past competitive behavior."[98] Thus, to predict the likelihood of a competitor's response to a current or planned action, the firm studies the responses that the competitor has taken previously when attacked—past behavior is assumed to be a reasonable predictor of future behavior.

Competitors are more likely to respond to either strategic or tactical actions that are taken by a market leader.[99] For example, Home Depot is the world's largest home improvement retailer and the second largest U.S. retailer (behind Wal-Mart). Known as an innovator in its core home improvement market as well as for having an ability to develop successful new store formats such as its EXPO Design Centers and Villager's Hardware Stores, Home Depot can predict that its competitors carefully study its actions, especially the strategic ones, and that they are likely to respond to them. Lowe's Companies, the second largest U.S. home improvement retailer and Home Depot's major competitor, is aware of Home Depot's actions. Lowe's also has both the motivation and ability to respond to actions by Home Depot. For example, partly in response to Home Depot's consistent focus on updating the retail concept of its core home improvement stores, Lowe's continues to transform ". . . its store base from a chain of small stores into a chain of destination of home improvement warehouses,"[100] increasing the similarity of its store design with Home Depot's as a result of doing so.

Other evidence suggests that commonly successful actions, especially strategic actions, will be quickly imitated, almost regardless of the actor's reputation. For example, although a second mover, IBM committed significant resources to enter the PC market. When IBM was immediately successful in this endeavor, competitors such as Dell, Compaq, and Gateway responded with strategic actions to enter the market. IBM's reputation as well as its successful strategic action strongly influenced entry by these competitors. Thus, in terms of competitive rivalry, IBM could predict that responses would follow its entry to the PC market if that entry proved successful. In addition, IBM could predict that those competitors would try to create value in slightly different ways, such as Dell's legendary decision to sell directly to consumers rather than to use storefronts as a distribution channel.

In contrast to a firm with a strong reputation, such as IBM, competitors are less likely to take responses against companies with reputations for competitive behavior that is risky, complex, and unpredictable. The firm with a reputation as a price predator (an actor that frequently reduces prices to gain or maintain market share) generates few responses to its pricing tactical actions. The reason is that price predators, which typically increase prices once their market share objective is reached, lack credibility with their competitors.[101] The opposite of a price predator in terms of reputation, Wal-Mart is widely recognized for its pricing integrity,[102] giving the firm a great deal of credibility when it launches a tactical action or response around the prices of its goods.

Dependence on the Market

Market dependence denotes the extent to which a firm's revenues or profits are derived from a particular market.[103] In general, firms can predict that competitors with high market dependence are likely to respond strongly to attacks threatening their market position.[104] Interestingly, the threatened firm in these instances tends not to respond quickly, suggesting the importance of an effective response to an attack on the firm's position in a critical market.

A firm such as Wm. Wrigley Company would be expected to respond aggressively, but not necessarily quickly to an attack. With well-known brands such as Spearmint, Doublemint, Juicy Fruit, Big Red, Extra, and Hubba Bubba bubble gum, Wrigley is the world's largest producer of chewing gum, accounting for roughly 50 percent of total chewing gum sales volume worldwide. Through its Amurol Confections subsidiary (which produces several products such as liquid gel candy, suckers, and hard roll candies), Wrigley has a minor amount of diversification. However, chewing gum accounts for more than 90 percent of the firm's total revenue as well as earnings.[105] Wrigley's dominant market position provides the flexibility needed to respond aggressively but carefully to actions that might be taken by a competitor, such as Adams. But, if Adams were to attack Wrigley's sugarless Extra gum through actions related to Adams's Trident, for example, it should understand that Wrigley's dependence on the chewing gum market will induce it to respond aggressively to protect its position in the sugarless gum market.

Competitive Dynamics

Whereas competitive rivalry concerns the ongoing actions and responses between a firm and its competitors for an advantageous market position, competitive dynamics concerns the ongoing actions and responses taking place among *all* firms competing within a market for advantageous positions.

To explain competitive rivalry, we described (1) factors that determine the degree to which firms are competitors (market commonality and resource similarity), (2) the drivers of competitive behavior for individual firms (awareness, motivation, and ability) and (3) factors affecting the likelihood a competitor will act or attack (first mover incentives, organizational size, and quality) and respond (type of competitive action, reputation, and market dependence). Building and sustaining competitive advantages are at the core of competitive rivalry, in that advantages are the link to an advantageous market position.

To explain competitive dynamics, we discuss the effects of varying rates of competitive speed in different markets (called slow-cycle, fast-cycle, and standard-cycle markets, defined below) on the behavior (actions and responses) of all competitors within a given market. Competitive behaviors as well as the reasons or logic for taking them are similar within each market type, but differ across market type.[106] Thus, competitive dynamics differs in slow-cycle, fast-cycle, and standard-cycle markets. The sustainability of the firm's competitive advantages is an important difference among the three market types.

As noted in Chapter 1, firms want to sustain their advantages for as long as possible, although no advantage is permanently sustainable. The degree of sustainability is affected by how quickly competitive advantages can be imitated and how costly it is to do so.

Slow-Cycle Markets

Slow-cycle markets are markets in which the firm's competitive advantages are shielded from imitation for what are commonly long periods of time and where imitation is costly.

Slow-cycle markets are markets in which the firm's competitive advantages are shielded from imitation for what are commonly long periods of time and where imitation is costly.[107] Competitive advantages are sustainable in slow-cycle markets.

Building a one-of-a-kind competitive advantage that is proprietary leads to competitive success in a slow-cycle market. This type of advantage is difficult for competitors to understand. As discussed in Chapter 3, a difficult-to-understand and costly-to-imitate advantage results from unique historical conditions, causal ambiguity, and/or social complexity. Copyrights, geography, patents, and ownership of an information resource are examples of what leads to one-of-a-kind advantages.[108] Once a proprietary advantage is developed, the firm's competitive behavior in a slow-cycle market is oriented to protecting, maintaining, and extending that advantage. Thus, the competitive dynamics in slow-cycle markets involve all firms concentrating on competitive actions and responses that enable them to protect, maintain, and extend their proprietary competitive advantage.

Walt Disney Co. continues to extend its proprietary characters, such as Mickey Mouse, Minnie Mouse, and Goofy. These characters have a unique historical development as a result of Walt and Roy Disney's creativity and vision for entertaining people. Products based on the characters seen in Disney's animated films are sold through Disney's theme park shops as well as self-standing, retail outlets called Disney Stores. The list of character-based products is extensive, including everything from the characters to clothing with the characters' images. Because patents shield it, the proprietary nature of Disney's advantage in terms of animated characters protects the firm from imitation by competitors.

Consistent with another attribute of competition in a slow-cycle market, Disney remains committed to protecting its exclusive rights to its characters and their use as shown by the fact that ". . . the company once sued a day-care center, forcing it to remove the likeness of Mickey Mouse from a wall of the facility."[109] As with all firms competing in slow-cycle markets, Disney's competitive actions (such as building theme parks in France and Japan and other potential locations such as China) and responses (such as lawsuits to protect its right to fully control use of its animated characters) maintain and extend its proprietary competitive advantage while protecting it. Disney has been able to establish through actions and defend through responses an advantageous market position as a result of its competitive behavior.

Patent laws and regulatory requirements such as those in the United States requiring FDA (Federal Drug Administration) approval to launch new products shield pharmaceutical companies' positions. Competitors in this market try to extend patents on their drugs to maintain advantageous positions that they (patents) provide. However, once a patent expires, the firm is no longer shielded from competition, a situation that has financial implications. For example, in describing Merck & Co.'s expected 2002 performance, some analysts observed that in that year, "Merck was expected to get rocked by the loss of revenue as the patent protection for some leading drugs—such as gastroesophageal reflux soother Prilosec, cholesterol drug Mevacor, and hypertension medication Prinivil—expires."[110] Based largely on these patent expirations, Merck announced in late 2001 that its earnings would be lower in 2002 than originally expected. Following the firm's announcement, some analysts lowered their recommendation on Merck stock from "buy" to "hold." In contrast, Pfizer Inc.'s position seemed to be shielded for a period of time according to analysts: "Unlike several of its competitors (including Merck), Pfizer faces little risk to product sales from impending patent expirations and thus for the next 3 to 4 years remains in a growth trajectory."[111]

Research and development (R&D) is the advantage that allows pharmaceutical companies to develop drugs that have the possibility of creating shielded market positions. Because of its importance as a competitive advantage, these firms invest heavily in R&D in hopes that the results of doing so will create additional positions that are shielded from competition. For example, Pfizer intended to increase its 2003 R&D expenditure by roughly 10 percent (from $4.8 billion to $5.3 billion) over 2002's amount. Competitor Merck also intended to increase its R&D expenditure during this time by as much as 16 percent. As with Disney, these actions are being taken to sustain for as long as possible (through patents) and extend in as many ways as possible (through R&D) the firms' proprietary advantages and the shielded market positions resulting from them.

The competitive dynamics generated by firms competing in slow-cycle markets are shown in Figure 5.4. In slow-cycle markets, firms launch a product (e.g., a new drug) that has been developed through a proprietary advantage (e.g., R&D) and then exploit it for as long as possible while the product is shielded from competition. Eventually, competitors respond to the action with a counterattack. In markets for drugs, this counterattack commonly occurs as patents expire, creating the need for another product launch by the firm seeking a shielded market position.

Fast-Cycle Markets

Fast-cycle markets are markets in which the firm's competitive advantages aren't shielded from imitation and where imitation happens quickly and somewhat inexpensively.

Fast-cycle markets are markets in which the firm's competitive advantages aren't shielded from imitation and where imitation happens quickly and somewhat inexpensively. Competitive advantages aren't sustainable in fast-cycle markets.

Reverse engineering and the rate of technology diffusion in fast-cycle markets facilitate rapid imitation. A competitor uses reverse engineering to quickly gain the knowledge required to imitate or improve the firm's products, usually in only a few months. Technology is diffused rapidly in fast-cycle markets, making it available to competitors in a short period of time. The technology often used by fast-cycle competitors isn't proprietary, nor is it protected by patents as is the technology used by

Figure 5.4 Gradual Erosion of a Sustained Competitive Advantage

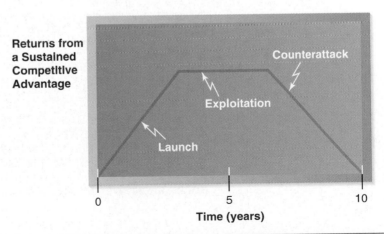

SOURCE: Adapted from I. C. MacMillan, 1988, Controlling competitive dynamics by taking strategic initiative, *Academy of Management Executive*, II(2): 111–118.

firms competing in slow-cycle markets. For example, only a few hundred parts, which are readily available on the open market, are required to build a PC. Patents protect only a few of these parts such as microprocessor chips.[112]

Fast-cycle markets are more volatile than slow-cycle and standard-cycle markets. Indeed, the pace of competition in fast-cycle markets is almost frenzied, as companies rely on ideas and the innovations resulting from them as the engines of their growth. Because prices fall quickly in these markets, companies need to profit quickly from their product innovations. For example, rapid declines in the prices of microprocessor chips produced by Intel and Advanced Micro Devices among others, make it possible for personal computer manufacturers to continuously reduce their prices to end users. Imitation of many fast-cycle products is relatively easy, as demonstrated by Dell and Gateway, along with a host of local PC vendors. All of these firms have partly or largely imitated IBM's initial PC design to create their products. Continuous declines in the costs of parts as well as the fact that the information and knowledge required to assemble a PC isn't especially complicated and is readily available, make it possible for additional competitors to enter this market without significant difficulty.[113]

The fast-cycle market characteristics described above make it virtually impossible for companies in this type of market to develop sustainable competitive advantages. Recognizing this, firms avoid "loyalty" to any of their products, preferring to cannibalize their own before competitors learn how to do so through successful imitation. This emphasis creates competitive dynamics that differ substantially from what is witnessed in slow-cycle markets. Instead of concentrating on protecting, maintaining, and extending competitive advantages as is the case for firms in slow-cycle markets, companies competing in fast-cycle markets focus on learning how to rapidly and continuously develop new competitive advantages that are superior to those they replace. In fast-cycle markets, firms don't concentrate on trying to protect a given competitive advantage because they understand that the advantage won't exist long enough to extend it.

The competitive behavior of firms competing in fast-cycle markets is shown in Figure 5.5. As suggested by the figure, competitive dynamics in this market type finds firms taking actions and responses in the course of competitive rivalry that are oriented to rapid and continuous product introductions and the use of a stream of ever-changing competitive advantages. The firm launches a product as a competitive

Figure 5.5 Obtaining Temporary Advantages to Create Sustained Advantage

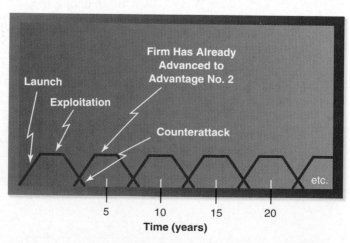

SOURCE: Adapted from I. C. MacMillan, 1988, Controlling competitive dynamics by taking strategic initiative, *Academy of Management Executive*, II(2): 111–118.

PART 2 /Strategic Actions: Strategy Formulation

action and then exploits the advantage associated with it for as long as possible. However, the firm also tries to move to another temporary competitive before competitors can respond to the first one (see Figure 5.5). Thus, competitive dynamics in fast-cycle markets, in which all firms seek to achieve new competitive advantages before competitors learn how to effectively respond to current ones, often result in rapid product upgrades as well as quick product innovations.[114]

As our discussion suggests, innovation has a dominant effect on competitive dynamics in fast-cycle markets. For individual firms, this means that innovation is a key source of competitive advantage. Through innovation, the firm can cannibalize its own products before competitors' successfully imitate them.

In the fast-cycle semiconductor market, Texas Instruments (TI) and Micron Technology Inc (Micron) both rely on innovation as a competitive advantage. There is evidence to suggest that the two companies are successful in this effort.

Recently *Technology Review Magazine* ranked ". . . Micron number one in the semiconductor market based on quality and quantity of patents and other key indicators including scientific papers cited and the ability to convert cutting edge technology into intellectual property."[115] TI publishes *Technology Innovations* (with subscriptions available through the firm's website) to describe its continuous stream of innovations.[116] Using innovation as the foundation for continuous attacks (launches) and counterattacks, TI increasingly is concentrating on digital signal processors and analog integrated circuits, while Micron is a leading supplier of dynamic random access memory chips, the most widely used semiconductor memory component in PCs.[117] Thus, although they aren't competitors in terms of these particular products, innovation allows each firm to continuously develop temporary competitive advantages that become the foundation for the development of still additional ones.

Standard-Cycle Markets

Standard-cycle markets are markets in which the firm's competitive advantages are moderately shielded from imitation and where imitation is moderately costly. Competitive advantages are partially sustainable in standard-cycle markets, but only when the firm is able to continuously upgrade the quality of its competitive advantages. The competitive actions and responses that form a standard-cycle market's competitive dynamics find firms seeking large market shares, trying to gain customer loyalty through brand names, and carefully controlling their operations to consistently provide the same usage experience for customers without surprises.[118]

Because of large volumes and the size of mass markets, the competition for market share is intense in standard-cycle markets. Procter & Gamble and Unilever compete in standard-cycle markets. A competitor analysis reveals that P&G and Unilever are direct competitors, in that they share multiple markets as they engage each other in competition in over 140 countries and they have similar types and amounts of resources and follow similar strategies. One of the product lines in which these two firms aggressively compete against each other for market share is laundry detergents. The market for these products is large, with an annual sales volume of over $6 billion in the United States alone. The sheer size of this market highlights the importance of market share, as a mere percentage point gain in share translates into a $60 million increase in revenues. As analysts have noted, in a standard-cycle market, "It's a death struggle to incrementally gain share." For P&G and Unilever, this means that the firms must ". . . slog it out for every fraction of every share in every category in every market where they compete."[119]

Standard-cycle companies serve many customers in competitive markets. Because the capabilities on which their competitive advantages are based are less specialized, imitation is faster and less costly for standard-cycle firms than for those competing in

Standard-cycle markets are markets in which the firm's competitive advantages are moderately shielded from imitation and where imitation is moderately costly.

slow-cycle markets. However, imitation is less quick and more expensive in these markets than in fast-cycle markets. Thus, competitive dynamics in standard-cycle markets rests midway between the characteristics of dynamics in slow-cycle and fast-cycle markets. The quickness of imitation is reduced and becomes more expensive for standard-cycle competitors when a firm is able to develop economies of scale by combining coordinated and integrated design and manufacturing processes with a large sales volume for its products.

Without scale economies, standard-cycle firms compete at a disadvantage. Recently, for example, some of Britain's well-known retailers such as Marks & Spencer reported continuing declines in sales volume. Entry to Britain by foreign competitors, including Sweden's Hennes & Mauritz, Spain's Zara, Japan's Uniqlo, and United States's Gap, is contributing to this decline. According to analysts, these competitors rely on their global fashion sense and economies of scale to quickly imitate their British competitors. The global presence and resulting sales volumes of these global competitors increase the likelihood that they will develop and benefit from economies of scale. In contrast, Britain's "home-grown retailers" lack the presence and volume required to develop economies of scale and to make imitation of their competitive advantage costly.[120]

Innovation can also drive competitive actions and responses in standard-cycle markets, especially when rivalry is intense. Thus, innovation has a substantial influence on competitive dynamics as it affects the actions and responses of all companies competing within a slow-cycle, fast-cycle, or standard-cycle market. We have emphasized the importance of innovation to the firm's strategic competitiveness in earlier chapters. Our discussion of innovation in terms of competitive dynamics extends the earlier discussions by showing its importance in all types of markets in which firms compete.

Innovation is vital to the competitive behavior of consumer goods competitor General Mills, especially as it competes against manufacturers of generic cereals. The world's largest cereal maker, this firm relies on its brand name as a source of advantage to successfully use the differentiation business-level strategy while competing in its standard-cycle market. Generic cereals, however, are a serious threat to General Mills' advantage as well as the strategy that is based on it. As an analyst noted, "Consumers just will not pay a 50–80 percent premium for General Mills Cheerios, for instance, now that the quality of store brands has become nearly indistinguishable from the original." General Mills is responding to attacks by generic manufacturers with product innovations, including Wheaties Energy Crunch, Milk 'n Cereal Bars, and Chex Morning Mix. To date, innovations have enabled General Mills to retain its sales volume.[121]

General Mills has built on its brand recognition by applying it to new products, and has also countered generic imitators by creating new varieties of its traditional cereals.

- Competitors are firms competing in the same market, offering similar products and targeting similar customers. Competitive rivalry is the ongoing set of competitive actions and competitive responses occurring between competitors as they compete against each other for an advantageous market position. The outcomes of competitive rivalry influence the firm's ability to sustain its competitive advantages as well as the level (average, below-average, or above-average) of its financial returns.

- For the individual firm, the set of competitive actions and responses it takes while engaged in competitive rivalry is called competitive behavior. Competitive dynamics is the set of actions taken by all firms that are competitors within a particular market.

- Firms study competitive rivalry in order to be able to predict the competitive actions and responses that each of its competitors likely will take. Competitive actions are either strategic or tactical in nature. The firm takes competitive actions to defend or build its competitive advantages or improve its market position. Competitive responses are taken to counter the effects of a competitor's competitive action. A strategic action or a strategic response requires a significant commitment of organizational resources, is difficult to successfully implement, and hard to reverse. In contrast, a tactical action or a tactical response requires fewer organizational resources and is easier to implement and reverse. For an airline company, for example, entering major new markets is an example of a strategic action or a strategic response while changing its prices in a particular market is an example of a tactical action or a tactical response.

- A competitor analysis is the first step the firm takes to be able to predict its competitors' actions and responses. In Chapter 2, we discussed what firms do to *understand* competitors. This discussion is extended further in this chapter as we described what the firm does to *predict* competitors' market-based actions. Thus, understanding precedes prediction. Market commonality (the number of markets with which competitors are jointly involved and their importance to each) and resource similarity (how comparable competitors' resources are in terms of type and amount) are studied to complete a competitor analysis. In general, the greater are market commonality and resource similarity, the more firms acknowledge that they are direct competitors.

- Market commonality and resource similarity shape the firm's awareness (the degree to which it and its competitor understand their mutual interdependence), motivation (the firm's incentive to attack or respond), and ability (the quality of the resources available to the firm to attack and respond). Having knowledge of a competitor in terms of these characteristics increases the quality of the firm's predictions about a competitor's actions and responses.

- In addition to market commonality and resource similarity and awareness, motivation and ability, three more specific factors affect the likelihood a competitor will take competitive actions. The first of these concerns first mover incentives. First movers, those taking an initial competitive action, often earn above-average returns until competitors can successfully respond to their action and gain loyal customers. Not all firms can be first movers in that they may lack the awareness, motivation, or ability required to engage in this type of competitive behavior. Moreover, some firms prefer to be a second mover (the firm responding to the first mover's action). One reason for this is that second movers, especially those acting quickly, can successfully compete against the first mover. By studying the first mover's product, customers' reactions to it and the responses of other competitors to the first mover, the second mover can avoid the early entrant's mistakes and find ways to improve upon the value created for customers by the first mover's good or service. Late movers though (those that respond a long time after the original action was taken), commonly are lower performers and much less competitive.

    Organizational size, the second factor, tends to reduce the number of different types of competitive actions that large firms launch while it results in smaller competitors' using a wide variety of actions. Ideally, the firm would like to initiate a large number of diverse actions when engaged in competitive rivalry.

    The third factor, quality, dampens firms' abilities to take competitive actions, in that product quality is a base denominator to successful competition in the global economy.

- The type of action (strategic or tactical) the firm took, the competitor's reputation for the nature of its competitor behavior, and its dependence on the market in which the action was taken are studied to predict a competitor's response to the firm's action. In general, the number of tactical responses taken exceeds the number of strategic responses. Competitors respond more frequently to the actions taken by the firm with a reputation for predictable and understandable competitive behavior, especially if that firm is a market leader. In general, the firm can predict that when its competitor is highly dependent for its revenue and profitability in the market in which the firm took a competitive action, that competitor is likely to launch a strong response. However, firms that are more diversified across markets are less likely to respond to a particular action that affects only one of the markets in which they compete.

- Competitive dynamics concerns the ongoing competitive behavior occurring among all firms competing in a market for advantageous positions. Market characteristics affect the set of actions and responses firms take while competing in a given market as well as the sustainability of firms' competitive advantages. In slow-cycle markets, where competitive advantages can be maintained, competitive dynamics finds firms taking actions and responses that are intended to protect, maintain, and extend their proprietary advantages. In fast-cycle markets, competition is almost frenzied as firms concentrate on developing a series of temporary competitive advantages. This emphasis is necessary because firms' advantages in fast-cycle markets aren't proprietary and as such, are subject to rapid and relatively inexpensive imitation. Standard-cycle markets are between slow-cycle and fast-cycle markets, in that firms are moderately shielded from competition in these markets as they use competitive advantages that are moderately sustainable. Competitors in standard-cycle markets serve mass markets and try to develop economies of scale to enhance their profitability. Innovation is vital to competitive success in each of the three types of markets. Firms should recognize that the set of competitive actions and responses taken by all firms differs by type of market.

Review Questions

1. Who are competitors? How are competitive rivalry, competitive behavior, and competitive dynamics defined in the chapter?

2. What is market commonality? What is resource similarity? What does it mean to say that these concepts are the building blocks for a competitor analysis?

3. How do awareness, motivation, and ability affect the firm's competitive behavior?

4. What factors affect the likelihood a firm will take a competitive action?

5. What factors affect the likelihood a firm will initiate a competitive response to the action taken by a competitor?

6. How is competitive dynamics in slow-cycle markets described in the chapter? In fast-cycle markets? In standard-cycle markets?

Competitive Rivalry

Part One. Define first mover and second mover, and provide examples of firms for each category.

First mover:

Second mover:

Part Two. In the following table, list the advantages and disadvantages of being the first mover and of being the second mover.

First Mover		Second Mover	
Advantages	Disadvantages	Advantages	Disadvantages

Part Three. Based on the above information, what are the most important issues that you feel first and second movers must consider before initiating a competitive move?

1. M.-J. Chen, 1996, Competitor analysis and interfirm rivalry: Toward a theoretical integration, *Academy of Management Review*, 21: 100–134.

2. S. Jayachandran, J. Gimeno, & P. R. Varadarajan, 1999, Theory of multimarket competition: A synthesis and implications for marketing strategy, *Journal of Marketing*, 63(3): 49–66.

3. R. E. Caves, 1984, Economic analysis and the quest for competitive advantage. In *Papers and Proceedings of the 96th Annual Meeting of the American Economic Association*, 127–132.

4. G. Young, K. G. Smith, C. M. Grimm, & D. Simon, 2000, Multimarket contact and resource dissimilarity: A competitive dynamics perspective, *Journal of Management*, 26: 1217–1236; C. M. Grimm & K. G. Smith, 1997, *Strategy as Action: Industry Rivalry and Coordination*, Cincinnati: South-Western College Publishing, 53–74.

5. H. A. Haveman & L. Nonnemaker, 2000, Competition in multiple geographic markets: The impact on growth and market entry, *Administrative Science Quarterly*, 45: 232–267.

6. G. Young, K. G. Smith, & C. M. Grimm, 1996, "Austrian" and industrial organization perspectives on firm-level competitive activity and performance, *Organization Science*, 73: 243–254.

7. K. G. Smith, W. J. Ferrier, & H. Ndofor, 2001, Competitive dynamics research: Critique and future directions, in M. A. Hitt, R. E. Freeman, & J. S. Harrison (eds.), *Handbook of Strategic Management*, Oxford, U.K.: Blackwell Publishers, 326.

8. G. S. Day & D. J. Reibstein, 1997, The dynamic challenges for theory and practice, in G. S. Day & D. J. Reibstein (eds.), *Wharton on Competitive Strategy*, New York: John Wiley & Sons, 2.

9. D. L. Deeds, D. DeCarolis, & J. Coombs, 2000, Dynamic capabilities and new product development in high technology adventures: An empirical analysis of new biotechnology firms, *Journal of Business Venturing*, 15: 211–299.

10. G. Khermouch, S. Holmes, & M. Iklwan, 2001, The best global brands, *Business Week*, August 6, 50–57.

11. C. Lederer & S. Hill, 2001, See your brands through your customers' eyes, *Harvard Business Review*, 79(6): 125–133.

12. S. Crainer, 2001, And the new economy winner is . . . . Europe, *Strategy & Business*, Second Quarter, 40–47.

13. J. E. Garten, 2001, The wrong time for companies to beat a global retreat, *Business Week*, December 17, 22.

14. Young, Smith, Grimm, & Simon, Multimarket contact and resource dissimilarity, 1230–1233.

15. D. R. Gnyawali & R. Madhavan, 2001, Cooperative networks and competitive dynamics: A structural embeddedness perspective, *Academy of Management Review*, 26: 431–445.

16. Young, Smith, Grimm, & Simon, Multimarket contact and resource dissimilarity, 1217; M. E. Porter, 1991, Towards a dynamic theory of strategy, *Strategic Management Journal*, 12: 95–117.

17. S. Godin, 2002, Survival is not enough, *Fast Company*, January, 90–94.

18. S. J. Marsh, 1998, Creating barriers for foreign competitors: A study of the impact of anti-dumping actions on the performance of U.S. firms, *Strategic Management Journal*, 19: 25–37; K. G. Smith, C. M. Grimm, G. Young, & S. Wally, 1997, Strategic groups and rivalrous firm behavior: Toward a reconciliation, *Strategic Management Journal*, 18: 149–157.

19. W. J. Ferrier, 2001, Navigating the competitive landscape: The drivers and consequences of competitive aggressiveness, *Academy of Management Journal*, 44: 858–877; M. E. Porter, 1980, *Competitive Strategy*, New York: Free Press.

20. Smith, Ferrier, & Ndofor, Competitive dynamics research, 319.

21. K. Ramaswamy, 2001, Organizational ownership, competitive intensity, and firm performance: An empirical study of the Indian manufacturing sector, *Strategic Management Journal*, 22: 989–998.

22. K. Cool, L. H. Roller, & B. Leleux, 1999, The relative impact of actual and potential rivalry on firm profitability in the pharmaceutical industry, *Strategic Management Journal*, 20: 1–14.

23. I. Sager, F. Keenan, C. Edwards, & A. Park, 2001, The mother of all price wars, *Business Week*, July 30, 32–35.

24. 2001, In the family's way, *The Economist*, December 15, 56.

25. Sager, Keenan, Edwards, & Park, The mother of all price wars, 33.

26. M. Williams, 2001, David Packard supports Hewlett family in opposing H-P's Compaq acquisition, *The Wall Street Journal Interactive*, http://www.interactive.wsj.com/articles, November 7; 2001, Hewlett deal launches family, board spats, *Reuters*, http://activequote100.fidelity.com, December 13.

27. P. Burrows, 2001, Carly's last stand? *Business Week*, December 24, 63–70.

28. A. Park, 2001, Can Compaq survive as a solo act? *Business Week*, December 24, 71.

29. C. Harrison, 2001, Compaq should discontinue its PC line, analysts say, *Dallas Morning News*, December 16, D1, D16.

30. W. P. Putsis, Jr., 1999, Empirical analysis of competitive interaction in food product categories, *Agribusiness*, 15(3): 295–311.

31. 2001, Dell Computer, *Standard & Poor's Stock Report*, http://www.standard&poor.com, December 8.

32. Chen, Competitor analysis, 108.

33. Ibid., 109.

34. E. Abrahamson & C. J. Fombrun, 1994, Macrocultures: Determinants and consequences. *Academy of Management Review*, 19: 728–755.

35. C. Salter, 2002, On the road again, *Fast Company*, January, 50–58.

36. Young, Smith, Grimm, & Simon, Multimarket contact, 1219.

37. Chen, Competitor analysis, 106.

38. J. Gimeno & C. Y. Woo, 1999, Multimarket contact, economies of scope, and firm performance. *Academy of Management Journal*, 42: 239–259.

39. K. MacArthur, 2001, McDonald's flips business strategy, *Advertising Age*, April 2, 1 & 36.

40. 2001, Prudential Financial Inc., *Standard & Poor's Stock Report*, http://www.standard&poor.com, December 27.

41. Young, Smith, Grimm, & Simon, Multimarket contact and resource dissimilarity, 1230.

42. J. Gimeno, 1999, Reciprocal threats in multimarket rivalry: Staking out 'spheres of influence' in the U.S. airline industry, *Strategic Management Journal*, 20: 101–128; N. Fernanez & P. L. Marin, 1998, Market power and multimarket contact: Some evidence from the Spanish hotel industry, *Journal of Industrial Economics*, 46: 301–315.

43. H. J. Korn & J. A. C. Baum, 1999, Chance, imitative, and strategic antecedents to multimarket contact, *Academy of Management Journal*, 42: 171–193.

44. Jayachandran, Gimeno, & Varadarajan, Theory of multimarket competition, 59; Chen, Competitor analysis, 107.

45. J. Gimeno & C. Y. Woo, 1996, Hypercompetition in a multimarket environment: The role of strategic similarity and multimarket contact on competitive de-escalation, *Organization Science*, 7: 322–341.

46. R. Berner, 2001, CVS: Will its growth elixir work? *Business Week*, July 9, 50–53.

47. Chen, Competitor analysis, 107–108.

48. Ibid., 110.

49. Ibid., 110; W. Ocasio, 1997, Towards an attention-based view of the firm, *Strategic Management Journal*, 18(Summer Special Issue): 187–206; Smith, Ferrier, & Ndofor, Competitive dynamics research, 320.

50. G. P. Hodgkinson & G. Johnson, 1994, Exploring the mental models of competitive strategists: The case for a processual approach, *Journal of Management Studies*, 31: 525–551; J. F. Porac & H. Thomas, 1994, Cognitive categorization and subjective rivalry among retailers in a small city, *Journal of Applied Psychology*, 79: 54–66.

51. 2001, Wal around the world, *The Economist*, December 8, 55–56.
52. Smith, Ferrier, & Ndofor, Competitive dynamics research, 320.
53. Chen, Competitor analysis, 113.
54. Grimm & Smith, *Strategy as Action*, 125.
55. 2002, Blue light blues, *The Economist*, January 29, 54; D. B. Yoffie & M. Kwak, 2001, Mastering strategic movement at Palm, *MIT Sloan Management Review*, 43(1): 55–63.
56. K. G. Smith, W. J. Ferrier & C. M. Grimm, 2001, King of the hill: Dethroning the industry leader, *Academy of Management Executive*, 15(2): 59–70.
57. G. S. Day, 1997, Assessing competitive arenas: Who are your competitors? In G. S. Day & D. J. Reibstein (eds.), *Wharton on Competitive Strategy*, New York: John Wiley & Sons, 25–26.
58. M. Ihlwan, L. Armstrong, & K. Kerwin, 2001, Hyundai gets hot, *Business Week*, December 17, 84–86.
59. J. Schumpeter, 1934, *The Theory of Economic Development*, Cambridge, MA.: Harvard University Press.
60. J. L. C. Cheng & I. F. Kesner, 1997, Organizational slack and response to environmental shifts: The impact of resource allocation patterns, *Journal of Management*, 23: 1–18.
61. F. Wang, 2000, Too appealing to overlook, *America's Network*, December, 10–12.
62. G. Hamel, 2000, *Leading the Revolution*, Boston: Harvard Business School Press, 103.
63. K. Belson, R. Hof, & B. Elgin, 2001, How Yahoo! Japan beat eBay at its own game, *Business Week*, June 4, 58.
64. Smith, Ferrier, & Ndofor, Competitive dynamics research, 331.
65. L. J. Bourgeois, 1981, On the measurement of organizational slack, *Academy of Management Review*, 6: 29–39.
66. M. B. Lieberman & D. B. Montgomery, 1988, First-mover advantages, *Strategic Management Journal*, 9: 41–58.
67. 2001, Older, wiser, webbier, *The Economist*, June 30, 10.
68. M. Shank, 2002, Executive strategy report, IBM business strategy consulting, http://www.ibm.com, March 14; W. Boulding & M. Christen, 2001, First-mover disadvantage, *Harvard Business Review*, 79(9): 20–21.
69. K. G. Smith, C. M. Grimm, & M. J. Gannon, 1992, *Dynamics of Competitive Strategy*, Newberry Park, CA.: Sage Publications.
70. H. R. Greve, 1998, Managerial cognition and the mimetic adoption of market positions: What you see is what you do, *Strategic Management Journal*, 19: 967–988.
71. Smith, Ferrier, & Ndofor, Competitive dynamics research, 327.
72. M.-J. Chen & D. C. Hambrick, 1995, Speed, stealth and selective attack: How small firms differ from large firms in competitive behavior, *Academy of Management Journal*, 38: 453–482.
73. D. Miller & M.-J. Chen, 1996, The simplicity of competitive repertoires: An empirical analysis, *Strategic Management Journal*, 17: 419–440.
74. Young, Smith, & Grimm, "Austrian" and industrial organization perspectives.
75. B. A. Melcher, 1993, How Goliaths can act like Davids, *Business Week*, Special Issue, 193.
76. 2001, Wal around the world, 55.
77. Ibid., 55.
78. P. B. Crosby, 1980, *Quality Is Free*, New York: Penguin.
79. W. E. Deming, 1986, *Out of the Crisis*, Cambridge, MA.: MIT Press.
80. T. Laseter, B. Long, & C. Capers, 2001, B2B benchmark: The state of electronic exchanges, *Strategy & Business*, Fourth Quarter, 32–42.
81. R. S. Kaplan & D. P. Norton, 2001, *The Strategy-Focused Organization*, Boston: Harvard Business School Press.
82. R. Cullen, S. Nicholls, & A. Halligan, 2001, Measurement to demonstrate success, *British Journal of Clinical Governance*, 6(4): 273–278.
83. K. E. Weick & K. M. Sutcliffe, 2001, *Managing the Unexpected*, San Francisco: Jossey-Bass, 81–82.
84. J. Aley, 1994, Manufacturers grade themselves, *Fortune*, March 21, 26.
85. J. Green & D. Welch, 2001, Jaguar may find it's a jungle out there, *Business Week*, March 26, 62.
86. J. Muller, 2001, Ford: Why it's worse than you think, *Business Week*, June 25, 80–89.
87. J. D. Westhpal, R. Gulati, & S. M. Shortell, 1997, Customization or conformity: An institutional and network perspective on the content and consequences of TQM adoption, *Administrative Science Quarterly*, 42: 366–394.
88. S. Sanghera, 1999, Making continuous improvement better, *Financial Times*, April 21, 28.
89. Muller, Ford, 82.
90. J. White, G. L. White, & N. Shirouzu, 2001, Soon, the big three won't be, as foreigners make inroads, *The Wall Street Journal*, August 13, A1, A12.
91. Ihlwan, Armstrong, & Kerwin, Hyundai gets hot, 84.
92. J. Hyde, 2001, In Detroit, a new definition of 'quality,' *Reuters Business News*, http://www.reuters.com, December 22.
93. Ihlwan, Armstrong, & Kerwin, Hyundai gets hot, 85.
94. J. Schumpeter, 1950, *Capitalism, Socialism and Democracy*, New York: Harper; Smith, Ferrier & Ndofor, Competitive dynamics research, 323.
95. M.-J. Chen & I. C. MacMillan, 1992, Nonresponse and delayed response to competitive moves, *Academy of Management Journal*, 35: 539–570; Smith, Ferrier, & Ndofor, Competitive dynamics research, 335.
96. M.-J. Chen, K. G. Smith, & C. M. Grimm, 1992, Action characteristics as predictors of competitive responses, *Management Science*, 38: 439–455.
97. M.-J. Chen & D. Miller, 1994, Competitive attack, retaliation and performance: An expectancy-valence framework, *Strategic Management Journal*, 15: 85–102.
98. Smith, Ferrier, & Ndofor, Competitive dynamics research, 333.
99. W. J. Ferrier, K. G. Smith, & C. M. Grimm, 1999, The role of competitive actions in market share erosion and industry dethronement: A study of industry leaders and challengers, *Academy of Management Journal*, 42: 372–388.
100. 2001, Lowe's Companies, *Standard & Poor's Stock Reports*, http://www.standard&poor.com, December 26.
101. Smith, Grimm, & Gannon, *Dynamics of Competitive Strategy*.
102. 2001, Retail Update 2001, *Argus Market Digest*, http://www.argusresearch.com, December 28.
103. A. Karnani & B. Wernerfelt, 1985, Research note and communication: Multiple point competition, *Strategic Management Journal*, 6: 87–97.
104. Smith, Ferrier, & Ndofor, Competitive dynamics research, 330.
105. 2001, Wrigley (Wm.) Jr., *Standard & Poor's Stock Report*, http://www.standard&poor.com, December 26.
106. J. R. Williams, 1999, *Renewable Advantage: Crafting Strategy through Economic Time*, New York: Free Press.
107. J. R. Williams, 1992, How sustainable is your competitive advantage? *California Management Review* 34(3): 29–51.
108. Ibid., 6.
109. Ibid., 57.
110. 2001, Fool take: Merck lurks, *Richmond Times-Dispatch*, December 30, D7.
111. 2001, Pfizer Inc., *Argus Company Report*, http://www.argusresearch.com, December 29.
112. Williams, *Renewable Advantage*, 8.
113. Ibid., 8.
114. R. Sanchez, 1995, Strategic flexibility in production competition, *Strategic Management Journal*, 16(Summer Special Issue): 9–26.
115. 2001, Industry awards, Micron Technology Inc. Home page, http://www.micron.com, December 30.
116. 2001, Technology innovations, Texas Instruments Home page, http://www.ti.com, December 30.
117. 2001, Micron Technology, *Standard & Poor's Stock Reports*, http://www.standard&poors.com, December 22; 2001, Texas Instruments, *Standard & Poor's Stock Reports*, http://www.standard&poors.com, December 22.
118. Williams, *Renewable Advantage*, 7.
119. K. Brooker, 2001, A game of inches, *Fortune*, February 5, 98–100.
120. 2001, High street woes, *The Economist*, July 28, 56.
121. 2001, General Mills Inc., *Argus Market Digest*, http:www.argusresearch.com, December 28.

6

Chapter Six

Corporate-Level Strategy

Knowledge Objectives

Studying this chapter should provide you with the strategic management knowledge needed to:

1. Define corporate-level strategy and discuss its importance to the diversified firm.

2. Describe the advantages and disadvantages of single- and dominant-business strategies.

3. Explain three primary reasons why firms move from single- and dominant-business strategies to more diversified strategies.

4. Describe how related diversified firms create value by sharing or transferring core competencies.

5. Explain the two ways value can be created with an unrelated diversification strategy.

6. Discuss the incentives and resources that encourage diversification.

7. Describe motives that can encourage managers to overdiversify a firm.

Cendant: A Diversified Service Conglomerate

Cendant Corporation was created in December 1997 by a merger between HFS, Inc., and CUC International. The merger combined a marketing company (CUC) with HFS, a diversified firm with franchising operations in several industries, including real estate, hospitality, and vehicle services. Henry Silverman, CEO of the former HFS, was appointed as chairman of the merged company. Massive accounting irregularities in CUC's businesses caused Cendant's shares to lose nearly half their market value four months after the merger and resulted in criminal charges against some of CUC's former executives.

Cendant Corporation owns a diversified set of services businesses, including its fee-for-services businesses—hotel, real estate, tax preparation, rental cars, fleet and fuel cards, mortgage origination, employee location, and vacation exchange and rental services. Cendant grows through acquisitions as well as through internal means, such as development of new product lines, to implement its related-linked corporate-level diversification strategy. Discussed in detail in the chapter, this strategy mixes related and unrelated diversification. Cendant also uses joint ventures and franchising (types of cooperative strategies that we discuss further in Chapter 9) to reach its growth objectives.

The focus of Cendant's corporate-level strategy is rapid growth through buying strong brands that are effectively positioned in the fee-for-service business area. Its businesses usually have low to moderate capital requirements but generate high margins and provide growing returns on capital and strong cash flows. Furthermore, Cendant seeks productivity improvements to lower costs by employing newer technologies.

Cendant's real estate franchises include Century 21, Coldwell Banker Commerce, and ERA—some of the most well-known franchises in the commercial and residential real estate brokerage market. Furthermore, it is one of the largest real estate retail mortgage originators in the United States. It also has a relocation service called Cendant Mobility. Real estate services generate approximately 40 percent of revenues for this diversified company.

Cendant Corporation implemented its strategic growth plan in 2001 and ended the year with revenues of $8.9 billion, a 90 percent increase over the previous year, and an increase in its share price by more than 100 percent. Cendant's real estate services, including Coldwell Banker Commercial Real Estate Services, with approximately 100 franchise offices and 1,000 U.S. sales agents, provided 21 percent of the firm's revenue for 2001.

In travel services, Cendant has a vast array of lodging franchises, including Days Inn, Howard Johnson's, Ramada Inn, Super 8, and Travel Lodge, among others. In fact, one in four customers in the budget segment stay in a Cendant franchised property. Because its customer base is budget conscious, the September 11, 2001 strikes on the United States were expected to have less of an effect on Cendant's revenues than on highly differentiated and more expensive lodging facilities. Cendant also owns Fairfield Communities, Inc., which operates a business through which vacation ownership interests are sold. To complement its travel business, it acquired Galileo International, a distributor of electronic global distribution services for the travel industry. Customers in 115 countries use Galileo's services to access schedule and fare information, make reservations, and issue tickets. Another recent Cendant acquisition, CheapTickets.com, provides additional opportunity in the online travel reservation segment. With the capability formed through its acquisitions, Cendant feels that it can effectively compete with online travel companies such as Travelocity.com and Priceline.com. Travel services generate approximately 28 percent of Cendant's revenues.

Cendant has a vehicle service division and is the leader in providing fleet and fuel management service cards. Avis Rental Service, National Car Parts, and Right Express form the core of this division. In total, this group of businesses accounts for roughly 17 percent of Cendant's sales revenue.

In regard to financial services, Cendant owns Jackson Hewitt Tax Service, the second largest U.S. tax preparation company, as well as Benefit Consultants, FISI-Madison Financial, and Long Term Preferred Care in the insurance and loyalty marketing area. On a combined basis, Cendant's financial services business unit contributes approximately 15 percent to the firm's total revenues.

Part of Cendant's related-linked diversification strategy is to acquire companies that complement its prestigious branded businesses. For instance, Galileo International, originally United Airlines' Apollo reservation system, has the second largest share of the electronic travel reservation business. Sabre Holdings Corporation, a competitor that operates the Sabre computer reservation system and also controls Travelocity.com, holds the largest share of this market. The Galileo network connects 43,000 travel agency sites to 550 airlines, 37 car rental companies, 47,000 hotel properties, 368 tour operators, and three major cruise lines. Thus, this acquisition creates a stronger link between its travel businesses.

A key objective of Cendant's acquisition strategy is to add companies that augment growth, strengthening the various businesses or segments where the firm has competitive advantages. Its best success with cross marketing has been in its array of real estate franchises. Although Cendant's businesses within each service type demonstrate some degree of relatedness, it has yet to realize the potential synergy between service categories. For example, Cendant hasn't developed a strong, value-creating relationship between car rentals and lodging. However, its acquisition of Galileo may provide more opportunity to exploit interrelatedness across Cendant's major strategic business units of travel, lodging, and vehicle service businesses. As is the case for all diversified business, Cendant must provide clear and transparent reports of its operations so investors and other stakeholders can fairly judge the value being created by exploiting interrelationships among the firm's business units.

SOURCES: 2002, Cendant Corp., *Standard & Poor's Stock Reports*, http://www.fidelity.com, April 1; A. Serwer, 2002, Dirty rotten numbers, *Fortune*, February 18, 74–84; A. Barrett & D. Brady, 2001, Just when it seems on the mend, *Business Week*, October 15, 75–76; 2001, Cendant home page, http://www.cendant.com; D. Colarusso, 2001, Wall Street is pondering Cendant's fresh start, *The New York Times*, http://www.nytimes.com, April 22; M. Rich, 2001, Cendant agrees to buy cheap tickets, *The Wall Street Journal*, August 14, B6; C. Rosen, 2001, Cendant ventures into travel, *Information Week*, June 25, 24; R. Sorkin & B. J. Feder, 2001, Owner of Avis and Day's Inn seen buying travel service, *The New York Times*, http://www.nytimes.com, June 18; A. Barrett, S. A. Forest, & T. Lowry, 2000, Henry Silverman's long road back, *Business Week*, February 28, 126–136.

Our discussions of business-level strategies (Chapter 4) and the competitive rivalry and competitive dynamics associated with them (Chapter 5) concentrate on firms competing in a single industry or product market.[1] When a firm chooses to diversify beyond a single industry and to operate businesses in several industries, it uses a corporate-level strategy of diversification. As explained in the Opening Case, Cendant operates in multiple industries while using a related-linked corporate-level strategy. A corporate-level strategy of diversification allows the firm to use its core competencies to pursue opportunities in the external environment.[2]

Diversification strategies play a major role in the behavior of large firms.[3] Strategic choices regarding diversification are, however, fraught with uncertainty.[4] The decision to merge CUC International with HFS seemed to have potential for improving the marketing capabilities of the merged firm, Cendant. However, because of accounting irregularities in some CUC businesses, the merger created significant difficulties, resulting in an initial precipitous decline in Cendant's market value.

A diversified company has two levels of strategy: business (or competitive) and corporate (or companywide).[5] Each business unit in the diversified firm chooses a business-level strategy as its means of competing in individual product markets. The firm's corporate-level strategy is concerned with two key questions: what businesses the firm should be in, and how the corporate office should manage the group of businesses.[6] Defined formally, **corporate-level strategy** specifies actions taken by the firm to gain a competitive advantage by selecting and managing a group of different businesses competing in several industries and product markets. In the current global environment, top executives should view their firm's businesses as a portfolio of core competencies when they select new businesses and decide how to manage them.[7] As with other strategic decisions that may not be as complex, speed is critical when executives make changes to this portfolio.[8]

Corporate-level strategy specifies actions taken by the firm to gain a competitive advantage by selecting and managing a group of different businesses competing in several industries and product markets.

A corporate-level strategy is expected to help the firm earn above-average returns by creating value, just as with the diversified firm's business-level strategies.[9] Some suggest that few corporate-level strategies actually create value.[10] A corporate-level strategy's value is ultimately determined by the degree to which "the businesses in the portfolio are worth more under the management of the company than they would be under any other ownership."[11] Thus, the effective corporate-level strategy creates, across all business units, aggregate returns that exceed what those returns would be without the strategy[12] and contributes to the firm's strategic competitiveness and its ability to earn above-average returns.[13]

Product diversification, a primary corporate-level strategy, concerns the scope of the industries and markets in which the firm competes as well as ". . . how managers buy, create and sell different businesses to match skills and strengths with opportunities presented to the firm."[14] Successful diversification is expected to reduce variability in the firm's profitability in that its earnings are generated from several different business units.[15] Because firms incur development and monitoring costs when diversifying, the ideal business portfolio balances diversification's costs and benefits.[16] Increasingly, a number of "traditional" economy firms are diversifying into Internet and e-commerce businesses in attempts to develop a properly balanced portfolio.[17]

Diversification requires the crafting of a multibusiness or corporate-level strategy. Multibusiness strategies often involve the firm with many different industry environments and product markets and, as explained in Chapter 11, require unique organizational structures. In the Opening Case, we describe Cendant's use of a multibusiness strategy to compete in the real estate, hospitality, travel, and vehicle services markets. The prevailing logic of diversification suggests that the firm should diversify into additional markets when it has excess resources, capabilities, and core competencies with multiple value-creating uses.[18] The probability of success increases when top-level managers verify that the firm has excess, value-creating resources, capabilities, and core competencies before choosing and trying to implement a corporate-level strategy.

We begin the chapter by examining different levels (from low to high) of diversification. Value-creating reasons for firms to use a corporate-level strategy are explored next. When diversification results in companies simultaneously competing against each other in multiple markets, they are engaging in multipoint competition.[19] For instance, the merger between Hewlett-Packard and Compaq Computer Corporation is expected to create a new firm that will be able to compete against IBM simultaneously in the attractive services market as well as in the PC and server markets.[20]

The chapter also describes using the vertical integration strategy as a means to gain power over competitors. Two types of diversification strategies denoting moderate to very high levels of diversification—related and unrelated—are then examined. The chapter also explores value-neutral incentives to diversify as well as managerial motives for diversification, which can be value destructive.

Levels of Diversification

Diversified firms vary according to their level of diversification and the connections between and among their businesses. Figure 6.1 lists and defines five categories of businesses according to increasing levels of diversification. In addition to the single- and dominant-business categories, more fully diversified firms are classified into related and unrelated categories. A firm is related through its diversification when there are several links between its business units; for example, units may share products or services, technologies, or distribution channels. The more links among businesses, the more "constrained" is the relatedness of diversification. Unrelatedness refers to the absence of direct links between businesses.

Low Levels of Diversification

A firm pursing a *low level of diversification* uses either a single or a dominant corporate-level diversification strategy. A single business diversification strategy is a corporate-level strategy wherein the firm generates 95 percent or more of its sales revenue from its core business area.[21] For example, focusing on the chewing-gum market, Wm. Wrigley Jr. Company uses a single business strategy while operating in relatively few product markets.[22] Wrigley's trademark chewing-gum brands include Spearmint, Doublemint, and Juicy Fruit. Sugarfree gums Hubba Bubba, Orbit, and Ice White were added in the 1990s. Its collaboration with Procter & Gamble to produce a dental chewing gum causes Wrigley to become slightly more diversified than it has been historically, although it is still using the single business diversification strategy. The dental chewing gum will be marketed under P&G's Crest brand.[23]

   With the dominant business corporate-level diversification strategy, the firm generates between 70 and 95 percent of its total revenue within a single business area. Smithfield Foods uses the dominant business diversification strategy as shown by the fact that the majority of its sales are generated from raising and butchering hogs. Recently, however, Smithfield diversified into beef packing by acquiring Moyer Packing Co., a smaller beef processor. Smithfield also attempted to acquire IBP, the largest beef packer, but was outbid by Tyson Foods.[24] Although it is still using the dominant business diversification strategy, the firm's addition of beef packing operations suggests that its portfolio of businesses is becoming more diversified. If Smithfield were to

---

Figure 6.1   Levels and Types of Diversification

Low Levels of Diversification

| Single business: | More than 95% of revenue comes from a single business. |  |

| Dominant business: | Between 70% and 95% of revenue comes from a single business. | 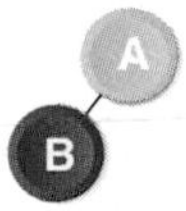 |

Moderate to High Levels of Diversification

| Related constrained: | Less than 70% of revenue comes from the dominant business, and all businesses share product, technological, and distribution linkages. | 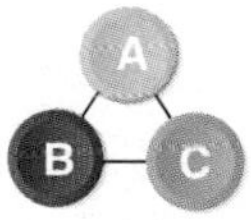 |

| Related linked (mixed related and unrelated): | Less than 70% of revenue comes from the dominant business, and there are only limited links between businesses. | 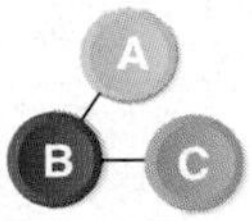 |

Very High Levels of Diversification

| Unrelated: | Less than 70% of revenue comes from the dominant business, and there are no common links between businesses. | 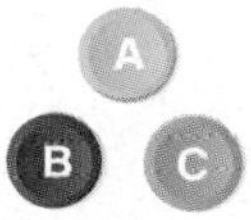 |

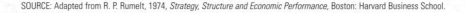

SOURCE: Adapted from R. P. Rumelt, 1974, *Strategy, Structure and Economic Performance*, Boston: Harvard Business School.

According to Wrigley CEO Bill Wrigley Jr., the firm's fourth-generation family leader, investments in new products "and other investments in sales infrastructure and global systems capability are consistent with our focus on long-term growth." In addition to the firm's typical products shown here, X-Cite, a combination chewing gum and mint, will be available throughout much of Europe and the Pacific region in 2003, and Eclipse Flash Strips—a dissolvable breath film, or mint strip—was introduced in the United States in 2002.

become even more diversified, its corporate-level strategy could find the firm more accurately described as one that is moderately diversified.

Moderate and High Levels of Diversification

A firm generating more than 30 percent of its sales revenue outside a dominant business and whose businesses are related to each other in some manner uses *a related diversification corporate-level strategy*. When the links between the diversified firm's businesses are rather direct, *a related constrained diversification strategy* is being used. Campbell Soup, Procter & Gamble, Xerox, and Merck & Company all use a related constrained strategy. A related constrained firm shares a number of resources and activities between its businesses.

The diversified company with a portfolio of businesses with only a few links between them is called a mixed related and unrelated firm and is using the *related linked diversification strategy* (see Figure 6.1). Johnson & Johnson, General Electric, and Schlumberger follow this corporate-level diversification strategy. Compared to related constrained firms, related linked firms share fewer resources and assets between their businesses, concentrating on transferring knowledge and competencies between the businesses instead.

A highly diversified firm, which has no relationships between its businesses, follows an unrelated diversification strategy. United Technologies, Textron, and Samsung are examples of firms using this type of corporate-level strategy.[25] Although many U.S. firms using the unrelated diversification strategy have refocused to become less diversified, a number continue to have high levels of diversification. In Latin America and other emerging economies such as China, Korea, and India, conglomerates (firms following the unrelated diversification strategy) continue to dominate the private sector.[26] For instance, in Taiwan, "the largest 100 groups produced one third of the GNP in the past 20 years."[27] Typically family controlled, these corporations account for the greatest percentage of private firms in India.[28] Similarly, the largest business groups in Brazil, Mexico, Argentina, and Colombia are family-owned, diversified enterprises.[29] However, questions are being raised as to the viability of these large diversified business groups, especially in developed economies such as Japan.[30]

Reasons for Diversification

There are many reasons firms use a corporate level diversification strategy (see Table 6.1). Typically, a diversification strategy is used to increase the firm's value by improving its overall performance. Value is created either through related diversification or through unrelated diversification when the strategy allows a company's business units to increase revenues or reduce costs while implementing their business-level strategies. Another reason for diversification is to gain market power relative to competitors. Often, this is achieved through vertical integration (see the discussion later in the chapter).

Other reasons for using a diversification strategy may not increase the firm's value; in fact, diversification could have neutral effects, increase costs, or reduce a firm's revenues and its value. These reasons include diversification to match and

PART 2 /Strategic Actions: Strategy Formulation

Table 6.1	Motives, Incentives, and Resources for Diversification

Motives to Enhance Strategic Competitiveness

- Economies of scope (related diversification)
  Sharing activities
  Transferring core competencies
- Market power (related diversification)
  Blocking competitors through multipoint competition
  Vertical integration
- Financial economies (unrelated diversification)
  Efficient internal capital allocation
  Business restructuring

Incentives and Resources with Neutral Effects on Strategic Competitiveness

- Antitrust regulation
- Tax laws
- Low performance
- Uncertain future cash flows
- Risk reduction for firm
- Tangible resources
- Intangible resources

Managerial Motives (Value Reduction)

- Diversifying managerial employment risk
- Increasing managerial compensation

thereby neutralize a competitor's market power (such as to neutralize another firm's advantage by acquiring a distribution outlet similar to its rival) and to expand a firm's portfolio of businesses to reduce managerial employment risk (if one of the businesses in a diversified firm fails, the top executive of the firm remains employed). Because diversification can increase a firm's size and thus managerial compensation, managers have motives to diversify a firm to a level that reduces its value. Diversification rationales that may have a neutral or negative effect on the firm's value are discussed in a later section.

To provide an overview of value-creating diversification strategies, Figure 6.2 illustrates operational relatedness and corporate relatedness. Study of these independent relatedness dimensions shows the importance of resources and key competencies.[31] The figure's vertical dimension indicates sharing activities (operational relatedness) while its horizontal dimension depicts corporate capabilities for transferring knowledge (corporate relatedness). The firm with a strong capability in managing operational synergy, especially in sharing assets between its businesses, falls in the upper left quadrant, which also represents vertical sharing of assets through vertical integration. The lower right quadrant represents a highly developed corporate capability for transferring a skill across businesses. This capability is located primarily in the corporate office. The use of either operational relatedness or corporate relatedness is based on a knowledge asset that the firm can either share or transfer.[32] Unrelated diversification is also illustrated in Figure 6.2 in the lower left quadrant. As shown, the unrelated diversification strategy creates value through financial economies rather than through either operational relatedness or corporate relatedness among business units.

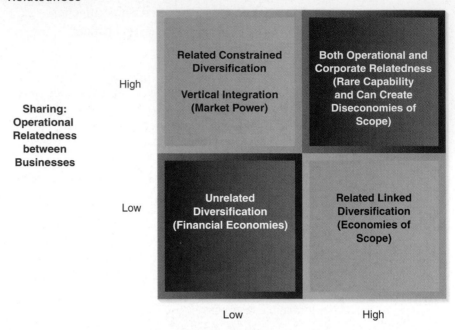

Related Constrained
Diversification

Vertical Integration
(Market Power)

Both Operational and
Corporate Relatedness
(Rare Capability
and Can Create
Diseconomies of
Scope)

Unrelated
Diversification
(Financial Economies)

Related Linked
Diversification
(Economies of
Scope)

Sharing:
Operational
Relatedness
between
Businesses

High

Low

Low   High

Corporate Relatedness: Transferring Skills into
Businesses through Corporate Headquarters

Related Diversification

With the related diversification corporate-level strategy, the firm builds upon or
extends its resources, capabilities, and core competencies to create value.[33] The company using the related diversification strategy wants to develop and exploit
economies of scope between its business units. Available to companies operating in
multiple industries or product markets,[34] **economies of scope** are cost savings that
the firm creates by successfully transferring some of its capabilities and competencies
that were developed in one of its businesses to another of its businesses.

As illustrated in Figure 6.2, firms seek to create value from economies of scope
through two basic kinds of operational economies: sharing activities (operational
relatedness) and transferring skills or corporate core competencies (corporate relatedness). The difference between sharing activities and transferring competencies is
based on how separate resources are jointly used to create economies of scope.
Tangible resources, such as plant and equipment or other business-unit physical
assets, often must be shared to create economies of scope. Less tangible resources,
such as manufacturing know-how, also can be shared. However, when know-how is
transferred between separate activities and there is no physical or tangible resource
involved, a corporate core competence has been transferred as opposed to operational sharing of activities having taken place.

Economies of scope are
cost savings that the firm
creates by successfully
transferring some of its
capabilities and competencies that were developed in
one of its businesses to
another of its businesses.

Operational Relatedness: Sharing Activities

Firms can create operational relatedness by sharing either a primary activity (such as
inventory delivery systems) or a support activity (for example, purchasing practices)
(see Chapter 3's discussion of the value chain). Sharing activities is quite common,

especially among related constrained firms. Procter & Gamble's paper towel business and baby diaper business both use paper products as a primary input to the manufacturing process. The firm's joint paper production plant that produces inputs for the two divisions is an example of a shared activity. In addition, these two businesses are likely to share distribution channels and sales networks, because they both produce consumer products.

Firms expect activity sharing among units to result in increased strategic competitiveness and improved financial returns. For example, PepsiCo purchased Quaker Oats for $12 billion on August 10, 2001. Pepsi has done well in the recent past, but sales growth in carbonated beverages—a staple for PepsiCo—may have reached a point of market saturation and could even decline, because medical studies have linked soft drink consumption to childhood obesity. With the purchase of Quaker Oats, the maker of sports drink Gatorade, Pepsi hopes it has found a reliable growth driver. Gatorade is the market leader in sports drinks and experienced a 13 percent annual growth rate in sales revenue between 1998 and 2001. Pepsi is integrating Gatorade into its distribution channels, partly to increase Gatorade's market share outside the United States. Thus, Pepsi soft drinks, such as Pepsi Cola and Mountain Dew, and Gatorade are sharing the firm's outbound logistics activity. Similarly, the same distribution channels could be used to distribute Quaker Oats' healthy snacks and Frito Lay's salty snacks.[35]

Other issues affect the degree to which activity sharing creates positive outcomes. For example, activity sharing requires sharing strategic control over business units. Moreover, one business unit manager may feel that another unit is receiving a disproportionate share of the gains. Such a perception could create conflicts between division managers.

Activity sharing also is risky because business-unit ties create links between outcomes. For instance, if demand for one business's product is reduced, there may not be sufficient revenues to cover the fixed costs required to operate the facilities being shared. Organizational difficulties such as these can prevent activity sharing success.[36]

Although activity sharing across business units isn't risk free, research shows that it can create value. For example, studies that examined acquisitions of firms in the same industry (called horizontal acquisitions), such as the banking industry, have found that sharing resources and activities and thereby creating economies of scope contributed to post-acquisition increases in performance and higher returns to shareholders.[37] Additionally, firms that sold off related units in which resource sharing was a possible source of economies of scope have been found to produce lower returns than those that sold off businesses unrelated to the firm's core business.[38] Still other research discovered that firms with more related units had lower risk.[39] These results suggest that gaining economies of scope by sharing activities across a firm's businesses may be important in reducing risk and in creating value. Further, more attractive results are obtained through activity sharing when a strong corporate office facilitates it.[40]

Corporate Relatedness: Transferring of Core Competencies

Over time, the firm's intangible resources, such as its know-how, become the foundation of core competencies. As suggested by Figure 6.2, corporate core competencies are complex sets of resources and capabilities that link different businesses, primarily through managerial and technological knowledge, experience, and expertise.[41]

Related linked firms often transfer competencies across businesses, thereby creating value in at least two ways. First, the expense of developing a competence has been incurred in one unit. Transferring it to a second business unit eliminates the need for the second unit to allocate resources to develop the competence. Resource intangibility is a second source of value creation through corporate relatedness. Intangible resources are difficult for competitors to understand and imitate. Because of this difficulty, the unit receiving a transferred competence often gains an immediate competitive advantage over its rivals.

Currently, McDonald's is attempting to create value by transferring an intangible resource among businesses it has acquired. Chipotle Mexican Grill (a small Colorado chain of Mexican food restaurants), Donatos Pizza (a pizza restaurant chain), Boston Market (a nationally known chain specializing in home-style cooking), and Prêt à Manger (a London chain with an eclectic food offering, such as sushi and salmon sandwiches) are now owned by McDonald's. Efforts are underway from the corporate level to transfer McDonald's knowledge about all phases of the fast food industry and restaurant operations to its newly acquired businesses. These actions demonstrate that McDonald's executives believe that the knowledge the company has gained from operating its core business can also create value in its other food venues—venues attracting customers who do not frequent McDonald's units. Interestingly, McDonald's stock price declined in early 2002 with questions surfacing about the firm's ability to maintain its historic growth and performance rates (this issue is further discussed in the Strategic Focus on page 136). Although all of these acquired businesses are small, McDonald's believes that each can profitably grow by applying its knowledge in their unique settings. Estimates are that the new units could add 2 percent to McDonald's growth rate within a few years.[42]

A number of firms have successfully transferred some of their resources and capabilities across businesses. Virgin Industries transferred its marketing skills across travel, cosmetics, music, drinks, and a number of other businesses. Thermo Electron uses its entrepreneurial skills to start new ventures and maintain a new-venture network. Coopers Industries manages a number of manufacturing-related businesses. Honda has developed and transferred its expertise in small and now larger engines for different types of vehicles, from motorcycles and lawnmowers to its range of automotive products.[43]

One way managers facilitate the transfer of competencies is to move key people into new management positions. However, a business-unit manager of an older division may be reluctant to transfer key people who have accumulated knowledge and experience critical to the business unit's success. Thus, managers with the ability to facilitate the transfer of a core competence may come at a premium, or the key people involved may not want to transfer. Additionally, the top-level managers from the transferring division may not want the competencies transferred to a new division to fulfill the firm's diversification objectives. Research suggests that transferring expertise in manufacturing-based businesses often does not result in improved performance.[44] Businesses in which performance does improve often demonstrate a corporate passion for pursuing skill transfer and appropriate coordination mechanisms for realizing economies of scope.

Market Power

Related diversification can also be used to gain market power. Market power exists when a firm is able to sell its products above the existing competitive level or to reduce the costs of its primary and support activities below the competitive level, or both.[45]

One approach to gaining market power through diversification is *multipoint competition*. Multipoint competition exists when two or more diversified firms simultaneously compete in the same product areas or geographic markets.[46] As mentioned earlier, the actions taken by Hewlett-Packard (HP) in its merger with Compaq Computer Corporation demonstrate multipoint competition. This merger allows the combined firm to compete with other larger companies, such as IBM and Sun

Microsystems. For example, HP and Compaq are now coordinating their efforts in PCs, servers, and services. The combined revenues of the two companies almost equal those of IBM. The merged firm will most likely compete directly with IBM in the server market and will continue to increase its services division as well.[47]

The preceding example illustrates the potential dynamics of multipoint competition. As a strategic action (see Chapter 5), HP and Compaq's decision to merge is partly a competitive response to IBM's success in servers and services.[48] Counterattacks are not common in multipoint competition because the threat of a counterattack may prevent strategic actions from being taken, or, more likely, firms may retract their strategic actions when faced with the threat of counterattack.[49] Using a matching strategy, where the responding firm takes the same strategic action as the attacker, is a prominent form of response because it signals a commitment to defend the status quo without escalating rivalry.[50] This can be seen in the responses of media firms to the AOL Time Warner merger, as illustrated in the Strategic Focus on page 192 about Disney and other media firms.

Some firms choose to create value by using vertical integration to gain market power (see Figure 6.2). **Vertical integration** exists when a company produces its own inputs (backward integration) or owns its own source of distribution of outputs (forward integration). In some instances, firms partially integrate their operations, producing and selling their products by using both company units and outside sources.

Vertical integration is commonly used in the firm's core business to gain market power over rivals. Market power is gained as the firm develops the ability to save on its operations, avoid market costs, improve product quality, and, possibly, protect its technology from imitation by rivals. Market power also is created when firms have strong ties between their assets for which no market prices exist. Establishing a market price would result in high search and transaction costs, so firms seek to vertically integrate rather than remaining separate businesses.[51]

Smithfield Foods, mentioned earlier, is a vertically integrated company with hog processing as its core business. Smithfield has vertically integrated backward by raising the hogs that it later processes in its plants. Most packaging plants operate profitably when the price of meat is low and suffer with high meat prices. In contrast, Smithfield can better control its costs because it owns facilities that provide the raw materials required for its core processing operations. This control often results in Smithfield having market power over its competitors because it typically produces products at below the average industry production cost. Recent acquisitions of ten U.S. and a few international meat-packaging companies are intended to support the firm's use of vertical integration to yield competitively attractive options to consumers.[52]

There are also limits to vertical integration. For example, an outside supplier may produce the product at a lower cost. As a result, internal transactions from vertical integration may be expensive and reduce profitability relative to competitors. Also, bureaucratic costs may occur with vertical integration. And, because vertical integration can require substantial investments in specific technologies, it may reduce the firm's flexibility, especially when technology changes quickly. Finally, changes in demand create capacity balance and coordination problems. If one division is building a part for another internal division, but achieving economies of scale requires the first division to manufacture quantities that are beyond the capacity of the internal buyer to absorb, it would be necessary to sell the parts outside the firm as well as to the internal division. Thus, although vertical integration can create value, especially through market power over competitors, it is not without risks and costs.

Many manufacturing firms no longer pursue vertical integration.[53] In fact, deintegration is the focus of most manufacturing firms, such as Intel and Dell, and even among large automobile companies, such as Ford and General Motors, as they develop independent supplier networks.[54] Solectron Corp., a contract manufacturer,

Vertical integration exists when a company produces its own inputs (backward integration) or owns its own source of distribution of outputs (forward integration).

Multipoint Competition among Media Firms: Content Is King at Disney

Following the announcement of the AOL Time Warner merger, other content-oriented media firms felt pressure to pursue distribution businesses. The merger provided a content company (AOL) with several distribution outlets (Time Warner). Time Warner already had distribution assets through its cable TV operations, and the merger with AOL added the largest Internet service provider (ISP). Vivendi Universal (discussed in a later Strategic Focus), created through the merger of French utility conglomerate Vivendi with Seagrams, which owned Universal Studios and Universal Music, is seeking to match the content and distribution strategy developed by AOL Time Warner.

Walt Disney Company, however, has resisted the pressure to imitate these competitive actions. The firm has been a strong force in the business of entertaining consumers for decades. True to its beginnings, Disney has grown to be one of the largest moviemakers in the industry—consistently producing hit movies. As the company grew and the media industry consolidated, it brought ABC and its affiliates under its corporate umbrella, becoming a major competitor in the television network business. The diversified entertainment behemoth also built theme parks all over the world. According to Disney CEO Michael Eisner, all of the firm's business segments focus on one main product offering: content. In his view, Disney provides content—an actual, intellectual product made for consumption by the consumer.

© FRED PROUSER/REUTERS NEWMEDIA INC./CORBIS.

According to Walt Disney corporate website (http://disney.go.com), the firm's key objective is to be the world's premier family entertainment company through the ongoing development of its powerful brand and character franchises. Shown here are performers Lebo M and Paulette Ivory from a production of the musical play, "The Lion King," which builds on the company's movie characters by the same name. Walt Disney once remarked about his company, "I only hope we don't lose sight of one thing—that it was all started by a mouse."

The AOL Time Warner merger resulted in a battle in which AOL Time Warner cut Disney-owned ABC off from 3.5 million subscribers for 39 hours because of disputes between the two companies. There is much pressure, both from outside investors and inside executives, to expand Disney's distribution options. Some content producers have approached the company about bidding for AT&T Broadband, but it has not done so. Disney hopes that its content offerings will be so strong that consumers would complain if the Disney-owned channels were taken off the air, as was the case during the disagreement with AOL Time Warner.

To support "content is king" as the foundation for its competition position, Disney completed a transaction with News Corporation and Saban Entertainment Inc. to buy Fox Family Worldwide. This acquisition added over 100 million subscribers to Disney's already vast cable operations, which include the Disney Channel, Toon Disney, SoapNet, and ESPN. Fox Family Worldwide also provides Disney with a rich library of content, including 6,500 episodes of animated shows such as *Digimon, Spider-Man,* and *Mighty Morphin Power Rangers.* The company plans to integrate the Fox Family Channel with ABC's operations to air reruns of shows originally aired on the ABC Network or other Disney-owned channels. This "repurposing" will allow viewers to see their favorite shows outside of the normal viewing time. It will also allow Disney to make extra revenue from the shows and the firm should be able to spread the cost across several outlets.

Disney sees itself as a creator of entertainment content rather than as a distribution channel for it. Consistent with its vision, Disney continues to diversify in ways that add content to its substantial library, such as its acquisition of Fox Family Worldwide, and resists the temptation to add distribution capabilities, such as cable businesses like AT&T

Broadband. Because of the multipoint competition for advertising, Disney may have to respond to the pressures for distribution assets. However, Disney encountered difficulties in its past attempts to do so, such as the go.com Internet portal. Thus, Disney feels pressure to move beyond its emphasis on content into new areas of competence to meet the competition, which is developing distribution channel capabilities.

SOURCES: B. Carter, 2001, Disney discusses strategy behind buying Fox Family, *The New York Times*, http://www.nytimes.com, July 24; N. Deogun, S. Beatty, B. Orwall, & J. Lippman, 2001, Disney plans to acquire Fox Family for $3 billion and debt assumption, *The Wall Street Journal Interactive*, http://www.interactive.wsj.com, July 23; G. Fabrikant & A. R. Sorkin, 2001, Disney is said to be close to acquiring Fox Family, *The New York Times*, http://www.nytimes.com, July 23; J. Flint & B. Orwall, 2001, 'ABC Family' cable channel will recycle network fare, *The Wall Street Journal Interactive*, http://www.interactive.wsj.com, July 24; R. Grover, 2001, Fox Family enters the Mouse House, *Business Week Online*, http://www.businessweek.com, July 24; J. Guyon, 2001, Can Messier make cash flow like water? *Fortune*, September 3, 148–150; R. Linnett, Leap frog, *Advertising Age*, 2001, July 30, S12; S. Schiesel, 2001, For Disney's Eisner, the business is content, not conduits, *The New York Times*, http://www.nytimes.com, July 2.

represents a new breed of large contract manufacturers that is helping to foster this revolution in supply-chain management. Such firms often manage their customers' entire product lines, and offer services ranging from inventory management to delivery and after-sales service. Performing business through e-commerce also allows vertical integration to be changed into "virtual integration."[55] Thus, closer relationships are possible with suppliers and customers through virtual integration or electronic means of integration, allowing firms to reduce the costs of processing transactions while improving their supply-chain management skills and tightening the control of their inventories. "The longer the supply chain, the bigger the potential gains from B2B e-commerce, since it allows firms to eliminate the many layers of middlemen that hamper economic efficiency."[56]

Simultaneous Operational Relatedness and Corporate Relatedness

As Figure 6.2 suggests, some firms simultaneously seek operational and corporate forms of economies of scope.[57] Because simultaneously managing two sources of knowledge is very difficult, such efforts often fail, creating diseconomies of scope.[58] For example, USA Networks Inc. has focused primarily on TV entertainment, owning networks such as USA, the Sci Fi channel, and the Home Shopping Network. CEO Barry Diller seeks to make the company a leader in the interactive-commerce market. In 2001, USA Networks bought a controlling interest in Expedia, the online travel website, from Microsoft and announced its intention of buying National Leisure Group, a small travel company. The firm plans to innovate by combining its acquired firms' travel capabilities with its current cable TV capabilities. Resulting from this integration of capabilities will be a new cable network that provides a travel-shopping channel allowing viewers to buy travel services over the phone. Thus, the firm will share the phone capabilities already in place for its shopping channels and also transfer its TV capabilities to its newly acquired online travel and travel service assets. The online-travel market was seen as having tremendous growth potential before the terrorist acts of September 11, and USA Networks wanted to establish a first-mover advantage in this market in combination with its TV capability.[59] Although this strategy is difficult to implement, if the firm is successful, it could create value that is hard for competitors to imitate.

Vivendi is trying to achieve both operational relatedness and corporate relatedness in the media business. Vivendi's strategy, as illustrated in the Strategic Focus on page 194, may be difficult to achieve because its distribution of content is focused on mobile web technology.

Vivendi: From Water Treatment to Media Might

With a foundation in the water treatment business, the French firm Vivendi has diversified into various media businesses. This movement into media became more pronounced with Vivendi's announcement of its merger with Seagram's Universal Studios and Universal Music Group. At the time of this transaction, Vivendi CEO, Jean-Marie Messier described his vision of the future. The vision is one in which consumers could use either their cellular telephones or handheld computers to purchase music through an online music site and view movies through broadband subscription services. To realize this vision, Vivendi Universal acquired MP3.com, an online music-sharing website. Messier asserted that it was "a big step forward for Vivendi Universal's priority to develop an aggressive, legitimate and attractive offering of our content to consumers." To overcome the powerful middle-men, such as Blockbuster video-rental chain and HBO cable network and to reach his vision, Vivendi Universal has formed a joint venture with other studios (including Sony Pictures, AOL Time Warner's Warner Brothers, Viacom's Metro-Goldwyn-Mayer) to create a digital video on demand platform. This service will allow direct broadband delivery of digital video to
consumers.

When Vivendi Universal purchased Houghton Mifflin, a U.S. educational publisher, Messier asserted that it was "another step forward for Vivendi Universal to achieve world leadership in key content segments." He also said that leveraging the acquired content and technologies assets of Houghton Mifflin would allow Vivendi Universal "to capitalize on the growth of the education sector" and to match the publishing and content assets of AOL Time Warner.

In June 2001, Vivendi Universal further extended its reach by acquiring a larger stake in Elektrim Telekomunikacja, the telecommunication assets of Polish conglomerate Elektrim, which gave it control over that company, and, in effect, control over Polska Telefonia Cyfrowa (PTC), Eastern Europe's largest mobile-telephone operator. Vivendi already is one of the largest providers of mobile phone service in Europe. Earlier, Vivendi joined forces with British telecommunications leader Vodafone to create Vizzavi, which was launched in France in June 2000. "Vizzavi would be Messier's distribution arm in Europe, beaming content over the wireless Web to Vivendi's eight million and Vodafone's 48 million mobile-phone customers." This additional acquisition gave Vivendi Universal a strong foothold into the mobile phone market in Eastern Europe, which fits nicely with its vision of the future.

The acquisition of MP3.com brought a number of things to Vivendi Universal. First, even though Vivendi had fought with the online music distributors, MP3.com gave it a well-known online brand. More importantly for Vivendi, however, is the technology and know-how that the acquisition provides. Vivendi Universal and Sony Music have announced that they will also enter into the online music distribution business through a music service named Pressplay. The purchase of MP3.com brings into the company the demonstrated technology and experience that will be essential to Pressplay's success.

Vivendi Universal's acquisitions have extended the company's content and distribution network. The merger with Universal and the acquisition of Houghton Mifflin provided the company with well-known brands to produce content. By purchasing an online music distributor, Vivendi expanded its ability to put its content in front of the consumer for purchase. The procurement of a controlling stake in PTC gives the company a high performing cellular phone company and is a step into the future where people "see a trailer for a film on [their] . . . mobile phone." By diversifying into different content and distribution areas, Vivendi Universal is building for a future in which it hopes to be a one-stop media outlet. In content businesses, it shares activities to produce movies, movie themes in its theme parks, and movie sound tracks. Additionally, it has the knowledge through its phone acquisitions and alliances and the MP3.com acquisition to transfer this expertise to improve distribution. However, because Vivendi's distribution is more dependent on mobile online technology than other large media firms, the success of Vivendi's approach remains an open question. Furthermore, it is hard to tell how the acquisitions are doing relative to the basic water treatment assets, given that the income streams from these assets are hard to distinguish in the accounting reports. The increased emphasis on transparency regarding how a firm is generating its revenue and profits suggests that this could become an important issue.

SOURCES: C. Matlack, 2002, Memo to Jean-Marie Messier, *Business Week,* March 4, 56; 2001, Associated Press, MP3.com adds 1 millionth song; launches new subscriber service, *The Detroit News Online,* http://www.detnews.com, June 14; D. Leonard, 2001, Mr. Messier is ready for his close-up, *Fortune,* September 3, 136–148; 2001, Dow Jones Newswire, France's Vivendi appears to win battle for mobile operator PTC in Poland, *The Wall Street Journal Interactive,* http://www.wsj.com, June 28; B. Orwall, 2001, Five Hollywood studios enter venture to offer feature films of the Internet, *The Wall Street Journal Interactive,* http://www.wsj.com, August 17; M. Richtel, 2001, Vivendi deal for MP3.com highlights trend, *The New York Times,* http://www.nytimes.com, May 22; S. Schiesel, 2001, Vivendi will acquire Houghton Mifflin for $1.7 billion, *The New York Times,* http://www.nytimes.com, June 2; A. R. Sorkin, 2001, Vivendi in deal to acquire MP3.com, *The New York Times,* http://www.nytimes.com, May 21; A. Weintraub, R. Grover, & C. Matlack, 2001, Vivendi faces the music on the Web, *Business Week,* June 4, 43.

As illustrated in the Strategic Focus about Vivendi, a critical aspect of achieving both operational relatedness and corporate relatedness is how well a firm manages the sharing of activities *and* the transferring of knowledge. Disney, another media firm, has been successful in using both operational relatedness and corporate relatedness, although it has not developed distribution capabilities.

Disney's strategy is especially successful compared to Sony when measured by revenues generated from successful movies. By using operational relatedness and corporate relatedness, Disney made $3 billion on the 150 products that were marketed with its movie, *The Lion King.* Sony's *Men in Black* was a super hit at the box office and earned $600 million, but box-office and video revenues were practically the entire success story. Disney was able to accomplish its great success by sharing activities regarding the *Lion King* theme within its movie and theme parks, music and retail products divisions, while at the same time transferring knowledge into these same divisions,

Pictured here are Vivendi CEO Jean-Marie Messier (left) with USA Networks CEO Barry Diller.

creating a music CD, *Rhythm of the Pride Lands,* and producing a video, *Simba's Pride.* In addition, there were *Lion King* themes at Disney resorts and Animal Kingdom parks.[60] However, as is the case with Vivendi Universal, it is difficult for analysts from outside the firm to fully assess the value-creating potential of the firm pursuing both operational relatedness and corporate relatedness. As such, Disney's and Vivendi Universal's assets have been discounted somewhat because "the biggest lingering questions is whether multiple revenue streams will outpace multiple-platform overhead."[61]

Unrelated Diversification

Firms do not seek either operational relatedness or corporate relatedness when using the unrelated diversification corporate-level strategy. An unrelated diversification strategy (see Figure 6.2) can create value through two types of financial economies.

Financial economies are cost savings realized through improved allocations of financial resources based on investments inside or outside the firm.

Financial economies are cost savings realized through improved allocations of financial resources based on investments inside or outside the firm.[62]

The first type of financial economy results from efficient internal capital allocations. This approach seeks to reduce risk among the firm's business units—for example, through the development of a portfolio of businesses with different risk profiles. The approach thereby reduces business risk for the total corporation. The second type of financial economy is concerned with purchasing other corporations and restructuring their assets. This approach finds the diversified firm buying other companies, restructuring their assets in ways that allows the purchased company to operate more profitably, and then selling the company for a profit in the external market.

Efficient Internal Capital Market Allocation

In a market economy, capital markets are thought to efficiently allocate capital. Efficiency results from investors' purchasing of firm equity shares (ownership) that have high future cash-flow values. Capital is also allocated through debt as shareholders and debtholders try to improve the value of their investments by taking stakes in businesses with high growth prospects.

In large diversified firms, the corporate office distributes capital to business divisions to create value for the overall company. Such an approach may provide gains from internal capital market allocation relative to the external capital market.[63] This happens because while managing the firm's portfolio of businesses, the corporate office may gain access to detailed and accurate information regarding those businesses' actual and prospective performance.

The corporate office needs to convey its ability to create value in this manner to the market. One way firms have been doing this is through tracking stocks, as General Motors has done for its Hughes Aerospace division.[64] GM created a new stock listing for the Hughes assets that conveyed better information to the market about this additional asset. This approach allows more scrutiny by the market and thus more transparency of increasingly complex and diversified internal operations.

Compared with corporate office personnel, investors have relatively limited access to internal information and can only estimate divisional performance and future business prospects. Although businesses seeking capital must provide information to potential suppliers (such as banks or insurance companies), firms with internal capital markets may have at least two informational advantages. First, information provided to capital markets through annual reports and other sources may not include negative information, instead emphasizing positive prospects and outcomes. External sources of capital have limited ability to understand the dynamics inside large organizations. Even external shareholders who have access to information have no guarantee of full and complete disclosure.[65] Second, although a firm must disseminate information, that information also becomes simultaneously available to the firm's current and potential competitors. With insights gained by studying such information, competitors might attempt to duplicate a firm's competitive advantage. Thus, an ability to efficiently allocate capital through an internal market may help the firm protect its competitive advantages.

If intervention from outside the firm is required to make corrections to capital allocations, only significant changes are possible, such as forcing the firm into bankruptcy or changing the top management team. Alternatively, in an internal capital market, the corporate office can fine-tune its corrections, such as choosing to adjust managerial incentives or suggesting strategic changes in a division. Thus, capital can be allocated according to more specific criteria than is possible with external market allocations. Because it has less accurate information, the external capital market may fail to allocate resources adequately to high-potential investments compared with corporate office investments. The corporate office of a diversified company can more effectively perform tasks such as disciplining underperforming management teams through resource allocations.[66]

Research suggests, however, that in efficient capital markets, the unrelated diversification strategy may be discounted.[67] "For years, stock markets have applied a 'conglomerate discount': they value diversified manufacturing conglomerates at 20 percent less, on average, than the value of the sum of their parts. The discount still applies, in good economic times and bad. Extraordinary manufacturers (like GE) can defy it for a while, but more ordinary ones (like Philips and Siemens) cannot."[68]

Some firms still use the unrelated diversification strategy.[69] These large diversified business groups are found in many European countries and throughout emerging economies as well. For example, research indicates that the conglomerate or unrelated diversification strategy has not disappeared in Europe, where the number of firms using it has actually increased.[70] Although many conglomerates, such as ITT and Hansen Trust, have refocused, other unrelated diversified firms have replaced them.

The Achilles heel of the unrelated diversification strategy is that conglomerates in developed economies have a fairly short life cycle because financial economies are more easily duplicated than are the gains derived from operational relatedness and corporate relatedness. This is less of a problem in emerging economies, where the absence of a "soft infrastructure" (including effective financial intermediaries, sound regulations, and contract laws) supports and encourages use of the unrelated diversification strategy.[71] In fact, in emerging economies such as those in India and Chile, diversification increases performance of firms affiliated with large diversified business groups.[72]

Restructuring

Financial economies can also be created when firms learn how to create value by buying and selling other companies' assets in the external market.[73] As in the real estate business, buying assets at low prices, restructuring them, and selling them at a price exceeding their cost generates a positive return on the firm's invested capital.

Under CEO Dennis L. Kozlowski, Tyco International, Ltd., gains financial economies through restructuring. Tyco focuses on two types of acquisitions: platform, which represent new bases for future acquisitions, and add-on, in markets Tyco currently has a major presence. As with many unrelated diversified firms, Tyco acquires mature product lines. "In Tyco's entrepreneurial culture, managers have enormous autonomy. Kozlowski relies on a computerized reporting system that gives him a detailed snapshot of how each business is performing. It's updated several times a week with information including sales, profit margins, and order backlog sliced by geography and product area. If he spots a problem, Kozlowski invariably uses the phone rather than e-mail."[74]

During Kozlowski's tenure, Tyco has created a significant amount of value by acquiring companies, restructuring their assets, and then selling them in the external market for a gain. Nonetheless, in the wake of the Enron disaster, Tyco's accounting has been called into question along with many other complex firms including GE. Large unrelated diversified firms creating value by buying, restructuring, and selling other companies' assets often complete a significant number of transactions. For example, "During the past decade Tyco has acquired hundreds of humdrum businesses—an astounding 700 in the past three years alone [1999–2001]."[75] Completing large numbers of complex transactions has resulted in accounting practices that aren't as transparent as stakeholders now demand. Actions being taken in 2002 suggest that firms creating value through financial economies are responding to the demand for greater transparency in their practices. Responding in this manner will provide the transparent information the market requires to more accurately estimate the value the diversified firm is creating when using the unrelated diversification strategy.[76]

Selling underperforming divisions and placing the rest under rigorous financial controls such as those described for Tyco increases a unit's value. Rigorous controls require divisions to follow strict budgets and account regularly for cash inflows and outflows to corporate headquarters. A firm creating financial economies at least partly through rigorous controls may have to use hostile takeovers or tender offers, because target firm managers often do not find this environment attractive and are less willing to be acquired. Hostile takeovers have the potential to increase the resistance of the target firm's top-level managers.[77] In these cases, corporate-level managers often are discharged, while division managers are retained, depending on how important each is to future operational success.

Creating financial economies by acquiring and restructuring other companies' assets requires an understanding of significant trade-offs. Success usually calls for a focus on mature, low-technology businesses because of the uncertainty of demand for high-technology products. Otherwise, resource allocation decisions become too complex, creating information-processing overload on the small corporate staffs of unrelated diversified firms. Service businesses with a client orientation are also difficult to buy and sell in this way, because of their client-based sales orientation.[78]

Sales staffs of service businesses are more mobile than those of manufacturing-oriented businesses and may seek jobs with a competitor, taking clients with them.[79] This is especially so in professional service businesses such as accounting, law, advertising, consulting, and investment banking. Sears, Roebuck & Co. discovered this problem after its 1981 diversification into financial services by acquiring Coldwell Banker and Dean Witter Reynolds, Inc. The anticipated synergies in financial services did not materialize, and Sears' retail performance deteriorated. In 1992, Sears announced the divestiture of financial services and a refocusing on retail operations.[80]

Diversification: Incentives and Resources

The economic reasons given in the last section summarize conditions under which diversification strategies can increase a firm's value. Diversification, however, is also often undertaken with the expectation that it will prevent reductions in firm value. Thus, there are reasons to diversify that are value neutral. In fact, some research suggests that all diversification leads to tradeoffs and some suboptimization.[81] Nonetheless, as we explain next, several incentives may lead a firm to pursue further diversification.

Incentives to Diversify

Incentives to diversify come from both the external environment and a firm's internal environment. The term "incentive" implies that managers have choices. External incentives include antitrust regulations and tax laws. Internal incentives include low performance, uncertain future cash flows, and an overall reduction of risk for the firm. Several of the incentives are illustrated in the Strategic Focus on page 199, where we highlight actions being taken at Boeing, PepsiCo, and Procter & Gamble.

As the discussion in the Strategic Focus indicates, there are incentives for the firm to use a diversification strategy. Diversification strategies taken in light of various incentives (such as PepsiCo's need to diversify its beverage line) sometimes increase the firm's ability to create value. Currently, it seems that Boeing and PepsiCo's diversification strategies are helping those firms create value. However, when a particular diversification strategy isn't creating the expected amount of value, which was determined to be the case by P&G upper-level decision makers, the firm must take corrective action to either reduce or increase the degree to which it is diversified.

Diversification Incentives Don't Always Lead to Success

Boeing was in trouble in the late 1990s after it acquired McDonnell Douglas. Besides performance problems associated with integrating the acquisition, Boeing's dominant segment—its civil-jet business—had slowed; the commercial jet market was only expanding by 5 percent per year. In response to these issues, Boeing decided to diversify.

In 2001, Boeing felt the effects of the airline industry's performance declines. Among other actions taken, the firm made the decision to lay off at least 30,000 employees before the end of 2002. However, because of the earlier performance problems and continuing uncertainty regarding the civilian airline industry, Boeing had already diversified over several years. Accordingly, the firm expects to benefit through its strong position as a space program supplier and particularly through its military and communications supply units. Because Boeing is a large producer of AWACS and C-17s for the U.S. Air Force, Boeing could benefit from the United States decision to enhance its air power after the September 11, 2001 terrorist attacks. Boeing expects that military sales could increase 10 percent and account for as much as 75 percent of sales increases in 2002 across its various business units. The company announced that no defense-related workers would be affected by the planned lay-offs.

Instead of focusing only on building jets and rockets, Boeing had also decided to move into services. In 2001, the firm won a $4 billion order from the U.S. Air Force to upgrade avionics on existing C-130 aircraft, which rival Lockheed Martin had built. Boeing recently entered the aircraft maintenance and services market and believes that it has significant growth potential in these two areas.

Boeing also released its plans for building air-traffic management systems, which it hopes to develop with the Federal Aviation Administration when the agency overhauls the air-traffic control system. If the FAA partners with Boeing, the company believes that the market may be worth $70 billion annually. Boeing is also delving into the broadband communications market, hoping to provide airline passengers with live television and high-speed data links. In addition, the company recently opened an office in Europe to facilitate expansion of its financing company. Because of the terrorist crisis, many of the airlines have asked Boeing to refinance their current accounts, which will increase the returns from the firm's financing unit.

Some firms diversify, as did Boeing, because of unexpected poor performance. Others diversify because they expect future growth to slow. As mentioned earlier, PepsiCo, maker of Pepsi, acquired Quaker Oats in order to gain access to the increased growth associated with Gatorade in the sports drink segment. Thus, there are a number of incentives for firms to diversify beyond their successful business areas. However, not all of these efforts create value.

Procter & Gamble (P&G) has been divesting its non-core brands. In recent years, P&G diversified in an effort to boost sales, because many of its products, such as Pantene shampoo, compete in mature markets. Some of the products resulting from the diversification, such as its Olay line of cosmetics and artificial cooking fat Olestra, have failed. New CEO A. G. Lafley has decided to sell off the performing poorly brands and refocus on P&G's core, higher-profit businesses by backing the company out of the food product business and other failed undertakings.

SOURCES: S. Holmes & S. Crock, 2002, The fortunes—and misfortunes—of war, *Business Week,* January 14, 90–91; 2001, Hard man Harry, *The Economist,* June 9, 68; S. Jaffe, 2001, Do Pepsi and Gatorade mix? *Business Week Online,* http://www.businessweek.com, August 14; J. Lunsford & A. Pasztor, 2001, Boeing Co.'s course in terror's wake seen as a wider U.S. test, *The Wall Street Journal,* September 20, A1, A8; E. Nelson, 2001, P&G expects to restore growth, Will pull the plug on failed projects, *The Wall Street Journal Interactive,* http://www.wsj.com, June 18.

Antitrust Regulation and Tax Laws

Government antitrust policies and tax laws provided incentives for U.S. firms to diversify in the 1960s and 1970s.[82] Antitrust laws to mergers that created increased market power (via either vertical or horizontal integration) were stringently enforced during that period.[83] As a result, many of the mergers during that time were unrelated, involving companies pursuing different lines of business. Thus, the merger wave of the 1960s was "conglomerate" in character. Merger activity that produced conglomerate diversification was encouraged primarily by the Celler-Kefauver Act, which discouraged horizontal and vertical mergers. For example, in the 1973–1977 period, 79.1 percent of all mergers were conglomerate.[84]

During the 1980s, antitrust enforcement lessened, resulting in more and larger horizontal mergers (acquisitions of target firms in the same line of business, such as a merger between two oil companies).[85] In addition, investment bankers became more open to the kinds of mergers they tried to facilitate; as a consequence, hostile takeovers increased to unprecedented numbers.[86] The conglomerates or highly diversified firms of the 1960s and 1970s became more "focused" in the 1980s and early 1990s as merger constraints were relaxed and restructuring was implemented.[87]

In the late 1990s and early 2000s, antitrust concerns emerged again with the large volume of mergers and acquisitions (see Chapter 7).[88] Thus, mergers are now receiving more scrutiny than they did in the 1980s and through the early 1990s.

The tax effects of diversification stem not only from individual tax rates, but also from corporate tax changes. Some companies (especially mature ones) generate more cash from their operations than they can reinvest profitably. Some argue that *free cash flows* (liquid financial assets for which investments in current businesses are no longer economically viable) should be redistributed to shareholders as dividends.[89] However, in the 1960s and 1970s, dividends were taxed more heavily than ordinary personal income. As a result, before 1980, shareholders preferred that firms use free cash flows to buy and build companies in high-performance industries. If the firm's stock value appreciated over the long term, shareholders might receive a better return on those funds than if they had been redistributed as dividends, because they would be taxed more lightly under capital-gains rules than dividends when they sell their stock.

Under the 1986 Tax Reform Act, however, the top individual ordinary income tax rate was reduced from 50 to 28 percent, and the special capital-gains tax was also changed, treating capital gains as ordinary income. These changes created an incentive for shareholders to stop encouraging firms to retain funds for purposes of diversification. These tax law changes also influenced an increase in divestitures of unrelated business units after 1984. Thus, while individual tax rates for capital gains and dividends created a shareholder incentive to increase diversification before 1986, they encouraged less diversification after 1986, unless it was funded by tax-deductible debt. The elimination of personal-interest deductions, as well as the lower attractiveness of retained earnings to shareholders, might prompt the use of more leverage by firms, for which interest expense is tax deductible.

Corporate tax laws also affect diversification. Acquisitions typically increase a firm's depreciable asset allowances. Increased depreciation (a non-cash-flow expense) produces lower taxable income, thereby providing an additional incentive for acquisitions. Before 1986, acquisitions may have been the most attractive means for securing tax benefits,[90] but the 1986 Tax Reform Act diminished some of the corporate tax advantages of diversification.[91] The recent changes recommended by the Financial Accounting Standards Board (FASB) regarding the elimination of the "pooling of interests" method for accounting for the acquired firm's assets and the elimination of the write-off for research and development in process reduce some of the incentives to make acquisitions, especially related acquisitions in high technology industries (these changes are discussed further in Chapter 7).[92]

Although there was a loosening of federal regulations in the 1980s and a retightening in the late 1990s, a number of industries have experienced increased merger activity due to industry specific deregulation activity, including banking, telecommunications, oil and gas, and electric utilities, among others. For example, the electric utilities industry is deregulating throughout the developed world.[93] German utility companies such as RWE are finding deregulation challenging, in that it has produced lower electricity prices and limited profit growth. RWE, which easily raised $17 billion for acquisitions, hoped to diversify into utility markets in the United States and Europe to buffer deregulation's effects. CFO Klaus Sturany explained that the company was looking to purchase firms in the company's "core businesses: electricity, gas, water, and waste management . . . [that] fit strategically."[94] Important to RWE is whether the acquisition is in a growth market, whether the quality of management is good, and whether existing profitability is high. RWE plans to find the most growth with water companies, but is also considering unregulated companies in the electricity generation sector. Such moves will require significant learning because most utilities have traditionally operated in slow-cycle markets.[95]

Low Performance

Some research shows that low returns are related to greater levels of diversification.[96] If "high performance eliminates the need for greater diversification,"[97] as in the case of Wm. Wrigley Jr. Co., then low performance may provide an incentive for diversification. Firms plagued by poor performance often take higher risks.[98] Poor performance may lead to increased diversification as it did with Boeing described in the Strategic Focus on page 199, especially if resources exist to do so.[99] Continued poor returns following additional diversification, however, may slow its pace and even lead to divestitures. Thus, an overall curvilinear relationship, as illustrated in Figure 6.3, may exist between diversification and performance.[100]

As mentioned in the Strategic Focus, Procter & Gamble may have diversified beyond its capabilities to manage the diversification. The company has had strong historical success in its consumer soaps, including Tide and Ivory, and in toothpaste (Crest). However, its Olay cosmetics and artificial cooking fat, Olestra, have not been

---

Figure 6.3 The Curvilinear Relationship between Diversification and Performance

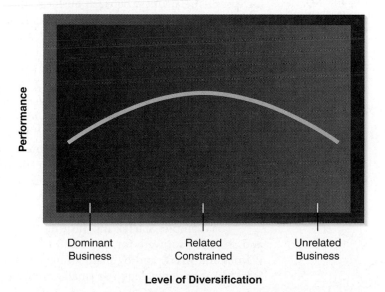

successful, resulting in the firm's recent decision to refocus on its "core" brands. P&G's refocusing may suggest that its diversification level was producing poor returns (see diversification-performance curve in Figure 6.3).

Uncertain Future Cash Flows

As a firm's product line matures or is threatened, diversification may be taken as an important defensive strategy.[101] Small firms and companies in mature or maturing industries sometimes find it necessary to diversify for long-term survival.[102] Certainly, this was one of the dominant reasons for diversification among railroad firms during the 1960s and 1970s. Railroads diversified primarily because the trucking industry was perceived to have significant negative effects for rail transportation and thus created demand uncertainty. Uncertainty, however, can be derived from supply, demand, and distribution sources. As explained earlier, PepsiCo acquired Quaker Oat to fortify its growth with Gatorade and healthy snacks. These products are projected to experience greater growth rates than Pepsi's soft drinks.

Tupperware also wanted to diversify its distribution due to uncertainty about demand for its products. Historically, Tupperware products were sold by independent sales agents sponsoring "Tupperware parties." Because more women have entered the workforce, the firm's traditional customer base—women in their homes—has eroded. Tupperware's response over the past few years has been to sell its products to new customers through different distribution channels. For example, in July 2001, the company reached an agreement with retailer Target to display Tupperware products in SuperTarget stores. To prevent problems with the traditional sales channel, Tupperware's independent sales agents staff the displays of the firm's products in SuperTarget stores. Tupperware products are also available through Target's website. Company officials estimated that 40 percent of sales would come from this and similar ventures (such as television, Internet, and mall ventures) within five years.[103] Thus, Tupperware is diversifying its distribution channels in order to reduce the uncertainty of its future cash flows.

Firm Risk Reduction

Diversified firms pursuing economies of scope often have investments that are too inflexible to realize synergy between business units. As a result, a number of problems may arise. **Synergy** exists when the value created by business units working together exceeds the value those same units create working independently. But, as a firm increases its relatedness between business units, it also increases its risk of corporate failure, because synergy produces joint interdependence between business units and the firm's flexibility to respond is constrained. This threat may force two basic decisions.

First, the firm may reduce its level of technological change by operating in more certain environments. This behavior may make the firm risk averse and thus uninterested in pursuing new product lines that have potential, but are not proven. Alternatively, the firm may constrain its level of activity sharing and forego synergy's benefits. Either or both decisions may lead to further diversification. The former would lead to related diversification into industries in which more certainty exists. The latter may produce additional, but unrelated, diversification.[104] Research suggests that a firm using a related diversification strategy is more careful in bidding for new businesses, whereas a firm pursuing an unrelated diversification strategy may be more likely to overprice its bid, because an unrelated bidder may not have full information about the acquired firm.[105]

For example, StarTek Inc. historically has generated its revenues by packaging and shipping software for Microsoft, by providing technical support to AOL Time Warner and AT&T, and by maintaining communications systems for AT&T. Because StarTek was so dependent on a small number of large customers, especially Microsoft,

Synergy exists when the value created by business units working together exceeds the value those same units create working independently.

it chose to diversify to reduce its dependence risk. In 1999, StarTek spent $12.4 million to acquire a 20 percent interest in Gifts.com, an online retailer selling gifts, home furnishings, and other merchandise. Reader's Digest Association Inc. also has an ownership position in Gifts.com, a firm that continues to lose money. If this doesn't soon change, StarTek could lose its investment in the venture. StarTek also invested in a mortgage-financing firm that has since been accused of defrauding investors, forcing StarTek to take a $3 million charge in 2001. Moreover, these problems were coming at a time when sales of software that StarTek handles for Microsoft, its biggest customer, were declining.[106] As the StarTek example shows, firms seeking to reduce risk by diversifying should fully understand the nature of the businesses they are entering through their diversification efforts.

Resources and Diversification

Although a firm may have incentives to diversify, it must also possess the resources required to create value through diversification.[107] As mentioned earlier, tangible, intangible, and financial resources all facilitate diversification. Resources vary in their utility for value creation, however, because of differences in rarity and mobility—that is, some resources are easier for competitors to duplicate because they are not rare, valuable, costly to imitate, and nonsubstitutable (see Chapter 3). For instance, free cash flows are a financial resource that may be used to diversify the firm. Because financial resources are more flexible and common, they are less likely to create value compared with other types of resources and less likely to be a source of competitive advantage.[108]

However, as a financial resource, cash can be used to invest in other resources that can lead to more valuable and less imitable advantages. For example, Microsoft had $30 billion in cash reserves in 2001, generated largely by its Windows and Office monopolies. Its cash reserves were growing by $1 billion every month.[109] With this much cash in reserve (more, by far, than any other company), Microsoft is able to invest heavily in R&D, to gradually build a market presence with products such as Xbox, Microsoft's video game machine, and to make diversifying acquisitions of other companies and new business ventures. This level of cash creates significant flexibility, allowing Microsoft to invest in R&D so that it has the support required for it to possibly become a competitive advantage. But, as this example suggests, excess cash can be the conduit the firm needs to create more sustainable advantages.[110]

Tangible resources usually include the plant and equipment necessary to produce a product and tend to be less flexible assets: Any excess capacity often can be used only for closely related products, especially those requiring highly similar manufacturing technologies. Excess capacity of other tangible resources, such as a sales force, can be used to diversify more easily. Again, excess capacity in a sales force is more effective with related diversification, because it may be utilized to sell similar products. The sales force would be more knowledgeable about related-product characteristics, customers, and distribution channels.[111] Tangible resources may create resource interrelationships in production, marketing, procurement, and technology, defined earlier as activity sharing. Intangible resources are more flexible than tangible physical assets in facilitating diversification. Although the sharing of tangible resources may induce diversification, intangible resources such as tacit knowledge could encourage even more diversification.[112]

Managerial Motives to Diversify

Managerial motives for diversification may exist independently of incentives and resources and include managerial risk reduction and a desire for increased compensation.[113] For instance, diversification may reduce top-level managers' employment risk (the risk of job loss or income reduction). That is, corporate executives may diversify a firm in order to diversify their own employment risk, as long as profitability does not suffer excessively.[114]

Diversification also provides an additional benefit to managers that shareholders do not enjoy. Diversification and firm size are highly correlated, and as size increases, so does executive compensation.[115] Large firms are more complex and difficult to manage; thus managers of larger firms usually receive more compensation.[116] Higher compensation may serve as a motive for managers to engage in greater diversification. Governance mechanisms, such as the board of directors, monitoring by owners, executive compensation, and the market for corporate control, may limit managerial tendencies to overdiversify. These mechanisms are discussed in more detail in Chapter 10.

On the other hand, governance mechanisms may not be strong, and in some instances managers may diversify the firm to the point that it fails to earn even average returns.[117] The loss of adequate internal governance may result in poor relative performance, thereby triggering a threat of takeover. Although takeovers may improve efficiency by replacing ineffective managerial teams, managers may avoid takeovers through defensive tactics, such as "poison pills," or may reduce their own exposure to them with "golden parachute" agreements. Therefore, an external governance threat, although restraining managers, does not flawlessly control managerial motives for diversification.[118]

Most large publicly held firms are profitable because managers are positive stewards of firm resources and many of their strategic actions (e.g., diversification strategies) contribute to the firm's success. As mentioned, governance devices should be designed to deal with exceptions to the norms of achieving strategic competitiveness and increasing shareholder wealth. Thus, it is overly pessimistic to assume that managers usually act in their own self-interest as opposed to their firm's interest.[119]

Managers may also be held in check by concerns for their reputation. If positive reputation facilitates power, a poor reputation may reduce it. Likewise, a strong external market for managerial talent may deter managers from pursuing inappropriate diversification.[120] In addition, a diversified firm may police other diversified firms to acquire those poorly managed firms in order to restructure its own asset base. Knowing that their firms could be acquired if they are not managed successfully encourages managers to use value-creating strategies.

Even when governance mechanisms cause managers to correct a problem of poorly implemented diversification or overdiversification, these moves are not without trade-offs. For instance, firms that are spun off may not realize productivity gains, even though spinning them off is in the best interest of the divesting firm.[121] Accordingly, the assumption that managers need disciplining may not be entirely correct, and sometimes governance may create consequences that are worse than those resulting from overdiversification. Governance that is excessive may cause a firm's managers to be overly cautious and risk averse.[122]

As shown in Figure 6.4, the level of diversification that can be expected to have the greatest positive effect on performance is based partly on how the interaction of resources, managerial motives, and incentives affects the adoption of particular diversification strategies. As indicated earlier, the greater the incentives and the more flexible the resources, the higher is the level of expected diversification. Financial resources (the most flexible) should have a stronger relationship to the extent of diversification than either tangible or intangible resources. Tangible resources (the most inflexible) are useful primarily for related diversification.

As discussed in this chapter, firms can create more value by effectively using diversification strategies. However, diversification must be kept in check by corporate governance (see Chapter 10). Appropriate strategy implementation tools, such as

Figure 6.4

Summary Model of the Relationship between Firm Performance and Diversification

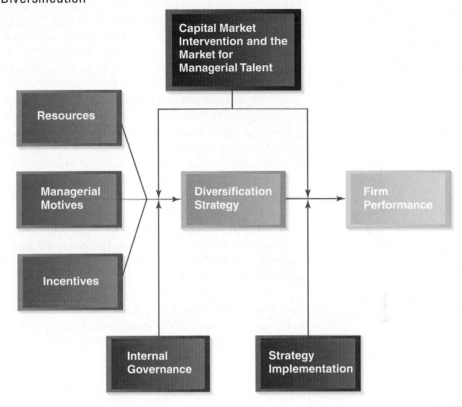

SOURCE: R. E. Hoskisson & M. A. Hitt, 1990, Antecedents and performance outcomes of diversification: A review and critique of theoretical perspectives, *Journal of Management*, 16: 498.

organizational structures, are also important (see Chapter 11), as shown by the experiences of a number of Internet-based firms.

CMGI Inc. is a diversified Internet company incubator that "bought up Internet businesses willy-nilly during the delirious days of hyperinflated dot.com stock prices, but has since failed to figure out a way to make its many companies work together for profits."[123] When this happens, the firm's board of directors must act decisively, in that the board of directors is largely responsible for making certain that its firm's top-level managers are making decisions that have a high probability of leading to competitive success and that are in shareholders' best interests. Unfortunately, because their boards tend to be fairly weak in terms of their composition, this isn't likely to happen in a fairly large number of new Internet-based ventures, especially those in which the CEO is also the firm's founder. In slightly different words, a weak board of directors working with strong top-level managers may result in decisions that aren't in shareholders best interests.[124] This might be the case at Internet Capital Group. An SEC investigation of this firm found that while many retail investors were still buying shares in the firm, managers and inside board members were selling their shares. Thus, top-level managers and board members may have benefited from information that was available to them but not to outside investors.[125]

We have described corporate-level strategies in this chapter. In the next one, we discuss the use of mergers and acquisitions as a prominent means of firms to diversify. These trends toward more diversification through acquisitions, which have been partially reversed due to restructuring (see Chapter 7), indicate that learning has taken place regarding corporate-level diversification strategies.[126] Firms performing well in their dominant business may not want to diversify, as shown by the effect of the U.S. economy in 2001 and 2002. Moreover, firms that diversify should do so cautiously, choosing to focus on a relatively few, rather than many, businesses.[127] In fact, research suggests that although unrelated diversification has decreased, related diversification has increased, possibly due to the restructuring that continued into the 1990s and early 21st century.[128]

Both in some emerging economies as well as in many industrialized countries, such as Germany, Italy and France, diversification has become the norm for the most successful firms. Subsequently, though, many of these diversified firms began to restructure. This sequence of diversification followed by restructuring mirrors actions of firms in the United States and the United Kingdom.[129]

In Europe, for example, many of the largest conglomerates are restructuring as a result of two elements' effects. First, deregulation across Europe is creating more competition, and the emergence of the European Union is causing firms to pursue pan-European strategies. Second, the realities of global competition are becoming prominent in Europe, resulting in corporate restructurings, and firms in several industries sectors are responding by restructuring to encourage long-term growth in both sales revenue and profitability.

As in the United States, these firms are finding that strategic competitiveness can be increased when they pursue a level of diversification that is appropriate for their resources (especially financial resources) and core competencies and the opportunities and threats in their external environment.[130]

Summary

- Using a single- or dominant-business corporate-level strategy may be preferable to seeking a more diversified strategy, unless a corporation can develop economies of scope or financial economies between businesses, or unless it can obtain market power through additional levels of diversification. These economies and market power are the main sources of value creation when the firm diversifies.

- Related diversification creates value through the sharing of activities or the transfer of core competencies.

- Sharing activities usually involves sharing tangible resources between businesses. Transferring core competencies involves transferring core competencies developed in one business to another one. It also may involve transferring competencies between the corporate office and a business unit.

- Sharing activities is usually associated with the related constrained diversification corporate-level strategy. Activity sharing is costly to implement and coordinate, may create unequal benefits for the divisions involved in the sharing, and may lead to fewer managerial risk-taking behaviors.

- Transferring core competencies is often associated with related linked (or mixed related and unrelated) diversification, although firms pursuing both sharing activities and transferring core competencies can use it.

- Efficiently allocating resources or restructuring a target firm's assets and placing them under rigorous financial controls are two ways to accomplish successful unrelated diversification. These methods focus on obtaining financial economies.

- The primary reason a firm diversifies is to create more value. However, diversification is sometimes pursued because of incentives from tax and anti-trust government policies, performance disappointments, uncertainties about future cash flow, or to reduce risk.

- Managerial motives to diversify (including to increase compensation) can lead to overdiversification and a reduction in the firm's value-creating ability. On the other hand, managers can also be good stewards of the firm's assets.

- Managers need to pay attention to their firm's internal environment and its external environment when making decisions about the optimum level of diversification for their company. Of course, internal resources are important determinants of the direction that diversification should take. However, conditions in the firm's external environment may facilitate additional levels of diversification as might unexpected threats from competitors.

Review Questions

1. What is corporate-level strategy? Why is it important to the diversified firm?

2. What are the advantages and disadvantages of single- and dominant-business strategies, compared with those of firms with higher levels of diversification?

3. What are three reasons that firms choose to become more diversified by moving away from either a single- or a dominant-business corporate-level strategy?

4. How do firms share activities or transfer core competencies to obtain economies of scope when using a related diversification strategy?

5. What are the two ways to obtain financial economies when using an unrelated diversification strategy?

6. What incentives and resources encourage diversification?

7. What motives might encourage managers to diversify the firm beyond an appropriate level?

Experiential Exercise

Diversification

As a member of the strategic management team for a very successful sporting goods firm that specializes in the manufacturing and marketing of soccer equipment, you have been asked to provide your thoughts as to whether the firm should diversify and to what extent.

Part One. List the advantages and disadvantages of diversification in the following table.

Part Two. Provide examples of related and unrelated diversification areas that you feel might be appropriate for the firm, including some specific advantages and disadvantages that the firm might find for each.

Advantages	Disadvantages

Notes

1. M. E. Porter, 1980, *Competitive Strategy*, New York: The Free Press, xvi.
2. R. E. Hoskisson, R. A. Johnson, D. Yiu, & W. P. Wan, 2001, Restructuring strategies of diversified business groups: Differences associated with country institutional environments. In M. A. Hitt, R. E. Freeman, J. S. Harrison (eds.), *Handbook of Strategic Management*, Oxford, U.K.: Blackwell Publishers, 433–463; Y. Luo, 2001, Determinants of entry in an emerging economy: A multilevel approach, *Journal of Management Studies*, 38: 443–472; T. B. Palmer & R. M. Wiseman, 1999, Decoupling risk taking from income stream uncertainty: A holistic model of risk, *Strategic Management Journal*, 20: 1037–1062.
3. E. H. Bowman & C. E. Helfat, 2001, Does corporate strategy matter? *Strategic Management Journal*, 22: 1–23; M. A. Hitt, R. E. Hoskisson, & H. Kim, 1997, International diversification: Effects on innovation and firm performance in product-diversified firms, *Academy of Management Journal*, 40: 767–798.
4. R. L. Simerly & M. Li, 2000, Environmental dynamism, capital structure and performance: A theoretical integration and an empirical test, *Strategic Management Journal*, 21: 31–49; D. D. Bergh & M. W. Lawless, 1998, Portfolio restructuring and limits to hierarchical governance: The effects of environmental uncertainty and diversification strategy, *Organization Science*, 9: 87–102.
5. M. E. Porter, 1987, From competitive advantage to corporate strategy, *Harvard Business Review*, 65(3): 43–59.
6. Porter, From competitive advantage to corporate strategy; C. A. Montgomery, 1994, Corporate diversification, *Journal of Economic Perspectives*, 8: 163–178.
7. G. H. Stonehouse, J. D. Pemberton, & C. E. Barber, 2001, The role of knowledge facilitators and inhibitors: Lessons from airline reservations systems, *Long Range Planning*, 34(2): 115–138; B. Wysocki, Jr., 1999, Corporate America confronts the meaning of a "core" business, *The Wall Street Journal*, November 9, A1, A4.
8. C. Meyer, 2001, The second generation of speed, *Harvard Business Review*, 79(4): 24–25.
9. M. Kwak, 2002, Maximizing value through diversification, *MIT Sloan Management Review*, 43(2): 10; R. A. Burgelman & Y. L. Doz, 2001, The power of strategic integration, *MIT Sloan Management Review*, 42(3): 28–38; C. C. Markides, 1997, To diversify or not to diversify, *Harvard Business Review*, 75(6): 93–99.
10. P. Wright, M. Kroll, A. Lado, & B. Van Ness, 2002, The structure of ownership and corporate acquisition strategies, *Strategic Management Journal*, 23: 41–53; C. C. Markides & P. J. Williamson, 1996, Corporate diversification and organizational structure: A resource-based view, *Academy of Management Journal*, 39: 340–367.
11. A. Campbell, M. Goold, & M. Alexander, 1995, Corporate strategy: The question for parenting advantage, *Harvard Business Review*, 73(2): 120–132.
12. T. H. Brush, P. Bromiley, & M. Hendrickx, 1999, The relative influence of industry and corporate on business segment performance: An alternative estimate, *Strategic Management Journal*, 20: 519–547; T. H. Brush & P. Bromiley, 1997, What does a small corporate effect mean? A variance components simulation of corporate and business effects, *Strategic Management Journal*, 18: 825–835.
13. J. B. Barney, 2002, *Gaining and Sustaining Competitive Advantage*, 2nd ed., Upper Saddle River, NJ.: Prentice-Hall.
14. D. D. Bergh, 2001, Diversification strategy research at a crossroads: Established, emerging and anticipated paths. In M. A. Hitt, R. E. Freeman, & J. S. Harrison (eds.), *Handbook of Strategic Management*, Oxford, UK: Blackwell Publishers, 363.
15. C. Kim, S. Kim, & C. Pantzalis, 2001, Firm diversification and earnings volatility: An empirical analysis of U.S.-based MNCs, *American Business Review*, 19(1): 26–38; W. Lewellen, 1971, A pure financial rationale for the conglomerate merger, *Journal of Finance*, 26: 521–537.
16. J. D. Fisher & Y. Liang, 2000, Is sector diversification more important than regional diversification? *Real Estate Finance*, 17(3): 35–40.
17. H. von Kranenburg, M. Cloodt, & J. Hagedoorn, 2001, An exploratory story of recent trends in the diversification of Dutch publishing companies in the multimedia and information industries, *International Studies of Management & Organization*, 31(10): 64–86.
18. B. S. Silverman, 1999, Technological resources and the direction of corporate diversification: Toward an integration of the resource-based view and transaction cost economics, *Administrative Science Quarterly*, 45: 1109–1124; D. Collis & C. A. Montgomery, 1995, Competing on resources: Strategy in the 1990s, *Harvard Business Review*, 73(4): 118–128; M. A. Peteraf, 1993, The cornerstones of competitive advantage: A resource-based view, *Strategic Management Journal*, 14: 179–191.
19. Bergh, Diversification strategy research at a crossroads, 369.
20. N. Deogun, G. McWilliams, & M. Williams, 2001, Hewlett-Packard nears pact to buy Compaq for 26 Billion in Stock, *The Wall Street Journal*, September 4, A1, A6.
21. R. P. Rumelt, *Strategy, Structure, and Economic Performance*, Boston: Harvard Business School, 1974; L. Wrigley, 1970, *Divisional autonomy and diversification* (Ph.D. dissertation), Harvard Business School.
22. W. Heuslein, 2001, Wm. Wrigley Jr. Co.: Getting unstuck, *Forbes*, January 8, 138–139.

23. T. Mason, 2001, Can gum and dental care mix? *Marketing*, August 23, 21.

24. S. Killman, 2001, Smithfield foods CEO welcomes backlash over its hog farms, *The Wall Street Journal*, August 21, B4; J. Forster, 2001, Who's afraid of a little mud? *Business Week*, May 21, 112–113.

25. M. Ihlwan, P. Engardio, I. Kunii, & R. Crockett, 1999, Samsung: How a Korean electronics giant came out of the crisis stronger than ever, *Business Week Online*, http://www.businessweek.com, December 20.

26. L. A. Keister, 2000, *Chinese Business Groups: The Structure and Impact of Inter-Firm Relations During Economic Development*, New York: Oxford University Press; T. Khanna & K. Palepu, 1997, Why focused strategies may be wrong for emerging markets, *Harvard Business Review*, 75(4): 41–50.

27. C. Chung, 2001, Markets, culture and institutions: The emergence of large business groups in Taiwan, 1950s–1970s, *Journal of Management Studies*, 38: 719–745.

28. S. Manikutty, 2000, Family business groups in India: A resource-based view of the emerging trends, *Family Business Review*, 13: 279–292.

29. 1997, Inside story, *The Economist*, December 6, 7–9.

30. K. Dewenter, W. Novaes, & R. H. Pettway, 2001, Visibility versus complexity in business groups: Evidence from Japanese keiretsus, *Journal of Business*, 74: 79–100.

31. M. Farjoun, 1998, The independent and joint effects of the skill and physical bases of relatedness in diversification, *Strategic Management Journal*, 19: 611–630.

32. R. E. Hoskisson & L.W. Busenitz, 2002, Market uncertainty and learning distance in corporate entrepreneurship entry mode choice. In M. A. Hitt, R. D. Ireland, S. M. Camp, & D. L. Sexton (eds.), *Strategic Entrepreneurship: Creating a New Mindset*, Oxford, U.K.: Blackwell Publishers, 150–172; R. Morck & B. Yeung, 1999, When synergy creates real value, Mastering Strategy (Part 7), *Financial Times*, November 8, 6–7.

33. B. Garette & P. Dussauge, 2000, Alliances versus acquisitions: Choosing the right option, *European Management Journal*, 18(1): 63–69; L. Capron, 1999, The long term performance of horizontal acquisitions, *Strategic Management Journal*, 20: 987–1018.

34. M. E. Porter, 1985, *Competitive Advantage*, New York: The Free Press, 328.

35. S. Jaffe, 2001, Do Pepsi and Gatorade mix? *Business Week Online*, http://www.businessweek.com, August 14.

36. M. L. Marks & P. H. Mirvis, 2000, Managing mergers, acquisitions, and alliances: Creating an effective transition structure, *Organizational Dynamics*, 28(3): 35–47.

37. G. Delong, 2001, Stockholder gains from focusing versus diversifying bank mergers, *Journal of Financial Economics*, 2: 221–252; T. H. Brush, 1996, Predicted change in operational synergy and post-acquisition performance of acquired businesses, *Strategic Management Journal*, 17: 1–24; H. Zhang, 1995, Wealth effects of U.S. bank takeovers, *Applied Financial Economics*, 5: 329–336.

38. D. D. Bergh, 1995, Size and relatedness of units sold: An agency theory and resource-based perspective, *Strategic Management Journal*, 16: 221–239.

39. M. Lubatkin & S. Chatterjee, 1994, Extending modern portfolio theory into the domain of corporate diversification: Does it apply? *Academy of Management Journal*, 37: 109–136.

40. A. Van Oijen, 2001, Product diversification, corporate management instruments, resource sharing, and performance, *Academy of Management Best Paper Proceedings* (on CD-ROM Business Policy and Strategy Division); T. Kono, 1999, A strong head office makes a strong company, *Long Range Planning*, 32(2): 225.

41. M. Y. Brannen, J. K. Liker, & W. M. Fruin, 1999, Recontextualization and factory-to-factory knowledge transfer from Japan to the US: The Case of NSK, In J. K. Liker, W. M. Fruin, & P. Adler (eds.) *Remade in America: Transplanting and Transforming Japanese Systems*, New York: Oxford University Press, 117–153; L. Capron, P. Dussauge, & W. Mitchell, 1998, Resource redeployment following horizontal acquisitions in Europe and the United States, 1988–1992, *Strategic Management Journal*, 19: 631–61; A. Mehra, 1996, Resource and market based determinants of performance in the U.S. banking industry, *Strategic Management Journal*, 17: 307–322; S. Chatterjee & B. Wernerfelt, 1991, The link between resources and type of diversification: Theory and evidence, *Strategic Management Journal*, 12: 33–48.

42. B. Horovitz, 2001, McDonald's tries a new recipe to revive sales, *USA Today*, July 10, 1–2.

43. M. Maremont, 2000, For plastic hangers, you almost need to go to Tyco International, *The Wall Street Journal*, February 15, A1, A10; R. Whittington, 1999, In praise of the evergreen conglomerate, Mastering Strategy (Part 6), *Financial Times*, November 1, 4–6; W. Ruigrok, A. Pettigrew, S. Peck, & R. Whittington, 1999, Corporate restructuring and new forms of organizing: Evidence from Europe, *Management International Review*, 39(Special Issue): 41–64.

44. C. St. John & J. S. Harrison, 1999, Manufacturing-based relatedness, synergy, and coordination, *Strategic Management Journal*, 20: 129–145.

45. W. G. Shepherd, 1986, On the core concepts of industrial economics, in H. W. deJong & W. G. Shepherd (eds.), *Mainstreams in Industrial Organization*, Boston: Kluwer Publications.

46. D. Genesove & W. P. Mullin, 2001. Rules, communication, and collusion: Narrative evidence from the Sugar Institute Case, *American Economic Review*, 91: 379–398; J. Gimeno & C. Y. Woo, 1999, Multimarket contact, economies of scope, and firm performance, *Academy of Management Journal*, 42: 239–259.

47. S. Lohr & S. Gaither, 2002, Hewlett Packard declares victory on the merger, *The New York Times*, http://www.nytimes.com, March 20; N. Deogun, G. McWilliams, & M. Williams, 2001 Hewlett-Packard nears pact to buy Compaq for $26 billion in stock, *The Wall Street Journal*, September 4: A1, A6.

48. A. Karnani & B. Wernerfelt, 1985, Multipoint competition, *Strategic Management Journal*, 6: 87–96.

49. H. A. Haveman & L. Nonnemaker, 2000, Competition in multiple geographic markets: The impact on growth and market entry, *Administrative Science Quarterly*, 45: 232–267.

50. Genesove & Mullin, Rules, communication, and collusion.

51. O. E. Williamson, 1996, Economics and organization: A primer, *California Management Review*, 38(2): 131–146.

52. S. Killman, 2001, Smithfield foods CEO welcomes backlash over its hog farms, *The Wall Street Journal*, August 21, B4.

53. K. R. Harrigan, 2001, Strategic flexibility in the old and new economies. In M. A. Hitt, R. E. Freeman, & J. S. Harrison (eds.) *Handbook of Strategic Management*, Oxford, U.K.: Blackwell Publishers, 97–123.

54. R. E. Kranton, & D. F. Minehart, 2001, Networks versus vertical integration, *The Rand Journal of Economics*, 3: 570–601.

55. P. Kothandaraman & D. T. Wilson, 2001, The future of competition: Value-creating networks, *Industrial Marketing Management*, 30: 379–389.

56. D. Stapleton, P. Gentles, J. Ross, & K. Shubert, 2001, The location-centric shift from marketplace to marketspace: Transaction cost-inspired propositions of virtual integration via an e-commerce model, *Advances in Competitiveness Research*, 9: 10–41.

57. K. M. Eisenhardt & D. C. Galunic, 2000, Coevolving: At last, a way to make synergies work, *Harvard Business Review*, 78(1): 91–111.

58. R. Schoenberg, 2001, Knowledge transfer and resource sharing as value creation mechanisms in inbound continental European acquisitions, *Journal of Euro-Marketing*, 10: 99–114.

59. M. Peers, 2001, USA Networks agrees to acquire control of Expedia from Microsoft, *The Wall Street Journal Interactive*, http://www.wsj.com, July 16.

60. Eisenhardt & Galunic, Coevolving, 94.

61. M. Freeman, 2002, Forging a model for profitability, *Electronic Media*, January 28, 1, 13.

62. Bergh, Predicting divestiture of unrelated acquisitions; C. W. L. Hill, 1994, Diversification and economic performance. Bringing structure and corporate management back into the picture, in R. P. Rumelt, D. E. Schendel, & D. J. Teece (eds.), *Fundamental Issues in Strategy*, Boston: Harvard Business School Press, 297–321.

63. O. E. Williamson, 1975, *Markets and Hierarchies: Analysis and Antitrust Implications*, New York: Macmillan Free Press.

64. M. T. Billet & D. Mauer, 2001, Diversification and the value of internal capital markets: The case of tracking stock, *Journal of Banking & Finance*, 9: 1457–1490.

65. R. Kochhar & M. A. Hitt, 1998, Linking corporate strategy to capital structure: Diversification strategy, type, and source of financing, *Strategic Management Journal*, 19: 601–610.

66. Ibid.; P. Taylor & J. Lowe, 1995, A note on corporate strategy and capital structure, *Strategic Management Journal*, 16: 411–414.

67. M. Kwak, 2001, Spinoffs lead to better financing decisions, *MIT Sloan Management Review*, 42(4): 10; O. A. Lamont & C. Polk, 2001, The diversification discount: Cash flows versus returns, *Journal of Finance*, 56: 1693–1721; R. Rajan, H. Servaes, & L. Zingales, 2001, The cost of diversity: The diversification discount and inefficient investment, *Journal of Finance*, 55: 35–79.

68. 2001, Spoilt for choice, *The Economist*, http://www.economist.com, July 5.

69. D. J. Denis, D. K. Denis, & A. Sarin, 1999, Agency theory and the reference of equity ownership structure on corporate diversification strategies, *Strategic Management Journal*, 20: 1071–1076; R. Amit & J. Livnat, 1988, A concept of conglomerate diversification, *Journal of Management*, 14: 593–604.

70. Whittington, In praise of the evergreen conglomerate, 4.

71. T. Khanna & J. W. Rivkin, 2001. Estimating the performance effects of business groups in emerging markets, *Strategic Management Journal*, 22: 45–74.

72. T. Khanna & K. Palepu, 2000, Is group affiliation profitable in emerging markets? An analysis of diversified Indian business groups, *Journal of Finance*, 55: 867–892; T. Khanna & K. Palepu, 2000, The future of business groups in emerging markets: Long-run evidence from Chile, *Academy of Management Journal*, 43: 268–285.

73. R. E. Hoskisson, R. A. Johnson, D. Yiu, & W. P. Wan, 2001. Restructuring strategies and diversified business groups: Differences associated with country institutional environments. In M. A. Hitt, R. E. Freeman & J. S. Harrison (eds.), *Handbook of Strategic Management*, Oxford, UK: Blackwell Publishers, 433–463; S. J. Chang & H. Singh, 1999, The impact of entry and resource fit on modes of exit by multibusiness firms, *Strategic Management Journal*, 20: 1019–1035.

74. W. C. Symonds & P. L. Moore, 2001, The most aggressive CEO, *Business Week*, May 28: 68–77.

75. H. Greenberg, 2002, Does Tyco play accounting games? *Fortune*, April 1, 83–86.

76. Ibid.

77. J. S. Harrison, H. M. O'Neill, & R. E. Hoskisson, 2000, Acquisition strategy and target resistance: A theory of countervailing effects of pre-merger bidding and post-merger integration. In C. Cooper & A. Gregory (eds.) *Advances in Mergers and Acquisitions*, Vol. 1, Greenwich, CT: JAI/Elsevier, Inc, 157–182.

78. T. A. Doucet & R. M. Barefield, 1999, Client base valuation: The case of a professional service firm, *Journal of Business Research*, 44: 127–133.

79. S. Nambisan, 2001, Why service businesses are not product businesses, *MIT Sloan Management Review*, 42(4): 72–80.

80. S. L. Gillan, J. W. Kensinger, & J. D. Martin, 2000, Value creation and corporate diversification: The case of Sears, Roebuck & Co., *Journal of Financial Economics*, 55: 103–137.

81. E. Stickel, 2001, Uncertainty reduction in a competitive environment, *Journal of Business Research*, 51: 169–177; S. Chatterjee & J. Singh, 1999, Are tradeoffs inherent in diversification moves? A simultaneous model for type of diversification and mode of expansion decisions, *Management Science*, 45: 25–41.

82. M. Lubatkin, H. Merchant, & M. Srinivasan, 1997, Merger strategies and shareholder value during times of relaxed antitrust enforcement: The case of large mergers during the 1980s, *Journal of Management*, 23: 61–81.

83. D. P. Champlin & J. T. Knoedler, 1999, Restructuring by design? Government's complicity in corporate restructuring, *Journal of Economic Issues*, 33(1): 41–57.

84. R. M. Scherer & D. Ross, 1990, *Industrial Market Structure and Economic Performance*, Boston: Houghton Mifflin.

85. A. Shleifer & R. W. Vishny, 1994, Takeovers in the 1960s and 1980s: Evidence and implications, in R. P. Rumelt, D. E. Schendel, & D. J. Teece (eds.), *Fundamental Issues in Strategy*, Boston: Harvard Business School Press, 403–422.

86. Lubatkin, Merchant, & Srinivasan, Merger strategies and shareholder value; D. J. Ravenscraft & R. M. Scherer, 1987, *Mergers, Sell-Offs and Economic Efficiency*, Washington, DC: Brookings Institution, 22.

87. D. A. Zalewski, 2001, Corporate takeovers, fairness, and public policy, *Journal of Economic Issues*, 35: 431–437; P. L. Zweig, J. P. Kline, S. A. Forest, & K. Gudridge, 1995, The case against mergers, *Business Week*, October 30, 122–130; J. R. Williams, B. L. Paez, & L. Sanders, 1988, Conglomerates revisited, *Strategic Management Journal*, 9: 403–414.

88. E. J. Lopez, 2001, New anti-merger theories: A critique, *Cato Journal*, 20: 359–378; 1998, The trustbusters' new tools, *The Economist*, May 2, 62–64.

89. M. C. Jensen, 1986, Agency costs of free cash flow, corporate finance, and takeovers, *American Economic Review*, 76: 323–329.

90. R. Gilson, M. Scholes, & M. Wolfson, 1988, Taxation and the dynamics of corporate control: The uncertain case for tax motivated acquisitions, in J. C. Coffee, L. Lowenstein, & S. Rose-Ackerman (eds.), *Knights, Raiders, and Targets: The Impact of the Hostile Takeover*, New York: Oxford University Press, 271–299.

91. C. Steindel, 1986, Tax reform and the merger and acquisition market: The repeal of the general utilities, *Federal Reserve Bank of New York Quarterly Review*, 11(3): 31–35.

92. M. A. Hitt, J. S. Harrison, & R. D. Ireland, 2001, *Mergers and Acquisitions: A Guide to Creating Value for Stakeholders*, New York: Oxford University Press.

93. R. F. Hirsh, 2000, *Power Loss: The Origins of Deregulation and Restructuring in the American Electric Power Industry*, Cambridge: MIT Press.

94. J. Ewing, 2001, Guten tag, America, *Business Week Online*, http://www.businessweek.com, July 27.

95. A. Lomi & E. Larsen, 2000, Strategic implications of deregulation and competition in the electricity industry *European Management Journal*, 17(2): 151–163.

96. Y. Chang & H. Thomas, 1989, The impact of diversification strategy on risk-return performance, *Strategic Management Journal*, 10: 271–284; R. M. Grant, A. P. Jammine, & H. Thomas, 1988, Diversity, diversification, and profitability among British manufacturing companies, 1972–1984, *Academy of Management Journal*, 31: 771–801.

97. Rumelt, *Strategy, Structure and Economic Performance*, 125.

98. M. N. Nickel & M. C. Rodriguez, 2002, A review of research on the negative accounting relationship between risk and return: Bowman's paradox, *Omega*, 30(1): 1–18; R. M. Wiseman & L. R. Gomez-Mejia, 1998, A behavioral agency model of managerial risk taking, *Academy of Management Review*, 23: 133–153; E. H. Bowman, 1982, Risk seeking by troubled firms, *Sloan Management Review*, 23: 33–42.

99. J. G. Matsusaka, 2001, Corporate diversification, value maximization, and organizational capabilities, *Journal of Business*, 74: 409–432.

100. L. E. Palich, L. B. Cardinal, & C. C. Miller, 2000, Curvilinearity in the diversification-performance linkage: An examination of over three decades of research, *Strategic Management Journal*, 21: 155–174.

101. Simerly & Li, Environmental dynamism, capital structure and performance.

102. J. C. Sandvig & L. Coakley, 1998, Best practices in small firm diversification, *Business Horizons*, 41(3): 33–40; C. G. Smith & A. C. Cooper, 1988, Established companies diversifying into young industries: A comparison of firms with different levels of performance, *Strategic Management Journal*, 9: 111–121.

103. S. Day, 2001, Tupperware to sell products in SuperTarget stores, *The New York Times*, http://www.nytimes.com, July 18.

104. N. M. Kay & A. Diamantopoulos, 1987, Uncertainty and synergy: Towards a formal model of corporate strategy, *Managerial and Decision Economics*, 8: 121–130.

105. R. W. Coff, 1999, How buyers cope with uncertainty when acquiring firms in knowledge-intensive industries: Caveat emptor, *Organization Science*, 10: 144–161.

106. M. Selz, 2001, StarTek expands beyond core services as falling demand halts financial growth, *The Wall Street Journal Interactive*, http://www.wsj.com, June 26.

107. Chatterjee & Singh, Are tradeoffs inherent in diversification moves?; S. J. Chatterjee & B. Wernerfelt, 1991, The link between resources and type of diversification: Theory and evidence, *Strategic Management Journal*, 12: 33–48.

108. Kochhar & Hitt, Linking corporate strategy to capital structure.

109. J. Greene, 2001, Microsoft: How it became stronger than ever, *Business Week*, June 4, 75–85.

110. K. Haanes & O. Fjeldstad, 2000, Linking intangible resources and competition, *European Management Journal*, 18(1): 52–62.

111. L. Capron & J. Hulland, 1999, Redeployment of brands, sales forces, and general marketing management expertise following horizontal acquisitions: A resource-based view, *Journal of Marketing*, 63(2): 41–54.

112. R. D. Smith, 2000, Intangible strategic assets and firm performance: A multi-industry study of the resource-based view, *Journal of Business Strategies*, 17(2): 91–117.

113. M. A. Geletkanycz, B. K. Boyd, & S. Finklestein, 2001, The strategic value of CEO external directorate networks: Implications for CEO compensation, *Strategic Management Journal*, 9: 889–898; W. Grossman & R. E. Hoskisson, 1998, CEO pay at the crossroads of Wall Street and Main: Toward the strategic design of executive compensation, *Academy of Management Executive*, 12(1): 43–57; S. Finkelstein & D. C. Hambrick, 1996, *Strategic Leadership: Top Executives and Their Effects on Organizations*, St. Paul, MN: West Publishing Company.

114. P. J. Lane, A. A. Cannella, Jr., & M. H. Lubatkin, 1998, Agency problems as antecedents to unrelated mergers and diversification: Amihud and Lev reconsidered, *Strategic Management Journal*, 19: 555–578; D. L. May, 1995, Do managerial motives influence firm risk reduction strategies? *Journal of Finance*, 50: 1291–1308; Y. Amihud and B. Lev, 1981, Risk reduction as a managerial motive for conglomerate mergers, *Bell Journal of Economics*, 12: 605–617.

115. S. R. Gray & A. A. Cannella, Jr., 1997, The role of risk in executive compensation, *Journal of Management*, 23: 517–540; H. Tosi & L. Gomez-Mejia, 1989, The decoupling of CEO pay and performance: An agency theory perspective, *Administrative Science Quarterly*, 34: 169–189.

116. R. Bliss & R. Rosen, 2001, CEO compensation and bank mergers, *Journal of Financial Economics*, 1:107–138; S. Finkelstein & R. A. D'Aveni, 1994, CEO duality as a double-

edged sword: How boards of directors balance entrenchment avoidance and unity of command, *Academy of Management Journal*, 37: 1070–1108.

117. J. W. Lorsch, A. S. Zelleke, & K. Pick, 2001, Unbalanced boards, *Harvard Business Review*, 79(2): 28–30; R. E. Hoskisson & T. Turk, 1990, Corporate restructuring: Governance and control limits of the internal market, *Academy of Management Review*, 15: 459–477.

118. R. C. Anderson, T. W. Bates, J. M. Bizjak, & M. L. Lemmon, 2000, Corporate governance and firm diversification, *Financial Management*, 29(1): 5–22; J. D. Westphal, 1998, Board games: How CEOs adapt to increases in structural board independence from management. *Administrative Science Quarterly*, 43: 511–537; J. K. Seward & J. P. Walsh, 1996, The governance and control of voluntary corporate spin offs, *Strategic Management Journal*, 17: 25–39; J. P. Walsh & J. K. Seward, 1990, On the efficiency of internal and external corporate control mechanisms, *Academy of Management Review*, 15: 421–458.

119. W. G. Rowe, 2001, Creating wealth in organizations: The role of strategic leadership, *Academy of Management Executive*, 15(1): 81–94; Finkelstein & D'Aveni, CEO duality as a double-edged sword.

120. E. F. Fama, 1980, Agency problems and the theory of the firm, *Journal of Political Economy*, 88: 288–307.

121. R. A. Johnson, 1996, Antecedents and outcomes of corporate refocusing, *Journal of Management*, 22: 439–483; C. Y. Woo, G. E. Willard, & U. S. Dallenbach, 1992, Spin-off performance: A case of overstated expectations, *Strategic Management Journal*, 13: 433–448.

122. M. Wright, R. E. Hoskisson, & L. W. Busenitz, 2001, Firm rebirth: Buyouts as facilitators of strategic growth and entrepreneurship, *Academy of Management Executive*, 15(1): 111–125; H. Kim & R. E. Hoskisson, 1996, Japanese governance systems: A critical review, in S. B. Prasad (ed.), *Advances in International Comparative Management*, Greenwich, CT: JAI Press, 165–189.

123. D. Lewis, 2000, CMGI ventures into the red, *Internetweek*, December 18, 34.

124. A. L. Ranft & H. M. O'Neill, 2001, Board composition and high-flying founders: Hints of trouble to come? *Academy of Management Executive*, 15(1): 126–138; P. Buxbaum, 2000, The trouble with dot-com boards, *Chief Executive*, October, 50–51.

125. A. Serwer & J. Boorstin, 2001, Following the money, *Fortune*, September 17, 102–114.

126. L. Capron, W. Mitchell, & A. Swaminathan, 2001, Asset divestiture following horizontal acquisitions: A dynamic view, *Strategic Management Journal*, 22: 817–844.

127. Bergh, Diversification strategy: Research at a crossroads, 370–371; W. M. Bulkeley, 1994, Conglomerates make a surprising come-back—with a '90s twist, *The Wall Street Journal*, March 1, A1, A6.

128. J. P. H. Fan & L. H. P. Lang, 2000, The measurement of relatedness: An application to corporate diversification, *Journal of Business*, 73: 629–660.

129. Khanna & Palepu, The future of business groups in emerging markets, 268–285; P. Ghemawat & T. Khanna, 1998, The nature of diversified business groups: A research design and two case studies, *Journal of Industrial Economics*, 46: 35–61.

130. W. P. Wan & R. E. Hoskisson, 2002, Home country environments, corporate diversification strategies, and firm performance, *Academy of Management Journal,* in press.

Chapter Seven

Acquisition and Restructuring Strategies

Knowledge Objectives

Studying this chapter should provide you with the strategic management knowledge needed to:

1. Explain the popularity of acquisition strategies in firms competing in the global economy.

2. Discuss reasons firms use an acquisition strategy to achieve strategic competitiveness.

3. Describe seven problems that work against developing a competitive advantage using an acquisition strategy.

4. Name and describe attributes of effective acquisitions.

5. Define the restructuring strategy and distinguish among its common forms.

6. Explain the short- and long-term outcomes of the different types of restructuring strategies.

Hewlett-Packard's Acquisition of Compaq: IBM Envy or Good Business Acumen?

In the summer of 2001, CEO Carly Fiorina of Hewlett-Packard (HP) and Compaq CEO Michael Capellas agreed that HP should acquire Compaq. In the following months this decision was debated on several fronts. In many ways, the decision represents classic arguments regarding the value of acquisitions. At the time of the acquisition announcement both firms were experiencing performance problems, although Compaq's problems were more severe than those of HP, which raised another question: can merging two poorly performing firms create one high performing firm?

There were several arguments in favor of the acquisition. First, because both firms compete in some of the same markets, their integration would create economies of scale and produce estimated cost savings of at least $2.5 billion. Second, merging the two companies would generate annual revenues of approximately $87 billion and a strong cash flow, providing the combined firm with financial and market power similar to IBM. Third, HP and Compaq also offer some different products, which could be sold to the other's customers. Finally, the companies have complementary technological capabilities, such as HP in Internet systems and Compaq in highly reliable servers and clustering software.

Arguments about the potential problems and disadvantages of the acquisition were also strong. Both firms operate in the highly competitive, volatile, and low margin personal computer market. The combined firm would derive about 25 percent of its revenues from this business. Moreover, the acquisition would require integrating two massive firms, a highly challenging task. Some analysts questioned Fiorina's ability to effectively integrate the businesses. Not only would the acquisition cost HP over $20-plus billion (with the final price determined by the firms' value when the transaction is finalized), there are concerns that it would cause HP to lose focus of its highly successful printer and other supplemental computing equipment businesses. For these reasons, a number of industry analysts and major shareholders of HP questioned the wisdom of the acquisition. Walter Hewlett and other members of the founders' families were particularly outspoken in their opposition.

HP's goal is to develop its services and software businesses to compete with IBM. IBM's services produce over $26 billion in annual revenue, but HP generates a little over $11 billion in annual revenue from its services

Shown here answering questions at the firm's headquarters, Walter Hewlett, Hewlett-Packard board member and son of founder William Hewlett, led a bitter eight-month public battle against the firm's merger with Compaq. When Hewlett filed a lawsuit after the merger was approved by shareholders, the company did not renominate him to the board because of his "ongoing adversarial relationship with the company" and "concerns about his lack of candor and issues of trust," according to an HP statement.

© REUTERS NEWMEDIA INC./CORBIS

business. Thus, HP is unlikely to challenge IBM in this arena, and the acquisition of Compaq is unlikely to help much. While Compaq does provide more services capabilities, additional capabilities are still needed for HP to compete effectively with IBM.

The stakes are high both for HP and for Fiorina. The acquisition will be expensive, and Fiorina's job may be on the line. In a close vote, the acquisition was approved by HP's shareholders at their March 2002 meeting, followed by Walter Hewlett's lawsuit against the results of the vote. Had a few major stockholders been able to stop the acquisition, Fiorina might have lost her job. Both U.S. and European regulators have approved the proposed transaction, eliminating one hurdle to its completion.

SOURCES: C. Gaither, 2002, Hewlett heir files lawsuit to overturn merger vote, *The New York Times Interactive*, http://www.nytimes.com, March 29; 2002, The new HP: The pros and cons of the merger, *BusinessWeek Online*, http://www.businessweek.com, December 24; R. Sidel & M. Williams, 2001, Hewlett's fight on Compaq turns heads; HP director's stance is unusually strong, *The Wall Street Journal*, December 31, C1, C13; S. Morrison, 2001, HP talks up Compaq computer revenue potential, *Financial Times*, http://www.ft.com, December 19; L. DiCarlo, 2001, HP's IBM envy, *Forbes*, http://www.forbes.com, December 14; 2001, Hewlett-Packard chief executive says integration process is key, *The Wall Street Journal Interactive*, http://interactive.wsj.com, September 4; R. Sidel & J. Wilke, 2001, Hewlett-Packard nears pact to buy Compaq for $26 billion, *The Wall Street Journal*, September 4.

In Chapter 6, we studied corporate-level strategies, focusing on types and levels of product diversification strategies that can build core competencies and create competitive advantage. As noted in that chapter, diversification allows a firm to create value by productively using excess resources.[1] In this chapter, we explore mergers and acquisitions, often combined with a diversification strategy, as a prominent strategy employed by firms throughout the world. The acquisition of Compaq by Hewlett-Packard (HP) is a horizontal acquisition, as Compaq competed with HP in several markets. Still, each firm markets some different products and has different strengths. As such, combining the two firms creates an opportunity for synergy to be developed beyond economies of scope as described in the chapter's Opening Case.

In the latter half of the 20th century, acquisitions became a prominent strategy used by major corporations. Even smaller and more focused firms began employing acquisition strategies to grow and enter new markets. However, acquisition strategies are not without problems; a number of acquisitions fail. Thus, we focus on how acquisitions can be used to produce value for the firm's stakeholders.[2] Before describing attributes associated with effective acquisitions, we examine the most prominent problems companies experience with an acquisition strategy. For example, when acquisitions contribute to poor performance, a firm may deem it necessary to restructure its operations. Closing the chapter are descriptions of three restructuring strategies, as well as the short- and long-term outcomes resulting from their use. Setting the stage for these topics is an examination of the popularity of mergers and acquisitions and a discussion of the differences among mergers, acquisitions, and takeovers.

The Popularity of Merger and Acquisition Strategies

Acquisitions have been a popular strategy among U.S. firms for many years. Some believe that this strategy played a central role in an effective restructuring of U.S. businesses during the 1980s and 1990s.[3] Increasingly, acquisition strategies are becoming more popular with firms in other nations and economic regions, including Europe. In fact, about 40–45 percent of the acquisitions in recent years have been made across country borders (i.e., a firm headquartered in one country acquiring a firm headquartered in another country).[4]

There were five waves of mergers and acquisitions in the 20th century with the last two in the 1980s and 1990s. There were 55,000 acquisitions valued at $1.3 trillion in the 1980s, but acquisitions in the 1990s exceeded $11 trillion in value.[5] World economies, particularly the U.S. economy, slowed in the new millennium, reducing the number of mergers and acquisitions completed.[6] The annual value of mergers and acquisitions peaked in 2000 at about $3.4 trillion and fell to about $1.75 trillion in 2001.[7] Slightly more than 15,000 acquisitions were announced in 2001 compared to over 33,000 in 2000.[8] The acquisition of Compaq by HP was the second largest acquisition announced in 2001.

Although acquisitions have slowed, their number remains high. In fact, an acquisition strategy is sometimes used because of the uncertainty in the competitive landscape. A firm may make an acquisition to increase its market power because of a competitive threat, to enter a new market because of the opportunity available in that market, or to spread the risk due to the uncertain environment.[9] In addition, a firm may acquire other companies as options that allow the firm to shift its core business into different markets as the volatility brings undesirable changes to its primary markets.[10]

The strategic management process (see Figure 1.1) calls for an acquisition strategy to increase a firm's strategic competitiveness as well as its returns to shareholders. Thus, an acquisition strategy should be used only when the acquiring firm will be able to increase its economic value through ownership and the use of an acquired firm's assets.[11]

Evidence suggests, however, that at least for acquiring firms, acquisition strategies may not result in these desirable outcomes. Studies by academic researchers have found that shareholders of acquired firms often earn above-average returns from an acquisition, while shareholders of acquiring firms are less likely to do so, typically earning returns from the transaction that are close to zero.[12] In approximately two-thirds of all acquisitions, the acquiring firm's stock price falls immediately after the intended transaction is announced. This negative response is an indication of investors' skepticism about the likelihood that the acquirer will be able to achieve the synergies required to justify the premium.[13] For example, some analysts question the value of the AOL Time Warner merger creating the world's largest media company. The firm's market value has continued to decline since the merger was announced. Executives at AOL Time Warner also predicted that the company would continue to be harmed by a major decline in advertising, a current market trend.[14]

Mergers, Acquisitions, and Takeovers: What Are the Differences?

A **merger** is a strategy through which two firms agree to integrate their operations on a relatively co-equal basis. There are not many true mergers, because one party is usually dominant. Entergy executives halted the planned merger between the FPL GROUP INC. and Entergy Corporation in 2001. They claimed that FPL was trying to dilute the leadership roles of Entergy managers in the planned integrated firm and thus would not be a merger of equals.[15]

An **acquisition** is a strategy through which one firm buys a controlling, or 100 percent, interest in another firm with the intent of making the acquired firm a subsidiary business within its portfolio. In this case, the management of the acquired firm reports to the management of the acquiring firm. While most mergers are friendly transactions, acquisitions include unfriendly takeovers. A **takeover** is a special type of an acquisition strategy wherein the target firm did not solicit the acquiring firm's bid.

A **merger** is a strategy through which two firms agree to integrate their operations on a relatively co-equal basis.

An **acquisition** is a strategy through which one firm buys a controlling, or 100 percent, interest in another firm with the intent of making the acquired firm a subsidiary business within its portfolio.

A **takeover** is a special type of an acquisition strategy wherein the target firm did not solicit the acquiring firm's bid.

Oftentimes, takeover bids spawn bidding wars. For example, TMP Worldwide thought it had an agreement to acquire HotJobs.com, but Yahoo! offered $81 million more and acquired HotJobs. The number of unsolicited takeover bids increased in the economic downturn in 2001–2002, a common activity in economic recessions, because the poorly managed firms that are undervalued relative to their assets are more easily identified.[16]

Many takeover attempts are not desired by the target firm's managers and are referred to as hostile. In a few cases, unsolicited offers may come from parties familiar to the target firm. For example, financier Kirk Kerkorian, who specializes in takeovers, has acquired Metro-Goldwyn-Mayer (MGM) five separate times. The value of his investment in MGM has grown considerably as well, outperforming the Standard & Poor's 500. Still, MGM has struggled against fierce competition in recent years, and Kerkorian is trying to sell it (again).[17]

On a comparative basis, acquisitions are more common than mergers and takeovers. Accordingly, this chapter focuses on acquisitions.

Reasons for Acquisitions

In this section, we discuss reasons that support the use of an acquisition strategy. Although each reason can provide a legitimate rationale for an acquisition, the acquisition may not necessarily lead to a competitive advantage.

Increased Market Power

A primary reason for acquisitions is to achieve greater market power.[18] Defined in Chapter 6, *market power* exists when a firm is able to sell its goods or services above competitive levels or when the costs of its primary or support activities are below those of its competitors. Market power usually is derived from the size of the firm and its resources and capabilities to compete in the marketplace.[19] It is also affected by the firm's share of the market. Therefore, most acquisitions designed to achieve greater market power entail buying a competitor, a supplier, a distributor, or a business in a highly related industry to allow exercise of a core competence and to gain competitive advantage in the acquiring firm's primary market. One goal in achieving market power is to become a market leader.[20] For example, the acquisition of Compaq by HP will result in the combined firm having 25 percent of the personal computer market and revenues comparable to IBM, a major competitor in technical (computer-based) services.

Firms use horizontal, vertical, and related acquisitions to increase their market power.

Horizontal Acquisitions. The acquisition of a company competing in the same industry in which the acquiring firm competes is referred to as a *horizontal acquisition.* Horizontal acquisitions increase a firm's market power by exploiting cost-based and revenue-based synergies.[21] Research suggests that horizontal acquisitions of firms with similar characteristics result in higher performance than when firms with dissimilar characteristics combine their operations. Examples of important similar characteristics include strategy, managerial styles, and resource allocation patterns. Similarities in these characteristics make the integration of the two firms proceed more smoothly.[22]

As shown in the Strategic Focus on page 218, horizontal acquisitions are often most effective when the acquiring firm integrates the acquired firm's assets with its assets, but only after evaluating and divesting excess capacity and assets that do not complement the newly combined firm's core competencies.[23] However, as also described in the following Strategic Focus, horizontal acquisitions do not guarantee success. Some are successful, such as McDonald's acquisition of Boston Market, but it seems to have been partially based on luck because McDonald's originally intended to close and convert all Boston Market restaurants. Some require a long time to achieve success, such as Daimler-Benz's acquisition of Chrysler. The potential success of others has been questioned, such as the Coors' acquisition of Bass Brewers and Amgen's acquisition of Immunex. It will take time to determine if the managers of Coors and Amgen can produce positive returns from these acquisitions.

Vertical Acquisitions. A *vertical acquisition* refers to a firm acquiring a supplier or distributor of one or more of its goods or services. A firm becomes vertically integrated through this type of acquisition, in that it controls additional parts of the value chain (see Chapter 3). Walt Disney Company's acquisition of Fox Family Worldwide is an example of vertical integration. This acquisition expands Disney's cable network while Disney remains focused on its core business of creating content. Thus, it has purchased important new distribution for the content it develops. Disney is also launching a new cable television channel targeting young children called Playhouse Disney. The downside for Disney relates to the cost ($5.3 billion) and new debt it had to assume to make the purchase.[24]

Related Acquisitions. The acquisition of a firm in a highly related industry is referred to as a *related acquisition*. The proposed acquisition of Honeywell by GE (see the Strategic Focus on page 230) can be classified as a highly related acquisition. Both firms operate businesses in the aerospace industry: GE is a major manufacturer of jet engines, while Honeywell manufactures other avionics equipment. Thus, they have complementary products. GE also has powerful businesses in aircraft leasing and financing. Jack Welch, CEO of GE at the time of the proposed acquisition, stated that "This is the cleanest deal you'll ever see . . . there is no product overlap. Everything is complementary."[25]

Acquisitions intended to increase market power are subject to regulatory review, as well as to analysis by financial markets. For example, Compaq suffered in the financial markets as a result of the fallout among HP investors, posing serious threats to the proposed acquisition.[26] Likewise as we know from the Strategic Focus on page 230, European regulators did not approve the GE acquisition of Honeywell, dooming this strategic action. Thus, firms seeking growth and market power through acquisitions must understand the political/legal segment of the general environment (see Chapter 2) in order to successfully use an acquisition strategy.

Overcoming Entry Barriers

Barriers to entry (introduced in Chapter 2) are factors associated with the market or with the firms currently operating in it that increase the expense and difficulty faced by new ventures trying to enter that particular market. For example, well-established competitors may have substantial economies of scale in the manufacture of their products. In addition, enduring relationships with customers often create product loyalties that are difficult for new entrants to overcome. When facing differentiated products, new entrants typically must spend considerable resources to advertise their goods or services and may find it necessary to sell at a price below competitors' to entice customers.

Facing the entry barriers created by economies of scale and differentiated products, a new entrant may find the acquisition of an established company to be more effective than entering the market as a competitor offering a good or service that is unfamiliar to current buyers. In fact, the higher the barriers to market entry, the greater the probability that a firm will acquire an existing firm to overcome them. Although an acquisition can be expensive, it does provide the new entrant with immediate market access.

Firms trying to enter international markets often face quite steep entry barriers.[27] In response, acquisitions are commonly used to overcome those barriers.[28] At

The Good, the Bad, and the Lucky
of Horizontal Acquisitions

Internet-based startups experienced a high rate of failure at the turn of the 21st century. In fact, many of them faced an imperative of combine or fail—they had to merge in order to have adequate resources to survive. These horizontal acquisitions were largely involuntary. Although biotechnology firms Amgen and Immunex are also similar, Amgen's acquisition of Immunex for approximately $18 billion was not necessary, and many analysts questioned its value. The acquisition should allow the resulting firm to capture economies of scale, particularly in selling each of the firm's major arthritis drugs, but the two firms are so similar that they are unlikely to capture synergies other than the efficiencies from economies of scale. Moreover, the acquisition and the similarity in the two firms' products may actually confuse the market. Additionally, Amgen may not be able to recapture the substantial premium it had to pay for the acquisition because of the lack of potential synergy.

Many analysts have questioned Adolph Coors Company's horizontal acquisition of Bass Brewers, a firm with major operations in the United Kingdom. Their concern is that the acquisition does little to help Coors compete in the much larger U.S. market and may, in fact, take its focus off this important market. Moreover, because of the physical distance between the two firms, some economies of scale, such as purchasing agricultural ingredients for the manufacture of the beer, may not be great.

DaimlerChrysler offerings range from the Mercedes SL (shown here with board member Juergen Hubbert in the driver's seat) to the Dodge pickup truck (pictured with DaimlerChrysler design executive Trevor Creed).

least for large multinational corporations, another indicator of the importance of entering and then competing successfully in international markets is the fact that five emerging markets (China, India, Brazil, Mexico, and Indonesia) are among the 12 largest economies in the world, with a combined purchasing power that is already one-half that of the Group of Seven industrial nations (United States, Japan, Britain, France, Germany, Canada, and Italy).[29]

Cross-Border Acquisitions. Acquisitions made between companies with headquarters in different countries are called *cross-border acquisitions*. These acquisitions are often made to overcome entry barriers. In Chapter 9, we examine cross-border alliances and the reason for their use. Compared to a cross-border alliance, a firm has more control over its international operations through a cross-border acquisition.[30]

Historically, U.S. firms have been the most active acquirers of companies outside their domestic market. However, in the global economy, companies throughout

The Daimler-Benz acquisition of Chrysler Corporation began with great promise because of the potentially complementary core businesses of the two firms—Chrysler's mid-priced autos and minivans and Daimler's luxury autos. However, because of major differences in the two firms' corporate cultures and operating processes, integration was difficult, and the performance of the merged firm suffered. But in 2001, DaimlerChrysler showed signs of producing more positive results and realizing its initial promise, following the total replacement of the top management of the firm's U.S. operations.

A major success story is McDonald's acquisition of Boston Market. McDonald's acquired the firm for its locations, intending to close the Boston Market restaurants and build other types of restaurants in their place. McDonald's named Jeffrey Kindler to oversee Boston Market as its CEO. While about 100 of the stores were closed and almost 60 were converted, Kindler also saw unrealized opportunities in a loyal clientele and managers with good ideas, and he negotiated a 10-year contract with Heinz to produce and market frozen dinners with the Boston Market brand. In 2001, Boston Market had sales of over $700 million and is now consistently profitable. As a result, McDonald's is keeping the remaining 700 plus Boston Market restaurants.

SOURCES: D. Ackman, 2002, Not much fizz in Coors deal, *Forbes*, http://www.forbes.com, January 2; P. T. Larson, 2001, Amgen agrees to buy Immunex for $16 billion, *Financial Times*, http://www.ft.com, December 12; A. Pollack & A. R. Sorkin, 2001, Amgen is said to make offer of $18 billion for Immunex, *The New York Times Interactive*, http://www.nytimes.com, December 17; M. Herper, 2001, Why Amgen should not buy Immunex, *Forbes*, http://www.forbes.com, December 15; M Arndt, 2001, There's life in the old bird yet, *Business Week*, May 14, 77–78; G. Anders, 2001, Weak companies, strong mergers, *Fast Company*, February, 182–186; J. Muller, J. Green, & C. Tierney, 2001, Chrysler's rescue team, *Business Week*, January 15, 49–50; J. Ball, J. B. White, & S. Miller, 2000, Earnings at DaimlerChrysler fall as trouble at U.S. division piles up, *The Wall Street Journal Interactive*, http://interactive.wsj.com, October 27.

the world are choosing this strategic option with increasing frequency. In recent years, cross-border acquisitions have represented as much as 45 percent of the total number of acquisitions made annually.[31] The Daimler-Benz acquisition of Chrysler Corporation provides an example of this activity. Because of relaxed regulations, the amount of cross-border activity among nations within the European community also continues to increase. Accounting for this growth in a range of cross-border acquisitions, some analysts believe, is the fact that many large European corporations have approached the limits of growth within their domestic markets and thus seek growth in other markets. Additionally, they are trying to achieve market power to compete effectively throughout the European Union and thus have made acquisitions in other European countries.

Firms in all types of industries are completing cross-border acquisitions. For example, in the cosmetics industry, Japan's Shiseido created a new division to pursue mergers and acquisitions. With its growth long fueled by acquisitions, the firm is now committed to emphasizing the cross-border variety, especially with European companies. In another segment of the consumer goods industry, Kimberly-Clark, the world's largest producer of tissue products, intends to acquire primarily non-U.S. companies to expand its disposable medical products lines and tissue and diaper businesses.[32]

Cost of New-Product Development and Increased Speed to Market

Developing new products internally and successfully introducing them into the marketplace often require significant investments of a firm's resources, including time, making it difficult to quickly earn a profitable return.[33] Also of concern to firms' managers is achieving adequate returns from the capital invested to develop and commercialize new products—an estimated 88 percent of innovations fail to achieve adequate returns. Perhaps contributing to these less-than-desirable rates of return is the successful imitation of approximately 60 percent of innovations within four years after the patents are obtained. Because of outcomes such as these, managers often perceive internal product development as a high-risk activity.[34]

Acquisitions are another means a firm can use to gain access to new products and to current products that are new to the firm. Compared to internal product development processes, acquisitions provide more predictable returns as well as faster market entry. Returns are more predictable because the performance of the acquired firm's products can be assessed prior to completing the acquisition.[35] For these reasons, extensive bidding wars and acquisitions are more frequent in high technology industries.[36]

Acquisition activity is also extensive throughout the pharmaceutical industry, where firms frequently use acquisitions to enter markets quickly, to overcome the high costs of developing products internally, and to increase the predictability of returns on their investments. Interestingly, Merck & Co. has chosen not to acquire new drugs but to develop them internally, a strategy that has been beneficial for most of the last 20 years as it became the world's largest and most successful pharmaceutical firm. However, in the new millennium, Merck has experienced problems and now trails Pfizer and GlaxoSmithKline in the industry. Some analysts suggest that Merck may be unable to return to its number one ranking unless it acquires another large successful pharmaceutical firm.[37]

As indicated previously, compared to internal product development, acquisitions result in more rapid market entries.[38] Acquisitions often represent the fastest means to enter international markets and help firms overcome the liabilities associated with such strategic moves.[39] Acquisitions provide rapid access both to new markets and to new capabilities. Using new capabilities to pioneer new products and to enter markets quickly can create advantageous market positions.[40] Pharmaceutical firms, for example, access new products through acquisitions of other drug manufacturers. They also acquire biotechnology firms both for new products and for new technological capabilities. Pharmaceutical firms often provide the manufacturing and marketing capabilities to take the new products developed by biotechnology firms to the market.[41]

Merck spent approximately $2.45 billion on research and development in 2001. In 2000 Merck began collaborating with Schering-Plough in what the companies call "a flexible, creative partnership." One group in this arrangement plots strategies for combining ezetimibe (under study for reduction of cholesterol) and Zocor, Merck's leading cholesterol-reducer. Another group oversees the development combining Singulair, the leading asthma drug in the United States, and Claritin to combat allergic rhinits. Pictured here is a researcher in a Merck lab.

Lower Risk Compared to Developing New Products

Because an acquisition's outcomes can be estimated more easily and accurately compared to the outcomes of an internal product development process, managers may view acquisitions as lowering risk.[42] The difference in risk between an internal product development process and an acquisition can be seen in the results of Merck's strategy and its competitors described above.

As with other strategic actions discussed in this book, the firm must exercise caution when using a strategy of acquiring new products rather than developing them internally. While research suggests that acquisitions have become a common means of avoiding risky internal ventures (and therefore risky R&D investments), they may also become a substitute for innovation.[43] Thus, acquisitions are not a risk-free alternative to entering new markets through internally developed products.

Increased Diversification

Acquisitions are also used to diversify firms. Based on experience and the insights resulting from it, firms typically find it easier to develop and introduce new products in markets currently served by the firm. In contrast, it is difficult for companies to develop products that differ from their current lines for markets in which they lack experience. Thus, it is uncommon for a firm to develop new products internally to diversify its product lines.[44] Using acquisitions to diversify a firm is the quickest and, typically, the easiest way to change its portfolio of businesses.[45]

Both related diversification and unrelated diversification strategies can be implemented through acquisitions. For example, Tyco International has been very aggressive in using acquisitions and building a conglomerate—a highly unrelated diversified firm.[46] Tyco's companies manufacture products as diverse as valves and garbage bags. In 2001, Tyco acquired a large commercial finance company, CIT Group, Inc. However, Tyco experienced problems in 2002 for making a number of acquisitions without reporting them or the debt they obtained to finance them.

Research has shown the more related the acquired firm is to the acquiring firm, the greater is the probability that the acquisition will be successful.[47] Thus, horizontal acquisitions (through which a firm acquires a competitor) and related acquisitions tend to contribute more to the firm's strategic competitiveness than acquiring a company that operates in quite different product markets from those in which the firm competes.[48] For example, firms in the financial services industry have become more diversified over time, often through acquisitions. One study suggests that these firms are diversifying not only to provide a more complete line of products for their customers but also to create strategic flexibility. In other words, they diversify into some product lines to provide options for future services they may wish to emphasize. As noted earlier, such acquisitions are a means of dealing with an uncertain competitive environment.[49]

Reshaping the Firm's Competitive Scope

As discussed in Chapter 2, the intensity of competitive rivalry is an industry characteristic that affects the firm's profitability.[50] To reduce the negative effect of an intense rivalry on their financial performance, firms may use acquisitions to reduce their dependence on one or more products or markets. Reducing a company's dependence on specific markets alters the firm's competitive scope.

One of the arguments against HP's acquisition of Compaq, described in the Opening Case, is that it increases the firm's dependence on the highly competitive and volatile personal computer market. Thus, rather than using acquisitions to avoid competition, HP is increasing its emphasis in a market characterized by substantial competitive rivalry. Some major shareholders and analysts believe that HP should emphasize its printers and computer accessories businesses.

GE reduced its emphasis in the electronics markets many years ago by making acquisitions in the financial services industry. Today, GE is considered a service firm because a majority of its revenue now comes from services instead of industrial products.[51]

Learning and Developing New Capabilities

Some acquisitions are made to gain capabilities that the firm does not possess. For example, acquisitions may be used to acquire a special technological capability. Research has shown that firms can broaden their knowledge base and reduce inertia through acquisitions.[52] Therefore, acquiring other firms with skills and capabilities that differ from its own helps the acquiring firm to learn new knowledge and remain agile. Of course, firms are better able to learn these capabilities if they share some similar properties with the firm's current capabilities. Thus, firms should seek to acquire companies with different but related and complementary capabilities in order to build their own knowledge base.[53]

One of Cisco System's primary goals in its acquisitions is to gain access to capabilities that it does not currently possess. Cisco executives emphasize the importance of learning throughout the organization.[54] Cisco has developed an intricate process to quickly integrate the acquired firms and their capabilities (knowledge) after an acquisition is completed. Cisco's processes account for its phenomenal success in the latter half of the 1990s and being named one of the top ten most admired firms by *Fortune* in 2000.[55] While it suffered in the collapsing value of Internet-based companies in 2001 and early 2002, Cisco is expected to bounce back strongly as the U.S. economy recovers.

Problems in Achieving Acquisition Success

Acquisition strategies based on legitimate reasons described in this chapter can increase strategic competitiveness and help firms to earn above-average returns. However, acquisition strategies are not risk-free. Reasons for the use of acquisition strategies and potential problems with such strategies are shown in Figure 7.1.

Research suggests that perhaps 20 percent of all mergers and acquisitions are successful, approximately 60 percent produce disappointing results, and the last 20 percent are clear failures.[56] Successful acquisitions generally involve a well-conceived strategy in selecting the target, avoiding paying too high a premium, and an effective integration process.[57] As shown in Figure 7.1, several problems may prevent successful acquisitions.

Integration Difficulties

Integrating two companies following an acquisition can be quite difficult. Integration challenges include melding two disparate corporate cultures, linking different financial and control systems, building effective working relationships (particularly when management styles differ), and resolving problems regarding the status of the newly acquired firm's executives.[58]

The importance of a successful integration should not be underestimated. Without it, an acquisition is unlikely to produce positive returns. Thus, as suggested by a researcher studying the process, "managerial practice and academic writings show that the post-acquisition integration phase is probably the single most important determinant of shareholder value creation (and equally of value destruction) in mergers and acquisitions."[59]

Integration is complex and involves a large number of activities. For instance, Intel acquired Digital Equipment Corporation's semiconductors division. Successful integration was crucial—on the day Intel began to merge the acquired division into its operations, hundreds of employees working in dozens of different countries needed to complete 6,000 deliverables.[60]

It is important to maintain the human capital of the target firm after the acquisition. Much of an organization's knowledge is contained in its human capital.[61] Turnover of key personnel from the acquired firm can have a negative effect on the performance of the merged firm.[62] The loss of key personnel, such as critical managers, weakens the acquired firm's capabilities and reduces its value.

If implemented effectively, the integration process can have a positive effect on target firm managers and reduce the probability that they will leave.[63] Cisco Systems, as noted earlier, has been highly effective in making acquisitions, partly because of its

Figure 7.1   Reasons for Acquisitions and Problems in Achieving Success

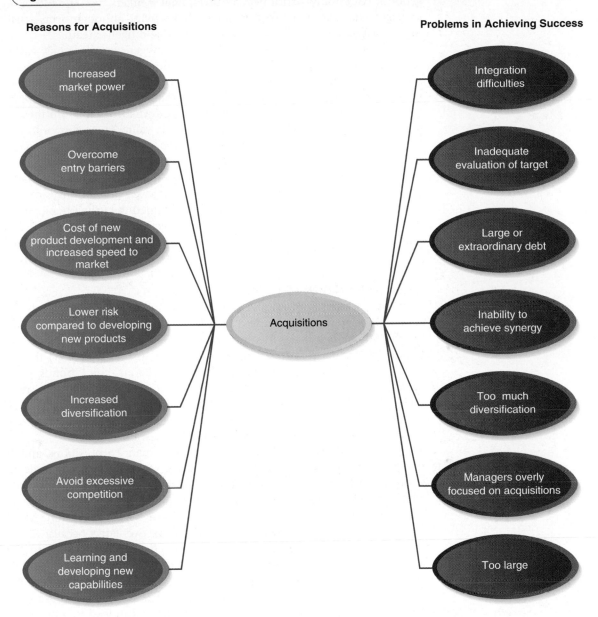

Reasons for Acquisitions

- Increased market power
- Overcome entry barriers
- Cost of new product development and increased speed to market
- Lower risk compared to developing new products
- Increased diversification
- Avoid excessive competition
- Learning and developing new capabilities

Acquisitions

Problems in Achieving Success

- Integration difficulties
- Inadequate evaluation of target
- Large or extraordinary debt
- Inability to achieve synergy
- Too much diversification
- Managers overly focused on acquisitions
- Too large

ability to quickly integrate its acquisitions into its existing operations. Focusing on small companies with products and services related closely to its own, Cisco uses a relatively large team charged with the responsibility to integrate key target firm personnel and processes into the firm. An important goal of the team is to make the acquired firm employees feel ownership in Cisco.[64]

Inadequate Evaluation of Target

Due diligence is a process through which a potential acquirer evaluates a target firm for acquisition. In an effective due-diligence process hundreds of items are examined in areas as diverse as the financing for the intended transaction, differences in cultures between the acquiring and target firm, tax consequences of the transaction, and actions that would be necessary to successfully meld the two workforces. Due diligence is commonly performed by investment bankers, accountants, lawyers, and management consultants specializing in that activity, although firms actively pursuing acquisitions may form their own internal due-diligence team.

The failure to complete an effective due-diligence process may easily result in the acquiring firm paying an excessive premium for the target company. In fact, research shows that without due diligence, "the purchase price is driven by the pricing of other 'comparable' acquisitions rather than by a rigorous assessment of where, when, and how management can drive real performance gains. [In these cases], the price paid may have little to do with achievable value."[65] As shown in the Strategic Focus on page 225, an effective due-diligence process may have revealed the true value of Enron to Dynegy, Inc., the firm that had agreed to acquire it.

In fact, as we discussed, Dynegy could have lost considerable value if it had completed the acquisition of Enron. It was saved because investors and lenders expressed concerns. Furthermore, Dynegy obtained the valuable pipeline assets for $1.5 billion. Under normal circumstances, effective due diligence would have identified Enron's problems, and Dynegy would not have entered into an agreement to acquire the company.

Large or Extraordinary Debt

To finance a number of acquisitions completed during the 1980s and 1990s, some companies significantly increased their levels of debt. A financial innovation called junk bonds helped make this increase possible. *Junk bonds* are a financing option through which risky acquisitions are financed with money (debt) that provides a large potential return to lenders (bondholders). Because junk bonds are unsecured obligations that are not tied to specific assets for collateral, interest rates for these high-risk debt instruments sometimes reached between 18 and 20 percent during the 1980s.[66] Some prominent financial economists viewed debt as a means to discipline managers, causing them to act in shareholders' best interests.[67]

Junk bonds are now used less frequently to finance acquisitions, and the conviction that debt disciplines managers is less strong. Nonetheless, some firms still take on significant debt to acquire companies. For example, Disney increased its total debt by $5.3 billion to approximately $15 billion to acquire Fox Family Worldwide. This action caused Moody's Investors Service to review Disney's debt condition.[68] Furthermore, some analysts believe that Disney is a potential takeover target because of its poor performance.[69] Analysts also question the amount of debt taken on by International Paper to finance several acquisitions. The firm built its total debt to $15.5 billion, equal to approximately 50 percent of its capital and 400 percent of its annual cash flow.[70]

High debt can have several negative effects on the firm. For example, because high debt increases the likelihood of bankruptcy, it can lead to a downgrade in the firm's credit rating by agencies such as Moody's and Standard & Poor's.[71] In addition, high debt may preclude needed investment in activities that contribute to the firm's long-term success, such as R&D, human resource training, and marketing.[72] Still, use of leverage can be a positive force in a firm's development, allowing it to take advantage of attractive expansion opportunities. However, too much leverage (such as extraordinary debt) can lead to negative outcomes, including postponing or eliminating investments, such as R&D expenditures, that are necessary to maintain strategic competitiveness over the long term.

Inability to Achieve Synergy

Derived from "synergos," a Greek word that means "working together," *synergy* exists when the value created by units working together exceeds the value those units could create working independently (see Chapter 6). That is, synergy exists when assets are

Dynegy Should Thank Its Lucky Stars

In November 2001 Dynegy, Inc., agreed to acquire its former rival Enron, the once highly successful, then highly troubled energy trading company. Only months before the merger was announced, Enron's market value was approximately $70 billion. When the firm announced that it had overstated earnings for several years, however, investors lost confidence. Dynegy accordingly agreed to purchase Enron for only $9 billion—far less than anticipated. In the next two weeks, serious financial problems continued to be revealed, and Enron's market value fell to less than $270 million. Dynegy claimed that Enron had failed to fully disclose the scope of its financial woes and withdrew its offer to acquire Enron. The U.S. Justice Department and Congress announced investigations into Enron's potential managerial improprieties, and the firm filed for bankruptcy shortly thereafter.

Enron also filed a lawsuit against Dynegy for withdrawing from the acquisition agreement, demanding $10 billion in damages. Dynegy countersued to acquire Enron's largest pipeline asset for $1.5 billion—an amount agreed upon earlier even if the acquisition was not consummated—and eventually received the asset.

Dynegy came out of the transaction the clear winner—the firm obtained a valued asset and dodged a bullet by not acquiring Enron. It is unclear, however, whether Dynegy conducted effective due diligence. If it had done so, it probably would not have agreed to buy Enron for $9 billion—or any other price. As it turned out, concerned major investors and lenders who forced Enron's disclosure of questionable financial practices helped Dynegy.

Enron executives likely created the firm's financial problems partially out of hubris, an exaggerated self-confidence. Its former CEO Jeffrey Skilling once remarked, "We're on the side of angels." Enron had built an envious energy trading operation and annual revenues of over $100 billion, but it experienced substantial losses in some trades when the economy turned sour in 2001 (such as its losses of over $127 million in trading of fiber-optic capacity). Substantial criticism has been aimed at Enron's auditor and board of directors for allowing unacceptable financial practices to occur. The full story of Enron's problems and practices may take years to discover.

SOURCES: N. Weinberg & D. Fisher, 2001, Power play, *Forbes*, December 24, 53–58; G. Robinson, 2001, Congressional probe into Enron intensifies, *Financial Times*, http://www.ft.com, December 17; R. Abelson, 2001, Enron board comes under a storm of criticism, *The New York Times Interactive*, http://www.nytimes.com, December 16; D. Ackman, 2001, Enron's mysterious, troubled core, *Forbes*, http://www.forbes.com, December 15; J. R. Emshwiller & R. Smith, 2001, Behind Enron's fall, a culture of secrecy which cost the firm its investors' trust, *The Wall Street Journal Interactive*, http://interactive.wsj.com, December 5; H. A. Upper, Jr. & A. R. Sorkin, 2001, Enron files largest U.S. claim for bankruptcy, *The New York Times Interactive*, http://www.nytimes.com, December 3; F. Norria, 2001, Gas pipeline is prominent as Dynegy seeks Enron, *The New York Times Interactive*, http://www.nytimes.com, November 13.

worth more when used in conjunction with each other than when they are used separately.[73] For shareholders, synergy generates gains in their wealth that they could not duplicate or exceed through their own portfolio diversification decisions.[74] Synergy is created by the efficiencies derived from economies of scale and economies of scope and by sharing resources (e.g., human capital and knowledge) across the businesses in the merged firm.[75]

A firm develops a competitive advantage through an acquisition strategy only when a transaction generates private synergy. *Private synergy* is created when the combination and integration of the acquiring and acquired firms' assets yield capabilities and core competencies that could not be developed by combining and integrating either firm's assets with another company. Private synergy is possible when firms' assets are complementary in unique ways; that is, the unique type of asset complementarity is not possible by combining either company's assets with another firm's assets.[76] Because of its uniqueness, private synergy is difficult for competitors to understand and imitate. However, private synergy is difficult to create.

A firm's ability to account for costs that are necessary to create anticipated revenue- and cost-based synergies affects the acquisition's success. Firms experience several expenses when trying to create private synergy through acquisitions. Called transaction costs, these expenses are incurred when firms use acquisition strategies to create synergy.[77] Transaction costs may be direct or indirect. Direct costs include legal fees and charges from investment bankers who complete due diligence for the acquiring firm. Indirect costs include managerial time to evaluate target firms and then to complete negotiations, as well as the loss of key managers and employees following an acquisition.[78] Firms tend to underestimate the sum of indirect costs when the value of the synergy that may be created by combining and integrating the acquired firm's assets with the acquiring firm's assets is calculated.

Too Much Diversification

Former Tyco CEO L. Dennis Kozolowski, center, answers questions following an investors' meeting. The firm had announced that it would split into four publicly traded companies to boost shareholder value and to erase $11 billion in debt. The firm's strategy of growth through acquisitions resulted in investors questioning its failure to fully disclose information about 700 acquisitions from 1998 to 2001, although the firm had accounted for their net cost. Tyco's later decision not to split into four separate companies shows the complexity of managing acquisition strategies.

As explained in Chapter 6, diversification strategies can lead to strategic competitiveness and above-average returns. In general, firms using related diversification strategies outperform those employing unrelated diversification strategies. However, conglomerates, formed by using an unrelated diversification strategy, also can be successful. For example, Virgin Group, the U.K. firm with interests ranging from cosmetics to trains, is successful. Tyco International, a highly diversified U.S. firm, has also been successful. Tyco was ranked by *Forbes* as the 25th-highest performing firm over the five-year period of 1997–2001, the highest ranking by a conglomerate firm. During this period, its stock price increased 341 percent.[79] However, Tyco's performance suffered in 2002, after it revealed unreported acquisitions and accumulated debt over the previous three years.

At some point, firms can become overdiversified. The level at which overdiversification occurs varies across companies because each firm has different capabilities to manage diversification. Recall from Chapter 6 that related diversification requires more information processing than does unrelated diversification. The need for related diversified firms to process more information of greater diversity is such that they become overdiversified with a smaller number of business units, compared to firms using an unrelated diversification strategy.[80] Regardless of the type of diversification strategy implemented, however, declines in performance result from overdiversification, after which business units are often divested.[81] The pattern of excessive diversification followed by divestments of underperforming business units acquired earlier was frequently observed among U.S. firms during the 1960s through the 1980s.[82]

Even when a firm is not overdiversified, a high level of diversification can have a negative effect on the firm's long-term performance. For example, the scope created by additional amounts of diversification often causes managers to rely on financial rather than strategic controls to evaluate business units' performances (financial and strategic controls are defined and explained in Chapters 11 and 12). Top-level executives often rely on financial controls to assess the performance of business units when they do not have a rich understanding of business units' objectives and strategies. Use of financial controls, such as return on investment (ROI), causes individual business-unit managers to focus on short-term outcomes at the expense of long-term investments. When long-term investments are reduced to increase short-term profits, a firm's overall strategic competitiveness may be harmed.[83]

Another problem resulting from too much diversification is the tendency for acquisitions to become substitutes for innovation. Typically, managers do not intend acquisitions to be used in that way. However, a reinforcing cycle evolves. Costs associated with acquisitions may result in fewer allocations to activities, such as R&D, that are linked to innovation. Without adequate support, a firm's innovation skills begin to atrophy. Without internal innovation skills, the only option available to a firm is to complete still additional acquisitions to gain access to innovation. Evidence suggests that a firm using acquisitions as a substitute for internal innovations eventually encounters performance problems.[84]

Managers Overly Focused on Acquisitions

Typically, a fairly substantial amount of managerial time and energy is required for acquisition strategies to contribute to the firm's strategic competitiveness. Activities with which managers become involved include (1) searching for viable acquisition candidates, (2) completing effective due-diligence processes, (3) preparing for negotiations, and (4) managing the integration process after the acquisition is completed.

Top-level managers do not personally gather all data and information required to make acquisitions. However, these executives do make critical decisions on the firms to be targeted, the nature of the negotiations, and so forth. Company experiences show that participating in and overseeing the activities required for making acquisitions can divert managerial attention from other matters that are necessary for long-term competitive success, such as identifying and taking advantage of other opportunities and interacting with important external stakeholders.[85]

For example, Case Corporation acquired New Holland to create CNH Global with annual sales of almost $11 billion, resulting in the second highest market share in the agricultural and construction equipment industry. However, the executives became preoccupied with integrating the two firms and largely ignored external economic events and competitors. The company's markets were rapidly changing and its competitors were taking away its customers. As a result, CNH's annual revenues in 2000 declined by $2.5 billion from the combined 1998 revenues of the two separate companies.[86] Thus, upper-level executives should avoid focusing on an acquisition strategy at the expense of the firm's long-term strategic competitiveness.

Acquisitions can consume significant amounts of managerial time and energy in both the acquiring and target firms. In particular, managers in target firms may operate in a state of virtual suspended animation during an acquisition.[87] Although the target firm's day-to-day operations continue, most of the company's executives are hesitant to make decisions with long-term consequences until negotiations have been completed. Evidence suggests that the acquisition process can create a short-term perspective and a greater aversion to risk among top-level executives in a target firm.[88]

Too Large

Most acquisitions create a larger firm that should help increase its economies of scale. These economies can then lead to more efficient operations—for example, the two sales organizations can be integrated using fewer sales reps because a sales rep can sell the products of both firms (particularly if the products of the acquiring and target firms are highly related).

Many firms seek increases in size because of the potential economies of scale and enhanced market power (discussed earlier). For example, when Daniel Brewster took the job as CEO of Gruner+Jahr USA Publishing, he announced that he had been given a mandate by the parent company, Bertelsmann, to double the firm's size in five years. With the resources provided by Bertelsmann, Brewster made $600 million in acquisitions in a six-month period, including the $342 million acquisition of *Fast Company*. Essentially, the goal given to Brewster by Bertelsmann was for Gruner+Jahr USA to become number one or two in the markets served. Thus, Brewster is trying to gain economies of scale and market power simultaneously.[89]

At some level, the additional costs required to manage the larger firm will exceed the benefits of the economies of scale and additional market power. In addition, the complexities generated by the larger size often lead managers to implement more bureaucratic controls to manage the combined firm's operations. Bureaucratic controls are formalized supervisory and behavioral rules and policies designed to ensure consistency of decisions and actions across different units of a firm. However, through time, formalized controls often lead to relatively rigid and standardized managerial behavior. Certainly, in the long run, the diminished flexibility that accompanies rigid and standardized managerial behavior may produce less innovation. Because of innovation's importance to competitive success, the bureaucratic controls resulting from a large organization (that is, built by acquisitions) can have a detrimental effect on performance.[90]

Effective Acquisitions

Earlier in the chapter, we noted that acquisition strategies do not consistently produce above-average returns for the acquiring firm's shareholders. Nonetheless, some companies are able to create value when using an acquisition strategy.[91] Results from a research study shed light on the differences between unsuccessful and successful acquisition strategies and suggest that there is a pattern of actions that can improve the probability of acquisition success.[92]

The study shows that when the target firm's assets are complementary to the acquired firm's assets, an acquisition is more successful. With complementary assets, integrating two firms' operations has a higher probability of creating synergy. In fact, integrating two firms with complementary assets frequently produces unique capabilities and core competencies.[93] With complementary assets, the acquiring firm can maintain its focus on core businesses and leverage the complementary assets and capabilities from the acquired firm. Oftentimes, targets were selected and "groomed" by establishing a working relationship sometime prior to the acquisition. As discussed in Chapter 9, strategic alliances are sometimes used to test the feasibility of a future merger or acquisition between the involved firms.[94]

The study's results also show that friendly acquisitions facilitate integration of the firms involved in an acquisition. Through friendly acquisitions, firms work together to find ways to integrate their operations to create synergy. In hostile takeovers, animosity often results between the two top-management teams, a condition that in turn affects working relationships in the newly created firm. As a result, more key personnel in the acquired firm may be lost, and those who remain may resist the changes necessary to integrate the two firms.[95] With effort, cultural clashes can be overcome, and fewer key managers and employees will become discouraged and leave.[96]

Additionally, effective due-diligence processes involving the deliberate and careful selection of target firms and an evaluation of the relative health of those firms (financial health, cultural fit, and the value of human resources) contribute to successful acquisitions. Financial slack in the form of debt equity or cash, in both the acquiring and acquired firms, also has frequently contributed to success in acquisitions. While financial slack provides access to financing for the acquisition, it is still important to maintain a low or moderate level of debt after the acquisition to keep debt costs low. When substantial debt was used to finance the acquisition, companies with successful acquisitions reduced the debt quickly, partly by selling off assets from the acquired firm, especially non-complementary or poorly performing assets. For these firms, debt costs do not prevent long-term investments such as R&D, and managerial discretion in the use of cash flow is relatively flexible.

Another attribute of successful acquisition strategies is an emphasis on innovation, as demonstrated by continuing investments in R&D activities. Significant R&D investments show a strong managerial commitment to innovation, a characteristic that is increasingly important to overall competitiveness, as well as acquisition success.

Flexibility and adaptability are the final two attributes of successful acquisitions. When executives of both the acquiring and the target firms have experience in managing change and learning from acquisitions, they will be more skilled at adapting their capabilities to new environments.[97] As a result, they will be more adept at integrating the two organizations, which is particularly important when firms have different organizational cultures.

Efficient and effective integration may quickly produce the desired synergy in the newly created firm. Effective integration allows the acquiring firm to keep valuable human resources in the acquired firm from leaving.[98]

The attributes and results of successful acquisitions are summarized in Table 7.1. Managers seeking acquisition success should emphasize the seven attributes that are listed.

As explained in the Strategic Focus on page 230, the attempted acquisition of Honeywell by GE had some but not all of the attributes of successful acquisitions summarized in Table 7.1.

Table 7.1	Attributes of Successful Acquisitions
Attributes	**Results**
1. Acquired firm has assets or resources that are complementary to the acquiring firm's core business	1. High probability of synergy and competitive advantage by maintaining strengths
2. Acquisition is friendly	2. Faster and more effective integration and possibly lower premiums
3. Acquiring firm conducts effective due diligence to select target firms and evaluate the target firm's health (financial, cultural, and human resources)	3. Firms with strongest complementarities are acquired and overpayment is avoided
4. Acquiring firm has financial slack (cash or a favorable debt position)	4. Financing (debt or equity) is easier and less costly to obtain
5. Merged firm maintains low to moderate debt position	5. Lower financing cost, lower risk (e.g., of bankruptcy), and avoidance of trade-offs that are associated with high debt
6. Sustained and consistent emphasis on R&D and innovation	6. Maintain long-term competitive advantage in markets
7. Has experience with change and is flexible and adaptable	7. Faster and more effective integration facilitates achievement of synergy

Was GE's Attempted Acquisition of Honeywell a Correct Strategy?

In 2001, Honeywell International agreed to be acquired by General Electric (GE). Even though the transaction was subject to approval by the European Union, GE and Honeywell executives likened the merger of these two firms to "a match made in heaven."

Analysts questioned the value of the acquisition by GE, however. The current Honeywell resulted from a previous acquisition of Honeywell by AlliedSignal. The integration of Honeywell and AlliedSignal had not gone well, and the firm's performance was suffering. United Technology made an offer to acquire Honeywell, but Honeywell executives and its board of directors rejected the offer.

Some considered GE as a "white knight" rescuing Honeywell from United Technologies. United Technologies had the last laugh—as it was one of four major firms that lobbied against the acquisition that was eventually disapproved by the European Union anti-trust regulators.

There seemed to be potential synergy between GE and Honeywell, especially in the aerospace businesses with GE's jet engines and Honeywell's avionic equipment. However, concern over potential dominance of this market is what led European regulators to disapprove the acquisition. It is unclear how much due diligence GE conducted prior to making its offer to acquire Honeywell. The fact that Honeywell and AlliedSignal had been unable to achieve an effective integration of their operations should have caused concerns for GE. Jack Welch, CEO of GE at the time, and Lawrence Bossidy, former CEO of AlliedSignal, were friends, but their two firms did not have major working relationships. GE also overlooked the possibility of disapproval by European regulators, conceding that its negotiated deal with Honeywell was completed so rapidly that no time had been allowed for consulting European lawyers on the regulatory concerns.

The deal had the trappings of managerial hubris. Welch was planning to retire, and some analysts touted this acquisition as his last great strategic move. In fact, he was writing a book planned for publication immediately after his retirement, and the last chapter was slated to cover the Honeywell acquisition. When the acquisition was disapproved, the last chapter of the book was hurriedly rewritten. When Bossidy came out of retirement to become CEO of Honeywell immediately after the deal fell through, speculation grew that he and Welch had an informal agreement to make the acquisition, with GE outbidding United Technologies.

Jeffrey Immelt, the new CEO of GE, predicted that although 2001 had not been a great year for the company, GE would continue to grow through acquisitions and that profits would increase by as much as 18 percent in 2002. There was no such positive prediction for Honeywell.

SOURCES: A. Hill, 2001, GE pins expansion plans on acquisitions, *Financial Times*, http://www.ft.com, December 19; D. Jones, 2001, Welch book trips on merger hurdle, *The Wall Street Journal*, July 24, D3; D. Hargreaves & A. Hill, 2001, GE accused of cold feet on Honeywell deal, *Financial Times*, http://www.ft.com, July 6; 2001, European foes stall merger with GE: Focus is misplaced in Honeywell deal, *Arizona Republic*, June 20, V4; L. Zuckerman & A. R. Sorkin, 2001, G.E. calls its $45 billion bid for Honeywell all but dead, *The New York Times Interactive*, http://www.nytimes.com, June 17; M. Murray, P. Shiskin, B. Davis, & A. Raghavan, 2001, As Honeywell deal goes awry for GE, fallout may be global, *The Wall Street Journal Interactive*, http://interactive.wsj.com, June 14.

It is unclear whether GE's acquisition of Honeywell would have succeeded if it had been approved. While it had some of the characteristics of effective acquisitions, such as potential complementary capabilities, and a friendly acquisition, reports suggest that the due diligence process was inadequate. Some analysts were concerned that it would have been difficult to integrate Honeywell into GE, and GE did not foresee the regulatory challenges.

As we have learned, some acquisitions enhance strategic competitiveness. However, the majority of acquisitions that took place from the 1970s through the 1990s did not enhance firms' strategic competitiveness. In fact, "history shows that anywhere between one-third [and] more than half of all acquisitions are ultimately divested or spun-off."[99] Thus, firms often use restructuring strategies to correct for the failure of a merger or an acquisition.

Restructuring

Restructuring is a strategy through which a firm changes its set of businesses or financial structure.

Defined formally, **restructuring** is a strategy through which a firm changes its set of businesses or financial structure.[100] From the 1970s into the 2000s, divesting businesses from company portfolios and downsizing accounted for a large percentage of firms' restructuring strategies. Restructuring is a global phenomenon.[101]

The failure of an acquisition strategy often precedes a restructuring strategy. Among the famous restructurings taken to correct for an acquisition failure are (1) AT&T's $7.4 billion purchase of NCR and subsequent spin-off of the company to shareholders in a deal valued at $3.4 billion, (2) Novell's purchase of WordPerfect for stock valued at $1.4 billion and its sale of the company to Corel for $124 million in stock and cash, and (3) Quaker Oats acquisition of Snapple Beverage Company for $1.7 billion, only to sell it three years later for $300 million.[102]

In other instances, however, firms use a restructuring strategy because of changes in their external and internal environments. For example, opportunities sometimes surface in the external environment that are particularly attractive to the diversified firm in light of its core competencies. In such cases, restructuring may be appropriate to position the firm to create more value for stakeholders, given the environmental changes.

As discussed next, there are three restructuring strategies that firms use: downsizing, downscoping, and leveraged buyouts.

Downsizing

Once thought to be an indicator of organizational decline, downsizing is now recognized as a legitimate restructuring strategy. *Downsizing* is a reduction in the number of a firm's employees and, sometimes, in the number of its operating units, but it may or may not change the composition of businesses in the company's portfolio. Thus, downsizing is an intentional proactive management strategy, whereas "decline is an environmental or organizational phenomenon that occurs involuntarily and results in erosion of an organization's resource base."[103]

In the late 1980s, early 1990s, and early 2000s, thousands of jobs were lost in private and public organizations in the United States. One study estimates that 85 percent of Fortune 1000 firms have used downsizing as a restructuring strategy.[104] Moreover, *Fortune* 500 firms laid off more than one million employees, or 4 percent of their collective workforce, in 2001 and into the first few weeks of 2002.[105]

Firms use downsizing as a restructuring strategy for different reasons. The most frequently cited reason is that the firm expects improved profitability from cost reductions and more efficient operations. For example, Ford announced a major downsizing and restructuring plan in 2002 that the company predicts will increase its operating profits by as much as $9 billion over the next few years. To reach this goal, Ford will lay off 35,000 employees worldwide, closing five manufacturing plants and cutting production at the remaining plants by an average of 16 percent. Because four of the five plants scheduled for closure are in the United States and the fifth is in

Canada, North American operations will be hit particularly hard. Ford executives felt forced to take this action because of poor financial performance and a loss of market share to competitors.[106]

Downscoping

Compared to downsizing, downscoping has a more positive effect on firm performance.[107] *Downscoping* refers to divestiture, spin-off, or some other means of eliminating businesses that are unrelated to a firm's core businesses. Commonly, downscoping is described as a set of actions that causes a firm to strategically refocus on its core businesses.

A firm that downscopes often also downsizes simultaneously. However, it does not eliminate key employees from its primary businesses in the process, because such action could lead to a loss of one or more core competencies. Instead, a firm that is simultaneously downscoping and downsizing becomes smaller by reducing the diversity of businesses in its portfolio.

By refocusing on its core businesses, the firm can be managed more effectively by the top management team. Managerial effectiveness increases because the firm has become less diversified, allowing the top management team to better understand and manage the remaining businesses.[108]

In general, U.S. firms use downscoping as a restructuring strategy more frequently than do European companies. In general, the trend in Europe, Latin America, and Asia has been to build conglomerates. In Latin America, these conglomerates are called *grupos*. Many Asian and Latin American conglomerates have begun to adopt Western corporate strategies in recent years and have been refocusing on their core businesses. This downscoping has occurred simultaneously with increasing globalization and with more open markets that have greatly enhanced the competition. By downscoping, these firms have been able to focus on their core businesses and improve their competitiveness.[109]

Among the U.S.-based firms using downscoping as a restructuring strategy, AT&T has refocused twice in the last ten years. Poor performance was the primary reason for both restructuring actions. In the first action, AT&T completed a trivestiture by spinning off Lucent Technologies and NCR. When AT&T's core long distance business began to lose market share, CEO Michael Armstrong diversified by acquiring cable companies at too high a price. He then provided high-speed Internet access and local telephone service over the cable-television network, but these services could not compensate for the poor performance in the core business. Therefore, in what is called "Armstrong's last stand," the downscoping restructuring was announced.[110]

In 2001, as part of his restructuring plan, AT&T CEO C. Michael Armstrong oversaw the auction of AT&T's cable television business, unwound an international joint venture with BT Group, and cut debt by $22 billion. Further cost-cutting measures in 2002 included the sale of AT&T's New Jersey headquarters property.

Leveraged Buyouts

Leveraged buyouts are commonly used as a restructuring strategy to correct for managerial mistakes or because the firm's managers are making decisions that primarily serve their own interests rather than those of shareholders.[111] A *leveraged buyout* (LBO) is a restructuring strategy whereby a party buys all of a firm's assets in order to take the firm private. Once the transaction is completed, the company's stock is no longer traded publicly.

Usually, significant amounts of debt are incurred to finance the buyout, hence the term "leveraged" buyout. To support debt payments and to downscope the company to concentrate on the firm's core businesses, the new owners may immediately sell a number of assets.[112] It is not uncommon for those buying a firm through an LBO to restructure the firm to the point that it can be sold at a profit within a five-year to eight-year period.

Management buyouts (MBOs), employee buyouts (EBOs), and whole-firm buyouts, in which one company or partnership purchases an entire company instead of a part of it, are the three types of LBOs. In part because of managerial incentives, MBOs, more so than EBOs and whole-firm buyouts, have been found to lead to downscoping, an increased strategic focus, and improved performance.[113] Research has shown that management buyouts can also lead to greater entrepreneurial activity and growth.

While there may be different reasons for a buyout, one is to protect against a capricious financial market, allowing the owners to focus on developing innovations and bringing them to the market.[114] As such, buyouts can represent a form of firm rebirth to facilitate entrepreneurial efforts and stimulate strategic growth.[115]

Restructuring Outcomes

The short-term and long-term outcomes resulting from the three restructuring strategies are shown in Figure 7.2. As indicated, downsizing does not commonly lead to a higher firm performance. Still, in free-market-based societies at large, downsizing has generated a host of entrepreneurial new ventures as individuals who are laid off start their own businesses.

Research has shown that downsizing contributed to lower returns for both U.S. and Japanese firms. The stock markets in the firms' respective nations evaluated downsizing negatively. Investors concluded that downsizing would have a negative

| Figure 7.2 | Restructuring and Outcomes |

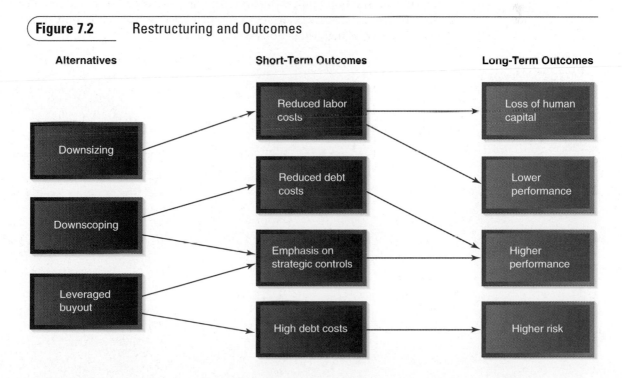

effect on companies' ability to achieve strategic competitiveness in the long term. Investors also seem to assume that downsizing occurs as a consequence of other problems in a company.[116] Ford's announcement in 2002 that it was downsizing by eliminating 35,000 jobs exemplifies this situation. Ford is experiencing significant performance problems due to its lack of competitiveness in the markets in which it competes.[117]

As shown in Figure 7.2, downsizing tends to result in a loss of human capital in the long term. Losing employees with many years of experience with the firm represents a major loss of knowledge. As noted in Chapter 3, knowledge is vital to competitive success in the global economy.[118] Thus, in general, research evidence and corporate experience suggest that downsizing may be of more tactical (or short-term) value than strategic (or long-term) value.

As Figure 7.2 indicates, downscoping generally leads to more positive outcomes in both the short and the long term than does downsizing or engaging in a leveraged buyout. Downscoping's desirable long-term outcome of higher performance is a product of reduced debt costs and the emphasis on strategic controls derived from concentrating on the firm's core businesses. In so doing, the refocused firm should be able to increase its ability to compete.

While whole-firm LBOs have been hailed as a significant innovation in the financial restructuring of firms, there can be negative trade-offs. First, the resulting large debt increases the financial risk of the firm, as is evidenced by the number of companies that filed for bankruptcy in the 1990s after executing a whole-firm LBO. Sometimes, the intent of the owners to increase the efficiency of the bought-out firm and then sell it within five to eight years creates a short-term and risk-averse managerial focus. As a result, these firms may fail to invest adequately in R&D or take other major actions designed to maintain or improve the company's core competence.[119] However, research also suggests that in firms with an entrepreneurial mind-set, buyouts can lead to greater innovation, especially if the debt load is not too great.[120] In a more recent action, AT&T was broken into four separate businesses: wireless, broadband, business services, and consumer service. Research has shown that refocusing is usually not successful unless the firm has adequate resources to have the flexibility to formulate the necessary strategies to compete effectively.[121] Thus, only time will tell if AT&T's latest restructuring efforts will be successful.

Summary

- Acquisition strategies are increasingly popular. Because of globalization, deregulation of multiple industries in many different economies, and favorable legislation, etc., the number and size of domestic and cross-border acquisitions continues to increase.

- Firms use acquisition strategies to (1) increase market power, (2) overcome entry barriers to new markets or regions, (3) avoid the costs of developing new products and increase the speed of new market entries, (4) reduce the risk of entering a new business, (5) become more diversified, (6) reshape their competitive scope by developing a different portfolio of businesses, and (7) enhance their learning, thereby adding to their knowledge base.

- Among the problems associated with the use of an acquisition strategy are (1) the difficulty of effectively integrating the firms involved, (2) incorrectly evaluating the target firm's value, (3) creating debt loads that preclude adequate long-term investments (e.g., R&D), (4) overestimating the potential for synergy, (5) creating a firm that is too diversified, (6) creating an internal environment in which managers devote increasing amounts of their time and energy to analyzing and completing the acquisition, and (7) developing a combined firm that is too large, necessitating extensive use of bureaucratic, rather than strategic, controls.

- Effective acquisitions have the following characteristics: (1) the acquiring and target firms have complementary resources that can be the basis of core competencies in the newly created firm, (2) the acquisition is friendly thereby facilitating integration of the two firms' resources, (3) the target firm is selected and purchased based on thorough due diligence, (4) the acquiring and target firms have considerable slack in the form of cash or debt capacity, (5) the merged firm maintains a low or moderate level of debt by

selling off portions of the acquired firm or some of the acquiring firm's poorly performing units, (6) the acquiring and acquired firms have experience in terms of adapting to change, and (7) R&D and innovation are emphasized in the new firm.

- Restructuring is used to improve a firm's performance by correcting for problems created by ineffective management. Restructuring by downsizing involves reducing a number of employees and hierarchical levels in the firm. Although it can lead to short-term cost reductions, they may be realized at the expense of long-term success, because of the loss of valuable human resources (and knowledge).

- The goal of restructuring through downscoping is to reduce the firm's level of diversification. Often, the firm divests unrelated businesses to achieve this goal. Eliminating unrelated businesses makes it easier for the firm and its top-level managers to refocus on the core businesses.

- Leveraged buyouts (LBOs) represent an additional restructuring strategy. Through an LBO, a firm is purchased so that it can become a private entity. LBOs usually are financed largely through debt. There are three types of LBOs: management buyouts (MBOs), employee buyouts (EBOs), and whole-firm LBOs. Because they provide clear managerial incentives, MBOs have been the most successful of the three. Oftentimes, the intent of a buyout is to improve efficiency and performance to point where the firm can be sold successfully within five to eight years.

- Commonly, restructuring's primary goal is gaining or reestablishing effective strategic control of the firm. Of the three restructuring strategies, downscoping is aligned the most closely with establishing and using strategic controls.

Review Questions

1. Why are acquisition strategies popular in many firms competing in the global economy?

2. What reasons account for firms' decisions to use acquisition strategies as one means of achieving strategic competitiveness?

3. What are the seven primary problems that affect a firm's efforts to successfully use an acquisition strategy?

4. What are the attributes associated with a successful acquisition strategy?

5. What is the restructuring strategy and what are its common forms?

6. What are the short- and long-term outcomes associated with the different restructuring strategies?

Mergers and Acquisitions

You are on the executive board of an information technology firm that provides trafficking software to the trucking industry. One of the firm's managers feels the company should grow and has suggested expanding by creating trafficking software for rail shipments or by offering trucking trafficking services online. You know your firm is in a position to expand but are not sure about the best way to do so.

Part One. Should the firm consider a merger with or an acquisition of a firm that offers the suggested services, or should it develop them internally? List the advantages and disadvantages of each strategic option.

Part Two. Based on your findings and other information, assume that your firm decides to obtain trafficking software for rail shipments through an acquisition of an existing firm. Predict some general problems your firm might encounter in an acquisition and how they might be resolved.

1. R. Whittington, 1999, In praise of the evergreen conglomerate, Mastering Strategy (Part Six), *Financial Times,* November 1, 4–6; P. Moran & S. Ghoshal, 1999, Markets, firms, and the process of economic development, *Academy of Management Review,* 24: 390–412; M. A. Hitt, R. E. Hoskisson, R. D. Ireland, & J. S. Harrison, 1991, Effects of acquisitions on R&D inputs and outputs, *Academy of Management Journal,* 34: 693–706.

2. M. A. Hitt, J. S. Harrison, & R. D. Ireland, 2001, *Mergers and Acquisitions: A Guide to Creating Value for Stakeholders,* New York: Oxford University Press.

3. 2000, How M&As will navigate the turn into a new century, *Mergers & Acquisitions,* January, 29–35.

4. J. A. Schmidt, 2002, Business perspective on mergers and acquisitions, in J. A. Schmidt (ed.), *Making Mergers Work,* Alexandria, VA: Society for Human Resource Management, 23–46.

5. M. A. Hitt, R. D. Ireland, & J. S. Harrison, 2001, Mergers and acquisitions: A value creating or a value destroying strategy? In M. A. Hitt, R. E. Freeman, & J. S. Harrison, *Handbook of Strategic Management,* Oxford, U.K.: Blackwell Publishers, 385–408.

6. L. Saigol, 2002, Thin pickings in dismal year for dealmaking, *Financial Times,* http://www.ft.com, January 2; 2001, Waiting for growth, *The Economist,* http://www.economist.com, April 27.

7. 2002, Mergers Snapshot: 2001 deal volume, *The Wall Street Journal,* January 4, C12; 2001, The great merger wave breaks, *The Economist,* January 27, 59–60.

8. R. Sidel, 2002, Volatile U.S. markets and global slowdown cool corporate desire to merge, *The Wall Street Journal,* January 2, R10.

9. P. Chattopadhyay, W. H. Glick, & G. P. Huber, 2001, Organizational actions in response to threats and opportunities, *Academy of Management Journal,* 44: 937–955.

10. H. T. J. Smit, 2001, Acquisition strategies as option games, *Journal of Applied Corporate Finance,* 14 (2): 79–89.

11. J. Anand, 1999, How many matches are made in heaven, Mastering Strategy (Part Five), *Financial Times,* October 25, 6–7.

12. M. C. Jensen, 1988, Takeovers: Their causes and consequences, *Journal of Economic Perspectives,* 1(2): 21–48.

13. A. Rappaport & M. L. Sirower, 1999, Stock or cash? *Harvard Business Review,* 77(6): 147–158.

14. C. Grimes, 2002, AOL Time Warner offers conservative 2002 outlook, *Financial Times,* http://www.ft.com, January 8; C. Yang, R. Grover, & A. T. Palmer, 2001, Show time for AOL Time Warner, *Business Week,* January 15, 57–64.

15. R. Sidel, 2001, FPL, Entergy blame each other as they call off $8 billion merger, *The Wall Street Journal Interactive,* http://www.interactive.wsj.com, April 2.

16. E. Thorton, F. Keesnan, C. Palmeri, & L. Himelstein, 2002, It sure is getting hostile, *Business Week,* January 14, 28–30.

17. J. Harding & C. Grimes, 2002, MGM owner sounds out possible suitors, *Financial Times,* http://www.ft.com, January 16; B. Pulley, 2001, The wizard of MGM, *Forbes,* 122–128.

18. P. Haspeslagh, 1999, Managing the mating dance in equal mergers, Mastering Strategy (Part Five), *Financial Times,* October 25, 14–15.

19. P. Wright, M. Kroll, & D. Elenkov, 2002, Acquisition returns, increase in firm size and chief executive officer compensation: The moderating role of monitoring, *Academy of Management Journal,* 45: in press.

20. G. Anders, 2002, Lessons from WaMU's M&A playbook, *Fast Company,* January, 100–107.

21. L. Capron, 1999, Horizontal acquisitions: The benefits and risks to long-term performance, *Strategic Management Journal,* 20: 987–1018.

22. M. Lubatkin, W. S. Schulze, A. Mainkar, & R. W. Cotterill, 2001, Ecological investigation of firm effects in horizontal mergers, *Strategic Management Journal,* 22: 335–357; K. Ramaswamy, 1997, The performance impact of strategic similarity in horizontal mergers: Evidence from the U.S. banking industry, *Academy of Management Journal,* 40: 697–715.

23. L. Capron, W. Mitchell, & A. Swaminathan, 2001, Asset divestiture following horizontal acquisitions: A dynamic view, *Strategic Management Journal,* 22: 817–844.

24. C. Parkes, 2001, Disney's debt climbs to $15 billion on Fox Family buy, *Financial Times,* http://www.ft.com, July 24; N. Deogun, B. Orwall, & J. Lippman, 2001, Disney plans to acquire Fox Family for $3 billion and debt assumption, *The Wall Street Journal Interactive,* http://interactive.wsj.com, July 23; N. Deogun & J. Lippman, 2001, Disney nears deal to buy Fox Family but AOL, Viacom continue talks, *The Wall Street Journal Interactive,* http://interactive.wsj.com, July 21.

25. M. Murray, P. Shiskin, B. Davis, & A. Raghavan, 2001, As Honeywell deal goes awry for GE, fallout may be global, *The Wall Street Journal Interactive,* http://interactive.wsj.com, June 14.

26. Q. Hardy, 2002, Compaq with the devil, *Forbes,* January 7, 40.

27. M. Lerner, 2001, Israeli Antitrust Authority's general director David Tadmor on corporate mergers, *Academy of Management Executive,* 15(1): 8–11.

28. S. J. Chang & P. M. Rosenzweig, 2001, The choice of entry mode in sequential foreign direct investment, *Strategic Management Journal,* 22: 747–776.

29. J. A. Gingrich, 1999, Five rules for winning emerging market consumers, *Strategy & Business,* 15: 19–33.

30. Hitt, Harrison, & Ireland, *Mergers and Acquisitions,* Chapter 10; D. Angwin & B. Savill, 1997, Strategic perspectives on European cross–border acquisitions: A view from the top European executives, *European Management Review,* 15: 423–435.

31. Schmidt, Business perspective on mergers and acquisitions.

32. 1999, Bloomberg News, Kimberly-Clark planning acquisitions, *Dallas Morning News,* December 1, D2; E. Robinson, 1999, Shiseido pursues M&A, *Financial Times,* July 27, 14.

33. J. K. Shank & V. Govindarajan, 1992, Strategic cost analysis of technological investments, *Sloan Management Review,* 34(3): 39–51.

34. Hitt, Harrison, & Ireland, *Mergers and Acquisitions.*

35. M. A. Hitt, R. E. Hoskisson, R. A. Johnson, & D. D. Moesel, 1996, The market for corporate control and firm innovation, *Academy of Management Journal,* 39: 1084–1119.

36. R. Coff, 2002, Bidding wars over R&D intensive firms: Knowledge, opportunism and the market for corporate control, *Academy of Management Journal,* 45: in press.

37. R. Langreth, 2002, Betting on the brain, *Forbes,* January 7, 57–59.

38. K. F. McCardle & S. Viswanathan, 1994, The direct entry versus takeover decision and stock price performance around takeovers, *Journal of Business,* 67: 1–43.

39. J. W. Lu & P. W. Beamish, 2001, The internationalization and performance of SMEs, *Strategic Management Journal,* 22(Special Issue): 565–586.

40. G. Ahuja & C. Lampert, 2001, Entrepreneurship in the large corporation: A longitudinal study of how established firms create breakthrough inventions, *Strategic Management Journal,* 22(Special Issue): 521–543.

41. F. Rothaermel, 2001, Incumbent's advantage through exploiting complementary assets via Interfirm cooperation, *Strategic Management Journal,* 22(Special Issue): 687–699.

42. G. Ahuja & R. Katila, 2001, Technological acquisitions and the innovation performance of acquiring firms: A longitudinal study, *Strategic Management Journal,* 22: 197–220. M. A. Hitt, R. E. Hoskisson, & R. D. Ireland, 1990, Mergers and acquisitions and managerial commitment to innovation in M-form firms, *Strategic Management Journal,* 11(Special Summer Issue): 29–47.

43. Hitt, Hoskisson, Johnson, & Moesel, The market for corporate control.

44. Hitt, Hoskisson, Ireland, & Harrison, Effects of acquisitions on R&D inputs and outputs, 693–706.

45. D. D. Bergh, 1997, Predicting divestiture of unrelated acquisitions: An integrative model of ex ante conditions, *Strategic Management Journal,* 18: 715–731.

46. P. L. Moore, 2001, The most aggressive CEO, *Business Week,* May 28, 67–77.

47. Hitt, Harrison, & Ireland, *Mergers and Acquisitions.*

48. J. Anand & H. Singh, 1997, Asset redeployment, acquisitions and corporate strategy in declining industries, *Strategic Management Journal,* 18(Special Summer Issue): 99–118.

49. M. Raynor, 2001, *Strategic Flexibility in the Financial Services Industry,* report published by Deloitte Consulting and Deloitte & Touche, Toronto, Canada.

50. W. J. Ferrier, 2001, Navigating the competitive landscape: The drivers and consequences of competitive aggressiveness, *Academy of Management Journal,* 44: 858–877.

51. 2002, General Electric, *Standard & Poor's Stock Report,* http://www.fidelity.com, April 4; R. E. Hoskisson & M. A. Hitt, 1994, *Downscoping: How to Tame the Diversified Firm,* New York: Oxford University Press.

52. F. Vermeulen & H. Barkema, 2001, Learning through acquisitions, *Academy of Management Journal,* 44: 457–476.

53. J. S. Harrison, M. A. Hitt, R. E. Hoskisson, & R. D. Ireland, 2001, Resource complementarities in business combinations: Extending the logic to organizational alliances, *Journal of Management,* 27: 679–690.

54. M. Killick, I. Rawoot, & G. J. Stockport, 2001, *Cisco Systems Inc–Growth Through Acquisitions*, case in the European Case Clearing House Collection; A. Muoio, 2000, Cisco's quick study, *Fast Company,* October, 287–295.

55. G. Colvin, 2000, America's most admired companies, *Fortune,* February 21, 108–111.

56. Schmidt, Business perspective on mergers and acquisitions.

57. Hitt, Harrison, & Ireland, *Mergers and Acquisitions.*

58. A. J. Viscio, J. R. Harbison, A. Asin, & R. P. Vitaro, 1999, Post-merger integration: What makes mergers work? *Strategy & Business,* 17: 26–33; D. K. Datta, 1991, Organizational fit and acquisition performance: Effects of post-acquisition integration, *Strategic Management Journal,* 12: 281–297.

59. M. Zollo, 1999, M&A—the challenge of learning to integrate, Mastering Strategy (Part Eleven), *Financial Times,* December 6, 14–15.

60. Ibid., 14.

61. M. A. Hitt, L. Bierman, K. Shimizu, & R. Kochhar, 2001, Direct and moderating effects of human capital on strategy and performance in professional service firms, *Academy of Management Journal,* 44: 13–28.

62. G. G. Dess & J. D. Shaw, 2001, Voluntary turnover, social capital and organizational performance, *Academy of Management Review,* 26: 446–456.

63. J. A. Krug & H. Hegarty, 2001, Predicting who stays and leaves after an acquisition: A study of top managers in multinational firms, *Strategic Management Journal,* 22: 185–196.

64. K. Ohmae, 1999, The Godzilla companies of the new economy, *Strategy & Business,* 18: 130–139.

65. Rappaport & Sirower, Stock or cash? 149.

66. G. Yago, 1991, Junk Bonds: How High Yield Securities Restructured Corporate America, New York: Oxford University Press, 146–148.

67. M. C. Jensen, 1986, Agency costs of free cash flow, corporate finance, and takeovers, *American Economic Review,* 76: 323–329.

68. C. Parkee, 2001, Disney's debt climbs to $15 billion on Fox Family buy, *Financial Times,* http://www.ft.com, July 24.

69. C. Grimes, 2002, Takeover talk grows at Disney amid frustration, *Financial Times,* http://www.ft.com, January 16.

70. N. Byrnes & M. Arndt, 2001, John Dillion's high-risk paper chase, *Business Week,* January 22, 58–60.

71. M. A. Hitt & D. L. Smart, 1994, Debt: A disciplining force for managers or a debilitating force for organizations? *Journal of Management Inquiry,* 3: 144–152.

72. Hitt, Harrison, & Ireland, *Mergers and Acquisitions.*

73. T. N. Hubbard, 1999, Integration strategies and the scope of the company, Mastering Strategy (Part Eleven), *Financial Times,* December 6, 8–10.

74. Hitt, Harrison, & Ireland, *Mergers and Acquisitions.*

75. Ibid.

76. Harrison, Hitt, Hoskisson, & Ireland, Resource complementarity; J. B. Barney, 1988, Returns to bidding firms in mergers and acquisitions: Reconsidering the relatedness hypothesis, *Strategic Management Journal,* 9(Special Summer Issue): 71–78.

77. O. E. Williamson, 1999, Strategy research: Governance and competence perspectives, *Strategic Management Journal,* 20: 1087–1108.

78. Hitt, Hoskisson, Johnson, & Moesel, The market for corporate control.

79. 2002, Forbes 400 best big companies, *Forbes,* http://www.forbes.com, January 14.

80. C. W. L. Hill & R. E. Hoskisson, 1987, Strategy and structure in the multiproduct firm, *Academy of Management Review,* 12: 331–341.

81. R. A. Johnson, R. E. Hoskisson, & M. A. Hitt, 1993, Board of director involvement in restructuring: The effects of board versus managerial controls and characteristics, *Strategic Management Journal,* 14(Special Issue): 33–50; C. C. Markides, 1992, Consequences of corporate refocusing: Ex ante evidence, *Academy of Management Journal,* 35: 398–412.

82. D. Palmer & B. N. Barber, 2001, Challengers, elites and families: A social class theory of corporate acquisitions, *Administrative Science Quarterly,* 46: 87–120.

83. Hitt, Harrison, & Ireland, *Mergers and Acquisitions.*

84. Ibid.

85. Hitt, Johnson, & Moesel, The market for corporate control.

86. M. Arndt, 2001, A merger's bitter harvest, *Business Week,* February 5, 112–114.

87. Hitt, Harrison, & Ireland, *Mergers and Acquisitions;* Hitt, Hoskisson, Ireland, & Harrison, The effects of acquisitions.

88. R. E. Hoskisson, M. A. Hitt, & R. D. Ireland, 1994, The effects of acquisitions and restructuring (strategic refocusing) strategies on innovation, in G. von Krogh, A. Sinatra, and H. Singh (eds.), *Managing Corporate Acquisitions,* London: Macmillan Press, 144–169.

89. T. Lowry, 2001, How many magazines did we buy today? *Business Week,* January 22, 98–99.

90. Hitt, Harrison, & Ireland, *Mergers and Acquisitions.*

91. Ibid.

92. M. A. Hitt, R. D. Ireland, J. S. Harrison, & A. Best, 1998, Attributes of successful and unsuccessful acquisitions of U.S. firms, *British Journal of Management,* 9: 91–114.

93. Harrison, Hitt, Hoskisson, & Ireland, Resource complementarity.

94. J. Reuer, 2001, From hybrids to hierarchies: Shareholder wealth effects of joint venture partner buyouts, *Strategic Management Journal,* 22: 27–44.

95. D. D. Bergh, 2001, Executive retention and acquisition outcomes: A test of opposing views on the influence of organizational tenure, *Journal of Management,* 27: 603–622; J. P. Walsh, 1989, Doing a deal: Merger and acquisition negotiations and their impact upon target company top management turnover, *Strategic Management Journal,* 10: 307–322.

96. M. L. Marks & P. H. Mirvis, 2001, Making mergers and acquisitions work: Strategic and psychological preparation, *Academy of Management Executive,* 15(2): 80–92.

97. Hitt, Harrison, & Ireland, *Mergers and Acquisitions;* Q. N. Huy, 2001, Time, temporal capability and planned change, *Academy of Management Review,* 26: 601–623; L. Markoczy, 2001, Consensus formation during strategic change, *Strategic Management Journal,* 22: 1013–1031.

98. R. W. Coff, 2002, Human capital, shared expertise, and the likelihood of impasse in corporate acquisitions, *Journal of Management,* in press.

99. Anand, How many matches, 6.

100. R. A. Johnson, 1996, Antecedents and outcomes of corporate refocusing, *Journal of Management,* 22: 437–481; J. E. Bethel & J. Liebeskind, 1993, The effects of ownership structure on corporate restructuring, *Strategic Management Journal,* 14(Special Issue, Summer): 15–31.

101. R. E. Hoskisson, R. A. Johnson, D. Yiu, & W. P. Wan, 2001, Restructuring strategies of diversified groups: Differences associated with country institutional environments, in M. A. Hitt, R. E. Freeman, and J. S. Harrison (eds.), *Handbook of Strategic Management,* Oxford, UK: Blackwell Publishers, 433–463; S. R. Fisher & M. A. White, 2000, Downsizing in a learning organization: Are there hidden costs? *Academy of Management Review,* 25: 244–251; A. Campbell & D. Sadtler, 1998, Corporate breakups, *Strategy & Business,* 12: 64–73; E. Bowman & H. Singh, 1990, Overview of corporate restructuring: Trends and consequences, in L. Rock & R. H. Rock (eds.), *Corporate Restructuring,* New York: McGraw-Hill.

102. Hitt, Harrison, & Ireland, *Mergers and Acquisitions.*

103. W. McKinley, J. Zhao, & K. G. Rust, 2000, A sociocognitive interpretation of organizational downsizing, *Academy of Management Review,* 25: 227–243.

104. W. McKinley, C. M. Sanchez, & A. G. Schick, 1995, Organizational downsizing: Constraining, cloning, learning, *Academy of Management Executive,* IX(3): 32–44.

105. P. Patsuris, 2002, Forbes.com layoff tracker surpasses 1M mark, *Forbes,* http://www.forbes.com, January 16.

106. 2002, Ford to cut 35,000 jobs, close five plants, slash production in broad restructuring, *The Wall Street Journal Interactive,* http://interactive.wsj.com, January 13.

107. Hoskisson & Hitt, *Downscoping.*

108. Johnson, Hoskisson, & Hitt, Board of directors' involvement; R. E. Hoskisson & M. A. Hitt, 1990, Antecedents and performance outcomes of diversification: A review and critique of theoretical perspectives, *Journal of Management,* 16: 461–509.

109. Hoskisson, Johnson, Yiu, & Wan, Restructuring strategies.

110. S. Rosenbush, 2001, Armstrong's last stand, *Business Week,* February 5, 88–96.

111. D. D. Bergh & G. F. Holbein, 1997, Assessment and redirection of longitudinal analysis: Demonstration with a study of the diversification and divestiture relationship, *Strategic Management Journal,* 18: 557–571; C. C. Markides & H. Singh, 1997, Corporate restructuring: A symptom of poor governance or a solution to past managerial mistakes? *European Management Journal,* 15: 213–219.

112. M. F. Wiersema & J. P. Liebeskind, 1995, The effects of leveraged buyouts on corporate growth and diversification in large firms, *Strategic Management Journal,* 16: 447–460.

113. A. Seth & J. Easterwood, 1995, Strategic redirection in large management buyouts: The evidence from post-buyout restructuring activity, *Strategic Management Journal,* 14: 251–274; P. H. Phan & C. W. L. Hill, 1995, Organizational restructuring and economic performance in leveraged buyouts: An ex-post study, *Academy of Management Journal,* 38: 704–739.

114. M. Wright, R. E. Hoskisson, L. W. Busenitz, & J. Dial, 2000, Entrepreneurial growth through privatization: The upside of management buyouts, *Academy of Management Review,* 25: 591–601.

115. M. Wright, R. E. Hoskisson, & L. W. Busenitz, 2001, Firm rebirth: Buyouts as facilitators of strategic growth and entrepreneurship, *Academy of Management Executive,* 15 (1): 111–125.

116. P. M. Lee, 1997, A comparative analysis of layoff announcements and stock price reactions in the United States and Japan, *Strategic Management Journal,* 18: 879–894.

117. Ford to cut 35,000 jobs.

118. Fisher & White, Downsizing in a learning organization.

119. W. F. Long & D. J. Ravenscraft, 1993, LBOs, debt, and R&D intensity, *Strategic Management Journal,* 14(Special Summer Issue): 119–135.

120. Wright, Hoskisson, Busenitz, & Dial, Entrepreneurial growth through privatization.

121. D. D. Dawley, J. J. Hoffman, & B. T. Lamont, 2002, Choice situation, refocusing and post-bankruptcy performance, *Journal of Management,* in press.

Chapter Eight

International Strategy

Knowledge Objectives

Studying this chapter should provide you with the strategic management knowledge needed to:

1. Explain traditional and emerging motives for firms to pursue international diversification.

2. Explore the four factors that lead to a basis for international business-level strategies.

3. Define the three international corporate-level strategies: multidomestic, global, and transnational.

4. Discuss the environmental trends affecting international strategy, especially liability of foreignness and regionalization.

5. Name and describe the five alternative modes for entering international markets.

6. Explain the effects of international diversification on firm returns and innovation.

7. Name and describe two major risks of international diversification.

8. Explain why the positive outcomes from international expansion are limited.

China Enters the World Trade Organization

On September 17, 2001, just a few days after the September 11 terrorist attacks, Beijing and its Chinese leaders formally accepted the requirements to enter the World Trade Organization (WTO). Over the next five years, this agreement portends to create a more open market and lower tariffs for importing and exporting goods into and out of China as the country increases its world trade and has more trading partners. Because of the size of the Chinese market, the agreement's effect on globalization is expected to be significant.

China's orientation toward increased trade actually began in 1979 when the late Chinese leader Deng Xiaoping introduced reforms leading towards a market economy. This change was phased in through a decentralization process, during which most enterprises were turned over to local government officials. At the same time, state-owned enterprises were gradually introduced to a market economy. Thus, Chinese leaders have been preparing for entrance into the WTO for over the last 20 years. However, because most Chinese firms are still all or partially state-owned, significant changes must occur in these firms as they encounter more efficient and competitive foreign firms in the global marketplace. In fact, Premier Zhu Rongji, the current leader of the reforms, said that to meet the competition, state-owned enterprises would need to reduce their work forces by "two-thirds." This reduction would result in 25 million people being added to China's unemployment rolls by 2006.

On the one hand, China seeks to compete strongly in high tech industries. For instance, the country hopes to supplant India as the number two software producer in the world after the United States. Currently, India holds this position, but like India, China also offers a well-educated, hardworking technology and engineering work force, but India exports $6.2 billion worth of software, while China has not yet reached the $1 billion mark.

To learn more about the Indian approach, the Chinese minister of higher education recently visited India's Bangalore software district, where Chinese software firm Huawei Technologies has a center. The firm's biggest operation outside of China, Huawei's Bangalore operation employs 536 people—180 Chinese workers work alongside Indian programmers to learn how the Indian employees approach the

In November 2001, China's Shi Guangsheng signed an agreement to join the World Trade Organization, which describes its purpose as "the only global international organization dealing with the rules of trade between nations. At its heart are the WTO agreements, negotiated and signed by the bulk of the world's trading nations and ratified in their parliaments. The goal is to help producers of goods and services, exporters, and importers conduct their business."

中国加入世界贸易组织签字仪式

SIGNING CEREMONY ON CHINA'S ACCESSION TO THE WTO

11 November 2001, Doha

development of software code. As a professor from China says, "They are learning how Indian programmers work together, how they coordinate."

On the other hand, however, China has a number of state-owned firms that are not competitive in world markets. Even though many firms have made significant changes during previous reforms, more change is necessary for them to be competitive. For instance, Angang Iron & Steel was listed in 1997 as a "red chip" firm on the Hong Kong exchange (only the best state-owned firms have qualified to be listed on Hong Kong or Shanghai stock exchanges). Since 1995, to make improvements in productivity, Angang has cut 30,000 people from its employment rolls (it still employs a total of 165,000). However, relative to South Korean steel producer Posco, Angang still needs to be more competitive. Posco produces 26 million tons of steel with 20,000 workers, while Angang produces 9.3 million tons with 43,000 workers— meaning that Posco is six times as productive as Angang. Even though Chinese wages are lower than those in South Korea, this example indicates that many of China's more productive employers have a long way to go to be competitive in world markets.

Still, China is a magnet for foreign direct investment and has an economy that has grown 8 percent per year in the recent past. In 2000, China's foreign direct investment was up 20 percent to a total of $27.4 billion, more than the combined investment received by the rest of Asia

As the Opening Case indicates, China's entry into the World Trade Organization (WTO) has put significant focus on this huge potential market. While more firms will enter China in the coming years, many foreign firms who have entered China have found it difficult to establish legitimacy.[1] This is most likely due to China's recent history.

"Collective property party" is the Chinese translation of the term *communist party*. Although law has established property rights, many Chinese (still under a Communist regime) do not share this mind-set. Their opposition to property rights is mainly of two types: ideological and practical. First, many local government and communist party officials feel that private enterprise is undermining the socialist ideal. As a result, many of the local policies (such as taxes, license fees, and so on) towards private firms are punitive. Second, as pointed out in the Opening Case, many officials fear that foreign private domestic competitors will undermine state-owned enterprises, which provide social, educational, medical, and retirement benefits to their employees. Although China's reforms include funds for social programs, there may be uncertainty as to how they will be distributed locally. Thus, private firms and those that are becoming more market oriented must work hard to establish legitimacy with local government officials, suppliers, and customers.

China and its entrance into the WTO clearly illustrate how entering international markets features both opportunities and threats for firms that choose to compete in global markets. This chapter examines opportunities facing firms as they seek to develop and exploit core competencies by diversifying into global markets. In (not including Japan). Although the country should grow and develop a strong middle class because of the direct foreign investment and its economic growth, it will also suffer from market liberalization. Thus, China's entrance into the WTO creates both a challenge and an opportunity for the country.

China will pursue its typical incremental strategy of change as it moves into world markets and is not likely to follow the WTO rules as strictly as preferred for new foreign entrants. In fact, China's decentralization from 1979 to the present will likely make implementation of the WTO rules somewhat difficult. Because local Chinese governments have more control now, the implementation will largely fall to local government officials, making the process of change more incremental than revolutionary. These local barriers are likely to facilitate an increase in foreign direct investment, however, because foreign firms will have to invest to overcome them. Consequently, although change represents an important opportunity with a significant risk of social upheaval, it will lead to more globalization both for China and for those investing in the nation's future.

SOURCES: S. Rai, 2002, Chinese race to supplant India software, *The New York Times*, http://www.nytimes.com, January 5; 2001, Asia: Ready for the competition? China and the WTO, *The Economist*, September 15, 35–36; B. Einhorn, C. Dawson, I. Kunii, D. Roberts, A. Webb, & P. Engardio, 2001, China: Will its entry into the WTO unleash new prosperity or further destabilize the world economy? *Business Week*, October 29, 38; 2001, Finance and economics: China's economy, celebration, and concern, *The Economist,* November 10, 102; D. Murphy, 2001, Riding the tiger of trade, *Far Economic Eastern Review*, November 22, 38–44; B. Powell, 2001, China's great step forward, *Fortune*, September 17, 128–142; A. Tanzer, 2001, Chinese walls, *Forbes*, November 12, 74–75.

addition, we discuss different problems, complexities, and threats that might accompany use of the firm's international strategies. Although national boundaries, cultural differences, and geographical distances all pose barriers to entry into many markets, significant opportunities draw businesses into the international arena. A business that plans to operate globally must formulate a successful strategy to take advantage of these global opportunities.[2] Furthermore, to mold their firms into truly global companies, managers must develop global mind-sets. Especially in regard to managing human resources, traditional means of operating with little cultural diversity and without global sourcing are no longer effective.[3]

As firms move into international markets, they develop relationships with suppliers, customers, and partners, and then learn from these relationships. Selling its products in 190 countries, Siemens, for example, uses 31 websites in 38 languages to facilitate development and use of relationships as well as opportunities to learn from them. Firms also learn from their competitors in international markets. In essence, they begin to imitate each other's policies in order to compete more effectively.[4] Such activity is evident in the pharmaceuticals industry as firms compete against each other in global markets.[5]

In this chapter, as illustrated in Figure 1.1, we discuss the importance of international strategy as a source of strategic competitiveness and above-average returns. The chapter focuses on the incentives to internationalize. Once a firm decides to compete internationally, it must select its strategy and choose a mode of entry into international markets. It may enter international markets by exporting from domestic-based operations, licensing some of its products or services, forming joint ventures with international partners, acquiring a foreign-based firm, or establishing a new subsidiary. Such international diversification can extend product life cycles, provide incentives for more innovation, and produce above-average returns. These benefits are tempered by political and economic risks and the problems of managing a complex international firm with operations in multiple countries.

Figure 8.1 provides an overview of the various choices and outcomes. The relationships among international opportunities, and the exploration of resources and capabilities that result in strategies and modes of entry that are based on core competencies, are explored in this chapter.

Identifying International Opportunities: Incentives to Use an International Strategy

An **international strategy** is a strategy through which the firm sells its goods or services outside its domestic market.

An **international strategy** is a strategy through which the firm sells its goods or services outside its domestic market.[6] One of the primary reasons for implementing an international strategy (as opposed to a strategy focused on the domestic market) is that international markets yield potential new opportunities.

Raymond Vernon captured the classic rationale for international diversification.[7] He suggested that, typically, a firm discovers an innovation in its home-country market, especially in an advanced economy such as that of the United States. Some demand for the product may then develop in other countries, and exports are provided by domestic operations. Increased demand in foreign countries justifies direct foreign investment in production capacity abroad, especially because foreign competitors also organize to meet increasing demand. As the product becomes standardized, the firm may rationalize its operations by moving production to a region with low manufacturing costs.[8] Vernon, therefore, suggests that firms pursue international diversification to extend a product's life cycle.

Another traditional motive for firms to become multinational is to secure needed resources. Key supplies of raw material—especially minerals and energy—are

---

Figure 8.1   Opportunities and Outcomes of International Strategy

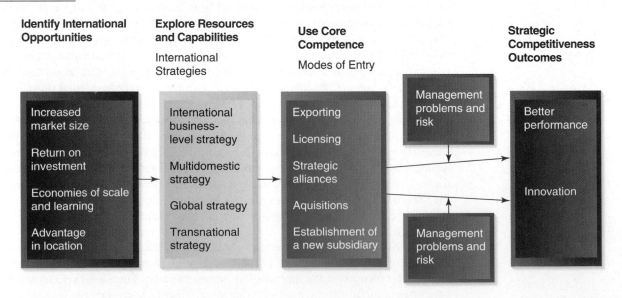

PART 2 / Strategic Actions: Strategy Formulation

important in some industries. For instance, aluminum producers need a supply of bauxite, tire firms need rubber, and oil companies scour the world to find new petroleum reserves. Other industries, such as clothing, electronics, watch making, and many others, seek low-cost factors of production, and have moved portions of their operations to foreign locations in pursuit of lower costs.

Research on China found that reasons for investing in China differ by the type of firm.[9] Large multinational firms invest primarily to gain access to the large demand potential of China's domestic market. Smaller firms from newly industrializing economies, such as Hong Kong, that use more mundane technologies are more interested in low-cost sources of inputs such as labor and land, to maintain their cost advantages.

Although these traditional motives persist, other emerging motivations also drive international expansion (see Chapter 1). For instance, pressure has increased for a global integration of operations, mostly driven by more universal product demand. As nations industrialize, the demand for some products and commodities appears to become more similar. This "nation-less," or borderless, demand for globally branded products may be due to similarities in lifestyle in developed nations. Increases in global communication media also facilitate the ability of people in different countries to visualize and model lifestyles in different cultures. Benetton, an Italian casual-wear apparel company, has used its global brand and well-established worldwide retail presence as the foundation needed to more effectively manage its supply and manufacturing networks with improved communications technology.[10]

In some industries, technology drives globalization because economies of scale necessary to reduce costs to the lowest level often require an investment greater than that needed to meet domestic market demand. The major Korean car manufacturers Daewoo and Hyundai certainly found this to be true.[11] There is also pressure for cost reductions, achieved by purchasing from the lowest-cost global suppliers. For instance, research and development expertise for an emerging business start-up may not exist in the domestic market.[12]

New large-scale, emerging markets, such as China and India, provide a strong internationalization incentive because of the potential demand in them.[13] Because of currency fluctuations, firms may also choose to distribute their operations across many countries, including emerging ones, in order to reduce the risk of devaluation in one country.[14] However, the uniqueness of emerging markets presents both opportunities and challenges.[15] While China, for example, differs from Western countries in many respects, including culture, politics, and the precepts of its economic system,[16] it also offers a huge potential market. Many international firms perceive Chinese markets as almost untouched markets, without exposure to many modern and sophisticated products. Once China is exposed to these products, these firms believe that demand will develop. However, the differences between China and Western countries pose serious challenges to Western competitive paradigms that emphasize the skills needed to manage financial, economic, and political risks.

A large majority of U.S.-based companies' international business is in European markets, where 60 percent of U.S. firms' assets that are located outside the domestic market are invested. Two-thirds of all foreign R&D spending by U.S. affiliates also takes place in Europe.[17] Companies seeking to internationalize their operations in Europe, as elsewhere, need to understand the pressure on them to respond to local, national, or regional customs, especially where goods or services require customization because of cultural differences or effective marketing to entice customers to try a different product.[18]

Of course, all firms encounter challenges when using an international strategy. For example, Unilever is a large European-centered global food and consumer products firm that adapts its products to local tastes as it moves into new national markets.

Its investors expect Unilever executives to create global mega-brands, which have the most growth potential and margins, even though most of Unilever's growth has come through acquisition and the selling of the acquired, unique local brands. Establishing mega-brands while also dealing with the forces for localization is difficult. As noted in Chapter 11, Unilever is restructuring to meet these challenges.[19]

Local repair and service capabilities are another factor influencing an increased desire for local country responsiveness. This localization may even affect industries that are seen as needing more global economies of scale, for example, white goods (home appliances, such as refrigerators). Alternatively, suppliers often follow their customers, particularly large ones, into international markets, which eliminates the firm's need to find local suppliers.[20] The transportation costs of large products and their parts, such as heavy earthmoving equipment, are significant, which may preclude a firm's suppliers following the firm to an international market.

Employment contracts and labor forces differ significantly in international markets. For example, it is more difficult to lay off employees in Europe than in the United States because of employment contract differences. In many cases, host governments demand joint ownership, which allows the foreign firm to avoid tariffs. Also, host governments frequently require a high percentage of procurements, manufacturing, and R&D to use local sources. These issues increase the need for local investment and responsiveness compared to seeking global economies of scale.[21]

We've discussed incentives influencing firms to use international strategies. When successful, firms can derive four basic benefits from using international strategies: (1) increased market size; (2) greater returns on major capital investments or on investments in new products and processes; (3) greater economies of scale, scope, or learning; and (4) a competitive advantage through location (for example, access to low-cost labor, critical resources, or customers). We examine these benefits in terms of both their costs (such as higher coordination expenses and limited access to knowledge about host country political influences[22]) and their managerial challenges.

Increased Market Size

Firms can expand the size of their potential market—sometimes dramatically—by moving into international markets. As part of its expansion efforts, Whirlpool learned how to be successful in emerging markets. In India, the firm conducted 14 months of research on local tastes and values. The company also provided incentives to Indian retailers to stock its products, and it uses local contractors to collect payments and deliver appliances throughout India. Since implementing this strategy in 1996, Whirlpool's sales in India had grown 80 percent by 2001. The ability to market its appliances overseas is important to Whirlpool because U.S. demand is forecast to stay flat through 2009, but international demand should grow 17 percent, to 293 million units.[23]

Although changing consumer tastes and practices linked to cultural values or traditions is not simple, following an international strategy is a particularly attractive option to firms (such as Whirlpool) competing in domestic markets that have limited growth opportunities. For example, the U.S. soft-drink industry is relatively saturated. Coca-Cola's case volume grew just about 1 percent per quarter in 2001 in North America, its largest market, but about 5 percent internationally.[24] PepsiCo hopes it has found a reliable growth driver with its purchase of Quaker Oats, the maker of the market leading sports drink Gatorade. PepsiCo plans to integrate Gatorade into its distribution systems and hopefully build market share outside of the United States.[25] Because most changes in domestic market share for any single firm come at the expense of competitors' shares, rivals Coca-Cola and PepsiCo entered international markets to take advantage of new growth opportunities instead of focusing on competing directly against each other to increase their share of their domestic, core soft drink market.[26]

The size of an international market also affects a firm's willingness to invest in R&D to build competitive advantages in that market. Larger markets usually offer higher potential returns and thus pose less risk for a firm's investments. The strength of the science base in the country in question also can affect a firm's foreign R&D investments. Most firms prefer to invest more heavily in those countries with the scientific knowledge and talent to produce value-creating products and processes from their R&D activities. However, research indicates that simultaneously pursuing R&D and collaborative foreign R&D joint ventures reduces effectiveness.[27]

Return on Investment

Large markets may be crucial for earning a return on significant investments, such as plant and capital equipment or R&D. Therefore, most R&D-intensive industries such as electronics are international. For example, significant R&D expenditures by multinational firms in Singapore's electronics industry must meet return on investment requirements. Besides meeting these requirements, the R&D project must also be "consistent with [regional] customer demands, the achievement of time-based competitiveness, the training of R&D manpower and the development of conducive innovation environments."[28] Thus, most firms investing in the Singapore electronics industry use approaches framed around the need to satisfy multiple project outcome requirements.

In addition to the need for a large market to recoup heavy investment in R&D, the development pace for new technology is increasing. As a result, new products become obsolete more rapidly. Therefore, investments need to be recouped more quickly. Moreover, firms' abilities to develop new technologies are expanding, and because of different patent laws across country borders, imitation by competitors is more likely. Through reverse engineering, competitors are able to take apart a product, learn the new technology, and develop a similar product that imitates the new technology. Because their competitors can imitate the new technology relatively quickly, firms need to recoup new-product development costs even more rapidly. Consequently, the larger markets provided by international expansion are particularly attractive in many industries such as computer hardware, because they expand the opportunity for the firm to recoup a large capital investment and large-scale R&D expenditures.[29]

Regardless of any other reason, however, the primary reason for making investments in international markets is to generate above-average returns on investments. For example, with domestic growth in the low single digits, Tricon Global Restaurants, owner of Kentucky Fried Chicken (KFC), Pizza Hut, and Taco Bell, has increased its overall growth by expanding globally. Tricon has around 5,000 KFC restaurants in the United States currently and has opened over 6,000 internationally. Overall the company operates more than 30,000 restaurants in over 100 countries worldwide—more than any other restaurant company. Even though the firm focused on growth, its global expansion realized an improved return on investment. Tricon's margin on its investments was up to just over 15 percent in 2001 from 11.6 percent in 1997, and the company's stock value doubled in 2001 compared to August of 2000. This success has come from the company's strategy of adapting to local tastes and preferences.[30]

Expected returns from the investments represent a primary predictor of firms moving into international markets. Still, firms from different countries have different expectations and use different criteria to decide whether to invest in international markets.[31]

Economies of Scale and Learning

By expanding their markets, firms may be able to enjoy economies of scale, particularly in their manufacturing operations. To the extent that a firm can standardize its products across country borders and use the same or similar production facilities, thereby coordinating critical resource functions, it is more likely to achieve optimal economies of scale.[32]

Economies of scale are critical in the global auto industry. China's decision to join the World Trade Organization will allow carmakers from other countries to enter the country and lower tariffs to be charged (in the past Chinese carmakers have had an advantage over foreign carmakers due to tariffs). Ford, Honda, General Motors, and Volkswagen are each producing an economy car to compete with the existing cars in China. Because of global economies of scale all of these companies are likely to obtain market share in China.[33] As a result, Chinese carmakers will have to change the way they do business to compete with foreign carmakers.

Firms may also be able to exploit core competencies in international markets through resource and knowledge sharing between units across country borders.[34] This sharing generates synergy, which helps the firm produce higher-quality goods or services at lower cost. In addition, working across international markets provides the firm with new learning opportunities. Multinational firms have substantial occasions to learn from the different practices they encounter in separate international markets. Even firms based in developed markets can learn from operations in emerging markets.[35]

Location Advantages

Firms may locate facilities in other countries to lower the basic costs of the goods or services they provide.[36] These facilities may provide easier access to lower-cost labor, energy, and other natural resources. Other location advantages include access to critical supplies and to customers.

Once positioned favorably with an attractive location, firms must manage their facilities effectively to gain the full benefit of a location advantage.[37] In Eastern Europe, Hungary is a prime location for many manufacturers. Flextronics, a large electronics contract manufacturer, is locating critical resources there. Hungary has good safety regulations and rapidly approves new projects. This small country borders seven nations and connects Europe to the emerging economies east of it. In 2001, 57 percent of Hungary's exports were in electronics equipment, providing a strong and growing market for Flextronics. Furthermore, it has lower labor costs than Ireland, another important electronic components producing country in Europe.[38]

In North America, Mexico has well-developed infrastructures and a skilled, though inexpensive, labor force, and it has received significant amounts of foreign direct investment. The costs of locating in Mexico are significantly lower than other countries regionally.[39] Flextronics found the country's reasonably low labor rate and proximity to its customers in North America ideal. As such, it located a 124-acre

KFC Corporation, based in Louisville, Kentucky, is the world's most popular chicken restaurant chain. Every day, nearly eight million customers are served around the world, choosing from the company's Original Recipe® chicken and also choosing among menu items tailored to the country, such as a salmon sandwich in Japan. Pictured here is one of the firm's restaurants in Quebec, Canada.

© MICHAEL S. YAMASHITA/CORBIS

industrial park in Guadalajara, Mexico, where everything from handheld computers to routers is manufactured.

International Strategies

Firms choose to use one or both of two basic types of international strategies: business-level international strategy and corporate-level international strategy. At the business level, firms follow generic strategies: cost leadership, differentiation, focused cost leadership, focused differentiation, or integrated cost leadership/differentiation. There are three corporate-level international strategies: multidomestic, global, or transnational (a combination of multidomestic and global). To create competitive advantage, each strategy must realize a core competence based on difficult-to-duplicate resources and capabilities.[40] As discussed in Chapters 4 and 6, firms expect to create value through the implementation of a business-level strategy and a corporate-level strategy.[41]

International Business-Level Strategy

Each business must develop a competitive strategy focused on its own domestic market. We discuss business-level generic strategies in Chapter 4 and competitive rivalry and competitive dynamics in Chapter 5. International business-level strategies have some unique features. In an international business-level strategy, the home country of operation is often the most important source of competitive advantage.[42] The resources and capabilities established in the home country frequently allow the firm to pursue the strategy into markets located in other countries. However, as a firm continues its growth into multiple international locations, research indicates that the country of origin diminishes in importance as the dominant factor.[43]

Michael Porter's model, illustrated in Figure 8.2, describes the factors contributing to the advantage of firms in a dominant global industry and associated with a specific country or regional environment.[44] The first dimension in Porter's model is *factors of production*. This dimension refers to the inputs necessary to compete in any industry—labor, land, natural resources, capital, and infrastructure (such as transportation, postal, and communication systems). There are basic (for example, natural and labor resources) and advanced (such as digital communication systems and a highly educated workforce) factors. Other production factors are generalized (highway systems and the supply of debt capital) and specialized (skilled personnel in a specific industry, such as the workers in a port that specialize in handling bulk chemicals). If a country has both advanced and specialized production factors, it is likely to serve an industry well by spawning strong home-country competitors that also can be successful global competitors.

Ironically, countries often develop advanced and specialized factors because they lack critical basic resources. For example, some Asian countries, such as South Korea, lack abundant natural resources but offer a strong work ethic, a large number of engineers, and systems of large firms to create an expertise in manufacturing. Similarly, Germany developed a strong chemical industry, partially because Hoechst and BASF spent years creating a synthetic indigo dye to reduce their dependence on imports, unlike Britain, whose colonies provided large supplies of natural indigo.[45]

The second dimension in Porter's model, *demand conditions*, is characterized by the nature and size of buyers' needs in the home market for the industry's goods or services. The sheer size of a market segment can produce the demand necessary to create scale-efficient facilities. This efficiency could also lead to domination of the industry in other countries. Specialized demand may also create opportunities beyond national

Figure 8.2   Determinants of National Advantage

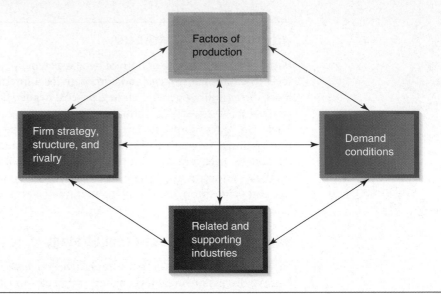

SOURCE: Adapted with the permission of The Free Press, an imprint of Simon & Schuster Adult Publishing Group, from *Competitive Advantage of Nations,* by Michael E. Porter, p. 72. Copyright ©1990, 1998 by Michael E. Porter.

boundaries. For example, Swiss firms have long led the world in tunneling equipment because of the need to tunnel through mountains for rail and highway passage in Switzerland. Japanese firms have created a niche market for compact, quiet air conditioners, which are important in Japan because homes are often small and located closely together.[46]

Related and supporting industries are the third dimension in Porter's model. Italy has become the leader in the shoe industry because of related and supporting industries; a well-established leather-processing industry provides the leather needed to construct shoes and related products. Also, many people travel to Italy to purchase leather goods, providing support in distribution. Supporting industries in leather-working machinery and design services also contribute to the success of the shoe industry. In fact, the design services industry supports its own related industries, such as ski boots, fashion apparel, and furniture. In Japan, cameras and copiers are related industries. Denmark's dairy products industry is related to an industry focused on food enzymes.

Firm strategy, structure, and rivalry make up the final country dimension and also foster the growth of certain industries. The dimension of strategy, structure, and rivalry among firms varies greatly from nation to nation. Because of the excellent technical training system in Germany, there is a strong emphasis on methodical product and process improvements. In Japan, unusual cooperative and competitive systems have facilitated the cross-functional management of complex assembly operations. In Italy, the national pride of the country's designers has spawned strong industries in sports cars, fashion apparel, and furniture. In the United States, competition among computer manufacturers and software producers has favored the development of these industries.

The four basic dimensions of the "diamond" model in Figure 8.2 emphasize the environmental or structural attributes of a national economy that contribute to national advantage. Government policy also clearly contributes to the success and failure of many firms and industries, as exemplified by the Turkish construction industry.[47] Relatively lower wages, the country's geographic and cultural proximity to several promising markets, the existence of a rivalrous home market and the accompanying pressures to continuously upgrade their capabilities have helped Turkish contractors achieve international success. Turkish government policy, however, has created financing difficulties for foreign projects. Related industries, such as the weak Turkish design, engineering, and consultant service industries, have also weakened Turkey's international position versus other international competitors.

Although each firm must create its own success, not all firms will survive to become global competitors—not even those operating with the same country factors that spawned the successful firms. The actual strategic choices managers make may be the most compelling reason for success or failure. Accordingly, the factors illustrated in Figure 8.2 are likely to produce competitive advantages only when the firm develops and implements an appropriate strategy that takes advantage of distinct country factors. Thus, these distinct country factors are necessary to consider when analyzing the business-level strategies (i.e., cost leadership, differentiation, focused cost leadership, focused differentiation, and integrated cost leadership/differentiation discussed in Chapter 4) in an international context.

International Corporate-Level Strategy

The international business-level strategies are based at least partially on the type of international corporate-level strategy the firm has chosen. Some corporate strategies give individual country units the authority to develop their own business-level strategies; other corporate strategies dictate the business-level strategies in order to standardize the firm's products and sharing of resources across countries.[48]

International corporate-level strategy focuses on the scope of a firm's operations through both product and geographic diversification.[49] International corporate-level strategy is required when the firm operates in multiple industries and multiple countries or regions.[50] The headquarters unit guides the strategy, although business or country-level managers can have substantial strategic input, given the type of international corporate level strategy followed. The three international corporate-level strategies are multidomestic, global, and transnational, as shown in Figure 8.3.

Multidomestic Strategy

A **multidomestic strategy** is an international strategy in which strategic and operating decisions are decentralized to the strategic business unit in each country so as to allow that unit to tailor products to the local market.[51] A multidomestic strategy focuses on competition within each country. It assumes that the markets differ and therefore are segmented by country boundaries. In other words, consumer needs and desires, industry conditions (e.g., the number and type of competitors), political and legal structures, and social norms vary by country. With multidomestic strategies, the firm can customize its products to meet the specific needs and preferences of local customers. Therefore, these strategies should maximize a firm's competitive response to the idiosyncratic requirements of each market.[52]

The use of multidomestic strategies usually expands the firm's local market share because the firm can pay attention to the needs of the local clientele.[53] However, the use of these strategies results in more uncertainty for the corporation as a whole, because of the differences across markets and thus the different strategies employed by local country units.[54] Moreover, multidomestic strategies do not allow for the achievement of economies of scale and can be more costly. As a result, firms employing a multidomestic strategy decentralize their strategic and operating decisions to the

A **multidomestic strategy** is an international strategy in which strategic and operating decisions are decentralized to the strategic business unit in each country so as to allow that unit to tailor products to the local market.

Figure 8.3 | International Corporate-Level Strategies

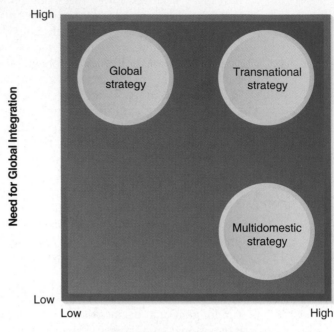

business units operating in each country. The multidomestic strategy has been more commonly used by European multinational firms because of the variety of cultures and markets found in Europe.

As mentioned earlier, Tricon has a strong incentive to compete internationally with its restaurant concepts (KFC, Taco Bell, and Pizza Hut). Tricon pursues a multidomestic strategy by trying to localize as much as possible. The firm does not open restaurants based solely on the U.S. model. It consistently adapts to local tastes and negotiates well when cultural and political climates change. "In Japan, for instance, KFC sells tempura crispy strips. In northern England, KFC stresses gravy and potatoes, while in Thailand it offers fresh rice with soy or sweet chili sauce. In Holland the company makes a potato-and-onion croquette. In France it sells pastries alongside chicken. And in China the chicken gets spicier the farther inland you travel. More and more, if it's only an American brand without a regional appeal, it's going to be difficult to market."[55] However, Tricon examines the distance from its American culture base and does better in those countries where it factors in how far its base culture is from the foreign culture it is considering to enter.[56] Thus, it sticks to high population areas, where American culture has some appeal as well.

Global Strategy

A **global strategy** is an international strategy through which the firm offers standardized products across country markets, with competitive strategy being dictated by the home office.

In contrast to a multidomestic strategy, a global strategy assumes more standardization of products across country markets.[57] As a result, a global strategy is centralized and controlled by the home office. The strategic business units operating in each country are assumed to be interdependent, and the home office attempts to achieve integration across these businesses. A **global strategy** is an international strategy through which the firm offers standardized products across country markets, with competitive strategy being dictated by the home office. Thus, a global strategy emphasizes economics of scale and offers greater opportunities to utilize innovations developed at the corporate level or in one country in other markets.

While a global strategy produces lower risk, the firm may forgo growth opportunities in local markets, either because those markets are less likely to identify opportunities or because opportunities require that products be adapted to the local market.[58] The global strategy is not as responsive to local markets and is difficult to manage because of the need to coordinate strategies and operating decisions across country borders. Consequently, achieving efficient operations with a global strategy requires sharing of resources and coordination and cooperation across country boundaries, which in turn require centralization and headquarters control. Many Japanese firms have successfully used the global strategy.[59]

Executives from Cemex opened the session of the New York Stock Exchange when the firm's initial listing of its shares took place in 1999. Cemex CEO Lorenzo Zambrano is fourth from the left.

Cemex, a Monterrey, Mexico-based cement maker, is the world's third largest cement manufacturer. Cemex acquired Southdown, the U.S. cement company for $3 billion at the end of 2001 and began to consolidate this operation with its other U.S. assets. Cemex has the leading market position in Spain with around 72 percent of the production capacity in the Spanish cement industry. Besides its significant assets in North and South America and southern Europe, the firm is also making inroads in Asia through acquisitions.

To integrate its businesses globally, Cemex uses the Internet as one way of increasing revenue and lowering its cost structure. The firm takes advantage of its dominant presence in Mexico and other Latin American locations by providing over 3,000 points of distribution through the Internet. Through its e-business subsidiary CxNetworks, Cemex launched the construction materials website Arkio.com; it expects to recoup the cost of implementation within a year and to add an additional $45 million in revenue by the end of 2002.

By using the Internet to improve logistics and manage an extensive supply network, Cemex can significantly reduce costs. With the savings derived from its Internet supply chain management efforts and by consolidating operations such as the Southdown acquisition into its existing U.S. operations, Cemex expects to cut $100 million from operating costs in the United States alone by 2003. Thus, Cemex is using a global strategy to integrate many aspects of its worldwide operations.[60]

Transnational Strategy

A **transnational strategy** is an international strategy through which the firm seeks to achieve both global efficiency and local responsiveness.

A **transnational strategy** is an international strategy through which the firm seeks to achieve both global efficiency and local responsiveness. Realizing these goals is difficult: one requires close global coordination while the other requires local flexibility. "Flexible coordination"—building a shared vision and individual commitment through an integrated network—is required to implement the transnational strategy.[61] In reality, it is difficult to successfully use the transnational strategy because of the conflicting goals (see Chapter 11 for more on implementation of this and other corporate-level international strategies). On the positive side, effective implementation of a transnational strategy often produces higher performance than does implementation of either the multidomestic or global international corporate-level strategies.[62]

The Strategic Focus on page 255 on the global automobile industry suggests that many large automobile manufacturers choose the transnational strategy to deal with global trends. DaimlerChrysler employed a transnational strategy to design and manufacture The Crossfire, a new product that is to be produced in 2003. The Crossfire has a sleek Chrysler design, but 40 percent of its components are from Mercedes-Benz. This global integration has facilitated lower costs for the vehicle—already engineered components were adapted from elsewhere and design enhancements produced a potentially attractive car for the U.S. market.[63] Thus, both General Motors (as described in the Strategic Focus) and DaimlerChrysler are using the transnational strategy to improve their competitiveness in the global automobile industry.

Environmental Trends

Although the transnational strategy is difficult to implement, emphasis on global efficiency is increasing as more industries begin to experience global competition. To add to the problem, there is also an increased emphasis on local requirements: global goods and services often require some customization to meet government regulations within particular countries or to fit customer tastes and preferences. In addition, most multinational firms desire coordination and sharing of resources across country markets to hold down costs, as illustrated by the Cemex example above. Furthermore, some products and industries may be more suited than others for standardization across country borders.

As a result, most large multinational firms with diverse products employ a multidomestic strategy with certain product lines and a global strategy with others. Many multinational firms may require this type of flexibility if they are to be strategically competitive, in part due to trends that change over time. Two important trends are the liability of foreignness which has increased after the terrorist attacks on September 11, 2001 and the trend towards regionalization.

Liability of Foreignness

The dramatic success of Japanese firms such as Toyota and Sony in the United States and other international markets in the 1980s was a powerful jolt to U.S. managers and awakened them to the importance of international competition in what were rapidly becoming global markets. In the 1990s, Eastern Europe and China represented potential major international market opportunities for firms from many countries, including the United States, Japan, Korea, and European nations.[64] However, as described in the Strategic Focus on page 257, there are legitimate concerns about the relative attractiveness of global strategies. Research showing that global strategies are not as prevalent as once thought and are very difficult to implement, even when using Internet based strategies,[65] as well as the September 11, 2001 attacks are sample explanations for these concerns.

In the 21st century, firms may focus less on truly global markets and more on regional adaptation. Although parallel developments in the Internet and mobile telecommunication facilitate communications across the globe, the implementation of web-based strategies also requires local adaptation.

The globalization of businesses with local strategies is demonstrated by the online operation of Lands' End, Inc., using local Internet portals to offer its products for sale. Lands' End, formally a direct-mail catalog business and now a part of Sears Roebuck and Company, launched its web-based business in 1995. The firm established websites in the U.K. and Germany in 1999, and in France, Italy, and Ireland in 2000 prior to initiating a catalog business in those countries. Not only are catalogs very expensive to print and mail outside the United States, they must also be sent to the

Large U.S. Auto Manufacturers and the Transnational Strategy

The Big Three automobile manufacturers—General Motors, Ford, and Chrysler (now part of DaimlerChrysler)—found their sales, market share, and revenues were hurt so much by the globalization of competition that their dominance in the crucial North American market was significantly diminished. For 60 years these three companies controlled the American car market, shaping consumer preferences as to which cars would be purchased and the price that would be paid for the cars. As recently as the late 1990s, these companies were earning record profits. However, the market shares of foreign car manufacturers have grown from their original, anemic level, and these firms are now serious competitors to domestic U.S. dominance. Toyota is close to the 13.8 percent market share held by Chrysler-branded products of DaimlerChrysler in the United States, and, as a group, Asian automakers hold 32 percent of the market.

Ford struggled when its main profit driver, the Explorer, received a reputation as being prone to roll over. Even as the firm attempted to fix this deficiency, problems on the production line forced a recall of the new Explorers that were supposed to be safer than the older models. General Motors has long fought an image that it does not build quality vehicles. Despite its ranking in a recent survey as being the most reliable domestic car maker in the 90 days after sales, GM still placed behind Toyota, Honda, and Nissan. For many consumers, quality is one of the major factors affecting their car purchase.

Although domestic companies are improving, some foreign car makers already have a good reputation and a known reliability rating. At the low end of the market, companies such as Hyundai and Kia are capturing market share. As price competition increases, domestic automakers have seen their market share shrink proportionately. Another problem is the cost of manufacturing. Even though in 2001 domestic carmakers had 61.2 percent of the American market and remained the largest auto sellers, this combined market share had fallen from the 73.5 percent share they held in 1995. Furthermore, profitability is down compared to Japanese carmakers, whose factories are more efficient than those of the U.S. firms.

In response to this situation, U.S. firms and other large automakers are using international corporate-level strategies. For example, General Motors has invested billions of dollars in foreign car companies, moving towards a more transnational strategy for its automobiles. The company owns Saab and Opel and also owns stakes in Fiat, Subaru, and Suzuki Motor. In the past, GM used a multidomestic strategy, where its foreign business units were managed in a decentralized way and each unit could decide what cars to design and build. This laissez-faire management approach resulted in poor financial results—GM's international operations lost almost $900 million in 2000, and its revenue remained flat at $35 billion.

GM CEO G. Richard Wagoner, Jr. decided to overcome this problem by implementing a transnational strategy. The senior managers from its partners' headquarters and product development centers now report directly to a top-ranking GM executive in the relevant region of the world. Thus, GM's top management team has more control over what happens in each of its foreign car companies but can continue to be responsive to regional or country needs. The result has been some successful products, such as the Suzuki-designed Opel Agila sold in Europe.

SOURCES: J. Ball, 2001, DaimlerChrysler sees net fall 58 percent, but says restructuring is on track, *The Wall Street Journal Interactive*, http://www.wsj.com, July 23; S. Freeman, 2001, Auto makers post slower sales in July amid continued economic uncertainty, *The Wall Street Journal Interactive*, http://www.wsj.com, August 2; S. Freeman, 2001, Auto sales rise despite Big Three as foreign brands gain ground, *The Wall Street Journal Interactive*, http://www.wsj.com, July 5; J. Muller, 2001, Ford, GM, and . . .Toyota, *Business Week*, January 14, 86–87; N. Shirouzu, 2001, Ford's loss widens in quarter due to sales incentives, recall, *The Wall Street Journal Interactive*, http://www.wsj.com, July 18; D. Welch, 2001, GM tries to show who's boss, *Business Week*, March 12, 54–55; G. L. White, 2001, GM net income tumbles 73 percent on weaker sales and prices, *The Wall Street Journal Interactive*, http://www.wsj.com, July 18; J. B. White, G. L. White, & N. Shirouzu, 2001, Soon, the Big Three won't be, as foreigners make inroads, *The Wall Street Journal Interactive*, http://www.wsj.com, August 13.

right people, and buying mailing lists is expensive. With limited online advertising and word-of-mouth, a website business can be built in a foreign country without a lot of initial marketing expenses. Once the online business is large enough, a catalog business can be launched with mailing targeted to customers who have used the business online.

Sam Taylor, vice president of international operations for Lands' End, suggested, "We've got a centralized Internet team based in Dodgeville, Wisconsin—all of our development, our designers. But you do need some local presence, so we have our local Internet manager . . . designers, marketing people and all that . . . because we don't know the nuances of the local markets."[66] He also indicated that each additional website was cheaper to implement. "Launching Ireland, France and Italy, we took the U.K. site, cloned it and partnered with Berlitz to translate it into French and into Italian. It was very cost effective. To launch the French site, it cost us 12 times less than the U.K. site, and to launch Italy, it cost us 16 times less."[67] Lands' End now derives 16 percent of its total revenues from Internet sales and ships to 185 countries, primarily from its Dodgeville, Wisconsin, corporate headquarters. Thus, even smaller companies can sell their goods and services globally when facilitated by electronic infrastructure without having significant (brick-and-mortar) facilities outside of their home location. But significant local adaptation is still needed in each country or region.

Regionalization

Regionalization is a second trend that has become more common in global markets. Because a firm's location can affect its strategic competitiveness,[68] it must decide whether to compete in all or many global markets, or to focus on a particular region or regions. Competing in all markets provides economies that can be achieved because of the combined market size. Research suggests that firms that compete in risky emerging markets can also have higher performance.[69]

However, a firm that competes in industries where the international markets differ greatly (in which it must employ a multidomestic strategy) may wish to narrow its focus to a particular region of the world. In so doing, it can better understand the cultures, legal and social norms, and other factors that are important for effective competition in those markets. For example, a firm may focus on Far East markets only rather than competing simultaneously in the Middle East, Europe, and the Far East. Or, the firm may choose a region of the world where the markets are more similar and some coordination and sharing of resources would be possible. In this way, the firm may be able not only to better understand the markets in which it competes, but also to achieve some economies, even though it may have to employ a multidomestic strategy. This is the case with Tricon, as we explained earlier.

Countries that develop trade agreements to increase the economic power of their regions may promote regional strategies. The European Union (EU) and South America's Organization of American States (OAS) in South America are country associations that developed trade agreements to promote the flow of trade across country boundaries within their respective regions.[70] Many European firms acquire and integrate their businesses in Europe to better coordinate pan-European brands as the EU creates more unity in European markets.

The North American Free Trade Agreement (NAFTA), signed by the United States, Canada, and Mexico, facilitates free trade across country borders in North America and may be expanded to include other countries in South America, such as Argentina, Brazil, and Chile.[71] NAFTA loosens restrictions on international strategies within a region and provides greater opportunity for international strategies. NAFTA does not exist for the sole purpose of U.S. businesses moving across its borders. In

Globalization Subsequent to Terrorist Attacks

The openness of economic policies that foster globalization in the post-Cold War era is counter to the increased concern for security after the terrorist attacks of September 11, 2001 in New York and Washington, D.C. Higher risks suggest higher cost of capital, and investors will not lend capital unless they get a higher return for foreign investment because the risks of such investments have increased. For instance, insurance and risk management costs will result in increased production prices, forcing e companies to reanalyze the risks of doing business in countries where security risks are higher.

Tighter immigration policies have also developed in the wake of the war on terrorism. For instance, these policies will increase labor costs that previously were reduced through foreign immigration. In the 1990s, two-thirds of the record inflow of 14 million nationals was legal immigrants, who accounted for 30 percent of the growth of the U.S. work force over the decade. Ethnic Chinese or Indians—who have been the backbone of new economy software innovations—founded 30 percent of Silicon Valley start-ups in the 1990s. "It is likely that the economic boom of the 1990s would not have happened if it had not been for immigrant flows," stated Mark M. Zandi, chief economist at the consulting firm Economy.com Inc.

Globalization helped disseminate investment capital, technology, and entrepreneurial ideas across borders. In globalization's wake, consumer goods manufacturers boosted productivity with just-in-time supply chains and pools of technical talent that immigrated into Silicon Valley. "Now, there is sand in the gears of cross border connectivity. That is a huge tectonic change in the global landscape," said Morgan Stanley Dean Witter's chief global economist, Steven S. Roach.

Although the events of September 11 created uncertainty about the progress of globalization, research also suggests that globalization is not as pervasive as once believed. In only a few sectors, such as consumer electronics, is a global strategy as defined above economically viable. For most manufacturing (such as automobiles), national responsiveness and implementation of the transnational strategy are increasingly important. In fact, even in a service sector such as banking, the more successful multinationals design their strategies on a regional basis, while the less successful multinationals pursue global strategies.

Business may need to rethink the globalization that was emphasized in the 1990s, not only as a result of events such as the terrorist attacks, but also because research on multinational firm strategy suggests that the global strategy isn't leading to competitive success in many industries. Stanley Fischer, a former executive at the International Monetary Fund, says, "It's hard to see that this [terrorism] is going to be a permanent setback." In fact, many have noted that the terrorists were themselves models of globalization, "using its tools—satellite telecommunications, the passenger jet—to turn the system on itself." Although Internet commerce has reduced the need for local sales outlets, research suggests that geography still matters in regard to competition and rivalry of firms who use the Internet. Thus, the events of September 11 are likely to slow the process of globalization—but not to reverse it.

SOURCES: S. R. Miller & A. Parkhe, 2002, Is there a liability of foreignness in global banking? An empirical test of banks' x-efficiency, *Strategic Management Journal*, 23: 55–75; P. Engardio, R. Miller, G. Smith, D. Brady, M. Kripalani, A. Borrus, & D. Foust, 2001, What's at stake: How terrorism threatens the global economy, *Business Week*, October 22, 34–37; K. Macharzina, 2001, Editorial: The end of pure global strategies? *Management International Review*, 41(2): 105; A. Rugman & R. Hodgetts, 2001, The end of global strategy, *European Management Journal*, 19(4): 333–343; S. Zaheer & A. Zaheer, 2001, Market microstructure in a global B2B network, *Strategic Management Journal*, 22: 859–873; J. Useem, 2001, Is it a small world after all? Terrorist attacks have ravaged our spirit, but not our global economy, *Fortune*, October 15, 38–42.

fact, Mexico is the number-two trading partner of the United States, and NAFTA greatly increased Mexico's exports to this country. In December 1999, the U.S. trade deficit with Mexico increased to its highest level, $1.7 billion; the catalyst for Mexico's export boom was NAFTA.[72] Although Vicente Fox's election as president of Mexico and Mexico's new spirit of democracy have created opportunity for change, the poor U.S. economy and the September 11, 2001 attacks have lowered the economic outlook for Mexico. Fox promised 1.3 million new export-led jobs annually, but Mexican employment instead was reduced by 500,000 jobs in 2001 because its trade was so closely tied to the U.S. economy.[73]

Most firms enter regional markets sequentially, beginning in markets with which they are more familiar. They also introduce their largest and strongest lines of business into these markets first, followed by their other lines of business once the first lines are successful.[74]

After the firm selects its international strategies and decides whether to employ them in regional or world markets, it must choose a market entry mode.[75]

Choice of International Entry Mode

International expansion is accomplished by exporting products, licensing arrangements, strategic alliances, acquisitions, and establishing new wholly owned subsidiaries. These means of entering international markets and their characteristics are shown in Table 8.1. Each means of market entry has its advantages and disadvantages. Thus, choosing the appropriate mode or path to enter international markets affects the firm's performance in those markets.[76]

Exporting

Many industrial firms begin their international expansion by exporting goods or services to other countries.[77] Exporting does not require the expense of establishing operations in the host countries, but exporters must establish some means of marketing and distributing their products. Usually, exporting firms develop contractual arrangements with host-country firms.

The disadvantages of exporting include the often high costs of transportation and possible tariffs placed on incoming goods. Furthermore, the exporter has less

Table 8.1	Global Market Entry: Choice of Entry Mode
Type of Entry	Characteristics
Exporting	High cost, low control
Licensing	Low cost, low risk, little control, low returns
Strategic alliances	Shared costs, shared resources, shared risks, problems of integration (e.g., two corporate cultures)
Acquisition	Quick access to new market, high cost, complex negotiations, problems of merging with domestic operations
New wholly owned subsidiary	Complex, often costly, time consuming, high risk, maximum control, potential above–average returns

control over the marketing and distribution of its products in the host country and must either pay the distributor or allow the distributor to add to the price to recoup its costs and earn a profit. As a result, it may be difficult to market a competitive product through exporting or to provide a product that is customized to each international market.[78] However, evidence suggests that cost leadership strategies enhance the performance of exports in developed countries, whereas differentiation strategies are more successful in emerging economies.[79]

Firms export mostly to countries that are closest to their facilities because of the lower transportation costs and the usually greater similarity between geographic neighbors. For example, U.S. NAFTA partners Mexico and Canada account for more than half of the goods exported from Texas. The Internet has also made exporting easier. Even small firms can access critical information about foreign markets, examine a target market, research the competition, and find lists of potential customers. Governments also use the Internet to facilitate applications for export and import licenses. Although the terrorist threat is likely to slow its progress, high-speed technology is still the wave of the future.[80]

Small businesses are most likely to use the exporting mode of international entry.[81] Currency exchange rates are one of the most significant problems small businesses face. While larger firms have specialists that manage the exchange rates, small businesses rarely have this expertise. On January 1, 2002, 12 countries began using Euro notes and coins for the first time. This change to a common currency in Europe is helpful to small businesses operating in European markets. Instead of 12 different exchange rates, these firms exporting to EU countries only have to obtain information on one, which should relieve tension and facilitate exports.[82]

Licensing

Licensing is one of the forms of organizational networks that are becoming common, particularly among smaller firms.[83] A licensing arrangement allows a foreign firm to purchase the right to manufacture and sell the firm's products within a host country or set of countries.[84] The licenser is normally paid a royalty on each unit produced and sold. The licensee takes the risks and makes the monetary investments in facilities for manufacturing, marketing, and distributing the goods or services. As a result, licensing is possibly the least costly form of international expansion.

Licensing is also a way to expand returns based on previous innovations. Even if product life cycles are short, licensing may be a useful tool. For instance, because the toy industry faces relentless change and an unpredictable buying public, licensing is used and contracts are often completed in foreign markets where labor may be less expensive.[85]

Licensing also has disadvantages. For example, it gives the firm very little control over the manufacture and marketing of its products in other countries. In addition, licensing provides the least potential returns, because returns must be shared between the licenser and the licensee. Worse, the international firm may learn the technology and produce and sell a similar competitive product after the license expires. Komatsu, for example, first licensed much of its technology from International Harvester, Bucyrus-Erie, and Cummins Engine to compete against Caterpillar in the earthmoving equipment business. Komatsu then dropped these licenses and developed its own products using the technology it had gained from the U.S. companies.[86]

In addition, if a firm wants to move to a different ownership arrangement, licensing may create some inflexibility. Thus, it is important that a firm thinks ahead and considers sequential forms of entry in international markets.[87]

Strategic Alliances

In recent years, strategic alliances have become a popular means of international expansion.[88] Strategic alliances allow firms to share the risks and the resources required to enter international markets.[89] Moreover, strategic alliances can facilitate the development of new core competencies that contribute to the firm's future strategic competitiveness.[90]

Most strategic alliances are formed with a host-country firm that knows and understands the competitive conditions, legal and social norms, and cultural idiosyncrasies of the country, which should help the expanding firm manufacture and market a competitive product. In return, the host-country firm may find its new access to the expanding firm's technology and innovative products attractive. Each partner in an alliance brings knowledge or resources to the partnership.[91] Indeed, partners often enter an alliance with the purpose of learning new capabilities. Common among those desired capabilities are technological skills.[92]

H.J. Heinz Co., for example, sought growth in the Asia-Pacific market as well as a way to reduce its operating costs there. The company decided to form an alliance with Japanese food company Kagome Co. The partners planned to use Heinz's existing retail network to enhance distribution of products, while Kagome would take the lead in research and production. For Kagome, whose food division had been struggling, the alliance could possibly help since Heinz has many strong food products, such as Boston Market frozen dinners and Ore-Ida frozen potatoes. Both companies felt that the alliance would help them cut operating costs as well as expand sales.[93]

Attracted by the huge Chinese market, Pearson PLC—the British education and publishing company that publishes the *Financial Times* and *The Economist,* among others—formed an alliance with CCTV, a unit of China State Television. The venture, named CTV Media Ltd., will provide "conversational English in an entertaining setting" to more than one billion viewers reached each day by CCTV. This venture opens up the Chinese television viewing market to Pearson and also to many international advertisers looking to promote their products in China.[94]

Not all alliances are successful; in fact, many fail. The primary reasons for failure include incompatible partners and conflict between the partners.[95] International strategic alliances are especially difficult to manage.[96] Several factors may cause a relationship to sour. Trust between the partners is critical and is affected by at least four fundamental issues: the initial condition of the relationship, the negotiation process to arrive at an agreement, partner interactions, and external events.[97]

Research has shown that equity-based alliances, over which a firm has more control, tend to produce more positive returns[98] (strategic alliances are discussed in greater depth in Chapter 9). However, if conflict in a strategic alliance or joint venture will not be manageable, an acquisition may be a better option. Research suggests that alliances are more favorable in the face of high uncertainty and where cooperation is needed to bring out the knowledge dispersed between partners and where strategic flexibility is important; acquisitions are better in situations with less need for strategic flexibility and when the transaction is used to maintain economies of scale or scope.[99]

Acquisitions

As free trade has continued to expand in global markets, cross-border acquisitions have also been increasing significantly. In recent years, cross-border acquisitions have comprised more than 45 percent of all acquisitions completed worldwide.[100] As explained in Chapter 7, acquisitions can provide quick access to a new market. In fact, acquisitions may provide the fastest, and often the largest, initial international expansion of any of the alternatives.

Although acquisitions have become a popular mode of entering international markets, they are not without costs. International acquisitions carry some of the disadvantages of domestic acquisitions (see Chapter 7). In addition, they can be expensive and often require debt financing, which also carries an extra cost. International negotiations for acquisitions can be exceedingly complex and are generally more complicated than for domestic acquisitions. For example, it is estimated that only 20 percent of the cross-border bids made lead to a completed acquisition, compared to 40 percent for domestic acquisitions.[101] Dealing with the legal and regulatory requirements in the target firm's country and obtaining appropriate information to negotiate an agreement frequently present significant problems. Finally, the problems of merging the new firm into the acquiring firm often are more complex than in domestic acquisitions. The acquiring firm must deal not only with different corporate cultures, but also with potentially different social cultures and practices. Therefore, while international acquisitions have been popular because of the rapid access to new markets they provide, they also carry with them important costs and multiple risks.

SERGIO DORANTES/CORBIS

Wal-Mart entered the international market for the first time in 1991 when it opened a store in Mexico City. In 1994, the Mexico City store pictured here was the firm's largest unit in the world.

Wal-Mart, the world's largest retailer, has used several entry modes to globalize its operations. For example, in China, the firm used a joint venture mode of entry. To begin its foray into Latin American countries, Wal-Mart also used joint ventures. But in some cases, such as in Mexico, it acquired its venture partner after entering the host country's market.

In Germany, Wal-Mart acquired a 21-store hypermarket chain in 1997 and acquired 74 Interspar stores in 1998. There were many problems with these acquisitions. None of these stores were profitable when Wal-Mart acquired them, and the amount of money needed to update them had been underestimated. The firm also encountered cultural problems. In the first year, the stores suffered significant losses, and it is expected to take many years before they show a profit—or break even—in Germany.

Wal-Mart learned from the German experience. When the firm bought a chain of British supermarket stores, it gave the managers running them the freedom to make necessary changes. Wal-Mart has learned that to be successful in foreign markets, it must have people in charge who understand the local culture and customers' needs.[102]

New Wholly Owned Subsidiary

The establishment of a new wholly owned subsidiary is referred to as a **greenfield venture.**

The establishment of a new wholly owned subsidiary is referred to as a **greenfield venture.** This process is often complex and potentially costly, but it affords maximum control to the firm and has the most potential to provide above-average returns. This potential is especially true of firms with strong intangible capabilities that might be leveraged through a greenfield venture.[103]

The risks are also high, however, because of the costs of establishing a new business operation in a new country. The firm may have to acquire the knowledge and expertise of the existing market by hiring either host-country nationals, possibly from competitors, or consultants, which can be costly. Still, the firm maintains control over the technology, marketing, and distribution of its products. Alternatively, the company must build new manufacturing facilities, establish distribution networks, and learn and implement appropriate marketing strategies to compete in the new market.

When British American Tobacco (BAT) decided to increase its market share in South Korea, a very tough market for imported cigarettes, it resolved to build a new greenfield cigarette factory there. The South Korean market is very protected, with a state-run monopoly, Korea Tobacco and Ginseng Corporation, controlling most of the market. Also, South Korea has said that it would impose increasingly high tariffs on imported tobacco, and there is a strong sentiment of antiforeignism among consumers. John Taylor, president of BAT Korea, hoped that its maneuver, which would produce cigarettes "made in Korea, by Koreans and for Koreans," would increase British American Tobacco's market share from 3.7 percent to 10 percent.[104]

Dynamics of Mode of Entry

A firm's choice of mode of entry into international markets is affected by a number of factors.[105] Initially, market entry will often be achieved through export, which requires no foreign manufacturing expertise and investment only in distribution. Licensing can facilitate the product improvements necessary to enter foreign markets, as in the Komatsu example. Strategic alliances have been popular because they allow a firm to connect with an experienced partner already in the targeted market. Strategic alliances also reduce risk through the sharing of costs. All three modes therefore are best for early market development tactics. Also, the strategic alliance is often used in more uncertain situations such as an emerging economy.[106] However, if intellectual property rights in the emerging economy are not well protected, the number of firms in the industry is growing fast, and the need for global integration is high, the wholly owned entry mode is preferred.[107]

To secure a stronger presence in international markets, acquisitions, or greenfield ventures may be required. Many Japanese automobile manufacturers, such as Honda, Nissan, and Toyota, have gained a presence in the United States through both greenfield ventures and joint ventures.[108] Toyota has particularly strong intangible production capabilities that it has been able to transfer through greenfield ventures.[109] Both acquisitions and greenfield ventures are likely to come at later stages in the development of an international strategy. In addition, both strategies tend to be more successful when the firm making the investment possesses valuable core competencies.[110] Large diversified business groups, often found in emerging economies, not only gain resources through diversification, but also have specialized abilities in managing differences in inward and outward flows of foreign direct investment. In particular, Korean *chaebols* have been adept at making acquisitions in emerging economies.[111]

Thus, to enter a global market, a firm selects the entry mode that is best suited to the situation at hand. In some instances, the various options will be followed sequentially, beginning with exporting and ending with greenfield ventures.[112] In other cases, the firm may use several, but not all, of the different entry modes, each in different markets. As explained above, this is how Wal-Mart has entered various international markets. The decision regarding which entry mode to use is primarily a result of the industry's competitive conditions, the country's situation and government policies, and the firm's unique set of resources, capabilities, and core competencies.

Strategic Competitiveness Outcomes

Once its international strategy and mode of entry have been selected, the firm turns its attention to implementation issues. It is important to do this, because as explained next, international expansion is risky and may not result in a competitive advantage (see Figure 8.1). The probability the firm will achieve success by using an international strategy increases when that strategy is effectively implemented.

International Diversification and Returns

As noted earlier, firms have numerous reasons to diversify internationally. **International diversification** is a strategy through which a firm expands the sales of its goods or services across the borders of global regions and countries into different geographic locations or markets. Because of its potential advantages, international diversification should be related positively to firms' returns. Research has shown that, as international diversification increases, firms' returns increase.[113] In fact, the stock market is particularly sensitive to investments in international markets. Firms that are broadly diversified into multiple international markets usually achieve the most positive stock returns.[114] There are also many reasons for the positive effects of international diversification, such as potential economies of scale and experience, location advantages, increased market size, and the opportunity to stabilize returns. The stabilization of returns helps reduce a firm's overall risk.[115] All of these outcomes can be achieved by smaller and newer ventures, as well as by larger and established firms. New ventures can also enjoy higher returns when they learn new technologies from their international diversification.[116]

Firms in the Japanese automobile industry (as indicated in the Strategic Focus on page 255) have found that international diversification may allow them to better exploit their core competencies, because sharing knowledge resources between operations can produce synergy. Also, a firm's returns may affect its decision to diversify internationally. For example, poor returns in a domestic market may encourage a firm to expand internationally in order to enhance its profit potential. In addition, internationally diversified firms may have access to more flexible labor markets, as the Japanese do in the United States, and may thereby benefit from global scanning for competition and market opportunities. Also, through global networks with assets in many countries, firms can develop more flexible structures to adjust to changes that might occur.[117]

Benetton, an Italian casual-wear company, developed a network structure over the years that has allowed it to improve its performance. "Without giving up the strongest aspects of its networked model, it is integrating and centralizing, instituting direct control over key processes throughout the supply chain. The company is also diversifying into sportswear, sports equipment and communications."[118] To manage the network, the firm has instituted state-of-the-art technology for communication and managing the supply chain. Accordingly, multinational firms with efficient and competitive operations are more likely to produce above-average returns for their investors and better products for their customers than are solely domestic firms. However, as explained later, international diversification can be carried too far.

International Diversification and Innovation

In Chapter 1, we note that the development of new technology is at the heart of strategic competitiveness. As noted in Porter's model (see Figure 8.2), a nation's competitiveness depends, in part, on the capacity of its industry to innovate. Eventually and inevitably, competitors outperform firms that fail to innovate and improve their operations and products. Therefore, the only way to sustain a competitive advantage is to upgrade it continually.[119]

International diversification provides the potential for firms to achieve greater returns on their innovations (through larger or more numerous markets) and lowers the often substantial risks of R&D investments. Therefore, international diversification provides incentives for firms to innovate.[120]

In addition, international diversification may be necessary to generate the resources required to sustain a large-scale R&D operation. An environment of rapid technological obsolescence makes it difficult to invest in new technology and the capital-intensive operations required to take advantage of such investment. Firms operating solely in domestic markets may find such investments problematic because of the length of time required to recoup the original investment. If the time is extended, it may not even be possible to recover the investment before the technology becomes obsolete.[121] As a result, international diversification improves a firm's ability to appropriate additional and necessary returns from innovation before competitors can overcome the initial competitive advantage created by the innovation. In addition, firms moving into international markets are exposed to new products and processes. If they learn about those products and processes and integrate this knowledge into their operations, further innovation can be developed.[122]

The relationship among international diversification, innovation, and returns is complex. Some level of performance is necessary to provide the resources to generate international diversification, which in turn provides incentives and resources to invest in research and development. The latter, if done appropriately, should enhance the returns of the firm, which then provides more resources for continued international diversification and investment in R&D.[123]

Because of the potential positive effects of international diversification on performance and innovation, such diversification may even enhance returns in product-diversified firms. International diversification would increase market potential in each of these firm's product lines, but the complexity of managing a firm that is both product diversified and internationally diversified is significant. Research suggests that firms in less developed countries gain from being product diversified when partnering with multinational firms from a more developed country that are looking to enter a less developed country in pursuit of increased international diversification.[124]

Asea Brown Boveri (ABB) demonstrates these relationships. This firm's operations involve high levels of both product and international diversification, yet ABB's performance is strong. Some believe that the firm's ability to effectively implement the transnational strategy contributes to its strategic competitiveness. One of ABB's latest moves was in North Korea; it had signed in Pyongyang (the capital of North Korea) "a wide-ranging, long-term co-operation agreement aimed at improving the performance of the country's electricity transmission network and basic industries."[125] To manage itself, ABB assembled culturally diverse corporate and divisional management teams that facilitated the simultaneous achievement of global integration and local responsiveness.

Another firm joins the New York Stock Exchange—executives from ABB open the session to celebrate their firm's listing on the exchange. ABB CEO Jorgen Cenerman is second from the left.

Evidence suggests that more culturally diverse top-management teams often have a greater knowledge of international markets and their idiosyncrasies[126] (top-management teams are discussed further in Chapter 12). Moreover, an in-depth understanding of diverse markets among top-level managers facilitates intrafirm coordination and the use of long-term, strategically relevant criteria to evaluate the performance of managers and their units.[127] In turn, this approach facilitates improved innovation and performance.[128]

PART 2 / Strategic Actions: Strategy Formulation

Complexity of Managing Multinational Firms

Although firms can realize many benefits by implementing an international strategy, doing so is complex and can produce greater uncertainty.[129] For example, multiple risks are involved when a firm operates in several different countries. Firms can grow only so large and diverse before becoming unmanageable, or the costs of managing them exceed their benefits. Other complexities include the highly competitive nature of global markets, multiple cultural environments, potentially rapid shifts in the value of different currencies, and the possible instability of some national governments.

Risks in an International Environment

International diversification carries multiple risks.[130] Because of these risks, international expansion is difficult to implement, and it is difficult to manage after implementation. The chief risks are political and economic. Taking these risks into account, highly internationally diversified firms are accustomed to market conditions yielding competitive situations that differ from what was predicted. Sometimes, these situations contribute to the firm's strategic competitiveness; on other occasions, they have a negative effect on the firm's efforts.[131] Specific examples of political and economic risks are shown in Figure 8.4.

Political Risks

Political risks are risks related to instability in national governments and to war, both civil and international. Instability in a national government creates numerous problems, including economic risks and uncertainty created by government regulation; the existence of many, possibly conflicting, legal authorities; and the potential nationalization of private assets. For example, as illustrated in the Strategic Focus on page 267 about Argentina, foreign firms that invest in another country may have concerns about the stability of the national government and what might happen to their investments or assets because of unrest and government instability.

Economic Risks

As illustrated in the Strategic Focus on page 267 about Argentina, economic risks are interdependent with political risks. Foremost among the economic risks of international diversification are the differences and fluctuations in the value of different currencies.[132] The value of the dollar relative to other currencies determines the value of the international assets and earnings of U.S. firms; for example, an increase in the value of the U.S. dollar can reduce the value of U.S. multinational firms' international assets and earnings in other countries. Furthermore, the value of different currencies can also, at times, dramatically affect a firm's competitiveness in global markets because of its effect on the prices of goods manufactured in different countries.

An increase in the value of the dollar can harm U.S. firms' exports to international markets because of the price differential of the products. It can also affect economies of other countries as in the case of Argentina, which had pegged its currency, the peso, one-for-one with the U.S. dollar. The devaluation caused a significant recession, 18 percent unemployment, and not many options for emerging from this morass.[133]

Limits to International Expansion: Management Problems

Firms tend to earn positive returns on early international diversification, but the returns often level off and become negative as the diversification increases past some point.[134] There are several reasons for the limits to the positive effects of international

Figure 8.4   Risk in the International Environment

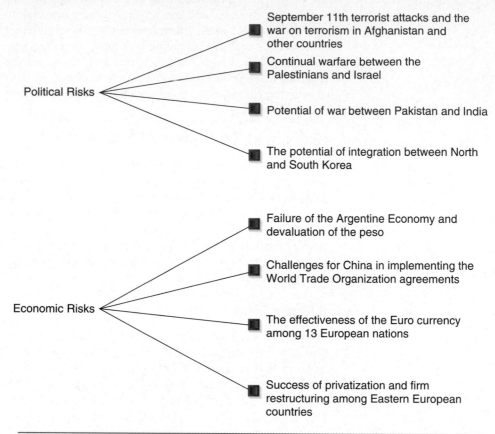

Political Risks
- September 11th terrorist attacks and the war on terrorism in Afghanistan and other countries
- Continual warfare between the Palestinians and Israel
- Potential of war between Pakistan and India
- The potential of integration between North and South Korea

Economic Risks
- Failure of the Argentine Economy and devaluation of the peso
- Challenges for China in implementing the World Trade Organization agreements
- The effectiveness of the Euro currency among 13 European nations
- Success of privatization and firm restructuring among Eastern European countries

SOURCES: E. Andrews, 2002, A smooth debut lifts Euro's value in money markets, *The New York Times on the web,* http://www.nytimes.com, January 3; M. Kripalani, N. Mangi, F. Balfour, P. Magnusson, & R. Brady, 2002, Now, will India and Pakistan get serious about peace? *Business Week,* January 14, 51; M. Wallin, 2002, Argentina grapples with postdevaluation, *The Wall Street Journal,* January 10, A8; B. Einhorn, C. Dawson, I. Kunii, D. Roberts, A. Webb, & P. Engardio, 2001, China: Will its entry into the WTO unleash new prosperity or further destabilize the world economy? *Business Week,* October 29, 38; P. Engardio, R. Miller, G. Smith, D. Brady, M. Kripalani, A. Borrus, & D. Foust, 2001, What's at stake: How terrorism threatens the global economy, *Business Week,* October 22, 33–34; D. Eisenberg, 2001, Arafat's dance of death, *Time,* December 24, 64–65; B. Fulford, 2001, Another enemy, *Forbes;* October 29, 117; K. E. Myer, 2001, Institutions, transaction costs, and entry model choice in Eastern Europe, *Journal of International Business Studies,* 32: 357–367.

diversification. First, greater geographic dispersion across country borders increases the costs of coordination between units and the distribution of products. Second, trade barriers, logistical costs, cultural diversity, and other differences by country (e.g., access to raw materials and different employee skill levels) greatly complicate the implementation of an international diversification strategy.[135]

Institutional and cultural factors can present strong barriers to the transfer of a firm's competitive advantages from one country to another. Marketing programs often have to be redesigned and new distribution networks established when firms expand into new countries. In addition, firms may encounter different labor costs and capital charges. In general, it is difficult to effectively implement, manage, and control a firm's international operations.[136]

Wal-Mart made significant mistakes in some Latin American markets. For example, its first Mexican stores carried ice skates, riding lawn mowers, fishing tackle—even

Currency Devaluation in Argentina

Since the early 1990s, the value of the Argentine peso had been an even exchange with the U.S. dollar. In January 2002, however, Argentina was forced to devalue the peso by approximately 40 percent after the country had defaulted on its $141 billion public debt. The devaluation created significant chaos for the people of Argentina. President Fernando de la Rúa had resigned on December 20, 2001, two years after being elected. Adolfo Rodrígues Saá replaced de la Rúa, but lasted only eight days in office. Eduardo Duhalde became Argentina's president on January 1, 2002.

Argentina policy makers, with the devaluation, changed the peso's association with the U.S. dollar. For the ten years before the devaluation, many foreign banks had invested over $10 billion in Argentina. After the devaluation, the Fleetwood Boston Financial Corporation showed an estimated $140 million loss and CitiGroup Chairman Sanford I. Weill indicated that his firm also would experience a significant loss. These losses may take place because the contracts for the firms allow their investments to be repaid in pesos rather than in U.S. dollars. In contrast, AES Corporation, a U.S. corporation that builds power plants in Argentina, had stipulated in its contracts that it must be paid in U.S. dollars.

Although many firms earn only a small percentage of their annual income from Argentina, such as Coca-Cola, their earnings will be decreased not only because of the devaluation but also because Argentina's economy has been in recession and will get worse due to the devaluation. Consumers will have less buying power due to the devaluation.

The one-to-one ratio of the peso for the U.S. dollar policy had been implemented in the early 1990s as a solution to the hyperinflation that Argentina experienced throughout the 1980s. Because the two currencies were linked, however, as the dollar increased in value in open currency markets, Argentina's exports also became more expensive. Thus, although the even exchange of pesos for dollars had blunted the earlier inflation problem, it contributed to the country's recession in the late 1990s.

In addition, Argentina's politics have not helped its economic situation. Although privatization of water, petroleum, airline firms, and other state-owned corporations presented an opportunity for increased economic growth, the patronage-based political system allowed top politicians to give the country's privatized assets to those which were not the best managers, leading to the dissipation of the value of the privatized firms. Thus, the privatization process did not lead Argentina's privatized firms to be competitive in world markets, and the politics involved did not facilitate improved economic growth.

The politicians also pursued policies that increased government spending. When significant deficits resulted, the International Monetary Fund (IMF), which oversees lending to emerging market countries, forced stringent fiscal policies on the Argentine government, further increasing Argentina's recessionary environment. Rather than being able to increase government spending at a critical juncture, the government was forced to tighten fiscal policy, which did not allow the country to emerge from recession quickly.

Although there are a number of causes for the economic and political crisis that resulted in the currency devaluation, all are hurt by the circumstance: the people of Argentina, the government, and the foreign investors who committed significant capital to build businesses in Argentina.

SOURCES: J. Fox, 2002, Argentina, *Fortune*, January 7, 26; 2002, Between the creditors and the streets, *The Economist*, January 5, 29–30; G. Smith, J. Goodman, C. Lindblad, & A. Robinson, 2002, A wrong turn in Argentina, *Business Week Online*, http://www. business-week.com, January 21; K. A. Dolan, 2001, Tails we win, *Forbes*, August 20, 54; J. Goodman, 2001, Thinking the unthinkable; Argentina could be forced to cut the peso's peg to the dollar, *Business Week*, November 19, 58; M. Wallin, Argentine leaders declare state of emergency, *The Wall Street Journal*, December 20, A8, A12.

clay pigeons for skeet shooting. To get rid of the clay pigeons they would be radically discounted "only to have automated inventory systems linked to Wal-Mart's corporate headquarters in Bentonville, Arkansas, order a fresh batch." Once Wal-Mart began to get the right mix of products, the Mexican currency was devalued in 1994. However, over time, Wal-Mart has become very successful in Latin America, especially Mexico. It has been able to increase its market share by taking advantage of local sourcing, especially by taking advantage of the lower wages in Mexico through NAFTA.[137]

The amount of international diversification that can be managed will vary from firm to firm and according to the abilities of each firm's managers. The problems of central coordination and integration are mitigated if the firm diversifies into more friendly countries that are geographically close and have cultures similar to its own country's culture. In that case, there are likely to be fewer trade barriers, the laws and customs are better understood, and the product is easier to adapt to local markets.[138] For example, U.S. firms may find it less difficult to expand their operations into Mexico, Canada, and Western European countries than into Asian countries.

Management must also be concerned with the relationship between the host government and the multinational corporation.[139] Although government policy and regulations are often barriers, many firms, such as Toyota and General Motors, have turned to strategic alliances to overcome those barriers. By forming interorganizational networks, such as strategic alliances, firms can share resources and risks but also build flexibility.[140]

- The use of international strategies is increasing not only because of traditional motivations, but also for emerging reasons. Traditional motives include extending the product life cycle, securing key resources, and having access to low-cost labor. Emerging motivations focus on the combination of the Internet and mobile telecommunications, which facilitates global transactions. Also, there is increased pressure for global integration as the demand for commodities becomes borderless, and yet pressure is also increasing for local country responsiveness.

- An international strategy usually attempts to capitalize on four benefits: increased market size; the opportunity to earn a return on large investments; economies of scale and learning; and advantages of location.

- International business-level strategies are usually grounded in one or more home-country advantages, as Porter's diamond model suggests. The diamond model emphasizes four determinants: factors of production; demand conditions; related and supporting industries; and patterns of firm strategy, structure, and rivalry.

- There are three types of international corporate-level strategies. A multidomestic strategy focuses on competition within each country in which the firm competes. Firms using a multidomestic strategy decentralize strategic and operating decisions to the business units operating in each country, so that each unit can tailor its goods and services to the local market. A global strategy assumes more standardization of products across country boundaries; therefore, competitive strategy is centralized and controlled by the home office. A transnational strategy seeks to combine aspects of both multidomestic and global strategies in order to emphasize both local responsiveness and global integration and coordination. This strategy is difficult to implement, requiring an integrated network and a culture of individual commitment.

- Although the transnational strategy's implementation is a challenge, environmental trends are causing many multinational firms to consider the need for both global efficiency and local responsiveness. Many large multinational firms—particularly those with many diverse products—use a multidomestic strategy with some product lines and a global strategy with others.

- The threat of terrorist attacks increases the risks and costs of international strategies. Furthermore, research suggests that the liability of foreignness is more difficult to overcome than once thought.

- Some firms decide to compete only in certain regions of the world, as opposed to viewing all markets in the world as potential opportunities. Competing in regional markets allows firms and managers to focus their learning on specific markets, cultures, locations, resources, etc.

- Firms may enter international markets in one of several ways, including exporting, licensing, forming strategic alliances, making acquisitions, and establishing new wholly owned subsidiaries, often referred to as greenfield ventures. Most firms begin with exporting or licensing, because of their lower costs and risks, but later may expand to strategic alliances and acquisitions. The most expensive and risky means of entering a new international market is through the establishment of a new wholly owned subsidiary. On the other hand, such subsidiaries provide the advantages of maximum control by the firm and, if they are successful, the greatest returns.

- International diversification facilitates innovation in a firm, because it provides a larger market to gain more and faster returns from investments in innovation. In addition, international diversification may generate the resources necessary to sustain a large-scale R&D program.

- In general, international diversification is related to above-average returns, but this assumes that the diversification is effectively implemented and that the firm's international operations are well managed. International diversification provides greater economies of scope and learning, which, along with greater innovation, help produce above-average returns.

- Several risks are involved with managing multinational operations. Among these are political risks (e.g., instability of national governments) and economic risks (e.g., fluctuations in the value of a country's currency).

- There are also limits to the ability to manage international expansion effectively. International diversification increases coordination and distribution costs, and management problems are exacerbated by trade barriers, logistical costs, and cultural diversity, among other factors.

1. What are the traditional and emerging motives that cause firms to expand internationally?

2. What four factors provide a basis for international business-level strategies?

3. What are the three international corporate-level strategies? How do they differ from each other? What factors lead to their development?

4. What environmental trends are affecting international strategy?

5. What five modes of international expansion are available, and what is the normal sequence of their use?

6. What is the relationship between international diversification and innovation? How does international diversification affect innovation? What is the effect of international diversification on a firm's returns?

7. What are the risks of international diversification? What are the challenges of managing multinational firms?

8. What factors limit the positive outcomes of international expansion?

Experiential Exercise

International Strategy

Coca-Cola's first international bottling plants opened in 1906 in Canada, Cuba, and Panama. Today the firm produces nearly 300 brands in almost 200 countries, and more than 70 percent of its income comes from outside the United States.

Coca-Cola's German operation began in 1929. Germany—Coke's first marketing success outside North America—is the firm's fifth-largest market. Nine bottlers with a total of 24 production plants serve Germany's population of 82 million people; and the firm has 13,000 German employees, and by 1939 was selling 4.5 million cases annually. Popular Coca-Cola products in Germany include Fanta (first introduced as a substitute to Coke during World War II) in several flavors, Mezzo Mix (a cola and orange-flavored beverage), Bonaqa table water, and Lift Apfelsaftschorle (apple juice with carbonated water).

Coca-Cola was introduced in Chile in 1941 with the opening of plants in Santiago and Valparaiso. Brands marketed in Chile include Coca-Cola, Coca-Cola Light, Sprite, Sprite Light, Fanta, Fanta Sabores, Lift, Vital mineral water, Nordic Mist Ginger Ale, and Nordic Mist Tonic Water. Juice brands are Kapo, Andifrut, and Nectar Andina. The Coca-Cola system in Chile has 11 bottling plants and employs more than 4,000 people.

1. Based on the above information, the cultural differences between Germany and Chile (as well as the obvious differences among the other countries in which Coca-Cola operates), and the type of product offered by the firm, compare and contrast the three generic international corporate level strategies illustrated in Figure 8.3 as they apply to Coca-Cola. Which strategy is best for this firm, and why?

2. Describe how Coca-Cola's country operations might be affected by the environmental trends of liability of foreignness and regionalization.

1. D. Ahlstrom & G. D. Bruton, 2001, Learning from successful local private firms in China: Establishing legitimacy, *Academy of Management Executive*, 15(4): 72–83.

2. A. K. Gupta & V. Govindarajan, 2001, Converting global presence into global competitive advantage, *Academy of Management Executive*, 15(2): 45–57.

3. A. McWilliams, D. D. Van Fleet, & P. M. Wright, 2001, Strategic management of human resources for global competitive advantage, *Journal of Business Strategies*, 18(1): 1–24; B. L. Kedia & A. Mukherji, 1999, Global managers: Developing a mindset for global competitiveness, *Journal of World Business*, 34(3): 230–251.

4. B. R. Koka, J. E. Prescott, & R. Madhaven, 1999, Contagion influence on trade and investment policy: A network perspective, *Journal of International Business Studies*, 30: 127–148.

5. G. Bottazzi, G. Dosi, M. Lippi, F. Pammolli, & M. Riccaboni, 2001, Innovation and corporate growth in the evolution of the drug industry, *International Journal of Industrial Organization*, 19: 1161–1187.

6. S. Tallman, 2001, Global strategic management, in M. A. Hitt, R. E. Freeman, & J. S. Harrison (eds.), *Handbook of Strategic Management*, Oxford, U.K.: Blackwell Publishers, 462–490; C. W. L. Hill, 2000, *International Business: Competing in the Global Marketplace*, 3d ed., Boston: Irwin/McGraw Hill, 378–380.

7. R. Vernon, 1996, International investment and international trade in the product cycle, *Quarterly Journal of Economics*, 80: 190–207.

8. H. F. Lau, C. C. Y. Kwok, & C. F. Chan, 2000, Filling the gap: Extending international product life cycle to emerging economies, *Journal of Global Marketing*, 13(4): 29–51.

9. Y. Shi, 2001, Technological capabilities and international production strategy of firms: The case of foreign direct investment in China, *Journal of World Business*, 18(4): 523–532.

10. A. Camuffo, P. Romano, & A. Vinelli, 2001, Back to the future: Benetton transforms its global network, *Sloan Management Review*, 43(1): 46–52.

11. B. Kim & Y. Lee, 2001, Global capacity expansion strategies: Lessons learned from two Korean carmakers, *Long Range Planning*, 34(3): 309–333.

12. K. Macharzina, 2001, The end of pure global strategies? *Management International Review*, 41(2): 105; W. Kuemmerle, 1999, Foreign direct investment in industrial research in the pharmaceutical and electronics industries—Results from a survey of multinational firms, *Research Policy*, 28:(2/3), 179–193.

13. Y. Luo, 2000, Entering China today: What choices do we have? *Journal of Global Marketing*, 14(2): 57–82.

14. C. C. Y. Kwok & D. M. Reeb, 2000, Internationalization and firm risk: An upstream-downstream hypothesis, *Journal of International Business Studies*, 31: 611–629; J. J. Choi & M. Rajan, 1997, A joint test of market segmentation and exchange risk factor in international capital markets, *Journal of International Business Studies*, 28: 29–49.

15. R. E. Hoskisson, L. Eden, C. M. Lau, & M. Wright, 2000, Strategy in emerging economies, *Academy of Management Journal*, 43: 249–267; D. J. Arnold & J. A. Quelch, 1998, New strategics in emerging markets, *Sloan Management Review*, 40: 7–20.

16. M. W. Peng, Y. Lu, O. Shenkar, & D. Y. L. Wang, 2001, Treasures in the China house: A review of management and organizational research on Greater China, *Journal of Business Research*, 52(2): 95–110; S. Lovett, L. C. Simmons, & R. Kali, 1999, Guanxi versus the market: Ethics and efficiency, *Journal of International Business Studies*, 30: 231–248.

17. J. P. Quinlan, 1998, Europe, not Asia, is corporate America's key market, *The Wall Street Journal*, January 12, A20.

18. W. Kuemmerle, 2001, Go global—or not? *Harvard Business Review*, 79(6): 37–49; Y. Luo & M. W. Peng, 1999, Learning to compete in a transition economy: Experience, environment and performance, *Journal of International Business Studies*, 30: 269–295.

19. R. Gray, 2001, Local on a global scale, *Marketing*, September 27, 22–23.

20. X. Martin, A. Swaminathan, & W. Mitchell, 1999, Organizational evolution in the interorganizational environment: Incentives and constraints on international expansion strategy, *Administrative Science Quarterly*, 43: 566–601.

21. P. Ghemawat, 2001, Distance still matters: The hard reality of global expansion, *Harvard Business Review*, 79(8): 137–147.

22. S. R. Miller & A. Parkhe, 2002, Is there a liability of foreignness in global banking? An empirical test of banks' x-efficiency, *Strategic Management Journal*, 23: 55–75; T. Kostova & S. Zaheer, 1999, Organizational legitimacy under conditions of complexity: The case of the multinational enterprise, *Academy of Management Review*, 24: 64–81; S. Zaheer & E. Mosakowski, 1997, The dynamics of the liability of foreignness: A global study of survival in financial services, *Strategic Management Journal*, 18: 439–464.

23. P. Engardio, 2001, Smart Globalization, *Business Week Online*, http://www.businessweek.com, August 27.

24. 2002, Coca-Cola, *Standard & Poor's Stock Report*, http://www.fidelity.com, March 28; H. Chura & R. Linnett, 2001, Coca-Cola readies global assault, *Advertising Age*, April 2, 1, 34.

25. S. Jaffe, 2001, Do Pepsi and Gatorade mix? *Business Week Online*, http://www.businessweek.com, August 14.

26. B. Morris & P. Sellers, 2000, What really happened at Coke? *Fortune*, January 10, 114–116.

27. R. C. Shrader, 2001, Collaboration and performance in foreign markets: The case of young high-technology manufacturing firms, *Academy of Management Journal*, 44: 45–60; W. Kuemmerle, 1999, The drivers of foreign direct investment into research and development: An empirical investigation, *Journal of International Business Studies*, 30: 1–24.

28. Z. Liao, 2001, International R&D project evaluation by multinational corporations in the electronics and IT industry of Singapore, *R & D Management*, 31: 299–307.

29. W. Shan & J. Song, 1997, Foreign direct investment and the sourcing of technological advantage: Evidence from the biotechnology industry, *Journal of International Business Studies*, 28: 267–284.

30. B. O'Keefe, 2001, Global brands, *Fortune*, November 26, 102–110.

31. W. Chung, 2001, Identifying technology transfer in foreign direct investment: Influence of industry conditions and investing firm motives, *Journal of International Business Studies*, 32: 211–229.

32. A. J. Mauri & A. V. Phatak, 2001, Global integration as inter-area product flows: The internalization of ownership and location factors influencing product flows across MNC units, *Management International Review*, 41(3): 233–249.

33. D. Roberts & A. Webb, 2001, China's carmakers: Flattened by falling tariffs, *Business Week*, December 3, 51.

34. W. Kuemmerle, 2002, Home base and knowledge management in international ventures, *Journal of Business Venturing*, 2: 99–122; H. Bresman, J. Birkinshaw, & R. Nobel, 1999, Knowledge transfer in international acquisitions, *Journal of International Business Studies*, 30: 439–462; J. Birkinshaw, 1997, Entrepreneurship in multinational corporations: The characteristics of subsidiary initiatives, *Strategic Management Journal*, 18: 207–229.

35. Ahlstrom & Bruton, Learning from successful local private firms in China; S. A. Zahra, R. D. Ireland, & M. A. Hitt, 2000, International expansion by new venture firms: International diversity, mode of market entry, technological learning, and performance, *Academy of Management Journal*, 43: 925–950.

36. Mauri & Phatak, Global integration as inter-area product flows.

37. J. Bernstein & D. Weinstein, 2002, Do endowments predict the location of production? Evidence from national and international data, *Journal of International Economics*, 56(1): 55–76.

38. D. Wilson, 2001, Turns to Diamond—Hungary glitters as Central Europe's choice manufacturing site, *Ebn*, January 29, 46.

39. R. Robertson & D. H. Dutkowsky, 2002, Labor adjustment costs in a destination country: The case of Mexico, *Journal of Development Economics*, 67: 29–54.

40. D. A. Griffith & M. G. Harvey, 2001, A resource perspective of global dynamic capabilities, *Journal of International Business Studies*, 32: 597–606; D. J. Teece, G. Pisano, & A. Shuen, 1997, Dynamic capabilities and strategic management, *Strategic Management Journal*, 18: 509–533.

41. Y. Luo, 2000, Dynamic capabilities in international expansion, *Journal of World Business*, 35(4): 355–378.

42. L. Nachum, 2001, The impact of home countries on the competitiveness of advertising TNCs, *Management International Review*, 41(1): 77–98.

43. Ibid.

44. M. E. Porter, 1990, *The Competitive Advantage of Nations*, New York: The Free Press.

45. Ibid., 84.

46. Ibid., 89.

47. O. Oz, 2001, Sources of competitive advantage of Turkish construction companies in international markets, *Construction Management and Economics*, 19(2): 135–144.

48. J. Birkinshaw, 2001, Strategies for managing internal competition, *California Management Review*, 44(1): 21–38.

49. W. P. Wan & R. E. Hoskisson, 2002, Home country environments, corporate diversification strategies and firm performance, *Academy of Management Journal*, in press;

J. M. Geringer, S. Tallman, & D. M. Olsen, 2000, Product and international diversification among Japanese multinational firms, *Strategic Management Journal*, 21: 51–80.

50. M. A. Hitt, R. E. Hoskisson, & R. D. Ireland, 1994, A mid-range theory of the interactive effects of international and product diversification on innovation and performance, *Journal of Management*, 20: 297–326.

51. A.-W. Harzing, 2000, An empirical analysis and extension of the Bartlett and Ghoshal typology of multinational companies, *Journal of International Business Studies*, 32: 101–120; S. Ghoshal, 1987, Global strategy: An organizing framework, *Strategic Management Journal*, 8: 425–440.

52. J. Sheth, 2000, From international to integrated marketing, *Journal of Business Research*, 51(1): 5–9; J. Taggart & N. Hood, 1999, Determinants of autonomy in multinational corporation subsidiaries, *European Management Journal*, 17: 226–236.

53. Y. Luo, 2001, Determinants of local responsiveness: Perspectives from foreign subsidiaries in an emerging market, *Journal of Management*, 27: 451–477.

54. M. Carpenter & J. Fredrickson, 2001, Top management teams, global strategic posture, and the moderating role of uncertainty, *Academy of Management Journal*, 44: 533–545; T. T. Herbert, 1999, Multinational strategic planning: Matching central expectations to local realities, *Long Range Planning*, 32: 81–87.

55. O'Keefe, Global brands.

56. Ghemawat, Distance still matters, 147.

57. Harzing, An empirical analysis and extension of the Bartlett and Ghoshal typology.

58. D. G. McKendrick, 2001, Global strategy and population level learning: The case of hard disk drives, *Strategic Management Journal*, 22: 307–334.

59. M. W. Peng, S. H. Lee, & J. J. Tan, 2001, The keiretsu in Asia: Implications for multilevel theories of competitive advantage, *Journal of International Management*, 7: 253–276; A. Bhappu, 2000, The Japanese family: An institutional logic for Japanese corporate networks and Japanese management. *Academy of Management Review*, 25: 409–415; J. K. Johaansson & G. S. Yip, 1994, Exploiting globalization potential: U.S. and Japanese strategies, *Strategic Management Journal*, 15: 579–601.

60 D. Ilott, 2002, Success story—Cemex: The cement giant has managed concrete earnings in a mixed year, *Business Mexico*, January(Special Edition), 34; 2001, Business: The Cemex way, *The Economist*, June 16, 75–76.

61. C. A. Bartlett & S. Ghoshal, 1989, *Managing Across Borders: The Transnational Solution*, Boston: Harvard Business School Press.

62. J. Child & Y. Yan, 2001, National and transnational effects in international business: Indications from Sino-foreign joint ventures, *Management International Review*, 41(1): 53–75.

63. J. Muller & C. Tierney, 2002, Daimler and Chrysler have a baby, *Business Week*, January 14, 36–37.

64. T. Isobe, S. Makino, & D. B. Montgomery, 2000, Resource commitment, entry timing and market performance of foreign direct investments in emerging economies: The case of Japanese international joint ventures in China, *Academy of Management Journal*, 43: 468–484.

65. S. Zaheer & A. Zaheer, 2001, Market microstructure in a global B2B network, *Strategic Management Journal*, 22: 859–873.

66. C. Sliwa, 2001, Clothing retailer finds worldwide business on the Web, *Computerworld*, April 30, 40–44.

67. Ibid.

68. F. X. Molina-Morales, 2001, European industrial districts: Influence of geographic concentration on performance of the firm, *Journal of International Management*, 7: 277–294; M. E. Porter & S. Stern, 2001, Innovation: Location matters, *Sloan Management Review*, 42(4): 28–36.

69. C. Pantzalis, 2001, Does location matter? An empirical analysis of geographic scope and MNC market valuation, *Journal of International Business Studies*, 32: 133–155.

70. R. D. Ludema, 2002, Increasing returns, multinationals and geography of preferential trade agreements, *Journal of International Economics*, 56: 329–358; L. Allen & C. Pantzalis, 1996, Valuation of the operating flexibility of multinational corporations, *Journal of International Business Studies*, 27: 633–653.

71. J. I. Martinez, J. A. Quelch, & J. Ganitsky, 1992, Don't forget Latin America, *Sloan Management Review*, 33(Winter): 78–92.

72. H. Przybyla, 2000, Strong U.S. economy pushing trade deficit with Latin America, *Houston Chronicle*, January 21, C1, C4.

73. C. Lindblad, 2001, Mexico: The Fox revolution is spinning its wheels, *Business Week*, December 10, 51.

74. J. Chang & P. M. Rosenzweig, 1998, Industry and regional patterns in sequential foreign market entry, *Journal of Management Studies*, 35: 797–822.

75. S. Zahra, J. Hayton, J. Marcel, & H. O'Neill, 2001, Fostering entrepreneurship during international expansion: Managing key challenges, *European Management Journal*, 19: 359–369.

76. Zahra, Ireland, & Hitt, International expansion by new venture firms.

77. M. W. Peng, C. W. L. Hill, & D. Y. L. Wang, 2000, Schumpeterian dynamics versus Williamsonian considerations: A test of export intermediary performance, *Journal of Management Studies*, 37: 167–184.

78. Luo, Determinants of local responsiveness.

79. M. A. Raymond, J. Kim, & A. T. Shao, 2001, Export strategy and performance: A comparison of exporters in a developed market and an emerging market, *Journal of Global Marketing*, 15(2): 5–29; P. S. Aulakh, M. Kotabe, & H. Teegen, 2000, Export strategies and performance of firms from emerging economies: Evidence from Brazil, Chile and Mexico. *Academy of Management Journal*, 43: 342–361.

80. B. Walker & D. Luft, 2001, Exporting tech from Texas, *Texas Business Review*, August, 1–5.

81. P. Westhead, M. Wright, & D. Ucbasaran, 2001, The internationalization of new and small firms: A resource-based view, *Journal of Business Venturing*, 16: 333–358.

82. D. Fairlamb & R. McNatt, 2002, The Euro: A shopper's best friend, *Business Week*, January 14, 8.

83. M. A. Hitt & R. D. Ireland, 2000, The intersection of entrepreneurship and strategic management research, in D. L. Sexton & H. Landstrom (eds.) *Handbook of Entrepreneurship*, Oxford, U.K.: Blackwell Publishers, 45–63.

84. A. Arora & A. Fosfuri, 2000, Wholly owned subsidiary versus technology licensing in the worldwide chemical industry, *Journal of International Business Studies*, 31: 555–572.

85. M. Johnson, 2001, Learning from toys: Lessons in managing supply chain risk from the toy industry, *California Management Review*, 43(3): 106–124.

86. C. A. Bartlett & S. Rangan, 1992, Komatsu limited, in C. A. Bartlett & S. Ghoshal (eds.), *Transnational Management: Text, Cases and Readings in Cross-Border Management*, Homewood, IL: Irwin, 311–326.

87. B. Petersen, D. E. Welch, & L. S. Welch, 2000, Creating meaningful switching options in international operations, *Long Range Planning*, 33(5): 688–705.

88. J. W. Lu & P. W. Beamish, 2001, The internationalization and performance of SMEs, *Strategic Management Journal*, 22(Special Issue): 565–586; M. Koza & A. Lewin, 2000, Managing partnerships and strategic alliances: Raising the odds of success, *European Management Journal*, 18(2): 146–151.

89. J. S. Harrison, M. A. Hitt, R. E. Hoskisson, & R. D. Ireland, 2001, Resource complementarity in business combinations: Extending the logic to organization alliances, *Journal of Management*, 27: 679–690; T. Das & B. Teng, 2000, A resource-based theory of strategic alliances, *Journal of Management*, 26: 31–61.

90. M. Peng, 2001. The resource-based view and international business, *Journal of Management*, 27: 803–829.

91. P. J. Lane, J. E. Salk, & M. A. Lyles, 2002, Absorptive capacity, learning, and performance in international joint ventures, *Strategic Management Journal*, 22: 1139–1161; B. L. Simonin, 1999, Transfer of marketing know-how in international strategic alliances: An empirical investigation of the role and antecedents of knowledge ambiguity, *Journal of International Business Studies*, 30: 463–490; M. A. Lyles & J. E. Salk, 1996, Knowledge acquisition from foreign parents in international joint ventures: An empirical examination in the Hungarian context, *Journal of International Business Studies*, 27(Special Issue): 877–903.

92. Shrader, Collaboration and performance in foreign markets; M. A. Hitt, M. T. Dacin, E. Levitas, J. L. Arregle, & A. Borza, 2000, Partner selection in emerging and developed market contexts: Resource based and organizational learning perspectives, *Academy of Management Journal*, 43: 449–467.

93. J. Eig, 2001, H.J. Heinz and Japan's Kagome are expected to form alliance, *The Wall Street Journal Interactive*, http://www.wsj.com, July 26.

94. C. Grande, 2001, Pearson plans to teach English on Chinese TV, *Financial Times*, November 20, 27.

95. Y. Gong, O. Shenkar, Y. Luo, & M-K. Nyaw, 2001, Role conflict and ambiguity of CEOs in international joint ventures: A transaction cost perspective, *Journal of Applied Psychology*, 86: 764–773.

96. D. C. Hambrick, J. Li, K. Xin, & A. S. Tsui, 2001, Compositional gaps and downward spirals in international joint venture management groups, *Strategic Management Journal*, 22: 1033–1053; M. T. Dacin, M. A. Hitt, & E. Levitas, 1997, Selecting partners for successful international alliances: Examination of U.S. and Korean Firms, *Journal of World Business*, 32: 3–16.

97. A. Arino, J. de la Torre, & P. S. Ring, 2001, Relational quality: Managing trust in corporate alliances, *California Management Review*, 44(1): 109–131.

98. Y. Pan & D. K. Tse, 2000, The hierarchical model of market entry modes, *Journal of International Business Studies*, 31: 535–554; Y. Pan, S. Li, & D. K. Tse, 1999, The

impact of order and mode of market entry on profitability and market share, *Journal of International Business Studies,* 30: 81–104.

99. W. H. Hoffmann & W. Schaper-Rinkel, 2001, Acquire or ally? A strategy framework for deciding between acquisition and cooperation, *Management International Review,* 41(2): 131–159.

100. M. A. Hitt, J. S. Harrison, & R. D. Ireland, 2001, *Creating Value through Mergers and Acquisitions,* New York: Oxford University Press.

101. 1999, French Dressing, *The Economist,* July 10, 53–54.

102. W. Zellner, K. A. Schimdt, M. Ihlwan, H. Dawley, 2001, How well does Wal-Mart travel? *Business Week,* September 3, 82–84.

103. A.-W. Harzing, 2002, Acquisitions versus greenfield investments: International strategy and management of entry modes, *Strategic Management Journal,* 23: 211–227; K. D. Brouthers & L. E. Brouthers, 2000, Acquisition or greenfield start-up? Institutional, cultural and transaction cost influences, *Strategic Management Journal,* 21: 89–97.

104. D. Kirk, 2001, British American Tobacco finds opening in South Korea, *The New York Times,* http://www.nytimes.com, August 9.

105. S.-J. Chang & P. Rosenzweig, 2001, The choice of entry mode in sequential foreign direct investment, *Strategic Management Journal,* 22: 747–776.

106. K. E. Myer, 2001, Institutions, transaction costs, and entry mode choice in Eastern Europe, *Journal of International Business Studies,* 32: 357–367.

107. Y. Luo, 2001, Determinants of entry in an emerging economy: A multilevel approach, *Journal of Management Studies,* 38: 443–472.

108. A. Takeishi, 2001, Bridging inter- and intra-firm boundaries: Management of supplier involvement in automobile product development, *Strategic Management Journal,* 22: 403–433.

109. D. K. Sobek, II, A. C. Ward, & J. K. Liker, 1999, Toyota's principles of set-based concurrent engineering, *Sloan Management Review,* 40(2): 53–83.

110. H. Chen, 1999, International performance of multinationals: A hybrid model, *Journal of World Business,* 34: 157–170.

111. S.-J. Chang & J. Hong, 2002, How much does the business group matter in Korea? *Strategic Management Journal,* 23: 265–274.

112. J. Song, 2002, Firm capabilities and technology ladders: Sequential foreign direct investments of Japanese electronics firms in East Asia, *Strategic Management Journal,* 23: 191–210.

113. M.Ramirez-Aleson & M. A. Espitia-Escuer, 2001, The effect of international diversification strategy on the performance of Spanish-based firms during the period 1991–1995, *Management International Review,* 41(3): 291–315; A. Delios & P. W. Beamish, 1999, Geographic scope, product diversification, and the corporate performance of Japanese firms, *Strategic Management Journal,* 20: 711–727.

114. C. Pantzalis, 2001, Does location matter? An empirical analysis of geographic scope and MNC market valuation, *Journal of International Business Studies,* 32: 133–155; C. Y. Tang & S. Tikoo, 1999, Operational flexibility and market valuation of earnings, *Strategic Management Journal,* 20: 749–761.

115. J. M. Geringer, P. W. Beamish, & R. C. daCosta, 1989, Diversification strategy and internationalization: Implications for MNE performance, *Strategic Management Journal,* 10: 109–119; R. E. Caves, 1982, *Multinational Enterprise and Economic Analysis,* Cambridge, MA: Cambridge University Press.

116. Zahra, Ireland, & Hitt, International expansion by new venture firms.

117. T. W. Malnight, 2002, Emerging structural patterns within multinational corporations: Toward process-based structures, *Academy of Management Journal,* 44: 1187–1210.

118. Camuffo, Romano, & Vinelli, Back to the future: Benetton transforms its global network.

119. G. Hamel, 2000, *Leading the Revolution,* Boston: Harvard Business School Press.

120. L. Tihanyi, R. A. Johnson, R. E. Hoskisson, & M. A. Hitt, 2002. Institutional ownership differences and international diversification: The effects of board of directors and technological opportunity, *Academy of Management Journal,* in press.

121. F. Bradley & M. Gannon, 2000, Does the firm's technology and marketing profile affect foreign market entry?, *Journal of International Marketing,* 8(4): 12–36; M. Kotabe, 1990, The relationship between off-shore sourcing and innovativeness of U.S. multinational firms: An empirical investigation, *Journal of International Business Studies,* 21: 623–638.

122. I. Zander & O. Solvell, 2000, Cross border innovation in the multinational corporation: A research agenda, *International Studies of Management and Organization,* 30(2): 44–67; Y. Luo, 1999, Time-based experience and international expansion: The case of an emerging economy, *Journal of Management Studies,* 36. 505–533.

123. Z. Liao, 2001, International R&D project evaluation by multinational corporations in the electronics and IT industry of Singapore, *R & D Management,* 31: 299–307; M Subramaniam & N. Venkartraman, 2001, Determinants of transnational new product development capability: Testing the influence of transferring and deploying tacit overseas knowledge, *Strategic Management Journal,* 22: 359–378.

124. Wan & Hoskisson, Home country environments, corporate diversification strategies and firm performance.

125. 2001, Business as usual, or for real? *Business Asia,* January 8, 3–5.

126. M. Carpenter & J. Fredrickson, 2001, Top management teams, global strategic posture, and the moderating role of uncertainty, *Academy of Management Journal,* 44: 533–545; S. Finkelstein & D. C. Hambrick, 1996, *Strategic Leadership: Top Executives and Their Effects on Organizations,* St. Paul, MN: West Publishing Company.

127. A. McWilliams, D. D. Van Fleet, & P. M. Wright, 2001, Strategic management of human resources for global competitive advantage, *Journal of Business Strategies,* 18(1): 1–24.

128. M. A. Hitt, R. E. Hoskisson, & H. Kim, 1997, International diversification: Effects on innovation and firm performance in product-diversified firms, *Academy of Management Journal,* 40: 767–798.

129. D. Rondinelli, B. Rosen, & I. Drori, 2001, The struggle for strategic alignment in multinational corporations: Managing readjustment during global expansion, *European Management Journal,* 19: 404–405; Carpenter & Fredrickson, Top management teams, global strategic posture, and the moderating role of uncertainty.

130. D. M. Reeb, C. C. Y. Kwok, & H. Y. Baek, 1998, Systematic risk of the multinational corporation, *Journal of International Business Studies,* 29: 263–279.

131. C. Pompitakpan, 1999, The effects of cultural adaptation on business relationships: Americans selling to Japanese and Thais, *Journal of International Business Studies,* 30: 317–338.

132. L. L. Jacque & P. M. Vaaler, 2001, The international control conundrum with exchange risk: An EVA framework, *Journal of International Business Studies,* 32: 813–832.

133. 2002, Argentina's ugly economic choices: No good options, *The Economist,* January 5, 30–31.

134. Wan & Hoskisson, Home country environments, corporate diversification strategies and firm performance; Hitt, Hoskisson, & Kim, International diversification; S. Tallman & J. Li, 1996, Effects of international diversity and product diversity on the performance of multinational firms, *Academy of Management Journal,* 39: 179–196; Hitt, Hoskisson, & Ireland, A mid-range theory of interactive effects; Geringer, Beamish, & daCosta, Diversification strategy.

135. A. K. Rose & E. van Wincoop, 2001, National money as a barrier to international trade: The real case for currency union, *American Economic Review,* 91: 386–390.

136. I. M. Manev & W. B. Stevenson, 2001, Nationality, cultural distance, and expatriate status: Effects on the managerial network in a multinational enterprise, *Journal of International Business Studies,* 32: 285–303.

137. D. Luhnow, 2001, How NAFTA helped Wal-Mart transform the Mexican market, *The Wall Street Journal,* August 31, A1, A2.

138. D. E. Thomas & R. Grosse, 2001, Country-of-origin determinants of foreign direct investment in an emerging market: The case of Mexico, *Journal of International Management,* 7: 59–79.

139. J. Feeney & A. Hillman, 2001, Privatization and the political economy of strategic trade policy, *International Economic Review,* 42: 535–556; R. Vernon, 2001, Big business and national governments: Reshaping the compact in a globalizing economy, *Journal of International Business Studies,* 32: 509–518; B. Shaffer & A. J. Hillman, 2000, The development of business-government strategies by diversified firms, *Strategic Management Journal,* 21: 175–190.

140. B. Barringer & J. Harrison, 2000, Walking the tightrope: Creating value through interorganizational relationships, *Journal of Management,* 26: 367–404.

9

Chapter Nine

Cooperative Strategy

Knowledge Objectives

Studying this chapter should provide you with the strategic management knowledge needed to:

1. Define cooperative strategies and explain why firms use them.

2. Define and discuss three types of strategic alliances.

3. Name the business-level cooperative strategies and describe their use.

4. Discuss the use of corporate-level cooperative strategies in diversified firms.

5. Understand the importance of cross-border strategic alliances as an international cooperative strategy.

6. Describe cooperative strategies' risks.

7. Describe two approaches used to manage cooperative strategies.

The S-92 Helicopter: A Product of a Cross-Border Alliance

Several factors, including product complexity and research and development costs, make it very difficult for a firm to undertake major projects on its own while competing in the 21st-century competitive landscape. A business analyst speaking about the nature of competition in the aerospace industry said, "If an aerospace company is not good at alliances, it's not in business." Similarly, the chief information officer of international food processor and distributor Cargill believes that successful product innovations require alliances: "To bring something new to the marketplace requires so much cooperation and integration of knowledge that you just can't get it done unless you pick partners."

Cross-border alliances are one type of cooperative strategy used to deal with the realities of the 21st-century competitive landscape and to develop product innovations. As discussed later in the chapter, a cross-border strategic alliance is a partnership formed between firms with headquarters in different nations. Firms use a cross-border alliance to uniquely combine their value-creating resources and capabilities to develop a competitive advantage that neither partner could form on its own.

Aerospace is one of the industries in which highly diversified United Technologies competes. The firm is involved with over 100 worldwide cooperative strategies, including cross-border alliances and joint ventures (defined later in the chapter). One of United Technologies' cooperative strategies is the cross-border alliance formed by the firm's Sikorsky business unit to produce the S-92 helicopter. Five firms from four continents joined with Sikorsky to form this alliance. Using its unique resource and capabilities, each partner assumed different responsibilities for the design and production of the S-92. The combination of the partners' resources and capabilities is thought to have resulted in a competitive advantage for the alliance.

The Sikorski S-92 demonstrates cooperation both in its creation and also in the end product. Following Canadian firm Cougar Helicopter's launch order, firms around the world have placed orders, including HeliJet of Vancouver, Aircontactgruppen AS of Norway, Copterline of Finland, and East Asia Airlines/Helicopter Hong Kong. The Irish Air Corps has ordered three S-92 SAR (search and rescue) variant helicopters and has an option for two more military transport variants. The craft also met Hollywood's demands—the Sikorski S-92 plays a part in *Mr. Deeds,* a 2002 comedy feature film, as a world-class executive transport helicopter owned by a fictional multimillion-dollar media firm.

Called "Team S-92," this alliance's partners and their responsibilities are: (1) Japan's Mitsubishi Heavy Industries (main cabin section), (2) Jingdezhen Helicopter Group/CATIC of the People's Republic of China (vertical tail fin

N392SA

and stabilizer), (3) Spain's Gamesa Aeronautica (main rotor pylon, engine nacelles AFT tail, transition section, and cabin interior), (4) Aerospace Industrial Development Corporation of Taiwan (the electrical harness, flight controls, hydraulic lines, and environmental controls forming the cockpit), and (5) Embraer of Brazil (main landing gear and fuel system). As the sixth member of the alliance, Sikorsky is responsible for the main and tail rotor head components and the S-92's transmissions. The "International Wide Area Network" connects alliance members via satellite. This connection enables real-time interactions among partners as they integrate their work.

Sikorsky has alliance responsibilities beyond those described above, including the final assembly of the S-92 and its certification as launch-ready. Following final assembly, the production program to commercially launch the S-92 was initiated in 1999. Commenting about the craft's potential, Sikorsky president Dean Borgman stated that, "The S-92 will be tops in its class in terms of cost and performance. We have numerous opportunities with this aircraft to sell to civil and government operators."

In 2000, Sikorsky, representing the Team S-92 alliance, formed a strategic relationship (called a launch agreement) with Canadian off-shore operator Cougar Helicopters, which intends to use the S-92 to support its offshore operations in St. John's, Newfoundland and Halifax, Nova Scotia. Sikorsky formed a strategic relationship with Cougar to facilitate the S-92's successful commercial launch. Through cooperative interactions with Cougar, Sikorsky is discovering possible S-92 modifications that it and its alliance partners may need to initiate for the project's long-term success.

Describing the benefits of this strategic relationship, a Sikorsky official stated that, "Cougar is an ideal launch customer. They are extremely professional and innovative. Further, they will put the aircraft to the test with very high utilization, actual icing conditions, and a requirement for the high service levels we have designed in. Sikorsky and our other customers will benefit greatly from the S-92's entry into service with Cougar." Cougar is scheduled to take delivery of the first two production runs of the S-92 in late 2002 and early 2003. Thus, Sikorsky formed a cross-border alliance to produce the S-92 and a strategic relationship (which essentially was another strategic alliance) to facilitate the product's commercial launch.

SOURCES: 2002, The S-92 program, United Technologies, http://www.utc.com; 2002, Cougar and Sikorsky work accord to launch S-92, Cougar Helicopters, http://www.cougar.com, March 14; D. Donovan, 2001, United Technologies, *Forbes Best of the Web*, May 21, 66; J. Fahey, 2001, Cargill, *Forbes Best of the Web*, May 21, 66.

Pursuing internal opportunities (doing better than competitors through strategic execution or innovation) and merging with or acquiring other companies are the two primary means by which firms grow that we have discussed to this point in the book. In this chapter, we examine cooperative strategies, which are the third major alternative firms use to grow, develop value-creating competitive advantages, and create differences between them and competitors.[1] Defined formally, a **cooperative strategy** is a strategy in which firms work together to achieve a shared objective.[2] Thus, cooperating with other firms is another strategy that is used to create value for a customer that exceeds the cost of constructing that value in other ways[3] and to establish a favorable position relative to competition (see Chapters 2, 4, 5, and 8).[4] The increasing importance of cooperative strategies as a growth engine shouldn't be underestimated. In fact, some believe that "in a global market tied together by the Internet, corporate partnerships and alliances are proving a more productive way to keep companies growing."[5] This means that effective competition in the 21st-century landscape results when the firm learns how to cooperate with as well as compete against competitors.[6]

A **cooperative strategy** is a strategy in which firms work together to achieve a shared objective.

Increasingly, cooperative strategies are formed by firms competing against one another,[7] as shown by the fact that more than half of the strategic alliances (a type of cooperative strategy) established within a recent two-year period were between competitors.[8] In an alliance between FedEx and the U.S. Postal Service (USPS), for example, FedEx transports roughly 3.5 million pounds of USPS packages daily on its planes and is allowed to place its drop boxes in post offices. ". . . The seven-year deal will earn [FedEx] more than $7 billion—$6.3 billion in transportation charges and $900 million in increased drop-box revenue."[9]

Because they are the primary type of cooperative strategy that firms use, strategic alliances (defined in the next section) are this chapter's focus. Although not frequently used, collusive strategies are another type of cooperative strategy discussed in this chapter. In a *collusive strategy*, two or more firms cooperate to raise prices above the fully competitive level.[10]

We examine several topics in this chapter. First, we define and offer examples of different strategic alliances as primary types of cooperative strategies. Next, we discuss the extensive use of cooperative strategies in the global economy and reasons for this use. In succession, we then describe business-level (including collusive strategies), corporate-level, international, and network cooperative strategies—most in the form of strategic alliances. The chapter closes with discussions of the risks of using cooperative strategies as well as how effective management of them can reduce those risks.

Strategic Alliances as a Primary Type of Cooperative Strategy

Strategic alliances are increasingly popular. Two researchers describe this popularity by noting that an "unprecedented number of strategic alliances between firms are being formed each year. [These] strategic alliances are a logical and timely response to intense and rapid changes in economic activity, technology, and globalization, all of which have cast many corporations into two competitive races: one for the world and the other for the future."[11]

A **strategic alliance** is a cooperative strategy in which firms combine some of their resources and capabilities to create a competitive advantage.

A **strategic alliance** is a cooperative strategy in which firms combine some of their resources and capabilities to create a competitive advantage.[12] Thus, as linkages between them, strategic alliances involve firms with some degree of exchange and sharing of resources and capabilities to co-develop or distribute goods or services.[13] Strategic alliances let firms leverage their existing resources and capabilities while

ANTONIO CALANNI/ASSOCIATED PRESS

A **joint venture** is a strategic alliance in which two or more firms create a legally independent company to share some of their resources and capabilities to develop a competitive advantage.

An **equity strategic alliance** is an alliance in which two or more firms own different percentages of the company they have formed by combining some of their resources and capabilities to create a competitive advantage.

working with partners to develop additional resources and capabilities as the foundation for new competitive advantages.[14]

Many firms, especially large global competitors, establish multiple strategic alliances. General Motors' alliances, for example, ". . . include collaboration with Honda on internal combustion engines, with Toyota on advanced propulsion, with Renault on medium- and heavy-duty vans for Europe and, in the U.S., with AM General on the brand and distribution rights for the incomparable Hummer."[15] Focusing on developing advanced technologies, Lockheed Martin has formed over 250 alliances with firms in more than 30 countries as it concentrates on its primary business of defense modernization.[16] In general, strategic alliance success requires cooperative behavior from all partners. Actively solving problems, being trustworthy, and consistently pursuing ways to combine partners' resources and capabilities to create value are examples of cooperative behavior known to contribute to alliance success.[17]

A competitive advantage developed through a cooperative strategy often is called a collaborative or relational advantage.[18] As previously discussed, particularly in Chapter 4, competitive advantages significantly influence the firm's marketplace success.[19] Rapid technological changes and the global economy are examples of factors challenging firms to constantly upgrade current competitive advantages while they develop new ones to maintain strategic competitiveness.[20]

The firms mentioned in the Opening Case combined their resources and capabilities to develop competitive advantages while working together as the Team S-92 alliance. No individual member of the alliance could have developed the *design* and *manufacturing* competitive advantages that were instrumental to the design and production of the S-92 helicopter—a product with size and cost benefits over competing helicopters.

Three Types of Strategic Alliances

There are three major types of strategic alliances—joint venture, equity strategic alliance, and nonequity strategic alliance.

A **joint venture** is a strategic alliance in which two or more firms create a legally independent company to share some of their resources and capabilities to develop a competitive advantage. Joint ventures are effective in establishing long-term relationships and in transferring tacit knowledge. Because it can't be codified, tacit knowledge is learned through experiences[21] such as those taking place when people from partner firms work together in a joint venture. As discussed in Chapter 3, tacit knowledge is an important source of competitive advantage for many firms.[22]

Typically, partners in a joint venture own equal percentages and contribute equally to its operations. Sprint and Virgin Group's joint venture, called Virgin Mobile USA, targets 15- to 30-year-olds as customers for pay-as-you-go wireless phone service. Brand (from Virgin) and service (from Sprint) are the primary capabilities the firms contribute to this joint venture.[23] In another example, Sony Pictures Entertainment, Warner Bros., Universal Pictures, Paramount Pictures, and Metro-Goldwyn-Mayer Inc. each have a 20 percent stake in a joint venture to use the Internet to deliver feature films on demand to customers.[24] Overall, evidence suggests that a joint venture may be the optimal alliance when firms need to combine their resources and capabilities to create a competitive advantage that is substantially different from any they possess individually and when the partners intend to enter highly uncertain markets.[25]

An **equity strategic alliance** is an alliance in which two or more firms own different percentages of the company they have formed by combining some of their resources and capabilities to create a competitive advantage. Many foreign direct investments such as those made by Japanese and U.S. companies in China are completed through equity strategic alliances.[26]

In another example, Cott Corporation, the world's largest retailer brand soft drink supplier, recently formed an equity strategic alliance with J. D. Iroquois Enterprises Ltd. to strengthen its reach into the spring water segment of its markets. With a 49 percent stake in the new venture, Cott gained exclusive supply rights for Iroquois' private label spring water products. Iroquois president Dan Villeneuve believes that the alliance ". . . will expand the Iroquois branded business in the West and Far East,"[27] which is the benefit his firm gains from its equity strategic alliance with Cott.

A **nonequity strategic alliance** is an alliance in which two or more firms develop a contractual relationship to share some of their unique resources and capabilities to create a competitive advantage. In this type of strategic alliance, firms do not establish a separate independent company and therefore don't take equity positions. Because of this, nonequity strategic alliances are less formal and demand fewer partner commitments than joint ventures and equity strategic alliances.[28] The relative informality and lower commitment levels characterizing nonequity strategic alliances make them unsuitable for complex projects where success requires effective transfers of tacit knowledge between partners.[29]

However, firms today increasingly use this type of alliance in many different forms such as licensing agreements, distribution agreements, and supply contracts.[30] For example, Ralph Lauren Company uses licensing agreements extensively. To support its flagship Polo brand, the firm currently uses 29 domestic licensing agreements, including West Point Stevens (bedding), Reebok (casual shoes), and ICI Paints (Ralph Lauren Home Products).[31] A key reason for the growth in types of cooperative strategies, as indicated by the Opening Case, is the complexity and uncertainty that characterize most global industries and make it difficult for firms to be successful without some sort of partnerships.[32]

Typically, outsourcing commitments take the form of a nonequity strategic alliance.[33] Discussed in Chapter 3, *outsourcing* is the purchase of a value-creating primary or support activity from another firm. Magna International Inc., a leading global supplier of technologically advanced automotive systems, components, and modules, has formed many nonequity strategic alliances with automotive manufacturers who have outsourced work to it. Magna's effectiveness with nonequity strategic alliances is suggested by the awards honoring the quality of its work that Magna has received from many of its customers, including General Motors, Ford Motor Company, Honda, DaimlerChrysler, and Toyota.[34]

Reasons Firms Develop Strategic Alliances

As previously noted, the use of cooperative strategies as a path to strategic competitiveness is on the rise[35] in for-profit firms of all sizes as well as in public organizations.[36] Thus, cooperative strategies are becoming more important to companies.[37] For example, recently surveyed executives of technology companies stated that strategic alliances are central to their firms' success.[38] Speaking directly to the issue of technology acquisition and development for these firms, a manager noted that, "You have to partner today or you will miss the next wave. You cannot possibly acquire the technology fast enough, so partnering is essential."[39]

Some even suggest that strategic alliances ". . . may be the most powerful trend that has swept American business in a century."[40] Among other benefits, strategic alliances allow partners to create value that they couldn't develop by acting independently[41] and to enter markets more quickly.[42] Moreover, most (if not virtually all) firms lack the full set of resources and capabilities needed to reach their objectives, which indicates that partnering with others will increase the probability of reaching them.[43]

The effects of the greater use of cooperative strategies—particularly in the form of strategic alliances—are noticeable. In large firms, for example, alliances now account for more than 20 percent of revenue.[44] Booz Allen Hamilton, Inc., predicted that by the end of 2002, alliances would account for as much as 35 percent of revenue for the one thousand largest U.S. companies.[45] Supporting this expectation is the belief of many senior-level executives that alliances are a prime vehicle for firm growth.[46]

In some industries, alliance versus alliance is becoming more prominent than firm against firm as a point of competition. In the global airline industry, for example, ". . . competition increasingly is between . . . alliances rather than between airlines."[47] This increased use of cooperative strategies and its results are not surprising in that the mid-1990s saw predictions that cooperative strategies were the wave of the future.[48]

The individually unique competitive conditions of slow-cycle, fast-cycle, and standard-cycle markets[49] find firms using cooperative strategies to achieve slightly different objectives (see Table 9.1). We discuss these three market types in Chapter 5 where we study competitive rivalry and competitive dynamics. *Slow-cycle markets* are markets where the firm's competitive advantages are shielded from imitation for relatively long periods of time and where imitation is costly. These markets are close to monopolistic conditions. Railroads and historically, telecommunications, utilities, and financial services are examples of industries characterized as slow-cycle markets. In *fast-cycle markets,* the firm's competitive advantages aren't shielded from imitation, preventing their long-term sustainability. Competitive advantages are moderately shielded from imitation in *standard-cycle markets,* typically allowing them to be sustained for a longer period of time compared to fast-cycle market situations, but for a shorter period of time than in slow-cycle markets.

Table 9.1	Reasons for Strategic Alliances by Market Type
Market	**Reason**
Slow-Cycle	• Gain access to a restricted market
	• Establish a franchise in a new market
	• Maintain market stability (e.g., establishing standards)
Fast-Cycle	• Speed up development of new goods or services
	• Speed up new market entry
	• Maintain market leadership
	• Form an industry technology standard
	• Share risky R&D expenses
	• Overcome uncertainty
Standard-Cycle	• Gain market power (reduce industry overcapacity)
	• Gain access to complementary resources
	• Establish better economies of scale
	• Overcome trade barriers
	• Meet competitive challenges from other competitors
	• Pool resources for very large capital projects
	• Learn new business techniques

Slow-Cycle Markets

Firms in slow-cycle markets often use strategic alliances to enter restricted markets or to establish franchises in new markets. For example, Paris-based steelmaker Usinor Group formed an equity strategic alliance with Dofasco, Canada's second-largest mill, to build a plant to supply car bodies for Honda, Toyota, General Motors, Ford, and DaimlerChrysler. For its 20 percent stake in the new venture, Usinor contributed $22 million in cash and technological know-how. Dofasco operates the North American–based plant and distributes its products. Through this alliance, Usinor and Dofasco were able to establish a new franchise ". . . in the import-averse U.S." steel market.[50]

In another example, the restricted entry to India's insurance market prompted American International Group (AIG) to form a joint venture—Tata AIG—with Mumbai-based Tata Group, ". . . which is one of the country's largest conglomerates and a trusted Indian brand name."[51] AIG executives believed that cooperative strategies were the only viable way for their firm to enter a market in which state-operated insurers had played a monopolistic role for decades.

Utility companies also use strategic alliances as a means of competing in slow-cycle markets. In the petrochemical industry, for example, Petróleos de Venezuela and Petrobras of Brazil formed a joint venture that calls for cross-investments between the partners. The eventual goal of this cooperative strategy is to form a pan–Latin American energy cooperative with firms in other countries. To reach the goal, the initial partners seek to expand the venture to add other state-owned oil companies in the region, including Colombia's Ecopetrol and Petróleos Mexicanos.[52]

Slow-cycle markets are becoming rare in the 21st-century competitive landscape for several reasons, including the privatization of industries and economies, the rapid expansion of the Internet's capabilities in terms of the quick dissemination of information, and the speed with which advancing technologies make quickly imitating even complex products possible.[53] Firms competing in slow-cycle markets should recognize the future likelihood that they'll encounter situations in which their competitive advantages become partially sustainable (in the instance of a standard-cycle market) or unsustainable (in the case of a fast-cycle market). Cooperative strategies can be helpful to firms making the transition from relatively sheltered markets to more competitive ones.

President of Polish Airlines LOT Jan Litwinski (left) and Lufthansa President Jan Weber (center) shake hands after signing a preliminary agreement in April 2002 for LOT to become a member of Star Alliance.

©AFP/CORBIS/LESZEK WROBLEWSKI

Fast-Cycle Markets

Fast-cycle markets tend to be unstable, unpredictable, and complex.[54] Combined, these conditions virtually preclude the establishment of long-lasting competitive advantages, forcing firms to constantly seek sources of new competitive advantages while creating value by using current ones. Alliances between firms with current excess resources and capabilities and those with promising capabilities help companies competing in fast-cycle markets to make an effective transition from the present to the future and also to gain rapid entry to new markets.

Sometimes, companies establish venture capital programs to facilitate these efforts.[55] Visa International formed a venture capital program to ". . . scout technologies and capabilities that will affect the future of financial services and the payments industry and enable (the firm) to deliver value to its more than 21,000 member institutions."[56] Visa International forms strategic alliances with firms that it believes have promising technologies and skills that, when shared with Visa's own resources and capabilities, have the potential to create new competitive advantages, providing the foundation for successfully entering new markets. In particular, Visa seeks partners to help create what it believes is the next generation of commerce—u-commerce, which is the ". . . merging and integration over time of the physical and the virtual world, where you may not be face-to-face, but still have the levels of trust, convenience, protection and security in addition to the ease in performing transactions even though you are physically far apart."[57]

Standard-Cycle Markets

In standard-cycle markets, which are often large and oriented toward economies of scale (e.g., commercial aerospace), alliances are more likely to be made by partners with complementary resources and capabilities. For example, Lufthansa (Germany) and United Airlines (United States) initially formed the Star Alliance in 1993. Since then, 13 other airlines have joined this alliance. Star Alliance partners share some of their resources and capabilities to serve almost 900 global airports. The goal of the Star Alliance is to ". . . combine the best routes worldwide and then offer seamless world travel through shared booking."[58]

Companies also may cooperate in standard-cycle markets to gain market power. As discussed in Chapter 6, market power allows the firm to sell its product above the existing competitive level or to reduce its costs below the competitive level, or both. Goodyear Tire recently spent $120 million to expand the tire plant in Dalian, China that was created through a 1994 joint venture between Goodyear and Dalian Rubber General Factory. The partners in the already successful venture want to expand the manufacturing facility to continue pursuing ". . . what is clearly destined to be one of the world's biggest long-term business opportunities."[59] Goodyear's investment is expected to increase plant efficiency and to provide even more differentiated and attractive products to those who demand top quality high performance tires and are willing to pay an above-average competitive price for them.

Business-Level Cooperative Strategy

A **business-level cooperative strategy** is used to help the firm improve its performance in individual product markets. As discussed in Chapter 4, business-level strategy details what the firm intends to do to gain a competitive advantage in specific product markets. Thus, the firm forms a business-level cooperative strategy when it believes that combining its resources and capabilities with those of one or more partners will create competitive advantages that it can't create by itself and that will lead to success in a specific product market. There are four business-level cooperative strategies (see Figure 9.1).

Complementary Strategic Alliances

Complementary strategic alliances are business-level alliances in which firms share some of their resources and capabilities in complementary ways to develop competitive advantages.[60] There are two types of complementary strategic alliances—vertical and horizontal (see Figure 9.1).

Vertical Complementary Strategic Alliance

In a *vertical complementary strategic alliance*, firms share their resources and capabilities from different stages of the value chain to create a competitive advantage (see Figure 9.2). McDonald's has formed vertical complementary alliances with major oil companies and independent store operators. With units located in these firms' storefronts, the customer can ". . . fill up (his or her) car, buy a meal, and pick up items for the home, with just one stop."[61] In another example, Boeing Company formed a vertical complementary alliance that included several partners to design and build the 777 plane, partly because of the project's scale and size. The partners, each of whom

---

A business-level cooperative strategy is used to help the firm improve its performance in individual product markets.

Complementary strategic alliances are business-level alliances in which firms share some of their resources and capabilities in complementary ways to develop competitive advantages.

Figure 9.1   Business-Level Cooperative Strategies

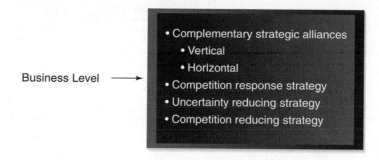

Business Level ⟶

- Complementary strategic alliances
  - Vertical
  - Horizontal
- Competition response strategy
- Uncertainty reducing strategy
- Competition reducing strategy

had superior resources and capabilities in a different part of the value chain, included United Airlines and five Japanese companies. According to an alliance partner, "The development of the 777 was the fastest and most efficient construction of a new commercial aircraft ever."[62]

Horizontal Complementary Alliance

A *horizontal complementary strategic alliance* is an alliance in which firms share some of their resources and capabilities from the same stage of the value chain to create a competitive advantage (see Figure 9.2). Commonly, firms use this type of alliance to focus on long-term product development and distribution opportunities.[63] Shin Caterpillar Mitsubishi Ltd. (SCM), for example, is a joint venture between Caterpillar Inc. and Mitsubishi Heavy Industries Ltd. that celebrates its 40th anniversary in 2003. These partners continue to share resources and capabilities to produce innovative products that neither firm could design and produce by itself. SCM is a leading supplier of earthmoving and construction equipment in Japan and also sells the products it produces on a global basis to other Caterpillar units.[64]

Two auto parts suppliers formed a horizontal complementary alliance to create a competitive advantage in terms of linking "bricks and clicks." CSK Auto Inc., which operates Checker Auto Parts, Shuck's Auto Supply, Kragen Auto Parts, and Advance Auto Parts, whose stores are called Advance Auto, joined forces to establish a separate company. Called PartsAmerica.com, the Web-based venture was launched in September 2000. The venture provides customers with easy access to nearly $1.5 billion in inventory and 3,000 locations in all 50 states. Customers can use either company's local stores to pick up and return parts ordered online.[65] The alliance's partners believe that sharing some of their resources and capabilities allows them to provide the "ultimate bricks and clicks" model in their industry.[66]

Competition Response Strategy

As discussed in Chapter 5, competitors initiate competitive actions to attack rivals and launch competitive responses to their competitors' actions. Strategic alliances can be used at the business level to respond to competitors' attacks. Because they can be

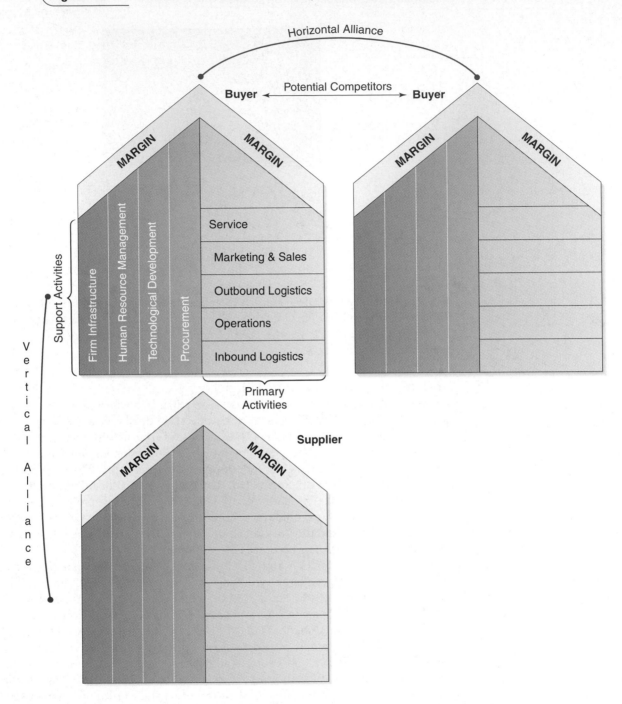

difficult to reverse and expensive to operate, strategic alliances are primarily formed to respond to strategic rather than tactical actions.

Recall from Chapter 5's Opening Case that UPS established its logistics business in 1994. Main rival FedEx responded to this strategic action by UPS when it too entered the logistics business. However, in 2002, UPS seemed to be outperforming its rival in this business area, at least as measured by sales growth. To improve its competitive position by responding to UPS, FedEx took several actions, including forming a strategic alliance with worldwide professional services firm KPMG. The alliance's intent is to deliver total, end-to-end supply-chain solutions to large and mid-sized companies. To reach this objective, the partners are combining some of their resources and capabilities to help firms improve their supply-chain planning and execution processes that connect suppliers and manufacturers with their end-customers. To form this alliance, FedEx committed what it believes are its industry-leading supply-chain-focused consulting, information-management systems, and transportation and logistics expertise. For its part, KPMG agreed to provide its supply-chain consulting and e-integration services.[67]

Strategic alliances are also sometimes used in the global oil industry to respond to competitors' actions, especially when those actions are strategic and were themselves products of strategic alliances. Recently, for example, Marathon Oil Co. (formerly a part of USX Corp.) completed a strategic alliance with Yukos, Russia's second largest oil company. The alliance was formed both to promote the two firms' international growth goals and as a response to the multitude of alliances formed by these companies' global competitors.[68] As a newly formed independent company, Marathon seeks to become recognized as a pacesetting firm in terms of sustainable growth for shareholders. According to company documents, unique cooperative partnerships such as the one with Yukos are critical to its efforts to reach this objective.[69]

Uncertainty Reducing Strategy

Particularly in fast-cycle markets, business-level strategic alliances are used to hedge against risk and uncertainty.[70] Global overcapacity and cost competition affected the capabilities of Siemens and Fujitsu to independently reach their objectives in the global PC market. To reduce the risk and uncertainty associated with their PC operations, the two firms formed a joint venture. Called Fujitsu Siemens Computers, this company was formally established on October 1, 1999. Evidence suggests that the formerly independent Fujitsu Computers (Europe) and Siemens Computer Systems are effectively sharing their technological resources and capabilities to create their joint venture. By uniquely combining what Fujitsu Siemens Computers believes is leading-edge technology from Fujitsu with manufacturing, marketing and logistics capabilities from Siemens, the joint venture has become Europe's top supplier of PCs for home users and small business firms.[71]

In other instances, firms form business-level strategic alliances to reduce the uncertainty associated with developing new product or technology standards. In the global automobile industry, for example, GM and Toyota formed a five-year R&D alliance that essentially makes the "no. 1 U.S. auto maker and the no. 1 Japanese auto maker partners in the competition to develop alternative-power green cars" for the 21st century. Through this alliance, the two firms expect to be able to set the industry standard for environmentally friendly vehicles.[72] At the same time, GM and Toyota joined Ford, DaimlerChrysler, and Renault SA in an alliance to develop an industrywide standard for accommodating communications and entertainment equipment being developed by automobile manufacturers.[73] Thus, the uncertainty and risk of the 21st-century landscape finds firms, such as those competing in the global automobile industry, forming multiple strategic alliances to increase their strategic competitiveness.

Competition Reducing Strategy

Collusive strategies are an often-illegal type of cooperative strategy, separate from strategic alliances, that are used to reduce competition. There are two types of collusive strategies—explicit collusion and tacit collusion.

"Powering the Information Age" is Fujitsu Siemens Computers vision. The vision combines the strength and innovation of its parent companies, Fujitsu Limited and Siemens AG. Fujitsu Siemens offers business customers products from PDAs, notebooks, PCs, and workstations to servers, mainframes, and enterprise storage solutions, and is the top supplier of computers for home users in Europe.

Explicit collusion ". . . exists when firms directly negotiate production output and pricing agreements in order to reduce competition."[74] Explicit collusion strategies are illegal in the United States and most developed economies (except in regulated industries).

Firms that use explicit collusion strategies may face litigation and may be found guilty of non-competitive actions. In a 1995 price-fixing scandal, for example, three Archer Daniels Midland (ADM) executives were convicted and sentenced to jail terms for cooperating with competitors to fix prices on farm commodity products.[75] Similarly, prominent toy retailer Toys 'R' Us was found in violation of U.S. federal trade laws for colluding with toy manufacturers to not sell their popular toy lines to Toys 'R' Us's primary competitors, such as Costco and Sam's Club warehouse clubs.[76]

Tacit collusion exists when several firms in an industry indirectly coordinate their production and pricing decisions by observing each other's competitive actions and responses. Tacit collusion results in below fully competitive production output and prices that are above fully competitive levels. Unlike explicit collusion, firms engaging in tacit collusion do not directly negotiate output and pricing decisions.

Discussed in Chapter 6, *mutual forbearance* is a form of tacit collusion ". . . in which firms avoid competitive attacks against those rivals they meet in multiple markets."[77] Rivals learn a great deal about each other when engaging in multimarket competition, including how to deter the effects of their rival's competitive attacks and responses. Given what they know about each other as a competitor, firms choose not to engage in what could be destructive competitions in multiple product markets.

Tacit collusion tends to be used as a business-level competition reducing strategy in highly concentrated industries, such as breakfast cereals. Firms in these industries recognize that they are interdependent and that their competitive actions and responses significantly affect competitors' behavior toward them. Understanding this interdependence and carefully observing competitors because of it tend to lead to tacit collusion.

Four firms (Kellogg, General Mills, Post, and Quaker) recently accounted for 84 percent of sales volume in the ready-to-eat segment of the U.S. cereal market. Some believe that this high degree of concentration results in ". . . prices for branded cereals that are well above (the) costs of production."[78] Prices above the competitive level in this industry suggest the possibility that the dominant firms were using a tacit collusion cooperative strategy.

At a broad level in free-market economies, governments need to determine how rivals can collaborate to increase their competitiveness without violating established regulations.[79] Reaching this determination is challenging when evaluating collusive strategies, particularly tacit ones. For example, the European Commission recently initiated an investigation of "suspicious price fixing" by the world's largest music producers and a few large retailers. A Commission spokesperson said, "We're trying to assess whether companies are trying to keep prices higher. It's sufficiently important to consumers to justify an investigation."[80] For individual companies, the issue is to understand the effect of a competition reducing strategy on their performance and competitiveness.

Assessment of Business-Level Cooperative Strategies

Firms use business-level strategies to develop competitive advantages that can contribute to successful positioning and performance in individual product markets. For a competitive advantage to be developed by using an alliance, the particular set of resources and capabilities that is combined and shared in a particular manner through the alliance must be valuable, rare, imperfectly imitable, and non-substitutable (see Chapter 3).

Evidence suggests that complementary business-level strategic alliances, especially vertical ones, have the greatest probability of creating a sustainable competitive advantage.[81] Strategic alliances designed to respond to competition and to reduce uncertainty can also create competitive advantages. However, these advantages tend to be more temporary than those developed through complementary (both vertical and horizontal) strategic alliances. The primary reason is that complementary alliances have a stronger focus on the creation of value compared to competition reducing and uncertainty reducing alliances, which tend to be formed to respond to competitors' actions rather than to attack competitors.

Of the four business-level cooperative strategies, the competition reducing strategy has the lowest probability of creating a sustainable competitive advantage. In the ready-to-eat breakfast cereal market, for example, annual household purchases of ready-to-eat cereals declined roughly 1.5 pounds between 1993 and 1997.[82] Even if the four largest cereal makers did use tacit collusion as a competition reducing strategy, the results likely failed to meet their performance expectations. The company using competition reducing business-level strategic alliances should carefully monitor them as to the degree to which they are facilitating the firm's efforts to develop and successfully use value-creating competitive advantages.

Corporate-Level Cooperative Strategy

A **corporate-level cooperative strategy** is used by the firm to help it diversify in terms of the products it offers or the markets it serves or both.

A **corporate-level cooperative strategy** is used by the firm to help it diversify in terms of the products it offers or the markets it serves or both. Diversifying alliances, synergistic alliances, and franchising are the most commonly used corporate-level cooperative strategies (see Figure 9.3).

Firms use diversifying alliances and synergistic alliances to grow and diversify their operations through a means other than a merger or acquisition.[83] When a firm seeks to diversify into markets in which the host nation's government prevents mergers and acquisitions, alliances become an especially appropriate option. Corporate-level strategic alliances are also attractive compared to mergers and particularly acquisitions, because they require fewer resource commitments[84] and permit greater flexibility in terms of efforts to diversify partners' operations.[85] An alliance can be used as well to determine if the partners might benefit from a future merger or acquisition

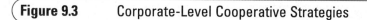

Figure 9.3   Corporate-Level Cooperative Strategies

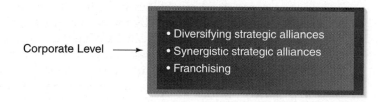

Corporate Level ⟶
- Diversifying strategic alliances
- Synergistic strategic alliances
- Franchising

between them. This "testing" process often characterizes alliances completed to combine firms' unique technological resources and capabilities.[86]

The collaboration that Wal-Mart, Seiyu Ltd. (a Japanese retail chain), and Sumitomo Corporation (a Japanese trading company) recently formed is partly an attempt to determine if there is a compelling reason for the firms to become more closely aligned in the future. Initially, Wal-Mart took a 6.1 percent interest in Seiyu, with Sumitomo owning 15.6 percent of the company. The firms intend to work together to study and develop retail business opportunities in Japan. If the collaboration is successful, Wal-Mart has the option of increasing its stake in Seiyu across time to as much as 66.7 percent.[87]

Diversifying Strategic Alliance

A **diversifying strategic alliance** is a corporate-level cooperative strategy in which firms share some of their resources and capabilities to diversify into new product or market areas. Boeing Company, for example, recently formed an alliance with the Insitu Group to develop a prototype for an unmanned aerial vehicle system to be called Scan Eagle. Insitu will incorporate Boeing's systems integration, communications technologies, and payload technologies into a version of its Seascan aircraft. Insitu is committed to designing and producing low-cost, long-endurance unmanned aerial vehicles—an earlier prototype of the Seascan flew 2,000 miles using 1.5 gallons of gasoline. Boeing's interest is gaining access to a product that can help it to further diversify into government and commercial markets. Involvement with some of Boeing's technological resources and capabilities is the benefit of this alliance for the Insitu Group.[88]

Synergistic Strategic Alliance

A **synergistic strategic alliance** is a corporate-level cooperative strategy in which firms share some of their resources and capabilities to create economies of scope. Similar to the business-level horizontal complementary strategic alliance, synergistic strategic alliances create synergy across multiple functions or multiple businesses between partner firms.

Cisco Systems, Inc. has formed many synergistic strategic alliances in the pursuit of profitable growth. Its synergistic alliance with Hewlett-Packard (HP) is intended to provide an optimized computing environment for Internet commerce players, such as telecom service operators and enterprise users. Synergy is expected from this alliance as HP integrates its state-of-the-art telecommunications management solutions with Cisco's industry-leading networking solutions. Working together through this alliance, the two firms anticipate melding ". . . the worlds of computing and networking, data and voice, and Unix and Windows NT."[89]

In the financial services sector, Rabobank and DG Bank, the Dutch and German cooperative institutions, have formed a joint venture as a synergistic strategic alliance. Called DG-Rabo International, this equally owned venture combines the unique resources and capabilities of each bank in the corporate and investment-banking business areas. Viewed by some as "one of the most important cross-border partnerships yet seen in European banking," the organizations intend to further meld their skills to cooperate in other areas (e.g., asset management transactions) in the future.[90] Thus, this synergistic strategic alliance is different from a complementary business-level alliance in that it diversifies both banks into a new business, but in a synergistic way.

A **diversifying strategic alliance** is a corporate-level cooperative strategy in which firms share some of their resources and capabilities to diversify into new product or market areas.

A **synergistic strategic alliance** is a corporate-level cooperative strategy in which firms share some of their resources and capabilities to create economies of scope.

Franchising

Franchising is a corporate-level cooperative strategy in which a firm (the franchisor) uses a franchise as a contractual relationship to describe and control the sharing of its resources and capabilities with partners (the franchisees).[91] A *franchise* is a "contractual agreement between two legally independent companies whereby the franchisor grants the right to the franchisee to sell the franchisor's product or do business under its trademarks in a given location for a specified period of time."[92]

Franchising is a popular strategy: companies using it account for $1 trillion in annual U.S. retail sales and compete in more than 75 industries. As the Cendant strategy outlined in Chapter 6 indicates, franchising can be used successfully across a number of businesses. Cendant has used franchising in real estate, for example, through its Century 21 and ERA brands. Already frequently used in developed nations, franchising is expected to account for significant portions of growth in emerging economies in the 21st century's first two decades.[93] As with diversifying and synergistic strategic alliances, franchising is an alternative to pursuing growth through mergers and acquisitions.

McDonald's, Hilton International, and Krispy Kreme are well-known examples of firms that use the franchising corporate-level cooperative strategy. Although franchising is its dominant corporate-level cooperative strategy, McDonald's also forms diversifying strategic alliances, such as its partnership with a Swiss firm to develop a Golden Arches Hotel.[94]

In the most successful franchising strategy, the partners (the franchiser and the franchisees) closely work together.[95] A primary responsibility of the franchisor is to develop programs to transfer to the franchisees the knowledge and skills that are needed to successfully compete at the local level.[96] In return, franchisees should provide feedback to the franchisor regarding how their units could become more effective and efficient.[97] Working cooperatively, the franchisor and its franchisees find ways to strengthen the core company's brand name, which is often the most important competitive advantage for franchisees operating in their local markets.[98]

Franchising is a particularly attractive strategy to use in fragmented industries, such as retailing and commercial printing. In fragmented industries, a large number of small and medium-sized firms compete as rivals; however, no firm or small set of firms has a dominant share, making it possible for a company to gain a large market share by consolidating independent companies through contractual relationships.[99] Recently La Quinta Inns decided to use franchising as a corporate-level cooperative strategy in order to increase its market share. Even though the lodging industry isn't as fragmented as it once was, La Quinta's decision to franchise has been viewed favorably. As one analyst observed, "La Quinta is in a situation where they don't have the ability to invest a lot of capital for growth, so finding franchisees is a lower-risk strategy of trying to grow the brand."[100]

Assessment of Corporate-Level Cooperative Strategies

Costs are incurred with each type of cooperative strategy.[101] Compared to those at the business-level, corporate-level cooperative strategies commonly are broader in scope and more complex, making them relatively more costly. Those forming and using cooperative strategies, especially corporate-level ones, should be aware of alliance costs and carefully monitor them.

In spite of these costs, firms can create competitive advantages and value when they effectively form and use corporate-level cooperative strategies.[102] The likelihood of this being the case increases when successful alliance experiences are internalized.

In other words, those involved with forming and using corporate-level cooperative strategies can also use them to develop useful knowledge about how to succeed in the future. To gain maximum value from this knowledge, firms should organize it and verify that it is always properly distributed to those involved with the formation and use of alliances.[103]

We explain in Chapter 6 that firms answer two questions to form a corporate-level strategy—the businesses in which the diversified firm will compete and how those businesses will be managed. These questions are also answered as firms form corporate-level cooperative strategies. Thus, firms able to develop corporate-level cooperative strategies and manage them in ways that are valuable, rare, imperfectly imitable and nonsubstitutable (see Chapter 3) develop a competitive advantage that is in addition to advantages gained through the activities of individual cooperative strategies. Later in the chapter, we further describe alliance management as a source of competitive advantage.

International Cooperative Strategy

A **cross-border strategic alliance** is an international cooperative strategy in which firms with headquarters in different nations combine some of their resources and capabilities to create a competitive advantage. Taking place in virtually all industries, the number of cross-border alliances being completed continues to increase,[104] in some cases at the expense of mergers and acquisitions.[105] This type of cooperative strategy is critical to Citigroup's positions in global markets: "If it wasn't for cross-border alliances with entities like the Japanese postal system, which gave the bank entry into the otherwise locked-up consumer banking market, Citi wouldn't be a highly regarded local operator with 100 million customers in 100 countries."[106]

There are several reasons for the increasing use of cross-border strategic alliances. In general, multinational corporations outperform firms operating on only a domestic basis,[107] so a firm may form cross-border strategic alliances to leverage core competencies that are the foundation of its domestic success to expand into international markets.[108] At Coca-Cola, efforts are underway to cut across the firm's geographic units to identify opportunities to leverage existing brands and competitive advantages. One result from these efforts was the decision to expand the firm's alliance with Nestlé. Called Beverage Partners Worldwide, this cross-border strategic alliance will add herbal beverages to its product line, which already includes Nestea and Nescafé, and will expand into additional global markets.[109]

Limited domestic growth opportunities is another reason firms use cross-border alliances. Diversified and globally oriented Sony Corporation, for example, has long relied on cross-border alliances (more than 100) to pursue growth objectives greater than its home market can support. One of the firm's recent alliances is with Ericsson to make cell phones.[110] In a different industry, General Mills formed Cereal Partners Worldwide with Nestlé partly in response to stagnating growth in General Mills' core breakfast cereal market in the United States. This joint venture (much like Coca-Cola and Nestlé's alliance) combines General Mills' cereal expertise with ". . . Nestlé's brand recognition and distribution throughout Europe."[111]

Another reason for forming cross-border alliances is government economic policies. As discussed in Chapter 8, local ownership is an important national policy objective in some nations. In India, for example, governmental policies reflect a strong preference to license local companies. Only recently did the South Korean government increase the ceiling on foreign investment in South Korean firms.[112] Thus, in some countries, the full range of entry mode choices that we describe in Chapter 8 may not be available to firms wishing to internationally diversify. Indeed, investment by foreign firms in these instances may be allowed only through a partnership with a

A **cross-border strategic alliance** is an international cooperative strategy in which firms with headquarters in different nations combine some of their resources and capabilities to create a competitive advantage.

Pictured here is Sony's nine-floor showroom in downtown Tokyo. Sony provides entertainment and electronic products and services to consumers around the world through its partnerships. Its major products are cutting-edge technology in audio components and systems, video equipment, televisions, information and communications products (including computer products), and other electronic components. Its principal US businesses include Sony Electronics Inc., Sony Pictures Entertainment, Sony Music Entertainment Inc., and Sony Computer Entertainment of America.

local firm, such as in a cross-border alliance. A cross-border strategic alliance can also be helpful to foreign partners from an operational perspective, because the local partner has significantly more information about factors contributing to competitive success such as local markets, sources of capital, legal procedures, and politics.[113]

Firms also use cross-border alliances to help transform themselves or to better use their competitive advantages to take advantage of opportunities surfacing in the rapidly changing global economy. For example, GEC, a U.K.-based company, seeks to move from "a broadly focused group deriving much of its revenues from the defence budget to a full range telecommunications and information systems manufacturer." The uncertainty characterizing many nations' defense budgets is influencing GEC's decision to develop cross-border alliances such as the one it formed with NEC, the Japanese electronics giant. The alliance has both a commercial and technological focus—NEC distributes GEC products through its extensive marketing channels and the two companies collaborate in their R&D efforts to develop new technologies.[114]

In general, cross-border alliances are more complex and risky than domestic strategic alliances. However, the fact that firms competing internationally tend to outperform domestic-only competitors suggests the importance of learning how to diversify into international markets. Compared to mergers and acquisitions, cross-border alliances may be a better way to learn this process, especially in the early stages of the firms' geographic diversification efforts. Careful and thorough study of a proposed cross-border alliance contributes to success[115] as do precise specifications of each partner's alliance role.[116] These points are explored later in our discussion of how to best manage alliances.

Network Cooperative Strategy

Increasingly, firms are involved with more than one cooperative strategy. Procter & Gamble (P&G), for instance, has formed over 120 strategic alliances. In a recent year, P&G ". . . teamed with Dana Undies to make Pampers cotton underwear, with Magla to make Mr. Clean disposable gloves and mops, and with GM to distribute its Tempo car clean-up towels" and agreed to partner with Whirlpool to develop a new "clothes refresher" product and appliance.[117]

A network cooperative strategy is a cooperative strategy wherein several firms agree to form multiple partnerships to achieve shared objectives.

In addition to forming their own alliances with individual companies, a growing number of firms are joining forces in multiple cooperative strategies. A **network cooperative strategy** is a cooperative strategy wherein several firms agree to form multiple partnerships to achieve shared objectives.

A network cooperative strategy is particularly effective when it is formed by firms clustered together,[118] as with Silicon Valley in California and Singapore's Silicon Island.[119] Effective social relationships and interactions among partners while sharing their resources and capabilities make it more likely that a network cooperative strategy will be successful,[120] as does having a productive *strategic center firm* (discussed further in Chapter 11). As explained in the Strategic Focus on page 292, Johnson Controls is a strategic center firm in its network cooperative strategy that the firm calls "Peer Partnering."[121]

From a financial perspective, Johnson Controls has been successful. Fiscal year 2001 was the firm's ". . . 55th consecutive year of sales increases and the 26th year of increased dividends. It was also the 11th consecutive year of increased income. (And), dividends have been paid consecutively since 1887."[122] The early evidence suggests that as a network cooperative strategy, Peer Partnering will be an increasingly important contributor to the 21st-century success of Johnson Controls. It is likely that the network resulting from the Peer Partnering strategy will grow as initial members identify other capabilities that the network needs.

Integrating Partners' Resources and Capabilities through a Network Cooperative Strategy

By emphasizing innovation to produce products and provide service exceeding customers' expectations, Johnson Controls, Inc. (JCI) has become a leading manufacturer of automotive interior systems, automotive batteries, and automated building control systems. A wide range of cooperative strategies has served as the engine of its growth. In its brand partnerships with LEGO InMotion, for example, it designs, develops, and engineers new co-branded products for vehicle interiors, offering 50 new LEGO-related features targeting active families. In its Packmate partnership with Jansport, JCI integrates a variety of Jansport luggage packs into the rear of fold-flat seats.

Given its success with other cooperative strategies such as co-branding and its belief in the value that can be achieved through collaboration, JCI established Peer Partnering—a network cooperative strategy—in 2000. JCI and its partners in the program (Gentex Corporation, Jabil Circuit, Inc., Microchip Technology, Inc. Royal Philips Electronics, SAGEM, Tokai Rika, and Yazaki North America) view vehicle interiors as an important source of differentiation for auto manufacturers and work with each other to develop and use advanced electronics as the foundation for innovative products to integrate into vehicle interiors. A JCI spokesperson says that through the Peer Partnering strategy, ". . . we deliver vehicle-integrated electronics that surprise and delight customers, and enable automakers to differentiate their products. This strategy, which accelerates the development process, increases innovation and reduces costs, is a winning one for our customers, our partners and for us as well." BMW, DaimlerChrysler, Ford, General Motors, Honda, Mazda, Mitsubishi, Nissan, Renault, Rover, Toyota, and Volkswagen are customers for JCI's automotive systems group (interiors and batteries) and also buy the products produced through the network cooperative strategy.

Headquartered in several nations (for example, SAGEM in France, Tokai Rika in Japan), the Peer Partnering members share some of their resources and capabilities. As the strategic center firm, JCI manages the relationships among all partners and holds each accountable in terms of the commitments it made to the network strategy and verifies that each firm benefits from its participation in the collaborative effort. The core contributions to the network are JCI's innovation and integration capabilities and its partners' capabilities in advanced, electronic-based technologies. The partners work through different combinations of their resources and capabilities with the shared objective of producing value-creating products for auto and truck interiors. A digital compass, upgraded audio equipment, and interior switches with optimized user interface capabilities are some of the first products from the Peer Partnering network.

The Peer Partnering network can also benefit as its members participate in other cooperative strategies. Tokai Rika, for example, has a strategic alliance with Toyoda Gosei to collaborate on the development, manufacture, and sale of automotive safety systems (such as air bags and seat belts) and components. Some of the skills Tokai Rika forms through this relationship may enhance the value of its contributions to the Peer Partnering network.

COURTESY JOHNSON CONTROLS

LEGO InMotion is a concept vehicle interior created by an exclusive partnership of LEGO Company & Johnson Controls, a supplier of automotive interior systems. The sports utility vehicle (SUV), designed for families, features luxurious front seat materials and bold colors and materials for the back seats, including Johnson Controls' removable AutoVision® video entertainment system DVD player with the LEGO Go Pad (a portable, hand-held digital device), and a LEGO digital camera.

SOURCES: 2002, Johnson Controls–Corporate Home, Recognition, http://www.johnsoncontrols.com, March 10; 2002, Johnson Controls, Corporate profile, http://www.johnsoncontrols.com, March 10; 2002, Johnson Controls, Johnson Controls partners with MatrixOne, http://www.johnsoncontrols.com, March 10; 2002, Johnson Controls, Peer partners, http://www.johnsoncontrols.com, March 10; 2002, Johnson Controls, *Standard & Poor's Stock Report*, http://www.fidelity.com, March 2; B. Berentson, 2001, Johnson Controls, *Forbes Best of the Web*, May 21, 70.

Alliance Network Types

An important advantage of a network cooperative strategy is that firms gain access "to their partners' partners."[123] As discussed in the Strategic Focus on page 292, JCI has access to other relationships with which Gentex, Jabil, Microchip, Philips, and Tokai Rika are involved, and those firms have access to JCI's other collaborative relationships. Having access to multiple collaborations increases the likelihood that additional competitive advantages will be formed as the set of resources and capabilities being shared expands. In turn, increases in competitive advantages further stimulate the development of product innovations that are so critical to strategic competitiveness in the global economy.[124]

The set of partnerships, such as strategic alliances, that result from the use of a network cooperative strategy is commonly called an *alliance network*. The alliance networks that companies develop vary by industry conditions. A *stable alliance network* is formed in mature industries where demand is relatively constant and predictable. Through a stable alliance network, firms try to extend their competitive advantages to other settings while continuing to profit from operations in their core, relatively mature industry. Thus, stable networks are built for *exploitation* of the economies (scale and/or scope) available between firms.[125] *Dynamic alliance networks* are used in industries characterized by frequent product innovations and short product life cycles. Believing that "no single company can hope to anticipate and fulfill all the challenges that are emerging today," Intel is involved with a number of e-business alliances in partnership with several firms, including BEA, Microsoft, i2, and BroadVision. This dynamic alliance network has been created to ". . . craft a new breed of computing solutions—open, flexible, scalable solutions that offer enterprise-grade reliability and outstanding value."[126] Thus, dynamic alliance networks are primarily used to stimulate rapid, value-creating product innovations and subsequent successful market entries, demonstrating that their purpose is often *exploration* of new ideas.[127]

Competitive Risks with Cooperative Strategies

Stated simply, many cooperative strategies fail.[128] In fact, evidence shows that two-thirds of cooperative strategies have serious problems in their first two years and that as many as 70 percent of them fail.[129] This failure rate suggests that even when the partnership has potential complementarities and synergies, alliance success is elusive.[130] We describe failed alliances in the Strategic Focus on page 294.

Although failure is undesirable, it can be a valuable learning experience. Companies willing to carefully study a cooperative strategy's failure may gain insights that can be used to successfully develop and use future cooperative strategies. Thus, companies should work equally hard to avoid cooperative strategy failure and to learn from failure if it were to occur.

As suggested in the Strategic Focus on page 294, the firm takes risk when it uses one or more cooperative strategies. Prominent cooperative strategy risks are shown in Figure 9.4.

One cooperative strategy risk is that a partner may act opportunistically. Opportunistic behaviors surface either when formal contracts fail to prevent them or when an alliance is based on a false perception of partner trustworthiness. Not infrequently, the opportunistic firm wants to acquire as much of its partner's tacit knowledge as it can.[131] Full awareness of what a partner wants in a cooperative strategy reduces the likelihood that a firm will suffer from another's opportunistic actions.[132]

Some cooperative strategies fail when it is discovered that a firm has misrepresented the competencies it can bring to the partnership. This risk is more common when the partner's contribution is grounded in some of its intangible assets. Superior

All Cooperative Strategies Aren't Made in Heaven

Firms are relying more and more on cooperative strategies as a means of achieving strategic competitiveness. To increase the probability of success, IBM is one of the growing number of firms assigning responsibility to oversee the development and use of cooperative strategies to a senior-level executive. However, in spite of all their good efforts, a number of firms find that their cooperative strategies fail. Announced with great fanfare, the Global One joint venture formed by Deutsche Telekom, Sprint, and France Telecom in 1996 is an example of a failed cooperative strategy. A senior-level executive set high expectations for this venture when he suggested that, "Global One (was) organized to respond to the customer, the technology and the marketplace (and) that no one else in the world (was) offering this unique level of service." Three years later, the partnership had ended and the venture is now run by France Telecom.

The joint venture's three-year history was filled with disagreements about many issues, including who would manage Global One's different divisions, who were its target customers, and where its headquarters should be located. Cultural differences were another issue. For example, during ". . . meetings the French would be on one side of the room, the Germans on the other. . . . ." However, cultural distinctions are to be expected when forming cooperative strategies. The most effective partners anticipate cultural differences and prepare to deal with them before they surface. Critical to this preparation is making certain that partners know how to appropriately change some of their deep-seated traditions to respect their collaborators.

Although culture differences were an issue in Global One's failure, corporate governance and control was the primary cause of it. Instead of a jointly chosen team of managers and workers who would collaborate on a day-to-day basis to successfully operate the venture, Global One was run by a high-level board of chief executives with layers of committees below it. This bureaucratic structure negatively affected decision making, particularly in response to "out-of-the-ordinary" requests from customers. The venture's decision structure forced specific customer requests ". . . to filter through layers of executives at Global One and also through executives at each parent." This centralization of decision making prevented Global One from developing the flexibility needed to use rapidly changing technologies to satisfy customers' quickly changing needs and from determining who should be responsible for meeting those needs.

The list of factors behind cooperative strategy failure is long. For example, the complexity of its strategic plan contributed to Pandesic's failure. Formed between Intel and German software firm SAP, this venture lasted only three years. Some believe that too many people were responsible for executing Pandesic's strategic plan and that the plan was too complicated, especially with respect to the venture's intended market position. Additional flexibility to those operating the venture would have allowed greater focus on meeting customers' needs rather than on executing an eloquent but overly detailed strategic plan.

In other instances, partners develop a product for which a target market of sufficient size doesn't exist. For example, Motorola and Cisco formed the joint venture Spectrapoint Wireless to become a leader in fixed wireless: "a medium where phone calls, Internet pages and television signals are beamed to a rooftop dish and then transported through the building via wires." After only a year, the partners concluded that while customers were impressed with the venture's product, they weren't willing to pay the high price necessary to buy it. As a result, the venture that started with much anticipation in 1999 was called off in 2000.

SOURCES: K. Eisenhardt, 2002, Has strategy changed? *MIT Sloan Management Review,* 43(2): 88–91; C. Ghosn, 2002, Saving the business without losing the company, *Harvard Business Review,* 80(1): 37–45; N. Hutheesing, 2001, *Forbes Best of the Web,* May 21, 30–32; L. Khosla, 2001, You say tomato, *Forbes Best of the Web,* May 21, 36; J. W. Michaels, 2001, Don't buy, bond instead, *Forbes Best of the Web,* May 21, 20.

Figure 9.4   Managing Competitive Risks in Cooperative Strategies

Competitive Risks

Risk and Asset Management
Approaches

Desired Outcome

- Inadequate contracts
- Misrepresentation of
  competencies
- Partners fail to use their
  complementary resources
- Holding alliance partner's
  specific investments hostage

- Detailed contracts and
  monitoring
- Developing trusting
  relationships

- Creating value

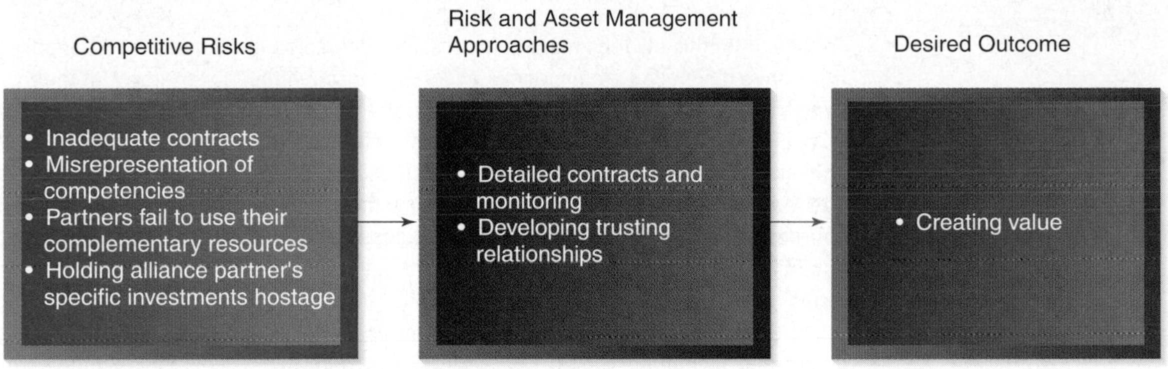

knowledge of local conditions is an example of an intangible asset that partners often fail to deliver. Asking the partner to provide evidence that it does possess the resources and capabilities (even when they are largely intangible) it is to share in the cooperative strategy may be an effective way to deal with this risk.

Another risk is that a firm won't actually make the resources and capabilities (such as its most sophisticated technologies) that it committed to the cooperative strategy available to its partners. This risk surfaces most commonly when firms form an international cooperative strategy.[133] In these instances, different cultures can result in different interpretations of contractual terms or trust-based expectations.

A final risk is that the firm may make investments that are specific to the alliance while its partner does not. For example, the firm might commit resources and capabilities to develop manufacturing equipment that can be used only to produce items coming from the alliance. If the partner isn't also making alliance-specific investments, the firm is at a relative disadvantage in terms of returns earned from the alliance compared to investments made to earn the returns.

Managing Cooperative Strategies

As our discussion has shown, cooperative strategies are an important option for firms competing in the global economy.[134] However, our study of cooperative strategies also shows that they are complex.[135]

Firms gain the most benefit from cooperative strategies when they are effectively managed. As discussed in the Strategic Focus on page 296, managing and flexibly adapting partnerships are crucial aspects of cooperative strategies.[136] The firm that learns how to manage cooperative strategies better than its competitors do may develop a competitive advantage in terms of this activity.[137] This is possible because the ability to effectively manage cooperative strategies is unevenly distributed across organizations.

In general, assigning managerial responsibility for a firm's cooperative strategies to a high-level executive or to a team improves the likelihood that the strategies will be well managed. IBM (see the following Strategic Focus), Johnson Controls, Coca-Cola, and Siebel Systems are four companies that have made such assignments. United Airlines has established an alliance division to monitor and create new partnerships and to manage the more than 100 cooperative strategies with which it is currently involved.[138]

Those responsible for managing the firm's set of cooperative strategies coordinate activities, categorize knowledge learned from previous experiences, and make

Managing Cooperative Strategies to Gain a Competitive Advantage

To date, effective alliance management skills seem to be in relatively short supply—few firms have developed a competitive advantage through the management of their cooperative strategies. A key reason is the need for the firm to simultaneously learn from its alliance partners while preventing its partners from learning too much from it. Another way of saying this is that as a partner, a company must develop the skills needed to manage the balance ". . . between trying to learn and trying to protect" its knowledge and sources of competitive advantages from excessive learning by partners. Finding ways to achieve this balance—a balance that is critical to developing a competitive advantage in terms of the management of cooperative strategies—seems to be difficult for most firms.

Global companies commonly compete against those with whom they are also collaborating. Toyota and General Motors, and Dell and IBM, are examples of companies that are both collaborators and competitors. While sharing some of their resources and capabilities in a partnership, firms exchange knowledge that may be related to a host of issues, including their technological skills, future plans, logistic systems, and hiring and training practices among many others. Part of the successful management of cooperative strategies is to follow procedures preventing partners from being disadvantaged in future competitions as a result of the resources, capabilities, and knowledge they share to use their cooperative strategy.

In spite of the difficulty, research findings and company experiences yield suggestions about knowledge protection and effective management of cooperative strategies. For example, assigning the responsibility to manage the firm's cooperative strategies to a group of people that reports to a senior-level official is vital. The charge to such a group is broad and should include responsibility to ". . . coordinate all alliance-related activity within the organization and (to institutionalize) processes and systems to teach, share, and leverage prior alliance-management experience and know-how throughout the company."

To manage its 70-plus cooperative strategies, IBM formed a strategic alliance team. Headed by an upper-level executive, the team handles all of IBM's collaborative ventures to create what it calls an alliance culture within the existing organizational structure. In the desired alliance culture, all parts of the company seek partners who could benefit from using IBM's marketing, sales, and solutions resources while leading with IBM's middleware, server platforms, and services to develop successful new market entries as outputs from each collaboration.

An important part of executing the broad charge given to teams (such as IBM's) that are expected to successfully manage their firm's cooperative strategies is their clear and detailed specification of the benefits of current cooperative strategies as well as those expected from the integration of new ones into the current set. Simultaneously, the team should closely work with all partners to specify the resources and capabilities that will be shared during the partnership and those that will not be shared. Part of this discussion must focus on knowledge that is to remain within the confines of the cooperative strategy, not leaking to other sections of the partner's organization. Collaborations based on trust have a higher probability of being successful in this effort.

SOURCES: R. D. Ireland, M. A. Hitt, & D. Vaidyanath, 2002, Alliance management as a source of competitive advantage, *Journal of Management*, in press; J. H. Dyer, P. Kale, & H. Singh, 2001, How to make strategic alliances work, *MIT Sloan Management Review*, 42(4): 37–43; A. C. Inkpen, 2001, Strategic alliances, in M. A. Hitt, R. E. Freeman, & J. S. Harrison (eds.), *Handbook of Strategic Management*, Oxford, U.K.: Blackwell Publishers, 409–432; 2001, IBM, IDC names IBM's strategic alliance program as a best practice in concept and implementation, http://www.ibm.com, December 1; D. Ernst & T. Halvey, 2000, When to think alliance, *McKinsey Quarterly*, 4, 46–55; P. Kale, H. Singh, & H. Perlmutter, 2000, Learning and protection of proprietary assets in strategic alliances: Building relational capital, *Strategic Management Journal*, 21: 217–237.

certain that what the firm knows about how to effectively form and use cooperative strategies is in the hands of the right people at the right time. Firms use one of two primary approaches to manage cooperative strategies—cost minimization and opportunity maximization[139] (see Figure 9.4). This is the case whether the firm has formed a separate cooperative strategy management function or not.

In the *cost minimization* management approach, the firm develops formal contracts with its partners. These contracts specify how the cooperative strategy is to be monitored and how partner behavior is to be controlled. The goal of this approach is to minimize the cooperative strategy's cost and to prevent opportunistic behavior by a partner. The focus of the second managerial approach—*opportunity maximization*—is on maximizing a partnership's value-creation opportunities. In this case, partners are prepared to take advantage of unexpected opportunities to learn from each other and to explore additional marketplace possibilities.[140] Less formal contracts, with fewer constraints on partners' behaviors, make it possible for partners to explore how their resources and capabilities can be shared in multiple value-creating ways.

Firms can successfully use either approach to manage cooperative strategies. However, the costs to monitor the cooperative strategy are greater with cost minimization, in that writing detailed contracts and using extensive monitoring mechanisms is expensive, even though the approach is intended to reduce alliance costs. Although monitoring systems may prevent partners from acting in their own best interests, they also preclude positive responses to those situations where opportunities to use the alliance's competitive advantages surface unexpectedly. Thus, formal contracts and extensive monitoring systems tend to stifle partners' efforts to gain maximum value from their participation in a cooperative strategy and require significant resources to put into place and use.

The relative lack of detail and formality that is a part of the contract developed by firms using the second management approach of opportunity maximization means that firms need to trust each other to act in the partnership's best interests. A psychological state, *trust* is a willingness to be vulnerable because of the expectations of positive behavior from the firm's alliance partner.[141] When partners trust each other, there is less need to write detailed formal contracts to specify each firm's alliance behaviors[142] and the cooperative relationship tends to be more stable.[143] On a relative basis, trust tends to be more difficult to establish in international cooperative strategies compared to domestic ones. Differences in trade policies, cultures, laws, and politics that are part of cross-border alliances account for the increased difficulty. When trust exists, partners' monitoring costs are reduced and opportunities to create value are maximized.

Research showing that trust between partners increases the likelihood of alliance success[144] seems to highlight the benefits of the opportunity maximization approach to managing cooperative strategies. Trust may also be the most efficient way to influence and control alliance partners' behaviors.[145] Research indicates that trust can be a capability that is valuable, rare, imperfectly imitable, and often nonsubstitutable.[146] Thus, firms known to be trustworthy can have a competitive advantage in terms of how they develop and use cooperative strategies. One reason is that it is impossible to specify all operational details of a cooperative strategy in a formal contract. Confidence that its partner can be trusted reduces the firm's concern about the inability to contractually control all alliance details.

- A cooperative strategy is one in which firms work together to achieve a shared objective. Strategic alliances, which are cooperative strategies in which firms combine some of their resources and capabilities to create a competitive advantage, are the primary form of cooperative strategies. Joint ventures (where firms create and own equal shares of a new venture that is intended to develop competitive advantages), equity strategic alliances (where firms own different shares of a newly created venture), and nonequity strategic alliances (where firms cooperate through a contractual relationship) are the three basic types of strategic alliances. Outsourcing, discussed in Chapter 3, commonly occurs as firms form nonequity strategic alliances.

- Collusive strategies are the second type of cooperative strategies (with strategic alliances being the other). In many economies and certainly developed ones, explicit collusive strategies are illegal unless sanctioned by government policies. With increasing globalization, fewer government-sanctioned situations of explicit collusion exist. Tacit collusion, also called mutual forbearance, is a cooperative strategy through which firms tacitly cooperate to reduce industry output below the potential competitive output level, thereby raising prices above the competitive level.

- Reasons firms use cooperative strategies vary by slow-cycle, fast-cycle, and standard-cycle market conditions. To enter restricted markets (slow-cycle), to move quickly from one competitive advantage to another (fast-cycle), and to gain market power (standard-cycle) demonstrate the differences among reasons by market type for use of cooperative strategies.

- There are four business-level cooperative strategies (a business-level cooperative strategy is used to help the firm improve its performance in individual product markets). Through vertical and horizontal complementary alliances companies combine their resources and capabilities to create value in different parts (vertical) or the same parts (horizontal) of the value chain. Competition responding strategies are formed to respond to competitors' actions, especially strategic ones. Competition reducing strategies are used to avoid excessive competition while the firm marshals its resources and capabilities to improve its competitiveness. Uncertainty reducing strategies are used to hedge against the risks created by the conditions of uncertain competitive environments. Complementary alliances have the highest probability of yielding a sustainable competitive advantage; competition reducing have the lowest probability of doing so.

- Corporate-level cooperative strategies are used when the firm wants to pursue product and/or geographic diversification. Through diversifying strategic alliances, firms agree to share some of their resources and capabilities to enter new markets or produce new products. Synergistic alliances are ones where firms share resources and capabilities to develop economies of scope. This alliance is similar to the business-level horizontal complementary alliance in which firms try to develop operational synergy whereas synergistic alliances are used to develop synergy at the corporate level. Franchising is a corporate-level cooperative strategy where the franchisor uses a franchise as a contractual relationship to describe the sharing of its resources and capabilities with franchisees.

- As an international cooperative strategy, cross-border alliances are used for several reasons, including the performance superiority of firms competing in markets outside their domestic market and governmental restrictions on growth through mergers and acquisitions. Cross-border alliances tend to be riskier than their domestic counterparts, particularly when partners aren't fully aware of each other's purpose for participating in the partnership.

- A network cooperative strategy is one wherein several firms agree to form multiple partnerships to achieve shared objectives. One of the primary benefits of a network cooperative strategy is the firm's opportunity to gain access "to its partner's other partnerships." When this happens, the probability greatly increases that partners will find unique ways to uniquely share their resources and capabilities to form competitive advantages. Network cooperative strategies are used to form either a stable alliance network or a dynamic alliance network. Used in mature industries, partners use stable networks to extend competitive advantages into new areas. In rapidly changing environments where frequent product innovations occur, dynamic networks are primarily used as a tool of innovation.

- Cooperative strategies aren't risk free. If a contract is not developed appropriately, or if a partner misrepresents its competencies or fails to make them available, failure is likely. Furthermore, a firm may be held hostage through asset-specific investments made in conjunction with a partner, which may be exploited.

- Trust is an increasingly important aspect of successful cooperative strategies. Firms recognize the value of partnering with companies known for their trustworthiness. When trust exists, a cooperative strategy is managed to maximize the pursuit of opportunities between partners. Without trust, formal contracts and extensive monitoring systems are used to manage cooperative strategies. In this case, the interest is to minimize costs rather than to maximize opportunities by participating in a cooperative strategy.

1. What is the definition of cooperative strategy and why is this strategy important to firms competing in the 21st-century competitive landscape?

2. What is a strategic alliance? What are the three types of strategic alliances firms use to develop a competitive advantage?

3. What are the four business-level cooperative strategies and what are the differences among them?

4. What are the three corporate-level cooperative strategies? How do firms use each one to create a competitive advantage?

5. Why do firms use cross-border strategic alliances?

6. What risks are firms likely to experience as they use cooperative strategies?

7. What are the differences between the cost-minimization approach and the opportunity-maximization approach to managing cooperative strategies?

Cooperative Strategy Risk

Your firm manufactures fasteners for industrial applications. As the senior vice president of sales, you have developed several long-term relationships with your customers. Your main competitor has recently approached you about establishing a strategic alliance with your firm.

1. Because you are not sure if this alliance would be beneficial to your firm, you decide to bring the proposal to your firm's executive committee for a preliminary discussion. You anticipate that the committee will ask several basic questions. What information should you be able to provide?

2. After several weeks of investigating the value of an alliance, your firm decides that it would be financially beneficial, but the executive committee now wants you to present the risks that an alliance might entail and how you would suggest minimizing them. What risks do you foresee? How can they be prevented?

3. Before a contract between your firm and your competitor can be signed, you begin negotiations with one of your competitor's largest customers to provide new products based on a new technology your firm has developed. In your opinion, does the alliance raise legal or ethical issues that your firm should consider before proceeding with your negotations?

1. K. M. Eisenhardt, 2002, Has strategy changed? *MIT Sloan Management Review*, 43(2): 88–91; T. B. Lawrence, C. Hardy, & N. Phillips, 2002, Institutional effects of interorganizational collaborations: The emergence of proto-institutions, *Academy of Management Journal*, 45: 281–290.

2. J. B. Barney, 2002, *Gaining and Sustaining Competitive Advantage*, 2nd ed., Upper Saddle River, NJ: Prentice-Hall, 339.

3. W. S. Desarbo, K. Jedidi, & I. Sinha, 2001, Customer value in a heterogeneous market, *Strategic Management Journal*, 22: 845–857.

4. C. Young-Ybarra & M. Wiersema, 1999, Strategic flexibility in information technology alliances: The influence of transaction cost economics and social exchange theory, *Organization Science*, 10: 439–459; M. E. Porter & M. B. Fuller, 1986, Coalitions and global strategy, in M. E. Porter (ed.), *Competition in Global Industries*, Boston: Harvard Business School Press, 315–344.

5. M. Schifrin, 2001, Partner or perish, *Forbes Best of the Web*, May 21, 26–28.

6. J. Bowser, 2001, Strategic co-opetition: The value of relationships in the networked economy, *IBM Business Strategy Consulting*, http://www.ibm.com, March 12.

7. M. A. Hitt, R. D. Ireland, S. M. Camp, & D. L. Sexton, 2002, Strategic entrepreneurship: Integrating entrepreneurial and strategic management perspectives, in M. A. Hitt, R. D. Ireland, S. M. Camp, & D. L. Sexton (eds.), *Strategic Entrepreneurship: Creating a New Mindset,* Oxford, U.K.: Blackwell Publishers, 8.

8. J. R. Harbison & P. Pekar, Jr., 1998, Institutionalizing alliance skills: Secrets of repeatable success, *Strategy & Business*, 11: 79–94.

9. S. Ulfelder, 2001, Partners in profit, http://www.computerworld.com, July/August, 24–28.

10. Barney, *Gaining and Sustaining Competitive Advantage*, 339.

11. Y. L. Doz & G. Hamel, 1998, *Alliance Advantage: The Art of Creating Value through Partnering*, Boston: Harvard Business School Press, xiii.

12. R. D. Ireland, M. A. Hitt, & D. Vaidyanath, 2002, Alliance management as a source of competitive advantage, *Journal of Management*, in press; J. G. Coombs & D. J. Ketchen, 1999, Exploring interfirm cooperation and performance: Toward a reconciliation of predictions from the resource-based view and organizational economics, *Strategic Management Journal*, 20: 867–888.

13. P. Kale, H. Singh, & H. Perlmutter, 2000, Learning and protection of proprietary assets in strategic alliances: Building relational capital, *Strategic Management Journal*, 21: 217–237.

14. D. F. Kuratko, R. D. Ireland, & J. S. Hornsby, 2001, Improving firm performance through entrepreneurial actions: Acordia's corporate entrepreneurship strategy, *Academy of Management Executive*, 15(4): 60–71; D. Ernst & T. Halevy, 2000, When to think alliance, *The McKinsey Quarterly*, Number 4: 46–55.

15. 2002, Borrego blurs traditional lines, *Dallas Morning News*, February 24, M4.

16. 2002, Lockheed Martin, Responsive global partnerships, http://www.lockheedmartin.com, March 17.

17. J. H. Tiessen & J. D. Linton, 2000, The JV dilemma: Cooperating and competing in joint ventures, *Revue Canadienne des Sciences de l'Administration*, 17(3): 203–216.

18. T. K. Das & B.-S. Teng, 2001, A risk perception model of alliance structuring, *Journal of International Management*, 7: 1–29; J. H. Dyer & H. Singh, 1998, The relational view: Cooperative strategy and sources of interorganizational competitive advantage, *Academy of Management Review*, 23: 660–679.

19. A. Afuah, 2002, Mapping technological capabilities into product markets and competitive advantage: The case of cholesterol drugs, *Strategic Management Journal*, 23: 171–179; A. Arino, 2001, To do or not to do? Noncooperative behavior by commission and omission in interfirm ventures, *Group & Organization Management*, 26(1): 4–23; C. Holliday, 2001, Sustainable growth, the DuPont Way, *Harvard Business Review*, 79(8): 129–134.

20. M. A. Geletkanycz & S. S. Black, 2001, Bound by the past? Experienced-based effects on commitment to the strategic status quo, *Journal of Management*, 27: 3–21.

21. S. L. Berman, J. Down, & C. W. L. Hill, 2002, Tacit knowledge as a source of competitive advantage in the National Basketball Association, *Academy of Management Journal*, 45: 13–31.

22. Tiessen & Linton, The JV dilemma, 206; P. E. Bierly, III & E. H. Kessler, 1999, The timing of strategic alliances, in M. A. Hitt, P. G. Clifford, R. D. Nixon, & K. P. Coyne (eds.), *Dynamic Strategic Resources: Development, Diffusion and Integration*, Chichester: John Wiley & Sons, 299–345.

23. 2001, Dow Jones Newswires and Bloomberg News Reports, Sprint, Virgin Group to create joint venture, *Dallas Morning News*, October 6, F3.

24. B. Orwall, 2001, Five Hollywood studios enter venture to offer feature films over Internet, *The Wall Street Journal*, http://www.wsj.com, August 17.

25. R. E. Hoskisson & L. W. Busenitz, 2002, Market uncertainty and learning distance in corporate entrepreneurship entry mode choice, in M. A. Hitt, R. D. Ireland, S. M. Camp, & D. L. Sexton (eds.), *Strategic Entrepreneurship: Creating a New Mindset*, Oxford, U.K.: Blackwell Publishers, 151–172.

26. A.-W. Harzing, 2002, Acquisitions versus Greenfield investments: International strategy and management of entry modes, *Strategic Management Journal*, 23: 211–227; S.-J. Chang & P. M. Rosenzweig, 2001, The choice of entry mode in sequential foreign direct investment, *Strategic Management Journal*, 22: 747–776; Y. Pan, 1997, The formation of Japanese and U.S. equity joint ventures in China, *Strategic Management Journal*, 18: 247–254.

27. 2002, Cott and J. D. Iroquois Enterprises Ltd. announce bottle water alliance, *Business Wire*, http://www.fidelity.com, February 26.

28. S. Das, P. K. Sen, & S. Sengupta, 1998, Impact of strategic alliances on firm valuation, *Academy of Management Journal*, 41: 27–41.

29. Bierly & Kessler, The timing of strategic alliances, 303.

30. Barney, *Gaining and Sustaining Competitive Advantage*, 339; T. B. Folta & K. D. Miller, 2002, Real options in equity partnerships, *Strategic Management Journal*, 23: 77–88.

31. J. McCullam, 2001, Polo Ralph Lauren, *Forbes Best of the Web*, May 21, 68.

32. A. C. Inkpen, 2001, Strategic alliances, in M. A. Hitt, R. E. Freeman, & J. S. Harrison (eds.), *Handbook of Strategic Management*, Oxford, U.K.: Blackwell Publishers, 409–432.

33. M. Delio, 1999, Strategic outsourcing, *Knowledge Management*, 2(7): 62–68.

34. 2002, Magna—Company information, http://www.magna.com, March 5.

35. J. J. Reuer, M. Zollo, & H. Singh, 2002, Post-formation dynamics in strategic alliances, *Strategic Management Journal*, 23: 135–151; P. Buxbaum, 2001, Making alliances work, *Computerworld*, 35(30): 30–31; Inkpen, Strategic alliances, 409.

36. D. Campbell, 2001, High-end strategic alliances as fundraising opportunities, *Nonprofit World*, 19(5): 8–12; M. D. Hutt, E. R. Stafford, B. A. Walker, & P. H. Reingen, 2000, Case study: Defining the social network of a strategic alliance, *Sloan Management Review*, 41(2): 51–62.

37. F. M. Lysiak, 2002, M&As create new competencies, *Best's Review*, 102(9): 32–33.

38. M. J. Kelly, J.-L. Schaan, & H. Jonacas, 2002, Managing alliance relationships: Key challenges in the early stages of collaboration, *R&D Management*, 32(1): 11–22.

39. A. C. Inkpen & J. Ross, 2001, Why do some strategic alliances persist beyond their useful life? *California Management Review*, 44(1): 132–148.

40. Schifrin, *Best of the Web*, 28.

41. Inkpen, Strategic alliances, 411.

42. L. Fuentelsaz, J. Gomez, & Y. Polo, 2002, Followers' entry timing: Evidence from the Spanish banking sector after deregulation, *Strategic Management Journal*, 23: 245–264.

43. K. R. Harrigan, 2001, Strategic flexibility in the old and new economies, in M. A. Hitt, R. E. Freeman, & J. S. Harrison (eds.), *Handbook of Strategic Management*, Oxford, U.K.: Blackwell Publishers, 97–123.

44. G. W. Dent, Jr., 2001, Gap fillers and fiduciary duties in strategic alliances, *The Business Lawyer*, 57(1): 55–104.

45. Ulfelder, Partners in profit, 24.

46. M. Gonzalez, 2001, Strategic alliances, *Ivey Business Journal*, 66(1): 47–51.

47. M. Johnson, 2001, Airlines rush for comfort alliances, *Global Finance*, 15(11): 119–120.

48. J. Child & D. Faulkner, 1998, *Strategies of Co-operation: Managing Alliances, Networks, and Joint Ventures*, New York: Oxford University Press.

49. J. R. Williams, 1998, *Renewable Advantage: Crafting Strategy Through Economic Time*, New York: The Free Press.

50. B. Nelson, Usinor Group, *Forbes Best of the Web*, May 21, 96.

51. V. Kumari, 2001, Joint ventures bolster credibility of new players in India, *National Underwriter*, 105(14): 46.

52. C. Hoag, 1999, Oil duo plan energy alliance, *Financial Times*, June 30, 17.

53. S. A. Zahra, R. D. Ireland, I. Gutierrez, & M. A. Hitt, 2000, Privatization and entrepreneurial transformation: Emerging issues and a future research agenda, *Academy of Management Review*, 25: 509–524.

54. Eisenhardt, Has strategy changed?, 88.

55. H. W. Chesbrough, 2002, Making sense of corporate venture capital, *Harvard Business Review*, 80(3): 90–99.

56. J. Strauss, 2001, Visa International: Creating the next generation of commerce, *Venture Capital Journal*, December 21, 40–41.

57. Ibid., 40.

58. B. Berentson, 2001, United Airlines, *Forbes Best of the Web*, May 21, 68.

59. 2002, Goodyear Tire—Press Releases, http://www.goodyear.com, March 5.

60. J. S. Harrison, M. A. Hitt, R. E. Hoskisson, & R. D. Ireland, 2001, Resource complementarity in business combinations: Extending the logic to organizational alliances, *Journal of Management*, 27: 679–699; S. H. Park & G. R. Ungson, 1997, The effect of national culture, organizational complementarity, and economic motivation on joint venture dissolution, *Academy of Management Journal*, 40: 297–307.

61. 2002, McDonald's, McDonald's USA—Oil Alliances, http://www.mcdonalds.com, March 6,

62. C. F. Freidheim, Jr., 1999, The trillion-dollar enterprise, *Strategy & Business*, 14: 60–66.

63. M. Kotabe & K. S. Swan, 1995, The role of strategic alliances in high technology new product development, *Strategic Management Journal*, 16: 621–636.

64. 2002, Caterpillar announces agreement with Mitsubishi Heavy Industries, http://www.caterpillar.com, March 5.

65. D. Clark, 2000, CSK, Advance Auto form firm to allow customers to purchase parts online, *The Wall Street Journal*, January 10, A8.

66. 2002, PartsAmerica.com Affiliate Program, http://www.partsamerica.com, March 6.

67. 2002, FedEx and KPMG join forces to deliver the next generation of global supply-chain services, http://www.fedex.com, March 7.

68. 2001, Marathon forms alliance with Russia's Yukos, *National Petroleum News*, 93(11): 10.

69. 2002, Marathon Oil Corporation outlines business strategy to security analysts, *PRNewswire*, http://www.prnewswire.com, February 28.

70. Hitt, Ireland, Camp, & Sexton, Strategic entrepreneurship, 9; R. G. McGrath, 1999, Falling forward: Real options reasoning and entrepreneurial failure, *Academy of Management Journal*, 22: 13–30.

71. 2002, Fujitsu Siemens Computers, Corporate profile, http://www. siemens.com, March 7.

72. J. Ball, 1999, To define future car, GM, Toyota say bigger is better, *The Wall Street Journal*, April 20, B4.

73. J. Ball, 1999, Five of the world's top auto makers agree to develop technology standard, *The Wall Street Journal*, April 28, B6.

74. Barney, *Gaining and Sustaining Competitive Advantage*, 339.

75. M. Freedman, 2000, Planting seeds, *Forbes*, February 7, 62–64.

76. J. M. Broder, 1997, Toys 'R' Us led price collusion, judge rules in upholding F.T.C. *The New York Times*, http://www.nytimes.com, October 1.

77. S. Jayachandran, J. Gimeno, & P. Rajan, 1999, Theory of multimarket competition: A synthesis and implications for marketing strategy, *Journal of Marketing*, 63(3): 49–66.

78. G. K. Price, 2000, Cereal sales soggy despite price cuts and reduced couponing, *Food Review*, 23(2): 21–28.

79. S. B. Garland & A. Reinhardt, 1999, Making antitrust fit high tech, *Business Week*, March 22, 34–36.

80. B. Mitchener & P. Shishkin, 2001, Price fixing by top five record companies, *The Wall Street Journal*, January 29, B1, B4.

81. G. Gari, 1999, Leveraging the rewards of strategic alliances, *Journal of Business Strategy*, 20(2): 40–43.

82. Price, Cereal sales soggy, 21.

83. Harrison, Hitt, Hoskisson, & Ireland, Resource complementarity, 684–685; S. Chaudhuri & B. Tabrizi, 1999, Capturing the real value in high-tech acquisitions, *Harvard Business Review*, 77(5): 123–130; J -F. Hennart & S. Reddy, 1997, The choice between mergers/acquisitions and joint ventures in the United States, *Strategic Management Journal*, 18: 1–12.

84. Inkpen, Strategic alliances, 413.

85. Young-Ybarra & Wiersema, Strategic flexibility, 439.

86. Folta & Miller, Real options, 77.

87. 2002, Wal-Mart Stores, Wal-Mart and Sumitomo agree to acquire strategic stake in Japan's Seiyu, http://www.walmart.com, March 16.

88. 2002, Boeing, Insitu to cooperatively develop unmanned vehicle prototype, Boeing News, http://www.boeing.com, March 8.

89. 2002, HP & Cisco, Cisco Strategic Alliances, http://www.cisco.com, March 8.

90. C. Harris & G. Cramb, 1999, Seeking wider co-operation, *Financial Times*, October 19, 20.

91. S. A. Shane, 1996, Hybrid organizational arrangements and their implications for firm growth and survival: A study of new franchisers, *Academy of Management Journal*, 39: 216–234.

92. F. Lafontaine, 1999, Myths and strengths of franchising, *Financial Times*, Mastering Strategy (Part Nine), November 22, 8–10.

93. L. Fenwick, 2001, Emerging markets: Defining global opportunities, *Franchising World*, 33(4): 54–55.

94. M. Sullivan, 2001, McDonald's, *Forbes Best of the Web*, May 21, 100.

95. R. P. Dant & P. J. Kaufmann, 1999, Franchising and the domain of entrepreneurship research, *Journal of Business Venturing*, 14: 5–16.

96. M. Gerstenhaber, 2000, Franchises can teach us about customer care, *Marketing*, March 16, 18.

97. P. J. Kaufmann & S. Eroglu, 1999, Standardization and adaptation in business format franchising, *Journal of Business Venturing*, 14: 69–85.

98. L. Wu, 1999, The pricing of a brand name product: Franchising in the motel services industry, *Journal of Business Venturing*, 14: 87–102.

99. Barney, *Gaining and Sustaining Competitive Advantage*, 110–111.

100. J. Higley, 2000, La Quinta jumps into franchising, *Hotel and Motel Management*, 215(13): 1, 54.

101. P. J. Buckley & M. Casson, 1996, An economic model of international joint venture strategy, *Journal of International Business Studies*, 27: 849–876; M. J. Dowling & W. L. Megginson, 1995, Cooperative strategy and new venture performance: The role of business strategy and management experience, *Strategic Management Journal*, 16: 565–580.

102. Ireland, Hitt, & Vaidyanath, Alliance management.

103. B. L. Simonin, 1997, The importance of collaborative know-how: An empirical test of the learning organization, *Academy of Management Journal*, 40: 1150–1174.

104. M. A. Hitt, M. T. Dacin, E. Levitas, J. -L. Arregle, & A. Borza, 2000, Partner selection in emerging and developed market contexts: Resource-based and organizational learning perspectives, *Academy of Management Journal*, 43: 449–467; M. D. Lord & A. L. Ranft, 2000, Organizational learning about new international markets: Exploring the internal transfer of local market knowledge, *Journal of International Business Studies*, 31: 73–589.

105. A. L. Velocci, Jr., 2001, U.S.-Euro strategic alliances will outpace company mergers, *Aviation Week & Space Technology*, 155(23): 56.

106. D. Kruger, 2001, Citigroup, *Forbes Best of the Web*, May 21, 71.

107. Ireland, Hitt, & Vaidyanath, Alliance management; M. A. Hitt, R. E. Hoskisson, & H. Kim, 1997, International diversification: Effects on innovation and firm performance in product diversified firms, *Academy of Management Journal*, 40: 767–798. R. N. Osborn & J. Hagedoorn, 1997, The institutionalization and evolutionary dynamics of interorganizational alliances and networks, *Academy of Management Journal*, 40: 261–278.

108. J. Hagedoorn, 1995, A note on international market leaders and networks of strategic technology partnering, *Strategic Management Journal*, 16: 241–250.

109. W. Heuslein, 2001, Coca-Cola, *Forbes Best of the Web*, May 21, 72.

110. P. Newcomb, 2001, Sony, *Forbes Best of the Web*, May 21, 84.

111. A. Gillies, General Mills, *Forbes Best of the Web*, May 21, 86.

112. M. Schuman, 1996, South Korea raises limit to 18% on foreign investment in firms, *The Wall Street Journal*, February 27, A12.

113. S. R. Miller & A. Parkhe, 2002, Is there a liability of foreignness in global banking? An empirical test of banks' X-efficiency, *Strategic Management Journal*, 23: 55–75; Y. Luo, 2001, Determinants of local responsiveness: Perspectives from foreign subsidiaries in an emerging market, *Journal of Management*, 27: 451–477.

114. A. Cane, 1999, GEC and NEC in alliance talks, *Financial Times*, May 11, 20.

115. P. Ghemawat, 2001, Distance matters: The hard reality of global expansion, *Harvard Business Review*, 79(8): 137–147.

116. J. K. Sebenius, 2002, The hidden challenge of cross-border negotiations, *Harvard Business Review*, 80(3): 76–85.

117. L. Kroll, 2001, Procter & Gamble, *Forbes Best of the Web*, May 21, 90.

118. C. B. Copp & R. L. Ivy, 2001, Networking trends of small tourism businesses in Post-Socialist Slovakia, *Journal of Small Business Management,* 39: 345–353.

119. S. S. Cohen & G. Fields, 1999, Social capital and capital gains in Silicon Valley, *California Management Review,* 41(2): 108–130; J. A. Matthews, 1999, A silicon island of the east: Creating a semiconductor industry in Singapore, *California Management Review,* 41(2): 55–78; M. E. Porter, 1998, Clusters and the new economics of competition, *Harvard Business Review,* 78(6): 77–90; R. Pouder & C. H. St. John, 1996, Hot spots and blind spots: Geographical clusters of firms and innovation, *Academy of Management Review,* 21: 1192–1225.

120. A. C. Cooper, 2001, Networks, alliances, and entrepreneurship, in M. A. Hitt, R. D. Ireland, S. M. Camp, & D. L. Sexton (eds.), *Strategic Entrepreneurship: Creating a New Mindset,* Oxford, U.K.: Blackwell Publishers, 203–222.

121. 2002, Johnson Controls, Corporate profile, http://www.johnsoncontrols com, March 10.

122. 2002, Johnson Controls, Corporate profile, http://www.johnsoncontrols. com, March 12.

123. R. S. Cline, 2001, Partnering for strategic alliances, *Lodging Hospitality,* 57(9): 42.

124. G. J. Young, M. P. Charns, & S. M. Shortell, 2001, Top manager and network effects on the adoption of innovative management practices: A study of TQM in a public hospital system, *Strategic Management Journal,* 22: 935–951.

125. F. T. Rothaermel, 2001, Complementary assets, strategic alliances, and the incumbent's advantage: An empirical study of industry and firm effects in the biopharmaceutical industry, *Research Policy,* 30: 1235–1251.

126. 2002, Intel, Strategic alliances, http://www.intel.com, March 10.

127. H. W. Volberda, C. Baden-Fuller, & F. A. J. van den Bosch, 2001, Mastering strategic renewal: Mobilising renewal journeys in multi-unit firms, *Long Range Planning,* 34(2): 159–178.

128. D. C. Hambrick, J. Li, K. Xin, & A. S. Tsui, 2001, Compositional gaps and downward spirals in international joint venture management groups, *Strategic Management Journal,* 22: 1033–1053; T. K. Das & B.-S. Teng, 2000, Instabilities of strategic alliances: An internal tensions perspective, *Organization Science,* 11: 77–101.

129. M. P. Koza & A. Y. Lewin, 1999, Putting the S-word back in alliances, Mastering Strategy (Part Six), *Financial Times,* November 1, 12–13; S. H. Park & M. Russo, 1996, When cooperation eclipses competition: An event history analysis of joint venture failures, *Management Science,* 42: 875–890.

130. A. Madhok & S. B. Tallman, 1998, Resources, transactions and rents: Managing value through interfirm collaborative relationships, *Organization Science,* 9: 326–339.

131. P. M. Norman, 2001, Are your secrets safe? Knowledge protection in strategic alliances, *Business Horizons,* November/December, 51–60.

132. M. A. Hitt, M. T. Dacin, B. B. Tyler, & D. Park, 1997, Understanding the differences in Korean and U.S. executives strategic orientations, *Strategic Management Journal,* 18: 159–168.

133. P. Lane, J. E. Salk, & M. A. Lyles, 2001, Absorptive capacity, learning, and performance in international joint ventures, *Strategic Management Journal,* 22: 1139–1161.

134. R. Larsson, L. Bengtsson, K. Henriksson, & J. Sparks, 1998, The interorganizational learning dilemma: Collective knowledge development in strategic alliances, *Organization Science,* 9: 285–305.

135. Ireland, Hitt, & Vaidyanath, Alliance management.

136. Reuer, Zollo, & Singh, Post-formation dynamics, 148.

137. J. H. Dyer, P. Kale, & H. Singh, 2001, How to make strategic alliances work, *MIT Sloan Management Review,* 42(4): 37–43.

138. Berentson, United Airlines, 68.

139. J. H. Dyer, 1997, Effective interfirm collaboration: How firms minimize transaction costs and maximize transaction value, *Strategic Management Journal,* 18: 535–556; M. H. Hansen, R. E. Hoskisson, & J. B. Barney, 1997, Trustworthiness in strategic alliances: Opportunism minimization versus opportunity maximization, Working paper, Brigham Young University.

140. Mitchell, Alliances, 7.

141. Hutt, Stafford, Walker, & Reingen, Defining the social network, 53.

142. D. F. Jennings, K. Artz, L. M. Gillin, & C. Christodouloy, 2000, Determinants of trust in global strategic alliances: Amrad and the Australian biomedical industry, *Competitiveness Review,* 10(1): 25–44.

143. H. K. Steensma, L. Marino, & K. M. Weaver, 2000, Attitudes toward cooperative strategies: A cross-cultural analysis of entrepreneurs, *Journal of International Business Studies,* 31: 591–609.

144. A. Arino & J. de la Torre, 1998, Learning from failure: Towards and evolutionary model of collaborative ventures, *Organization Science,* 9: 306–325; J. B. Barney & M. H. Hansen, 1994, Trustworthiness: Can it be a source of competitive advantage? *Strategic Management Journal,* 15(Special Winter Issue): 175–203.

145. R. Gulati & H. Singh, 1998, The architecture of cooperation: Managing coordination costs and appropriation concerns in strategic alliances, *Administrative Science Quarterly,* 43: 781–814; R. Gulati, 1996, Social structure and alliance formation patterns: A longitudinal analysis, *Administrative Science Quarterly,* 40: 619–652.

146. J. H. Davis, F. D. Schoorman, R. C. Mayer, & H. H. Tan, 2000, The trusted general manager and business unit performance: Empirical evidence of a competitive advantage, *Strategic Management Journal,* 21: 563–576; R. C. Mayer, J. H. Davis, & F. D. Schoorman, 1995, An integrative model of organizational trust, *Academy of Management Review,* 20. 709–734.

Strategic Actions: Strategy Implementation

10

Chapter Ten

Corporate Governance

Knowledge Objectives

Studying this chapter should provide you with the strategic management knowledge needed to:

1. Define corporate governance and explain why it is used to monitor and control managers' strategic decisions.

2. Explain how ownership came to be separated from managerial control in the modern corporation.

3. Define an agency relationship and managerial opportunism and describe their strategic implications.

4. Explain how three internal governance mechanisms—ownership concentration, the board of directors, and executive compensation—are used to monitor and control managerial decisions.

5. Discuss trends among the three types of compensation executives receive and their effects on strategic decisions.

6. Describe how the external corporate governance mechanism—the market for corporate control—acts as a restraint on top-level managers' strategic decisions.

7. Discuss the use of corporate governance in international settings, in particular in Germany and Japan.

8. Describe how corporate governance fosters ethical strategic decisions and the importance of such behaviors on the part of top-level executives.

Corporate Governance and CEO Pay

Top executive pay increased by 571 percent between 1990 and the end of 2000. Even in 2000, the year in which the Standard & Poor's stock index of 500 firms suffered a loss of 10 percent, this trend of increased CEO pay continued. In comparison, the average worker's pay barely outpaced inflation over this same decade; worker pay increased 37 percent versus inflation of 32 percent. In an age where pay for performance has been prominently featured in the business press, this discrepancy seems to defy logic. What caused this disparity?

The board of directors of any large publicly owned corporation makes executive pay decisions, typically through an executive compensation committee. In the 1990s, competitive benchmarking—setting standards based on those of competitors—became widespread. It is estimated that 96 percent of the companies in Standard & Poor's 500 stock index used such benchmarking to set pay. Executive compensation committees rationalize that if their CEOs do not earn as much as their peers, they may seek a position with another firm. By using this benchmarking trend instead of *directly* tying pay to performance, firms seem to be using alternative mechanisms for corporate governance. In fact, some research has suggested that this approach has led to underperforming executives getting increased pay regardless of the performance of the firm they manage.

Cash compensation for CEOs in the year 2000 increased 18 percent, while total pay increased 6.3 percent—the smallest total increase in compensation in 5 years. This increase far exceeds the 4.3 percent increase received by salaried workers in 2000, however, and the gap is even wider between the CEO and the average rank-and-file worker. Some hard-hit companies continued to increase their CEOs' pay even though the companies they managed underperformed their competitors. Net income at Walt Disney Company, for example, fell from $1.9 billion in 1997 to $920 million in the year 2000, but Disney increased Michael Eisner's salary and awarded him 2 million stock option shares valued at $37.7 million and a $11.5 million bonus.

At a minority of companies, however, the board of directors lowered a top executive's pay when the company did not perform well. For instance, at Dana Corporation, CEO Joseph M. Magliochetti had his pay reduced to $948,363 in 2000, a 63 percent drop from 1999. The auto parts maker had a poor year in 2000 as

In spite of being ranked the fifth most powerful person in Hollywood, Walt Disney chairman Michael Eisner's annual compensation for 2001 fell to $1 million in salary and no bonus at all, reflecting the economic downturn and the effect on travel and entertainment from the events of September 11. In one of Disney's strongest years, Eisner's annual compensation from salary, bonuses, and stock option came to $40 million.

sales dropped 6 percent, profits fell by 44 percent, and Dana's stock lost more than half of its value, which accordingly made Magliochetti's stock options worthless in addition to his salary decrease.

Other companies may have reduced CEO salary but have increased CEO stock options grants when the price of the stock is considerably lower than in previous years. For example, if a stock declines to $2.00 from $10.00, a firm will give significantly more stock options to meet a certain CEO compensation goal. As the economy expands, these managers will then receive a windfall thanks to a booming economy for which they were not responsible.

The bottom line is that even though mid-year 2002 found the economy and the stock market retreating from their then-recent high levels, few firms seemed willing to reduce executive pay in proportions mirroring declines in the performance of the firm for which they were responsible. Of course, it is more costly for a firm that has had performance problems to hire a top flight CEO, because it is a high-risk situation for the executive. Nonetheless, even though a firm will have to pay significantly more for a CEO for a turnaround situation, additional efforts to more closely align executive pay with firm performance appear necessary.

SOURCES: G. Colvin, 2001, The great CEO pay heist, *Fortune*, June 25, 64–70; J. Fox, 2001, The amazing stock option sleight of hand, *Fortune*, June 25, 86–92; L. Lavelle & F. F. Jespersen, 2001, Executive pay, *Business Week*, April 16, 76–80; C. J. Loomis, 2001, This stuff is wrong, *Fortune*, June 25, 73–84; D. Nichols & C. Subramaniam, 2001, Executive compensation; Excess or equitable? *Journal of Business Ethics*, 29: 339–351; R. C. Anderson, T. W. Bates, J. M. Bizjak, & M. L. Lemmon, 2000, Corporate governance and firm diversification, *Financial Management*, 29(1): 5–22.

As the Opening Case illustrates, corporate governance is an increasingly important part of the strategic management process.[1] If the board makes the wrong decision in compensating the firm's strategic leader, the CEO, the whole firm suffers, as do its shareholders. Compensation is used to motivate CEOs to act in the best interests of the firm—in particular, the shareholders. When they do, the firm's value should increase.

What are a CEO's actions worth? The Opening Case suggests that they are worth a significant amount in the United States. While some critics argue that U.S. CEOs are paid too much, the hefty increases in their compensation in recent years ostensibly have come from linking their pay to their firms' performance, and U.S. firms have performed better than many firms in other countries. However, research suggests that firms with a smaller pay gap between the CEO and other top executives perform better, especially when collaboration among top management team members is more important.[2] The performance improvement is attributed to better cooperation among the top management team members. Other research suggests that CEOs receive excessive compensation when corporate governance is the weakest.[3] Also, as noted in the Opening Case, benchmarking—basing CEO compensation on that paid to peers at other companies—appears to be a prevalent cause of excessive compensation.

Corporate governance represents the relationship among stakeholders that is used to determine and control the strategic direction and performance of organizations.[4] At its core, corporate governance is concerned with identifying ways to ensure

Corporate governance represents the relationship among stakeholders that is used to determine and control the strategic direction and performance of organizations.

that strategic decisions are made effectively.[5] Governance can also be thought of as a means corporations use to establish order between parties (the firm's owners and its top-level managers) whose interests may be in conflict. Thus, corporate governance reflects and enforces the company's values.[6] In modern corporations—especially those in the United States and the United Kingdom—a primary objective of corporate governance is to ensure that the interests of top-level managers are aligned with the interests of the shareholders. Corporate governance involves oversight in areas where owners, managers, and members of boards of directors may have conflicts of interest. These areas include the election of directors, the general supervision of CEO pay and more focused supervision of director pay, and the corporation's overall structure and strategic direction.[7]

Corporate governance has been emphasized in recent years because, as the Opening Case illustrates, corporate governance mechanisms occasionally fail to adequately monitor and control top-level managers' decisions. This situation has resulted in changes in governance mechanisms in corporations throughout the world, especially with respect to efforts intended to improve the performance of boards of directors. A second and more positive reason for this interest is that evidence suggests that a well-functioning corporate governance and control system can create a competitive advantage for an individual firm.[8] For example, one governance mechanism—the board of directors—has been suggested to be rapidly evolving into a major strategic force in U.S. business firms.[9] Thus, in this chapter, we describe actions designed to implement strategies that focus on monitoring and controlling mechanisms, which can help to ensure that top-level managerial actions contribute to the firm's strategic competitiveness and its ability to earn above-average returns.

Effective corporate governance is also of interest to nations.[10] As stated by one scholar, "Every country wants the firms that operate within its borders to flourish and grow in such ways as to provide employment, wealth, and satisfaction, not only to improve standards of living materially but also to enhance social cohesion. These aspirations cannot be met unless those firms are competitive internationally in a sustained way, and it is this medium- and long-term perspective that makes good corporate governance so vital."[11]

Corporate governance, then, reflects company standards, which in turn collectively reflect societal standards.[12] In many individual corporations, shareholders hold top-level managers accountable for their decisions and the results they generate. As with these individual firms and their boards, nations that effectively govern their corporations may gain a competitive advantage over rival countries. For example, during the 1997 currency crisis in Asia, weak governance in the emerging economies resulted in asset prices falling lower than would have been the case had there been strong governance.[13]

In a range of countries, but especially in the United States and the United Kingdom, the fundamental goal of business organizations is to maximize shareholder value.[14] Traditionally, shareholders are treated as the firm's key stakeholders, because they are the company's legal owners. The firm's owners expect top-level managers and others influencing the corporation's actions (for example, the board of directors) to make decisions that will result in the maximization of the company's value and, hence, of the owners' wealth.[15]

In the first section of this chapter, we describe the relationship providing the foundation on which the modern corporation is built: the relationship between owners and managers. The majority of this chapter is used to explain various mechanisms owners use to govern managers and to ensure that they comply with their responsibility to maximize shareholder value.

Three internal governance mechanisms and a single external one are used in the modern corporation (see Table 10.1). The three internal governance mechanisms we

Table 10.1 | Corporate Governance Mechanisms

Internal Governance Mechanisms

Ownership Concentration

- Relative amounts of stock owned by individual shareholders and institutional investors

Board of Directors

- Individuals responsible for representing the firm's owners by monitoring top-level managers' strategic decisions

Executive Compensation

- Use of salary, bonuses, and long-term incentives to align managers' interests with shareholders' interests

External Governance Mechanism

Market for Corporate Control

- The purchase of a company that is underperforming relative to industry rivals in order to improve the firm's strategic competitiveness

describe in this chapter are (1) ownership concentration, as represented by types of shareholders and their different incentives to monitor managers, (2) the board of directors, and (3) executive compensation. We then consider the market for corporate control, an external corporate governance mechanism. Essentially, this market is a set of potential owners seeking to acquire undervalued firms and earn above-average returns on their investments by replacing ineffective top-level management teams.[16] The chapter's focus then shifts to the issue of international corporate governance. We briefly describe governance approaches used in German and Japanese firms whose traditional governance structures are being affected by the realities of global competition. In part, this discussion suggests the possibility that the structures used to govern global companies in many different countries, including Germany, Japan, the United Kingdom, and the United States, are becoming more, rather than less, similar. Closing our analysis of corporate governance is a consideration of the need for these control mechanisms to encourage and support ethical behavior in organizations.

Importantly, the mechanisms discussed in this chapter can positively influence the governance of the modern corporation, which has placed significant responsibility and authority in the hands of top-level managers. The most effective managers understand their accountability for the firm's performance and respond positively to corporate governance mechanisms.[17] In addition, the firm's owners should not expect any single mechanism to remain effective over time. Rather, the use of several mechanisms allows owners to govern the corporation in ways that maximize strategic competitiveness and increase the financial value of their firm.[18] With multiple governance mechanisms operating simultaneously, however, it is also possible for some of the governance mechanisms to conflict.[19] Later, we review how these conflicts can occur.

Separation of Ownership and Managerial Control

Historically, the founder-owners and their descendants managed U.S. firms. In these cases, corporate ownership and control resided in the same persons. As firms grew larger, "the managerial revolution led to a separation of ownership and control in most large corporations, where control of the firm shifted from entrepreneurs to professional managers while ownership became dispersed among thousands of unorganized stockholders who were removed from the day-to-day management of the firm."[20] These changes created the modern public corporation, which is based on the efficient separation of ownership and managerial control. Supporting the separation is a basic legal premise suggesting that the primary objective of a firm's activities is to increase the corporation's profit and, thereby, the financial gains of the owners (the shareholders).[21]

The separation of ownership and managerial control allows shareholders to purchase stock, which entitles them to income (residual returns) from the firm's operations after paying expenses. This right, however, requires that they also take a risk that the firm's expenses may exceed its revenues. To manage this investment risk, shareholders maintain a diversified portfolio by investing in several companies to reduce their overall risk.[22] As shareholders diversify their investments over a number of corporations, their risk declines. The poor performance or failure of any one firm in which they invest has less overall effect. Thus, shareholders specialize in managing their investment risk.

In small firms, managers often are high percentage owners, so there is less separation between ownership and managerial control, but as these firms grow and become more complex, their owners-managers may contract with managerial specialists. These managers oversee decision making in the owner's firm and are compensated on the basis of their decision-making skills. As decision-making specialists, managers are agents of the firm's owners and are expected to use their decision-making skills to operate the owners' firm in ways that will maximize the return on their investment.[23]

Without owner (shareholder) specialization in risk bearing and management specialization in decision making that we have described, a firm probably would be limited by the abilities of its owners to manage and make effective strategic decisions. Thus, the separation and specialization of ownership (risk bearing) and managerial control (decision making) should produce the highest returns for the firm's owners.

Shareholder value is reflected by the price of the firm's stock. As stated earlier, corporate governance mechanisms, such as the board of directors or compensation based on the performance of a firm, is the reason that CEOs show general concern about the firm's stock price. For example, Cisco earned the dubious honor in 2001 of losing the most in shareholder value: $156 billion for the year. Furthermore, it lost $456 billion between March 2000 and December 2001. Although Cisco CEO John Chambers had been considered an excellent CEO, mid-2002 was a time during which the firm's losses since early 2000 as well as its possible future prospects caused some to begin questioning this belief.[24] On a more positive note, it is fair to report that over its lifetime, Cisco has created significant wealth for its investors and managers; it ranks 11th overall in regard to wealth creation.[25] Moreover, study of 2001's business landscape shows that Cisco's performance in that year was not unlike that of many other U.S. companies, which lost a combined total of $2.5 trillion in shareholder wealth.

Agency Relationships

An **agency relationship** exists when one or more persons (the principal or principals) hire another person or persons (the agent or agents) as decision-making specialists to perform a service.

The separation between owners and managers creates an agency relationship. An **agency relationship** exists when one or more persons (the principal or principals) hire another person or persons (the agent or agents) as decision-making specialists to perform a service.[26] Thus, an agency relationship exists when one party delegates decision-making responsibility to a second party for compensation (see Figure 10.1).[27] In addition to shareholders and top executives, other examples of agency

Figure 10.1   An Agency Relationship

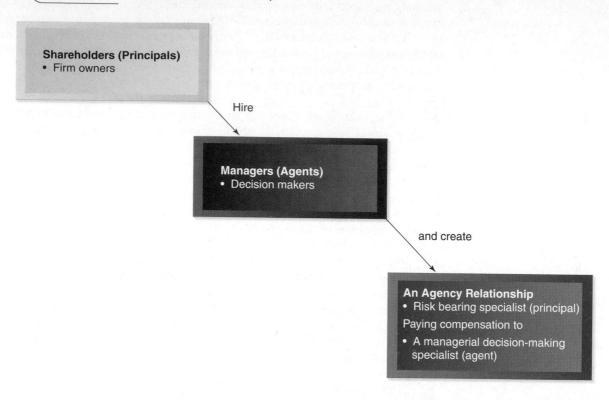

relationships are consultants and clients and insured and insurer. Moreover, within organizations, an agency relationship exists between managers and their employees, as well as between top executives and the firm's owners.[28] In the modern corporation, managers must understand the links between these relationships and the firm's effectiveness.[29] Although the agency relationship between managers and their employees is important, in this chapter we focus on the agency relationship between the firm's owners (the principals) and top-level managers (the principals' agents), because this relationship is related directly to how the firm's strategies are implemented.

The separation between ownership and managerial control can be problematic. Research evidence documents a variety of agency problems in the modern corporation.[30] Problems can surface because the principal and the agent have different interests and goals, or because shareholders lack direct control of large publicly traded corporations. Problems also arise when an agent makes decisions that result in the pursuit of goals that conflict with those of the principals. Thus, the separation of ownership and control potentially allows divergent interests (between principals and agents) to surface, which can lead to managerial opportunism.

Managerial opportunism is the seeking of self-interest with guile (i.e., cunning or deceit).[31] Opportunism is both an attitude (e.g., an inclination) and a set of behaviors (i.e., specific acts of self-interest).[32] It is not possible for principals to know beforehand which agents will or will not act opportunistically. The reputations of top executives are an imperfect predictor, and opportunistic behavior cannot be observed until it has occurred. Thus, principals establish governance and control mechanisms to prevent agents from acting opportunistically, even though only a few are likely to

Managerial opportunism is the seeking of self-interest with guile (i.e., cunning or deceit).

do so.[33] Any time that principals delegate decision-making responsibilities to agents, the opportunity for conflicts of interest exist. Top executives, for example, may make strategic decisions that maximize their personal welfare and minimize their personal risk.[34] Decisions such as these prevent the maximization of shareholder wealth. Decisions regarding product diversification demonstrate these possibilities.

Product Diversification as an Example of an Agency Problem

As explained in Chapter 6, a corporate-level strategy to diversify the firm's product lines can enhance a firm's strategic competitiveness and increase its returns, both of which serve the interests of shareholders and the top executives. However, product diversification can result in two benefits to managers that shareholders do not enjoy, so top executives may prefer more product diversification than do shareholders.[35]

First, diversification usually increases the size of a firm, and size is positively related to executive compensation. Also, diversification increases the complexity of managing a firm and its network of businesses and may thus require more pay because of this complexity.[36] Thus, increased product diversification provides an opportunity for top executives to increase their compensation.[37]

Second, product diversification and the resulting diversification of the firm's portfolio of businesses can reduce top executives' employment risk.[38] Managerial employment risk is the risk of job loss, loss of compensation, and loss of managerial reputation.[39] These risks are reduced with increased diversification, because a firm and its upper-level managers are less vulnerable to the reduction in demand associated with a single or limited number of product lines or businesses. For example, Gemplus International named Antonio Perez as its CEO in 2000. With his 25-year career at Hewlett-Packard, Perez had a good reputation in the business world and his Hewlett-Packard experience seemed to be perfect preparation for his new position. Gemplus, headquartered in France, is the world's top producer of smart cards, "microchip-embedded cards used for everything from phone calls to credit-card transactions," and is very focused on a narrow product market. Perez's appointment was met with outrage by the French media over the $97 million worth of stock and options he received when he was hired. When demand for the Gemplus smart cards dropped sharply with slowing sales of mobile phones that used Gemplus chips, the company, worth approximately $3 billion in December 2000, lost more than 65 percent of its worth in the ensuing 15 months. Perez cut his own pay by 20 percent, but his decision to cut some of the company's 7,800-person workforce and the ensuing battle with Marc Lassus, company founder and chairman, led to both being forced by the firm's major shareholders to resign. Perez's employment risk was higher because the firm lacked significant product diversification, which is probably why he received significant compensation in the form of stock and options when he began his tenure with Gemplus.[40]

Another concern that may represent an agency problem is a firm's free cash flows over which top executives have control. Free cash flows are resources remaining after the firm has invested in all projects that have positive net present values within its current businesses.[41] In anticipation of positive returns, managers may decide to invest these funds in products that are not associated with the firm's current lines of business to increase the firm's level of diversification. The managerial decision to use free cash flows to overdiversify the firm is an example of self-serving and opportunistic managerial behavior. In contrast to managers, shareholders may prefer that free cash flows be distributed to them as dividends, so they can control how the cash is invested.[42]

Curve S in Figure 10.2 depicts the shareholders' optimal level of diversification. Owners seek the level of diversification that reduces the risk of the firm's total failure while simultaneously increasing the company's value through the development of economies of scale and scope (see Chapter 6). Of the four corporate-level diversification strategies shown in Figure 10.2, shareholders likely prefer the diversified position noted by point A on curve S—a position that is located between the dominant business and related–constrained diversification strategies. Of course, the optimum level of diversification owners seek varies from firm to firm.[43] Factors that affect shareholders' preferences include the firm's primary industry, the intensity of rivalry among competitors in that industry, and the top management team's experience with implementing diversification strategies.

As do principals, upper-level executives—as agents—also seek an optimal level of diversification. Declining performance resulting from too much product diversification increases the probability that corporate control of the firm will be acquired in the market. Once a firm is acquired, the employment risk for the firm's top executives increases substantially. Furthermore, a manager's employment opportunities in the external managerial labor market (discussed in Chapter 12) are affected negatively by a firm's poor performance. Therefore, top executives prefer diversification, but not to a point that it increases their employment risk and reduces their employment opportunities.[44] Curve M in Figure 10.2 shows that executives prefer higher levels of product diversification than shareholders. Top executives might prefer the level of diversification shown by point B on curve M.

In general, shareholders prefer riskier strategies and more focused diversification. They reduce their risk through holding a diversified portfolio of equity investments. Alternatively, managers obviously cannot balance their employment risk by working for a diverse portfolio of firms. Therefore, top executives may prefer a level of diversification that maximizes firm size and their compensation and that reduces their employment risk. Product diversification, therefore, is a potential agency problem that could result in principals incurring costs to control their agents' behaviors.

Figure 10.2 Manager and Shareholder Risk and Diversification

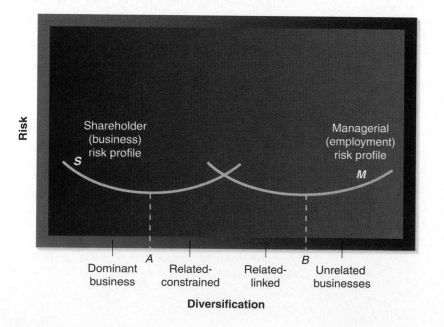

PART 3 /Strategic Actions: Strategy Implementation

Agency Costs and Governance Mechanisms

The potential conflict illustrated by Figure 10.2, coupled with the fact that principals do not know which managers might act opportunistically, demonstrates why principals establish governance mechanisms. However, the firm incurs costs when it uses one or more governance mechanisms. **Agency costs** are the sum of incentive costs, monitoring costs, enforcement costs, and individual financial losses incurred by principals, because governance mechanisms cannot guarantee total compliance by the agent. If a firm is diversified, governance costs increase because it is more difficult to monitor what is going on inside the firm.[45]

In general, managerial interests may prevail when governance mechanisms are weak, as is exemplified by allowing managers a significant amount of autonomy to make strategic decisions. If, however, the board of directors controls managerial autonomy, or if other strong governance mechanisms are used, the firm's strategies should better reflect the interests of the shareholders.

Recent research suggests that even using more governance mechanisms may produce major changes in strategies. Firms acquired unrelated businesses at approximately the same rate in the 1980s as they did in the 1960s, even though more governance mechanisms were employed in the 1980s. Thus, governance mechanisms are an imperfect means of controlling managerial opportunism.[46] Alternatively, other current evidence suggests that active shareholders, especially institutional investors, are more willing to try to remove the CEO leading a firm that is performing poorly. The actions taken at Gemplus International, as explained above, demonstrate this willingness.[47]

Next, we explain the effects of different governance mechanisms on the decisions managers make about the choice and the use of the firm's strategies.

Ownership Concentration

Both the number of large-block shareholders and the total percentage of shares they own define **ownership concentration**. **Large-block shareholders** typically own at least 5 percent of a corporation's issued shares. Ownership concentration as a governance mechanism has received considerable interest because large-block shareholders are increasingly active in their demands that corporations adopt effective governance mechanisms to control managerial decisions.[48]

In general, diffuse ownership (a large number of shareholders with small holdings and few, if any, large-block shareholders) produces weak monitoring of managers' decisions. Among other problems, diffuse ownership makes it difficult for owners to effectively coordinate their actions. Diversification of the firm's product lines beyond the shareholders' optimum level might result from weak monitoring of managers' decisions. Higher levels of monitoring could encourage managers to avoid strategic decisions that do not create greater shareholder value. In fact, research evidence shows that ownership concentration is associated with lower levels of firm diversification.[49] Thus, with high degrees of ownership concentration, the probability is greater that managers' strategic decisions will be intended to maximize shareholder value.

Ownership concentration is a natural consequence of deregulated industries. For example, after the airline industry was deregulated in the United States, the ownership of the airlines became more concentrated.[50] A similar pattern has occurred in the banking industry, where there has been substantial consolidation through acquisitions.[51] Much of this concentration has come from increasing equity ownership by institutional investors.

Agency costs are the sum of incentive costs, monitoring costs, enforcement costs, and individual financial losses incurred by principals, because governance mechanisms cannot guarantee total compliance by the agent.

Ownership concentration is defined by both the number of large-block shareholders and the total percentage of shares they own.

Large-block shareholders typically own at least 5 percent of a corporation's issued shares.

The Growing Influence of Institutional Owners

A classic work published in the 1930s argued that the "modern" corporation had become characterized by a separation of ownership and control.[52] This change occurred primarily because growth prevented founders-owners from maintaining their dual positions in their increasingly complex companies. More recently, another shift has occurred: Ownership of many modern corporations is now concentrated in the hands of institutional investors rather than individual shareholders.[53]

Institutional owners are financial institutions such as stock mutual funds and pension funds that control large-block shareholder positions. Because of their prominent ownership positions, institutional owners, as large-block shareholders, are a powerful governance mechanism. Institutions of these types now own more than 50 percent of the stock in large U.S. corporations, and of the top 1,000 corporations, they own, on average, 59 percent of the stock.[54] Pension funds alone control at least one-half of corporate equity.[55]

These ownership percentages suggest that as investors, institutional owners have both the size and the incentive to discipline ineffective top-level managers and can significantly influence a firm's choice of strategies and overall strategic decisions.[56] Research evidence indicates that institutional and other large-block shareholders are becoming more active in their efforts to influence a corporation's strategic decisions. Initially, these shareholder activists and institutional investors concentrated on the performance and accountability of CEOs and contributed to the ouster of a number of them. They are now targeting what they believe are ineffective boards of directors.[57]

For example, CalPERS provides retirement and health coverage to over 1.3 million current and retired public employees.[58] One of the largest public employee pension funds in the United States, CalPERS is generally thought to act aggressively to promote decisions and actions that it believes will enhance shareholder value in companies in which it invests. To pressure boards of directors to make what it believes are needed changes, CalPERS has advocated for board reform. In 1990, 66 percent of all directors on U.S. company boards were outsiders; by 2000 the level had risen to 78 percent. CalPERS believes that all but the CEO should be outsiders, "which translates into 92 percent of all company directors should be independent non-executives."[59] The largest institutional investor, TIAA-CREF, has taken actions similar to those of CalPERS, but with a less publicly aggressive stance (furthermore, as the Strategic Focus on page 318 suggests, CalPERS may not be as aggressive in regard to governance as it has been historically). To date, research suggests that these institutions' activism may not have a direct effect on firm performance, but that its influence may be indirect through its effects on important strategic decisions, such as those concerned with innovation.[60]

Shareholder Activism: How Much Is Possible?

The U.S. Securities and Exchange Commission (SEC) has issued several rulings that support shareholder involvement and control of managerial decisions. For example, the SEC eased its rule regarding communications among shareholders. Historically, shareholders could communicate among themselves only through a cumbersome and expensive filing process. Now, with a simple notification to the SEC of an upcoming meeting, shareholders can convene to discuss a corporation's strategic direction. If a consensus on an issue exists, shareholders can vote as a block. "In 2000, we saw 24 proxy fights—of those, management won 14 and dissidents won 10, which means that management was victorious in 58 percent of them and the dissident group was victorious in 42 percent."[61] Among these 24 proxy fights, management proposals receiving significant opposition from institutional investors included "executive compensation, stock options and anti-takeover devices." The Internet has also facilitated proxy battles because "the Web makes it easier and cheaper to contact and organize other investors."[62]

Some argue that greater latitude should be extended to those managing the funds of large institutional investor groups, believing that allowing these individuals to hold positions on boards of firms in which their organizations have significant investments might enable fund managers to better represent the interests of those they serve.[63] However, the actions of traditionally activist institutional investor CalPERS were potentially compromised by investments it had in Enron (see the Strategic Focus on page 332 on Enron's governance and ethics and Chapter 7's Strategic Focus on page 225 about the failed acquisition of Enron by Dynegy). Institutional activism should create a premium for companies with good corporate governance. However, trustees for these funds sometimes have other relationships that compromise their effectiveness, as apparently was the case for CalPERS. It is more often the case that large *private* pension funds, which have other business relationships with companies in their fund's portfolio, reduce effective monitoring.[64]

Also, the degree to which institutional investors can effectively monitor the decisions being made in all of the companies in which they have investments is questionable. Historically, CalPERS targeted 12 companies at a time for improvement. The New York Teachers Retirement Fund, another activist institutional investor, focuses on 25 of the 1,300-plus companies in its portfolio. Given limited resources, even large-block shareholders tend to concentrate on corporations in which they have significant investments. Thus, although shareholder activism has increased, institutional investors face barriers to the amount of active governance they can realistically employ.[65] Furthermore, at times, activist institutional shareholders may have conflicting goals.[66] Other means of corporate governance are needed.

Besides institutional owners, other owners are able to influence the decisions managers make as agents. Although other investors have significant influence, battles are not likely to be won or lost unless institutional investors are involved because they currently are such significant shareholders. Texas billionaire Sam Wyly sold his company, Sterling Software, to Computer Associates in 2000. Wyly fought to elect a new Computer Associates board that would in turn elect him to be Computer Associates chairman. He argued that Computer Associates, the fourth largest software company in the world, had not performed well since 1996 and had alienated customers and employees.[67] As part of his leadership proposal, Wyly sought to break the company into four small companies. Influential shareholders who considered it "too radical" did not support this proposal and Walter Haefner, who is the largest shareholder in the company, supported the current management. Wyly was unsuccessful in his attempt to take over the leadership of Computer Associates, but his revised plan won the support of CalPERS and other investors. Even though Wyly lost his attempt at leadership, Computer Associates will likely improve its corporate governance procedures.[68]

Corporate governance may also by affected by the recent phenomenon of increased managerial ownership of the firm's stock. There are many positive reasons for managerial ownership, including the use of stock options to link managerial pay to the performance of a firm. However, an unexpected outcome of managerial ownership has been reduced support for shareholder-sponsored proposals to repeal anti-takeover provisions. Institutional owners generally support the repeal of these provisions because shareholder wealth is typically increased if a takeover is offered, while managerial owners, whose jobs are at risk if a takeover is executed,

Sam Wyly founded his first company—University Computing Company—with $1,000 in 1963. The firm went public in 1965 and earned its investors an astounding 100 to 1 return in the next four years, eventually merging with Computer Associates. Sterling Software, which he founded in 1983, was sold to Computer Associates for $8 billion in 2000.

CalPERS, Institutional Investor Activism, and Conflict of Interest

Although large active institutional investors, such as the California Public Employees Retirement System (CalPERS), have been significant advocates of improved corporate governance and better board oversight of large corporations, they have also pursued a trend of private placement of equity investments.

CalPERS' private placement of equity in Enron partnerships may be cause for concern because of a potential conflict of interest. CalPERS' December 2000 board proceedings show that the institution was a substantial shareholder and partner with Enron in a set of private partnerships that ultimately was the impetus for Enron's failure. Because these partnerships were guaranteed by Enron stock and thus represented off-balance sheet liabilities, the investments were riskier than common shareholders realized because the accounting for these liabilities was not transparent in annual reports.

Records indicate that the CalPERS board was considering an additional proposed private equity investment in LJM3, an Enron-sponsored partnership proposed by Andrew Fastow, Enron's former chief financial officer. Although CalPERS had received a good return from previous partnerships with Enron, the CalPERS board declined to invest in this partnership. The Pacific Corporate Group, an investment advisor for CalPERS on private equity deals such as the LJM3 partnership, indicated that there were potential conflicts of interest for Fastow and others at Enron. A memo from Pacific indicated that the visibility and "duality" of Fastow's roles as a partner in the private partnership as well as serving as Enron's chief financial officer were of concern. Accordingly, Pacific alerted the CalPERS board to these potential difficulties.

Pacific reported further that "CalPERS should have been deeply concerned that the Enron board would approve something that could seriously endanger the company's reputation." CalPERS had in the past been known to actively lobby against a corporate governance issue such as this, and had symbolized such activism for shareholders. In this case, CalPERS seems to have put its own interest ahead of the shareholders of Enron because of the previous private partnership investments that CalPERS had pursued with Enron and some of its top-level managers. These earlier investments may have constituted a conflict of interest for CalPERS against protecting Enron shareholders. At the time, CalPERS simply declined to participate in LJM3 rather than going directly to the Enron board and seeking to correct the problem identified by Pacific. Because of this lapse in activism, CalPERS' board is now debating whether it should again be more proactive in board governance issues, as it had been in the past. It remains to be seen whether CalPERS will continue to be as effective as it once was in advocating board governance reforms. It appears that because of its private placement and involvement with Enron and its reduced emphasis on governance reforms, it is less proactive in pursuing shareholder rights and information disclosure.

In many ways, this conflict of interest and lack of action by CalPERS hurt other pension systems significantly. After CalPERS realized a $132.5 million profit on a $250 million investment in Enron's joint energy development investments (JEDI), it poured an additional $175 million into another Enron partnership called JEDI II, which has returned $171.7 million so far and actually expects to break even. However, other public pension funds that invested in Enron's stock (not in its private equity partnerships) have lost significant amounts. For instance, six of California's other public pension funds lost $250 million when the market devalued Enron's stock. Florida's state retirement system lost $325 million as a result of losses on Enron's stock.

CalPERS' profits from its investments in the JEDI partnerships came about because of opportunities created by measures such as deregulation in California's energy market. This windfall opportunity for Enron and its private placement partners that took advantage of high-priced energy also significantly increased California's debt and contributed to the bankruptcy proceedings of its largest utility. Although Enron was not responsible for deregulation and energy prices, it is responsible for its own corporate governance and strategic leadership, just as CalPERS is responsible for management of its assets. In both situations, an improved focus on corporate governance would have contributed to significantly lower losses and may have helped prevent the financial disaster associated with Enron's collapse.

SOURCES: M. Benson, 2002, Two large pension funds may adopt tougher corporate-governance policies, *The Wall Street Journal Interactive,* http://www.wsj.com, January 16; G. Colvin, 2002, The boardroom follies, *Fortune,* January 7, 32; J. Schwartz, 2002, Darth Vader. Machiavelli. Skilling set intense pace, *The New York Times,* http://www.nytimes.com, February 7; A. Felo, 2001, Ethics programs, board involvement, and potential conflicts of interest in corporate governance, *Journal of Business Ethics,* 32: 205–218; D. B. Henriques, 2002, Even a watchdog is not always fully awake, *The New York Times,* http://www.nytimes.com, February 5; 2002, California pension funds hurt by Enron downfall, *The Wall Street Journal Interactive,* http://www.wsj.com, January 29.

generally oppose their repeal. Thus, managerial ownership provides managers with power to protect their own interests.[69]

Board of Directors

Typically, shareholders monitor the managerial decisions and actions of a firm through the board of directors. Shareholders elect members to their firm's board. Those who are elected are expected to oversee managers and to ensure that the corporation is operated in ways that will maximize its shareholders' wealth. As we have described, the practices of large institutional investors have resulted in an increase in ownership concentration in U.S. firms. Nonetheless, diffuse ownership still describes the status of most U.S. firms,[70] which means that monitoring and control of managers by individual shareholders is limited in large corporations. Furthermore, large financial institutions, such as banks, are prevented from directly owning stock in firms and from having representatives on companies' boards of directors, although this is not the case in Europe and elsewhere.[71] These conditions highlight the importance of the board of directors for corporate governance. Unfortunately, over time, boards of directors have not been highly effective in monitoring and controlling top management's actions.[72] While boards of directors are imperfect, they can positively influence both managers and the companies they serve.[73]

The **board of directors** is a group of elected individuals whose primary responsibility is to act in the owners' interests by formally monitoring and controlling the corporation's top-level executives.[74] Boards have power to direct the affairs of the organization, punish and reward managers, and protect shareholders' rights and interests.[75] Thus, an appropriately structured and effective board of directors protects owners from managerial opportunism. Board members are seen as stewards of their company's resources, and the way they carry out these responsibilities affects the society in which their firm operates.[76]

Generally, board members (often called directors) are classified into one of three groups (see Table 10.2). *Insiders* are active top-level managers in the corporation who are elected to the board because they are a source of information about the firm's day-to-day operations.[77] *Related outsiders* have some relationship with the firm, contractual or otherwise, that may create questions about their independence, but these individuals are not involved with the corporation's day-to-day activities. *Outsiders*

The **board of directors** is a group of elected individuals whose primary responsibility is to act in the owners' interests by formally monitoring and controlling the corporation's top-level executives.

provide independent counsel to the firm and may hold top-level managerial positions in other companies or may have been elected to the board prior to the beginning of the current CEO's tenure.[78]

Some argue that many boards are not fulfilling their primary fiduciary duty to protect shareholders. Among other possibilities, it may be that boards are a managerial tool: they do not question managers' actions, and they readily approve managers' self-serving initiatives.[79] In general, those critical of boards as a governance mechanism believe that inside managers dominate boards and exploit their personal ties with them. A widely accepted view is that a board with a significant percentage of its membership from the firm's top executives tends to provide relatively weak monitoring and control of managerial decisions.[80]

Critics advocate reforms to ensure that independent outside directors represent a significant majority of the total membership of a board.[81] For instance, Interpublic, a global marketing communications and marketing services company, had six inside and six outside directors when it announced a change in early 2002 to a majority of outside directors—two inside and seven outside directors, with the arrival of a new outside director, Michael I. Roth, chief executive at the MONY Group. "The interests of Interpublic shareholders will be best served by a board that is primarily made up of independent, outside directors, consistent with that of other leading public companies," said John J. Dooner Jr., Interpublic's chairman and CEO.[82]

Because successful high-tech startup firms usually operate in a dynamic environment, they often have strong entrepreneurial leaders or founders who guide them through rapid changes. However, such entrepreneurs often put together weak boards of directors. By creating strong boards with independent outsiders who can help foster the entrepreneurial spirit, such "high-flying" firms can maintain their momentum and profitability if and when their founders leave. Some examples of these strong leaders are Jeff Bezos at Amazon, Stephen Case at AOL Time Warner, and Bill Gates at Microsoft.[83]

One criticism of boards has been that some have not been vigilant enough in hiring and then monitoring the behavior of CEOs. For example, Albert Dunlap, the former CEO at Sunbeam, agreed to settle a shareholder lawsuit brought against him (and other former executives) for $15 million out of his own pocket. A number of questionable acquisitions had been made by the Dunlap team, ultimately spreading the company too thin and causing Sunbeam to file for Chapter 11 bankruptcy. Although Dunlap and his colleagues claimed that they did nothing wrong, there were significant performance problems and the accounting at the company lacked transparency.[84] The Sunbeam board must share the blame in the failure for two reasons. First, it selected the CEO. Second, the board should have been actively involved in the development of the firm's strategy—if the strategy fails, the board has failed.[85]

Other issues, in addition to criticisms of their work, affect today's corporate

Table 10.2	Classifications of Boards of Directors' Members

Insiders
- The firm's CEO and other top-level managers

Related outsiders
- Individuals not involved with the firm's day-to-day operations, but who have a relationship with the company

Outsiders
- Individuals who are independent of the firm in terms of day-to-day operations and other relationships

boards. For example, there is some disagreement about the most appropriate role of outside directors in a firm's strategic decision-making process.[86] Because of external pressures, board reforms have been initiated. To date, these reforms have generally called for an increase in the number of outside directors, relative to insiders, serving on a corporation's board. For example, in 1984, the New York Stock Exchange started requiring that listed firms have board audit committees composed solely of outside directors.[87] As a result of external pressures, boards of large corporations have more outside members. Research shows that outside board members can influence the strategic direction of companies.[88] Therefore, there are potential strategic implications associated with the movement toward having corporate boards dominated by outsiders.

Alternatively, a large number of outside board members can create some issues. Outsiders do not have contact with the firm's day-to-day operations and typically do not have easy access to the level of information about managers and their skills that is required to effectively evaluate managerial decisions and initiatives. Outsiders can, however, obtain valuable information through frequent interactions with inside board members, during board meetings and otherwise. Insiders possess such information by virtue of their organizational positions. Thus, boards with a critical mass of insiders typically are better informed about intended strategic initiatives, the reasons for the initiatives, and the outcomes expected from them.[89] Without this type of information, outsider-dominated boards may emphasize the use of financial, as opposed to strategic, controls to gather performance information to evaluate managers' and business units' performances. A virtually exclusive reliance on financial evaluations shifts risk to top-level managers, who, in turn, may make decisions to maximize their interests and reduce their employment risk. Reductions in R&D investments, additional diversification of the firm, and the pursuit of greater levels of compensation are some of the results of managers' actions to achieve financial goals set by outsider dominated boards.[90]

Enhancing the Effectiveness of the Board of Directors

Because of the importance of boards of directors in corporate governance and as a result of increased scrutiny from shareholders—in particular, large institutional investors—the performances of individual board members and of entire boards are being evaluated more formally and with greater intensity.[91] Given the demand for greater accountability and improved performance, many boards have initiated voluntary changes. Among these changes are (1) increases in the diversity of the backgrounds of board members (for example, a greater number of directors from public service, academic, and scientific settings; a greater percentage of boards with ethnic minorities and women; and members from different countries on boards of U.S. firms), (2) the strengthening of internal management and accounting control systems, and (3) the establishment and consistent use of formal processes to evaluate the board's performance.[92]

Boards have become more involved in the strategic decision-making process, so they must work collaboratively. Research shows that boards working collaboratively make higher-quality strategic decisions, and they make them faster.[93] Sometimes, as the Strategic Focus on page 322 about the merger between Hewlett-Packard (HP) and Compaq illustrates, there is conflict among board members regarding the appropriate strategic direction for a company. In addition, because of the increased pressure from owners and the potential conflict, procedures are necessary to help boards function effectively in facilitating the strategic decision-making process.[94] (See also Chapter 7's Opening Case on page 213, where we consider the HP/Compaq transaction from the perspective of acquisitions and mergers.)

Hewlett-Packard Board of Directors
Versus Walter Hewlett, Board Member

The merger between Hewlett-Packard Company (HP) and Compaq Computer Corp. was the largest high-tech merger in history. Almost as noteworthy, however, was the resulting battle among board members.

While industry analysts questioned the merger because of past problems in merging two large technology and computer companies, the most significant opposition regarding the transaction came from a board member. Walter Hewlett, son of Hewlett-Packard founder William Hewlett and member of HP's board of directors, fought the merger as a representative of a group who collectively represent 18 percent of HP's ownership. At the end of 2001, he filed a preliminary proxy filing with the SEC trying to block the proposed deal.

In his proxy filing, Hewlett said that the acquisition of Compaq was overpriced and unnecessarily risky. He also stated that he had expressed similar doubts since learning of the possibility of a deal in May 2001. He argued that combining the two firms would damage the value of shareholders' investments, noting that HP's market capitalization diminished by $12.3 billion from the announcement of the deal until the day he came out in opposition; that day, shares rose 7 percent, adding $5.7 billion in value. His reason for filing the proxy was to convince other shareholders to vote against the merger.

Interestingly, Hewlett had originally voted in favor of the merger when it came before the board. Carly Fiorina, HP's CEO, speaking about Mr. Hewlett's actions, said that she was surprised, and that "there [was] a big difference between an individual managing his own personal assets and the assets of the foundation and a board member going out and actively soliciting against a board's decision." She believed that the transaction would strengthen the combined firm's sales of personal computers, servers, and technology consulting, putting the company in a stronger position to compete with market leaders IBM and Dell Computer. Among the shareholders, both sides had their strong supporters. Together with Hewlett, the other heirs of HP founders, as mentioned, control 18 percent of the company's stock through foundations and came out in opposition to the merger. Board members in favor of the merger noted that the internal rate of return following the 1998 merger of DEC and Compaq was a very high 29 percent. These board members believed that this fact swayed some shareholders to their side in the shareholder vote.

The battle between the board members was fought quite publicly. Each side ran full-page newspaper ads addressed to each other and to shareholders, and both established websites to further their reach (http://www.votethehpway.com for the corporation and http://www.votenohpcompaq.com for the opposition). Following the vote on March 19, 2002, Walter Hewlett filed suit against the apparent passage of the merger, citing shareholders were allowed to change their votes and to vote twice, and records of two large institutional shareholders—Deutschebank and Northern Trust—were being investigated. However, even if these votes were thrown out, there were enough votes for the merger to pass because of a 3 percent margin of victory. With the transaction approved, the challenge for the newly created firm's board of directors is to make decisions that will maximize shareholders' wealth.

SOURCES: M. Kane, 2002, Government examining HP vote, http://www.cnet.com, April 15; S. Lohr, 2002, Hewlett's chief says count confirms victory, *The New York Times,* http://www.nytimes.com, April 18; S. Lohr, 2002, 2 computer giants hope to avoid pitfalls of past mergers, *The New York Times,* http://www.nytimes.com, January 1; S. Thurm, 2002, A lion's capital throws its support behind HP proposal to buy Compaq, *The Wall Street Journal Interactive,* http://www.wsj.com, January 21; P. Burrows & K. Rebello, 2001, Q&A: Fiorina: The deal is "the right thing for shareholders," *Business Week Online,* http://businessweek.com, December 24; C. Gaither, 2001, Hewlett heir in new action against merger, *The New York Times,* http://nytimes.com, December 28; S. Lohr, 2001, Hewlett chief battles for her deal and her career, *The New York Times,* http://nytimes.com, December 10; A. Park, 2001, Can Compaq survive as a solo act?, *Business Week Online,* http://businessweek.com, December 24; R. Sidel & M. Williams, 2001, Hewlett's opposition to Compaq deal is strong statement for board member, *The Wall Street Journal Interactive,* http://wsj.com, December 31; M. Williams, 2001, Walter Hewlett files SEC proxy materials urging deal's rejection, defending stance, *The Wall Street Journal Interactive,* http://wsj.com, December 28.

Besides being increasingly involved in important strategic decisions such as the HP/Compaq combination, boards also are becoming more active in expressing their view about CEO succession, as opposed to readily supporting the incumbent's choice. In general, however, boards have relied on precedence (past decisions) for guidance in the selection process. Also, they are most likely to consider inside candidates before looking for outside candidates.[95] Outside directors have the power to facilitate the firm's transition to a new CEO. When an internal heir apparent CEO candidate is associated with a high performing firm, outside directors are likely to help the heir apparent make the transition. However, if firm performance is problematic, outside directors are less likely to support the chosen successor and are often skeptical of someone chosen to follow in the footsteps of the former CEO.[96]

Increasingly, outside directors are being required to own significant equity stakes as a prerequisite to holding a board seat. In fact, some research suggests that firms perform better if outside directors have such a stake.[97] Another study suggests that the performance of inside directors also improves if they hold an equity position. Therefore, an inside director's knowledge of the firm can be used appropriately. Finally, an inside director's relationship to the CEO does not necessarily lead to entrenchment of that CEO if the inside director has a strong ownership position.[98] One activist concludes that boards need three foundational characteristics to be effective: director stock ownership, executive meetings to discuss important strategic issues, and a serious nominating committee that truly controls the nomination process to strongly influence the selection of new board members.[99]

Executive Compensation

As the Opening Case illustrates, the compensation of top-level managers, and especially of CEOs, generates a great deal of interest and strongly held opinions. One reason for this widespread interest can be traced to a natural curiosity about extremes and excesses. Another stems from a more substantive view, that CEO pay is tied in an indirect but very tangible way to the fundamental governance processes in large corporations: Who has power? What are the bases of power? How and when do owners and managers exert their relative preferences? How vigilant are boards? Who is taking advantage of whom?[100]

Executive compensation is a governance mechanism that seeks to align the interests of managers and owners through salaries, bonuses, and long-term incentive compensation, such as stock options.[101] Stock options are a mechanism used to link executives' performance to the performance of their company's stock.[102] Increasingly, long-term incentive plans are becoming a critical part of compensation packages in U.S. firms. The use of longer-term pay helps firms cope with or avoid potential agency problems.[103] Because of this, the stock market generally reacts positively to the introduction of a long-range incentive plan for top executives.[104]

Sometimes the use of a long-term incentive plan prevents major stockholders (e.g., institutional investors) from pressing for changes in the composition of the board of directors, because they assume that the long-term incentives will ensure that top executives will act in shareholders' best interests. Alternatively, stockholders largely assume that top-executive pay and the performance of a firm are more closely aligned when firms have boards that are dominated by outside members.[105]

Effectively using executive compensation as a governance mechanism is particularly challenging to firms implementing international strategies. For example, the interests of owners of multinational corporations may be best served when there is less uniformity among the firm's foreign subsidiaries' compensation plans.[106] Developing an array of unique compensation plans requires additional monitoring and increases the firm's agency costs. Importantly, levels of pay vary by regions of the world. For example, managers receive the highest compensation in the United States,

Executive compensation is a governance mechanism that seeks to align the interests of managers and owners through salaries, bonuses, and long-term incentive compensation, such as stock options.

while managerial pay is much lower in Asia. Compensation is lower in India partly because many of the largest firms have strong family ownership and control.[107] As corporations acquire firms in other countries, the managerial compensation puzzle becomes more complex and may cause additional executive turnover.[108] For instance, when Daimler-Benz acquired Chrysler, the top executives of Chrysler made substantially more than the executives at Daimler-Benz—but the Chrysler executives ended up reporting to the Daimler executives.[109]

A Complicated Governance Mechanism

For several reasons, executive compensation—especially long-term incentive compensation—is complicated. First, the strategic decisions made by top-level managers are typically complex and nonroutine, so direct supervision of executives is inappropriate for judging the quality of their decisions. The result is a tendency to link the compensation of top-level managers to measurable outcomes, such as the firm's financial performance. Second, an executive's decision often affects a firm's financial outcomes over an extended period, making it difficult to assess the effect of current decisions on the corporation's performance. In fact, strategic decisions are more likely to have long-term, rather than short-term, effects on a company's strategic outcomes. Third, a number of other factors affect a firm's performance besides top-level managerial decisions and behavior. Unpredictable economic, social, or legal changes (see Chapter 2) make it difficult to discern the effects of strategic decisions. Thus, although performance-based compensation may provide incentives to top management teams to make decisions that best serve shareholders' interests,[110] such compensation plans alone are imperfect in their ability to monitor and control managers.[111] Still, annual bonuses as incentive compensation represent a significant portion of many executives' total pay. For example, annual bonuses compose an average of about 60 percent of the CEO's total compensation in the United States, about 45 percent in the United Kingdom, approximately 30 percent in Canada, while only 19 percent in France.[112]

Although incentive compensation plans may increase the value of a firm in line with shareholder expectations, such plans are subject to managerial manipulation. For instance, annual bonuses may provide incentives to pursue short-run objectives at the expense of the firm's long-term interests. Supporting this conclusion, some research has found that bonuses based on annual performance were negatively related to investments in R&D when the firm was highly diversified, which may affect the firm's long-term strategic competitiveness.[113] In high tech firms, where uncertainty is higher, short-term (salary and bonus) compensation was related to innovation, but no such relationship was found in low tech firms. However, no relationship between innovation and long-term compensation was found among either high tech or low tech firms.[114]

Although long-term performance-based incentives may reduce the temptation to under invest in the short run, they increase executive exposure to risks associated with uncontrollable events, such as market fluctuations and industry decline. The longer the focus of incentive compensation, the greater are the long-term risks borne by top-level managers. Also, because long-term incentives tie a manager's overall wealth to the firm in a way that is inflexible, such incentives and ownership may not be valued as highly by a manager as by outside investors who have the opportunity to diversify their wealth in a number of other financial investments.[115] Thus, firms may have to overcompensate managers using long-term incentives, especially stock options, as the next section suggests.

The Effectiveness of Executive Compensation

The compensation recently received by some top-level managers, especially CEOs, has angered many stakeholders, including shareholders. Table 10.3 lists the compensation received by the highest-paid U.S. CEOs in the 1990s, and Table 10.4 shows the

Table 10.3 | Highest-Paid U.S. CEOs, 1990–2000

Year	CEO, *Company*	Compensation (in $millions)
1990	Steven Ross, *Time Warner*	$75
1991	Roberto Goizueta, *Coca-Cola*	$61
1992	Alan Greenberg, *Bear Stearns*	$16
1993	George Fisher, *Eastman Kodak*	$29
1994	Lawrence Bossidy, *AlliedSignal*	$34
1995	Lawrence Coss, *Green Tree Financial*	$66
1996	Michael Eisner, *Walt Disney*	$194
1997	Henry Silverman, *Cendant*	$194
1998	Michael Dell,* *Dell Computer*	$94
1999	Charles Wang, *Computer Associates*	$507
2000	Steven Jobs, *Apple Computer*	$381

Note: "Compensation" includes salary, bonuses, restricted stock granted (regardless of when it vests), long-term payouts, "other" compensation, and an estimate of the present value of options grants.
*Though reported in fiscal year 1999, Dell's options were granted in March and July 1998.
SOURCE: From "The Great CEO Pay Heist" by G. Covin in *Fortune*, June 25, 2001, pp. 66–67. Copyright © 2001 Time Inc. All rights reserved. Reprinted by permission.

largest value of stock options for CEOs for the same time period. As the tables show, in 2000, Steven Jobs, CEO of Apple Computer, had both the highest total compensation and value of stock options granted at $381 and $872 million, respectively.[116]

As Tables 10.3 and 10.4 indicate, stock and stock options are the primary component of large compensation packages. In fact, the average amount of the stock held by top executives and directors of firms reached 21 percent in the 1990s. This trend

Table 10.4 | Largest Options Grants, 1990–2000

Year	CEO, *Company*	Grants (in $millions)
1990	Steven Ross, *Time Warner*	$215
1991	Leon Hirsch, *U.S. Surgical*	$170
1992	Roy Vagelos, *Merck*	$35
1993	George Fisher, *Eastman Kodak*	$67
1994	Lawrence Bossidy, *AlliedSignal*	$63
1995	Millard Drexler, *Gap*	$79
1996	Michael Eisner, *Walt Disney*	$506
1997	Henry Silverman, *Cendant*	$570
1998	Michael Dell,* *Dell Computer*	$272
1999	Joseph Nacchio, *Qwest Communications*	$257
2000	Steven Jobs, *Apple Computer*	$872

Note: These figures reflect the face value of the options at the time they were granted—that is, the then-current price of the stock multiplied by the number of shares optioned. Options, of course, don't automatically deliver wealth. For that to happen, the stock must increase in value.
*Though reported in fiscal year 1999, Dell's options were granted in March and July 1998.
SOURCE: From "The Great CEO Pay Heist" by G. Covin in *Fortune*, June 25, 2001, pp. 66–67. Copyright © 2001 Time Inc. All rights reserved. Reprinted by permission.

Apple CEO Steve Jobs, who cofounded Apple in 1976 and returned to the firm in 1997. His business philosophy is, "It's not about the money. It's about the people you have, how you're led and how much you get it." It may also be about the options he holds, which have an estimated value of up to $1.4 billion, and the $9 million Gulfstream jet he received as his 1999 bonus.

has continued into the 21st century, partly because of the long-term incentive plans that compensate executives in stock options and stock.[117]

The primary reasons for compensating executives in stock is that the practice affords them with an incentive to keep the stock price high and hence aligns managers' interests with shareholders' interests. However, there may be some unintended consequences. Managers who own greater than 1 percent of their firm's stock may be less likely to be forced out of their jobs, even when the firm is performing poorly.[118] Furthermore, a review of the research suggests "that firm size accounts for more than 40 percent of the variance in total CEO pay, while firm performance accounts for less than 5 percent of the variance."[119] Thus, the effectiveness of pay plans as a governance mechanism is suspect.

Another way that boards may compensate executives is through loans with favorable, or no, interest for the purpose of buying company stock. If appropriately used, this practice can be a governance tool, since it aligns executives' priorities with the shareholders in that the executives hold stock, not just options on the stock. They gain or lose money along with the shareholders. "When people exercise most stock options, they pay the regular income-tax rate—close to 40 percent for executives—on the difference between the option's exercise price and the share price at that time. But if executives buy shares with borrowed money instead of receiving options, the government considers their profit to be an investment gain, not a part of their salary, and they pay only the capital-gains tax of 20 percent or less."[120]

Despite the positive benefits of providing loans for buying stock, it can also be devastating if the value of the stock falls. For example, in 1998, Comdisco lent 106 executives an average of $1 million to buy company stock; the price of the stock at that time was $20 a share. At the beginning of 2002, the stock traded at about 50 cents per share and $104 million of the original $109 million in loans is still outstanding. A loan to buy stock seems effective only when the upside is considered. But when stocks fall, and thus the executive's ability to pay back the loan decreases, companies can be seriously affected.[121]

To foster improved performances from their companies during the recessionary year 2001, many boards granted more stock options to executives than they had in the past. This trend of increasing stock options to compensate managers after a bad year seems to run counter to the concept of pay for performance. For example, Larry Ellison, CEO of Oracle, cashed in options for 23 million shares of stock worth $700 million in January 2001. To make good on these options and provide Ellison with 23 million shares, Oracle must issue that many new shares of stock, repurchase that amount from investors, or do a mixture of the two. No matter which approach Oracle takes, shareholder value or available cash decreases (this phenomenon is often called shareholder dilution).

While some stock option-based compensation plans are well designed with option strike prices substantially higher than current stock prices, too many have been designed simply to give executives more wealth that will not immediately show up on the balance sheet.[122] Research of stock option repricing where the strike price value of the option has been changed to lower than it was originally set suggests that step is taken more frequently in high risk situations. However, it also happens when firm performance was poor to restore the incentive effect for the option. But evidence also suggests that politics are often involved.[123] Again, this evidence shows that no internal governance mechanism is perfect.

Market for Corporate Control

The **market for corporate control** is an external governance mechanism that becomes active when a firm's internal controls fail.

The **market for corporate control** is an external governance mechanism that becomes active when a firm's internal controls fail.[124] The market for corporate control is composed of individuals and firms that buy ownership positions in or take over potentially undervalued corporations so they can form new divisions in established diversified companies or merge two previously separate firms. Because the undervalued firm's executives are assumed to be the party responsible for formulating and implementing the strategy that led to poor performance, that team is usually replaced. For instance, HP has performed better than Compaq recently, and the merger between the two firms described in the Strategic Focus on page 322 may turn out to be controlled by HP. Thus, when the market for corporate control operates effectively, it ensures that managers who are ineffective or act opportunistically are disciplined.[125]

The market for corporate control governance mechanism should be triggered by a firm's poor performance relative to industry competitors. A firm's poor performance, often demonstrated by the firm's earning below-average returns, is an indicator that internal governance mechanisms have failed; that is, their use did not result in managerial decisions that maximized shareholder value. This market has been active for some time. As noted in Chapter 7, the 1980s were known as a time of merger mania, with almost 55,000 acquisitions valued at approximately $1.3 trillion. However, there were many more acquisitions in the 1990s, and the value of mergers and acquisitions in that decade was more than $10 trillion.[126]

During the economic downturn of 2001–2002, unsolicited takeover bids increased. In a recession, poorly managed firms are more easily identified.[127] In a few cases, unsolicited offers may come from familiar parties. Ford made an offer to buy back at $30 per share the Hertz stock it sold to the public at $24 per share a few years ago. The stock had reached $64 per share but then fell drastically. Even though it sold a substantial amount of stock, Ford retained significant ownership control. Critics think that Ford has taken advantage of Hertz investors by offering only $30 when they felt it was worth at least $40 per share at the time. The directors of Hertz, who owned only 6,000 shares, did not have much control over whether to sell or keep the stock. In this case, minority stakeholders had little or no say in decision making because of Ford's strong ownership position.[128]

Managerial Defense Tactics

Hostile takeovers are the major activity in the market for corporate control governance mechanism. Not all hostile takeovers are prompted by poorly performing targets, and firms targeted for hostile takeovers may use multiple defense tactics to fend off the takeover attempt. Historically, the increased use of the market for corporate control has enhanced the sophistication and variety of managerial defense tactics that are used to reduce the influence of this governance mechanism. The market for corporate control tends to increase risk for managers. As a result, managerial pay is often augmented indirectly through golden parachutes (wherein a CEO can receive up to three years' salary if his or her firm is taken over).

Among other outcomes, takeover defenses increase the costs of mounting a takeover, causing the incumbent management to become entrenched, while reducing the chances of introducing a new management team.[129] Some defense tactics require asset restructuring created by divesting one or more divisions in the diversified firm's portfolio. Others necessitate only changes in the financial structure of the firm, such as repurchasing shares of the firm's outstanding stock.[130] Some tactics (e.g., reincorporation of the firm in another state) require shareholder approval, but the greenmail tactic, wherein money is used to repurchase stock from a corporate raider to avoid the takeover of the firm, does not. These defense tactics are controversial, and the research on their effects is inconclusive. Alternatively, most institutional investors oppose the use of defense tactics. TIAA-CREF and CalPERS have taken actions to have several firms' poison pills eliminated.[131]

As an example, when Alltel Corp. decided to try to take over CenturyTel Inc., a smaller competitor in the telecommunications industry, CenturyTel rejected Alltel's offer to purchase the company despite the large premium Alltel was willing to pay. For Alltel to succeed in a hostile takeover bid, it would have had to overcome many defenses. For example, CenturyTel staggered its board elections—new board members are elected on a staggered schedule, meaning a bid to take control of the board of directors could take years. In addition, company bylaws required a supermajority of shares to support a takeover bid. The company also had arranged to provide significant voting power to long-term shareholders and employees, who are expected to be more loyal to a company. Finally, CenturyTel also boasted a poison pill: as soon as a company or investor gained control of more than 15 percent of the stock, the board would automatically reject a merger. Because the board would have rejected a merger, Alltel would then need to have a shareholder vote taken and would have needed to receive 80 percent support to be successful. Thus, the bid by Alltel was not successful.[132]

A potential problem with the market for corporate control is that it may not be totally efficient. A study of several of the most active corporate raiders in the 1980s showed that approximately 50 percent of their takeover attempts targeted firms with above-average performance in their industry—corporations that were neither undervalued nor poorly managed.[133] The targeting of high-performance businesses may lead to acquisitions at premium prices and to decisions by managers of the targeted firm to establish what may prove to be costly takeover defense tactics to protect their corporate positions.[134]

Although the market for corporate control lacks the precision of internal governance mechanisms, the fear of acquisition and influence by corporate raiders is an effective constraint on the managerial-growth motive.[135] The market for corporate control has been responsible for significant changes in many firms' strategies and, when used appropriately, has served shareholders' interests.[136] But this market and other means of corporate governance vary by region of the world and by country. Accordingly, we next address the topic of international corporate governance.

International Corporate Governance

Understanding the corporate governance structure of the United Kingdom and the United States is inadequate for a multinational firm in today's global economy.[137] The governance of German and Japanese corporations, and corporations in other countries, illustrate that the nature of corporate governance throughout the world has been affected by the realities of the global economy and its competitive challenges.[138] While the stability associated with German and Japanese governance structures has historically been viewed as an asset, some believe that it may now be a burden.[139] And the governance in Germany and Japan is changing, just as it is changing in other parts of the world.

For example, shareholder activism is increasing in South Korea. Small shareholders won a lawsuit against the heads of Samsung Group, the parent company of Samsung Electronics. The suit alleged that the company was misusing funds; profits from the successful businesses in the corporation were diverted to poorly performing sister companies so as to make them appear to be more successful than they were. Although the $7 million that ten company officers must pay back to the company does not greatly reduce their personal worth, the ruling is a large victory for small shareholders in this Southeast Asian country.[140]

Corporate Governance in Germany

In many private German firms, the owner and manager may still be the same individual. In these instances, there is no agency problem.[141] Even in publicly traded German corporations, there is often a dominant shareholder. Thus, the concentration of ownership is an important means of corporate governance in Germany, as it is in the United States.[142]

Historically, banks have been at the center of the German corporate governance structure, as is also the case in many other European countries, such as Italy and France. As lenders, banks become major shareholders when companies they financed earlier seek funding on the stock market or default on loans. Although the stakes are usually under 10 percent, the only legal limit on how much of a firm's stock banks can hold is that a single ownership position cannot exceed 15 percent of the bank's capital. Through their shareholdings, and by casting proxy votes for individual shareholders who retain their shares with the banks, three banks in particular—Deutsche, Dresdner, and Commerzbank—exercise significant power. Although shareholders can tell the banks how to vote their ownership position, they generally do not do so. A combination of their own holdings and their proxies results in majority positions for these three banks in many German companies. Those banks, along with others, monitor and control managers, both as lenders and as shareholders, by electing representatives to supervisory boards.

German firms with more than 2,000 employees are required to have a two-tiered board structure. Through this structure, the supervision of management is separated from other duties normally assigned to a board of directors, especially the nomination of new board members. Germany's two-tiered system places the responsibility for monitoring and controlling managerial (or supervisory) decisions and actions in the hands of a separate group.[143] While all the functions of direction and management are the responsibility of the management board (the Vorstand), appointment to the Vorstand is the responsibility of the supervisory tier (the Aufsichtsrat). Employees, union members, and shareholders appoint members to the Aufsichtsrat.

Because of the role of local government (through the board structure) and the power of banks in Germany's corporate governance structure, private shareholders rarely have major ownership positions in German firms. Large institutional investors, such as pension funds and insurance companies, are also relatively insignificant owners of corporate stock. Thus, at least historically, German executives generally have not been dedicated to the maximization of shareholder value that is occurring in many countries.

Volkswagen (VW) made an amazing turnaround in the latter half of the 1990s. The company became much more profitable than it had been, and it appeared to be headed to new heights. Despite these promising signs, many investors had uneasy feelings about VW. The company would not release financial data including operating profits that investors wanted to examine. Plus, it was difficult to learn how VW calculates earnings. Some people wondered whether the earnings were real or "pumped-up." As a result, VW's stock price has changed little since the spring of 1997. In 2001, VW's market capitalization was less than Bayerische Motoren Werke's (BMW's), another German carmaker, in spite of the fact that VW generated twice as much revenue as BMW.

Investors suspected that VW management cared little for profit margins. This might be because the largest stakeholder in VW was the government of Lower Saxony, in which five of VW's seven German factories are located. These five factories are among the least productive in Europe. "The government of Lower Saxony . . . worries more about jobs than shareholder value."[144] Thus, the stock price of Volkswagen should have been higher, but problems with productivity (because of government ownership of stock) and investor trust kept it low.

Corporate governance in Germany is changing, at least partially, because of the increasing globalization of business. Many German firms are beginning to gravitate toward the U.S. system. For example, German drug maker Bayer experienced a 40 percent decline in its stock price on the Frankfurt Exchange throughout 2001. While some of this decline can be attributed to the failure of Baycol, a cholesterol-lowering drug that was implicated in 52 deaths, much can be ascribed to investor discontent with the company's strategy. Activist shareholders have tried to convince management to sell off under-performing parts of the company and focus on the lucrative pharmaceutical business. One London analyst indicated, "This is a classic case of a company that should be broken up to get some value out of it, but management clearly doesn't agree."[145] However, it will be difficult for Bayer not to refocus because it is listed on the New York Stock Exchange and will feel continued pressure to sell off under-performing divisions.

Timothy Collins (right), in 1995 founded Ripplewood Holdings LLC, named after his grandfather's Kentucky tobacco farm. In March 2000 his New-York based private equity company became the first overseas investor to buy a Japanese bank (the Long Term Credit Bank (LTCB), which it relaunched as Shinsei with Masamoto Yashiro (left) serving as its president). Ripplewood also bought the biggest share of 93-year-old Japanese music company Nippon Columbia Co. and purchased Seagaia, Japan's sprawling golf-and-beach resort.

Corporate Governance in Japan

Attitudes toward corporate governance in Japan are affected by the concepts of obligation, family, and consensus.[146] In Japan, an obligation "may be to return a service for one rendered or it may derive from a more general relationship, for example, to one's family or old alumni, or one's company (or Ministry), or the country. This sense of particular obligation is common elsewhere but it feels stronger in Japan."[147] As part of a company family, individuals are members of a unit that envelops their lives; families command the attention and allegiance of parties throughout corporations. Moreover, a *keiretsu* (a group of firms tied together by cross-shareholdings) is more than an economic concept; it, too, is a family. Consensus, an important influence in Japanese corporate governance, calls for the expenditure of significant amounts of energy to win the hearts and minds of people whenever possible, as opposed to issuing edicts from top executives. Consensus is highly valued, even when it results in a slow and cumbersome decision-making process.

As in Germany, banks in Japan play an important role in financing and monitoring large public firms. The bank owning the largest share of stocks and the largest amount of debt—the main bank—has the closest relationship with the company's top executives. The main bank provides financial advice to the firm and also closely monitors managers. Thus, Japan has a bank-based financial and corporate governance structure, whereas the United States has a market-based financial and governance structure.

Aside from lending money, a Japanese bank can hold up to 5 percent of a firm's total stock; a group of related financial institutions can hold up to 40 percent. In many cases, main-bank relationships are part of a horizontal keiretsu. A keiretsu firm usually owns less than 2 percent of any other member firm; however, each company typically has a stake of that size in every firm in the keiretsu. As a result, somewhere between 30 and 90 percent of a firm is owned by other members of the keiretsu. Thus, a keiretsu is a system of relationship investments.

As is the case in Germany, Japan's structure of corporate governance is changing. For example, because of their continuing development as economic organizations, the role of banks in the monitoring and control of managerial behavior and firm outcomes is less significant than in the past.[148] The Asian economic crisis in the latter part of the 1990s made the governance problems in Japanese corporations apparent. The problems were readily evidenced in the large and once-powerful Mitsubishi keiretsu. Many of its core members lost substantial amounts of money in the late 1990s.[149]

Still another change in Japan's governance system has occurred in the market for corporate control, which was nonexistent in past years. Japan experienced three recessions in the 1990s and is facing another one at the start of the 21st century. Many managers are unwilling to make the changes necessary to turn their companies around. As a result, many firms in Japan are performing poorly, but could, under the right guidance, improve their performance. Timothy Collins, CEO of Ripplewood Holdings LLC, is acquiring companies that he feels are greatly undervalued, which is a risky move in Japan. Among his takeovers is Shinsei Bank Ltd., formerly Long Term Credit Bank, which was one of the financiers of Japan's post-World War II recovery. This takeover has been good for the bank, which recorded a profit for the year ending March 31, 2001 of $730 million, the company's first profit in over three years.[150]

Global Corporate Governance

The 21st-century competitive landscape is fostering the creation of a relatively uniform governance structure that will be used by firms throughout the world.[151] As markets become more global and customer demands more similar, shareholders are becoming the focus of managers' efforts in an increasing number of companies. Investors are becoming more and more active throughout the world.

Changes in governance are evident in many countries and are moving the governance models closer to that of the United States. For example, in France, very little information about top executives' compensation has traditionally been provided. However, this practice has come under pressure with increasing foreign investment in French companies.[152] One report recommended that the positions of CEO and chairman of the board be held by different individuals; it also recommended reducing the tenure of board members and disclosing their pay.[153] In South Korea, changes went much further: Principles of corporate governance were adopted that "provide proper incentives for the board and management to pursue objectives that are in the interests of the company and the shareholders and facilitate effective monitoring, thereby encouraging firms to use resources more efficiently."[154]

Even in transitional economies, such as those of China and Russia, changes in corporate governance are occurring.[155] However, changes are implemented much slower in these economies. Chinese firms have found it helpful to use stock-based compensation plans, thereby providing an incentive for foreign companies to invest in China.[156] Because Russia has reduced controls on the economy and on business activity much faster than China has, the country needs more effective governance systems to control its managerial activities. In fact, research suggests that ownership concentration leads to lower performance in Russia, primarily because minority shareholder rights are not well protected through adequate governance controls.[157]

Governance Mechanisms and Ethical Behavior

The governance mechanisms described in this chapter are designed to ensure that the agents of the firm's owners—the corporation's top executives—make strategic decisions that best serve the interests of the entire group of stakeholders, as described in Chapter

The Enron Disaster:
The Importance of Ethics in Governance

Enron, the large energy-trading firm, headquartered in Houston, filed for bankruptcy in late 2001. Huge losses were suffered not only by Enron's shareholders, employees, and managers, but also by other stakeholders in the energy industry. These losses were the result of a disaster created by the poor ethics of Enron's top executives and its board of directors. Not only were Enron and other energy firms affected, but the entire accounting and auditing industry was also tarnished by the misconduct of Enron's auditor Arthur Andersen and Enron executives. Beyond Andersen and Enron, any firm that has less transparent accounting practices has been called into question. The magnitude of this disaster and its effect on the U.S. economy were underscored by President Bush in his 2002 State of the Union address when he indicated that accounting reform would be on the national agenda.

Enron's problems started with its decisions to create off balance sheet partnerships or private equity placement with pension funds, such as those mentioned in an earlier Strategic Focus about CalPERS. Andrew Fastow, Enron's former chief financial officer, formed a number of these private placements, enriching him and other Enron employees through these partnership deals. The problem was that many of these partnerships were underwritten by Enron stock and thus were potential liabilities for Enron shareholders.

Enron's board of directors should have ensured that private partnerships such as these were not approved because they represented a conflict of

Kenneth Lay, former Enron CEO, was called before Congress in February 2002, but invoked his Fifth Amendment rights and did not testify. Although his wife proclaimed tearfully that "Everything we had was mostly in Enron stock. . . . We are struggling for liquidity," Lay had sold 18 million shares of Enron for $101 million between October 1998 and November 2001.

1. In the United States, shareholders are recognized as a company's most significant stakeholder. Thus, governance mechanisms focus on the control of managerial decisions to ensure that shareholders' interests will be served, but product market stakeholders (e.g., customers, suppliers, and host communities) and organizational stakeholders (e.g., managerial and nonmanagerial employees) are important as well.[158] Therefore, at least the minimal interests or needs of all stakeholders must be satisfied through the firm's actions. Otherwise, dissatisfied stakeholders will withdraw their support from one firm and provide it to another (for example, customers will purchase products from a supplier offering an acceptable substitute).

The firm's strategic competitiveness is enhanced when its governance mechanisms take into consideration the interests of all stakeholders. Although the idea is subject to debate, some believe that ethically responsible companies design and use governance mechanisms that serve all stakeholders' interests. There is, however, a more critical relationship between ethical behavior and corporate governance mechanisms. The Strategic Focus on the Enron disaster illustrates the devastating effect of poor ethical behavior not only on a firm's stakeholders, but also on other firms.

interest for Fastow and other key executives. Even if Enron had a reason to pursue private placement of equity investments, the transactions and their effects for shareholders should have been transparent in accounting reports. Because they were not transparent, Enron's auditor, Arthur Andersen, shared Enron's culpability by its approval of the financial reports Enron provided to the public. An Andersen partner was fired and later prosecuted for authorizing the destruction of thousands of e-mails and paper documents related to its auditing of Enron's finances—after learning that federal regulators were probing Enron's finances and accounting practices. Thus, both Enron and Andersen employees contributed to Enron's ethical failure.

As a result of this disaster, regulatory procedures regarding financial reporting will be strengthened and enforced. Auditing firms will also tighten their reporting requirements. Another outcome will be the further separation between consulting and auditing. Even though Arthur Andersen's consulting business had broken from the firm and renamed itself Accenture as an independent firm in a highly publicized action several years earlier, Andersen continued to offer non-auditing consulting services to its clients. As such, in addition to serving as Enron's auditor, Andersen also had a significant consulting relationship with Enron—and a contributing conflict of interest with the firm. Andersen may not survive as an independent company due to this crisis.

Because ethical governance had not been implemented by Enron or by Andersen, the resulting financial disaster devastated not only Enron's stakeholders and those closely associated with them, but, by implication, many other firms—even those only remotely associated with Enron.

SOURCES: N. Byrnes, 2002, Paying for the sins of Enron, *Business Week*, February 11, 35; 2002, A chronology of Enron's recent woes, *The Wall Street Journal Interactive*, http://www.wsj.com, February 5; G. Colvin, 2002, You're on your own, *Fortune*, February 4, 42; 2002, Enron and stock market jitters; The good Lay, *The Economist*, February 2, 70; J. D. Glater, 2002, Lone ranger of auditors fellow slowly out of the saddle, *The New York Times*, http://www.nytimes.com, April 20; D. B. Henriques, 2002, Even a watchdog is not always fully awake, *The New York Times*, http://www.nytimes.com, February 5; S. Lubov & E. McDonald, 2002, *Forbes*, February 18, 56–57; A. Barrionuevo, 2001, Williams Cos. seeks stronger balance sheet among jitters concerning energy traders, *The Wall Street Journal*, December 20, B2; A. J. Felo, 2001, Ethics programs board involvement and potential conflicts of interest in corporate governance, *Journal of Business Ethics*, 32: 205–218; G. Morgenson, 2001, After Enron's failure should Calpine investors worry? *The New York Times* http://www.nytimes.com, December 9.

As the Strategic Focus about Enron demonstrates, all corporate owners are vulnerable to unethical behaviors by their employees, including top-level managers—the agents who have been hired to make decisions that are in shareholders' best interests. The decisions and actions of a corporation's board of directors can be an effective deterrent to these behaviors. In fact, some believe that the most effective boards participate actively to set boundaries for their firms' business ethics and values.[159] Once formulated, the board's expectations related to ethical decisions and actions of all of the firm's stakeholders must be clearly communicated to its top-level managers. Moreover, as shareholders' agents, these managers must understand that the board will hold them fully accountable for the development and support of an organizational culture that results in ethical decisions and behaviors. As explained in Chapter 12, CEOs can be positive role models for ethical behavior.

Only when the proper corporate governance is exercised can strategies be formulated and implemented that will help the firm achieve strategic competitiveness and earn above-average returns. As the discussion in this chapter suggests, corporate governance mechanisms are a vital, yet imperfect, part of firms' efforts to select and successfully use strategies.

- Corporate governance is a relationship among stakeholders that is used to determine a firm's direction and control its performance. How firms monitor and control top-level managers' decisions and actions affects the implementation of strategies. Effective governance that aligns managers' decisions with shareholders' interests can be a competitive advantage.

- There are three internal governance mechanisms in the modern corporation—ownership concentration, the board of directors, and executive compensation. The market for corporate control is the single external governance mechanism influencing managers' decisions and the outcomes resulting from them.

- Ownership is separated from control in the modern corporation. Owners (principals) hire managers (agents) to make decisions that maximize the firm's value. As risk-bearing specialists, owners diversify their risk by investing in multiple corporations with different risk profiles. As decision-making specialists, owners expect their agents (the firm's top-level managers) to make decisions that will lead to maximization of the value of their firm. Thus, modern corporations are characterized by an agency relationship that is created when one party (the firm's owners) hires and pays another party (top-level managers) to use its decision-making skills.

- Separation of ownership and control creates an agency problem when an agent pursues goals that conflict with principals' goals. Principals establish and use governance mechanisms to control this problem.

- Ownership concentration is based on the number of large-block shareholders and the percentage of shares they own. With significant ownership percentages, such as those held by large mutual funds and pension funds, institutional investors often are able to influence top executives' strategic decisions and actions. Thus, unlike diffuse ownership, which tends to result in relatively weak monitoring and control of managerial decisions, concentrated ownership produces more active and effective monitoring. An increasingly powerful force in corporate America, institutional investors actively use their positions of concentrated ownership to force managers and boards of directors to make decisions that maximize a firm's value.

- In the United States and the United Kingdom, a firm's board of directors, composed of insiders, related outsiders, and outsiders, is a governance mechanism that shareholders expect to represent their collective interests. The percentage of outside directors on many boards now exceeds the percentage of inside directors. Outsiders are expected to be more independent of a firm's top-level managers compared to those selected from inside the firm.

- Executive compensation is a highly visible and often criticized governance mechanism. Salary, bonuses, and long-term incentives are used to strengthen the alignment between managers' and shareholders' interests. A firm's board of directors is responsible for determining the effectiveness of the firm's executive compensation system. An effective system elicits managerial decisions that are in shareholders' best interests.

- In general, evidence suggests that shareholders and boards of directors have become more vigilant in their control of managerial decisions. Nonetheless, these mechanisms are insufficient to govern managerial behavior in many large companies. Therefore, the market for corporate control is an important governance mechanism. Although it, too, is imperfect, the market for corporate control has been effective in causing corporations to combat inefficient diversification and to implement more effective strategic decisions.

- Corporate governance structures used in Germany and Japan differ from each other and from that used in the United States. Historically, the U.S. governance structure has focused on maximizing shareholder value. In Germany, employees, as a stakeholder group, have a more prominent role in governance. By contrast, until recently, Japanese shareholders played virtually no role in the monitoring and control of top-level managers. However, all of these systems are becoming increasingly similar, as are many governance systems in both developed countries, such as France and Italy, and transitional economies, such as Russia and China.

- Effective governance mechanisms ensure that the interests of all stakeholders are served. Thus, long-term strategic success results when firms are governed in ways that permit at least minimal satisfaction of capital market stakeholders (e.g., shareholders), product market stakeholders (e.g., customers and suppliers), and organizational stakeholders (managerial and nonmanagerial employees, see Chapter 2). Moreover, effective governance produces ethical behavior in the formulation and implementation of strategies.

1. What is corporate governance? What factors account for the considerable amount of attention corporate governance receives from several parties, including shareholder activists, business press writers, and academic scholars? Why is governance necessary to control managers' decisions?

2. What does it mean to say that ownership is separated from control in the modern corporation? Why does this separation exist?

3. What is an agency relationship? What is managerial opportunism? What assumptions do owners of modern corporations make about managers as agents?

4. How is each of the three internal governance mechanisms—ownership concentration, boards of directors, and executive compensation—used to align the interests of managerial agents with those of the firm's owners?

5. What trends exist regarding executive compensation? What is the effect of the increased use of long-term incentives on executives' strategic decisions?

6. What is the market for corporate control? What conditions generally cause this external governance mechanism to become active? How does the mechanism constrain top executives' decisions and actions?

7. What is the nature of corporate governance in Germany and Japan?

8. How can corporate governance foster ethical strategic decisions and behaviors on the part of managers as agents?

Corporate Governance and the Board of Directors

The composition and actions of the firm's board of directors have a profound effect on the firm. "The most important thing a board can ask itself today is whether it is professionally managed in the same way that the company itself is professionally managed," says Carolyn Brancato, director of the Global Corporate Governance Research Center at The Conference Board, which creates and disseminates knowledge about management and the marketplace. "The collegial nature of boards must give way to a new emphasis on professionalism, and directors must ask management the hard questions."

Following are several questions about boards of directors and corporate governance. Break into small groups and use the content of this chapter to discuss these questions. Be prepared to defend your answers.

1. How can corporate governance keep a company viable and maintain its shareholders' confidence?

2. How should boards evaluate CEOs? How can the board learn of problems in the CEO's performance? How does a board decide when a CEO needs to be replaced? How should succession plans be put in place?

3. Who should serve on a board? What human factors affect board members' interactions with each other, and how can those factors be used to best advantage?

4. Should independent directors meet on a regular basis without management present? Does the board have a role in setting corporate strategy?

5. What should a CEO expect of directors? How can a CEO move unproductive participants off a board?

6. What processes can be put in place to help make the board more aware of problems in company operations? How can the board be assured of receiving appropriate information? How can the board fulfill its monitoring role while relying on information provided by management and external accountants?

1. M. Carpenter & J. Westphal, 2001, Strategic context of external network ties: Examining the impact of director appointments on board involvement in strategic decision making, *Academy of Management Journal*, 44: 639–660.

2. A. Henderson & J. Fredrickson, 2001, Top management team coordination needs and the CEO pay gap: A competitive test of economic and behavioral views, *Academy of Management Journal*, 44: 96–117.

3. F. Elloumi & J.-P. Gueyie, 2001, CEO compensation, IOS and the role of corporate governance, *Corporate Governance*, 1(2): 23–33; J. F. Core, R. W. Holthausen, & D. F. Larcker, 1999, Corporate governance, chief executive officer compensation, and firm performance, *Journal of Financial Economics*, 51: 371–406.

4. A. J. Hillman, G. D. Keim, & R. A. Luce, 2001, Board composition and stakeholder performance: Do stakeholder directors make a difference? *Business and Society*, 40: 295–314; R. K. Mitchell, B. R. Agle, & D. J. Wood, 1997, Toward a theory of stakeholder identification and salience: Defining the principle of who and what really counts, *Academy of Management Review*, 22: 853–886.

5. P. Stiles, 2001, The impact of the board on strategy: An empirical examination, *Journal of Management Studies*, 38: 627–650; J. H. Davis, F. D. Schoorman, & L. Donaldson, 1997, Toward a stewardship theory of management, *Academy of Management Review*, 22: 20–47.

6. D. Finegold, E. E. Lawler III, & J. Conger, 2001, Building a better board, *Journal of Business Strategy*, 22(6): 33–37.

7. E. F. Fama & M. C. Jensen, 1983, Separation of ownership and control, *Journal of Law and Economics*, 26: 301–325.

8. R. Charan, 1998, *How Corporate Boards Create Competitive Advantage*, San Francisco: Jossey-Bass.

9. A. Cannella Jr., A. Pettigrew, & D. Hambrick, 2001, Upper echelons: Donald Hambrick on executives and strategy, *Academy of Management Executive*, 15(3): 36–52; J. D. Westphal & E. J. Zajac, 1997, Defections from the inner circle: Social exchange, reciprocity and diffusion of board independence in U.S. corporations, *Administrative Science Quarterly*, 42: 161–212; Ward, 21st Century Corporate Board.

10. J. McGuire & S. Dow, 2002, The Japanese keiretsu system: An empirical analysis, *Journal of Business Research*, 55: 33–40.

11. J. Charkham, 1994, *Keeping Good Company: A Study of Corporate Governance in Five Countries*, New York: Oxford University Press, 1.

12. A. Cadbury, 1999, The future of governance: The rules of the game, *Journal of General Management*, 24: 1–14.

13. S. Johnson, P. Boone, A. Breach, & E. Friedman, 2000, Corporate governance in the Asian financial crisis, *Journal of Financial Economics*, 58: 141–186.

14. Cadbury Committee, 1992, *Report of the Cadbury Committee on the Financial Aspects of Corporate Governance*, London: Gee.

15. C. K. Prahalad & J. P. Oosterveld, 1999, Transforming internal governance: The challenge for multinationals, *Sloan Management Review*, 40(3): 31–39.

16. M. A. Hitt, R. A. Harrison, & R. D. Ireland, 2001, *Creating Value through Mergers and Acquisitions: A Complete Guide to Successful M&As*, New York: Oxford University Press; M. A. Hitt, R. E. Hoskisson, R. A. Johnson, & D. D. Moesel, 1996, The market for corporate control and firm innovation, *Academy of Management Journal*, 39: 1084–1119; J. P. Walsh & R. Kosnik, 1993, Corporate raiders and their disciplinary role in the market for corporate control, *Academy of Management Journal*, 36: 671–700.

17. Davis, Schoorman & Donaldson, Toward a stewardship theory of management.

18. R. C. Anderson, T. W. Bates, J. M. Bizjak, & M. L. Lemmon, 2000, Corporate governance and firm diversification, *Financial Management*, 29(1): 5–22; C. Sundaramurthy, J. M. Mahoney, & J. T. Mahoney, 1997, Board structure, antitakeover provisions, and stockholder wealth, *Strategic Management Journal*, 18: 231–246; K. J. Rediker & A. Seth, 1995, Boards of directors and substitution effects of alternative governance mechanisms, *Strategic Management Journal*, 16: 85–99.

19. R. E. Hoskisson, M. A. Hitt, R. A. Johnson, & W. Grossman, 2002, Conflicting voices: The effects of ownership heterogeneity and internal governance on corporate strategy, *Academy of Management Journal*, in press.

20. G. E. Davis & T. A. Thompson, 1994, A social movement perspective on corporate control, *Administrative Science Quarterly*, 39: 141–173.

21. R. Bricker & N. Chandar, 2000, Where Berle and Means went wrong: A reassessment of capital market agency and financial reporting, *Accounting, Organizations and Society*, 25: 529–554; M. A. Eisenberg, 1989, The structure of corporation law, *Columbia Law Review*, 89(7): 1461 as cited in R. A. G. Monks & N. Minow, 1995, *Corporate Governance*, Cambridge, MA: Blackwell Business, 7.

22. R. M. Wiseman & L. R. Gomez-Mejia, 1999, A behavioral agency model of managerial risk taking, *Academy of Management Review*, 23: 133–153.

23. E. E. Fama, 1980, Agency problems and the theory of the firm, *Journal of Political Economy*, 88: 288–307.

24. J. A. Byrne & B. Elgin, 2002, Cisco: Behind the hype, *Business Week*, January 21, 56–61.

25. D. Stires, 2001, America's best & worst wealth creators, *Fortune*, December 10, 137–142.

26. M. Jensen & W. Meckling, 1976, Theory of the firm: Managerial behavior, agency costs, and ownership structure, *Journal of Financial Economics*, 11: 305–360.

27. L. R. Gomez-Mejia, M. Nunez-Nickel, & I. Gutierrez, 2001, The role of family ties in agency contracts, *Academy of Management Journal*, 44: 81–95; H. C. Tosi, J. Katz, & L. R. Gomez Mejia, 1997, Disaggregating the agency contract: The effects of monitoring, incentive alignment, and term in office on agent decision making, *Academy of Management Journal*, 40: 584–602.

28. M. G. Jacobides & D. C. Croson, 2001, Information policy: Shaping the value of agency relationships, *Academy of Management Review*, 26: 202–223.

29. R. Mangel & M. Useem, 2001, The strategic role of gainsharing, *Journal of Labor Research*, 2: 327–343; T. M. Welbourne & L. R. Gomez-Mejia, 1995, Gainsharing: A critical review and a future research agenda, *Journal of Management*, 21: 577.

30. Jacobides & Croson, Information policy: Shaping the value of agency relationships.

31. O. E. Williamson, 1996, *The Mechanisms of Governance*, New York: Oxford University Press, 6; O. E. Williamson, 1993, Opportunism and its critics, *Managerial and Decision Economics*, 14: 97–107.

32. C. C. Chen, M. W. Peng, & P. A. Saparito, 2002, Individualism, collectivism, and opportunism: A cultural perspective on transaction cost economics, *Journal of Management*, in press; S. Ghoshal & P. Moran, 1996, Bad for practice: A critique of the transaction cost theory, *Academy of Management Review*, 21: 13–47.

33. K. H. Wathne & J. B. Heide, 2000, Opportunism in interfirm relationships: Forms, outcomes, and solutions, *Journal of Marketing*, 64(4): 36–51.

34. Y. Amihud & B. Lev, 1981, Risk reduction as a managerial motive for conglomerate mergers, *Bell Journal of Economics*, 12: 605–617.

35. Anderson, Bates, Bizjak & Lemmon, Corporate governance and firm diversification; R. E. Hoskisson & T. A. Turk, 1990, Corporate restructuring: Governance and control limits of the internal market, *Academy of Management Review*, 15: 459–477.

36. M. A. Geletkanycz, B. K. Boyd, & S. Finklestein, 2001, The strategic value of CEO external directorate networks: Implications for CEO compensation, *Strategic Management Journal*, 9: 889–898.

37. P. Wright, M. Kroll, & D. Elenkov, 2002, Acquisition returns, increase in firm size and chief executive officer compensation: The moderating role of monitoring, *Academy of Management Journal*, 45: in press; S. Finkelstein & D. C. Hambrick, 1989, Chief executive compensation: A study of the intersection of markets and political processes, *Strategic Management Journal*, 16: 221, 239; H. C. Tosi & L. R. Gomez-Mejia, 1989, The decoupling of CEO pay and performance: An agency theory perspective, *Administrative Science Quarterly*, 34: 169–189.

38. Hoskisson & Turk, Corporate restructuring.

39. Gomez-Mejia, Nunez-Nickel, & Gutierrez, The role of family ties in agency contracts.

40. C. Matlack, 2001, Gemplus: No picnic in Provence, *Business Week Online*, http://www.businessweek.com, August 6; C. Matlack, 2001, A global clash at France's Gemplus, *Business Week Online*, http://www.businessweek.com, December 21.

41. M. S. Jensen, 1986, Agency costs of free cash flow, corporate finance, and takeovers, *American Economic Review*, 76: 323–329.

42. T. H. Brush, P. Bromiley, & M. Hendrickx, 2000, The free cash flow hypothesis for sales growth and firm performance, *Strategic Management Journal*, 21: 455–472; H. DeAngelo & L. DeAngelo, 2000, Controlling stockholders and the disciplinary role of corporate payout policy: A study of the Times Mirror Company, *Journal of Financial Economics*, 56: 153–207.

43. K. Ramaswamy, M. Li, & R. Veliyath, 2002, Variations in ownership behavior and propensity to diversify: A study of the Indian corporate context, *Strategic Management Journal*, 23: 345–358.

44. P. Wright, M. Kroll, A. Lado, & B. Van Ness, 2002, The structure of ownership and corporate acquisition strategies, *Strategic Management Journal*, 23: 41–53.

45. R. Rajan, H. Servaes, & L. Zingales, 2001, The cost of diversity: The diversification discount and inefficient investment, *Journal of Finance*, 55: 35–79; A. Sharma, 1997, Professional as agent: Knowledge asymmetry in agency exchange, *Academy of Management Review*, 22: 758–798.

46. P. Lane, A. A. Cannella, Jr., & M. H. Lubatkin, 1999, Agency problems as antecedents to unrelated mergers and diversification: Amihud and Lev reconsidered, *Strategic Management Journal*, 19: 555–578.

47. David Champion, 2001, Off with his head? *Harvard Business Review*, 79(9): 35–46.

48. J. Coles, N. Sen, & V. McWilliams, 2001, An examination of the relationship of governance mechanisms to performance, *Journal of Management*, 27: 23–50.

49. S.-S. Chen & K. W. Ho, 2000, Corporate diversification, ownership structure, and firm value: The Singapore evidence, *International Review of Financial Analysis*, 9: 315–326; R. E. Hoskisson, R. A. Johnson, & D. D. Moesel, 1994, Corporate divestiture intensity in restructuring firms: Effects of governance, strategy, and performance, *Academy of Management Journal*, 37: 1207–1251.

50. S. R. Kole & K. M. Lehn, 1999, Deregulation and the adaptation of governance structure: The case of the U.S. airline industry, *Journal of Financial Economics*, 52: 79–117.

51. K.C. Banning, 1999, Ownership concentration and bank acquisition strategy: An empirical examination, *International Journal of Organizational Analysis*, 7(2): 135–152.

52. A. Berle & G. Means, 1932, *The Modern Corporation and Private Property*, New York: Macmillan.

53. P. A. Gompers & A. Metrick, 2001, Institutional investors and equity prices, *Quarterly Journal of Economics*, 116: 229–259; M. P. Smith, 1996, Shareholder activism by institutional investors: Evidence from CalPERS, *Journal of Finance*, 51: 227–252.

54. M. Useem, 1998, Corporate leadership in a globalizing equity market, *Academy of Management Executive*, 12(3): 43–59.

55. Hoskisson, Hitt, Johnson, & Grossman, Conflicting Voices; C. M. Dailey, 1996, Governance patterns in bankruptcy reorganizations, *Strategic Management Journal*, 17: 355–375.

56. Hoskisson, Hitt, Johnson, & Grossman, Conflicting Voices; Useem, Corporate leadership in a globalizing equity market; R. E. Hoskisson & M. A. Hitt, 1994, *Downscoping: How to Tame the Diversified Firm*, New York: Oxford University Press.

57. K. Rebeiz, 2001, Corporate governance effectiveness in American corporations: A survey, *International Management Journal*, 18(1): 74–80;

58. 2002, CalPERS at a glance, http://www.calpers.com, April 24.

59. 2001, The fading appeal of the boardroom series, *The Economist*, February 10 (Business Special): 67–69.

60. Hoskisson, Hitt, Johnson & Grossman, Conflicting voices; P. David, M. A. Hitt, & J. Gimeno, 2001, The role of institutional investors in influencing R&D, *Academy of Management Journal*, 44: 144–157; B. J. Bushee, 2001, Do institutional investors prefer near-term earnings over long-run value? *Contemporary Accounting Research*, 18: 207–246.

61. 2001, Shareholder activism is rising, *Investor Relations Business*, August 6, 8.

62. 2000, Now, a gadfly can bite 24 hours a day, *Business Week*, January 24, 150.

63. M. J. Roe, 1993, Mutual funds in the boardroom, *Journal of Applied Corporate Finance*, 5(4): 56–61.

64. R. A. G. Monks, 1999, What will be the impact of active shareholders? A practical recipe for constructive change, *Long Range Planning*, 32(1): 20–27.

65. B. S. Black, 1992, Agents watching agents: The promise of institutional investor's voice, *UCLA Law Review*, 39: 871–893.

66. Hoskisson, Hitt, Johnson, & Grossman, Conflicting voices; T. Woidtke, 2002, Agents watching agents?: Evidence from pension fund ownership and firm value, *Journal of Financial Economics*, 63, 99–131.

67. A. Berenson, 2001, The fight for control of Computer Associates, *The New York Times*, http://www.nytimes.com, June 25.

68. A. Park, 2001, If at first you don't succeed, *Business Week*, September 3, 39.

69. C. Sandaramurthy & D. W. Lyon, 1998, Shareholder governance proposals and conflict of interests between inside and outside shareholders, *Journal of Managerial Issues*, 10: 30–44.

70. Wright, Kroll, Lado, & Van Ness, The structure of ownership and corporate acquisition strategies.

71. S. Thomsen & T. Pedersen, 2000, Ownership structure and economic performance in the largest European companies, *Strategic Management Journal*, 21: 689–705.

72. D. R. Dalton, C. M. Daily, A. E. Ellstrand, & J. L. Johnson, 1998, Meta-analytic reviews of board composition, leadership structure, and financial performance, *Strategic Management Journal*, 19: 269–290; M. Huse, 1998, Researching the dynamics of board-stakeholder relations, *Long Range Planning*, 31: 218–226.

73. A. Dehaene, V. De Vuyst, & H. Ooghe, 2001, Corporate performance and board structure in Belgian companies, *Long Range Planning*, 34(3): 383–398;

74. Rebeiz, Corporate governance effectiveness in American corporations; J. K. Seward & J. P Walsh, 1996, The governance and control of voluntary corporate spinoffs, *Strategic Management Journal*, 17: 25–39.

75. S. Young, 2000, The increasing use of non-executive directors: Its impact on UK board structure and governance arrangements, *Journal of Business Finance & Accounting*, 27(9/10): 1311–1342; P. Mallete & R. L. Hogler, 1995, Board composition, stock ownership, and the exemption of directors from liability, *Journal of Management*, 21: 861–878.

76. J. Chidley, 2001, Why boards matter, *Canadian Business*, October 29, 6; D. P. Forbes & F. J. Milliken, 1999, Cognition and corporate governance: Understanding boards of directors as strategic decision-making groups, *Academy of Management Review*, 24: 489–505.

77. Hoskisson, Hitt, Johnson, & Grossman, Conflicting voices; B. D. Baysinger & R. E. Hoskisson, 1990, The composition of boards of directors and strategic control: Effects on corporate strategy, *Academy of Management Review*, 15: 72–87.

78. Carpenter & Westphal, Strategic context of external network ties: Examining the impact of director appointments on board involvement in strategic decision making; E. J. Zajac & J. D. Westphal, 1996, Director reputation, CEO-board power, and the dynamics of board interlocks, *Administrative Science Quarterly*, 41: 507–529.

79. A. Hillman, A. Cannella Jr., & R. Paetzold, 2000, The resource dependence role of corporate directors: Strategic adaptation of board composition in response to environmental change, *Journal of Management Studies*, 37: 235–255; J. D. Westphal & E. J. Zajac, 1995, Who shall govern? CEO/board power, demographic similarity, and new director selection, *Administrative Science Quarterly*, 40: 60–83.

80. J. Westphal & L. Milton, 2000, How experience and network ties affect the influence of demographic minorities on corporate boards, *Administrative Science Quarterly*, June, 45(2): 366–398; R. P. Beatty & E. J. Zajac, 1994, Managerial incentives, monitoring, and risk bearing: A study of executive compensation, ownership, and board structure in initial public offerings, *Administrative Science Quarterly*, 39: 313–335.

81. The fading appeal of the boardroom series. A. Bryant, 1997, CalPERS draws a blueprint for its concept of an ideal board, *The New York Times*, June 17, C1.

82. 2002, Interpublic board to add outsiders, *The New York Times*, http://www.nytimes.com, February 12.

83. A. L. Ranft & H. M. O'Neill, 2001, Board composition and high-flying founders: Hints of trouble to come? *Academy of Management Executive*, 15(1): 126–138.

84. K. Greene, 2002, Dunlap agrees to settle suit over Sunbeam, *The Wall Street Journal*, January 15, A3, A8.

85. Stiles, The impact of the board on strategy; J. A. Byrne, 1999, Commentary: Boards share the blame when the boss fails, *Business Week Online*, http://www.businessweek.com, December 27.

86. E. Perotti & S. Gelfer, 2001, Red barons or robber barons? Governance and investment in Russian financial-industrial groups, *European Economic Review*, 45(9): 1601–1617; I. M. Millstein, 1997, Red herring over independent boards, *The New York Times*, April 6, F10; W. Q. Judge, Jr. & G. H. Dobbins, 1995, Antecedents and effects of outside directors' awareness of CEO decision style, *Journal of Management*, 21: 43–64.

87. I. E. Kesner, 1988, Director characteristics in committee membership: An investigation of type, occupation, tenure and gender, *Academy of Management Journal*, 31: 66–84.

88. T. McNulty & A Pettigrew, 1999, Strategists on the board, *Organization Studies*, 20: 47–74.

89. J. Coles & W. Hesterly, 2000, Independence of the Chairman and board composition: Firm choices and shareholder value, *Journal of Management*, 26: 195–214; S. Zahra, 1996, Governance, ownership and corporate entrepreneurship among the Fortune 500: The moderating impact of industry technological opportunity, *Academy of Management Journal*, 39: 1713–1735.

90. Hoskisson, Hitt, Johnson & Grossman, Conflicting Voices.

91. A, Conger, E.E. Lawler, & D.L. Finegold, 2001, *Corporate Boards: New Strategies for Adding Value at the Top*, San Francisco: Jossey-Bass; J. A. Conger, D. Finegold, & E. E. Lawler, III, 1998, Appraising boardroom performance, *Harvard Business Review*, 76(1): 136–148.

92. J. Marshall, 2001, As boards shrink, responsibilities grow, *Financial Executive*, 17(4): 36–39.

93. C. A. Simmers, 2000, Executive/board politics in strategic decision making, *Journal of Business and Economic Studies*, 4: 37–56.

94. Hoskisson, Hitt, Johnson, & Grossman, Conflicting voices.

95. W. Ocasio, 1999, Institutionalized action and corporate governance, *Administrative Science Quarterly*, 44: 384–416.

96. A. A. Cannella, Jr. & W. Shen, 2001, So close and yet so far: Promotion versus exit for CEO heirs apparent, *Academy of Management Journal*, 44: 252–270.

97. M. Gerety, C. Hoi, & A. Robin, 2001, Do shareholders benefit from the adoption of incentive pay for directors?, *Financial Management*, 30: 45–61; D. C. Hambrick & E. M. Jackson, 2000, Outside directors with a stake: The linchpin in improving governance, *California Management Review*, 42(4): 108–127.

98. S. Rosenstein & J. G. Wyatt, 1997, Inside directors, board effectiveness, and shareholder wealth, *Journal of Financial Economics*, 44: 229–250.

99. J. Kristie, 2001, The shareholder activist: Nell Minow, *Directors and Boards*, 26(1): 16–17.

100. D. C. Hambrick & S. Finkelstein, 1995, The effects of ownership structure on conditions at the top: The case of CEO pay raises, *Strategic Management Journal*, 16: 175.

101. J. S. Miller, R. M. Wiseman, & L. R. Gomez-Mejia, 2002, The fit between CEO compensation design and firm risk, *Academy of Management Journal*, in press; L. Gomez-Mejia & R. M. Wiseman, 1997, Reframing executive compensation: An assessment and outlook, *Journal of Management*, 23: 291–374.

102. J. G. Combs & M. S. Skill, 2002, Managerialist and human capital explanations for key executive pay premiums: A Contingency, *Academy of Management Journal*, in press; S. Finkelstein & B. K. Boyd, 1998, How much does the CEO matter? The role of managerial discretion in the setting of CEO compensation, *Academy of Management Journal*, 41: 179–199.

103. W. G. Sanders & M. A. Carpenter, 1998, Internationalization and firm governance: The roles of CEO compensation, top team composition and board structure, *Academy of Management Journal*, 41: 158–178.

104. N. T. Hill & K. T. Stevens, 2001, Structuring compensation to achieve better financial results, *Strategic Finance*, 9: 48–51; J. D. Westphal & E. J. Zajac, 1999, The symbolic management of stockholders: Corporate governance reform and shareholder reactions, *Administrative Science Quarterly*, 43: 127–153.

105. Elloumi & Gueyie, CEO compensation, IOS and the role of corporate governance; M. J. Conyon & S. I. Peck, 1998, Board control, remuneration committees, and top management compensation, *Academy of Management Journal*, 41: 146–157; Westphal & Zajac, The symbolic management of stockholders.

106. S. O'Donnell, 2000, Managing foreign subsidiaries: Agents of headquarters, or an interdependent network? *Strategic Management Journal*, 21: 521–548; K. Roth & S. O'Donnell, 1996, Foreign subsidiary compensation: An agency theory perspective, *Academy of Management Journal*, 39: 678–703.

107. K. Ramaswamy, R. Veliyath, & L. Gomes, 2000, A study of the determinants of CEO compensation in India, *Management International Review*, 40(2): 167–191.

108. J. Krug & W. Hegarty, 2001, Predicting who stays and leaves after an acquisition: A study of top managers in multinational firms, *Strategic Management Journal*, 22: 185–196.

109. S. Fung, 1999, How should we pay them? *Across the Board*, June, 37–41.

110. M. A. Carpenter & M. G. Sanders, 2002, Top management team compensation: The missing link between CEO pay and firm performance, *Strategic Management Journal*, in press.

111. S. Bryan, L. Hwang, & S. Lilien, 2000, CEO stock-based compensation: An empirical analysis of incentive-intensity, relative mix, and economic determinants, *Journal of Business*, 73: 661–693.

112. C. Peck, H. M. Silvert, & K. Worrell, 1999, Top executive compensation: Canada, France, the United Kingdom, and the United States, *Chief Executive Digest*, 3: 27–29.

113. R. E. Hoskisson, M. A. Hitt, & C. W. L. Hill, 1993, Managerial incentives and investment in R&D in large multiproduct firms, *Organization Science*, 4: 325–341.

114. D. B. Balkin, G. D. Markman, & L. Gomez-Mejia, 2000, Is CEO pay in high-technology firms related to innovation? *Academy of Management Journal*, 43: 1118–1129.

115. L. K. Meulbroek, 2001, The efficiency of equity-linked compensation: Understanding the full cost of awarding executive stock options, *Financial Management*, 30(2), 5–44.

116. G. Colvin, 2001, The great CEO pay heist, *Fortune*, June 25, 67.

117. S. Strom, 2002, Even last year, option spigot was wide open, *The New York Times*, http://www.nytimes.com, February 3; C. G. Holderness, R. S. Kroszner, & D. P. Sheehan, 1999, Were the good old days that good? Changes in managerial stock ownership since the Great Depression, *Journal of Finance*, 54: 435–469.

110. J. Dahya, A. A. Lonie, & D. A. Power, 1998, Ownership structure, firm performance and top executive change: An analysis of UK firms, *Journal of Business Finance & Accounting*, 25: 1089–1118.

119. H. Tosi, S. Werner, J. Katz, & L. Gomez-Mejia, 2000, How much does performance matter? A meta-analysis of CEO pay studies, *Journal of Management*, 26: 301–339.

120. D. Leonhardt, 2002, It's called a 'loan,' but it's far sweeter, *The New York Times*, http://www.nytimes.com, February 3.

121. Ibid.

122. Strom, Even last year, Option spigot was wide open.

123. T. G. Pollock, H. M. Fischer, & J. B. Wade, 2002, The role of politics in repricing executive options, *Academy of Management Journal*, in press; M. E. Carter, L. J. Lynch, 2001, An examination of executive stock option repricing, *Journal of Financial Economics*, 2: 207–225; D. Chance, R. Kumar, & R. Todd, 2001, The 'repricing' of executive stock options, *Journal of Financial Economics*, 57: 129–154.

124. R. Coff, 2002, Bidding wars over R&D intensive firms: Knowledge, opportunism and the market for corporate control, *Academy of Management Journal*, in press; Hitt, Hoskisson, Johnson, & Moesel, The market for corporate control and firm innovation; Walsh & Kosnik, Corporate raiders.

125. D. Goldstein, 2000, Hostile takeovers as corporate governance? Evidence from 1980s, *Review of Political Economy*, 12: 381–402.

126. Hitt, Harrison, & Ireland, *Creating Value through Mergers and Acquisitions.*

127. E. Thorton, F. Keesnan, C. Palmeri, & L. Himelstein, 2002, It sure is getting hostile, *Business Week*, January 14, 28–30.

128. R. Barker, 2000, Hijacking Hertz shareholders, *Business Week*, October 16, 214.

129. Sundaramurthy, Mahoney, & Mahoney, Board structure, antitakeover provisions, and stockholder wealth.

130 J. Westphal & E. Zajac, 2001, Decoupling policy from practice: The case of stock repurchase programs, *Administrative Science Quarterly*, 46: 202–228.

131. J. A. Byrne, 1999, Poison pills: Let shareholders decide, *Business Week*, May 17, 104.

132. 2001, Reuters, Alltel bid encounters takeover defenses, *The New York Times*, http://www.nytimes.com, August 15.

133. Walsh & Kosnik, Corporate raiders.

134. A. Chakraborty & R. Arnott, 2001, Takeover defenses and dilution: A welfare analysis, *Journal of Financial and Quantitative Analysis*; 36: 311–334.

135. A. Portlono, 2000, The decision to adopt defensive tactics in Italy, *International Review of Law and Economics*, 20: 425–452.

136. C. Sundaramurthy, 2000, Antitakeover provisions and shareholder value implications: A review and a contingency framework. *Journal of Management*, 26: 1005–1030.

137. B. Kogut, G. Walker, & J. Anand, 2002, Agency and institutions: National divergence in diversification behavior, *Organization Science*, 13: 162–178; D. Norburn, B.K. Boyd, M. Fox, & M. Muth, 2000, International corporate governance reform, *European Business Journal*, 12(3): 116–133; Useem, Corporate leadership in a globalizing equity market.

138. Monks & Minow, *Corporate Governance*, 271–299; J. Charkham, *Keeping Good Company: A Study of Corporate Governance in Five Countries*, 6–118.

139. Y. Yafeh, 2000, Corporate governance in Japan: Past performance and future prospects. *Oxford Review of Economic Policy*, 16(2): 74–84; H. Kim & R. E. Hoskisson, 1996, Japanese governance systems: A critical review, in B. Prasad (ed.), *Advances in International Comparative Management*, Greenwich, CT: JAI Press, 165–189.

140. D. Kirk, 2001, Court order tells 10 executives to pay $75 million to Samsung, *The Wall Street Journal Interactive*, http://www.wsj.com, December 28.

141. S. Klein, 2000, Family businesses in Germany: Significance and structure, *Family Business Review*, 13: 157–181.

142. J. Edwards & M. Nibler, 2000, Corporate governance in Germany: The role of banks and ownership concentration, *Economic Policy*, 31: 237–268; E. R. Gedajlovic & D. M. Shapiro, 1998, Management and ownership effects: Evidence from five countries, *Strategic Management Journal*, 19: 533–553.

143. S. Douma, 1997, The two-tier system of corporate governance, *Long Range Planning,* 30(4): 612–615.

144. C. Tierney, 2001, Volkswagen, *Business Week Online,* http://www.businessweek. com, July 23.

145. K. Capell, 2002, Can Bayer cure its own headache?, *Business Week Online,* http://www.businessweek.com, January 28.

146. T. Hoshi, A.K. Kashyap, & S. Fischer, 2001, *Corporate Financing and Governance in Japan,* Boston: MIT Press.

147. Charkham, *Keeping Good Company,* 70.

148. B. Bremner, 2001. Cleaning up the banks—finally, *Business Week,* December 17: 86; 2000, Business: Japan's corporate-governance u-turn, *The Economist,* November 18, 73.

149. B. Bremner, E. Thornton, & I. M. Kunii, 1999, Fall of a keiretsu, *Business Week,* March 15, 87–92.

150. B. Bremner & J. Lichtblau, 2001, Gaijin at the gate, *Business Week Online,* http://www.businessweek.com, December 10.

151. J. B. White, 2000, The company we'll keep, *The Wall Street Journal Interactive,* http://www.wsj.com, January 17.

152. A. Alcouffe & C. Alcouffe, 2000, Executive compensation-setting practices in France, *Long Range Planning,* 33(4): 527–543.

153. J. Groenewegen, 2001, European integration and changing corporate governance structures: The case of France, *Journal of Economic Issues,* 34: 471–479.

154. C. P. Erlich & D.-S. Kang, 1999, South Korea: Corporate governance reform in Korea: The remaining issues—Part I: Governance structure of the large Korean firm, *East Asian Executive Reports,* 21: 11–14+.

155. P. Mar & M. Young, 2001, Corporate governance in transition economies: A case study of 2 Chinese airlines, *Journal of World Business,* 36(3): 280–302; M. W. Peng, 2000, *Business Strategies in Transition Economies,* Thousand Oaks, CA: Sage.

156. L. Chang, 1999, Chinese firms find incentive to use stock-compensation plans, *The Wall Street Journal*, November 1, A2.; T. Clarke & Y. Du, 1998, Corporate governance in China: Explosive growth and new patterns of ownership, *Long Range Planning*, 31(2): 239–251.

157. I. Filatotchev, R. Kapelyushnikov, N. Dyomina, & S. Aukutsionek, 2001, The effects of ownership concentration on investment and performance in privatized firms in Russia, *Managerial and Decision Economics*, 22(6): 299–313; E. Perotti & S. Gelfer, 2001, Red barons or robber barons? Governance and investment in Russian financial-industrial groups, *European Economic Review*, 45(9): 1601–1617; T Buck, I. Filatotchev, & M. Wright, 1998, Agents, stakeholders and corporate governance in Russian firms, *Journal of Management Studies*, 35: 81–104.

158. Hillman, Keim, & Luce, Board composition and stakeholder performance; R. Oliver, 2000, The board's role: Driver's seat or rubber stamp?, *Journal of Business Strategy*, 21: 7 9.

159. A. Felo, 2001, Ethics programs, board involvement, and potential conflicts of interest in corporate governance, *Journal of Business Ethics*, 32: 205–218.

Chapter Eleven

Organizational Structure and Controls

Knowledge Objectives

Studying this chapter should provide you with the strategic management knowledge needed to:

1. Define organizational structure and controls and discuss the difference between strategic and financial controls.

2. Describe the relationship between strategy and structure.

3. Discuss the functional structures used to implement business-level strategies.

4. Explain the use of three versions of the multidivisional (M-form) structure to implement different diversification strategies.

5. Discuss the organizational structures used to implement three international strategies.

6. Define strategic networks and strategic center firms.

Aligning Strategy and Structure at Zurich Financial Services

Zurich Financial Services was founded in Switzerland in 1872, primarily as a property and casualty insurer and re-insurer. Part of the reason for Zurich's historical success was the firm's rapid movement into markets outside its home nation. International expansion intensified during the early 1990s when Rolf Hüppi, Zurich CEO, concluded that the dynamic global economy created significant opportunities for firms to profitably sell financial products and services to customers in different regions of the world.

Convinced that acquisition was the route for Zurich to become a diversified, global financial powerhouse, Hüppi acted quickly and boldly. In 1996, Zurich gained a strong presence in the asset management business by spending $2 billion to acquire Kemper, a U.S. life insurer and asset manager. Paying an additional $2 billion one year later to buy Scudder, Stevens & Clark, a U.S. fund manager, significantly expanded Zurich's asset management position. The two acquisitions were then combined to form Zurich Scudder Investments, which became Zurich's global fund management arm. Zurich's size doubled in 1998 when it merged with the financial service arm of British American Tobacco.

Study of Zurich's transactions shows that by 2000, the firm had become a diversified, global financial corporation with 70,000-plus employees and operations in more than 60 countries, serving more than 35 million customers. By this time, a new organizational structure was formed. This structure grouped the firm's diversified businesses into five segments: non-life insurance (e.g., property, accident, and car and liability); life insurance; reinsurance; farmers management services; and asset management. Investors responded favorably to Zurich's diversification, as shown by the company's quick growth to a $50 billion-plus market capitalization.

Hüppi touted the merits of what Zurich had become and confidently claimed that the company should be worth $100 billion because of its large, lucrative customer base. However, all was not well at Zurich. In fact, in 2001, the company surprised investors when it issued a series of profit warnings and hints of unexpected and significant losses in its fund management business unit.

Rolf Hüppi, CEO and chairman of Zurich Financial Services, announced in late spring 2002 that he would leave the firm, which reported a large loss for 2001. Huppi had urged Zurich managers to develop technology projects like a "field of one thousand flowers," resulting in heavy spending and duplication According to a former manager, "The problem was overextension into areas which were not their core business, and undoubtedly a worry that too much scrutiny is coming its way. It can't get worse than that."

Zurich's market value quickly tumbled by half to $25 billion. In response, Zurich announced plans to divest several large holdings to raise $4 billion to reduce the firm's debt and the burden of servicing that debt.

What caused Zurich's problems? How could the value of a firm that appeared to have effectively diversified its operations tumble so quickly? In the words of a business analyst, "It was not Zurich's expansion (diversification strategy) that got it into trouble. It was its failure to adapt its structure to its new incarnation (strategy)."

Throughout the time Zurich was quickly diversifying its operations, Hüppi focused on driving top line sales revenue growth, but little attention was paid to the company's organizational structure. In fact, the structure in place prior to diversification—a hybrid of centralization and decentralization designed to coordinate and control roughly a dozen business units—remained relatively unchanged as Zurich became more diversified. This structure could not accommodate the complexity of the 350 or so business units that resulted from rapid growth and diversification. Without an organizational structure that could support the firm's new and more diversified corporate-level strategy, decisions about how to best integrate Zurich's recently acquired businesses with existing units were slow in the making.

The lack of integration was particularly pronounced in the Scudder Investments division. Kemper and Scudder, Stevens & Clark were combined to form Zurich's asset management business, but the two firms had very different cultures. Well-known in the midwestern United States, Kemper sold funds through brokers and financial advisors. Scudder, on the other hand, was an old-line Boston-based money manager selling mutual funds directly to investors. The decision to have Scudder executives run the asset management unit complicated things, as these executives had little experience in convincing brokerage firms and banks to sell mutual funds. The decisions made by inexperienced decision makers appear to have contributed to former Kemper investors withdrawing $7 billion in assets in 1999 and another $5.3 billion in 2000.

Convinced that a lack of fit between its diversification strategy and organizational structure was contributing to its financial difficulties, in late 2001, Zurich's top-level managers changed their firm's structure while simultaneously reshaping its portfolio of businesses (for example, Zurich left the reinsurance business by spinning off Converium, its reinsurance operation formerly known as Zurich Re). In the new organizational structure, 11 global and regional businesses were grouped into five business units, each headed by an executive reporting directly to Hüppi. As shown in the chart, four of the units are organized across geographic lines with the fifth framed around global asset and investment businesses. An eight-member Group Executive Committee, consisting of Hüppi, the five unit heads, the chief financial officer, and the chief operating officer, considers strategic and financial issues for all of Zurich. The 25-person Group Management Board is an information and networking body working to ensure horizontal collaboration across the segments.

By creating these larger, regional geographic business units, Zurich intends to capitalize on economies of scale in purchasing and back office functions, and it also plans to customize its product offerings to satisfy the needs of local clientele. Scale economies should help Zurich reduce its costs, while local product customization should increase revenue. Hüppi believes in the new structure's value, suggesting that it ". . . is an important step in creating the platform for an efficient and focused development of our Group (business firm)." In mid-2002, new CEO James J. Schiro remained committed to using the structure shown here.

SOURCES: B. Rigby & T. Johnson, 2002, Zurich scraps plan to sell U.S. unit, *Reuters Business News*, http://www.fidelity.com, January 9; 2001, Zurich Financial Services and Deutsche Bank have signed definitive agreements, Zurich Financial Services, http://www.zurich.com/newsmedia, December 4; 2001, Zurich Financial Services: Refining the management structure and streamlining the organization, Zurich Financial Services, http://www.zurich.com/newsmedia, July 9; 2001, Re structure, The Swiss group badly needs a structure to fit its strategy, *The Economist*, September 8, 80–82; H. Deogun & T. Lauricella, 2001, Zurich Financial seeks a merger to reinvigorate its Scudder unit, *The Wall Street Journal*, April 23; 2001, W. Hall, 2001, Zurich financial profits fall amid fund management fears, *Financial Times*, September 6; S. Tuckey, 2001, Zurich CEO sees consolidation, *Insurance Accounting*, December 3; 2000, Analyst's day presentation, Zurich Financial Services, http://www.zurich.com/presentations, November; 2000, Zurich Financial Services Group: New organizational structure, Zurich Financial Services, http://www.zurich.com/newsmedia, October 31.

As described in Chapter 4, all firms use one or more business-level strategies. In Chapters 6–9, we discuss the other strategies that might be used (corporate-level, international, and cooperative strategies). Once selected, strategies can't be implemented in a vacuum. Organizational structure and controls, this chapter's topic, provide the framework within which strategies are used. However, as we explain, separate structures and controls are required to successfully implement different strategies. Top-level managers have the final responsibility for ensuring that the firm has matched each of its strategies with the appropriate organizational structure and that changes to both take place when needed.[1] The match or degree of fit between strategy and structure influences the firm's attempts to earn above-average returns.[2] Thus, the ability to select an appropriate strategy and match it with the appropriate structure is an important characteristic of effective strategic leadership.[3]

This chapter opens with an introduction to organizational structure and controls. We then provide more details about the need for the firm's strategy and structure to be properly matched. Critical to this match is the fact that strategy and structure influence each other.[4] As we discuss, strategy has a more important influence on structure, although once in place, structure influences strategy.[5]

The chapter then describes the relationship between growth and structural change that successful firms experience. This is followed with discussions of the different organizational structures that firms use to implement the separate business-level, corporate-level, international, and cooperative strategies. A series of figures highlights the different structures firms match with strategies. Across time and based on their experiences, organizations, especially large and complex ones, customize these general structures to meet their unique needs.[6] Typically, the firm tries to form a structure that is complex enough to facilitate use of its strategies but simple enough for all to effectively implement.[7] The chapter closes with brief discussions of alternative organizational structures and controls.

Organizational Structure and Controls

Research shows that organizational structure and the controls that are a part of it affect firm performance.[8] In particular, when the firm's strategy isn't matched with the most appropriate structure and controls, performance declines.[9] This relationship is shown in the Opening Case: the mismatch between strategy and structure contributed to Zurich Financial Services' declining performance. Recognizing this mismatch, the firm is changing its structure and controls to form a better match with strategy. Even though mismatches between strategy and structure do occur, the evidence suggests that managers try to act rationally when forming or changing their firm's structure.[10]

Organizational Structure

Organizational structure specifies the firm's formal reporting relationships, procedures, controls, and authority and decision-making processes.[11] Developing an organizational structure that will effectively support the firm's strategy is difficult, especially because of the uncertainty about cause-effect relationships in the global economy's rapidly changing and dynamic competitive environments.[12] When a structure's elements (e.g., reporting relationships, procedures, and so forth) are properly aligned with one another, that structure facilitates effective implementation of the firm's strategies.[13]

Organizational structure influences how managers work and the decisions resulting from that work.[14] As explained in the Opening Case, in Zurich's structure prior to diversification, former CEO Hüppi's decisions were oriented to driving the firm's growth through sales volume increases. However, greater diversification created a need for Huppi and the top management team to choose a structure that facilitated coordination and integration among the firm's rapidly growing number of business units.

A firm's structure specifies the work to be done and how to do it, given the firm's strategy or strategies.[15] Supporting the implementation of strategies,[16] structure is concerned with processes used to complete organizational tasks.[17] Effective struc-

> **Organizational structure** specifies the firm's formal reporting relationships, procedures, controls, and authority and decision-making processes.

tures provide the stability a firm needs to successfully implement its strategies and maintain its current competitive advantages, while simultaneously providing the flexibility to develop competitive advantages that will be needed for its future strategies.[18] Thus, *structural stability* provides the capacity the firm requires to consistently and predictably manage its daily work routines,[19] while *structural flexibility* provides the opportunity to explore competitive possibilities and then allocate resources to activities that will shape the competitive advantages the firm will need to be successful in the future.[20] An effective organizational structure allows the firm to *exploit* current competitive advantages while *developing* new ones.[21]

Modifications to the firm's current strategy or selection of a new strategy call for changes to its organizational structure. As explained in the Opening Case, Zurich's existing structure —developed when Zurich had far fewer business units and when it was much less diversified— became incapable of supporting implementation of the firm's new corporate-level diversification strategy. However, Zurich's structure wasn't changed until the firm's performance had dramatically declined.

Research shows that Zurich's experience with strategy and structure isn't unusual. Once in place, organizational inertia often inhibits efforts to change structure, even when the firm's performance suggests that it is time to do so.[22] In his pioneering work, Alfred Chandler found that organizations change their structures only when inefficiencies force them to do so.[23] Firms seem to prefer the structural status quo and its familiar working relationships until the firm's performance declines to the point where change is absolutely necessary. In addition, top-level managers hesitate to conclude that there are problems with the firm's structure (or its strategy, for that matter), in that doing so suggests that their previous choices weren't the best ones.[24]

Because of these inertial tendencies, structural change is often induced instead by the actions of stakeholders who are no longer willing to tolerate the firm's performance. For example, continuing losses of customers who have become dissatisfied with the value created by the firm's products could force change, as could reactions from capital market stakeholders (see Chapter 2). In Zurich's case, changes were made to form a match between strategy and structure when the firm's shareholders and debt holders became quite dissatisfied with the firm's financial performance.

In spite of the timing of structural change described above, many companies make changes prior to substantial performance declines. Appropriate timing of structural change happens when top-level managers quickly recognize that a current organizational structure no longer provides the coordination and direction needed for the firm to successfully implement its strategies.[25] Effective organizational controls help managers recognize when it is time to change the firm's structure.

Organizational Controls

Organizational controls are an important aspect of structure. **Organizational controls** guide the use of strategy, indicate how to compare actual results with expected results, and suggest corrective actions to take when the difference between actual and expected results is unacceptable. The fewer are the differences between actual and expected outcomes, the more effective are the organization's controls.[26] It is hard for the company to successfully exploit its competitive advantages without effective organizational controls.[27] Properly designed organizational controls provide clear insights regarding behaviors that enhance firm performance.[28] Firms rely on strategic controls and financial controls as part of their structures to support use of their strategies.[29]

Strategic controls are largely subjective criteria intended to verify that the firm is using appropriate strategies for the conditions in the external environment and the company's competitive advantages. Thus, strategic controls are concerned with examining the fit between what the firm *might do* (as suggested by opportunities in its

Organizational controls guide the use of strategy, indicate how to compare actual results with expected results, and suggest corrective actions to take when the difference between actual and expected results is unacceptable.

Strategic controls are largely subjective criteria intended to verify that the firm is using appropriate strategies for the conditions in the external environment and the company's competitive advantages.

external environment) and what it *can do* (as indicated by its competitive advantages) (see Figure 3.1). Effective strategic controls help the firm understand what it takes to be successful.[30] Strategic controls demand rich communications between managers responsible for using them to judge the firm's performance and those with primary responsibility for implementing the firm's strategies (such as middle- and first-level managers). These frequent exchanges are both formal and informal in nature.[31]

Strategic controls are also used to evaluate the degree to which the firm focuses on the requirements to implement its strategies. For a business-level strategy, for example, the strategic controls are used to study primary and support activities (see Tables 3.8 and 3.9) to verify that those critical to successful execution of the business-level strategy are being properly emphasized and executed. With related corporate-level strategies, strategic controls are used to verify the sharing of appropriate strategic factors such as knowledge, markets, and technologies across businesses. To effectively use strategic controls when evaluating related diversification strategies, executives must have a deep understanding of each unit's business-level strategy.[32]

Partly because strategic controls are difficult to use with extensive diversification,[33] financial controls are emphasized to evaluate the performance of the firm following the unrelated diversification strategy. The unrelated diversification strategy's focus on financial outcomes (see Chapter 6) requires the use of standardized financial controls to compare performances between units and managers.[34] **Financial controls** are largely objective criteria used to measure the firm's performance against previously established quantitative standards. Accounting-based measures, such as return on investment and return on assets, and market-based measures, such as economic value added, are examples of financial controls.

When using financial controls, firms evaluate their current performance against previous outcomes as well as their performance compared to competitors and industry averages. In the global economy, technological advances are being used to develop more sophisticated financial controls, making it possible for firms to more thoroughly analyze their performance results.[35] Pfizer Inc.'s expectations of sophisticated financial controls are that they will: "(1) safeguard the firm's assets, (2) ensure that transactions are properly authorized, and (3) provide reasonable assurance, at reasonable cost, of the integrity, objectivity, and reliability of the financial information."[36]

Without effective financial controls, the firm's performance can deteriorate. PSINet, for example, grew rapidly into a global network providing Internet services to 100,000 business accounts in 27 countries. However, expensive debt instruments such as junk bonds were used to fuel the firm's rapid expansion. According to a member of the firm's board of directors, PSINet spent most of its borrowed money "without the financial controls that should have been in place."[37] With a capital structure unable to support its rapidly growing and financially uncontrolled operations, PSINet and 24 of its U.S. subsidiaries filed for bankruptcy in June 2001.[38]

Both strategic and financial controls are important aspects of each organizational structure, and any structure's effectiveness is determined by using a combination of strategic and financial controls. However, the relative use of controls varies by type of strategy. For example, companies and business-units of large diversified firms using the cost leadership strategy emphasize financial controls (such as quantitative cost goals), while companies and business units using the differentiation strategy empha-

Financial controls are largely objective criteria used to measure the firm's performance against previously established quantitative standards.

Pfizer Inc. is a global pharmaceutical and consumer products company that discovers, develops, manufactures, and markets innovative medicines for humans, and animals. Its 2000 merger with Warner-Lambert for $90 billion made it the world's second largest pharmaceutical company.

size strategic controls (such as subjective measures of the effectiveness of product development teams).[39] As explained above, a corporatewide emphasis on sharing among business units (as called for by related diversification strategies) results in an emphasis on strategic controls while financial controls are emphasized for strategies in which activities or capabilities aren't shared (e.g., in an unrelated diversification).

Relationships between Strategy and Structure

Strategy and structure have a reciprocal relationship.[40] This relationship highlights the interconnectedness between strategy formulation (Chapter 4 and Chapters 6–9) and strategy implementation (Chapters 10–13). In general, this reciprocal relationship finds structure flowing from or following the selection of the firm's strategy. Once in place, structure can influence current strategic actions as well as choices about future strategies. The general nature of the strategy/structure relationship means that changes to the firm's strategy create the need to change how the organization completes its work. In the "structure influences strategy" direction, firms must be vigilant in their efforts to verify that how their structure calls for work to be completed remains consistent with the implementation requirements of chosen strategies. Research shows, however, that ". . . strategy has a much more important influence on structure than the reverse."[41]

Regardless of the strength of the reciprocal relationships between strategy and structure, those choosing the firm's strategy and structure should be committed to matching each strategy with a structure that provides the stability needed to use current competitive advantages as well as the flexibility required to develop future advantages. This means, for example, that when changing strategies, the firm should simultaneously consider the structure that will be needed to support use of the new strategy. Moreover, a proper strategy/structure match can be a competitive advantage.[42] Based on the four criteria of sustainability discussed in Chapter 3, the firm's strategy/structure match is a competitive advantage when that match is valuable, rare, imperfectly imitable, and nonsubstitutable. When the firm's strategy/structure combination is a competitive advantage, it contributes to the earning of above-average returns.[43]

Recent actions at Charles Schwab & Co. demonstrate these issues. A premier discount broker, Schwab has been challenged by declines in its online trading volume and its overall financial performance. At least partly as a result of uncertainty created by the events of September 11, 2001, Schwab's average daily trades in the third quarter of 2001 fell 26 percent compared to the same period a year earlier. In turn, revenue declines were instrumental in the 50.6 percent fall in year-to-year (2000–2001) net income. Following analysis of these data as well as current and possible future conditions in the global financial industry, Schwab concluded that its website and discount trades could no longer be the foundation for the firm's strategy in what were rapidly changing financial markets. Supporting this conclusion was feedback indicating that an increasing number of investors want a relationship in the form of financial advice, in addition to low trading costs, when making their investment choices. This feedback is not surprising—recent evidence suggests that customers for all types of firm services want to receive them through relationships rather than through encounters.[44] Commenting about the importance of the trend of customers wanting personal relationships, one analyst noted, "If Schwab doesn't offer advice, it risks losing the customer relationship altogether."[45] As a result of Schwab's evaluation of its current situation and future possibilities, the firm decided to change its cost leadership strategy as a discount broker to an integrated cost leadership/differentiation strategy. This change was made so Schwab could offer relatively low-cost financial advice while simultaneously becoming more of a full-service brokerage house.

Schwab's decision makers recognize that the firm's structure will have to change to support the new strategy. Historically, the firm's strategy called for Schwab brokers to take orders rather than sell them. In that structure the brokers served as intermediaries between customers who had decided what they want to buy with the sellers of those products. The firm's new structure must now support brokers' efforts to find customers and sell advice and a broad array of products. Work in the previous structure was largely centralized and dictated by rules and procedures. To support a marketing, advice-driven strategy, Schwab's structure needs to be more decentralized with greater decision responsibility at the individual broker level.

Efforts are underway at Schwab to match structure with the new strategy. If that match proves to be valuable, rare, imperfectly imitable, and nonsubstitutable, the firm will have a competitive advantage based on its integration between strategy and structure.

Evolutionary Patterns of Strategy and Organizational Structure

Research suggests that most firms experience a certain pattern of relationships between strategy and structure. Chandler[46] found that firms tended to grow in somewhat predictable patterns: "first by volume, then by geography, then integration (vertical, horizontal) and finally through product/business diversification."[47] (See Figure 11.1). Chandler interpreted his findings to indicate that the firm's growth patterns determine its structural form.

As shown in Figure 11.1, sales growth creates coordination and control problems that the existing organizational structure can't efficiently handle. Organizational growth creates the opportunity for the firm to change its strategy to try to become even more successful. However, the existing structure's formal reporting relationships, procedures, controls, and authority and decision making processes lack the sophistication required to support use of the new strategy. A new structure is needed that can help decision makers gain access to the knowledge and understanding required to effectively coordinate and integrate the actions to implement the new strategy.[48]

Three major types of organizational structures are used to implement strategies: simple structure, functional structure, and multidivisional structure.

Simple Structure

The **simple structure** is a structure in which the owner-manager makes all major decisions and monitors all activities while the staff serves as an extension of the manager's supervisory authority.[49] Typically, the owner-manager actively works in the business on a daily basis. Informal relationships, few rules, limited task specialization, and unsophisticated information systems describe the simple structure. Frequent and informal communications between the owner-manager and employees make it relatively easy to coordinate the work that is to be done. The simple structure is matched with focus strategies and business-level strategies as firms commonly compete by offering a single product line in a single geographic market. Local restaurants, repair businesses, and other specialized enterprises are examples of firms relying on the simple structure to implement their strategy.

As the small firm grows larger and becomes more complex, managerial and structural challenges emerge. For example, the amount of competitively relevant information requiring analysis substantially increases, placing significant pressure on the owner-manager. Still additional growth and success may cause the firm to change its strategy. Even if the strategy remains the same, the firm's larger size dictates the need for more sophisticated workflows and integrating mechanisms. At this evolu-

The **simple structure** is a structure in which the owner-manager makes all major decisions and monitors all activities while the staff serves as an extension of the manager's supervisory authority.

Figure 11.1   Strategy and Structure
Growth Pattern

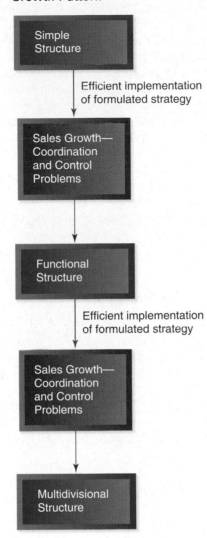

The **functional structure** is
a structure consisting of a
chief executive officer and
a limited corporate staff,
with functional line man-
agers in dominant organi-
zational areas such as
production, accounting,
marketing, R&D, engineer-
ing, and human resources.

The **multidivisional
(M-form) structure** con-
sists of operating divisions,
each representing a sepa-
rate business or profit center in which the top
corporate officer delegates
responsibilities for day-to-
day operations and
business-unit strategy to
division managers.

tionary point, firms tend to move from the simple structure
to a functional organizational structure.[50]

This move may soon be made by Casketfurniture.
com, a firm mentioned in Chapter 4 as an example of a
company using the focus differentiation strategy. Family-
owned and managed, this venture is a new part of MHP
Enterprises Ltd.'s operations. As a small family firm, MHP
has long been managed through the simple structure. In
1997, MHP decided to expand its distribution by establishing Casketfurniture.com. Using the Internet, this venture
sells what it believes are creative products throughout the
world. The continuing success of Casketfurniture.com
could create coordination and control problems for MHP
that may be solved only by the firm changing from the simple to the functional structure.[51]

Functional Structure

The **functional structure** is a structure consisting of a chief
executive officer and a limited corporate staff, with functional line managers in dominant organizational areas such
as production, accounting, marketing, R&D, engineering,
and human resources.[52] This structure allows for functional
specialization,[53] thereby facilitating active sharing of knowledge within each functional area. Knowledge sharing facilitates career paths as well as the professional development of
functional specialists. However, a functional orientation can
have a negative effect on communication and coordination
among those representing different organizational functions. Because of this, the CEO must work hard to verify that
the decisions and actions of individual business functions
promote the entire firm rather than a single function.[54] The
functional structure supports implementation of business-
level strategies and some corporate-level strategies (e.g., single or dominant business) with low levels of diversification.

Multidivisional Structure

With continuing growth and success firms often consider greater levels of diversification. However, successful diversification requires analysis of substantially greater
amounts of data and information when the firm offers the same products in different
markets (market or geographic diversification) or offers different products in several
markets (product diversification). In addition, trying to manage high levels of diversification through functional structures creates serious coordination and control
problems.[55] Thus, greater diversification leads to a new structural form.[56]

The **multidivisional (M-form) structure** consists of operating divisions, each
representing a separate business or profit center in which the top corporate officer
delegates responsibilities for day-to-day operations and business-unit strategy to division managers. Each division represents a distinct, self-contained business with its
own functional hierarchy.[57] As initially designed, the M-form was thought to have
three major benefits: "(1) it enabled corporate officers to more accurately monitor the
performance of each business, which simplified the problem of control; (2) it facilitated comparisons between divisions, which improved the resource allocation
process; and (3) it stimulated managers of poorly performing divisions to look for

ways of improving performance."[58] Active monitoring of performance through the M-form increases the likelihood that decisions made by managers heading individual units will be in shareholders' best interests. Diversification is a dominant corporate-level strategy in the global economy, resulting in extensive use of the M-form.[59]

Used to support implementation of related and unrelated diversification strategies, the M-form helps firms successfully manage the many demands (including those related to processing vast amounts of information) of diversification.[60] Chandler viewed the M-form as an innovative response to coordination and control problems that surfaced during the 1920s in the functional structures then used by large firms such as DuPont and General Motors.[61] Research shows that the M-form is appropriate when the firm grows through diversification.[62] Partly because of its value to diversified corporations, some consider the multidivisional structure to be one of the 20th century's most significant organizational innovations.[63]

No organizational structure (simple, functional, or multidivisional) is inherently superior to the other structures.[64] Because of this, managers concentrate on developing proper matches between strategies and organizational structures rather than searching for an "optimal" structure.

We now describe the strategy/structure matches that evidence shows positively contribute to firm performance.

Matches between Business-Level Strategies and the Functional Structure

Different forms of the functional organizational structure are used to support implementation of the cost leadership, differentiation, and integrated cost leadership/differentiation strategies. The differences in these forms are accounted for primarily by different uses of three important structural characteristics or dimensions—*specialization* (concerned with the type and number of jobs required to complete work[65]), *centralization* (the degree to which decision-making authority is retained at higher managerial levels), and *formalization* (the degree to which formal rules and procedures govern work[66]).

Using the Functional Structure to Implement the Cost Leadership Strategy

Firms using the cost leadership strategy want to sell large quantities of standardized products to an industry's or a segment's typical customer. Simple reporting relationships, few layers in the decision-making and authority structure, a centralized corporate staff, and a strong focus on process improvements through the manufacturing function rather than the development of new products through an emphasis on product R&D characterize the cost leadership form of the functional structure.[67] (See Figure 11.2). This structure contributes to the emergence of a low cost culture—a culture in which all employees constantly try to find ways to reduce the costs incurred to complete their work.

In terms of centralization, decision-making authority is centralized in a staff function to maintain a cost-reducing emphasis within each organizational function (for example, engineering, marketing, etc.). While encouraging continuous cost reductions, the centralized staff also verifies that further cuts in costs in one function won't adversely affect the productivity levels in other functions.

Jobs are highly specialized in the cost leadership functional structure. Job specialization is accomplished by dividing work into homogeneous subgroups. Organizational functions are the most common subgroup, although work is sometimes batched on the basis of products produced or clients served. Specializing in their work allows employees to increase their efficiency, reducing the firm's costs as a

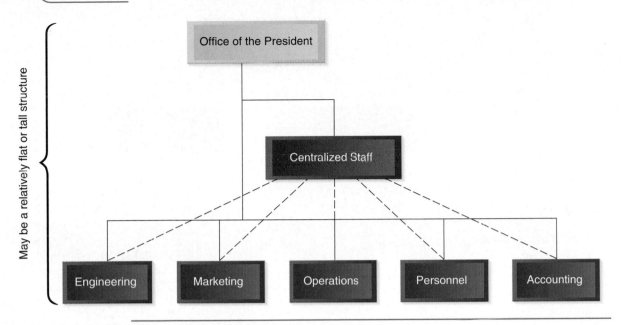

Notes: • Operations is the main function
   • Process engineering is emphasized rather than new product R&D
   • Relatively large centralized staff coordinates functions
   • Formalized procedures allow for emergence of a low-cost culture
   • Overall structure is mechanical; job roles are highly structured

result. Highly formalized rules and procedures, often emanating from the centralized staff, guide the work completed in the cost leadership form of the functional structure. Predictably following formal rules and procedures creates cost-reducing efficiencies. Known for its commitment to EDLP ("everyday low price"), Wal-Mart's functional organizational structures in both its retail (e.g., Wal-Mart Stores, Supercenters, Sam's Club) and specialty (e.g., Wal-Mart Vacations, Used Fixture Auctions) divisions are formed to continuously drive costs lower.[68] As discussed in Chapter 4, competitors' efforts to duplicate the success of Wal-Mart's cost leadership strategies have failed, partly because of Wal-Mart's effective strategy/structure configurations in its business units.

Using the Functional Structure to Implement the Differentiation Strategy

Firms using the differentiation strategy produce products that customers perceive as being different in ways that create value for them. With this strategy, the firm wants to sell nonstandardized products to customers with unique needs. Relatively complex and flexible reporting relationships, frequent use of cross-functional product development teams, and a strong focus on marketing and product R&D rather than manufacturing and process R&D (as with the cost leadership form of the functional structure) characterize the differentiation form of the functional structure (see Figure 11.3). This structure contributes to the emergence of a development-oriented culture—a culture in which employees try to find ways to further differentiate current products and to develop new, highly differentiated products.

Continuous product innovation demands that people throughout the firm be able to interpret and take action based on information that is often ambiguous,

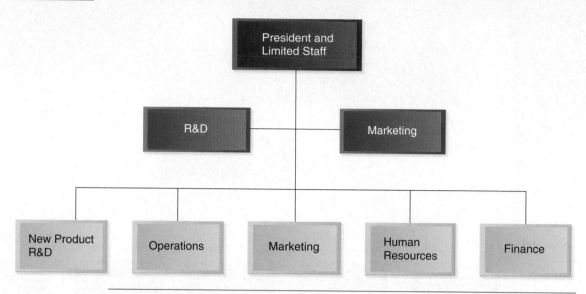

Notes: • Marketing is the main function for keeping track of new product ideas
   • New product R&D is emphasized
   • Most functions are decentralized, but R&D and marketing may have centralized staffs that work closely with each other
   • Formalization is limited so that new product ideas can emerge easily and change is more readily accomplished
   • Overall structure is organic; job roles are less structured

incomplete, and uncertain. With a strong focus on the external environment to identify new opportunities, employees often gather this information from people outside
the firm, such as customers and suppliers. Commonly, rapid responses to the possibilities indicated by the collected information are necessary, suggesting the need for
decision-making responsibility and authority to be decentralized. To support creativity and the continuous pursuit of new sources of differentiation and new products,
jobs in this structure are not highly specialized. This lack of specialization means that
workers have a relatively large number of tasks in their job descriptions. Few formal
rules and procedures are also characteristics of this structure. Low formalization,
decentralization of decision-making authority and responsibility, and low specialization of work tasks combine to create a structure in which people interact frequently
to exchange ideas about how to further differentiate current products while developing ideas for new products that can be differentiated to create value for customers.

Using the Functional Structure to Implement
the Integrated Cost Leadership/Differentiation Strategy
Firms using the integrated cost leadership/differentiation strategy want to sell products that create value because of their relatively low cost and reasonable sources of differentiation. The cost of these products is low "relative" to the cost leader's prices
while their differentiation is "reasonable" compared to the clearly unique features of
the differentiator's products.

The integrated cost leadership/differentiation strategy is used frequently in the
global economy, although it is difficult to successfully implement. This difficulty is
due largely to the fact that different primary and support activities (see Chapter 3)
must be emphasized when using the cost leadership and differentiation strategies. To
achieve the low-cost position, emphasis is placed on production and process engineering, with infrequent product changes. To achieve a differentiated position, mar-

keting and new-product R&D are emphasized while production and process engineering are not. Thus, use of the integrated strategy results when the firm successfully combines activities intended to reduce costs with activities intended to create additional differentiation features. As a result, the integrated form of the functional structure must have decision-making patterns that are partially centralized and partially decentralized. Additionally, jobs are semi-specialized, and rules and procedures call for some formal and some informal job behavior.

Matches between Corporate-Level Strategies and the Multidivisional Structure

As explained earlier, Chandler's research showed that the firm's continuing success leads to product or market diversification or both.[69] The firm's level of diversification is a function of decisions about the number and type of businesses in which it will compete as well as how it will manage the businesses (see Chapter 6). Geared to managing individual organizational functions, increasing diversification eventually creates information processing, coordination, and control problems that the functional structure can't handle. Thus, use of a diversification strategy requires the firm to change from the functional structure to the multidivisional structure to develop an appropriate strategy/structure match.

As defined in Figure 6.1 in Chapter 6, corporate-level strategies have different degrees of product and market diversification. The demands created by different levels of diversification highlight the need for each strategy to be implemented through a unique organizational structure (see Figure 11.4).

Using the Cooperative Form of the Multidivisional Structure to Implement the Related-Constrained Strategy

The **cooperative form** is a structure in which horizontal integration is used to bring about interdivisional cooperation.

The **cooperative form** is a structure in which horizontal integration is used to bring about interdivisional cooperation. The divisions in the firm using the related-constrained diversification strategy commonly are formed around products, markets or both. The objective of related-constrained firm Procter & Gamble (P&G), to "think globally, act locally," for example, is supported by a cooperative structure of five global business product units (baby, feminine and family care, fabric and home care, food

---

Figure 11.4   Three Variations of the Multidivisional Structure

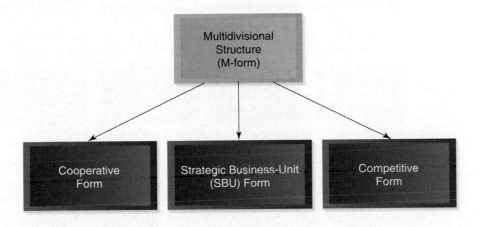

and beverage, and health and beauty care) and seven market development organizations (MDOs), each formed around a region of the world, such as Northeast Asia. Using the five global product units to create strong brand equities through ongoing innovation is how P&G thinks globally; interfacing with customers to ensure that a division's marketing plans fully capitalize on local opportunities is how P&G acts locally. Information is shared between the product-oriented and the marketing-oriented efforts to enhance the corporation's performance. Indeed, some corporate staff members are responsible for focusing on making certain that knowledge is meaningfully categorized and then rapidly transferred throughout P&G's businesses.[70]

In Figure 11.5, we use product divisions as part of the representation of the cooperative form of the multidivisional structure, although as the P&G example suggests, market divisions could be used instead of or in addition to product divisions to develop the figure. Thus, P&G has slightly modified the core cooperative form of the multidivisional structure to satisfy its unique strategy/structure match requirements.

All of the related-constrained firm's divisions share one or more corporate strengths. Production competencies, marketing competencies, or channel dominance are examples of strengths that the firm's divisions might share.[71] Production expertise is one of the strengths shared across P&G's divisions. At Halliburton Co., the world's largest oilfield services company, the firm's competence in the development and application of sophisticated technologies is shared between its two major divisions.[72]

The sharing of divisional competencies facilitates the corporation's efforts to

Figure 11.5   Cooperative Form of the Multidivisional Structure for Implementation of a Related–Constrained Strategy

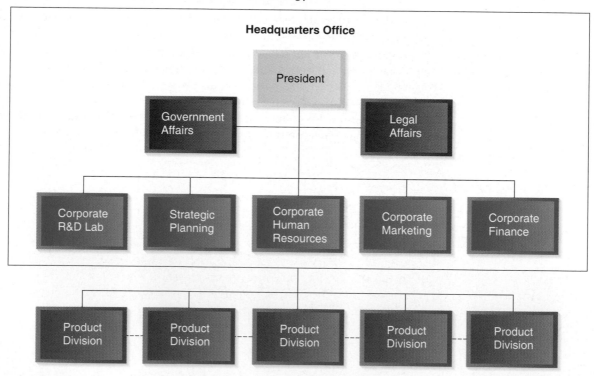

Notes: • Structural integration devices create tight links among all divisions
   • Corporate office emphasizes centralized strategic planning, human resources, and marketing to foster cooperation between divisions
   • R&D is likely to be centralized
   • Rewards are subjective and tend to emphasize overall corporate performance in addition to divisional performance
   • Culture emphasizes cooperative sharing

PART 3 /Strategic Actions: Strategy Implementation

develop economies of scope. As explained in Chapter 6, economies of scope (cost savings resulting from the sharing of competencies developed in one division with another division) are linked with successful use of the related–constrained strategy. Interdivisional sharing of competencies depends on cooperation, suggesting the use of the cooperative form of the multidivisional structure.[73] Increasingly, it is important that the links resulting from effective use of integration mechanisms support the cooperative sharing of both intangible resources (such as knowledge) as well as tangible resources (such as facilities and equipment).[74]

Different characteristics of structure are used as integrating mechanisms by the cooperative structure to facilitate interdivisional cooperation. Defined earlier in the discussion of functional organizational structures, centralization is one of these mechanisms. Centralizing some organizational functions (human resource management, R&D, marketing, and finance) at the corporate level allows the linking of activities among divisions. Work completed in these centralized functions is managed by the firm's central office with the purpose of exploiting common strengths among divisions by sharing competencies. The intent is to develop a competitive advantage in the divisions as they implement their cost leadership, differentiation, or integrated cost leadership/differentiation business-unit strategies that exceeds the value created by the advantages used by undiversified rivals' implementation of these strategies.[75]

Frequent, direct contact between division managers, another integrating mechanism, encourages and supports cooperation and the sharing of either competencies or resources that have the possibility of being used to create new advantages. Sometimes, liaison roles are established in each division to reduce the amount of time division managers spend integrating and coordinating their unit's work with the work taking place in other divisions. Temporary teams or task forces may be formed around projects whose success depends on sharing competencies that are embedded within several divisions. Formal integration departments might be established in firms frequently using temporary teams or task forces. Ultimately, a matrix organization may evolve in firms implementing the related–constrained strategy. A *matrix organization* is an organizational structure in which there is a dual structure combining both functional specialization and business product or project specialization. Although complicated, an effective matrix structure can lead to improved coordination among a firm's divisions.[76]

The success of the cooperative multidivisional structure is significantly affected by how well information is processed among divisions. But because cooperation among divisions implies a loss of managerial autonomy, division managers may not readily commit themselves to the type of integrative information-processing activities that this structure demands. Moreover, coordination among divisions sometimes results in an unequal flow of positive outcomes to divisional managers. In other words, when managerial rewards are based at least in part on the performance of individual divisions, the manager of the division that is able to benefit the most by the sharing of corporate competencies might be viewed as receiving relative gains at others' expense. Strategic controls are important in these instances, as divisional managers' performance can be evaluated at least partly on the basis of how well they have facilitated interdivisional cooperative efforts. Furthermore, using reward systems that emphasize overall company performance, besides outcomes achieved by individual divisions, helps overcome problems associated with the cooperative form.

Using the Strategic-Business-Unit Form of the Multidivisional Structure to Implement the Related–Linked Strategy

When the firm has fewer links or less constrained links among its divisions, the related–linked diversification strategy is used. The strategic business-unit form of the multidivisional structure supports implementation of this strategy. The **strategic**

Figure 11.6 SBU Form of the Multidivisional Structure for Implementation of a
Related–Linked Strategy

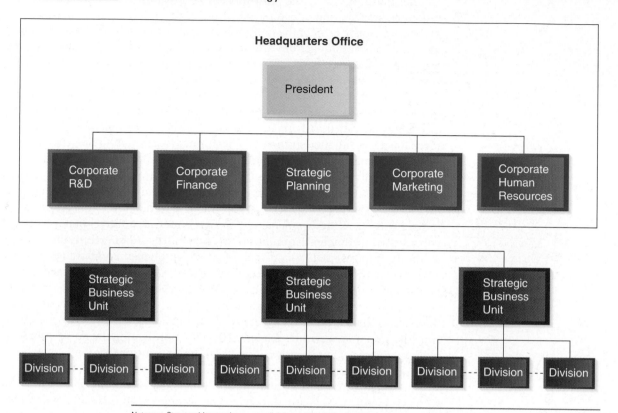

Headquarters Office

President

Corporate R&D | Corporate Finance | Strategic Planning | Corporate Marketing | Corporate Human Resources

Strategic Business Unit | Strategic Business Unit | Strategic Business Unit

Division - - - Division - - - Division | Division - - - Division - - - Division | Division - - - Division - - - Division

Notes: • Structural integration among divisions within SBUs, but independence across SBUs
• Strategic planning may be the most prominent function in headquarters for managing the strategic planning approval process of SBUs for the president
• Each SBU may have its own budget for staff to foster integration
• Corporate headquarters staff serve as consultants to SBUs and divisions, rather than having direct input to product strategy, as in the cooperative form

The **strategic business unit (SBU) form** is a structure consisting of three levels: corporate headquarters, strategic business units (SBUs), and SBU divisions.

business unit (SBU) form is a structure consisting of three levels: corporate headquarters, strategic business units (SBUs), and SBU divisions (see Figure 11.6).

The divisions within each SBU are related in terms of shared products or markets or both, but the divisions of one SBU have little in common with the divisions of the other SBUs. Divisions within each SBU share product or market competencies to develop economies of scope and possibly economies of scale. The integration mechanisms used by the divisions in a cooperative structure can be equally well used by the divisions within the individual strategic business units that are part of the SBU form of the multidivisional structure. In the SBU structure, each SBU is a profit center that is controlled and evaluated by the headquarters office. Although both financial and strategic controls are important, on a relative basis, financial controls are vital to headquarters' evaluation of each SBU; strategic controls are critical when the heads of SBUs evaluate their divisions' performance. Strategic controls are also critical to the headquarters' efforts to determine if the company has chosen an effective portfolio of businesses and if those businesses are being effectively managed.

Used by large firms, the SBU structure can be complex, with the complexity reflected by the organization's size and product and market diversity. Related–linked firm GE, for example, has 28 strategic business units, each with multiple divisions. GE Aircraft Engines, Appliances, Power Systems, NBC, and GE Capital are a few of the firm's SBUs. As is frequently the case with large diversified corporations, the scale of GE's business units is striking. GE Aircraft Engines, for example, is the world's leading manufacturer of jet engines for civil and military aircraft. With almost 30 divisions, GE Capital is a diversified financial services company creating comprehensive solutions to increase client productivity and efficiency. The GE Power Systems business unit has 21 divisions including GE Energy Rentals, GE Distributed Power, and GE Water Technologies.[77]

In many of GE's SBUs, efforts are undertaken to form competencies in services and technology as a source of competitive advantage. Recently technology was identified as an advantage for the GE Medical Systems SBU, as that unit's divisions share technological competencies to produce an array of sophisticated equipment, including computed tomography (CT) scanners, magnetic resonance imaging (MRI) systems, nuclear medicine cameras, and ultrasound systems.[78] Once a competence is developed in one of GE Medical Systems' divisions, it is quickly transferred to the other divisions in that SBU so that the competence can be leveraged to increase the unit's overall performance.[79]

Eastman Kodak also uses the SBU structure. In the Strategic Focus on page 360, we describe this firm's evolution to the SBU structure. To date, it is not clear whether the diversification strategy and structure are now properly matched at Kodak. This latest structural change occurred under Patricia Russo's leadership as CEO. However, Russo departed after only 8 months at Kodak to accept the CEO position at Lucent Technologies.[80] In spite of this disruption to the firm's operations, Kodak's current leadership is confident that it has the strategy and structure in place that will lead to competitive success.

Using the Competitive Form of the Multidivisional Structure to Implement the Unrelated Diversification Strategy

Firms using the unrelated diversification strategy want to create value through efficient internal capital allocations or by restructuring, buying, and selling businesses.[81] The competitive form of the multidivisional structure supports implementation of this strategy.

The **competitive form** is a structure in which there is complete independence among the firm's divisions.

The **competitive form** is a structure in which there is complete independence among the firm's divisions (see Figure 11.7). Unlike the divisions included in the cooperative structure, the divisions that are part of the competitive structure do not share common corporate strengths (e.g., marketing competencies or channel dominance). Because strengths aren't shared, integrating devices aren't developed for use by the divisions included in the competitive structure.

The efficient internal capital market that is the foundation for use of the unrelated diversification strategy requires organizational arrangements that emphasize divisional competition rather than cooperation.[82] Three benefits are expected from the internal competition that the competitive form of the multidivisional structure facilitates. First, internal competition creates flexibility—corporate headquarters can have divisions working on different technologies to identify those with the greatest future potential. Resources can then be allocated to the division that is working with the most promising technology to fuel the entire firm's success. Second, internal competition challenges the status quo and inertia, because division heads know that future resource allocations are a product of excellent current performance as well as superior positioning of their division in terms of future performance. Lastly, internal competition motivates effort. The challenge of competing against internal peers can be as great as the challenge of competing against external marketplace competitors.[83]

Kodak Implements the Strategic-Business-Unit Form to Regain Growth

The world's largest manufacturer of photographic film, Kodak has struggled recently with intense competitive pressures from several sources. Kodak is engaged in a fierce price war with Fuji Photo Film, its biggest competitor, to maintain its market share in film sales both in the United States and in international markets. Even more potentially competitively threatening are the revolutionary changes taking place in photography with the advent of digital technology. In growing numbers, consumers are abandoning traditional film in favor of digital cameras.

Shareholder concerns about future performance pushed Kodak's stock price down from near $70 in late 2000 to the $30–$35 range in mid-2002. Contributing to shareholders' actions were recent earnings per share figures. Kodak's third-quarter 2001 earnings were $0.15 per share, significantly below the expected $0.46 per share. Although the firm's fourth-quarter 2001 earnings of $0.12 per share beat analysts' expectation of $0.09, shareholders remained unimpressed. The September 11 events may have influenced these results somewhat when consumers canceled or curtailed their travel plans (less travel leads to fewer film purchases). In addition, Hollywood studios canceled film projects and commercials, negatively affecting Kodak's entertainment business. Even Kodak's traditionally dependable medical imaging business suffered as hospitals banded together to demand lower prices from their suppliers.

For years, Kodak used the cooperative form of the multidivisional structure to implement the related–constrained diversification strategy. In this structure, primary organizational functions such as manufacturing, customer care, and strategic planning were centralized, which allowed their expertise to be shared among its seven product divisions. Consistent with the cooperative structure's mandates, headquarters personnel encouraged interdivisional cooperation. In addition to the product divisions, Kodak also maintained separate divisions organized according to geographic region.

The cooperative structure worked well for Kodak as it used the related–constrained strategy to compete in what for many years had been relatively stable markets. However, innovative technologies and increased competition disrupted these markets, making the sharing of the firm's technologies and related skills across product divisions less competitively valuable. Moreover, sharing key resources and their corresponding costs across many business units with increased competition in unstable markets made it difficult for Kodak to assess the profitability of its product divisions. The inability to pinpoint the firm's revenue and profitability sources was an issue, as Kodak had decided that it wanted to develop "anything that helps people capture, use or store images, including digital technology." However, the firm also concluded that being able to pinpoint the revenue and profitability outcomes of all new product offerings would influence these attempts to improve its overall financial performance.

Study of its external environment and its competitive advantages found Kodak concluding that it should reduce the number of links between its business units and their products and services. In October 2000, Kodak moved to the SBU structure. As shown in the figure, this structure combined seven previous product divisions into two broad customer-oriented SBUs, Consumer and Commercial. Global Operations, the third SBU included in the structure, continued to handle Kodak's supply chain and operational needs.

Although this SBU structure halved the number of direct reports to the CEO, the structure did not yield the robust feedback needed to assess products on a stand-alone profitability basis, as competencies were shared within individual SBU product divisions. Furthermore, the customer groupings were too broad to generate scope and scale economies among the product divisions. Executives concluded that another form of the SBU structure was necessary.

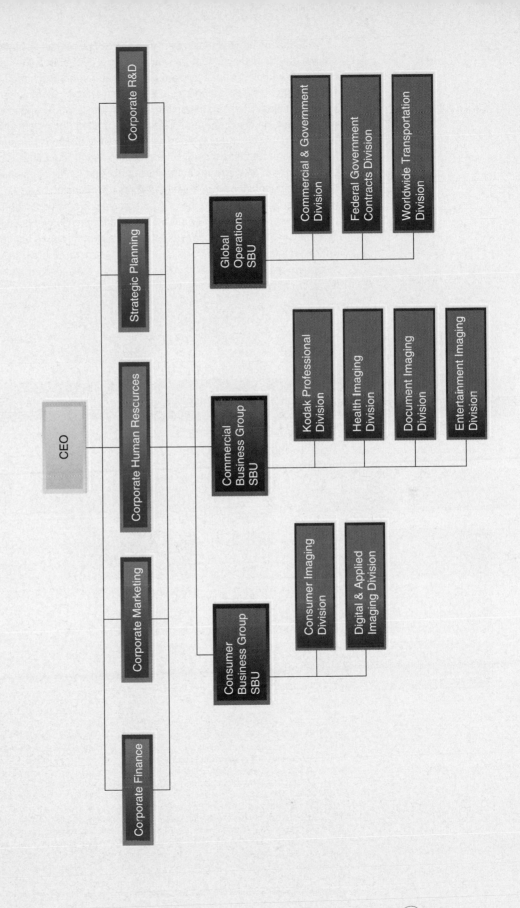

Kodak completed a new version of its SBU structure in November 2001, as shown below. The firm believes that this version is a proper match with its newly selected related–linked diversification strategy and that it offers the benefits it had been seeking. Each product division is now responsible for managing all activities that affect earnings, including supply chain management, inventory, marketing, and customer service. Each product division also generates its own independent financial statements. Financial controls can be used to measure performance within divisions, creating the data required to identify the profitability of individual products and product lines. The additional autonomy this form of the SBU structure provides to division heads should allow product-related decisions to be made more quickly. The rapidly changing nature of Kodak's competitive arena affords a premium to the firm able to quickly satisfy consumers' emerging needs with new products. Finally, Kodak's product divisions should be able to realize scope and possible scale economies because they have been grouped based on a similar customer orientation, technology platform, and channel structure. Strategic controls can be used to determine the degree to which divisions are effectively sharing common competencies in terms of customers, technologies, and distribution channels.

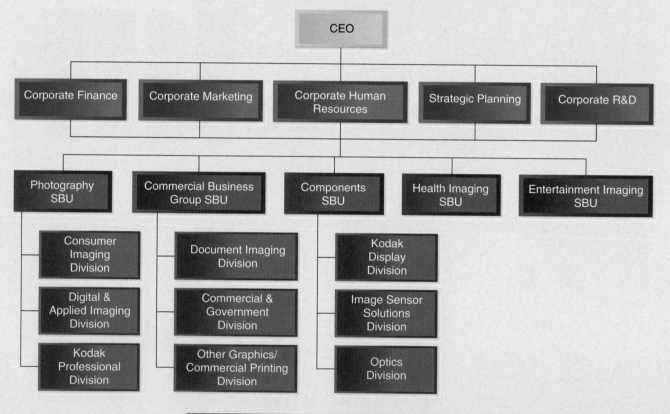

SOURCES: 2002, Kodak press center, http://www.kodak.com, January 15; S. Rosenbush, 2002, A lengthy honeymoon at Lucent? *Business Week*, January 31, 34; 2001, Kodak's Eric Steenburgh announces retirement, *Business Wire*, November 14; C. Deutsch, 2001, Kodak realigns operations as slump in demand persists, *The New York Times*, http://www.nyt.com, November 15; 2001, Eastman Kodak restructures business units, *Reuters*, November 14; A. Hill & P. Russo, 2001, Kodak puts its faith in group reorganization, *Financial Times*, http://www.ft.com, November 15; 2001, Eastman Kodak Company, *Hoovers Online*, http://www.hoovers.com, December 12; A. Tsao, 2001, Kodak: Not enough positive developments? Its shares are off their lows, but long term question marks over its transition to a digital world linger, *Business Week Online*, http://www.businessweek.com, November 26; 2001, Kodak aligns business units to focus on growth, simplification: New structure designed to improve customer satisfaction, drive growth, Eastman Kodak Company press release, http://www.kodak.com, October 23; 2001, Kodak announces new operating model, business alignment to build profitable growth, businesses given more direct responsibility for sales and profits, Eastman Kodak Company press release, http://www.kodak.com, November 14; 2001, Kodak reports third quarter 2001 sales and earnings; Operating results within expectations, economic downturn deepens, Eastman Kodak Company press release, http://www.kodak.com, October 24; D. Shook, 2000, Why Kodak is worth focusing on again: The company's plausible digital strategy could slowly start to improve its image on the Street, *Business Week Online*, http://www.businessweek.com, June 27.

Figure 11.7

Competitive Form of the Multidivisional Structure for Implementation of an Unrelated Strategy

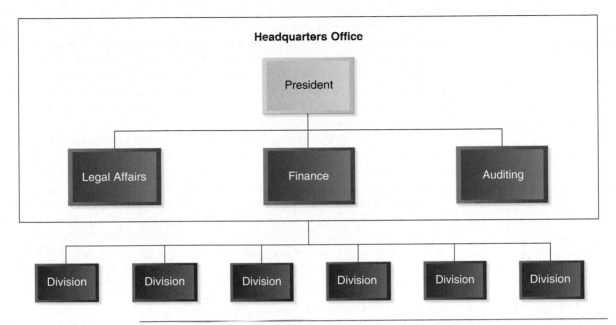

Notes:
- Corporate headquarters has a small staff
- Finance and auditing are the most prominent functions in the headquarters office to manage cash flow and assure the accuracy of performance data coming from divisions
- The legal affairs function becomes important when the firm acquires or divests assets
- Divisions are independent and separate for financial evaluation purposes
- Divisions retain strategic control, but cash is managed by the corporate office
- Divisions compete for corporate resources

Independence among divisions, as shown by a lack of sharing of corporate strengths and the absence of integrating devices, allows the firm using the unrelated diversification strategy to form specific profit performance expectations for each division to stimulate internal competition for future resources. The benefits of internal capital allocations or restructuring cannot be fully realized unless divisions are held accountable for their own independent performance. In the competitive structure, organizational controls (primarily financial controls) are used to emphasize and support internal competition among separate divisions and as the basis for allocating corporate capital based on divisions' performances.

To emphasize competitiveness among divisions, the headquarters office maintains an arms-length relationship with them and does not intervene in divisional affairs, except to audit operations and discipline managers whose divisions perform poorly. In this situation, the headquarters office relies on strategic controls to set rate-of-return targets and financial controls to monitor divisional performance relative to those targets. The headquarters office then allocates cash flow on a competitive basis, rather than automatically returning cash to the division that produced it. Thus, the focus of the headquarters' work is on performance appraisal, resource allocation, and long-range planning to verify that the firm's portfolio of businesses will lead to financial success.[84]

Textron Inc. is an industrial conglomerate using the unrelated diversification strategy.[85] Textron has grown through the "volume, geography, vertical or horizontal integration, diversification" pattern we mention earlier in the chapter. The seed for Textron was Special Yarns Corporation, a small textile company founded in 1923 with first year revenues of $75,000. Special Yarns Corporation became the world's first conglomerate. Its evolution started when the firm vertically integrated in 1943 to gain control of declining revenues and underutilized production capacity. Facing another revenue decline in 1952, the CEO received board approval to diversify the firm by acquiring businesses in unrelated industries. Today, Textron has five divisions—aircraft, automotive, industrial products, fastening systems, and finance. Return on invested capital is the financial control Textron uses as the primary measure of divisional performance. According to the firm, "return on invested capital serves as both a compass to guide every investment decision and a measurement of Textron's success."[86]

The three major forms of the multidivisional structure should each be paired with a particular corporate-level strategy. Table 11.1 shows these structures' characteristics. Differences are seen in the degree of centralization, the focus of the performance appraisal, the horizontal structures (integrating mechanisms), and the incentive compensation schemes. The most centralized and most costly structural form is the cooperative structure. The least centralized, with the lowest bureaucratic costs, is the competitive structure. The SBU structure requires partial centralization and involves some of the mechanisms necessary to implement the relatedness between divisions. Also, the divisional incentive compensation awards are allocated according to both SBUs and corporate performance.

An early Textron facility and its Providence, R.I. headquarters.

© COURTESY OF TEXTRON INC.

© COURTESY OF TEXTRON INC./POTOGRAPHER: FRANK GUILIANNI

Table 11.1

Characteristics of the Structures Necessary to Implement the Related–Constrained, Related–Linked, and Unrelated Diversification Strategies

Structural Characteristics	Overall Structural Form		
	Cooperative M-Form (Related–Constrained Strategy)[a]	SBU M-Form (Related–Linked Strategy)[a]	Competitive M-Form (Unrelated Diversification Strategy)[a]
Centralization of operations	Centralized at corporate office	Partially centralized (in SBUs)	Decentralized to divisions
Use of integration mechanisms	Extensive	Moderate	Nonexistent
Divisional performance appraisals	Emphasize subjective (strategic) criteria	Use a mixture of subjective (strategic) and objective (financial) criteria	Emphasize objective (financial) criteria
Divisional incentive compensation	Linked to overall corporate performance	Mixed linkage to corporate, SBU, and divisional performance	Linked to divisional performance

[a]Strategy implemented with structural form.

Matches between International Strategies and Worldwide Structures

As explained in Chapter 8, international strategies are becoming increasingly important for long-term competitive success.[87] Among other benefits, international strategies allow the firm to search for new markets, resources, core competencies, and technologies as part of its efforts to outperform competitors.[88]

As with business-level and corporate-level strategies, unique organizational structures are necessary to successfully implement the different international strategies. Forming proper matches between international strategies and organizational structures facilitates the firm's efforts to effectively coordinate and control its global operations.[89] More importantly, recent research findings confirm the validity of the international strategy/structure matches we discuss here.[90]

Using the Worldwide Geographic Area Structure to Implement the Multidomestic Strategy

The *multidomestic strategy* decentralizes the firm's strategic and operating decisions to business units in each country so that product characteristics can be tailored to local preferences. Firms using this strategy try to isolate themselves from global competitive forces by establishing protected market positions or by competing in industry segments that are most affected by differences among local countries. The worldwide geographic area structure is used to implement this strategy. The **worldwide geographic area structure** is a structure emphasizing national interests and facilitating the firm's efforts to satisfy local or cultural differences (see Figure 11.8).

Because using the multidomestic strategy requires little coordination between different country markets, integrating mechanisms among divisions in the worldwide

The **worldwide geographic area structure** is a structure emphasizing national interests and facilitating the firm's efforts to satisfy local or cultural differences.

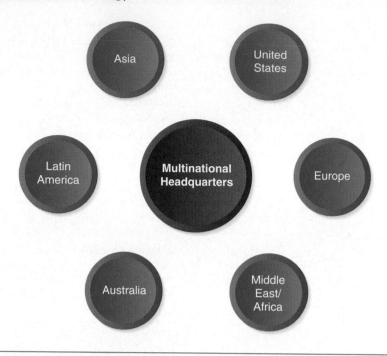

Notes: • The perimeter circles indicate decentralization of operations
• Emphasis is on differentiation by local demand to fit an area or country culture
• Corporate headquarters coordinates financial resources among independent subsidiaries
• The organization is like a decentralized federation

geographic area structure aren't needed. Hence, formalization is low, and coordination among units in a firm's worldwide geographic area structure is often informal.

The multidomestic strategy/worldwide geographic area structure match evolved as a natural outgrowth of the multicultural European marketplace. Friends and family members of the main business who were sent as expatriates into foreign countries to develop the independent country subsidiary often implemented this type of structure for the main business. The relationship to corporate headquarters by divisions took place through informal communication among "family members."[91]

As mentioned in Chapter 6, Unilever, the giant Dutch consumer products firm, has refocused its business operations. As a result, the firm grouped its worldwide operations into two global divisions—foods and home and personal care. The firm uses the worldwide geographic area structure. For the foods division (known as Unilever Bestfoods), regional presidents are responsible for results from operations in the region to which they have been assigned. Asia, Europe, North America, Africa, Middle East and Turkey, and Latin America are the regions of the foods division. The firm describes the match between the multidomestic strategy and Unilever's worldwide geographic structure (in terms of the firm's foods division): "Unilever Bestfoods' strength lies in our ability to tailor products to different markets as well as to anticipate consumer trends and demands. This comes from our deep understanding of the countries in which we operate and our policy of listening to our customers."[92]

A key disadvantage of the multidomestic strategy/worldwide geographic area structure match is the inability to create global efficiency. With an increasing emphasis on lower-cost products in international markets, the need to pursue worldwide economies of scale has also increased. These changes have fostered the use of the global strategy and its structural match, the worldwide product divisional structure.

Using the Worldwide Product Divisional Structure to Implement the Global Strategy

With the corporation's home office dictating competitive strategy, the *global strategy* is one through which the firm offers standardized products across country markets. The firm's success depends on its ability to develop and take advantage of economies of scope and scale on a global level. Decisions to outsource some primary or support activities to the world's best providers are particularly helpful when the firm tries to develop economies of scale.

The **worldwide product divisional structure** is a structure in which decision-making authority is centralized in the world-wide division headquarters to coordinate and integrate decisions and actions among divisional business units.

The worldwide product divisional structure supports use of the global strategy. In the **worldwide product divisional structure,** decision-making authority is centralized in the worldwide division headquarters to coordinate and integrate decisions and actions among divisional business units (see Figure 11.9). This structure is often used in rapidly growing firms seeking to manage their diversified product lines effectively, as in Japan's Kyowa Hakko. With businesses in pharmaceuticals, chemicals, bio-chemicals and liquor and food, this company uses the worldwide product divisional structure to facilitate its decisions about how to successfully compete in what it believes are rapidly shifting global competitive environments.[93]

Figure 11.9   Worldwide Product Divisional Structure for Implementation of a Global Strategy

Notes: • The headquarters' circle indicates centralization to coordinate information flow among worldwide products
      • Corporate headquarters uses many intercoordination devices to facilitate global economies of scale and scope
      • Corporate headquarters also allocates financial resources in a cooperative way
      • The organization is like a centralized federation

Integrating mechanisms are important to effective use of the worldwide product divisional structure. Direct contact between managers, liaison roles between departments, and temporary task forces as well as permanent teams are examples of these mechanisms. One researcher describes the use of these mechanisms in the worldwide structure, "There is extensive and formal use of task forces and operating committees to supplement communication and coordination of worldwide operations."[94] The evolution of a shared vision of the firm's strategy and how structure supports its implementation is one of the important outcomes resulting from these mechanisms' effective use. The disadvantages of the global strategy/worldwide structure combination are the difficulty involved with coordinating decisions and actions across country borders and the inability to quickly respond to local needs and preferences.

Using the Combination Structure to Implement the Transnational Strategy

The *transnational strategy* calls for the firm to combine the multidomestic strategy's local responsiveness with the global strategy's efficiency. Thus, firms using this strategy are trying to gain the advantages of both local responsiveness and global efficiency.[95] The combination structure is used to implement the transnational strategy. The **combination structure** is a structure drawing characteristics and mechanisms from both the worldwide geographic area structure and the worldwide product divisional structure.

The **combination structure** is a structure drawing characteristics and mechanisms from both the worldwide geographic area structure and the worldwide product divisional structure.

The fits between the multidomestic strategy and the worldwide geographic area structure and between the global strategy and the worldwide product divisional structure are apparent. However, when a firm wants to implement both the multidomestic and the global strategy simultaneously through a combination structure, the appropriate integrating mechanisms for the two structures are less obvious. The structure used to implement the transnational strategy must be simultaneously centralized and decentralized; integrated and nonintegrated; formalized and nonformalized. These seemingly opposite characteristics must be managed by an overall structure that is capable of encouraging all employees to understand the effects of cultural diversity on a firm's operations.

This requirement highlights the need for a strong educational component to change the whole culture of the organization. If the cultural change is effective, the combination structure should allow the firm to learn how to gain competitive benefits in local economies by adapting its core competencies, which often have been developed and nurtured in less culturally diverse competitive environments. As firms globalize and move toward the transnational strategy, the idea of a corporate headquarters has become increasingly important in fostering leadership and a shared vision to create a stronger company identity.[96]

Matches between Cooperative Strategies and Network Structures

As discussed in Chapter 9, a network strategy exists when partners form several alliances together in order to improve the performance of the alliance network itself through cooperative endeavors.[97] The greater levels of environmental complexity and uncertainty companies face in today's competitive environment are causing increasing numbers of firms to use cooperative strategies such as strategic alliances and joint ventures.[98]

The breadth and scope of firms' operations in the global economy create many opportunities for firms to cooperate.[99] In fact, the firm can develop cooperative relationships with many of its stakeholders, including customers, suppliers, and competitors.[100] When the firm becomes involved with combinations of cooperative relationships, it is part of a strategic network.

A *strategic network* is a group of firms that has been formed to create value by participating in multiple cooperative arrangements, such as alliances and joint ventures. An effective strategic network facilitates the discovery of opportunities beyond those identified by individual network participants.[101] A strategic network can be a source of competitive advantage for its members when its operations create value that is difficult for competitors to duplicate and that network members can't create by themselves.[102] Strategic networks are used to implement business-level, corporate-level, and international cooperative strategies.

Commonly, a strategic network is a loose federation of partners who participate in the network's operations on a flexible basis. At the core or center of the strategic network, the *strategic center firm* is the one around which the network's cooperative relationships revolve (see Figure 11.10).

Because of its central position, the strategic center firm is the foundation for the strategic network's structure. Concerned with various aspects of organizational structure, such as formal reporting relationships and procedures, the strategic center firm manages what are often complex, cooperative interactions among network partners. The strategic center firm is engaged in four primary tasks as it manages the strategic network and controls its operations:[103]

> *Strategic outsourcing.* The strategic center firm outsources and partners with more firms than do other network members. At the same time, the strategic center firm requires network partners to be more than contractors. Members are expected to find opportunities for the network to create value through its cooperative work.
>
> *Competencies.* To increase network effectiveness, the strategic center firm seeks ways to support each member's efforts to develop core competencies that can benefit the network.

Figure 11.10   A Strategic Network

Technology. The strategic center firm is responsible for managing the development and sharing of technology-based ideas among network members. The structural requirement that members submit formal reports detailing the technology-oriented outcomes of their efforts to the strategic center form facilitates this activity.

Race to learn. The strategic center firm emphasizes that the principal dimensions of competition are between value chains and between networks of value chains. Because of this, the strategic network is only as strong as its weakest value-chain link. With its centralized decision-making authority and responsibility, the strategic center firm guides participants in efforts to form network-specific competitive advantages. The need for each participant to have capabilities that can be the foundation for the network's competitive advantages encourages friendly rivalry among participants seeking to develop the skills needed to quickly form new capabilities that create value for the network.[104]

Implementing Business-Level Cooperative Strategies

As noted in Chapter 9, there are two types of business-level complementary alliances: vertical and horizontal. Firms with competencies in different stages of the value chain form a vertical alliance to cooperatively integrate their different, but complementary skills. Firms who agree to combine their competencies to create value in the same stage of the value chain form a horizontal alliance. Vertical complementary strategic alliances, such as those developed by Toyota Motor Company, are formed more frequently than horizontal alliances. Acting as the strategic center firm, Toyota fashioned its lean production system around a network of supplier firms.[105]

A strategic network of vertical relationships, such as the network in Japan between Toyota and its suppliers, often involves a number of implementation issues. First, the strategic center firm encourages subcontractors to modernize their facilities and provides them with technical and financial assistance to do so, if necessary. Second, the strategic center firm reduces its transaction costs by promoting longer-term contracts with subcontractors, so that supplier-partners increase their long-term productivity. This approach is diametrically opposed to that of continually negotiating short-term contracts based on unit pricing. Third, the strategic center firm enables engineers in upstream companies (suppliers) to have better communication with those companies with whom it has contracts for services. As a result, suppliers and the strategic center firm become more interdependent and less independent.[106]

The lean production system pioneered by Toyota has been diffused throughout the Japanese and U.S. automobile industries. However, no automobile company has learned how to duplicate the manufacturing effectiveness and efficiency Toyota derives from the cooperative arrangements in its strategic network.[107] A key factor accounting for Toyota's manufacturing-based competitive advantage is the cost other firms would incur to imitate the structural form used to support Toyota's application. In part, then, the structure of Toyota's strategic network that it created as the strategic center firm facilitates cooperative actions among network participants that competitors can't fully understand or duplicate.

In vertical complementary strategic alliances, such as the one between Toyota and its suppliers, the strategic center firm is obvious, as is the structure that that firm establishes. However, this is not always the case with horizontal complementary strategic alliances where firms try to create value in the same part of the value chain, as with airline alliances that are commonly formed to create value in the marketing and sales primary activity segment of the value chain (see Table 3.8).

From left: Aeromexico chairman Alfonso Pasquel, Delta Air Lines chairman Leo Mullin, Korean Air President Yi-Taek Shim, and Air France chairman Jean-cyril Spinetta announce the Sky Team alliance of their airlines.

As strategic networks, airline alliances have not been very stable. An airline may decide to change alliances, as when Delta left a network with Swiss Air and Sabena, its primary partners, to join Air France, Korean Air, and Aero Mexico to form the Sky Team alliance (Alitalia has since joined this network).[108] Or, an airline may simultaneously participate in several strategic networks. American Airlines (AA) and British Airways (BA) are members of the Oneworld alliance of eight airlines. However, BA formed another network (and serves as the strategic center firm) to provide region-specific service to customers and to extend its reach by offering a broader set of destination choices to its customers. Called Franchise Carriers, its partners (including British Mediterranean Airways, Brymon Airlines, Loganair, and Maersk Air) fly aircraft featuring the BA cabin interior and in-flight service is provided by personnel wearing BA uniforms.[109] In addition, BA has a separate partnership with AA and Iberia Airlines, all of whom are also members of Oneworld.[110] Participating in multiple networks makes it difficult to select the strategic center firm and may cause firms to question partners' true loyalties and intentions. For these reasons, horizontal complementary alliances are used less frequently than their vertical counterpart.

As explained in the Strategic Focus on page 372, strategic networks have been important to Cisco Systems, Inc. The worldwide leader in networking for the Internet, Cisco provides a broad line of solutions for transporting data, voice, and video in multiple settings[111] and has been involved with a number of strategic networks in its pursuit of competitive success. Cisco recently announced that it was changing its organizational structure. Historically, the firm's structure featured three primary business units—enterprise, service provider, and commercial. In late 2001, Cisco changed its structure to create 11 technology areas.[112] Will cooperative strategies be as critical to the firm as it completes its work through the dictates of a new organizational structure? In all likelihood, this will be the case, although the evolution of strategy and structure at Cisco will ultimately decide this issue.

Implementing Corporate-Level Cooperative Strategies

Corporate-level cooperative strategies (such as franchising) are used to facilitate product and market diversification. As a cooperative strategy, franchising allows the firm to use its competencies to extend or diversify its product or market reach, but without completing a merger or acquisition. For example, McDonald's, the largest fast-food company in the world, has more than 50 percent of its almost 30,000 restaurants outside the United States and serves more than 45 million customers daily.[113]

The McDonald's franchising system is a strategic network. McDonald's headquarters office serves as the strategic center firm for the network's franchisees. The headquarters office uses strategic controls and financial controls to verify that the franchisees' operations create the greatest value for the entire network. One strategic control issue is the location of franchisee units. McDonald's believes that its greatest expansion opportunities are outside the United States. Density percentages seem to

Cisco Utilizes Strategic Networks to Achieve Success

Networks of cooperative relationships, including vertical complementary alliances, are critical to Cisco Systems, Inc. For example, Cisco long ago decided that its suppliers should be partners who were fully integrated into Cisco's supply chain. Cisco's goal was to ultimately create a "single enterprise," providing a seamless, unified front to customers despite multiple suppliers managing major portions of the firm's supply chain. To accomplish this level of mutual interdependence, Cisco removed barriers that would impede the flow of information within the strategic network that it had formed between itself and its suppliers. Cisco also encouraged its suppliers to adopt the Internet and created Cisco Online, a standardized platform across which network participants interact.

Cisco and its suppliers are able to exchange critical information about customers, products, schedules, inventories, and costs in real time, which has resulted in significant time savings for performing key aspects of the manufacturing process. For example, Cisco discovered that as many as four to five iterations, each taking one to two weeks, were required when building prototypes of new products. By automating the information-gathering process and simulating the manufacturability of a product's design, Cisco was able to reduce the number of supplier interactions by half and identify 98 percent of manufacturing problems before beginning the actual production process.

Based on its success with vertical complementary alliances, Cisco has also formed a series of "ecosystems." An ecosystem is a web of business partnerships that includes everything from product sales and distribution to e-learning. The ecosystems make it possible for Cisco to provide end-to-end solutions to its customers without expending significant resources to develop the required capabilities. Instead, Cisco relies on its partners to provide complementary products and services. Cisco also has access to a greater array of customers through leveraging its partners' business contacts. Finally, Cisco is better able to cope with the rapid evolution of new technologies by sharing knowledge and different perspectives with its partners.

Cisco's entry into the Japanese market demonstrates the firm's success with its ecosystem model. Despite a sagging Japanese economy, Cisco was able to grow its business in Japan from almost nothing in the early 1990s to nearly $1 billion in annual sales ten years later. This achievement was largely a function of Cisco's understanding that cooperative relationships were critical to its success in Japan. Thus, with full support of the Japanese government, Cisco formed cooperative ventures with 14 Japanese partners. These relationships gave Cisco the local credibility required to compete in what was a challenging economy.

Because of its positive experience in Japan as well as in other areas, Cisco has forged alliances with hundreds of companies. To enhance the benefits gained from its cooperative arrangements, Cisco works hard to ensure their success. Partners are carefully chosen, with consideration given to those with similar corporate cultures. In addition, Cisco's partners must be strongly committed to providing superior customer service. In this context, once an ecosystem has been established, Cisco assumes an active leadership role, requiring its partners to have at least one technology specialization and meet annual customer satisfaction targets. Cisco then strives to ensure that every ecosystem benefits financially as a result of its decision to partner with Cisco. The company also provides non-financial incentives such as free on-line training and marketing and sales support to partners generating high sales volume or demonstrating superior technical expertise. These measures reflect the strong commitment to building mutually beneficial relationships that has enabled Cisco to achieve success via its ecosystem strategy.

SOURCES: 2002, News @ Cisco, http://www.cisco.com, February 5; D. R. Beresford, 2002, Getting to the bottom of Cisco's numbers, *Business Week*, February 11, 18; R. Hacki & J. Lighton, 2001, The future of the networked company, *The McKinsey Quarterly*, September, 3; R. Nolan, W. Harding, K. Porter, C. Akers, & C. Darwall, 2001, Cisco Systems: Web-enablement, *Harvard Business School Case*, April 6; R. Preston, 2000, Vendor partners stand by you when things go south, *Internetweek*, http://www.internetwk.com, November 13, 9; D. Strausl, 2001, Four stages to building an effective supply chain network, *EBN*, http://www.ebnonline.com, February 26, 43; G. Anders, 2001, After the deluge, *Fast Company*, July, 100–110; L. Hooper, 2001, Chairman & CEO, Cisco, *Jericho*, November 12, 82–84.

support this conclusion. "While in the United States there are 22,000 people per McDonald's, in the rest of the world there is only one McDonald's for every 605,000 people."[114] As a result, as the strategic center firm, McDonald's is devoting its capital expenditures (over 70 percent in the last three years) primarily to develop units in non-U.S. markets. Financial controls are framed around requirements an interested party must satisfy to become a McDonald's franchisee as well as performance standards that are to be met when operating a unit.[115]

As the strategic center of its cooperative network of franchisees, McDonald's concentrates on finding ways for all network units to improve their performance. Currently, the headquarters office is developing an evaluation system to improve customer service, especially in the U.S. units. Increased training for personnel and simplification of processes used to take and deliver orders are actions that the strategic center firm is requiring all network members to take. In addition, the financial controls used to determine the bonuses for regional teams are being changed. The intent is to increase managers' accountability for the performance of units for which they are responsible.

Improving service throughout a strategic network as large as the McDonald's franchise system is challenging.[116] However, being able to do this is necessary for the strategic center firm to increase the value created by its corporate-level cooperative franchising strategy.

Implementing International Cooperative Strategies

Jan Wareby (left), president of Ericcson Consumer Products, and Katsumi Ihara, president of Sony Digital Telecommunications Network Company are pictured here. Wareby and Ihara lead their firms' joint venture company, Sopny Ericsson Mobil Communications.

© BETIL ERICSON/AFP/CORBIS

Strategic networks formed to implement international cooperative strategies result in firms competing in several countries.[117] Differences among countries' regulatory environments increase the challenge of managing international networks and verifying that at a minimum, the network's operations comply with all legal requirements.[118]

Distributed strategic networks are the organizational structure used to manage international cooperative strategies. As shown in Figure 11.11, several regional strategic center firms are included in the distributed network to manage partner firms' multiple cooperative arrangements.[119] Strategic centers for Ericsson (telecommunications exchange equipment) and Electrolux (white goods, washing machines) are located in countries throughout the world, instead of only in Sweden where the firms are headquartered. Ericsson, for example, is active in more than 140 countries and employs more than 90,000 people. Using the SBU structure, Ericsson has five strategic business units and has formed cooperative agreements with companies throughout the world in each unit. As a founding member of an Ethernet alliance (Intel and Cisco are also members), Ericsson acts as the strategic center firm for this cooperative arrangement, which seeks to solve the wireline access bottleneck by promoting open industry standards.[120]

Organizational Structure and Controls: An Additional Perspective

As noted in Chapter 4, no business-level strategy is inherently superior to the others. In this chapter, we note that the same is true for organizational structures. The objective when dealing with strategy and structure is to design a way for the firm's work to be completed as called for by a strategy's focus and details. Peter Drucker's words address this matter: "There is no one right organization anymore. Rather, the task . . . is to select the organization

Figure 11.11 A Distributed Strategic Network

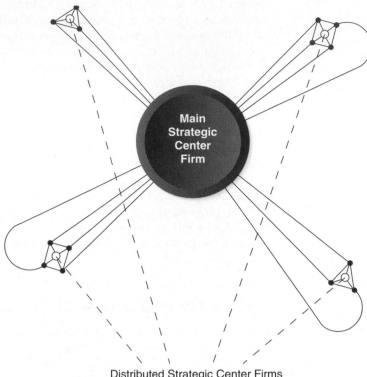

Distributed Strategic Center Firms

for the particular task and mission at hand."[121] In our context, Drucker is saying that the firm must select a structure that is "right" for the particular strategy that has been chosen to pursue the firm's strategic intent and strategic mission.

The increasingly competitive global economy finds firms continuously modifying the use of their strategies to improve performance. An important theme of this chapter is that once a strategy has been modified, the firm should also change how its work is to be done. Thus, 21st-century companies, especially global competitors, are in a stream of strategy and structure changes. In all cases, the outcome sought is to develop an effective match between what the firm intends to do (as indicated by strategy) with how it intends to do it (as indicated by structure).

There is no inherently superior strategy or structure, and there is no inherently superior strategy/structure match. In the Strategic Focus on page 375 about Semco, we describe an informal structure that seems to be effectively matched with a firm's strategy.

How appropriate are Semco's organizational structure and controls for other companies? For similar firms (that is, for relatively small companies committed to resource sharing across somewhat diversified product lines and markets) there are lessons to be learned. However, the primary message remains the same—firms must match strategy and structure to increase the probability of competitive success. Not set in concrete, strategy/structure matches evolve with changes in the firm's external and internal environments and should be grounded in the core matches discussed in this chapter.

Semco's Unique Organizational Structure

Semco is a diversified Brazilian manufacturing company specializing in marine and food service equipment. The firm's strategy is to grow by sharing ideas, people, technologies, and distribution channels. Thus, Semco essentially follows a dominant-business diversification strategy (one in which there is some, but not extensive product and market diversification). Supporting the use of this strategy is a unique organizational structure that appears to be effectively matched with the firm's strategy.

Semco was teetering on the brink of bankruptcy in the early 1980s when Ricardo Semler, the founder's son, became president at the age of 22. Semler thought that management control in the form of pyramidal hierarchy stifled creativity and flexibility. He believed that employees should be treated as adults and managed by common sense rather than rules, procedures, and formal decision-making processes. To implement his unconventional ideas, Semler streamlined Semco's organizational structure into an organizational "circle." Pictured here, this structure consists of three concentric circles, each representing a management level. One level is corporate and the other two are operating levels.

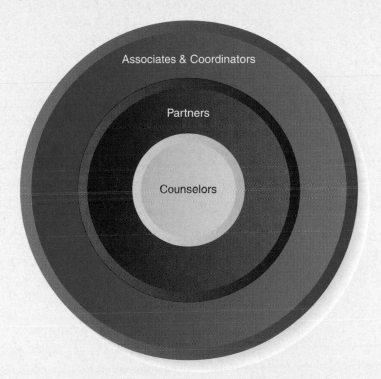

The smaller circle depicts the corporate level, containing the six individuals (called counselors) who are jointly responsible for coordinating Semco's operations. Rather than having a permanent CEO, Semco rotates each counselor into the CEO position for a six-month period. This structural characteristic allows responsibility for the firm's performance to be shared rather than isolated to one key executive. In Semler's view, "When financial performance is one person's problem, then everyone else can relax. In our system, no one can relax. You get to pass on the baton, but it comes back again two-and-a-half years later." The middle circle depicts the operating level of Semco's divisions and includes the division heads (called partners). The outer, largest circle also depicts an operating level and holds Semco's remaining employees, the majority of whom are classified as associates. Without direct reports, associates perform the research, design, sales, and manufacturing work at Semco. They select their own permanent and temporary task leaders, called coordinators, who are openly evaluated every six months. Depending on the uniqueness of their skill sets, associates often earn greater compensation than coordinators and partners. Moreover, associates can increase their corporate status and compensation through continuing excellence in their work, unlike employees at other firms, who more commonly must move into managerial positions to increase their status and total compensation.

The amount of authority and responsibility given to individual employees also differentiates Semco's structure from more traditional ones. Examples of empowerment by the firm's structure include the absence of a dress code, set work hours, assigned offices, and employee manuals. Indeed, employees determine their own hours, decide when to take holidays, and chose how they will be compensated. Staff functions such as human resources and marketing also are not part of Semco's structure. The firm feels that its turnover rate of roughly 1 percent precludes the need to allocate resources to examine personnel issues, and marketing is the responsibility of every employee. To support individuals' marketing efforts, all employees are provided cost and pricing information for the firm's products.

Semco does not hire individuals for specific jobs. Instead, it allows employees to chose their work and the location in which they'll perform it. All entry-level new hires participate in a program called "Lost in Space," in which they spend six months to a year rotating through at least 12 different business units and job functions until a preferred position is found. Employees are also encouraged to rotate positions at least every five years to "prevent boredom" and develop new skills.

Finally, Semco does not have a corporate mission and refuses to define its business. "Once you say what business you are in," explains Semler, "you put your employees in a mental straitjacket. You place boundaries around their thinking and, worst of all, you hand them a ready-made excuse for ignoring new opportunities."

Despite Semco's success, critics aren't convinced that the firm's unique structure is transferable. At present, Semco operates with approximately 1,000 employees and generates about $40 million in annual sales. This relatively small size, some argue, requires a less formal structure and fewer organizational controls compared to those needed by large organizations. In addition, its smaller size facilitates communication within the firm as well as between the firm and its stakeholders. As a privately held company with Semler holding the majority ownership position, Semco encounters minimal pressure for growth from investors. Although the applicability of Semco's ideas to mainstream businesses is debatable, Semco is an interesting example of an efficient and successful organization built and operated without conventional rules and controls.

SOURCES: G. Colvin, 2001, The anti-control freak, *Fortune,* November 26, 60; R. Semler, 2000, How we went digital without a strategy, *Harvard Business Review,* 78(5): 51–58; J. F. Wolff, 1999, In the organization of the future, competitive advantage will lie with inspired employees, *Research Technology Management,* 42(4): 2–4; R. Semler, 1994, Why my former employees still work for me, *Harvard Business Review,* 72(1): 64–74; R. Semler, 1989, Managing without managers, *Harvard Business Review,* 89(5): 76–84.

- Organizational structure specifies the firm's formal reporting relationships, procedures, controls, and authority and decision-making processes. Influencing managerial work, structure essentially details the work to be done and how that work is to be accomplished. Organizational controls guide the use of strategy, indicate how to compare actual and expected results, and suggest actions to take to improve performance when it falls below expectations. When properly matched with the strategy for which they were intended, structure and controls can be a competitive advantage.

- Strategic controls (largely subjective criteria) and financial controls (largely objective criteria) are the two types of organizational controls used to successfully implement the firm's chosen strategy. Both types of controls are critical, although their degree of emphasis varies based on individual matches between strategy and structure.

- Strategy and structure influence each other, although strategy has an overall stronger influence on structure. Research indicates that firms tend to change structure when declining performance forces them to do so. Effective managers anticipate the need for structural change, quickly modifying structure to better accommodate the firm's strategy implementation needs when evidence calls for that action.

- Business-level strategies are implemented through the functional structure. The cost leadership strategy requires a centralized functional structure—one in which manufacturing efficiency and process engineering are emphasized. The differentiation strategy's functional structure decentralizes implementation-related decisions, especially those concerned with marketing, to those involved with individual organizational functions. Focus strategies, often used in small firms, require a simple structure until such time that the firm diversifies in terms of products and/or markets.

- Unique combinations of different forms of the multidivisional structure are matched with different corporate-level diversi-

fication strategies to properly implement these strategies. The cooperative M-form, used to implement the related–constrained corporate-level strategy, has a centralized corporate office and extensive integrating mechanisms. Divisional incentives are linked to overall corporate performance. The related–linked SBU M-form structure establishes separate profit centers within the diversified firm. Each profit center may have divisions offering similar products, but the centers are unrelated to each other. The competitive M-form structure, used to implement the unrelated diversification strategy, is highly decentralized, lacks integrating mechanisms, and utilizes objective financial criteria to evaluate each unit's performance.

- The multidomestic strategy, implemented through the worldwide geographic area structure, emphasizes decentralization and locates all functional activities in the host country or geographic area. The worldwide product divisional structure is used to implement the global strategy. This structure is centralized in order to coordinate and integrate different functions' activities so as to gain global economies of scope and scale. Decision-making authority is centralized in the firm's worldwide division headquarters.

- The transnational strategy—a strategy through which the firm seeks the local responsiveness of the multidomestic strategy and the global efficiency of the global strategy—is implemented through the combination structure. Because it must be simultaneously centralized and decentralized, integrated and nonintegrated, and formalized and nonformalized, the combination structure is difficult to organize and manage successfully.

- Increasingly important to competitive success, cooperative strategies are implemented through organizational structures framed around strategic networks. Strategic center firms are critical to the management of strategic networks.

Review Questions

1. What is organizational structure and what are organizational controls? What are the differences between strategic controls and financial controls?

2. What does it mean to say that strategy and structure have a reciprocal relationship?

3. What are the characteristics of the functional structures that are used to implement the cost leadership, differentiation, integrated cost leadership/differentiation, and focused business-level strategies?

4. What are the differences among the three versions of the multidivisional (M-form) organizational structures that are used to implement the related–constrained, related–linked, and unrelated corporate-level diversification strategies?

5. What organizational structures are used to implement the multidomestic, global, and transnational international strategies?

6. What is a strategic network? What is a strategic center firm?

Organizational Structure and Controls

As an executive board member for a successful 50-partner firm that provides accounting services to corporate clients, you are interested in expanding to offer management consulting services to these clients. Another possibility for your firm is offering both types of services to smaller clients.

Part One. You are concerned about how your organizational structure may need to change to support these services. Based on the material in the chapter, use the chart to rank each type of organizational structure against the activities—information processing, coordination, and control—that you anticipate will need to be strengthened.

Part Two. You are also very concerned that there may be a potential conflict of interest if your firm provides both accounting and management consulting services to the same client. In small groups, discuss whether it is possible for a firm to use organizational structure and controls to achieve its strategic objectives but also to prevent conflicts of interest among its divisions.

	Information Processing	Coordination	Control
Simple structure			
Functional structure			
Multidivisional structure			

1. R. J. Herbold, 2002, Inside Microsoft: Balancing creativity and discipline, *Harvard Business Review,* 80(1): 73–79.

2. R. E. Miles & C. C. Snow, 1978, *Organizational Strategy, Structure and Process,* New York: McGraw-Hill.

3. M. van Clieaf, 2001, Leading & creating value in the knowledge economy, *Ivey Business Journal,* 65(5): 54–59.

4. T. Amburgey & T. Dacin, 1994, As the left foot follows the right? The dynamics of strategic and structural change, *Academy of Management Journal,* 37: 1427–1452.

5. B. Keats & H. O'Neill, 2001, Organizational structure: Looking through a strategy lens, in M. A. Hitt, R. E. Freeman, & J. S. Harrison (eds.), *Handbook of Strategic Management,* Oxford, U.K.: Blackwell Publishers, 520–542.

6. R. E. Hoskisson, C. W. L. Hill, & H. Kim, 1993, The multidivisional structure: Organizational fossil or source of value? *Journal of Management,* 19: 269–298.

7. F. Warner, 2002, Think lean, *Fast Company,* February, 40–42.

8. T. Burns & G. M. Stalker, 1961, *The Management of Innovation,* London: Tavistok; P. R. Lawrence & J. W. Lorsch, 1967, *Organization and Environment,* Homewood, IL.: Richard D. Irwin; J. Woodward, 1965, *Industrial Organization: Theory and Practice,* London: Oxford University Press.

9. P. Jenster & D. Hussey, 2001, *Company Analysis: Determining Strategic Capability,* Chichester: John Wiley & Sons, 135–171; D. J. Teece, G. Pisano, & A. Shuen, 1997, Dynamic capabilities and strategic management, *Strategic Management Journal,* 18: 509–533.

10. B. Keats & H. O'Neill, 2001, Organizational structure: Looking through a strategy lens, in M. A. Hitt, R. E. Freeman & J. S. Harrison (eds.), *Handbook of Strategic Management,* Oxford, U.K.: Blackwell Publishers, 520–542; J. R. Galbraith, 1995, *Designing Organizations,* San Francisco: Jossey-Bass, 6.

11. Keats & O'Neill, Organizational structure, 533; Galbraith. *Designing Organizations,* 6.

12. V. P. Rindova & S. Kotha, 2001, Continuous "morphing": Competing through dynamic capabilities, form, and function, *Academy of Management Journal,* 44: 1263–1280.

13. J. G. Covin, D. P. Slevin, & M. B. Heeley, 2001, Strategic decision making in an intuitive vs. technocratic mode: Structural and environmental consideration, *Journal of Business Research,* 52: 51–67.

14. M. A. Schilling & H. K. Steensma, 2001, The use of modular organizational forms: An industry-level analysis, *Academy of Management Journal,* 44: 1149–1168.

15. Jenster & Hussey, *Company Analysis,* 169; L. Donaldson, 1997, A positivist alternative to the structure-action approach, *Organization Studies,* 18: 77–92.

16. D. C. Hambrick & J. W. Fredrickson, 2001, Are you sure you have a strategy? *Academy of Management Executive,* 15(4): 48–59.

17. G. G. Dess & G. T. Lumpkin, 2001, Emerging issues in strategy process research, in M. A. Hitt, R. E. Freeman, & J. S. Harrison (eds.), *Handbook of Strategic Management,* Oxford, U.K.: Blackwell Publishers, 3–34.

18. C. A. de Kluyver, 2000, *Strategic Thinking: An Executive Perspective,* Upper Saddle River: Prentice Hall, 52.

19. G. A. Bigley & K. H. Roberts, 2001, The incident command system: High-reliability organizing for complex and volatile task environments, *Academy of Management Journal,* 44: 1281–1299.

20. J. Child & R. M. McGrath, 2001, Organizations unfettered: Organizational form in an information-intensive economy, *Academy of Management Journal,* 44: 1135–1148.

21. T. W. Malnight, 2001, Emerging structural patterns within multinational corporations: Toward process-based structures, *Academy of Management Journal,* 44: 1187–1210; A. Sharma, 1999, Central dilemmas of managing innovation in firms, *California Management Review,* 41(3): 146–164; H. A. Simon, 1991, Bounded rationality and organizational learning, *Organization Science,* 2: 125–134.

22. B. W. Keats & M. A. Hitt, 1988, A causal model of linkages among environmental dimensions, macroorganizational characteristics, and performance, *Academy of Management Journal,* 31: 570–598.

23. A. Chandler, 1962, *Strategy and Structure,* Cambridge, MA.: MIT Press.

24. Keats & O'Neill, Organizational structure, 535.

25. C. H. Noble, 1999, The eclectic roots of strategy implementation research, *Journal of Business Research,* 45: 119–134.

26. S. Venkataraman & S. D. Sarasvathy, 2001, Strategy and entrepreneurship: Outlines of an untold story, in M. A. Hitt, R. E. Freeman & J. S. Harrison (eds.), *Handbook of Strategic Management,* Oxford, U.K.: Blackwell Publishers, 650–668.

27. J. Matthews, 1999, Strategic moves, *Supply Management,* 4(4): 36–37.

28. D. F. Kuratko, R. D. Ireland, & J. S. Hornsby, 2001, Improving firm performance through entrepreneurial actions: Acordia's corporate entrepreneurship strategy, *Academy of Management Executive,* 15(4): 60–71.

29. J. S. Harrison & C. H. St. John, 2002, *Foundations in Strategic Management* (2nd ed.), Cincinnati: South-Western College Publishing, 118–129.

30. D. Incandela, K. L. McLaughlin, & C. S. Shi, 1999, Retailers to the world, *The McKinsey Quarterly,* 3: 84–97.

31. R. E. Hoskisson, M. A. Hitt, & R. D. Ireland, 1994, The effects of acquisitions and restructuring strategies (strategic refocusing) on innovation, in G. von Krogh, A. Sinatra, & H. Singh (eds.), *Managing Corporate Acquisition,* London: MacMillan Press, 144–169.

32. M. A. Hitt, R. E. Hoskisson, R. A. Johnson, & D. D. Moesel, 1996, The market for corporate control and firm innovation, *Academy of Management Journal,* 39: 1084–1119.

33. R. E. Hoskisson & M. A. Hitt, 1988, Strategic control and relative R&D investment in multiproduct firms, *Strategic Management Journal,* 9: 605–621.

34. D. J. Collis, 1996, Corporate strategy in multibusiness firms, *Long Range Planning,* 29: 416–418.

35. K. Massaro, 2000, FTI and PeopleSoft ally to offer financial control solution, *Wall Street & Technology,* 18(11): 84.

36. 2002, Pfizer Inc., Management's report, http://www.pfizer.com, January 27.

37. S. Woolley, 2001, Digital hubris, *Forbes,* May 28, 66–70.

38. 2001, PSINet announces NASDAQ delisting, http://www.psinet.com, June 1.

39. J. B. Barney, 2002, *Gaining and Sustaining Competitive Advantage* (2nd ed.), Upper Saddle River: Prentice Hall.

40. M. Sengul, 2001, Divisionalization: Strategic effects of organizational structure, Paper presented during the 21st Annual Strategic Management Society Conference.

41. Keats & O'Neill, Organizational structure, 531.

42. K. J. Euske & A. Riccaboni, 1999, Stability to profitability: Managing interdependencies to meet a new environment, *Accounting, Organizations & Society,* 24: 463–481; D. Miller & J. O. Whitney, 1999, Beyond strategy: Configuration as a pillar of competitive advantage, *Business Horizons,* 42(3): 5–17.

43. S. Tallman, 2001, Global strategic management, in M. A. Hitt, R. E. Freeman, & J. S. Harrison (eds.), *Handbook of Strategic Management,* Oxford, U.K.: Blackwell Publishers, 464–490.

44. B. A. Gutek & T. Welsh, 2000, *The Brave New Service World,* New York: AMACOM.

45. L. Lee, 2002, Will investors pay for Schwab's advice? *Business Week,* January 21, 36.

46. Chandler, *Strategy and Structure.*

47. Keats & O'Neill, Organizational structure, 524.

48. G. M. McNamara, R. A. Luce, & G. H. Thompson, 2002, Examining the effect of complexity in strategic group knowledge structures on firm performance, *Strategic Management Journal,* 23: 153–170; J. P. Walsh, 1995, Managerial and organizational cognition: Notes from a trip down memory lane, *Organization Science,* 6: 280–321.

49. C. Levicki, 1999, *The Interactive Strategy Workout* (2nd ed.), London: Prentice-Hall.

50. J. J. Chrisman, A. Bauerschmidt, & C. W. Hofer, 1998, The determinants of new venture performance: An extended model, *Entrepreneurship Theory & Practice,* 23(3): 5–29; H. M. O'Neill, R. W. Pouder, & A. K. Buchholtz, 1998, Patterns in the diffusion of strategies across organizations: Insights from the innovation diffusion literature, *Academy of Management Review,* 23: 98–114.

51. 2002, Casketfurniture.com, About our company, http://www.casketfurniture.com, February 2.

52. Galbraith, *Designing Organizations,* 25.

53. Keats & O'Neill, Organizational structure, 539.

54. Lawrence & Lorsch, *Organization and Environment.*

55. O. E. Williamson, 1975, *Markets and Hierarchies: Analysis and Anti-trust Implications,* New York: The Free Press.

56. Chandler, *Strategy and Structure.*

57. J. Greco, 1999, Alfred P. Sloan, Jr. (1875–1966): The original organizational man, *Journal of Business Strategy,* 20(5): 30–31.

58. Hoskisson, Hill, & Kim, The multidivisional structure, 269–298.

59. W. G. Rowe & P. M. Wright, 1997, Related and unrelated diversification and their effect on human resource management controls, *Strategic Management Journal,* 18: 329-338; D. C. Galunic & K. M. Eisenhardt, 1996, The evolution of intracorporate domains: Divisional charter losses in high-technology, multidivisional corporations, *Organization Science,* 7: 255–282.

60. A. D. Chandler, 1994, The functions of the HQ unit in the multibusiness firm, in R. P. Rumelt, D. E. Schendel, & D. J. Teece (eds.), *Fundamental Issues in Strategy*, Cambridge, MA: Harvard Business School Press, 327.

61. O. E. Williamson, 1994, Strategizing, economizing, and economic organization, in R. P. Rumelt, D. E. Schendel, & D. J. Teece (eds.), *Fundamental Issues in Strategy*, Cambridge, MA: Harvard Business School Press, 361–401.

62. R. M. Burton & B. Obel, 1980, A computer simulation test of the M-form hypothesis, *Administrative Science Quarterly*, 25: 457–476.

63. O. E. Williamson, 1985, *The Economic Institutions of Capitalism: Firms, Markets, and Relational Contracting*, New York: MacMillan.

64. Keats & O'Neill, Organizational structure, 532.

65. R. H. Hall, 1996, *Organizations: Structures, Processes, and Outcomes* (6th ed.), Englewood Cliffs: Prentice-Hall, 13; S. Baiman, D. F. Larcker, & M. V. Rajan, 1995, Organizational design for business units, *Journal of Accounting Research*, 33: 205–229.

66. Hall, *Organizations*, 64–75.

67. Barney, *Gaining and Sustaining Competitive Advantage*, 257.

68. 2002, Wal-Mart stores pricing policy, http://www.walmart.com, February 2.

69. Chandler, *Strategy and Structure*.

70. 2002, Procter & Gamble corporate structure, http://www.procter&gamble.com, January 26.

71. R. Rumelt, 1974, *Strategy, Structure and Economic Performance*, Boston: Harvard University Press.

72. 2002, Halliburton Co., http://www.halliburton.com, February 1.

73. C. C. Markides & P. J. Williamson, 1996, Corporate diversification and organizational structure: A resource-based view, *Academy of Management Journal*, 39: 340–367; C. W. L. Hill, M. A. Hitt, & R. E. Hoskisson, 1992, Cooperative versus competitive structures in related and unrelated diversified firms, *Organization Science*, 3: 501–521.

74. P. F. Drucker, 2002, They're not employees, they're people, *Harvard Business Review*, 80(2): 70–77; J. Robins & M. E. Wiersema, 1995, A resource-based approach to the multibusiness firm: Empirical analysis of portfolio interrelationships and corporate financial performance, *Strategic Management Journal*, 16: 277–299.

75. C. C. Markides, 1997, To diversify or not to diversify, *Harvard Business Review*, 75(6): 93–99.

76. J. G. March, 1994, *A Primer on Decision Making: How Decisions Happen*, New York: The Free Press, 117–118.

77. 2002, GE businesses, http://www.ge.com, February 4.

78. 2002, General Electric Co., Argus Research, http://argusresearch.com, February 4.

79. J. Welch with J. A. Byrne, 2001, *Jack: Straight from the Gut*, New York: Warner Business Books.

80. S. Rosenbush, 2002, A lengthy honeymoon at Lucent? *Business Week*, January 21, 34.

81. R. E. Hoskisson & M. A. Hitt, 1990, Antecedents and performance outcomes of diversification: A review and critique of theoretical perspectives, *Journal of Management*, 16: 461–509.

82. Hill, Hitt, & Hoskisson, Cooperative versus competitive structures, 512.

83. J. Birkinshaw, 2001, Strategies for managing internal competition, *California Management Review*, 44(1): 21–38.

84. T. R. Eisenmann & J. L. Bower, 2000, The entrepreneurial M-form: Strategic integration in global media firms, *Organization Science*, 11: 348–355.

85. C. Scott, 2001, Enterprising values, *The Wall Street Journal Sunday*, December 23, D5.

86. 2002, Textron profile, http://www.textron.com, February 4.

87. Y. Luo, 2002, Product diversification in international joint ventures: Performance implications in an emerging market, *Strategic Management Journal*, 23: 1–20.

88. Tallman, Global strategic management, 467.

89. Malnight, Emerging structural patterns, 1188.

90. J. Wolf & W. G. Egelhoff, 2002, A reexamination and extension of international strategy-structure theory, *Strategic Management Journal*, 23: 181–189.

91. C. A. Bartlett & S. Ghoshal, 1989, *Managing across Borders: The Transnational Solution*, Boston: Harvard Business School Press.

92. 2002, Unilever today, http://www.unilever.com, February 5.

93. 2001, Kyowa Hakko, Semiannual report, September 30.

94. Malnight, Emerging structural patterns, 1197.

95. Barney, *Gaining and Sustaining Competitive Advantage*, 533.

96. R. J. Kramer, 1999, Organizing for global competitiveness: The corporate headquarters design, *Chief Executive Digest*, 3(2): 23–28.

97. Y. L. Doz & G. Hamel, 1998, *Alliance Advantage: The Art of Creating Value through Partnering*, Boston: Harvard Business School Press, 222.

98. A. C. Inkpen, 2001, Strategic alliances, in M. A. Hitt, R. E. Freeman, & J. S. Harrison (eds.), *Handbook of Strategic Management*, Oxford, U.K.: Blackwell Publishers, 409–432.

99. Luo, Product diversification in international joint ventures, 2.

100. R. Gulati, N. Nohira, & A. Zaheer, 2000, Strategic networks, *Strategic Management Journal*, 21(Special Issue): 203–215; B. Gomes-Casseres, 1994, Group versus group: How alliance networks compete, *Harvard Business Review*, 72(4): 62–74.

101. C. Lee, K. Lee, & J. M. Pennings, 2001, Internal capabilities, external networks, and performance: A study on technology-based ventures, *Strategic Management Journal* 22(Summer Special Issue): 615–640.

102. M. B. Sarkar, R. Echambadi, & J. S. Harrison, 2001, Alliance entrepreneurship and firm market performance, *Strategic Management Journal*, 22(Summer Special Issue): 701–711.

103. S. Harrison, 1998, *Japanese Technology and Innovation Management*, Northampton, MA: Edward Elgar.

104. P. Dussauge, B. Garrette, & W. Mitchell, 2000, Learning from competing partners: Outcomes and duration of scale and link alliances in Europe, North America and Asia, *Strategic Management Journal*, 21: 99–126; G. Lorenzoni & C. Baden-Fuller, 1995, Creating a strategic center to manage a web of partners, *California Management Review*, 37(3): 146–163.

105. J. H. Dyer & K. Nobeoka, 2000, Creating and managing a high-performance knowledge-sharing network: The Toyota case, *Strategic Management Journal*, 21(Special Issue): 345–367; J. H. Dyer, 1997, Effective interfirm collaboration: How firms minimize transaction costs and maximize transaction value, *Strategic Management Journal*, 18: 535–556.

106. T. Nishiguchi, 1994, *Strategic Industrial Sourcing: The Japanese Advantage*, New York: Oxford University Press.

107. W. M. Fruin, 1992, *The Japanese Enterprise System*, New York: Oxford University Press.

108. 2002, About Delta, http://www.delta.com, February 10.

109. 2002, British Airways' Extended Network, http://www.ba.com, February 10.

110. 2002, Iberia's History, http://www.iberia.com, February 10.

111. 2002, News @ Cisco, http://www.cisco.com, February 10.

112. 2002, Q&A with John Chambers, http://www.cisco.com, February 10.

113. 2002, McDonald's Corp., *Standard & Poor's Stock Report*, http://www.fidelity.com, January 26.

114. Ibid.

115. 2002, McDonald's USA franchising, http://www.mcdonalds.com, February 9.

116. 2002, Argus Company Report, McDonald's Corp, http://argusresearch.com, February 10.

117. C. Jones, W. S. Hesterly, & S. P. Borgatti, 1997, A general theory of network governance: Exchange conditions and social mechanisms, *Academy of Management Review*, 22: 911–945.

118. J. M. Mezias, 2002, Identifying liabilities of foreignness and strategies to minimize their effects: The case of labor lawsuit judgments in the United States, *Strategic Management Journal*, 23: 229–244.

119. R. E. Miles, C. C. Snow, J. A. Mathews, G. Miles, & J. J. Coleman, Jr., 1997, Organizing in the knowledge age: Anticipating the cellular form, *Academy of Management Executive*, 11(4): 7–20.

120. 2002, Ericsson NewsCenter, http://www.ericsson.com, February 10.

121. M. F. Wolff, 1999, In the organization of the future, competitive advantage will be inspired, *Research Technology Management*, 42(4): 2–4.

Chapter Twelve
Strategic Leadership

Knowledge Objectives

Studying this chapter should provide you with the strategic management knowledge needed to:

1. Define strategic leadership and describe top-level managers' importance as a resource.

2. Define top management teams and explain their effects on firm performance.

3. Describe the internal and external managerial labor markets and their effects on developing and implementing strategies.

4. Discuss the value of strategic leadership in determining the firm's strategic direction.

5. Explain strategic leaders' role in exploiting and maintaining core competencies.

6. Describe the importance of strategic leaders in developing human capital.

7. Define organizational culture and explain what must be done to sustain an effective culture.

8. Explain what strategic leaders can do to establish and emphasize ethical practices.

9. Discuss the importance and use of organizational controls.

IBM and Strategic Leadership: Transitioning from Gerstner to Palmisano

Louis V. Gerstner left his position of CEO of IBM (remaining as chairman of the board) at the end of February 2002, and Samuel J. Palmisano, who had served as the firm's president, took over as CEO on March 1. Gerstner came to IBM as an outsider. During his 10 years as CEO, he turned the fading hardware-based company around by becoming more focused on services and software.

When Gerstner was hired as CEO, IBM's primary business of mainframe computers was slipping, and the company seemed to have lost its competitive edge. With experience as CEO for RJ Reynolds (tobacco and food) and American Express (financial services) he did not have a strong technical background, but was instead hired because of his skill in general management. IBM's board of directors had ascertained that the problem with the company was not its technology, but its culture and focus. As CEO, Gerstner guided the company away from a pure focus on hardware, particularly PCs and mainframes, and into the services market. Under his leadership, the company's stock market value increased to more than $180 billion, and profits increased more than $3.5 billion. According to one analyst, "A $10,000 investment made in IBM the day Gerstner took over is worth $92,060 today."

Unlike Gerstner, Palmisano has spent his entire 28-year career with IBM, having joined the company out of college. He is known as a strong salesman who is not afraid to take risks and push the company in new directions. With positive results being generated by using the firm's current strategies, Palmisano seems to be a good choice to follow Gerstner. He is an insider, and current performance outcomes suggest that at least in the short run, he should keep IBM focused on effectively implementing its strategies. On the other hand, he is not afraid to take risks, so he should be able to continue to promote innovation at IBM. For example, when Palmisano became head of IBM's computer servers business in 1999 he aggressively changed the way business had been done, and made it more profitable. "He assigned his top people to key bids and freed the sales staff to dazzle customers with discounts of up to 70 percent—untouchable by other computer makers." By the first quarter of 2000, IBM was number one in the servers market with a 25 percent share.

Samuel J. Palmisano (left) succeeded Lous V. Gerstner as IBM's CEO in spring 2002. One of Palmisano's first strategic actions was cutting IBM's work force to reduce costs and help the firm maintain productivity.

Palmisano's achievement in the servers business mirrored his success as head of Integrated Systems Solutions Corp. beginning in 1992; this group became the core of Global Services, now IBM's largest revenue generating unit. By changing the way people were paid—basing their commissions on the profitability instead of the size of contracts—he led the group as revenues increased from $14.9 billion in 1993 to $22.9 billion in 1996.

When Palmisano became IBM's CEO in 2002, the firm's sales and earnings were flat because of the downturn in the economy. It will be interesting to see his strategic approach. It may be a difficult challenge to find opportunities of new growth, because Gerstner did such a good job in turning IBM around and as a result of changing the firm's strategies. As Andrew Grove, former CEO of Intel, said about Gerstner, "The key to IBM's success with its services business is that it wraps things around commodity products that differentiate them. Every other computer company has now adopted as its primary objective to be more IBM-like. It's kind of interesting that this service-driven strategy, an idea that everyone else is now copying, came from an outsider to this industry."

So far, Palmisano has maintained that IBM's sectors, including computer servers, data storage devices, database software, and middleware programs, are still in good shape, but it is obvious that he will have to focus on increasing revenue. Although some insiders thought that Palmisano should make some large acquisitions in the beginning to bolster revenue growth, he made it clear such actions were not in the near future for the company. It will be interesting to see if Palmisano can boost revenues at IBM and maintain high growth levels while steering the firm towards continued success.

SOURCES: S. E. Ante & I. Sager, 2002, IBM's new boss, *Business Week,* February 11, 66–72; W. Bulkeley, 2002, As PC industry slumps, IBM hands off manufacturing of desktops, *The Wall Street Journal,* January 9, B1, B4; W. Bulkeley & J. Guidera, 2002, IBM taps its president to succeed Gerstner as CEO, *The Wall Street Journal,* January 30, B1, B4; L. DiCarlo, 2002, A successor for IBM's silent man, *Forbes,* http://www.forbes.com, January 29; D. Kirkpatrick, 2002, The future of IBM, *Fortune,* February 18, 60–64; S. Lohr, 2002, Gerstner to step down as IBM. chief, *The New York Times,* http://www.nytimes.com, January 29; B. J. Feder, 2001, Waiting to call plays for IBM, *The New York Times,* http://www.nytimes.com, August 15.

As the Opening Case illustrates, the selection of a new CEO can make a significant difference in how a firm performs. If a new leader can create a strategic vision for the firm and energize its human capital, positive outcomes can be achieved, as was the case at IBM under Louis V. Gerstner's leadership as the firm's CEO. Although the challenge of strategic leadership is significant, as it will be for Samuel Palmisano who took Gerstner's position at IBM, the outcomes of strategic leadership are potentially significant. However, it is difficult to build and maintain success over a sustained period of time.

As this chapter makes clear, it is through effective strategic leadership that firms are able to successfully use the strategic management process. As strategic leaders, top-level managers must guide the firm in ways that result in the formation of a strategic intent and strategic mission. This guidance may lead to goals that stretch everyone in the organization to improve their performance.[1] Moreover, strategic leaders must facilitate the development of appropriate strategic actions and determine how to implement them. These actions on the part of strategic leaders culminate in strategic competitiveness and above-average returns,[2] as shown in Figure 12.1.

This chapter begins with a definition of strategic leadership and its importance as a potential source of competitive advantage. Next, we examine top management teams and their effects on innovation, strategic change, and firm performance. Following this discussion is an analysis of the internal and external managerial labor markets from which strategic leaders are selected. Closing the chapter are descriptions of the six key components of effective strategic leadership: determining a strategic

Figure 12.1   Strategic Leadership and the Strategic Management Process

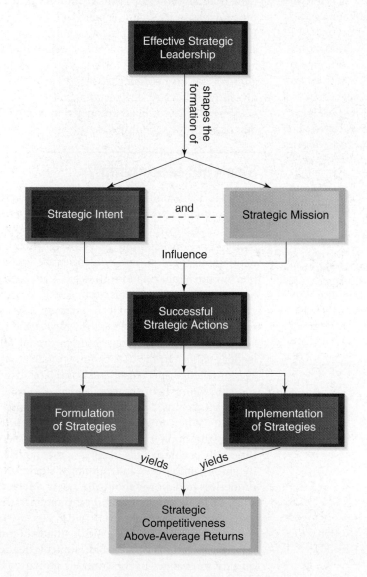

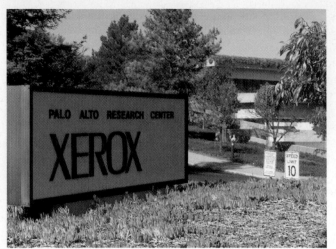

AP PHOTO/XEROX, DOUG KANTER

Xerox recently set up an independent company at the firm's Palo Alto Research Center (pictured here), where the graphical user interface and mouse were invented, to commercialize more of Xerox's non-core innovation. CEO and chairman Anne Mulcahy said, "The nature of this research is that you capitalise on some of it in your own business and some of it you don't. For as many examples of innovation that have migrated to other places, there are great examples of innovation that stays."

Strategic leadership is the ability to anticipate, envision, maintain flexibility, and empower others to create strategic change as necessary.

direction, exploiting and maintaining core competencies, developing human capital, sustaining an effective organizational culture, emphasizing ethical practices, and establishing balanced organizational control systems.

The impermanence of success is well documented by the frequent changes in leadership at Xerox. Xerox's board of directors promoted Anne Mulcahy to president in May 2000, after it ousted CEO G. Richard Thoman, who lasted 13 months. Thoman had followed Paul A. Allaire as CEO, who remained chairman of the board. Even though Xerox invented the idea of the personal computer and was the innovator of the copier machine, it was not able to capitalize on the computer and has stumbled in copiers. For example, Hewlett-Packard's division that manufactures and sells laser printers (based on the same technology as the copier) has more total revenue than all of Xerox. Even with these strategic blunders, Xerox has enjoyed significant success in its digital copiers (see the Strategic Focus on page 10 in Chapter 1).[3] However, because of significant weakness in its many businesses "the company was close to floundering after years of weak sales and high costs; employees were as disgruntled as customers."[4] Mulcahy, who was named CEO and chairman in July 2001 after several unsuccessful leaders, is trying to turn the situation at Xerox around by divesting businesses, such as financial services, and not only selling copiers and printers, but also by strengthening its services and solutions business as IBM did, as described in the Opening Case.

Strategic Leadership

Strategic leadership is the ability to anticipate, envision, maintain flexibility, and empower others to create strategic change as necessary. Multifunctional in nature, strategic leadership involves managing through others, managing an entire enterprise rather than a functional subunit, and coping with change that seems to be increasing exponentially in the 21st-century competitive landscape. Because of this landscape's complexity and global nature, strategic leaders must learn how to effectively influence human behavior in what is an uncertain environment. By word or by personal example, and through their ability to envision the future, effective strategic leaders meaningfully influence the behaviors, thoughts, and feelings of those with whom they work.[5]

The ability to manage human capital may be the most critical of the strategic leader's skills.[6] In the 21st century, intellectual capital, including the ability to manage knowledge and create and commercialize innovation, affects a strategic leader's success.[7] Competent strategic leaders also establish the context through which stakeholders (such as employees, customers, and suppliers) can perform at peak efficiency.[8] "When a public company is left with a void in leadership, for whatever reason, the ripple effects are widely felt both within and outside the organization. Internally, a company is likely to suffer a crisis of morale, confidence and productivity among employees and, similarly, stockholders may panic when a company is left rudderless and worry about the safety and future of their investment."[9] The crux of strategic leadership is the ability to manage the firm's operations effectively and sustain a high performance over time.[10]

A firm's ability to achieve strategic competitiveness and earn above-average returns is compromised when strategic leaders fail to respond appropriately and quickly to changes in the complex global competitive environment. As mentioned, the failure to respond quickly resulted in problems at Xerox. Research suggests that a firm's "long-term competitiveness depends on managers' willingness to challenge continually their managerial frames" and that global competition is more than product versus product or company versus company: It is also a case of "mind-set versus mind-set, managerial frame versus managerial frame."[11] Competing on the basis of mind-sets demands that strategic leaders learn how to deal with diverse and cognitively complex competitive situations. One author labels this ability strategic intelligence, which consists of five interrelated elements or competencies: "foresight, systems thinking, visioning, motivating, and partnering."[12]

Effective strategic leaders are willing to make candid and courageous, yet pragmatic, decisions—decisions that may be difficult, but necessary—through foresight as they reflect on external conditions facing the firm. They also need to understand how such decisions will affect the internal systems currently in use in the firm. Effective strategic leaders use visioning to motivate employees. They often solicit corrective feedback from peers, superiors, and employees about the value of their difficult decisions and vision. Ultimately, they develop strong partners internally and externally to facilitate execution of their strategic vision.[13]

The primary responsibility for effective strategic leadership rests at the top, in particular, with the CEO. Other commonly recognized strategic leaders include members of the board of directors, the top management team, and divisional general managers. Regardless of their title and organizational function, strategic leaders have substantial decision-making responsibilities that cannot be delegated.[14] Strategic leadership is an extremely complex, but critical, form of leadership. Strategies cannot be formulated and implemented to achieve above-average returns without effective strategic leaders. Because strategic leadership is a requirement of strategic success, and because organizations may be poorly led and overmanaged, firms competing in the 21st-century competitive landscape are challenged to develop effective strategic leaders.[15]

Managers as an Organizational Resource

As we have suggested, top-level managers are an important resource for firms seeking to formulate and implement strategies effectively.[16] The strategic decisions made by top-level managers influence how the firm is designed and whether goals will be achieved. Thus, a critical element of organizational success is having a top-management team with superior managerial skills.[17]

Managers often use their discretion (or latitude for action) when making strategic decisions, including those concerned with the effective implementation of strategies.[18] Managerial discretion differs significantly across industries. The primary factors that determine the amount of decision-making discretion a manager (especially a top-level manager) has include (1) external environmental sources (such as the industry structure, the rate of market growth in the firm's primary industry, and the degree to which products can be differentiated), (2) characteristics of the organization (including its size, age, resources, and culture), and (3) characteristics of the manager (including commitment to the firm and its strategic outcomes, tolerance for ambiguity, skills in working with different people, and aspiration levels) (see Figure 12.2). Because strategic leaders' decisions are intended to help the firm gain a competitive advantage, how managers exercise discretion when determining appropriate strategic actions is critical to the firm's success.[19] Top executives must be action oriented; thus, the decisions that they make should spur the company to action.

In addition to determining new strategic initiatives, top-level managers develop the appropriate organizational structure and reward systems of a firm. In Chapter 11, we describe how the organizational structure and reward systems affect strategic actions taken to implement different strategies. Top executives also have a major

Figure 12.2   Factors Affecting Managerial Discretion

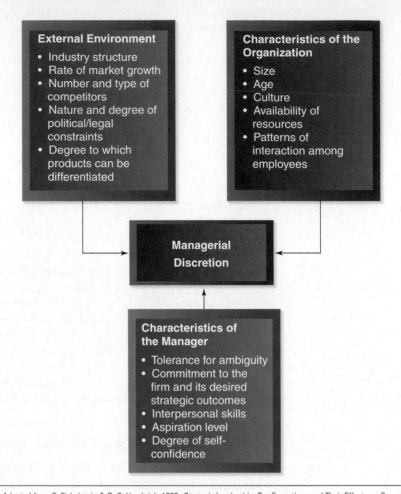

SOURCE: Adapted from S. Finkelstein & D. C. Hambrick, 1996, *Strategic Leadership: Top Executives and Their Effects on Organizations*, St. Paul, MN: West Publishing Company.

effect on a firm's culture. Evidence suggests that managers' values are critical in shaping a firm's cultural values.[20] Accordingly, top-level managers have an important effect on organizational activities and performance.[21]

The potential effect of strategic leadership is illustrated by Mitt Romney's successful turnaround of the 2002 Winter Olympic Games. When Romney took over as CEO of the Salt Lake Organizing Committee in 1999, it had a $379 million deficit resulting from the loss of sponsors following the Olympic bid scandal and allegations of bribery. Romney's ability not only to cut costs but also to attract new sponsors saved the games financially. Moreover, his approach and integrity won over many and helped heal the wounds from the bid controversy. "If we do our job well, people will go away feeling like they have had a fire lit within them or they've been inspired by the athletes and by the people they've met here and by their fellow citizens from around the world."[22] Romney's leadership was very effective in accomplishing this aspiration.

The decisions and actions of strategic leaders can make them a source of competitive advantage for the firm. In accordance with the criteria of sustainability discussed in Chapter 3, strategic leaders can be a source of competitive advantage only

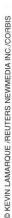

Mitt Romney, pictured here with the 2002 Olympic torch, oversaw the Salt Lake Olympic Games. Following a six-year position as vice president of Boston-based management consulting firm Bain & Company, he founded Bain Capital. He later served as interim CEO of Bain & Company during a period of financial turmoil and led the firm's highly successful turnaround. In 2002, he became a candidate for governor of Massachusetts.

The **top management team** is composed of the key managers who are responsible for selecting and implementing the firm's strategies.

A **heterogeneous top management team** is composed of individuals with different functional backgrounds, experience, and education.

when their work is valuable, rare, costly to imitate, and nonsubstitutable. Effective strategic leaders become a source of competitive advantage when they focus their work on the key issues that ultimately shape the firm's ability to earn above-average returns.[23] Accordingly, managerial beliefs affect strategic decisions that in turn affect the firm's performance.[24] For example, Mitt Romney certainly believed that the 2002 Winter Olympic Games could be turned into a success. However, Romney's vision was achieved through a team of leaders.

Top Management Teams

The complexity of the challenges faced by the firm and the need for substantial amounts of information and knowledge require teams of executives to provide the strategic leadership of most firms. The **top management team** is composed of the key managers who are responsible for selecting and implementing the firm's strategies. Typically, the top management team includes the officers of the corporation, defined by the title of vice president and above or by service as a member of the board of directors.[25] The quality of the strategic decisions made by a top management team affects the firm's ability to innovate and engage in effective strategic change.[26]

Top Management Team, Firm Performance, and Strategic Change

The job of top-level executives is complex and requires a broad knowledge of the firm's operations, as well as the three key parts of the firm's external environment—the general, industry, and competitor environments, as discussed in Chapter 2. Therefore, firms try to form a top management team that has the appropriate knowledge and expertise to operate the internal organization, yet also can deal with all the firm's stakeholders as well as its competitors.[27] This normally requires a heterogeneous top management team. A **heterogeneous top management team** is composed of individuals with different functional backgrounds, experience, and education. The more heterogeneous a top management team is, with varied expertise and knowledge, the more capacity it has to provide effective strategic leadership in *formulating* strategy.

Members of a heterogeneous top management team benefit from discussing the different perspectives advanced by team members. In many cases, these discussions increase the quality of the top management team's decisions, especially when a synthesis emerges from the diverse perspectives that is generally superior to any one individual perspective.[28] For example, heterogeneous top management teams in the airline industry have the propensity to take stronger competitive actions and reactions than do more homogenous teams.[29] The net benefit of such actions by heterogeneous teams has been positive in terms of market share and above-average returns. Research shows that more heterogeneity among top management team members promotes debate, which often leads to better strategic decisions. In turn, better strategic decisions produce higher firm performance.[30]

It is also important that the top management team members function cohesively. In general, the more heterogeneous and larger the top management team is, the more difficult it is for the team to effectively implement strategies.[31] Comprehensive and long-term strategic plans can be inhibited by communication difficulties among top executives who have different backgrounds and different cognitive skills.[32] As a result, a group of top executives with diverse backgrounds may inhibit the process of decision making if it is not effectively managed. In these cases, top management teams may fail to comprehensively examine threats and opportunities, leading to a suboptimal strategic decision.

Having members with substantive expertise in the firm's core functions and businesses is also important to the effectiveness of a top management team. In a high-technology industry, it may be critical for a firm's top management team to have R&D expertise, particularly when growth strategies are being implemented.[33]

The characteristics of top management teams are related to innovation and strategic change.[34] For example, more heterogeneous top management teams are associated positively with innovation and strategic change. The heterogeneity may force the team or some of the members to "think outside of the box" and thus be more creative in making decisions.[35] Therefore, firms that need to change their strategies are more likely to do so if they have top management teams with diverse backgrounds and expertise. A top management team with various areas of expertise is more likely to identify environmental changes (opportunities and threats) or changes within the firms that require a different strategic direction.[36]

CEO Daniel Vasella, chairman of Novartis, formed through the merger of Swiss drugmakers Sandoz and Ciba-Geigy in 1996, runs the world's seventh-largest pharmaceutical company.[37] Vasella, formerly a physician, has transformed the once stodgy Swiss conglomerate into an aggressive innovator, partly by putting together an energetic but diverse top management team. One analyst noted, "Although the top executives at Novartis contain a diversity of strong personalities, their oft-used term 'alignment' rings true in their teamwork. . . . Yet, each team member carries a different charge and perspective."[38]

The CEO and Top Management Team Power

As noted in Chapter 10, the board of directors is an important governance mechanism for monitoring a firm's strategic direction and for representing stakeholders' interests, especially those of shareholders. In fact, higher performance normally is achieved when the board of directors is more directly involved in shaping a firm's strategic direction.[39]

Boards of directors, however, may find it difficult to direct the strategic actions of powerful CEOs and top management teams.[40] It is not uncommon for a powerful CEO to appoint a number of sympathetic outside board members or have inside board members who are on the top management team and report to the CEO.[41] In either case, the CEO may have significant control over the board's actions. "A central question is whether boards are an effective management control mechanism . . . or whether they are a 'management tool,' . . . a rubber stamp for management initiatives . . . and often surrender to management their major domain of decision-making authority, which includes the right to hire, fire, and compensate top management."[42]

As mentioned earlier, Xerox has stumbled, partly due to its board. *Fortune* named it one of the "dirty half dozen" in 2001: "Xerox is a textbook example of a high-profile board asleep at the wheel . . . the once proud document giant has been plagued by everything short of locusts: missed earnings estimates, plummeting stock, mounting debt, and an SEC investigation of dodgy accounting practices in Xerox's Mexican operations. What have the venerable directors done? Very little—perhaps because they were busy at other meetings (most of Xerox's directors serve on at least four other boards)."[43]

Alternatively, recent research shows that social ties between the CEO and board members may actually increase board members' involvement in strategic decisions. Thus, strong relationships between the CEO and the board of directors may have positive or negative outcomes.[44]

DaimlerChrysler Corporation President and CEO Dieter Zetsche, pictured here, believes firms should take marketing risks. "We are willing to cause just a bit of controversy, if it creates products that resonate with our customers," Zetsche said. "We also want to find ways not to be driven to middle ground, the `no man's land' of ultraconservative products ."

CEOs and top management team members can achieve power in other ways. A CEO who also holds the position of chairman of the board usually has more power than the CEO who is not simultaneously serving as chairman of the firm's board.[45] Although this practice of CEO duality (when the CEO and the chairperson of the board are the same) has become more common in U.S. businesses, it has come under heavy criticism. Duality has been blamed for poor performance and slow response to change in a number of firms.[46]

DaimlerChrysler CEO Jergen Schrempp, who holds the dual positions of chairman of the board and CEO, has substantial power in the firm. In fact, insiders suggest that he was purging those individuals who are outspoken and who represent potential threats to his dominance. In particular, former Chrysler executives are leaving the firm, although research suggests that retaining key employees after an acquisition contributes to improved post acquisition performance.[47] Thus, it has been particularly difficult to turn around the US operations.[48] Dieter Zetsche, a German who is likely next in line to be CEO at DaimlerChrysler, is leading the team that is seeking to reverse Chrysler's fortunes. Schrempp's future may depend on how Zetsche's team does. It is ironic that six of the turnaround team members are former Chrysler executives. The loss of some of these key executives, such as Thomas Stallkamp, has been blamed in part for the poor performance.

Although it varies across industries, duality occurs most commonly in the largest firms. Increased shareholder activism, however, has brought CEO duality under scrutiny and attack in both U.S. and European firms. Historically, an independent board leadership structure in which the same person did not hold the positions of CEO and chair was believed to enhance a board's ability to monitor top-level managers' decisions and actions, particularly in terms of the firm's financial performance.[49] Stewardship theory, on the other hand, suggests that CEO duality facilitates effective decisions and actions. In these instances, the increased effectiveness gained through CEO duality accrues from the individual who wants to perform effectively and desires to be the best possible steward of the firm's assets. Because of this person's positive orientation and actions, extra governance and the coordination costs resulting from an independent board leadership structure would be unnecessary.[50]

Top-management team members and CEOs who have long tenure—on the team and in the organization—have a greater influence on board decisions.[51] Long tenure is known to restrict the breadth of an executive's knowledge base. With the limited perspectives associated with a restricted knowledge base, long-tenured top executives typically develop fewer alternatives to evaluate in making strategic decisions.[52] However, long-tenured managers also may be able to exercise more effective strategic control, thereby obviating the need for board members' involvement because effective strategic control generally produces higher performance.[53]

To strengthen the firm, boards of directors should develop an effective relationship with the firm's top management team. The relative degrees of power held by the board and top management team members should be examined in light of an individual firm's situation. For example, the abundance of resources in a firm's external environment and the volatility of that environment may affect the ideal balance of power between boards and top-management teams.[54] Moreover, a volatile and uncertain environment may create a situation where a powerful CEO is needed to move quickly, but a diverse top management team may create less cohesion among team members and prevent or stall a necessary strategic move.[55] Through the development of effective working relationships, boards, CEOs, and other top management team members are able to serve the best interests of the firm's stakeholders.[56]

Managerial Labor Market

The choice of top executives—especially CEOs—is a critical organizational decision with important implications for the firm's performance.[57] Many companies use leadership screening systems to identify individuals with managerial and strategic leadership potential. The most effective of these systems assess people within the firm and gain valuable information about the capabilities of other companies' managers, particularly their strategic leaders.[58] Based on the results of these assessments, training and development programs are provided for current managers in an attempt to preselect and shape the skills of people who may become tomorrow's leaders. The "ten-step talent" management development program at GE, for example, is considered one of the most effective in the world.[59]

Organizations select managers and strategic leaders from two types of managerial labor markets—internal and external.[60] An **internal managerial labor market** consists of the opportunities for managerial positions within a firm, whereas an **external managerial labor market** is the collection of career opportunities for managers in organizations other than the one for which they work currently. Several benefits are thought to accrue to a firm when the internal labor market is used to select an insider as the new CEO. Because of their experience with the firm and the industry environment in which it competes, insiders are familiar with company products, markets, technologies, and operating procedures. Also, internal hiring produces lower turnover among existing personnel, many of whom possess valuable firm-specific knowledge. When the firm is performing well, internal succession is favored to sustain high performance. It is assumed that hiring from inside keeps the important knowledge necessary to sustain the performance.

Given the phenomenal success of GE and its highly effective management development program, an insider, Jeffrey Immelt, was chosen to succeed Jack Welch.[61] Similarly, as the Opening Case illustrates, an insider, Samuel Palmisano, was selected to replace Louis Gerstner, who was an outsider when he was chosen as IBM's CEO. Gerstner was selected to change the strategic direction of the firm, which was suffering at the time of his hire. Since IBM's performance has improved considerably, investors do not want a change in strategic direction. For an inside move to the top to occur successfully, however, firms must develop and implement effective succession management programs. In that way, managers can be developed so that one will eventually be prepared to ascend to the top.[62]

It is not unusual for employees to have a strong preference for the internal managerial labor market to be used to select top management team members and the CEO.[63] This preference for insiders to fill top-level management positions reflects a desire for continuity and a continuing commitment to the firm's current strategic intent, strategic mission, and chosen strategies.[64] Thus, internal candidates tend to be valued over external candidates[65] in the selection of a firm's CEO and other top-level managers. In fact, outside succession to the CEO position "is an extraordinary event for business firms [and] is usually seen as a stark indicator that the board of directors wants change."[66]

Alternatively, firms often have valid reasons to select an outsider as its new CEO. For example, research evidence suggests that executives who have spent their entire career with a particular firm may become "stale in the saddle."[67] Long tenure with a firm seems to reduce the number of innovative ideas top executives are able to develop to cope with conditions facing their firm. Given the importance of innovation for a firm's success in today's competitive landscape (see Chapter 13), an inability to innovate or to create conditions that stimulate innovation throughout a firm is a liability in a strategic leader. Figure 12.3 shows how the composition of the top

An **internal managerial labor market** consists of the opportunities for managerial positions within a firm.

An **external managerial labor market** is the collection of career opportunities for managers in organizations other than the one for which they work currently.

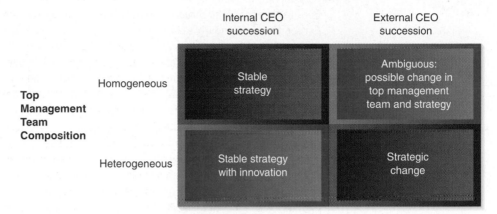

management team and CEO succession (managerial labor market) may interact to
affect strategy. For example, when the top-management team is homogeneous (its
members have similar functional experiences and educational backgrounds) and a
new CEO is selected from inside the firm, the firm's current strategy is unlikely to
change.

On the other hand, when a new CEO is selected from outside the firm and the
top management team is heterogeneous, there is a high probability that strategy will
change. When the new CEO is from inside the firm and a heterogeneous top management team is in place, the strategy may not change; but, innovation is likely to
continue. An external CEO succession with a homogeneous team creates a more
ambiguous situation.

To have an adequate number of top managers, firms must take advantage of a
highly qualified labor pool, including one source of managers that has often been
overlooked: women. Firms are beginning to utilize women's potential managerial talents with substantial success, as described in the Strategic Focus on page 394.

The early years of the 21st century find women being more frequently
appointed to the boards of directors for organizations in both the private and public
sectors. These additional appointments suggest that women's ability to represent
stakeholders' and especially shareholders' best interests in for-profit companies at the
level of the board of directors is being more broadly recognized. However, in addition to appointments to the board of directors, firms competing in the complex and
challenging global economy—an economy demanding the best of an organization—
may be well served by adding more female executives to their top management teams.

Key Strategic Leadership Actions

Several identifiable actions characterize strategic leadership that positively contributes to effective use of the firm's strategies.[68] We present the most critical of these
actions in Figure 12.4. Many of the actions interact with each other. For example,

Opportunities for Women as Top-Level Managers

Is there a "glass ceiling" keeping women from becoming CEOs? Only 1.2 percent of CEOs in the *Fortune* 500 are women, while 20.6 percent of federal judges are women, as are 13 percent of U.S. senators. Women have also made significant progress in top positions in Europe. A recent *Wall Street Journal* survey of the top 25 women managers across firms in Europe found that nearly a third of the entrepreneurs starting new business are women (although Germany had no women in the CEO position).

The small percentage of women holding top-level managers' positions typically receives more media attention than do many of their male counterparts. The attention is generally positive when a woman succeeds, such as is the case with eBay's Meg Whitman. It can also be very negative when a woman fails, as did Linda Wachner, former CEO of Warnaco. Positive media attention about a woman CEO can also help a company's image, as when Carly Fiorina became head of the respected Silicon Valley firm, Hewlett-Packard. If the 2002 merger between HP and Compaq is unsuccessful, Fiorina may become another failure story, which could make it more difficult for other women to get significant corporate leadership opportunities. Each time a woman executive succeeds, all women executives seem to receive some new measure of respect, while each time one fails, the others are studied with a more critical eye.

Lucent's new CEO, Patricia Russo, is only the ninth woman to run one of the 1,000 largest companies. She is not new to Lucent, even though she was only recently hired from Kodak. Most of her career had been spent working for a division of AT&T, which subsequently became Lucent after the AT&T break up. She had left Lucent for a position at Kodak, and she was rehired by Lucent as its CEO only eight months later, in January 2002. It was likely that Russo would have been named CEO of Kodak after a few years of service as the firm's COO (chief operating officer). Lucent has struggled in the last two years and is looking for help from its new CEO. Russo claims that she will continue to use former Lucent CEO Schacht's plan for the company. She also claims that no significant changes in management will occur. Some critics worry that this inaction could make the situation worse for Lucent and that the lack of new blood could cause the company to become stagnant. Russo will make an estimated base salary of at least $1.1 million per year, and she could receive more than four million stock options within her first year.

eBay, headed by President and CEO Meg Whitman, pictured here, has $300 exchanged every second on its website. During the late 1990s, Whitman was upstaged by the heads of other Internet firms, but eBay was profitable from the start under her disciplined management.

A study examining the gender compensation gap among high-level executives in the United States found that women, who represented about 2.5 percent of the sample, earned about 45 percent less than men. However, "as much as 75 percent of this gap can be explained by the fact that women managed smaller companies and were less likely to be CEO, chair, or company president." In fact, the gap decreases to less than 5 percent when the study results are controlled for the younger average age and lower average seniority of the female executives. Also, the gap was reduced between 1992 and 1997, the timeframe of one study, because women's participation in the top executive ranks nearly tripled and their relative compensation also strongly improved, mostly by their increased representation in larger corporations.

Still, female CEOs earned far less than their male CEO counterparts in 2000. In fact, even when compared to women executives in other positions, female CEOs earned less, partly because they cashed in fewer stock options than other female executives. Another,

PART 3 /Strategic Actions: Strategy Implementation

possibly more important, reason was that companies led by women CEOs had a rough year in 2000. Women CEOs also are found more often at so-called "old economy" companies, which do a better job of promoting women but do not consistently compensate upper-level executives as generously as have many "new economy" companies. However, the compensation practices of new economy companies is coming under increasing scrutiny as a result of the declining performances recorded by many of them in the first few years of the 21st century.

SOURCES: D. Berman & J. Lublin, 2002, Russo's goal as Lucent's new chief: Restore luster, *The Wall Street Journal*, January 8, B1, B4; A. Stanley, 2002, For women, to soar is rare, to fall is human, *The New York Times,* http://www.nytimes.com, January 13;. E. Williamson, 2002, List of leading female executives doesn't include German women, *The Wall Street Journal Interactive*, http://www.wsj.com, February 27; M. Bertrand & K. F. Hallock, 2001, The gender gap in top corporate jobs, *Industrial & Labor Relations Review,* 55: 3–21; L. Lavelle, 2001, For female CEOs, it's stingy at the top, *Business Week,* April 23, 70–71; J. G. Oakley, 2000, Gender-based barriers to senior management positions: Understanding the scarcity of female CEOs, *Journal of Business Ethics,* 27: 321–334.

developing human capital through executive training contributes to establishing a strategic direction, fostering an effective culture, exploiting core competencies, using effective organizational control systems, and establishing ethical practices.

Determining Strategic Direction

Determining the strategic direction of a firm involves developing a long-term vision of the firm's strategic intent.

Determining the strategic direction of a firm involves developing a long-term vision of the firm's strategic intent. A long-term vision typically looks at least five to ten years into the future. A philosophy with goals, this vision consists of the image and character the firm seeks.[69]

Figure 12.4   Exercise of Effective Strategic Leadership

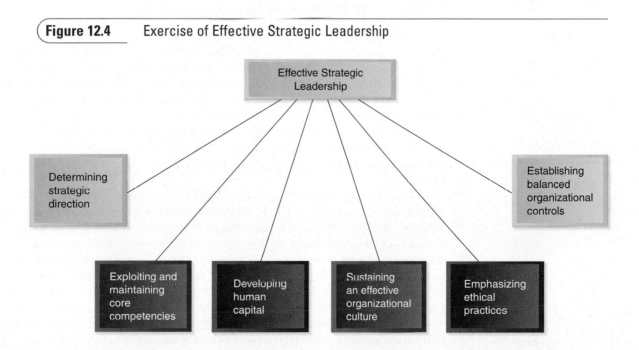

The ideal long-term vision has two parts: a core ideology and an envisioned future. While the core ideology motivates employees through the company's heritage, the envisioned future encourages employees to stretch beyond their expectations of accomplishment and requires significant change and progress in order to be realized.[70] The envisioned future serves as a guide to many aspects of a firm's strategy implementation process, including motivation, leadership, employee empowerment, and organizational design.

Matthew D. Heyman came out of Harvard Business School in 1993 with a vision of building lavish movie theaters in Mexico City, a city with 20 million inhabitants. The Mexican theater industry was in shambles because of government price controls, and so a vacuum existed for quality movie theaters. For six months, Heyman and his partners, Miguel Angel Dávila and Adolfo Fastlicht, were told by investors that their idea was too risky. After finding financial backing for their company, Cinemex, they began constructing movie theaters, but then the Mexican economy crashed. Heyman decided to push through anyway, as much of his competition disappeared as a result of the crash. He decided early on to target the largest market in Mexico City, the working poor. His theaters charged about half as much for tickets in poor areas of the city compared to the price charged by theaters in wealthy areas, even though these theaters were just as extravagant. In 2001, Cinemex was expected to generate a profit of approximately $40 million.[71] This accomplishment is largely due to Heyman's vision and the employees of Cinemex who were inspired by Heyman's leadership to implement his vision.

A charismatic CEO may foster employees' commitment to a new vision and strategic direction. Nonetheless, it is important not to lose sight of the strengths of the organization in making changes required by a new strategic direction. Most top executives obtain inputs regarding their vision from many people with a range of skills to help them analyze various aspects of the firm's operations. In addition, executives must structure the firm effectively to help achieve their vision.[72] The goal is to balance the firm's short-term need to adjust to a new vision while maintaining its long-term survivability by emphasizing its current and valuable core competencies.

Exploiting and Maintaining Core Competencies

Examined in Chapters 1 and 3, *core competencies* are resources and capabilities that serve as a source of competitive advantage for a firm over its rivals. Typically, core competencies relate to an organization's functional skills, such as manufacturing, finance, marketing, and research and development. As shown by the descriptions that follow, firms develop and exploit core competencies in many different functional areas. Strategic leaders must verify that the firm's competencies are emphasized in strategy implementation efforts. Intel, for example, has core competencies of *competitive agility* (an ability to act in a variety of competitively relevant ways) and *competitive speed* (an ability to act quickly when facing environmental and competitive pressures).[73]

In many large firms, and certainly in related diversified ones, core competencies are effectively exploited when they are developed and applied across different organizational units (see Chapter 6). For example, PepsiCo purchased Quaker Oats, which makes the sports drink Gatorade. Pepsi plans to use its competence in distribution systems to build market share outside the United States. Accordingly, Pepsi soft drinks (e.g., Pepsi Cola and Mountain Dew) and Gatorade will share the logistics activity. Similarly, Quaker Oats' healthy snacks and Frito Lay's salty snacks (already owned by Pepsi) can use this competence and be distributed through the same channels.[74]

In making a number of acquisitions, Cisco became skilled at integrating the new businesses into the firm's operating culture, especially in building its main business in routers, which was a critical part of building the Internet infrastructure. In light of new opportunities, Cisco is now trying to diversify into new businesses of "voice-over-Internet systems, wireless networking gear, storage-networking devices and optical equipment."[75] The degree to which Cisco will be able "to pluck promising technology after someone else had borne the development risk" using an acquisition strategy as the foundation for how it competes in its new business areas is unknown. Other competitors exist in these new markets with already established capabilities. Cisco's human capital will play a critical role in the firm's attempt to develop the core competencies that are required to successfully compete in the markets Cisco is now targeting.

Developing Human Capital

Human capital refers to the knowledge and skills of a firm's entire workforce.

Human capital refers to the knowledge and skills of a firm's entire workforce. From the perspective of human capital, employees are viewed as a capital resource that requires investment.[76] These investments are productive, in that much of the development of U.S. industry can be attributed to the effectiveness of its human capital,[77] leading to the conviction in many business firms today that "as the dynamics of competition accelerate, people are perhaps the only truly sustainable source of competitive advantage."[78] Human capital's increasing importance suggests a significant role for the firm's human resource management activities.[79] As a support activity (see Chapter 2), human resource management practices facilitate people's efforts to successfully select and especially to use the firm's strategies.[80]

Finding the human capital necessary to run an organization effectively is a challenge that many firms attempt to solve by using temporary employees. Other firms try to improve their recruiting and selection techniques. Solving the problem, however, requires more than hiring temporary employees; it requires building effective commitment to organizational goals as well. Hiring star players is also insufficient; rather, a strategic leader needs to build an effective organizational team committed to achieving the company's vision and goals.[81]

Increasingly, international experience has become essential to the development necessary for strategic leaders. Because nearly every industry is targeting fast-growing foreign markets, more companies are requiring "global competency" among their top managers.[82] Thus, companies trying to learn how to compete successfully in the global economy should find opportunities for their future strategic leaders to work in locations outside of their home nation.[83] When multinational corporations invest in emerging economies, they are also wise to invest in human capital in foreign subsidiaries.[84] Also, because international management capabilities are becoming important, managing "inpatriation" (the process of transferring host-country or third-country national managers into the domestic market of multinational firms) has become an important means of building global core competencies.[85]

Effective training and development programs increase the probability that a manager will be a successful strategic leader. These programs have grown progressively important as knowledge has become more integral to gaining and sustaining a competitive advantage.[86] Additionally, such programs build knowledge and skills, inculcate a common set of core values, and offer a systematic view of the organization, thus promoting the firm's strategic vision and organizational cohesion. The programs also contribute to the development of core competencies.[87] Furthermore, they help strategic leaders improve skills that are critical to completing other tasks associated with effective strategic leadership, such as determining the firm's strategic direction, exploiting and maintaining the firm's core competencies, and developing an organizational culture that supports ethical practices. Thus, building human capital is vital to the effective execution of strategic leadership.[88]

© MICHAEL NICHOLSON/CORBIS

Barclays Bank headquarters in London. Currently, Barclays is emphasizing human capital and strategic leadershp to create competitive advantages the firm believes are linked to its success.

Strategic leaders must acquire the skills necessary to help develop human capital in their areas of responsibility. This challenge is important, given that most strategic leaders need to enhance their human resource management abilities. For example, firms that place value on human resources and have effective reward plans for employees obtained higher returns on their initial public offerings.[89] When human capital investments are successful, the result is a workforce capable of learning continuously. Continuous learning and leveraging the firm's expanding knowledge base are linked with strategic success.[90]

Although Barclays Group lost its position among the world's largest banks in the 1980s (it was ranked fifth in the world in assets in the early 1980s), its prestige was rising again in 2000. Barclays' return on equity was 23 percent in fiscal year 2000, up from 15 percent in 1997, thanks to the leadership of Barclays' Matthew Barrett, named CEO in October 1999. Much of Barrett's accomplishments can be attributed to hiring significant leadership talent away from other firms to form formidable top management teams for Barclays' various business groups. For instance, he hired Robert Diamond from Morgan Stanley to lead Barclays' capital unit. Barrett has developed a new long-term vision of the firm's strategic intent by taking the position that: "I want us to be the premier European investment bank for debt finance." While competitors are downsizing, Barclays is adding key people, partly by raiding its German rival Deutsche Bank for additional talent. The firm has also hired 25 senior investment bankers for its New York unit and hired Michael O'Neill from Bank of America to be the chief executive of its long-term capital management group. In summary, Barrett is relying on Barclay's human capital to pursue the firm's newly determined strategic direction.[91]

Programs that achieve outstanding results in the training of future strategic leaders become a competitive advantage for a firm. As noted earlier, General Electric's system of training and development of future strategic leaders is comprehensive and thought to be among the best.[92] Accordingly, it may be a source of competitive advantage for the firm.

Because of the economic downturn in 2001 and early 2002, many firms are laying off key people. Layoffs can result in a significant loss of the knowledge possessed by a firm's human capital. Although it is also not uncommon for restructuring firms to reduce their expenditures on, or investments in, training and development programs, restructuring may actually be an important time to increase investments in these programs. Restructuring firms have less slack and cannot absorb as many errors; moreover, the employees who remain after layoffs may find themselves in positions without all of the skills or knowledge they need to perform the required tasks effectively.[93] Improvements in information technology can facilitate better use of human resources when a downsizing event occurs.[94]

Viewing employees as a resource to be maximized rather than a cost to be minimized facilitates the successful implementation of a firm's strategies. The implementation of such strategies also is more effective when strategic leaders approach layoffs in a manner that employees believe is fair and equitable.[95]

Sustaining an Effective Organizational Culture

An **organizational culture** consists of a complex set of ideologies, symbols, and core values that is shared throughout the firm and influences the way business is conducted.

An **organizational culture** consists of a complex set of ideologies, symbols, and core values that is shared throughout the firm and influences the way business is conducted. Evidence suggests that a firm can develop core competencies in terms of both the capabilities it possesses and the way the capabilities are used to produce strategic

PART 3 /Strategic Actions: Strategy Implementation

actions. In other words, because the organizational culture influences how the firm conducts its business and helps regulate and control employees' behavior, it can be a source of competitive advantage.[96] Thus, shaping the context within which the firm formulates and implements its strategies—that is, shaping the organizational culture—is a central task of strategic leaders.[97]

Entrepreneurial Orientation

An organizational culture often encourages (or discourages) the pursuit of entrepreneurial opportunities, especially in large firms.[98] Entrepreneurial opportunities are an important source of growth and innovation.[99] In Chapter 13, we describe how large firms use strategic entrepreneurship to pursue entrepreneurial opportunities and to gain first-mover advantages. Medium and small firms also rely on strategic entrepreneurship when trying to develop innovations as the foundation for profitable growth. In firms of all sizes, strategic entrepreneurship is more likely to be successful when employees have an entrepreneurial orientation. Five dimensions characterize a firm's entrepreneurial orientation: autonomy, innovativeness, risk taking, proactiveness, and competitive aggressiveness.[100] In combination, these dimensions influence the activities of a firm to be innovative and launch new ventures.

The first of an entrepreneurial orientation's five dimensions, *autonomy*, allows employees to take actions that are free of organizational constraints and permits individuals and groups to be self-directed. The second dimension, *innovativeness*, "reflects a firm's tendency to engage in and support new ideas, novelty, experimentation, and creative processes that may result in new products, services, or technological processes."[101] Cultures with a tendency toward innovativeness encourage employees to think beyond existing knowledge, technologies, and parameters in efforts to find creative ways to add value. *Risk taking* reflects a willingness by employees and their firm to accept risks when pursuing entrepreneurial opportunities. These risks can include assuming significant levels of debt and allocating large amounts of other resources (e.g., people) to projects that may not be completed. The fourth dimension of an entrepreneurial orientation, *proactiveness*, describes a firm's ability to be a market leader rather than a follower. Proactive organizational cultures constantly use processes to anticipate future market needs and to satisfy them before competitors learn how to do so. Finally, *competitive aggressiveness* is a firm's propensity to take actions that allow it to consistently and substantially outperform its rivals.[102]

James Farrell, CEO of Illinois Tool Works (ITW), uses an unorthodox method for creating an entrepreneurial culture among ITW's businesses, most of which were acquired. In many organizations, acquisitions are consolidated with other business units, but Farrell does not consolidate the businesses he purchases. In fact, ITW usually breaks up acquisitions into smaller units so business managers can be closer to their customers. Farrell gives these managers a large amount of autonomy, which encourages them to act like entrepreneurs. Farrell suggests that his success with acquisitions is how he focuses management on what ITW calls the "80/20 process." This means that the division should aggressively focus on the 20 percent of customers or products that provide 80 percent of sales, and forget about the rest, which are seen as a distraction. Usually, the firms ITW acquires experience an increase in their operating margin, from an average of 9 percent to an average of 19 percent.[103]

Changing the Organizational Culture and Business Reengineering

Changing a firm's organizational culture is more difficult than maintaining it, but effective strategic leaders recognize when change is needed. Incremental changes to the firm's culture typically are used to implement strategies.[104] More significant and, sometimes, even radical changes to organizational culture are used to support the selection of strategies that differ from those the firm has implemented historically. Regardless of the reasons for change, shaping and reinforcing a new culture require effective communication and problem solving, along with the selection of the right people (those who have the values desired for the organization), effective performance appraisals (establishing goals and measuring individual performance toward goals that fit in with the new core values), and appropriate reward systems (rewarding the desired behaviors that reflect the new core values).[105]

Evidence suggests that cultural changes succeed only when the firm's CEO, other key top management team members, and middle-level managers actively support them.[106] To effect change, middle-level managers in particular need to be highly disciplined to energize the culture and foster alignment with the strategic vision.[107]

As noted earlier, selecting new top management team members from the external managerial labor market is a catalyst for changes to organizational culture. This is illustrated in the Strategic Focus about Carlos Ghosn on page 401. A Brazilian-born manager working for Renault, Ghosn was charged with turning around Nissan, partially owned by Renault, which was suffering from lost market share. As this Strategic Focus about illustrates, transforming an organization and its culture is challenging. For example, William W. George, CEO until June 2001 of Medtronic, a medical device company, spent years building Medtronic into a "mission driven" company that creates long-term value for shareholders. He has built a culture that has a goal of deriving 70 percent of its revenue from products launched in the previous two years. George argues that making decisions based solely on financial considerations leads to poor market place competitiveness and customer satisfaction, because such decisions only enhance the wealth of the top officers and do not engage the rest of the employees—in fact, they create cynicism.[108] He argues that a customer-focused culture, which is mission-driven, based on a clear set of widely used values and an adaptable business strategy, has allowed Medtronic and other firms to create successful and innovation-oriented cultures.[109]

Emphasizing Ethical Practices

The effectiveness of processes used to implement the firm's strategies increases when they are based on ethical practices. Ethical companies encourage and enable people at all organizational levels to act ethically when doing what is necessary to implement the firm's strategies. In turn, ethical practices and the judgment on which they are based create "social capital" in the organization in that "goodwill available to individuals and groups" in the organization increases.[110] Thus, while "money motivates, it does not inspire" as social capital can.[111] Alternately, when unethical practices evolve in an organization, they become like a contagious disease.[112]

To properly influence employees' judgment and behavior, ethical practices must shape the firm's decision-making process and be an integral part of an organization's culture. In fact, research has found that a value-based culture is the most effective means of ensuring that employees comply with the firm's ethical requirements.[113] As discussed in chapter 10, in the absence of ethical requirements, managers may act opportunistically, making decisions that are in their own best interests, but not in the firm's best interests. In other words, managers acting opportunistically take advantage of their positions, making decisions that benefit them to the detriment of the firm's owners (shareholders).[114]

Managerial opportunism may explain the behavior and decisions of a few key executives at Enron, where stockholders lost almost all the value in their Enron stock in the firm's bankruptcy proceeding. The bankruptcy seems to have been precipitated by off-balance sheet partnerships formed by Enron managers (see the Strategic Focus on page 332 in Chaper 10).[115] Accounting firm Arthur Andersen, Enron's auditor, was

An Outsider from Brazil Facilitates Change at Nissan

In 1999, Renault assumed $5.4 billion of Nissan's debt in return for 36.6 percent of Nissan's equity, giving it a controlling stake in the Japanese automaker. The combined assets of Renault and Nissan made them the fourth largest carmaker in the world. However, Nissan was struggling with shrinking market share, both domestically in Japan and worldwide. Renault turned to Carlos Ghosn to lead a turnaround for the Japanese carmaker.

Ghosn came to Renault from Michelin's Brazilian subsidiary. He was given a complex challenge—not only did he face the difficulty of overcoming conservatism among Nissan car designers, which had allowed engineers to dominate for the past decade of slow market share loss, but he also had to face the cultural challenge of being an outsider in the homogeneous Japanese culture. Although the challenge was daunting, Ghosn was able to win over key Japanese inside managers necessary to implement his plan, as well as suppliers and labor leaders who might have been expected to resist more intensely. Furthermore, the car designs created under Ghosn's leadership had much more flare than in the recent past. As a result, in 2001, Nissan posted a profit of $2.7 billion; its largest in its 68-year history and its first annual profit in 4 years.

How was Ghosn, a manager who was selected from the external managerial labor market, able to accomplish this significant strategic turnaround? Although he continues to indicate that his strategic change agenda is not complete because facilitating a change in the organization culture takes time, several actions can be identified. For example, he charged Itaru Koeda with the task of drastic cost reduction with specific targets and tactics. To accomplish this reduction, Ghosn brought together a younger set of Nissan managers, "thirty-five- and forty-five-year-old managers," to participate in identifying issues to focus on in the cost reduction. Although this action may not sound that unusual outside of Japan, it was revolutionary to have "young people in the company to debate things and propose what we should do."

Next, he changed the way the supply chain was managed by reducing the number of suppliers and, at the same time, sought to create deeper partnerships with them. To fund this new way of managing the supply chain, Ghosn dismantled the cross shareholding associated with Nissan's keiretsu investments. Ghosn found that $4 billion was tied up in cross shareholdings with keiretsu partner companies, which often had no relationship with Nissan. Following this action, Nissan allowed suppliers to specialize in what they do best, and suppliers became part of cross-functional teams for new model development. Because of this fresh outside influence, the car designs have become much more sleek and exciting.

Another difficult action Ghosn took was to close a number of plants, although in Japan lifetime employment is still seen as an important labor movement objective. To facilitate closure of a plant in a Tokyo suburb, Ghosn worked with Nissan's unions to show that no matter how painful, in the long run such actions would be good for workers as well. He negotiated a generous one-time bonus of 5.2 months pay for those workers who were laid off. Because other companies were challenging the practice of lifetime employment, Ghosn's efforts had some legitimacy.

Although Nissan knew such actions were needed before it put Ghosn in charge, it needed someone like him to "push the button." Kenichi Ohmae, a Japanese management expert, has indicated that a large majority of Japanese companies face problems similar to Nissan's. However, few have the "power to heal themselves from within." In Ghosn's words, "a good corporate culture taps into the productive aspects of a country's culture,

Nissan CEO Carlos Ghosn oversaw the development of the new Micra subcompact, a result of the Nissan/Renault partnership.

and in Nissan's case we have been able to exploit the uniquely Japanese combination of keen competitiveness and sense of community that has driven the likes of Sony and Toyota—and Nissan itself in earlier times." A Japanese manager will likely take over Nissan after Ghosn leaves. However, he will have left a legacy of significant cultural change that will likely foster success in the future.

SOURCES: C. Dawson, 2002, Nissan bets big on small, *Business Week Online,* http://www.businessweek.com, March 4; C. Ghosn, 2002, Saving the business without losing the company, *Harvard Business Review,* 80(1): 37–45; M. S. Mayershon, 2002, Nissan's u-turn to profits, *Chief Executive,* January, 12–16; A. Raskin, 2002, Voulez-dous completely overhaul this big, slow company and start making some cars people actually want avec moi? *Business 2.0,* January, 61–67; G. S. Vasilash, 2002, Managing design; Design management, *Automotive Design and Production,* February, 34–35; C. Ahmadjian & P. Robinson, 2001, Safety in numbers: Downsizing and the deinstitutionalization of permanent employment in Japan, *Administrative Science Quarterly,* 46: 622–654; C. Dawson & S. Prasso, 2001, Pow! Bam! Zap! Meet Nissan's super hero, *Business Week,* April 30, 12; L. P. Norton, 2001, Meet Mr. Nissan, *Barron's,* November 19, 17–19.

also severely damaged by the disaster. The SEC, other federal agencies, and several different Congressional committees have investigated Enron's financial reporting. Andersen fired partner David Duncan and put two others from the firm's Houston office on administrative leave. Duncan had ordered the destruction of documents regarding accounting practices at Enron. Due to the unethical practices of both the company and the auditor, many accounting firms and other firms unrelated to Enron but with aggressive accounting methods have not only been criticized, but have lost customers or been devalued by investors.[116] Firms that have been reported to have poor ethical behavior, such as fraud or having to restate financial results, see their overall corporate value in the stock market drop precipitously.[117]

These incidents suggest that firms need to employ ethical strategic leaders—leaders who include ethical practices as part of their long-term vision for the firm, who desire to do the right thing, and for whom honesty, trust, and integrity are important.[118] Strategic leaders who consistently display these qualities inspire employees as they work with others to develop and support an organizational culture in which ethical practices are the expected behavioral norms.[119]

Unfortunately, not all people in positions of strategic leadership display the ethical approach described. The actions explained in the next Strategic Focus about Global Crossing suggests the need for vigilance in guarding against unethical actions taken by those in key managerial positions.

Strategic leaders are challenged to take actions that increase the probability that an ethical culture will prevail in their organizations. One action that has gained favor is to institute a formal program to manage ethics. Operating much like control systems, these programs help inculcate values throughout the organization.[120] Therefore, when these efforts are successful, the practices associated with an ethical culture become institutionalized in the firm; that is, they become the set of behavioral commitments and actions accepted by most of the firm's employees and other stakeholders with whom employees interact.

Additional actions strategic leaders can take to develop an ethical organizational culture include (1) establishing and communicating specific goals to describe the firm's ethical standards (e.g., developing and disseminating a code of conduct); (2) continuously revising and updating the code of conduct, based on inputs from people throughout the firm and from other stakeholders (e.g., customers and suppliers); (3) disseminating the code of conduct to all stakeholders to inform them of the firm's ethical standards and practices; (4) developing and implementing methods and procedures to use in achieving the firm's ethical standards (e.g., using internal auditing practices that are consistent with the standards); (5) creating and using

The Cost of Poor Ethical Decisions by Strategic Leaders

As Internet use expanded, telecom firm Global Crossing went public and accumulated debt to finance the expansion of its long-haul fiber optics networks across the ocean in order to carry increased traffic. The firm ran into trouble when the price of long-haul traffic dropped dramatically as companies overbuilt this capacity. An additional problem was that, although Global Crossing had a good long-haul network, there was no way to facilitate metropolitan connectivity. Only firms that had the connectivity, such as Qwest, which had acquired U.S. West, a local phone system operator with lots of local connectivity, could use its capacity effectively. Global Crossing had to sell its capacity on the unfavorable open market and was left with a very low-margin business. It could not pay the debt that had accumulated to fund the fixed assets of laying fiber optic cable thousands of feet under the world's oceans to link networks across countries.

Although there were strategic errors by Global Crossing's leaders, significant ethical issues are also a part of this story. As with Enron, some insiders at Global Crossing had enriched themselves to the detriment not only of shareholders, but also of employees. On January 28, 2002, Global Crossing declared bankruptcy. The company's stock dropped from a high of $64 to below $.30, and many workers lost nearly all of the value in their 401k accounts. Although many employees received a severance package, the company cannot pay them until it emerges from bankruptcy proceedings, as these severance packages are considered accounting liabilities. However, some Global Crossing top-level managers, including Gary Winnick, Barry Porter, Lodwrick Cook, and Joseph Clayton, sold over a billion dollars worth of stock options in the months leading to their firm's bankruptcy. Although selling these options is not a crime, it is unethical. In addition, many loans made to executives were forgiven before the firm declared bankruptcy. Because upper-level Global Crossing managers likely had knowledge about the firm's impending failure, investors were at a significant disadvantage, as were employees who weren't members of the top management team. Poor ethical behavior by executives, such as Global Crossing's, undermines the confidence of investors and employees and damages the firm's attempts to earn above-average returns.

Because of Global Crossing's bankruptcy and loss of confidence in the industry, other firms have also experienced difficulties. Level 3 Communications, Williams Communications, and 360Networks are under pressure. Because of the excess telecommunications capacity, these competitors are not only competing against each other, but also more established carriers, such as AT&T and WorldCom. The competition against the more established competitors is difficult because they are more financially stable than are firms such as Level 3 Communications, Williams Communications, and 360Networks that are concentrating on developing additional network capacity.

In addition to affecting competitors throughout an industry such as the telecommunications industry, a lapse in ethics across a number of firms creates a crisis of confidence in financial institutions. This crisis of confidence because of unethical behavior makes banks leery of lending money, makes investors leery of investing, and makes employees leery of working for firms with a reputation for poor ethical behavior. After all, if you can't trust managers as decision-making specialists (see Chapter 10) to make ethical decisions that are in stakeholders' and especially shareholders' best interests, the efficiency of separating ownership from the making of decisions in the modern corporation is undermined and governance or monitoring costs are increased for all stakeholders.

SOURCES: A. Borrus & L. Woellert, 2002, Global Crossing: Where's the outrage on Capitol Hill? *Business Week*, February 25, 53; R. Blumestein, D. Soloman, & K. Chen, 2002, As Global Crossing crashed, executives got loan relief, pension payouts, *The Wall Street Journal*, February 21, B1, B4; J. Creswell, 2002, First going for broke, *Fortune*, February 18, 24–25, L. H. LaBarba, 2002, Global blunder, *Telephony*, February 4, 25; G. Fabrikant & S. Romero, 2002, How executives prospered as Global Crossing collapsed, *The New York Times*, http://www.nytimes.com, February 11; K. Fitchard, 2002, Global Crossing bombshell creates fallout among IXCs, *Telephony*, February 4, 12; S. Romero & G. Fabrikant, 2002, Another twist at Global as chairman quits board, *The New York Times*, http://www.nytimes.com, February 23; M. Weisskopf, 2002, Equal-opportunity crisis, *Time*, February 25, 45.

explicit reward systems that recognize acts of courage (e.g., rewarding those who use proper channels and procedures to report observed wrongdoings); and (6) creating a work environment in which all people are treated with dignity.[121] The effectiveness of these actions increases when they are taken simultaneously, thereby making them mutually supportive. When managers and employees do not engage in such actions—perhaps because an ethical culture has not been created—problems are likely to occur. As we discuss next, formal organizational controls can help prevent further problems and reinforce better ethical practices.

Establishing Balanced Organizational Controls

Organizational controls have long been viewed as an important part of strategy implementation processes. Controls are necessary to help ensure that firms achieve their desired outcomes.[122] Defined as the "formal, information-based . . . procedures used by managers to maintain or alter patterns in organizational activities," controls help strategic leaders build credibility, demonstrate the value of strategies to the firm's stakeholders, and promote and support strategic change.[123] Most critically, controls provide the parameters within which strategies are to be implemented, as well as corrective actions to be taken when implementation-related adjustments are required. In this chapter, we focus on two organizational controls—strategic and financial—that are introduced in Chapter 11. Our discussion of organizational controls here emphasizes strategic and financial controls because strategic leaders are responsible for their development and effective use.

Evidence suggests that, although critical to the firm's success, organizational controls are imperfect. *Control failures* have a negative effect on the firm's reputation and divert managerial attention from actions that are necessary to effectively use the strategic management process.

As explained in Chapter 11, financial control focuses on short-term financial outcomes. In contrast, strategic control focuses on the *content* of strategic actions, rather than their *outcomes*. Some strategic actions can be correct, but poor financial outcomes may still result because of external conditions, such as a recession in the economy, unexpected domestic or foreign government actions, or natural disasters.[124] Therefore, an emphasis on financial control often produces more short-term and risk-averse managerial decisions, because financial outcomes may be caused by events beyond managers' direct control. Alternatively, strategic control encourages lower-level managers to make decisions that incorporate moderate and acceptable levels of risk because outcomes are shared between the business-level executives making strategic proposals and the corporate-level executives evaluating them.

The Balanced Scorecard

The **balanced scorecard** is a framework that firms can use to verify that they have established both strategic and financial controls to assess their performance.

The **balanced scorecard** is a framework that firms can use to verify that they have established both strategic and financial controls to assess their performance.[125] This technique is most appropriate for use when dealing with business-level strategies, but can also apply to corporate-level strategies.

The underlying premise of the balanced scorecard is that firms jeopardize their future performance possibilities when financial controls are emphasized at the expense of strategic controls,[126] in that financial controls provide feedback about outcomes achieved from past actions, but do not communicate the drivers of the firm's future performance.[127] Thus, an overemphasis on financial controls could promote organizational behavior that has a net effect of sacrificing the firm's long-term value creating potential for short-term performance gains.[128] An appropriate balance of strategic controls and financial controls, rather than an overemphasis on either, allows firms to effectively monitor their performance.

Four perspectives are integrated to form the balanced scorecard framework: *financial* (concerned with growth, profitability, and risk from shareholders' perspective), *customer* (concerned with the amount of value customers perceive was created by the firm's products), *internal business processes* (with a focus on the priorities for various business processes that create customer and shareholder satisfaction), and *learning and growth* (concerned with the firm's effort to create a climate that supports change, innovation, and growth). Thus, using the balanced scorecard's framework allows the firm to understand how it looks to shareholders (financial perspective), how customers view it (customer perspective), the processes it must emphasize to successfully use its competitive advantage (internal perspective), and what it can do to improve its performance in order to grow (learning and growth perspective).[129] Generally speaking, strategic controls tend to be emphasized when the firm assesses its performance relative to the learning and growth perspective, while financial controls are emphasized when assessing performance in terms of the financial perspective. Study of the customer and internal business processes perspectives often is completed through virtually an equal emphasis on strategic controls and financial controls.

Firms use different criteria to measure their standing relative to the scorecard's four perspectives. Sample criteria are shown in Figure 12.5. The firm should select the number of criteria that will allow it to have both a strategic understanding and a

| Figure 12.5 | Strategic Controls and Financial Controls in a Balanced Scorecard Framework |

Perspectives	Criteria
Financial	• Cash flow • Return on equity • Return on assets
Customer	• Assessment of ability to anticipate customers' needs • Effectiveness of customer service practices • Percentage of repeat business • Quality of communications with customers
Internal Business Processes	• Asset utilization improvements • Improvements in employee morale • Changes in turnover rates
Learning and Growth	• Improvements in innovation ability • Number of new products compared to competitors' • Increases in employees' skills

financial understanding of its performance without becoming immersed in too many details.[130]

Strategic leaders play an important role in determining a proper balance between strategic controls and financial controls for their firm. This is true in single business firms as well as in diversified firms. A proper balance between controls is important, in that, "Wealth creation for organizations where strategic leadership is exercised is possible because these leaders make appropriate investments for future viability [through strategic control], while maintaining an appropriate level of financial stability in the present [through financial control]."[131] In fact, most corporate restructuring is designed to refocus the firm on its core businesses, thereby allowing top executives to reestablish strategic control of their separate business units.[132] Thus, as emphasized in Chapter 11, both strategic controls and financial controls support effective use of the firm's corporate-level strategy.

Successful use of strategic control by top executives frequently is integrated with appropriate autonomy for the various subunits so that they can gain a competitive advantage in their respective markets.[133] Strategic control can be used to promote the sharing of both tangible and intangible resources among interdependent businesses within a firm's portfolio. In addition, the autonomy provided allows the flexibility necessary to take advantage of specific marketplace opportunities. As a result, strategic leadership promotes the simultaneous use of strategic control and autonomy.[134]

Balancing strategic and financial controls in diversified firms can be difficult. Failure to maintain an effective balance between strategic controls and financial controls in these firms often contributes to a decision to restructure the company. For example, following the 1997 Southeast Asian currency crisis, Samsung Electronics, a large Korean firm, was heading into a significant crisis in its Chinese operations. It was a large diversified firm, which had businesses throughout the world. Its Chinese operations were selling everything from washing machines to VCRs. Each product division had established Chinese factories and a nationwide sales organization by the mid-1990s. However, in China, these divisions encountered significant losses, losing $37 million in 1998.

When Yun Jonong Yong took over as Samsung's CEO in 1997, he shut down all 23 sales offices and declared that each of the seven mainland factories would have to become profitable on its own to survive. Thus, he instituted strong financial controls that were to be followed to verify that each division was operating profitably. Additionally, based on market survey results, Samsung executives decided that the firm would focus on 10 major cities in China. Furthermore, the firm carefully selected products and supported them with intense marketing. Thus, the firm improved strategic controls using a "top-down marketing strategy." As a result, in 2001, Samsung sold products worth $1.81 billion in China, a fivefold increase since 1998, and profits increased over 70 percent to $228 million. A more effective balance between strategic and financial controls has helped Samsung to improve its performance and to make progress towards its goal of establishing marquee brands in China, comparable to Sony and Motorola.[135]

PART 3 /Strategic Actions: Strategy Implementation

- Effective strategic leadership is a prerequisite to successfully using the strategic management process. Strategic leadership entails the ability to anticipate events, envision possibilities, maintain flexibility, and empower others to create strategic change.

- Top-level managers are an important resource for firms to develop and exploit competitive advantages. In addition, when they and their work are valuable, rare, imperfectly imitable, and nonsubstitutable, strategic leaders can themselves be a source of competitive advantage.

- The top management team is composed of key managers who play a critical role in the selection and implementation of the firm's strategies. Generally, they are officers of the corporation or members of the board of directors.

- There is a relationship among the top management team's characteristics, a firm's strategies, and its performance. For example, a top management team that has significant marketing and R&D knowledge positively contributes to the firm's use of growth strategies. Overall, most top management teams are more effective when they have diverse skills.

- When the board of directors is involved in shaping a firm's strategic direction, that firm generally improves its performance. However, the board may be less involved in decisions about strategy formulation and implementation when CEOs have more power. CEOs increase their power when they appoint people to the board and when they simultaneously serve as the CEO and board chair.

- Strategic leaders are selected from either the internal or the external managerial labor market. Because of their effect on performance, the selection of strategic leaders has implications for a firm's effectiveness. There are valid reasons to use either the internal or the external market when choosing the firm's strategic leaders. In most instances, the internal market is used to select the firm's CEO. Outsiders often are selected to initiate needed change.

- Effective strategic leadership has six major components: determining the firm's strategic direction, exploiting and maintaining core competencies, developing human capital, sustaining an effective organizational culture, emphasizing ethical practices, and establishing balanced organizational controls.

- A firm must develop a long-term vision of its strategic intent. A long-term vision is the driver of strategic leaders' behavior in terms of the remaining five components of effective strategic leadership.

- Strategic leaders must ensure that their firm exploits its core competencies, which are used to produce and deliver products that create value for customers, through the implementation of strategies. In related-diversified and large firms in particular, core competencies are exploited by sharing them across units and products.

- A critical element of strategic leadership and the effective implementation of strategy is the ability to develop a firm's human capital. Effective strategic leaders and firms view human capital as a resource to be maximized, rather than as a cost to be minimized. Resulting from this perspective is the development and use of programs intended to train current and future strategic leaders to build the skills needed to nurture the rest of the firm's human capital.

- Shaping the firm's culture is a central task of effective strategic leadership. An appropriate organizational culture encourages the development of an entrepreneurial orientation among employees and an ability to change the culture as necessary.

- In ethical organizations, employees are encouraged to exercise ethical judgment and to behave ethically at all times. Improved ethical practices foster social capital. Setting specific goals to describe the firm's ethical standards, using a code of conduct, rewarding ethical behaviors, and creating a work environment in which all people are treated with dignity are examples of actions that facilitate and support ethical behavior within the firm.

- Developing and using balanced organizational controls is the final component of effective strategic leadership. An effective balance between strategic and financial controls allows for the flexible use of core competencies, but within the parameters indicated by the firm's financial position. The balanced scorecard is a tool used by the firm and its strategic leaders to develop an appropriate balance between its strategic and financial controls.

1. What is strategic leadership? In what ways are top executives considered important resources for an organization?

2. What is a top-management team, and how does it affect a firm's performance and its abilities to innovate and make appropriate strategic changes?

3. What are the differences between the internal and external managerial labor markets? What are the effects of each type of labor market on the formulation and implementation of strategies?

4. How does strategic leadership affect the determination of the firm's strategic direction?

5. Why is it important for strategic leaders to make certain that their firm exploits its core competencies in the pursuit of strategic competitiveness and above-average returns?

6. What is the importance of human capital and its development for strategic competitiveness?

7. What is organizational culture? What must strategic leaders do to develop and sustain an effective organizational culture?

8. As a strategic leader, what actions could you take to establish and emphasize ethical practices in your firm?

9. What are organizational controls? Why are strategic controls and financial controls important parts of the strategic management process?

Strategic Leadership

The executive board for a large company is concerned that the firm's future leadership needs to be developed. Several top-level managers are expected to leave the firm in the next three to seven years. You have been put in charge of a committee to determine how the firm should prepare for these departures.

Part 1 (individual) Use the information provided within this chapter and your own perceptions to complete the following chart. Be prepared to discuss in class.

Candidates	Internal Managerial Labor Market	External Managerial Labor Market
Strengths		
Weaknesses		

Part 2 (Individually or in small groups) The firm's executive board feels that the external managerial labor market is beyond its control—the managerial resources the firm will need may or may not be available when they are needed. The board has then asked your committee to consider a program that would develop the firm's internal managerial labor market. Outline the objectives that you want your program to achieve, the steps you would take to reach them, and the time frame involved. Also consider potential problems in such a program and how they could be resolved.

1. R. D. Ireland, M. A. Hitt, S. M. Camp, & D. L. Sexton, 2001, Integrating entrepreneurship and strategic management actions to create firm wealth, *Academy of Management Executive*, 15(1): 49–63; K. R. Thompson, W. A. Hochwarter, & N. J. Mathys, 1997, Stretch targets: What makes them effective? *Academy of Management Executive*, 11(3): 48–59.

2. A. Cannella Jr., A. Pettigrew, & D. Hambrick, 2001, Upper echelons: Donald Hambrick on executives and strategy, *Academy of Management Executive*, 15(3): 36–52; R. D. Ireland & M. A. Hitt, 1999, Achieving and maintaining strategic competitiveness in the 21st century: The role of strategic leadership, *Academy of Management Executive*, 12(1): 43–57; D. Lei, M. A. Hitt, & R. Bettis, 1996, Dynamic core competencies through meta-learning and strategic context, *Journal of Management*, 22: 547–567.

3. A. Bianco & P. L. Moore, 2001, Downfall: The inside story of the management fiasco at Xerox, *Business Week*, March 5, 82–92.

4. P. A. Moore, 2001, She's here to fix the Xerox: Can Anne Mulcahy pull off an IBM-style makeover? *Business Week*, August 6, 47–48.

5. T. J. Peters, 2001, Leadership: Sad facts and silver linings, *Harvard Business Review*, 79(11): 121–128.

6. J. Collins, 2001, Level 5 Leadership: The triumph of humility and fierce resolve, *Harvard Business Review*, 79(1): 66–76; M. A. Hitt, B. W. Keats, & S. DeMarie, 1998, Navigating in the new competitive landscape: Building competitive advantage and strategic flexibility in the 21st century, *Academy of Management Executive*, XI(4): 22–42; J. B. Quinn, P. Anderson, & S. Finkelstein, 1996, Managing professional intellect: Making the most of the best, *Harvard Business Review*, 74(2): 71–80.

7. D. J. Teece, 2000, *Managing Intellectual Capital: Organizational, Strategic and Policy Dimensions*, Oxford: Oxford University Press.

8. M. F. R. Kets de Vries, 1995, *Life and Death in the Executive Fast Lane*, San Francisco: Jossey-Bass.

9. D. C. Carey & D. Ogden, 2000, *CEO Succession: A Window on How Boards Can Get It Right When Choosing a New Chief Executive*, New York: Oxford University Press.

10. M. Maccoby, 2001, Making sense of the leadership literature, *Research Technology Management*, 44(5): 58–60; T. Kono, 1999, A strong head office makes a strong company, *Long Range Planning*, 32: 225–246.

11. G. Hamel & C. K. Prahalad, 1993, Strategy as stretch and leverage, *Harvard Business Review*, 71(2): 75–84.

12. M. Maccoby, 2001, Successful leaders employ strategic intelligence, *Research Technology Management*, 44(3): 58–60.

13. Ibid.; M. Hammer & S. A. Stanton, 1997, The power of reflection, *Fortune*, November 24, 291–296.

14. S. Finkelstein & D. C. Hambrick, 1996, *Strategic Leadership: Top Executives and Their Effects on Organizations*, St. Paul, MN: West Publishing Company, 2.

15. Collins, Level 5 Leadership.

16. R. Castanias & C. Helfat, 2001, The managerial rents model: Theory and empirical analysis, *Journal of Management*, 27: 661–678; H. P. Gunz & R. M. Jalland, 1996, Managerial careers and business strategy, *Academy of Management Review*, 21: 718–756.

17. M. Beer & R. Eisenstat, 2000, The silent killers of strategy implementation and learning, *Sloan Management Review*, 41(4): 29–40; C. M. Christensen, 1997, Making strategy: Learning by doing, *Harvard Business Review*, 75(6): 141–156; M. A. Hitt, B. W. Keats, H. E. Harback, & R. D. Nixon, 1994, Rightsizing: Building and maintaining strategic leadership and long-term competitiveness, *Organizational Dynamics*, 23: 18–32.

18. M. Wright, R. E. Hoskisson, L. W. Busenitz, & J. Dial, 2000. Entrepreneurial growth through privatization: The upside of management buyouts, *Academy of Management Review*, 25: 591–601; M. J. Waller, G. P. Huber, & W. H. Glick, 1995, Functional background as a determinant of executives' selective perception, *Academy of Management Journal*, 38: 943–974; N. Rajagopalan, A. M. Rasheed, & D. K. Datta, 1993, Strategic decision processes: Critical review and future directions, *Journal of Management*, 19: 349–384.

19. W. Rowe, 2001, Creating wealth in organizations: The role of strategic leadership, *Academy of Management Executive*, 15(1): 81–94; Finkelstein & Hambrick, *Strategic Leadership*, 26–34; D. C. Hambrick & E. Abrahamson, 1995, Assessing managerial discretion across industries: A multimethod approach, *Academy of Management Journal*, 38: 1427–1441; D. C. Hambrick & S. Finkelstein, 1987, Managerial discretion: A bridge between polar views of organizational outcomes, in B. Staw & L. L. Cummings (eds.), *Research in Organizational Behavior*, Greenwich, CT: JAI Press, 369–406.

20. J. A. Petrick & J. F. Quinn, 2001, The challenge of leadership accountability for integrity capacity as a strategic asset, *Journal of Business Ethics*, 34: 331–343; R. C. Mayer, J. H. Davis, & F. D. Schoorman, 1995, An integrative model of organizational trust, *Academy of Management Review*, 20: 709–734.

21. J. J. Sosik, 2001, Self-other agreement on charismatic leadership: Relationships with work attitudes and managerial performance, *Group & Organization Management*, 26: 484–511; D. A. Waldman & F. Yammarino, 1999, CEO charismatic leadership: Levels of management and levels of analysis effects, *Academy of Management Review*, 24: 266–285.

22. J. Call, 2002, The fire within, *BYU Magazine*, Winter, 34–39.

23. J. E. Dutton, S. J. Ashford, R. M. O'Neill, & K. A. Lawrence, 2001, Moves that matter: Issue selling and organizational change. *Academy of Management Journal*, 44: 716–736.

24. W. Ferrier, 2001, Navigating the competitive landscape: The drivers and consequences of competitive aggressiveness, *Academy of Management Journal*, 44: 858–877; P. Chattopadhyay, W. H. Glick, C. C. Miller, & G. P. Huber, 1999, Determinants of executive beliefs: Comparing functional conditioning and social influence, *Strategic Management Journal*, 20: 763–789.

25. I. Goll, R. Sambharya, & L. Tucci, 2001, Top management team composition, corporate ideology, and firm performance, *Management International Review*, 41(2): 109–129.

26. L. Markoczy, 2001, Consensus formation during strategic change, *Strategic Management Journal*, 22: 1013–1031; A. L. Iaquito & J. W. Fredrickson, 1997, Top management team agreement about the strategic decision process: A test of some of its determinants and consequences, *Strategic Management Journal*, 18: 63–75.

27. C. Pegels, Y. Song, & B. Yang, 2000, Management heterogeneity, competitive interaction groups, and firm performance, *Strategic Management Journal*, 21: 911–923; N. Athanassiou & D. Nigh, 1999, The impact of U.S. company internationalization on top management team advice networks: A tacit knowledge perspective, *Strategic Management Journal*, 20: 83–92.

28. Markoczy, Consensus formation during strategic change; D. Knight, C. L. Pearce, K. G. Smith, J. D. Olian, H. P. Sims, K. A. Smith, & P. Flood, 1999, Top management team diversity, group process, and strategic consensus, *Strategic Management Journal*, 20: 446–465.

29. D. C. Hambrick, T. S. Cho, & M. J. Chen, 1996, The influence of top management team heterogeneity on firms' competitive moves, *Administrative Science Quarterly*, 41: 659–684.

30. J. J Distefano & M. L. Maznevski, 2000, Creating value with diverse teams in global management, *Organizational Dynamics*, 29(1): 45–63; T. Simons, L. H. Pelled, & K. A. Smith, 1999, Making use of difference, diversity, debate, and decision comprehensiveness in top management teams, *Academy of Management Journal*, 42: 662–673.

31. Finkelstein & Hambrick, *Strategic Leadership*, 148.

32. S. Barsade, A. Ward, J. Turner, & J. Sonnenfeld, 2000, To your heart's content: A model of affective diversity in top management teams, *Administrative Science Quarterly*, 45: 802–836; C. C. Miller, L. M. Burke, & W. H. Glick, 1998, Cognitive diversity among upper-echelon executives: Implications for strategic decision processes, *Strategic Management Journal*, 19: 39–58.

33. U. Daellenbach, A. McCarthy, & T. Schoenecker, 1999, Commitment to innovation: The impact of top management team characteristics, *R & D Management*, 29(3): 199–208; D. K. Datta & J. P. Guthrie, 1994, Executive succession: Organizational antecedents of CEO characteristics, *Strategic Management Journal*, 15: 569–577.

34. S. Wally & M. Becerra, 2001, Top management team characteristics and strategic changes in international diversification: The case of U.S. multinationals in the European community, *Group & Organization Management*, 26: 165–188; W. Boeker, 1997, Strategic change: The influence of managerial characteristics and organizational growth, *Academy of Management Journal*, 40: 152–170.

35. A. Tomie, 2000, Fast Pack 2000, *Fast Company Online*, http://www.fastcompany.com, March 1.

36. Wally & Becerra, Top management team characteristics and strategic changes in international diversification; L. Tihanyi, C. Daily, D. Dalton, & A. Ellstrand, 2000, Composition of the top management team and firm international diversification, *Journal of Management*, 26: 1157–1178; M. E. Wiersema & K. Bantel, 1992, Top management team demography and corporate strategic change, *Academy of Management Journal*, 35: 91–121; K. Bantel & S. Jackson, 1989, Top management and innovations in banking: Does the composition of the top team make a difference? *Strategic Management Journal*, 10: 107–124.

37. 2002, The top 25 managers: Daniel Vasella, *Business Week*, January 14, 58.

38. W. Koberstein, 2001, Executive profile: Novartis inside out, *Pharmaceutical Executive*, November, 36–50.

39. B. Taylor, 2001, From corporate governance to corporate entrepreneurship, *Journal of Change Management*, 2(2): 128–147; W. Q. Judge, Jr. & C. P. Zeithaml, 1992, Institutional and strategic choice perspectives on board involvement in the strategic decision process, *Academy of Management Journal*, 35: 766–794; J. A. Pearce II & S. A. Zahra, 1991, The relative power of CEOs and boards of directors: Associations with corporate performance, *Strategic Management Journal*, 12: 135–154.

40. B. R. Golden & E. J. Zajac, 2001, When will boards influence strategy? Inclination times power equals strategic change, *Strategic Management Journal*, 22: 1087–1111.

41. M. Carpenter & J. Westphal, 2001, Strategic context of external network ties: Examining the impact of director appointments on board involvement in strategic decision making, *Academy of Management Journal*, 44: 639–660.

42. J. D. Westphal & E. J. Zajac, 1995, Who shall govern? CEO/board power, demographic similarity, and new director selection, *Administrative Science Quarterly*, 40: 60.

43. M. Boyle, 2001, The dirty half-dozen: America's worst boards, *Fortune*, May 14, 249–252.

44. J. D. Westphal, 1999, Collaboration in the boardroom: Behavioral and performance consequences of CEO-board social ties, *Academy of Management Journal*, 42: 7–24.

45. Ibid., 66; J. Roberts & P. Stiles, 1999, The relationship between chairmen and chief executives: Competitive or complementary roles? *Long Range Planning*, 32(1): 36–48.

46. J. Coles, N. Sen, & V. McWilliams, 2001, An examination of the relationship of governance mechanisms to performance, *Journal of Management*, 27: 23–50; J. Coles & W. Hesterly, 2000, Independence of the chairman and board composition: Firm choices and shareholder value, *Journal of Management*, 26: 195–214; B. K. Boyd, 1995, CEO duality and firm performance: A contingency model, *Strategic Management Journal*, 16: 301.

47. D. D. Bergh, 2001, Executive retention and acquisition outcomes: A test of opposing views on the influence of organizational tenure, *Journal of Management*, 27: 603–622.

48. J. Muller, J. Green, & C. Tierney, 2001, Chrysler's Rescue Team, *Business Week*, January 15, 48–50.

49. C. M. Daily & D. R. Dalton, 1995, CEO and director turnover in failing firms: An illusion of change? *Strategic Management Journal*, 16: 393–400.

50. R. Albanese, M. T. Dacin, & I. C. Harris, 1997, Agents as stewards, *Academy of Management Review*, 22: 609–611; J. H. Davis, F. D. Schoorman, & L. Donaldson, 1997, Toward a stewardship theory of management, *Academy of Management Review*, 22: 20–47.

51. M. A. Carpenter, 2002, The implications of strategy and social context for the relationship between top management team heterogeneity and firm performance, *Strategic Management Journal*, 23: 275–284; J. D. Westphal & E. J. Zajac, 1997, Defections from the inner circle: Social exchange, reciprocity and diffusion of board independence in U.S. corporations, *Administrative Science Quarterly*, 161–183.

52. Rajagopalan & Datta, CEO characteristics, 201.

53. R. A. Johnson, R. E. Hoskisson, & M. A. Hitt, 1993, Board involvement in restructuring: The effect of board versus managerial controls and characteristics, *Strategic Management Journal*, 14(Summer Special Issue): 33–50.

54. Boyd, CEO duality and firm performance: A contingency model.

55. M. Carpenter & J. Fredrickson, 2001, Top management teams, global strategic posture, and the moderating role of uncertainty, *Academy of Management Journal*, 44: 533–545.

56. M. Schneider, 2002, A stakeholder model of organizational leadership, *Organization Science*, 13: 209–220.

57. M. Sorcher & J. Brant, 2002, Are you picking the right leaders? *Harvard Business Review*, 80(2): 78-85; D. A. Waldman, G. G. Ramirez, R. J. House, & P. Puranam, 2001, Does leadership matter? CEO leadership attributes and profitability under conditions of perceived environmental uncertainty, *Academy of Management Journal*, 44: 134–143; R. Charan & G. Colvin, 2000, The right fit, *Fortune*, April 17, 226–238.

58. A. Kakabadse & N. Kakabadse, 2001, Dynamics of executive succession, *Corporate Governance*, 1(3): 9–14.

59. R. Charan, 2000, GE's ten-step talent plan, *Fortune*, April 17, 232.

60. R. E. Hoskisson, D. Yiu, & H. Kim, 2000, Capital and labor market congruence and corporate governance: Effects on corporate innovation and global competitiveness. In S. S. Cohen & G. Boyd (eds.), *Corporate Governance and Globalization*, Northampton, MA: Edward Elgar, 129–154.

61. S. B. Shepard, 2002, A Talk with Jeff Immelt: Jack Welch's successor charts a course for GE in the 21st century, *Business Week*, January 28, 102–104.

62. D. C. Carey & D. Ogden, 2000, *CEO Succession: A Window on How Boards Can Get It Right When Choosing a New Chief Executive*, New York: Oxford University Press.

63. A. A. Cannella, Jr. & W. Shen, 2001, So close and yet so far: Promotion versus exit for CEO heirs apparent, *Academy of Management Journal*, 44: 252–270.

64. V. Kisfalvi, 2000, The threat of failure, the perils of success and CEO character: Sources of strategic persistence, *Organization Studies*, 21: 611–639.

65. Datta & Guthrie, Executive succession, 570.

66. Finkelstein & Hambrick, *Strategic Leadership*, 180–181.

67. D. Miller, 1991, Stale in the saddle: CEO tenure and the match between organization and environment, *Management Science*, 37: 34–52.

68. B. Dyck, M. Mauws, F. Starke, & G. Mischke, 2002, Passing the baton: The importance of sequence, timing, technique and communication in executive succession, *Journal of Business Venturing*, 17: 143–162.

69. J. J. Rotemberg & G. Saloner, 2000, Visionaries, managers, and strategic direction, *RAND Journal of Economics*, 31: 693–716.

70. I. M. Levin, 2000, Vision revisited, *Journal of Applied Behavioral Science*, 36: 91–107; J. C. Collins & J. I. Porras, 1996, Building your company's vision, *Harvard Business Review*, 74(5): 65–77.

71. G. Gori, 2001, An American directs Mexico City's cinema revival, *The New York Times*, http://www.nytimes.com, July 15.

72. P. W. Beamish, 1999, Sony's Yoshihide Nakamura on structure and decision making, *Academy of Management Executive*, 13(4): 12–16; R. M. Hodgetts, 1999, Dow Chemical's CEO William Stavropoulos on structure and decision making, *Academy of Management Executive*, 13(4): 29–35.

73. R. A. Burgelman, 2001, *Strategy Is Destiny: How Strategy-Making Shapes a Company's Future*, New York: The Free Press.

74. S. Jaffe, 2001, Do Pepsi and Gatorade mix? *Business Week Online*, http://www.businessweek.com, August 14.

75. J. Byrne & B. Elgin, 2002, Cisco: Behind the hype, *Business Week Online*, http://www.businessweek.com, January 21.

76. C. A. Lengnick-Hall & J. A. Wolff, 1999, Similarities and contradictions in the core logic of three strategy research streams, *Strategic Management Journal*, 20: 1109–1132.

77. M. A. Hitt, L. Bierman, K. Shimizu, & R. Kochhar, 2001, Direct and moderating effects of human capital on strategy and performance in professional service firms: A resource-based perspective, *Academy of Management Journal*, 44:13–28;

78. S. A. Snell & M. A. Youndt, 1995, Human resource management and firm performance: Testing a contingency model of executive controls, *Journal of Management*, 21: 711–737.

79. P. Caligiuri & V. Di Santo, 2001, Global competence: What is it, and can it be developed through global assignments? *Human Resource Planning*, 24(3): 27–35; D. Ulrich, 1998, A new mandate for human resources, *Harvard Business Review*, 76(1): 124–134.

80. A. McWilliams, D. D. Van Fleet, & P. M. Wright, 2001, Strategic management of human resources for global competitive advantage, *Journal of Business Strategies* 18(1): 1–24; J. Pfeffer, 1994, *Competitive Advantage through People*, Cambridge, MA: Harvard Business School Press.

81. L. Gratton, 2001, *Living Strategy: Putting People at the Heart of Corporate Purpose*, London: Financial Times/Prentice Hall, London.

82. Caligiuri & Di Santo, Global competence.

83. M. W. McCall & G. P. Hollenbeck, 2001, *Developing Global Executives: The Lessons of International Experience*, Boston: Harvard Business School Press.

84. C. F. Fey & I. Bjorkman, 2001, The effect of human resource management practices on MNC subsidiary performance in Russia, *Journal of International Business Studies*, 32: 59–75.

85. M. G. Harvey & M. M. Novicevic, 2000, The influences of inpatriation practices on the strategic orientation of a global organization, *International Journal of Management*, 17: 362–371; M. G. Harvey & M. R. Buckley, 1997, Managing inpatriates: Building a global core competency, *Journal of World Business*, 32(1): 35–52.

86. C. A. Bartlett & S. Ghoshal, 2002, Building competitive advantage through people, *MIT Sloan Management Review*, 43(2): 34–41; D. M. DeCarolis & D. L. Deeds, 1999, The impact of stocks and flows of organizational knowledge on firm performance: An empirical investigation of the biotechnology industry, *Strategic Management Journal*, 20: 953–968.

87. J. Sandberg, 2000, Understanding human competence at work: An interpretative approach, *Academy of Management Journal*, 43: 9–25.

88. J. Lee & D. Miller, 1999, People matter: Commitment to employees, strategy and performance in Korean firms, *Strategic Management Journal*, 20: 579–593.

89. T. M. Welbourne & L. A. Cyr, 1999, The human resource executive effect in initial

public offering firms, *Academy of Management Journal,* 42: 616–629; J. Pfeffer & J. F. Veiga, 1999, Putting people first for organizational success, *Academy of Management Executive,* 13(2): 37–48.

90. Bartlett & Ghoshal, Building competitive advantage through people.

91. J. H. Christy, 2001, Eagle aloft, *Forbes,* August 6, 60.

92. H. Collingwood & D. L. Coutu, 2002, Jack on Jack, *Harvard Business Review,* 80(2): 88–94.

93. J. Di Frances, 2002, 10 reasons why you shouldn't downsize, *Journal of Property Management,* 67(1): 72–73; M. A. Hitt, R. E. Hoskisson, J. S. Harrison, & B. Summers, 1994, Human capital and strategic competitiveness in the 1990s, *Journal of Management Development,* 13(1): 35–46.

94. A. Pinsonneault & K. Kraemer, 2002, The role of information technology in organizational downsizing: A tale of two American cities, *Organization Science,* 13: 191–208.

95. M. David, 2001, Leadership during an economic slowdown, *Journal for Quality and Participation,* 24(3): 40–43; C. L. Martin, C. K. Parsons, & N. Bennett, 1995, The influence of employee involvement program membership during downsizing: Attitudes toward the employer and the union, *Journal of Management,* 21: 879–890.

96. A. K. Gupta & V. Govindarajan, 2000, Knowledge management's social dimension: Lessons from Nucor steel, *Sloan Management Review,* 42(1): 71–80; C. M. Fiol, 1991, Managing culture as a competitive resource: An identity-based view of sustainable competitive advantage, *Journal of Management,* 17: 191–211; J. B. Barney, 1986, Organizational culture: Can it be a source of sustained competitive advantage? *Academy of Management Review,* 11: 656–665.

97. V. Govindarajan & A. K. Gupta, 2001, Building an effective global business team, *Sloan Management Review,* 42(4): 63–71; S. Ghoshal & C. A. Bartlett, 1994, Linking organizational context and managerial action: The dimensions of quality of management, *Strategic Management Journal,* 15: 91–112.

98. D. F. Kuratko, R. D. Ireland, & J. S. Hornsby, 2001, Improving firm performance through entrepreneurial actions: Acordia's corporate entrepreneurship strategy, *Academy of Management Executive,* 15(4): 60–71.

99. T. E. Brown, P. Davidsson, & J. Wiklund, 2001, An operationalization of Stevenson's conceptualization of entrepreneurship as opportunity-based firm behavior, *Strategic Management Journal,* 22: 953–968.

100. G. T. Lumpkin & G. G. Dess, 1996, Clarifying the entrepreneurial orientation construct and linking it to performance, *Academy of Management Review,* 21: 135–172.

101. Ibid., 142.

102. Ibid., 137.

103. M. Arndt, 2001, The rules of James Farrell's game, *Business Week Online,* http://www.businessweek.com, August 6.

104. R. R. Sims, 2000, Changing an organization's culture under new leadership, *Journal of Business Ethics,* 25: 65–78.

105. R. A. Burgelman & Y. L. Doz, 2001, The power of strategic integration, *Sloan Management Review,* 42(3): 28–38; P. H. Fuchs, K. E. Mifflin, D. Miller, & J. O. Whitney, 2000, Strategic integration: Competing in the age of capabilities, *California Management Review,* 42(3): 118–147.

106. J. S. Hornsby, D. F. Kuratko, & S. A. Zahra, 2002, Middle managers' perception of the internal environment for corporate entrepreneurship: Assessing a measurement scale, *Journal of Business Venturing,* 17: 253–273; J. E. Dutton, S. J. Ashford, R. M. O'Neill, E. Hayes, & E. E. Wierba, 1997, Reading the wind: How middle managers assess the context for selling issues to top managers, *Strategic Management Journal,* 18: 407–425.

107. B. Axelrod, H. Handfield-Jones, & E. Michaels, 2002, A new game plan for C players, *Harvard Business Review,* 80(1): 80–88.

108. J. E. Garten, 2001, *The Mind of the CEO,* New York: Basic Books.

109. W. W. George, 2001, Medtronic's chairman William George on how mission-driving companies create long-term shareholder value, *Academy of Management Executive,* 15(4): 39–47.

110. P. S. Adler & S.-W. Kwon, 2002, Social capital: Prospects for a new concept, *Academy of Management Review,* 27: 17–40.

111. T. A. Stewart, 2001, Right now the only capital that matters is social capital, *Business 2.0,* December, 128–130.

112. D. J. Brass, K. D. Butterfield, & B. C. Skaggs, 1998, Relationships and unethical behavior: A social network perspective, *Academy of Management Review,* 23: 14–31.

113. L. K. Trevino, G. R. Weaver, D. G. Toffler, & B. Ley, 1999, Managing ethics and legal compliance: What works and what hurts, *California Management Review,* 41(2): 131–151.

114. C. W. L. Hill, 1990, Cooperation, opportunism, and the invisible hand: Implications for transaction cost theory, *Academy of Management Review*, 15: 500–513.

115. S. Forest, W. Zellner, & H. Timmons, 2001, The Enron debacle, *Business Week*, November 12, 106–110.

116. K. Brown, G. Hitt, S. Liesman, & J. Weil, 2002, Andersen fires partner it says led shredding of Enron documents, *The Wall Street Journal*, January 16, A1, A18.

117. W. Wallace, 2000, The value relevance of accounting: The rest of the story, *European Management Journal*, 18(6): 675–682.

118. E. Soule, 2002, Managerial moral strategies—In search of a few good principles, *Academy of Management Review*, 27: 114–124; J. Milton-Smith, 1995, Ethics as excellence: A strategic management perspective, *Journal of Business Ethics,* 14: 683–693.

119. L. M. Leinicke, J. A. Ostrosky, & W. M. Rexroad, 2000, Quality financial reporting: Back to the basics, *CPA Journal*, August, 69–71.

120. J. R. Cohen, L. W. Pant, & D. J. Sharp, 2001, An examination of differences in ethical decision-making between Canadian business students and accounting professionals, *Journal of Business Ethics*, 30: 319–336; G. R. Weaver, L. K. Trevino, & P. L. Cochran, 1999, Corporate ethics programs as control systems: Influences of executive commitment and environmental factors, *Academy of Management Journal*, 42: 41–57.

121. P. E. Murphy, 1995, Corporate ethics statements: Current status and future prospects, *Journal of Business Ethics*, 14: 727–740.

122. J. H. Gittell, 2000, Paradox of coordination and control, *California Management Review*, 42(3): 101–117; L. J. Kirsch, 1996, The management of complex tasks in organizations: Controlling the systems development process, *Organization Science*, 7: 1–21.

123. M. D. Shields, F. J. Deng, & Y. Kato, 2000, The design and effects of control systems: Tests of direct- and indirect-effects models, *Accounting, Organizations and Society*, 25: 185–202; R. Simons, 1994, How new top managers use control systems as levers of strategic renewal, *Strategic Management Journal*, 15: 170–171.

124. K. J. Laverty, 1996, Economic "short-termism": The debate, the unresolved issues, and the implications for management practice and research, *Academy of Management Review*, 21: 825–860.

125. R. S. Kaplan & D. P. Norton, 2001, The strategy-focused organization, *Strategy & Leadership*, 29(3): 41–42; R. S. Kaplan & D. P. Norton, 2000, *The Strategy-Focused Organization: How Balanced Scorecard Companies Thrive in the New Business Environment*, Boston: Harvard Business School Press.

126. B. E. Becker, M. A. Huselid, & D. Ulrich, 2001, *The HR Scorecard: Linking People, Strategy, and Performance*, Boston: Harvard Business School Press, 21.

127. Kaplan & Norton, The strategy-focused organization; Kaplan & Norton, *The Strategy-Focused Organization*.

128. R. S. Kaplan & D. P. Norton, 2001, Transforming the balanced scorecard from performance measurement to strategic management: Part I, *Accounting Horizons*, 15(1): 87–104.

129. R. S. Kaplan & D. P. Norton, 1992, The balanced scorecard—measures that drive performance, *Harvard Business Review*, 70(1): 71–79.

130. M. A. Mische, 2001, *Strategic Renewal: Becoming a High-Performance Organization*, Upper Saddle River: Prentice Hall, 181.

131. Rowe, Creating wealth in organizations: The role of strategic leadership.

132. R. E. Hoskisson, R. A. Johnson, D. Yiu, & W. P. Wan, 2001, Restructuring strategies of diversified business groups: Differences associated with country institutional environments. In M. A. Hitt, R. E. Freeman, J. S. Harrison (eds.), *Handbook of Strategic Management*, Oxford, U.K.: Blackwell Publishers, 433–463; R. A. Johnson, 1996, Antecedents and outcomes of corporate refocusing, *Journal of Management*, 22: 437–481; R. E. Hoskisson & M. A. Hitt, 1994, *Downscoping: How to Tame the Diversified Firm*, New York: Oxford University Press.

133. J. Birkinshaw & N. Hood, 2001, Unleash innovation in foreign subsidiaries, *Harvard Business Review*, 79(3): 131–137.

134. Ireland & Hitt, Achieving and maintaining strategic competitiveness.

135. M. Ihlwan, & D. Roberts, 2002, How Samsung plugged into China, *Business Week Online*, http://www.businessweek.com, March 4.

Chapter Thirteen

Strategic Entrepreneurship

Knowledge Objectives

Studying this chapter should provide you with the strategic management knowledge needed to:

1. Define and explain strategic entrepreneurship.

2. Describe the importance of entrepreneurial opportunities, innovation, and entrepreneurial capabilities.

3. Discuss the importance of international entrepreneurship and describe why it is increasing.

4. Describe the two forms of internal corporate venturing: autonomous and induced strategic behaviors.

5. Discuss how cooperative strategies such as strategic alliances are used to develop innovation.

6. Explain how firms use acquisitions to increase their innovations and enrich their innovative capabilities.

7. Describe the importance of venture capital and initial public offerings to entrepreneurial activity.

8. Explain how the practice of strategic entrepreneurship creates value for customers and shareholders of all types of firms, large and small, new and established.

What Makes Entrepreneurs Successful?

There is a wide variety of types of entrepreneurs, but no one formula for success. However, there are many successful entrepreneurs. For example, Marion McCaw Garrison was one of the first female accounting graduates of the University of Washington in 1939. While she was told that it was unlikely she could ever earn her CPA because she was a woman, she completed her degree in accounting anyway. At 22 years of age, she bought 40 acres of land and became a real estate developer, one of the first women to do so. After she married, she helped her husband manage their businesses, including radio and television stations and real estate. When her husband died suddenly, she took over the management of the businesses. She moved out of the radio business and entered cable television and wireless communications. The company went public in 1987, and in 1994, McCaw Cellular Communications was sold to AT&T for more than $11 billion. Garrison was successful because of her strong business knowledge and determination.

Anatoly Karachinsky originally had no thoughts of starting his own business. In 1992, he was invited to attend a conference in Arizona, where he met the CEO of EDS, Mort Myerson. After a several-hour conversation with Myerson, Karachinsky returned to Russia and took over a friend's computer consulting firm. In 1994, Karachinsky met Michael Dell and became the exclusive distributor of Dell computers in Russia. Several U.S. investors became impressed with his company, Informatsionniye Biznes Sistemy (IBS), and how he managed it, and Citigroup and AIG Brunswick Millennium Fund invested $30 million of capital in his firm. IBS has continued to grow and now controls much of the IT market in Russia. In 2001, IBS earned more than $5 million of pretax income on total revenues of $200 million. Karachinsky was successful because he had a good idea and implemented it without help from the Russian government or the "black market." He was able to obtain the critical venture capital for these reasons.

A visionary leader, Jonathan Coon started his business in 1995. By 2001, his mail order contact lens business—the name of the business is also its phone number: 1-800 CONTACTS—had become the largest direct-to-consumer contact lens business in the world. It stocks 9 million lenses, selling over 100,000 per day. Before he started the business, Coon developed an effective business plan that has

Anatoly Karachinsky, CEO and founder of Informatsionniye Biznes Sistemy (IBS).

produced a strong cash flow. He also has an effective distribution system and built-in repeat business because the product is disposable. Coon's employees are empowered to do whatever is necessary to satisfy customers. He also allows them to participate in developing company policies and provides stock options to all employees. Because of his firm's success, he was named the National Ernst & Young Retail Entrepreneur of the Year.

Each of these three successful entrepreneurs took some unique actions and had some special traits, but they all had a passion for the businesses they developed. According to Michael Dell, passion must be the driving force for starting a company. Dell also emphasizes the importance of identifying and exploiting opportunities. All of the entrepreneurs described identified opportunities and obviously were passionate about exploiting them.

SOURCES: T. Singer, 2002, What business would you start? *INC*, March, 68–76; 2001, Direct-to-consumer visionary Jonathan Coon of mail order giant, 1-800 CONTACTS, named Ernst & Young Retail Entrepreneur of the Year, Ernst & Young newsroom, http://www.ey.com/global, October 30; 2001, Marion McCaw Garrison: An entrepreneurial woman, *Business*, University of Washington Business School, Fall, 40; T. Kellner, 2001, Entrepreneurs, *Forbes*, April 30, 116–117.

The Opening Case provides examples of three successful entrepreneurs. While the descriptions are brief, several factors can be identified as important for each person's success. They all have a passion for their business. Furthermore, they had strong business knowledge and planned well (for example, they developed a business plan). Each identified opportunities and exploited them. Other factors, such as determination (Marion McCaw Garrison), strong values and independence (Anatoly Karachinsky), and creativity and empowering employees (Jonathan Coon) also contributed to their success.

Understanding why some entrepreneurs succeed while others fail is important to help future entrepreneurs in their efforts to be successful. Entrepreneurship is the economic engine driving many nations' economies in the global competitive landscape. Entrepreneurship and innovation have become important for young and old and for large and small firms in all types of industries. Research conducted by the Center for Entrepreneurial Leadership at the Kauffman Foundation has shown that in recent years almost 100 percent of the new jobs in the United States were created by entrepreneurial firms of less than two years of age.[1] As a result, this chapter focuses on strategic entrepreneurship. **Strategic entrepreneurship** is taking entrepreneurial actions using a strategic perspective. More specifically, it involves engaging in simultaneous opportunity seeking and competitive advantage seeking behaviors to design and implement entrepreneurial strategies to create wealth.[2] These actions can be taken by individuals or by corporations. Such activity is particularly important in the evolving 21st-century landscape.

The competitive landscape that has evolved in the 21st century presents firms with substantial change, a global marketplace, and significant complexity and uncertainty.[3] Because of this uncertain environment, firms cannot easily predict the future. As a result, they must develop strategic flexibility to have a range of strategic alternatives that they can implement as needed. To do so, they must acquire resources and

Strategic entrepreneurship is taking entrepreneurial actions using a strategic perspective.

build the capabilities that allow them to take necessary actions to adapt to a dynamic environment or to proact in that environment.[4] In this environment, entrepreneurs and entrepreneurial managers design and implement actions that capture more of existing markets from less aggressive and innovative competitors while creating new markets.[5] In effect, they are trying to create tomorrow's businesses.[6]

Creating tomorrow's businesses requires identifying opportunities, as argued by Michael Dell in the Opening Case, and developing innovation. In other words, firms must be entrepreneurial and innovative. Innovations are critical to companies' efforts to differentiate their goods or services from competitors in ways that create additional or new value for customers.[7] Thus, entrepreneurial competencies are important for firms to achieve and sustain competitive advantages for a period of time.[8]

To describe how firms produce and manage innovation, we examine several topics in this chapter. To set the stage, we first examine entrepreneurship and innovation in a strategic context. Next, we discuss international entrepreneurship, a phenomenon reflecting the increased use of entrepreneurship in countries throughout the world. Internally, firms innovate through either autonomous or induced strategic behavior. After our descriptions of these internal corporate venturing activities, we discuss actions taken by firms to implement the innovations resulting from those two types of strategic behavior. In addition to innovating through internal activities, firms can gain access to other companies' innovations or innovative capabilities through strategic alliances and acquisitions. Following our discussion of these topics is a description of entrepreneurship in start-up ventures and smaller firms. This section closes both the chapter and our analysis of actions that firms take to successfully implement strategies.

Strategic Entrepreneurship and Innovation

Joseph Schumpeter viewed entrepreneurship as a process of "creative destruction," through which existing products or methods of production are destroyed and replaced with new ones.[9] Thus, entrepreneurship is "concerned with the discovery and exploitation of profitable opportunities."[10] Entrepreneurial activity is an important mechanism for creating changes, as well as for helping firms adapt to changes created by others. Firms that encourage entrepreneurship are risk takers, are committed to innovation, and act proactively in that they try to create opportunities rather than waiting to respond to opportunities created by others.[11]

Entrepreneurial opportunities represent conditions in which new products or services can satisfy a need in the market. The essence of entrepreneurship is to identify and exploit these opportunities.[12] Importantly, entrepreneurs or entrepreneurial managers must be able to identify opportunities not perceived by others. Identifying these opportunities in a dynamic and uncertain environment requires an entrepreneurial mind-set that entails the passionate pursuit of opportunities.[13] Matthew Heyman and two Harvard classmates found opportunity in the chaos of Mexico City's movie theater industry. The movie theaters were all in bad shape and largely unprofitable. All of the major theater companies gave up and departed the Mexico City market. However, Heyman and his colleagues saw opportunity and started Cinemex in 1994. They received venture capital from J.P. Morgan and used it to attract other investors. After raising almost $22 million in capital, Cinemex built attractive theaters and now dominates the market with approximately 90,000 viewers and revenues of $140 million in 2001.[14] In the previous chapter, we described the long-term vision (one of the actions associated with effective strategic leadership) that supported Heyman and his partners as they started their entrepreneurial venture. As we now see, these strategic leaders were successful in their pursuit of what they recognized to be an entrepreneurial opportunity.

Entrepreneurial opportunities represent conditions in which new products or services can satisfy a need in the market.

After identifying the opportunities, entrepreneurs take actions to exploit them and establish a competitive advantage. The process of identifying and pursuing opportunities is entrepreneurial, but this activity alone is rarely enough to create maximum wealth or even to survive over time. Actions must be valuable, rare, difficult to imitate, and non-substitutable to create and sustain a competitive advantage (as described in Chapter 3). Without the competitive advantage, success will be only temporary (as explained in Chapter 1). An innovation may be valuable and rare early in its life, if a market perspective is used in its development. However, strategic actions must be taken to introduce the new product to the market and protect its position in the market against competitors (difficult to imitate) to gain a competitive advantage. These actions combined represent strategic entrepreneurship.

Peter Drucker argues that "innovation is the specific function of entrepreneurship, whether in an existing business, a public service institution, or a new venture started by a lone individual." Moreover, Drucker suggests that innovation is "the means by which the entrepreneur either creates new wealth-producing resources or endows existing resources with enhanced potential for creating wealth."[15] Thus, entrepreneurship and the innovation resulting from it are important for large and small firms, as well as for start-up ventures, as they compete in the 21st-century competitive landscape. Therefore, we can conclude that, "Entrepreneurship and innovation are central to the creative process in the economy and to promoting growth, increasing productivity and creating jobs."[16]

Innovation

Innovation is a key outcome firms seek through entrepreneurship and is often the source of competitive success. In Rosabeth Moss Kanter's words, "Winning in business today demands innovation. Companies that innovate reap all the advantages of a first mover."[17] For example, research results show that firms competing in global industries that invest more in innovation also achieve the highest returns.[18] In fact, investors often react positively to the introduction of a new product, thereby increasing the price of a firm's stock. Innovation, then, is an essential feature of high-performance firms.[19] Furthermore, "innovation may be required to maintain or achieve competitive parity, much less a competitive advantage in many global markets."[20]

Invention is the act of creating or developing a new product or process.

Innovation is the process of creating a commercial product from an invention.

Imitation is the adoption of an innovation by similar firms.

In his classic work, Schumpeter argued that firms engage in three types of innovative activity.[21] **Invention** is the act of creating or developing a new product or process. **Innovation** is the process of creating a commercial product from an invention. Thus, an invention brings something new into being, while an innovation brings something new into use. Accordingly, technical criteria are used to determine the success of an invention, whereas commercial criteria are used to determine the success of an innovation.[22] Finally, **imitation** is the adoption of an innovation by similar firms. Imitation usually leads to product or process standardization, and products based on imitation often are offered at lower prices, but without as many features.

In the United States in particular, innovation is the most critical of the three types of innovative activity that occur in firms. Many companies are able to create ideas that lead to inventions, but commercializing those inventions through innovation has, at times, proved difficult. Approximately 80 percent of R&D occurs in large firms, but these same firms produce fewer than 50 percent of the patents.[23]

Corporate entrepreneurship is a process whereby an individual or a group in an existing organization creates a new venture or develops an innovation.

Innovations produced in large established firms are often referred to as corporate entrepreneurship. **Corporate entrepreneurship** is a process whereby an individual or a group in an existing organization creates a new venture or develops an innovation. Overall, corporate entrepreneurship is the sum of a firm's innovation, renewal, and venturing efforts. Evidence suggests that corporate entrepreneurship practices are facilitated through the effective use of a firm's strategic management

process and effectively using the firm's human capital.[24] Determining how to harness the ingenuity of a firm's employees and how to reward them for it while retaining some of the rewards of the entrepreneurial efforts for the shareholders' benefit facilitates the emergence of value-creating corporate entrepreneurship.[25]

Cinemex founder Matthew Heyman saw a market in Mexico City and created Cinemex. His theaters offer moviegoers in Mexico an enjoyable experience, including luxurious facilities, as shown here, and first-run films for a reasonable price.

Entrepreneurs are individuals, acting independently or as part of an organization, who create a new venture or develop an innovation and take risks entering them into the marketplace.

Entrepreneurs and Entrepreneurial Capabilities

Entrepreneurs are individuals, acting independently or as part of an organization, who create a new venture or develop an innovation and take risks entering them into the marketplace. Entrepreneurs can be independent individuals or surface in an organization at any level. Thus, top-level managers, middle- and first-level managers, staff personnel, and those producing the company's good or service can all be entrepreneurs.

Firms need employees who think entrepreneurially. Top-level managers should try to establish an entrepreneurial culture that inspires individuals and groups to engage in corporate entrepreneurship.[26] Apple Computer's Steve Jobs is committed to this effort, believing one of his key responsibilities is to help Apple become more entrepreneurial. And, Apple has introduced some innovatively designed products, such as its recent iMac with its 15-inch liquid crystal display attached to the base computer with a chrome swivel bar.[27] Some believe that it looks more like a desk lamp. Apple is using the new design to capture a larger share of the PC market.

Of course, to create and commercialize products such as the iMac requires not only intellectual capital, but an entrepreneurial mind-set as well. It also requires entrepreneurial competence. Returning to the Opening Case, entrepreneurial competence involves effective knowledge of the business and technology, a passion for the business, and a risk orientation.[28] In most cases, knowledge must be transferred to others in the organization, even in smaller ventures, to enhance the entrepreneurial competence of the firm. The transfer is likely to be more difficult in larger firms. Research has shown, however, that units within firms are more innovative if they have access to new knowledge.[29]

Transferring knowledge can be difficult, because the receiving party must have adequate absorptive capacity to learn the knowledge.[30] This requires that the new knowledge be linked to the existing knowledge. Thus, managers will need to develop the capabilities of their human capital to build on their current knowledge base while incrementally expanding that knowledge.[31]

Developing innovations and achieving success in the marketplace requires effective human capital. In particular, firms must have strong intellectual capital in their R&D organization.[32] However, a firm must have strong human capital throughout its workforce if employees are to be innovative. For example, Winspec West Manufacturing Inc. credits its positive market position to innovation produced by its strong employee base. In fact, the managers are very careful in hiring. Even in jobs with seemingly low challenges, they try to hire high potential employees. For one secretarial position, the managers hired a person with an MBA in finance; that person went on to serve as the acting chief financial officer.[33]

Having the intellectual talent is only part of the challenge. The management of the talent to realize its potential is critical for a firm to be entrepreneurial.[34] Managers must develop the culture and infuse it with the values espoused by successful entrepreneurs such as those discussed in the Opening Case. Additionally, managers should empower employees at all levels to act independently, as Jonathan Coon of 1-800 CONTACTS did, described in the Opening Case.[35]

International Entrepreneurship

Entrepreneurship is a global phenomenon.[36] It is at the top of public policy agendas in many of the world's countries, including Finland, Germany, Israel, Ireland, and France, among others. In Northern Ireland, for example, the minister for enterprise, trade, and investment told businesspeople that their current and future commercial success would be affected by the degree to which they decided to emphasize R&D and innovation (critical components of entrepreneurship).[37]

According to some researchers who are studying economies throughout the world, virtually all industrial nations "are experiencing some form of transformation in their economies, from the dramatic move from centrally planned to market economies in East-central Europe . . . to the efforts by Asian countries to return to their recent high growth levels."[38] Entrepreneurship can play central roles in those transformations, in that it has a strong potential to fuel economic growth, create employment, and generate prosperity for citizens.[39]

While entrepreneurship is a global phenomenon, there are differences in the rate of entrepreneurship across countries. A recent study of 29 countries found that the percentage of adults involved in entrepreneurial activity ranged from a high of more than 20 percent in Mexico to a low of approximately 5 percent in Belgium. The United States had a rate of about 13 percent. Importantly, this study also found a strong positive relationship between the rate of entrepreneurial activity and economic development in the country.[40]

Culture is one of the reasons for the differences in rates of entrepreneurship among different countries. For example, the tension between individualism and collectivism is important for entrepreneurship; research shows that entrepreneurship declines as collectivism is emphasized. Simultaneously, however, research results suggest that exceptionally high levels of individualism might be dysfunctional for entrepreneurship. Viewed collectively, these results appear to call for a balance between individual initiative and a spirit of cooperation and group ownership of innovation. For firms to be entrepreneurial, they must provide appropriate autonomy and incentives for individual initiative to surface, but also promote cooperation and group ownership of an innovation if it is to be implemented successfully. Thus, entrepreneurship often requires teams of people with unique skills and resources, especially in cultures where collectivism is a valued historical norm.[41]

Another important dimension of international entrepreneurship is the level of investment outside of the home country made by young ventures. In fact, with increasing globalization, a greater number of new ventures have been 'born global.'[42] Research has shown that new ventures that enter international markets increase their learning of new technological knowledge and thereby enhance their performance.[43] Because of these outcomes, the amount of international entrepreneurship has been increasing in recent years.[44]

The probability of entering international markets increases when the firm has top executives with international experience. Furthermore, the firm has a higher likelihood of successfully competing in international markets when its top executives have international experience.[45] Because of the learning and economies of scale and scope afforded by operating in international markets, both young and established internationally diversified firms often are stronger competitors in their domestic market as well. Additionally, internationally diversified firms are generally more innovative, as research has shown.[46]

International entrepreneurship has been an important factor in the economic development of Asia. In fact, private companies owned by Chinese families outside of China compose the fourth largest economic power in the world. Significant learning from their international ventures occurs in these businesses, and this learning enhances their success with future ventures.[47] The learning that occurs contributes to a firm's knowledge of operating in international markets.[48] It also contributes knowledge that can enhance a firm's new product development, on which we focus in the next section.

The outcomes of effective new product development are described in the Strategic Focus on page 422. These processes render outstanding and smartly designed new products, such as those chosen as the best new products of 2001.

New Product Development and Internal Corporate Ventures

Most corporate innovation is developed through research and development (R&D). In many industries, the competitive battle for the market begins in the R&D labs. In fact, R&D may be the most critical factor in gaining and sustaining a competitive advantage in some industries, such as pharmaceuticals. Larger, established firms use R&D labs to create the competence-destroying new technology and products envisioned by Schumpeter. Such radical innovation has become an important component of competition in many industries.[49]

Incremental and Radical Innovation

Firms can create incremental or more radical innovations. Most innovations are *incremental*—that is, they build on existing knowledge bases and provide small improvements in the current product lines. Alternatively, *radical innovations* usually provide significant technological breakthroughs and create new knowledge.[50]

Radical innovations are rare because of the difficulty and risk involved in developing them. There is substantial uncertainty with radical innovation regarding the technology and the market opportunities.[51] Because radical innovation creates new knowledge and uses only some or little of a firm's current product or technological knowledge, creativity is required. However, creativity does not create something from nothing. Rather, creativity discovers, combines, or synthesizes current knowledge, often from diverse areas.[52] This knowledge is then used to develop new products or services that can be used in an entrepreneurial manner to move into new markets, capture new customers, and gain access to new resources.[53] Such innovations are often developed in separate units that start internal ventures.[54]

Internal corporate venturing is the set of activities used to create inventions and innovations through internal means.[55] Spending on R&D is linked to success in internal corporate venturing. Put simply, firms are unable to invent or innovate without significant R&D investments. Because of the importance of innovation to the competitiveness of multinational firms, the effectiveness of their internal venturing process is critical.

Internal corporate venturing is the set of activities used to create inventions and innovations through internal means.

Strategic Focus

Developing the Best New Products on the Market

The best new products for 2001 range from high technology to food. They include the Apple PowerBook G4 laptop, Harmony, a new low-fat cereal for women offered by General Mills, and Visa's plastic paycheck. Using the plastic paycheck, consumers can have their pay deposited into their Visa accounts and then use their Visa card to pay for goods, similar to a debit card.

Hitachi's new DZ-MV100A camcorder can be used to edit home movies. Equator developed the Round Refrigerator that features pull-out shelves that operate similar to a "lazy susan." Listerine introduced stamp-sized strips to freshen your breath.

While the Samsung 1300 phone, combining wireless phone functions with those of a palm organizer, was selected as a best product, Nokia brought to the market the Nokia 8270a phone, named one of the "cutest" wireless phones. Nokia's phone offers code division multiple access (CDMA) technology, supports a wireless Internet browser, enables two-way text messaging, and serves as an alarm clock and calendar. Analysts believe the new fashion-sensitive phone will compete well with Samsung and Motorola products.

Intel is well known as one of the most innovative firms in any industry. Intel invests $4 billion annually in R&D and does not let up during recessions. In fact, Intel has learned that it can gain ground on competitors during recessions. Intel's laboratories are developing the semi-conductor chips of the future. Intel is now designing a new way to manufacture chips, which could not be built much smaller or faster using the firm's existing manufacturing technology. This process innovation will facilitate further product innovation.

Innovation is increasing at GM. Because of its emphasis on planning and analysis in prior years, GM autos were perceived as boring, with only incremental innovations added to new models. Its designs were "criteria-ed to death," and its market share had markedly decreased. However, Robert Lutz, formerly of Chrysler, was hired as GM's new product czar in late 2001 and has changed the system that he described as producing a lot of bunts, singles, and walks, but no home runs. Lutz is changing the culture to promote inspiration and the development of new ideas, which hopefully will lead to innovative GM products in future years.

SOURCES: G. Anders, 2002, How Intel puts innovation inside, *Fast Company,* March, 122–124; A. Hesseidahl, 2002, Nokia has fashion sense, *Forbes,* http://www.forbes.com, February 19; L. Armstrong, 2001, The best products of 2001, *Business Week,* December 17, 116–124; J. Flint, 2001, A breath of fresh air, *Forbes,* http://www.forbes.com, November 11.

As shown in Figure 13.1, there are two forms of internal corporate venturing: autonomous strategic behavior and induced strategic behavior.

Autonomous Strategic Behavior

Autonomous strategic behavior is a bottom-up process in which product champions pursue new ideas, often through a political process, by means of which they develop and coordinate the commercialization of a new good or service until it achieves success in the marketplace. A *product champion* is an organizational member with an entrepreneurial vision of a new good or service who seeks to create support for its commercialization. Evidence suggests that product champions play critical roles in moving innovations forward.[56] Autonomous strategic behavior is based on a firm's wellsprings of knowledge and resources that are the sources of the firm's innovation. Thus, a firm's technological capabilities and competencies are the basis for new products and processes.[57]

Autonomous strategic behavior is a bottom-up process in which product champions pursue new ideas, often through a political process, by means of which they develop and coordinate the commercialization of a new good or service until it achieves success in the marketplace.

Figure 13.1   Model of Internal Corporate Venturing

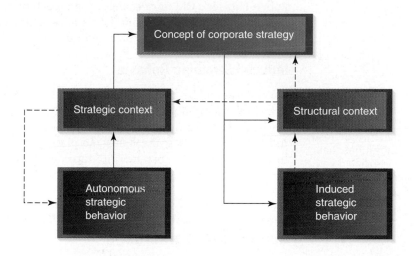

SOURCE: Adapted from R. A. Burgelman, 1983, A model of the interactions of strategic behavior, corporate context, and the concept of strategy, *Academy of Management Review*, 8: 65.

GE depends on autonomous strategic behavior on a regular basis to produce innovations. Essentially, "the search for marketable services can start in any of GE's myriad businesses. [For example], an operating unit seeks out appropriate technology to better do what it already does. Having mastered the technology, it then incorporates it into a service it can sell to others." In response to frequent crisis calls and requests from customers, GE's Industrial Systems division took six months to develop a program that uses artificial intelligence to help assign field engineers to customer sites. Quite sophisticated, the program handles thousands of constraints while making assignments. The division's customer relationship manager was a champion for this product. The manager observed that the program "reduced the average time to dispatch an engineer from 18 hours to 4 hours."[58] In addition to facilitating the operations of one of GE's units, the program is being sold as a marketable item that developed through autonomous strategic behavior.

Changing the concept of corporate-level strategy through autonomous strategic behavior results when a product is championed within strategic and structural contexts (see Figure 13.1). The strategic context is the process used to arrive at strategic decisions (often requiring political processes to gain acceptance). The best firms keep changing their strategic context and strategies because of the continuous changes in the current competitive landscape. Thus, some believe that the most competitively successful firms reinvent their industry or develop a completely new one across time as they engage in competition with current and future rivals.[59]

To be effective, an autonomous process for developing new products requires that new knowledge be continuously diffused throughout the firm. In particular, the diffusion of tacit knowledge is important for development of more effective new products.[60] Interestingly, some of the processes important for the promotion of autonomous new product development behavior vary by the environment and country in which a firm operates. For example, the Japanese culture is high on uncertainty avoidance. As such, research has found that Japanese firms are more likely to engage in autonomous behaviors under conditions of low uncertainty.[61]

GM is trying to develop a process that resembles autonomous strategic behavior as explained in the Strategic Focus on page 422 about the best new products. Robert Lutz feels GM must change its approach in order to develop more competitive products and break away from the tradition of incremental innovations. To do so, it must change older practices that are more similar to induced strategic behavior.

Induced Strategic Behavior

Induced strategic behavior is a top-down process whereby the firm's current strategy and structure foster product innovations that are closely associated with that strategy and structure.

The second of the two forms of internal corporate venturing, **induced strategic behavior,** is a top-down process whereby the firm's current strategy and structure foster product innovations that are closely associated with that strategy and structure. In this form of venturing, the strategy in place is filtered through a matching structural hierarchy. Some of the best new products described in the Strategic Focus on page 422 were developed through induced strategic behavior.

Implementing New Product Development and Internal Ventures

To be innovative and develop internal ventures requires an *entrepreneurial mind-set*. In Chapter 12, we discuss an entrepreneurial orientation that includes several dimensions, such as risk propensity. Clearly, firms and individuals must be willing to take risks in order to commercialize new products. While they must continuously attempt to identify opportunities, they must also select and pursue the best opportunities and do so with discipline. Thus, employing an *entrepreneurial mind-set* entails not only developing new products and markets but also an emphasis on execution. According to Rita McGrath and Ian MacMillan, those with an entrepreneurial mind-set "engage the energies of everyone in their domain," both inside and outside the organization.[62]

Having processes and structures in place through which a firm can successfully implement the outcomes of internal corporate ventures and commercialize the innovations is critical. The successful introduction of innovations into the marketplace reflects implementation effectiveness.[63] In the context of internal corporate ventures, processes are the "patterns of interaction, coordination, communication, and decision making employees use" to convert the innovations resulting from either autonomous or induced strategic behaviors into successful market entries.[64] As we described in Chapter 11, organizational structures are the sets of formal relationships supporting organizational processes.

Effective integration of the various functions involved in innovation processes—from engineering to manufacturing and, ultimately, market distribution—is required to implement (that is, to effectively use) the innovations that result from internal corporate ventures.[65] Increasingly, product development teams are being used to integrate the activities associated with different organizational functions. Product development teams are commonly used to produce cross-functional integration. Such coordination involves coordinating and applying the knowledge and skills of different functional areas in order to maximize innovation.[66]

Cross-Functional Product Development Teams

Cross-functional teams facilitate efforts to integrate activities associated with different organizational functions, such as design, manufacturing, and marketing. In addition, new product development processes can be completed more quickly and the products more easily commercialized when cross-functional teams work effectively.[67] Using cross-functional teams, product development stages are grouped into parallel or overlapping processes to allow the firm to tailor its product development efforts to its unique core competencies and to the needs of the market.

Horizontal organizational structures support the use of cross-functional teams in their efforts to integrate innovation-based activities across organizational functions.[68] Therefore, instead of being built around vertical hierarchical functions or departments, the organization is built around core horizontal processes that are used to produce and manage innovations. Some of the core horizontal processes that are critical to innovation efforts are formal; they may be defined and documented as procedures and practices. More commonly, however, these processes are informal: "They are routines or ways of working that evolve over time."[69] Often invisible, informal processes are critical to successful product innovations and are supported properly through horizontal organizational structures more so than through vertical organizational structures. Two primary barriers that may prevent the successful use of cross-functional teams as a means of integrating organizational functions are independent frames of reference of team members and organizational politics.[70]

GM's president of North America operations and vice chairman of product development, Robert Lutz, is pictured here with the Pontiac Solstice roadster concept vehicle.

Team members working within a distinct specialization (i.e., a particular organizational function) may have an independent frame of reference typically based on common backgrounds and experiences. They are likely to use the same decision criteria to evaluate issues such as product development efforts as they do within their functional units. Research suggests that functional departments vary along four dimensions: time orientation, interpersonal orientation, goal orientation, and formality of structure.[71] Thus, individuals from different functional departments having different orientations on these dimensions can be expected to perceive product development activities in different ways. For example, a design engineer may consider the characteristics that make a product functional and workable to be the most important of the product's characteristics. Alternatively, a person from the marketing function may hold characteristics that satisfy customer needs most important. These different orientations can create barriers to effective communication across functions.[72]

Organizational politics is the second potential barrier to effective integration in cross-functional teams. In some organizations, considerable political activity may center on allocating resources to different functions. Interunit conflict may result from aggressive competition for resources among those representing different organizational functions. This dysfunctional conflict between functions creates a barrier to their integration.[73] Methods must be found to achieve cross-functional integration without excessive political conflict and without changing the basic structural characteristics necessary for task specialization and efficiency.

Facilitating Integration and Innovation

Shared values and effective leadership are important to achieve cross-functional integration and implement innovation.[74] Highly effective shared values are framed around the firm's strategic intent and mission, and become the glue that promotes integration between functional units. Thus, the firm's culture promotes unity and internal innovation.[75]

Strategic leadership is also highly important for achieving cross-functional integration and promoting innovation. Leaders set the goals and allocate resources. The goals include integrated development and commercialization of new goods and services. Effective strategic leaders remind organizational members continuously of the value of product innovations. In the most desirable situations, this value-creating potential becomes the basis for the integration and management of functional department activities.

Effective strategic leaders also ensure a high quality communication system to facilitate cross-functional integration. A critical benefit of effective communication is the sharing of knowledge among team members.[76] Effective communication thus helps create synergy and gains team members' commitment to an innovation throughout the organization. Shared values and leadership practices shape the communication systems that are formed to support the development and commercialization of new products.[77]

Creating Value from Innovation

The model in Figure 13.2 shows how the firm can create value from the internal processes it uses to develop and commercialize new goods and services. An entrepreneurial mind-set is necessary so that managers and employees will consistently try to identify entrepreneurial opportunities that the firm can pursue by developing new goods and services and new markets. Cross-functional teams are important to promote integrated new product design ideas and commitment to their implementation thereafter. Effective leadership and shared values promote integration and vision for

Figure 13.2 Creating Value through Internal Innovation Processes

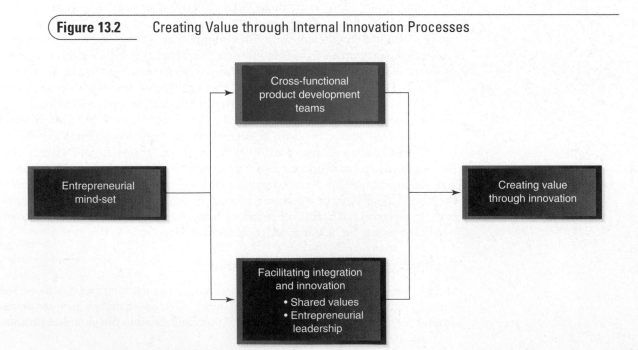

PART 3 /Strategic Actions: Strategy Implementation

innovation and commitment to it. The end result for the firm is the creation of value for the customers and shareholders through development and commercialization of new products.[78]

Cooperative Strategies for Entrepreneurship and Innovation

It is unlikely that a firm possesses all the knowledge and resources required for it to be entrepreneurial and innovative in dynamic competitive markets. Knowledge and resources are needed to develop new products and serve new markets.[79] To successfully commercialize inventions, firms may therefore choose to cooperate with other organizations and integrate their knowledge and resources. Entrepreneurial new ventures, for example, may seek investment capital as well as the distribution capabilities of more established firms to implement a new product idea and introduce it to the market.[80] Alternatively, more established companies may need new technological knowledge and can gain access to it through alliances with newer entrepreneurial firms.[81] Alliances between large pharmaceutical firms and biotechnology companies have increasingly been formed to integrate the knowledge and resources of both to develop new products and bring them to market.[82] With increasing frequency, alliances are used to produce or manage innovations. To innovate through a cooperative relationship, firms must share their knowledge and skills.[83]

Microsoft and Intel—two corporations that have earned considerable profits from the personal computer markets with their software and computer chips, respectively— formed an alliance to develop similar innovations in the mobile phone market. They are creating the same "Wintel duopoly" that they used in the PC market in an attempt to replicate their business model for the high end of the mobile phone market. In 2002, the two companies announced that they were cooperating to provide their software and chips to allow other firms to enter the market and compete successfully against the industry leader, Nokia. Essentially, they are developing complementary new products that will make mobile phones more like computers. Through this alliance, Microsoft and Intel are combining their technological expertise (knowledge) in an attempt to develop the standard technology for cell phones. In this case, both firms are integrating their technological expertise to successfully commercialize their complementary technologically-based products for cell phones.[84]

Because of the importance of alliances, particularly in the development of new technology and in commercializing innovations, firms are beginning to build networks of alliances that represent a form of social capital to them. This social capital in the form of relationships with other firms helps them to obtain the knowledge and other resources necessary to develop innovations.[85] Knowledge from these alliances helps firms develop new capabilities.[86] Some firms now even allow external firms to participate in their internal new product development processes. It is not uncommon for firms to have supplier representatives on their cross-functional innovation teams because of the importance of the suppliers' input to ensure quality materials for any new product developed.[87]

However, alliances formed for the purpose of innovation are not without risks. An important risk is that a partner will appropriate a firm's technology or knowledge and use it to enhance its own competitive abilities.[88] To prevent or at least minimize this risk, firms, particularly new ventures, need to select their partners carefully. The ideal partnership is one in which the firms have complementary skills, as well as compatible strategic goals.[89] However, because firms are operating in a network of firms and thus may be participating in multiple alliances simultaneously, they encounter challenges in managing the alliances.[90] Research has shown that firms can become involved in too many alliances, which can harm rather than facilitate their innovation capabilities.[91] Thus, effectively managing the cooperative relationships to produce innovation is critical.

Seeking Growth through Internal Development or Acquisitions

The capital market values growth, and firms therefore seek growth in multiple ways. Creating new products through invention and commercializing them through innovation are important means of organizational growth. For example, innovation has been a primary means of growth for 3M; it has developed a reputation for being an innovative company. However, 3M CEO Jim McNerney has a goal of doubling 3M's rate of growth in sales and earnings in 10 years. He does not believe that it can be accomplished only through new products developed by 3M's 7,000-strong R&D work force that operates with an annual budget of $1 billion. McNerney suggests that he will have to make several acquisitions to supplement the innovations produced by 3M's R&D operations.

While acquisitions can be expensive, as explained in Chapter 7, R&D is costly as well. For example, Campbell Soup's CEO, Doug Conant, announced in 2002 that the company was cutting dividends to shareholders in order to increase its investment in R&D. The firm's intent is to develop new products and improve the quality of Campbell's existing product lines in soups and snacks. Analysts expressed concern with the time required for Conant's strategy to work. Computer Associates, long known for its growth through acquisitions, announced in 2002 that it was foregoing major acquisitions in order to invest more in internal development of new products.

Acquisitions can provide access to new products more quickly than additional investments in R&D. For example, Carlos Gutierrez, CEO of Kellogg, dramatically changed his firm's product mix with its acquisition of Keebler Foods for $4.4 billion. Before the acquisition, 75 percent of Kellogg's sales revenues came from cereal products. After the acquisition, 60 percent of the firm's sales came from non-cereal products. The acquisition of Keebler provided Kellogg with faster growth products along with an effective distribution system.

Merck traditionally has had a policy of growth through internally developed new products. Merck faces the expiration of patents on several of its primary drug products, which will reduce its sales revenues (and profits) if it does not introduce new drugs to replace them. Its new pain reliever drug, Vioxx, has not done as well in the market as hoped. Accordingly, in 2001–2002, Merck faced increasing pressure from its shareholders to acquire a firm with several new drugs. However, Merck CEO Raymond Gilmartin considers the firm's core competence to be the capability to "turn cutting-edge science into medical breakthroughs." Merck's future may rest on its continued ability to introduce valuable pharmaceutical innovations without making acquisitions.

SOURCES: S. Hamm, 2002, A long climb out of a deep rut, *Business Week*, February 25, 124–125; M. Kwak, 2002, Shopping for R&D, *MIT Sloan Management Review*, 43(2): 9–10; G. Dyer & A. Michaels, 2002, Merck in need of fix to get off the sick list, *Financial Times*, http://www.ft.com, January 22; M. Arndt, 2002, 3M: A lab for growth, *Business Week*, January 21, 50–51; A. Edgecliffe-Johnson, 2001, Campbell cuts to revive its brands, *Financial Times*, http://www.ft.com, July 29; J. Muller, 2001, Thinking outside of the cereal box, *Business Week*, January 15, 54–55.

Acquisitions to Buy Innovation

The Strategic Focus above describes several situations where firms have made or plan to make acquisitions to supplement their product line. One of the reasons that firms turn to acquisitions is the capital market values growth; acquisitions provide a means to rapidly extend the product line and increase the firm's revenues. 3M likely cannot achieve its growth goals without acquiring other companies. Kellogg changed its product mix quickly by acquiring Keebler. Firms can acquire firms with new products or new product development capability. Usually, investing in R&D does not produce new products rapidly. Analysts are concerned that Campbell Soup's new investments in R&D may not achieve new products and growth fast enough to satisfy the capital market.

Similar to internal corporate venturing and strategic alliances, acquisitions are not a risk-free approach to producing and managing innovations. A key risk of acquisitions is that a firm may substitute an ability to buy innovations for an ability to produce innovations internally. In support of this contention, research shows that firms engaging in acquisitions introduce fewer new products into the market.[92] This substitution may take place because firms lose strategic control and focus instead on financial control of their original and especially of their acquired business units. This outcome is evident on page 428 in the Strategic Focus description of Merck, which chose to avoid acquisitions to emphasize its R&D process to develop innovations.

We noted in Chapter 7 that firms can also learn new capabilities from acquired firms. As such, firms can gain capabilities to produce innovation from an acquired firm. Additionally, firms that emphasize innovation and carefully select companies for acquisition that also emphasize innovation are likely to remain innovative.[93]

Capital for Entrepreneurial Ventures

Venture capital is a resource that is typically allocated to entrepreneurs who are involved in projects with high growth potential. The intent of venture capitalists is to achieve a high rate of return on the funds they invest.[94] In the late 1990s, the number of venture capital firms and the amount of capital invested in new ventures reached unprecedented levels. The amount of venture capital invested in new ventures reached a high of $46.1 billion in 1999.[95] Venture capitalists desire to receive large returns on their investments and take major risks by investing in new ventures. Research has shown that venture capitalists may earn large returns or experience significant losses. For example, one study found that 34 percent of venture capitalists experienced a loss, while 23 percent gained a rate of return on their investments of 50 percent or greater.[96]

For the decade of the 1990s, the top quintile of performers in the *Standard & Poor 500* had average annual growth in revenues and earnings of 20.6 percent and 29.3 percent, respectively. Furthermore, these firms provided average annual returns to their shareholders of 34 percent.[97] Additional research showed that 90 percent of these high-performing firms had created and successfully commercialized a radical innovation or developed a fundamental new business model in an existing industry, both indicative of an entrepreneurial firm.[98]

Venture capitalists place weight on the competence of the entrepreneur or the human capital in the firms in which they consider investing. They also weigh the expected scope of competitive rivalry the firm is likely to experience and the degree of instability in the market addressed.[99] However, the characteristics of the entrepreneur or firm in which venture capitalists invest as well as the rate of return expected will vary with the type of venture in which investments are made.[100]

Increasingly, venture capital is being used to support the acquisition of innovations. To provide such support, some firms establish their own venture-capital divisions. These divisions carefully evaluate other companies to identify those with innovations or innovative capabilities that might yield a competitive advantage. In other instances, a firm might decide to serve as an internal source of capital for innovative product ideas that can be spun off as independent or affiliated firms. New enterprises that are backed by venture capital provide an important source of innovation and new technology. The amount of corporate venture capital invested grew exponentially at the end of the 1990s and in 2000. For example, it grew from about

$2 billion in 1998 to almost $11 billion in 1999. In 2000, the amount of corporate venture capital invested was slightly over $18 billion.[101]

Some relatively new ventures are able to obtain capital through initial public offerings (IPOs). Firms that offer new stock in this way must have high potential in order to sell their stock and obtain adequate capital to finance the growth and development of the firm. This form of capital can be substantial and is often much larger than the amounts obtained from venture capitalists. Investment bankers frequently play major roles in the development and offering of IPOs. Research has shown that founder-managed firms generally receive lower returns from IPOs than professionally managed firms.[102] The IPO market values experienced managers more than founders who frequently do not have substantial managerial experience. JetBlue Airways created a lot of interest from investors because of its low costs, strong customer demand, and highly experienced CEO (who also happens to be the firm's founder).[103] Investors believe that the firm with an experienced CEO is more likely to succeed. Also, firms that have received venture capital backing usually receive greater returns from IPOs.[104]

The Strategic Focus on page 431 explains that the capital for new ventures was difficult to obtain in 2001–2002, when the downturn in the stock market dried up the IPO market. Moreover, the substantial losses by venture capitalists in the high technology sector reduced the amount of capital available for investment in new ventures. Still, some capital was available, and these investors were able to obtain attractive terms for their capital investments.

JetBlue Airways founder and CEO David Neeleman speaks at the firm's highly successful initial public offering of stock in his firm. Neeleman, who refers to his company not as an airline but as a services company, says of his employees, "We don't want jaded people working here. If you don't like people or can't deal with rude customers, you'll be fired."

AP PHOTO/RICHARD DREW

Creating Value through Strategic Entrepreneurship

Newer entrepreneurial firms often are more effective than larger firms in identifying opportunities. Some believe that these firms tend to be more innovative as well because of their flexibility and willingness to take risks. Alternatively, larger and well-established firms often have more resources and capabilities to exploit opportunities that are identified.[105] So, younger, entrepreneurial firms are generally opportunity seeking, and more established firms are advantage seeking. However, to compete effectively in the landscape of the 21st century, firms must identify and exploit opportunities but do so while achieving and sustaining a competitive advantage.[106] Thus, newer entrepreneurial firms must learn how to gain a competitive advantage, and older more established firms must relearn how to identify entrepreneurial opportunities. The concept of strategic entrepreneurship suggests that firms can be simultaneously entrepreneurial and strategic regardless of their size and age.

To be entrepreneurial, firms must develop an entrepreneurial mind-set among their managers and employees. Managers must emphasize the development of their resources, particularly human capital and social capital. The importance of knowledge to identify and exploit opportunities as well as to gain and sustain a competitive advantage suggests that firms must have strong human capital.[107] Social capital is critical for access to comple-

Sources of Capital for Entrepreneurial Ventures

Early in their development, biotechnology firms received strong support from the capital market and several of them were able to raise significant capital through IPOs. When the stock market entered a downturn in late 2000 and 2001, biotech firms needing capital had to turn instead to venture capitalists. The investors obtained attractive terms from these firms to provide them with needed capital.

IPOs provided biotech firms with between $10 billion and $11 billion in 2000 but provided only about $3 billion in 2001. Alternatively, biotech firms received about $5 billion from venture capitalists in 1998-1999, but received about $17 billion in 2000-2001. Many other new venture high technology firms also received venture capital in the late 1990s and into 2000. For example, venture capitalists invested $98 billion in U.S. new ventures in 2000. Such amounts were prompted by results such as the approximately 100,000 percent return earned by venture capitalists that invested early in eBay. A McKinsey study, however, showed that in the 1990s venture capitalists earned an average return of 13.4 percent, compared to 12.1 percent earned by public equity firms. The difference is not large, considering the significant difference in risk taken by the two on their investments.

In 2001, many venture capitalists were hurting. The rapid decline in 2001–2002 of the dot.com firms in which they had invested substantial venture capital placed many venture capitalists in a crisis mode. Thus, new venture firms experienced difficulty in obtaining the necessary capital to survive and grow.

One unique form of venture capital fund is the Markle Foundation. President Zoe Baird invests the funds to create social change. The funds are invested in for-profit companies, usually as foundation investments in firms that are developing interactive media that will improve people's lives. Example investments include projects to reunite missing children with their families in West Africa and other projects in Kosovo. The foundation has invested in Global Forest Watch. This program tracks the degradation of old forests and firms working in them and posts the results on the Internet to stop companies (and governments) from cheating on the amount of trees that are cut. Another investment by the Markle Foundation supports a polling organization on issues of interest to women.

Most venture capitalists invest to earn a good return, but events beyond recessions and stock market downturns can harm the venture capital markets. For example, the events on September 11 had a negative effect on venture capital investments. The financial services firm of Cantor Fitzgerald, with its offices on the top five floors of one of the World Trade Center towers, was literally destroyed when the airliner struck the tower. This event severely harmed new ventures that were to receive venture capital from the firm, such as Livewire International. Craig Souser, the entrepreneur who started Livewire, was to receive the first payment of $1 million in cash from Cantor Fitzgerald on September 11. It did not come, and Livewire was able to persevere only by making substantial reductions in its operations.

SOURCES: A. Barrett & E. Licking, 2002, In biotech, private cash is king, *Business Week*, February 18, 90; J. Harwood & B. Gruley, 2001, How Sept. 11 upended the life and work of one entrepreneur, *The Wall Street Journal*, December 28, A4; 2001, Silicon Valley's venture capitalists face cash burn, *Financial Times*, http://www.ft.com, August 18; J. Reingold, 2001, Fast foundation, *Fast Company*, February, 124–133.

mentary resources from partners in order to compete effectively in domestic and international markets.[108]

There remain many entrepreneurial opportunities in international markets. Thus, firms should seek to enter and compete in international markets. Firms can learn new technologies and management practices from international markets and diffuse this knowledge throughout the firm. Furthermore, the knowledge firms gain can contribute to their innovations. Research has shown that firms operating in international markets tend to be more innovative.[109] Small and large firms are now regularly moving into international markets. Both types of firms must also be innovative to compete effectively. Thus, developing resources (human and social capital), taking advantage of opportunities in domestic and international markets, and using the resources and knowledge gained in these markets to be innovative, firms achieve competitive advantages. In so doing, they create value for their customers and shareholders.

Firms that practice strategic entrepreneurship contribute to a country's economic development. In fact, some countries such as Ireland have made dramatic economic progress by changing the institutional rules for business operating in the country. This could be construed as a form of institutional entrepreneurship. Likewise, firms that seek to establish their technology as a standard, also representing institutional entrepreneurship, are engaging in strategic entrepreneurship because creating a standard produces a sustainable competitive advantage for the firm.[110]

Research shows that because of its economic importance and individual motives, entrepreneurial activity is increasing across the globe. Furthermore, more women are becoming entrepreneurs because of the economic opportunity entrepreneurship provides and the individual independence it affords.[111] In future years, entrepreneurial activity may increase the wealth of less affluent countries and continue to contribute to the economic development of the more affluent countries. Regardless, the companies that practice strategic entrepreneurship are likely to be the winners in the 21st century.[112]

Summary

- Strategic entrepreneurship is taking entrepreneurial actions using a strategic perspective. More specifically, it involves engaging in simultaneous opportunity seeking and competitive advantage seeking behaviors to design and implement entrepreneurial strategies to create wealth.

- The concepts of entrepreneurial opportunity, innovation, and capabilities are important to firms. Entrepreneurial opportunities represent conditions in which new products or services can satisfy a need in the market. The essence of entrepreneurship is to identify and exploit these opportunities. Innovation is the process of commercializing the products or processes that surfaced through invention. Entrepreneurial capabilities include building an entrepreneurial culture, having a passion for the business, and having a desire for measured risk.

- Increasingly, entrepreneurship is being practiced in many countries. As used by entrepreneurs, entrepreneurship and corporate entrepreneurship are strongly related to a nation's economic growth. This relationship is a primary reason for the increasing use of entrepreneurship and corporate entrepreneurship in countries throughout the global economy.

- Three basic approaches are used to produce and manage innovation: internal corporate venturing, strategic alliances, and acquisitions. Autonomous strategic behavior and induced strategic behavior are the two processes of internal corporate venturing. Autonomous strategic behavior is a bottom-up process through which a product champion facilitates the commercialization of an innovative good or service. Induced strategic behavior is a top-down process in which a firm's current strategy and structure facilitate product or process innovations that are associated with them. Thus, induced strategic behavior is driven by the organization's current corporate strategy, structure, and reward and control systems.

- To create incremental and radical innovation requires effective innovation processes and practices. Increasingly, cross-functional integration is vital to a firm's efforts to develop and implement internal corporate venturing activities and to commercialize the resulting innovation. Additionally, integration and innovation can be facilitated by the development of shared values and the practice of entrepreneurial leadership.

- In the complex global economy, it is difficult for an individual firm to possess all the knowledge needed to innovate consistently and effectively. To gain access to the kind of specialized knowledge that often is required to innovate, firms may form a cooperative relationship such as a strategic alliance with other firms, sometimes even with competitors.

- Acquisitions provide another means for firms to produce and manage innovation. Innovation can be acquired through direct acquisition, or firms can learn new capabilities from an acquisition, thereby enriching their internal innovation processes.

- Entrepreneurial activity requires capital for development. Venture capitalists are a prime source for this capital. The amount of venture capital available increased dramatically in the decade of the 1990s. While it decreased recently due to economic problems, it remains much higher than in earlier years. Initial public offerings (IPOs) also have become a common means of obtaining capital for new ventures.

- The practice of strategic entrepreneurship by all types of firms, large and small, new and more established, creates value for all stakeholders, especially for shareholders and customers. Strategic entrepreneurship also contributes to the economic development of entire nations. Thus, entrepreneurial activity is increasing throughout the world.

Review Questions

1. What is strategic entrepreneurship? What is its importance for firms competing in the global economy?

2. What are entrepreneurial opportunities, innovation, and entrepreneurial capabilities, and what is their importance?

3. Why is international entrepreneurship important and why is it increasing across the globe?

4. What is autonomous strategic behavior? What is induced strategic behavior?

5. How do firms use strategic alliances to help them produce innovation?

6. How can a firm use acquisitions to increase the number of innovations it produces and improve its capability to produce innovations?

7. What is the importance of venture capital and initial public offerings to entrepreneurial activity?

8. How does strategic entrepreneurship create value for customers and shareholders and contribute to economic development?

Experiential Exercise

Strategic Entrepreneurship

Assume that you are a partner in a new venture energy company called Currence. You have approached an investor group for capital to fund the first three years of your operation. Following the preliminary presentation, you find that the group is very impressed by Currence and by its six start-up partners, each of whom brings unique, yet critical skills, experience, contacts, and other knowledge to the venture. Before the investor group decides to fund your company, however, it has asked for a brief presentation about how the Currence partners will be rewarded.

Part 1 (complete individually). Indicate how Currence will determine the approximate salary, fringe benefits, and shares of stock (as a percentage) each partner will be allocated upon closing the financing of your new venture. Also indicate your rationale for these amounts.

Part 2 (in small groups). Compare your responses to Part 1 with others in your small group. Reach a consensus on the criteria your small group would use to determine how to reward each partner. Appoint one small group member to present your consensus and how your team reached it to the class.

Part 3 (in small groups). Following the presentations in Part 2, discuss the following issues and indicate any important lessons and implications:

1. Why would an entrepreneurial venture such as Currence be asked to provide this type of information to an investor group?

2. What criteria did the groups use concerning salaries and stock? Why?

3. What patterns did you perceive in the approaches taken by each team?

4. Did the groups make salaries or stock equal for all Currence partners? Why or why not? What reasons would there be for providing different rewards for different partners?

5. How difficult was it for the small groups to reach a consensus?

Notes

1. S. M. Camp, L. W. Cox, & B. Kotalik, 2001, *The Hallmarks of Entrepreneurial Excellence: 2001 Survey of Innovative Practices*, Kauffman Center for Entrepreneurial Leadership, Ewing Marion Kauffman Foundation.
2. M. A. Hitt, R. D. Ireland, S. M. Camp, & D. L. Sexton, 2002, Strategic entrepreneurship: Integrating entrepreneurial and strategic management perspectives. In M. A. Hitt, R. D. Ireland, S. M. Camp, & D. L. Sexton (eds.), *Strategic Entrepreneurship: Creating a New Mindset*, Oxford, U.K.: Blackwell Publishers, 1–16; M. A. Hitt, R. D. Ireland, S. M. Camp, & D. L. Sexton, 2001, Strategic entrepreneurship: Entrepreneurial strategies for wealth creation, *Strategic Management Journal*, 22(Special Issue): 479–491; R. D. Ireland, M. A. Hitt, S. M. Camp, & D.L. Sexton, 2001, Integrating entrepreneurship and strategic management actions to create firm wealth, *Academy of Management Executive*, 15(1): 49–63.
3. R. D. Ireland & M. A. Hitt, 1999, Achieving and maintaining strategic competitiveness in the 21st century: The role of strategic leadership, *Academy of Management Executive*, 13(1): 43–57.
4. H. Lee, M. A. Hitt, & E. K. Jeong, 2002, The impact of CEO and TMT characteristics on strategic flexibility and firm performance, working paper, University of Connecticut; M. E. Raynor, 2001, *Strategic Flexibility in the Financial Services Industry: Creating Competitive Advantage Out of Competitive Turbulence*, New York: Deloitte Research.
5. G. Hamel, 2000, *Leading the Revolution*, Boston, MA: Harvard Business School Press.
6. S. Michael, D. Storey, & H. Thomas, 2002, Discovery and coordination in strategic management and entrepreneurship. In M. A. Hitt, R. D. Ireland, S. M. Camp, & D. L. Sexton (eds.), *Strategic Entrepreneurship: Creating a New Mindset*, Oxford, U.K.: Blackwell Publishers, 45-65.
7. M. A. Hitt, R. D. Nixon, P. G. Clifford, & K. P. Coyne, 1999, The development and use of strategic resources. In M. A. Hitt, P. G. Clifford, R. D. Nixon, & K. P. Coyne (eds.), 1999, *Dynamic Strategic Resources: Development, Diffusion and Integration*, Chichester: John Wiley & Sons, Ltd., 1–14.
8. T. W. Y. Man, T. Lau, & K. F. Chan, 2002, The competitiveness of small and medium enterprises: A conceptualization with focus on entrepreneurial competencies, *Journal of Business Venturing*, 17: 123–142.
9. J. Schumpeter, 1934, *The Theory of Economic Development*, Cambridge, MA: Harvard University Press.
10. S. Shane & S. Venkataraman, 2000, The promise of entrepreneurship as a field of research, *Academy of Management Review*, 25: 217-226.
11. B. R. Barringer & A. C. Bluedorn, 1999, The relationship between corporate entrepreneurship and strategic management, *Strategic Management Journal*, 20: 421–444.
12. G. D. Meyer, H. M. Neck, & M. D. Meeks, 2002, The entrepreneurship-strategic management interface. In M. A. Hitt, R. D. Ireland, S. M. Camp & D. L. Sexton (eds.), *Strategic Entrepreneurship: Creating a New Mindset*, Oxford, U.K.: Blackwell Publishers, 19–44; I. Kirzner, 1997, Entrepreneurial discovery and the competitive market process: An Austrian approach, *Journal of Economic Literature*, 35 (1): 60–85.
13. R. G. McGrath & I. MacMillan, 2000, *The Entrepreneurial Mindset*, Boston, MA: Harvard Business School Press.
14. G. Gori, 2001, An American directs Mexico City's cinema revival, *The New York Times*, http://www.nytimes.com, July 15.
15. P. F. Drucker, 1998, The discipline of innovation, *Harvard Business Review*, 76(6): 149–157.
16. P. D. Reynolds, M. Hay, & S. M. Camp, 1999, *Global Entrepreneurship Monitor, 1999 Executive Report*, Babson Park, MA.: Babson College.
17. R. M. Kanter, 1999, From spare change to real change: The social sector as beta site for business innovation, *Harvard Business Review*, 77(3): 122–132.
18. Hamel, *Leading the Revolution*; R. Price, 1996, Technology and strategic advantage, *California Management Review*, 38(3): 38–56; L. G. Franko, 1989, Global corporate competition: Who's winning, who's losing and the R&D factor as one reason why, *Strategic Management Journal*, 10: 449–474.
19. G. T. Lumpkin & G. G. Dess, 1996, Clarifying the entrepreneurial orientation construct and linking it to performance, *Academy of Management Review*, 21: 135–172; K. M. Kelm, V. K. Narayanan, & G. E. Pinches, 1995, Shareholder value creation during R&D innovation and commercialization stages, *Academy of Management Journal*, 38: 770–786.
20. M. A. Hitt, R. D. Nixon, R. E. Hoskisson, & R. Kochhar, 1999, Corporate entrepreneurship and cross-functional fertilization: Activation, process and disintegration of a new product design team, *Entrepreneurship: Theory and Practice*, 23(3): 145–167.
21. Schumpeter, *The Theory of Economic Development*.
22. P. Sharma & J. L. Chrisman, 1999, Toward a reconciliation of the definitional issues in the field of corporate entrepreneurship, *Entrepreneurship: Theory and Practice*, 23(3): 11–27; R. A. Burgelman & L. R. Sayles, 1986, *Inside Corporate Innovation: Strategy, Structure, and Managerial Skills*, New York: Free Press.
23. R. E. Hoskisson & L. W. Busenitz, 2002, Market uncertainty and learning distance in corporate entrepreneurship entry mode choice. In M. A. Hitt, R. D. Ireland, S. M. Camp, & D. L. Sexton (eds.), *Strategic Entrepreneurship: Creating a New Mindset*, Oxford, U.K.: Blackwell Publishers, 151–172.
24. J. S. Hornsby, D. F. Kuratko, & S. A. Zahra, 2002, Middle managers' perception of the internal environment for corporate entrepreneurship: Assessing a measurement scale, *Journal of Business Venturing*, 17: 253–273.
25. S. D. Sarasvathy, 2000, Seminar on research perspectives in entrepreneurship (1997), *Journal of Business Venturing*, 15: 1–57.
26. D. F. Kuratko, R. D. Ireland, & J. S. Hornsby, 2001, Improving firm performance through entrepreneurial actions: Acordia's corporate entrepreneurship strategy, *Academy of Management Executive*, 15(4): 60–71; J. Birkinshaw, 1999, The determinants and consequences of subsidiary initiative in multinational corporations, *Entrepreneurship: Theory and Practice*, 24(1): 9–36.
27. 2002, Apple unveils its latest iMac, *The Arizona Republic*, January 8, D8; P.-W. Tam, 2002, Apple unveils sleek new iMac design, hoping to revive struggling business, *The Wall Street Journal Interactive*, http://www.wsj.com, January 8.
28. T. Erickson, 2002, Entrepreneurial capital: The emerging venture's most important asset and competitive advantage, *Journal of Business Venturing*, 17: 275–290.
29. W. Tsai, 2001, Knowledge transfer in intraorganizational networks: Effects of network position and absorptive capacity on business unit innovation and performance, *Academy of Management Journal*, 44: 996–1004.
30. S. A. Zahra & G. George, 2002, Absorptive capacity: A review, reconceptualization, and extension, *Academy of Management Review*, 27: 185–203.
31. M. A. Hitt, L. Bierman, K. Shimizu, & R. Kochhar, 2001, Direct and moderating effects of human capital on strategy and performance in professional service firms: A resource-based perspective, *Academy of Management Journal*, 44: 13–28.
32. I. Bouty, 2000, Interpersonal and interaction influences on informal resource exchanges between R&D researchers across organizational boundaries, *Academy of Management Journal*, 43: 5–65.
33. 2001, Some like it hot, *Entrepreneur.com*, October 30.
34. T. W. Brailsford, 2001, Building a knowledge community at Hallmark Cards, *Research Technology Management*, 44 (5): 18–25.
35. R. G. McGrath, 2001, Exploratory learning, innovative capacity, and managerial oversight, *Academy of Management Journal*, 44: 118–131.
36. J. W. Lu & P. W. Beamish, 2001, The internationalization and performance of SMEs, *Strategic Management Journal*, 22(Special Issue): 565–585.
37. 2000, Staff reporter, Business innovation urged, *Irish Times*, 23.
38. J. E. Jackson, J. Klich, & V. Kontorovich, 1999, Firm creation and economic transitions, *Journal of Business Venturing*, 14: 427–450.
39. M. Kwak, 2002, What's the best commercialization strategy for startups? *MIT Sloan Management Review*, 43(3): 10.
40. P. D. Reynolds, S. M. Camp, W. D. Bygrave, E. Autio, & M. Hay, 2002, *Global Entrepreneurship Monitor*, Kauffman Center for Entrepreneurial Leadership, Ewing Marion Kauffman Foundation.
41. M. H. Morris, 1998, *Entrepreneurial Intensity: Sustainable Advantages for Individuals, Organizations, and Societies*, Westport, CT: Quorum Books, 85–86. M. H. Morris, D. L. Davis, & J. W. Allen, 1994, Fostering corporate entrepreneurship: Cross-cultural comparisons of the importance of individualism versus collectivism, *Journal of International Business Studies*, 25: 65–89.
42. S. A. Zahra & G. George, 2002, International entrepreneurship: The sate of the field and future research agenda. In M. A. Hitt, R. D. Ireland, S. M. Camp, & D. L. Sexton (eds.), *Strategic Entrepreneurship: Creating a New Mindset*, Oxford, U.K.: Blackwell Publishers, 255–288.
43. S. A. Zahra, R. D. Ireland, & M. A. Hitt, 2000, International expansion by new venture firms: International diversity, mode of market entry, technological learning and performance, *Academy of Management Journal*, 43: 925–950.
44. P. P. McDougall & B. M. Oviatt, 2000, International entrepreneurship: The intersection of two paths, *Academy of Management Journal*, 43: 902–908.
45. H. Barkema & O. Chvyrkov, 2002, What sort of top management team is needed at the helm of internationally diversified firms? In M. A. Hitt, R. D. Ireland, S. M. Camp & D. L. Sexton (eds.), *Strategic Entrepreneurship: Creating a New Mindset*, Oxford, U.K.: Blackwell Publishers, 290–305.
46. T. S. Frost, 2001, The geographic sources of foreign subsidiaries' innovations, *Strategic Management Journal*, 22: 101–122.

47. E. W. K. Tsang, 2002, Learning from overseas venturing experience: The case of Chinese family businesses, *Journal of Business Venturing,* 17: 21–40.

48. W. Kuemmerle, 2002, Home base and knowledge management in international ventures, *Journal of Business Venturing,* 17: 99–12.

49. R. Leifer, G. Colarelli, & M. Rice, 2001, Implementing radical innovation in mature firms: The role of hubs, *Academy of Management Executive,* 15(3): 102–113.

50. G. Ahuja & M. Lampert, 2001, Entrepreneurship in the large corporation: A longitudinal study of how established firms create breakthrough inventions, *Strategic Management Journal,* 22(Special Issue): 521–543.

51. Leifer, Collarelli, & Rice, Implementing radical innovation.

52. R. I. Sutton, 2002, Weird ideas that spark innovation, *MIT Sloan Management Review,* 43(2): 83–87.

53. K. G. Smith & D. Di Gregorio, 2002, Bisociation, discovery, and the role of entrepreneurial action. In M. A. Hitt, R. D. Ireland, S. M. Camp & D. L. Sexton (eds.), *Strategic Entrepreneurship: Creating a New Mindset,* Oxford, U.K.: Blackwell Publishers, 129–150.

54. Hoskisson & Busenitz, Market uncertainty and learning distance.

55. R. A. Burgelman, 1995, *Strategic Management of Technology and Innovation,* Boston: Irwin.

56. R. Leifer & M. Rice, 1999, Unnatural acts: Building the mature firm's capability for breakthrough innovation. In M. A. Hitt, P. G. Clifford, R. D. Nixon, & K. P. Coyne (eds.), *Dynamic Strategic Resources: Development, Diffusion and Integration,* Chichester: John Wiley & Sons, 433–453.

57. M. A. Hitt, R. D. Ireland, & H. Lee, 2000, Technological learning, knowledge management, firm growth and performance, *Journal of Engineering and Technology Management,* 17: 231–246; D. Leonard-Barton, 1995, *Wellsprings of Knowledge: Building and Sustaining the Sources of Innovation,* Cambridge, MA: Harvard Business School Press.

58. S. S. Rao, 2000, General Electric, software vendor, *Forbes,* January 24, 144–146.

59. H. W. Chesbrough, 2002, Making sense of corporate venture capital, *Harvard Business Review,* 80(3): 90–99; G. Hamel, 1997, Killer strategies that make shareholders rich, *Fortune,* June 23: 70–88.

60. M. Subramaniam & N. Venkatraman, 2001, Determinants of transnational new product development capability: Testing the influence of transferring and deploying tacit overseas knowledge, *Strategic Management Journal,* 22: 359–378.

61. M. Song & M. M. Montoya-Weiss, 2001, The effect of perceived technological uncertainty on Japanese new product development, *Academy of Management Journal,* 44: 61–80.

62. McGrath and MacMillan, *Entrepreneurial Mindset.*

63. 2002, Building scientific networks for effective innovation, *MIT Sloan Management Review,* 43(3): 14.

64. C. M. Christensen & M. Overdorf, 2000, Meeting the challenge of disruptive change, *Harvard Business Review,* 78(2): 66–77.

65. L. Yu, 2002, Marketers and engineers: Why can't we just get along? *MIT Sloan Management Review,* 43 (1):13.

66. P. S. Adler, 1995, Interdepartmental interdependence and coordination: The case of the design/manufacturing interface, *Organization Science,* 6: 147–167.

67. B. L. Kirkman & B. Rosen, 1999, Beyond self-management: Antecedents and consequences of team empowerment, *Academy of Management Journal,* 42: 58–74; A. R. Jassawalla & H. C. Sashittal, 1999, Building collaborative cross-functional new product teams, *Academy of Management Executive,* 13(3): 50–63.

68. Hitt, Nixon, Hoskisson, & Kochhar, Corporate entrepreneurship.

69. Christensen & Overdorf, 2000, Meeting the challenge of disruptive change.

70. Hitt, Nixon, Hoskisson, & Kochhar, Corporate entrepreneurship.

71. A. C. Amason, 1996, Distinguishing the effects of functional and dysfunctional conflict on strategic decision making: Resolving a paradox for top management teams, *Academy of Management Journal,* 39: 123–148; P. R. Lawrence & J. W. Lorsch, 1969, *Organization and Environment,* Homewood, IL: Richard D. Irwin.

72. D. Dougherty, L. Borrelli, K. Muncir, & A. O'Sullivan, 2000, Systems of organizational sensemaking for sustained product innovation, *Journal of Engineering and Technology Management,* 17: 321–355; D. Dougherty, 1992, Interpretive barriers to successful product innovation in large firms, *Organization Science,* 3: 179–202.

73. Hitt, Nixon, Hoskisson, & Kochhar, Corporate entrepreneurship.

74. E. C. Wenger & W. M. Snyder, 2000, Communities of practice: The organizational frontier, *Harvard Business Review,* 78(1): 139–144.

75. Hamel, *Leading the Revolution.*

76. McGrath & MacMillan, *Entrepreneurial Mindset.*

77. Hamel, *Leading the Revolution.*

78. Hitt, Ireland, Camp, & Sexton, Strategic entrepreneurship; S. W. Fowler, A. W. King, S. J. Marsh, & B. Victor, 2000, Beyond products: New strategic imperatives for developing competencies in dynamic environments, *Journal of Engineering and Technology Management,* 17: 357–377.

79. R. K. Kazanjian, R. Drazin, & M. A. Glynn, 2002, Implementing strategies for corporate entrepreneurship: A knowledge-based perspective. In M. A. Hitt, R. D. Ireland, S. M. Camp, & D. L. Sexton (eds.), *Strategic Entrepreneurship: Creating a New Mindset,* Oxford, U.K.: Blackwell Publishers, 173–199.

80. A. C. Cooper, 2002, Networks, alliances and entrepreneurship. In M. A. Hitt, R. D. Ireland, S. M. Camp & D. L. Sexton (eds.), *Strategic Entrepreneurship: Creating a New Mindset,* Oxford, U.K.: Blackwell Publishers, 204–222.

81. S. A. Alvarez & J. B. Barney, 2001, How entrepreneurial firms can benefit from alliances with large partners, *Academy of Management Executive,* 15(1): 139–148; F. T. Rothaermel, 2001, Incumbent's advantage through exploiting complementary assets via interfirm cooperation, *Strategic Management Journal,* 22(Special Issue): 687–699.

82. J. Hagedoorn & N. Roijakkers, 2002, Small entrepreneurial firms and large companies in inter-firm R&D networks—the international biotechnology industry. In M. A. Hitt, R. D. Ireland, S. M. Camp, & D. L. Sexton (eds.), *Strategic Entrepreneurship: Creating a New Mindset,* Oxford, U.K.: Blackwell Publishers, 223–252.

83. P. Kale, H. Singh, & H. Perlmutter, 2000, Learning and protection of proprietary assets in strategic alliances: Building relational capital, *Strategic Management Journal,* 21: 217–237.

84. D. Pringle, 2002, Wintel duo targets the cellphone, *The Wall Street Journal,* February 19, B1.

85. H. Yli-Renko, E. Autio, & H. J. Sapienza, 2001, Social capital, knowledge acquisition and knowledge exploitation in young technology-based firms, *Strategic Management Journal,* 22(Special Issue): 587–613.

86. C. Lee, K. Lee, & J. M. Pennings, 2001, Internal capabilities, external networks and performance: A study of technology-based ventures, *Strategic Management Journal,* 22(Special Issue): 615–640.

87. A. Takeishi, 2001, Bridging inter- and intra-firm boundaries: Management of supplier involvement in automobile product development, *Strategic Management Journal,* 22: 403–433.

88. R. D. Ireland, M. A. Hitt, & D. Vaidyanath, 2002, Strategic alliances as a pathway to competitive success, *Journal of Management,* in press.

89. M. A. Hitt, M. T. Dacin, E. Levitas, J.-L. Arregle, & A. Borza, 2000. Partner selection in emerging and developed market contexts: Resource-based and organizational learning perspectives, *Academy of Management Journal,* 43: 449–467.

90. J. J. Reuer, M. Zollo, & H. Singh, 2002, Post-formation dynamics in strategic alliances, *Strategic Management Journal,* 23: 135–151.

91. F. Rothaermel & D. Deeds, 2002, More good things are not always necessarily better: An empirical study of strategic alliances, experience effects, and new product development in high-technology start-ups. In M. A. Hitt, R. Amit, C. Lucier, & R. Nixon (eds.) *Creating Value: Winners in the New Business Environment,* Oxford, U.K.: Blackwell Publishers, 85–103.

92. M. A. Hitt, R. E. Hoskisson, R. A. Johnson, & D. D. Moesel, 1996, The market for corporate control and firm innovation, *Academy of Management Journal,* 39: 1084–1119.

93. M. A. Hitt, J. S. Harrison, & R. D. Ireland, 2001, *Mergers and Acquisitions: A Guide to Creating Value for Stakeholders,* New York: Oxford University Press.

94. J. A. Timmons, 1999, *New Venture Creation: Entrepreneurship for the 21st Century* (5th ed.), New York: Irwin/McGraw-Hill.

95. R. Amit, C. Lucier, M. A. Hitt, & R. D. Nixon, 2002, Strategies for the entrepreneurial millennium. In M. A. Hitt, R. Amit, C. Lucier & R. Nixon (eds.) *Creating Value: Winners in the New Business Environment,* Oxford, U.K.: Blackwell Publishers, 1–12.

96. C. M. Mason & R. T. Harrison, 2002, Is it worth it? The rates of return from informal venture capital investments, *Journal of Business Venturing,* 17: 211–236.

97. Amit, Lucier, Hitt, & Nixon, Strategies for the entrepreneurial millennium.

98. C. E. Lucier, L. H. Moeller, & R. Held, 1997, 10X value: The engine powering long-term shareholder returns, *Strategy & Business,* 8: 21–28.

99. D. A. Shepherd & A. Zacharakis, 2002, Venture capitalists' expertise: A call for research into decision aids and cognitive feedback, *Journal of Business Venturing,* 17: 1–20.

100. S. Manigart, K. de Waele, M. Wright, K. Robbie, P. Desbrieres, H. J. Sapienza, & A. Beekman, 2002, Determinants of required return in venture capital investments: A

five-country study, *Journal of Business Venturing*, 17: 291–312.

101. M. Maula & G. Murray, 2002, Corporate venture capital and the creation of U. S. public companies: The impact of sources of capital on the performance of portfolio companies. In M. A. Hitt, R. Amit, C. Lucier, & R. Nixon (eds.) C*reating Value: Winners in the New Business Environment*, Oxford, U.K.: Blackwell Publishers, 164–187.

102. S. T. Certo, J. G. Covin, C. M. Daily, & D. R. Dalton, 2001, Wealth and the effects of founder management among IPO-stage new ventures, *Strategic Management Journal*, 22(Special Issue): 641–658.

103. L. DeCarlo, 2002, JetBlue IPO will fly right for investors, *Forbes*, http://www.forbes.com, February, 13.

104. Maula & Murray, Corporate venture capital.

105. Amit, Lucier, Hitt, & Nixon, Strategies for the entrepreneurial millennium.

106. Hitt, Ireland, Camp, & Sexton, Strategic entrepreneurship.

107. Hitt, Bierman, Shimizu, & Kochhar, Direct and moderating effects of human capital.

108. M. A. Hitt, H. Lee, & E. Yucel, 2002, The importance of social capital to the management of multinational enterprises: Relational networks among Asian and Western firms, *Asia Pacific Journal of Management*, in press.

109. M. A. Hitt, R. E. Hoskisson, & H. Kim, 1997, International diversification: Effects on innovation and firm performance in product diversified firms, *Academy of Management Journal*, 40: 767–798.

110. R. Garud, S. Jain, & A. Kumaraswamy, 2002, Institutional entrepreneurship in the sponsorship of common technological standards: The case of Sun Microsystems and JAVA, *Academy of Management Journal*, 45: 196–214.

111. Reynolds, Camp, Bygrave, Autio, & Hay, *Global Entrepreneurship Monitor*.

112. Hitt, Ireland, Camp, & Sexton, Strategic entrepreneurship; Amit, Lucier, Hitt, & Nixon, Strategies for the entrepreneurial millennium.

Case Studies

Introduction

Preparing an Effective Case Analysis

In most strategic management courses, cases are used extensively as a teaching tool.[1] A key reason is that cases provide active learners with opportunities to use the strategic management process to identify and solve organizational problems. Thus, by analyzing situations that are described in cases and presenting the results, active learners (i.e., students) become skilled at effectively using the tools, techniques, and concepts that combine to form the strategic management process.

The cases that follow are concerned with actual companies. Presented within the cases are problems and situations that managers and those with whom they work must analyze and resolve. As you will see, a strategic management case can focus on an entire industry, a single organization, or a business unit of a large, diversified firm. The strategic management issues facing not-for-profit organizations also can be examined using the case analysis method.

Basically, the case analysis method calls for a careful diagnosis of an organization's current conditions (as manifested by its external and internal environments) so that appropriate strategic actions can be recommended in light of the firm's strategic intent and strategic mission. Strategic actions are taken to develop and then use a firm's core competencies to select and implement different strategies, including business-level, corporate-level, acquisition and restructuring, international, and cooperative strategies. Thus, appropriate strategic actions help the firm to survive in the long run as it creates and uses competitive advantages as the foundation for achieving strategic competitiveness and earning above-average returns. The case method that we are recommending to you has a rich heritage as a pedagogical approach to the study and understanding of managerial effectiveness.[2]

As an active learner, your preparation is critical to successful use of the case analysis method. Without careful study and analysis, active learners lack the insights required to participate fully in the discussion of a firm's situation and the strategic actions that are appropriate.

Instructors adopt different approaches in their application of the case analysis method. Some require active learners/students to use a specific analytical procedure to examine an organization; others provide less structure, expecting students to learn by developing their own unique analytical method. Still other instructors believe that a moderately structured framework should be used to analyze a firm's situation and make appropriate recommendations. Your professor will determine the specific approach you take. The approach we are presenting to you is a moderately structured framework.

We divide our discussion of a moderately structured case analysis method framework into four sections. First, we describe the importance of understanding the skills active learners can acquire through effective use of the case analysis method. In the second section, we provide you with a process-oriented framework. This framework can be of value in your efforts to analyze cases and then present the results of your work. Using this framework in a classroom setting yields valuable experiences that can, in turn, help you successfully complete assignments that you will receive from your employer. The third section is where we describe briefly what you can expect to occur during in-class case discussions. As this description shows, the relationship and interactions between instructors and active learners/students during case discussions are different than they are during lectures. In the final section, we present a moderately structured framework that we believe can help you prepare effective oral and written presentations. Written and oral communication skills also are valued highly in many organizational settings; hence, their development today can serve you well in the future.

Skills Gained Through Use of the Case Analysis Method

The case analysis method is based on a philosophy that combines knowledge acquisition with significant involvement from students as active learners. In the words of Alfred North Whitehead, this philosophy "rejects the doctrine that students had first learned passively, and then, having learned should apply knowledge."[3] In contrast to this philosophy, the case analysis method is based on principles that were elaborated upon by John Dewey:

> Only by wrestling with the conditions of this problem at hand, seeking and finding his own way out, does [the student] think. . . . If he cannot devise his own solution (not, of course, in isolation, but in correspondence with the teacher and other pupils) and find his own way out he will not learn, not even if he can recite some correct answer with a hundred percent accuracy.[4]

The case analysis method brings reality into the classroom. When developed and presented effectively, with rich and interesting detail, cases keep conceptual discussions grounded in reality. Experience shows that simple fictional accounts of situations and collections of actual organizational data and articles from public sources are not as effective for learning as fully developed cases. A comprehensive case presents you with a partial clinical study of a real-life situation that faced managers as well as other stakeholders including employees. A case presented in narrative form provides motivation for involvement with and analysis of a specific situation. By framing alternative strategic actions and by confronting the complexity and ambiguity of the practical world, case analysis provides extraordinary power for your involvement with a personal learning experience. Some of the potential consequences of using the case method are summarized in Exhibit 1.

As Exhibit 1 suggests, the case analysis method can assist active learners in the development of their analytical and judgment skills. Case analysis also helps you learn how to ask the right questions. By this we mean questions that focus on the core strategic issues that are included in a case. Active learners/students with managerial aspirations can improve their ability to identify underlying problems rather than focusing on superficial symptoms as they develop skills at asking probing yet appropriate questions.

The collection of cases your instructor chooses to assign can expose you to a wide variety of organizations and decision situations. This approach vicariously broadens your experience base and provides insights into many types of managerial situations, tasks, and responsibilities. Such indirect experience can help you make a more informed career decision about the industry and managerial situation you believe will prove to be challenging and satisfying. Finally, experience in analyzing cases definitely enhances your problem-solving skills, and research indicates that the case method for this class is better than the lecture method.[5]

Furthermore, when your instructor requires oral and written presentations, your communication skills will be honed through use of the case method. Of course, these added skills depend on your preparation as well as your instructor's facilitation of learning. However, the primary responsibility for learning is yours. The quality of case discussion is generally acknowledged to require, at a minimum, a thorough mastery of case facts and some independent analysis of them. The case method there-

| Exhibit 1 | Consequences of Student Involvement with the Case Method |

1. Case analysis requires students to practice important managerial skills—diagnosing, making decisions, observing, listening, and persuading—while preparing for a case discussion.

2. Cases require students to relate analysis and action, to develop realistic and concrete actions despite the complexity and partial knowledge characterizing the situation being studied.

3. Students must confront the *intractability of reality*—complete with absence of needed information, an imbalance between needs and available resources, and conflicts among competing objectives.

4. Students develop a general managerial point of view—where responsibility is sensitive to action in a diverse environmental context.

SOURCE: C. C. Lundberg and C. Enz, 1993, A framework for student case preparation, *Case Research Journal*, 13 (Summer): 134.

fore first requires that you read and think carefully about each case. Additional comments about the preparation you should complete to successfully discuss a case appear in the next section.

Student Preparation for Case Discussion

If you are inexperienced with the case method, you may need to alter your study habits. A lecture-oriented course may not require you to do intensive preparation for *each* class period. In such a course, you have the latitude to work through assigned readings and review lecture notes according to your own schedule. However, an assigned case requires significant and conscientious *preparation before class*. Without it, you will be unable to contribute

meaningfully to in-class discussion. Therefore, careful reading and thinking about case facts, as well as reasoned analyses and the development of alternative solutions to case problems, are essential. Recommended alternatives should flow logically from core problems identified through study of the case. Exhibit 2 shows a set of steps that can help you familiarize yourself with a case, identify problems, and propose strategic actions that increase the probability that a firm will achieve strategic competitiveness and earn above-average returns.

Gaining Familiarity

The first step of an effective case analysis process calls for you to become familiar with the facts featured in the case and the focal firm's situation. Initially, you should

Exhibit 2	An Effective Case Analysis Process

Step 1: *Gaining Familiarity*	a. In general—determine who, what, how, where, and when (the critical facts of the case). b. In detail—identify the places, persons, activities, and contexts of the situation. c. Recognize the degree of certainty/uncertainty of acquired information.
Step 2: *Recognizing Symptoms*	a. List all indicators (including stated "problems") that something is not as expected or as desired. b. Ensure that symptoms are not assumed to be the problem (symptoms should lead to identification of the problem).
Step 3: *Identifying Goals*	a. Identify critical statements by major parties (e.g., people, groups, the work unit, etc.). b. List all goals of the major parties that exist or can be reasonably inferred.
Step 4: *Conducting the Analysis*	a. Decide which ideas, models, and theories seem useful. b. Apply these conceptual tools to the situation. c. As new information is revealed, cycle back to substeps a and b.
Step 5: *Making the Diagnosis*	a. Identify predicaments (goal inconsistencies). b. Identify problems (discrepancies between goals and performance). c. Prioritize predicaments/problems regarding timing, importance, etc.
Step 6: *Doing the Action Planning*	a. Specify and prioritize the criteria used to choose action alternatives. b. Discover or invent feasible action alternatives. c. Examine the probable consequences of action alternatives. d. Select a course of action. e. Design an implementation plan/schedule. f. Create a plan for assessing the action to be implemented.

SOURCE: C. C. Lundberg and C. Enz, 1993, A framework for student case preparation, *Case Research Journal*, 13 (Summer): 144.

become familiar with the focal firm's general situation (e.g., who, what, how, where, and when). Thorough familiarization demands appreciation of the nuances as well as the major issues in the case.

Gaining familiarity with a situation requires you to study several situational levels, including interactions between and among individuals within groups, business units, the corporate office, the local community, and the society at large. Recognizing relationships within and among levels facilitates a more thorough understanding of the specific case situation.

It is also important that you evaluate information on a continuum of certainty. Information that is verifiable by several sources and judged along similar dimensions can be classified as a *fact*. Information representing someone's perceptual judgment of a particular situation is referred to as an *inference*. Information gleaned from a situation that is not verifiable is classified as *speculation*. Finally, information that is independent of verifiable sources and arises through individual or group discussion is an *assumption*. Obviously, case analysts and organizational decision makers prefer having access to facts over inferences, speculations, and assumptions.

Personal feelings, judgments, and opinions evolve when you are analyzing a case. It is important to be aware of your own feelings about the case and to evaluate the accuracy of perceived "facts" to ensure that the objectivity of your work is maximized.

Recognizing Symptoms

Recognition of symptoms is the second step of an effective case analysis process. A symptom is an indication that something is not as you or someone else thinks it should be. You may be tempted to correct the symptoms instead of searching for true problems. True problems are the conditions or situations requiring solution before the performance of an organization, business unit, or individual can improve. Identifying and listing symptoms early in the case analysis process tends to reduce the temptation to label symptoms as problems. The focus of your analysis should be on the *actual causes* of a problem, rather than on its symptoms. Thus, it is important to remember that symptoms are indicators of problems, subsequent work facilitates discovery of critical causes of problems that your case recommendations must address.

Identifying Goals

The third step of effective case analysis calls for you to identify the goals of the major organizations, business units, and/or individuals in a case. As appropriate, you should also identify each firm's strategic intent and strategic mission. Typically, these direction-setting state-ments (goals, strategic intents, and strategic missions) are derived from comments made by central characters in the organization, business unit, or top management team as described in the case and/or from public documents (e.g., an annual report).

Completing this step successfully sometimes can be difficult. Nonetheless, the outcomes you attain from this step are essential to an effective case analysis because identifying goals, intent, and mission helps you to clarify the major problems featured in a case and to evaluate alternative solutions to those problems. Direction-setting statements are not always stated publicly or prepared in written format. When this occurs, you must infer goals from other available factual data and information.

Conducting the Analysis

The fourth step of effective case analysis is concerned with acquiring a systematic understanding of a situation. Occasionally cases are analyzed in a less-than-thorough manner. Such analyses may be a product of a busy sched-ule or the difficulty and complexity of the issues described in a particular case. Sometimes you will face pressures on your limited amounts of time and may believe that you can understand the situation described in a case without systematic *analysis* of all the facts. However, experience shows that familiarity with a case's facts is a necessary, but insufficient, step in the development of effective solu-tions—solutions that can enhance a firm's strategic com-petitiveness. In fact, a less-than-thorough analysis typically results in an emphasis on symptoms, rather than problems and their causes. To analyze a case effectively, you should be skeptical of quick or easy approaches and answers.

A systematic analysis helps you understand a situation and determine what can work and probably what will not work. Key linkages and underlying causal networks based on the history of the firm become apparent. In this way, you can separate causal networks from symptoms.

Also, because the quality of a case analysis depends on applying appropriate tools, it is important that you use the ideas, models, and theories that seem to be use-ful for evaluating and solving individual and unique sit-uations. As you consider facts and symptoms, a useful theory may become apparent. Of course, having famil-iarity with conceptual models may be important in the effective analysis of a situation. Successful students and successful organizational strategists add to their intellec-tual tool kits on a continual basis.

Making the Diagnosis

The fifth step of effective case analysis—diagnosis—is the process of identifying and clarifying the roots of the problems by comparing goals to facts. In this step, it is useful to search for predicaments. Predicaments are situations in which goals do not fit with known facts. When you evaluate the actual performance of an organization, business unit, or individual, you may identify over- or underachievement (relative to established goals). Of course, single-problem situations are rare. Accordingly, you should recognize that the case situations you study probably will be complex in nature.

Effective diagnosis requires you to determine the problems affecting longer term performance and those requiring immediate handling. Understanding these issues will aid your efforts to prioritize problems and predicaments, given available resources and existing constraints.

Doing the Action Planning

The final step of an effective case analysis process is called action planning. Action planning is the process of identifying appropriate alternative actions. In the action planning step you select the criteria you will use to evaluate the identified alternatives. You may derive these criteria from the analyses; typically, they are related to key strategic situations facing the focal organization. Furthermore, it is important that you prioritize these criteria to ensure a rational and effective evaluation of alternative courses of action.

Typically, managers "satisfice" when selecting courses of action; that is, they find *acceptable* courses of action that meet most of the chosen evaluation criteria. A rule of thumb that has proved valuable to strategic decision makers is to select an alternative that leaves other plausible alternatives available if the one selected fails.

Once you have selected the best alternative, you must specify an implementation plan. Developing an implementation plan serves as a reality check on the feasibility of your alternatives. Thus, it is important that you give thoughtful consideration to all issues associated with the implementation of the selected alternatives.

What to Expect From In-Class Case Discussions

Classroom discussions of cases differ significantly from lectures. The case method calls for instructors to guide the discussion, encourage student participation, and solicit alternative views. When alternative views are not forthcoming, instructors typically adopt one view so students can be challenged to respond to it thoughtfully. Often students' work is evaluated in terms of both the quantity and the quality of their contributions to in-class case discussions. Students benefit by having their views judged against those of their peers and by responding to challenges by other class members and/or the instructor.

During case discussions, instructors listen, question, and probe to extend the analysis of case issues. In the course of these actions, peers or the instructor may challenge an individual's views and the validity of alternative perspectives that have been expressed. These challenges are offered in a constructive manner; their intent is to help students develop their analytical and communication skills. Instructors should encourage students to be innovative and original in the development and presentation of their ideas. Over the course of an individual discussion, students can develop a more complex view of the case, benefiting from the diverse inputs of their peers and instructor. Among other benefits, experience with multiple-case discussions should help students increase their knowledge of the advantages and disadvantages of group decision-making processes.

Student peers as well as the instructor value comments that contribute to the discussion. To offer *relevant* contributions, you are encouraged to use independent thought and, through discussions with your peers outside of class, to refine your thinking. We also encourage you to avoid using "I think," "I believe," and "I feel" to discuss your inputs to a case analysis process. Instead, consider using a less emotion-laden phrase, such as "My analysis shows." This highlights the logical nature of the approach you have taken to complete the six steps of an effective case analysis process.

When preparing for an in-class case discussion, you should plan to use the case data to explain your assessment of the situation. Assume that your peers and instructor know the case facts. In addition, it is good practice to prepare notes before class discussions and use them as you explain your view. Effective notes signal to classmates and the instructor that you are prepared to engage in a thorough discussion of a case. Moreover, thorough notes eliminate the need for you to memorize the facts and figures needed to discuss a case successfully.

The case analysis process just described can help you prepare to effectively discuss a case during class meetings. Adherence to this process results in consideration of the issues required to identify a focal firm's problems and to propose strategic actions through which the firm can increase the probability that it will achieve strategic competitiveness.

In some instances, your instructor may ask you to prepare either an oral or a written analysis of a particular case. Typically, such an assignment demands even more thorough study and analysis of the case contents. At your instructor's discretion, oral and written analyses may be completed by individuals or by groups of two or more people. The information and insights gained through completing the six steps shown in Exhibit 2 often are of value in the development of an oral or written analysis.

However, when preparing an oral or written presentation, you must consider the overall framework in which your information and inputs will be presented. Such a framework is the focus of the next section.

Preparing an Oral/Written Case Strategic Plan

Experience shows that two types of thinking are necessary to develop an effective oral or written presentation (see Exhibit 3). The upper part of the model in Exhibit 3 outlines the *analysis* stage of case preparation.

In the analysis stage, you should first analyze the general external environmental issues affecting the firm. Next your environmental analysis should focus on the particular industry (or industries, in the case of a diversified company) in which a firm operates. Finally, you

should examine the competitive environment of the focal firm. Through study of the three levels of the external environment, you will be able to identify a firm's opportunities and threats. Following the external environmental analysis is the analysis of the firm's internal environment, which results in the identification of the firm's strengths and weaknesses.

As noted in Exhibit 3, you must then change the focus from analysis to *synthesis*. Specifically, you must *synthesize* information gained from your analysis of the firm's internal and external environments. Synthesizing information allows you to generate alternatives that can resolve the significant problems or challenges facing the focal firm. Once you identify a best alternative, from an evaluation based on predetermined criteria and goals, you must explore implementation actions.

Exhibit 4 and Exhibit 5 outline the sections that should be included in either an oral or a written strategic plan presentation: introduction (strategic intent and

---

Exhibit 3   Types of Thinking in Case Preparation: Analysis and Synthesis

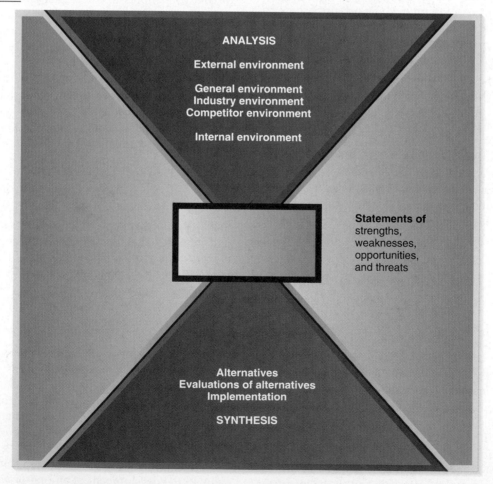

ANALYSIS

External environment

General environment
Industry environment
Competitor environment

Internal environment

Statements of strengths, weaknesses, opportunities, and threats

Alternatives
Evaluations of alternatives
Implementation

SYNTHESIS

Exhibit 4 Strategic Planning Process

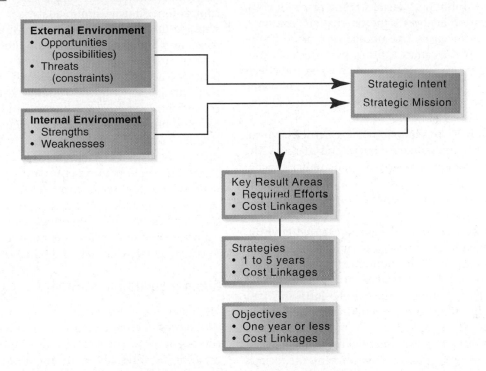

Exhibit 5 Strategic Planning and Its Parts

- *Strategic planning* is a *process* through which a firm determines what it seeks to accomplish and the actions required to achieve desired outcomes
  - ✓ *Strategic planning*, then, is a *process* that we use to determine *what* (outcomes to be reached) and how (actions to be taken to reach outcomes)
- The effective *strategic plan* for a firm would include statements and details about the following:
  - ✓ *Opportunities* (possibilities) and *threats* (constraints)
  - ✓ *Strengths* (what we do especially well) and *weaknesses* (deficiencies)
  - ✓ *Strategic intent* (an indication of a firm's ideal state)
  - ✓ *Strategic mission* (purpose and scope of a firm's operations in product and market terms)
  - ✓ *Key result areas* (KRAs) (categories of activities where efforts must take place to reach the mission and intent)
  - ✓ *Strategies* (actions for each KRA to be completed within one to five years)
  - ✓ *Objectives* (specific statements detailing actions for each strategy that are to be completed in one year or less)
  - ✓ *Cost linkages* (relationships between actions and financial resources)

mission), situation analysis, statements of strengths/ weaknesses and opportunities/threats, strategy formulation, and implementation plan. These sections, which can be completed only through use of the two types of thinking featured in Exhibit 3, are described in the following discussion. Familiarity with the contents of this book's 13 chapters is helpful because the general outline for an oral or a written strategic plan shown in Exhibit 5 is based on an understanding of the strategic management process detailed in these chapters.

External Environment Analysis

As shown in Exhibit 5, a general starting place for completing a situation analysis is the external environment. The *external environment* is composed of outside (external) conditions that affect a firm's performance. Your analysis of the environment should consider the effects of the *general environment* on the focal firm. Following that evaluation, you should analyze the *industry and competitor environmental* trends.

These trends or conditions in the external environment shape the firm's strategic intent and mission. The external environment analysis essentially indicates what a firm *might choose to do*. Often called an *environmental scan,* an analysis of the external environment allows a firm to identify key conditions that are beyond its direct control. The purpose of studying the external environment is to identify a firm's opportunities and threats. *Opportunities* are conditions in the external environment that appear to have the potential to contribute to a firm's success. In essence, opportunities represent *possibilities*. *Threats* are conditions in the external environment that appear to have the potential to prevent a firm's success. In essence, threats represent potential *constraints*.

When studying the external environment, the focus is on trying to *predict* the future (in terms of local, regional, and international trends and issues) and to *predict* the expected effects on a firm's operations. The external environment features conditions in the broader society *and* in the industry (area of competition) that influence the firm's possibilities and constraints. Areas to be considered (to identify opportunities and threats) when studying the general environment are listed in Exhibit 6. Many of these issues are explained more fully in Chapter 2.

Once you analyze the general environmental trends, you should study their effect on the focal industry. Often the same environmental trend may have a significantly different impact on separate industries. Furthermore, the same trend may affect firms within the same industry differently. For instance, with deregulation of the airline industry, older, established airlines had a significant decrease in profitability, while many smaller airlines such as Southwest Airlines, with lower cost structures and greater flexibility, were able to aggressively enter new markets.

Porter's five forces model is a useful tool for analyzing the specific industry (see Chapter 2). Careful study of how the five competitive forces (i.e., supplier power, buyer power, potential entrants, substitute products, and rivalry among competitors) affect a firm's strategy is important. These forces may create threats or opportunities relative to the specific business-level strategies (i.e., differentiation, cost leadership, focus) being imple-

mented. Often a strategic group's analysis reveals how different environmental trends are affecting industry competitors. Strategic group analysis is useful for understanding the industry's competitive structures and firm constraints and possibilities within those structures.

Firms also need to analyze each of their primary competitors. This analysis should identify competitors' current strategies, strategic intent, strategic mission, capabilities, core competencies, and a competitive response profile. This information is useful to the focal firm in formulating an appropriate strategic intent and mission. Sources that can be used to gather information about a general environment, industry, and companies with whom the focal firm competes are listed in Appendix I. Included in this list is a wide range of web sites; publications, such as periodicals, newspapers, bibliographies, and directories of companies; industry ratios; forecasts; rankings/ratings; and other valuable statistics.

Internal Environment Analysis

The *internal environment* is composed of strengths and weaknesses internal to a firm that influence its strategic competitiveness. The purpose of completing an analysis of a firm's internal environment is to identify its strengths and weaknesses. The strengths and weaknesses in a firm's internal environment shape the strategic intent and strategic mission. The internal environment essentially indicates what a firm *can do*. Capabilities or skills that allow a firm to do something that others cannot do or that allow a firm to do something better than others do it are called strengths. *Strengths* can be categorized as something that a firm does especially well. Strengths help a firm take advantage of external opportunities or overcome external threats. Capabilities or skill deficiencies that prevent a firm from completing an important activity as well as others do it are called weaknesses. *Weaknesses* have the potential to prevent a firm from taking advantage of external opportunities or succeeding in efforts to overcome external threats. Thus, *weaknesses* can be thought of as something the firm needs to improve.

Analysis of the primary and support activities of the value chain provides opportunities to understand how external environmental trends affect the specific activities of a firm. Such analysis helps highlight strengths and weaknesses (see Chapter 3 for an explanation of the value chain). For purposes of preparing an oral or written presentation, it is important to note that strengths are internal resources and capabilities that have the potential to be core competencies. Weaknesses, on the other hand, have the potential to place a firm at a competitive disadvantage relative to its rivals.

| **Exhibit 6** | Sample General Environmental Categories |

Technology	• Information technology continues to become cheaper and have more practical applications
	• Database technology allows organization of complex data and distribution of information
	• Telecommunications technology and networks increasingly provide fast transmission of all sources of data, including voice, written communications, and video information
Demographic Trends	• Computerized design and manufacturing technologies continue to facilitate quality and flexibility
	• Regional changes in population due to migration
	• Changing ethnic composition of the population
	• Aging of the population
	• Aging of the "baby boom" generation
Economic Trends	• Interest rates
	• Inflation rates
	• Savings rates
	• Trade deficits
	• Budget deficits
	• Exchange rates
Political/Legal Environment	• Anti-trust enforcement
	• Tax policy changes
	• Environmental protection laws
	• Extent of regulation/deregulation
	• Developing countries privatizing state monopolies
	• State-owned industries
Sociocultural Environment	• Increasing number of women in the work force
	• Awareness of health and fitness issues
	• Concern for the environment
	• Concern for customers
Global Environment	• Currency exchange rates
	• Free trade agreements
	• Trade deficits
	• New or developing markets

When evaluating the internal characteristics of the firm, your analysis of the functional activities emphasized is critical. For instance, if the strategy of the firm is primarily technology-driven, it is important to evaluate the firm's R&D activities. If the strategy is market-driven, marketing functional activities are of paramount importance. If a firm has financial difficulties, critical financial ratios would require careful evaluation. In fact, because of the importance of financial health, most cases require financial analyses. Appendix II lists and operationally defines several common financial ratios. Included are exhibits describing profitability, liquidity, leverage, activity, and shareholders' return ratios. Other firm characteristics that should be examined to study the internal environment effectively include leadership, organizational culture, structure, and control systems.

Identification of Strategic Intent and Mission

Strategic intent is associated with a mind-set that managers seek to imbue within the company. Essentially, a mind-set captures how we view the world and our intended role in it. Strategic intent reflects or identifies a firm's ideal state. Strategic intent flows from a firm's opportunities, threats, strengths, and weaknesses. However, the major influence on strategic intent is a firm's *strengths*. Strategic intent should reflect a firm's intended character and reflects a commitment to "stretch" available resources and strengths in order to reach what may seem to be unattainable strategies and objectives in terms of Key Result Areas (KRAs). When established effectively, strategic intent can cause each employee to perform in ways never imagined possible.

Strategic intent has the ability to reflect what may be the most worthy goal of all: to unseat the best or to be the best on a regional, national, or even international basis. Examples of strategic intent include:

- The relentless pursuit of perfection (Lexus).
- It's our strategic intent that customers worldwide view us as their most valued pharmaceutical partner (Eli Lilly).
- To be the top performer in everything that we do (Phillips Petroleum).
- To become a high performance multinational energy company—not the biggest, but the best (Unocal Corporation).
- We are dedicated to being the world's best at bringing people together (AT&T).
- Ben & Jerry's is dedicated to the creation and demonstration of a new corporate concept—linked prosperity.
- Our intent is to be better than the best (Best Products).
- The Children's Defense Fund exists to provide a strong and effective voice for the children of America who cannot vote, lobby, or speak for themselves.
- We build homes to meet people's dreams (Kaufman & Broad).
- We will be a leader in the emerging energy services industry by challenging conventional wisdom and creating superior value in a safe and environmentally responsible manner (PSI Energy, Inc.).
- We intend to become the single source of information technology for the home (Dell Computer Corporation).
- To be a premier provider of services and products that contribute to the health and well-being of people (MDS Health Group Limited).
- We seek to set the standard for excellence, leadership and integrity in the utility industry (New York State Electric & Gas Corp.).

The strategic mission flows from a firm's strategic intent; it is a statement used to describe a firm's unique intent and the scope of its operations in product and market terms. In its most basic form, the strategic mission indicates to stakeholders what a firm seeks to accomplish. An effective strategic mission reflects a firm's individuality and reveals its leadership's predisposition(s). The useful strategic mission shows how a firm differs from others and defines boundaries within which the firm intends to operate. Examples of strategic missions include:

- To make, distribute, and sell the finest quality all-natural ice cream and related products in a wide vari-

ety of innovative flavors made from Vermont dairy products (Ben & Jerry's).
- To serve the natural and LP needs of the customers in the Clearwater and surrounding Florida SunCoast area in the most safe, reliable and economical manner possible while optimizing load growth, customer satisfaction, financial return to the City of Clearwater and the equity value of the Clearwater Gas System (Clearwater Gas System).
- Public Service Company of Colorado is an energy company that primarily provides gas, electricity and related services to present and potential markets.
- Our mission is to understand and satisfy customer expectations for quality and energy and energy-related products and services and profitably serve Oklahoma markets (Public Service Company of Oklahoma).
- Children's Hospital Medical Center is dedicated to serving the health-care needs of infants, children, and adolescents and to providing research and teaching programs that ensure delivery of the highest quality pediatric care to our community, the nation, and the world (Children's Hospital Medical Center).
- To provide services and products which will assist physicians, health care institutions, corporations, government agencies, and communities to improve the health and well-being of the people for whom they are responsible (MDS Health Group Limited).
- The William Penn Foundation is a private grant making organization created in 1945 by Otto Haas and his wife, Phoebe. The principal mission of the Foundation is to help improve the quality of life in the Delaware Valley (William Penn Foundation).

Key Result Areas (KRAs)

Once the strategic intent and mission have been defined, the analysis can turn to defining KRAs to help accomplish the intent and mission. *Key result areas* are categories of activities that must receive attention if the firm is to achieve its strategic intent and strategic mission. A rationale or justification and specific courses of action for each KRA should be specified. Typically, a firm should establish no more than six KRAs. KRAs should suggest (in broad terms) a firm's concerns and intended directions.

Flowing from the nature of a firm's KRAs, *strategies* are courses of action that must be taken to satisfy the requirements suggested by each KRA. Strategies typically have a one-, two-, or three-year time horizon (although it can be as long as five years). Strategies are developed to describe approaches to be used or methods to follow in order to attain the strategic intent and strategic mission (as suggested by the KRAs). Strategies reflect a group's action intentions. Flowing from individual strategies, *objectives* are specific and measurable statements describing actions that are to be completed to implement individual strategies. Objectives, which are more specific in nature than strategies, usually have a one-year or shorter time horizon.

Strategic planning should also result in cost linkages to courses of action. Once key cost assumptions are specified, these financial requirements can be tied to strategies and objectives. Once linked with strategies and objectives, cost or budgetary requirements can be related back to KRAs.

Hints for Presenting an Effective Strategic Plan

There may be a temptation to spend most of your oral or written case analysis on results from the analysis. It is important, however, that you make an equal effort to develop and evaluate KRA alternatives and to design implementation for the chosen alternatives. In your presentation, the *analysis* of a case should not be overemphasized relative to the *synthesis* of results gained from your analytical efforts (see Exhibit 3).

Strategy Formulation: Choosing Key Result Areas

Once you have formulated a strategic intent and mission, choosing among alternative KRAs is often one of the most difficult steps in preparing an oral or written presentation. Each alternative should be feasible (i.e., it should match the firm's strengths, capabilities, and especially core competencies), and feasibility should be demonstrated. In addition, you should show how each alternative takes advantage of the environmental opportunity or avoids/buffers against environmental threats. Developing carefully thought out alternatives requires synthesis of your analyses and creates greater credibility in oral and written case presentations.

Once you develop strong alternative KRAs, you must evaluate the set to choose the best ones. Your choice should be defensible and provide benefits over the other alternatives. Thus, it is important that both the alternative development and evaluation of alternatives be thorough. The choice of the best alternative should be explained and defended.

Key Result Area Implementation

After selecting the most appropriate KRAs (that is, those with the highest probability of enhancing a firm's strategic competitiveness), you must consider effective implementation. Effective synthesis is important to ensure that you have considered and evaluated all critical implementation issues. Issues you might consider include the structural changes necessary to implement the new strategies and objectives associated with each KRA. In addition, leadership changes and new controls or incentives may be necessary to implement these strategic actions. The implementation actions you recommend should be explicit and thoroughly explained. Occasionally, careful evaluation of implementation actions may show the strategy to be less favorable than you originally thought. A strategy is only as good as the firm's ability to implement it effectively. Therefore, expending the effort to determine effective implementation is important.

Process Issues

You should ensure that your presentation (either oral or written) has logical consistency throughout. For example, if your presentation identifies one purpose, but your analysis focuses on issues that differ from the stated purpose, the logical inconsistency will be apparent. Likewise, your alternatives should flow from the configuration of strengths, weaknesses, opportunities, and threats you identified through the internal and external analyses.

Thoroughness and clarity also are critical to an effective presentation. Thoroughness is represented by the comprehensiveness of the analysis and alternative generation. Furthermore, clarity in the results of the analyses, selection of the best alternative KRAs, and design of implementation actions are important. For example, your statement of the strengths and weaknesses should flow clearly and logically from the internal analyses presented.

Presentations (oral or written) that show logical consistency, thoroughness, and clarity of purpose, effective analyses, and feasible recommendations are more effective and will receive more positive evaluations. Being able to withstand tough questions from peers after your presentation will build credibility for your strategic plan presentation. Furthermore, developing the skills necessary to make such presentations will enhance your future job performance and career success.

Appendix I: Sources for Industry and Competitor Analyses

Strategic Management Web Sites

Search Engines (may be the broadest sources of information on companies and industries)	Alta Vista—*http://www.altavista.digital.com* Excite—*http://www.excite.com* InfoSeek—*http://www.infoseek.com* Lycos—*http://www.lycos.com* WebCrawler—*http://www.webcrawler.com* Yahoo!—*http://www.yahoo.com*
Professional Societies	Academy of Management <*http://www.aom.pace.edu*> publishes *Academy of Management Journal, Academy of Management Review, and Academy of Management Executive,* three publications that often print articles on strategic management research, theory, and practice. The Academy of Management is the largest professional society for management research and education and has a large Business Policy and Strategy Division. Strategic Management Society <*http://www.smsweb.org*> publishes the *Strategic Management Journal* (a top academic journal in strategic management).
Government Sources of Company Information and Data	Census Bureau <*http://www.census.gov*> provides useful links and information about social, demographic, and economic information. Federal Trade Commission <*http://www.ftc.gov*> includes discussion on several antitrust and consumer protection laws useful to businesses looking for accurate information about business statutes. Free EDGAR <*http://www.freeedgar.com*> provides free, unlimited access to real-time corporate data filed with the Securities and Exchange Commission (SEC). Better Business Bureau <*http://www.bbb.org*> provides a wide variety of helpful publications, information, and other resources to both consumers and businesses to help people make informed marketplace decisions.
Publication Web Sites	Business Week <*http://www.businessweek.com*> allows search of *Business Week* magazine's articles by industry or topic, such as strategy. Forbes <*http://www.forbes.com*> provides searching of *Forbes* magazine business articles and data. Fortune <*http://www.fortune.com*> allows search of *Fortune* magazine and other articles, many of which are focused on strategy topics. Financial Times <*http://www.ft.com*> provides access to many *Financial Times* articles, data, and surveys. Wall Street Journal <*http://www.wsj.com*> *The Wall Street Journal Interactive* edition provides an excellent continuing stream of strategy-oriented articles and announcements.

Abstracts and Indexes

Periodicals	*ABI/Inform* *Business Periodicals Index* *InfoTrac (CD-ROM computer multidiscipline index)* *Investext (CD-ROM)* *Predicasts F&S Index United States* *Predicasts Overview of Markets and Technology (PROMT)* *Predicasts R&S Index Europe* *Predicasts R&S Index International*

Public Affairs Information Service Bulletin (PAIS)
Reader's Guide to Periodical Literature
Newspapers   NewsBank
Business NewsBank
New York Times Index
Wall Street Journal Index
Wall Street Journal/Barron's Index
Washington Post Index

Bibliographies

Encyclopedia of Business Information Sources
Handbook of Business Information

Directories

Companies—General

America's Corporate Families and International Affiliates
Hoover's Handbook of American Business
Hoover's Handbook of World Business
Million Dollar Directory
Standard & Poor's Corporation Records
Standard & Poor's Register of Corporations, Directors, and Executives
Ward's Business Directory

Companies—International

America's Corporate Families and International Affiliates
Business Asia
Business China
Business Eastern Europe
Business Europe
Business International
Business International Money Report
Business Latin America
Directory of American Films Operating in Foreign Countries
Directory of Foreign Firms Operating in the United States
Hoover's Handbook of World Business
International Directory of Company Histories
Moody's Manuals, International (2 volumes)
Who Owns Whom

Companies—Manufacturers

Manufacturing USA: Industry Analyses, Statistics, and Leading Companies
Thomas Register of American Manufacturers
U.S. Office of Management and Budget, Executive Office of the President, *Standard Industrial Classification Manual*
U.S. Manufacturer's Directory

Companies—Private

Million Dollar Directory
Ward's Directory

Companies—Public

Annual Reports and 10-K Reports
Disclosure (corporate reports)
Q-File
Moody's Manuals:
  Moody's Bank and Finance Manual
  Moody's Industrial Manual
  Moody's International Manual
  Moody's Municipal and Government Manual
  Moody's OTC Industrial Manual
  Moody's OTC Unlisted Manual
  Moody's Public Utility Manual
  Moody's Transportation Manual

Standard & Poor Corporation, *Standard Corporation Descriptions*:
   Standard & Poor's Handbook
   Standard & Poor's Industry Surveys
   Standard & Poor's Investment Advisory Service
   Standard & Poor's Outlook
   Standard & Poor's Statistical Service

Companies—Subsidiaries and Affiliates

America's Corporate Families and International Affiliates
Ward's Directory
Who Owns Whom
Moody's Industry Review
Standard & Poor's Analyst's Handbook
Standard & Poor's Industry Report Service
Standard & Poor's Industry Surveys (2 volumes)
U.S. Department of Commerce, *U.S. Industrial Outlook*

Industry Ratios

Dun & Bradstreet, *Industry Norms and Key Business Ratios*
Robert Morris Associates Annual Statement Studies
Troy Almanac of Business and Industrial Financial Ratios

Industry Forecasts

International Trade Administration, *U.S. Industrial Outlook*
   Predicasts Forecasts

Rankings & Ratings

Annual Report on American Industry in *Forbes*
Business Rankings and Salaries
Business One Irwin Business and Investment Almanac
Corporate and Industry Research Reports (CIRR)
Dun's Business Rankings
Moody's Industrial Review
Rating Guide to Franchises
Standard & Poor's Industry Report Service
Value Line Investment Survey
Ward's Business Directory

Statistics

American Statistics Index (ASI) Bureau of the Census, U.S.
   Department of Commerce, *Economic Census Publications*
Bureau of the Census, U.S. Department of Commerce,
   Statistical Abstract of the United States
Bureau of Economic Analysis, U.S. Department of Commerce,
   Survey of Current Business
Internal Revenue Service, U.S. Treasury Department, *Statistics of Income: Corporation Income Tax Returns*
Statistical Reference Index (SRI)

Appendix II: Financial Analysis in Case Studies

Exhibit A-1 — Profitability Ratios

Ratio	Formula	What It Shows
1. Return on total assets	$\dfrac{\text{Profits after taxes}}{\text{Total assets}}$ or $\dfrac{\text{Profits after taxes + interest}}{\text{Total assets}}$	The net return on total investment of the firm or The return on both creditors' and shareholders' investments
2. Return on stockholders' equity (or return on net worth)	$\dfrac{\text{Profits after taxes}}{\text{Total stockholders' equity}}$	How effectively the company is utilizing shareholders' funds
3. Return on common equity	$\dfrac{\text{Profit after taxes − preferred stock dividends}}{\text{Total stockholders' equity− par value of preferred stock}}$	The net return to common stockholders
4. Operating profit margin (or return on sales)	$\dfrac{\text{Profits before taxes and before interest}}{\text{Sales}}$	The firm's profitability from regular operations
5. Net profit margin (or net return on sales)	$\dfrac{\text{Profits after taxes}}{\text{Sales}}$	The firm's net profit as a percentage of total sales

Exhibit A-2 — Liquidity Ratios

Ratio	Formula	What It Shows
1. Current ratio	$\dfrac{\text{Current assets}}{\text{Current liabilities}}$	The firm's ability to meet its current financial liabilities
2. Quick ratio (or acid-test ratio)	$\dfrac{\text{Current assets − inventory}}{\text{Current liabilities}}$	The firm's ability to pay off short-term obligations without relying on sales of inventory
3. Inventory to net working capital	$\dfrac{\text{Inventory}}{\text{Current assets − current liabilities}}$	The extent of which the firm's working capital is tied up in inventory

Exhibit A-3   Leverage Ratios

Ratio	Formula	What It Shows
1. Debt-to-assets	$\dfrac{\text{Total debt}}{\text{Total assets}}$	Total borrowed funds as a percentage of total assets
2. Debt-to-equity	$\dfrac{\text{Total debt}}{\text{Total shareholders' equity}}$	Borrowed funds versus the funds provided by shareholders
3. Long-term debt-to-equity	$\dfrac{\text{Long-term debt}}{\text{Total shareholders' equity}}$	Leverage used by the firm
4. Times-interest-earned (or coverage ratio)	$\dfrac{\text{Profits before interest and taxes}}{\text{Total interest charges}}$	The firm's ability to meet all interest payments
5. Fixed charge coverage	$\dfrac{\text{Profits before taxes and interest + lease obligations}}{\text{Total interest charges + lease obligations}}$	The firm's ability to meet all fixed-charge obligations including lease payments

Exhibit A-4   Activity Ratios

Ratio	Formula	What It Shows
1. Inventory turnover	$\dfrac{\text{Sales}}{\text{Inventory of finished goods}}$	The effectiveness of the firm in employing inventory
2. Fixed assets turnover	$\dfrac{\text{Sales}}{\text{Fixed assets}}$	The effectiveness of the firm in utilizing plant and equipment
3. Total assets turnover	$\dfrac{\text{Sales}}{\text{Total assets}}$	The effectiveness of the firm in utilizing total assets
4. Accounts receivable turnover	$\dfrac{\text{Annual credit sales}}{\text{Accounts receivable}}$	How many times the total receivables have been collected during the accounting period
5. Average collection period	$\dfrac{\text{Accounts receivable}}{\text{Average daily sales}}$	The average length of time the firm waits to collect payments after sales

Ratio	Formula	What It Shows
1. Dividend yield on common stock	$$\frac{\text{Annual dividends per share}}{\text{Current market price per share}}$$	A measure of return to common stockholders in the form of dividends.
2. Price-earnings ratio	$$\frac{\text{Current market price per share}}{\text{After-tax earnings per share}}$$	An indication of market perception of the firm. Usually, the faster-growing or less risky firms tend to have higher PE ratios than the slower-growing or more risky firms.
3. Dividend payout ratio	$$\frac{\text{Annual dividends per share}}{\text{After-tax earnings per share}}$$	An indication of dividends paid out as a percentage of profits.
4. Cash flow per share	$$\frac{\text{After-tax profits + depreciation}}{\text{Number of common shares outstanding}}$$	A measure of total cash per share available for use by the firm.

Endnotes

1. M. A. Lundberg, B. B. Levin, & H. I. Harrington, 2000, *Who Learns What From Cases and How? The Research Base for Teaching and Learning with Cases* (Englewood Cliffs, New Jersey: Lawrence Erlbaum Associates).
2. L. B. Barnes, A. J. Nelson, & C. R. Christensen, 1994, *Teaching and the Case Method: Text, Cases and Readings* (Boston: Harvard Business School Press); C. C. Lundberg, 1993, Introduction to the case method, in C. M. Vance (ed.), *Mastering Management Education* (Newbury Park, Calif.: Sage); C. Christensen, 1989, *Teaching and the Case Method* (Boston: Harvard Business School Publishing Division).
3. C. C. Lundberg, & E. Enz, 1993, A framework for student case preparation, *Case Research Journal*, 13 (Summer): 133.
4. J. Solitis, 1971, John Dewey, in L. E. Deighton (ed.), *Encyclopedia of Education* (New York: Macmillan and Free Press).
5. F. Bocker, 1987, Is case teaching more effective than lecture teaching in business administration? An exploratory analysis, *Interfaces*, 17(5): 64–71.

Acer in Canada

Jaideep Anand

The University of Western Ontario

Prescott C. Ensign

The University of Western Ontario

In late summer 1996, Anthony Lin, general manager of Acer America's Canadian operation, believed that if the right approach and line of products were introduced and the right market segments focused on, the firm could have a prosperous future. Lin, after having been in Mississauga, Ontario, only a few weeks, knew that he had just two more days before he flew to Acer America headquarters in San Jose, California, to deliver his proposal for the future of the Canadian operation. He had to decide whether the Canadian market was worth pursuing, and if so, in what manner. He was contemplating the various markets to target and the channels by which the firm could reach these markets. Although he had determined that assembly in Canada was a real possibility, such a move would require solid justification.

Anthony Lin

Since joining the Acer group (a multinational enterprise in the global personal computer [PC] industry) in 1982, Lin had held a variety of positions. Most recently, he had been in Copenhagen, Denmark, as the managing director of Acer Scandinavia A/S, and as the general manager of Acer North Europe. Lin had turned around the firm to a profitable position with significant sales revenue growth in the Scandinavian countries. From an internal report, Acer Scandinavia had 80 percent growth in sales revenue in 1995. Further, according to Dataquest, Acer moved from the eighth to the fifth position among PC vendor market share in Denmark during early 1996. Lin had also spent two years at Acer America's headquarters, where he had become well acquainted with the executives as well as the firm's logistics and operations. For example, he knew that the flow of materials handled in California would not place the highest priority on processing smaller orders such as those "drop shipments" coming from Canada. Lin knew that Acer would permit him to seize opportunities, but he also realized that the firm wouldn't pour money into Canada without justification.

Though Lin had been in Canada only a few weeks, he was looking forward to the task ahead. He had been charged with the responsibility of overseeing all the sales and marketing activities across Canada, as well as customer service and support. If all went well, he would be in Canada for three to five years, at which point the local people he had helped would be entrusted with the business. Although he was fully charged with generating and executing a strategic plan for the Canadian organization, his role was one of assistance. Lin was to ensure that the Acer operation in Canada developed within the local PC industry network. He knew that there were incentives for the entire Acer workforce in Canada and he was excited about an additional employee who would be joining his team of 10. A goal had been set—double revenue by the end of 1996 and, within two years, to be in the top 10 in terms of Canadian PC market share.

Anthony Lin recognized that real and substantial differences existed between Canada and the United States. For example, Acer America did not worry about AST because it was not considered to be a serious competitor in the United States, whereas AST had developed a strong reputation and market position in Canada and was a significant player in the Canadian PC industry. Lin knew that even though government sales appeared to be marginal, in reality, government was a major buyer which purchased through a variety of channels. He was certain that Canadian assembly would improve Acer's profile and might even be necessary to satisfy government and Quebec orders. He also recognized that the "clones" were very strong in Canada. In general, mail order was a viable means of distribution in the United States (e.g., Dell and Gateway focused efforts on this channel), whereas Canadians were more reluctant to make purchases through the mail. Such differences needed to be articulated and considered in whatever action was undertaken.

Lin knew that assembly to order offered a variety of benefits: it would shorten delivery time, MRP (materials requirement planning) would be much smoother, and lower transport costs would make the operation more competitive. The ability to control inventory was high on his list of reasons for Canadian assembly. Local production would also assist in configuration of bilingual PCs, would shorten the reaction time to the ever changing market, and would take into consideration the corporate image of assembly in Canada. However, Lin knew that there were costs and other disadvantages involved with Canadian production.

Stan Shih and the History of Acer

Acer was founded in Taiwan in 1976 as Multitech International by Stan Shih, his wife (who still plays a major role at Acer), and a handful of friends. Multitech International began with registered capital of US$25,000 and 11 employees. Shih, reflecting on his impetus to start a business, said, "Traditional Chinese family companies often mix up company money and family money. Little information is shared with employees. I knew there had to be a better way of running a business." Prior to the 1976 venture, Shih had learned a few difficult lessons while working for others. He had directed the development of Taiwan's first pen-watch and had managed Taiwan's largest manufacturer of calculators.

Multitech International prospered in the late 1970s and early 1980s, and continued to innovate and increase its level of PC technology. During the firm's first 10 years, average sales grew by 100 percentage points per year. The period from 1981 to 1988 was a transition from a domestic to an international firm. Until 1989, Multitech International's products were manufactured only in Taiwan. Shih encouraged a corporate culture based on his belief that "human nature is basically good" and that people must be dealt with honestly. Reportedly, Shih's patience with managers included the allowance for mistakes to be written off as a "tuition payment" for educational development.

Shih and his creative engineers continuously strove to develop original products, breaking out of the typically Taiwanese "pattern of copycat manufacturers." Multitech International sought to free itself of the mold where unrecognized production of components and entire computers were produced, only to have the moniker of a famous brand placed on the finished good. In 1982 Multitech International launched a Chinese home computer. (China was expected to become the world's largest PC market by the turn of the century.) In 1983 it introduced its first IBM compatible computer, and in 1986 unveiled a PC based on the Intel 386 microprocessor before IBM did. With revenues of US$530 million in 1988, the business was renamed Acer (Latin for active, sharp, clever, and incisive). Shih took the firm public in 1989, offering shares on the Taiwanese stock exchange. By 1990 Acer was the 13th-largest PC maker in the world, with revenue of US$1 billion. The following year, due to a slowdown in the economy and overcapacity, Acer recorded its first loss (US$22.7 million after taxes) and cut 400 jobs in Taiwan. Despite the ensuing upheaval, ISO 9000 certification was obtained in 1992. The following year Acer recorded sales of US$1.7 billion, and by 1994 was the world's seventh-largest PC brand.

In late 1995 Acer reported that it expected to produce four million PCs that year, twice the previous year's figure. As well, it anticipated a 60 percent leap in revenues for 1995 to US$5 billion, which would be accompanied by a 50 percent jump in earnings. Actual 1995 revenues for Acer exceeded that estimate, reaching US$5.8 billion by year-end. Such growth, occurring with only a few acquisitions, was considered remarkable by most observers.

By 1996 Acer had become the seventh-largest PC manufacturer worldwide, the second-largest monitor maker, and the fourth-largest keyboard maker. The firm

Exhibit 1 | Acer Corporate Revenue and Net Income (US$ Millions)

	1984	1985	1986	1987	1988	1989	1990	1991	1992	1993	1994	1995
Revenue	55	100	180	330	530	680	970	1,000	1,200	1,900	3,200	5,800
Net income	1.0	5.0	4.5	16.0	26.5	5.8	2.4	-22.7	2.4	80.0	205.0	310.0

SOURCE: Acer documents.

operated 80 offices in 38 countries, had more than 15,000 employees, and supported dealers in over 100 countries. Exhibit 1 provides an overview of Acer's revenue and net income.

Acer Organizational Characteristics

2000 in 2000—In 1994, Acer "Vision 2000" was to have over NT$2,000 *yi* (US$8 billion) in annual revenue by the year 2000. When 1995 revenue reached US$5.7 billion, Vision 2000 was revised upward to US$10 billion a year in revenue by the turn of the century.

21 in 21—Acer proclaimed that it would have 21 publicly-owned businesses worldwide by the 21st century and be among the top five in the information technology industry by the turn of the century. Lin knew that two more Acer units had gone public in the past two weeks and that more were scheduled to go public shortly.

Operating Strategy

To remain competitive and take advantage of efficiencies in manufacturing and engineering, as well as make swift marketing decisions locally, Acer decentralized control. In 1990 it reorganized into a "federation of companies" with world headquarters in Taipei, strategic business units organized along product lines, and five regional business units organized along geographic lines (see Appendix A). Each of these units operated as a profit centre, and managed itself as if it were a self-owned corporation. Shih indicated that, "Technology markets change too fast and Acer has too broad a product line to afford the luxury of centralized control." In 1992 Acer made the decision to re-engineer "in the face of strong competition" to "reach economies-of-scale in low-cost manufacturing." Two re-engineering programs were introduced: fast food and client server.

Fast Food

This business model was similar to that used by fast-food restaurants. "Components" were prepared in large, centralized mass-manufacturing facilities and then shipped to assembly sites close to local customers. This process made it possible to enjoy production economies-of-scale and tailor each product to suit the needs of the individual customer. This was reflected in a new corporate mission statement, "fresh technology enjoyed by everyone, everywhere," and also by standardized quality, customized products, and lower inventory costs. Inventory turnover of more than 12 times per year assisted in a return on equity of 70 to 126 percentage points above industry average. At Acer, fresh meant the "best"—proven, high-value, low-risk technology which was affordable and had a long, useful lifespan. The "fresh" concept was not applied only to technology. Shih claimed that "Fresh ideas are very powerful when applied to business strategy. Keeping the company fresh is the only way to compete successfully in this rapidly changing industry."

Client Server

Borrowing from the terminology of computer networks, this management model let each business unit act independently but also coordinated each unit's efforts to gain maximum benefit from use of Acer's international resources. At the heart of Acer's "client server" organization was a closely linked network of mature and experienced managers who were committed to the success of their own part of the Acer group as well as to Acer's overall long-term growth.

Lin knew that distributive manufacturing played an important role in global operations. Acer considered itself to be one of the most vertically integrated microcomputer manufacturers in the world, with product assembly separated into three stages.

1. Components whose prices did not fluctuate (housing, power supply, fans, and keyboards) were shipped in bulk via boat.
2. Components that were price or technology sensitive, such as motherboards, were shipped via aircraft.
3. Components such as microprocessors, hard disk drives, and memory were sourced locally on a just-in-time basis to meet individual tastes.

In response to market turbulence, components with very unstable prices such as DRAMs and CPUs were purchased and installed at the last moment, ideally a few days before delivery to the market.

Final assembly at more than 30 sites around the world was made easy by a modular design in which assembly of various parts took only a few minutes. The housing for both desktop and laptop allowed for various physical configurations. With the interchangeability of sub-assemblies (components), a number of arrangements were possible. Acer's production operation allowed regional units to receive volume discounts on purchases under the Acer umbrella yet produce the exact quantity and models based on local market demand.

Global Brand—Local Touch

As part of Shih's plan to avoid Acer's being perceived as a Taiwanese firm, the business units cooperated but were free to buy from sources outside the organization network. In fact, a business unit was able to establish its own business partners—through spin-offs, joint venture, or some other type of relationship-building strategy. These independent business units were to be owned by local investors and managed by the local workforce. Because he believed in decentralization of control and ownership, Shih hoped that the local distributors, who were permitted to buy shares, would be motivated to promote Acer products. It was Shih's intent to have the majority of ownership held in the local country. In his view, this would prevent claims that Acer was a Taiwanese firm. He believed that corporate control was not gained through ownership but by intangible means—a common interest in brand name and technology.

Freedom at Acer Hong Kong

Acer's operation in Hong Kong serves as a point of reference. In 1986 Michael Mak was a partner in Altos Far East Ltd. In 1990 Acer bought Altos America and gained control of Altos Far East Ltd. As of 1996, Acer Far East Ltd. was under the auspices of Acer Computer International Ltd. (headquartered in Singapore and responsible for Asia, Middle East, Africa, and Pacifica). Mak was entrepreneurial by nature and his personality was congruent with the freedom Acer corporate allowed.

Although he did not receive any financial assistance from the Acer group (his operation was self-financing), Mak believed he was given credit for what he had built up in Hong Kong. Top management at Acer was open-minded and trusted him personally; he had the autonomy to run the business as if it were his own.

Developing relationships with the value-added resellers (distributors who supplied the network of PC dealers) was considered challenging. Mak characterized the channel development process as "Talk, talk, and more talk—you must keep communicating." There was an exciting independent distributor for Acer in Hong Kong prior to the Acer purchase of Altos Far East Ltd., but Mak continued building more channels. Because the distributors were not dedicated to a single firm, staying in a favorable position with them was important.

In 1995 the Hong Kong channel structure changed in response to new market conditions. Acer Hong Kong moved from supplying the conventional network exclusively and added mass merchandising and department stores as avenues for sales. These channels relied directly on the vendor for support; the customer could not get help from the point of purchase but had to rely on the manufacturer. Acer Hong Kong was well-situated to provide such support to the end user. Building on abilities and resources, Mak's group was able to provide help lines necessary for customer support.

Distribution was vital in the Hong Kong business environment. Acer Hong Kong utilized approximately 30 reseller channels. Mak described the situation as follows:

> The channels are not exclusive—they're biased and so are we. We favour those that are devoted, and consequently work more closely with those with whom we have good relationships. The channel is very important—in terms of an ongoing relationship; for things to work it must be win-win. With any change we make, we must not take advantage of the channels.

Local Touch

There were competitors based in Hong Kong that only competed locally. It was estimated that 30 to 40 percent of the overall market was satisfied by generic products. Mak viewed the progress from a starting point of zero in 1991 and subsequent "stealing of market share" as an accomplishment. Working with different types of channels, as the operation grew in scope and scale, and meeting the necessity of support from the vendor required much attention to detail. Channel structure had changed and brand perception was important; this required great local knowledge of the home environment. Mak's assessment was that:

> We have to know their lifestyle, we have become part of their daily life. Because the kitchen is so close to the customer, we can react effectively—we can react dynamically. If you have the right person in the right place, that's more important. If the person isn't right, flexibility is lost; that

person shouldn't be on the job. Only through know-how and know-who can you make use of ideas from other places.

Opportunities for Learning

The various Acer subsidiaries (Singapore, Indonesia, Malaysia, Hong Kong, etc.) were all linked electronically. Contact was reported on a day-to-day basis and best practices were often exchanged between subsidiaries. The heads of the various geographic operations met every three to four months. Mak indicated that it was the small things that were taken away, many things that could not be easily articulated or even identified. For example, he had personally borrowed from a Mexican video commercial—adopting some of it and adapting some of it.

The Global Information Technology Industry

A general consensus existed that dramatic changes were occurring in the global information technology industry. Many problems were linked to the supply of components. Margins in this highly segmented industry attracted many new players, resulting in what was generally regarded as fierce competition. Competitors tried to outdo each other by lowering price, or skimming, by being the first to market with the introduction of the newest, most advanced generation of components. With component prices extremely unstable, introductions of new generations of components were more frequent. Oversupply of product or even components could quickly turn to losses passed on through the value chain. In North America, the leading distribution firms were considered to be in good position because they had price protection as well as return capabilities.

Acer manufactured more PCs, keyboards, and monitors for the 30 largest computer firms than any other OEM PC producer in the world. OEM accounted for 29 to 39 percent of Acer's sales. As of April 1995, Acer held third position in the United States retail channel. Shih's understanding of the global information technology industry and its key success factors are provided in Appendix B.

The Global Market for PCs

From a geographic perspective, the Asia-Pacific region, including Japan, was expected to be the fastest-growing market. In the more mature areas of North America and Western Europe, the home market was forecast to become the largest single segment of the market, larger than the business segment and far ahead of education and government markets. In some markets, the home segment would account for as much as half of all PC demand in units. With the proliferation of multimedia, some expected the home PC to continue evolving as an indispensable educational tool. Others pointed to the Web and Internet as the new domain that might act as a catalyst for PC sales; but with the advent of a US$500 Web/Net browser, the multimedia PC could become obsolete for many.

Dataquest forecast 71.7 million in unit shipments, a 19.1 percent unit growth in the worldwide PC market for 1996 (13.6 percent growth in the United States market in 1996). This represents a decline from the previous year's 25.6 percent growth to a US$125 billion market. According to 1996 Dataquest reports, the world market for PCs was expected to grow at a compound annual rate of 15.9 percent in unit shipments and 14.3 percent in revenues until 1999—the year the market was expected to reach 100 million units shipped per year.

Estimated worldwide PC growth was 71.2 million units, up 22 percent from 1995, noting opportunities outside the United States. In 1995, the percentage of the populations owning a PC was: 26 in the United States, less than 12 in Western Europe, less than 8 in Japan, and less than 1 percent in Asia-Pacific countries. The percentage growth forecast for 1996 was: 18 in the United States, 15 in Western Europe, 36 in Asia-Pacific countries, 38 in Japan, and 25 in the rest of the world.

Hambrecht & Quist's figures and estimates are shown in Exhibit 2.

PC vendor Compaq, which held the top position worldwide (as well as in the United States) with 1995 sales of 1.2 million more units than in 1994, decided in March 1996 it would lower the pricing grid, changing industry rivalry. Some expected many of the smaller suppliers would exit the market. Nearly 50 percent of the PC industry was supplied by firms that individually maintained less than a 2 percent share of the market. Industry watchers conjectured that Apple and Packard Bell, both in financial difficulty, would be absorbed by even larger suppliers. More secure firms such as AT&T and Digital Equipment exited all or part of the PC industry. In 1995 Packard Bell was the leader in the desktop market in the United States, but its gamble on low price rather than value at the high end left the firm with cash flow problems. Exhibit 3 provides information on worldwide PC shipments by vendor.

The Canadian Information Technology Industry

Canadian Distributors

With regard to the information technology industry in Canada, a significant proportion of lower-priced consumer products had moved directly to mass merchandisers and

Exhibit 2

Worldwide PC Unit Shipments in Millions

	1993	1994	1995	1996*	1997*	1998*
North America corporate	10.9	12.6	14.2	16.0	17.9	19.1
North America consumer	5.2	7.3	9.7	11.8	14.1	16.6
Europe	10.3	11.4	13.9	16.4	19.1	21.2
Japan/ROW	12.3	16.0	21.4	27.0	33.9	36.3
Total	38.8	47.4	59.2	71.2	85.0	93.2

*Estimated

bypassed the distributors. Distributor sales to mass merchandisers continued to rise; ultimately, growth in the mass merchandising channel would have come at the expense of the traditional retail outlets who were struggling to compete against mass merchandisers' rock-bottom pricing strategies. The home market was acknowledged to be driving growth in microcomputer sales. Home users were not only projected to buy in greater number but were choosing expensive, feature-rich machines. Typical configurations included large hard drives, multimedia components, fax modems, and large software bundles. Aggregate distributor sales for 1993 were CDN$2.6 billion and CDN$3.1 billion for 1994. Total distributor revenues were CDN$3.9 billion

for 1995. Projected distributor sales were CDN$4.4 billion for 1996 and CDN$4.7 billion for 1997. Distributors were estimated to receive a markup of 7 to 10 percentage points on sales to dealers and resellers whose margin was approximately 10 to 15 percent on sales to end users. Retailers, who sold directly to end users, could expect a margin of 18 to 20 percent (3 to 5 percent above that in the United States). In the United States, among vendors selling branded PCs, 60 percent of sales were to retailers with the remaining 40 percent sold to distributors. In Europe, among a similar group of firms, 20 percent of sales were to retailers with 80 percent sold to distributors. Exhibit 4 provides distributor revenues by product segment.

Exhibit 3

Worldwide PC Unit Shipments in Millions (Market Share)

Vendor	1995		1996*	
Compaq	5.8	(9.9%)	7.2	(10.0%)
Apple	5.0	(8.5%)	5.7	(7.9%)
IBM	4.5	(7.7%)	5.4	(7.5%)
Packard Bell	3.3	(5.6%)	3.9	(5.4%)
NEC	2.7	(4.6%)	3.4	(4.7%)
HP	2.5	(4.3%)	3.6	(5.0%)
Dell	2.0	(3.4%)	2.7	(3.8%)
Acer	1.8	(3.1%)	2.3	(3.2%)
Fujitsu	1.8	(3.1%)	1.3	(1.8%)
Toshiba	1.5	(2.6%)	1.9	(2.6%)
Other	27.9	(47.4%)	33.2	(46.3%)
Total market	58.8	(100.0%)	71.7	(100.0%)

*Estimated.
Totals may not add up due to rounding errors.
SOURCE: Dataquest

Exhibit 4 — Distributor Revenues by Product Segment in Canada

	1994	1995	1996*	1997*
Peripheral products	30%	26%	24%	23%
Central processing units	18%	22%	23%	25%
Software	21%	20%	19%	18%
Storage	11%	12%	13%	14%
Communication products	10%	11%	12%	12%
Other (e.g., supplies and accessories)	10%	9%	9%	8%

*Projected. Columns sum to 100%.
SOURCE: *Evans Report*.

Throughout 1995, mass merchandisers (e.g., Future Shop and London Drugs) continued to grow in importance. There was a clear trend away from small local retailers to the national mass merchandise chains. Maximizing sales to the mass merchandise sector was a major priority with most manufacturers and distributors. Both groups had set up special detailing teams that visited stores to arrange displays, organize shelf facings, take stock, and train salespeople. A few distributors performed such a role with smaller retailers. Mass merchandisers received significant "market development funds." Manufacturers provided these funds because of high volumes through these mass outlets and because mass merchandisers had formal marketing entities that could maximize effectiveness of such funds. Large system integrators were expanding their marketing departments so that they might be able to take greater advantage of "market development funds" offered by manufacturers. Lacking the resources to implement formal programs, smaller systems integrators and retailers were unlikely to see increases in "market development funds" opportunities.

In 1995, distributor revenue by customers was: 29 percent from value-added resellers and regional systems integrators; 25 percent from national system integrators (e.g., SHL and Hamilton); 21 percent from smaller and local retailers; 18 percent from mass merchandisers; 5 percent from other sources; and 2 percent from original equipment manufacturers. Distributor revenues were expected to decline at least a full percentage point each year through 1997, whereas distributor revenues from mass merchandisers were expected to increase over 1.5 percentage points per year through 1997.

With regard to sales by geographic region, distributors in 1995 made 49 percent of all sales in Ontario. Western Canada, which accounted for 24 percent in 1995, was expected to account for 25 percent by 1997. Quebec, with a 20 percent share in 1995, was expected to have 19 percent by 1997. Eastern Canada had a 6 percent share in 1994 and a 7 percent share in 1995.

Distributor revenue broken down by product segment and customer is reported in Exhibit 5. These figures cover sales by distributors only and do not include sales made by manufacturers which may also sell directly to these channels.

Peripherals—Value-added resellers and regional systems integrators topped the list of distributors' customers purchasing peripherals. These buyers lacked the volume to deal with manufacturers directly. National systems integrators tended to deal directly with laser printer vendors, but usually dealt with distributors for lower volume products such as inkjet printers, scanners, and monitors (the one product Acer produced in this category).

CPUs—Value-added resellers and regional systems integrators were distributors' leading group of customers for CPUs. These firms bought from distributors because they lacked the volume required to buy from "tier one" CPU manufacturers. National systems integrators bought from distributors in situations where they could not meet the required volume commitments to buy direct or when manufacturers were unable to fulfill orders on a timely basis. For distributors to get mass merchandiser business, they often had to match the manufacturers and allow the chains to negotiate "market development funds" directly with the manufacturers.

Communication—Most value-added resellers bought from distributors because they lacked the internal technical resources to sell and support the products. Two types of distributors existed to service the networking requirements of customers. There were specialized

	Peripherals	CPUs	Software	Storage	Communication
Value-added resellers and regional systems integrators	30%	28%	21%	34%	47%
National system integrators (e.g., SHL and Hamilton)	22%	26%	32%	24%	19%
Smaller retailers/local retailers	21%	25%	21%	12%	17%
Mass merchandisers	19%	20%	26%	12%	5%
Direct	5%	0%	0%	0%	8%
Original equipment manufacturer	3%	1%	0%	18%	4%
Value of segment (CDN$ millions)	1,000	869	793	458	415

Columns sum to 100%.
SOURCE: *Evans Report.*

networking distributors with support groups to assist with network and cabling solutions, and more broadly focused distributors who had set up special support groups for more technical products such as Unix-based systems.

Canadian Distributors and Vendors

Data on revenue by product segment and customer are presented in Exhibit 6. The figures represent the combined revenue of both computer vendors and the previously analyzed distributors.

CPUs—Large manufacturers tended to pursue a "two-pronged" strategy, using distributors to address the needs of retail channels and small value-added retailers and regional systems integrators while employing direct sales to address large corporate accounts. The rationale was that consumers demanded that the product be in the store; corporate accounts would accept lead times of a month or more. Small manufacturers employed a different approach. These firms hardly ever used distributors but instead relied on dealing directly with hundreds of small value-added resellers, regional systems integrators, and retail outlets across Canada.

Canadian Vendors

In 1995, 32 percent of sales by PC manufacturers were made to dealers. This channel was a particular favourite of the Canadian-based PC manufacturers. Distributors accounted for 18 percent of sales; a direct sales force was used for 15 percent of sales. Mass merchandisers were responsible for 13 percent of manufacturers' sales in 1994. Mass merchandisers accounted for 14 percent of sales in 1995 and were expected to be 16 percent of sales in 1996 and 17 percent of sales in 1997. Value-added resellers and regional systems integrators accounted for 8 percent of sales; original equipment manufacturers accounted for the remaining 4 percent of sales.

Although distributors could offer savings in the areas of administration and logistics, the direct relationship between dealer and manufacturer facilitated close collaboration in the areas of sales, marketing, and training. The direct approach provided the greatest control, but dealers could expect discounts if relationships were good. If logistically efficient, the manufacturer could obtain superior rents. Service delivery and support might also give cause to sell directly. Large or otherwise important accounts might merit such attention. The possible danger with such treatment was that relations with other channels could be disrupted.

The Canadian Market for PCs

In 1995 the home and home-office segment represented 28 percent of the PC market in Canada. This segment was expected to account for 31 percent of the market by 1996, and 32 to 33 percent by 1997. In the business market, large firms represented 23 percent of sales in 1995 and were expected to decline to 20 or 21 percent by 1997.

	Peripherals	CPUs	Software	Storage	Communication
Value-added resellers and regional systems integrators	17%	13%	24%	19%	45%
National system integrators (e.g., GE Capital, SHL, and Hamilton)	26%	14%	30%	18%	19%
Smaller retailers/local retailers	19%	37%	18%	6%	4%
Mass rerchandisers	20%	17%	24%	6%	1%
Direct	2%	15%	4%	0%	30%
Original equipment manufacturer	16%	4%	0%	51%	1%
Value of segment (CDN$ Millions)	2,300	3,800	960	1,300	1,600

Columns sum to 100%.
SOURCE: *Evans Report.*

Small and mid-size firms represented 18 percent and 14 percent of shipments, respectively, in 1995. Government agencies accounted for 9 percent of shipments, and educational institutions 8 percent. By 1997, these latter four market segments were expected to decline collectively by 3 percentage points. Vendors were aware that home and commercial markets had developed distinct characteristics. The home market was not only growing rapidly but was particularly lucrative, with consumers choosing expensive, full-featured products. PC vendors anticipated increasing funds on advertising and store-level promotions to increase sales in this particular market.

Analysts had estimated that there were 5.23 million PCs in Canada compared with 74.24 million PCs operating in the United States. This amounted to .188 computers per person in Canada and .287 computers per person in the United States. Computing power, measured in millions of instructions per second (mips), was 10,533 mips in Canada and 173,676 mips in the United States. This was 379.2 mips per thousand people in Canada and 672.9 mips per thousand people in the United States.

Geographic Region—In 1995, Ontario received 51 percent of PC shipments, Quebec received 23 percent, the West received 22 percent, and the East received 4 percent. Manufacturers did not anticipate this pattern changing in the foreseeable future.

Price—In the early 1980s, prices decreased on an annual basis of 15 percent or more. In the latter half of that decade, prices fell 5 to 10 percentage points per year. In 1993 there was a decline of 3 percentage points—the last year prices fell. That year the average PC cost CDN$1,750 and the average home model cost CDN$1,900. Prices rose 6 percent in 1994 to an average of CDN$1,849 for a typical PC and CDN$2,040 for a typical home unit. A dramatic 11 percent increase in 1995 brought the average PC price to CDN$2,052 and CDN$2,358 for the average home PC. The average PC was expected to sell for CDN$2,113 in 1996 and CDN$2,000 in 1997. By 1997 the price differential between home and business PCs was expected to be CDN$500. This trend in prices began in 1993; prior to that time, business PCs cost more on average than home PCs. In the mid-1980s, an average business PC typically sold for CDN$1,000 to CDN$2,000 more than a home PC.

Sales—Microcomputer sales approached CDN$2.7 billion in 1994, up 17 percent from the previous year. Sales in 1995 reached CDN$3.395 billion. Revenues for 1996 were expected to be CDN$3.877 billion and CDN$4.001 billion in 1997. Unit shipments for 1995 were 1,654,191—a 15 percent increase over 1994. The number of units shipped in 1996 was expected to be 1,835,296. Shipments in 1997 were anticipated to be 2,000,473 units.

Retirement—In 1995, 18 percent of PCs were retired. The retirement rate was expected to be 20 percent for 1996 and 22 percent for 1997.

Data on unit shipments and revenue in the Canadian PC market are provided in Exhibit 7. The desktop portion of units shipped was expected to decline, although revenue from these sales was expected to increase.

With regard to vendors, Exhibit 8 provides a breakdown of the 12 leaders in the PC market in Canada based on unit shipments. This includes unit shipments for all markets (commercial, home, and non-profit).

Compared to share of unit shipments, 1995 revenues provide a different picture. Compaq and IBM each accounted for 21 percent of 1995 industry revenue. Apple captured 16 percent and AST 8 percent of industry revenue. NEC received 6 percent of industry revenue, Toshiba had 5 percent, and Sidus had 3 percent.

With regard to the home market for PCs, Apple captured 18 percent of this lucrative market in 1995. Compaq was next with an 11 percent share. IBM and AST followed with 10 percent each. Packard Bell held a 6 percent share of the home market. The industry watched closely as an additional competitor, Hewlett-Packard, entered the home PC market in Canada.

Anthony Lin had kept his eye on what competitors in North America were doing. NEC was phasing out PC manufacturing in the United States. Apple, too, was cutting back manufacturing worldwide, including Canada. Digital Equipment, with Canada's largest computer and manufacturing assembly plant, was holding its course. Sidus was expanding operations and purchasing land for a manufacturing plant to open in Austin, Texas. Likewise, Gateway was planning an US$18 million manufacturing facility in the United States. AT&T was moving out of the PC business, while MCI had just acquired SHL. On the ninth of August Compaq announced intentions to "build to order," something the generic/clone builders had already been doing. Compaq's impetus was the threat of losing business. IBM already built to order for Canada. With light assembly capabilities, IBM's build to order program pursued its major dealers first and its distributors second. AST supported a Canadian configuration centre which focused on direct dealers. Sidus had recently retrenched, freeing up resources, in order to concentrate on its core computer manufacturing business. Distributors such as Merisel and Ingram Micro had even added configuration facilities. Lin contemplated competitors' actions and wondered if assembly in Canada wasn't so much an extra or added feature, but a necessity.

Acer's Operation in North America— Acer America

Ronald Chwang was the president and CEO of Acer America Corporation, the eighth-largest computer manufacturer in the United States. Chwang held a Ph.D. in electrical engineering, was a Canadian citizen, and a graduate of McGill University. According to him, Acer America, headquartered in San Jose, California, had successfully managed key technology transitions to the latest Intel Pentium processors and provided the first consumer PCs pre-loaded with Microsoft Windows 95.

Acer America posted revenues of US$1.44 billion in 1995 and US$858 million in 1994. Prior to that, Acer America had been credited for pushing Acer corporate toward negative earnings from 1990 through 1992. Acer America accounted for about 10 percent of all Acer employees worldwide and was responsible for engineering, manufacturing, and marketing operations in the

Exhibit 7	Canadian PCs by Type: Unit Shipments (and Revenue)			
	1994	1995	1996*	1997*
Portables—units shipped in thousands	192	229	293	331
(and revenue in $ millions CDN)	(500)	(575)	(625)	(675)
Desktops—units shipped in thousands	1,193	1,360	1,469	1,587
(and revenue in $ millions CDN)	(1,515)	(2,030)	(2,375)	(2,470)
Servers—units shipped in thousands	43	58	68	75
(and revenue in $ millions CDN)	(675)	(810)	(875)	(925)

*Projected.
SOURCE: *Evans Report.*

Exhibit 8   Leading Vendors in Canada by Market Share

	Pre–1993	1993	1994	1995
Compaq	#6 in 1990, #4 in 1991, #3 in 1992	7.6%	12.0%	12.7%
IBM	#1 in 1992	14.8%	14.6%	12.6%
Apple	#1 in 1991, #2 in 1992	11.1%	11.0%	9.8%
AST	#18 in 1991, #5 in 1992	5.0%	5.7%	7.7%
Sidus*	#11 in 1991, #6 in 1992	4.7%	7.3%	5.5%**
NEC				5.0%
3D*	#8 in 1991, #4 in 1992	3.7%	3.7%	
Dell	#7 in 1992	2.8%	2.7%	
Seanix*		2.7%	2.5%	
Empac*		2.6%	2.6%	
STD*		2.5%	2.5%	
Mynix*		2.2%	2.5%	

*Canadian-based firms.
**Sidus' share drops to 4 percent if OEM shipments are excluded.
SOURCE: *Evans Report*.

United States, and now, in Canada. The United States was one of five countries with manufacturing; the others were the Netherlands, Taiwan, Malaysia, and the Philippines.

Chwang knew that Acer America, with clear financial visibility, was preparing for the next stage of business growth and an eventual initial public offering in the United States. In formal company documents, Chwang stated that "Mr. Lin has demonstrated the ability to consistently generate business opportunities for Acer, as well as to develop strategies for future growth." In 1996 Acer America's sales were 60 percent consumer and 40 percent commercial. Exhibit 9 provides the top PC vendors in the United States.

Lin knew that there had been a change in channel structure after NAFTA, and that the North American market was vastly different than it had been. With an open border, product could move easily north or south as long as 50 percent or more of the product value was added in one of the three member countries. As a result, most warehousing of PCs was in the United States. It was primarily national and was centralized, with logistics being the major concern. Lin considered distributors to be very strong in the United States. For a vendor to succeed, developing a direct relationship with distributors was vital. Distributors achieved economies by having more than one vendor. Exhibit 10 provides United States

PC sales in units and Exhibit 11 provides United States PC revenues.

Acer's Current Situation in Canada

Acer operations in Canada served as a conduit for Acer America to deliver products to Canadian distributors. The Canadian facility handled only shipment and repair of Acer products for customers in Canada, and at this point was selling no products directly to consumers in Canada, but was providing repair and shipment of all Acer products to Canadian customers. The intent of Anthony Lin, general manager of Acer America's operation in Canada, was to have a full line of products sold via different channels to different target groups—commercial, home, and non-profit (government and education).

Lin was fully aware of Acer's philosophy to utilize local distributors because their past experience, knowledge of the existing environment, and an understanding of the market placed them in the best position to access markets. Lin, with assistance from a veteran of the Canadian computer industry, believed he had a strong understanding of what was and was not possible. He readily recognized many of the usual problems associated with taking a product into Canada; for example, bilingual requirements for packaging. Technical support lines would also have to be in English and French.

Exhibit 9 | Top 10 United States PC Vendors

Vendor	Shipments in Millions	(Market Share)
Compaq	2.198	(11.8%)
Apple	2.153	(11.5%)
Packard Bell	2.125	(11.4%)
IBM	1.640	(8.8%)
Gateway 2000	.934	(5.0%)
Dell	.787	(4.2%)
AST	.721	(3.9%)
Toshiba	.618	(3.3%)
Acer	.464	(2.5%)
Hewlett-Packard	.445	(2.4%)
Other	6.615	(35.4%)
United States total	18.700	(100.0%)

SOURCE: *International Data Corp.*

Exhibit 10 | United States PC Unit Sales by Distributor (in Thousands)

Distributor	1991	1992	1993	1994	1995	1996*	1997*
Computer specialty stores	3,726	3,952	4,231	4,385	4,477	4,512	4,540
Computer superstores	330	564	835	1,159	1,505	1,832	2,166
VARs/system integrators	942	1,023	1,067	1,111	1,155	1,200	1,243
Local assemblers	1,033	1,215	1,382	1,560	1,669	1,764	1,844
Office product superstores	134	253	357	473	593	732	878
Consumer electronics stores	722	809	898	990	1,086	1,189	1,296
Consumer electronics superstores	225	378	540	733	944	1,154	1,325
Warehouse slubs	174	233	292	342	410	479	537
Other mass merchants	336	511	632	773	927	1,085	1,244
Direct marketing/mail order	1,220	1,650	1,985	2,185	2,370	2,550	2,720
Direct sales force	772	654	572	514	466	430	410
Other distribution channels	399	420	439	458	477	497	518
Total United States PC unit sales	10,014	11,663	13,229	14,681	16,079	17,425	18,721
Yearly growth rate	6.7%	16.5%	13.4%	11.0%	9.5%	8.4%	7.4%

*Estimated.
SOURCE: *Evans Report.*

Exhibit 11 | United States PC Revenues (in US$ Millions)

Distributor	1991	1992	1993	1994	1995	1996*	1997*
Computer specialty stores	9,885	10,764	11,527	12,100	12,410	12,733	12,989
Computer superstores	637	1,209	1,988	2,751	3,499	4,226	4,848
VARs/system integrators	3,917	4,195	4,472	4,741	5,014	5,221	5,426
Local assemblers	2,064	2,544	3,057	3,615	3,900	4,011	4,110
Office product superstores	226	495	815	1,077	1,308	1,583	1,881
Consumer electronics stores	1,166	1,429	1,806	2,042	2,212	2,385	2,571
Consumer electronics superstores	348	694	1,128	1,540	1,907	2,319	2,671
Warehouse clubs	269	415	593	702	817	941	1,061
Other mass merchants	509	899	1,262	1,564	1,823	2,108	2,397
Direct marketing/mail order	2,770	4,129	5,061	5,764	6,193	6,613	7,036
Direct sales force	2,108	1,836	1,632	1,515	1,390	1,310	1,283
Other distribution channels	839	938	1,019	1,102	1,147	1,193	1,214
Total United States PC unit sales	24,738	29,548	34,360	38,514	41,622	44,642	47,488
Yearly growth rate	0.5%	19.4%	16.3%	12.1%	8.1%	7.3%	6.4%

*Estimated.
SOURCE: *Evans Report.*

As a veteran of the Acer organization, Lin knew that decision making had been characterized as informal but following a consistent pattern. The process took into account seniority, rank, and professionalism, as well as recognized expertise and dedication to Acer.

Lin believed that Canadian service, both to resellers, and, ultimately, to customers, could be improved by local PC assembly, which would offer "an immense opportunity." Dealers wanted no inventory because PCs depreciated so rapidly; therefore, both they and their customers would appreciate the short cycle times afforded through local assembly. As well, the short lead times for components would give Acer local control over the "on/off switch," thereby increasing the firm's local competitiveness. Lin considered a PC's primary ingredients to be: microprocessor, hard disk, and memory. Acer made memory from scratch but neither of the other two components. With an understanding of Shih's smiling curve, Lin viewed the cost structure for the PC industry from producer to consumer as comprising three parts: raw materials, assembly, and developing and sustaining channels. Raw materials and channel management were high costs, whereas assembly was comparatively lower.

In the era of liberalized trade, some multinational enterprises were consolidating operations and withdraw-ing from Canada, with the result that the Canadian market was increasingly being served from the United States. Currently, Acer's Canadian operations—an office in Mississauga, Ontario—was an intermediary between Acer America and the Canadian market. Acer had always gone against the flow, but should its operation in Canada be a satellite sales office or a self-sufficient entity? The latter option would require Lin to devise strategy, structure, and control mechanisms.

Appendix A

World headquarters:

Acer Incorporated, Taipei, Taiwan

Regional headquarters:

Acer America Corporation, (North America), San Jose, California, US

Acer Computer B.V., (Europe), The Netherlands

Acer Computer International Ltd., (Asia, Middle East, Africa, Pacifica), Singapore

Acer Computec Latin America, (Latin America), Mexico

Acer Sertek Incorporated, (Taiwan and Greater China), Taipei, Taiwan

Worldwide operations:

Asia:

Acer Computer International, CIS, Moscow, Russia

Acer Computer (Far East) Ltd., Hong Kong

Acer Computer (M.E.) Ltd., Dubai, United Arab Emirates

Acer Computer Turkey, Istanbul, Turkey

Acer Japan Corporation, Tokyo, Japan

Acer Korea Co. Ltd., Seoul, South Korea

Acer Market Services Ltd., Beijing, Peoples Republic of China

Acer Sales & Services Sdn Bhd, Kuala Lumpur, Malaysia

Acer Sertek Incorporated, Taipei, Taiwan

Australia & New Zealand:

Acer Computer Australia Pty Ltd., North Ryde, New South Wales, Australia

Sales offices in South Australia, Western Australia, Australian Capital Territory, Victoria, and Queensland

Acer Computer New Zealand Ltd., Auckland, New Zealand

Sales office in Wellington

Latin America:

Acer Latin America, Miami, Florida

Sales offices:

Acer Argentina, Buenos Aires, Argentina

Acer Chile, Santiago, Chile

Acer Columbia, Bogota, Columbia

Acer de Venezuela, Caracas, Venezuela

Europe:

Acer Belgium NV, Antwerpen, Belgium

Acer Computer B.V., The Netherlands

Acer Computer France, Paris, France

Acer Computer GmbH, Hamburg, Germany

Acer Computer HandelsgmbH, Wien, Austria

Acer Computer Norway A/S, Asker, Norway

Acer Computer Representative Hungary, Budapest, Hungary

Acer Computer Iberica, S.A., Barcelona, Spain

Acer Italy s.r.l., Milan, Italy

Acer Scandinavia A/S, Denmark

Acer UK Limited, United Kingdom

North America:

Acer America, San Jose, California

Sales offices in: Mississauga, Ontario (Canada); Boston, Massachusetts (Boston); Rolling Meadows, Illinois (North Central West); Farmington Hills, Michigan (Midwest); Dallas, Texas (South Central); Duluth, Georgia (Southeast); Wyckoff, New Jersey (North Mid-Atlantic); Bayville, New York (New York Metro); Issaquah, Washington (Northwest); Akron, Ohio (North Central East); Costa Mesa, California (Southwest); Vienna, Virginia (Government Sales)

Africa:

Acer Africa (Pty) Ltd., South Africa

Appendix B
PC Industry Value-Added Curve

The primary key to success in today's industry is providing value. By doing well in "value-added" business segments, companies can succeed in the current disintegrated business environment. To explain the disintegration trend, Shih came up with this chart that looks like a big smile; he calls it his "smiling curve." Value is added in component production on the left side and marketing/distribution on the right.

Today, there is no longer any value added in assembling computers—everyone can make a PC. To succeed in the new IT age, you have to gain a top position in component segments, like software, CPUs, DRAM, ASICs, monitors, storage, etc., or else as a distribution leader in a country or region.

The key to success on the components side of the chart is global competitiveness. Universal standards in components mean global competition, so if you're going to pursue a segment along the left side, you need technology and a strong manufacturing capability for economies of scale. On the distribution side, where competition is local, you can succeed through a good image, brand name awareness, well-managed channels, and effective logistics.

Note that in today's disintegrated industry environment there is one simple rule: if you are not one of a market segment's leaders, you cannot survive. Whether on the right side or the left side of the curve, speed and cost are two main factors for success in such an environment. "Speed" means fast time to market with new products and fast responses to change in the industry. "Cost" includes minimizing overhead, inventory reduction, and risk management. Only the leaders of each segment will

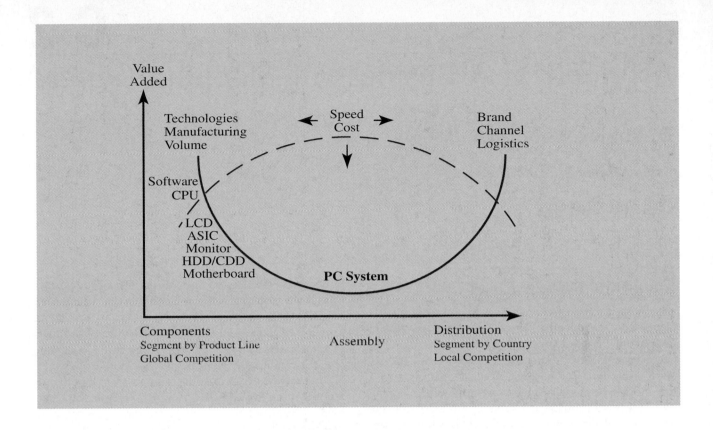

survive, so whoever understands this curve will end up smiling in the future.

In today's PC industry, a lot of the leading companies are "computerless computer companies." They primarily concentrate on marketing, and have little or no involvement on the components side of the business. Speed is the primary factor that will determine the success or failure of these companies in the future. Cost is also an important long-term factor for success. On the compo- nent side, Acer is among the top five worldwide in all the segments we currently pursue. On the distribution side, Acer is currently the seventh-largest PC brand in the world, ninth-largest in the United States, and number one in the Middle East, Latin America, and Southeast Asia. Already enjoying top-level status in so many developing countries, the company's current target is to achieve a top ten position in Europe, and top five status worldwide.

The Richard Ivey School of Business gratefully acknowledges the generous support of the Richard and Jean Ivey Fund in the development of this case as part of the RICHARD AND JEAN IVEY FUND ASIAN CASE SERIES.

Affymetrix: A Business of Mapping Genes

D. Robley Wood, Jr.

Virginia Commonwealth University

Gerard George

University of Wisconsin-Madison

Synopsis of Case

Affymetrix is a biotechnology firm providing diagnostic equipment (biochips) to research human genes and understand the ailments that afflict humans. The case traces the history of the entrepreneur-scientist and the creation of the firm in the early 1990s. Affymetrix enjoys a first-mover advantage with its strong employee base, quality product, and intellectual capital. In 2001, with the unraveling of the human genome, the biochip industry takes the spotlight with new entrants such as Motorola and Corning. This case allows students to understand (1) evolution of high-technology firms, (2) strategy in uncertain environments, and (3) formulating strategy to compete with larger resource-endowed firms.

The year 2001 was a watershed year. The human genome was finally sequenced, opening up new opportunities to comprehend and derive meaning from the three billion letters that comprise the "Book of Life." Affymetrix Inc. is a key player in an industry dedicated to understanding how human genes are encoded and their specific functions. Fully processing this information could pave the way to cure diseases and prevent maladies that afflict the human race. Affymetrix is the market leader in the production and sales of DNA probe arrays (also known as *biochips*) and peripherals. Affymetrix's biochips and systems allow researchers to study the activities of genes. Consequently, it markets its products to pharmaceutical and biotechnology firms, academic research centers, and clinical reference laboratories.

The past few years have been good to Affymetrix. In 1999, it more than doubled its biochip shipments, doubled its installed base, doubled its number of employees, and tripled its manufacturing capacity. In 2000, on the heels of a glorious 1999 fiscal year, it tripled its customer base and doubled its shipments. In early 2001, it had more than 100 patents and 300 pending patents in the US, employed over 700 people, and its revenues almost doubled to $200 million, up from $110 million in 1999. Its market capitalization topped $3 billion by the end of the year 2000. The CEO of Affymetrix, Stephen Fodor, summarizing the firm's tremendous potential, said, ". . . this is an extraordinary opportunity for Affymetrix and its customers to use this unique technology to conduct whole genome-based experiments. These studies are key to deciphering the immense complexity of human and other genomes, leading to the development of products that will ultimately revolutionize our quality of life."

Affymetrix's efforts have not gone unnoticed and recently its market niche has attracted the attention of Fortune 100 companies such as Motorola and Corning. The market for biochips is expected to quickly become a billion-dollar market and Corning's management has stated that it intends to be the future market leader. Meanwhile, Affymetrix continues to ramp-up production in a second plant that began production in 1999. Affymetrix continues to make substantial investments in R&D. Affymetrix's patent estate has the potential to become its most valuable asset. Revenue from license fees and royalties for 2000 was $21.5 million, an increase of over 650 percent from 1999. Affymetrix continued to

Reprinted with permission of the author.
Contact Author:
Gerard George
Weinert Center for Entrepreneurship
University of Wisconsin-Madison
School of Business
Room 5252 Grainger Hall
975 University Avenue
Madison, WI 53706-1323
ggeorge@bus.wisc.edu
(608) 265-3544

We would like to thank Affymetrix Inc. for its cooperation and to our graduate students for their assistance. The authors gratefully acknowledge the support of the Weinert Center for Entrepreneurship at the University of Wisconsin-Madison School of Business.

expand its product offerings through internal development and acquisitions. In 2000, Affymetrix purchased Genetic Microsystems, a privately held Massachusetts company that specialized in making the instruments for spotting micro-array systems that are the low-cost alternative to the Affymetrix GeneChip® system. Affymetrix also acquired California-based Neomorphic, a privately held bioinformatics company that is developing new products based on information from the Human Genome Project. Also in 2000, Affymetrix formed a subsidiary company, Perlegen Sciences, to identify genetic variations between individuals and subsequently market the information to pharmaceutical companies.

In spite of such astounding growth and potential, Affymetrix's management faces considerable challenges in the future. First, its market space is becoming increasingly competitive with large and resource-rich firms such as Motorola and Corning joining the fray such that Affymetrix's first-mover advantage and sources of competitive advantage were being eroded. In 2000, biochips worth millions of dollars had to be replaced because they did not meet certain quality specifications. Second, Affymetrix is a party to significant intellectual property litigation with key competitors, and it is expected that the litigation will consume substantial financial and managerial resources. Finally, questions about sustainability of manufacturing capacity and growth abound, along with the softening of the US economy in 2001, as pharmaceutical and biotech customers postpone their capital equipment purchases from Affymetrix due to soft demand conditions for their own products. Also, its two main manufacturing sites in California could face increased power prices and rolling blackouts. The company incurred operating losses every year since its inception, including a loss of $54.0 million for the fiscal year 2000. However, with over $450 million in cash and securities, it has the resources to compete. The issues that face the CEO are complex. Affymetrix has to devise an agenda, define its strategies, and execute plans for sustained growth in an increasingly competitive and uncertain market in the future. To chart a plan for the future, one needs to understand the past; below is a description of the firm's evolution, its industry, and its market.

The Evolution of Affymetrix: Entrepreneurship and the Scientist

Company History

Affymetrix is a product of the California technology revolution and entrepreneurial spirit. Affymetrix began operations in 1991 as a division of Affymax, which was

founded in 1988 by entrepreneur Dr. Alejandro Zaffaroni. Previously, Dr. Zaffaroni helped to launch Syntex (birth control pills) and had started Alza (nicotine patches). In 1988, he founded Affymax to automate chemical synthesis in order to increase the speed of generating drug candidates. Affymetrix was incorporated as a wholly owned subsidiary of Affymax in 1992 to focus on DNA probe arrays (now known as biochips) that had been developed from work on peptide synthesis. In 1993, Affymax completed a spin-off of Affymetrix that now operates as an independent firm. Glaxo Wellcome later acquired the parent company, Affymax, in 1995. Headquartered in Santa Clara, California, Affymetrix successfully completed its initial public offering in June of 1996.

The Early Biochip Scientists

Work on DNA biochips started in the late 1980s when physician Leighton Read suggested that it should be possible for Affymax researchers to mimic semiconductor manufacturers who use light to manipulate molecules in solid structures. Stanford University biochemists worked with Dr. Stephen Fodor, current CEO of Affymetrix, to make Dr. Read's idea into a commercial product. They were recognized for their work in 1993 when their team won the Intellectual Property Owners Association Distinguished Inventor Award. The driving force behind the technological breakthroughs and commercial success of Affymetrix's DNA biochips was Dr. Fodor.

Dr. Fodor, son of a Seattle physician, delayed college in order to work on a potato farm and pursue his love for fly-fishing. "Going to college," he said, "would have been conforming to people's expectations." Toiling in the spud patch soon lost its charm, though, so he enrolled at Washington State University to earn a degree in agriculture. While at Washington State, he mastered the art of taking pictures with an electron microscope. He liked working with electron microscopes. "It was the first time I got my hands on something a little higher tech and I was able to do something real. I started having fun," he said. Later, he enrolled at Princeton University and earned his Ph.D. He continued his formal education at the University of California at Berkeley where he did postdoctoral research. It was at Berkeley that Dr. Fodor was spotted by Dr. Zaffaroni's scouts, though initially he resisted, stating that his "hands weren't for hire." Eventually, he gave in to the lure of working with stellar scientists in a rewarding industry environment. Once on Dr. Zaffaroni's talented staff, innovations in their labs led to ideas that formed the basis of Affymetrix.

The Biotechnology Industry: Human Diagnostics and Therapeutics

More than 250 million people worldwide have been helped by the more than 117 biotechnology drug products and vaccines approved by the US Food and Drug Administration over the past 25 years. There are more than 350 biotechnology drug products and vaccines currently in human clinical trials and hundreds more in early development in the United States. These medicines are designed to treat various cancers, Alzheimer's, heart disease, multiple sclerosis, AIDS, obesity, and other conditions. There were 1,273 biotechnology companies in the United States in 2000, of which 300 are publicly held. The US biotechnology industry has created more than 150,800 high-wage, high-value jobs. Biotechnology is one of the most research-intensive industries in the world. The U.S. biotech industry spent $10.7 billion on research and development in 2000. The top five biotechnology companies spent an average of $89,400 per employee on R&D. This compares with an average of $37,200 per employee for the top pharmaceutical companies. Market capitalization grew from $52 billion in 1995 to $353 billion in 2000 and revenues estimated at $22 billion.[1] As the biotechnology industry evolves, the estimated potential for growth is substantial (refer to Exhibit 1).

Understanding Genes and Disease

So much of who we are ultimately can be traced to our genes and to the deoxyribonucleic acid (DNA) that encodes genetic instructions and determines heredity and disease. Increased knowledge of how DNA molecules encode the functions of living organisms generated a worldwide effort to identify and sequence the genes of many organisms. Begun in 1990, the US Human Genome Project was a three billion-dollar effort coordinated by the US Department of Energy and the National Institutes of Health. Its purpose was to identify all the estimated 100,000 genes in human DNA and determine the sequences of the three billion chemical bases that make up human DNA. The US Human Genome Project finished and published its draft of the human genome sequence in February 2001. A major discovery of the project was that the number of genes in the human genome is close to 30,000, not the previously estimated 100,000.

Knowing the order of DNA bases tells an investigator where genes are located, as well as what instructions are carried in a piece of DNA. This information is critical to understanding the function of genes and how they cause or prevent disease. Knowledge of gene functions continues to grow as researchers analyze the genetic causes of disease at the molecular level and associate specific gene alterations with an individual's risk for disease. An immediate spin-off of disease-gene discovery is the development of genetic tests that may indicate an individual's predisposition to disease. The ability to test for disease genes will make it possible to design medical programs for individuals that include lifestyle, diet, and medical surveillance to alleviate or prevent disease. Eventually, new treatments will be developed for many diseases that result from gene malfunctions such as cancer.

Exhibit 1	US Biotechnology Products Sales Forecast (Millions of 1998 US Dollars)			
	Base Year	Forecasts		Average Annual Growth Rate
	1998	2003	2008	1998–2008(%)
Human therapeutics	9,120	16,100	27,000	11
Human diagnostics	2,100	3,100	4,300	7
Agriculture	420	1,000	2,300	19
Specialties	390	900	2,000	18
Non-medical diagnostics	270	400	600	8

SOURCE: Consulting Resources Corp (1998). Op Cit. *The Outlook of the Biotechnology Industry.* http://www.biotechnav.com/outlook.shtml.

Affymetrix and the BioChip Technology

One of the keys to expanding our knowledge of the human genome lies in accelerating the ability to identify DNA sequences, which are composed of many different combinations of the A, C, G, and T nucleotide bases that act as the chemical building blocks of DNA. Until recently, the process of identifying these sequences was extremely laborious and time-consuming. But the interplay of computer hardware engineering and biotechnology is changing the ways in which large amounts of genetic information are analyzed. The integration of semiconductor wafer manufacturing with computer software and biological research technologies has emerged as an important factor in helping to advance the frontiers of genomics. In essence, a combination of Silicon Valley's "high-technology" disciplines is now finding application in the biotechnology arena, and the differences they will make have the potential to transform biological research. Complex sequencing analyses performed in traditional "wet biology" laboratories, for example, can now be accomplished in a small fraction of the time by using new methods.

Affymetrix's Product: The GeneChip® Technology

The Affymetrix product line is built around the GeneChip® system, a unique platform for acquiring, analyzing, and managing complex genetic information. Consisting of disposable DNA probe arrays containing selected gene sequences on a chip, instruments to process the arrays, and software to manage the information, GeneChip® technology enables researchers to analyze large amounts of genetic information more rapidly and efficiently. The system has been developed as a tool to help understand the human genome, and to improve the diagnosis, monitoring, and treatment of disease. Combining the disciplines of biotechnology and semiconductor manufacturing, GeneChip® technology takes advantage of the fact that the DNA double helix is built like a "zipper" that consists of four distinct nucleotides that join together in strict sequence. Guanine (G) binds only to cytosine (C), while adenine (A) binds only to thymine (T). Affymetrix's GeneChip® system provides one half of the zipper by assembling a series of vertical DNA "probe arrays" of known sequence on a silica wafer. A biological sample obtained from a research experiment or a patient provides the other half of the zipper to complete an assay.

To create a GeneChip® array, a silica wafer is alternately illuminated through a lithographic mask in defined patterns and washed with a solution of synthetic nucleotides. This creates single strands of synthetic DNA that rise up from the wafer in an array that contains genetic information. These sequences or probes contain only half the DNA code; the other half—which will bind along the probe where the sequences form a complementary match—resides in a test sample, such as a patient's blood. Assume, for example, that probes were placed on a GeneChip® array, which conform to half of the zipper for a gene associated with a particular virus. To determine if a person was suffering from that specific type of viral infection, a sample of DNA from the patient would be passed over the GeneChip® array. The DNA in the sample would adhere to its complementary counterparts on the chip, which would then be scanned by a laser reader to reveal genetic sequence matches. The locations of these points of contact would then be read and analyzed by the GeneChip® scanner and GeneChip® software, respectively. In a matter of minutes, a clinician could identify the bacteria or virus, paving the way for the prescription of a specific treatment. This same process could also be used to analyze DNA sequences from other organisms or to answer questions about mutations in the genetic sequence of a cancer biopsy. Attempting such a feat with traditional methods of gene analysis would be expensive, due to the time and labor involved in such a process. The simplicity and high-information content of the GeneChip® platform places Affymetrix in a position to have a significant impact on the future of genomic research and diagnostics.

Setting the Dominant Design: Application Areas and Collaborations

Affymetrix has selected three application areas for emphasis. The first is gene expression profiling which allows researchers to identify and validate targets for drug discovery. Gene expression is the term for a gene being switched on so its protein product is produced. An Affymetrix biochip can monitor thousands of genes at a time and thus monitor which genes are switching on and off during the body's performance of various tasks. It is estimated that this business could be a $100 million annual revenue opportunity for Affymetrix.

The second application area is polymorphism discovery that enables genetic sequence variations to be identified for correlation with disease and therapeutic responses. Polymorphism discovery requires scientists to compare the genes of many individuals at different times in life and under different conditions. It requires the screening of large samples of affected and unaffected humans. To support this application, Affymetrix launched a program to discover sequence variations in human genes in 1997. In 2000, Affymetrix created a new company called Perlegen Sciences to focus specifically on variations in human genes. These sequence variations are being compiled into a large database that could establish a new paradigm in therapeutic and disease management.

The third application area targeted is disease management. This is the area with the largest long-term potential. Management believes that its GeneChip® probe arrays have the potential to correlate genetic variation with successful treatment strategies. This could result in a new generation of diagnostic tests that make use of the GeneChip® DNA probe-array technology. Management believes that the expression patterns and polymorphism associations being examined using the GeneChip® technology will lead to a pipeline of disease management products for the future. In 1996, to accelerate the discovery and development of new products, Affymetrix proposed a strategy of expanding its collaboration and research partners. The intent was to gain acceptance of its biochip technology before its competitors could gain a foothold in this emerging market. Five years later, this strategy has paid off with many well-established pharmaceutical and biotech firms using Affymetrix technology for their in-house R&D. Also, in order to gain the acceptance of the scientific community, Affymetrix established collaborative research partners with non-profit research institutions that are the leaders in drug research (refer to Exhibit 2).

Affymetrix and Its Competitors

Affymetrix has competitors working on similar biochip technologies. Affymetrix may be the farthest along in perfecting this technology, but others are very close and some may even be ahead when it comes to specific applications.

Nanogen Inc. is one competitor developing a complete DNA-chip based system for diagnostic and research applications. Microchip arrays with 25 to 10,000 test sites are being designed for diagnostic, drug discovery, and gene expression applications. The integrated microelectronics system is being designed to carry out detection, data analysis, and presentation. Dr. Michael J. Heller, Chief Technical Officer at Nanogen, stated that their system can analyze samples of double-stranded DNA targets which skips the step in the process of isolating single-stranded targets before carrying out the analysis on the chips. Nanogen's researchers are also using DC positive bias electric fields to transport and concentrate negatively charged nucleic acid molecules over selected locations on its chips. This results in increases in speed, sensitivity, and selectivity, which means that chips with fewer test sites can be used. Nanogen reported that it has used its

electric field microchips to complete in seconds the same analysis that takes hours under the typical passive techniques. Nanogen is selling its biochips under the trade name NanoChip. Nanogen ended the fiscal year 2000 with a net loss of $18 million on revenues of $11 million. Cash reserves totaled over $95 million with total assets of $111 million.

Hyseq Inc. is another competitor developing a complete integrated platform to conduct analyses such as gene identification, diagnostic testing, and genetic mapping. Hyseq's DNA array system has been demonstrated to determine the DNA sequence more rapidly and precisely than gel sequencing in a controlled experiment. Hyseq's system is similar to Affymetrix' in that it takes advantage of DNA's ability to hybridize with a complementary sequence. DNA hybridization provides a powerful tool for diagnostics and nucleic acid sequencing. Improvements in this technique are being researched at the Lawrence Berkeley National Laboratory. Hyseq's patented system uses its proprietary chips that contain probes (sequences) of known content onto which a DNA sample of unknown sequence is placed and subsequently identified. Hyseq has worked with the Perkin-Elmer Corporation to develop and commercialize its HyChip DNA sequencing chips. Hyseq ended the fiscal year 2000 with a net loss of $22 million on revenues of $16 million. Cash reserves totaled about $3 million with total assets of $21 million.

Incyte Pharmaceuticals has concentrated on building gene databases that can be used in drug discovery. It generates the gene sequences for its databases and has developed the supporting bioinformatics software to scan and analyze data on gene expression. It has a joint venture with Affymetrix to commercialize chips in the gene expression-monitoring field. However, in January of 1998, Incyte completed an acquisition of Synteni that held the exclusive worldwide rights from Stanford University to commercialize chip-making technology that Stanford scientists had helped develop. Incyte is using the technology it obtained from Synteni to manufacture and sell biochips. It now has available single biochips that contain up to 10,000 unique genes from its proprietary database. It also builds custom biochips and offers all of the software tools for processing and displaying data resulting from the use of its biochips. In 1998, Affymetrix filed patent infringement lawsuits against Incyte/Synteni. At this time, though Affymetrix received some favorable rulings, it is too early to know the potential outcome and impact of these lawsuits. In 1998, Incyte acquired Hexagen PLC of Cambridge, U.K., a leader in the technology of identifying genetic variations that could enable pharmaceutical firms to tailor drugs for individuals. Incyte ended the fiscal year 2000

Exhibit 2 Affymetrix' Alliance Partners and Interactions

Partners (partial list only)	Purpose of Alliance	Type of Interaction
bioMérieux Vitek	DNA probes/HIV	License/collaborative research
Eli Lilly & Co.	Platform and service access	License/technology use
F. Hoffmann-La Roche	Bacterial research	Option/collaborative research
Glaxo Wellcome	GeneChip® for HIV	Collaborative R&D/equity position
Hewlett-Packard	DNA chip	Co-development & supply
Merck & Co.	Technology use in own R&D	License
Novartis Pharma AG	GeneChip® database	Access license
Parke-Davis	Technology use in own R&D	License
Pfizer	Technology use in own R&D	License
Roche Molecular Systems	Disease management	Research/technology sharing

Other collaborative research partners (non-profit research institutions)
Harvard University
National Institutes of Health
Princeton University
Salk Institute
Stanford University
UC Berkeley
UC San Francisco
Whitehead Institute

with a net loss of $29 million on revenues of $194 million. Cash reserves totaled over $580 million with total assets of $886 million.

Other Potential Competitors. Due to numerous applications of biochips, other firms also have invested heavily in development of this technology. Competition also comes from existing technologies used to perform many of the same functions for which Affymetrix plans to market its GeneChip® systems. In the diagnostic field, established diagnostic companies such as Abbott Laboratories, Boehringer, Mannheim GmbH, Roche, Johnson & Johnson, and SmithKline Beecham provide these technologies. These technologies include a variety of established assays, such as immunoassays, histochemistry, flow cytometry and culture, and newer DNA probe diagnostics to analyze certain limited amounts of genetic information. In the genomics field, competitive technologies include gel-based sequencing using instruments provided by companies such as the Applied Biosystems division of Perkin Elmer and Pharmacia Biotech AB. In order to compete against existing technologies, Affymetrix will need to demonstrate to potential customers that the GeneChip® system provides improved performance and capabilities. Additional competition arises from large companies just entering the diagnostic markets.

Motorola and Corning Enter the Biochip Business

Motorola, Inc.'s BioChip Systems Unit built a pilot line in Phoenix that produced biochip prototypes in the year 2000. Motorola licensed technology from Argonne National Laboratories and from the Engelhardt Institute in Moscow. One biochip process Motorola scientists have worked on uses a gel solution to provide a three-dimensional area for molecular reactions. The three-dimensional space allows for more reactions than the two-dimensional surface of Affymetrix's biochips. Motorola also has joint ventures or investments in pioneer companies in the field of molecular diagnostics. It hopes to develop portable instruments that a doctor would drop biochips into and then read out the results. Motorola provides significant competition to Affymetrix through the development of new products. Motorola has a strategic commitment to biochips, the financial and other resources to invest in new technologies, substantial intellectual property portfolios, substantial experience in new product development, regulatory expertise, manufacturing capabilities, and the distribution channels to deliver products to customers. Motorola's biochip processes and products will not be compatible with the GeneChip® system. In addition, Motorola has formed alliances with genomics companies such as Incyte to gain access to genetic information to incorporate into its diagnostic tests. In 2000, Motorola revenues from multiple businesses topped $37 billion, held about $3 billion in cash, and assets of $42 billion.

Corning went into commercial production of biochips in early 2001. Corning estimates the market for biochips will soon expand to one billion dollars annually, and it wants to have the potential to capture the leadership position in the market by 2005. Corning believes that researchers have been hampered by an inadequate supply of affordable high-quality biochips. Corning believes that it can use its high-volume processes to manufacture biochips 10 to 20 times faster than Affymetrix. In 2000, Corning revenues from its diverse businesses topped $7.2 billion, held cash equivalents of nearly $2 billion, and assets of $17 billion.

Financial Conditions and Results of Operations 1998–2000

Affymetrix stock has seen both incredible highs and depressing lows. This erratic behavior is somewhat explained by investor enthusiasm for technology stocks and a promise of substantial future revenues once this industry sector becomes central to pharmaceutical and biotechnology research and development. The stock has touched a high of $162 in 2000, up from a low of nearly $12 in 1999. In 2001, the stock appeared to mirror the rest of the NASDAQ stock market with a steady downtrend in prices (refer to Exhibit 3). To fully understand this cycle, an analysis of the promise held by this stock can be gleaned from its financial statements.

In 1998, revenue increased 163 percent to $52 million up from $19.8 million in 1997 (refer to Exhibit 4). Also, commercial contract and grant revenues grew from $19.8 million to $57.4 million for a 204 percent increase in one year. Total costs and expenses in 1998 increased to $85.3 million compared to $47.9 million in 1997. The increase in operating expenses for 1998 resulted primarily from expansion and higher legal costs

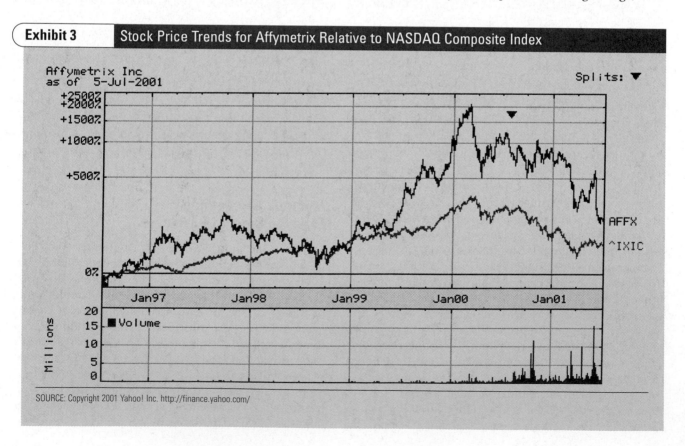

Exhibit 3 Stock Price Trends for Affymetrix Relative to NASDAQ Composite Index

SOURCE: Copyright 2001 Yahoo! Inc. http://finance.yahoo.com/

Assets	2000	1999	1998	1997	1996
Current assets:					
Cash and cash equivalents	436,030	226,440	80,568	71,573	108,982
Accounts receivable	53,104	24,646	8,919	6,216	1,888
Inventories	17,234	12,792	3,276	2,637	1,901
Other current assets	2,524	4,159	2,184	748	523
Total current assets	508,892	268,037	94,947	81,174	113,294
Property and equipment, net	56,245	40,775	30,865	19,088	5,397
Acquired technology rights	10,014	8,965	—	—	—
Goodwill & other intangible assets	26,788	—	—	—	—
Notes receivable from employees	2,113	1,074	—	—	—
Other assets	16,728	7,736	10,616	908	209
Total assets	620,780	326,587	136,428	101,170	118,900
Liabilities & stockholders' equity					
Current liabilities	90,590	36,655	14,560	9,621	5,626
Obligation to Beckman Coulter, Inc.	5,000	5,000	5,000	—	—
Convertible subordinated notes	375,000	150,000	—	—	—
Convertible preferred stock	—	—	49,857	—	—
Common stock purchase rights	3,000	3,000	—	—	—
Other liabilities	60	—	261	513	741
Stockholders' equity:	—	—	—	—	—
Common stock and paid-in-capital	342,112	257,010	159,377	158,924	158,687
Notes receivable from stockholders	(994)	(150)	—	—	—
Deferred stock compensation	(27,875)	(119)	—	—	—
Accumulated other comprehensive Income	12,080	(606)	93	(619)	(1,411)
Accumulated deficit	(178,193)	(124,203)	(92,720)	(67,269)	(44,743)
Total stockholders' equity	147,130	131,932	66,750	91,036	112,533
Total liabilities & stockholders' equity	620,780	326,587	136,428	101,170	118,900

(Continued)

arising from ongoing patent litigation. Extensive expansion was completed in the Santa Clara chip production facilities in 1998 which increased the annual rate to more than 400,000, up from 80,000 GeneChip® DNA biochips in 1997. Affymetrix's cash and short-term investments totaled over $80 million at the end of 1998. During 1998, it sold preferred stock to Glaxo Wellcome plc. for approximately $50 million, which was later converted into 1.26 million shares of Affymetrix common stock. Affymetrix had no long-term debt in 1999 and was able to obtain $32.5 million in a private placement of its common stock to an institutional investor.

For 1999, revenue increased to $109 million, up from $52 million for 1998. Product sales increased 144 percent to $98 million for 1999. In the second half of 1999, Affymetrix obtained a substantial increase in manufacturing capacity with the completion of its second manufacturing facility in West Sacramento, California. The West Sacramento plant contains 51,000 square feet and could eventually employ 300 people. Total costs and expenses increased to $139.3 million, compared to $85.3 million for 1998 due primarily to the expansion of manufacturing and commercial activities as well as increased legal costs arising from its ongoing litigation.

Revenue	2000	1999	1998	1997	1996
Product	173,546	98,168	36,932	4,789	1,389
Research	5,780	8,059	14,522	14,976	10,583
License fees and royalties	21,504	2,847	959	—	—
Total revenue	200,830	109,074	52,413	19,765	11,972
Cost and expenses					
Cost of product revenue	70,884	42,219	15,226	4,559	2,178
Research and development	57,384	43,524	38,433	28,590	18,762
Selling, general and administrative	113,429	53,590	31,640	14,756	7,569
Merger related costs	2,395	—	—	—	—
Amortization of deferred stock compensation	2,118	—	—	—	—
Amortization of purchased intangibles	997	—	—	—	—
Charge for in-process technology	14,989	—	—	—	—
Total costs and expenses	262,196	139,333	85,299	47,905	28,509
Loss from operations	(61,366)	(30,259)	(32,886)	(28,140)	(16,537)
Interest income, net	7,976	4,755	4,817	5,190	4,310
Loss before income tax benefit	(53,390)	(25,504)	(28,069)	(22,950)	(12,227)
Income tax provision/benefit	(600)	—	1,269	170	—
Net loss	(53,990)	(25,504)	(26,800)	(22,780)	(12,227)
Preferred stock dividends		(2,055)	(2,321)	—	—
Net loss attributable to common stockholders	(53,990)	(27,559)	(29,121)	(22,780)	(12,227)
Basic and diluted net loss per common share	(0.98)	(0.54)	(0.62)	(0.50)	(0.30)
Shares used in computing basic and diluted net loss per common share	55,035	51,167	46,932	45,294	40,262

The company reported a net loss of $27.6 million, or $0.54 per diluted share. Affymetrix had cash and short-term investments of $226.4 million and approximately 51 million shares of common stock outstanding. For the year, Affymetrix shipped more than 100,000 GeneChip® DNA biochips to customers and collaborators and ended the year with an installed base of more than 220 GeneChip® systems. The Affymetrix biochips' costs range from $90 to $2,500. The complete GeneChip® system, which includes instruments to read and analyze results, costs approximately $200,000.

In 2000, total revenue increased by 84 percent to $200.8 million with the shipment of more than 200,000 GeneChip® DNA biochips and the sale of more than 150 complete GeneChip® Systems. Licensing fees and royalties increased by 655 percent to $21.5 million as the company worked to generate revenue and gain widespread adoption of its platform. Total costs and expenses increased to $262.2 million and resulted in a net loss of $54.0 million for the year ending December 31, 2000. Affymetrix did have one profitable quarter in 2000 and its cash and securities increased by 93 percent to $436 million.

Management and Organization

Affymetrix ended 2000 with 744 full-time employees, most of whom were engaged in engineering, manufacturing, bioinformatics, and basic research. The intellectual property of the company includes 105 issued US patents, 300 pending US patent applications, and extensive foreign filings. Affymetrix and the press continue to report on new applications for its GeneChip® technology. In May of 1999, the company reported working on DNA biochip technology that could be used to test water quality. Affymetrix expects its system to be faster, more accurate, and cheaper than tests that are currently available. If the GeneChip® system should become the standard for the identification of disease-causing waterborne microbes, the international market could be substantial in size.

In August of 1999, scientists at the University of Wisconsin-Madison reported that they had identified changes in 6,000 genes that play critical roles in the aging process. Using GeneChip® technology supplied by Affymetrix, they were able to study the activity levels for thousands of individual genes when mice were fed different diets. The research is considered a milestone in research on aging as it analyzed more genes with regard to aging than all previous studies combined. Also in August 1999, Susan Siegel was promoted to the position of President of Affymetrix. Dr. Fodor remained as CEO and also assumed the role of Chairman of the Board. Dr. John Diekman, former Chairman of the Board of Affymetrix, now serves as Vice-Chairman of the Board. Ms. Siegel has extensive world-class sales and marketing experience and has worked for Affymetrix since 1998 as Senior Vice President of Marketing. Prior to joining Affymetrix, Ms. Siegel had worked for Amersham Biotech, DuPont, Bio Image/Kodak, and Bio Rad Laboratories. This is a continuation in the evolution of the management team as Affymetrix moves into commercialization of its technology.

Looking Forward: Addressing Problems and Forging Ahead

Despite the increase in competition, Dr. Fodor does not perceive a major threat at this time. He believes that Affymetrix's strong patent position and manufacturing capabilities should allow Affymetrix to remain the leader in the biochip business. In 2001, Affymetrix spun off subsidiary Perlegen Sciences which is using biochips to study the genomes contained in both chromosomes of fifty people to detect the subtle variations both within and among them. In Fodor's own words, "In these patterns, we will find the signature of human evolution. The potential for scientific discovery is fantastic."

However, not all investors shared the same level of enthusiasm for Affymetrix. Its share price tumbled from

a high in the $150s range per share to the $20–$30 range by July 2001. Though Affymetrix has consistently outperformed the NASDAQ (Exhibit 3), it joined scores of companies that warned the investment community that their revenues would fall short of expectations due to weak demand in their customer base. Also, revenues were off because of a recall of one of Affymetrix' chip products due to a design error. The recall and replacement of the chip will hurt sales into the third quarter of the year, dropping 2001 revenue to the low end of projections, now forecast to be $260 million to $290 million. Even if other chips meet target revenue expectations, the design error could possibly hurt their product quality image. Compounding this issue are the changes in its industry. Turning industry profit potential into firm revenues and profits is a difficult step. Previously, Affymetrix was the first mover in its field, which allowed the firm to develop a range of quality products that cater to a market niche. The industry has now evolved to include several new and capable players. Whether the firm succeeds in maintaining its position or not would depend on its future strategy.

With an unanticipated turn in the economy and a decreasing demand for its genechip products, the near-term future of Affymetrix is far from certain. The emergence of new and stronger competitors with extensive research, production, and marketing capabilities poses a significant change to the dynamics of competition within the industry. Though the CEO downplayed the long-term impact of these new entrants, the strategic changes that need to be in place to effectively compete is yet to be defined and an agenda for the future clearly spelt out. Clearly, Affymetrix has the intellectual capital of its employees, a progressive patent base, ample cash resources of about $450 million, and a committed top management and employee team to make it work in the long run.

Endnotes

1. Biotechnology Industry Organization (2001). *Editors and Reporters Guide to Biotechnology.* http://www.bio.org/aboutbio/guide2001/letter.pdf

Air Power in Mexico

Stephen Jenner

California State University, Dominguez Hills

"Our traditional customers are gone," declared Henry, the President of Air Power of San Diego, California. It was a really desperate situation, and the firm was facing the prospect of bankruptcy. In 1994, sales were $10 million but rapidly declining; however, Henry was very aware of the booming industrial development taking place in Tijuana just across the border and other major cities in Northern Baja California, Mexico. Henry had to figure out a way to save the family business, and he wondered whether Air Power should enter the Mexican market, and if so, how? What were the opportunities and threats in the business environment for Air Power in the future? Baja California was booming, but doing business in Mexico was controversial and risky. Was a strategy for entering the Mexican market the hope for Henry Jr.'s future?

On a clear day, Tijuana's hillsides were visible from adjacent San Diego, and it was possible to drive from downtown San Diego to the Mexican border in 20 minutes. Business, labor, and government leaders in San Diego had debated the passage of the North American Free Trade Agreement (NAFTA), but Henry was not concerned with the trade issues covered in the media. The national governments acting in the name of their countries develop policies, which set the pre-conditions for trade and investment, but ultimately managers of companies make the decisions to make it happen. Companies, not countries, decide to invest and trade.

Company Profile

Air Power sold and serviced a line of Ingersoll-Rand (I/R) 100–300 horsepower air compressors as well as a range of other industrial products. Air Power compressors were used in a variety of industrial and agricultural applications, often to power handtools. For example, air compressors were used to power drills or paint sprayers. The firm did not manufacture any of its products—instead sales and service, including sales of replacement parts, represented their core business.

San Diego Market Segments

Air Power's historical market segment was large ships—for 40 years they worked with the US Navy and the tuna fleet in San Diego. Historically, Air Power and the machine shop serviced the San Diego and nearby Ensenada tuna fleets, as well as the defense industry (including the US Navy). However, the entire tuna fleet moved from San Diego to the western Pacific, and the US trade embargo on Mexican tuna which was not "dolphin-safe" reduced the Ensenada fleet from 200 to 30 boats. Air compressor sales rapidly declined even further due to the major aerospace manufacturers moving out of the area with the downsizing of defense industry. The Navy was also buying much less, and the rest of Southern California was outside Air Power's territory as a distributor, effectively boxing them in against the Pacific Ocean and the Mexican border.

Competitive Forces

Ingersoll-Rand is a large US multinational corporation with a Mexican subsidiary based in Mexico City. Even though IR had a distributor in Mexico City, their coverage of the large Mexican market was limited and did not

This case was prepared by Stephen Jenner, School of Management, California State University, Dominguez Hills, as a basis for class discussion rather than to illustrate either effective or ineffective handling of administrative situations.

Not for quotation without prior written permission from author.

include Baja California. This was a typical situation because the Baja California peninsula was isolated from the Mexican mainland by the Sea of Cortez. For example, there was no Mexican railroad to Tijuana and vehicular traffic had to climb from the desert near Mexicali over the mountains to reach Tijuana.

"All of our competitors in Baja California were three I/R distributors from Los Angeles and another from Orange County. We will all end up duplicating our marketing efforts and cutting prices so nobody can make money. Our normal gross profit margin was 28–40 percent for equipment, 30–40 percent for parts, and we could charge US$35 per hour in Tijuana, whereas we charge US$65 per hour in San Diego. Our rival distributors were cutting prices to 10 percent over cost, and leaving us to service the accounts. I/R should have controlled the situation better—they had a policy that distributors who sold into another territory should pay 5 percent of their net profit to the distributor in that territory for compressors of at least 50 horsepower."

There were no Mexican competitors that Henry was aware of, and he felt that Air Power's reputation for reliable service and the agreement with I/R would serve as formidable entry barriers for potential new competitors.

Mexican Market Segments

Possible market segments were manufacturing companies, agribusiness, the Mexican government, small retailers, and more. Other possible Mexican customers ran small auto repair and upholstery shops, construction companies, agricultural segments including tomato farming and vineyards. Given Air Power's history, the Mexican Navy and the remaining fishing fleet were also possibilities. US-, Asian-, and some Mexican-owned maquiladora factories were churning out televisions, computers, and other electronics, as well as apparel, wood furniture, food and beverages, sports equipment, shoes, all to be exported to the US. IR granted exclusive territories to distributors, but these were not enforced, and there was little support from headquarters in resolving conflicts between Air Power and other IR distributors. Asian rivals had an edge with Asian maquilas. (See Appendix 1, "Maquiladoras and NAFTA," and Appendix 2, 'The "Twin Cities' and the Development of Their Industrial Base.")

Business Risks in Mexico

Henry recognized the multiple risks associated with doing business in Mexico. Internally, operating two facilities would result in much higher costs, and there could be a negative impact on jobs in San Diego.

In Mexico, getting paid can be a big problem, particularly with smaller firms. Accounts receivable often waited six months or more, and many small accounts had to be written off if they were offered credit terms.

Personal safety was a growing concern since kidnappings and robberies were increasingly common in Tijuana. There were also environmental pressures on companies which translated into more visits by Mexican government inspectors and higher costs. There were "toxic cemeteries" of 55 gallon drums at many sites, as well as dumping of these drums in the canyons surrounding the industrial city. In addition to issues related to unionization, gender issues such as pregnancy testing and sexual harassment were widely publicized. Henry was aware of many of the ethical issues related to globalization and "exploitation" of cheap labor abroad.

Strategic Options

Henry Jr. wanted to continue to run the business succeeding his father, and Henry Jr. was willing to go into Mexico. Border delays could last hours due to waiting lines for US Customs inspection northbound. Henry was not fluent in Spanish and he and his son did not know Mexico very well.

The firm had a very small long-term debt and a little cash. Financial resources were very limited, and cash flow was always a problem.

Air Power could not move backward in its supply chain to design and/or make air compressors (with their own maquiladora). Their business was the final part of the supply chain, sell-move-after sales service and parts.

Some of Air Power's strategic options for serving these Mexican market segments included the following:

1. Export and service from San Diego, including all sales force and service employees.
2. Establish a wholly-US owned facility in Baja to provide local service using local employees supported by San Diego. Possible locations included Tijuana, Ensenada, Mexicali, and Tecate. Four legal forms are possible in Mexico: corporation (usually a "sociedad anonima de capital variable," or SA de CV), partnership, a hybrid, or a branch.
3. Form a strategic alliance with suppliers other than IR which has their Mexican headquarters located in Mexico City (Federal District or DF), and it is not a factor in Baja. Locations too far away include Guadalajara and Monterrey. Air Power could also form alliances with rival IR distributors.
4. Find a Mexican partner and form a joint venture.
5. Sell to a rival distributor from Orange County or Los Angeles.
6. Stay in San Diego and do not try to enter Mexico.

Appendix 1 Maquiladoras and NAFTA

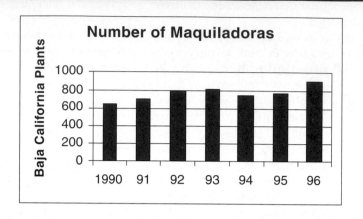

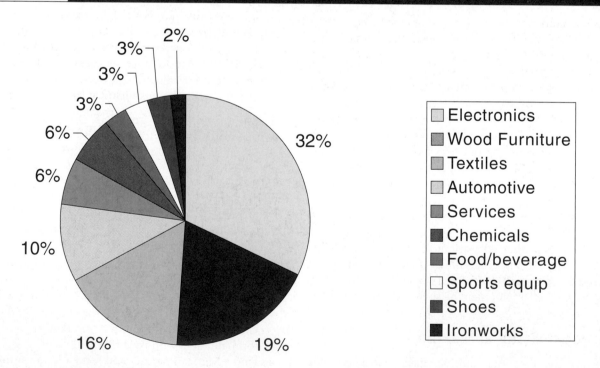

US trade laws (Harmonized Tariff Schedule [HTS] 9802) had long allowed companies to temporarily export US components for assembly in foreign countries. US companies exporting components and reimporting those same components paid duty only on the value added abroad. Mexico created the Border Industrialization Program (BIP) in 1965 to help ease border unemployment after the end of the US Bracero Program ("brazo" means "arm" in Spanish, so "bracero" is a man with arms employed by US farmers as a field hand). Also known as the "maquiladora" program (a "maquila" was the portion of corn flour withheld by a mill as a commission for grinding the corn in colonial days) or in-bond assembly, it exempted foreign firms from Mexican foreign investment law requiring 51% Mexican ownership. The BIP was also intended to bring back US production subcontracted in Hong Kong, Taiwan, and other East Asian countries. Tijuana began attracting Japanese television (TV) assemblers in the late 1970s, and there was a major TV industry investment boom following the Mexican peso devaluation of 1982.

One of the most visible forms of these cross-border economic linkages is the so-called "twin plant" form of the maquiladora program. Twin plants are maquiladora co-production systems with capital intensive operations and specialized tasks performed north of the border, and the labor intensive assembly plants located south of the border. After the product is assembled in Mexico, it is usually sent back to the US for further processing or distribution.

Maquiladoras have also contributed to transboundary linkages by creating a constant flow of commuters. Most top executives and higher level staff in the maquiladora industry lived in San Diego and commuted to Tijuana for their work. According to a study by San Diego Dialogue in 1994, 5,000–6,000 Americans were crossing the border each day to work in Tijuana. This number was expected to grow as more maquiladoras were built, and even more important, as more plants were shifting their activities on the Mexican side from assembly only, to more technological, sophisticated manufacturing, which requires higher skill levels. For many maquiladoras in Tijuana, the term assembly plant was no longer appropriate. Instead, "component manufacturing" has become a better term to describe the activities of those plants. This trend was also reflected in the value added per employee.

Between 1991 and 1993 the value added per employee increased in the Tijuana maquiladora industry. Some of this increase in value added was also due to increased production, increased productivity of workers, increased local sourcing of inputs, and increased prices of some local inputs. The value added per employee in the Tijuana maquiladoras grew from $1,600 New Pesos (NP) in 1991 to $3,000 NP in 1993 as more component manufacturing requiring higher skill levels was added to assembly operations. In addition to paying Mexican wages (entry level jobs paid about US$1.50 per hour) and payroll taxes, maquiladoras purchased many services locally, including transportation and distribution, customs brokerage, financial services, and repairs and maintenance.

NAFTA

Assessing the situation in 1994, Henry knew that it was getting easier to do business in Baja California, Mexico, with or without the passage of NAFTA.

The North American Free Trade Agreement (NAFTA) was the result of years of negotiation between host governments. In June, 1991, the governments of Canada, the U.S. and Mexico began negotiating a free trade agreement that would over time reduce or eliminate barriers to trade and investment flows. NAFTA, which became operative on January 1, 1994, created a $7.8 billion market with a population of 370 million people. This trilateral pact combined the world's first (U.S.), eighth (Canada) and twelfth (Mexico) largest economies into the largest unified market in the world. Under NAFTA guidelines, all tariffs on goods originating in Canada, Mexico and the United States will be eliminated over a transition period of fifteen years.

NAFTA's "Rules of Origin" require companies to have a higher percentage of local content or inputs originating in North America to qualify for reduced tariffs. The percentage of North American content required varies greatly depending on the product. For example, televisions must contain 33 percent North American content, including the picture tube, and be sufficiently transformed in North America so as to undergo a change in tariff classification. This part of the NAFTA is expected to have a major positive impact on regional sourcing. The purpose of the rules is to ensure that NAFTA benefits are given only to goods that are produced inside the NAFTA region.

"Sourcing Strategies of Asian Manufacturers and the Development of Local Linkages in San Diego and Tijuana," (Stephen Jenner [CSUDH], and Wim Douw and Boudewijn Koops [both graduate students in the Faculty of Geographical Sciences at the University of Utrecht, The Netherlands]), Journal of Borderland Studies, 8:2:19–48, San Diego, CA: San Diego State University, Fall, 1998.

Appendix 2
The "Twin Cities" and the Development of Their Industrial Base

In 1994, San Diego County's gross regional product (GRP) was $66.8 billion and Tijuana's was $12 billion. When the GRPs of San Diego and Tijuana were combined, the transborder region ranked 36th in the world, with an economy of $78.8 billion, above Malaysia, and below Israel. San Diego's per capita GRP was $24,680 in 1994. This placed the County's standard of living among the highest in the world, ranking ninth for national economies. This was in great contrast to its Mexican twin city, Tijuana, where per capita income was only $3,200.

About 42 percent of all border crossings between Tijuana and San Diego were for the purpose of shopping. In 1995, Mexican visitors spent $2.8 billion in San Diego (San Diego Dialogue. 1996. *The San Diego/Tijuana Binational Region*. San Diego, CA: University of California). Despite the international boundary and inherent differences between the two cities, a significant cross-border economic relationship existed. This relationship has been an especially important element in the development of this binational region as it has become functionally integrated through its economic linkages in several sectors.

Prior to the growth of the maquila industry, manufacturing activity in the northern border region was limited and small in scale, essentially serving the needs of the border population that were not met by imports from the United States or, to a much lesser extent, central Mexico. A large proportion of the labor force and entrepreneurial resources were dedicated to small-scale provision of services from foreign tourists. Mexican border cities simply did not possess the entrepreneurial vision, industrial base, or market size that would have permitted local suppliers to compete with foreign sources in a wide spectrum of materials and inputs. (Brannon, Jeffrey, D. James, and G. Lucker. 1994. "Generating and Sustaining Backward Linkages Between Maquiladoras and Local Suppliers in Northern Mexico." *World Development* 22(12): 1933–1945.)

AmBev, The Dream Project: A Brazilian–Based Multinational Beverage Company with Global Scale

Lourdes Casanova

INSEAD

Fernando Rodrigues

INSEAD

Introduction

1 July 1999 was one of the most important days ever for Marcel Telles, Brahma's CEO and one of its major shareholders.[1] For years, he had thought of developing Brahma into a serious global beverage player, but although his company dominated the Brazilian market, it still looked like a potential target for acquisition by any global player such as Coca-Cola or Pepsi.

On 1 July 1999, the beverage sector made headline news throughout the Brazilian press. Antarctica (see company profile in Exhibit 3) and Brahma (see company profile in Exhibit 4) were merging to create a major player in the Brazilian and Latin American markets. It represented the largest merger deal in the history of Brazil. The largest Brazilian company had been created by bringing together Antarctica's US$3,3 billion and Brahma's US$7 billion in sales revenues. They would have 16,500 employees, 50 factories with an 8.9 billion hectoliters (hl) production capacity, and more than 70 percent market share of the Brazilian beer market.[2]

The executive summary of the press release is shown here:

American Beverage Company
Compañia de Bebidas de Las Américas
Companhia de Bebidas das Américas
AmBev
Antarctica and Brahma Combine to Create AmBev
A Brazilian-Based Multinational Beverage Company with Global Scale
1 July 1999

Executive Summary:

Companhia Antarctica Paulista ("Antarctica") and Companhia Cervejaria Brahma ("Brahma") are announcing their combination, resulting in the creation of Companhia de Bebidas das Américas—AmBev ("AmBev," American Beverage Company). The newly formed entity will be a Brazilian beverage company with the capacity to compete successfully in the global beverage arena and take advantage of global consolidation trends.

AmBev's strategy is to utilize its Brazilian base of operations, as well as its presence in Argentina, Uruguay, Venezuela, and exports to over 15 countries, in order to pursue expansion opportunities that will arise in Latin America as the continent's markets become more integrated with the creation of the Free Trade Zone of the Americas. By the year 2005, there will be one single market that will span from the United States to the Southern Cone, in which products will cross borders free of trade tariffs following the successful example of the European Union.

AmBev is created as a diversified beverage company. Through its existing proprietary brands as well as its partnerships with other global players, AmBev will operate in the beer, soft drinks, juices, mineral water, sports drinks, and iced tea beverage segments. AmBev will maintain independent distribution and marketing channels for its major brands, thus promoting a competitive environment for consumers.

The numbers that emerge from the creation of AmBev are significant. Based on pro-forma year-end 1998 figures, the company's total assets amounted to R$8.1 billion and its net worth would have exceeded R$2.8 billion. The 1998 revenues would have been R$4.5 billion with a consolidated EBITDA (earnings before interest and taxes, plus depreciation and amortization) of approximately R$873 million. In 1998, the combined entity would have sold 64 million hl of beer and 25 million hl of soft drinks, which would have ranked it as the world's fifth largest beverage company in terms of volume, on a pro-forma basis.

Brahma and Antarctica are convinced that AmBev is uniquely positioned to take advantage of regional consolidation opportunities and economies of scale, while being better protected from the higher cost of capital associated with Brazil. All of this will be to the benefit of consumers and shareholders alike.

The establishment of AmBev is being submitted for approval to the Brazilian anti-trust authorities.

Some years before, during a press conference, Marcel Telles had said: "Fifteen years from now there will be only five major beer companies in the world and Brahma will be one of them." He had maintained his strong belief in global consolidation but now seemed to acknowledge the importance of merging with a strong local player in order to achieve the final goal: "I don't think there will be more than four to six players per industry [in the world] five to ten years from now. If we merge, we would be one of them. If not, I don't see how."[3]

Kaiser, the third largest Brazilian beverage company (with 16 percent market share) after Brahma and Antarctica, reacted promptly to the news. According to Kaiser's CEO, Humberto Pandolpho, a monopoly was being created and the Government should take measures to stop such a high concentration move: "I am an optimist. I believe everyone will understand that we can't have an 80 percent concentration in the Brazilian beverage market." Kaiser also told the press that 8,000 jobs at AmBev (see Exhibit 1 for AmBev pro-forma financials) would be lost due to the merger, but AmBev answered that such a plan had no basis.[4]

In order to proceed, the merger needed the authorization of the Brazilian government. In fact, what was at stake was far more important than a mere "beer deal." Behind the scenes a bigger controversy was going on with the potential to change the face of Brazilian business. Brazil had been able to regain international investors' confidence over recent years and had attracted important Foreign Direct Investment Funds (more than US$56 billion in 1998 and 1999), which had helped the economy to grow. At the same time, Brazil had seen several major European and US corporations enter the market and relegate local players to secondary positions, while leading Brazilian-owned firms seemed to have become an endangered species. Therefore, there was a growing trend towards the creation of "Brazilian multinationals," stricter laws designed to keep foreign competitors at bay and increased support for local companies to expand across Mercosul[5] and gain market share in the emerging regional markets.

The Brazilian government had a tough decision to make:

- Should AmBev be allowed to pursue its dominant role in the Brazilian market and from there create a sustainable basis for becoming a global company?
- Should it defend Brazilian consumers from the risk of a monopoly and therefore not allow the creation of what could be the first truly global Brazilian company?
- Was the merger a defensive one to avoid becoming a potential acquisition target?

The decision process promised to be long and bumpy, with Brahma and Antarctica trying to influence decision-makers and the general public to accept the huge benefits that could be obtained from AmBev's creation, while Kaiser would champion the cause against monopoly and the potential exploitation of Brazilian consumers by AmBev. Global beverage players would also become involved, with Pepsi allied with Brahma and Antarctica (see Pepsi-AmBev distribution deal in Exhibit 2) while Coke supported Kaiser.

The "Dream Project": The Merger Process

In May 1999, Marcel Telles met Victorio de Marchi, CEO of Antarctica, in São Paulo, in a trendy, noisy restaurant called Gero. Their meetings were common and would always take place in public places, so both CEOs could avoid speculation about any attempt at collusion or secretive moves. On that day, the two men discussed the world market and how a Brazilian company could become a global player. Telles launched the initial idea about merging the two companies and how they could capture substantial benefits from it. Victorio de Marchi

	Brahma	Antarctica	AmBev
Cash	$1,081,026	$196,391	$1,277,417
Total current assets	1,997,203	761,544	2,758,747
Net PR&E	2,115,962	1,950,027	4,065,989
Total assets	$4,669,322	$3,402,148	$8,071,470
ST debt	898,749	468,427	1,367,176
LT debt	981,169	570,129	1,551,298
Total liabilities	$3,190,456	$1,480,721	$4,671,177
Stockholders' equity	$1,478,866	$1,921,427	$3,400,293
Total liabilities and equities	$4,669,322	$3,402,148	$8,071,470
Net revenues	$3,155,674	$1,381,874	$4,537,548
COGS	1,799,726	929,889	2,729,615
Gross profit	$1,355,948	$451,985	$1,807,933
Selling and marketing expenses	695,622	186,966	882,588
G&A	319,342	202,809	522,151
EBIT	$389,916	$128,286	$518,202
EBITDA	$666,614	$205,981	$872,595
Net income (before minorities)	318,395	64,200	
Net income	$329,098	$26,552	

was a bit surprised but promised to consider and analyze it. The "Dream Project" was born.

Brahma's executives had been considering the need to become a global player for some time. The merger had been debated but seemed like an impossible idea. As Marcel Telles says: "We talked about that, but it seemed impossible—like dating Sharon Stone." However, 40 days after the restaurant meeting, the creation of AmBev would be announced to the market and Telles' dream would come true.

The financial markets viewed Brahma's search for additional scale without surprise. For a long time, Brahma had considered that acquisitions were the way to go to establish itself as a significant Latin American player. In 1994, Brahma acquired Cervecera Nacional, Venezuela's second largest brewer, and opened a factory in Argentina. In early 1999, Brahma came very close to buying Bavaria (the largest brewer group in Colombia) for US$2 billion, but with the devaluation of the *real*, the price went up and the deal did not go ahead.

Brahma's efforts to expand abroad were not enough. It had to move faster and take bolder steps. A merger between Brahma and Antarctica would be a surprise as the two companies were direct and aggressive competitors, each with very specific cultures. For many years, Antarctica and Brahma had regarded each other as enemies in the Brazilian beverage war. But the time had come to get together—otherwise they would become easy acquisition targets for global players.

Right after the lunch in São Paulo, each company assigned a two-member team to act as a task force to debate operational questions and other details concerning the merger. The group spent a month debating in absolute secrecy. Not even their families knew about it. (In the companies themselves only 10 people knew about the merger one week before the public announcement.) They were arriving home late with no excuses to offer. Adilson Miguel, Brahma's sales director, said: "My wife was getting suspicious—she thought I was having an affair." Meetings took place in a neutral location: GP Investimentos (Brazilian I-bank) and at the offices of Morgan Stanley where members of the negotiation team wore badges with a single identification number—no names or company logos were used.

The "Dream Project" was supposed to go public on 7 July, but 10 days before, Brahma's and Antarctica's stock

| Exhibit 2 | Pepsi-AmBev Distribution Deal |

September 1999 Press Release

AmBev and Pepsi Take Guaraná Antarctica to the World

Guaraná Antarctica will be bottled and distributed throughout the world by PepsiCo. The signing of an international licensing agreement will be communicated to President Fernando Henriques Cardoso this Wednesday by the joint Presidents of AmBev—Companhia de Bebidas das Américas—Victório Carlos De Marchi and Marcel Hermann Telles, and by the President of PepsiCo Inc., Steve Reinemund, during an audience at the Palácio do Planalto.

The agreement is the first step in the internationalization of AmBev, a company created on 1 July through the merger of Antarctica with Brahma, forming the fifth largest drinks company in the world. "It is the taste of Brazil for the world," says Victório De Marchi, joint President of AmBev and also the general manager of Antarctica, in reference to the slogan adopted by the new company.

"The unique taste, the fact that guaraná is a product of the Amazon region, grown with respect for ecology and the environment, together with Pepsi's distribution reach, are all excellent tools to support Guaraná Antarctica's claim for a slice of the world soft drink market," says the president of PepsiCo, Steve Reinemund. PepsiCo is one of the world's largest consumer product companies, operating in 175 countries. The company's worldwide sales in 1998 were US$22,3 billion and the operating profit was US$2,6 billion. The company consists of Frito-Lay, the leader in snack chips; Pepsi-Cola, the world's second largest beverage company; and Tropicana Products, the world's largest marketer and producer of juices.

The companies plan to launch Guaraná Antarctica in many of the international markets starting in the second half of 2000.

The agreement will be submitted to CADE which is still examining the merger of the two companies, but it is expected that a favorable ruling will be announced before the international operation begins. "Obviously, we will not take any action that goes against the CADE's rulings. CADE, as far as we can tell from its most recent decisions, has a modern outlook on the globalized economy and its dynamics, and it will understand the advantages of this association for consumers and for Brazil," believes Marcel Telles, joint President of AmBev and Chairman of Brahma's Board of Directors. Guaraná Antarctica is the leading soft drink in the guaraná segment, with a 25 percent market share, according to the Nielsen Market Research Institute, reaching a million points of sale throughout Brazil.

Today, Guaraná Antarctica is ranked the 15th best-selling soft drink in the world with annual sales of 800 million liters.

It is projected that Guaraná Antarctica will be one of the top 10 soft drink brands worldwide within five years of signing the contract with PepsiCo. AmBev's Antarctica division will export guaraná extract from the Amazon to PepsiCo's worldwide production and distribution operations. "This contract with PepsiCo is a concrete example of what Antarctica and Brahma promised when they created AmBev: opening up the external market for Brazilian drinks," says Marcel Telles.

---

prices rose unusually high, creating suspicion about an information leakage and it was decided to move the announcement date to 1 July and catch everyone by surprise.

The final step was to ensure that the communication process with the financial markets was clear and well supported—the press release was re-written 30 times and the AmBev logo went through 15 versions during a long night. A crucial detail was to get Marcel Telles and Victorio de Marchi a private audience with Fernando Henriques Cardoso (FHC), President of Brazil, to tell him what was about to happen. Lobbying, old contacts, and relationships proved to very effective.

On 1 July 1999, more than 70 reporters attended a press conference in São Paulo given by Marcel Telles and Victorio de Marchi. Before the press conference, they had answered more than a hundred anticipated questions over two hours and so they were well prepared to handle the media attacks. When the press conference finished only one doubt persisted in Marcel Telles' mind: "How will I explain the merger to my son? I have forbidden him to ever drink Guaraná Antarctica—what will I tell him now?"

Exhibit 3 Antarctica's Company Profile

Historical Background

Antarctica was founded in 1885, but initially the company was a food and ice producer. Only in 1888 did Antarctica start producing beer, using a German method. Its first factory was located in Agua Branca in São Paulo. This region became known as Parque (Park) Antarctica. In 1904, Antarctica acquired Cervejaria Bavaria, a leading beverage company at the time. In 1911, it inaugurated its first subsidiary company in Ribeirão Preto, in the interior of the São Paulo state.

Antarctica has always been a pioneer in terms of product innovation and development. As a result, it launched the first tonic water product and the first Guaraná drink in Brazil.

In 1944, Antarctica entered a growth phase, increasing production capacity and revamping the technology used. It launched new factories and acquired others, with a special attention to Cervejaria Bohemia, the oldest in Brazil.

Antarctica kept introducing new products and driving the market. It launched the first premium beer (Bavaria) and the first non-alcoholic beer (Kronenbier) in the Brazilian market.

In 1996, Antarctica made an agreement with Anheuser-Busch, which produces the Budweiser brand, to produce and distribute this product in Brazil.

1997 was a crucial year for Antarctica. It launched Bavaria Pilsen, a light beer, which was positioned as the "Beer for Friends" and had major success: 10 months after its market introduction, it had already 7 percent of national market share.

In 1998, Antarctica re-positioned most of its products and changed its logos and advertising. For instance, the traditional Bohemia and Polar beers had their logos changed and soft drinks, such as Guaraná and Soda, were also changed to give a more dynamic, modern look.

Internationalization and Alliance Strategy

Antarctica's most recent goal is to increase its global reach, especially in the US market. For this reason, the alliance with Anheuser-Busch is particularly important. The commitment to developing the US market is such that Antarctica created a specific affiliated company with that specific purpose in mind. Antarctica USA Inc. is an affiliated company focused on distributing Antarctica's products in the US and currently US-based production is not being considered.

Anheuser-Busch currently has 5 percent of Antarctica's equity, but holds the option to increase its participation to a maximum of 30 percent by 2002. The alliance has already provided significant steps forward:

- A company in which Antarctica holds 49 percent and Anheuser-Busch holds 51 percent of the equity, produces Budweiser beer in Brazil.
- Antarctica created a specific beer brand (Rio Cristal) to be distributed in the US in the imported beers segment. Currently, it is only distributed in Florida and California, but there are plans to expand its distribution coverage across the US.
- It supported the development of an international expansion plan through franchising for the Guaraná soft drink product line.

This franchising plan implies establishing agreements with international bottlers. Antarctica supplies the concentrate and local bottlers invest in production and distribution in each local market. It is a strategy quite similar to the one used by Coca-Cola in worldwide terms.

For now, only the US and Japan are using a franchise system, while the rest of the world receives Antarctica's Guaraná through export:

Table 1	Antarctica and Its International Presence in 1998

Exports	Franchise
Lebanon, Portugal, France, Germany, Italy, Switzerland, Paraguay, Bolivia, Uruguay, Venezuela, Argentina, and Chile	USA and Japan

Recent Performance

Antarctica Group has US$3,3 billion in sales revenues and more than 7,500 employees. It controls 15 breweries, 16 soft drink factories and seven franchised soft drinks factories. Its annual production capacity is

(Continued)

| Exhibit 3 | Antarctica's Company Profile *(Continued)* |

around 57,7 million hl of beer and soft drinks. It uses a distribution network of more than 400 wholesale distributors, which cover more than one million points of sale across Brazil. In the last 10 years, Antarctica has invested more than US$1,6 billion to obtain a 133 percent increase in production capacity.

Antarctica has also been involved in a productivity improvement effort, which has been quite successful: productivity per employee has increased 151 percent since 1990.

As a result, Antarctica holds a 26 percent market share in the Brazilian market. Antarctica Pilsen is one of the leading beer brands in the Brazilian market. In the soft drinks market Antarctica has a 15 percent market share. Guaraná Antarctica, Soda Antarctica, and Tonic Water Antarctica have had a leadership position in their specific segments for many years.

Antarctica also possesses very strong brand awareness. According to "top of mind" market research, Antarctica is the brand with highest customer recall in the beer and non-cola soft drink segments.

Competition's Initial Reaction

Kaiser's reaction only came on 2 July. Soon after the press conference, Humberto Pandolpho heard the news on the radio. He was shocked and a bit lost. He became unreachable by the media and tried to design a fight-back strategy. The following day, a short press release from Kaiser condemned the merger which was also supported by an advertisement campaign. Kaiser formed a six-strong task-force to tackle the critical issues raised by the merger. They worked every day for a week until 2 a.m. to produce a 15-page report that defined Kaiser's strategy. Its main points were to:

- Focus the discussion on the Brazilian market and not on the global market, as AmBev would prefer.
- Emphasize the monopoly risk by having a player with a 73 percent market share in the Brazilian beer market.
- Argue that AmBev could push for abusive price increases, based on monopolistic behavior.
- Mention that AmBev would cut several thousands of jobs in Brahma and Antarctica.
- Show consumers needed to be aware of potential repercussions and that Kaiser was trying to defend the natural interests of the majority of Brazilians.

Anti-Trust Regulations in Brazil

According to the 1994 anti-trust law, any "concentration act" that builds a 20 percent or higher market share needs the approval of government to become effective. It must go through three main stages in the decision process:

- Secretary of Economic Monitoring (Secretaria de Acompanhamento Económico [SAEE])—a unit of the Tax Ministry (Ministério da Fazenda)—that provides an opinion regarding the impact on the financial markets.
- Secretary of Economic Defense (Secretaria de Defesa Económica [SDE])—a unit of the Justice Ministry (Ministério da Justiça)—that provides an opinion regarding the legal aspects of the business.
- Council of Economic Management (Conselho de Administração Economica [CADE])—also a unit of the Justice Ministry (Ministério da Justiça)—which is the only institution with power to approve or veto the business.

The first two stages simply provide qualified opinions which may help CADE in taking the final decision. The process only comes to an end when CADE announces its decision. However, influencing SAEE and especially SDE can prove to be useful as they can have some influence on the final decision.

The first step taken by CADE was to freeze any major decision that Brahma and Antarctica could take in order to make AmBev a *fait accompli*. The rationale for this move was to provide some reassurance to workers, unions, and competitors that feared that the usual slow pace of Brazilian bureaucracy would allow Brahma and Antarctica to move ahead without waiting for a final legal decision.

In 1995, CADE was also called to decide upon a very high "concentration act" when the multinational Colgate-Palmolive paid US$780 million for Kolynos, a toothpaste brand. The acquisition would have given Colgate a 79 percent market share in Brazil. CADE did not approve the deal and asked Colgate to take the Kolynos brand off the market for four years. Colgate launched a new brand substitute for Kolynos called

"Sorriso" (meaning Smile), which also became a success, based on low price strategy (20 percent to 30 percent discount). Gessy-Lever, a Colgate competitor, argued that the new brand was very similar to Kolynos in its packaging and advertising, but that did not change CADE's decision. In the end, CADE's decision evidently benefited the consumer as toothpastes' prices over five years rose only 26 percent, compared to the 77 percent inflation rate.

Lobbying and Influencing Government

Initially, AmBev adopted a low profile regarding the anti-trust decision process. However, Kaiser started to move very aggressively, trying to get more influence over the general public and politicians. Kaiser published a brochure publicizing its arguments against the merger. One of its main arguments was the loss of jobs as a consequence of the merger—Kaiser mentioned 8,000 jobs being lost in the process. This figure was unrealistic given that Antarctica had less than 8,000 employees at that time. Nevertheless, the "8,000" figure was a powerful message that increased general public awareness of the problem, albeit in a populist, sensational way. Kaiser also got a private audience with FHC and tried to win several politicians to its side.

In October, 90 days after the public announcement of the merger, the process was still under analysis by SEAE (the first consulting unit that supports CADE with an opinion). Kaiser was winning over public opinion. AmBev needed to do something.

The Guaraná factor was used. On 20 October 1999, Steve Reinemund, CEO of Pepsi, visited Brazil to announce that Pepsi would internationally distribute Guaraná Antarctica. It was the first practical result from the creation of AmBev. Analysts expected Guaraná to capture 1 percent of the global soft drinks market, valued at US$70 billion per year. AmBev also tried to match Kaiser's influence among politicians and Marcel Telles started a small road show in Brazilia to convey his ideas about the benefits of the merger.

AmBev's First Defeat

On 11 November, SEAE came out with its report: it was favorable to the merger but with restrictions. It recommended that AmBev should be reduced in size and its main beer brand (Skol) should be sold. Skol had belonged to Brahma since 1980 and was the largest single beer brand in Brazil. According to SEAE, AmBev could not have more than 70 percent of the beer market and control the three main brands: Skol, Brahma, and Antarctica.

AmBev was prompt to answer and issued a press release in which it attacked the report's technical quality. In addition, AmBev had reason to believe that Kaiser already knew about the report's content before the public announcement. On 11 November, Kaiser had installed a TV studio outside the SEAE building to support journalists and broadcast a video-conference with Humberto Pandolpho, right after SEAE announced its decision. AmBev was surprised by such a move from a competitor and became even more suspicious about the content of the report.

The recommendation to sell the Skol brand and its supporting assets was a complete surprise for AmBev, as it implied a major cut in its aspirations. AmBev's internal assessment forecast the need to sell only two factories (Manaus e Cuiabá) and a two year suspension of the Polar brand (very strong in the southern Brazil). AmBev argued that selling Skol would lead to a very strange situation in the beer market: Brahma (controlling Skol and Brahma brands) would have had a higher market share before the merger than AmBev after the merger (if Skol had to be sold). SEAE's argument was that they had to cut somewhere and it wouldn't make sense to force AmBev to drop Antarctica or Brahma brands in the beer market, as they also had a presence in the soft drinks markets. Skol was only present in the beer market.

Obviously, Kaiser showed an immediate interest in acquiring Skol.

AmBev's Second Defeat

SDE, the second entity to advise CADE, issued a report with a line of reasoning very close to that already presented by SEAE. On 1 February 2000, SDE told Brahma and Antarctica that they should sell one of their three main beer brands—Skol (27 percent market share), Brahma (22 percent market share), or Antarctica (22 percent market share)—and its factories, distributing firms, and other assets. Soft drinks and mineral water were left out of SDE's recommendation, which focused only on the beer market, similarly to SEAE's report. Regarding the soft drinks, SDE saw the merger as a positive move as it could create a stronger national player to compete against Coca-Cola.

SDE argued that without this divesture, Brazilian consumers could be hurt by AmBev. For example, a price increase in Skol would lead to a migration of consumers mostly to Brahma or Antarctica. Therefore AmBev could raise prices in one or two of its main brands without a major risk of losing market share.

Once again, Kaiser's CEO received the report with satisfaction. He said that SDE followed the opinion expressed by SEAE and the main problem with the

Exhibit 4   Brahma's Company Profile

Historical Background

In 1808, beer reached Brazil from Europe, brought by the Portuguese royal family when it moved to the then colony, Brazil. Following the opening up of ports by nations friendly to Portugal, Britain was the first to introduce beer to the former colony. Nonetheless, in the first half of the 19th century beer was still restricted to a small portion of the population and, in practice, only imported brands were sold.

"Cerveja Barbante," after the brand of the same name, was the generic denomination given to Brazilian beers, which, with their rudimentary manufacture, produced a large amount of carbonic gas, the string (or *barbante*) serving to prevent the cork from bursting out of the bottle.

In 1888, a Swiss immigrant, Joseph Villiger, accustomed to the taste of European beers, decided to open his own business and started making beer at home. Savored first by his friends, this beer found favor with various palates and eventually became so famous that Villiger founded the "Manufatura de Cerveja Brahma Villiger & Companhia," at 128, Rua Visconde de Sapucahi. In the beginning, 32 employees were involved in the manufacture of 12,000 liters of beer a day.[a]

The word "Brahma" has three possible meanings as the origin of the brand:

- An Indian god worshipped mainly near Lake Pushkar, where legend has it that those who bathe in its waters will have all their sins forgiven, no matter how serious.
- It derives from the composer Brahms.
- The Brahmin religion (Brahmanism), which is centered on breaking out of the endless cycle of successive incarnations (samsara). Brahma is considered the creating principle by this religion.

Months later, on 6 September 1888, the Board of Trade of the Capital of the Empire granted Villiger & Cia the registration of the Brahma brand. In this document, a woman wrapped in the flowery branches of hops and barley symbolized the main image of the first Brahma label. Companhia Cervejaria Brahma was formed by the merger of Georg Maschke & Cia, Cervejaria Brahma, and Preiss Häussler & Cia.

Cervejaria Teutonia. According to the press, the new company's IPO amounted to 25,000 shares.

The new company kept growing until the 1970s, mainly focused on the beer market but it also went into soft drinks. However the major step forward came in the early 1970s, when Brahma started growing through associations and alliances with powerful groups. In 1972, it formed an association with Grupo Fratelli Vita and as a result the company added three brands of non-alcoholic drinks to its product line: Sukita, Guraná Fratelli, and Gasosa Limão. By 1974, the company already had nine factories, one malt plant, and an experimental barley plantation.

In 1980 Brahma beer was considered the "best imported beer in the United States," which was a recognition of its product quality abroad.

Also in 1980, the company needed to grow and it acquired a controlling interest in Cervejarias Skol Caracu. It added the brands Cerveja Skol, Chopp Claro Skol, canned beer made for export, Ouro Fino, and the historical Caracu beer.

In 1984, an agreement was signed with Pepsi Cola International for the production, sale, and distribution of the Pepsi Cola soft drink in Rio de Janeiro and the operation of three factories in Rio Grande do Sul. On 27 October 1984, the Garantia Group acquired the shareholding control of Companhia Cervejaria Brahma.

1995 was a very full year for Brahma. The new Guaraná Brahma was launched in the state of São Paulo and the interior of Minas Gerais. At the same time, the Company launched the Brahma Bock beer in the states of São Paulo, Rio Grande do Sul, Rio de Janeiro, the federal District, and Mato Grosso do Sul. The product was launched simultaneously in Argentina, Paraguay, and Uruguay as a beer appropriate for drinking in the winter months because it is stronger and full-bodied. In the light of the results of surveys it carried out, the American company Miller Brewing Company observed that the beer market was growing, especially in South America. As a result, it entered into a joint venture with the Company for the distribution of Miller Genuine Draft. The agreement provided for the possibility of manufacturing the beer in Brazil to compete in the domestic market.

As of 1996, when Argentine consumers heard the name Brahma they no longer thought just of beer, because this was the year the Company launched its

---

[a]The word "Chopp," the generally used Brazilian expression for beer, means "measure." In drinking establishments, Germans would order a chopp of beer or wine, which would be equivalent to ordering a glass of beer or a chopp in modern times.

Exhibit 4   Brahma's Company Profile *(Continued)*

line of soft drinks: Guaraná Brahma, Limón Brahma, Naranja Brahma, and Pomelo Brahma. The difference lay in the Guaraná taste, previously unknown in the region, and in Pomelo, a citrus-flavored soft drink based on grapefruit, specifically developed for the Argentine market.

Also in 1996, the "Brahma Reciclarte" project was launched in the Rio de Janeiro Botanical Gardens, in a playful and practical manner, applying the concepts of recycling, reusing, and reducing waste to people's day-to-day lives. For the event, artists and designers were invited to create objects using Brahma packs.

Companhia Cervejari Brahma is one of the most aggressive marketing companies, always seeking innovation with regard to its brand image. With the Atlanta Olympics in 1996, the Company, traditionally associated with soccer, became official sponsor of the Brazilian Olympic Committee.

In 1998, the Company hired Ronaldinho, the Brazilian football star, to launch a campaign centered on beer and the football World Cup. The campaign emphasizes Brahma as the irresistible number one flavor. Brahma is also concerned with becoming more sales and customer-oriented. On 17 September 1998 all employees, with the exception of the production staff, became salespersons. They went out into the streets with a single purpose: making the Company more sales-focused. They all worked at points of sale throughout Brazil to learn a little more about customers and their needs, as part of an event called "GENTE QUE VENDE" (People That Sell).

Recent Performance

Today, Brahma is the dominant player in the Brazilian beer market. It controls the top two Brazilian brands: Skol and Brahma. It is licensed to produce premium brands: Miller and Carlsberg. It is the second most important player in the Brazilian soft drinks market, by being a Pepsi bottler and also from its position with its own brand of soft drinks. It has expanded into Argentina and Venezuela, and is therefore starting to have a growing international presence, at least in South America. Its market capitalization is over US$3.9 billion and Brahma is listed in São Paulo (Bovespa) and New York (NYSE). It has achieved an extraordinary stock market performance, as can be seen from the following chart.

Over the last 10 years, it has implemented an aggressive restructuring plan with very positive results:

Brahma in 1989	Brahma in 1999
25,000 employees	10,700 employee
36 plants	29 plants
43 million hl capacity	89 million hl capacity
50,3% market share	49,1% market share
760,000 retail outlets	Over 1,000,000 retail outlets
957 distributors	358 distributors
1,200 hl/employee	8.700 hl/employee
Net income of US$36 million	Net income of US$272 million

Brahma followed a forceful productivity improvement plan with very significant gains. It reduced the workforce and number of plants but increased capacity and productivity per employee. Profitability went up dramatically, while market share remained close to the 50 percent level. Its distribution network was rationalized (less distributors) but it was able to achieve higher capillarity at the retail level (more presence in retail outlets), which means that Brahma is now able to reach more markets and has better distribution coverage.

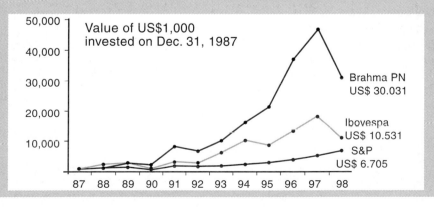

merger was the monopolistic risk. He was very active in giving media interviews, while AmBev's top executives preferred to remain silent on this subject.

On 2 February, AmBev expressed its point of view on SDE's report: "AmBev does not accept the SDE recommendation and believes that CADE will eliminate these restrictions." Once again, AmBev argued that, according to the report's recommendation, AmBev would become a smaller beer player than Brahma alone had been.

Next Steps

After the SDE decision, CADE had 60 days to decide. The final decision remained with CADE as SEAE and SDE had a purely consulting function and their recommendations were not mandatory. The CADE board was composed of seven members sourced from universities and the Justice Ministry.

They came under very high pressure throughout the process. In fact, it was already evident on 31 January 2000, when Gesner de Oliveira, the CADE chairman, called a press conference to announce that the Federal Police were investigating a bribery charge against one of the CADE's seven members. According to some rumors it was Kaiser who paid the bribe, while others pointed to AmBev as the source of the bribe.

Until then, AmBev had kept a low profile in this process, while Kaiser had used the media extensively to convey its opinions to the general public. According to Marcel Telles, "This case is not supposed to be a media war" but until then the advantage seemed to be with Kaiser.

There were signs of change in AmBev's strategy. Marcel Telles gave an interview to the New York Times on 4 February 2000 in which he tried to convey the message that Coca-Cola was strongly backing Kaiser, as it controlled 10 percent of the company and Coca-Cola bottlers controlled more than 60 percent. Marcel Telles said, "Kaiser is trying to portray itself as David when it is in fact a Goliath." Coca-Cola denied the accusation.

AmBev tried to use an external and stronger enemy such as Coca-Cola to gain backing from the general public, accusing Coca-Cola of being opposed to the merger's success. By picking a foreign enemy, the thesis related to creating a truly Brazilian multinational became more compelling. Antarctica's CEO, Victorio de Marchi, told the press that Coca-Cola had tried to buy Guaraná Antarctica in 1997 to launch it on the international market. Now, under AmBev, Pepsi was about to start distributing Guaraná Antarctica on a worldwide basis.

Opportunities for the Future

Brazil still represents a major opportunity that needs to be further developed. Despite having a stable 50 percent market share, Brahma believed very strongly in the potential for market growth. This belief was supported by favorable demographics and a low *per capita* consumption. Its association with Miller and Carlsberg in the local market seemed to have high potential, as premium beers were still largely unexplored in the Brazilian market.

Despite Brazil's market potential, Brahma recognized the need to go further and build a more solid presence in the international marketplace. Up to now, its focus had been South America, but the future may lead to more audacious moves.

AmBev Strategic Blueprint
Market Dominance and Financial Strength

AmBev is a formidable giant in the Brazilian market. It controls more than 70 percent of the Brazilian beer market through its three main brands: Skol (27 percent); Brahma (22 percent) and Antarctica (22 percent). Jointly, Antarctica and Brahma have 39 percent of Brazil's beverage market, including beer, soft drinks, mineral water, health drinks and iced tea. It would be the third largest beer company and the fifth largest beverage company in the world.[6]

Beer Company	Sales Revenues in US$Billion (1998)
Anheuser-Busch (USA)	11,2
Heineken (Holland)	7,3
AmBev (Brazil)	6,6
South African Breweries (RSA)	6,4
Carlsberg (Denmark)	4,6
Kirin (Japan)	4,5
Interbrew (Belgium)	4,2
Miller (USA)	4,1
Foster's (Australia)	3,0
Modelo (Mexico)	2,0

Internationalization Goals

Although a local market giant, AmBev is still far from a global player. Its international presence is still limited to South America and most of it is in the form of direct exports. A stronger presence has only been obtained in some of the South American countries, such as Argentina or Venezuela.

AmBev relies on truly global players to support the globalization challenge, such as Pepsi. Its guaraná international distribution agreement is clear evidence of

AmBev's difficulty in shaping and developing a world-wide scale distribution structure on its own. In summary, AmBev will sell concentrated guaraná to Pepsi, which will distribute it in 175 countries (based on Pepsi's global bottlers network). The target is to achieve 1 percent market share in the global beverage market over the next five years. Guaraná Antarctica is currently the 15th largest soft drink brand in the world (annual sales of more than 8 million hl). If the proposed target is accomplished, Guaraná Antarctica will rank among the top 10 soft drink brands.[7]

Operating Structure

According to AmBev's first press release, AmBev's operating structure is defined in the following way:

> Mr. Victório de Marchi and Mr. Marcel Telles, the current Chairmen of Antarctica and Brahma, respectively, will be co-Chairmen of the Board of Directors of the new company. Mr. Magim Rodriguez, the current President of Brahma, will be the President of AmBev. Mr. Rodriguez will be responsible for conducting day-to-day operations of AmBev and will also lead the transition team during the restructuring process. Mr. Rodriguez joined Brahma in 1989, and was responsible for the implementation of the Company's successful restructuring process. He has been serving as President since 1996.

> AmBev will operate with three separate domestic distribution networks for Antarctica, Brahma, and Skol, respectively. Combined, these networks will be comprised of 770 independent distributors that will continue to operate in a competitive environment. Furthermore, the commercial and marketing policies of each of these brands will remain separate in order to preserve their independence, with autonomous advertising, promotional, and marketing campaigns.

> Brahma's and Antarctica's best practices will lead to the development of one of the most efficient companies on a global scale. Furthermore, the creation of AmBev will allow for further dilution of fixed costs associated with increased economies of scale. The impact of AmBev's increased efficiency, coupled with the maintenance of independent distribution channels for the Antarctica, Brahma, and Skol brands, should create value for consumers and shareholders.

It seems that AmBev will be strongly influenced by Brahma's way of doing things. Some analysts prefer to mention the word acquisition instead of merger, as Brahma is expected to have full control over AmBev. That can be understood from several facts:

- It is Brahma that is really pushing the merging process forward and its executives are occupying key positions

in AmBev—Magim Rodriquez (former president of Brahma) is a typical case, as he becomes the president of AmBev, with day-to-day responsibilities.
- Brahma is much larger than Antarctica and also seems to be more efficient.
- Brahma's culture is much more aggressive and informal than Antarctica's (see Brahma's mission, culture, and values in Exhibit 5).

In the last 10 years, Antarctica has had serious difficulties defending its market position, while Brahma has accumulated cash flows and increased market share, clearly showing an appetite for growth and success. Antarctica has tried to copy Anheuser-Busch's best practices but with modest results.

Therefore, it is no surprise that Brahma's stock market performance clearly beats that of Antarctica. In 1992, the stock market valued Antarctica at R$2,5 billion[8] and Brahma at R$2,2 billion. In 1998, Brahma was worth R$3,7 billion, while Antarctica had a mere R$330 million.

AmBev was created from two very different companies. In Antarctica, variable remuneration was still not very common, while in Brahma almost everyone received stock options and had their pay indexed to some measure of performance. In Antarctica, unions tended to be more powerful and employees had better fringe benefits, whereas Brahma preferred to be more restricted in terms of fringe benefits but performance was key for higher remuneration. Finally, casual dress was the norm at Brahma, with virtually nobody wearing a tie while Antarctica was just the opposite in terms of dress code.

Bearing this in mind, Antarctica's employees will need some time to adapt to the new rules that seem to be on the way.

General Post-Merger Strategy

AmBev is expected to focus on cost savings, especially at the corporate level, and some jobs may be lost. Some less efficient factories may be closed. There is no estimate available in terms of cost savings expected for AmBev.

One should also anticipate that international partners might change. Currently, there are rumors about Anheuser-Busch leaving Brazil and terminating its relationship with Antarctica. Pepsi, which had close links with Brahma, is expected to have a stronger role in the future.

AmBev is expected to rapidly move more aggressively into Latin America and to build a stronger presence in neighboring countries. In the medium term, AmBev intends to become a major player across Latin America and leverage its strategic partners to help the worldwide

Exhibit 5   Brahma's Mission, Culture, and Values

A summary view of Brahma would show that it is a top performing company, with a very strict ethical code, focused on winning and having a leadership position in the market.

Brahma defines itself as a "Total Beverage Company," whose mission is to "lead or reach leadership in segments of the beverage market which have synergies with our existing distribution network and access to smaller points of sale influenced by breadth of product line." As one can see, it is a mission clearly focused on increasing size and importance of its operations always going further to sell its products.

Brahma's values and culture are visibly oriented towards speed, effectiveness, and customer service, with employee initiative being highly rewarded and demanded: "A sense of urgency, non-complacency, and thirst for results are the cornerstones of Brahma's corporate culture. An informal work environment and a lack of physical barriers facilitate communication and agility. Remuneration policies encourage employees to act like owners. The ultimate goal of all employees is to satisfy our consumers."

It is no surprise that people policies are seen as crucial for Brahma's development and growth. Human capital is a strong priority for the Company, for example:

- Intensive training and professional education programs.
- Meritocracy system: performance is rewarded with variable bonuses.
- 100 percent of employees are eligible for stock ownership plans.
- A Trainee Program is an important source of young talent.

(mostly Europe and United States) distribution of certain products (Guaraná and select beer brands, possibly).

Rationalizing distribution channels will also be a priority for AmBev, as considerable overlap exists between Antarctica's and Brahma's structures. Brands will continue to be managed in an independent and competitive way, each one being left to manage its own resources. Just as Skol used to compete with Brahma brands, now AmBev's three main beer brands are expected to act in the same way.

Endnotes

1. The most important sources used here were two Exame (Brazilian business magazine) articles: "Saúde—14 July 1999—and "A Guerra das Cervejas"—12 January 2000.
2. Some basic financial data on Brahma and Antarctica are shown in Exhibit 1.
3. "Brazil's Breweries: The More Mergers the Merrier?" *Business Week International Edition,* 27 March 2000.
4. "Kaiser Dá Sugestão Para Ambev"; Agencia do Estado, 2 March 2000; "Kaiser Considera Fusão de Cervejarias Inaceitável"; O'Globo; 3 July 1999 and "Fusão das Gigantes da Cerveja Causará 8.000 demissões," CNNemPortugues, 20 September 1999.
5. Mercosul (in Spanish Mercosur) is the free trade agreement signed by Argentina, Brazil, Paraguay, and Uruguay. Chile and Bolivia are associated countries.
6. Refer to Exhibit 1 for detailed 1998 pro-forma financials (balance sheet and income statement) for AmBev as presented on 1 July 1999 when the merger was announced.
7. For details of the Pepsi-AmBev deal, refer to Exhibit 2—Press release published in September 1999.
8. 1 Brazilian real = 0.5256US$, 1US$ = 1.8990 Brazilian real (November 1, 2000).

The Strategic Alliance of Bang & Olufsen and Philips N.V.

Arthur Stonehill

Thunderbird, The American Graduate School of International Management

During September 1991, Anders Knutsen, President, and Povl U. Skifter, Chief Financial Officer, the top management team of Bang & Olufsen A/S (B&O), were reviewing the performance of Denmark's premier consumer electronics company and contemplating its future strategy. During the period 1978 to mid-1991, under the dynamic leadership of Vagn Andersen, B&O had survived with good future prospects, even though many observers had expected the company would die. Intense global competition had caused a host of other companies to drop out or merge, leaving a relatively few large multinational firms to dominate the worldwide consumer electronics industry in the 1990s.

During the past four years, two unexpected external shocks had a very negative impact on B&O's sales and financial results. The worldwide stock market crash of October 1987 and the Gulf War crisis of August 1990–March 1991 had each caused consumers to cut back on their purchases. This was especially true for the consumer electronics industry as a whole and for B&O's market niche in particular.

Mainly as a result of the Gulf War crisis, B&O had just reported a DKK74 million loss after taxes and minority interests for the fiscal year ending May 31, 1991. Although the operating loss was painful to report, it did not seriously endanger B&O's financial health. B&O's liquidity was adequate and its debt burden manageable due in part to an equity infusion from the Dutch concern, Philips Consumer Electronics (Philips), as part of a strategic alliance in 1990.

Unfortunately, more serious problems existed that could impact the long-run health of B&O. Most of the problems were structural and could be traced to B&O's small size relative to its large multinational competitors. Anders Knutsen and Povl Skifter could identify at least eight problems of major concern.

- **Niche Strategy.** Because of its small size, B&O did not compete across the board in consumer electronics, but rather followed a niche strategy. This emphasized outstanding design, systems solutions, and rapid response to changing customer tastes. Despite heavy emphasis on research and development, it was becoming increasingly difficult to get new products to market in a timely manner.
- **Economies of Scale.** Although B&O designed and produced some proprietary components for its own use, it lacked economies of scale relative to its competitors. B&O purchased the rest of its components from others but lacked the buying power to get the best volume discounts.
- **Dependence on Competition for Supply.** Most of the purchased components were bought from Philips, and to a lesser extent from other possible competitors. This left B&O potentially vulnerable to delivery schedules over which it had no control. If component shipments were delayed for even a few months, it would seriously impair B&O's strategy of timely introduction of a constant stream of new products. On the other hand, B&O's long-time purchasing experience with Philips had always been highly satisfactory.
- **Economies of Scope.** Following a niche strategy meant that B&O could not offer its sales outlets a complete line of products. Thus, the products of competitors were nearly always displayed side-by-side with B&O's products, competing for floor space and the sales force's attention.

- **Price.** Since B&O needed to cover heavy investments in research and development with relatively modest sales volume, its products were always high-priced compared to the competition .
- **Sensitivity to Business Cycles.** B&O's sales were extremely sensitive to business cycles. On the other hand, its cost structure was not flexible enough to adjust quickly to variable sales volume. The result was periodic losses with even modest swings in sales.
- **Foreign Exchange Exposure.** Since B&O produced nearly all of its products in Denmark but sold 77 percent outside of Denmark, it was potentially very sensitive to foreign exchange economic and transaction exposures. For example, when foreign currencies strengthened relative to the Danish krone, B&O's exported products could become more price competitive. This would be only partially offset by the higher foreign exchange costs of imported components. The reverse was also true. If foreign currencies weakened, B&O could face a negative foreign exchange effect. With respect to transaction exposure, B&O hedged most exposures with forward contracts.
- **Shareholder Strength.** Although B&O's B-shares were listed on the Copenhagen Stock Exchange, the controlling A-shares were held by foundations, representing descendants of the founders, and group of five Danish institutional investors.[1] An investment agreement among the A-shareholders ensured that no unfriendly takeover could occur. However, the family members, in particular, did not have outside funds that could be used to finance additional A- or B-share issues. B&O's modest financial results during the 1980s also precluded significant internal financing for growth and would make it difficult to attract new investors if a public equity issue should be attempted.

The Consumer Electronics Industry

The worldwide consumer electronics industry was characterized by rapid technological development and obsolescence, significant economies of scale and scope, a high degree of capital intensity, declining unit prices, and fierce global competition among multinational firms. The main audio/video product lines in the 1990s were derivatives of the old television, video recorder, phonograph, and radio industries. About 80 percent of B&O's sales were of products first introduced in the two preceding fiscal years. This was typical of the industry worldwide. Thus, the technological pace placed a heavy emphasis on timely research and development, which necessitated heavy capital investment costs.

The Competition

B&O's main competitors included six large Japanese and three large European companies. Notably absent were any significant U.S. competitors since they had been mostly eliminated by intense Japanese competition during the 1980s. The main Japanese competitors were Sony, Sanyo, Hitachi, Toshiba, Yamaha, and Matsushita.

The three main European competitors were survivors of an ongoing consolidation process in Europe. Phillips, Thomson CSF, and Nokia were the survivors of 16 European companies in the television sector of consumer electronics.[2] In addition, the two principal British competitors, GEC and Rank, had been taken over by Hitachi and Toshiba, respectively.

The nature of consumer electronics products lends itself to mass production and mass distribution methods. Gaining economics of scale and scope, while denying these to competitors, is a critical determinant of competitive advantage. However, a few niche companies, such as B&O, managed to survive despite lacking such economies.

Ownership and Control

B&O was founded in 1925 by Peter Bang and Svend Olufsen. It remained a privately owned company until 1977, when B-shares were sold to the public and B&O listed on the Copenhagen Stock Exchange. In the following years, public ownership was gradually increased with a participating preferred share issue sold to institutional investors in 1981, and a public B-share issue in 1983. In 1988 the family heirs and institutional investors signed an investment agreement which gave the right of first refusal to each other on A-share transfers. An important objective of both the heirs and institutional investors was to maintain control in order to ensure that B&O could continue to pursue its long-range strategy while remaining a Danish-owned company.

Finance

B&O's historical financial results prior to the strategic alliance were typified by extreme volatility both in operating results and share price development. The cumulative returns to stockholders were also quite modest. Exhibit 1 shows the key financial results for the period 1986–1991. Exhibit 2 shows the share price development during the period 1983–1991. Cumulatively, Exhibits 1 and 2 capture the financial situation before and after the strategic alliance (June 1990).

	1986/87	1987/88	1988/89	1989/90	1990/91
TURNOVER					
Turnover	1,902.1	1,955.7	2,098.8	2,279.5	2,180.1
Turnover outside Denmark	1,451.9	1,472.9	1,591.1	1,729.4	1,677.8
as % of total	76.3	75.3	75.8	75.9	77.0
EARNINGS					
Operating earnings	137.8	39.5	85.3	91.1	(47.1)
Earnings before extraordinary items	81.1	(19.5)	47.6	28.5	(115.5)
Earnings before tax	81.1	(19.5)	48.8	68.0	(135.5)
Earnings after tax & minority interests	53.1	(8.6)	32.3	55.3	(74.4)
TOTAL ASSETS					
Total assets	1,332.9	1,337.2	1,459.4	1,715.6	1,685.2
Shareholders' funds	478.3	477.9	505.3	603.5	656.5
Minority shareholders	—	—	—	—	183.4
Asset cover, %	35.9	35.7	34.6	35.2	49.8
Return on investment on 1/16/90, %	18.4	(4.1)	10.2	13.5	(22.5)
SHARE CAPITAL					
Share capital	100.0	124.0	124.0	124.0	124.0
Earnings after tax per 100 shares (kroner)*	43	(/)	26	45	(60)
Dividend, % of nominal value	10	0	10	10	0
Quoted share price at May 31	432	432	277	402	530
EMPLOYMENT					
Number of employees at year end	3,177	2,856	3,357	3,200	3,301

*Adjusted for share capital increases under market price. Asset cover includes shares held by minority shareholders.

Marketing

B&O produced a line of audio/video products, such as televisions, video recorders, and stereo systems, which could be easily connected into a coordinated household entertainment system. B&O products had a worldwide reputation for advanced design, ease of use, and systems integration. In addition to excellent technical qualities, B&O products were designed to appear as ultramodern furniture pieces.

B&O marketed its products worldwide through its own sales subsidiaries and independent distributors. In the United States it experimented with franchised outlets selling exclusively B&O products. About 77 percent of B&O's sales were outside of Denmark. Although it had a

Exhibit 2 | Share Price Development 1983–1991

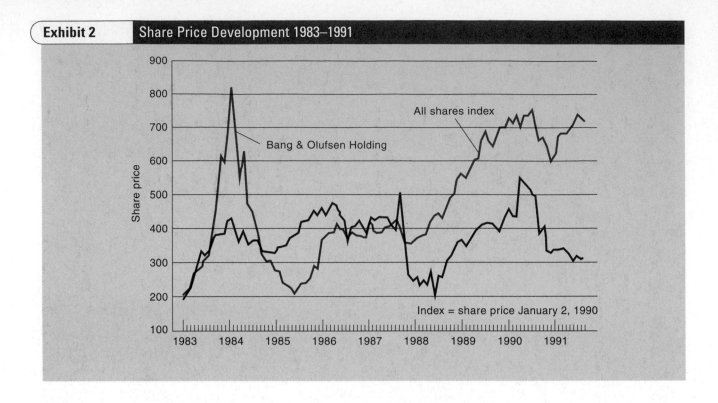

respectable share of the Danish audio/video market, it had a relatively small share of its other geographic markets.

B&O products appealed to those who placed a high value on lifestyle. Its customers were willing to pay a premium price for high-quality, user-friendly products featuring a futuristic design. B&O had a rather large global share of this narrow product market niche.

Production

Most of B&O's production was located in Jutland, Denmark, in the towns of Struer, Lemvig, and Skive. B&O employed about 3,300 persons, of which about 85 percent were located in Denmark. The rest were located in numerous sales and service subsidiaries abroad. About 10 percent of the Danish employees were engaged in product development.

B&O produced a significant share of the components it needed. Some of these were proprietary products based on B&O's own research and development. The rest were standard items but were self-produced in order to guarantee quality and assurance of delivery. The balance of components were sourced outside. Philips was a major European supplier. Some of the Japanese electronic firms were also suppliers.

B&O assembled all of its products at its manufacturing locations in Jutland. Although labor was relatively

costly in Denmark, its reliability and productivity were also high. The direct labor content of most of B&O's products is modest, but the research and development overhead was quite significant because of the relatively small production runs of each product.

Restructuring the Corporate Organization

In anticipation of future cooperative agreements, during 1989 B&O, in cooperation with its financial advisors, Gudme Raaschou Investment Bank, devised a creative reorganization plan which became effective on June 1, 1990. B&O A/S changed its name to B&O Holding A/S and continued as the listed company. A new company was established by B&O Holding A/S as a 100 percent-owned subsidiary. It was called B&O A/S and took over the audio/video activities, comprising about 85 percent of the group's activities. Exhibit 3 shows B&O's corporate organization before and after the change.

The new corporate organization had several advantages over the old one:

- B&O's fundamental image, product concepts, management situation, and strategies were preserved.
- B&O Holding remained controlled by the existing shareholders and had the same Board of Directors as B&O A/S.

Exhibit 3 | Bang & Olufsen's Corporate Reorganization of June 1, 1990

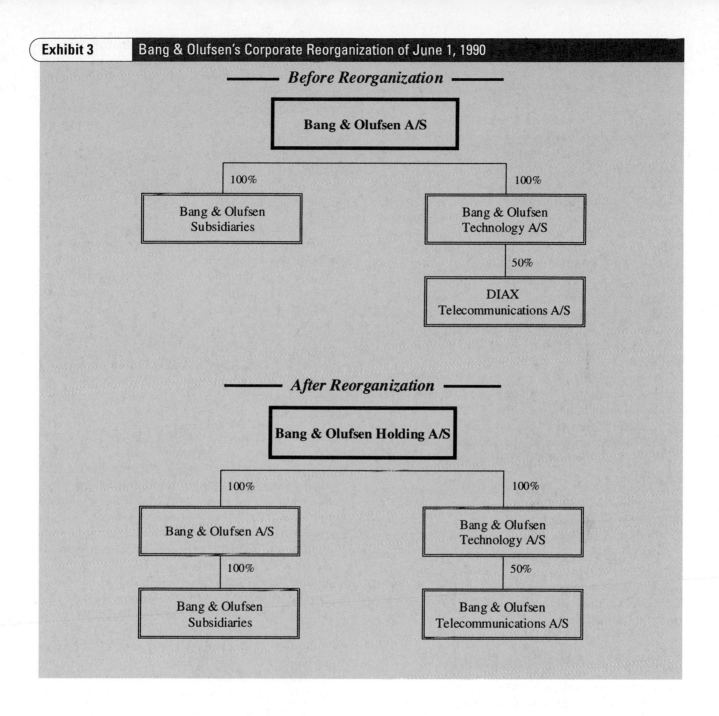

Before Reorganization

Bang & Olufsen A/S

100% — Bang & Olufsen Subsidiaries

100% — Bang & Olufsen Technology A/S

50% — DIAX Telecommunications A/S

After Reorganization

Bang & Olufsen Holding A/S

100% — Bang & Olufsen A/S

100% — Bang & Olufsen Subsidiaries

100% — Bang & Olufsen Technology A/S

50% — Bang & Olufsen Telecommunications A/S

- In the future, new subsidiaries of B&O Holding could be easily established to exploit new technologies or products unrelated to the existing product line. These new subsidiaries could then form alliances or joint ventures with whatever companies were appropriate for their activities.
- The terms of equity participation in the new subsidiaries could vary with market conditions and their synergistic value to specific partners without reference to the share price of B&O Holding or its other subsidiaries.
- Potential partners could buy into just those activities that were valuable to them and not to be forced to invest in less suitable activities.
- In the future, B&O Holding could sell off subsidiaries that it no longer wanted, perhaps to its partner, or to another company acceptable to its partner.

Joint Venture with L. M. Ericsson

During the 1980s, B&O had received numerous feelers from companies attracted by its upscale market niche. Some were interested in acquiring B&O. Some wanted to conduct cooperative activities, while others proposed joint ventures or strategic alliances. Among the most interesting of these possibilities were proposals from L. M. Ericsson (Sweden) and Philips.

During 1989 a joint venture to develop and market products in the telecommunications industry was proposed by L. M. Ericsson, one of the leading multinational firms in the world in the industry. L. M. Ericsson was particularly interested in a small digital telephone concentrator which had been developed by B&O. This product was complementary to the telephone exchanges for which L. M. Ericsson was famous. Although the B&O digital telephone concentrator was not fully developed, it represented potential future competition for L. M. Ericsson, particularly if B&O could find another strong partner.

The proposed joint venture was attractive to B&O because it would have had difficulties financing further development and improvement of the digital telephone concentrator. Moreover, this product would be sold through different marketing channels and to a different type of customer than B&O's existing audio/video product line.

The proposal was that B&O provide the technology and product, while L. M. Ericsson would provide access to its worldwide marketing network. L. M. Ericsson would invest DKK 50 million in return for 50 percent of a newly formed corporate joint venture, Diax. Agreement was reached and Diax began operations January 1, 1990. B&O's interest was placed under B&O Technology A/S, a subsidiary of B&O Holding, as part of the June 1990 reorganization.

Strategic Alliance with Philips

As a major supplier of components to B&O for nearly 60 years, Philips was very comfortable with B&O and its management. Several times Philips had approached B&O about acquiring an equity interest or cooperating in various activities. Both companies were ripe for something positive to happen when negotiations were opened in 1989.

Philips was eager to join forces with B&O in the upscale consumer electronics market. Philips had a product designed for this market but it did not possess the high-quality image of B&O's products. Philips was also worried that if financial pressure continued, B&O might choose a competitor as a partner. A Japanese competitor would be very damaging. Philips had always been supported politically by B&O in its efforts to gain national and EU support to make the remaining European companies more competitive vis-à-vis Japanese competitors. Philips was also interested in cementing relations with B&O as a major customer for Philips' components.

B&O was interested in Philips because a closer relationship could partially solve some of B&O's long-run problems. In particular, Philips could give B&O the following advantages:

- More rapid access to new technology,
- Assistance in converting Philips' technology into B&O product applications,
- Assurance of component supplies at large volume discounts from Philips itself, as well as from its large network of suppliers,
- Equity financing from Philips.

During the course of 1989–1990 a strategic alliance between B&O and Philips was agreed upon. It went into effect on June 1, 1990, simultaneously with B&O's corporate reorganization. The main features of the alliance were:

- Philips would provide B&O with instant access to its new technology, but not vice-versa.
- Philips would give B&O access to its supplier network to take advantage of the discounts and delivery terms that Philips enjoyed. However, B&O was not forced to buy from Philips or its suppliers.
- Philips invested DKK342 million in an equity increase for B&O A/S in return for a 25 percent ownership of the expanded company.
- Philips agreed not to be represented on the Board of Directors of B&O A/S or B&O Holding but was given the right to veto the choice for President of B&O A/S. However, it could not choose the President.
- Philips was given the right to buy another 25 percent of the equity in B&O A/S for net book value if the B&O Holding A-shares should in the future be sold to investors outside of the present group. This protected Philips from having a competitor overseeing its activities with B&O A/S.
- B&O was given the right to buy back its shares from Philips at net book value if the alliance did not live up to expectations.

When B&O's strategic alliance with Philips was announced to the public on May 3, 1990, the reaction was instantaneously favorable both in the press and in the stock market. B&O's share price jumped by 35 percent during the next two days and remained at the new level until the Gulf War crisis depressed the share price

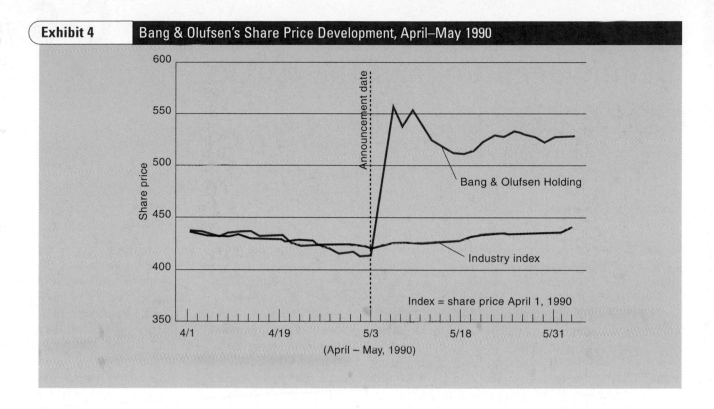

once again. Exhibit 4 shows B&O's share price development before and after the announcement.

The Future

As Anders Knutsen and Povl Skifter contemplated the future from the perspective of September 1991, they could look back with satisfaction on the steps taken during the last two years to solve some of B&O's long-run problems. In particular:

- The equity base was considerably strengthened by the Philips investment.
- B&O had gained more rapid access to new technology.
- B&O had improved its access to components at a better price.
- B&O's organization had been rationalized to encourage more joint ventures of the type illustrated by DIAX with L. M. Ericsson and the Philips alliance.

On the other hand, the DKK74 million loss, which had just been announced, reminded them that certain long-run problems remained. Indeed, even in the short run, B&O had not yet taken full advantage of the possibilities opened up by the Philips alliance and the new organization structure.

At the time of the strategic alliance, Franz Timmer, Managing Director of Philips Electronics (subsidiary of Philips N.V.), had made several suggestions to B&O's management about the future strategic path for B&O A/S. They were:

- Focus on design and systems integration, where B&O A/S had a comparative advantage.
- Outsource more of B&O A/S's component production, where it did not have economies of scale.

Endnotes

1. In Denmark and a number of other European countries, it is common to have more than one class of voting shares. The Danish tradition is to maintain control of a company through continued possession of A-shares, each of which has 10 votes. B-shares are sold to the public. They have one vote each.
2. Although Grudig was controlled by Philips, which owned 32 percent of its shares, it would be considered a fourth European competitor because it competed as if it were an independent company.

Beijing Jeep Co. and the WTO

Michael N. Young
University of Western Ontario

Justin Tan
Creighton University

In May of 2000, the Beijing Jeep Corporation, Ltd. (BJC) faced one of the most challenging periods of its relatively short, tumultuous history. Founded in China in 1984, BJC was a pioneer in the Chinese automotive industry. It was one of the first joint ventures between an American company and a Chinese enterprise. At its initial founding, it was hailed with great fanfare by the American media as a potential savior of the American automobile industry, which at that time was being battered by Japanese competition. This was to be a "beachhead" by which the Americans could access the Asian market and beat the Japanese on their own turf. Early in its operations, BJC was given preferential treatment on tariffs and foreign exchange. The company had also spent many years cultivating relationships with senior government officials — what the Chinese refer to as guanxi — to help it achieve its objectives. And since over 40 percent of its product's content was produced in China, BJC had operated as a local manufacturer under heavy protection from imports for all of its short life.[1]

All of this appeared to be on the brink of changing. Trade negotiators for the United States and the People's Republic of China had reached an agreement the previous November after 13 years of on-again-off-again negotiations, where they announced the agreement of terms for China's entry into the World Trade Organization

(WTO). Although the Chinese authorities still needed the approval of the major European countries of the WTO, the blessing of the US negotiating team was seen as the major hurdle. Now that the hurdle had been cleared, it meant that China's entry was probably just a matter of time. The terms of the agreement called for a steep reduction in tariffs for imported automobiles from nearly 100 percent to 25 percent by 2006.[2] This would lower the entry barriers to the Chinese automotive industry in which BJC already competed. However, the news was not all bad for BJC, for it meant BJC would pay lower tariffs on components of its Jeep Cherokees that were imported from the United States. Still, these lower tariffs were not enough to offset the potential flood of imported vehicles that could pose serious competition for BJC. As one analyst for the Chinese auto industry stated: "The entire auto industry is under attack from the WTO." This was in addition to the loss of market share and falling profits of the previous three years.

To make matters worse, the more formidable of BJC's two partners, DaimlerChrysler, was beset with its own problems and was in no position to assist BJC. DaimlerChrysler was the world's third largest car company. It had come into existence a little over a year earlier when Daimler Benz of Germany merged with the Chrysler Corporation of the United States. This international merger had created a whole host of unforeseen integration problems, and the company was preoccupied with sorting out its own affairs.[3] Thus, on the threshold of the 21st century, BJC was beset with unprecedented challenges that appeared to threaten its very survival.

Beijing Jeep's History

A British writer declared more than 150 years ago: "If only we could persuade every person in China to lengthen his shirt tails by a foot, we could keep the mills of Lancashire working round the clock."[4] In the early

1980s, American Motors Corporation (AMC), along with other foreign enterprises, wished to tap into the vast Chinese Market. Todd Clare, AMC's vice-president (VP) for international operations who directed the China operation, stated that the volume of cars sold in the United States was stable at about 15 million a year. The Western European market was also saturated. Thus, in the United States or Western Europe, one could only sell more cars by stealing another firm's market share — a "zero sum" game. Latin America's economies were showing little promise, and Africa's economies were worse. Yet China's market, with over a billion people, had been largely unexplored. The potential seemed enormous, for China covered about 20 percent of the world's land mass and was home to a quarter of the world's population.[5]

Thus, AMC initiated the pioneering Sino-American joint venture with Beijing Automotive Works (BAW) shortly after China opened its doors in 1978 under the economic reforms of the late paramount leader Deng Xiaoping. At this time, the PRC was attracting worldwide attention because of its large potential market, low labor cost, newly introduced economic reforms, and its strategic location. AMC was not alone; Mercedes-Benz, Fiat, British Leyland, Volkswagen and Ford, following the lead of Japanese companies such as Toyota, Nissan, Mitsubishi and Daihatsu, soon sent emissaries to evaluate business prospects in China. In May 1983, after four years of negotiations, AMC and the Beijing Automotive Works agreed to form a joint venture, the Beijing Jeep Corporation Limited (BJC), to produce jeeps in the Chinese capital city of Beijing.

The deal was a landmark. It was the largest manufacturing agreement up to that time between a foreign corporation and a Chinese enterprise. AMC would own a 31.35 percent stake by contributing US$8 million in cash and another US$8 million in technology. The Chinese agreed to put up the equivalent of US$35 million in cash and assets for 68.65 percent of the new company. The board of directors of BJC would consist of seven Chinese members and four Americans. For the first three years, an American would hold the title of president and CEO, and then the job would alternate between the Chinese and Americans. The American media seemed pleased with the deal.[6] China was still seen as a land of limitless potential and serious obstacles to profitability were often overlooked. Although AMC had reported major losses for the three years before the deal, investors brushed that aside; AMC's stock increased 40 percent within two weeks of the announcement. At a press conference, Joseph E. Cappy, AMC's executive vice-president, said AMC would reinvest profits to increase AMC's equity share to 49 percent. "For American Motors, [Beijing Jeep]

has meant not only an entry into the Chinese market, but the establishment of a strategic manufacturing base in the Pacific rim of Asia," Cappy said.[7]

The euphoria of both sides soon gave way to reality as the two sides attempted to get down to the business of producing automobiles. First of all, bringing the two sides together was not an easy task, because of cultural differences. In addition, the two sides did not share the same goals. The Chinese hoped to assimilate the sophisticated technology and eventually rank among the world's most advanced auto producers, while the Americans hoped to establish a base in Asia that would enable them to manufacture cars at low cost and compete in this growing region.[8] Also, the Americans learned that although the deal was signed, the "real" negotiations had just begun. Chinese business people were much more accustomed to doing business based on personal relationships and the charisma of business leaders and tended to view contracts nonchalantly. The Americans on the other hand viewed contracts as binding, and put much less emphasis on the aspects of personality in business.[9]

After the venture started in January 1984, the two sides disagreed over the product to be produced. According to the initial agreement, BJC was to continue manufacturing the old BJ series (based on a Soviet version of the American Second World War Jeep) while developing a new generation of Jeeps. The Americans wanted the new product to be similar to AMC's existing line of jeeps, but the Chinese wanted a military jeep for the army, historically BAW's most important customer. The army wanted a four-door vehicle with a removable top so that soldiers could open fire from inside the car and quickly hop in and out. Such a vehicle could not be designed based on AMC's existing jeeps, and developing the vehicle would cost at least US$700 million. Neither China nor AMC had that kind of money. So AMC officials tried to convince the Chinese to assemble AMC's newest product — the Jeep Cherokee — from parts kits imported from the United States. The Chinese partners reluctantly agreed. Thus, AMC switched its objective from "making money selling cars" to "making money-selling kits." But a new problem emerged: Where would BJC obtain the foreign exchange for the kits? Whenever large-scale foreign exchange was conducted, a special license was required. BJC had not formally cleared this with the Chinese government.

Thus, later in 1985, AMC had hundreds of Cherokee kits in the United States ready to ship to China, but BJC had trouble getting a government import license and no hard currency to pay for the kits. Moreover, housing costs for AMC's staff rose 38 percent when luxury hotels increased their rates. BJC was virtually broke, and the plant was shut down for two months in early 1986.[10] Don St. Pierre, then BJC's American president, appealed to the top Chinese leaders. It took special intervention by then-Premier Zhao Ziyang. Large loans, new capital funds and foreign exchange were provided under a special, confidential agreement. BJC was also given preferential import tariffs and was given special permission to convert AMC's share of dividends into US dollars and send them back to the United States. In return, the company was expected to spread good news worldwide about China. Chinese officials held BJC up as a "model joint venture." That is, the officials held up BJC to lure other companies to invest much-needed foreign exchange and transfer-advanced technology. All along, the foreign firms were not aware of the special deals.[11]

Given the resolution of these problems, the company was back in business. In early 1986, the venture had about 4,300 employees, including 800 administrators, engineers and technicians. Its main activities were producing chassis frames and body panels, welding, painting and final assembly. Labor costs were low: wages at the BJC plant were US$.60 cents an hour, compared to labor costs (including fringe benefits) of about US$22 an hour in the United States and US$12 an hour in Japan. In 1985, United States Vice-President George Bush visited the factory and gave his blessing.

From AMC to Chrysler

Although things were running smoothly for BJC, AMC continued to lose money and market share. It was becoming apparent that the situation could not continue, and in 1987, Chrysler acquired AMC. Chrysler's CEO, Lee Iacocca, made it clear that AMC's Jeep was one of the main reasons for the acquisition. "For Chrysler, the attractions are Jeep, the best-known automotive brand name in the world. . . ," Iacocca said. The Jeep division gave Chrysler an instant entry into the booming 4WD truck market.[12] Chrysler bought the Jeep name and gained overseas operations in Egypt, Venezuela and China. Chrysler announced that it had no intention of altering operations at BJC. Nonetheless, the Chinese were concerned, since they had little knowledge of Chrysler, and they were also unaccustomed to the takeovers and other aspects of American-style capitalism.

To alleviate China's potential fears, Chrysler hinted that because it had more financial resources and more people at its disposal, it may be willing to invest more. In 1988, in accordance with the initial joint venture, Don St. Pierre handed the presidency of BJC over to Chen Xulin, his hand-picked successor, and Chrysler continued to hold out the prospect of big plans for

China. In mid-1987, Chrysler's vice president Bob Lutz signed a deal under which Chrysler sold new engine technology to China. Chinese officials were discussing the possibility of manufacturing passenger cars in Changchun, and Chrysler hoped to land that contract. In addition, Chrysler began discussing the possibility of a major expansion of BJC. There was even talk of manufacturing trucks. At one point the Chinese suggested that Chrysler invest as much as US$80 to US$100 million for the expansion. Yet Chrysler officials moved cautiously, avoiding any commitment of new money. The First Automotive Corp. of Changchun gave the contract for passenger cars to Audi, a subsidiary of Volkswagen.

Still, Chrysler continued to be a good corporate citizen. After the Tiananmen Square incident on June 4, 1989, Chrysler was among the first Western companies to send executives and their families back to Beijing, after they had been relocated temporarily to Chrysler's Tokyo office.[13] Thereafter, Chrysler continued to show a commitment to the joint venture, and in the process, cultivated much-valued good relations with the Chinese authorities. In October 1988, then Chairman and CEO Lee Iacocca visited China. He inspected BJC and said, "I really have a feeling that they are creating history." In 1990, BJC began producing engines at a new engine facility. And from 1990 to 1992, annual Cherokee production went from 7,100 units to 20,808 units while production of the BJ-2000 series went from 34,300 to 37,070 units. Exhibit 1 shows production volumes of BJC since its inception. In 1993, an enhanced version of the BJ-2020 was launched. The Chinese president, Jiang Zemin, who had trained in China and the Soviet Union as an automotive and electrical engineer and had an in-depth knowledge of the automobile industry, inspected the company in 1995. In 1996 the venture acquired ISO-9000 certification. Exhibit 2 displays a time line of major events in BJC's history.

The Daimler Benz-Chrysler Merger

In November 1998, Daimler Benz merged with Chrysler Corporation to form the world's third largest car company, DaimlerChrysler. The company had since been beset with merger problems, such as the exodus of many top executives from Chrysler.[14] Professor E. Han Kim, an expert on mergers and acquisitions, believed that the merger was a good decision, but that the culture clash first needed to be addressed. He stated:

> If they can somehow overcome this huge difference in corporate culture, which is the problem that they are really facing, they can achieve their full potential of synergistic gains. It's not only the savings, but greater revenue, increased perception in terms of quality, and growth in the

Case 6 / Beijing Jeep Co. and the WTO

Exhibit 1   Production History—Production Volume

Calendar Year	Cherokee	BJ-series	Total
1984	n/a	16,400	16,400
1985	300	20,600	20,900
1986	1,500	22,800	24,300
1987	3,500	23,700	27,200
1988	5,000	26,700	31,700
1989	6,600	32,500	39,100
1990	7,100	34,300	41,400
1991	15,797	35,000	50,797
1992	20,808	37,070	57,878
1993	10,400	33,300	43,700
1994	15,500	46,000	61,500
1995	26,127	55,024	80,151
1996	26,051	45,282	71,333
1997	19,700	31,883	51,583
1998 (thru Nov.)	8,236	19,552	27,788

SOURCE: DaimlerChrylser fact sheet.

product line. I think that could be perhaps as big, or bigger, than the savings in cost.

Kim believed that the company's United States operations had lost good executives wary of a German takeover.

I think that was in part due to this culture clash between the German style of management and the American style of management, or the dominance of the Germans. When we look at these companies, really the biggest asset they have is people, and if you lose the people, that's it.[15]

Investors were not optimistic about the merger prospects. In January 1999, DaimlerChrysler's average closing share price was around US$108; by late May 2000, the share was trading at around US$55.[16] This represents a loss of nearly 50 percent of value in a year and four months. Thus, the Chinese feared that DaimlerChrysler, beset with merger problems, might not focus much attention on BJC, which played a relatively small role in its corporate structure. DaimlerChrysler owned 42.4 percent of BJC; the other 57.6 percent was owned by Beijing Automobile Works. In 1998, Beijing Jeep's total revenues were approximately equivalent to US$399 million, of which DaimlerChrylser's share was about US$169 million. This represented about one-tenth of 1 percent of DaimlerChrysler's US$131,782 billion total sales.

The Political and Economic Climate in China

In 2000, China's political economy was still undergoing a major transformation, begun in 1978 by Deng Xiaoping. China planned to achieve "socialist modernization" through economic reform and opening up to the outside world. This included the use of financial markets and the establishment of joint ventures. Thus, China was the first communist nation in the world to have stock exchanges and the only socialist country to initiate building a "market style modern enterprise system"through a corporatization and shareholding framework.[17] As a result of economic reforms and the introduction of market mechanisms, provincial and local administrators and managers had more decision-making autonomy and new profit-sharing incentives had been put into place. Even though economic activities were still subject to a substantial amount of state intervention, the Chinese economy moved a step closer to a market system.

Exhibit 2	Time Line—DaimlerChrysler in China

- May 5, 1983 Joint venture agreement is signed between Beijing Automobile Works and AMC, including a total original investment of US$152 million.
- January 1984 The Beijing Jeep Corporation (BJC) begins business operations.
- September 1985 Jeep Cherokee production begins at BJC, with 4,300 local employees.
- October 1985 vice-president George Bush visits BJC.
- 1987 Chrysler Corporation purchases American Motors and continues joint venture agreement with Beijing Automobile Works, the first joint venture between a Chinese and an American automotive company.
- October 1990 An engine plant is added to Beijing Jeep facilities.
- June 1993 Enhanced version of BJ-2020, a locally-produced utility vehicle is launched.
- April 1994 Chrysler's Beijing business office opens.
- November 1995 Chinese President Jiang Zemin inspects BJC.
- June 1996 BJC passes the ISO9000 certification.
- July 1997 Chrysler announces it will close the Beijing business office.
- Nov. 1998 Chrysler merges with Daimler-Benz to form DaimlerChrysler.

SOURCE: DaimlerChrysler fact sheet.

It was still not clear what the end result of the process of reforms would be. There was political conflict between the hard-liners and the reformers during the transition of the power structure, and there was likely to be political and social unrest during this process. While industrial enterprises had acquired more autonomy, the central government still had substantial power and influence over business activities, due to its control of the majority of raw materials and the distribution system. The government was also the largest customer and product distributor.[18]

From 1992 to 1996, China attracted more total foreign investment than any other developing country. During the latter part of the 1990s, however, foreign investors began to doubt China's commitment to market reforms. In the first 10 months of 1999, contracted foreign investment in the mainland was about US$40 billion, down 35 percent on the corresponding period the previous year and the first such fall since Beijing started its open-door policy in 1979. Although this was partly due to over-capacity in certain industries, it was also caused by slowing economic growth, inadequate laws and regulatory protection, and lack of access to markets. These factors were causing foreign firms to reconsider investing in China.[19]

One representative of a United States telecommunications was quoted as saying:

Foreign companies made major commitments to China over the past four years on assumptions of continuing lib-

eralization of the investment climate and a market of 1.2 billion consumers. Now there is a perception that the process of liberalization, of reducing bureaucratic procedures, taxes, and obstacles to doing business has come to a halt. There is a question about China's real commitment to a market economy.

Some believed that there was a policy battle within the Chinese leadership between those who wanted a market economy and those who wanted a South Korean-style system dominated by big state corporations.[20]

China's Entry into the World Trade Organization

On November 15, 1999, US trade representative Charlene Barshefsky and China Trade Minister Shi Guangsheng reached an agreement on terms for China's entry into the WTO. The agreement had followed 13 years of stalemated negotiations that seemed to follow the general ebbs and flows of Sino-US relations. For example, the negotiations were postponed by the bombing of the Chinese Embassy in Belgrade, Yugoslavia, by American military pilots in May of 1999.

In order to join the WTO, China had to agree to liberalize its financial markets. It also had to allow for more foreign investment in firms engaged in electronic commerce, entertainment, travel and tourism and other industries. In addition, trade tariffs had to be reduced on a wide range of agricultural and manufactured products

— including a reduction in the tariffs on imported automobiles from 100 percent to 25 percent by 2006.[21] Barshefsky stated: "This deal is crucial to China's economic reform because investment dollars will flow to other countries if China remains mired in rules and inefficiencies." Indeed, it was difficult to overestimate the importance of WTO entry to China's economic landscape. Political analyst Wang Shan called entry into the WTO the most important political event in China since Deng Xiaoping launched his ground-breaking reforms. The terms of the deal would reverberate deep inside Chinese society. If handled well, the WTO's terms would help China become more competitive, more modern, even more pluralistic. If managed poorly, the country could face an explosion of rural poverty and the disintegration of central control, warned an economist in Beijing.[22]

The Chinese Automotive Industry

In 2000, most cars in China were publicly owned or used as taxis, and were either imported or joint venture models. The proportion of old vehicles still in daily use was much higher than in Western countries, and the government wished to see these older vehicles replaced to improve safety and energy efficiency. There were about 1.7 million township enterprises and 150,000 urban collectively owned enterprises that were more autonomous than state-owned enterprises. As these enterprises developed, it was anticipated that more vehicles would be needed. Owners of private cars were mainly business people, especially private entrepreneurs.

A survey of the residents of Beijing, Shanghai, Guangzhou, Chengdu, Nanjing and nine other major cities conducted in early 2000, indicated that private purchases of sedans would reach 910,000 that year. This represented an increase of around 390 percent over the same period in 1999, in which 2.6 percent of households surveyed indicated they had purchased vehicles. These optimistic projections were gaining the attention of car makers from all around the world. According to the same survey, 7.8 percent of households in those cities already owned vehicles, with 4.2 percent owning sedans and 0.4 percent owning Jeeps.[23] Thus, it appeared that the industry was poised for dramatic growth.

The situation was particularly attractive for Jeep, as China was perhaps the world's biggest potential market for four-wheel drive (4WD) vehicles because of its rugged, rural landscape and heavy emphasis on agriculture. Although there had been a road-building campaign and the government was committed to developing the highways system in its western, more rural areas, the need for Jeeps would likely continue to be great. Compared to the United States, China had less-rigid emission control and safety standards, but it was in the process of upgrading the standards. As in other parts of the world, the Chinese government had tried to regulate car sales by raising and lowering taxes and third-party motor vehicle insurance had been mandatory since February 15, 1989.

Major Domestic Competitors

In 2000, the Chinese automotive industry could be described as fragmented. There were around 136 domestic producers. Yet, some 40 percent of the capacity lay idle, and about half of all vehicle manufacturers were losing money.[24] But there was likely to be major consolidation in the next few years as import tariffs were reduced, and the remaining firms attempted to improve efficiency through increasing economies of scale.[25] In July of 1999, the State Council of the Central Government announced intentions to accelerate the restructuring of the auto sector. The State Machine-Building Industry Bureau would be in charge of the restructuring, with the goal of merging China's top 13 largest auto manufacturers into three conglomerates. The State Council hoped to transform the automobile sector into a "pillar industry." The three conglomerates would be based on Changchun's First Automobile Works (Group) Corp. (FAW), Shanghai Automobile Manufacturing Corp., and Wuhan's Dongfeng Motor Co. Together, the top 13 domestic automakers produced roughly 1.4 million units, or 92 percent of national output in 1998.[26]

According to a source at the United States-China Business Council, the new restructuring policy was based on supporting strong companies and closing struggling ones. The policy aimed initially to close small township and village enterprises that received funding from local governments and produced substandard vehicles and parts. Provincial authorities would work to identify enterprises operating under poor manufacturing conditions and violating intellectual property rights. By late 1999, the list of enterprises slated for closure was announced. Small joint venture players that had already developed a niche in the China market by producing mini-buses and automobiles, such as Nanjing-based Yuejin Auto (Group) Co. and Jiangxi based Jiangxi Jiangling Auto Co., were unlikely to be affected by the new policy.[27]

Now that China's entry into the WTO seemed likely, government planners realized that China's domestic industry was ill-prepared for global competition. They hoped that the new plan would reinvigorate ongoing efforts to eliminate duplicate investment and spur consolidation. The new plan coincided with the promulgation of China's 10th "Five-Year Plan" and the announcement of a new "Guiding Catalogue for Foreign Investment" which was to be released in year 2000. Both of these documents would reportedly be critical in setting the future course of the industry.[28] However, local governments viewed auto manufacturing as an important source of tax revenue and employment. This hindered central government efforts to consolidate the scattered and inefficient industry.

Foreign Joint Ventures

Chinese consumers were demanding better cars, and this was putting increasing pressure on domestic producers, while opening doors for high-quality foreign companies. "I see a watershed point in the auto industry here," said Michael Dunne, the managing director of Automotive Resources Asia LTD, a Beijing- and Bangkok-based consulting firm.[29] Volkswagen, Audi, Honda, Daimler-Chrysler, Citroen, Daihatsu, Suzuki and Subaru all had joint venture manufacturing plants in China.[30] Japanese auto makers had been selling in China since the early 1970s. Toyota decided that China was beginning to prosper and begun to sell trucks, buses, luxury cars, taxis, and motorcycles. Soon after, Nissan, Daihatsu, Suzuki, Mitsubishi and others followed. Between 1983 and 1984, Japan's auto exports to China increased sevenfold, from 10,800 to 85,000, and China became Japan's second largest foreign car market after the United States. The massive imports of vehicles resulted in rapid depletion of foreign currency reserves and resulted in cancellations of further import licenses. The Chinese government had established some incentives, including taxes, bank loans and foreign exchange, to encourage foreign companies operating in China to reinvest earnings or export their product. For example, a new tax law allowed a joint venture to avoid import tariffs when 40 percent of the value of a vehicle was produced in China.

General Motors

General Motors used the marketing and sales strategy from its Saturn division in the United States to produce and sell new Buicks in China that were manufactured by a 50/50 joint venture with Shanghai Automotive Industry Co. in Shanghai. The strategy seemed to be working; the new cars were selling well and there was a long waiting list despite a price that was the equivalent of about US$45,000 at the official exchange rate.[31] General Motors' Philip Murtaugh, executive vice president for Shanghai GM, was fiercely proud of his operation and the respect it showed for the Chinese people. "The growth forecast for the Asian auto market was 15 to

20 percent a year. Some economists believe somewhere around 2025, China's auto industry will be the same size as North America's. [GM Chairman Jack Smith] is intent on the company participating in that growth," Murtaugh said. GM's investment in the project was around US$1.5 billion, and the joint venture was capable of producing about 100,000 units per year. Shanghai GM was planning to add a second vehicle, a minivan in 2000, and a small car later if approved by the government.[32]

This was not the first time that GM had sold cars to the Chinese; the last emperor owned a Buick and so did Communist leader Chou En-Lai. And Buick had sold 10,000 to 15,000 cars per year in China in the 1920s and 1930s, said Jay Hunt, Shanghai GM director of marketing and distribution.[33] GM demanded that Chinese suppliers match United States quality standards. Forty percent of the vehicle's value was produced by Chinese labor and parts, a requirement for reducing duties on imported parts. GM expected to hit 60 percent local content in the second year and 80 percent in the third or fourth year.[34]

At the Shanghai plant, 1,800 workers were needed to staff one eight-hour shift. The workers received training and wages well above the local norm, earning an average US$350 per month, plus benefits worth the same amount, including a housing subsidy, health care, company-provided breakfasts and lunches, shuttle service to and from work and incentive bonuses. The plant employed a few more employees than it normally would in the United States.

The 200,000 square-metre integrated plant was built in 1997 and 1998 on a 500,000 square-metre site. It was laid out for efficiency and was similar to GM plants in Argentina, Thailand and Poland. The plant contained areas for stamping, storage, a body shop, engine, transmission, trim, chassis, general assembly lines, a paint booth and a small sales showroom. The Shanghai operation built its own automatic transmissions and 2.98 litre V6 engines on site (the central government levied heavy taxes on cars with engines 3.0 litres or larger and did not allow for low-level bureaucrats to own them).

Supplier costs were higher than they probably should have been, partly because many state-run companies and joint ventures had not traditionally been concerned with costs or profits. "The biggest challenge the industry faces here in China is cost and quality competitiveness," said vice-president Murtaugh. "We are showing we can compete on quality. But our costs are still 25 percent to 30 percent above North America." General Motors had also teamed up with another partner, Jinbei Automotive GM, to make a version of its Chevrolet Blazer in the northeastern city of Shenyang. This would compete directly with BJC. Yet, at 300,000 yuan, the cars cost about 10 percent more than BJC's Cherokee.[35]

Volkswagen

Volkswagen (VW) dominated the China auto market with about 55 percent of sales. The company was bringing on production of five modern vehicles over the next three years, including the luxury Audi A6 and the VW Passat and Jetta. The No. 1 German automaker was doubling its investment in China to six billion marks ($3.28 billion). Still, Volkswagen was not resting on its laurels. "China is becoming much more competitive, with demand more like it is in Western markets," said Stefan Jacoby, the VW vice-president in charge of the Asian-Pacific region.[36]

Much of Volkswagen's success had been in supplying China's demand for taxicabs, as anyone who visited the mainland in 2000 could determine; most of the taxis in use in the urban areas were Santanas or Jettas. Shanghai Volkswagen catered to this large market segment. For example, in June 1999, Shanghai Volkswagen began a new policy to expand its sales to the taxi service sector. Under the new policy, any local taxi company that bought 100 units of Santana cars or 50 units of Santana 2000GLS would get an extra unit of the same model. Also, the sales corporation offered a 15,000 kilometre (km), third-class, free maintenance warranty in addition to the 7,500 km, first-class, free maintenance for any Santana 2000GLS used as a taxi. Approximately 40 percent of Santanas made in 1998 went to the taxi sector. VW Santanas accounted for over 80 percent of the taxis in Shanghai. Volkswagen did not offer a sports utility vehicle, and thus did not compete directly with the Cherokee or BJ models.

Honda

Honda was Japan's third-largest automaker. It manufactured its Accord in China at a joint venture with Denway Investment in Guangzhou. In December of 1999, the joint venture, named Guangzhou Honda, announced it would add models, raise output and sales of passenger cars and increase the ratio of locally purchased parts to 80 percent within three years. A spokesman for the company said it wanted to boost local sales amid rising competition as rival automakers expanded vehicle production.

From March 2000, Guangzhou Honda began producing 2000 cubic centimeters (cc) Accords in addition to the 2300cc model it was already producing.[37] Honda said it hoped to increase government sales with the addition of the new model as Chinese officials can use only cars with low exhaust emission levels. Honda said it was also aiming to boost Accord sales to individual buyers as

the model was favored by China's growing business community. The company said the ratio of locally sourced parts used at Honda Guangzhou reached 45 percent in November and that the next target was 60 percent, ahead of an eventual goal of 80 percent. "We adhere to the concept of producing cars where the demand is and meeting customer needs directly," a Honda official said.

Higher local-content ratios allowed the carmaker to avoid taxes on imported parts, the company said. Honda was producing 10,000 sedans at the joint-venture plant, which it acquired from Peugeot Citroen in 1997. The factory was scheduled to reach full capacity of 30,000 within two years, Guangzhou Honda president Koji Kadowaki said in June 1999. At that time Honda also announced a boost in annual output to 50,000, as low prices and a crackdown on smuggling sparked demand for its China-made Accords.[38]

Toyota

Although Toyota had been reluctant to enter the Chinese market, it hoped to control 10 percent of the Chinese market within five to 10 years of starting local production, according to Koji Hasegawa, managing director in charge of Asian operations. "The China market is still very young, but the potential is huge," said Hasegawa. "If we can offer an attractive vehicle to these customers, we can compete with Volkswagen."[39]

In 1998, Toyota shipped 27,000 cars and trucks to China, giving it a 1.7 percent market share. In November of 1999, Toyota was still awaiting approval from the Chinese government to start local production, most likely with local partner Tianjin Automotive Works. It was thought they would produce compact cars similar to the popular Vitz model in Japan. In preparation, Toyota had built up a network of more than 60 service stations, which it hoped to turn into dealerships. Hasegawa said Toyota planned eventually to offer three vehicles to the Chinese market: a compact car, a van and a pick-up truck.[40] Exhibit 3 shows the market share of the major competitors in the Chinese Automotive Industry.

Beijing Jeep's Operations

Jeep was the second most recognizable foreign brand name in China, after Coca-Cola and before Head and Shoulders shampoo.[41] Still, the late 1990s was not a good period for BJC's performance. Profits fell from $216 million yuan in 1996 to $20 million yuan in 1997,[42] and for 1998, there was a loss.[43] Andy Okab, the vice-president of Chrysler Corp's Beijing Jeep said that during 1999, the company cut its workforce from 7,100 to 4,800, through early retirement, lay-offs and by moving staff from permanent to contract basis, and reduced its bank loans by 25 percent and inventory from more than 800 million yuan to 350 million yuan. Okab added: "We were below break-even last year."

Beijing Jeep's current top management team consisted of one American, F. B. Krebs, as the general manager. The deputy general manager was Yunde Zhu, followed by the senior executives, Yaunzhu Li, Kaiying Zhou and Meidong Wang.[44]

Thus, BJC was continually losing market share. After its foundation in 1984, its total output was allocated to state companies and little sales or marketing was required. Sales to the army still accounted for 30 percent of the total, but industry growth was concentrated in taxi companies and the wealthy, mostly in the cities, who wanted comfortable passenger cars like the Santana, the Citreon ZX and Jetta.[45] On top of that, a road-building campaign that had included 4,735 kilometres of highways had lessened the need for jeeps. Yet the company maintained that there was enormous potential demand for its vehicles in rural and mountainous areas. Unfortunately these were poor areas where people did not have the money to buy the company's vehicles.[46]

In the longer term, there was a question mark over the company's place in the mainland's overall car strategy. Following Chrysler's merger with Daimler-Benz, BJC was undergoing an evaluation by the new company. There had even been rumors that DaimlerChrysler may try to get out of its China operations to focus on the more immediate concerns of its merger integration problems. One analyst stated that the venture was looking like a lost cause. It was "saddled with an aged plant, bloated workforce and two outdated models," and that "even confirmed optimists are discouraged by the plethora of problems confronting the company."[47]

Still, DaimlerChrysler denied that it was thinking of pulling out. "No one in his right mind can recommend packing up and leaving," Okab said. "So much has changed in the past five years and so much could change in the next five years."[48] Jerry Hsu, vice-president for sales and marketing for Chrysler Asia-Pacific said that in the last quarter of 1999, Chrysler sent teams to redirect sales and marketing. To reduce costs, the firm had in the past six months reduced the workforce from 8,100 to 7,000. He denied rumors that Chrysler was considering leaving the mainland. Said Okab: "We remain firmly committed to China as a key part of our strategy. We believe in the economy and in the future."

Conor O'Clery, another Chinese automotive industry analyst, believed that BJC had been left behind by changes in the mainland's car market from being dominated by companies and state institutions to one in

Exhibit 3 Production Statistics by Model for China's Automotive Industry

Model Names	Sales Sept. 1999	Sales Sept. 1998	% Change in Sales	Market Share	Production in 1999	Production in 1998	% Change in Production
Santana (VW)	31,421	17,584	78.7	45.08	20,502	17,377	18.0
Jetta (VW)	7,622	5,358	42.3	10.93	7,840	5,235	49.8
Audi 2000	480	730	−34.2	0.69	102	654	−84.4
Buick (GM)	3,788	0	0.0	5.43	4,069	0	0.0
Small Hongqi	1,710	478	257.7	2.45	1,662	387	329.5
Fukang–Citroen	4,743	4,564	3.9	6.80	4,066	4,600	−11.6
Charade (Daihatsu)	12,542	7,585	65.4	17.99	11,262	10,069	11.8
Alto	5,254	3,274	60.5	7.54	6,464	3,417	89.2
Guangzhou Honda	1,251	0	0.0	1.8	1,199	0	0.0
Beijing Jeep	816	907	−10.0	1.17	520	723	−28.1
Subaru	86	0	0.0	0.12	0	0	0.0
Total	69,713	40,480	72.2	100.00	57,686	42,462	35.9

SOURCE: ASIA PULSE, November 22, 1999.

which the individual was becoming the most important customer. BJC's production scale was too small to allow price cuts to match those of its competitors and the high petrol consumption of its vehicles deterred many potential urban buyers. The previous year, private buyers had purchased about 40 percent of national output of 1.57 million vehicles, including 470,000 passenger cars, up from 1.45 million in 1996, and were expected to account for 50 percent in 1999.[49]

The lowest price for the Cherokee Jeep was 128,000 yuan (approximately US$15,000).[50] Research had shown there was demand for this vehicle without some luxury features, so BJC planned a third-quarter launch of a model priced at less than $100,000 yuan.[51] The Cherokee assembled in China was powered by a 2.5 liter AMC petrol engine from the United States. There was a question, however, of whether the Cherokee was really suitable for China, or whether the more basic BJ200 series was better (see Exhibits 4 and 5). For example, Erming Xu, professor of strategic management and dean of the business school at the People's University in Beijing, stated the Cherokee was not an ideal model choice for China in that it did not fit a broad market niche. It was a bit too plush for the rural areas, and yet it was not as smooth riding as a sedan, which was popular in urban areas. He goes further to state that the Cherokee seemed to be produced for United States residents living in suburbs who like to go exploring on the weekends; among these residents, sport utility vehicles (SUVs), as the Cherokee is often classified, were typically second cars which supplemented their primary model of transportation, which was a sedan. The suburbs were still in the infant stages of development in China, and most people could not afford a first car, much less a second. In fact, the Cherokee had been modified to suit the Chinese market. BJC engineers made design changes on the chassis frame and suspension to make it more sturdy, and optional extras had been deleted. In short, the vehicle was not as luxurious as the United States version. BJC officials announced in February of 1999, that they were introducing a new "no-frills" version of the Cherokee.[52]

O'Clery, a Beijing-based analyst, stated that,

> Like many other foreigners in China, I drive a Beijing Jeep. Actually there isn't much choice. The huge duty on foreign imports makes other cars extremely expensive. The Cherokee is considered to be a high-class vehicle.

Beijing Jeeps were produced in different versions, but they were all based on a relatively heavy-gauge chassis frame, which gave the vehicle strength and a stiff base on which to mount the sturdy mechanicals: engine, a three-speed manual gearbox, 4WD transmission, long travel, semi-elliptic leaf spring suspension, and a high- and low-speed transfer box. Both the BJ212 and the civilian version BJ212A were not fuel-efficient. The BJ212 had been exported from China to the Netherlands, France and Australia in small numbers. Some had to be modified and upgraded to meet current safety regulations applying to those export markets. The original BJ212 design was later replaced by a modified version, BJ212L. The entire BJ series was originally based on a Soviet commander car. The BJ121K version had all the features of the BJ121A plus a canvas top with side windows, which covered the whole vehicle; it could also double as a 10-seat rural bus.

The local Beijing officials were trying to help the ailing carmaker since it was a major supplier of good paying jobs in the city—an indication that BJC still has some connections with powerful people. For example, in 1999, city authorities issued an edict that all sports utility vehicles—except those manufactured by BJC—would be barred from driving on the second and third ring roads between Monday and Friday. Any Beijing resident knew that trying to get anywhere without being able to drive on the city's two main circular arteries would amount to a considerable test of patience and ingenuity. Therein, historically, lies one of the main appeals of the Beijing Jeep. However, such anti-tariff tactics barriers appeared to be on the way out with WTO on the horizon. Yet there was the question of how well the WTO changes could be enforced, at least in the short-run.[53]

Strategic Challenges

Thus, as the year 2000 got under way, the managers of Beijing Jeep were faced with challenges and opportunities. On one hand, as the Asian crisis faded, the Chinese economy promised growth rates that would put more consumers within reach of owning an automobile. Total private automobile sales were projected to nearly quadruple over that of 1999; thus, the dream of the vast Chinese market appeared to be becoming a reality.[54] Yet on the other hand, the competition for that market was steadily intensifying, and the WTO promised to lower the barriers on, what had been for BJC, a somewhat protected market.

As the first major foreign joint venture, BJC had learned to do things the hard way. They had painstakingly cultivated guanxi with central and local government officials over the years. Guanxi is sometimes said to be a response to poorly developed market and regulatory institutions. Yet if the WTO improved the institutional and regulatory structure, it was possible that BJC's guanxi advantage would count for less in the future. As China was being pulled into the world economy, competition in its markets would more closely resemble that of the rest of the world. Until recently, BJC had been the

Exhibit 4   Advertisement for Beijing Jeep Cherokee BJ7250 EL

Safety

We thought about Safety—with each and every passenger in mind. We've incorporated double-sided galvanized steel for 24 percent increased stiffness and durability. The collision absorbing steering column and the buffer zone work synergistically to reduce frontal impact injury. The three point safety belts are available for all seats and provide effective protection for passengers. Parents can relax while the "rear door child protection locks" are engaged improving their children's safety.

New Safety Features

- Increased stiffness
- Collision absorbing steering column and buffer zone
- Three point safety belts
- Rear door child protection locks

Utilization

We thought about Versatility—and developed a vehicle adaptable for various road terrains. Understanding the desires of our customers to carry everything from groceries to heavy equipment, we included the rear-folding seat to give a spacious luggage/cargo area. Cherokee's comfortable interior design is a result of our dedication to fully meet the ergonomic requirements and provide a luxurious ride.

Performance

We thought about overall performance—and succeeded in designing the Super Cherokee for quick response and all-round drive-ability. The available engines provide our customers with the power they want (standard 2.5L or more powerful 4.0L). Our off-road ability is ensured by the outstanding break-over angle approach angle and departure angle. Our state-of-the-art international suspension system adapts to the different Chinese road conditions as well as to different travelling speeds. The optional full-time 4WD shift-on-the-fly can be left in the four FULL-TIME mode over any road surfaces, including dry, paved road without damaging the drive train or reducing fuel economy all 4WD models have. Shift-on-the fly capability allows the customer to shift from 2WD to 4WD without slowing down or getting out of the vehicle to lock the hubs.

Value

We thought about value—and designed a vehicle with priceless capabilities. The comfort and convenience of the Super Cherokee go above and beyond customer expectations. Our guarantee is to passenger safety and superior performance. The exceptional value far exceeds the price of the Super Cherokee.

Environmental Protection

We thought about the environment—and equipped the Super Cherokee with an R134a air conditioner to ensure environmental protection. The addition of a catalytic converter to the electronic fuel injection engine insures compliance with the requirements of China's strict emission regulations.

Multiple Utilizations of the Super Cherokee

We thought of multiple utilizations of the Super Cherokee—and made it adaptable to an infinite range of roads, including: city, mountain, village, high sloping fields, low-lying land, forest, wilderness, grasslands, deserts, snow covered, rain slick, mud covered, etc. We designed the Super Cherokee to accommodate a vast number of different professional and trade uses, including:

- Engineering
- Fire fighting
- Irrigating work
- Rescuing
- Banking

- Electric power works
- Military functions
- Medical and health works
- Security jobs, procurator
- Court functions

- Farming
- Forestry work
- Animal husbandry
- Fishery work

Exhibit 4 Advertisement for Beijing Jeep Cherokee BJ7250 EL *(Continued)*

The Super Cherokee accommodates all personality styles, including: natural, unrestrained, tenacious, determined, fashion-minded, thrill seeking, distinguished, family-minded, business-minded, pleasure seekers, etc.

- Adaptable to an infinite range of roads
- Accommodates a vast number of different professions
- Accommodates all personality styles

We thought about everything—and built a Jeep vehicle that is perfect for you. Take the keys to a legendary Jeep and you've taken ownership of something much bigger: rugged off-road trails, scenic mountaintops, freedom previously unknown and the company of like minds whose common bonds are adventure, discovery, comfort, convenience, and prestige, all at an affordable price. The confidence a Jeep provides in all places at all times allows a peace of mind you've never known.

SOURCE: BJC Web Site—Company URL: http://www.Beijing-jeep.com/.

darling of the government policy makers in Beijing, and it was once held up as a model joint venture. That honeymoon period was now over. American, German and Japanese automobile companies had all expressed their intentions to create or expand joint venture plans in the near future. BJC was no longer the "only game in town" when it came to joint ventures. It would be forced to compete with the best that the world had to offer.

It appeared that the venture could benefit from more technology, management expertise and investment from its major foreign partner, DaimlerChrysler. BJC was losing money and market share, and it had two outdated models and 15-year old-technology. But how could it get more commitment from this organization, which was facing disgruntled investors and merger problems of its own? Also, DaimlerChrysler was reluctant to transfer technology due to the historically weak record of property rights protection in China. There was even open speculation among some Chinese auto analysts that DaimlerChrysler was considering pulling out of the BJC venture totally.

Another point worth considering was the product

Exhibit 5 Advertisement for Beijing Jeep BJ2020SY

China is a country with a vast land mass area with every possible terrain and climate. The numerous complex road conditions (i.e., dry Gobi desert, sandy lands of Inner Mongolia and summertime seasonal rivers, the long winters that bring snow and ice in the Northeast, the rolling hills and narrow roads in the hot, humid climates of Yunnan, Guizhou and Sichuan Provinces) put any vehicle to the test of endurance. Despite the complex roads and inclement weather, Beijing Jeep Corporation, Ltd. provides a variety of models to take you where you want to go.

Highly skilled Beijing Jeep Corporation, Ltd. engineers have developed the hard-top Kuangchao Series, BJ2020SY, BJ2020SM and the BJ2020SMW, by using the most advanced technology. The option of an air conditioner is available to improve passenger comfort. There is always a model to meet your needs.

The BJ2020SY is equipped with a reinforced fibreglass removable hardtop. The robust hardtop is resistant to corrosion, resistant to aging, resistant to impact, durable and lightweight. Enjoy warm, sunny weather with the wind in your hair when the hardtop is removed.

BJ2020SM has a metal roof, which seals out the environmental elements, such as rain, cold in the winter and heat in the summer. In addition to the BJ2020SM's metal roof, the BJ2020SMW is designed with a lift gate for easy loading and unloading. Fold the rear seat forward for a spacious cargo area.

SOURCE: BJC Web site—Company URL: http://www.Beijing-jeep.com/.

line. Should BJC attempt to leverage the guanxi it had built up with Chinese authorities over the years and focus on government contracts, or should it concentrate on the growing middle class and market to individual consumers? Should the company focus more on the old BJ Jeeps that seemed to be more suitable for the masses, or should it attempt to go upscale and try to sell Grand Cherokees?

Thus, BJC was at a crossroads in the organization's history. Whichever path they took was going to be full of challenges and opportunities, as the vast Chinese economy was in the midst of making a major historical transformation.

Endnotes

1. J. Mann, *Beijing Jeep: A Case Study of Western Business in China*, Westview Press, Boulder Colorado, 1997.
2. D. Roberts. and P. Mangusson, "Welcome to the Club: China's deal to join the WTO holds both promise and peril," *Business Week*. November 29, 1999, p. 34.
3. K. Bradsher, "A Struggle Over Culture and Turf at Auto Giant," *New York Times*, September 24, 1999, p. C1.
4. C. O'Clery, "Making China Good for US Motors," *The Irish Times*, July 20, 1998, p. 10.
5. Mann, *Beijing Jeep*.
6. *Ibid*.
7. *Ibid*.
8. *Ibid*.
9. *Ibid*.
10. N. Fletcher, "Chrysler China Venture Finds Road to Success," *Journal of Commerce and Commercialization*, May 12, 1989, p. A1.
11. Mann, *Beijing Jeep*, p. 223.12. O'Clery, "Making China Good for U.S. Motors," p. 10.
12. O'Clery, "Making China Good for U.S. Motors," p. 10.
13. Mann, *Beijing Jeep*.
14. B. Klayman, "Year Later, DaimlerChrysler Struggles With Identity," *Toronto Star*, November 13, 1999.
15. R. Kisiel, "DaimlerChrysler Turns 1: Bigger . . . But Better?" *Automotive News*, November 15, 1999, p. 1.
16. Invest-O-Rama, http://home.sprintmail.com/, 2000.
17. C. Yao, *Stock Market and Futures in the People's Republic of China*. Oxford University Press, New York, 1998.
18. *China Against the Tide: The Succession Struggle and Prospects for Reform in China After the Peking Spring*, The Economist Intelligence Unit, London, 1990 (Special Report 2025).
19. M. O'Neill, "Foreign Ventures Lose Allure: Outside Investors Begin to Doubt the Mainland's Free-Market Dream," *South China Morning Post*. December 11, 1999.
20. *Ibid*.
21. Roberts, "Welcome to the Club."
22. M. Liu et al, "A Tale of Two Cities: Beijing," *Newsweek*, November 29, 1999, p. 54.
23. "China Car Sales Forecast to Jump 390 percent," *Junrong Shibao (Financial News)*, April 25, 2000, Beijing.
24. R. Jacob, and T. Burt, "China's Walls will Crumble but only one Brick at a Time", *Financial Times*, May 30, 2000, p. 12.
25. Roberts, "Welcome to the Club."
26. "Chinese Automobile Industry will be Restructured," *Modern Plastic*, November, 1999 (No. 76), p. A24.
27. *Ibid*.
28. *Ibid*.
29. R. L. Simison, "Nascent Demand in China for Better Cars Buoys Buick," *Asian Wall Street Journal*, October 25, 1999.
30. C. W. Craig, "As the Sun Sets on the 20th Century, it is Rising on the Chinese Automotive Market," *Detroit Free Press*, October 27,1999.
31. Simison, "Nascent Demand."
32. *Ibid*.
33. T. Lassa, "Shanghai Century; When Better Buicks Are Built, China Will Build 'Em," *Auto Week*, November 25, 1999, p. 4.
34. Simison, "Nascent Demand."
35. "GM to Sell Expensive Sports Vehicles in China," *Business Day*, June 4, 1999.
36. Simison, "Nascent Demand."
37. "Honda Gears up for Competition," *Hong Kong Standard*, December 8, 1999.
38. *Ibid*.
39. A. Harney, "Toyota Targets Chinese Market," *Financial Times*, November 24, 1999, p. 31.
40. *Ibid*.
41. O'Clery, "Making China Good."
42. Mann, *Beijing Jeep*.
43. M. O'Neill, "Beijing Jeep on Rocky Roads as Profits Tumble," *South China Morning Post*, January 21, 1998, p. B4.
44. Graham & Whiteside Ltd. The Major Company Database 2000.
45. O'Clery, "Making China Good."
46. *Ibid*.
47. M. Chrysler, "Is DaimlerChrylser Racking off from Beijing Jeep?," *Ward's Auto World*, 1999, 35(10), p. 63.
48. O'Clery, "Making China Good."
49. *Ibid*.
50. Mann, *Beijing Jeep*.
51. M. O'Neill, "Beijing Jeep Races After Sales with Few-Frills Cherokee," *South China Morning Post*, February 18, 1999, p. B3.
52. *Ibid*.
53. Jacob, "China's Wall Will Crumble."
54. "China Car Sales," *Junrong Shibao (Financial News)*, 2000.

Case 7

Philip Condit and the Boeing 777: From Design and Development to Production and Sales

Isaac Cohen

San Jose State University

Following his promotion to Boeing CEO in 1988, Frank Shrontz looked for ways to stretch and upgrade the Boeing 767—an eight year old wide-body twin jet—in order to meet Airbus competition. Airbus had just launched two new 300-seat wide-body models, the two-engine A330 and the four-engine A340. Boeing had no 300-seat jetliner in service, nor did the company plan to develop such a jet.

To find out whether Boeing's customers were interested in a double-decker 767, Philip Condit, Boeing Executive Vice President and future CEO (1996) met with United Airlines Vice President Jim Guyette. Guyette rejected the idea outright, claiming that an upgraded 767 was no match to Airbus new model transports. Instead, Guyette urged Boeing to develop a brand new commercial jet, the most advanced airplane of its generation. Shrontz had heard similar suggestions from other airline carriers. He reconsidered Boeing's options, and decided to abandon the 767 idea in favor of a new aircraft program. In December 1989, accordingly, he announced the 777 project and put Philip Condit in charge of its management. Boeing had launched the 777 in 1990, delivered the first jet in 1995, and by February 2001, 325 B-777s were flying in the services of the major international and US airlines.[1]

Condit faced a significant challenge in managing the 777 project. He wanted to create an airplane that was preferred by the airlines at a price that was truly competitive. He sought to attract airline customers as well as cut production costs, and he did so by introducing several innovations—both technological and managerial—in aircraft design, manufacturing, and assembly. He looked for ways to revitalize Boeing's outmoded engineering production system, and update Boeing's manufacturing strategies. And to achieve these goals, Condit made continual efforts to spread the 777 program-innovations company wide.

Looking back at the 777 program, this case focuses on Condit's efforts. Was the 777 project successful and was it cost effective? Would the development of the 777 allow Boeing to diffuse the innovations in airplane design and production beyond the 777 program? Would the development of the 777s permit Boeing to revamp and modernize its aircraft manufacturing system? Would the making and selling of the 777 enhance Boeing competitive position relative to Airbus, its only remaining rival?

The Aircraft Industry

Commercial aircraft manufacturing was an industry of enormous risks where failure was the norm, not the exception. The number of large commercial jet makers had been reduced from four in the early 1980s — Boeing, McDonnell Douglas, Airbus and Lockheed — to two in late 1990s, turning the industry into a duopoly, and pitting the two survivors — Boeing and Airbus — one against the other. One reason why aircraft manufacturers so often failed was the huge cost of product development.

Developing a new jetliner required an up front investment of up to $15 billion (2001 dollars), a lead time of 5 to 6 years from launch to first delivery, and the ability to sustain a negative cash flow throughout the development phase. Typically, to break even on an entirely new jetliner, aircraft manufacturers needed to sell a minimum of 300 to 400 planes and at least 50 planes per year. Only a few commercial airplane programs had ever made money.[2]

The case was presented in the October 2000, meeting of the North American Case Research Association at San Antonio, Texas.

Copyright Isaac Cohen, 2000. I am grateful to the San Jose State University College of Business for its support.

The price of an aircraft reflected its high development costs. New model prices were based on the average cost of producing 300 to 400 planes, not a single plane. Aircraft pricing embodied the principle of learning by doing, the so called "learning curve":[3] workers steadily improved their skills during the assembly process, and as a result, labor cost fell as the number of planes produced rose.

The high and increasing cost of product development prompted aircraft manufacturers to utilize subcontracting as a risk-sharing strategy. For the 747, the 767, and the 777, the Boeing Company required subcontractors to share a substantial part of the airplane's development costs. Airbus did the same with its own latest models. Risk sharing subcontractors performed detailed design work and assembled major subsections of the new plane while airframe integrators (i.e. aircraft manufacturers) designed the aircraft, integrated its systems and equipment, assembled the entire plane, marketed it, and provided customer support for 20 to 30 years. Both the airframe integrators and their subcontractors were supplied by thousands of domestic and foreign aircraft components manufacturers.[4]

Neither Boeing, nor Airbus, nor any other post-war commercial aircraft manufacturer produced jet engines. A risky and costly venture, engine building had become a highly specialized business. Aircraft manufacturers worked closely with engine makers—General Electric, Pratt and Whitney, and Rolls Royce—to set engine performance standards. In most cases, new airplanes were offered with a choice of engines. Over time, the technology of engine building had become so complex and demanding that it took longer to develop an engine than an aircraft. During the life of a jetliner, the price of the engines and their replacement parts was equal to the entire price of the airplane.[5]

A new model aircraft was normally designed around an engine, not the other way around. As engine performance improved, airframes were redesigned to exploit the engine's new capabilities. The most practical way to do so was to stretch the fuselage and add more seats in the cabin. Aircraft manufacturers deliberately designed flexibility into the airplane so that future engine improvements could facilitate later stretching. Hence the importance of the "family concept" in aircraft design, and hence the reason why aircraft manufacturers introduced families of planes made up of derivative jetliners built around a basic model, not single, standardized models.[6]

The commercial aircraft industry, finally, gained from technological innovations in two other industries. More than any other manufacturing industry, aircraft construction benefited from advances in material applications and electronics. The development of metallic and non-metallic composite materials played a key role in improving airframe and engine performance. On the one hand, composite materials that combined light weight and great strength were utilized by aircraft manufacturers; on the other, heat-resisting alloys that could tolerate temperatures of up to 3,000 degrees were used by engine makers. Similarly, advances in electronics revolutionized avionics. The increasing use of semiconductors by aircraft manufacturers facilitated the miniaturization of cockpit instruments, and more important, it enhanced the use of computers for aircraft communication, navigation, instrumentation, and testing.[7] The use of computers contributed, in addition, to the design, manufacture, and assembly of new model aircraft.

The Boeing Company

The history of the Boeing company may be divided into two distinct periods: the piston era and the jet age. Throughout the piston era, Boeing was essentially a military contractor producing fighter aircraft in the 1920s and 1930s, and bombers during World War II. During the jet age, beginning in the 1950s, Boeing had become the world's largest manufacturer of commercial aircraft, deriving most of its revenues from selling jetliners.

Boeing's first jet was the 707. The introduction of the 707 in 1958 represented a major breakthrough in the history of commercial aviation; it allowed Boeing to gain a critical technological lead over the Douglas Aircraft Company, its closer competitor. To benefit from government assistance in developing the 707, Boeing produced the first jet in two versions: a military tanker for the Air Force (k-135) and a commercial aircraft for the airlines (707-120). The company, however, did not recoup its own investment until 1964, six years after it delivered the first 707, and twelve years after it had launched the program. In the end, the 707 was quite profitable, selling 25 percent above its average cost.[8] Boeing retained the essential design of the 707 for all its subsequent narrow-body single-aisle models (the 727, 737, and 757), introducing incremental design improvements, one at a time.[9] One reason why Boeing used shared design for future models was the constant pressure experienced by the company to move down the learning curve and reduce overall development costs.

Boeing introduced the 747 in 1970. The development of the 747 represented another breakthrough; the 747 wide body design was one of a kind; it had no real competition anywhere in the industry. Boeing bet the entire company on the success of the 747, spending on the project almost as much as the company's total net worth in 1965, the year the project started.[10] In the short-run, the outcome was disastrous. As Boeing began delivering its 747s, the company was struggling to avoid bankruptcy. Cutbacks in orders as a result of a deep recession, coupled with production inefficiencies and escalating costs, created a severe cash shortage that pushed the company to the brink. As sales dropped, the 747's break-even point moved further and further into the future.

Yet, in the long run, the 747 program was a triumph. The Jumbo Jet had become Boeing's most profitable aircraft and the industry's most efficient jetliner. The new plane helped Boeing solidify its position as the industry leader for years to come, leaving McDonnell Douglas far behind, and forcing the Lockheed Corporation to exit the market. The new plane, furthermore, contributed to Boeing's manufacturing strategy in two ways. First, as Boeing increased its reliance on outsourcing, six major subcontractors fabricated 70 percent of the value of the 747 airplane,[11] thereby helping Boeing reduce the project's risks. Second, for the first time, Boeing applied the family concept in aircraft design to a wide-body jet, building the 747 with wings large enough to support a stretched fuselage with bigger engines, and offering a variety of other modifications in the 747's basic design. The 747-400 (1989) is a case in point. In 1997, Boeing sold the stretched and upgraded 747-400 in three versions, a standard jet, a freighter, and a "combi" (a jetliner whose main cabin was divided between passenger and cargo compartments).[12]

Boeing developed other successful models. In 1969, Boeing introduced the 737, the company's narrow-body flagship, and in 1982 Boeing put into service two additional jetliners, the 757 (narrow-body) and the 767 (wide-body). By the early 1990s, the 737, 757, and 767 were all selling profitably. Following the introduction of the 777 in 1995, Boeing's families of planes included the 737 for short-range travel, the 757 and 767 for medium range travel, and the 747 and 777 for medium to long range travel (Exhibit 1).

In addition to building jetliners, Boeing also expanded its defense, space and information businesses. In 1997, the Boeing Company took a strategic gamble, buying the McDonnell Douglas Company in a $14 billion stock deal. As a result of the merger, Boeing had become the world's largest manufacturer of military aircraft, NASA's largest supplier, and the Pentagon's second largest contractor (after Lockheed). Nevertheless, despite the growth in its defense and space businesses, Boeing still derived most of its revenues from selling jetliners. Commercial aircraft revenues accounted for 59 percent of Boeing's $49 billion sales in 1997 and 63 percent of Boeing's $56 billion sales in 1998.[13]

Following its merger with McDonnell, Boeing had one remaining rival: Airbus Industrie.[14] In 1997, Airbus booked 45 percent of the worldwide orders for commercial jetliners[15] and delivered close to 1/3 of the worldwide industry output. In 2000, Airbus shipped nearly 2/5 of the worldwide industry output (Exhibit 2).

Airbus' success was based on a strategy that combined cost leadership with technological leadership. First, Airbus distinguished itself from Boeing by incorporating the most advanced technologies into its planes. Second, Airbus managed to cut costs by utilizing a flexible, lean production manufacturing system that stood in a stark contrast to Boeing's mass production system.[16]

| Exhibit 1 | Total Number of Commercial Jetliners Delivered by the Boeing Company, 1958–2/2001* |

Model	No. Delivered	First Delivery
B-707	1,010 (retired)	1958
B-727	1,831 (retired)	1963
B-737	3,901	1967
B-747	1,264	1970
B-757	953	1982
B-767	825	1982
B-777	325	1995
B-717	49	2000
Total:	10,159	

*McDonnell Douglas commercial jetliners (the MD-11, MD-80, and MD-90) are excluded.
SOURCES: Boeing Commercial Airplane Group, *Announced Orders and Deliveries as of 12/31/97; The Boeing Company 1998 Annual Report*, p. 35. "Commercial Airplanes: Order and Delivery Summary," http://www.Boeing.com/commercial/orders/index.html. Retrieved from Web 3/20/2001.

	1992	1993	1994	1995	1996	1997	1998	1999	2000
Boeing	61%	61%	63%	54%	55%	67%	71%	68%	61%
MD	17	14	9	13	13				
Airbus	22	25	28	33	32	33	29	32	39

SOURCES: *Aerospace Facts and Figures, 1997–98,* p. 34; *Wall Street Journal,* December 3, 1998, and January 12, 1999; *The Boeing Company 1997 Annual Report,* p. 19; Data supplied by Mark Luginbill, Airbus Communication Director, November 16, 1998, February 1, 2000, and March 20, 2001.

As Airbus prospered, the Boeing company was struggling with rising costs, declining productivity, delays in deliveries, and production inefficiencies. Boeing Commercial Aircraft Group lost $1.8 billion in 1997 and barely generated any profits in 1998.[17] All through the 1990s, the Boeing Company looked for ways to revitalize its outdated production manufacturing system, on the one hand, and to introduce leading edge technologies into its jetliners, on the other. The development and production of the 777, first conceived of in 1989, was an early step undertaken by Boeing managers to address both problems.

The 777 Program

The 777 program was Boeing's single largest project since the completion of the 747. The total development cost of the 777 was estimated at $6.3 billion and the total number of employees assigned to the project peaked at nearly 10,000. The 777's twin-engines were the largest and most powerful ever built (the diameter of the 777's engine equaled the 737's fuselage), the 777's construction required 132,000 uniquely engineered parts (compared to 70,000 for the 767), the 777's seat capacity was identical to that of the first 747 that had gone into service in 1970, and its manufacturer empty weight was 57 percent greater than the 767's. Building the 777 alongside the 747 and 767 at its Everett plant near Seattle, Washington, Boeing enlarged the plant to cover an area of 76 football fields.[18]

Boeing's financial position in 1990 was unusually strong. With a 21 percent rate of return on stockholder equity, a long term debt of just 15 percent of capitalization, and a cash surplus of $3.6 billion, Boeing could gamble comfortably.[19] There was no need to bet the company on the new project as had been the case with the 747, or to borrow heavily, as had been the case with the 767. Still, the decision to develop the 777 was defi-

nitely risky; a failure of the new jet might have triggered an irreversible decline of the Boeing Company and threatened its future survival.

The decision to develop the 777 was based on market assessment—the estimated future needs of the airlines. During the 14-year period, 1991-2005, Boeing market analysts forecasted a +100 percent increase in the number of passenger miles traveled worldwide, and a need for about 9,000 new commercial jets. Of the total value of the jetliners needed in 1991-2005, Boeing analysts forecasted a $260 billion market for wide body jets smaller than the 747. An increasing number of these wide body jets were expected to be larger than the 767.[20]

A Consumer Driven Product

To manage the risk of developing a new jetliner, aircraft manufacturers had first sought to obtain a minimum number of firm orders from interested carriers, and only then commit to the project. Boeing CEO Frank Shrontz had expected to obtain 100 initial orders of the 777 before asking the Boeing board to launch the project, but as a result of Boeing's financial strength, on the one hand, and the increasing competitiveness of Airbus, on the other, Schrontz decided to seek the board's approval earlier. He did so after securing only one customer: United Airlines. On October 12, 1990, United had placed an order for 34 777s and an option for an additional 34 aircraft, and two weeks later, Boeing's board of directors approved the project.[21]

Negotiating the sale, Boeing and United drafted a hand written agreement (signed by Philip Condit and Richard Albrecht, Boeing's executive vice presidents, and Jim Guyette, United's Executive Vice President) that granted United a larger role in designing the 777 than the role played by any airline before. The two companies pledged to cooperate closely in developing an aircraft with the "best dispatch reliability in the industry" and the "greatest customer appeal in the industry." "We will endavor to do it right the first time with the highest degree of professionalism" and with "candor, honesty, and respect" [the agreement read]. Asked to comment on the agreement, Philip Condit, said: "We are going to listen to our customers and understand what they want. Everybody on the program has that attitude."[22] Gordon McKinzie, United's 777 program director agreed: "In the past we'd get brochures on a new airplane and its options . . . wait four years for delivery, and hope we'd get what we ordered. This time Boeing really listened to us."[23]

Condit invited other airline carriers to participate in the design and development phase of the 777. Altogether, eight carriers from around the world (United, Delta, America, British Airways, Qantas, Japan Airlines, All Nippon Airways, and Japan Air System) sent full time representatives to Seattle; British Airways alone assigned 75 people at one time. To facilitate interaction between its design engineers and representatives of the eight carriers, Boeing introduced an initiative called "Working Together." "If we have a problem," a British Airways production manager explained, "we go to the source — design engineers on the IPT [Integrated Product Teams], not service engineer(s). One of the frustrations on the 747 was that we rarely got to talk to the engineers who were doing the work."[24]

"We have definitely influenced the design of the aircraft," a United 777 manager said, mentioning changes in the design of the wing panels that made it easier for airline mechanics to access the slats (slats, like flaps, increased lift on takeoffs and landings), and new features in the cabin that made the plane more attractive to passengers.[25] Of the 1,500 design features examined by

representatives of the airlines, Boeing engineers modified 300 (Exhibit 3). Among changes made by Boeing was a redesigned overhead bin that left more stand-up headroom for passengers (allowing a six-foot-three tall passenger to walk from aisle to aisle), "flattened" side walls which provided the occupant of the window seat with more room, overhead bin doors which opened down and made it possible for shorter passengers to lift baggage into the overhead compartment, a redesigned reading lamp that enabled flight attendants to replace light bulbs, a task formerly performed by mechanics, and a computerized flight deck management system that adjusted cabin temperature, controlled the volume of the public address system, and monitored food and drink inventories.[26]

More important were changes in the interior configuration (layout plan) of the aircraft. To be able to reconfigure the plane quickly for different markets of varying travel ranges and passengers loads, Boeing's customers sought a flexible plan of the interior. On a standard commercial jet, kitchen galleys, closets, lavatories, and bars were all removable in the past but were limited to fixed positions where the interior floor structure was reinforced to accommodate the "wet" load. On the 777, by contrast, such components as galleys and lavatories could be positioned anywhere within several "flexible zones" designed into the cabin by the joint efforts of Boeing engineers and representatives of the eight airlines. Similarly, the flexible design of the 777's seat tracks made it possible for carriers to increase the number of seat combinations as well as reconfigure the seating arrangement quickly. Flexible configurations resulted, in

Exhibit 3	The 777: Selected Design Features Proposed by Boeing Airline Customers and Adapted by The Boeing Company

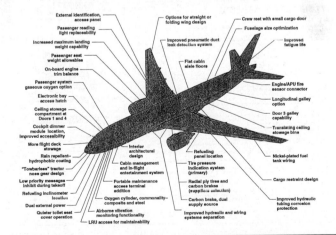

SOURCE: The Boeing Company.

turn, in significant cost savings; airlines no longer needed to take the aircraft out of service for an extended period of time in order to reconfigure the interior.[27]

The airline carriers also influenced the way in which Boeing designed the 777 cockpit. During the program definition phase, representatives of United Airlines, British Airways and Quantas—three of Boeing's clients whose fleets included a large number of 747-400s—asked Boeing engineers to model the 777 cockpit on the 747-400's. In response to these requests, Boeing introduced a shared 747/777 cockpit design that enabled its airline customers to use a single pool of pilots for both aircraft types at a significant cost savings.[28]

Additionally, the airline carriers urged Boeing to increase its use of avionics for in-flight entertainment. The 777, as a consequence, was equipped with a fully computerized cabin. Facing each seat on the 777, and placed on the back of the seat in front, was a combined computer and video monitor that featured movies, video programs, and interactive computer games. Passengers were also provided with a digital sound system comparable to the most advanced home stereo available, and a telephone. About 40 percent of the 777's total computer capacity was reserved for passengers in the cabin.[29]

The 777 was Boeing's first fly by wire (FBW) aircraft, an aircraft controlled by a pilot transmitting commands to the moveable surfaces (rudder, flaps, etc.) electrically, not mechanically. Boeing installed a state of the art FBW system on the 777 partly to satisfy its airline customers, and partly to challenge Airbus' leadership in flight con-

trol technology, a position Airbus had held since it introduced the world's first FBW aircraft , the A-320, in 1988.

Lastly, Boeing customers were invited to contribute to the design of the 777's engine. Both United Airlines and All Nippon Airlines assigned service engineers to work with representatives of Pratt and Whitney (P&W) on problems associated with engine maintenance. P&W held three specially scheduled "airline conferences." At each conference, some 40 airline representatives clustered around a full scale mock-up of the 777 engine and showed Pratt and Whitney engineers gaps in the design, hard-to-reach points, visible but inaccessible parts, and accessible but invisible components. At the initial conference, Pratt and Whitney picked up 150 airline suggestions, at the second, 50, and at the third, 10 more suggestions.[30]

A Globally Manufactured Product

Twelve international companies located in 10 countries, and 18 more US companies located in 12 states, were contracted by Boeing to help manufacture the 777. Together, they supplied structural components as well as systems and equipment. Among the foreign suppliers were companies based in Japan, Britain, Australia, Italy, Korea, Brazil, Singapore, and Ireland; among the major US subcontractors were the Grumman Corporation, Rockwell (later merged with Boeing), Honeywell, United Technologies, Bendix, and the Sunstrand Corporation (Exhibits 4 and 5). Of all foreign participants, the

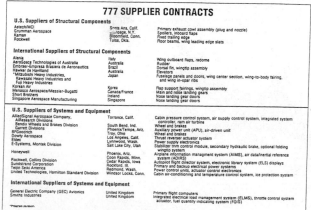

| Exhibit 4 | Global Suppliers |

SOURCE: James Woolsey, "777: Boeing's New Large Twinjet," *Air Transport World*, April 1994, p. 24.

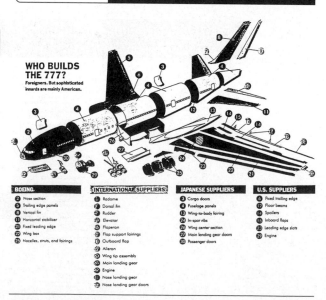

| Exhibit 5 | Global Components |

SOURCE: Jeremy Main, "Corporate Performance: Betting on the 21st Century Jet," *Fortune* April 20, 1992, p. 104.

Case 7 / Philip Condit and the Boeing 777: From Design and Development to Production and Sales

Japanese played the largest role. A consortium made up of Fuji Heavy Industries, Kawasaki Heavy Industries, and Mitsubishi Heavy Industries had worked with Boeing on its wide-body models since the early days of the 747. Together, the three Japanese subcontractors produced 20 percent of the value of the 777's airframe (up from 15 percent of the 767's). A group of 250 Japanese engineers had spent a year in Seattle working on the 777 alongside Boeing engineers before most of its members went back home to begin production. The fuselage was built in sections in Japan and then shipped to Boeing's huge plant at Everett, Washington for assembly.[31]

Boeing used global subcontracting as a marketing tool as well. Sharing design work and production with overseas firms, Boeing required overseas carriers to buy the new aircraft. Again, Japan is a case in point. In return for the contact signed with the Mitsubishi, Fuji, and Kawasaki consortium — which was heavily subsidized by the Japanese government — Boeing sold 46 777 jetliners to three Japanese air carriers: All Nippon Airways, Japan Airlines, and Japan Air System.[32]

A Family of Planes

From the outset, the design of the 777 was flexible enough to accommodate derivative jetliners. Because all derivatives of a given model shared maintenance, training, and operating procedures, as well as replacement parts and components, and because such derivatives enabled carriers to serve different markets at lower costs, Boeing's clients were seeking a family of planes built around a basic model, not a single 777. Condit and his management team, accordingly, urged Boeing's engineers to incorporate the maximum flexibility into the design of the 777.

The 777's design flexibility helped Boeing manage the project's risks. Offering a family of planes based on a single design to accommodate future changes in customers' preferences, Boeing spread the 777 project's risks among a number of models all belonging to the same family.

The key to the 777's design efficiency was the wing. The 777 wings, exceptionally long and thin, were strong enough to support vastly enlarged models. The first model to go into service, the 777-200, had a 209 foot-long fuselage, was designed to carry 305 passengers in three class configurations, and had a travel range of 5,900 miles in its original version (1995), and up to 8,900 miles in its extended version (1997). The second model to be introduced (1998), the 777-300, had a stretched fuselage of 242 ft (10 foot longer than the 747) was configured for 379 passengers (3-class), and flew to destinations of up to 6,800 miles away. In the all-tourist class configuration, the stretched 777-300 could carry as many as 550 passengers.[33]

Digital Design

The 777 was the first Boeing jetliner designed entirely by computers. Historically, Boeing had designed new planes in two ways: paper drawings and full-size models called mock-ups. Paper drawings were two dimensional and therefore insufficient to account for the complex construction of the three dimensional airplane. Full scale mock-ups served as a backup to drawings.

Boeing engineers used three classes of mock-ups. Made up of plywood or foam, class 1 mock-ups were used to construct the plane's large components in three dimensions, refine the design of these components by carving into the wood or foam, and feed the results back into the drawings. Made partly of metal, class 2 mock-ups addressed more complex problems such as the wiring and tubing of the airframe, and the design of the machine tools necessary to cut and shape the large components. Class 3 mock-ups gave the engineers one final opportunity to refine the model and thereby reduce the need to keep on changing the design during the actual assembly process or after delivery.[34]

Despite the engineers' efforts, many parts and components did not fit together on the final assembly line but rather "interfered" with each other, that is, over-lapped in space. The problem was both pervasive and costly; Boeing engineers needed to rework and realign all overlapping parts in order to join them together.

A partial solution to the problem was provided by the computer. In the last quarter of the 20th Century, computer aided design was used successfully in car manufacture, building construction, machine production and several other industries; its application to commercial aircraft manufacturing came later, both in the United States and in Europe. Speaking of the 777, Dick Johnson, Boeing chief engineer for digital design, noted the "tremendous advantage" of computer application:

> With mock-ups, the . . . engineer had three opportunities at three levels of detail to check his parts, and nothing in between. With Catia [Computer aided three dimensional, interactive application] he can do it day in and day out over the whole development of the airplane.[35]

Catia was a sophisticated computer program that Boeing bought from Dassault Aviation, a French fighter planes builder. IBM enhanced the program to improve image manipulation, supplied Boeing with eight of its largest mainframe computers, and connected the mainframes to 2,200 computer terminals that Boeing distributed among its 777 design teams. The software program showed on a screen exactly how parts and components fit together before the actual manufacturing process took place.[36]

A digital design system, Catia had five distinctive advantages. First, it provided the engineers with 100 percent visualization, allowing them to rotate, zoom, and "interrogate" parts geometrically in order to spotlight interferences. Second, Catia assigned a numerical value to each drawing on the screen and thereby helped engineers locate related drawings of parts and components, merge them together, and check for incompatibilities. Third, to help Boeing's customers service the 777, the digital design system created a computer simulated human—a Catia figure playing the role of the service mechanic—who climbed into the three dimensional images and showed the engineers whether parts were serviceable and entry accessible. Fourth, the use of Catia by all 777 design teams in the US, Japan, Europe, and elsewhere facilitated instantaneous communication between Boeing and its subcontractors and ensured the frequent updating of the design. And fifth, Catia provided the 777 assembly line workers with graphics that enhanced the narrative work instructions they received, showing explicitly on a screen how a given task should be performed.[37]

Design-Build Teams (DBT)

Teaming was another feature of the 777 program. About 30 integrated-level teams at the top and more than 230 design-build teams at the bottom worked together on the 777.[38] All team members were connected by Catia. The integrated-level teams were organized around large sections of the aircraft; the DBTs around small parts and components. In both cases, teams were cross-functional, as Philip Condit observed:

> If you go back . . . to earlier planes that Boeing built, the factory was on the bottom floor, and Engineering was on the upper floor. Both Manufacturing and Engineering went back and forth. When there was a problem in the factory, the engineer went down and looked at it. . . .
>
> With ten thousand people [working on the 777], that turns out to be really hard. So you start devising other tools to allow you to achieve that — the design-build team. You break the airplane down and bring Manufacturing, Tooling, Planning, Engineering, Finance, and Materials all together [in small teams].[39]

Under the design-build approach, many of the design decisions were driven by manufacturing concerns. As manufacturing specialists worked alongside engineers, engineers were less likely to design parts that were difficult to produce and needed to be re-designed. Similarly, under the design-build approach, customers' expectations as well as safety and weight considerations were all incorporated into the design of the aircraft; engineers no longer needed to "chain saw"[40] structural components and systems in order to replace parts that did not meet customers expectations, were unsafe, or were too heavy.

The design of the 777's wing provides an example. The wing was divided into two integration-level teams, the "leading edge" (the foreword part of the wing) and the "trailing edge" (the back of the wing) team. Next, the trailing edge team was further divided into ten design-build teams, each named after a piece of the wing's trailing edge (Exhibit 6). Membership in these DBTs extended to two groups of outsiders: representatives of the customer airlines and engineers employed by the foreign subcontractors. Made up of up to 20 members, each DBT decided its own mix of insiders and outsiders, and each was led by a team leader. Each DBT included representatives from six functional disciplines: engineering, manufacturing, materiel, customer support, finance, and quality assurance. The DBTs met twice a week for two hours to hear reports from team members, discuss immediate goals and plans, divide responsibilities, set time lines, and take specific notes of all decisions taken.[41] Described by a Boeing official as "little companies," the DBTs enjoyed a high degree of autonomy from management supervision; team members designed their own tools, developed their own manufacturing plans,

Exhibit 6	The Ten DBTs ("little companies") Responsible for the Wing's Trailing Edge

Flap Supports Team
Inboard Flap Team
Outboard Flap Team
Outboard Fixed Wing Team
Flaperon* Team
Aileron* Team
Inboard Fixed Wing and Gear Support Team
Main Landing Gear Doors Team
Spoilers** Team
Fairings*** Team

* The Flaperon and Aileron were moveable hinged sections of the trailing edge that helped the plane roll in flight. The Flaperon was used at high speed, the Aileron at low speed.
** The spoilers were the flat surfaces that lay on top of the trailing edge and extended during landing to slow down the plane.
*** The fairings were the smooth parts attached to the outline of the wing's trailing edge. They helped reduce drag.
SOURCE: Karl Sabbagh, *21st Century Jet: The Making and Marketing of the Boeing 777* (New York: Scribner, 1996), p. 73.

Case 7 / Philip Condit and the Boeing 777: From Design and Development to Production and Sales

and wrote their own contracts with the program management, specifying deliverables, resources, and schedules. John Monroe, a Boeing 777 senior project manager remarked:

> The team is totally responsible. We give them a lump of money to go and do th[eir] job. They decide whether to hire a lot of inexpensive people or to trade numbers for resources. It's unprecedented. We have some $100 million plus activities led by non-managers.[42]

Employees' Empowerment and Culture

An additional aspect of the 777 program was the empowering of assembly line workers. Boeing managers encouraged factory workers at all levels to speak up, offer suggestions, and participate in decision making. Boeing managers also paid attention to a variety of "human relations" problems faced by workers, problems ranging from child care and parking to occupational hazards and safety concerns.[43]

All employees entering the 777 program — managers, engineers, assembly line workers, and others — were expected to attend a special orientation session devoted to the themes of team work and quality control. Once a quarter, the entire "777 team" of up to 10,000 employees met off site to hear briefings in the aircraft status. Dressed casually, the employees were urged to raise questions, voice complaints, and propose improvements. Under the 777 program, managers met frequently to discuss ways to promote communication with workers. Managers, for example, "fire fought" problems by bringing workers together and empowering them to offer solutions. In a typical "firefight" session, Boeing 777 project managers learned from assembly line workers how to improve the process of wiring and tubing the airframe's interior: "staffing" fuselage sections with wires, ducts, tubs, and insulation materials before joining the sections together was easier than installing the interior parts all at once in a preassembled fuselage.[44]

Under the 777 program, in addition, Boeing assembly line workers also were empowered to appeal management decisions. In a case involving middle managers, a group of Boeing machinists sought to replace a non-retractable jig (a large device used to hold parts) with a retractable one in order to ease and simplify their jobs. Otherwise they had to carry heavy equipment loads up and down stairs. Again and again, their supervisors refused to implement the change. When the machinists eventually approached a factory manager, he inspected the jig personally, and immediately ordered the change.[45]

Under the 777 program, work on the shop floor was ruled by the "Bar Chart." A large display panel placed at different work areas, the Bar Chart listed the name of each worker, his or her daily job description, and the time available to complete specific tasks. Boeing had utilized the Bar Chart system as a "management visibility syatem" in the past, but only under the 777 program was the system fully computerized. The chart showed whether assembly line workers were meeting or missing their production goals. Boeing industrial engineers estimated the time it took to complete a given task and fed the information back to the system's computer. Workers ran a scanner across their ID badges and supplied the computer with the data necessary to log their job progress. Each employee "sold" his/her completed job to an inspector, and no job was declared acceptable unless "bought" by an inspector.[46]

Leadership and Management Style

The team in charge of the 777 program was led by a group of five vice presidents, headed by Philip Condit, a gifted engineer who was described by one Wall Street analyst as "a cross between a grizzly bear and a teddy bear. Good people skills, but furious in the marketplace."[47] Each of the five vice presidents rose through the ranks, and each had a 25–30 years experience with Boeing. All were men.[48]

During the 777 design phase, the five VPs met regularly every Tuesday morning in a small conference room at Boeing's headquarters in Seattle in what was called the "Muffin Meeting." There were no agendas drafted, no minutes drawn, no overhead projectors used, and no votes taken. The home-made muffins, served during the meeting, symbolized the informal tone of the forum. Few people outside the circle of five had ever attended these weekly sessions. Acting as an informal chair, Condit led a freewheeling discussion of the 777 project, asking each VP to say anything he had on his mind.[49]

The weekly session reflected Boeing's sweeping new approach to management. Traditionally, Boeing had been a highly structured company governed by engineers. Its culture was secretive, formal, and stiff. Managers seldom interacted, sharing was rare, divisions kept to themselves, and engineers competed with each other. Under the 777 program, Boeing made serious efforts to abandon its secretive management style. Condit firmly believed that open communication among top executives, middle managers, and assembly line workers was indispensable for improving morale and raising productivity. He urged employees to talk to each other and share information, and he used a variety of management tools to do so: information sheets, orientation sessions, question and answer sessions, leadership meetings, regular managers' meetings, and "all team" meetings. To empower shop floor workers as well as middle managers, Condit introduced a three-way performance review procedure whereby managers were evaluated by their supervisors, their peers, and their subordinates.[50] Most important, Condit made team work the hallmark of the 777 project. In an address entitled "Working Together: The 777 Story" and delivered in December 1992 to members of the Royal Aeronautics Society in London,[51] Condit summed up his team approach:

> [T]eam building is . . . very difficult to do well but when it works the results are dramatic. Teaming fosters the excitement of a shared endeavor and creates an atmosphere that stimulates creativity and problem solving.
>
> But building team[s] . . . is hard work. It doesn't come naturally. Most of us are taught from an early age to compete and excel as individuals. Performance in school and performance on the job are usually measured by individual achievement. Sharing your ideas with others, or helping others to enhance their performance, is often viewed as contrary to one's self interest.
>
> This individualistic mentality has its place, but . . . it is no longer the most useful attitude for a workplace to possess in today's world. To create a high performance organization, you need employees who can work together in a way that promotes continual learning and the free flow of ideas and information.

The Results of the 777 Project

The 777 entered revenue service in June 1995. Since many of the features incorporated into the 777's design reflected suggestions made by the airline carriers, pilots mechanics and flight attendants were quite enthusiastic about the new jet. Three achievements of the program, in airplane interior, aircraft design, and aircraft manufacturing, stood out.

Configuration Flexibility

The 777 offered carriers enhanced configuration flexibility. A typical configuration change took only 72 hours on the 777 compared to three weeks in competing aircraft. In 1992, the Industrial Design Society of America granted Boeing its Excellence Award for building the 777 passenger cabin, honoring an airplane interior for the first time.[52]

Digital Design

The original goal of the program was to reduce "change, error, and rework" by 50 percent, but engineers building the first three 777's managed to reduce such modification by 60 percent to 90 percent. Catia helped engineers identify more than 10,000 interferences that would have otherwise remained undetected until assembly, or until after delivery. The first 777 was only 0.023 inch short of perfect alignment, compared to as much as 0.5 inch on previous programs.[53] Assembly line workers confirmed the beneficial effects of the digital design system. "The parts snap together like Lego blocks," said one mechanic.[54] Reducing the need for reengineering, replanning, retooling, and retrofitting, Boeing's innovative efforts were recognized yet again. In 1993, the Smithsonian Institution honored the Boeing 777 division with its Annual Computerworld Award for the manufacturing category.[55]

Empowerment

Boeing 777 assembly line workers expressed a high level of job satisfaction under the new program. "It's a whole new world," a 14 year Boeing veteran mechanic said, "I even like going to work. It's bubbly. It's clean. Everyone has confidence."[56] "We never used to speak up," said another employee, "didn't dare. Now factory workers are treated better and are encouraged to offer ideas."[57] Although the Bar Chart system required Boeing 777 mechanics to work harder and faster as they moved down the learning curve, their principal union organization, the International Association of Machinists, was pleased with Boeing's new approach to labor-management relations. A union spokesman reported that under the 777 program, managers were more likely to treat problems as opportunities from which to learn rather than mistakes for which to blame. Under the 777 program, the union representative added, managers were more respectful of workers' rights under the collective bargaining agreement.[58]

Unresolved Problems and Lessons Learned

Notwithstanding Boeing's success with the 777 project, the cost of the program was very high. Boeing did not publish figures pertaining to the total cost of Catia. But a company official reported that under the 777 program, the 3D digital design process required 60 percent more engineering resources than the older, 2D drawing-based design process. One reason for the high cost of using digital design was slow computing tools: Catia's response time often lasted minutes. Another was the need to update the design software repeatedly. Boeing revised Catia's design software four times between 1990 and 1996, making the system easier to learn and use. Still, Catia continued to experience frequent software problems. Moreover, several of Boeing's outside suppliers

Case 7 / Philip Condit and the Boeing 777: From Design and Development to Production and Sales

were unable to utilize Catia's digital data in their manufacturing process.[59]

Boeing faced training problems as well. One challenging problem, according to Ron Ostrowski, Director of 777 engineering, was "to convert people's thinking from 2D to 3D. It took more time than we thought it would. I came from a paper world and now I am managing a digital program."[60] Converting people's thinking required what another manager called an "unending communication" coupled with training and retraining. Under the 777 program, Ostrowski recalled, "engineers had to learn to interact. Some couldn't, and they left. The young ones caught on" and stayed.[61]

Learning to work together was a challenge to managers too. Some managers were reluctant to embrace Condit's open management style, fearing a decline in their authority. Others were reluctant to share their mistakes with their superiors, fearing reprisals. Some other managers, realizing that the new approach would end many managerial jobs, resisted change when they could, and did not pursue it whole heartedly when they could not. Even top executives were sometimes uncomfortable with Boeing's open management style, believing that sharing information with employees was likely to help Boeing's competitors obtain confidential 777 data.[62]

Team work was another problem area. Working under pressure, some team members did not function well within teams and had to be moved. Others took advantage of their new-born freedom to offer suggestions, but were disillusioned and frustrated when management either ignored these suggestions, or did not act upon them. Mangers experienced different team-related problems. In several cases, managers kept on meeting with their team members repeatedly until they arrived at a solution desired by their bosses. They were unwilling to challenge senior executives, nor did they trust Boeing's new approach to teaming. In other cases, managers distrusted the new digital technology. One engineering manager instructed his team members to draft paper drawings alongside Catia's digital designs. When Catia experienced a problem, he followed the drawing, ignoring the computerized design, and causing unnecessary and costly delays in his team's part of the project.[63]

Extending the 777 Revolution

Boeing's learning pains played a key role in the company's decision not to implement the 777 program companywide. Boeing officials recognized the importance of team work and Catia in reducing change, error, and rework, but they also realized that teaming required frequent training, continuous reinforcement, and ongoing monitoring, and that the use of Catia was still too expensive, though its cost was going down (in 1997, Catia's "penalty" was down to 10 percent). Three of Boeing's derivative programs, the 737 Next Generation, the 757-300, and the 767-400, had the option of implementing the 777's program innovations, and only one, the 737, did so, adopting a modified version of the 777's cross-functional teams.[64]

Yet the 777's culture was spreading in other ways. Senior executives took broader roles as the 777 entered service, and their impact was felt through the company. Larry Olson, director of information systems for the 747/767/777 division, was a former 777 manager who believed that Boeing 777 employees "won't tolerate going back to the old ways." He expected to fill new positions on Boeing's next program—the 747X—with former 777 employees in their 40s.[65] Philip Condit, Boeing CEO, implemented several of his own 777's innovations, intensifying the use of meeting among Boeing's managers, and promoting the free flow of ideas throughout the company. Under Condit's leadership, all mid level managers assigned to Boeing Commercial Airplane Group, about sixty people, met once a week in to discuss costs, revenues, and production schedules, product by product. By the end of the meeting — which sometimes ran into the evening — each manager had to draft a detailed plan of action dealing with problems in his/her department.[66] Under Condit's leadership, more importantly, Boeing developed a new "vision" that grew out of the 777 project. Articulating the company's vision for the next two decades (1996-2016), Condit singled out "Customer satisfaction," "Team leadership," and "A participatory workplace," as Boeing's core corporate values.[67]

Conclusion: Boeing, Airbus and the 777

Looking back at the 777 program 11 years after the launch and six years after first delivery, it is now (2001) clear that Boeing produced the most successful commercial jetliner of its kind. Airbus launched the A330 and A340 in 1987, and McDonnell Douglas launched a new 300-seat wide body jet in the mid 1980s, the three-engine MD11. Coming late to market, the Boeing 777 soon outsold both models. The 777 had entered service in 1995, and within a year Boeing delivered more than twice as many 777s as the number of MD11s delivered by McDonnell Douglas. In 1997, 1998, and 1999, Boeing delivered a larger number of 777s than the combined number of A330s and A340s delivered by Airbus, and in 2000 the 777 outsold each of its two Airbus competitors (Exhibit 7). A survey of nearly 6,000 European airline passengers who had flown both the 777 and the A330/A340 found that the 777 was preferred by more than three out of four passengers.[68] In the end, a key

	1996	1997	1998	1999	2000
McDonnell Douglas/Boeing MD11	15	12	12	8	4
Airbus A330	10	14	23	44	43
Airbus A340	28	33	34	20	19
Boeing 777	32	59	74	83	55

SOURCES: For Airbus, Mark Luginbill, Airbus Communication Director, February 1, 2000, and March 20, 2001. For Boeing, *The Boeing Company Annual Report*, 1997, p. 35, 1998, p. 35; "Commercial Airplanes: Order and Delivery, Summary," http://www.boeing.com/commercial/order/index.html. Retrieved from Web, February 2, 2000 and February 2, 2001.

element in the 777's triumph was its popularity with the traveling public.

Appendix A
Selected Features of the 777
Aerodynamic Efficiency

Aircraft operating efficiency depended, in part, on aerodynamics: the smoother the surface of the plane and the more aerodynamic the shape of the plane, the less power was needed to overcome drag during flight. To reduce aerodynamic drag, Boeing engineers sought to discover the optimal shape of the plane's major components, namely, the wings, fuselage, nose, tails, and nacelles (engine protective containers). Speaking of the 777's "airfoil," the shape of the wing, Alan Mulally, the 777's director of engineering (he later succeeded Condit as the project manager), explained:

> The 777 airfoil is a significant advance in airfoil design over . . . past airplanes . . . We arrived at this shape by extensive analysis in wind tunnel. . . . [W]e learned new things by testing the airfoil at . . . near flight conditions as far as temperature . . . pressures, and air distribution are concerned. And . . . we've ended up with an airfoil that is a new standard at maximizing lift versus drag.[69]

The 777's advanced wing enhanced its ability to climb quickly and cruise at high altitudes. It also enabled the airplane to carry full passenger payloads out of many high elevation airfields served by Boeing customers. Boeing engineers estimated that the design of the 777

lowered its aerodynamic drag by 5-10 percent compared to other advanced jetliners.[70]

A Service Ready Aircraft

A two-engine plane needed special permission from the Federal Aviation Administration (FAA) to fly long over water routes. Ordinarily, the FAA first certified a twin-jet for one hour of flight away from an airport, then two hours, and only after two years in service, three hours across water anywhere in the world. For the 767, Boeing attained the three hours certification, known as ETOPS (extended range twin-engine operations) approval, after two years in service. For the 777, Boeing customers sought to obtain an ETOPS approval right away, from day one of revenue operations. Boeing 777 costumers also expected the new jet to deliver a high level of schedule reliability from the start (Boeing 767 customers experienced frequent mechanical and computer problems as the 767 entered service in 1982).[71]

To receive an early ETOPS approval, as well as minimize service disruptions, Boeing engineers made special efforts to produce a "service ready" plane. Using advanced computer technology, Boeing tested the 777 twice as much as the 767, improved and streamlined the testing procedure, and checked all systems under simulated flight conditions in a new $370 million high-tech lab called Integrated Aircraft System Laboratory. The Boeing Company, in addition, conducted flight tests for an extended period of time, using United pilots as test pilots. Following a long validation process that included taking off, flying, and landing on one engine, the FAA certified the 777 in May 1995.[72]

The 777 proved highly reliable. During the first three months of its revenue service, United Airlines experienced a schedule reliability of 98 percent, a level the 767 took 18 months to reach. British Airways' first 777 was in service five days after delivery, a company record for a new aircraft. The next three 777s to join British Airways fleet went into service a day after they arrived at Heathrow.[73]

The Use of Composite Materials

Advanced composite materials accounted for 9 percent of the 777's total weight, the comparable figure for Boeing's other jetliners was 3 percent. Improved Alcoa aluminum alloys that saved weight and reduced corrosion and fatigue were used for the construction of the 777's upper wing skin; other non-metallic composites were used for the 777's rudder, fines and the tails. To help reduce corrosion around the lavatories and galleys, Boeing pioneered the use of composite materials for the construction of the floor beam structure. Boeing made a larger use of titanium alloys on the 777 than on any previous aircraft. Substituting steel with titanium cut weight by half, and space by one quarter; titanium was also 40 percent less dense than steel, yet of equal strength. The use of heat resisting titanium in the 777's engine nacelle saved Boeing 180 pounds per engine, or 360 pounds per plane; the use of titanium rather than steel for building the 777's landing gear saved Boeing 600 pounds per plane. Although titanium was more expensive than steel or aluminum, the choice of its application was driven by eco-nomics: for each pound of empty weight Boeing engineers squeezed out of the 777, Boeing airline customers saved hundreds of dollars worth of fuel during the lifetime of the plane.[74]

Appendix B
The 777's Choice of Engines

Pratt and Whitney (P&W), General Electric (GE), and Rolls Royce (RR) had all developed the 777 jet engine, each offering its own make. Boeing required an engine that was more powerful, more efficient, and quieter than any jet engine in existence; the 777 engine was designed to generate close to 80,000 pounds of thrust (the forward force produced by the gases escaping backward from the engine) or 40 percent more power than the 767's.[75]

All three engine makers had been selected by Boeing airline customers (Exhibit 8). United Airlines chose the Pratt & Whitney engine. Partly because P&W supplied engines to United 747 and 767 fleets, and also because the design of the 777 engine was an extension of the 747's and 767's design, United management sought to retain P&W as its primary engine supplier.[76] British Airways, on the other hand, selected the GE engine. A major consideration in British Airways' choice was aircraft efficiency: fuel consumption of the GE engine was 5 percent lower than that of the two competing engines. Other carriers selected the RR engine for their reasons pertaining to their own needs and interests.

Exhibit 8	The Choice of Engines: Boeing 777's Largest Customers		
Air France	GE	Japan Air System	P&W
All Nippon Airways	P&W	Japan Airlines	P&W
American Airlines	RR	Korea Airlines	P&W
British Airways	GE	Malaysia Airlines	RR
Cathay Pacific Airways	RR	Saudi Airlines	GE
Continental Airlines	GE	Singapore Airlines	RR
Delta Airlines	RR	Thai Airways International	RR
International Lease Finance Corp.	GE	United Airlines	P&W

SOURCE: Boeing Commercial Airplane Group, *777 Announced Order and Delivery Summary . . . As of 9/30/99.*

Exhibit 9	Selected Financial Data (Dollars in Millions Except per Share Data)				
Operation	2000	1999	1998	1997	1996
Sales and Revenues					
Commercial Airplanes	$31,171	38,475	36,998	27,479	19,916
Defense and Space*	20,236	19,015	19,879	18,125	14,934
Other	758	771	612	746	603
Accounting Differences	(844)	(304)	(1,335)	(550)	
Total	$51,321	57,993	56,154	45,800	35,453
Net Earnings (Loss)	$2,128	2,309	1,120	(178)	1,818
Earnings (Loss) per share	2.48	2.52	1.16	(0.18)	1.88
Cash dividends	$504	537	564	557	480
Per Share	0.59	0.56	0.56	0.56	0.55
Other income (interest)	386	585	283	428	388
Research and Development	1,441	1,341	1,895	1,924	1,633
Capital expenditure	932	1,236	1,665	1,391	971
Depreciation	1,159	1,330	1,386	1,266	1,132
Employee salaries and wages	11,614	11,019	12,074	11,287	9,225
Year-end workforce	198,000	197,000	231,000	238,000	211,000
Financial Position at 12/31					
Total assets	$42,028	36,147	37,024	38,293	37,880
Working capital	(2,425)	2,056	2,836	5,111	7,783
Plant and Equipment	8,814	8,245	8,589	8,391	8,266
Cash and Short-term Investments	1,010	3,454	2,462	5,149	6,352
Total debt	8,799	6,732	6,972	6,854	7,489
Customer and commercial financing assets	6,959	6,004	5,711	4,600	3,888
Shareholders' equity	11,020	11,462	12,316	12,953	13,502
Per share	13.18	13.16	13.13	13.31	13.96
Contractual Backlog					
Commercial airplanes	$89,780	72,972	86,057	93,788	86,151
Defense and Space*	30,820	26,276	26,839	27,852	28,022
Total	$120,600	99,248	112,896	121,640	114,173

*Including Information

SOURCE: *The Boeing Company 2000 Annual Report*, pp. 8, 98.

A special note: For additional financial data, as reported in the company's annual reports and other financial documents, check out Boeing's Web site at www.boeing.com

Endnotes

1. Eugene Rodgers, *Flying High: The Story of Boeing* (New York: *Atlantic Monthly Press*, 1996), pp. 423–15; Michael Dornheim, "777 Twinjet will Grow to Replace 747-200," *Aviation Week and Space Technology*, June 3, 1991, p. 43.

2. "Commercial Airplanes: Order and Delivery, Summary," http://www.boeing.com/commercial/ orders/index.html. Retrieved from Web, February 2, 2000.

3. J. P. Donlon, "Boeing's Big Bet" (an interview with CEO Frank Shrontz), *Chief Executive*, November/ December 1994, p. 42; Michael Dertouzos, Richard Lester, and Robert Solow, *Made in America: Regaining the Productive Edge* (New York: Harper Perennial, 1990), p. 203.

4. John Newhouse, *The Sporty Game* (New York: Alfred Knopf, 1982), p. 21, but see also pp. 10–20.

5. David C. Mowery and Nathan Rosenberg, "The Commercial Aircraft Industry," in Richard R. Nelson, ed., *Government and Technological Progress: A Cross Industry Analysis* (New York: Pergamon Press, 1982), p. 116; Dertouzos et. al, *Made in America*, p. 200.

6. Dertouzos, et. al, *Made in America*, p. 203.

7. Newhouse, *Sporty Game*, p. 188. Mowery and Rosenberg, "The Commercial Aircraft Industry," pp. 124–125.

8. Mowery and Rosenberg, "The Commercial Aircraft Industry," pp. 102–103, 126–128.

Case 7 / Philip Condit and the Boeing 777: From Design and Development to Production and Sales

9. John B. Rae, *Climb to Greatness: The American Aircraft Industry, 1920–1960* (Cambridge, Mass.: MIT Press, 1968), pp. 206–207; Rodgers, *Flying High,* pp. 197–198.

10. Frank Spadaro, "A Transatlantic Perspective," *Design Quarterly,* Winter 1992, p. 23.

11. Rodgers, *Flying High,* p. 279; Newhouse, *Sporty Game,* Ch. 7.

12. M. S. Hochmuth, "Aerospace," in Raymond Vernon, ed., *Big Business and the State* (Cambridge: Harvard University Press, 1974), p. 149.

13. Boeing Commercial Airplane Group, *Announced Orders and Deliveries as of 12/31/97,* Section A 1.

14. *The Boeing Company 1998 Annual Report,* p. 76.

15. Formed in 1970 by several European aerospace firms, the Airbus Consortium had received generous assistance from the French, British, German, and Spanish governments for a period of over two decades. In 1992, Airbus had signed an agreement with Boeing that limited the amount of government funds each aircraft manufacturer could receive, and in 1995, at long last, Airbus had become profitable. "Airbus 25 Years Old," *Le Figaro,* October 1997 (reprinted in English by Airbus Industrie); Rodgers, *Flying High,* Ch. 12; *Business Week,* December 30, 1996, p. 40.

16. Charles Goldsmith, "Re-Engineering, After Trailing Boeing for Years, Airbus Aims for 50 percent of the Market," *Wall Street Journal,* March 16, 1998.

17. "Hubris at Airbus, Boeing Rebuild," *Economist,* November 28, 1998.

18. *The Boeing Company 1997 Annual Report, p. 19; The Boeing Company 1998 Annual Report,* p. 51.

19. Donlon, "Boeing's Big Bet," p. 40; John Mintz, "Betting It All on 777," *Washington Post,* March 26, 1995; James Woolsey, "777: A Program of New Concepts," *Air Transport World,* April 1991, p. 62; Jeremy Main, "Corporate Performance: Betting on the 21st Century Jet," *Fortune,* April 20, 1992, p. 104; James Woolsey, "Crossing New Transport Frontiers," *Air Transport World,* March 1991, p. 21; James Woolsey, "777: Boeing's New Large Twinjet," *Air Transport World,* April 1994, p. 23; Michael Dornheim, "Computerized Design System Allows Boeing to Skip Building 777 Mockup," *Aviation Week and Space Technology,* June 3, 1991, p. 51; Richard O'Lone, "Final Assembly of 777 Nears," *Aviation Week and Space Technology,* October 2, 1992, p. 48.

20. Rodgers, *Flying High,* p. 42.

21. *Air Transport World,* March 1991, p. 20; *Fortune,* April 20, 1992, pp. 102–103.

22. Rodgers, *Flying High,* pp. 416, 420–24.

23. Richard O'Lone and James McKenna, "Quality Assurance Role Was Factor in United's 777 Launch Order," *Aviation Week and Space Technology,* October 29, 1990, pp. 28–29; *Air Transport World,* March 1991, p. 20.

24. Quoted in the *Washington Post,* March 25, 1995.

25. Quoted in Bill Sweetman, "As Smooth as Silk: 777 Customers Applaud the Aircraft's First 12 Months in Service," *Air Transport World,* August 1996, p. 71, but see also *Air Transport World,* April 1994, pp. 24, 27.

26. Quoted in *Fortune,* April 20, 1992, p. 112.

27. Rodgers, *Flying High,* p. 426; *Design Quarterly,* Winter 1992, p. 22; Polly Lane, "Boeing Used 777 to Make Production Changes," *Seattle Times,* May 7, 1995.

28. *Design Quarterly,* Winter 1992, p. 22; The Boeing Company, *Backgrounder: Pace Setting Design Value-Added Features Boost Boeing 777 Family,* May 15, 1998.

29. Boeing, *Backgrounder,* May 15, 1998; Sabbagh, *21st Century Jet,* p. 49.

30. Karl Sabbagh, *21st Century Jet: The Making and Marketing of the Boeing 777* (New York: Scribner, 1996), pp. 264, 266.

31. Sabbagh, *21st Century Jet,* pp. 131–132.

32. *Air Transport World,* April 1994, p. 23; *Fortune,* April 20, 1992, p. 116.

33. *Washington Post,* March 26, 1995; Boeing Commercial Airplane Group, 777 Announced Order and Delivery Summary . . . As of 9/30/99.

34. Rodgers, *Flying High,* pp. 420–426; *Air Transport World,* April 1994, pp. 27, 31; "Leading Families of Passenger Jet Airplanes," Boeing Commercial Airplane Group, 1998.

35. Sabbagh, *21st Century Jet,* p. 58.

36. Quoted in Sabbagh, *21st Century Jet,* p. 63.

37. *Aviation Week and Space Technology,* June 3, 1991, p. 50, October 12, 1992, p. 49; Sabbagh *21st Century Jet,* p. 62.

38. George Taninecz, "Blue Sky Meets Blue Sky," *Industry Week,* December 18, 1995, pp. 49–52; Paul Proctor, "Boeing Rolls Out 777 to Tentative Market," *Aviation Week and Space Technology,* October 12, 1992, p. 49.

39. *Aviation Week and Space Technology,* April 11, 1994, p 37, and June 3, 1991, p. 35.

40. Quoted in Sabbagh, *21st Century Jet,* pp. 68–69.

41. This was the phrase used by Boeing project managers working on the 777. See Sabbagh, *21st Century Jet,* Ch. 4.

42. *Fortune* April 20, 1992, p. 116; Sabbagh, *21st Century Jet,* pp. 69–73; Wolf L. Glende, "The Boeing 777: A Look Back," The Boeing Company, 1997, p. 4.

43. Quoted in *Air Transport World,* August 1996, p. 78.

44. Richard O'Lone, "777 Revolutionizes Boeing Aircraft Development Process," *Aviation Week and Space Technology,* June 3, 1992, p. 34.

45. O. Casey Corr. "Boeing's Future on the Line: Company's Betting its Fortunes Not Just on a New Jet, But on a New Way of Making Jets," *Seattle Times,* August 29, 1993; Polly Lane, "Boeing Used 777 to Make Production Changes, Meet Desires of Its Customers," *Seattle Times,* May 7, 1995; *Aviation Week and Space Technology,* June 3, 1991, p. 34.

46. *Seattle Times,* August 29, 1993.

47. *Seattle Times,* May 7, 1995, and August 29, 1993.

48. Quoted in Rodgers, *Flying High,* pp. 419–420.

49. Sabbagh, *21st Century Jet,* p. 33.

50. Sabbagh, *21st Century Jet,* p. 99.

51. Dori Jones Young, "When the Going Gets Tough, Boeing Gets Touchy-Feely," *Business Week,* January 17, 1994, pp. 65–67; *Fortune,* April 20, 1992, p. 117.

52. Reprinted by The Boeing Company, Executive Communications, 1992.

53. Boeing, *Backgrounder,* May 15, 1998.

54. *Industry Week,* December 18, 1995, pp. 50–51; *Air Transport World,* April 1994, p. 24.

55. *Aviation Week and Space Technology,* April 11, 1994, p. 37.

56. Boeing, *Backgrounder,* "Computing & Design/Build Process Help Develop the 777." Undated.

57. *Seattle Times,* August 29, 1993.

58. *Seattle Times,* May 7, 1995.

59. *Seattle Times,* August 29, 1993.

60. Glende, "The Boeing 777: A Look Back," 1997, p. 10; *Air Transport World,* August 1996, p. 78.

61. *Air Transport World,* April 1994, p. 23.

62. *Washington Post,* March 26, 1995.

63. *Seattle Times,* May 7, 1995; Rodgers, *Flying High,* p. 441.

64. *Seattle Times,* May 7, 1995; Rodgers, *Flying High,* pp. 441–442.

65. Glende, "The Boeing 777: A Look Back," 1997, p. 10.

66. *Air Transport World,* August 1996, p. 78.

67. "A New Kind of Boeing," *Economist,* January 22, 2000, p. 63.

68. "Vision 2016," The Boeing Company 1997.

69. "Study: Passengers Voice Overwhelming Preference for Boeing 777," http://www.boeing.com/news/ releases/1999. Retrieved from Web, 11/23/99.

70. Quoted in Sabbagh, *21st Century Jet,* pp. 46–47.

71. Boeing *Backgrounder,* May 25, 1998; Michael Dornmeim, "777 Twinjet Will Grow to Replace 747-200," *Aviation Week and Space Technology,* June 3, 1991, p. 43; Sabbagh *21st Century Jet,* pp. 286–87.

72. *Air Transport World,* April 1994, p. 27; *Fortune,* April 20, 1992, p. 117; Sabbagh, *21st Century Jet,* pp. 139–140.

73. *Industry Week,* December 18, 1995, p. 52; *Aviation Week and Space Technology,* April 11, 1994, p. 39; *Seattle Times,* May 7, 1995; Boeing, *Backgrounder,* May 15, 1998; Sabbagh, *21st Century Jet,* Ch. 24.

74. *Industry Week,* December 18, 1995, p. 52; *Air Transport World,* August 1996, p. 71.

75. Steven Ashley, "Boeing 777 Gets a Boost from Titanium," *Mechanical Engineering,* July 1993, pp. 61, 64–65; *Aviation Week and Space Technology,* June 3, 1991, p. 49; Boeing, *Backgrounder,* May 15, 1998; *Air Transport World,* March 1991, pp. 23–24.

76. Boeing, *Backgrounder,* May 15, 1998.

77. Sabbagh, *21st Century Jet,* pp. 12–122.

78. Arthur Reed, "GE90 Lives Up to Promises," *Air Transport World,* August 1996, p. 72.

The British Broadcasting Corporation

Clive Helm

Westminster Business School, University of Westminster

Introduction

The British Broadcasting Corporation (BBC) is one of the oldest broadcasting organisations in the world and a British institution. Known to many insiders and longer term employees simply as "the Corporation," it was founded and began broadcasting in 1922 in Britain not long after the invention and early development of radio around the beginning of the century. The BBC was also arguably the first organisation in the world to begin broadcasting high (by 1930s standards) definition television pictures which began on a regular basis from its transmitter at Alexandra Palace in the suburbs of north London in 1936. At the beginning of the year 2000, however, the BBC faces a very different world to that of the 1920s and 30s. One of the main questions now facing it is how its role as a British "public service" broadcaster can fit into the rapidly changing and increasingly competitive and globalised communications industry of the twenty-first century.

Outline History of the BBC and the British Broadcasting Industry: Origins and Early History

In June 1896 Guglielmo Marconi filed the first patent at the British Patent Office for "wireless telegraphy appara-

tus" and in the following month gave the first public demonstration of his new invention at the headquarters of the General Post Office in London. Use of radio, or "wireless" as it was commonly called in those days, spread rapidly, and the British government responded by quickly introducing a system of controls and regulation in 1904. After the First World War ended in 1918, popular interest in the new medium increased, particularly with a growing number of enthusiasts or "radio hams," many of whom built their own equipment as radio sets at that time were only just beginning to become commercially available and were expensive to buy.

In October 1922 the government sanctioned the formation of the British Broadcasting Company with a share capital of £100,000 owned jointly by a number of major radio manufacturers of the time, notably the Marconi, Western Electric, and General Electric companies. It began regular daily broadcasts in November, and in the following year was granted an exclusive licence to broadcast in the UK by the Postmaster General of Great Britain.

In December 1922 John (later Lord) Reith was appointed as the first General Manager. Born in 1896 with a strong Presbyterian Scottish background and upbringing, Reith had very definite views on the role that the new medium of broadcasting should play. His vision of the BBC was of a broadcaster with a strong mission and social purpose to "educate, inform, and entertain," while being imbued with a firmly moral ethic and making, as he put it, "no concessions to the vulgar." He also felt strongly that broadcasting in Britain should be kept as a monopoly with what he described as a "unity of control." Funding for the BBC was to be principally by means of a compulsory "licence fee" payable by anyone using a radio in Britain and collected by the Post Office, together with a levy of 10 percent on the sales of all new radio sets sold.

This case was written by Clive Helm, Westminster Business School. It is intended to be used as the basis for class discussion rather than to illustrate either effective or ineffective handling of a management situation.

The case was compiled from published sources.

© 2001 C. Helm, Westminster Business School, University of Westminster, London, UK.

Distributed by The European Case Clearing House, England and USA.

North America, phone: +1 781 239 5884, fax: +1 781 239 5885, e-mail: ECCHBabson@aol.com.

Rest of the World, phone: +44 (0)1234 750903, fax: +44 (0)1234 751125, e-mail: ECCH@cranfield.ac.uk.

All rights reserved. Printed in UK and USA. Web Site: http://www.ecch.cranfield.ac.uk.

In the months following these early beginnings the BBC's output began to grow to several hours a day to include news bulletins, talks, religious addresses, plays, orchestral concerts, children's programmes, and variety shows. In 1923, a government committee—the first of many over the years to come—met to discuss the future of broadcasting in Britain. In line with Reith's wishes, the committee rejected the idea of allowing the financing of the new medium of radio by advertising as had happened in the United States, and decided on the continuation of the licence fee. They also concluded that, "the control of such a potential power over public opinion and the life of the nation ought to remain with the state." In the same year, the first edition of the Radio Times, a magazine published by the BBC listing its programmes, went on sale.

As the cost of radio receivers fell rapidly, sales boomed. The number of licenses priced at 10 shillings (50 pence) issued rose rapidly from just over 35,000 in 1922 to around 600,000 in 1923 and continued to grow. Despite the high-minded ideals espoused by Reith, however, from the outset the BBC was not immune to criticism. While it may have sought to inform, educate, and entertain, there were those who felt that some of its output was somewhat highbrow and intellectual for popular tastes. As an organisation, some viewed the BBC as elitist and paternalistic, a criticism that was to echo down the years to the present day. A visitor to its offices near the Savoy Hotel in London, described them as ". . . next to the House of Commons, quite the most pleasant club in London—there were coal fires and visitors were welcomed by a most distinguished gentleman who would conduct them to a private room and offer whisky and soda." In the early days, radio announcers were reputedly expected to wear evening dress while on air and to speak according to a set of conventions and with a style of pronunciation that came to be known as "BBC English." One contemporary observer noted that at that time, "most employees had very little experience of broadcasting . . . mainly they were a mixture of enthusiasts who believed in the possibilities of radio."

On 1st January 1927 the BBC became a public body, the British Broadcasting Corporation, constituted under a Charter which was to be reviewed by the government periodically after a number of years. The Charter's purpose was to set out the role and standards for the BBC while at the same time giving it a separation from direct state influence, a system of public obligation and government regulation that came to be known as the "public service" model of broadcasting. A Board of Governors was appointed whose role was to see that the BBC was properly managed and accountable both to the government and licence fee payers. John Reith was appointed as the first Director General.

During the 1930s radio ownership continued to grow rapidly so that by the end of the decade almost all the population of Britain could receive programmes. In 1932 the BBC moved into Broadcasting House, a large, imposing, purpose designed building located in a prominent position in central London which housed all its facilities and offices and from where the King, George V, gave the first Christmas message on radio to the nation. In the same year, the "Empire Service" began short wave broadcasts to Australia, India, parts of Africa, and Canada. This was followed by the introduction of foreign language broadcasts to other parts of the world. These networks, which came to be called External Services, were financed by a grant directly from the government and not from the licence fee.

The Birth of Television

During the early 1930s, the BBC had been collaborating closely with Electrical and Musical Industries (EMI), a company with interests in music publishing and recording as well as radio manufacturing and electronics, to develop a workable technology for television. In November 1936, after several years of experimenting with different systems, the first regular television broadcasts began from the BBC's transmitter at Alexandra Palace in the suburbs of north London. Initially, television was only available in the London area and, as with the beginnings of radio, very few people owned television sets due to their low availability and high cost. Like radio, the new television service was also funded by a licence fee. John Reith, however, was uncertain about the new medium and apparently showed little enthusiasm for it. In his diary he wrote, ". . . to Alexandra Palace for the television opening. I declined to be televised or take part." In 1938, having set the tone of British broadcasting for years to come, he left the BBC to become the first government appointed chairman of the new British state airline, Imperial Airways.

Television broadcasting was stopped by the Second World War in 1939 when a Mickey Mouse cartoon that was showing was abruptly blacked out. Radio continued, however, encouraged by the government, both as a means of entertainment and morale raising, as well as a source of news and government information. English and foreign language services were expanded and continued to broadcast news and information throughout war torn Europe and many other parts of the world in over 45 different languages. These wartime broadcasts, together with the BBC's perceived freedom from direct state control, helped create and foster an international reputation for the quality and impartiality of its news reporting.

After war ended in 1946, television in Britain resumed—with the same Mickey Mouse cartoon that had been interrupted in 1939—and gradually spread to most of the country as ownership of sets increased, although progress in building a transmitter network was slowed by post war materials shortages. By the end of the 1940s, as well as its single television channel, the BBC was operating three radio networks; the "Home Service" carrying primarily news and speech, the "Light Programme" delivering popular music and light entertainment, and the "Third programme" which was almost exclusively dedicated to classical music.

The 1950s and the Launch of Commercial Television

The first competition in British broadcasting came in 1954 with the government's passing of an Act of Parliament allowing commercial television—television paid for by carrying advertising—to begin operating in the UK. The system of "Independent Television" (ITV) was to be regulated by an Independent Television Authority (ITA) which would own the transmitters, select and appoint which television companies would be allowed to operate, set standards for programmes, and regulate the standards and amount of advertising on the new network.

The ITV system was set up on a regional basis with a different television contracting company covering each of 14 different areas of Britain, as well as Independent Television News (ITN), which was jointly owned by all the regional companies and provided a news service to the whole network. The franchisees who bid for the contracts to run the new ITV regions were in the main consortia of companies who already had interests in businesses such as newspaper publishing, film production and distribution, ownership of theatres and cinemas, and other areas of the entertainment industry. In order to try and avoid complete regional monopolies, the franchise for the Greater London area, which was seen as being the most financially attractive, was split between two contractors, Associated-Rediffusion Television, which operated on weekdays, and Associated Television, which operated on weekends. These two companies, together with the two others which gained the contracts for the other most heavily populated and therefore most lucrative franchise areas, became the main "network companies" which produced and provided most of the programming to the rest of the ITV system. The smaller regional companies acted mainly as distributors of this material but had a contractual obligation to produce a certain amount of locally oriented news and programming. The first ITV broadcast took place on the evening of 22nd September 1955 and the first television commercial seen by the British public was for "tingling fresh" Gibbs SR toothpaste.

For a commercial broadcaster whose income comes from advertising revenue, the price that advertisers can be charged for airtime is usually directly related to the size of the audience watching—audience ratings are therefore all important. The ITV system, however, was quite strictly regulated by the ITA in terms of programme quality and content and the amount and type of advertising that could be carried. Direct sponsorship of television shows by advertisers, as happened in the United States, was not allowed. Initially programmes could only be broadcast after 7:00 pm. However, this was soon changed so that the TV companies could transmit between 9:00 am and 11:00 pm, but only to a maximum of 35 hours a week. There was also a short-lived restriction on broadcasting between 6:00 pm and 7:00 pm, which was known as "toddler's time" and which was intended to allow parents time to put small children to bed.

Many advertisers jumped at the new opportunity offered to promote their products directly to an audience of British consumers sitting in the comfort of their living rooms through the powerful medium of television for the first time. Following some initial losses after start up, several of the ITV franchisees quickly became very profitable: one of the smaller companies' shares, for example, multiplied in value 28 fold after two years, and owning a commercial television station at this time was famously described by one investor as "a licence to print money."

The advent of commercial television was seen by some of the senior management at the BBC as a major threat not only to the Corporation but also to the standard of British broadcasting as a whole. One executive at the time dismissively criticised ITV's output as being, "a collection of wiggle dances, giveaways, panel games, and light entertainment." From the beginning, although the commercial system was highly regulated, its programming was determinedly more populist and innovative than the BBC's, some of which now seemed staid by comparison. There was a greater emphasis on light entertainment and comedy on formats copied from American television, such as quiz and talent shows. By this time there was also a growing international trade in television programming and ITV, as well as producing its own shows, also tended to import more of its output from the United States—American police series such *Seventy Seven Sunset Strip* and westerns such as *Bonanza* proved to be particularly successful with British and other European audiences.

The popular success of ITV posed BBC executives at that time with a dilemma: should they try to fight back and get into an audience ratings battle with the commercial network or try to stay truer to Reith's founding ideals of public service broadcasting? Eventually it was decided that the BBC would not try to compete with the commercial network head on, but would instead be prepared to let its average share of audience ratings fall to one third of the total. To the surprise of many however, this did not happen—after an initial swing to ITV, the audience settled down to a roughly even split. Eventually the BBC responded to the commercial channels' challenge to a degree by introducing its own versions of some of the kinds of shows that ITV had made popular and by buying in more American programming of its own.

The beginning of commercial television also revived the public, political, and media debate that had been going on for many years, indeed since the BBC began, about the role of public service broadcasting. The BBC still viewed itself, and was seen by many, to be an integral part of the fabric of British national culture. It tended to be the natural channel to broadcast occasions of national importance such as addresses by the Queen or Prime Minister, the opening of Parliament, or major sporting and cultural events. Critics, however, questioned whether it was now necessary to have a public service broadcaster financed by a compulsory fee at all when a commercial system could now provide television for free. The ITV companies in particular argued fiercely that the licence fee gave the BBC an unfair advantage. There were those who thought that it amounted to a compulsory tax on the viewing public, some of whom, with the beginning of choice in broadcasting, might not actually want to watch the BBC's programmes at all. There was also a body of opinion that the BBC could be funded in other ways, perhaps by subscription or advertising, or a combination of both. This debate was to carry on and intensify over the decades to come.

Broadcasting in Other Parts of the World

In contrast to the public service, monopoly type of model that characterised the birth of broadcasting in Britain, the development of radio and television in the United States had followed a very different pattern. Radio station KDKA, which started transmitting in November 1920 from a shack on the roof of the Westinghouse company's plant in East Pittsburgh, is generally claimed to be the first commercial station to begin regular broadcasts in America. By 1922, 600 commercial stations were operating either independently or in chains and licenced by the US Federal Communications Commission. In 1926 the National Broadcasting Company (NBC) was founded as a subsidiary of the Radio Corporation of America. It rapidly acquired existing chains of stations as well as setting up more of its own. The Columbia Broadcasting System (CBS), which also operated a string of stations, was founded in the following year.

The first television broadcast in America was made by NBC from the World's Fair in 1939. Large-scale introduction of television was delayed by the Second World War, but by 1954 there were around 400 stations operating across the United States. By the beginning of the 1980s this number had grown to around 10,000 radio and 1,200 commercial television stations, a large majority of which were either directly owned by or affiliated to the three major networks, NBC, CBS, and their newer and smaller rival, the American Broadcasting Company (ABC).

Television in the United States was therefore almost wholly commercial, unlike in Britain. Advertisers in the US were also allowed to directly produce and sponsor radio and television shows which often prominently featured their products, a practice which was not allowed in the UK. Criticisms of American television tended to be that it was overly commercial and that its programming sometimes aimed at the lowest common denominator in terms of quality and content. In 1967 the Public Broadcasting System (PBS) was created as the first alternative network, financed by a mixture of public and private funding, and carrying a range of programmes that attempted to be less commercial and in some cases educational. British programming from both the BBC and ITV networks formed a significant part of PBS's output.

In most western European countries, broadcasting generally developed along lines broadly similar to those in Britain—a public service or state broadcaster funded by a licence fee alongside a fairly tightly regulated single or number of commercial channels, although in some countries the public service broadcaster also carried advertising. In Russia and Eastern Europe all the official broadcasting organisations were very much more directly under the control of the state.

Radio and television in Australia, Canada, New Zealand, and South Africa, all countries with a historic and cultural link to the UK, also tended to follow the same duopolistic form of a public service network, sometimes financed directly from the government, alongside a number of regulated commercial channels. In Australia and New Zealand in particular, the Australian Broadcasting Corporation and the Broadcasting Corporation of New Zealand were to some extent modelled directly on the BBC, whose personnel had been drafted in to help set them up with technology and expertise in their early days.

The 1960s and 70s

By the middle of the 1960s the BBC had learned to live with the challenge posed by ITV in Britain as both channels vied for the attentions of the British television audience. They both produced a range of popular, generalist programming that tried to appeal to most sections of the public at some time, including news and current affairs, light entertainment and comedy, sport, drama, and feature films. Both channels also had an obligation to produce a certain amount of educational programmes for schools. In 1964 the BBC was given permission by the government to begin a second channel, BBC2, which aimed at a more upmarket audience and had more of a bias towards factual and arts programming than the existing channel, which now became BBC1.

The International Marketplace

Although some programming on both the BBC and ITV networks was imported, particularly from the United States, much of it was produced directly by the BBC and the ITV companies themselves for the British home audience and therefore tended to have a distinctive British quality and cultural slant. Both the BBC and ITV exported programmes to a large number of foreign markets, most notably to western Europe, Australia, Canada, New Zealand, and also to the United States.

Among broadcasters around the world, the BBC had developed a reputation for producing high quality programming, particularly in areas like historical and classic drama, and factual programming in subjects such as natural history and popular science. Some of these programmes were co-productions which tended to be large, prestige projects which would be expensive for one network to undertake alone and which were therefore financed, produced, and possibly distributed jointly by the BBC and one or more other broadcasters in other countries. In the United States, the world's largest television market, some of the BBC's output tended to be seen as being more educational in nature rather than as entertainment. Although some programme material was sold to the major networks, a significant proportion of the BBC's American sales was therefore either to the PBS system or one of the other US public networks which had appeared to provide less purely commercially driven programming. On the whole, British comedy and light entertainment, although selling well in some countries like Australia and New Zealand, did not transfer well to the US mainstream market, probably due to cultural differences. Some British comedy shows, however, did sell successfully to smaller American stations and networks where they tended to find a specialist audience, sometimes achieving a cult status.

The job of selling programmes abroad was handled by the wholly owned commercial arm of the Corporation, BBC Enterprises, which had been formed in 1962. As well as exporting programmes, BBC Enterprises' other main activities included the exploitation of copyrights held by the BBC through sales of records and cassette tapes, film library material, and character merchandising. Selling programming in foreign markets was not always a very profitable activity, especially in some smaller countries where sales did not always cover costs. Revenues from BBC Enterprises were £3.7m in 1973 against total income from the licence fee of £128m.

The BBC in the 1960s and 70s

By this time, the BBC had grown to become a large organisation employing around 24,000 people full time which had come to see itself not just as a broadcaster but in some ways as a national institution. With a management structure organised largely along the lines of a hierarchical bureaucracy, it was now based not only in Broadcasting House and various other buildings around the centre of London, but also in a new, large, specially built complex spread over several acres of west London known as Television Centre, which is still the main headquarters of its television operations. Television Centre had been designed to house all the administrative offices, studios, technical resources, and many other kinds of facilities needed for television production—the scenery department alone reportedly covered more than one acre. There were also similar but smaller specially built facilities centres in several other British cities.

At this time, the BBC was also maintaining 12 orchestras, a full-time choral society and choir, and a training academy for musicians. Although some creative people involved in programme production such as performers, directors, and technicians worked on a freelance or contract basis, the majority of staff were employed permanently and paid on a system of fixed, graded salary scales. A significant proportion of employees, especially in managerial grades, tended to be graduates from leading universities, particularly Oxford and Cambridge. Recruitment and promotion for many posts tended to be carried out following appraisal processes and procedures that were similar to those in the British civil service. It was (and still is) customary for the Director General to be knighted by the Queen and given the title "Sir" in the New Year Honours list.

During the 1960s television became the dominant broadcasting medium as radio listening went into decline. In 1964 the BBC's radio division had also faced a further threat from a new breed of broadcaster, a number of offshore, unlicenced "pirate" radio stations that had begun to transmit continuous pop music to a growing and increasingly affluent young audience. The BBC at this time had no pop music station. Pirate stations were illegal under British regulations but avoided legal action by operating from ships moored just outside UK territorial waters. After strong lobbying of the British government by the BBC, offshore broadcasting was outlawed under an Act of Parliament in 1967. In the same year, three years after the first pirate station went on the air, the BBC started its own pop station, Radio One, and the other three radio networks were renamed Radios Two, Three, and Four. Shortly afterwards the first of a chain of around 20 BBC local radio stations around Britain was launched. This was both to fulfill a public service obligation to local, community broadcasting and also in response to what was seen as a need for more locally rather than nationally based programming based on differing needs throughout the country. Legitimate independent commercial radio began in Britain in 1973.

The 1980s

The 1980s saw many further rapid changes in British broadcasting including further deregulation and the growth of new technologies such as satellite and cable television and the internet, all resulting in ever increasing competition for the BBC.

New Rivals

Channel 4, a second terrestrial ITV channel, began broadcasting in November 1982 and in early 1983 the BBC's new breakfast time television show, the first in Britain, was closely followed by its new commercial rival, TV-am, a channel devoted solely to breakfast TV. In January 1984, Sky Television, the majority of which was owned by Rupert Murdoch's News International, a multinational media corporation, was launched as the first pay satellite television service in Britain. Sky offered several channels for a monthly fee to subscribers who also needed to buy a satellite dish and decoder box in order to receive its programmes.

In 1985 the government's Cable Authority began granting local franchises to operators to begin installing networks in British towns and cities and connecting up subscribers to cable. Up till this time, cable television in Britain had been limited to about 14 percent of households, but over the next few years it spread rapidly throughout the country. This followed the example of the United States where by 1984, 44 percent of all homes had been cabled. In the same year, Cable News Network (CNN), and American based, round the clock news channel, became available in Britain for the first time.

Over the next few years, many more satellite and cable channels were launched in the UK, as shown in Exhibit 6, many of them carrying specialist types of programming such as feature films, music, or sport. As had happened earlier in the US, there was much industry talk about the fragmentation of audiences and speculation that perhaps this was the end of broadcasting and the beginning of the era of "narrowcasting."

There were also changes in the ITV network that had now become known as Channel 3. Over the years, several of the original franchisees had changed and while the regional structure remained intact, a relaxation in the regulation on takeovers within the industry had led to a number of mergers between some of the ITV companies, a process of consolidation that seemed likely to continue.

Government Policy

In 1985, yet another government committee was formed under Professor Sir Alan Peacock as chairman to once again consider the future of broadcasting in Britain, and in particular alternative ways of financing of the BBC. A series of opinion polls had shown that around two-thirds of the British public were actually in favour of funding the BBC through advertising rather than by paying the compulsory licence fee. The Peacock committee concluded that the BBC should not have to carry advertising in the immediate future, but that there should be further moves to deregulate the broadcasting industry and that government broadcasting policy should seek to "enlarge both the consumers' choice and programme makers' opportunities."

Part of this policy was a requirement that by 1990 both the BBC and ITV companies should aim to commission around 25 percent of their original programming from outside contractors rather than produce it in-house. Although a small proportion of programme production had always been made by external, independent producers, this move hastened the growth of an independent television production industry in the UK making programming primarily for the BBC and commercial networks. Channel 4, the newest commercial channel, in fact had few production facilities of its own: instead it commissioned most of its original output from independent production companies or bought in programmes from the international marketplace, making it a model of what came to be called in the industry a "publisher broadcaster." Many of the newer cable and satellite channels, some of which had very low programming budgets compared to the traditional terrestrial broadcasters, also relied primarily on low cost, bought in material.

The BBC in the 1980s

By the late 1980s, there was a growing awareness amongst senior managers that the BBC would have to respond to the rapid changes that were happening in their industry. As if deregulation and the rapidly increasing competition from satellite and cable were not enough, there were also two other major threats that faced the Corporation towards the end of the 1980s. Firstly, for many decades it had enjoyed a steadily increasing revenue from licence fees as the number of households with television grew and also as viewers switched from black and white television to the higher priced licence for colour: by the end of the 1980s this growth had come to an end. Secondly, the BBC's Charter, which was periodically reviewed by the government, was due for renewal in 1996. With the explosion of television channels that had occurred, once again there was growing public and media debate about whether a publicly funded broadcaster was really necessary, throwing the future renewal of the Charter into doubt.

The BBC's Governors and top management realised that they would have to respond quickly to these challenges both in order to justify the continuation of the licence fee to both the government and the public and also to convince them that it was money well spent. In 1988, in conjunction with proposals put forward by consultants, a wide ranging five-year plan for restructuring and reorganising large parts of the BBC was formulated. Broadly its objectives were:

- to cut costs through reductions in overheads, staffing, and disposal of unnecessary premises
  and
- to reduce in house production capacity and make greater use of outside services and suppliers.

In addition, another set of goals was developed as the basis on which it was hoped the Corporation could move into the nineties and beyond. These were:

- to seek to maximise income from sources other than the license fee
- to investigate opportunities for commercial partnerships and
- to seek to compete in global markets.

Into the 90s

In 1992 John Birt became Director General of the BBC having been deputy since 1987. Birt had had a long career in British television, both in programme making and in management, and had formerly been Director of Programmes at London Weekend Television, the ITV weekend contractor for the London area.

A Period of Change: The Introduction of "Producer Choice"

Faced with the goals set out in the plan, Birt set about attempting the major task of restructuring large parts of the BBC, particularly the areas concerned with programme production. Over the next few years, working with external consultants, Birt and a team of senior managers began to spearhead moves to increase efficiency under a wide ranging set of new initiatives that were branded under the label "Producer Choice."

The main thrust of Producer Choice was to create an internal market in programme making resources by separating the purchasing and supply of these resources within the BBC. This meant that the internal purchasing of in house facilities used to make programmes such as studios, lighting, editing suites, and so on, as well as personnel, would be now financially distinct from the cost of providing them from within the organisation. A price would now be put on these facilities so that in house users and purchasers, in this case BBC producers (who are responsible for the overall production and delivery of finished programmes), would have greater flexibility and a more accurate and accountable way of budgeting and monitoring the production costs of their shows. Previously, the costs of providing and using BBC internal production facilities had never been fully assessed or quantified: costing and pricing these facilities would now enable programming to be costed and budgeted more accurately. Producers could now also shop around. They could compare the price of the in house facilities offered by "BBC Resources," as the newly created division was to be called, with those offered by outside suppliers which they now had the discretion to use if they felt that these offered better value.

At the same time, BBC Resources were encouraged to actively market and sell their programme making facilities to outside customers as well as internally within the BBC. Alongside this system of "market testing," a wide range of other internal overhead and support services were also set with stringent efficiency targets that were based on comparisons with the outside private sector.

The greater accountability offered by Producer Choice also enabled other production and administrative areas where there appeared to be overcapacity to be slimmed down. By 1996 the number of permanent jobs in BBC Resources was reduced from around 11,000 to around 6,800, with a reduction of several hundred other jobs in other general administrative and support functions. At the end of the same year, BBC Resources as a unit reported a trading surplus of £15m while supplying 78 percent of the BBC's facilities requirement while in the British production facilities market as a whole, it was reportedly the biggest provider of television and radio facilities in the UK, and had gained a 22 percent share of the total market.

Some radio and television production departments where there was thought to be overlap and duplication were also merged. This was particularly the case in one of the BBC's largest and most prestigious departments, news, which was responsible for producing the BBC's output of newscasts for all its television and radio channels. This was now merged with another department called current affairs, which was more concerned with the production of lengthier feature programmes devoted to news analysis and issues of current interest. Television and radio news operations were also combined. Journalists who had previously worked exclusively either in radio or television were now expected to work in both media as required by production schedules. Technical staff were also required to work more flexibly and in some cases adopt a wider range of roles and skills, a process known as "multi-skilling." The trend to multi-skilling was to some extent facilitated by developments in technology, which meant that some of the hardwear and equipment used in television and radio production was becoming easier and required less specialised training to use.

The productivity and efficiency gains achieved by these changes, as well as the sale and disposal of over one million square feet of surplus buildings and floor space over the same period, were estimated at over £100m with annual savings of more than £50m expected in years to follow. At the same time, both the BBC and ITV were given permission by the government to sell off their transmitter networks, and in 1997 the BBC's transmission system was sold to Castle Transmission Services for £244m resulting in the transfer to Castle of about 500 BBC staff.

Not unnaturally, the wide ranging changes and restructuring brought about by Producer Choice attracted criticism and reaction from some of the employees affected, as well as the in-house union that represented them within the BBC. However, although there were some relatively minor instances of resistance such as short strikes and "go slows" in some areas, on the whole there was no large scale industrial action.

There was a general move within BBC Resources towards employing production staff more on fixed term contracts or a freelance basis as needed by programme making schedules, and away from full time, permanent, salaried employment. Some full time staff were offered and chose to take redundancy payments that were calculated on the basis of the number of years that they had been in employment. Many of these people then become re-employed by the BBC in similar roles on flexible, short term contracts or as self employed freelancers, who could also work elsewhere in the industry.

Some of these employees, however, particularly those who had been with the BBC for a large part of their working lives, disliked the change from a culture characterised by a stable employment and clearly defined roles to one where they might have to undertake varying tasks and employment was less certain. They resented what they saw as the lessening of career security and the uncertainties presented by the new, more flexible structure, ways of working, and employment practices. Many felt that the BBC was no longer the organisation it once was. There were reports that morale among some staff had fallen to an all time low in the Corporation's history. In this new, more commercial climate, producers also claimed to be increasingly unsure about what their goals now were in making programmes—were they supposed to be going all out to chase audiences and ratings or aiming to make shows that aimed for something higher, more in the public service BBC tradition?

The decision to merge the news and current affairs departments and combine radio and television news was also generally unpopular with many of the journalists employed there. There was widespread dissatisfaction and claims that these moves would undermine the quality of news output, supposedly one of the BBC's main strengths. Several journalists, some of whose names were familiar to British audiences, took the opportunity to express their views by publishing articles in other newspapers, and one well known television newscaster, Martyn Lewis, left the BBC after many years.

John Birt also came in for criticism of his management style. To most BBC staff, the Director General was traditionally a remote and lofty figure. Birt, however, reportedly exacerbated this by communicating to employees through circulars and reports in a style loaded with management jargon that was deridedly dubbed "Birtspeak." Other critics, including producers and programme makers who felt that they had borne the brunt of the cost savings and efficiencies imposed by Producer Choice, also pointed to his apparent increasing like for using management and design consultancies and advertising agencies as well as the growing cost and amount of executives' time being reportedly taken up with exercises such as ongoing strategy reviews and management "awaydays." The cost of management consultants to the BBC had now risen to around £8m a year—money that could, they claimed, have been better spent on creating programming. It was pointed out that even after all the restructuring of the last few years, the BBC still employed around 23,000, although not all full time, and while there were now many less people involved in programme making, there had been a rapid growth in the number of managers in some areas, notably a department of around 300 corporate policy makers. Even a former BBC chairman, Marmaduke (now Lord) Hussey, took the opportunity to make a speech in the House of Lords, the upper chamber of the British parliament, lambasting the present BBC for "too much bureaucracy, over-bloated policy units, and too much time spent on expansion in management."

There were also problems with the implementation of some Producer Choice initiatives, which did not also always go smoothly or achieve the intended result. Apart from employees' reluctance to change working practices and the difficulties in designing and putting into practice new processes and procedures, it was found that anomalies sometimes occurred in trying to make the internal market actually work. Transactions and trading between various BBC departments, for example, could become inordinately time consuming, complex, and bureaucratic, causing frustration and increased costs. There was also the issue of whether it was really appropriate to compare and benchmark efficiency and performance measures derived from an examination of private sector industry firms with the internal departments of a large organisation like the BBC.

The BBC's Charter was renewed in 1996 for a further ten years, but as well as seeking cost savings and efficiencies, Birt's new strategy also encompassed longer-term plans to try and ensure the longer term future of the Corporation. Among these was the formation in 1994 of a new commercial and international division, BBC Worldwide, to replace BBC Enterprises. Worldwide's prime, stated purpose was to ensure that licence payers benefitted fully from the BBC's assets and to engage in commercial activities generating sustainable, increasing cash flow which could be passed back to the BBC. An important consideration was that Worldwide was to be financed and managed quite separately from licence fee funded activities in order not to breach the terms of the BBC's public service Charter.

The Dawn of Digital

The nineties also saw the beginnings of the digital revolution in television. As well as holding out the promise of better quality pictures and sound, digital technology meant that many more TV channels—potentially up to several hundred—could now be sent either by terrestrial signals or by cable or satellite to those who had digitally equipped sets.

In the BBC's 1997 Annual Report, John Birt wrote,

The entire broadcasting industry is experiencing massive changes and so far we have seen only the tip of the iceberg. Digital technology will allow choice and encourage competition on an unprecedented scale. Broadcasting

will become more disparate and more global, and certainly more commercial. The BBC cannot live in isolation from those changes. We have repeatedly said that we must adapt or die. We intend to take a leading role in exploiting the new technology, pioneering new services in the future as we have done in the past.

As well as an explosion of new channels, digital and cable also offered the possibility of delivering a whole host of other telecommunication, information, and interactive services into the home. Another major trend was the convergence of digital, internet, and telecoms technologies which offered a multitude of new "infotainment" possibilities. Not so long before, the internet had been seen by some broadcasters as a threat—an alternative source of home information and entertainment, particularly with the young and computer literate. The potential outcomes of these technologies coming together, such as the development of internet television, brought about the possibility of partnerships with other operators in these rapidly evolving industries.

Between 1992 and 1998, the BBC's annual audience share in the UK dropped from 32 percent to 29.5 percent, the first time it had fallen below what was considered to be the psychologically significant figure of 30 percent. Over the same period ITV's share fell from 42 percent to 32 percent. This followed the pattern in the US where the major terrestrial networks now had less than 50 percent of the audience following the growth of satellite and cable.

New Products and Services

In the late 1990s, the BBC launched a plethora of new services. As well as the existing BBC1 and 2 channels, several new licence fee funded channels were launched on digital terrestrial, cable, and satellite platforms free to licence payers: "News 24," a round-the-clock, rolling news channel, "BBC Choice," a selection of the best shows from the two existing networks, and "BBC Inform," an information and data service. At the same time, BBC Worldwide launched several new commercial pay channels and entered into various partnerships and international distribution deals. Among these were:

- "BBC World," a wholly owned round-the-clock news and information channel
- "BBC Prime," a wholly owned channel featuring the "best of the BBC"
- a joint venture with Flextech plc, a British-based pay TV operator, to begin three new subscription channels in Britain: "UK Horizons" (factual programming), Arena (arts), and "UK Style" (living and leisure)

- a partnership with the Discovery Channel in the US, which specialises in nature and wildlife programming, to co-produce and distribute programmes and also start three new pay channels in America: BBC America, Animal Planet, and People and Arts on satellite and cable
- BBC Online, the BBC's website and online news service, including 140,000 pages of information and over 50,000 news stories
- the publication of a growing number of new magazines and CD ROM titles based on BBC shows, as well as 120 book titles, 151 video titles, and 126 audio titles
- a 20 percent stake in UK TV Australia, a pay TV channel joint venture with Pearson plc, a British media group, and Fox Television of the United States.

By 1998, the BBC World channel was available on cable or satellite in 187 countries and claimed 52 million subscribers worldwide, while BBC Online claimed to be the UK's most visited site on the internet. Other new channels and online services were also planned for the future. In 1998 BBC Worldwide's total sales had grown to £409 with profits before tax of £12m.

BBC Worldwide and Its Brands

At the beginning of 1999, the new chief executive of BBC Worldwide, Rupert Gavin, who had recently been recruited from the internet and multimedia division of British Telecom, announced his aggressive new commercial strategy for BBC Worldwide. The strategy was to be that Worldwide would be first and foremost driven by the creation of programme brands for the global TV market, which could then be exploited and fed through a "brand pipeline" to channels and other media formats around the world. This development and international commercialisation of branded entertainment products followed an approach long followed by major Hollywood studios such as Disney. At this time, one of the BBC's most successful programmes was Teletubbies, a morning show for pre-school children featuring four lovable, cuddly toy characters which had been a great hit in the UK. Another BBC success story was TV cook Delia Smith, who was enormously popular and had a very large following in Britain. Both Teletubbies and Delia Smith had generated very large sales of spin-offs such as books and other licenced merchandise. Gavin described Worldwide's "battle plan" as "to take all the brands, whether it is Delia, Teletubbies . . . or new brands in the pipeline, and apply the same process: build the brand, get it on TV, exploit it internationally, and make it happen over a wide range of formats." Both Delia Smith's show and Teletubbies were made by independent production companies—Teletubbies was the creation of independent producers Ragdoll Productions, who had an interest in the ultimate copyright and licencing rights to the Teletubby characters. The Teletubbies had also been a hit in the US, where revenue from merchandising in the first year alone reportedly amounted to over US $800m.

In the rapidly changing and internationalising television and media industry, however, John Birt was of the opinion that one of the BBC's main assets was the BBC brand itself, which was considered to be well known and highly regarded throughout the world. He had been quoted as saying;

> The best values of the BBC lie in a dedication to programme quality. The BBC will concentrate on the kind of broadcasting most at risk in a commercial marketplace—original entertainment, intelligent news and current affairs, a comprehensive service of education, and the full reflection of our national culture. These are the BBC's historic broadcasting strengths, by which our audiences judge us, and where we believe we lead the field.

Conclusion

There were those who were not so sure about the Corporation's future. Both media commentators and politicians once again raised the issue of the conflict that seemed to be growing between public accountability to licence payers and commercialism while the BBC pursued what seemed to be an increasingly aggressive, commercial strategy through its Worldwide arm. Critics rounded on the fact that the new digital "News 24" channel, which had cost £30m of licence fee payer's money to set up, was as yet only available to the very few who had digital TV and at the end of 1998 was attracting a small audience of only 120,000. As for the digital revolution, while some analysts were predicting that by the year 2003 around 45 percent of British households would be equipped for digital TV, the signs were that its launch in early 1999 had been met with what seemed to be a general apathy by the British public. Writing in the "Guardian" newspaper in February 1999 under the headline, "Dawning of the Digital Age Is One Big Yawn to the British Viewer," one journalist reported the findings of a market survey which suggested that many consumers were confused by all the new media choices on offer and, although generally open to the idea of pay television, thought that digital TV had in fact little new to offer.

There were also accusations that, in a more competitive television environment, there had been some "dumbing down" of programmes and in particular that the BBC1 channel had gone downmarket in an attempt to chase ratings. There were also those who feared that in becoming more commercial and international, the BBC was in danger of losing its public service ethic and purpose. Former prominent British film producer David (now Lord) Puttnam, who was also chairman of the National Endowment for Science, Technology, and the Arts, had been quoted as saying,

> . . . No public service broadcaster can hope to be involved in every single aspect of the digital economy. [The BBC] must play to its strengths, its specific and very well honed strengths. In an increasingly expensive and fragmented broadcasting environment, the BBC, well led and well motivated, has to re-establish the argument for the universal licence fee as one of the most equitable and truly sustainable forms of social justice of the modern era.
>
> Its core role, its mission, needs to be defined as tightly as possible. To use a metaphor I've become increasingly fond of, the BBC needs to be more of a "keep" than a "castle" possibly a smaller organisation, but one with higher walls, guarding a unique national treasure house of innovative talent, critical standards, and, most important of all, truth.
>
> . . . Creativity drives everything that's good about the BBC. At its best, it's the lifeblood of the Corporation. . . . In my experience, creativity becomes stifled as soon as you attempt to over-manage it, if you constrain it too tightly within structures against which it will constantly, and for the most part unproductively, chafe.
>
> . . . Public service broadcasting was born out of passion, and a commitment to an ideal of "quality" in the first half of this century—I believe that only similar passion will sustain it in the increasingly hostile environment of the next century.

On the other hand, there were others who questioned why it should be assumed that the BBC was the sole bastion of quality broadcasting in Britain and who argued that, as in other forms of media, there was no reason why quality could not just as well be delivered by the commercial sector as by a public service broadcaster whose compulsory licence fee was now an anachronism. Writing in the national press, politician Gerald Kaufman, chairman of the government's Culture, Media, and Sports Select Committee expressed his view that:

> . . . As a smaller and smaller proportion of households watch BBC television, the outcry against the licence fee will grow angrier. . . . an organisation whose existence depends upon a regressive "poll tax" is, in the long run, unviable. . . . The Chancellor should do the decent thing. He should privatise the BBC, use the income from its sale to finance tax cuts to the present licence payers, (a double

vote winner), and force this increasingly weird anomaly to enter the real world of competitive broadcasting.

Even among some of the most ardent supporters of public service broadcasting, there were doubts as to whether the BBC, positioning itself as a "quality" broadcaster with a distinctive British heritage, could compete globally in an increasingly competitive environment against some of the world's biggest, diversified media companies such as Time Warner, Disney, and Viacom, all of whom were aggressively pursuing the new opportunities presented by the changing world of digital communications and entertainment. In a rapidly shifting and evolving industry, developments in early 1999 had included the purchase by Microsoft for $500m of a 5 percent stake in NTL, the British cable operator and owner of the former ITV transmitter network, and the acquisition of Flextech by TCI, a $50bn international cable giant headed by John Malone, who had been described by US Vice President Al Gore as "The Darth Vader of the information age."

Further denting the BBC's credibility at the end of the nineties was its loss of the rights to broadcast two major British sporting events. It was outbid by Sky for the UK football Premier League, and by Channel 4 for the English Test Match cricket series which had traditionally been shown on the BBC for many years. Sky was also eagerly pursuing other major sports events and had made a bid to buy Manchester United, one of the UK's leading football clubs. It seemed increasingly likely that in the future, major sporting occasions would be appearing on pay channels like Sky, which were also beginning to charge viewers extra to watch these events on a "pay per view" basis.

John Birt's tenure as Director General was due to end in the year 2000. With growing uncertainties hanging over the next renewal of the BBC's Charter by the government in 2006, it was announced in June 1999 that his successor was to be Greg Dyke, an executive with a long career in British commercial television and with a reputedly strong commercial and populist instinct. Dyke was quoted as saying that he wished to maintain and develop the ethos of public service broadcasting by "re-igniting the great traditions of the BBC," while at the same time aggressively developing the profit making potential of the Worldwide division by giving it greater autonomy and freedom to operate separately from licence fee funded activities.

In the conclusion of his statement in the BBC's 1998 annual report, John Birt wrote the following:

> The nature of broadcasting is changing rapidly. If the BBC is to continue to offer distinctive but genuinely pop-

ular service it must adapt. It is already doing so, but the challenges are immense, in terms of funding, technology, and competition. . . .

In the digital world of multi-channel choice, the need for the BBC will be greater, not less. Real choice means genuine programme diversity that guarantees something for everyone. That is what the BBC exists to deliver. We will sustain the services that audiences know and trust, but we will also launch new ones and so continue to extend choice. . . .

In striving to bring the benefits of the new technologies to every home in the land, the BBC will remain true to its long standing public service values and principles. The BBC in 1998 is a confident and dynamic institution. We are serving our audiences better than ever. We are alert to the world around us. We are ready to face the formidable challenges to come. We are, and intend to remain, one of the great cultural institutions in the world.

Macdonald, B.: "Broadcasting in the UK," Mansell, 1994.

Head, S.: "World Broadcasting Systems—A Comparative Analysis," Wadsworth, 1986.

Rosen, P. (ed.): "International Handbook of Broadcasting Systems," Greenwood, 1988.

Financial Times, London: 11.2.1999, 21.4.1999.

Sunday Times, London: 13.6.1999.

Guardian, London: 26.1.1999, 17.2.1999, 19.2.1999, 4.3.1999, 24.3.1999, 25.6.1999.

BBC Report and Accounts: 1973–74, 1993–94, 1994–95, 1995–96, 1996–97, 1997–98, 1998–99.

BBC Worldwide Report and Accounts: 1998–99.

Sources:

Briggs, A.: "The BBC: The First Fifty Years," Oxford University Press, 1985.

Exhibit 1	Opening Statement from the BBC Report and Accounts 1998–99

"We aim to be the world's most trusted broadcaster and programme maker, seeking to satisfy all our audiences in the UK with services that inform, educate and entertain, and enrich their lives in ways that the market alone will not. We aim to be guided by our public purposes; to encourage the UK's most innovative talents; to act independently of all interests; to aspire to the highest ethical standards; to offer the best value for money; to be accountable to our licence payers; to endeavour to be the world's leading broadcaster; to be the best—or learn from the best—in everything we do."

Exhibit 2   The BBC's Objectives

The Governors have endorsed the following key objectives for the BBC in 1998–99;

1   Secure the BBC's role as a standard setter of programme quality, in new as well as existing services, continuously innovating, developing, and refreshing output across all genres.

2   Serve the whole audience effectively, responding to the needs of the different groups of licence payers and communicating the value of the BBC's services to them.

3   In the light of the BBC's strong commitment to education, embrace opportunities presented by new initiatives and new broadcast technologies and ensure that educational purposes underpin programming on a broad front.

4   Strengthen popular drama, entertainment, and situation comedy on television.

5   Demonstrate increased value for money throughout the BBC.

6   Maximise the potential for creativity and efficiency of digital production.

7   Agree and implement plans for responding to new political institutions in Scotland, Wales, Northern Ireland, and London.

8   Secure the position of the World service within the context of a global strategy for the BBC in television, radio, and online.

9   Continue to improve the effectiveness of the BBC's two main commercial businesses, BBC Worldwide and BBC Resources, while trading fairly.

10 Build on the improvement in two way communication between staff and management and ensure that all who work for the BBC play their part in delivering BBC goals and strategies.

SOURCE: BBC Report and Accounts, 1998–99.

Exhibit 3   BBC Top Organisational Structure, 1935

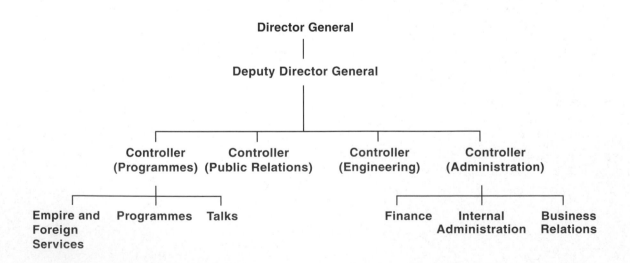

Exhibit 4   BBC Top Organisational Structure, 1994

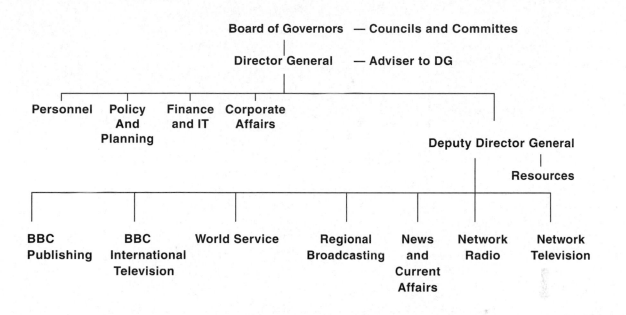

SOURCE: BBC Report and Accounts, 1994–95.

Exhibit 5   ITV Companies Ownership, March 1995

Owner	Company	Area of UK Covered
Granada Group	Granada TV	North West England
	Yorkshire TV	Yorkshire
	Tyne Tees TV	North East England
	GMTV (share)	UK Breakfast time
Carlton Communications	Carlton TV	London (weekdays)
	Central TV	East and West Midlands
	Westcountry TV	South West England
	GMTV (share)	UK Breakfast time
United News and Media	Anglia TV	East of England
	Meridian TV	Southern England
	HTV	Wales and West of England
Scottish Media Group	Scottish TV	Central Scotland
	Grampian TV	Northern Scotland
	GMTV (share)	UK Breakfast time
Ulster	Ulster TV	Northern Ireland
Border and Cumbrian Newspaper Group	Border TV	Scottish Borders

Exhibit 6 Selected UK Satellite and Cable Channels, 1984–93

Start:	Channel:	Start:	Channel:
1984	Sky One	1989	Eurosport
1984	Screensport	1989	Sky Movies
1984	The Children's Channel	1989	Sky News
1985	Premiere*	1990	The Movie Channel
1985	Bravo	1990	Sky Sports
1985	Home Video Channel	1991	Sportscast
1985	The Arts Channel	1991	The Comedy Channel*
1985	Lifestyle	1992	The Adult Channel
1986	Indra Dhnush (Asia Vision)	1992	The Parliamentary Channel
1986	Vision	1992	The Learning Channel
1987	Super Channel	1992	The European Family Christian Network
1987	MTV Europe	1992	UK Gold
1987	CNN International	1992	TV Asia
1987	Cable Jukebox	1993	UK Living
1988	The Landscape Channel	1993	The Family Channel
1989	Japansat	1993	QVC The Shopping Channel
1989	The Discovery Channel		

*No longer operating

Exhibit 7 BBC Licence Fee Income, 1996–97 through 1998–99

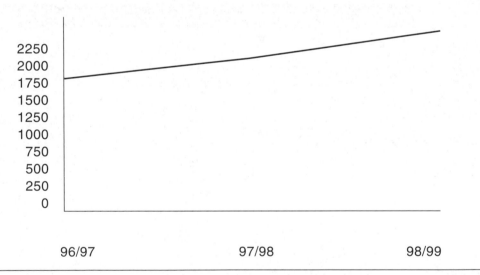

SOURCE: BBC Report and Accounts, 1998–99.

Exhibit 8   BBC Licence Fee Expenditure, 1998–99

Total Expenditure	£2155m
Expenditure (£m)	
BBC1	752
BBC2	406
National and regional television	185
National, regional, and local radio	149
BBC Radio 1	37
BBC Radio 2	42
BBC Radio 3	62
BBC Radio 4	89
BBC Radio 5 Live	55
BBC1 & BBC2 Widescreen	30
BBC Choice	34
BBC News 24	50
BBC Parliament	2
Digital Radio	6
BBC Online	23
Digital development costs	9
Restructuring	31
Corporate centre	60
Licence fee collection costs	133

SOURCE: BBC Report and Accounts, 1998–99.

Exhibit 9   BBC Worldwide Sales History Excluding Joint Ventures, 1993–94 through 1998–99

1993–94	1994–95	1995–96	1996–97	1997–98	1998–99
£239m	£274m	£338m	£334m	£409m	£429m

Exhibit 10   BBC Worldwide Cash Flow to the BBC, 1996–97 through 1998–99

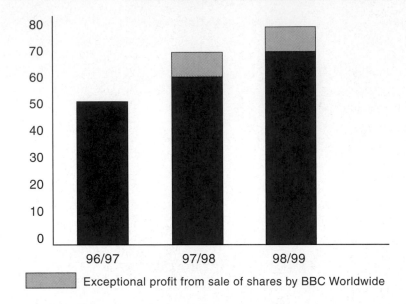

SOURCE: BBC Report and Accounts, 1998–99.

Exhibit 11   BBC Worldwide Joint Ventures, 1997–98

Name of Entity	Type of Entity	Partner	Date Entered
UK Channel Management Ltd.	Joint Venture	Flextech	April 1997
UK Gold Holdings	Joint Venture	Flextech	April 1997
Animal Planet (Latin America)	Associate	Discovery	March 1998
People and Arts (Latin America)	Associate	Discovery	March 1998
Animal Planet LLC	Associate	Discovery	March 1998
JV Programmes	Joint Venture	Discovery	March 1998
JV Network LLC	Associate	Discovery	March 1998

To year end 31st March:	1999	1998 £m
Turnover (including share of joint ventures)	446.3	422.0
Less: Share of joint ventures	(26.0)	(13.1)
Group turnover	420.3	408.9
Cost of sales	(264.6)	(274.8)
Gross profit	155.7	134.1
Distribution costs	109.4	106.3
Administration expenses	(34.9)	(35.6)
Group operating profit/loss	11.4	7.8
Share of operating profit in joint ventures	—	—
Share of operating profit in associates	0.6	0.6
Total operating profit (loss)	12.0	(7.2)
Profit on sale of investments	8.4	20.7
Profit before interest and taxation	20.4	13.5
Interest receivable	8.5	0.5
Interest payable	(1.3)	(2.2)
Profit on ordinary activities before taxation	19.9	11.8
Tax on profit on ordinary activities	(7.8)	(8.5)
Profit on ordinary activities after taxation	12.1	3.3
Equity minority interest	(0.1)	(0.1)
Retained profit for the financial year	12.0	3.2

Exhibit 13 BBC Worldwide Consolidated Balance Sheet, 1998–99

As at 31st March	1999	1998
Fixed assets		
Tangible fixed assets	9.6	8.4
Investment in programmes for future sale	95.2	85.3
Investments and interests in associated undertakings	0.2	0.1
	105.0	93.8
Current assets		
Stock	13.7	13.2
Debtors	116.1	119.6
Cash at bank	21.1	13.0
	150.9	145.8
Creditors falling due within one year	(167.9)	(166.5)
Net current liabilities	(17.0)	(20.7)
Total assets less current liabilities	88.0	73.1
Creditors falling due after more than one year	(16.9)	(16.9)
Provisions for liabilities and charges	(1.5)	—
Net assets	69.6	56.2
Capital and reserves		
Called up share capital	0.2	0.2
Profit and loss account	69.1	55.8
Equity shareholder's fund	69.3	56.0
Equity minority interest	0.3	0.2
	69.6	56.2

Exhibit 14 BBC Worldwide Board Profiles, 1998

Peter Teague, BBC Worldwide's Director of Finance and Information Technology, is Acting Chief Executive of BBC Worldwide until Rupert Gavin takes up the post of Chief Executive on 1st July 1998. At that point Peter becomes Managing Director of the UK Region and Deputy Chief Executive. Peter, a qualified chartered accountant, joined BBC Worldwide in January 1997 from AT&T Unisource Communications Services. He began his career at Peat Marwick Mitchell as an Audit Senior. After spending the majority of his post qualification career in venture capital and corporate finance advisory roles, he joined ISTEL in 1987 as Director, Finance.

Mike Phillips is Director of the Rights Agency, which provides a link between BBC Worldwide and BBC programme makers in the exploitation of commercial rights and handles all BBC co-productions. Mike joined BBC Worldwide Television as Deputy Managing Director in June 1996 from his post as Managing Director of Thames Television. He was also a director of the parent company, Pearson Television.

Peter Phippen is BBC Worldwide's Managing Director, UK Region, with responsibility for magazine, book, video, and spoken word publishing and BBC Worldwide's television joint venture with Flextech. He joined IPC Magazines in 1982 as a graduate trainee, leaving five years later to join BBC Magazines as Marketing Director. From 1 July Peter becomes President and Chief Executive Officer of BBC Worldwide Americas Inc., to drive forward our business throughout the Americas.

Mark Young is the Managing Director for BBC Worldwide's activities in Europe, the Middle East, Africa, and India. He was appointed Finance and Commercial Director in June 1994 and was Managing Director of BBC Worldwide until November 1997. Mark joined the BBC in 1993 as Chief Assistant to the Deputy Director General. Prior to that, he was Head of Business Affairs at Independent Television News. He previously spent five years with the publishers William Collins.

Sam Younger took up his post as Managing Director of BBC World Service in November 1994. He is responsible for BBC World Service's international radio broadcasts in 44 languages, listened to by 140 million people each week. Sam was Assistant Editor of Middle East International before joining BBC External Services as a talks writer in 1979. His career with BBC World Service has included time as Director of Broadcasting, Controller of Overseas Services, Head of the Arabic Service, and head of Current Affairs, World Service in English. Sam has been a director of BBC Worldwide since December 1995.

Carolyn Fairbairn is BBC Worldwide's Director of Strategy devising strategies to maximise BBC Worldwide's commercial opportunities both in the UK market and in key territories around the world. Previously Carolyn was a member of the Downing Street Policy Unit with responsibility for policy development in health and social issues. Previous to this, she spent seven years working as a Management Consultant with McKinsey and Company with a particular focus on the information technology and broadcasting sectors.

Jeff Taylor is BBC Worldwide's Director of Global Brand Development, the division which develops and markets properties with multiple media global potential. Jeff joined BBC Worldwide in February 1996 as Director of Consumer Publishing. He joined from Sony where he was European Marketing Manager for Consumer Video, responsible for Western and Eastern Europe.

Jeremy Mayhew is BBC Worldwide's Director of New Media. Jeremy joined BBC Worldwide in 1995 as Director of Strategy and New Media Development. Jeremy joined from the BBC where he was Head of Strategy Development, Corporate Strategy, advising the Director of General and Board of Management on major policy and managerial issues. Previously he was Special Adviser at the Departments of Trade and Industry and Social Security and was a consultant in the communications practice of Booz, Allen, and Hamilton. Jeremy has also worked as a producer on current affairs and documentary television programmes.

SOURCE: BBC Worldwide Annual Report and Accounts, 1998–99.

The Comeback of Caterpillar, 1985–2001

Isaac Cohen

San Jose State University

For three consecutive years, 1982, 1983, and 1984, the Caterpillar Company lost one million dollars a day. Caterpillar's major competitor was a formidable Japanese company called Komatsu. Facing a tough global challenge, the collapse of its international markets, and an overvalued dollar, Caterpillar had no choice. It had to reinvent itself, or die.

Caterpillar managed to come back as a high-tech, globally competitive, growth company. Over a period of 15 years, and throughout the tenure of two CEOs — George Schaefer (1985-1990) and Donald Fites (1990-1999) — Caterpillar had transformed itself. George Schaefer introduced cost-cutting measures and employee involvement programs, outsourced machines, parts, and components, and began modernizing Caterpillar's plants. Donald Fites diversified Caterpillar's product line and reorganized the company structurally. He also completed Caterpillar's plant modernization program, revitalized Caterpillar's dealership network, and altered radically Caterpillar's approach to labor relations.

As Donald Fites retired in February 1999, Glen Barton was elected CEO. Barton was in an enviable position. The world's largest manufacturer of construction and mining equipment, and a Fortune 100 company, Caterpillar generated 21 billion dollars in revenues in 1998, the sixth consecutive record year. Leading its industry while competing globally, Caterpillar recorded a $1.5 billion profit in 1998, the second best ever.[1]

Notwithstanding Caterpillar's dramatic comeback, Barton could not count on the continual prosperity of the company because the US construction industry was moving into a grinding economic downturn. At the time Barton completed his first year as CEO, on February 1,

2000, the company announced its 1999 result: sales declined by 6 percent and earnings by 37 percent. In March 2000, Caterpillar share price was trading close to its 52 week low ($36 against a high of $66) and one industry analyst declared: "The stock for the foreseeable future is dead money."[2]

What should Barton do? Should Burton follow the strategies implemented by Schaefer and Fites to enhance Caterpillar's competitive position relative to its principal rivals, Komatsu, John Deere, and CNH Global (CNH was the product of a 2000 merger between the Case Corp. and New Holland)? Should he, instead, reverse some of the policies introduced by his predecessors? Or should he, rather, undertake whole new strategies altogether?

To assess Barton's strategic choices in improving Caterpillar's results, the case looks back at the experience of his two predecessors. How precisely did both Schaefer and Fites manage to turn Caterpillar around?

The Heavy Construction Equipment Industry

The heavy construction equipment industry supplied engineering firms, construction companies, and mine operators. The industry's typical product line included earthmovers (bulldozers, loaders, and excavators), road building machines (pavers, motor graders, and mixers), mining related equipment (off-highway trucks, mining shovels), and large cranes. Most machines were offered in a broad range of sizes, and a few were available with a choice of wheels or crawler tracks. Most were used for the construction of buildings, power plants, manufacturing plants, and infra-structure projects such as roads, airports, bridges, tunnels, dams, sewage systems, and water lines. On a global basis, earthmoving equipment accounted for about half of the industry's total sales in

---

This case was presented in the October 2001 meeting of the North American Case Research Association at Memphis, Tennessee. Copyright Isaac Cohen, 2001.

the 1990s (Exhibit 1). Among earthmovers, hydraulic excavators accounted for 45 percent of the sales. Excavators were more productive, more versatile, and easier to use in tight spaces than either bulldozers or loaders. Off-highway trucks that hauled minerals, rocks, and dirt, were another category of fast selling equipment.[3]

Global demand for heavy construction machinery grew at a steady rate of 4.5 percent in the 1990s. The rate of growth, however, was faster among the developing nations of Asia, Africa, and Latin America than among the developed nations. In the early 2000s, North America and Europe were each expected to account for 25 percent of the industry's sales, Japan for 20 percent, and the developing nations for the remaining 30 percent.[4]

The distinction between original equipment and replacement parts was an essential feature of the industry. Replacement parts and "attachments" (work tools) made up together over a quarter of the total revenues of the heavy construction equipment industry (Exhibit 1), but accounted for a substantially larger share of the industry's earnings for two reasons: first, the sale of replacement parts was more profitable than that of whole machines; and second, the market for replacement parts was less cyclical than that for original equipment.[5] As a rule of thumb, the economic life of a heavy construction machine was 10 to 12 years, but in many cases, especially in developing countries, equipment users kept their machines in service much longer, perhaps 20 to 30 years, thus creating an ongoing stream of revenues for parts, components, and related services.[6]

Another characteristic of the industry was the need to achieve economies of scale. According to industry observers, the optimal scale of operation was about 90,000 units annually. In other words, up to a produc-tion level of 90,000 units a year, average equipment unit cost declined as output increased, and therefore capturing a large market share was critical for benefitting from economies of scale.[7] The relatively low volume of global sales—200,000 to 300,000 earthmoving equipment units per year (1996)[8]—further intensified competition over market share among the industry's leading firms.

Successful marketing also played an important role in gaining competitive advantage. A widespread distribution and service network had always been essential for competing in the heavy construction equipment industry because "downtime" resulting from the inability to operate the equipment at a construction site was very costly. Typically, manufacturers used a worldwide network of dealerships to sell machines, provide support, and offer after sales service. Dealerships were independent, company owned, or both, and were normally organized on an exclusive territorial basis. Since heavy construction machines operated in a tough and inhospitable environment, equipment wore out and broke down frequently, parts needed to be rebuilt or replaced often, and therefore manufacturers placed dealers in close proximity to equipment users, building a global service network that spread all over the world.

Manufacturers built alliances as well. Intense competition over market share drove the industry's top firms to form three types of cooperative agreements. The first were full scale joint ventures to share production. Caterpillar's joint venture with Mitsubishi Heavy Industries was a notable case in point. The second were technology sharing agreements between equipment manufacturers and engine makers to ensure access to the latest engine technology. The joint venture between Komatsu and Cummins Engine, on the one hand, and the Case Corporation and Cummins, on the other, provided two examples. The third type of agreements were

| Exhibit 1 | Global Demand of Heavy Construction Equipment by Major Categories, 1985–2005 |

Item	1985	1994	2000	2005*
Earthmoving Equipment	50%	49%	49%	49%
Off Highway Trucks	8%	7%	7%	7%
Construction Cranes	9%	11%	10%	10%
Mixers, Pavers, and Related Equipment	6%	6%	7%	7%
Parts & Attachments	27%	27%	27%	26%
Total Demand (billions)	$38	$56	$72	$90

*Percentages do not add up to 100 because of rounding.
Source: Andrew Gross and David Weiss, "Industry Corner: The Global Demand for Heavy Construction Equipment," *Business Economics*, July 1996, p. 56.

technology sharing alliances between major global firms and local manufacturers whereby the former gained access to new markets, and in return, supplied the latter with advanced technology. Caterpillar utilized such an arrangement with Shanghai Diesel in China, and Komatsu did so with the BEML company in India.[9]

History of Caterpillar

At the turn of the century, farmers in California faced a serious problem. Using steam tractors to plow the fine delta land of the San Joaquin valley, California farmers fitted their tractors with large drive wheels to provide support on the moist soil; nevertheless, despite their efforts, the steamer's huge wheels—measuring up to 9 feet high—sank deeply into the soil. In 1904, Benjamin Holt, a combine maker from Stockton California, solved the protractor's weight on a broader surface. Holt, in addition, replaced the heavy steam engine with a gasoline engine, thus improving the tractor's mobility further by reducing its weight (a steam tractor weighed up to 20 tons). He nicknamed the tractor "Caterpillar", acquired the "Caterpillar" trade mark, and applied it to several crawler-type machines that his company manufactured and sold. By 1915 Holt tractors were sold in 20 countries.[10]

Outside agriculture, crawler tractors were first used by the military. In 1915, the British military invented the armor tank, modeling it after Holt's machine, and during World War I, the United States and its allies in Europe utilized Holt's track-type tractors to haul artillery and supply wagons. In 1925, the Holt Company merged with another California firm, the Best Tractor Company, to form Caterpillar (Cat). Shortly thereafter, Caterpillar moved its corporate headquarters and manufacturing plants to Peoria, Illinois. The first company to introduce a diesel engine on a moving vehicle (1931), Caterpillar discontinued its combine manufacturing during the 1930s and focused instead on the production of road-building, construction, logging, and pipelaying equipment. During World War II, Caterpillar served as the primary supplier of bulldozers to the US Army; its sales volume more than tripled between 1941 and 1944 to include motor graders, diesel engines, and electric generators, apart from tractors and wagons.[11]

Demand for Caterpillar products exploded in the early post-war years. Cat's equipment was used to reconstruct Europe, build the US interstate highway system, erect the giant dams of the Third World, and lay out the major airports of the world. The company managed to differentiate itself from its competitors by producing reliable, durable and high quality equipment, offering a quick after-sales service, and providing a speedy delivery of replacement parts. As a result, during the 1950s and 1960s, Caterpillar had emerged as the uncontested leader of the heavy construction equipment industry, far ahead of any rival. By 1965, Caterpillar had established foreign manufacturing subsidiaries—either wholly owned or joint ventures—in Britain, Canada, Australia, Brazil, France, Mexico, Belgium, India, and Japan. Caterpillar's 50/50 joint venture with Mitsubishi in Japan, established in 1963, had become one of the most successful, stable, and enduring alliances among all American-Japanese joint ventures.[12]

Caterpillar's distribution and dealership network also contributed to the company's worldwide success. From the outset, the company's marketing organization rested on a dense network of independent dealers who sold and serviced Cat equipment. Strategically located throughout the world, these dealers were self sustaining entrepreneurs who invested their own capital in their business, derived close to 100 percent of their revenues from selling and supporting Cat equipment, and cultivated close relationships with Caterpillar customers. On average, a Caterpillar dealership had remained in the hands of the same family—or company—for over 50 years. Indeed, some dealerships, including several located overseas, predated the 1925 merger that gave birth to Caterpillar.[13] In 1981, on the eve of the impending crisis, the combined net worth of Cat dealers equaled that of the company itself, the total number of employees working for Cat dealers was slightly lower than the company's own workforce.[14]

The Crisis of the Early 1980s

Facing weak competition both at home and abroad, Caterpillar charged premium prices for its high quality products, paid its production workers, union-scale wages, offered its shareholders high rates of return on their equity, and enjoyed superior profits. Then, in 1982, following a record year of sales and profits, Caterpillar suddenly plunged into three successive years of rising losses totaling nearly 1$ billion. "Quite frankly, our long years of success made us complacent, even arrogant,"[15] Pierre Guerindon, an executive vice president at Cat conceded.

The crisis of 1982-84 stemmed from three sources: a global recession, a costly strike, and unfavorable currency exchange rates. First, the steady growth in demand for construction machinery, dating back to 1945, came to an end in 1980, as highway construction in the US slowed down to a halt while declining oil prices depressed the world-wide market for mining, logging, and pipelaying equipment. Second, Caterpillar's efforts to freeze wages and reduce overall labor cost triggered a seven month strike (1982-83) among its US employees.

Case 9 / The Comeback of Caterpillar, 1985–2001

Led by the United Auto Workers (UAW) union, the strike accounted for a sizable portion of the company's three year loss. The third element in Caterpillar's crisis was a steep rise in the value of the dollar (relative to the Yen and other currencies) that made US exports more expensive abroad, and US imports (shipped by Caterpillar's competitors) cheaper at home. "The strong dollar is a prime factor in Caterpillar's reduced sales and earning . . . [and] is undermining manufacturing industries in the United States,"[16] said Cat's annual reports for 1982 and 1984.

Taking advantage of the expensive dollar, Komatsu Limited had emerged as Caterpillar's principal rival. Komatsu ("little pine tree" in Japanese) had initially produced construction machinery for the Japanese and Asian markets, then sought to challenge Caterpillar's dominance in the markets of Latin America and Europe, and eventually penetrated the United States to rival Caterpillar in its domestic market. Attacking Caterpillar head-on, Komatsu issued a battle cry, "Maru C," meaning "encircle Cat." Launching a massive drive to improve quality while reducing costs, Komatsu achieved a 50 percent labor productivity advantage over Caterpillar, and in turn, underpriced Caterpillar's products by as much a 30 percent. The outcome was a dramatic change in market share. Between 1979 and 1984 Komatsu global market share more than doubled to 25 percent while Caterpillar's fell by almost a quarter to 43 percent.[17]

Turnaround: George Schaefer's Caterpillar, 1985-1990

Competition with Komatsu and the crisis of 1982-84 forced Caterpillar to reexamine its past activities. Caterpillar's new CEO (1985), George Schaefer, was a congenial manager who encouraged Cat executives to openly admit the company's past mistakes. "We have experienced a fundamental change in our business — it will never again be what it was," Schaefer said as he became CEO. "We have no choice but to respond, and respond vigorously, to the new world in which we find ourselves."[18] Under Schaefer's direction, Caterpillar devised and implemented a series of strategies that touched upon every important function of the company, including purchasing, manufacturing, marketing, personnel, and labor relations.

Global Outsourcing

Traditionally, Caterpillar functioned as a vertically integrated company that relied heavily on in-house production. To ensure product quality as well as an uninterrupted supply of parts, Cat self-produced two-thirds of its parts and components, and assembled practically all of its finished machines. Under the new policy of "shopping around the world," Caterpillar sought to purchase parts and components from low-cost suppliers who maintained high quality standards. Working closely with its suppliers, Caterpillar moved towards the goal of outsourcing 80 percent of its parts and components.[19]

An additional goal of the policy was branding, that is, the purchase of final products for resale. Through its branding program, Caterpillar sold outsourced machines under its own brand name, taking advantage of its superior marketing organization, and keeping production costs down. Beginning in the mid 1980s, Cat contracted to buy lift trucks from a Norwegian company, hydraulic excavators from a West German manufacturer, paving machines from an Oklahoma corporation, off-highway trucks from a British firm, and logging equipment from a Canadian company, and resell them all under the Cat nameplate. Ordinarily, Caterpillar outsourced product manufacturing but not product design. By keeping control over the design of many of its outsourced products, Caterpillar managed to retain in-house design capability, and ensure quality control.[20]

Broader Product Line

For nearly a decade, the DC10 bulldozer had served as Caterpillar's signature item. It stood 15 feet tall, weighed 73 tons, and sold for more than $500,000 (1988). It had no competitors. But as demand for highway construction projects dwindled, Caterpillar needed to reevaluate its product mix because heavy equipment was no longer selling well. Sales of light construction equipment, on the other hand, were fast increasing. Between 1984 and 1987, accordingly, Caterpillar doubled its product line from 150 to 300 models of equipment, introducing many small machines that ranged from farm tractors to backhoe loaders (multi-purpose light bulldozers), and diversified its customer base. Rather than focusing solely on large clients, i.e. multinational engineering and construction firms like the Bechtel corporation — a typical user of heavy bulldozers — Cat began marketing its light-weight machines to a new category of customers: small-scale owner operators and emerging contractors. Still, the shift in Cat's product mix had a clear impact on the company's bottom line. Unlike the heavy equipment market where profit margins were wide, intense competition in the market for light products kept margins slim and pitted Caterpillar against John Deere and the Case corporation, the light equipment market leaders.[21]

Labor Relations

To compete successfully, Caterpillar also needed to repair its relationship with the union. In 1979, following the expiration of its collective bargaining agreement, Caterpillar experienced an 80 days strike, and three years later, in 1982, contract negotiations erupted in a 205 days strike, the longest company-wide work stoppage in the UAW history.[22] Named CEO in 1985, George Schaefer led the next two rounds of contract negotiations.

Schaefer's leadership style was consensual. By contrast to the autocratic style of his predecessors, Schaefer advocated the free flow of ideas between officers, managers, and production workers, and promoted open communication at all levels of the company. A low-key CEO who often answered his own phone, Schaefer possessed exceptional people skills. Asked to evaluate Schaefer's performance, John Stark, editor of *Off Highway Ledger,* a trade journal, said: "Schaefer is probably the best manager the construction machinery industry has ever had."[23]

Schaefer's social skills led to a significant improvement in Cat's relations with the UAW. Not a single strike broke out over contract negotiations during Schaefer's tenure; on the contrary, each cycle of bargaining was settled peacefully. Under Schaefer's direction, furthermore, the union agreed to reduce the number of labor grades and job classifications, and to streamline seniority provisions, a move that enhanced management flexibility in job assignment, and facilitated the cross utilization of employees.[24] More important, improved labor relations contributed to the success of two programs that played a critical role in Caterpillar's turnaround strategy, namely, an employee involvement plan based on team work, and a reengineering effort of plant modernization and automation.

Employee Involvement

An industry-wide union famous for its cooperative labor-management efforts at the Saturn corporation, the NUMMI plant (a GM-Toyota joint-venture in Fremont California), and elsewhere, the UAW lent its support to Caterpillar's employee involvement program. Called the Employee Satisfaction Process (ESP), and launched by Schaefer in 1986, the program was voluntary. ESP members were organized in work teams, met weekly with management, and offered suggestions that pertained to many critical aspects of the manufacturing process, including production management, workplace layout, and quality enhancement. Implemented in a growing number of US plants, the program resulted (1990) in productivity gains, quality improvements, and increased employee satisfaction. At the Cat plant in Aurora Illinois, for example, the local ESP chairman recalled: the ESP program "changed everything: the worker had some say over his job. . . . [and t]op management was very receptive. We zeroed in on quality, anything to make the cus-

tomer happy." Management credited the ESP teams at Aurora with a steep fall in the rate of absenteeism, a sharp decline in the number of union grievances filed, and cost savings totaling $10 million.[25] At another ESP plant, a Cat assembly-line worker told a *Fortune* reporter in 1988: "Five years ago the foreman wouldn't even listen to you, never mind the general foreman or plant supervisor. . . . Now everyone will listen." Caterpillar applied the ESP program to outside suppliers as well. Typically, ESP teams made up of Caterpillar machinists visited suppliers' plants to check and certify equipment quality. The certified vendors received preferential treatment, mostly in the form of reduced inspection, counting, and other controls. Only 0.6 percent of the parts delivered by certified suppliers were rejected by Caterpillar compared to a reject rate of 2.8 percent for non-certified suppliers.[26]

Plant with a Future

Caterpillar's employee involvement plan went hand in hand with a $1.8 billion plant modernization program launched by Schaefer in 1986.[27] Dubbed "Plant with a Future" (PWAF), the modernization program combined just-in-time inventory techniques, a factory automation scheme, a network of computerized machine tools, and a flexible manufacturing system. Several of these innovations were pioneered by Komatsu late in the 1970s. The industry's technological leader, Komatsu had been the first construction equipment manufacturer to introduce both the just-in-time inventory system, and the "quick changeover tooling," technique, a flexible tooling method designed to produce a large variety of equipment models in a single plant.[28]

To challenge Komatsu, top executives at Caterpillar did not seek to merely imitate the Japanese. This was not enough. They studied, instead, the modernization efforts of several manufacturing companies, and arrived at two important conclusions: it was necessary 1) to change the layout of an entire plant, not just selected departments within a plant; and 2) to implement the program company-wide, that is, on a global basis both at home and abroad. Implementing such a comprehensive program took longer than expected, however, lasting seven years: four under Schaefer's direction, and three more under the direction of his successor, Donald Fites.[29]

The traditional manufacturing process at Caterpillar, known as "batch" production, was common among U.S. assembly plants in a number of industries. Under batch production, subassembly lines produced components (radiators, hydraulic tanks, etc.) in small lots. Final assembly lines put together complete models, and the entire production system required large inventories of parts and components owing to the high level of "work in process" (models being built at any one time). Under batch production, furthermore, assembly tasks were highly specialized, work was monotonous and dull, and workers grew lax and made mistakes. Correcting assembly mistakes, it should be noted, took more time than the assembly process itself because workers needed to disassemble components in order to access problem areas. Parts delivery was also problematic. Occasionally, delays in delivery of parts to the assembly areas forced workers to leave the line in order to locate a missing part. Occasionally, the early arrival of parts before they were needed created its own inefficiencies.[30]

To solve these problems, Caterpillar reconfigured the layout of its manufacturing plants into flexible work "cells." Grouped in cells, workers used computerized machine tools to perform several manufacturing steps in sequence, processing components from start to finish and sending them "just-in-time" to an assembly area, as the following example suggests. To manufacture steel tractor-tread under the batch production layout, Cat workers were required to cut, drill, and heat-treat steel beams on three distinct assembly lines. Under cellular manufacturing, by contrast, all three operations were carried out automatically in single tractor-tread cells linked together by computers.[31]

Caterpillar, in addition, reduced material handling by means of an automated electrified monorail which delivered parts to storage and assembly areas, traveling on a long aluminum track throughout the modernized plant. When parts arrived at the delivery point, a flash light alerted the assembly line workers, semi-automatic gates (operated by infrared remote control) opened, and a lift lowered the components directly onto an assembly. Don Western, a manufacturing manager at Cat Aurora plant, observed: "Materials now [1990] arrive at the assembly point only when required—and in the order required. At most, we hold about a 4 hour supply of large parts and components on the line."[32]

Caterpillar, finally, improved product quality. Formerly, components moved down the assembly line continuously, not intermittently, and therefore workers were unable to respond quickly to quality problems. Managers alone controlled the speed of the line. Under the new assembly plan, on the other hand, components moved automatically between work areas and remained stationary during the actual assembly operation. More important, under the PWAF plan, managers empowered production workers to change the speed of the assembly line at will, granting them the flexibility necessary to resolve quality and safety problems.[33]

The PWAF program resulted in productivity and quality gains across the board in many of Caterpillar plants.

At the Aurora plant in Illinois, for instance, factory workers managed to reduce the assembly process time fourfold, building and shipping a customer order in four rather than 16 days, and cutting product defects by one-half in four years (1986-1990).[34] At the Cat plant in Grenoble, France, to mention another case, workers slashed the time it took to assemble machinery parts from 20 to 8 days in three years (1986-1989). Company wide changes were equally impressive: collectively, Caterpillar's 30 worldwide plants cut inventory levels by 50 percent and manufacturing space by 21 percent in three years.[35]

Looking back at Schaefer's five year-long tenure, Caterpillar had reemerged as a globally competitive company, lean, flexible, and technologically advanced. Caterpillar's world market share rebounded from 43 percent to 50 percent (1984-1990),[36] revenues increased by 66 percent (1985-1989), and the company was profitable once again. As Caterpillar prospered, Komatsu was retrenching. In 1989, Caterpillar's sales totaled over $11 billion or nearly twice the sales reported by Komatsu, Caterpillar's profit margins exceeded Komatsu's, and the gap between the two companies—in terms of both market share and income on sales—was growing (Exhibit 2).

The Transformation Continued: Donald Fites' Caterpillar, 1990-1999

Notwithstanding Schaefer's achievements, the transformation of Caterpillar was far from over. For one thing, the company stock lagged far behind its earnings; Cat shares underperformed the S&P 500 index by over 50 percent for five years (1987-1992).[37] For another, Caterpillar was facing an industry-wide downturn in both its domestic and international markets. Partly as a result of the cyclical nature of the construction equipment industry, and also as a result of an increase in the value of the dollar (a weak dollar in the late 1980s helped Caterpillar's foreign sales), Caterpillar revenues and profits fell. During the two years following Schaefer's retirement, the company actually lost money (Exhibit 5).

Replacing Schaefer in the winter of 1990, Donald Fites viewed Caterpillar's financial troubles as an opportunity to introduce change: "I certainly didn't count on . . . [a] recession . . . but [the recession] made it easier to accept the fact that we needed to change."[38] "It's hard to change an organization when you're making record profits."[39]

Leadership

Fites leadership style stood in a stark contrast to Schaefer's. "George was . . . a consensus builder" while

"[Don] expects people to challenge him forcefully,"[40] one Cat executive said, and another (former Cat CEO Lee Morgan) described Fites as "one of the most determined men I've ever met."[41] Fites was a hard line executive, feared by his subordinates, respected by his peers, and cheered by Wall Street. An imposing man standing six feet five, Fites led by explicit command rather than persuasion, asserted the company's "right to manage" in face of mounting union opposition, and did not hesitate to cut thousands of management and production jobs at a stroke.

The son of a subsistence corn farmer, Fites had joined Caterpillar in 1956, rising through the ranks, and spending 16 years overseas. A career marketeer, he worked for Cat in South Africa, Germany, Switzerland, Brazil, Japan, and other countries. In 1971, Fites had earned an MBA from MIT, writing a thesis entitled "Japan Inc.: Can US Industry Compete?" and soon thereafter, he received an assignment in Japan, serving nearly five years as the marketing director of Caterpillar-Mitsubishi joint venture. Fites' Japanese experience resonated throughout the remainder of his career. He was impressed, first of all, by the ways in which the Japanese trained their managers, rotating executives through functional departments in order to educate them in all aspects of the business. Returning from Japan to Peoria in the mid 1970s, Fites revamped Cat's product development process, utilizing an integrated approach based on Japanese-style functional teams. He also admired Japanese labor relations. Historically, American unions had been organized on an industry-wide basis and therefore labor relations in the United States were often adversarial. Trade unions in Japan, by contrast, were company-based organizations, loyal, cooperative, and in Fites' words, "deeply dedicated to the success of the [firm]."[42] Leading Caterpillar in the 1990s, Fites sought to bring Caterpillar's labor relations closer to the Japanese model.

Reorganization

A marketing manager, Fites was convinced that Caterpillar did not pay sufficient attention to customer needs because global pricing decisions were made at the company's headquarters in Peoria with little knowledge of the local market conditions around the world. In 1985, as he took charge of Cat's worldwide marketing organization, Fites delegated district offices the authority to set prices, thereby pushing responsibility down the chain of command to the lowest possible level. Promoted to President in 1989, Fites applied the same principle to Caterpillar's entire structure, developing a company-wide reorganization plan under Schaefer's direction.[43]

Caterpillar's old organizational structure was archaic. It was a functional structure suitable for a small company that operated just a few plants, all located within the United States. A centralized body with only four primary functions — engineering, manufacturing, marketing, and finance — the old structure served Caterpillar well until World War II, but as the company expanded globally in subsequent decades, the limitations of such a structure had become apparent. First, decisions were made at the top of each functional unit, and executives were reluctant to delegate authority to mid-level or low-level managers. Second, each functional unit tended to focus on its own goal rather than the enterprise's objectives (marketing was preoccupied with market share, engineering with product safety, manufacturing with assembly problems, etc.), making it difficult for top management to coordinate functional goals.[44] And third, the bureaucratization of the decision making

Exhibit 2		George Schaefer's Caterpillar Highlights of Financial Data: Caterpillar versus Komatsu		
	CAT		KOMATSU	
	Sales ($Bil.)	Income as % of Sales	Sales ($Bil.)	Income as % of Sales
1985	$6.7	2.9%	_____*	1.8%
1986	$7.3	1.0%	_____*	2.8%
1987	$8.2	3.9%	$5.1	1.3%
1988	$10.4	5.9%	$6.2	0.4%
1989	$11.1	4.5%	$6.0	2.6%

*Sales are available only in Yen: 1985, 796 billion Yen; 1986, 789 billion Yen.
SOURCE: For Caterpillar, *Hoover's Handbook of American Business, 1995*, p. 329; For Komatsu, *Hoover's Handbook of World Business, 1995–96*, p. 291.

Case 9 / The Comeback of Caterpillar, 1985–2001

process impaired effective communication. Under the old structure, Fites recalled, the flow of information upwards was "so filtered with various prejudices — particularly functional prejudice[s] — that you didn't know whether you were really looking at the facts or looking at someone's opinion."[45]

To equip Caterpillar with the flexibility, speed, and agility necessary to operate in the global economy, Fites broke the company into 17 semi-autonomous divisions or "profit centers," 13 responsible for products (tractors, engines, etc.), and four for services.[46] He then required each division to post a 15 percent rate of return on assets, and threatened to penalize any division that fell behind. He stood by his words. When Caterpillar's forklift division failed to improve its return on assets in 1992, Fites transferred it into an 80 percent-20 percent joint venture controlled by Mitsubishi.[47]

Caterpillar's new divisional structure facilitated downsizing. Under the new structure, Caterpillar cut 10,000 jobs in three years, 1990-1993 (Exhibit 3). Of the 7,500 employees who lost their jobs between January 1990 and August 1992, 2,000 were salaried managers and 5,500 hourly workers.[48] As Caterpillar's sales grew from $10 billion to $15 billion in the first half of the 1990s, the number of managers employed by the company fell by 20 percent.[49] In addition, the move from a functional into a divisional structure, coupled with the drive for profit making, brought about a change in the methods of managerial compensation. Traditionally, Cat managers were paid in proportion to the size of the budget they controlled or the number of employees they supervised. Under the new plan, Caterpillar based all its incentive compensation schemes on return on assets.[50] Lastly, Caterpillar decentralized its research and development activities. With each division controlling its own product development programs and funding, R&D activities under the new plan were more customer driven than at any other period in the past.[51]

Marketing and Dealerships

Caterpillar's reorganization plan affected the company's distribution network as well. Under the new structure, dealers seeking assistance could contact any of the 17 product and service profit-centers directly, saving time and money; they no longer needed to call the General Office in their search for assistance within the company.[52] The new structure also facilitated a more frequent interaction between Caterpillar's managers and dealers, a development which resulted in "[v]irtually everyone from the youngest design engineer to the CEO" having "contact with somebody in [a] dealer organization [wrote Fites]." Ordinarily, low level managers at Caterpillar communicated daily with their counterparts at Cat dealerships; senior corporate executives, several times a week.[53]

Caterpillar's network of dealerships was extensive. In 1999, 207 independent dealers served Caterpillar, 63 of whom were stationed in the US and 144 abroad. The number of employees working for Cat dealers exceeded the company's own workforce (67,000) by nearly one third; the combined net worth of Cat dealers surpassed Caterpillar's stockholders' equity ($5.5 billion)[54] by nearly one quarter (Exhibit 4). Many of Caterpillar's dealerships were privately owned, a few were public companies. On average, the annual sales of a Caterpillar dealership amounted to $150 million (1996); several of the large dealerships, however, generated annual revenues of up to $1 billion.

To Caterpillar, the informal relationships between the company and its dealers were far more important than the formal contractual relations. Dealership agreements ran only a few pages, had no expiration date, and allowed each party to terminate the contract at will, following a 90-days notice. Notwithstanding the open ended nature of the contract, turnover among Cat dealerships was extremely low. Caterpillar actively encouraged its dealers to keep the business in their families, running seminars on tax issues and succession plans for dealers, holding regular conferences in Peoria for the sons and daughters of "dealer Principals" (dealership owners), and taking concrete steps to encourage a proper succession from one generation to another.[55]

Exhibit 3	Donald Fites' Caterpillar: Employment and Sales	
	Number of Employees	Sales ($Bil.)
1990	60,000	$11.4
1991	56,000	10.2
1992	52,000	10.2
1993	50,000	11.6
1994	54,000	14.3
1995	54,000	16.1
1996	57,000	16.5
1997	60,000	18.9
1998	64,000	21.0

SOURCE: for 1990–1997, *Hoover's Handbook of American Business*, 1999, p. 329; for 1998, Caterpillar Inc. 1999 *Annual Report*, p. 1.

Exhibit 4   Caterpillar Dealerships, 1999

	Inside U.S.	Outside U.S.	Worldwide
Dealers	63	144	207
Branch Stores	382	1,122	1,504
Employees	34,338	54,370	88,709
Service Bays	6,638	5,529	12,167
Estimated Net Worth	$3.22 bil.	$3.54 bil.	$6.77 bil.

SOURCE: Caterpillar Inc. 1999 *Annual Report*, p. 43.

While Caterpillar had always protected its dealers against failure, under Fites' direction, Caterpillar did so more aggressively than before, assisting individual dealers who were subjected to intense price competition by rival manufacturers. To help a dealer, Caterpillar sometimes offered discounted prices, sometimes helped reduce the dealer's costs, and occasionally launched a promotion campaign in the dealer's service territory, emphasizing the lower lifetime cost of a Cat machine relative to a competitor's. Caterpillar also protected dealers during recessions. Despite the company's loses during the industry slump of 1991-92, Fites' Caterpillar helped vulnerable Cat dealers survive the downturn, stay in the business, and order equipment in advance of the 1993 upturn. Caterpillar's competitors, in contrast, saw several of their dealers go out of business during the recession.[56]

Fites' Caterpillar cooperated with dealers in other ways. During the 1990s, Caterpillar worked together with its dealers to conduct surveys among customers in order to improve customer service and parts delivery. Sending out 90,000 survey forms annually, Cat received a response rate of nearly 40 percent. Through its "Partners in Quality" program, Caterpillar involved dealers in quality control discussions, linking personnel at Cat plants and dealerships, and sponsoring quarterly meetings. Periodically, Caterpillar invited its entire body of independent dealers to a week long conference in Peoria to review corporate strategy, manufacturing plants, and marketing policies. A firm believer in strong personal business ties, Fites explained:

> Dealers can call me or any senior corporate officer at any time, and they do. Virtually any dealer in the world is free to walk in my door. I'll know how much money he made last year and his market position. And I'll know what is happening in his family. I consider the majority of dealers personal friends. Of course, one reason I know the dealers so well is that I rose through our distribution organization.[57]

Caterpillar's worldwide distribution system, according to Fites, was the company's single greatest advantage over its competitors. It was a strategic asset whose importance was expected to grow in the future: "[u]ntil about 2010," Fites predicted, "distribution" — that is, after-sales support, product application, and service information — "will be what separates the winners from the losers in the global economy."[58] Contrasting American and Japanese manufacturing firms, Fites elaborated:

> Although many Japanese companies had the early advantage in manufacturing excellence, US companies may have the edge this time around. . . . [T]hey know more about distribution than anyone else. . . . Quite frankly, distribution traditionally has not been a strength of Japanese companies. Marketing people and salespeople historically have been looked down upon in Japanese society.[59]

Information Technology

Fites' Caterpillar invested generously in expanding and upgrading Caterpillar's worldwide computer network — a system linking together factories, distribution centers, dealers, and large customers. By 1996, the network connected 1,000 locations in 160 countries across 23 time zones, providing Caterpillar with the most comprehensive and fastest part delivery system in the industry. Although Caterpillar had long guaranteed a 48-hours delivery of parts anywhere in the world, by 1996, Cat dealers supplied 80 percent of the parts a customer needed at once; the remaining 20 percent — not stocked by the dealers — was shipped by the company on the same day the parts were ordered. With 22 distribution centers spread all around the world, Caterpillar serviced a total of 500,000 different parts, keeping over 300,000 in stock, and manufacturing the remainder on demand.[60]

A critical element in Caterpillar's drive for technological leadership was an electronic alert information system the company was developing under Fites. The new system was designed to monitor machines remotely, identify parts which needed to be replaced, and replace them before they failed. Once fully operational in the early 2000's, the new IT system was expected first, to help dealers repair machines before they broke down, thereby reducing machine downtime, on the one hand, and saving repair costs, on the other; and second, provide Caterpillar and its dealers with the opportunity to slash their inventory costs. In 1995, the value of the combined inventories held by Caterpillar and its dealers amounted to $2 billion worth of parts.[61]

Diversification

Fites' Caterpillar expanded its sales into farm equipment, forest products, and compact construction machines, introducing new lines of products, one at a time. Between 1991 and 1999, Caterpillar entered a total of 38 mergers and joint venture agreements, many of which contributed to the company's efforts to diversify.[62]

The growth in Caterpillar's engine sales was the company's largest. Caterpillar had traditionally produced engines for internal use only, installing them on Cat machines, but beginning in the mid 1980s, as the company was recovering from its most severe crisis, Cat embarked on a strategy of producing engines for sale to other companies. In 1999, engine sales accounted for 35 percent of Cat's revenues, up from 21 percent in 1990, and Cat engines powered about one-third of the big trucks in the United States. Apart from trucking companies, Caterpillar produced engines for a variety of other customers including petroleum firms, electric utility companies, and shipbuilding concerns (Exhibit 6). Only 10 percent of the diesel engines manufactured by Caterpillar in 1999 were installed on the company's own equipment.[63]

Two important acquisitions by Caterpillar helped the company compete in the engine market. In 1996, Donald Fites purchased the MaK Company — a German maker of engines for power generation. Partly because governments of developing countries were reluctant to build large power plants, and partly because the utility industry in the United States deregulated and new electrical suppliers entered the market, worldwide demand for generators was fast increasing. The rise in demand helped Caterpillar increase its sales of power generators by 20 percent annually between 1995 and 1999.[64]

Similarly, in 1998, Fites bought Britain's Perkins Engines, a manufacturer of engines for compact construction machinery, for $1.3 billion. The new acquisition contributed to Caterpillar's efforts to increase its share in the small equipment market which was growing at a rate of 10 percent a year. Perkins' best selling engine powered the skid steer loader. A compact wheel tractor operated by one person and capable of maneuvering in tight spaces, the skid dug ditches, moved dirt, broke up asphalt, and performed a wide variety of other tasks.[65]

Labor Relations

Perhaps no other areas of management had received more attention than Caterpillar's labor relations under Fites. For nearly seven years, 1991-1998, Fites fought the UAW in what had become the longest U.S. labor dispute in the 1990s. On the one side, a union official described the UAW relationship with Fites as "the single most contentious . . . in the history of the union;" on the other, a Wall Street analyst called Fites "the guy who broke the union, pure and simple."[66]

In part, Fites' opposition to the UAW was ideological: it "is not so much a battle about economics as it is a battle about who's going to run the company."[67] Yet economics did matter, and Fites was determined to ensure Caterpillar's global competitiveness by cutting the company's labor cost. His principal target was a UAW "pattern" agreement, a collective bargaining contract modeled on agreements signed by the UAW and Caterpillar's domestic competitors, John Deere, the Case Corporation, and others (a pattern agreement tied separate labor contracts together so that changes in one led to similar changes in others within the same industry). Fites rejected pattern bargaining because Caterpillar was heavily dependent on the export of domestically manufactured products, selling over 50 percent of its American-made equipment in foreign markets, and thus competing head-to-head with foreign-based, global companies like Komatsu. Cat's US-based competitors, by contract, exported a far smaller proportion of their domestically made goods. Because Cat's global competitors paid lower wages overseas than the wages paid by Cat's American-based competitors at home, Fites argued, Caterpillar could not afford paying the UAW pattern of wages.[68]

The first Caterpillar strike erupted in 1991, at a time Caterpillar's 17,000 unionized employees were working under a contract. The contract was set to expire on September 30, and Fites was prepared. He had built up enough inventory to supply customers for six months, giving Cat dealers special incentives to buy and stock parts and equipment in case a strike shut down the company's US plants. Caterpillar's contract offer included three principal demands: no pattern on wages, flexible work schedules, and a two-tier wage system. The union rejected the offer outright and staged a strike. About 50 percent of the strikers were within six years of retirement, and as the strike prolonged, 30 percent of the strikers crossed the picket line. Five months into the strike, Fites threatened to replace the strikers permanently if they did not return to work within a week. Shortly thereafter, the union called off the strike, the strikers went back to work "unconditionally," and Cat's unionized employees continued working without a contract under the terms of the rejected offer.[69]

One casualty of the 1991-1992 strike was Caterpillar's Employee Satisfaction Process. The strike effectively put an end to Cat's ESP program which George Schaefer had launched in 1986 and strove so painstakingly to perverse. As the climate of labor relations at Caterpillar deteriorated, the number of unresolved grievances increased. At the Aurora plant at Illinois, the number of grievances at the final stage before arbitration rose from less than 20 prior to the strike to over 300 in the year following the end of the strike. When Cat employees began wearing their own ESP buttons to read "Employee Stop Participating," Caterpillar terminated the program altogether.[70]

During 1992-94, Caterpillar's unionized employees continued to resist Fites' hard-line stand against the UAW. They organized shopfloor disruptions ("informational picketing"), slowdowns ("Work to Rule"), wildcat strikes in selected plants, and picket lines at Cat's dealerships.[71] Fites, in the meantime, trained managers and office workers to operate factory machinery and reassigned many of them to the shopfloor of plants undergoing short-term work-stoppages. Once again, he was fully prepared for a long strike.

The 1994-95 strike broke out in June 1994, lasted 17 months, was bitterly fought by the striking unionists, and came to an abrupt end when the UAW ordered its members to return to work "immediately and unconditionally" in order to save their jobs.[72] During the strike, Caterpillar supplemented its workforce with 5,000 reassigned white color employees, 3,700 full-time and part-time new hires, 4,000 union members who crossed the picket line, and skilled workers borrowed from its dealerships. The company, furthermore, shifted work to non-union plants in the South. Additionally, Caterpillar supplied the US market with equipment imported from its plants in Europe, Japan, and Brazil.[73]

Operating effectively all through the strike, Caterpillar avoided massive customer defection, and managed to keep up production, expand sales, increase profits, and drive up the company stock price. In 1995, the company earned record profits for the second year in a row (Exhibit 5). During the two years following the end of the strike, the shopfloor struggle between Cat management and the union resumed. Caterpillar issued strict rules of workplace conduct, limiting employees' behavior as well as speech. Union activists, in response, launched a work-to-rule campaign in Cat's unionized

plants. The UAW, in addition, filed numerous charges with the National Labor Relations Board (NLRB), alleging that the company committed unfair labor practices. Accepting many of these charges, the NLRB issued formal complaints.[74] Meanwhile, in 1997, Caterpillar racked up record profits for the fourth year in a row (Exhibit 5).

In February 1998, at long last, Caterpillar and the union reached an agreement. The terms of the 1998 agreement clearly favored Caterpillar. First and most important, the contract allowed Caterpillar to break away from the long-standing practice of pattern bargaining. Second, the contract allowed Caterpillar to introduce a two-tier wage system and pay new employees 70 percent of the starting union scale. A third clause of the contract provided for a more flexible work schedule, allowing management to keep employees on the job longer than eight hours a day and during weekends (without paying overtime). The contract also granted management the right to hire temporary employees at certain plants without the union's approval, and reduce the number of union jobs below a certain level. Running for six years rather than the typical three years, the contract was expected to secure Caterpillar with a relatively long period of industrial peace.[75]

Several provisions of the contract were favorable to the union. The contract's key economic provisions included an immediate wage increase of 2-4 percent and future increases of 3 percent in 1999, 2001, and 2003; cost of living allowances; and substantial gains in pension benefits (the average tenure of the 1994-95 strikers was 24 years). Another provision favorable to the UAW was a moratorium on most plant closings. But perhaps the most significant union gain was simply achieving a contract, as AFL-CIO Secretary Treasurer Rich Trumka observed: "The message to corporate America is this: Here's one of the biggest companies, and they couldn't walk away from the union."[76]

Why, then, was Fites willing to sign a contract? Why did a company which operated profitably year after year without a contract, and operated effectively during strikes, suddenly seek to reach an agreement with the UAW?

Fites' decision was influenced by two developments. First, Caterpillar's record revenues and profits during 1993-97 came to an end in 1998-99, as the industry was sliding into a recession. Revenues and profits were declining as a result of a strong dollar coupled with a weak demand for Cat products. Caterpillar, therefore needed a flexible wage agreement, stable employment relations, and a more cooperative workforce in order to smooth its ride during the impending downturn. Another reason why Fites sought accommodation with the union was the need to settle some 400 unfair labor

	Sales ($Mil.)	Net Income ($Mil.)	Income as % of Sales	Stock Price FY Close
1991	$10,182	$ (404)	—	$10.97
1992	10,194	(2,435)	—	13.41
1993	11,615	652	5.6%	22.25
1994	14,328	955	6.7%	27.56
1995	16,072	1,136	7.1%	29.38
1996	16,522	1,361	8.2%	37.63
1997	18,925	1,665	8.8%	48.50

SOURCE: *Hoover's Handbook for American Business*, 1999, p. 329.

practice charges filed by the NLRB against the company during the dispute. These charges were not only costly to adjudicate but could have resulted in huge penalties which the company had to pay in cases where the NLRB ruled in favor of the UAW. One of Caterpillar's principal demands in the 1998 settlement — to which the UAW agreed — was dropping these unfair labor practice charges.[77]

The Future: Glen Barton's Caterpillar 1999-

As Fites retired in February 1999, Glen Barton, a 39-year Cat veteran, assumed the company's leadership. During his first year in office, Barton lost two potential allies on the Cat Board of Directors, Glen Schaefer and Donald Fites. In January 2000, Caterpillar's Board of Directors revised the company's corporate governance guidelines to prohibit retired Cat employees from sitting on the board. The move was intended to safeguard the interests of stockholders and prevent the company's inside directors from opposing swift actions proposed by the board's outside members.[78]

Barton faced other difficulties. In 1999, Caterpillar's profits fell 37 percent to $946 million, the worst results since 1993, and its North American market, which accounted for half of Cat's sales and nearly 2/3 of its profits, was in a slump.[79]

Barton believed that the downturn in the US construction market could be offset by an upturn in the international market. He thought that Caterpillar could take advantage of it global positioning to cushion the US decline by increasing sales in Asia and Latin America whose economies were rebounding. But being cautious, Barton also realized that he needed to ensure the future of Caterpillar in the long run. He therefore embarked on four growth strategies: the expansion into new markets; diversification; the development of a new distribution channel; and the build up of alliances with global competitors.

New Markets

In 1999, 80 percent of the world's population lived in developing countries, and Caterpillar's sales to developing nations accounted for only 23 percent of the total company's sales. Developing countries had limited access to water, electricity, and transportation, and therefore needed to invest in building highways, bridges, dams, and waterways. Under Barton's leadership, increased sales of Caterpillar's equipment to the developing nations of Asia, Latin America, Eastern Europe, and the Commonwealth of Independent States (the former Soviet Union) was a top strategic priority.[80]

Diversification

Just as globalization protected Caterpillar from the cyclical movements of boom and bust, so did diversification. Cat's expansion into the engine business is a case in point. In 1999, Caterpillar's overall sales fell by 6 percent, yet its engine sales rose by 5 percent. Cat's engine business itself was further diversified, with truck-engine sales making up just over one-third of all Cat's engine sales in 1999 (Exhibit 6). Such a diversification, according to Barton, ensured the company that any future decline in truck engine sales could be offset, at least in

| Exhibit 6 | Cat Engine Sales to End Users, 1999, 2000 |

	1999	2000
Trucks	34%	27%
Electric Power Generators	26%	33%
Oil Drilling Equipment	20%	19%
Industrial Equipment	11%	13%
Ships and Boats	9%	8%

SOURCE: Caterpillar Inc. 1999 *Annual Report*, p. 24; and 2000 *Annual Report*.

| Exhibit 7 | Caterpillar's Sales of Power Generators |

	Power Generators Sales ($Bil.)	Power Generators As % of Total Revenues
1996	$1.2	7.3%
1997	1.3	6.9%
1998	1.6	7.6%
2000	1.8	9.1%
2001	2.3	11.4%

SOURCE: David Barboza, "Cashing In On the World's Energy Hunger," *The New York Times*, May 22, 2001.

part, by an increase in sales of non-truck engines. By 2010, Caterpillar's total engine sales were expected to double to nearly $14 billion.[81]

Of all Cat engine sales, the growth in sales of electric diesel generators — 20 percent a year since 1996 — had been the fastest (Exhibit 7). Caterpillar's energy business clearly benefitted from the energy crisis. Large corporations, manufacturing facilities, internet server centers, and utility companies had installed back up diesel generators for standby or emergency use; in the nine months ending May 2001, Cat sales of mobile power modules (trailer equipped with a generator) quadrupled.[82]

The world's largest manufacturer of diesel generators, Caterpillar nevertheless faced a serious challenge in its efforts to transform itself into an ET (energy technology) company: diesel generators produced far more pollution than other sources of power. To address this problem, Barton's Caterpillar accelerated its shift towards cleaner micro power. In 2001, only 10 percent of Caterpillar's generators were powered by natural gas; in 2011, the corresponding figure was expected to climb to 50 percent.[83]

To diversify the company in still another way, Barton planned to double its farm equipment sales in five years (1999-2004).[84] In the agricultural equipment market, caterpillar needed to compete head-to-head with the John Deere Co. and the CNH Corporation (former Case Corp. and New Holland), the leading U.S. manufacturers.

A New Distribution Channel

Under Barton's direction, Caterpillar expanded its rental equipment business, reaching a new category of customers both at home and abroad. Formerly, Caterpillar sold or rented equipment to rental centers, and these centers, in turn, re-rented the equipment to end-users. Rarely did Caterpillar rent directly to customers. Now Barton was making aggressive efforts to help Cat dealers diversify into rentals. Nearly half of all Cat's machines sold in North America in 2000 entered the market through the rental distribution channel, and the fastest growing segment of the business was short-term rentals. Implemented by Barton in 1999-2000, the Cat Rental Store Program was designed to assist dealers in operating a one-stop rental shop that offered a complete line of rental equipment from heavy bulldozers and tractors, to light towers, work platforms, and hydraulic tools.[85]

Joint Ventures

Increasingly, Caterpillar had used joint ventures to expand into new markets and diversify into new products. In November 2000, Barton's Caterpillar announced a plan to form two joint ventures with DaimlerChrysler, the world's leading manufacturer of commercial vehicles. One was for building medium-duty engines, the other was for manufacturing fuel systems. The combined share of the two companies in the medium-duty engine market was only 10 percent, yet the medium-duty engine market generated world-wide sales of $10 billion annually.

The sales of fuel systems were even more promising. Fuel systems were designed to increase the efficiency of diesel engines and thereby reduce diesel emissions. Participating in the two joint ventures were Cat and DaimlerChrysler plants in four US states (South Carolina, Georgia, Illinois, and Michigan) and at least five other countries.[86]

Future Prospects

Notwithstanding their initial prospects, Barton's strategic initiatives failed to addressed adequately two major concerns that could have effected the company's future.

Case 9 / The Comeback of Caterpillar, 1985–2001

Exhibit 8

Caterpillar: Five Year Financial Summary ($Mil. except per share data)

	2000	1999	1998	1997	1996
Sales and Revenues	$20,175	$19,702	$20,977	$18,925	$16,522
Profits	1,053	946	1,513	1,665	1,361
As % of Sales & Rev.	5.2%	4.8%	7.2%	8.8%	8.2%
Profits per Share	$3.04	$2.66	$4.17	$4.44	$3.54
Dividends per Share	1.345	1.275	1.150	0.950	0.775
Return on Equity	19.0%	17.9%	30.9%	37.9%	36.3%
Capital Expenditures, Net	$723	$790	$925	$824	$506
R&D Expenses	854	814	838	700	570
As % of Sales & Rev.	4.2%	4.1%	4.0%	3.7%	3.4%
Wage, Salaries & Employee Benefits	$4,029	$4,044	$4,146	$3,773	$3,437
Number of Employees	67,200	66,225	64,441	58,366	54,968
December 31					
Total assets Consolidated	$28,464	$26,711	$25,128	$20,756	$18,728
Machinery & Engines	16,554	16,158	15,619	14,188	13,066
Financial Products	14,618	12,951	11,648	7,806	6,681
Long term debt Consolidated	11,334	9,928	9,404	6,942	5,087
Machinery & Engines	2,854	3,099	2,993	2,367	2,018
Financial Products	8,480	6,829	6,411	4,575	3,069
Total debt Consolidated	15,067	13,802	12,452	8,568	7,459
Machinery & Engines	3,427	3,317	3,102	2,474	2,176
Financial Products	11,957	10,796	9,562	6,338	5,433

SOURCE: *Caterpillar Inc. 2000 Annual Report*, p. 39.

A Special Note: For additional financial data, as reported in the company's annual reports and other financial documents, check out Caterpillar's web site at www.caterpillar.com

One had to do with the state of labor relations, particularly Cat's employee satisfaction program which Schaefer had introduced and Fites terminated. Implemented effectively by Schaefer, the ESP program, we have seen, contributed to increased labor productivity, improved product quality, enhanced employee satisfaction, and reduced employee absenteeism. Should Barton, then, reintroduce Cat's employee satisfaction program and thereby improve the climate of labor relations at the company's US plants? Would Barton be able to cooperate closely with the local union leadership to persuade shopfloor employees to join the program?

Another challenge Barton faced pertained to the impact of E-commerce. How could Caterpillar take advantage of the opportunities offered by E-commerce without undermining its distribution system? How, in other words, could Caterpillar benefit from utilizing the internet for the marketing, distribution, and service of its products without weakening its strong dealers' networks? Barton wondered, "What should I do next?"

Endnotes

1. *The Caterpillar Company 1999 Annual Report*, p. 39.
2. Michael Arndt, "This Cat Isn't so Nimble," *Business Week*, February 21, 2000, Start p. 148. Online. Lexis-Nexis. Academic Universe; Mark Tatge, "Caterpillar's Truck-Engine Sales May Hit Some Breaking," *Wall Street Journal*, March 13, 2000.
3. Andrew Gross and David Weiss, "Industry Corner: The Global Demand for Heavy Construction Equipment," *Business Economics*, 31:3 (July 1996), pp. 54–55.
4. Gross and Weiss, "Industry Corner," p. 54.
5. Ibid.
6. Donald Fites, "Making Your Dealers Your Partners," *Harvard Business Review*, March–April 1996, p. 85.
7. U. Srinivasa Rangan, "Caterpillar Tractor Co.," in Christopher Bartlett and Sumantra Ghoshal, *Transatlantic Management: Text, Cases, and Readings in Cross Border Management* (Homewood IL.: Irwin, 1992), p. 296.
8. Fites, "Making Your Dealers Your Partners," p. 85.
9. Gross and Weiss, "Industry Corner," p. 58.
10. William L. Naumann, *The Story of Caterpillar Tractor Co.* (New York: The Newcomen Society, 1977), pp. 7–9.

11. "Caterpillar Inc.," *Hoover's Handbook of American Business 1999* (Austin: Hoover Business Press, 1999), p. 328; "The Story of Caterpillar." Online. Caterpillar.Com. Retrieved March 9, 2000.

12. Michael Yoshino and U. Srinivasa Rangan, *Strategic Alliances: An Entrepreneurial Approach to Globalization* (Boston: Harvard Business School Press, 1995), p. 93; Naumann, *"Story of Caterpillar,"* pp. 12–14; William Haycraft, *Yellow Power: The story of the Earthmoving Equipment Industry* (Urbana, Illinois: University of Illinois Press, 2000), pp. 118–122, 159–167, 196–203.

13. Fites, "Making your Dealers Your Partners," p. 94.

14. Rangan, "Caterpillar Tractor Co.," p. 304; James Risen, "Caterpillar: A Test of U.S. Trade Policy," *Los Angeles Times,* June 8, 1986. Online. Lexis-Nexis. Academic Universe.

15. Cited in Kathleen Deveny, "For Caterpillar, the Metamorphosis Isn't Over," *Business Week,* August 31, 1987, p. 72.

16. Cited in Dexter Hutchins, "Caterpillar's Triple Whammy," *Fortune,* October 27, 1986, p. 91. See also Robert Eckley, "Caterpillar's Ordeal: Foreign Competition in Capital Goods," *Business Horizons,* March–April 1989, pp. 81–83.

17. James Abegglen and George Stalk, *Kaisha, the Japanese Corporation* (New York: Basic Books, 1985), pp. 62, 117–118; Yoshino and Rangan, *Strategic Alliances,* pp. 94–95; "Komatsu Ltd.," *Hoover's Handbook of World Business,* 1999, p. 320.

18. Quoted in Yoshino and Rangan, *Strategic Alliances,* p. 96.

19. Yoshino and Rangan, *Strategic Alliances,* p. 97; Eckley, "Caterpillar's Ordeal," p. 84.

20. Eckley, "Caterpillar's Ordeal," p. 84; *Business Week,* August 31, 1987, p. 73; Yoshino and Rangan, *Strategic Alliances,* p. 97.

21. Ronald Henkoff, "This Cat is Acting like a Tiger," *Fortune,* December 19, 1988, pp. 67, 72, 76; *Business Week,* August 31, 1987, p. 73.

22. Eckley, "Caterpillar's Ordeal," pp. 81, 83.

23. Quoted in *Fortune,* December 19, 1988, p. 76.

24. Eckley, "Caterpillar's Ordeal," p. 84, *Fortune,* December 19, 1988, p. 76; Alex Kotlowitz, "Caterpillar Faces Shutdown with UAW," *Wall Street Journal,* March 5, 1986. Online. ABI data base.

25. Barry Bearak, "The Inside Strategy: Less Work and More Play at Cat," *Los Angeles Times,* May 16, 1995. Online. Lexis-Nexis. Academic Universe.

26. *Fortune,* December 19, 1988, p. 76.

27. Brian Bremner, "Can Caterpillar Inch its Way Back to Heftier Profits?" *Business Week,* September 25, 1989, p. 75.

28. Abegglen and Stalk, *Kaisha,* p. 118.

29. *Fortune,* December 19, 1988, pp. 72, 74; *Business Week,* September 25, 1989, p. 75.

30. Karen Auguston, "Caterpillar Slashes Lead Times from Weeks to Days," *Modern Materials Handling,* February 1990, p. 49.

31. Barbara Dutton, "Cat Climbs High with FMS," *Manufacturing Systems,* November 1989, pp. 16–22; *Business Week,* August 31, 1987, p. 73, September 25, 1989, p. 75.

32. Quoted in Auguston, "Caterpillar Slashes Lead Times," p. 49.

33. Auguston, "Caterpillar Slashes Lead Times," pp. 50–51.

34. Auguston, "Caterpillar Slashes Lead Times," pp. 49, 51.

35. *Business Week,* September 25, 1989, p. 75.

36. Yoshino and Rangan, *Strategic Alliances,* p. 98.

37. Jennifer Reingold, "CEO of the Year," *Financial World,* March 28, 1995, p. 68.

38. Quoted in "An Interview with Caterpillar Inc. Chairman and CEO Donald V. Fites," *Inter-Business Issues,* December 1992, p. 32.

39. Quoted in Tracy Benson, "Caterpillar Wakes Up," *Industry Week,* May 20, 1991, p. 36.

40. Quoted in Reingold, "CEO of the Year," p. 74.

41. Quoted in Kevin Kelly, "Caterpillar's Don Fites: Why He Didn't Blink," *Business Week,* August 10, 1992, p. 56.

42. Quoted in *Business Week,* August 10, 1992, pp. 56–57.

43. *Business Week,* August 10, 1992, p. 57.

44. Quoted in Benson, "Caterpillar Wakes Up," p. 32.

45. "An Interview with Fites," *Inter Business Issues,* p. 32.

46. Benson, "Caterpillar Wakes Up," p. 33.

47. *Business Week,* August 10, 1992, p. 56.

48. J. P. Donlon, "Heavy Metal," *Chief Executive,* September 1995, p. 50.

49. Andrew Zadoks, "Managing Technology at Caterpillar," *Research Technology Management,* January 1997, pp. 49–51. Online. Lexis-Nexis. Academic Universe.

50. *Business Week,* August 10, 1992, p. 56.

51. Donlon, "Heavy Metal," p. 50.

52. Benson, "Caterpillar Wakes Up," p. 36.

53. Fites, "Make Your Dealers Your Partners," p. 93.

54. *Caterpillar Inc. 1999 Annual Report,* p. 34.

55. Fites, "Make Your Dealers Your Partners." pp. 89, 91–92, 94.

56. Fites, "Make Your Dealers Your Partners," pp. 92–93.

57. Quoted in Fites, "Make Your Dealers Your Partners," P. 94, but see also pp. 90, 93.

58. Quoted in Donlon. "Heavy Metal," p. 50.

59. Quoted in Fites, "Make Your Dealers Your Partners," p. 86.

60. Myron Magnet, "The Productivity Payoff Arrives," *Fortune,* June 27, 1994, pp. 82–83; Benson, "Caterpillar Wakes Up," p. 36; Fites, "Making Your Dealers Your Partners," pp. 88–89.

61. Quoted in Steven Prokesch, "Making Global Connections in Caterpillar," *Harvard Business Review,* March–April 1996, p. 89, but see also p. 88, and Donlon, "Heavy Metals," p. 50.

62. "Caterpillar's Growth Strategies," Copyright 1999. Online. Caterpillar.Com.

63. *Wall Street Journal,* March 13, 2000; David Barboza, "Aiming for Greener Pastures," *New York Times,* August 4, 1999.

64. De'Ann Weimer, "A New Cat on the Hot Seat," *Business Week,* March 9, 1998, p. 61, *Wall Street Journal,* March 13, 2000.

65. *Business Week,* March 9, 1998; *Wall Street Journal,* March 13, 2000.

66. The quotations, in order, are from Reingold, "CEO of the Year," p. 72; Carl Quintanilla, "Caterpillar Chairman Fites to Retire," *Wall Street Journal,* October 15, 1998. Online. ABI data base.

67. Quoted in Reingold, "CEO of the Year," p. 72.

68. "An Interview with Fites," *Inter Business Issues,* pp. 34–35; "What's Good for Caterpillar," *Forbes,* December 7, 1992. Online. ABI data base.

69. Michael Cimini, "Caterpillar's Prolonged Dispute Ends," *Compensation and Working Conditions,* Fall 1998, pp. 5–6; Kevin Kelly, "Cat May be Trying to Bulldoze the Immovable," *Business Week,* December 2, 1991, p. 116, "Cat VS. Labor: Hardhats, Anyone?" *Business Week,* August 26, 1991, Start p. 48. Lexis-Nexis. Academic Universe.

70. Michael Verespej, "Bulldozing Labor Peace at Caterpillar," *Industry Week,* February 15, 1993, Start p. 19. Online. ABI data base.

71. "Caterpillar: Union Bull," *Economist,* January 9, 1993, Start P. 61. Online. Lexis-Nexis. Academic Universe; Cimini "Caterpillar's Prolonged Dispute Ends," pp. 7–9.

72. Cimini, "Caterpillar's Prolonged Dispute Ends," p. 9; Robert Rose, "Caterpillar Contract with UAW May be Tough to Sell to Workers," *Wall Street Journal,* February 17, 1998. Online. ABI data base; Reingold, "CEO of the Year," p. 72.

73. Cimini, "Caterpillar's Prolonged Dispute Ends," pp. 8–9.

74. Ibid.

75. Carl Quintanilla, "Caterpillar Touts Its Gains as UAW Battle Ends," *Wall Street Journal,* March 24, 1998; Dirk Johnson, "Auto Union Backs Tentative Accord with Caterpillar," *New York Times,* February 14, 1998.

76. Quoted in Philip Dine, "Gulf Remains Wide in Caterpillar's Home," *St. Louis Post Dispatch,* March 29, 1998. Online. Lexis-Nexis. Academic Universe. See also Cimini, "Caterpillar's Prolonged Dispute Ends," P. 11.

77. "The Caterpillar Strike: Not Over Till It's Over," *Economist,* February 28, 1998.

78. *Business Week,* February 21, 2000, Start p. 148.

79. Ibid.

80. "Growth Strategies." Caterpillar.Com, p. 2.

81. *Wall Street Journal,* March 13, 2000.

82. David Barboza, "Cashing In On the World's Energy Hunger," *New York Times,* May 22, 2001.

83. *New York Times* May 22, 2001; "Energy Technology: Beyond the Bubble," *Economist,* April 21, 2001.

84. Heather Landy, "Putting More Cats Down on the Farm," *Chicago Sun Times,* March 28, 1999. Online. Lexis-Nexis. Academic Universe.

85. Michael Roth, "Seeing the Light," *Rental Equipment Register,* January 2000. Online. Lexis-Nexis. Academic Universe; Nikki Tait, "Cat Sharpens Claws to Pounce Again," *Financial Times,* November 8, 2000. Online. Lexis-Nexis. Academic Universe.

86. Joseph Hallinan, "Caterpillar, DaimlerChrysler Team Up," *Wall Street Journal,* November 23, 2000.

Case 9 / The Comeback of Caterpillar, 1985–2001

The Chicagotribune.com: Creating a Newspaper for the New Economy (A)

Nina Ziv

Polytechnic University

I. Background

As he sat in his office in *The Tribune* Tower in downtown Chicago on a sunny morning in August, 1999, Owen Youngman, Director of Interactive Media for *The Chicago Tribune*, reflected on what it was like to manage the Chicagotribune.com:

> The big deal is that you get up in the morning and come to work and you are on the bus and you know you'll make a mistake today. You don't know what it is and you may not know for a long time. Whereas in the newspaper business, there's a lot more certainty regardless of what part of the business you are talking about. And adjusting to that reality is different. And so you manage differently as a result. Some things you hedge; other you don't.[1]

Youngman, a seasoned veteran of *The Chicago Tribune* for over 28 years, was used to a culture which valued innovation, but was steeped in 150 years of tradition. He now found himself managing in an environment characterized by constant change, instantaneous feedback from readers, a volatile marketplace, and competitors who had never been on his radar screen. True, in its foray into the online world, *The Tribune* had been very successful. As a leader and innovator in developing an online newspaper, *The Tribune* had not only developed a distinctive persona for its online paper but had also been innovative at

This case was written by Professor Nina Ziv, Institute for Technology and Enterprise, Polytechnic University. It is intended to be used as the basis for class discussion rather than to illustrate either effective or ineffective handling of a management situation.

The case was made possible by the cooperation of The Tribune Company.

Reprinted with permission. © Nina Ziv, Polytechnic University.

Distributed by The European Case Clearing House, England and USA.

North America, phone: +1 781 239 5884, fax: +1 781 239 5885, e-mail: ECCHBabson@aol.com.

Rest of the World, phone: +44 (0)1234 750903, fax: +44 (0)1234 751125, e-mail: ECCH@cranfield.ac.uk.

All rights reserved. Printed in UK and USA. Web Site: http://www.ecch.cranfield.ac.uk.

integrating the digital and physical aspects of the paper and providing unique online offerings for its readers. It had been recognized for its efforts by such prestigious organizations as the Newspaper Association of America (NAA) as well as the "bible" of the newspaper business, *Editor & Publisher* magazine. In the summer of 1997, it was named "Best Newspaper site" (in the largest circulation category) by the NAA. In 1998, *Editor & Publisher* honored the Chicagotribune.com as 1998's Best Online newspaper among publications with print circulations of more than 100,000. The online newspaper also won awards for the best business section and the best design.

But clearly, the Chicagotribune.com faced significant challenges in its fourth year of operation. Perhaps the most important challenge was creating a digital brand which would build on the reputation of the print newspaper but offer its readers features they could not get in print. Most online news sites obtained up to 70 percent of their online content simply by re-using and reformatting print stories for the online market, a practice known in the industry as 'shoveling'.[2] Rather than just providing its readers with an electronic version of the print edition, Youngman and his staff were committed to exploiting the strength of each medium and constantly fine tuning the interaction between them. In order to do this, the organization currently in place would need to be restructured to accommodate the new medium and the right kind of talent would need to be recruited which could adapt to this hybrid environment.

Closely linked to the development of the brand was the challenge of defining what business the newspaper should be in as it positioned itself in the NewMedia industry. Should the Chicagotribune.com be in the business of providing news to its readership, or should it become an e-commerce business with news as just one of its many products? Unlike many new media companies which operate independently, the Chicagotribune.

Exhibit 1   Tribune Company Structure

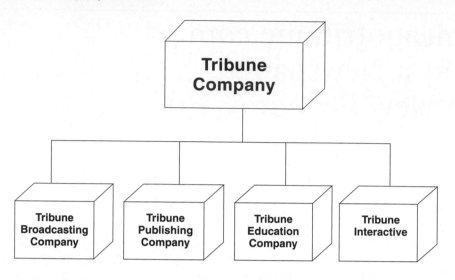

com is part of the Tribune Company, a media conglomerate, and thus its development as an online entity is linked to the overall strategy of the parent company. In May 1999, the Tribune Company consolidated its national and local online businesses into one business unit, a move which could have a significant impact on the development of the Chicagotribune.com. Tribune Interactive, which joined publishing, broadcasting, and education as the Tribune Company's fourth line of business (Exhibit 1), brought together the interactive functions of *The Tribune's* four newspapers and 17 television stations. In addition, other Internet products and services such as BlackVoices, Go2Orlando and Digital City sites for Chicago, Hampton Roads, Orlando and South Florida, were placed under the umbrella of the business unit (Exhibit 2).

The purpose of the consolidation was to enable *The Tribune* to develop new products for the online environment more rapidly and achieve economies of scale. Yet Jeff Scherb, the CTO of *The Tribune* and President of Tribune Interactive (TI), stated on numerous occasions, that the "goal is for TI to be an e-commerce company enabled by great content."[3] Scherb understands that the mission of the newspaper is to focus on coverage of events and breaking news, but his vision also entails building Internet businesses which would provide consumers with the utility and convenience of "one-stop" shopping on the web.

Whether or not the e-commerce mission of the online edition delineated by Scherb will be realized, executives at *The Tribune* see the Chicagotribune.com as one part of

their plan to leverage the rich content of old media newspapers and evolve the Tribune Company into a cross-media company with multiple outlets serving a wide-ranging audience. Indeed, with the acquisition of the Times Mirror Company, which owns several newspapers in major cities such as Los Angeles and New York City, the Tribune Company will be in a strong position to develop what John Madigan, Chairman and President of the company, calls a "national platform rich in content and the ability to develop e-commerce."[4,5]

As the Tribune Company redefines its role in the media industry on a national level, another challenge for the Chicagotribune.com will be how best to serve its Chicago-based readership in a complex environment where competitors are emerging from nontraditional sectors of the community and where making the right partnerships and alliances is essential. For example, new media companies such as Yahoo! have emerged over the pas few years which are providing news services and thus making inroads on the audiences that had traditionally been considered in *The Tribune's* domain. With the proliferation of cellular phones and PDAs, technology companies could also play a major role in shaping the way information is distributed and formatted for the "small screen." During the past nine years, The Tribune Company has made numerous investments in online companies and formed alliances and partnerships with these companies. The Chicagotribune.com now has the task of cultivating these relationships and integrating the offerings of these companies in a way that will enhance the online edition and differentiate it from its competitors.

Exhibit 2 | Tribune Company Holdings By Business Unit[33]

Tribune Broadcasting Company

Television

WPIX (WB)
New York
KWGN (WB)
Denver
KTLA (WB)
Los Angeles
KTXL (FOX)
Sacramento
WGN (WB)
Chicago
KSWB (WB)
San Diego
WATL (WB)
Atlanta
WNOL (WB)
New Orleans

WLIV (WB)
Boston
WTIC (FOX)
Hartford
KDAF (WB)
Dallas
WXMI (FOX)
Grand Rapids
WBDC (WB)
Washington
WGNO (ABC)
New Orleans
WBZL (WB)
Miami

KHWB (WB)
Houston
WPMT (FOX)
Harrisburg
KCPQ (FOX)
Seattle
WEWB (WB)
Albany
KTWB
Seattle
WPHL (WB)
Philadelphia
WXIN (FOX)
Indianapolis

Radio

WGN-AM
Chicago
KKHK-FM
Denver

KEZW-AM
Denver

KOSI-FM
Denver

TV Programming

Tribune Entertainment Company, Los Angeles—develops and distributes first-run television programming for the Tribune station group and national syndication

Baseball

Chicago National Ball Club Inc. (Chicago Cubs)

Investments

The WB Television Network (25 percent stake), TV Food Network (29 percent stake)

Tribune Publishing Company

Daily Newspapers

| *Chicago Tribune* | *Sun-Sentinel* | *The Orlando Sentinel* | *Daily Press* |
| Chicago | South Florida | Orlando | Hampton Roads, VA |

Weekly Newspapers

Sun-Sentinel Community News Group   *Exito*

(Continued)

Exhibit 2   Tribune Company Holdings By Business Unit[33] *(Continued)*

Entertainment Listings and Syndications

Tribune Media Services, Chicago—TV, cable, and movie listings; comics, features and opinion columns; online and wire services; advertising networks

Cable Programming

CLTV News, Chicago; Central Florida News 13, Orlando, a 50 percent partnership with Time Warner Communications

Other Products and Services

Chicago, Illinois

Auto Finder	Job Finder	Mature Adult	New Homes Guide	Silicon Prairie
RELCON Apartment Guide	Tribune Direct Marketing			

Orlando, Florida

Auto Finder	Black Family Today	Central Florida Family	Hot Properties
O Arts	The Orlando City Book	RELCON Apt. Renter's Book	Sentinel Direct

South Florida

Florida New Homes & Condominium Guides	Gold Coast Shopper South
Florida Parenting	Vital Signs

Newport News, Virginia

Hampton Roads Gardening and Home

Investments

BrassRing Inc. (36 percent owned); CareerPath.com (16 percent); Classified Ventures (17 percent); Knight Ridder/Tribune Information Services (50 percent)
Tribune Education Company

Educational Products for Schools

The Wright Group
Everyday Learning/Creative Publications Group
NTC/Contemporary Publishing Group
Instructional Fair Group

Educational Products for Consumers

NTC/Contemporary Publishing Group

Instructional Fair Group

Landoll

Investments

Discourse Technologies (19 percent owned)

ImageBuilder Software (22 percent)

| Exhibit 2 | Tribune Company Holdings By Business Unit[33] *(Continued)* |

Tribune Interactive

National Businesses

BlackVoices.com

Cubs.com

Go2Orlando.com

Local Businesses

Chicagotribune.com

Dailypress.com

Orlandosentinel.com

Sun-sentinenel.com

Showtimeinteractive.com

HRticket.com

ChicagoSports.com

Web sites for all Tribune television and radio stations

Classified Businesses

Automotive—cars.com

Real Estate—apartments.com, newhomenetwork.com

Recruitment—BlackVoices.com, BrassRing.com, CareerPath.com, Siliconprairie.com, thepavement.com

General Merchandise—Auctions.com

How the online newspaper will deal with the challenges outlined above remains to be seen. Will the Chicagotribune.com remain a strong, forward-looking pioneer in the NewMedia industry or will it struggle to survive in the vast media network of the Tribune Company?

II. The Tribune as Innovator

The Chicago Tribune was founded in 1847 and during its 150 year history has been an innovative pioneer in the media industry. Very early in its history, Colonel Robert McCormick, who took over *The Tribune* in 1911, expanded the reach of the newspaper to include the *Washington Times-Herald* and the *Daily News* of New York. In 1924, when radio was a new medium, McCormick bought WDAP, one of the first radio stations in Chicago because he viewed it as another way to reach his audience. Later *The Tribune* invested in television stations even though most major newspapers saw television as a threat (Exhibit 3).

With its history of innovation, ". . . it was really no big leap for the Tribune company to view interactive media as another way to do what it had done successfully so many times before," said Owen Youngman. Moreover, key members of senior management were very much in favor of moving in this direction. Jack Fuller, President of The Tribune Company, recognized early on that the Internet would be a positive force for the newspaper industry and promoted this idea in his 1996 book, *News Values*. Fuller's vision of the convergence between this

new medium and the traditional newspaper business proved to be a driving force in enabling the culturally conservative *Tribune* to develop its online offering. Charles Brumback, the Chairman of the Tribune Company from the late 70's until 1995, also believed that computer services would be crucial to the development of newspapers and it was he who initiated the Tribune Company's investments in various online ventures.[6]

The Tribune Company began to amass its portfolio of online companies in 1991 when it bought a 10 percent share in America Online then known as Quantum. Over time, the newspaper sold off its shares and invested the money into other NewMedia opportunities. As of August 1999, the Tribune's portfolio, which includes stakes in public companies like AOL, *Excite@home*, iVillage, and Peapod, Inc., and private companies such as WB Network, Lightspan Partnership, and Digital City Inc, was valued at more than $812 million.[7] (Exhibit 4).

In addition to the potential financial gains from making such investments, John Madigan, the Tribune's chairman, president and Chief Executive Officer, said the investments were "our form of R&D."[8] Owen Youngman elaborated on Madigan's idea:

> *Being an early investor in AOL gave the company an up-close view of the mind set that it takes to be successful in this space. AOL, first and foremost, is a great marketer. And so, seeing their marketing techniques up close and the speed with which they'd both move and with which they would change, helped us to make decisions about what we should be doing. No, we're not spending the*

Exhibit 3 History of the Chicago Tribune [34]

1847—*The Chicago Tribune* newspaper is founded by 2 newspapermen—John E. Wheeler and Joseph K. C. Forrest and a leather merchant—James Kelly. The first edition was a 4-page newspaper—The *Chicago Daily Tribune*. 400 copies were printed.

1848—*The Tribune* becomes the first paper in the west to receive regular news by wire. By the end of 1849 circulation was near 1000.

1852—The subscription price for *The Tribune* is raised to 15¢.

July 1, 1858—The *Chicago Daily Tribune* and the *Democratic Press* merge to become the *Chicago Daily Press and Tribune*.

1861—*The Tribune* takes over Chicago's oldest paper *The Daily Democrat*.

1871—The Great Chicago Fire. The buildings housing the paper are totally destroyed by the fire.

1897—The newspaper prints its first half-tone image.

1903—The first daily spot color begins running.

1912—*The Tribune* builds its first paper mill in Ontario.

1924—The paper expands into local radio.

1925—The Tribune Tower is dedicated.

1931—The "Dick Tracy" comic strip begins publishing.

1939—*The Tribune* prints the first-ever full-color spot news photo.

1948—*The Tribune*'s television station—WGN—begins broadcasting.

1981—The Tribune Company purchases the Chicago Cubs baseball team.

1983—The Tribune Company goes public.

1991—The Tribune Company makes a $5 million investment in America Online.

1992—*The Tribune* goes digital with Chicago Online—available via America Online.

October, 1995—CareerPath is formed as an employment information service—in conjunction with *The Boston Globe, Los Angeles Times, The New York Times, San Jose Mercury News,* and *The Washington Post.*

March, 1996—*The Tribune* launches its Web site, the Chicagotribune.com.

September, 1996—Digital City Arlington Heights is unveiled—Chicago's first 'virtual community.'

June 10, 1997—*The Tribune* marks its 150th anniversary with a free public celebration. *The Tribune* is older than *The New York Times* (146 years old), *The Washington Post* (120), *The Los Angeles Time* (116), and *The Wall Street Journal* (108).

July, 1997—Community Web sites are expanded to 20.

February, 1998—The Chicagotribune.com web site is redesigned so that news and advertising are divided into 7 categories.

December, 1998—The *Chicago Tribune*'s Media Services launch FanStand. This site provides online shopping for film and television related merchandise.

March, 1999—The Tribune Company announces that it will digitize its entire archive of news clippings (1985 to date is already online). The completed database will house over 15 million images and include content from as early as 1920. Images and full text of every front page since 1849 will also be available, as will obituaries and death notices.

April, 1999—Tribune Ventures makes an investment in SuperMarkets Online.

May, 1999—Tribune Interactive is created.

November, 1999—*The Tribune* announces it will no longer produce a special edition for AOL.

---

same percentage of revenues on promotion that AOL did, but it's a good leading indicator that spending promotional money early on can help to build a powerful brand down the line.

Thus, the newspaper viewed its investments in NewMedia companies as an avenue for learning about how to operate effectively in the NewMedia environment and understand how some of these companies could affect the long-term development of the newspaper. Indeed, some of these companies were threatening one of the newspaper's most important sources of revenue—advertising. In an August 1999 report, Forrester Research predicted that by 2003, newspapers would lose over 23 percent of their total ad revenues.[9] Yet The Tribune Company's strategy was to incorporate these online opportunities and use them to enhance their own media offerings.

For example, last year, the newspaper invested in Supermarkets Online. The company, which is based in

Exhibit 4 | Tribune Ventures As Of April, 2000[35]

Public Investments

America Online—America's largest online service, with more than 14 million subscribers.

Exactis—Customizable, scalable e-mail marketing solutions for business.

Excite@Home—Leading provider of broadband Web services and open access to the Internet via cable.

iVillage—A leading online network targeted to women, with top brands Parent Soup and Better Health.

Lightspan—Developer of electronic education curriculum products. Products used in more than 500 school districts.

Peapod—Online grocery shopping service, with more than 75,000 customers and operations in eight U.S. cities.

VarsityBooks.com—Nation's premier online college bookstore.

Private Investments

BlackVoices.com—The leading online African American community.

Food.com—The Internet's largest takeout and delivery service.

iExplore—One stop resource for adventure and experiential travel.

iOwn.com—Online mortgage broker and real estate service.

Legacy.com—Publisher of online memorials and related information.

Pseudo Programs—Online entertainment network. Produces more than 40 Internet-television programs.

Replay Networks—Creators of next-generation television products using advanced digital technologies.

SocialNet.com—Destination site to meet people for work, leisure, housing and romance.

Teach.com—Premier provider of training solutions focused on improving knowledge worker productivity.

ValuPage—A website service where consumers receive coupon savings on leading national brands at local supermarkets.

Greenwich, Connecticut, provides electronic coupons which are accepted at over 9,000 brick and mortar grocery stores nationwide. In making this investment, Andy Oleszczuk, Tribune Venture president said:

> With Supermarkets Online, we see a company that represents the future of consumer packaged goods promotion and helps our traditional media properties serve the needs of our consumers and advertisers.[10]

For *The Tribune*, a company such as Supermarkets Online, which offers digital coupons, could potentially threaten the supermarket advertising business which had been so lucrative for the newspaper in the past. However, rather than view this as a threat, newspaper executives saw it as an opportunity to integrate the content offerings of the newspaper with advertising and create a richer online experience, especially for the local consumer.

The Tribune Company's investments and innovative strategies appeared to have paid off. The company's 1999 Annual Report indicates that the Tribune has continued to be profitable (Exhibit 5). In a press release detailing the full year results of the Tribune Company's operations in 1999, John W. Madigan reported:

> "This is our eighth consecutive year of earnings growth. In our media businesses, we increased our operating cash flow margins once again in 1999. Our daily newspapers' operating cash flow margins of 35 percent are among the best in the industry. And operating cash flow margins from our television stations expanded to more than 41 percent. Our television group—the largest station group not owned by a network—has been the most significant driver of earnings growth. The fundamentals of all of our businesses are strong, and we're looking forward to continued growth in 2000."[11]

III. Organizational Challenges for The Chicagotribune.com

The first online edition of *The Tribune* was launched in 1992 and could be accessed only through America Online. As the World Wide Web became more pervasive, *The*

Exhibit 5 Financial Highlights

For the Year *(in thousands, except per share data)*	1999	1998	Change
Operating revenues	$3,221,890	$2,980,889	+8%
Operating profit	$770,440	$702,289	+10%
Net income			
Before non-operating items	$415,446	$350,809	+18%
Including non-operating items	1,483,050	414,272	*
Cumulative effect of accounting change, net	(3,060)	-	*
Total	$1,479,990	$414,272	*
Diluted earnings per share			
Before non-operating items	$1.54	$1.27	+21%
Including non-operating items	5.62	1.50	*
Cumulative effect of accounting change, net	(.01)	-	*
Total	$5.61	$1.50	*
Common dividends per share:	$.36	$.34	+6%
Common stock price per share:			
high	$60.88	$37.53	
low	$30.16	$22.38	
close	$52.56	$33.32	

At Year End	Dec. 26, 1999	Dec. 27, 1998	Change
Total assets	$8,797,691	$5,935,570	+48%
Total debt	$2,724,881	$1,646,161	+66%
Shareholders' equity	$3,469,898	$2,356,617	+47%
Common shares outstanding	237,792	238,004	—

Common Stock Eleven Year Price History
(Dollars based on closing price each quarter)

Operating Revenues
(Dollars in billions)

Operating Profits
(Dollars in millions)

SOURCE: *Tribune Annual Report*, 1999.

Tribune launched its own website in March 1996, the Chicagotribune.com, which featured stories from the daily paper as well as original content such as election news.

Even with Jack Fuller and the rest of the senior management behind the effort, Youngman, who was charged with the developing the new online edition, described his role as a mediator between two cultures:

There is a culture of innovation that suffuses the newspaper. That is helpful. There is a willingness to take measured risks. That's helpful. On the other hand, there are elements of the culture that are very hide bound and traditional. It's a balancing act and one of my key roles is sort of mediating and juggling all that stuff and deciding when to push and when not to push.

As he juggled these two disparate cultures, one of Youngman's immediate tasks was to develop an organization that could successfully produce an online edition of the newspaper. While the standard departments such as marketing, finance, advertising, and customer services would all continue to exist in the new online organization, the old ways of gathering, validating, and presenting the news were no longer suitable, and the organization as well as the people in it would have to reflect this.

Many newspapers faced with developing news in two media simply used their print reporters to staff their online editions and "integrated" their print and on-line operations.[12] In contrast, *The Tribune* was the first newspaper to build a team of reporters whose primary responsibility was to produce online content. By mid 1997, the newspaper had hired 130 "digital journalists," the largest staff of any online newspaper.[13] While these online reporters worked in a separate unit, they were just as adept at posting a breaking story on the newspaper's website as writing a long article about the same issue for the print edition. Indeed, the expansion of the online staff was initially intended to help not only the Chicagotribune.com but also to enhance the market share for the print edition of the paper, especially in the area of local news. This hybrid organizational model has continued to evolve because the management at *The Tribune* has ensured that the two organizations interact at various levels. Thus, the top online editors attend news meetings with the print editors and reporters and work with their print counterparts to post early versions of print stories on the website.[14]

Youngman soon discovered that aside from the ability to be conversant in both print and online media, the most successful new hires had other attributes that enabled them to thrive in this new environment.

We started off early—because there was not much of an established Internet model for employees in 1995—hiring people with skills that were going to translate into the new medium. But over time what we've learned is that flexibility and adaptability are more important than almost any other skills and when we hire people we say now this is what we're hiring you for today but three months, three days from now we might ask you to do something different. The business is changing rapidly. We're trying to learn from our mistakes, leverage our success and there are really very few people in the whole organization,

two to three at most, that are doing the same thing today that they were originally hired to do. And you have to be comfortable with that amount of change and to some degree comfortable with the ambiguity in order to thrive.

Along with finding the right people who could work in an environment that was constantly undergoing change, Youngman suggested that a significant challenge for a traditional media company like *The Tribune* was trying to understand the nature of the NewMedia workforce. Not only were NewMedia employees more mobile and less likely to stay at *The Tribune* for the length of their careers; the competition for top-notch human talent was coming from unexpected quarters. Instead of *The Chicago Sun Times*, technology companies such as Sun Microsystems, AOL, and Microsoft were luring away *The Tribune*'s people:

For old media companies that are in the NewMedia space, the biggest differences are workforce issues. The Chicago Tribune, The New York Times, The Washington Post, The LA Times are destination newspapers. People will generally go there and that is where they stay. In the Internet space, it's a different competitive set. We are not competing with The Sun Times for people. We're competing with Sun or AOL or Excite. And we've lost people to those companies and more. Adjusting to the sort of rent-a-player mentality, where you know when you hire somebody they are not likely to be a career employee but you want to help them. You want to keep them as long as you can, help them build their skills knowing they are ultimately going to leave but wanting to get as much value out of them as you can.

Indeed, Madigan is concerned about the constant turnover and whether there will be enough of the right kind of people to manage the newspaper in the future.

I worry about whether we have the right people in the right places to deal with the issues that will be most significant in the future. Are you are growing the right people, hiring at entry and middle management level, the kind of people who will develop into the positions of the future? Are you recruiting enough from the outside to immediately provide the management talent for tomorrow's needs? It's something I think about every day.[15]

IV. Building a Brand

While the Chicagotribune.com was able to capitalize on the brand name of its print counterpart, *The Chicago Tribune*, it was important that the online organization build a brand that went beyond this legacy. Instead of being merely an electronic version of the newspaper, the online edition would have to offer stories and information not readily available in the print edition.

In order to differentiate itself, the Chicagotribune.com began to experiment with producing various content which was unique to the web. One of the most successful features it implemented was "Metro Daywatch" a breaking news feature, which was launched in January, 1999. This feature exploits the unique capabilities of the online edition. For unlike the print edition, which has one production cycle, the online version has a constant deadline cycle which enables online reporters to deliver the news in a timely fashion even after the print newspaper edition has been finalized. For example, when an Amtrak train crashed in a Chicago suburb, online reporters were able to go to the scene immediately and post stories throughout the night. The crash occurred after midnight, long after the print edition had been "put to bed." In the morning, the website had fresh information about the crash while the print edition had none.

Ben Estes, editor of the Chicagotribune.com believes that features like breaking news are important for developing a readership for the online newspaper: "We have a lot to offer the reader who wants to know the latest. That's where our future is".[16] In fact, the ability of the Chicagotribune.com to provide in-depth coverage on breaking news stories has enabled the online newspaper to significantly increase its user base. When Walter Payton died in November, 1999, the Chicagotribune.com had extensive coverage on Payton within hours of his death. In just three days, there were over 600,000 page views on that story line alone.

One of the keys to the development of the unique online features which characterize the Chicagotribune.com's brand is the incorporation of various technologies into the newspaper's infrastructure. Early in the development of the Chicagotribune.com, a major investment was made in a technology called Story Server, a content management system for the Web. CNET had originally developed this technology called PRISM (Presentation of Real-Time Interactive Service Material) to maintain high volume Web sites. CNET sold this technology to Vignette, an Austin, Texas based company in mid 1996. After becoming a beta test site for the new technology, the Chicagotribune.com implemented Story Server in the spring of 1997. Mike Guilino, The Tribune's manager of interactive technology, viewed the acquisition of Story Server as a way to improve the handling of the vast amount of information that existed on line. "There's no way to support our efforts statically," he said. "Discrete, independent files live in the directory structures and the larger they get, the more difficult it becomes."[17]

The first Tribune operation to use Story Server was Silicon Prairie http://www.chicagotribune.com/tech/, a feature which focuses on delivering the latest technology news and job listings to Chicago's high tech professionals. With the help of Story Server, the majority of the stories on the Silicon Prairie site are original with only two columns coming from the print Tribune. Writers send the editor stories by e-mail which are edited before being posted on the website. In addition to holding the stories on the site, Story Server creates relationships between articles. Thus in several Silicon Prairie columns, headlines for the previous ten are available at the end.[18]

In addition to providing technical improvements for managing the online content, Owen Youngman sees technologies such as Story Server as a way of harnessing the productivity of his employees and making some sections of the print newspaper more efficient:

> One of my goals in building Metromix was to move the newspaper away from its inefficient way of putting listings in the paper which is Rudy gets a press release and opens up a file. And types in the information and next week he gets another press release, opens it up, deletes last week's, and types in another one. Awful. So we built a database for Metromix of events so that Rudy can now get the press release, type in a whole year's worth of events, and it's fielded. So every week we just do a dump from the database to create the nine zone listing for the newspaper which is localized. We've decreased the error rate in them from 12 per page to 3 per page, typos and so on. Because it's all databased, it's only typed once. Huge deal. Huge deal.

Technology has also been used to enhance the online edition by providing readers with access to vast amounts of information in easy-to-use formats. For example, the online newspaper offered data on Illinois school districts which included statistics on standardized tests in math and reading. In addition to articles on the results, an interface to the database was designed so that the readers were able to access not only their own district statistics but also do comparisons with the statistics of other school districts in Chicago.

Another example of the use of technology is the online paper's ability to provide in-depth coverage of elections. Along with the standard information that is usually provided about candidates, the Chicagotribune.com provides all the contribution records and the paper's endorsements of the candidates. In addition, the online edition provides copies of the questionnaires that the candidates filled out in seeking the paper's endorsement so that voters can understand the paper's rationale in endorsing a particular candidate. Youngman said that this type of information could not be offered in the print edition because "there's no room in the newspaper to do that. Print is expensive and there is just no space for it. But here [in the Chicagotribune.com] we can do that and do it powerfully."

Case 10 / The Chicagotribune.com: Creating a Newspaper for the New Economy (A)

The technology has also enabled reporters to tell their stories in non-traditional innovative ways that invariably enhanced what they could have done in the print edition. Using a process called "nonlinear story telling," reporters can provide a variety of ways for viewing and reading a story. Since the web is structured so that links from one computer page location can lead to another, a story can be told in components or from several points of view, and can encompass different media such as video, audio, and text.

Thus, during the 1996 Democratic convention, Tribune reporter Darnell Little developed a historical tour of some of the previous 25 political conventions in the city. Little, who holds a degree in both engineering and journalism used a variety of media and devised three parallel tours which included tours of some of the conventions, a behind-the-scenes look at what was happening in Chicago at the time of the conventions, and archives and cartoons of the various periods. Little also used a technique called "layering" which guides the reader from one section of the story to the next. Unlike a print newspaper page which usually has ample space for a story, a computer screen might only contain the first "layer" of a digital story in the form of a headline, photograph, or text. The reader is given the option to click on the first "layer" and proceed in a logical order to the other aspects of the story.[19]

While the use of technology has had a significant impact on the type of information offered to the readers of the Chicagotribune.com, the Chicagotribune.com's competitive edge lies in part in its ability to provide solid reporting and compelling writing just as its print counterpart has done for 150 years. In a well publicized thrust into the NewMedia business, Microsoft developed a group of web entries called Sidewalk. Aimed at providing an entertainment guide for cities around the country including Chicago, Sidewalk was poised to be a significant threat to online ventures like the Chicagotribune.com. Microsoft even tried to recruit away editorial people from the Tribune to work on Sidewalk.

The Tribune responded by developing Metromix, http://metromix.com/top/1,1419,M-Metromix-Home-X!Front.00.html, which Youngman said was far superior to Sidewalk in terms of content and focus on the Chicago market. Though Microsoft's technological capabilities far outweighed that of an online newspaper like the Chicagotribune.com, according to Jack Fuller, the newspaper could respond to this threat because of the news values which are part of the newspaper's culture and define its brand. Fuller believes that though people can get information from anywhere, they still need filters for selecting and creating meaning out of the vast amount of information that they have been given and the newspaper can act as such a filter. In a discussion of the role of the newspaper in the NewMedia environment, Fuller wrote:

> Whether delivered on paper or electronically, the newspaper must have human editors. It must continue to embody the complexities of human personality, to demonstrate judgment and character, to have a distinctive voice that relates well to the community it serves. All these elements come together in what the marketers like to call brand identity, which in a fragmented, targeted environment, will be vital to differentiating one source of information from another. . . . Out of the welter of products on a supermarket shelf, a few stand out because of their comfortable familiarity. Organizations with the most brand loyalty—earned by staying close to their communities and by adhering strictly to proper new values—will be the ones that thrive.[20]

Fuller's vision of a brand which garners loyalty by espousing particular values and catering to its constituent communities, may not be viable in a future characterized by a proliferation of content, and a variety of news media that provide coverage on the Web. It remains to be seen whether the vast audience of users will be interested in a comprehensive newspaper like the Chicagotribune.com or prefer more Yahoo-type short takes on newsworthy events.

V. Content, Community, and Commerce

As the Chicagotribune.com developed, it became apparent that if the newspaper was going to succeed, it would need to rethink its strategy vis a vis the various stakeholders both traditional and nontraditional, who were becoming an influential part of the community in which *The Tribune* operated. Indeed, the management of *The Tribune* realized that the nature of the interactive medium had changed the way the newspaper related to its partners, its competitors and its readers. Owen Youngman pointed out that the competitive landscape had changed dramatically: "The nature of this business is changing so much that our best customers are turning into competitors, and our competitors are turning into potential collaborators."[21] For example, some of the local media and publishing organizations that used to be competitors of *The Tribune* are now forming alliances with the Chicagotribune.com. *Crain's Chicago Business* now has a relationship with the online newspaper as do several radio stations which have online presences. Conversely, real estate agencies which used to be a traditional source of classified ad revenues for the newspaper, were now setting up websites that bypassed the newspaper and offered property directly to the consumer.

Because of this dramatic shift in alliances, Youngman spent much of his time seeking out a variety of strategic partners with whom the newspaper could form mutually beneficial alliances. When he realized that cultivating relationships was an intrinsic part of the new online business, Youngman created a position in his organization, the strategic relationship manager, which would focus on managing such strategic partnerships. Youngman considers this to be one of the most important jobs in his organization:

> Going it alone did not make any sense. Six months into this, it became clear to me that we needed to have a focus in the digital arena on this. If you are going to make these relationships, someone is going to have to manage them and make sure they work for everybody. Sorting it out is a full-time thing, and making sure that those relationships accrue to the benefit of our organization and our partners' organization requires a full-time focus.[22]

In addition, Jack Fuller appointed a vice president for acquisitions and alliances at the newspaper itself. In another iteration of the hybrid organization that has evolved at *The Tribune*, the two relationship managers work closely together and meet regularly with Youngman.

The thrust of the newspaper toward reaching out to the larger community of partners echoed Jeff Scherb's tripartite strategy of "content, community, and commerce." Scherb, who recently became President of Tribune Interactive, believes that while the first goal of the newspaper is to be the premier provider of local news and information, this is only one aspect of a newspaper's mission. Providing up-to-the-minute news through such features as Metrowatch, also drives traffic to local e-commerce sites thus serving the local community in a multidimensional way. An example of this blend of content, community, and commerce is the news coverage and related advertising which appeared before and during Hurricane Floyd in September 1999. Along with weather updates and breaking news stories, the Chicagotribune.com teamed up with Lowe's, a home products retailer, who provided information on the availability of supplies that would be useful during the storm.[23]

The importance of the community of readers for *The Tribune* is also reflected in several features of the Chicagotribune.com website. There is Metromix, a site devoted to providing up-to-the-minute information on movies, restaurants, art exhibits, and other entertainment events; a network of community websites devoted to local events and groups; and most recently, the addition of Chicagosports.com http://www.chicagosports.com, a website devoted exclusively to in-depth coverage on Chicago sports teams and events which is linked to the Chicagotribune.com home page.

Because of the nature of the interactive medium, the community of readers has not only been passive receivers of information; they have become active participants in content creation on several levels. For example, a decision was made in early 1998 to change the newspaper page metaphor that was *The Tribune*'s home page and redesign it so that it looked like a television screen with content in different channels. Because of the overwhelming negative response to the redesign from the user community, the newspaper switched back so that it would look like the other newspaper sites such as *The New York Times* and *The Wall Street Journal*. In addition, readers have become active participants within their own online communities. Using a self-publishing software tool, local community groups can post news and events on their particular community websites.

VI. Emerging Issues

On March 14, 2000, The Tribune Company and the Times-Mirror Company announced that they would merge. The combined company, which would own 11 daily newspapers, 22 television stations and 4 radio stations, would have a combined circulation of 3.6 million copies, ranking the new company third among newspaper companies after Gannett and Knight Ridder.[24] Along with a more powerful presence on the print side, the addition of the Times-Mirror web sites would give Tribune Interactive an audience of 34 million unique visitors, more than the web site of *The New York Times* (www.nytimes.com) and USA.com (www.usa.com) combined.[25]

While the creation of a nationwide website is something Tribune executives envision, the company has no immediate plans to combine content on any of the web sites. Instead, the company will create a national network of locally focused sites and focus on how it can leverage the advertising, promotional and technological possibilities that the merger will bring. For example, the company will explore how to manage the technology of its entire group of web sites more efficiently and see if common content management platforms and search engines can be developed.[26]

For the Chicagotribune.com, the proposed merger may have an effect on its development as a strong local online newspaper. Clearly, there will be more opportunities for online advertisers both locally and nationally and the emphasis on advertising at the expense of good content could threaten the brand that Owen Youngman and his staff have been building over the last four years. Even before the merger, there were organizational changes that were seen by many as a step in the wrong direction. Indeed, after the creation of Tribune Interactive in March 1999, more than 15 percent of the Chicagotribune.com's staff left, including Howard Witt, associate managing editor of the paper. Staffers say they left because the company was de-emphasizing writing and journalism and focusing more on promotion and profit.[27]

Yet in an interview in December 1999 with *The Digital Edge*, Digby Solomon, who had just been appointed as the new general manager of Tribune Interactive's Chicago division, defended the focus on e-commerce and suggested that the content needed to be changed in order to compete with pure Internet companies such as AOL and Yahoo!: "Let's face it—we created many products that audiences didn't want to read and that advertisers wouldn't pay for, because they were legacies of our traditional newspaper businesses. We needed to focus on content that drove ratings . . ."[28] Solomon also insisted that the editorial quality of the online newspaper would not suffer and that "our properties will still follow the journalistic values of our newspaper and television newsrooms."[29]

While the conflict between profitability and good journalism continues, online newspapers such as the Chicagotribune.com must search for additional sources of revenue to sustain their operations. One such potential revenue source is subscriptions. With the exception of *The Wall Street Journal Interactive*, which has had a subscription fee since its inception, other online newspapers have not charged for access to their sites. Moreover, in a recent survey released by ScreamingMedia.com, 89 percent of the 1232 respondents said that they had never paid for news or information on the Web and 83 percent said that they were not willing to pay.[30] Nevertheless, Owen Youngman thinks that this should change and is investigating what users will pay for: "We're conducting research on what people will pay for and what they won't and how much they'll pay for it. We're looking at what [content] is highly commoditized."[31] Another potential source of revenue may be subscriptions to mobile services. *The New York Times* already has a free service which provides daily updated coverage of top stories that are downloadable to handheld devices. However, users may be willing to pay for subscriptions to such features as breaking news and stock reports.

After four years of operation, the Chicagotribune.com remains one of the premier online newspapers. Yet its leadership knows that in the rapidly changing business environment, flexibility, adaptability, and constantly reassessing the competitive landscape, are key if the newspaper is going to continue to be recognized for its high quality reporting and features. Owen Youngman knows this very well:

It's literally true that, every day I question whether what we're doing is going to continue next week, next month next year or in five years. If you let a week go by without evaluating what you're doing, you can be left behind.[32]

Endnotes

1. The remarks by Owen Youngman throughout this case study were taken from a taped interview with Mr. Youngman in Chicago on August 10, 1999.
2. Martha Stone, "Print to Web: It Takes Teamwork," *Editor & Publisher Online*, July 10, 1999.
3. Press Release, "PaineWebber Media Conference," December 8, 1999, http://www.tribune.com/about/ news/1999/pw.htm.
4. Mark Fitzgerald, "The Team Riding the Tiger", *Editor and Publisher Online*, March 27, 2000.
5. For further discussion on the merger with the Times-Mirror, see *The Chicagotribune.com: Creating a Newspaper for the New Economy (B)*, Institute for Technology and Enterprise, November 2000
6. Mark Fitzgerald, "The Team Riding the Tiger," *Editor and Publisher Online*, March 27, 2000.
7. Jeff Borden, "Trib Co. buys low, flies high with shrewd Internet buys", *Crain's Chicago Business*, August 30, 1999, www.pcreprints.com/eprint/tribune/buylow.htm
8. James P. Miller, "How Tribune Grabbed a Media Prize", *Wall Street Journal*, March 14, 2000.
9. Charlene Li, "Internet Advertising Skyrockets", *Forrester Research Report*, August 1999.
10. Staff reporters, "Chicago Media Company Increases Internet Investments" *Editor & Publisher Online*, April 9, 1999.
11. "Tribune Reports Record 4Q and Full Year Earnings" Chicago, Friday January 21, 2000, Press Release, http://www.tribune.com/about/news/ 2000/4q99.htm
12. Rob Runett, "Study. Joint Newsrooms Still Dominate", *The Digital Edge*, April 2000, www. digitaledge.org/monthly/2000/04/mediaincyberspace.html
13. Scott Kirsner, "Explosive Expansion at Tribune Website", *Editor & Publisher Online*, July 7, 1997.
14. Martha Stone, "Print to Web: It Takes Teamwork," *Editor & Publisher Online*, July 10, 1999.
15. Jeff Borden, "A Collision of Media," *Crain's Chicago Business*, June 7, 1999, www.pcreprints.com/eprint/ tribune.
16. Martha Stone, Print to Web: It Takes Teamwork, *Editor & Publisher Online*, July 10, 1999.
17. Staff Editors, "Web Databasics", *NAA Presstime*, July/August 1997, www.naa.org/presstime/9707/ wb2.html
18. Staff Editors, "Web Databasics", *NAA Presstime*, July/August 1997, www.naa.org/presstime/9707/ wb2.html
19. Christopher Harper, "Journalism in a Digital Age", Lecture given at the Democracy and Digital Media Conference held at MIT, May 8–9, 1998. For a discussion about content innovation at the Chicagotribune.com, see George Szarka. "Chicago Tribune Internet Edition", Unpublished paper, Institute for Technology and Enterprise, Polytechnic University, Spring 1999.
20. Jack Fuller, *News values: Ideas for an Information Age*, Chicago: University of Chicago Press, 1996, p. 229—230.
21. Staff Editors, "Meeting The Online Competition", *Editor & Publisher Online*, January 8, 1997.
22. Staff Editors, "Meeting The Online Competition," *Editor & Publisher Online*, January 8, 1997.
23. Paine Webber Media Conference, December 8, 1999.
24. Felicity Barringer and Laura M. Holson, "Tribune Company Agrees to Buy Times Mirror", *The New York Times*, March 14, 2000, p. A1.
25. Jason Williams, "The New Spider in the Web", *Editor & Publisher Online*, March 20, 2000.
26. Jim Benning, "Mergers—Times Mirror and Tribune: A Powerhouse is Born?", *Online Journalism Review*, March 14, 2000, www.oir.usc.edu/content/ print.cfm?print=346.
27. Martha L. Stone, "Defections Hit Tribune Co.'s Interactive Unit", *Editor & Publisher Online*, September 8, 1999.
28. Rob Runett, "Solomon Grabs Point Position as Tribune Restructures Sites", *The Digital Edge*, December, 1999, www.digitaledge.org/monthly/ 1999_12/digbyprofile.html

29. Rob Runett, "Solomon Grabs Point Position as Tribune Restructures Sites", *The Digital Edge,* December, 1999, www.digitaledge.org/monthly/ 1999_12/digbyprofile.html

30. Felicity Barringer, "Web Surfers Want the News Fast and Free", *The New York Times,* May 1, 2000, p. C12.

31. Martha L. Stone, "Chicago Tribune Web site Moving to Registration", *Editor & Publisher Online,* March 3, 1999.

32. Jeff Borden, "A Collision of Media", *Crain's Chicago Business,* June 7, 1999, www.pcreprints.com/eprint/ tribune

33. *Tribune Company Annual Report,* 1999.

34. Lloyd Wendt, *Chicago Tribune: The Rise of a Great American Newspaper.* Chicago: Rand McNally & Company, 1979.

35. *Tribune Company Annual Report,* 1999.

Cisco Systems Inc.– Growth Through Acquisitions

Mike Killick
University of Cape Town
Isack Rawoot
University of Cape Town
Gary J. Stockport
University of Western Australia

INTRODUCTION

"We're paranoid. A lot of companies are arrogant. They're on top and they believe they belong there. We've got almost the reverse attitude. We've got a tremendous fear of failing. We make Andy Grove at Intel look relaxed."

(Cisco CEO - John Chambers in an interview in 1997).

Cisco Systems is one of the most successful companies in the global Internet industry. From its beginnings at Stanford University in 1984 and the shipping of its first product in 1986, the company has grown to be one of the most valuable companies in Silicon Valley. Cisco Systems passed a capitalisation mark of $100 billion in 1998 only 14 years after it was founded. On 10th December 1999, Cisco became only the third company in history (following *General Electric* and *Microsoft*) to go past the $300 billion mark in market capitalisation. Since going public in 1990, Cisco's annual revenue has increased from $69 million to $18.9 billion in fiscal 2000 – nearly 275 fold in 10 years.

Despite a sharp decline in their stock price from March to November 2000, from a value around $80 to

about $52, Cisco shows no signs of retreating from its long-running strategy of buying other companies to foster its growth. Acquisitions have been the *"lifeblood"* of Cisco's growth from 1993, and it is on-track to acquire 20 to 25 companies during the year 2000. In a decade where most technology-based acquisitions are not successful, Cisco has achieved unprecedented successes and has acquired and successfully integrated 70 companies into its fold as at 2nd December 2000. Dataquest Analyst Tim Smith believed that Cisco would not hesitate to make an acquisition if it needed the technology and states the following about Cisco's acquisition intentions:

"With their stock price being less valuable, it might be a tougher nut to swallow, but they can still do it and won't hesitate if an acquisition opportunity has a long term benefit. Cisco is very adept at making acquisitions and turning them into money-makers."

Cisco operates in a market that at the beginning of 2000 was estimated at $500 billion. The market consists of three different kinds of networks: phone networks, local and wide area networks for data, and the broadcast networks for video. The company controls more than three-quarters of the global market for products that link networks and power the Internet, including routers and switches. It also manufactures dial-up access servers and network management software. Cisco has established strategic partnerships worldwide, including alliances with leading technology companies such as *IBM*, *Motorola*, and *Sun Microsystems*. Chambers believes that the companies that will emerge as industry leaders are those that have the ability to acquire other companies, partner with industry leaders and develop products internally. But the question remained, would acquisitions further fuel the growth of Cisco in the future?

Early History of Cisco

The Company Start-Up

Cisco was founded by Leonard Bosack and Sandy Lerner, a husband and wife team of computer scientists who worked in two different departments at Stanford University. The couple was frustrated by the fact that their computers situated in different departments at the University ran on different operating systems and, as a result, they could not send e-mail messages to each other. To solve this problem, the couple built an IP[A] router (Internet protocol router), which enabled the connection of normally incompatible networks. After the University denied them permission to continue their business on the University campus or to use school resources for making routers for their colleagues at other Universities and Research Centres, Leonard and Sandy left Stanford in 1984 and formed their own company, Cisco. The company name was based on the last few letters of the city, San Francisco. At the time Cisco was founded, the Internet had only 1000 computers connected to it.

To finance the business, Len and Sandy mortgaged their home and Sandy took on an additional job at *Schlumberger,* an international technical company. They transformed their home living room into the headquarters for the design and manufacture of their network products. During 1985, the business grew and eventually they ran out of production space at their home. In 1986, Cisco moved its operation to a rented office space in Menlo Park, Silicon Valley.

Getting Funded

By 1987, Cisco Systems encountered competition from other networking companies such as *Bridge* and *3COM.* In order to regain and increase market share, Cisco needed additional financing. Sandy and Leonard approached Don Valentine, a venture capitalist who agreed to take a 32 percent stake in the company for $2.5 million. The venture capital firm would provide financing, recruitment and other important management support functions that were required to grow the Cisco business. After signing the contract, without any involvement of lawyers, Sandy became Vice President of customer service and Leonard became Chief Technology Officer. The timing of the receipt of the venture capital funds coincided with the commercialisation of the Internet being made a reality by the USA Congress in 1987.

The demand for routers increased dramatically during late 1988, as personal computers became popular amongst corporations worldwide. It was at the same time that businesses were pushing for networking their organisations, thereby making the router commercially viable. Cisco's cash resources quickly accumulated as sales of routers to the PC industry grew. Cisco eventually ended up not using the $2.5 million venture capital as cash resources were sufficient to fund the operations of the business.

Financing Cisco

In 1988, Don Valentine exercised his right to choose the executive management team. He began replacing members of the management team with people he could trust. He did not, however, change Sandy's and Leonard's positions. The staff replacements resulted in animosity between Don Valentine and the founding members, particularly Sandy. She thought that Valentine was killing the original culture and systematically pushing her and her husband out. Valentine also decided to recruit a CEO for Cisco. He was looking for an industry veteran and a proven leader. Valentine made John P. Morgridge, then President of *Grid Systems*, a portable computer manufacturer, an offer to become CEO of Cisco, which Morgridge accepted in mid 1988.

Morgridge's Appointment as CEO

Before accepting Cisco's offer, Morgridge investigated the company's background. He did this by interviewing and calling a number of Cisco's customers and enquiring about three things:

1. Are you currently using the Cisco product?
2. Do you like it?
3. Are you going to buy more?

All the customers he contacted answered *"yes"* to all three questions and Morgridge took the job. Morgridge's experience included being President of *Grid Systems* for two years, a marketing Vice President position at *Stratus Computers,* and many years of experience as a salesman at *Honeywell.* Morgridge was also a graduate from the University of Wisconsin School of Business. Morgridge's experience was as a small company executive and his management style was typical of that environment. He made sure that he was involved in all decision making by establishing a strong central management team that reported directly to him. Morgridge was also very frugal with the company's money, but he was prepared to spend huge sums for things that he felt were crucial to the company's success. Morgridge's mission was to centralise the whole organisation as it offered him more comfort knowing that he would have more control.

Morgridge frequently lectured his executives on indulgences such as travelling first class on business trips. He believed that business was about attitude and not about luxury. Morgridge did not like executives to believe that they deserved better than everyone else and commented:

> "Someone flies first class, no one else does; he gets a suite, no one else does. You can run the company that way but don't expect the employees to get excited about it."

Morgridge himself would fly on senior discount coupons and get upgrades only when he attained enough frequent flyer miles. This philosophy of Morgridge was the centre of Cisco's organisational culture. During Morgridge's years as CEO, Cisco had no 5-year plan but rather followed a 1-year plan as Morgridge believed that it kept morale high and the company's goals in focus. According to Morgridge:

> "At Cisco we build a one year plan with 80 to 90 percent assurance we'll meet our goals, so it's not a stretch."

The IPO

By late 1989, Cisco was developing industry standards and had a list of customers including the *US Army, Boeing, Hewlett Packard, General Electric* and *Morgan Stanley*. In fiscal year 1989, Cisco reported profits of $4.2 million and $2.5 million in the first quarter of 1990. Cisco was now expanding and Morgridge and his executive team considered going public to raise funds for the further expansion of the business. Cisco made its Initial Public Offering (IPO) in 1990 and the stock opened at $18 and closed that day at around $22.50.

The Founders Sell Out

Six months after the IPO, several Cisco executives approached Morgridge with complaints about Sandy, stating that they found her intolerable to work with. The executives advised Morgridge that either Sandy "*go*" or they would resign. The executives approached Don Valentine with the same complaints. On August 28th 1990, Sandy was dismissed and soon thereafter Leonard resigned as a member of the Board, later resigning from the company altogether. In August 1990, Sandy and Leonard sold their two-thirds of Cisco stocks for $170 million.

In the period 1991 through to 1993, following the withdrawal by Sandy and Leonard, Morgridge set the tone for Cisco's culture and operational methods. Morgridge ran the business focusing on cutting costs and establishing a strong central team beneath him. He also made sure that Cisco continued its strong customer focus that enabled it to progress so speedily in the mid 1980's. Under Morgridge, Cisco sold routers mainly directly to large corporations and they sold them to upper management as opposed to technical staff. This sales strategy quickly created a name for Cisco in the market.

Leadership Under John Chambers
Chambers Becomes CEO

Chambers joined Cisco in 1991 as Senior Vice President, worldwide sales and operations and second in command to John Morgridge. At that time, Cisco had $70 million in annual revenues, 300 employees and a market capitalisation of $600 million. For four years, Chambers operated as Morgridge's right hand man and, as such, played a key role in Cisco's early acquisitions, their acquisition strategy, and the development of Cisco's overall long term goals and objectives. Chambers was promoted to Executive Vice President of worldwide operations in 1994 and a few months later in 1995 to Chief Executive Officer replacing Morgridge. Morgridge remained at Cisco serving as Chairman of the Board.

Background

John Chambers was born in 1949 in Charleston, West Virginia. Both his parents were physicians, his mother a psychiatrist and his father an obstetrician. From an early age, Chambers' career goal was either to be a doctor or to run his own business. John Chambers grew up with a disadvantage of having a mild form of dyslexia which made reading difficult. His mother took him to a reading coach, Lorena Anderson Walters, who had the following to say about Chambers:

> "Oh, I loved Johnny. He knew that he had a problem, and he had no doubt in his mind that he was going to do something about it. He made no excuses for not being able to read, and that's very rare."

In spite of the dyslexia, he graduated second in his class at high school through perseverance, hard work and tutoring. Even today, Chambers dislikes reading and never does it for pleasure. In order to compensate for his disability, Chambers relies upon his remarkable memory, in which he recalls virtually everything he hears. Chambers attended West Virginia University after high school and graduated with a BS/BA in Business Administration in 1971 and JD (Law) degree in 1974. As an undergraduate he played basketball, a sport which required an intensive team spirit. Chamber's father said the following about his son's participation in sport at the time:

"John played a lot of sports, but he was never the star. He liked to organise teams and expected them to win. He wouldn't have played if he didn't."

In 1975, Chambers also graduated with an MBA in Finance and Management from Indiana University.

Work Experience Prior to Cisco

After graduating, Chambers accepted a position in the sales department at *IBM* in 1977, after being impressed by his interviewer's sale pitch: *"You're not selling technology; you're selling a dream."* Whilst gaining hands-on experience, Chambers also learnt the lesson of how to sell at multiple levels within an organisation. Aggressive customer satisfaction was another lesson which Chambers learnt, and his team at *IBM* would move heaven and earth not to let a customer down. Chambers left *IBM* partly due to the organisation's bureaucracy and partly due to being chided by management for only meeting 9 out of his 10 set promised goals, this in spite of the fact that *IBM* only required that employees set and attain 3 goals. In 1983, Chambers left *IBM* for *Wang Laboratories,* then a high-flying maker of minicomputers that threatened the dominance of *IBM's* mainframes. Unfortunately, *Wang* was unsuccessful in adapting its proprietary word processing system to customer demand and technological change and Chambers, who had been promoted in 1990 to Senior Vice President of US sales, had to oversee 5 separate layoffs totalling over 4,000 people. This was a traumatic experience for Chambers and he has stated that he never wanted to be involved in layoffs again. Chambers made the comment:

"Laying off people was the toughest thing I ever did. I'll move heaven and earth to avoid doing that again."

Another important lesson which Chambers learnt from both *IBM* and *Wang* was that a company had to adapt with the flow of technology and not resist it. In 1991, Chambers resigned from *Wang Laboratories* as he did not like the direction in which *Wang* was heading.

Teamwork a Priority

One of the first things Chambers did after his appointment as CEO was to establish a compensation system tied to team successes and to instil a policy of open communication. Chambers rates the ability to work as part of a team essential and has said:

"In our organisation if I've got a leader who can't be a team player, they're gone. That does not mean that we don't want healthy disagreement, but regardless of how well they're performing, if they can't learn over time to be part of a team and to challenge when appropriate, they

really aren't going to fit into our long term culture."

One of the reasons why Chambers insists on teamwork was so that he could enact his key plan for decentralisation. Chambers knew that decentralisation was the only way in which he could sustain a path of high growth for the business and allow the business to be flexible enough to adapt to a fast-moving technological environment. Decentralisation also allowed Chambers to eliminate the layers of management between himself and the customer, thus enabling him to get closer to the customer. Chambers empowered his Vice Presidents with decision-making capabilities and powers thereby also allowing more people in the organisation to have the capability to make a difference. Chambers invariably makes the CEO of an acquired company a Vice President. During interviews, Chambers frequently accredits his Vice Presidents and the teams of people working underneath them for Cisco's successes. President Clinton once made the following anecdotal comment about Chambers:

"I always liked John Chambers, until I found out that he had 70 Vice Presidents. I don't know what to make of that. That he's more important than I am? He's less efficient than I am?"

Customer Focus

Chambers is known to be a relentless competitor who is fanatical about putting the customer first. Chambers is known to spend as much as 55 percent of his time with customers and hands out his personal contact details to all the customers he meets. Chambers continuously listens to what his customers are telling him and believes that his customers' needs and wants help guide and shape the future strategy and direction of Cisco. In an interview in February 2000, Chambers made the following comment:

"Each time our customers changed what was important to them, we changed the company. So over the last decade, we've literally changed several times. . . . We built a culture of changing every time customer ways of buying changed."

Chambers also believes in trust and prefers to make agreements with a handshake rather than a written contract. Chambers emphasises the following on priorities:

"The two things that get companies into trouble is that they get too far away from their customers and too far away from their employees."

One of the key factors for Chambers' success is his people skills. He has driven Cisco's strategy for growth while recognising the crucial role played by employees.

Chambers believes in retaining human capital and this is evident in his approach to acquisitions. Chambers' strategy on how to manage organisational growth reflects his personal management style, and his personality and approach are intrinsically linked to Cisco's success. Exhibit 1 outlines Chambers philosophy on managing growth within a company. Chambers is considered as one of the most innovative and dynamic leaders in global business and has received leadership recognition from various sources including being named CEO of the year by *Worth* magazine. Exhibit 2 shows the leadership recognition which Chambers has received. John Chamber's vision is simple: *"We can change the way people live and work, play and learn."* He has set his sights beyond data networking and has made himself into an e-commerce ambassador, travelling the globe to sell corporate leaders and government officials on the virtues of the Internet. Chambers spends half of his time on the road, meeting heads of state and countless executives.

Early Growth Years (1993 to 1996)

Revision of Business Plan

In 1993, Cisco's market capitalisation reached $6.4 billion. The growth of the Internet world-wide created a demand for other technology in addition to merely routers. Morgridge and Chambers realised that the market pressures to move beyond routers presented an opportunity for Cisco to expand its range of products. Morgridge and Chambers made a conscious decision to attempt to shape the future of the entire industry. They decided that they wanted to dominate the networking industry in the same way that *Microsoft* had dominated the PC industry and *IBM* had dominated the mainframe industry. In order to achieve this, Cisco decided to compete across the entire internetworking market place, from Internet hardware and software to asynchronous transfer mode switches and routers. The Cisco management decided to adopt the General Electric mentality of striving to be either the No.1 or No.2 player in each market segment in which they chose to compete. Cisco had three choices: 1). either to achieve it themselves, 2). by a merger with an equal, or 3). by partnering and acquiring other companies.

Morgridge, John Chambers and Ed Kozel (Chief Technology Officer), set about revising the business plan which was originally drawn up in 1988. Their new business plan focused on four areas:

- Providing a complete solution for businesses
- Make acquisitions a structured process
- Define the industry-wide networking software protocols and
- Form the right strategic alliances

Exhibit 1	John Chambers' Lessons on Managing Growth

1. *Make your customers the center of your culture.*
   Customer satisfaction is Cisco's number one priority so we tie our employee compensation programs directly to our customer satisfaction ratings. Although it may take 12-18 months to see the results, there is a 1-to-1 correlation between customer satisfaction and revenues and profits.
2. *Empower every employee.*
   Empowering employees will increase productivity and improve retention within your company. Cisco has an unusual culture in that we believe we can do anything, yet we also realize that we could quickly lose our leadership position if we mis-execute or if our competition executes well.
3. *Thrive on change.*
   Turning change into a competitive advantage is necessary for survival in today's fast-paced Internet economy. Cisco is committed to helping our customers implement the Internet applications that will help them compete successfully in the future.
4. *Teamwork requires Open Communication and Trust.*
   You must establish open, two-way communication to create a truly empowered workforce. We work closely with our employees and customers to develop annual goals and initiatives and I ask all 30,000 employees to carry this information on their badges to ensure our common vision.
5. *Build strong partnerships.*
   Leading companies in the 80s focused on internal development, and in the 90s, on internal development and acquisitions. This decade, leading companies will be those that develop internally, acquire effectively and form ecosystem partnerships in a horizontal business model.

SOURCE: Cisco Connection Online, 2000.

The rise of the Internet and personal computing reshaped Cisco's business. The Internet had shifted Cisco's focus from building routers for allowing one network to talk to another, to connecting the whole world via the Internet. Morgridge realised that Cisco's 80 percent market share of routers would be of little value if the market decided to move to new technologies and that product diversification was therefore essential. An acquisition strategy would enable Cisco to own, develop and market an array of network products and standards as the market demanded them. Chambers also heard from his large accounts that they wanted single-vendor servicing in the networking arena. In line with the philosophy of always listening to their customers, Cisco had as one of its objectives a plan to provide a complete solution for businesses.

First Acquisition

In early 1993, Cisco started negotiations with *Boeing* for a $10 million router order. *Boeing*, however, preferred the low cost simplified product produced by one of Cisco's competitors, *Crescendo Communications*. *Crescendo* was one of a few companies that came out with an alternative networking technology based on switches - devices that increasingly competed with Cisco's routers. With these switches, companies could build large LAN'S[B] (local area networks) that were robust, fast and inexpensive, as opposed to building collections of smaller networks using hubs connected by Cisco routers. The dealmakers at *Boeing* indicated to Chambers that Cisco would not get the contract unless they worked with *Crescendo*, either through partnership or through acquisition. At around the same time, *Ford Motor Company* also opted to purchase the switches manufactured by *Crescendo* as opposed to Cisco's routers. Morgridge, Chambers and Kozel believed that it was essential for Cisco to diversify and persuaded the Board to proceed with the acquisition of *Crescendo*. On the 21st of September 1993, Cisco acquired *Crescendo* for $89 million. When the acquisition was announced, Cisco's stock price fell, the first time in the history of the company that the stock price had fallen as analysts could not believe that Cisco would acquire a company that only made $10 million revenue per year for a price of $89 million.

Acquisitions between 1994 and 1996

After Cisco's acquisition of *Crescendo Communications* in September 1993, it proceeded to acquire *Newport Systems Solutions*, *Kalpana* and *Lightstream Corporation* in 1994. Exhibit 4 gives a summary of Cisco's acquisitions from September 1993 to November 2000. *Lightstream*, which was purchased by Cisco for $120 million, had developed one of the most advanced enterprise-level ATM[C] switches on the market and would make Cisco the only networking company able to offer its customers a choice of all the key technologies needed for the switched Internetworks of the future.

Cisco's acquisition trail continued in 1995 with four additional companies being acquired. Cisco's revenue grew from $1.3 billion in 1994 to $2.2 billion in 1995 and its market capitalisation grew from $5.5 billion to $17.2 billion. Table 1 gives the financial history of Cisco from the period 1993 through to 2000. The table also shows that Cisco funded their acquisitions by means of equity finance as opposed to debt finance.

(Text continues on page C.138)

Exhibit 4	Summary of Cisco's Acquisitions from September 1993 to November 2000					
Acquisition Number	Name of Acquired Company	Date Acquired	Approx. Value millions $	Approx. Value Employees	No. of Location	Market Opportunity
70	Radiata Inc	14–Nov–00	$295	53	Australia/ San Jose, California	High performance Wireless Networks
69	Active Voice Corporation	10–Nov–00	$266		Seattle, Washington	IP based unified messaging Solution (VoIP)
68	CAIS	20–Oct–00	$170	65	San Diego, California	Broadband connectivity management software
67	Vovida Networks, Inc.	28–Sep–00	$369	65	San Jose, California	Voice over IP (VoIP)
66	IPCell Technologies, Inc.	28–Sep–00		110	Texas, USA	Voice and Data Integrated Access Services
65	PixStream, Inc.	31–Aug–00	$369	156	Canada	Distribute and Manage Digital Video
64	IPMobile, Inc.	01–Aug–00	$425	81	Texas, USA	Mobile Wireless Internet
63	NuSpeed Internet Systems, Inc.	27–Jul–00	$450	56	Minnesota, USA	IP-enable Storage Area Networking Technology
62	Komodo Technology, Inc.	25–Jul–00	$175	25	Los Gatos, California	VoIP Devices for Analogue Phones
61	Netiverse, Inc.	07–July–00	$210	34	San Jose, California	Content Aware Switches
60	HyNEX, Ltd.	05–Jun–00	$127	49	Israel	ATM and IP solutions
59	Qeyton Systems	12–May–00	$800	52	Sweden	Metropolitan DWDM Technology
58	ArrowPoint Communications, Inc.	05–May–00	$5,700	337	Massachusetts, USA	Content Networking Technology
57	Seagull Semiconductor, Ltd.	12–Apr–00	$19	17	Israel	High-speed Silicon for Terabit Routers
56	PentaCom Ltd.	11–Apr–00	$118	48	Israel	Metro IP Networks
55	SightPath, Inc.	29–Mar–00	$800	76	Massachusetts, USA	Content Delivery Optimisers
54	InfoGear Technology Corp.	16–Mar–00	$301	74	Redwood City, California	Software to Manage Information Appliances

Acquisition Number	Name of Acquired Company	Date Acquired	Approx. Value millions $	Approx. Value Employees	No. of Location	Market Opportunity
53	JetCell, Inc.	16–Mar–00	$200	46	Menlo Park, California	In-building Wireless Technology
52	Atlantech Technologies Ltd.	01–Mar–00	$180	120	Scotland	Network Element Management Software
51	Growth Networks, Inc.	16–Feb–00	$355	53	Mountain View, California	Internet Switching Fabrics
50	Altiga Networks	19–Jan–00	$567	76	MA	Enterprise VPN Solutions
49	Compatible Systems Corp.	19–Jan–00		68	CO	Service Provider VPN Solutions
48	Pirelli Optical Systems	20–Dec–99	$2,150	701	Italy	Optical Internetworking
47	Internet Engineering Group, LLC	17–Dec–99	$25	13	Michigan, USA	Optical Internetworking
46	Worldwide Data Systems, Inc.	16–Dec–99	$25.5		New Jersey, USA	Customery Advocacy
45	V-Bus, Inc.	11–Nov–99	$128	30	San Jose, California	Cable
44	Aironet Wireless Communications, Inc.	09–Nov–99	$799	131	Ohio, USA	Wireless LANs
43	Tasmania Network Systems, Inc.	26–Oct–99	$25	16	San Jose, California	Network Caching Software technology (Web Scaling)
42	WebLine Communications Corp.	22–Sep–99	$325	120	MA	Intelligent Contact Management
41	Cocom A/S	15–Sep–99	$65.6	66	Denmark	Cable
40	Cerent Corporation	26–Aug–99	$6,900	287	Petaluma, California	Optical Internetworking
39	Monterey Networks, Inc.	26–Aug–99	$500	132	Texas, USA	Optical Internetworking
38	MaxComm Technologies, Inc.	18–Aug–99	$143	35	MA	Broadband Internet technology (DSL)
37	Calista, Inc.	16–Aug–99	$55		England/California	IP Telephony

Case 11 / Cisco Systems Inc.—Growth Through Acquisitions

Acquisition Number	Name of Acquired Company	Date Acquired	Approx. Value millions $	Approx. Value Employees	No. of Location	Market Opportunity
36	StratumOne Communications, Inc.	29–June–99	$435	78	Santa Clara, California	Optical Internetworking
35	TransMedia Communications, Inc.	17–Jun–99	$407	66	San Jose, California	Media Gateway Technology
34	Amteva Technologies, Inc.	28–Apr–99	$170	144	Virginia, USA	IP-based unified communications software
33	GeoTel Communications Corp.	13–Apr–99	$2,000	310	MA	Network-based call routing solutions for distributed call centers
32	Sentient Networks, Inc.	08–Apr–99	$445	102	Milpitas, California	ATM Circuit Emulation Services Gateway
31	Fibex Systems	08–Apr–99		100	Petaluma, California	Integrated Access Digital Loop Carrier
30	PipeLinks, Inc.	02–Dec–98	$126	73	San Jose, California	ISR Products
29	Selsus Systems, Inc.	14–Oct–98	$145	51	Texas, USA	IP Telephony solutions
28	Clarity Wireless Corporation	15–Sep–98	$157	39	Belmont, California	Last Mile Wireless Technology
27	American Internet Corporation	21–Aug–98	$56	50	MA	Cisco Network Registrar
26	Summa Four, Inc.	28–Jul–98	$116	210	Manchester, New Hampshire	Programmable Switches
25	CLASS Data Systems	04–May–98	$50	34	Israel	Policy-based Networking Solutions
24	Precept Software, Inc.	11–Mar–98	$84	50	Palo Alto, California	IP/TV
23	NetSpeed, Inc.	10–Mar–98	$236	140	Texas, USA	605 Personal PCI ADSL Modem, 675 SOHO/ Telecommuter
22	WheelGroup Corporation	18–Feb–98	$124	75	Texas, USA	NetSonar, NetRanger

Acquisition Number	Name of Acquired Company	Date Acquired	Approx. Value millions $	Approx. Value Employees	No. of Location	Market Opportunity
21	LightSpeed International, Inc.	22–Dec–97	$160	70	Virginia, USA	Signalling Controller CS2200
20	Dagaz (Integrated Network Corporation)	28–Jul–97	$124.5	30	New Jersey, USA	6200 Series Advanced DSL Access Multiplexers
19	Ardent Communications Corp.	24–Jun–97	$156	40	San Jose, California	3800 Multiservice Access Platform
18	Global Internet Software Group	24–Jun–97	$40	20	Palo Alto, California	Firewall Solutions
17	SkyStone Systems Corp	09–Jun–97	$89.1	40	Canada	Sonet Technologies
16	Telesend	26–Mar–97				Cisco 901 IDSL Channel Unit
15	Metaplex, Inc	01–Dec–96				Enterprise SNA Solutions
14	Netsys Technologies, Inc.	14–Oct–96	$79	50	Palo Alto, California	Netsys Service-Level Management Suite
13	Granite Systems, Inc.	03–Sep–96	$220	50	Palo Alto, California	Gigabit Ethernet Solutions
12	Nashoba Networks, Inc.	06–Aug–96	$100	40	Massachusetts, USA	Token Ring Switching Solutions
11	Telebit's MICA Technologies	22–Jul–96	$200		Massachusetts, USA	Universal Access Servers
10	Stratacom, Inc.	22–Apr–96	$4,000		San Jose, California	WAN Switching Solution
9	TGV Software, Inc.	23–Jan–96	$115	130	Santa Cruz, California	Security Products and Technologies
8	Network Translation, Inc.	27–Oct–95	(not disclosed)		Palo Alto, California	PIX Firewall, Web Cache Engine, Local Director
7	Grand Junction Networks, Inc.	27–Sep–95	$348	85	Fremont, California	Catalyst 2900 Series 10/100 Switching Solutions, Catalyst 1900/2820 Ethernet Switching

Exhibit 4 Summary of Cisco's Acquisitions from September 1993 to November 2000 (*Continued*)

Acquisition Number	Name of Acquired Company	Date Acquired	Approx. Value millions $	Approx. Value Employees	No. of Location	Market Opportunity
6	Internet Junction, Inc.	06–Sep–95	$5.5	10	Mountain View, California	Internet/Extranet Solutions
5	Combinet, Inc.	10–Aug–95	$114.2	100	Sunnyvale, California	Cisco 700 Series ISDN Access Routers, Cisco 800 Series ISDN Access Routers
4	LightStream Corporation	08–Dec–94	$120	60	Massachusetts, USA	Campus ATM Switching Solutions
3	Kalpana, Inc.	24–Oct–94	$203	150	Sunnyvale, California	Catalyst 3000 Stackable Switching Solutions
2	Newport Systems Solutions	12–Jul–94		55	Newport Beach, California	Cisco Dial Access System Solutions
1	Crescendo Communications, Inc.	21–Sep–93	$89	60	Sunnyvale, California	Catalyst 5000 Switching Solutions

Notes:

1. Where the information concerning the acquisition is ommitted in the exhibit, the information was undisclosed or unavailable.

2. The locations of all the acquisitions made by CISCO outside the USA have been bolded.

SOURCE: Cisco Connection Online, 2000.

Table 1   Cisco 1993–2000

	Jul–00	Jul–99	Jul–98	Jul–97	Jul–96	Jul–95	Jul–94	Jul–93
Income Statement $m								
Sales	18,928	12,154	8,488	6,452	4,096	2,232	1,334	649
Cost of Sales	7,037	4,240	2,924	2,243	1,409	743	450	210
Gross Profit	11,891	7,914	5,564	4,209	2,686	1,489	884	438
Net Income available to ordinary shareholders	2,668	2,096	1,355	1,051	913	456	323	172
Earnings per share (EPS)	0.36	0	0.21	0.17	0.15	0.08	0.06	0.04
Dividends per share (DPS)	0	0	0	0	0	0	0	0
Gross Margin %	62.80%	65.10%	65.60%	65.20%	65.60%	66.70%	66.20%	67.60%
Net Profit Margin	14.10%	17.25%	15.96%	16.29%	22.29%	20.43%	24.21%	26.50%
Balance Sheet								
Total Assets	32,870	14,893	8,972	5,452	3,630	1,991	1,053	595
Common Equity	26,497	11,811	7,148	4,289	2,819	1,562	848	475
Long-Term Debt	0	0	0	0	0	0	0	0
Shares Issued	7,138	6,821	6,304	6,037	5,843	5,554	4,638	4,453
Market Capitalization	458,306	203,214	100,599	53,367	33,600	17,202	5,413	6,418
Ratio Analysis								
Return on Equity (ROE)	13.90%	22.30%	23.70%	29.60%	41.70%	37.90%	48.80%	47.70%
Debt/Equity	0.00%	0.00%	0.00%	0.00%	0.00%	0.00%	0.00%	0.00%

SOURCE: Multex, 2000.

Before 1996, over 80 percent of Cisco's business came from the router market. Each acquisition Cisco made represented a small strategic step away from Cisco's core business of routers. Chambers was determined in his desire to diversify and he firmly believed that a company must accept technological change. According to Chambers:

> *"The companies that get into trouble are those that fall in love with 'religious technologies'. The key to success is having a culture with the discipline to accept change and not fight the religious wars."*

Cisco is not afraid of any specific technology or product becoming obsolete. Unlike many networking companies, Cisco has no fixed ideas when it comes to which technology is best and does not take a rigid approach that favours one technology over another. Cisco can afford such indifference, as they compete with a wide product range and can always acquire and integrate a new company with a promising technology into Cisco. By 1996, the revenue from *Crescendo*, Cisco's first acquisition, had risen from $10 million when it was acquired to more than $500 million per year and it was this phenomenal success that paved the way for the big acquisitions to come. Chambers believed that in order to remain a market leader, Cisco would have to continue buying ideas and companies rather than rely on internal development. Cisco had moved from being an innovation leader to being a technology acquirer. During the course of 1996, Cisco realised that the ATM market had changed quicker than it had originally anticipated and that in order to maintain market share in the long term it would have to acquire a bigger ATM manufacturer such as *Stratacom.* Cisco acquired *Stratacom* for $4 billion on 22nd April 1996, the largest acquisition in Silicon Valley's history at the time. *Stratacom* was at the time the leading supplier of ATM and Frame Relay high-speed wide area network (WAN[D]) switching equipment that would integrate and transport a wide variety of information, including voice, data and video. The acquisition of *Stratacom* enabled Cisco to become the first vendor to provide advanced networking infrastructure for the Intranet and Internet environments and the only vendor able to provide end to end solutions across public, private or hybrid networks. Cisco stock rose 10 percent the week following the announcement of the *Stratacom* acquisition, a sign that the market agreed upon the strategic path which Cisco was following. By the end of 1996, Cisco had acquired a total of 15 companies.

Cisco Grows Globally

Change in Focus 1997

Towards the end of 1996, Chambers started publicly discussing his belief that the Internet could be utilised to carry telephone calls. He believed that the future of telephony was over IP networks, a technology called *voice over* IP (VoIP[E]). Chambers became a proponent of free phone calls on the Internet and decided to start selling Cisco's Internet technology to phone companies. Chambers classified digital data as *New World* and the circuits of voice infrastructure as *Old World.* Chambers believed that the *New World Network* would converge the Internet with telecom's high-speed fibre-optic, cable and wireless systems. He envisaged Cisco as forming the backbone of the communications industry as well as the Internet. In order to ensure that Cisco would be able to prepare for the future, Chambers reorganised Cisco in 1997 from a decentralised structure into a line of business structure. This reorganisation also allowed Cisco to focus more strongly on a customer orientated rather than a product orientated strategy and to deliver on Chambers' Seven Strategic Initatives (see below). The three lines of business were: 1). Service Provider, headed by Don Listwin, 2). Enterprise, headed by Mario Mazzola, and 3). Small/Medium Businesses, headed by Howard Charney.

The seven Strategic Initiatives were:

- To become a leader in providing end-to-end networking solutions
- To succeed in each individual line-of-business segment targeted
- To forge strategic partnerships

- To spearhead data/voice/video integration efforts
- To recruit, retain and develop the top 10 percent of technology employees
- To become number one in sales of high-end networking products and
- To promote Cisco's IOS[F] (Internetworking Operating System) as the leading network services architecture

In the Service Provider Market, Cisco sold its technology and services to companies that provide information services including telecommunication carriers. The Enterprise business unit serviced large organisations with complex networking needs usually spanning multiple locations and types of communication systems. In their Small/Medium business line, Cisco targeted companies with a need for data networks of their own and connections to the Internet and/or to business partners.

Cisco decided on a long-term strategy of moving into all areas of telecommunications from the end-user to the network backbone. The new emerging market opportunities which Cisco decided to focus on were: 1). Digital Subscriber Lines (DSL[G]), 2). Multi-service products, and 3) Fibre-Optic equipment.

Digital Subscriber Lines (DSL)

DSL is a technology that allows high speed data connections over existing phone lines. In the space of 18 months, through acquiring smaller companies, Cisco went from having no DSL capabilities to becoming a major provider of DSL equipment to big companies like *US West.* The first DSL company which Cisco acquired was *Telesend* in March 1997. Only 23 days after this acquisition, Cisco was able to release its new product on the market. In July 1997, Cisco acquired *Dagaz,* a subsidiary of *Integrated Network corporation,* for $124.5 million and with this acquisition Cisco was able to extend its capabilities into international markets.

The CEO of *US West,* a major telecommunication carrier, informed Chambers that it liked the products which a start-up company called *Netspeed International* was manufacturing but they did not want to buy from a start-up. As a result, Cisco purchased *Netspeed International* for $326 million in March 1998. Cisco further complemented its DSL range by purchasing *MaxComm Technologies* for $143 million in August 1999.

Multi-Service

Cisco's multi-service initiative was aimed at providing clients with voice and video services over its data networks. Cisco's first acquisition in this field was that of *Ardent Communication Corporation* in June 1997 for $156 million. This was followed by the acquisition of

LightSpeed International in December 1997. From the period March 1998 through to August 1998, Cisco acquired a further four companies which it believed might give it a viable VoIP (voice over Internet Protocol) package. The sum of the purchase price for these acquisitions amounted to approximately $307 million. By November 1998, Cisco had through these acquisitions the ability to handle multi-service networks serving approximately 100 people. This capacity was sufficient for Cisco to start selling their product but it fell far short of the long-term goal and vision. On the 14th October 1998, Cisco acquired *Selsius,* a Texas based company for $145 million. This acquisition enabled Cisco to handle Legacy phone systems. From the period April through to August 1999, Cisco acquired an additional several companies. The acquisition of *Calista,* a company based in Chalfont Saint Peter in England, gave Cisco the ability to emulate traditional private phone systems on an IP network. By September 1999, Cisco was able to connect small IP voice, video and data networks to traditional phone networks. The Internet industry has developed rapidly and at the expense of reliability and tolerance of flaws which would not be acceptable in the telecommunication industry. The two major problems and challenges which Cisco and its competitors face are, firstly, the overall unreliability of computer equipment and, secondly, connection quality. In telephony, a split second delay in transmission would effect the quality of a conversation. Cisco has still a long way to go to achieve the quality-of-service standards required to ensure clean uninterrupted phone conversations.

Fibre-Optic Equipment

In 1997, Cisco took a decision to transform itself into a credible supplier of high-end fibre-optic equipment. This objective like its other initiatives would be achieved through a combination of internal research and carefully selected acquisitions.

Cisco made its intentions clear in the optical network industry when in late 1997 it worked with *Ciena Corporation,* a pioneer in WDM[H] (Wave Division Multiplexing) equipment, to establish the Optical Internetworking Forum, an industry Group exploring unique protocol stacks.

The growth of the Internet is encouraging telecommunication companies to increasingly build fibre-optic networks which carry more information than the traditional copper telephone lines by converting the information into pulses of light. Cisco realised that the next generation network operators would have to focus on increasing the capacity and intelligence of the optical portion of high speed networks in order to accommo-

date the rapid growth of the Internet and electronic commerce. Cisco's first acquisition in the Fiber-Optic field was that of *Skystone Systems* for $92 million in June 1997. Acquiring *Skystone Systems* enabled Cisco to connect its routers and switches to fibre-optic lines. In December 1998, Cisco acquired *Pipelinks* for $126 million in order to enable the integration of the optical network protocols into Cisco routers. A company on the forefront of optical internetworking at the time was *Cerent Corporation.* In 1998, in line with their policy of making minority equity investments in start-up firms, to buy a closer look at potential acquisitions, Cisco bought a 9 percent share in Cerent Corporation. In order to avoid being potentially shut out of this huge potential market Cisco, on 26th August 1999, acquired both *Cerent Corporation* and *Monterey Network.* These acquisitions added optical networking equipment to Cisco's extensive data-orientated product portfolio and positioned Cisco to grab a giant share of this emerging market. It took Cisco a period of two years with over $8 billion in acquisitions and an undisclosed expenditure on internal research to be able to enter the fibre-optic market. At a Conference in 1999, Chambers expressed the following view of the fibre-optic market:

> *"Anyone who understands our market understands that the optical transport business in going to explode. The companies that can't partner and acquire will be left behind. Getting everything connected is everything."*

On the 20th December, 1999 Cisco purchased *Pirelli Optical systems* which was based in Milan Italy for $2.15 billion. *Pirelli's* optical networking unit complimented Cisco's product line and gave Cisco an important credibility boost in the European telecommunications market.

From 1997 through to 2000, Cisco's revenues increased from $6,452 million to $18,928 million. Table 2 gives Cisco's cash flows from the period 1996 through to 2000.

The Acquisition Process

The management of Cisco realised in 1993 that Cisco could not develop everything that it needed inside the company and that an acquisition strategy would enable Cisco to own, develop and market an array of network products and standards as the market demanded them. Cisco investigates buying start-ups if it decides that it is too far behind its competitors to take the time to build a product from scratch. In April 1999, Mike Volpi, Vice President in charge of Business Development had the following to say:

> *"Time to market is crucial to us. But so is being able to identify emerging technologies that are going to be*

Case 11 / Cisco Systems Inc.—Growth Through Acquisitions

Table 2	Cash Flow Statements of Cisco (1996–2000)				
	Jul–00	Jul–99	Jul–98	Jul–97	Jul–96
Net Income $m	2,668	2,023	1,331	1,051	913
Depreciation	863	489	329	214	133
Deferred Taxes	(782)	(247)	(76)	(186)	(74)
Non-Cash Items	4,043	1,387	1,062	672	270
Changes in Working Capital	(651)	673	219	(303)	(179)
Total Cash from Operating Activities	6,141	4,325	2,865	1,448	1,063
Capital Expenditures	(1,530)	(697)	(429)	(332)	(283)
Other Investment Items	(2,847)	(4,288)	(2,674)	(1,075)	(775)
Total Cash from Investment Activities	(4,377)	(4,985)	(3,103)	(1,407)	(1,058)
Financing Cashflow Items	(7)	(7)	(7)	(5)	(11)
Insurance/(Retirement) of stock	1,564	947	555	(15)	1
Total Cash from Financing Activities	1,557	954	548	(20)	10

important and grabbing them. We couldn't possibly develop all the pieces on our own, nor would we want to. At a start-up a small team of folks will work 20-hour days for months to get a product out the door, and take a shot at a big financial reward. Those are the type of people we want to join us. We use our stock to give them the big pay-off and get a jump on getting to the market."

Cisco targets companies for potential acquisitions that usually have complementary technologies to Cisco and are companies that give Cisco a significant time-to-market advantage over internal development. Even though Cisco is renowned for its strategy of acquisition, approximately 70 percent of product development is still carried out internally. Cisco's acquisition strategy focuses on start-ups, companies that are old enough to have finished and tested a product, but are still young enough to be privately held and flexible. According to Mike Volpi:

"If you buy a company with customers, product flows, and entrenched enterprise resource systems, you have to move very gingerly. Otherwise you risk customer dissatisfaction. Figuring out how to integrate this type of company could take nine months."

Don Listwin compared Cisco's acquisition to the strategy of one of their rivals, *Lucent Technologies* by saying:

"Lucent wants the smartest group of people in Bell Labs. But if we are not good at something, we've got Silicon Valley. It's our Lab."

If Cisco is unsure whether a potential acquisition would be successful, it embarks on a policy of minority equity investment whereby it will acquire a small share of the company and wait for market forces to determine the outcome. Cisco will acquire the firm if it proves to be successful. This minority investment strategy allows Cisco to hedge its bets in a market of future uncertainty, rapid innovations and market turbulence. Acquiring high technology companies is crucial to Cisco's growth strategy in order for them to gain a competitive edge over competitors like *Lucent Technologies* and *Nortel Networks*. Cisco buys technology that can be incorporated into their existing equipment because it is not feasible for Cisco to modernise their routers and switches by replacing them with newer models. The technology which Cisco acquires must go into its existing products to make them more efficient.

Cisco's Four-Step Plan   To ensure that acquisitions are successful, Cisco employs a structured and carefully designed business process, which is carried out by cross-functional integration teams. Cisco manages and measures its integration process and strives for continuous improvement in merging the culture, technology and management of new acquisitions into Cisco. The secret to Cisco's acquisition blueprint is a four-step plan and the steps are as follows:

Step 1: Evaluate the prospective company

Step 2: Persuade the company of the benefits of working together (called the Cisco sell)

Step 3: Appraise the potential acquisition

Step 4: Integrate the company into Cisco

Step 1: Evaluation

Cisco's profile of a target acquisition usually follows a number of guidelines. The company must share a common vision about where the industry was heading. The target acquisitions are usually fast-growing, focused and highly entrepreneurial companies with strong teams in the technical and marketing areas. Within Cisco potential acquisitions are known as *"Cisco Kids"*. The potential acquisition must be culturally compatible with Cisco. As the acquired executives would become part of Cisco's management, Chambers studied the new companies management philosophy in order to determine the solidity of the management team and to decide whether the chemistry was right and whether the new company would be able to meld with Cisco. Cisco's first acquisition outside Silicon Valley was that of a company called *Lightstream*, situated in Massachusetts. *Lightstream* had a different culture to Cisco as it started out of an East Coast academic culture of companies that had originated at MIT. This culture was not compatible with the almost fanatical pragmatism of Silicon Valley. After struggling with the integration of this acquisition, Cisco ensured that in the future a tight cultural fit and extra care with integration became high priorities.

The potential acquisition should be able to deliver a positive return for Cisco immediately. A priority for Chambers was that the newly acquired companies be no more than a couple of months away from delivering a product to the market place. Chambers was aware that his acquisitions would be closely scrutinised by shareholders but his overarching philosophy was, however, the future. The potential acquisitions must be able to provide a long-term strategic win for Cisco's shareholders, customers, employees and business partners. Chambers did not like making acquisitions that did not benefit the employees of the newly acquired company and would not make an acquisition if it involved layoffs of staff. Cisco ensured that employees from newly acquired companies did not lose out financially by the acquisition and their stock options were vested at the acquired company's old rate, but for Cisco stock. The potential acquisition must be located in a geographically desirable position relative to the location of Cisco. 8 of the first 9 companies acquired were in Silicon Valley, on the West Coast of California, close to Cisco. Chambers' attitude was that he did not want to have to board a plane to solve any problems which could arise as a result of the acquisition. Chambers has likened Cisco's acquisition selection process to a marriage selection and in an interview in 1997 he said:

> *"I think that the most important decision in your acquisition is your selection process. If you select right, with the criteria we set, your probabilities of success are extremely high. Its tough enough to make a marriage work. If you don't spend a fair amount of time on the evaluation of what the key ingredients are for that, your probability of having a successful marriage after one date is pretty small. We spend a lot of time on the upfront."*

Step 2: The Cisco Sell

Cisco does not consider hostile takeovers, and if the CEO of a potential company is not interested in a deal then Cisco does not pursue the matter any further. Cisco's acquisitions were designed to accommodate the people first and then the product, as the only way to ensure a successful acquisition was to ensure that the target company's staff wanted to work for Cisco. The CEO of *Internet Junction*, Krish Ramakrishnan, which Cisco acquired for $5.5 million in September 1995, described his company's acquisition by Cisco as a very pleasant one. He described it as follows:

> *"Cisco approached us. The Chief Technical Officer (Ed Kozel) came and had lunch, told us about his vision and wanted to hear ours. Then I had a one-hour lunch with Chambers at Cisco. John put me at ease. What he was trying to figure out was whether we would be successful in this environment. He asked me about my vision for the company. John's opinion is that if the people fit, everything else would work out. At the end of the lunch there was a handshake and the deal was done in a couple of days. We made a deal, not like what you'd imagine when you're trying to sell a company. I was interviewing for a job rather than selling my company."*

Step 3: The Appraisal

The appraisal part of the process was an exercise in due diligence. A team drawn from every major department of Cisco would determine if Cisco could integrate the new company's upper management and the line-level employees successfully into Cisco. Engineers in Cisco examined the technology, while financiers examined the company's books. Cisco's acquisition team would typically spend two weeks in a *"war room"* to determine if the potential target acquisition complied with Cisco's guidelines for evaluation. The guidelines were tested from the perspective of every department within Cisco and this whole process of critical examination was central to

Cisco's acquisition successes. The Cisco team also examined the depth of the company's talent, the quality of its management and its venture funding. Besides acquiring companies for their technology, Cisco also acquired companies for their intellectual talent. For this reason, Cisco focused on the *"people"* issues early on and they relied upon stock options as their primary incentive in buying prospective companies and for retaining newly acquired employees. The stock options which Cisco offered its new employees became *"golden handcuffs"* locking the employees firmly in place when the Cisco stock price increased. During the due diligence phase, a lot of time was spent on looking at stock equity issues. During the appraisal process of the prospective company, Chambers took into account the long-term security of all parties involved. Chambers was not willing to acquire a company if there were numerous layoffs involved. During the appraisal process, Dan Scheiman, Vice President of Legal Affairs and Cisco's *"culture cop"*, evaluates how well the potential acquisitions would fit into Cisco. Some of the issues he looks at prior to approving a potential acquisition are:

- *Look for a bad deal* – Scheiman believes that if a start-up company has not made one glaring mistake which it has learnt from, then it is not daring enough.
- *Role Play* - Go over the historical decisions made by management and see if Cisco would have arrived at the same conclusion. If so, then the company's executives think along similar lines to the management of Cisco.

Scheiman also believed that Cisco's strength is that it is not afraid to terminate a potential deal at the last moment and has backed off from as many acquisitions as it has acquired companies. It would be prepared to cease the negotiations with a company at any point before the actual stock transfer. It believed that a poor choice of a company will lead to acquisition failure irrespective of how good the integration process was. Similarly, the acquisition of a well-chosen company would also fail if it was not properly integrated and the employees retained. In order to streamline the process, the full Board of Cisco is not involved in Cisco's early decisions of acquiring a company. The decision as to whether to acquire another company was made by Chambers, Morgridge and Valentine alone and this ensured that the acquisition process was simple, fast and foolproof.

Step 4: Integration

The biggest risks and challenges associated with acquisitions are the product line integration, operations integration and risks inherent in entering any new market.

Cisco has a transition team to oversee every detail of an acquisition assimilation into Cisco. The team was headed by Mimi Gigoux, Cisco's Human Resources Director of acquisition integration and is comprised of about 40 staff who work full-time at integrating the new employees into Cisco. Mimi Gigoux joined Cisco when Cisco acquired *Kalpana*, their third acquisition, in 1994. At the time she thought that Cisco did a poor job integrating the new employees of *Kalpana* into Cisco and recalled the following:

> *"They didn't have anyone especially responsible for integration. There were these very long and complex meetings with no one tracking progress. It took months before everyone from Kalpana knew what their role was at Cisco and months after that before everyone was moved and located at Cisco."*

Gigoux assembles a customised packet of information for each separate acquisition. This package contained descriptions of Cisco's structure and employee benefits, staff contact details within Cisco and an explanation stating the strategic importance of the newly acquired company to Cisco. On the day the acquisition is announced, Cisco's Human Resources and Business Development teams meet in small groups with employees of the acquired company to set expectations and answer questions. Cisco's integration team collaborates with the newly acquired company's management in *"mapping"* employees into new jobs. It tries to ensure that the newly acquired staff retain their current jobs and bosses and it is only where there is duplication with Cisco's existing staff that new employees are reassigned. On the day after the deal is finally closed, Gigoux's Department offers a tailor-made orientation. Managers are schooled in Cisco's hiring practices, sales people in Cisco's products, and the engineers in Cisco's development projects. Once the deal has been signed, Cisco's Information Technology Department starts an aggressive integration of the new company's technology. A 6 person IT team is typically dedicated to the task and follows a strict methodology integrating all the systems including toll-free support numbers, electronic mail, sales automation, web sites and product order systems. The acquired company is usually presented to the public as being part of Cisco within 100 days of officially acquiring the company.

Acquisition Employee Retention

Cisco complies with what is known as the *"Mario rule,"* whereby the services of any employee of a newly acquired company can be terminated only if both Chambers and the former CEO give their consent. The *"Mario rule"* was named after Mario Mazzola, who was

CEO of *Crescendo* when it was bought by Cisco and it was under the abovementioned terms that this acquisition took place. Acquired employees usually continue to report to their former CEOs. Mr. Giancarlo, the Senior Vice President of the Small/Business Line, states that Cisco works hard at retaining the CEO of the acquired company for at least six months after the deal is closed: *"If you don't retain executive management, you don't retain the rank and file."*

According to Mike Volpi:

> *"Even in acquisitions we focus very much on bringing in talent that can evolve the technology. Keep in mind when you buy a company and you spend a lot of money . . . let's say you spend a billion dollars on an acquisition, it takes you many, many years to recover that investment. And the only way you recover it is if the smart people who came with the acquisition stay at Cisco, grow what they've built and create a business that then returns on that investment."*

Cisco's corporate culture contributes to its success at acquiring and integrating other companies. From the beginning, Cisco built a culture that accepted people from different environments and backgrounds as it focused more on intellectual capacity than cultural differences. Cisco's culture not only accepted new ideas and people but actually thrives on it.

Jayshree Ullal, the founder of *Cresecendo Communications,* Cisco's first acquisition in 1993 had the following to say about Chambers and the integration of *Crescendo* in Cisco:

> *"If we hadn't been welcomed, supported, funded, and smoothly integrated into Cisco, I wouldn't have stayed. But John appreciates what individual people bring. It's not like he chops everyone up in a blender. He makes Cisco more like a tossed green salad, full of different flavours."*

Chambers believes that after 6-12 months, he is able to tell if an acquisition is successful. He judges this by, customer satisfaction, revenue, market share and on retention rate (by department, position and level of management). According to Chambers:

> *"When we acquire a company, we aren't simply acquiring its current products, we're acquiring the next generation of products through its people. If you pay between $500,000 and $3 million per employee, and all that you are doing is buying the current research and the current market share, you're making a terrible investment"*

Two Examples of Acquisitions

Two of Cisco's bigger acquisitions, namely that of *Stratacom* in 1996 and *Cerent* in 1999 are described in more detail below. The acquisition of *Stratacom* was invaluable to Cisco as it helped them refine and develop their acquisition process. *Cerent* is Cisco's largest acquisition as at November 2000.

Stratacom: Challenges Encountered

Stratacom was Cisco's largest acquisition at the time. Handling an acquisition the size of *Stratacom* enabled Cisco to learn important lessons about the integration process. Morgridge, the Chairman of Cisco's Board, said the following about the *Stratacom* acquisition:

> *"It was good because we gained insight on the unique challenges of doing a big deal versus a small one. We felt pretty good with the small deals. Whenever you feel like that you had better watch out."*

The integration of *Stratacom* into Cisco took longer than the 90 days which Cisco had publicly stated. The divergent products of the two companies created a great deal of initial confusion and Cisco found leveraging the ATM technology through its existing sales channels a difficult task. An internal challenge for Cisco was to get the company as a whole to embrace ATM technology. Cisco, in their 9 acquisitions prior to *Stratacom*, was able discard the acquired companies marketing plan, replace the products label with a Cisco product label and then sell the new products through existing Cisco channels. The integration of *Sratacom*, however, was not as simple as *Stratacom* had a well-known line of switches with an ATM bias and an established sales and support organisation of their own. Another problem which Cisco faced following the integration was to convince its 1,800 strong sales force to push the sale of Stratacom switches as the commissions received from the sale of the Stratacom equipment was much lower than that which they received for the sale of Cisco's routers. Many of the Stratacom sales force were dissatisfied with the Cisco sales approach and resigned from Cisco. After the acquisition of *Stratacom*, Cisco also discontinued one of its previous acquisition products (the *Lightstream* 20/20 ATM switch) with *Stratacom's* IGX platform. Customers who had recently installed the *Lightstream* 20/20 switch were angered by this action. Cisco however, placated its customers by agreeing to compensate them for the full value of the old switches when they upgraded their networks and also by providing them with the necessary training and assistance.

Cerent: The Negotiation Process and Integration

During August 1999, Cisco acquired *Cerent Corporation* for $6.9 billion. *Cerent* was a two-year old company that had only introduced its first product to market eight months prior to being acquired by Cisco. Cisco acquired *Cerent* for its technology that could take bits of data from old copper-wire telephone networks and transfer the data to fibre-optic networks.

At a Conference in May 1999 Chambers met the *Cerent* CEO, Carl Russo and began a game of poker. An extract from their conversation went as follows: *"I don't think I can afford you guys,"* Chambers told Russo. *"I don't think you can afford not to"* Russo replied. In July, Chambers decided to make an offer for *Cerent*. On the 11th August, Volpi met with Russo at San Francisco International Airport and made an offer of $4 billion for *Cerent*. Mr Russo declined the offer demanding $6.9 billion. On the 13th August, Chambers, Volpi and Russo met in Cisco's offices and the acquisition deal was concluded for $6.3 billion. At the time the deal was concluded, *Cerent* was only 30 days away from finalising its IPO listing. In the 2.5 years that *Cerent* had been in business, it had totalled $10 million in sales, never posted a profit and had accumulated $60 million in losses. *Cerent* had received offers for their company prior to Cisco approaching them but the offer made by Cisco was the first offer that was made at the right time for the right amount. The following factors led to *Cerent* accepting Cisco's proposal:

- Cisco would give *Cerent* accelerated access to existing markets
- Cisco would give *Cerent* access to markets that they had not been previously pursuing
- The deal would allow accelerated integration of technology into the *Cerent* platform and
- The deal would give the ability to offer customers end-to-end solutions

On the afternoon of the 25th August 1999, Russo informed his staff that *Cerent* would be acquired by Cisco. This came as surprising news to the majority of the staff as they were expecting an update regarding their anticipated IPO listing. Nevertheless, some of *Cerent's* staff working at their loading dock had a forewarning of what was going to happen as they had opened a box of coffee mugs supporting the Cisco logo and the inscription *"Welcome to the team"*, which had inadvertently been sent to *Cerent* a day early. The staff at *Cerent* were placated, however, when they heard that they would be receiving 1.445 Cisco shares for every *Cerent* share which they held. Directly after the acquisition announcement, Gigi Gigoux and two assistants handed each *Cerent* employee a folder containing basic information about Cisco, including phone numbers and e-mail addresses of several Cisco executives and an 8 page chart comparing the vacation, medical and retirement benefits at *Cerent* and at Cisco. The next 2 days Cisco hosted a question

and answer session to allay any fears which the *Cerent* employees might have had. Cisco's reasoning behind the information sessions was aimed at reducing staff uncertainty over the transition period in order not to effect productivity. Chambers also told the *Cerent* staff that he there would be no layoffs resulting from the acquisition. Russo also agreed with Chambers that none of his original staff would be fired or reassigned without Russo's prior approval.

On the 26th August 1999, Cisco's integration team began plotting *Cerent's* transformation and started *"mapping"* each of the 266 *Cerent* employees into a Cisco job. On the 29th August, Russo and Terry Brown, head of the *Cerent* sales team, flew to Nashville Tennessee to attend a Cisco sales meeting. On 31st August, Cisco's IT team arrived at Cerent to plan the conversion of *Cerent's* computer systems. By the 25th September, when Cisco's 23-member integration team met with *Cerent* executives most of the big decisions concerning *Cerent* had been made. It was decided that *Cerent* would continue to manufacture its products at the factory that it was currently using. Cisco learned from their earlier mistakes when it had acquired *Stratacom* where approximately one-third of *Stratacom's* sales force resigned within a few months as they lost accounts to existing Cisco sales staff and as a consequence of changes to their commission plan. In order to avoid resignations from *Cerent* staff, Cisco decided that the sales staff were to remain independent and that they would keep their own accounts.

Towards the end of September, Cisco's transition team had completed the employee mapping exercise. In line with their policy, most employees kept their jobs and bosses. Of the 266 employees, approximately only 30 were reassigned in order to avoid job duplication with existing Cisco staff. 8 of *Cerent's* employees were relocated to the Cisco's headquarters. On the 2nd November, the morning Cisco formally took control of *Cerent*, *Cerent's* staff had photos taken for new ID cards and 2 days later most of the staff had new business cards. The following weekend Cisco's technical experts worked around the clock installing new software on *Cerent's* system. *Cerent's* Internet connection was also redirected through Cisco's internal network and the voice mail was linked to the Cisco system. There were times after the acquisition that *Cerent* employees referred to Cisco as *"the Borg"*, a reference to *"Star Trek"* villains who forcibly assimilate their victims into a technology obsessed collective consciousness. This impression, however, faded as Cisco's rule proved to be more benign than anticipated. After the acquisition, work continued as normal for the former *Cerent* employees. Mr Russo, the former CEO, commented that the atmosphere was more sober and said: *"It's feeling more like a business and less like a start-up."*

Alliances and Partnerships

With the fast growth in the Internet market, Cisco was not able to get out products fast enough. According to Selby Wellman, the Senior Vice-President of Cisco Business Units:

"The networking segment of the industry is enjoying the biggest growth rate in the history of high technology, we can't get the products out fast enough, so we had to partner."

The demand for Cisco's products was growing internationally, but Cisco lacked the worldwide sales and service presence to capitalise on it. Exhibit 3 gives a list of Cisco's products debuts. Morgridge started a strategy of forming alliances and partnering companies that had complimentary products. In most instances, companies that produced products outside Cisco's core competencies would be a target for an alliance and alliances with industry giants helped Cisco quickly gain a global presence. By 1994 Cisco had major deals with 13 Japanese firms including, *NEC, Hitachi* and *Fujitsu* who had all invested $40 million in Cisco's Japanese subsidiary, *Nihon* Cisco. Other deals with global companies such as *IBM* and *Hewlett Packard* gave Cisco worldwide service capabilities.

Chamber's rules for strategic alliances were threefold:

1. It has to benefit the customer
2. It has to result, within 3 years, in $500 million to $1 billion in incremental revenue per year

3. It needs to be a competitive landscape change for both partners

Cisco's first alliance was with a competitor, *Synoptics,* a company manufacturing network hubs – devices that retransmit incoming signals without analysis or redirection. *Synoptics* products did not compete directly with Cisco as Cisco promoted router-based networks, whereas *Synoptics* promoted hub-based networks. This alliance ended in a failure as the two companies could not agree on the same strategic direction because of differences in their products. The failure prompted Cisco to conclude that all future alliances would be with companies that were not direct competitors. Cisco also enters into strategic alliances with industry leaders where collaboration can produce industry advancement acceleration of new markets. Cisco's goals and objectives for a strategic alliance can include one or more of the following: technology exchange, product development, joint sales and marketing, and, new market creation. As Cisco has now become a global player in its own right, it currently uses alliances more to manage its potential competition.

Cisco's Competition - 2000

As Cisco competes in different market segments, it has numerous competitors. In the traditional router and switch market, it competes against companies such as *Cabletron* and *3 Com* and Juniper. In the Enterprise line of business, Cisco's major competitor is *Cabletron*. In the service provider marketplace, Cisco's major competitors are *Lucent* and *Nortel* Networks in Northern America and, potentially, *Alcatel, Ericsson* and *Siemens* in Europe.

In so far as Cisco's competition is concerned, Chambers fears start-ups such as *Juniper,* which has an internet router that's faster than Cisco's best, more than he does the bigger companies and says:

"I have a list of a dozen little companies that I'm tracking very closely, Guys who start from a fresh sheet of paper have an enormous advantage technologically. We have to carefully integrate new capabilities into our existing product lines, and that is tougher. They keep us on our toes."

Figure 1 gives Cisco's share price performance between 1990 and 2000. Figure 2 shows the relative performance of Cisco against the Nasdaq between 1996 and 2000. Figure 4 shows Cisco's market share in the line of businesses in which it competes. Figure 5 shows that Cisco's revenues from their Router and Switch Markets in 1999 comprises 77 percent of their total revenue. Table 3 gives industry comparisons of financial indicators based on a 5 year average.

Exhibit 3	Cisco's Product Debuts

Product Name (Date of debut)
Routers (1986)
Dial-in access servers (1992)
Switches (1993)
WAN Switches (1994)
Hubs (1995)
Firewalls and caching engines (1995)
Cable Boxes (1996)
Cable head-ends (1996)
DSL head-ends (1997)
Internet phones (1998)
Home modems (1999)
Wireless LANs (2000)

SOURCE: Cisco Connection Online, 2000.

Figure 1   Cisco's Share Price Performance (1990–2000)

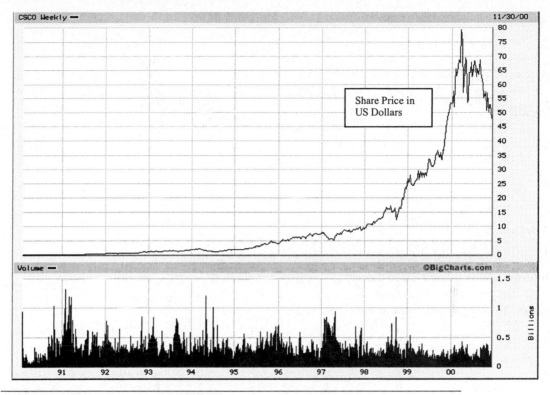

SOURCE: BigCharts, 2000.

Figure 2   Relative Performance of Cisco against the Nasdaq (1996–2000)

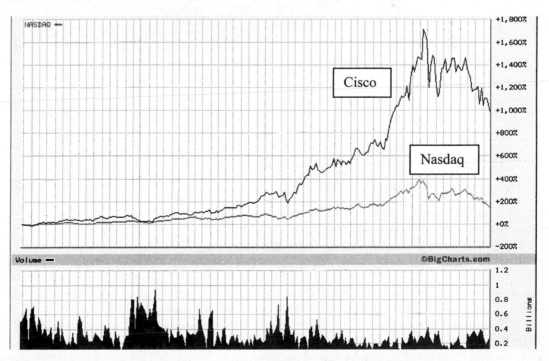

SOURCE: BigCharts, 2000.

Figure 4

Figure 4   Cisco's Share of Business in Different Markets - 2000

Corporations	40%
Small/Medium Corporations	18%
Internet Service Providers	33%
Telephone Companies	1%
Consumer Networking	10%

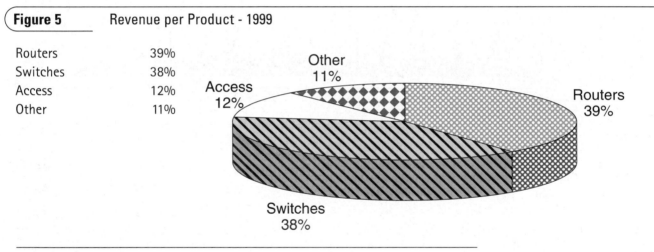

SOURCE: Barker 2000.

Figure 5   Revenue per Product - 1999

Routers	39%
Switches	38%
Access	12%
Other	11%

SOURCE: Serwer, 2000.

Telecommunication Industry - 2000

Alcatel, Cisco, *Ericsson, Lucent, Nortel Networks* and *Siemens* (the *Big 6* equipment vendors) all subscribe to the notion of all-purpose networks, but do not agree on whether the migration path to those converged networks will take the form of IP technology or ATM technology and whether Dense Wavelength Division Multiplexing[l] (DWDM) will replace SONET[j] as the transport technology used for carrying information in very high capacity backbone networks. In order to stay ahead in the race of *"getting products out"* and signing up the big customers, all of the *Big 6* make use of an acquisition strategy. Kevin

Oye, *Lucent's* Vice President of Strategic and Business Development for data networking, described the future as follows:

> *"I could draw a map of different product segments that are supported today, but I think all of that is going to get thrown up in the air. What protocols are going to be riding over the network of the future and the services that are delivered will see an awful lot of evolution. I don't think there's a lot of people saying that any of the protocols that are around today will absolutely be the protocol five years from now."*

Table 3 Industry Comparisons of Financial Indicators

	Cisco	Computer Network Industry	Technology Sector	S&P 500
Growth Rates (%)				
Sales – 5 Yr. Growth Rate	53.34	55.42	37.67	20.92
EPS – 5 Yr. Growth Rate	35.02	36.76	38.67	21.49
Capital Spending – 5 Yr Growth	58.73	59.42	33.66	20.24
Profitability Ratios (%)				
Gross Margin – 5 Yr. Average	65.15	61.77	51.58	48.25
EBITD – 5 Yr. Average	26.68	20.73	17.41	21.30
Operating Margin – 5 Yr. Average	24.91	19.69	10.69	16.87
Net Profit Margin – 5 Yr. Average	17.00	13.09	7.94	10.23
Dividends				
Dividend Yield – 5 Yr. Average	–	0.01	0.20	1.20
Management Effectiveness (%)				
Return on Assets – 5 Yr. Average	20.44	18.81	9.81	8.58
Return on Equity – 5 Yr. Average	25.96	23.8	19.05	21.81
Efficiency				
Revenue/Employee	556,706	553,581	398,057	616,016
Net Income/Employee	78,471	80,774	85,139	94,289

SOURCE: Marketguide, 2000.

Cisco's major competitors in North America, *Lucent* and *Nortel* are formidable rivals. In 1999, *Lucent* was three times as big as Cisco in revenues and *Nortel* was twice as big. *Lucent* is the leader in fibre-optic technology and also became a major competitor in the data networking arena when it acquired *Ascend* for $24 billion in early 1999. Between 1996 and 1999, *Lucent* purchased 11 data-networking companies in a bid to stake its claim in the race towards data convergence and the Internet. *Nortel*, based in Canada, purchased *Bay Networks*, then one of Cisco's closest competitors, for $9.1 billion in 1998. *Nortel* benefited from the acquisition by gaining instant legitimacy in the data networking arena. *Alcatel, Siemens* and *Ericsson*, hampered by the slow-moving networking market in Europe, are starting to make acquisitions in the USA in order to stay competitive. Figure 3 shows the market capitalisation of Cisco compared to its major competitors in the telecommunication industry.

Future Outlook

Chambers' goal is to triple Cisco's revenue over the next 10 year period to 2010. In order to reach this goal, Cisco has to make inroads in the $225 billion telecommunication market, in which Cisco currently has less than a 1 percent share. Chambers believed that the market for *Cerent* type equipment could grow from the $4 billion in 2000 to $10 billion by 2002 and that Cisco depending on its execution could capture 25 percent to 70 percent of the market. It was expected that Internet traffic will grow exponentially over the next 10 years and will soon need a network twice as large as the voice network capacity in 2000. This would leave voice with only 1 percent of the telephone lines in the future while data will dominate the rest. Cisco products currently form the backbone of the Internet and Cisco is positioning itself to be the company that benefits most when the Internet finally migrates to all-optical fibre networks. Don Listwin considered Cisco's role in the future as more than just a supplier of router and he thought that Cisco will be the driving force of a revolution that is re-shaping the world. According to Don Listwin:

"Within the next two years, China will have the biggest Internet in the world. We estimate that the internet is a $523 billion business now, and is growing

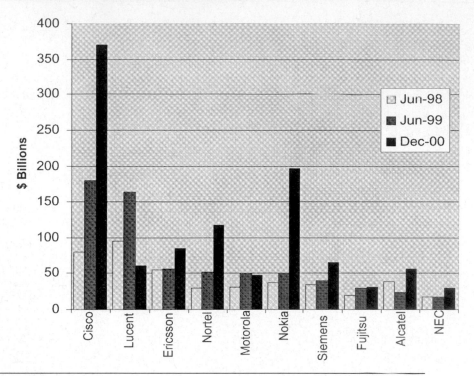

SOURCE: Marketguide, 2000.

exponentially thanks to breakthroughs in fiber-optic technology – a technology that is developing faster than Moore's Law."

Beyond the strategic goal of being No.1 or No.2 in every market in which they compete, Chambers also believed that the new rules of competition demanded that organisations be built on change and not on stability, that they are organised around networks, alliances and the interdependency of partners and not on rigid hierarchy and self sufficiency. Finally, that organisations are constructed on technological advantage and not only on the old fashioned *"bricks and mortar."*

Chambers predicts that it is home use, and specifically devices attached to the Internet, which will drive future Internet growth in what he defined as the Internet's *"third phase"* or the *"consumer phase."* Chambers believes that home networking which would connect refrigerators, microwaves, pianos, stereos and other devices to the Internet will become a reality very soon. Chambers pondered whether growth through acquisitions would continue to be the pathway to the future?

Glossary of Terms

[A]IP: Internet Protocol: The Internet Protocol (IP) is the method or protocol by which data is sent from one computer to another on the Internet.

[B]LAN: Local Area Network: A telecommunications network that requires its own dedicated channels and that encompasses a limited distance, usually one building or several buildings in close proximity.

[C]ATM: Asynchronous transfer mode: A networking technology that parcels information into 8-byte cells, allowing data to be transmitted between computers from different vendors at different speeds.

[D]WAN: Wide Area Network: A telecommunications network that spans a large geographical distance. It may consist of a variety of cable satellite and microwave technologies.

[E]VoIP: Voice over IP is a term used in IP telephony for a set of facilities for managing the delivery of voice information using the Internet Protocol (IP).

[F]IOS: Internetworking Operating system : Cisco's IOS software is a common networking software platform deployed across a broad range of Cisco products.

[G]DSL: Digital Subscriber Line. Public network technology that delivers high bandwidth over conventional copper wiring at limited distances.

[H]WDM: Wave Division Multiplexing: WDM is a technology that transmits multiple data signals using different wavelengths of light through a single fiber.

[I]DWDM: Dense Wave Division Multiplexing: DWDM is the ability to transmit 16 wavelength channels through a single fiber (See WDM).

[J]SONET: Synchronous optical network. SONET is the U.S standard for synchronous data transmission on optical media. SONET ensures standards so that digital networks can interconnect internationally and that existing conventional transmission systems can take advantage of optical media through tributary attachments.

Bibliography

Barker, C. 2000. "Cisco switches on to new strategy". Computing,
http://thebusiness.vnunet.com/Features/1109305

Bhuvnesh, C. June 1999. *A Fine Web of Business Relationships*. *Voice and Data*,
www.voicendata.com/jun99/cisco.html

Bunnell, D. 2000. Making the Cisco Connection. USA: John Wiley and Sons Inc

Byrne, J. 1998. "The Corporation of the Future". BusinessWeek,
www.cisco.com/warp/public/146/2041.html

Chowdhary. S. 2000. "The New Money-spinners". Computers Today,
www.india-today.com/ctoday/20000616/master.html

Cope, J. 2000, "Integrating Acquisitions Key to Cisco's Growth Strategy". ComputerWorld.com
http://www.itdd.co.uk/latest/strategycwd.html

Daly, J. 1999. "John Chambers: The Art of the Deal". Business2.0,
www.business2.com/content/magazine/indepth/1999/10/01/12769

Donlon, J.P. "Why John Chambers is the CEO of the Future". Chief Executive,
www.chiefexecutive,net/mag/157/cover1a.htm

Fryer, B. 1999. " Cooking with Cisco". Equity, about Women and Money, www.equitymag.com

Goldblatt, H. 1999. "Cisco's Secrets". Fortune Archives,
http://library.northernlight.com/PN19991029040000150.html?cb=13&sc=0

Goldstein, H. 2000. "As the Internet Grows, So Cisco Goes". GreenMagazine,
www.greenmagazine.com/2000/01/000120b.asp

Higgins, K.J. 1996. "Cisco's $4.5 billion gamble – Will Stratacom products, culture fit in?". Internet Week,
www.techweb.com/se/directlink.cgi?CWK19960826SS0002

Korzeniowski, P. 2000. "Internet Growth Shakes Network Core", WebServer Online,
http://webserver.cpg.com/news/5.2/n1.shtml

Kupfer, A. 1988. "The Real King of the Internet". Fortune Archives,
http://library.northernlight.com/SG19990714120008354.html?cb=13&sc=0

LaPlante, A. 1997. "The Man behind Cisco". Electronic Business,
http://www.eb-mag.com/eb-mag/issues/1997/9712/1297ceo.asp

Lindstrom, A. 1999. "A Funny Thing Happened on the Way to the IPO", Telecom Investor Magazine,
www.telecominvestormag.com/issues/9910/9910_funny.htm

Lundquist,E. 1999. "The Last Word: Cisco head sees the big picture". ZDNet.eWEEK,
www.zdnet.com/pcweek/stories/columns/0,4351,2345765,00.html

Neilson, Pasternack and Viscio. 2000. "Focus: Cisco Systems, The paradigm of an e.org", Strategy. Management.Competition,
http://www.strategy-business.com/strategy/00106/page5.html

O'Keefe, Masud. 1999. " Who Has the Winning Strategy?". Telecommunications,
www.telecommagazine.com/issues/199904/tcs/winners.html

Reardon, M. 2000. " Sizzling Cisco". InformationWeek,
www.techweb.com/se/directlink.cgi?IWK20000228S0031

Reardon, M. 2000. "Sizzling Cisco: IT takes a Starring Role in Cisco's Acquisition Adventures". Information Week,
http://www.informationweek.com/775/cisc2.htm

Reinhardt, A. 1999. "Meet Cisco's Mr Internet". BusinessWeek Online,
www.businessweek.com/1999/99_37/b3646001.htm

Reinhardt, R. 1997. "Cisco: Crunch Time for a High-Tech Wiz". Business Week,
www.businessweek.com/1997/17/b3524136.htm

Rifkin, G. 1997. Growth by Acquisition. Strategy and Business. Booz Allen & Hamilton, pp1-12
www.strategy-business.com/thoughtleaders/97209/page1.html

Sanchez, J. 1999. "Update: Cisco CEO says consumers will drive Net Growth". IDG News Service, London Bureau.

Serwer, A, "There's something about Cisco", Fortune, 05/15/2000, Vol 141, No 10, pp114. http://library.northernlight.com/LH20000505020000188.html?cb=13&sc=0

Sosinsky,B. 2000. "Cisco sees the Light". Windows 2000 Magazine, www.winntmag.com/Articles/Index.cfm?ArticlesID=7905

Staff Reporter. 2000. "Cisco still hungry overseas", CNNfn, http://cnnfn.cnn.com/2000/10/26/europe/cisco/index.htm

Staff Reporter, "Top exec talks strategy inside Cisco", CNET News.Com, 4.07/2000, http://news.cnet.com/news/0-1004-200-2200430.html

Thurm, S. 2000 ."Cisco Defies the Odds With Mergers That Work". Wall Street Journal, www.benchmarkingreports.com/articles/wsj_merger_article/wsj_merger_article.htm

Wong, W. 2000. " Can Cisco keep up its shopping spree?". CNET News.com, http://news.cnet.com/news/0-1004-200-3412402.html?tag=st.ne.1430735

Wuebker, R., Navoth, Z., Rao, B., Horwitch, M. & Ziv, N. 1998. "Cisco Systems: The Internetworking Company of the Future". Institute for Technology and Enterprise, pp1-13, www.ite.poly.edu/htmls/Cisco_case_3.html

Young, J.S. 1999. " The Next Net". Wired, http://fox.rollins.edu/~tlairson/ecom/CISCO.HTML

Cisco Connection Online Whiz Kid: Young deal maker is the force behind a Company's Growth http://www.cisco.com/warp/public/750/acquisition/articles/volpi.html

Cisco Connection Online, Corporate News and Information Acquisition Summary http://www.cisco.com/warp/public/750/acquisition/summarylist.html

Cisco Connection Online, Corporate News and Information Cisco Systems 1999 Annual Report http://www.cisco.com/warp/public/749/ar99/

Cisco Connection Online, Cisco Systems Fact Sheet http://www.cisco.com/warp/public/750/corpfact.html

Press Release. 1998. "Remarks by the President and the Vice President at Electronic Commerce Event". The White House, Office of the Press Secretary, www.npr.gov/library/speeches/rmk.selec.html

BigCharts, www.bigcharts.com

Investorguide: Analysis of Cisco Systems (CSC0) http://www.investorguide.com/CSCO.htm

Market Guide, www.marketguide.com

Multex, www.multex.com

Dell: Selling Directly, Globally

Pauline Ng, P. Lovelock, and Ali F. Farhoomand

The University of Hong Kong

"I believe we have the right business model for the Internet age."

- Michael Dell, CEO, Dell Computer Corporation[1]

Dell Computer Corporation was into its fifteenth year of operation and had expanded from a US$6.2 million US-based business in 1985 to a US$21.7 billion international business in 1999. In 1999 it ranked second in both the US and the worldwide PC market. Its success was founded on the direct business-to-customer model, which revolutionised the PC industry, at first in the US and then in over 170 countries around the world. The Company had been setting the standards for pricing and performance worldwide, despite analysts repeatedly saying that, "This is an American concept. It cannot work here!" Then in 1996, Dell again rocked the PC industry by making its direct approach even more direct through the Internet. *Dell On-line* seemed a natural progression for Dell. In the first quarter of 1997, Dell reported daily on-line sales of US$1 million. For the month of August 1999, daily on-line sales had reached US$30 million, translating to US$11 billion per annum. By the end of 2000, Dell targeted to conduct half of its business in each region on-line.

Pauline Ng prepared this case in conjunction with P. Lovelock under the Supervision of Dr. Ali F. Farhoomand for class discussion. This case is not intended to show effective or ineffective handling of decision or business processes.

Reprinted with permission. Ali F. Farhoomand Centre for Asian Business Cases, University of Hong Kong. This case is part of a project funded by the University Grants Committee (UGC) of Hong Kong.

Ref. 99/53C

Distributed by The European Case Clearing House, Cranfeld University, Wharley End, Bedford MK43 0JR, England. To order copies, phone: +44 (0)1234 750903, fax: +44 (0)1234 751125, e mail: ECCH@cranfeld.ac.uk. All rights reserved. Printed in UK.

However, despite its remarkable growth and global expansion, there were still many regions Dell needed to break into to ensure its future position in the ranks, notably China. Analysts predicted that China would soon become the second largest PC market after the US, generating revenues of US$25 billion by 2002. In September 1999, Dell ranked number seven in China's PC market. The Company had ambitions to achieve approximately 10 percent of its global sales through the China market by 2002, which would secure number two ranking in China. The China market would thus account for 50 percent of regional sales by 2002. Fifty percent of sales were also to be achieved through the Internet. Was this timescale realistic? Was the market mature enough to handle its business on-line direct? Aaron Loke, Director of Marketing, was contemplating the expansion strategy for Dell to pursue in China. Could the "American model" work in China?

Dell Direct

From Glory to Glory

"I definitely felt that I was diving into something pretty major without knowing most of the details. . . . But I did know one thing. I knew what I wanted to do: build better computers than IBM, and become number one in the industry."

- Michael Dell[2]

In 1983, at the age of 18 and with US$1,000, Michael Dell realised his life ambition and started out selling upgraded PCs and add-on components from his dormitory room at the University of Texas, Austin. This dorm-room business officially became Dell Computer Corporation in May 1984. With the rapid growth of the Company, Dell went public in June 1988. Ten years on, Dell was ranked number two and the fastest growing among all major computer systems companies worldwide, with more than 26,000 employees around the globe [see Exhibit 1]. Michael Dell earned the reputation of being the youngest CEO ever of a Fortune 500 company. Furthermore, he was named one of the *Business Week*'s "Top 25 Managers of the Year" in 1997, "Entrepreneur of the Year" by *Inc.* magazine, "Man of the Year" by *PC Magazine,* and "CEO of the Year" by *Financial World.* The success of Michael Dell and the Dell Computer Corporation was founded on the direct business-to-consumer model [see Exhibit 2].

The Direct Model

The Company was founded on a simple concept: that by selling personal computers directly to customers, Dell could best understand their needs and provide the most effective computing solutions to meet those needs. Dell sold directly to customers, dealt directly with suppliers and communicated directly with employees, all without the unnecessary interference of intermediaries. To the customer, whether a regular consumer or a multinational corporation, Dell was their single point of contact and accountability.

Dealing directly with customers meant that Dell knew exactly what its customers wanted. While IBM's PC was an open box designed to allow for expansion, reconfigu-

---

Exhibit 1 — US and Worldwide PC Shipments 2nd Quarter, 1998

Top Five Vendors, US PC Shipments

Rank	Vendor	2nd Qtr, 1998 Shipments (000's Units)	Market Share
1	Compaq	1,157	14.4%
2	Dell	1,143	14.3%
3	IBM	511	6.4%
4	Gateway	623	7.8%
5	Hewlett-Packard	628	7.8%
	Others	3,952	49.3%
	All Vendors	8,014	100.0%

Top Five Vendors, Worldwide PC Shipments

Rank	Vendor	2nd Qtr, 1998 Shipments (000's Units)	Market Share
1	Compaq	2,819	14.0%
2	Dell	1,818	9.1%
3	IBM	1,573	7.8%
4	Hewlett-Packard	1,239	6.2%
5	NEC/PBNEC	1,295	6.5%
	Others	11,333	56.4%
	All Vendors	20,077	100.0%

Notes:
* Shipments are branded shipments and exclude OEM sales for all vendors.
* Data for NEC/PBNEC includes shipments for Packard Bell, NEC, NEC Japan, NEC China and ZDS.
* Data for Compaq includes shipments for Compaq, Digital Equipment and Tandem.
SOURCE: International Data Corporation, Q3 1999.

Case 12 / Dell: Selling Directly, Globally

Exhibit 2   Dell's Build-To-Customer Order

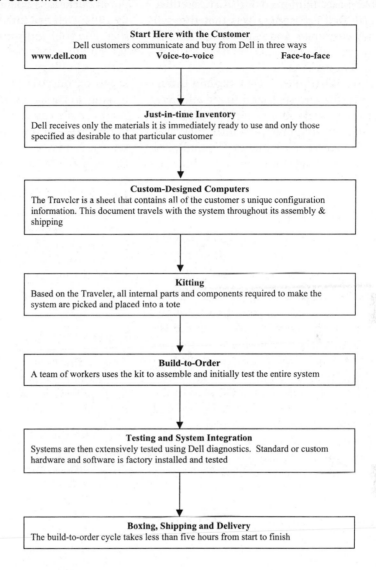

Start Here with the Customer
Dell customers communicate and buy from Dell in three ways
www.dell.com   Voice-to-voice   Face-to-face

Just-in-time Inventory
Dell receives only the materials it is immediately ready to use and only those specified as desirable to that particular customer

Custom-Designed Computers
The Traveler is a sheet that contains all of the customer's unique configuration information. This document travels with the system throughout its assembly & shipping

Kitting
Based on the Traveler, all internal parts and components required to make the system are picked and placed into a tote

Build-to-Order
A team of workers uses the kit to assemble and initially test the entire system

Testing and System Integration
Systems are then extensively tested using Dell diagnostics. Standard or custom hardware and software is factory installed and tested

Boxing, Shipping and Delivery
The build-to-order cycle takes less than five hours from start to finish

ration and continual upgrading, Dell chose to build PCs to order. Dell was the first PC manufacturer to offer free installation of applications software as a standard service option. By using patented technology, it installed network cards to customers' proprietary, in-house applications, right on the manufacturing line. Thus, Dell claimed that it offered its customers more powerful, more richly configured systems for their money than competitors. Rather than pursuing technology for technology's sake, customers got only what they wanted. Many PC manufacturers had fallen into the trap of guessing what their customers might want.

Dealing directly with suppliers was essential for the successful application of Dell's direct model. Just-in-time inventory control created advantages that had an immediate impact on customers. Inventory costs were kept to a minimum, new technological breakthroughs (e.g., faster chips, bigger disk drives) could be delivered to customers within a week as opposed to two months, and obsolete and dated stock holdings were minimised. The threat of being caught in a transition to a next-generation product with an inventory of obsolete stock was a perpetual problem in the industry, but one that the direct model could avoid. Dell was able to pass along to its customers the savings from reductions in system component costs quickly because it maintained very low inventories. This was of paramount importance in the PC industry as the rate of development of new technology dictated PC prices. Dealing directly with a few main suppliers on a global basis reinforced Dell's competitive advantage. Michael Dell's reasoning was that through closer contact with customers and with more information about customer needs, there was less need for massive amounts of inventory.

There were three golden rules at Dell: disdain inventory, always listen to the customer and never sell indirectly. The formula worked well for Dell. Its build-to-order manufacturing operation for the US was located in Texas, for Europe in Limerick (Ireland), for Asia Pacific in Penang (Malaysia) and for China in Xiamen.

Growth and Expansion Beyond the US

"Our success was, in fact, something of a crisis point."
                                        - Michael Dell[3]

Rapid growth and expansion were necessary if the Company was to survive. The Company started out targeting the small- to medium-size businesses in the US market. While its competitors were aiming at the top end of the market (i.e., the large corporations), Dell chose to lead a price/performance revolution from the bottom up, bringing new technology at affordable prices to the widest possible group of customers. The strategy worked well in the US. By the end of 1986, Dell had achieved US$60 million in sales. Michael Dell was concerned about the next step for his Company because staying small would make them vulnerable to the consolidation that was taking place in the PC industry. In the fall of 1986, he called together the executives of the Company and held a brainstorming meeting. Three key realisations materialised that were to map the course that Dell was to take:

1. Dell had to target large companies if the business was to grow;
2. To do this, they had to offer the best support in the industry;
3. Despite the fact the Company was only two-and-a-half years old, it needed to expand globally and to grow beyond the US.

"Many people told us the direct model would fail in virtually every country we expanded into. . . . The message was always the same: Our country is different, your business model won't work here."
                                        - Michael Dell[4]

In June 1987, Dell ventured out of the US for the first time and started business in the UK. Journalists and analysts speculated that Dell's direct model might work in the US, but not in Europe. However, 11 more international operations opened over the period 1987 to 1991. By 1994, Dell had international subsidiaries in 14 countries, and sold and supported its products in more than 100 additional markets through partnering agreements with technology distributors. In 1995, construction began on the Asia Pacific Customer Centre (APCC) in Penang, Malaysia. In the first half of 1995, Dell opened offices in six countries in the region. Malaysia became the hub of a comprehensive Asia Pacific management, sales and marketing network that included Australia, China, Hong Kong, India, Indonesia, Korea, Malaysia, New Zealand, the Philippines, Singapore, Taiwan and Thailand. The intention was to begin on a selected basis and to extend out from country to country over time. In 1998, the Xiamen manufacturing and service centre (China Customer Centre) was opened. The regional headquarters of Dell Asia Pacific remained in Hong Kong. In 1998, Dell operated sales offices in 33 countries and served customers in more than 170 countries and territories around the world.

Results that Spoke for Themselves

"Dell Computer Corporation defies gravity. Whether you measure its growth in sales, profits, market share, or stock price, the Company is simply weightless."
                                        - Business Week, 2 November, 1998

Dell went through extremely rapid growth throughout the Company's history [see Exhibit 3]. Its build-to-order, direct-sales approach allowed it to far outpace industry growth rates. In 1995, a Company press release reported that Dell's stock value had appreciated by more than 700 percent since the Company's first public offering in 1988.[5] In the same year, Fortune Magazine ranked Dell for "best investment" with an 81.2 percent "total return to investors" over the previous year. By December 1997, Dell had overtaken IBM and became the second-largest supplier of desktop PCs worldwide, with a 9.7 percent share of the market and a 10-15 percent price advantage over its major competitors who distributed their products through indirect channels.[6] [See Exhibit 1.] Between 1988 to 1998 the Company's stock value increased by 36,000 percent. In the same period, it had grown from a US$159 million company to a US$18 billion company.[7]

By February 1998, the Company reported a sales increase in Europe of 61 percent in the fourth quarter of the 1998 financial year, bringing sales close to US$1 billion. Sales from Asia Pacific increased by 79 percent in the 1998 financial year compared to the previous year, an increase that was more than in any other Dell regional business, albeit from a small base. In August

Exhibit 3   Dell Computer Corporation Financial Years Ended 1995–1998

US$ millions/ Percentage of net revenue	Financial Year Ended				
	29 Jan., 1999	1 Feb., 1998	1 Feb., 1997	28 Jan., 1996	29 Jan., 1995
Operating Results					
Net revenue	18,243	12,327	7,759	5,296	3,475
Gross margin	4,106	2,722	1,666	1,067	738
Operating income	2,046	1,316	714	377	249
Net income	1,460	944	518	272	149
Net revenue by product line					
Desktops	64%	71%	78%	81%	87%
Enterprise	13%	9%	4%	3%	5%
Portables	23%	20%	18%	16%	8%
Nonsystem net revenue, percentage of total system net revenue	7%	9%	10%	11%	12%

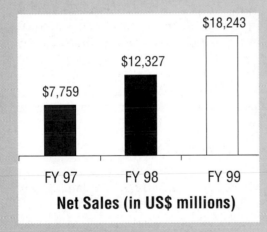

Net Sales (in US$ millions)

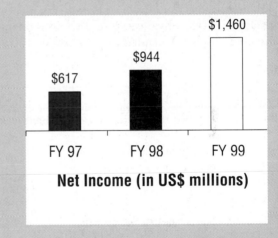

Net Income (in US$ millions)

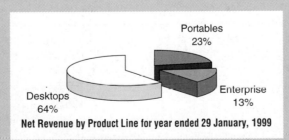

Net Revenue by Product Line for year ended 29 January, 1999

Net Revenue by Product Line for year ended 29 January, 1999

SOURCE: URL: http://www.dell.com/...financials/financialSummReport.htm, August 1999.

1999, the Company announced that it was number one in PC shipments within the UK. [See Exhibit 4 for a breakdown of revenue by geographic region.]

For the quarter ended 31 July, 1999, the Company reported revenue of US$21.7 billion. It became the number one PC vendor to businesses in the US. Dell again led industry growth in unit shipments, revenue and earnings. Shipments increased by 55 percent, two times analysts' estimates of total industry growth. Dell's operating income was 11.3 percent of revenue, and operating expenses declined by nearly one percentage point. Return on investment was 260 percent, four times higher than that of Dell's nearest major competitor. At quarter end, Dell held six days of inventory. [See Exhibit 5 for details of Dell's achievements.]

Selective Expansion

Dell had applied an expansion strategy that involved selective introduction of the direct model, country by country. The strategy followed the same pattern in each country: in the first instance, Dell would make use of distributors (e.g., currently in India). The benefits of the direct model over the indirect model (such as reduced costs and increased attention to customer experience and satisfaction) were obviously lost. The decision to apply the direct model depended on the "readiness" of the country/region and would rest on a number of factors, including:

- The size of the market, current and potential.
- The availability of resources, especially a sales force that was capable of applying the direct-sales model: the PC industry was dominated by vendors selling through indirect channels. The skills-set required for relating to customers needs and translating those needs into customised products and services was not readily available.
- Sufficient management resources at the local level: senior management required knowledge of the behaviour of the local market, the training potential and needs of the local labour force, as well as other cultural, physical and political limitations that had to be overcome.
- Local acceptance of Dell's direct model: potential customers who had not heard of the Dell brand would find it difficult to pick up the telephone and order Dell PCs without having seen one. This applied even more so in countries/regions where the cost of a PC was two or three times an individual's monthly salary. From Dell's experience, customer trust had to be earned. This would initially entail significant resources mobilised to ensure face-to-face contact with potential customers. However, once trust was

---

| Exhibit 4 | Dell Computer Corporation Revenue by Region |

US$ millions/
Percentage of net revenue

Financial Year Ended

	29 Jan., 1999	1 Feb., 1998	1 Feb., 1997	28 Jan., 1996	29 Jan., 1995
Net revenue, by region					
Americas	68%	69%	68%	66%	69%
Europe	26%	24%	26%	28%	27%
Asia-Pacific & Japan	6%	7%	6%	6%	4%

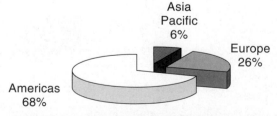

Asia Pacific 6%

Europe 26%

Americas 68%

Net Revenue by Region for year ended 29 January, 1999

SOURCE: URL: http://www.dell.com/...financials/financialSummReport.htm, August 1999.

Case 12 / Dell: Selling Directly, Globally

established through product and service satisfaction, customers were happy to make repeat orders through the telephone.

- Suppliers' ability to deliver parts at short notice: Dell's direct model was dependent to a large extent on just-in-time inventory management.
- Adequate arrangements with carriers to ensure timely delivery of orders: Dell's average order-to-delivery time was six days. Dell had made arrangements with authorised carriers (American, Airborne, Conway, Eagle, First Air, FedEx, RPS, UPS and Watkins) to expedite deliveries around the globe. DHL, FedEx and Bax Global were used extensively in the Asia Pacific region.
- Operating costs.

Timing for entry to new markets was therefore essential given all the factors that had to be considered. However, the underlying motivating force at Dell was that, given the right timing and the readiness of the market, all countries/regions in the world would accept the direct model for selling PCs. The PC had become a commodity and the globalisation of the PC market would, in the future, be comparable to purchasing a can of Coca Cola or a pizza. In the past, major barriers for Dell have included government regulations, lack of human resources, inadequate telecommunications and transportation infrastructures, and unavailability or inaccessibility of parts.

While planning for global expansion, the impact of the Internet explosion rippled through Dell.

www.dell.com

"Dell, the Company, seems to have been born and evolved with an anticipation of the Internet age."
- *Andrew S. Grove, Chairman, Intel Corporation*

Exhibit 5	Dell's Ranking Achievements

No.1 supplier of PCs to the US corporate market segment (2Q 1997)

No.1 supplier of PCs to the US federal, state and government market segment (2Q 1997)

No.2 for shipment of PCs to large and medium businesses worldwide (2Q 1997)

No.3 supplier of notebooks in the US (June 1998)

No.3 supplier of servers worldwide (1998)

No.2 supplier of servers in the US (1998)

No.1 supplier of workstations in the US (1998)

No.1 supplier of PCs in the UK (1999)

Dell's Accolades of Industry and Business Awards

- The "Readers' Choice" Award for Overall Service and Reliability, *Fortune Technology Buyer's Guide*
- The "Readers' Choice" award for Service and Reliability for both desktops and notebooks, *PC Magazine*
- No. 1 in Web-based support, *ComputerWorld*
- The "Reliability and Service Award" for work PCs, home PCs and notebooks, *PC World*
- Highest customer satisfaction rating for servers, desktops and notebooks from industry analyst firm, Technology Business Research
- "Delivering the Best Return on Investment to Shareholders" award among the Fortune 500 (1994)
- The "Most Admired Companies" award since 1995, *Fortune*
- The "Best Performing Information Technology Company" in the world award, 1998, *Business Week*
- Top performing stock among the Standard & Poor's 500 and Nasdaq 100 in 1996 and 1997, and top performing US stock on the Dow Jones World Stock Index

---

Note: This list is not conclusive.
SOURCE: "Dell Redefines the Low-cost Consumer PC Market", 15 June, 1999, URL: http://www.dell.com/corporate/media/newsreleases/99/9906/15.htm, August 1999; "Major Publications, Independent Surveys Declare Dell a Winner," 16 December, 1998, URL: http://www.dell.com/corporate/media/newsreleases/98/9812/16.htm, August 1999; Dell Direct World – Access: Dell Management (M. Dell), URL: http://www.dell.com/corporate/acce...1mgnt/offcceo/mdell/mdellbiojr.htm, August 1999.

"Our PC consumer shipments grew more than 100 percent in the quarter [ended 31 July, 1999], and about one-half of those sales were generated on-line, through www.dell.com."

- Michael Dell[8]

Very early on Dell saw the advantages of the Internet and exploited them before others in the industry. For Dell, this new technology presented a medium through which it could get even closer to its customers and enhance its direct-sales approach. It was a logical extension to the direct model, making it even more direct.

In June 1994, Dell launched www.dell.com. This was phase one of Dell's plan to link with its customers through the Net. The site presented customers with simple product and price lists, almost like an on-line catalogue.

Since July 1996, Dell customers could configure and order a computer directly through Dell's Website. This was phase two of Dell's plan. Within a year, daily sales over the Net totalled over US$3 million [see Exhibit 6]. Dell was the first computer company to provide a comprehensive on-line purchasing tool.

Phase three included on-line technical support, order status information and on-line downloading of software. Dell's electronic commerce strategy was beginning to take shape [see Exhibit 7 for the sitemap of www.dell.com]. It was developed to work seamlessly with the Company's existing systems, providing real-time pricing and order status. Its goal was to make the internal operations of the Company agile enough to respond to the ever-increasing and ever-changing needs of customers. On average in 1998, Dell responded to over 120,000 technical support queries a week through its Website. Interestingly, 90 percent of sales through the Net were placed by small businesses and consumers. Corporate customers chose to use the Website for gath-

ering product information, order status and technical help rather than to place orders.

For Dell, the benefits of the Internet were enormous. Eighty percent of the consumers and half of the small businesses who purchased on Dell's Website were first-time buyers. Undoubtedly, www.dell.com brought in additional revenues. Providing product information, pricing and technical support on-line helped to lower sales and marketing costs. Basic customer service and technical support functions provided through the Internet helped to lower service and support costs. Dell estimated that 20,000 customers who would check their order status on-line would present savings for Dell of between US$6,000 to US$10,000 per week, and 30,000 software requests that could be downloaded on-line would save Dell US$150,000 per week.[9]

By mid-1998, all Dell customers had individual files of their system configurations on-line. Customers were able to take advantage of the very latest technology and immediate component price reductions. In addition, it offered 24-hour on-line service and support. It removed inter-company boundaries and achieved speed-to-market in ways that were not possible before. In April 1997, Dell established a new joint-venture leasing company called Dell Financial Services, which provided a range of flexible leasing options directly to Dell customers in the US and eventually worldwide. Its Internet offerings included more than 6,500 products from its DellWare catalogue.

Dell's application of Internet technology to its direct model created a fully integrated value chain. It allowed a three-way "information partnership" with suppliers and customers by treating each player as a collaborator to improve efficiency across the entire supply and demand chain, thus sharing the benefits. For example, at Dell's manufacturing site in Ireland, orders were received via the Web and call centres, Dell would relay to its suppliers details of the components required, all the compo-

| Exhibit 6 | Dell's Daily On-line Sales and Weekly Technical Support Volumes 1997 |

	1st Qtr 1997	2nd Qtr 1997	3rd Qtr 1997	4th Qtr 1997
Sales per day	US$1 m	US$2 m	US$3 m	US$3 m++
Tech. support/ queries per week	30,000	45,000	60,000	120,000
Visitors per week	213,000	225,000	250,000	400,000
% sales outside the US	0%	5%	10%	17%

SOURCE: US Department of Commerce, "The Emerging Digital Economy", 15 April, 1998, URL: http://www.ecommerce.gov/emerging.htm, August 1999.

Case 12 / Dell: Selling Directly, Globally

Exhibit 7   www.dell.com Sitemap

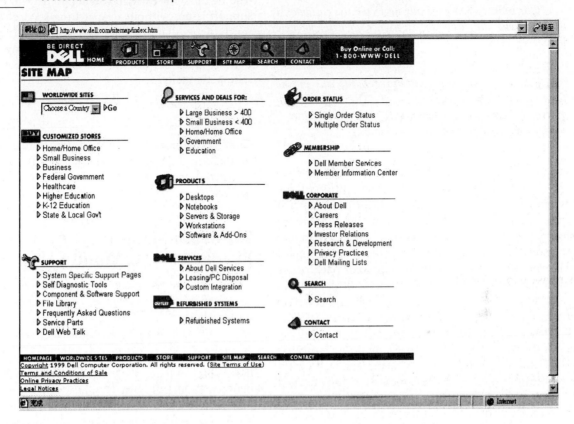

nents were delivered to the site, and complete computers would be shipped out, all within a few hours.

Customisation

The Internet also provided great potential for enhancing customer relations and opened up new selling possibilities. Through its Website, Dell refined the services tailored to its customer segments. Dell offered capabilities, service and content tailored to the needs of its customers, including large commercial accounts, government, educational institutions, small/medium businesses and home buyers. To attract the corporate clientele, Dell created customised "Premier Pages" that allowed them to make purchases from the company's own Intranet. Microsoft was one company that made use of its customised Premier Page.

Typically, the company would receive its configured systems in about four days from the day of order. The on-line paperless purchase orders and electronic invoicing capabilities saved Microsoft an estimated US$1 million in procurement costs in the first year alone. Another large company estimated that it had saved US$2 million in technical support costs and another estimated 15 percent savings from Internet procurement efficiencies.

Later on, the Company introduced "My Dell" Web pages that were customised pages for small-business and home-office consumers.

Realising the Full Potential of the Internet

In August 1999, the Company reported sales of more than US$30 million in products each day over the Net. The Website attracted more than 25 million visitors per quarter and had unique Web pages for 44 countries in 21 languages. The Company had more than 27,000 customer-specific Premier Pages within www.dell.com. In June 1999, 70 percent of Dell's Internet sales came through Premier Pages. By the end of 2000, Dell anticipated that half of its total business (sales, service and support) would be conducted on-line. The Internet had the potential to change the face of the PC industry. Dell aimed to assume a leadership position in Internet commerce, defining the Internet business model as an extension of the direct model rather than simply an adjunct to some reseller relationship.

". . . we enjoy the advantage of continuing to refine our model while others retrofit theirs."

- Michael Dell[10]

E-Support Direct

"Our industry has generally neglected the customer. I want to take the customer experience to a whole new level."

- *Michael Dell*[11]

"Service is the new competitive battlefield in the information technology industry . . . The largest global enterprise customers are demanding more – and better – service and support from systems vendors."

- *Michael Dell*[12]

E-Support Direct was the fourth phase of Dell's electronic commerce strategy. The Internet improved the speed and flow of information at much lower costs. It was the natural tool for Dell to deliver the ultimate in customer experience, the direct-service model. In the early years of the industry it was driven by technological breakthroughs. As competition gathered pace, price became an increasingly significant driver of demand in the market place. For Dell, price and time to the market had become the huge differentiators. However, Michael Dell foresaw that building a business solely on pricing was not a sustainable advantage. Maintaining customer loyalty became a primary focus. This marked Dell's gradual evolution from a simple box-mover to a fully fledged service provider, yielding the powers of the Internet to build on the competitive advantages of the direct model.

In 1998, Dell announced that it intended to focus on creating a new direct-service model for building the business of the future. In August 1999, Dell unveiled E-Support-Direct. The plan involved creating computing environments where a PC or server would be capable of maintaining itself. E-Support would provide tailored services designed to achieve higher levels of system uptime, streamline the customer support process and decrease the total cost of system ownership.

Just as Dell had revolutionised the PC industry with its direct model and with www.dell.com, Dell intended to use the Internet to revolutionise the customer support experience. Internet-enabled support was to provide customised capability to easily automate and speed up the support process. These included Dell On-line Knowledge Base, Ask Dudley, Resolution Assistant and HelpTech. Support information was unique to each system and could be found at support.dell.com [see Exhibits 8a-8c for details of E-Support services].

Dell was named as one of 1999's Ten Best Web Support Sites by the Association of Support Professionals, a national body that examined industry support trends. Dell was the only PC vendor to win the award. In the same year, Dell was also awarded an "A" in Web Support by the CNET Editor's Choice for Service

and Support. The Company also announced that it was leading the industry by resolving 80 percent of technical support issues without despatching service technicians, much higher than the industry average of 27 percent.

Within the industry, there was growing consensus that the focus of business was shifting beyond the box-selling mentality.

"The old model of making PCs is no longer viable."
- *Mr. Anderson, IDC*[13]

Global expansion through the Internet, however, had its limitations. This was especially true for regions where Internet usage was still low in terms of population density.

The Second-largest PC Market in the World

"If we're not in what will soon be the second-biggest PC market in the world, then how can Dell possibly be a global player?"

- *John Legere, President, Dell Asia Pacific*[14]

The PC market in the Mainland had seen rapid growth. [See Exhibit 9 for growth of China's computer industry between 1990-1996.] In 1996, PC vendors sold 2.1 million desktop PCs, notebooks and servers in China, an increase of nearly 40 percent from the previous year. The total value of the market in 1996 was US$3.34 billion, an increase of over 20 percent from the previous year. In three years' time, it was estimated that China's market size would be around 10 million PCs. The major Chinese PC makers, such as Legend, Founder and Great Wall, ranked within the top 10 in terms of PC shipments. All PC vendors competing in China sold through distributors who carried many brands. For example, Compaq had engaged 21 distributors at one point during 1996.

In June 1998, the Market Information Centre (MIC) reported its prediction that by the year 2000, Mainland China's annual PC production would reach 7.6 million, making it the third-largest in the world after the US and Japan. Furthermore, if Japan's economic slump continued, China could take second place in global PC production. If PC shipments in China continued to grow at 30 percent per annum (as it had between 1996-1999), China's PC market would surpass Japan's by 2004. Not even the Asian financial crisis had slowed down this growth. As at June 1999, China was the fifth-largest PC market behind the US, Japan, Germany and Britain.

However, China and her PC market were characterised by a number of factors:

- Retail buyers only accounted for 10 percent of sales.[15]

Exhibit 8a   Dell Computer Corporation E-Support Services

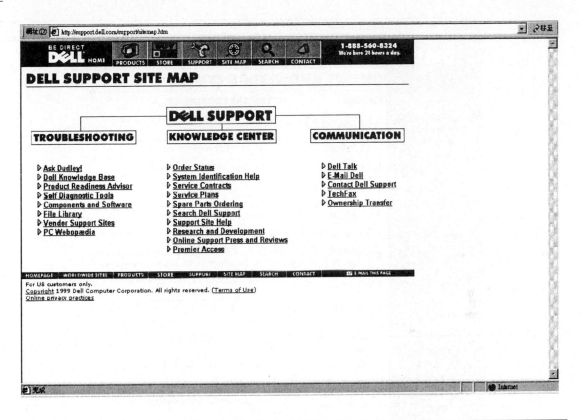

Exhibit 8b   Dell Computer Corporation E-Support Services

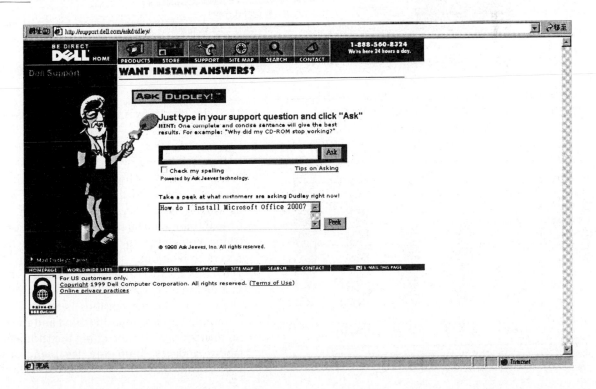

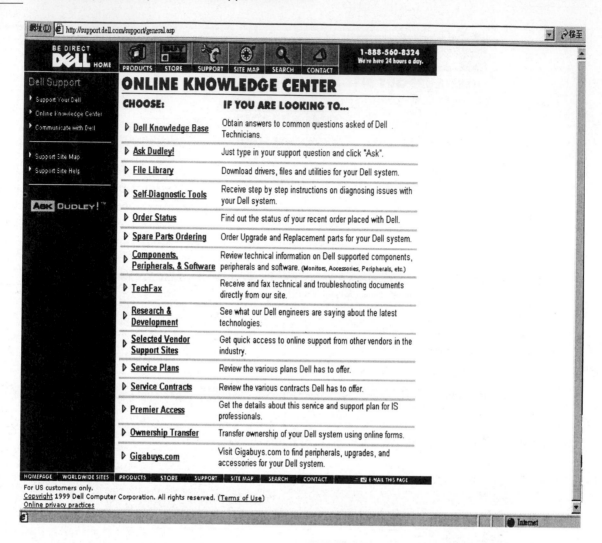

Exhibit 9   Growth Of China's Computer Industry Between 1990–1996

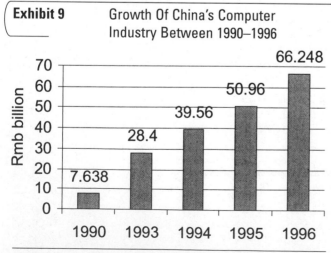

SOURCE: Buchel, B., & Raub, S., (1999), "Legend Group and the Chinese Computer Industry", *Asian Case Research Journal*, Vol. 3, Issue 1, May 1999, p. 51.

- The price of a PC was the equivalent of two years of a person's savings.[16]
- Chinese managers were becoming more and more tech-savvy on their own.
- The problem of software piracy in China was rife: Microsoft estimated that 95 percent of the software used in Chinese corporations was stolen.
- China's nationalistic politics made US companies in China vulnerable to the ups and downs of Sino-American relations.
- The Chinese Government made no secret of the fact that national PC vendors would be promoted.
- There remained the tensions between the immense economic opportunities in China and the constraints on business activity, including the shortage of skilled labour and the immature legal and institutional frameworks.

- In 1995, *PCWeek On-line* reported in an article that "... building close and trusting relationships is critical to succeeding in China."[17] However, five years on, times had changed and many foreign companies in China were succeeding without having the connections.

- The government required users of the Internet to register with the police when opening an account, and there was widespread belief that user activity was monitored by the government. Many commentators predicted that one of the key obstacles to future growth of Internet usage in China was the issue of government control.

- The credit payment system: China's Ninth Five-Year Plan made it a priority to establish a series of "Golden" projects, one of which was the "Golden Card". This project was aimed at developing a nationwide credit-card network that would also provide debit and electronic purse facilities in China. It was reported in 1997 that the smart cards were scheduled to be operational before the end of 2002, and that 250-300 million cards would be in use by then.[18] China had embarked on the largest smart bank card in the world. Having said that, it seemed unlikely that the smart card would be readily issued to the average citizen, but mainly to corporate bodies and people of high social standing.

- On the Internet front, Chinese Internet usage was proliferating. Between 1997 and 1998, according to IDC, the number of Internet users increased by 71 percent to more than 2 million.

- Analysts predicted that China would contribute the largest Internet growth in the first part of the 21st Century.[19]

Dell in China

Dell Takes the Direct Model to China

In February 1998, Dell announced its intention to extend into the world's most populous country, China. Reporters and analysts told the Company that the Western concept would not work in China. China's regulation was that if goods were not manufactured in China they could not be sold directly in the Mainland. Hence in August, a new 135,000 square-foot facility was opened and a China Customer Centre (CCC) was established to produce, sell and provide service and technical support. The intention was to place the Company closer to its customers in markets that presented long-term potential. In the previous three years, Dell's business in the Chinese market had grown steadily and sales of computer systems were through distributors.

Xiamen was chosen for its ideal location, half way between Hong Kong and Shanghai on China's southeastern coast in Fujian Province. It was one of China's first four Special Economic Zones established in 1981. Xiamen was a rapidly growing city with a vigorous economy and a fully-modern infrastructure. It boasted of excellent highway connections to major cities in China and an efficient domestic airport. Furthermore, it had a number of reputable universities and over 20 percent of Xiamen's population were graduates of higher education. The telecommunications network in Xiamen was excellent, providing over 1,000 telephone lines to the CCC. Through negotiations with the government, two power grids supplied electricity directly to the CCC.

The CCC mirrored the manufacturing and professional functions found at the Asia Pacific Customer Centre (APCC) in Penang. The CCC allowed Dell to pass on the benefits of the direct model to its customers in China, including cutting out the costs of the distributors, being able to make-to-order within three to four days and providing upgraded systems to customers within a week. An order could be off the production line within two days. Most deliveries, using contracted carriers, were by road. Furthermore, 70 percent of Dell's parts were supplied from within the Mainland through manufacturers who had global agreements with Dell. Quality was therefore not sacrificed.

In August 1998, direct sales and technical support operations began in nine areas of China, including Beijing, Shanghai, Guangzhou and Xiamen. Through these locations, Dell covered over 80 percent of the potential user population. The Company also launched toll-free sales and technical-support telephone numbers to provide immediate local-language assistance to customers. The Xiamen operation employed a little under 500 people. Around 200 were "outside sales" staff, engaged in door-to-door visits, looking after corporate customers. The balance worked at the CCC and included engineers, production staff as well as "inside sales" staff. The latter engaged in taking on-line and telephone orders. Staffing was a major challenge for Dell. It was difficult to find experienced direct sales people, because direct sales was a new profession in China. Despite this, 96 percent of the workforce were recruited locally, the remainder consisting of management level staff who were mostly from Hong Kong. Over 60 percent were university graduates.

Another problem encountered in China was the bureaucracy and red tape involved in securing government contracts, the government and government-owned corporations being major customers in China's PC market. The negotiation process could be extremely lengthy while the terms of the contracts were often one sided and non-negotiable in any case.

Dell's range of OptiPlex desktops and Latitude notebook computers and PowerEdge network servers were made available to customers in all nine areas [see Exhibit 10 for a full list of Dell's systems]. Additional products and services were to be introduced in response to market demand and technology advancements. In fact, in April 1999, Dell introduced its award-winning range of Dimension desktops specifically targeted at home and small business customers.

Contrary to popular belief, most of Dell's sales in China and Asia were not to consumers buying over the telephone. While many vendors were targeting the general market, Dell resolved to focus initially on corporate customers. It was, therefore, questionable whether a like-for-like application of the direct model could be achieved in China. This tactic rattled Chinese PC vendors such as Legend and Founder by nibbling into their most valuable client base: state-owned enterprises. Unlike the US market, where two in 10 PCs sold by Dell were to consumers, the consumer segment in China was very different. The price of a PC could cost the equivalent of three months of a person's wages. The average consumer could not afford the investment and very few had a bank account let alone a credit card. If consumers wanted to buy a Dell PC, they would often visit the nearest Dell office to see one first. Alternatively, they could refer to Dell's Website or newspaper advertisements. Although Dell had stopped using distributors, retailers were purchasing direct from Dell and selling systems on to consumers at marked-up prices.

Dell's customer groups were divided into three segments:

Exhibit 10   Dell Computer Corporation Product List

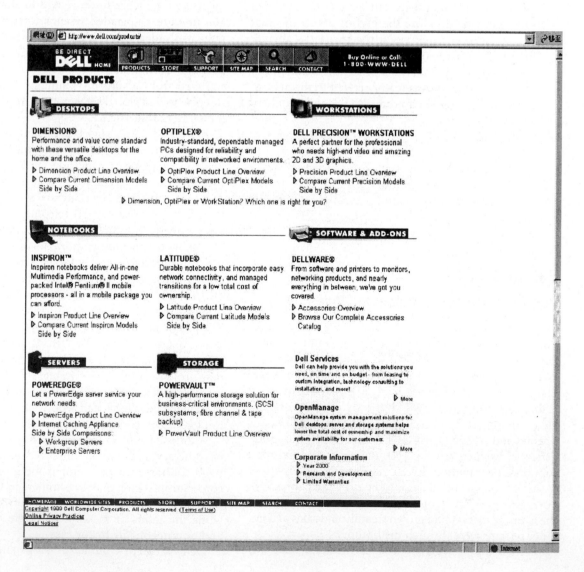

- Large Corporate Accounts (LCA): companies with 1,500-plus employees.
- Preferred Accounts Division (PAD): companies with 500-1,500 employees.
- Home and Small Businesses (HSB): establishments with fewer than 500 employees.

The segment in which Dell was seeing some repeat buyers was in the corporate accounts. Initially, resources were mobilised towards maximising face-to-face contact, establishing good customer relations and promoting the Dell brand on a personal level. This "relationship sales" strategy was required for the LCA and PAD segments to hone business deals. Some business deals were made through customer relationships and recommendations, while others were made purely through pricing advantages. Once trust and confidence were established, Dell expected that these segments would require less face-to-face contact and that more orders would be placed through the telephone or even through the Net, thus reducing Dell's operating costs. Within corporations,

Dell targeted the IT managers who seemed to have some knowledge of the latest PC technology and knew what specifications were required for their companies.

Within the LCA segment, four main industries or sectors accounted for 50 percent of Dell's business: government, education, telecommunications and power, and finance/banking. Two-thirds of Dell's corporate customers in China were state-owned enterprises. Dell Asia Pacific had targeted for revenues in China to constitute approximately 10 percent of global sales (representing 50 percent of sales for the region) by 2002, making it the second largest PC vendor (in terms of volume) and possibly the largest supplier to LCAs. But to achieve this target, senior managers at the CCC debated the need to further segment the market to better serve their customers.

In 1999, Dell ranked seventh in China [see Exhibit 11 for rankings in China's PC market in 1999]. Dell saw orders coming in from nearly 100 of the Mainland's biggest cities via the telephone, the Internet and from the sales staff, which was still the most common method of

| Exhibit 11 | Rankings In China's PC Industry In 1999 |

Ranking		Q2, 1998	Market Share (%)
1st	Legend	117,468	11.5
2nd	IBM	66,944	6.5
3rd	Hewlett–Packard	61,500	6.0
4th	Compaq	56,045	5.5
5th	Tontru	42,379	4.1
11th	Dell	7,340	0.7
	Others	671,875	65.6
	Total	1,023,551	100.0

Ranking		Q2, 1999	Market Share (%)
1st	Legend	208,841	17.3
2nd	IBM	82,330	6.8
3rd	Hewlett–Packard	71,287	5.9
4th	Founder	67,920	5.6
5th	Great Wall	38,755	3.2
7th	Dell	27,955	2.3
	Others	706,863	58.7
	Total	1,203,951	100.0

SOURCE: International Data Corporation, Hong Kong.

selling. In the fourth quarter of 1998, Dell's sales in the Mainland grew by 100 percent, albeit from a small base. In the second quarter of 1999, Dell recorded year-on-year unit growth of 561 percent. If Dell could sustain that pace of growth, it was anticipated that it would achieve sales of more than US$100 million in 1999.

China On-line?

However, just as Dell had been careful to identify the timeliness of making the transition from using distributors to using the direct model, so the timing and market readiness for electronic commerce had to be assessed from country to country. Dell anticipated that, whereas 50 percent of its business (by volume) in the US would be conducted on-line within one to two years, this same target would be achieved in two to three years in Asia Pacific. [See Exhibit 12 for details of Internet usage in the US and Asia-Pacific.] The majority of Dell's business in Asia Pacific came from large- and medium-sized corporations. Dell's Website supported 16 country-specific sites for Asia Pacific, using three languages, including Chinese and Japanese.

Part of the problem was that the Chinese were uncomfortable with credit card sales, especially of high-price-ticket products that could not be viewed before purchase. Many resources had therefore been invested in door-to-door sales calls to corporations. The operating costs were obviously higher for Dell in China than in, say, Europe or the US, where the majority of sales were placed through the telephone or on-line. Until China caught up with the West in terms of Internet penetration and credit card usage, the costs of enforcing the direct model would continue to take a tidy chunk out of Dell's earnings. Furthermore, these limitations would restrict the potential reach of the direct model.

Some large corporations in China had Premier Pages. These preferred to buy through the Net as it was convenient and fast. While the majority of customers could buy through www.dell.com, there were limitations. Payment had to be made by credit card, cheque or telegraphic transfer. Apart from large corporations who were given credit facilities, other customers had to pay up-front. This created complications and delayed the ordering process. Also, access to the Internet was expensive, and only senior executives were granted usage.

Exhibit 12	Internet Usage in the US and Asia-Pacific			
Country (1997)	Internet Hosts People	Hosts/1,000 (1997*)	Number of Internet Users	Users/1,000 People
United States	11,829,141	45.8	54,680,000	212.0
Japan	955,688	7.7	7,970,000	64.0
Australia	707,611	40.2	3,350,000	190.3
New Zealand	155,678	44.5	210,000	60.0
Korea	123,370	2.8	155,000	3.5
Taiwan	40,706	1.9	590,000	27.6
Singapore	60,674	21.7	150,000	53.6
Hong Kong	48,660	8.4	200,000	34.5
Malaysia	40,533	2.1	90,000	4.7
Indonesia	10,861	0.06	60,000	0.3
Thailand	12,794	0.22	80,000	1.4
Philippines	4,309	0.07	40,000	0.6
India	4,794	0.005	40,000	0.04
China	25,594	0.02	70,000	0.06

*1996 for New Zealand, Korea, Taiwan, Singapore, Hong Kong, Malaysia, Indonesia, Thailand, the Philippines, India and China.
SOURCE: Dedrick, J., & Kraemer, K. L., "Competing in Computers in the Network Era", in *Asia's Computer Challenge: Threat or Opportunity for the United States and the World?*, Oxford University Press, 1998, p. 288.

Case 12 / Dell: Selling Directly, Globally

In 1999, Internet sales accounted for less than two percent of total sales in China, compared to 25 percent worldwide. Undoubtedly, the future potential for Internet growth was huge. However, the timing remained uncertain. So far, only Premier Pages and DellWare had been launched on the Net.

Copy-Cats

"Yes, we're using Dell's direct-selling model when we target Chinese government companies or multinationals in China."

- Mary Ma, Chief Financial Officer, Legend [20]

Competition in the Mainland PC market was intense. Legend, the government-backed company, remained in number one position and looked set to remain there for a while yet. All the major vendors, such as IBM, Hewlett Packard and Compaq, were vying for position, while a growing number had established manufacturing plants in China. Still others felt the best way to do business in China was to form joint ventures with local companies (e.g., Digital and Founder).

Dell was hoping that its experience and knowledge with the direct model, particularly with the leadership it had in on-line direct-selling, would give them a clear run in the medium term at least. However, with the insignificant volume of on-line sales in China and the simplicity of the direct model, it was only a matter of time before the competition would try to beat them at their own game. Legend announced to *Fortune Magazine* that it was rapidly adopting the just-in-time delivery model, selling directly to its corporate customers and being able to cut costs and reduce inventory holdings in the process. [See Exhibit 13 for details of Legend's sales growth.]

Compaq, on the other hand, opted to selectively adopt the direct model. In May 1999, the company announced that it had slashed its US distributors from 40 to four to cut costs, in an attempt to better manage inventory and as a positive step towards applying the direct model. In China, however, Compaq continued to sell through distributors and value-added resellers.

"The US is a whole different market and it requires a different model to be efficient. Here in Greater China, we will continue to be committed to our channel partners."
- Tony Leung, Marketing Director – Greater China, Compaq [21]

However, in June, Compaq cut its list of resellers in Greater China from 30 to 10. In July 1999, Mr Leung conceded that "The trend to go direct is inevitable…".[22] But unlike the Dell direct model, Compaq chose not to bypass its resellers. Instead, the "partner-direct" model linked Compaq to its partners' systems so that orders could be input from its customers on-line. In this way, access to customers would not be limited, said Compaq's chief executive.

In June 1999, IBM announced that it would open a new assembly plant in Shekou at the end of 2000. This was a joint venture between IBM and Great Wall. Being the second-largest PC vendor after Legend, IBM hoped

---

Exhibit 13   Legend's Sales Growth

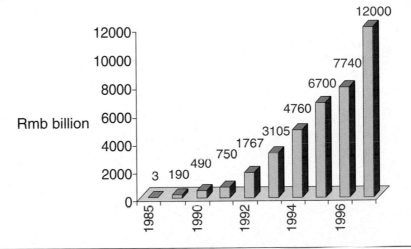

SOURCE: Buchel, B., & Raub, S., (1999), "Legend Group and the Chinese Computer Industry", *Asian Case Research Journal*, Vol. 3, Issue 1, May 1999, p. 59.

that the new facility would help to reduce inventory holdings to less than four days. While IBM had announced that it would apply the direct model to its North American market, company officials commented that it would take some time before the direct model would be adopted in Asia, where 80 percent of its PCs were sold through traditional channels.

Talking about the potential for taking their business on-line, an IBM official said:

> *"We have to look at market readiness. The environment here is different from the one in the US. And Asia-Pacific is not as comfortable right now with e-commerce the way the US is."*[23]

IBM reported Internet sales of US$3.3 billion in 1998, and the company anticipated that this figure would grow to US$10 billion for 1999.

In the midst of a tense PC market in China and bearing in mind that Dell's three golden rules (disdain inventory, listen to customers and never sell indirectly) were not to be broken, Aaron Loke was to report to the Asia-Pacific regional head office on the strategy for expansion. Could the direct model take Dell to the number two position? Was the target for on-line sales realistic and how could this be achieved? Was Dell to be a box-seller in China or was there a demand for services and support? How should Dell pursue its on-line global strategy?

Endnotes

1. "Dell Paves the Way for a New Level of Direct Economics and Customer Benefits", 14 April, 1997, URL:http://www.dell.com/corporate/media/newsreleases/97/9704/14.htm, August 1999.

2. Dell, M., & Fredman, C., (1999), *Direct from Dell: Strategies that Revolutionized an Industry*, London: HarperCollinsPublishers, p. 11.

3. Dell, M., & Fredman, C., (1999), p. 26.

4. Dell, M., & Fredman, C., (1999), p. 28.

5. "Be Quick and Focused; Global Markets Surging Ahead, Dell CEO Says", (27 January, 1995), URL: www.dell.com/corporate/media/newsreleases/95/9501/27.htm, August 1999.

6. US Department of Commerce, "The Emerging Digital Economy", 15 April, 1998, URL: http://www.ecommerce.gov/emerging.htm, August 1999.

7. Dell, M., & Fredman, C., (1999), p. 225.

8. "Internet Benefits to Customers, Company Expanding; Online Sales Reach $30 Million Per Day", Dell Computer Corporation, URL: http://www.dell.com/corporate/media/newsreleases/99/9908/17.htm, September 1999.

9. US Department of Commerce, (1999).

10. "Dell Paves the Way for a New Level of Direct Economics and Customer Benefits", 14 April, 1997, URL: http://www.dell.com/corporate/media/newsreleases/97/9704/14.htm, August 1999.

11. "What does No. 1 do for an Encore?", *Newsweek*, 2 November, 1998.

12. "Dell Joins with Unisys and Wand Global to Expand Service Offering for Global Customers", 11 May, 1998, URL: http://www.dell.com/corporate/media/newsreleases/98/9805/11.htm, August 1999.

13. Ong, C., "Crunch Time for Resellers as Direct PC Selling Grows", *South China Morning Post*, 20 April, 1999.

14. Chowdhury, N., "Dell Cracks China", *Fortune*, 21 June, 1999.

15. Chowdhury, (1999).

16. Chowdhury, (1999).

17. Hamm, S., (1995), "Sound the Gong", *PCWeek On-line*, URL: http://www.zdnet.com/~pcweek/inside/0724/tgong.html, September 1999.

18. Tse, S., & Tsang, P., (Last Update 2 July, 1997) "Internet and WWW in China: All the Right Connections", AUG95 & Asia-Pacific World Wide Web '95 Conference & Exhibition, URL: http://www.csu.edu.au/special/conference/apwww95/papers95/stse/stse.html, September 1999.

19. Tse, S., & Tsang, P., (Last Update 2 July, 1999).

20. Chowdhury, N., (1999).

21. Ong, C., "Compaq Axes US Retail Outlets, but Keeps China Plan", *South China Morning Post*, 11 May, 1999.

22. Ong, C., "Crunch Time for Resellers as Direct PC Selling Grows', *South China Morning Post*, 20 April, 1999.

23. Ong, C., "Asia Not Affected by IBM Direct-Sales Plan," *South China Morning Post*, 13 April, 1999.

eBay.com—Profitably Managing Growth from Start-up to 2000

Dale Pudney and Marius van der Merwe
University of Cape Town

Gary J. Stockport
University of Western Australia

Introduction

It was the 21st of November 2000, and Meg Whitman was considering the events of the last few days. As the Chief Executive Officer (CEO), she had led eBay.com to its position as the world's largest person-to-person (P2P) trading community, but the share price had just fallen 20 percent to US$34.75 when eBay's share was downgraded from a *"buy"* to a *"neutral"* by Lehman Brothers, a global investment bank because of concerns over eBay's aggressive sales forecasts. The previous day, eBay had announced the launch of a new product, application programming interface software that would enable other web companies to display eBay auctions on their sites.

The company had experienced explosive growth from start-up when the founder and current Chairman, Pierre Omidyar, launched eBay in September 1995. Whilst most e-commerce companies were making significant losses by spending aggressively to build their customer and revenue bases, eBay had remained profitable since the beginning. In the 3-month period to September 2000, US$1.4 billion worth of goods were transacted on eBay with items listed in more than 4,320 categories. The company had 18.9 million registered users at the end of the period and eBay had captured over 80 percent of the

on-line auction market with its closest competitors being Yahoo! and Amazon.com.

Background to eBay

Pierre Omidyar

Pierre Omidyar was born in Paris, France in 1967 and moved to Washington, D.C. USA, with his parents at the age of 6. From an early age he was interested in computers and he wrote a program to print catalogue cards for the school library at the age of 14. In 1988, he graduated with a Bachelors degree in Computer Science from Tufts University. He initially worked as a developer of consumer application software such as MacDraw, for Claris, a software subsidiary of Apple Computer. In 1991, he was one of the founders of Ink Development which later became eShop, an early e-commerce site that was bought by Microsoft in 1996.

Person-to-Person (P2P) Trading prior to 1995

In traditional P2P trading forums, it is sometimes difficult for buyers to find pricing benchmarks to ensure that the prices that they pay correspond to the proper value of the item. It was estimated that in 1995, US$100 billion was traded annually in the following forums:

- *Newspaper classifieds* – Users listed items that were for sale or wanted, normally in locally distributed newspapers. The classifieds typically generated more than 50 percent of local newspaper's revenues from listing fees. The buyers usually inspected the items before purchasing and may have collected and paid for the items in person. As a consequence of the proximity of buyers and sellers, the items could have been larger items that were difficult to transport over long distances.

This case study was written by Dale Pudney and Marius van der Merwe, MBA students at the University of Cape Town, under the supervision of Professor Gary J. Stockport, Graduate School of Management, University of Western Australia. It is intended to be used as the basis for class discussion rather than to illustrate either effective or ineffective handling of a management situation.

This case was compiled from published sources.

© 2001 G J Stockport, University of Western Australia, Perth, Australia.

Distributed by The European Case Clearing House, England and USA.

North America, phone: +1 781 239 5884, fax: +1 781 239 5885, e-mail: ECCHBabson@aol.com.

Rest of the World, phone: +44 (0)1234 750903, fax: +44 (0)1234 751125, e-mail: ECCH@cranfield.ac.uk.

All rights reserved. Printed in UK and USA. Web Site: http://www.ecch.cranfield.ac.uk.

- *Flea markets and garage sales* – Sellers stocked items for sale either at their homes or at organised markets. Buyers were typically looking for bargains or interesting artefacts. The buyers were able to inspect the items and needed to pay for them before they could collect.
- *Auction houses* – Sellers took items that were for sale to auction houses where buyers could inspect them before the auction. Buyers needed to pay a registration fee in order to bid and were required to be at the auction or have a proxy bidder. The highest bidder won the auction and normally paid the auction house. The auction house typically deducted a percentage of the sale price and paid the balance to the seller.

The Opportunity

In the early 1990s, Silicon Valley was quickly turning its attention away from electronics manufacturers towards new Internet-based start-ups that married existing technology to new business models. Internet usage growth and the provision of the infrastructure required to ensure acceptable data transmission speeds were however uncertain. Analysts were also unsure whether people would buy goods of value from distant strangers without seeing them beforehand. Omidyar was writing code for communications-software maker General Magic in 1995 when he started to think about the possibility of online auctions. He said the following about his idea:

> *"I had been thinking about how to create an efficient marketplace – a level playing field, where everyone had access to the same information and could compete on the same terms as everyone else. Not just a site where big corporations sold stuff to consumers and bombarded them with ads, but rather one where people "traded" with each other. . . . I thought, if you could bring enough people together and let them pay whatever they thought something was worth . . . real values could be realised and it could ultimately be a fairer system – a win-win for buyers and sellers."[2]*

Start-Up in 1995

eBay (then AuctionWeb) was launched on Labour Day, 1st September 1995, using a web site that was hosted by Omidyar's US$30 per month Internet Service Provider (ISP). The site was located at *www.ebay.com*. The company operated from Omidyar's apartment with only the web site, a filing cabinet, an old school desk and a laptop computer. The site was not much more than a simple marketplace where sellers listed items and buyers bid for them. Omidyar made no guarantees about the goods

being sold, took no responsibility and settled no disputes. There were no fees, no registration, no search engine and for the first month, no customers.

Omidyar's only attempt at marketing was to list eBay on the National Centre for Supercomputing Applications' *"What's Cool"* site. Despite this, so many people visited the site that by February 1996 Omidyar had to institute a fee of 10c per listing to recoup the ISP costs which by then had risen to US$250 per month. By the end of March 1996, eBay showed a profit. Omidyar had kept his day job at General Magic but the traffic to the site became so intense that he had to concentrate on eBay full-time and the ISP asked him to take the site elsewhere. He therefore bought his own web server and installed it in his apartment.

Omidyar developed software that was capable of supporting a robust scalable web site and transaction processing system to provide real-time reporting on the current auctions. The system was scalable to reduce the initial investment but enabled expansions when an increasing number of auctions demanded it. A copy of the eBay home page in 2000 is given in Exhibit 1.

By July 1996, Omidyar needed to move the operation to a one-room office and hire a part-time employee. The risks that the business faced at that stage were substantial and with barriers to entry being low there was nothing to stop the large Internet players such as America Online (AOL) (ISP and Internet portal), Amazon.com (on-line book retailer) and Yahoo! (search engine and Internet portal) from stealing the opportunity. As the business was based on collectors' items, changes in the current fads could have affected the revenues significantly. At one stage, trading of Beanie Babies generated 7 percent of eBay's revenues.

The Business Concept

Omidyar asked one of his friends, Jeff Skoll, to join the company as its first President in August 1996 and his role was to turn the concept into a business. He had a Masters in Business Administration (MBA) degree from Stanford University and had wide experience in managing distribution channels of on-line news information, computer-consulting and computer rentals.

The business concept was to provide P2P auctions on the Internet. Using the Internet, buyers and sellers could access a larger market which was important for those collectors who could not find people with similar interests in their areas. By providing a marketplace for buyers and sellers to trade their collectibles on the Internet in an auction format, the buyers set the price for items based on demand. When more potential buyers bid on the items, sellers received higher prices. As the buyers and

Exhibit 1   eBay's Home Page

SOURCE: www.ebay.com (11/2000).

sellers may be from different parts of the US and even the world, the items that were sold were typically collectibles that were easy to deliver long distances.

The eBay process was simple and easy to understand. Sellers could list items for sale and pay a small listing fee which depended on where and how the listing was presented and whether the seller required a reserve price. The seller chose the auction duration during which buyers could bid for the item. At the end of the auction, eBay notified the seller and the winning bidder following which, they made their own arrangements for payment and delivery of the goods. The seller was also charged a percentage of the final value of the transaction. Over time, eBay added services to this simple model to improve the user experience and thereby increase user loyalty and retention. eBay has been profitable from start-up and although eBay's business was seasonal with volatile revenues, the company had maintained high gross margins of about 70-80 percent (see Table 1). The only costs of goods sold were computing infrastructure and customer service expenses. eBay's business model did not require it to keep any inventory, establish an extensive distribution network or have a large staff complement. Its product range was also determined by the size of its community and their listings and not by eBay's product development staff.

The listing fees and final value fees charged by eBay are shown in Tables 2 and 3. For example, if a seller

| Table 1 | Quarterly Financial Results and Statistics |

	1998				1999				2000		
	Q1	Q2	Q3	Q4	Q1	Q2	Q3	Q4	Q1	Q2	Q3
Financial data											
Revenue ('000s)	US$13,988	US$19,480	US$21,731	US$30,930	US$42,801	US$49,479	US$58,525	US$73,919	US$85,753	US$97,399	US$113,377
Gross profit ('000)		US$16,194	US$17,364	US$24,980	US$34,824	US$38,534	US$41,444	US$52,334	US$62,481	US$73,756	US$89,465
Gross margin		83.1%	79.9%	80.8%	81.4%	77.9%	70.8%	70.8%	72.9%	75.7%	78.9%
Operating expenses ('000s)		US$11,996	US$15,504	US$21,365	US$27,063	US$43,166	US$46,478	US$51,883	US$62,029	US$65,026	US$75,149
Net income ('000s)		US$2,729	US$461	US$2,639	US$3,765	US$816	US$1,186	US$4,895	US$6,288	US$11,590	US$15,211
Net profitability		14.0%	2.1%	8.5%	8.8%	1.6%	2.0%	6.6%	7.3%	11.9%	13.4%
Registered users		0.85 m	1.3 m	2.2 m	3.8 m	5.6 m	7.7 m	10.0 m	12.6 m	15.8 m	18.9 m
No. of auctions		6.6 m	9.2 m	13.6 m	22.9 m	29.3 m	36.2 m	41.0 m	53.6 m	62.5 m	68.5 m
Growth											
Revenue (per quarter)		39%	12%	42%	38%	16%	18%	26%	16%	14%	16%
Net income			−83%	472%	43%	−78%	45%	313%	28%	84%	31%
Registered users			53%	69%	73%	47%	38%	30%	26%	25%	20%
No. of auctions			39%	48%	68%	28%	24%	13%	31%	17%	10%
Auctions / registered user		7.1	6.2	6.0	5.2	4.7	4.1	4.3	4.0	3.6	
Revenue / auction		US$2.95	US$2.36	US$2.27	US$1.87	US$1.69	US$1.62	US$1.80	US$1.60	US$1.56	US$1.66

Notes: The registered users figures include everyone who had ever registered on the site and does not reflect currently active users.
The growth figures are growth per quarter.
Revenue figures exclude refunds to seller due to site outages.
SOURCE: eBay financial statements.

listed a collection of rare stamps on eBay and the maximum bid is US$24, they would have paid a 50¢ insertion fee when they listed the item, assuming that the listing was not *emphasised* in any way. They would also have paid 5 percent of the final sale price if the item was sold. eBay would have received US$1.60 for the listing if the auction closed. If the seller had a reserve price of US$24.50 on the item, the auction would not have closed, so eBay would have received the insertion fee and a 50¢ fee for the reserve price which was only payable if the item did not sell.

Building the Team

In June 1997, Omidyar and Skoll realised that they would need capital and management expertise if eBay was to realise its full potential. They approached venture capitalists Benchmark Capital who invested US$5 million for stock and warrants worth 22 percent of the company. Bob Kagle, a partner at Benchmark Capital, became a Board member of eBay. This money was never used but the agreement gave them access to Benchmark's network of potential CEOs, marketing gurus, consultants and bankers. eBay needed this to help them build the business and recruit talented management. One of the first members of the management team was Gary Bengier, who was hired in November 1997 as the Chief Financial Officer (CFO). He was responsible for developing the financial strategy and vision of the company and maintaining a corporate culture of financial discipline and prudence and for equipping eBay for an eventual public offering of its shares.

Benchmark persuaded Meg Whitman to leave her job as General Manager of Hasbro's pre-school division to become President and CEO of eBay. She was a strong and decisive executive without the need to dominate personality which meant that there was a good fit with eBay's existing culture of being open to the voices of customers and employees. Whitman was impressed by the fact that eBay was doing something that could not be done effectively off-line and by the emotional connection between the eBay users and the service. Whitman brought global marketing and brand management experience with her when she joined in February 1998. Her previous work included being a Vice President at Bain & Company and developing Stride Rite's Internet strategy. She had an MBA from Harvard Business School and a BA in Economics from Princeton.

Whitman recognised the need for other advisors on the Board who understood the challenges of expanding into new markets and could provide advice and feedback. Again, Benchmark was instrumental in finding people such as Howard Schultz, Chairman and CEO of

Starbucks, and Scott Cook, Chairman of Intuit. Whitman also went on to build her management team and details of the other top-level management at eBay are given in Exhibit 2.

Exhibit 2	Summary of eBay Management at November 2000

Pierre Omidyar (33), Founder and Chairman, oversees strategic direction and growth, model and site development and community advocacy. He has a B.S. in Computer Science from Tufts University. His previous jobs include founder, Ink Development Corp., developer of consumer applications for Claris, a subsidiary of Apple Computer and General Magic.

Meg Whitman (43), President and CEO, responsible for building a successful business while delivering on customer needs and expectations. Her focus is on the user experience, creating a fun, efficient and safe forum for on-line person-to-person trading. She develops the work ethic and culture of eBay as a fun, open and trusting environment and keeps the organisation focused on the big-picture objectives and key priorities. She has an MBA from Harvard and a BA in Economics from Stanford. Previous jobs include General Manager for Hasbro Inc.'s pre-school division, global marketing of Playskool and Mr. Potato Head brands; President and CEO of Florists Transworld Delivery, President of Stride Rite division, Executive Vice President at Keds Division, Senior Vice President of Marketing for the Walt Disney Company's consumer products, Vice President at Bain & Co; and Brand Manager at Procter & Gamble.

Gary Bengier (45), Chief Financial Officer, responsible for developing the financial strategy and vision as well as maintaining a corporate culture of financial discipline and prudence for eBay. He has an MBA from Harvard and a BBA in Computer Science and Operations Research, Kent State University. Previous jobs include CFO, Vxtreme, Financial Officer at Compass Design Automation and senior financial posts at Kenetech Corp. and Qume Corp.

Brian Swette (45) Chief Operating Officer, helps build the eBay community as well as creating an environment for trade by responding to the community and introducing new categories. He has a BA in Economics degree from Arizona State University. His previous jobs include Executive Vice President and Chief Marketing Officer, Pepsi-Cola Company responsible for world-wide marketing and advertising efforts for Pepsi and Brand Manager at Procter & Gamble.

Maynard Webb (43) President, eBay Technologies, oversees eBay's technology strategies, engineering, architecture and site operations. He has a BA from Florida Atlantic University. Previous jobs include Senior Vice President and CIO at Gateway, Inc.

Mike Wilson, Chief Scientist, responsible for site architecture. Previous jobs include Chief Architect and Project Manager at Ink Development Corp.

Jeff Skoll (35), Vice President, Strategic Planning and Analysis, responsible for competitive analysis, new business planning and incubation as well as overall strategic direction. He has an MBA from Stanford University and a B.S. in Electrical Engineering from the University of Toronto. His previous jobs include manager of the distribution channels of on-line news information for Knight-Ridder Information and founder of Skoll Engineering.

Steve Westly, Senior Vice President, International and General Manager of Premium Services responsible for business development, corporate communications, mergers, acquisitions and partnerships. He has an MBA and B.A. from Stanford University. Previous jobs include Vice President, WhoWhere?

Jeff Jordan, Vice President and General Manager of Regionals and Services, oversees eBay's regional business and end-to-end services which has the goal of making it easier to trade on the site. He has an MBA from Stanford University and a B.A. Political Science and Psychology from Amherst College. Previous jobs include President of Reel.com.

SOURCE: www.ebay.com (11/2000).

Building the Community of Users

Many of eBay's early customers were the result of referrals. eBay's loyal customers performed the marketing and sales function through word of mouth to bring new customers *to the community*. eBay undertook limited marketing but had entered into cross promotional agreements with the following:

- Banner advertisement on Web Portals such as Netscape, Excite and Yahoo!.
- America Online (AOL) – provided an auction service for AOL's classified section which gave eBay access to AOL's more than 10 million users.
- ZAuction, a vendor-sourced auction site which was a leading provider of computer products, electronic equipment and other brand name consumer goods.

Omidyar created a platform where *"anybody could sell anything"* and did not interfere in the user transactions. Most of eBay's sellers were serious collectors and small traders who used eBay as their storefront to access a large market across the US and the world. eBay provided a facility whereby users could interact with each other through the use of discussion boards and later through a chat room called the *eBay Café*. The *eBay Café* was similar to a traditional coffee shop where users could relax, catch up on news and hearsay and exchange information. It brought users back to the site every day and they sometimes communicated directly with each other. One frequent user of the *eBay Café* described it as follows:

> *"At the eBay Café you will meet a bunch of caring and friendly folks talking, helping, laughing, and at times even complaining about varied subjects. I have found and met some great folks here. If you ever need help with almost ANYTHING, if you have some tips, tricks or a good story or two to share . . . the Café is the place."*[2]

When eBay tried to impose changes on users such as pricing changes, the users expressed their disappointment through these discussion forums. It trusted the users for suggestions to improve the site and by giving the customers what they wanted, eBay was improving both customer retention and loyalty. One analyst commented that eBay's community was critical for attracting and retaining buyers and sellers:

> *"eBay has found a natural feedback loop where creating a critical mass of bidders increases the price obtained by sellers, which increases the number of sellers, which attracts more bidders, et cetera."*[2]

Initially, there was no way to ensure that what was being bought was real or that the goods would be paid for. The anonymity and physical distance between buyers and sellers on the Internet encouraged counterfeiting and fraud. In message-board postings to Omidyar, the eBay users suggested that he set up a system for buyers and sellers to rate each other. This became known as the Feedback Forum and was a peer-review reporting system. Buyers and sellers rated each other and comment on how their business together went. When launching this, Omidyar laid out eBay's guiding philosophy:

> *"eBay wouldn't exist if it wasn't for our community. . . . At eBay, our customer experience is based on how our customers deal with our other customers. They rarely deal directly with the company. So how do you control the customer-to-customer experience? We can't control how one person treats another. . . . The only thing we can do is to influence customer behaviour by encouraging them to adopt certain values. And those values are to assume that people are basically good, to give people the benefit of the doubt, and to treat people with respect."*[2]

Company Values

Omidyar hoped that his auction community would reflect the values of honesty, openness, equality, empowerment, trust, mutual respect and mutual responsibility. eBay's Mission Statement says:

> *"eBay was founded with the belief that people are honest and trustworthy. We believe that each of our customers, whether a buyer or a seller, is an individual who deserves to be treated with respect."*[45]

To instil these values into the community, Omidyar maintained that they had to be embraced by the company and its employees because everything that the company did such as the web site, press releases and strategic partnerships indirectly influenced the community. When Meg Whitman joined eBay her challenge was to develop the work ethic and culture of eBay as a fun, open and trusting environment and keep the organisation focused on the big-picture objectives and key priorities. eBay had a *"no penalty"* operating culture where there were no penalties for making mistakes or being on the wrong side of an issue which could *muzzle* employees or suppress new ideas. Whitman met with all new recruits and other staff on Mondays to tell them about the culture and make sure that they knew what was expected of them. eBay also brought some of its customers to the head offices regularly to talk to employees about their experiences.

Coping with Customer Service

By the end of 1997, more than 3 million items worth US$94 million had been sold on eBay resulting in total revenues of US$5.7 million and US$900,000 profit. eBay had achieved these results with only 76 employees. The average value of each item sold was about US$31 with 6 percent of this going to eBay's revenues. The number of auctions per day had increased from 1,500 at the end of 1996 to about 150,000 at the end of 1997. As the number of users increased, eBay started to find it difficult to provide customer service to the members of the community. Simple questions such as *"How do I list an item?"* or *"How do I buy an item?"* were answered using a self-service on-line help function which had prominent links from the eBay home page. Other queries were more difficult and needed knowledgeable users or service agents to answer. Users placed queries on bulletin boards dedicated to the discussion of specific issues of the business such as help, registration, listing and shipping, which were sometimes answered by other members of the community and at other times by eBay. As part of building their on-line community, eBay had contracted active, enthusiastic and knowledgeable users of the site to respond to requests for help. These independent contractors worked from home to answer emailed questions and those that were posted on the bulletin boards. eBay also decided to employ and supervise the customer service representatives directly to better understand the customer problems and control the quality of customer service. Nevertheless, not all of the users were satisfied with the customer service that eBay offered.

Building Trust and Loyalty

To work with the community to improve the services which were offered and develop trust and loyalty, eBay launched *SafeHarbor* in February 1998. *SafeHarbor* included the following elements:

- *Verified User Program* – eBay verified user information during registration and had partnered with Equifax to provide a higher level of verification if required.
- *Feedback Forum* - buyers and sellers rated their experience with each other as positive, neutral or negative. The user profile followed the user everywhere on eBay. Estimates suggested that users were willing to pay up to 30 percent more in certain markets for items sold by someone with a high feedback rating.
- *Insurance* - Lloyds of London provided insurance for users with a net non-negative feedback rating on their auctions up to US$200 subject to an excess of US$25.
- *Shill Bidding Policy* – suspended users who bid on an item with the intent to drive up the price without buying it.
- *Non-paying Bidder Policy* – non-paying bidders were warned and then suspended.

eBay's policies and service had helped them to develop a loyal community of buyers and sellers. One user described the eBay experience as follows.

"I visit eBay to transact auction business because it has a superior universe of sellers and bidders and quality and quantity of listings. The people visiting eBay are generally loyalists, while the average person visiting Amazon.com is there to buy a book, but I'd hazard a guess that he isn't going to stick around for an hour."[27]

eBay also provided facilities that users could personalise and these were the *"My eBay"* and *"About Me"* sections. *"My eBay"* was a tool that users could personalise to keep track of their favourite categories, view items they were selling or bidding on, check their recent account balance and feedback or up-date their contact information. An *"About Me"* page could be set up by users to tell other eBay users about themselves and their feedback rating which helped to improve the credibility and trust amongst the users. Not all users were however happy with the services and this can be seen in the following message taken from the discussion boards.

"Am I the only one that thinks the "Watch This Item" link in auctions is driving sellers to the poorhouse? Geez . . . Bidding is bad enough without encouraging bidders not to bid."[2]

Exhibit 3 contains a typical auction listing which indicates the auction listing and details the seller's and bidders' details, feedback ratings and links to their home pages and the bid history.

Brand Building

In a company that had always disdained advertising, Whitman employed Pepsi's Head of Marketing, Brian Swette, as Senior Vice President of Marketing in October 1998 to oversee international expansion, marketing and customer support efforts for eBay. He had worldwide brand building experience with both the Pepsi-Cola Company and Proctor & Gamble. His focus was on increasing brand awareness both nationally and internationally and to make eBay one of the most accessible and successful e-commerce sites on the Internet.

eBay found that serious collectors and small traders were the most active site users. Many of the traders were small businesses who had used eBay as their storefront or as a supplement to their existing stores. These users contributed 80 percent of the total revenues but only constituted 20 percent of the registered users. As a result, eBay decided to reduce its presence in broadband portals and concentrate its marketing and brand building resources on these users. This included advertising in many niche publications read by serious collectors and exhibiting at collectors' Trade Shows. eBay subsequently launched its first national print and broadcast advertising campaign in October 1998 in order to increase awareness of the company's brand with *The Acme Idea Company*, a strategic and creative consultancy committed exclusively to the building of brands. The national radio campaign was aired on more than 12,000 stations across the US for 5 weeks. The print campaign included adverts in Parade, People, Entertainment Weekly, Newsweek and Sports Illustrated and over 70 distinct collecting publications, reaching people who had an active passion, for example, for coins, stamps, dolls and photography.

eBay also instituted the *PowerSellers program* to benefit the bulk sellers. The *PowerSellers program* was designed to meet the needs of users who were running a full-time on-line trading business on eBay with benefits and privileges designed to make selling easier and more profitable. There were 3 different program levels namely: Bronze, Silver and Gold, which were achieved with minimum monthly sales on eBay of US$2,000, US$10,000 and US$25,000 respectively. eBay offered these users additional services depending upon the level that they had achieved. These benefits included the PowerSellers Logo to distinguish users on the site, dedicated email customer support, participation in eBay Success Stories Program (to be profiled for use in press-related events), invitations to special events, specialist customer phone support, dedicated account managers and support hotlines.

A member of the *PowerSeller* customer-service program complained that her e-mail and phone calls regularly went unanswered:

> *"I feel like I'm in a co-dependent relationship. I write to them, I get no response. I e-mail them, nothing. I'm being abused."*[2]

On 25th March 1999, eBay and AOL expanded their existing relationship and announced a 4-year strategic alliance to expand person-to-person commerce and community building on AOL and its family of brands. The agreement gave eBay prominent presence across the domestic and international AOL family of brands including AOL, AOL.com, CompuServe, Netscape's Netcenter, ICQ and Digital City. According to the agreement, eBay was to pay AOL US$75 million over the term of the agreement and AOL was entitled to all advertising revenues generated by the co-branded sites and to act as the exclusive third-party advertising sales force for advertising sold on eBay's web site. They created customised and co-branded sites for AOL's multiple brands that included comprehensive listings, feedback and ratings, message boards and select content from eBay. eBay was to promote AOL as its preferred Internet ISP and enabled its users to download ICQ (communication software that enables chat, voice, message board, data conferencing, file transfer or games on the Internet) on its web site as well as integrate AOL's *"My News"* feature into its *"My eBay"* feature. AOL, in return, undertook to promote eBay to its member community of over 16 million members. As a part of the agreement, the companies were to work together to facilitate eBay's expansion into international markets and AOL helped launch eBay's expansion into regional markets through the promotion of eBay on Digital City, a complete guide to activities in the US's largest cities.

The Challenges of Growth

Table 1 contains eBay's key quarterly financial results from the beginning of 1998 to the 3rd quarter of 2000, indicating its growth and profitability during this period. eBay never had any formal plan to develop the business but rather took advantage of opportunities as they arose. Opportunistic behaviour was bound by a clear goal to be *"the world's largest P2P online auction company"* and a focused strategy with 5 elements:

- Strengthening the eBay brand
- Expanding the user base
- Broadening the trading platform by increasing product categories and promoting new ones
- Fostering community affinity
- Enhancing site features and functionality

International Expansion

While the Internet was available to users around the world, trading goods across borders involved difficulties such as currency conversions, different duties, taxes and regulations, as well as high delivery costs. To build their user base and access the users in other countries, eBay needed to open country specific sites and started to expand into the international markets early in 1999. The company identified the following possible strategies to enter these new markets:

- Building a new user community
- Acquiring a company that was already in the local trading market
- Partnering with strong local companies

eBay started its international expansion in the UK and Canada (*www.ca.ebay.com*). eBay's community in the UK (*www.ebay.co.uk*) was built from grassroots by local management with on-line marketing and local events. eBay rolled this service out to Germany (*www.ebay.de*),

Exhibit 3   Typical Auction Listing

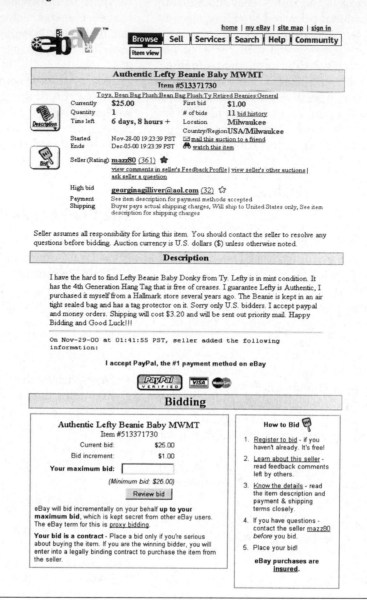

SOURCE: www.ebay.com (11/2000).

Australia (*www.ebay.com.au*), Japan (*www.ebayjapan.co.jp*) and France (*www.fr.ebay.com*).

In March 1999, some German entrepreneurs copied eBay's source code and set up a mirror image of the eBay site under the name of *Alando.de* in Germany. The site quickly established itself as the leading on-line trading company among Germany's 10 million Internet users and soon attracted eBay's attention. When it acquired *Alando* on 22nd June 1999, it had 50,000 registered users and 80,000 items listed in 500 categories. The site was later renamed *www.ebay.de*, which gave German users

access to eBay's worldwide community of active buyers and sellers.

eBay launched its local site in Australia in October 1999 in a joint venture with a leading Internet media company in Australia, PBL Online. To promote the launch of the web site, eBay Australia waived all listing fees for a limited period and this provided sellers with an even greater reason to list their items on www.ebay.com.au. In February 2000, eBay Japan was launched as a joint venture with NEC. The deal brought together eBay's unrivalled trading presence and NEC, one of the world's most innovative technology companies with a commanding presence in the Japanese market. As part of the agreement, NEC took an equity stake in eBay Japan and promoted the site in many ways including through its BIGLOBE Internet Service Provider (ISP), personal computer products and off-line marketing campaigns. The international sites contain:

- Country-specific categories and content, reflecting popular local collectibles.
- The ability to trade local items in the local currency with content in the local language
- Access to a worldwide community of traders. International sellers can list their item so that it can be viewed from any eBay site and buyers can view items listed anywhere in the world, with items denominated in the local currency and in US$s.
- Local discussion boards that allow the country's community to get the most out of the web site and a country specific chat room.

Amazon.com Enters the On-line Auction Market

New competitors in the on-line auction market were surfacing everyday, encouraged by the low barriers to entry and eBay's success. The first major competitor was Onsale which was already an established B2C site. Yahoo!, Lycos, Excite, Microsoft's MSN and many smaller niche competitors followed but all of them found that attracting buyers and sellers was difficult. Table 4 compares a few of the major on-line auctions sites as at October 2000 by their inventory of listed items, bidding activity, services and fees, design and functionality, customer support and the community.

In April 1999, Amazon.com launched its auction site which was remarkably similar to eBay's and made it easy for buyers and sellers to move across to Amazon. Amazon did not charge any fees for the first few months and offered additional services such as cross promotion to relevant Amazon retail sites, credit card payments and buyer guarantees by underwriting the risks of a seller failing to send an item or where the item is *"materially different"* from the description. Amazon achieved 100,000 auctions per day within a few months but the number of listings started to fall when Amazon introduced charges. Whilst the services they offered were superior to eBay's, they were not able to break into the market that was already dominated by eBay. One of the sellers summarised his reasons for staying with eBay:

"I've posted auctions on just about every site you can imagine (but) I pretty much stick with eBay. The buyers are there. I'm established there. My feedback rating establishes
me as an upstanding member of the community. I don't have those ratings on other sites because I don't do much business on any of them. I'd rather stay where I'm known."[2]

By being the first on-line auction to be able to scale up and acquire a critical mass of buyers and sellers in its community of users, eBay was able to successfully fend off attacks from Internet brands that were better recognised and offered better services. eBay's *community of buyers* meant that sellers were less likely to move to competitor sites.

Improved Customer Service Required

Following Amazon's launch with superior services, eBay launched services to assist their community with shipping (April 1999), credit card payments, escrow services, electronic stamps and a customer support centre (May 1999). These services were offered by entering into alliances with:

- iShip.com provided information to e-merchants and buyers regarding shipping costs and options
- MBE provided the bricks-and-mortar support for packing and shipping
- Billpoint facilitated person-to-person credit card payments on the Internet
- iEscrow enabled buyers to pay an escrow service when they bought an item. This was when a buyer placed money in the custody of a trusted escrow service. The money was then paid to the seller once a specified set of conditions was met such as the buyer receiving and approving the goods.
- e-Stamp allowed people to buy and print postage online to avoid queues at post offices where sellers needed to hand letters that weigh more than 16 ounces directly to a postal clerk.

eBay established its first remote customer support centre in Salt Lake City in order to stay ahead of the needs of the on-line community. Their main responsibility was to interact via email with the eBay community on a 24-hour basis and provide live customer support on eBay's customer support bulletin boards, such as the *"Support Q&A Board"*, *"Support Q&A For New Users"* and *"Help with Images and HTML"*. One user described his experience of eBay's customer support.

"I think we should spread the word for people to start using Amazon.com. Maybe then eBay will increase their customer service and see to it that their system is working instead of pissing people off. No wonder they are offering Billpoint for free. You can't count on it. eBay is not there to help. At least not readily. I have sent 3 emails to support and have heard NOTHING."[1]

Table 4 — Auction Site Competitor Comparison

Auction Site	Inventory	Bidding Activity	Services & Fees	Customer Support	Design & Functionality	Community
321Gone	○	○	○	●	●	○
Amazon.com	■	○	■	●	■	○
AuctionAddict.com	○	·	●	●	○	○
Auctions.com	●	○	●	●	●	·
Bid.com	·	·	●	●	○	N/A
BidBay.com	○	·	●	●	○	○
BoxLot	○	○	●	●	○	○
CityAuction	○	○	●	●	●	○
CNET Auctions	●	○	○	○	●	·
Collecting Nation	○	○	●	●	○	●
Comic Exchange	●	○	●	○	●	○
Dell Auction	○	○	●	●	●	·
eBay	■	●	●	●	●	■
edeal	○	○	●	●	○	●
eHammer	●	■	●	●	○	·
eOrbis.com	○	·	●	■	●	·
eRock.net	○	·	○	○	●	●
eWanted.com	○	○	●	●	●	○
Excite Auctions	○	○	■	●	○	·
First Auction	○	●	○	●	●	N/A
Gavelnet.com	○	·	●	●	●	○
GoAuction	●	○	●	●	●	·
Gold's Auction	○	·	■	●	●	●
Go Network Auction	○	·	●	●	●	○
Haggle Online	○	○	●	○	●	○
Lycos Auctions	○	○	●	■	●	○
MSN Auctions	●	○	●	○	○	○
Musichotbid.com	●	·	○	■	○	·
Onsale	●	●	○	●	○	N/A
Popula	○	●	●	●	○	●
Pottery Auction	○	○	●	■	●	○
Sothebys.com	■	●	●	●	●	N/A
SportsAuction	●	N/A	○	●	●	N/A
Teletrade	○	N/A	●	●	○	N/A
uBid	●	●	●	■	●	N/A
Up4Sale	●	○	○	○	●	○
Wantads.com	●	○	●	●	●	·
Xoom.com Auctions	●	○	●	●	●	○
Yahoo Auctions	■	●	●	·	■	○
Yahoo Store	●	N/A	●	○	■	N/A
ZDNet Auctions	●	●	●	○	○	○

■ = excellent; ● = good; ○ = average; · = below average
SOURCE: www.auctionwatch.com/awdaily/reviews/ratings.html (11/2000).

Case 13 / eBay.com—Profitably Managing Growth from Start-up to 2000 eBay still did not have its customer support up to the level of its competitors and this remained a problem for the users.

eBay Acquires Bricks-and-Mortar Businesses

With the on-line auction market being so competitive, eBay found it difficult to increase its fees. The only way to increase its revenues was to improve the traffic volumes by deepening the penetration into the North American market, expand internationally and raise the average price of goods sold. On 26th April 1999, eBay announced that it had agreed to acquire San Francisco based Butterfield & Butterfield (B&B), one of the world's largest and most prestigious auction houses. This acquisition enabled eBay to accelerate its penetration into higher priced items on a global basis because of B&B's expertise in premium markets and extensive relationships with dealers, auction houses and individuals throughout North America, Europe and Asia. B&B had begun providing auctions over the Internet through its relationship with a local company, but ended the arrangement 3 weeks prior to the announcement in order to work with eBay. eBay used this acquisition to start its *"great collections"* speciality site and other antique categories. Prior to this acquisition, eBay's average auction closed at only about US$47, of which eBay's fee was about US$3. The average B&B auction closed at US$1,400, of which the house's fee was almost US$400. Buying into the high-end auction business might not have increased the amount of interaction on the discussion boards or chat rooms but it promised to boost eBay's revenues. Shortly afterwards, on the 18th May 1999, eBay announced that it had acquired Kruse International, one of the world's most respected and well-established brands in the collector automobile market. This strategic acquisition enabled eBay to move into this market and continue to offer higher priced items to its community. Kruse participated in approximately 40 car auctions each year and had held events in 46 US states, the United Kingdom and Japan. eBay used expertise gained through this acquisition and other alliances with CarClub.com and Autotrader.com to introduce a new automotive section on the eBay site for collectable and other used cars and offer users related additional services.

eBay Introduces Local Sites

To further increase eBay's penetration into higher priced goods, eBay accessed the market for goods that were difficult to ship long distances such as cars and large appliances that would have normally been sold through the local newspaper classifieds owing to their size or fragile nature. Late in 1999, eBay launched *"eBay: Go Local"* with a campaign called *"from our homepage to your hometown"* whereby eBay toured 30 communities across the US, and introduced a pilot site in Los Angeles. At the end of 1999, there was a local site for 63 cities in the US and others internationally, with a regional flavour in order to connect local buyers and sellers. Buyers could also inspect the goods before they bid. The separate local sites were accessible through the "Go Local" area on the eBay home page.

Exhibit 4 gives a picture of eBay's Miami local page. eBay Local featured local categories and allowed members to browse through and trade items of local interest such as memorabilia from popular regional sports teams, political collectibles and antique postcards celebrating the region's heritage. The local site was completely integrated into eBay's worldwide listings so sellers could list locally while everyone on eBay could see the item.

Computing Infrastructure

The aggressive marketing and expansion during late 1998 and early 1999 resulted in rapid increases in demand upon the computing infrastructure that supported the on-line auctions. By the end of June 1999, eBay had 5.6 million registered users and had conducted 29.4 million auctions (about 250,000 per day) with gross merchandise sales of US$622 million during the previous 3-month period. The increasing traffic to the web site required constant expansion and up-grading of the technology. Frequent site outages and downtime for maintenance was a serious problem for the growing company. A number of the small traders, who depended on eBay for a living, attributed the *"downs"* in their business to site crashes, pages not loading, system slowdowns and slow end-of-auction notices. During June 1999, eBay experienced a 3-day string of outages because of problems with eBay's server operating system software which corrupted their databases. A report of the event even appeared on the front page of the New York Times and it was estimated that these outages cost the company between US$3-5 million in refunds to sellers. The share price fell by 25 percent and the web page viewing figures halved for the week after the outage. Other costs that could not be quantified were the lost revenues from those customers who got frustrated with the site and defected to competitors' sites. eBay instituted an automatic auction extension policy which meant that any outage lasting for 2 hours or more, resulted in an automatic lengthening in the time allowed to place bids. As a result of the outages, Whitman decided to build excess

Exhibit 4   eBay Miami Home Page

SOURCE: www.ebay.com (11/2000).

capacity but she decided that the additional cost would be small when compared to the cost of outages and poor site performance. She set the goal of building the infrastructure to 10* the required capacity.

In October 1999, eBay outsourced its backend Internet technology to AboveNet Communications and Exodus Communications. It outsourced their web servers, database servers and Internet routers and relied on the companies to provide increased network bandwidth for its millions of active buyers and sellers. These companies had front-end web servers which were linked to eBay's proprietary database and application servers and were all located at AboveNet's and Exodus's locations. The servers were located in temperature-controlled facilities with superior fire control, security and redundant power systems and were housed in seismically braced racks. These companies were also the primary service provider for Yahoo!, Lycos and other major on-line companies.

Expanding the Product Range

As of August 1999, eBay's brand was recognised by 91 million US adults compared to 118 million for Amazon.com. eBay's challenge was however to turn this awareness of its brand into registered users (7.7 million at the time) and revenues. This was becoming more difficult as new competition was entering the market all the time. In September 1999, FairMarket.com announced that it would form an auction network including Microsoft's MSN, Excite@Home and Lycos. Alta Vista, Xoom.com, Outpost.com, ZDNet, CompUSA and Ticketmaster soon joined the network. Each of the networked sites accessed a single database so any auction that was listed on one of the sites was automatically listed on all of the other partner sites which increased the number of buyers that was available for each member. The FairMarket network was intended to appeal to the big brand names that did not want their items listed next to collectibles and other "*junk*". The eBay share price dropped 7 percent on the news. Amazon had also launched their zshops whereby merchants could retail their goods in a fixed price format which competed with the many small traders who used eBay as their storefront but did not require the sale to be in an auction format.

In order to increase its revenues with this increased competition, eBay acquired Half.com in June 1999, a fixed-price, person-to-person trading marketplace to broaden the buying and selling choices for eBay's trading community and expand eBay's trading platform. Half.com had created an efficient, user-friendly marketplace where buyers and sellers could trade used books, CDs, movies and video games at fixed prices that were at least half of the list price. In the first quarter of 2000, eBay also launched its Business Exchange site which was to enable small businesses to trade with each other in business related categories such as computer and industrial equipment, power tools, office furniture and consumables like printer toner. While some business-to-business trading had always taken place on the site, the intention of this site was to expand this and further increase eBay's reach into higher priced goods.

On the 8th February 2000, eBay and the Walt Disney Corporation announced a comprehensive 4-year agreement in which eBay would ultimately become the on-line trading service across all of Disney's Internet properties, including the GO Network portal. The companies intended to develop, implement and promote a co-branded person-to-person trading site for the GO Network at *www.ebay.go.com*. In addition, the companies collaborated on the development of several merchant-to-person trading sites in an auction format for Disney.com, ESPN.com and ABC.com that showcase unique, exclusive and authenticated products, props and memorabilia from throughout The Walt Disney Company, including Walt Disney Studios, Disneyland and Walt Disney World, ESPN Cable Networks and ABC Television.

On the 20th November 2000, eBay launched its Application Programming Interface (API) that would allow other companies to display eBay auctions on their independent web sites. Companies would be able to subscribe to specific auction and fixed price categories on the eBay site. eBay had developed the software themselves and the software made it easier for programmers to create software applications without having to write all the code for basic features like screen menus and printing capabilities. eBay executives believed that the syndicated listings would appeal to other Internet commerce and media sites that wanted to give users more shopping options without building their own stores. Web sites that wanted eBay listings would not receive any fees of transactions executed through their site unless they owned the listed items. The company believed that it would eventually be able to persuade some sites that already sold goods to replace their in-house e-commerce systems with eBay's technology.

eBay at the End of 2000

eBay had created a convenient, efficient and entertaining marketplace where buyers and sellers could list, bid for and trade goods. eBay was the intermediary and only provided the marketspace for buyers and sellers to trade and did not take any responsibility for the actual transaction. To attract and retain buyers and sellers, eBay gave users access to value added services that made the transaction simpler. To improve loyalty to the site, eBay had also developed an on-line community where collectors and other users could interact. The site created excitement for buyers who searched for and bid on items that they hoped would be bargain buys. As one customer noted:

> "I'd recommend eBay Auction services to everyone! I attend many estate auctions on a regular basis in the Kentucky area. I have found the same thrills on eBay as I do at the real estate public auctions."[45]

Most trading took place in an auction format where the trade took place between the seller and the highest bidder, if the bid was above the reserve price (where applicable). More details of the different auction formats are contained in Exhibit 5. eBay did not take any ownership in or agency for the goods. Their neutrality eliminates some of the concerns that face other businesses, such as sourcing and supplying goods, inventory, responsibility, payment collections or shipping. This was important for eBay to maintain as implementing systems to perform these functions would have significant costs associated with them and would require additional resources.

Auction Aggregators Introduce a New Threat

At the end of 1999, auction aggregators such as AuctionWatch.com started to pose a threat to individual on-line auctions like eBay. These sites acted as a portal and they collected data on the auctions that were available on the individual auction sites and displayed similar

Exhibit 5 | Comparison of Auction Formats

Dutch Auction: The seller places one or more identical items on sale for a minimum price for a set time. When the auction ends, the highest bidder wins the item(s) at their bid price. Remaining items are sold to other bidders in order of price, quality and time.

Reserve Price: The seller lists a *"reserve bid price."* Buyers are allowed to place bids for any amount above or below the reserve price but the seller has the option to disregard any of the bids below the reserve price. The bidders do not normally know the reserve price.

Express Auction: Short timed auctions generally lasting between one-half to one hour. The quick turn-around offers a heightened auction experience.

Reverse Auction: The seller and not the buyer bears the risk of not being successful. The buyer lists what is required at the price they are willing to pay for it. Sellers bid for the business. The bidder can remain anonymous, and a maximum price can be established to maintain the price within a budget. This type of auction format is not offered by eBay. Priceline.com is well known for offering reverse auctions.

Sealed Bid Auctions: Bidders are only aware of the reserve price and bid without knowing the amounts of other incoming bids. All bids are automatically opened at the end date of the auction and the highest bidder wins.

Sniping: Placing a bid in the closing minutes or seconds of an auction. Any bid placed before the auction ends is allowed on eBay but not on some other sites.

Proxy Bidding: Placing a proxy bid at the maximum limit users are willing to bid for an item, will result in the system bidding on the bidders behalf each time a new bidder places a bid. The system will ensure that the proxy bidder's bid is one increment higher than the previous bid until the user's maximum limit is reached.

SOURCE: Various.

---

items from the competing sites together. Buyers could therefore see all of the required items at one time and compare prices. This was a significant threat to eBay as their success in the past was because of its established community of buyers and sellers ensured that they chose eBay over other competitors. eBay installed technical measures to try to block AuctionWatch servers from accessing its web site. This only worked for about a month until AuctionWatch designed software to get through the security features. eBay consequently threatened legal action claiming that these sites were illegally accessing its site, making unauthorised copies of its content and displaying the content in incomplete and confusing ways. While the users provided most of the content on its site such as item descriptions and photographs, eBay maintained that the content that it generated (number of bids, length of the auction etc.) was its property.

Counterfeit, Illegal and Other Questionable Listings

Whilst on-line publishers are responsible for the content of their sites as an on-line venue, eBay was not according to the Digital Millennium Copyright Act (DMCA) of 1998. People were, however, selling illegal items such as human kidneys, marijuana, counterfeit software, controversial items such as Nazi memorabilia and pornographic material. Whilst eBay had adopted a hands-off approach to what its customers sold on the site, Shultz advised the Board that these items affected the character of the company and Bay consequently changed its description to a *"venue where anybody can sell practically anything on earth"* and issued a list of items that were restricted on the site.

eBay had faced several lawsuits questioning the eBay business model where people claimed that eBay should take responsibility for the authenticity of items sold on the site. An example of this was where eBay was sued by someone who bought a collectors baseball card that turned out to be a fake. Checking every item that is listed on the site would have required an army of content checkers and if eBay had tried to verify the legality of all of the items it probably would have been liable for those items that slipped through its inspections. On 21st November 2000, a French judge ordered Yahoo! to block French users from visiting web sites that sold Nazi memorabilia. This ruling meant that all web sites would be subject to the laws and norms of all other countries in the world, which was a move away from the US inspired openness and freedom ethos. Critics suspected that this ruling may have prompted other governments to police web sites in an attempt to get them to comply with their local laws.

The Future

In the 3rd quarter of 2000, US$1.4 billion worth of goods were traded on eBay in 68.5 million auctions, which generated US$113.4 million of revenues and US$15.2 million in net income for the company. At the end of September 2000, eBay had 18.9 million registered users. When releasing these results, eBay announced a revenue goal of US$3 billion in 2005 with sites in 25 countries, representing the majority of the world's Internet users. Table 5 gives the Nielsen NetRatings of the top 25 web sites for October 2000, where eBay received 17 million unique visitors who spent an average of 2 hours 10 minutes on the site for the month. What was important to Whitman was the fact that eBay was making a profit whilst many other e-commerce companies were making significant losses while building their user base and establishing distribution networks (see Table 6).

However, on the 20th November 2000, Lehman Brothers downgraded eBay's share from a *"buy"* to a *"neutral"* citing eBay's "aggressive 2005 sales projection" as a concern. The share price fell 20 percent on the news and the analyst at Lehman Brothers said that eBay's core business was slowing down and that the new business initiatives were more costly than initial estimates. The staff complement had increased with the growth which meant that the company was being challenged to maintain the culture and values among the new recruits. Whitman knew that her greatest challenge would be to keep eBay focused while growing the company. Considering the share downgrade, Whitman was sure that the analyst was over-reacting on the forecasts. Over the past 5 years, eBay had been an example of e-commerce success for Internet and bricks-and-mortar companies.

They had transformed the auction business which had allowed them to become the world's largest P2P online auction company, achieving a higher value than many established Fortune 500 companies. Overcoming challenges was an everyday part of the environment for which eBay had set the example. But the future may bring as many threats as there were opportunities.

Bibliography

eBay Web Site

1. www.ebay.com

Books

2. Bunnell, D. (2000). *The eBay Phenomenon: Business Secrets Behind the World's Hottest Internet.* John Wiley & Sons, Inc. USA.

Articles and Web Sites

3. Alsop. S. (1999). "Contemplating eBay's Funeral". *Fortune Magazine.* Vol. 139. No. 11.
4. Amazon.com Auctions. (2000). <http://www.amazon.com>
5. AuctionGuide.com. (2000). <http://www.auctionguide.com/dir/index.htm>
6. AuctionWatch. (2000). <http://www.auctionwatch.com/awdaily/reviews/>
7. Bloomberg News. (1999). 'eBay founders give up billions to repay loans'. Cnet.com. June <http://www.cnet.com> (23 Sept 2000)
8. Butterfield & Butterfield. (2000). <http://www.butterfields.com/>
9. CiscoWorld. (2000). Case Study: 'Keeping Outages at bay at eBay.' <http://www.ciscoworldmagazine.com/bsonline/outages.htm> (5 October 2000)
10. Clampet, E. (1999). 'eBay Enhances Services with Acquisitions'. May. <http://www.internews.com> (23 Sept 2000)
11. Cohen, A. (1999) "The eBay Revolution: How the online auctioneer triggered a revolution of its own." *Time Magazine.* <http://www.time.com> (16 Oct 2000)
12. Dayal, S., Landesberg, H. & Zeisser, M. (2000). "Building Digital Brands". *The McKinsey Quarterly.* Number 2, pp. 42–51.
13. eBay Annual Report. (1999). *Form 10-K: Annual Report for eBay Inc. for fiscal year ended December 31, 1998*
14. eBay Annual Report. (2000). *Form 10-K: Annual Report for eBay Inc. for fiscal year ended December 31, 1999*

Table 5 — Web Sites Audience and Average Time per Month

Ranking	Web Site	Unique Audience '000s	Time Per Person (hrs:min:sec)
1	AOL Websites	64,744	00:43:29
2	Yahoo!	63,720	01:41:00
3	MSN	51,424	01:19:37
4	Microsoft	34,614	00:12:31
5	Lycos Network	33,708	00:21:28
6	Excite@Home	32,085	00:35:09
7	Walt Disney Internet Group	27,076	00:33:41
8	Time Warner	23,250	00:24:14
9	About The Human Internet	22,262	00:10:45
10	Amazon	21,837	00:16:23
11	AltaVista	18,560	00:21:41
12	CNET Networks	18,525	00:16:06
13	NBC Internet	18,243	00:14:51
14	**eBay**	**17,010**	**02:10:49**
15	eUniverse Network	16,003	00:18:01
16	LookSmart	15,840	00:07:39
17	Ask Jeeves	14,671	00:10:30
18	Real Network	12,625	00:06:46
19	American Greetings	11,856	00:11:49
20	EarthLink	11,602	00:17:15
21	AT&T	11,196	00:15:45
22	Uproar	11,113	00:42:35
23	The Go2Net Network	10,752	00:13:25
24	GoTo.com	10,564	00:04:15
25	Viacom International	10,178	00:14:21

SOURCE: Nielsen NetRatings.

Case 13 / eBay.com—Profitably Managing Growth from Start-up to 2000

Table 6 — Comparison of Financial Performance Dot-Coms

Performance measure	eBay	Yahoo!	Priceline	Amazon
Revenues[1] (US$ million)	113.4	295.5	341.3	637.9
Net income[1] (US$ million)	15.2	47.7	(191.9)	(240.5)
Gross margin[2] (%)	74.58	85.45	15.40	21.06
Operating margin[2] (%)	2.35	27.46	−97.04	−33.08
Profit margin[2] (%)	7.50	21.33	−96.18	−35.79
Recent share price[3] (US$)	36.94	40.88	2.53	28.94
Market capitalisation[3] (US$ million)	9,895.62	22,825.54	426.50	10,306.96
Number of employees[4]	138	1,992	373	7,600

Notes: 1. Revenue and net income for three months to 30 September 2000.
2. Margins for 12 months to 30 September 2000.
3. Share price as at 24 November 2000.
4. Employees as at 31 December 1999.
SOURCE: www.marketguide.com (11/2000).

Exhibit 6 — A Brief History of Auctions

The auction format of selling emerged almost from the beginning of time, when man first began to barter trade with each other. The word "auction" is derived from a Latin word, which means a gradual increase.

The earliest record of an organised auction was of the annual marriage market of Babylon in about 500 BC. Once a year the men of Babylon would gather around while a herald (auctioneer) would accept bids for maidens. The herald would begin the auction with the most *"beautiful"* girls and work his way through to the *"ugliest"*. Ancient Romans also auctioned goods. One of the most astonishing auctions in history occurred in the year AD 193 when no less than the entire Roman Empire was *'tossed on the block'* by the Praetorian Guard. First they killed Pertinax, the Emperor, and then they announced that the highest bidder could claim the Empire. As the Roman Empire came to an end, there were fewer and fewer auctions.

The earliest reference to the auction, as practised in Great Britain, is from 1595, but there are no more references until the end of the 17th century. At that time, auctions were held in taverns and coffee houses to sell art. In the beginning of the 17th century, four types of auctions developed which shaped how current auctions are conducted today. The four types were:

1. Auctions using a *'hammer'* as we know it today.
2. *Hourglass Auctions* - Bids were accepted until the last grain of sand was left at the top of the hourglass. The last bid called before the glass was empty, won.
3. *Candle Auction* - The same idea as the hourglass auction.
4. *Dutch Auction* -This is when the auctioneer begins at a high price and quotes smaller and smaller bids until there is a buyer.

Sotheby's and Christies were founded in 1744 and 1766 respectively.

SOURCES: http://www.bendisauctions.com/origin.htm
http://iml.jou.ufl.edu/projects/Spring2000/McKonzie/History.html
http://www.webcom.com/agorics/auctions/auction9.html

15. eBay Quarterly Financial Statements. (2000). *Form 10-Q: Quarterly Report for eBay Inc. for the quarterly period ended June 30, 2000.*

16. eBay Quarterly Financial Statements. (2000). *Form 10-Q: Quarterly Report for eBay Inc. for the quarterly period ended March 31, 2000.*

17. eBay Quarterly Financial Statements. (2000). *Form 10-Q: Quarterly Report for eBay Inc. for the quarterly period ended September 30, 2000.*

18. eBay.com (2000) http://www.ca.ebay.com (Canada).

19. eBay.com (2000) http://www.ebay.co.uk (United Kingdom).

20. eBay.com (2000) http://www.ebay.com.au (Australia).

21. eBay.com (2000) http://www.ebayjapan.co.jp (Japan).

22. eBay.com (2000) http://www.fr.ebay.com (France).

23. Ellington, D., Ficeli, D., Jaturaputpaibul P. & Kellam, K. (1999) *Issues Facing Consumer-Oriented Online Auctions.* MBA. Owen Graduate School of Management, Vanderbilt University <http://mba99.vanderbilt.edu/pitakj/group1/Auctions.htm> (17 Oct 2000).

24. Forrester Research. (2000). 'Forrester Findings: Internet Commerce'. September. <http://www.forrester.com/er/press/0,1772,0,FF.html> (17 September 2000).

25. Fortune (2000). "America's Forty under 40". Fortune Magazine. June. <http://www.fortune.com> (23 Oct 2000)

26. Fortune. (1999) e50. Company Index. <http://www.fortune.com/fortune/e50/> (29 Sept 2000).

27. Harrod, K. (1999) 'Amazon.com vs. eBay'. Letter to Fortune, 5 July 1999 <http://www.fortune.com> (23 Oct 2000).

28. Himelstein, L. (1999). 'Q&A with Meg Whitman: What's Behind the Boom at eBay.' Business Week <http://www.businessweek.com>

29. Interagency Government Asset Sales Team (IGAST). (2000). 'The Vendor Pilot Asset Sales and Auction'. US Chief Financial Officer's Council Auction White Paper. <http://www.financenet.gov/financenet/fed/cfo/salesteam/docs/whitepaper2.htm> (13 October 2000).

30. InternetNews Staff. (1998). 'eBay gets Personal'. InterNews.com. October. <http://www.internews.com> (23 Sept. 2000).

31. InternetNews Staff. (1998). 'eBay Launches National Advertising Campaign.' InterNews.com. October. <http://www.internews.com> (23 Sept 2000).

32. Jannarkar, S. (1999). 'eBay buys Butterfield & Butterfield.' Cnet.com. April <http://www.cnet.com> (26 Sept 2000).

33. Kruse International. (2000). <http://www.kruseinternational.com/>

34. Lee, J. (1998). "Why eBay is Flying." *Fortune Magazine.* Vol. 138. No. 11.

35. Moran, S. (1999). 'The Pro: Meg Whitman'. Business 2.0. June. <http://www.business2.com> (2 Oct 2000).

36. Nielsen/NetRatings Global Internet Index. (2000). 'Top 25 Web Sites by Property'. October. <http://www.nielsen-netratings.com/> (28 Nov 2000).

37. Reichheld F. R and Schefter P. (2000). "E-Loyalty: Your Secret Weapon on the Web." *Harvard Business Review.* Jul–Aug, pp. 105–113.

38. Roberts, L. (2000). 'eBay thinks global, big-time'. <http://www.marketwatch.com> (25 Sept 2000).

39. Roth, D. (1999). "Meg Muscles eBay Uptown." *Fortune Magazine.* Vol. 140. No. 1.

40. Sellers, P. (1999). "Powerful Women: These Women Rule." *Fortune Magazine.* Vol. 140. No. 8.

41. Silicon Valley (1999). 'Return to 1st Person: Pierre Omidyar'. Siliconvalley.com <http://www.sv.com> (23 Sept 2000).

42. Street, D. (1999) *Amazon.com: from start-up to the new millennium.* MBA Research Report, University of Cape Town.

43. Tedeschi, R. (1999). 'Using Discounts to Build a Client Base'. *New York Times.* 31 May.

44. The Standard. (1999). 'Profile: Pierre Omidyar'. <http://www.thestandard.com> (15 Sept 2000).

45. Various (2000) Epinions.com—Reviews of eBay . <http://www.epinions.com/cmsw_auctions-ebay> (21 November 2000).

46. Wall Street Journal (2000). 'Stocks Declined, Dragged Down by Analyst Downgrades, Election'. *Wall Street Journal.* <http://www.wsj.com> (20 Nov 2000).

47. Wingfield, N. (2000). 'eBay Aims to be Operating System for All E-Commerce on the Internet'. *Wall Street Journal.* <http://www.wsj.com> (20 Nov 2000).

48. Yahoo! Auctions. (2000).< http://auctions.yahoo.com/>.

Case 13 / eBay.com—Profitably Managing Growth from Start-up to 2000

Embraer 2000 Regional Jet Aircraft

Richard C. Scamehorn

Ohio University

Abstract
Embraer 2000 Regional Jet Aircraft

This case demonstrates the rapid growth of the regional aircraft industry. The regional jet aircraft market segment (which did not exist even ten years ago), in particular, is now a multi-billion dollar market and growing rapidly.

Brazil's Embraer becomes the world's largest producer of regional jet aircraft in this hot market, designing and manufacturing the industry's broadest range of products from the smallest to the largest. The case follows the company's history, demonstrating how Embraer successfully designed larger and larger aircraft to meet the commercial airlines demands in both Europe and North America.

The case presents significant qualitative and quantitative information for the student to benchmark past and current performance and competencies. Information concerning present and possible future competition is presented for the student to evaluate Embraer's strengths and weaknesses against competitive threats. Detailed financial information is presented, following Embraer's privatization by the Brazilian Government.

The case concludes with the question of defining the company's strategy and market mix for the future.

A RESEARCH TEACHING CASE
  Richard C. Scamehorn
  College of Business
  Ohio University
  304 Copeland Hall
  Athens, Ohio 45701 U.S.A.
  scamehorn@ouvaxa.cats.ohiou.edu
  /40-687-1842 (H)
  740-793-1388 FAX

This case is suitable for use in graduate (MBA) or senior-level undergraduate courses in business strategy and in graduate (MBA) courses in international business.

Embraer 2000

One of Embraer's customers, Mr. Paul Lidbury, Technical Manager for Qantas Airlines of Australia stated relative to Embraer's development of the ERJ-170 and ERJ-190 aircraft programs, "It is very important to participate from the beginning in the discussions about the aircraft's basic specifications. This way we can ensure our needs and those of our passengers will be satisfied." Other attendees at the October, 1999 Paris meeting of the Embraer's Advisory Board were equally enthusiastic.

Embraer: A Proud History

Embraer was founded in 1969 as a Brazilian, state-owned company with a mission to develop the necessary aeronautical technology to support the Brazilian military. Embraer's first aircraft, developed in 1979 for the Brazilian Air Force, was the EMB-110 *Bandeirante*. This versatile 19-seat airplane also became the first successful commercial commuter aircraft, since prior to that time, the smallest aircraft available was the DC-9 (with 125 seats) manufactured by Douglas Aircraft Company.

The EMB-110 *Bandeirante* had its shortcomings, the most significant being that it lacked passenger cabin pressurization, yielding two significant negative outcomes: 1) it's cruise altitude was limited to about 8,000 feet since breathing at higher altitudes becomes difficult and 2) because of this altitude limitation, it was forced to fly through (rather than over) storms and turbulent weather. Notwithstanding these shortfalls, the EMB-110 *Bandeirante* created two new industries: a commuter or regional air-route structure for the commercial airlines and thereby a regional aircraft manufacturing industry as well.

Recognizing the desires of the regional airlines as well as the flying passengers, Embraer designed, and in 1985 produced, the *EMB-120 Brasilia*. This new 30-seat aircraft incorporated two new significant improvements: full cabin pressurization and turboprop powerplants. The benefits of cabin pressurization were obvious, offering increased comfort and safety to passengers. Although the benefit of turboprop engines was less obvious to the average passenger, it was clearly recognized by the airlines.

Turboprop engines replaced the traditional internal-combustion, piston-driven engines that had been the powerplants for all aircraft since the Wright Brothers' Wright Flyer. Through years of development, piston engines had been refined to develop high horsepower with relatively light-weights, but achieving this desirable goal required extensive and expensive engine mainte-nance. Turboprop engines utilized a gas-turbine to drive the propeller which offered an improved horsepower to weight relationship and it also offered reduced mainte-nance requirements and reduced fuel consumption. Thus, turboprop aircraft had the extra power to provide cabin pressurization as a benefit for passengers and operating economies to the airlines.

The EMB-110 *Bandeirante* had started the regional air-line industry and now the *EMB-120 Brasilia* capitalized on this start. Passengers could now cruise as high as 32,000 feet: well above any bad weather. This issue, standing alone, was enough to cause the regional airline concept to mushroom. The airlines could now equip their fleets to expand their "hub-and-spoke" networks to an additional level. These successful hub-and-spoke net-works operated with the large, jumbo-jets flying long distances from hub to hub, e.g., Chicago O'Hare (ORD) to Los Angeles International (LAX). The spokes, feeding into these hubs, were serviced by smaller aircraft, such as Boeing's 737 or McDonnell-Douglas' MD-80. Both of these aircraft had at least 135 seats. The airlines would not service small airports where the passenger volume would not fill these 135-seat aircraft to at least the break-even point. Even when service was offered with piston-engine regional aircraft, many passengers preferred to drive to an existing spoke rather than suffer the trauma of flying through stormy weather.

With the benefits of the *EMB-120 Brasilia*, all the lim-itations, to both passenger and airline were eliminated. Airlines rushed to purchase the *EMB-120 Brasilia* as they further extended their spokes with the addition of "mini-spokes." These new "mini-spokes" provided service to passengers at small airports for the first time and allowed the airlines to provide the service profitably. Everybody won. As the year 2000 approached, Embraer had deliv-ered more than 350 *EMB-120 Brasilia* aircraft.

The Spokes Spawn Mini-Spokes

The new mini-spokes became the major growth segment in the commercial aircraft market in Western countries. In North America and Western Europe, most major air-lines had staked-out both their hubs and their primary "feeder-spokes" by the late 1980's. The situation between Western Europe and the USA differed in cause, but was similar in its result.

In Western Europe, each country had a dominate air-line which had staked-out its home base, typically in its home country: e.g., Lufthansa at Frankfurt, British Air at London's Heathrow, KLM in Amsterdam, Air France in Paris, etc. In addition, these major carriers developed spokes both within and outside their countries to feed passengers into their hub. The two largest in Western Europe became London and Frankfurt, to the benefit of British Air and Lufthansa, respectfully. London was a natural because it was the nearest to North America when the Boeing-707's range made it the first non-stop to New York. Frankfurt was also a natural, being the cen-ter of Europe's economic activity.

Within the USA, home bases developed in Dallas-Fort Worth for American Airlines, Miami for United, Atlanta for Delta, Houston for Continental, Minneapolis for Northwest and St. Louis for TWA. Each of these airlines then developed "feeder-spokes"— to funnel passengers into and out of their hubs. The larger airlines developed secondary hubs: both United and American in Chicago, Northwest in Detroit and Memphis, and Delta in Cincinnati.

By the late 1980's, growth from the serviceable spokes into the hubs was slowing. This problem was exacer-bated since development of additional spokes was lim-ited by load-factors (the percentage of occupied seats to total seat miles flown) at marginal spoke locations. As a result, the major airlines could not profitably fly large aircraft to these marginal cities. But, they discovered that it was profitable to develop "mini-spokes" utilizing a new form of aircraft, called "commuter-aircraft" such as the *EMB-120 Brasilia*.

Following a surge of orders for *EMB-120 Brasilia* and similar aircraft, the airlines started switching to regional jet aircraft. This action was driven by three significant issues:

1) **Customer demand;** passengers liked the regional jets much better than the slower, noisier prop planes. There was also an esthetic issue: jets (even

small, regional ones) were perceived by passengers as "real" transport planes.

2) **New markets;** jets could fly faster, and thus, further in the same amount of time. Ergo, four "mini-spoke" locations could now be serviced in the same time-span as only three with prop aircraft.

3) **Limited growth;** the new "mini-spokes" offered high growth potential as the established hub-and-spoke network's growth rate was substantially less, as shown below;

Annual Growth Rate	
Central Hubs and Spokes	Regional "Mini Spokes"
4–4½%	7–8%

A Major Step Forward

Even with a winning product such as the *EMB-120 Brasilia*, Embraer was not to rest on its laurels. In 1993, it committed to design and manufacture a regional turbo-jet (pure jet engine) aircraft. Named the *ERJ-145* (Embraer Regional Jet), the first aircraft was delivered in December, 1996. With seating for 50 passengers, the *ERJ-145* provided additional benefits to both passengers and airlines: the widest aisle in its class, better stand-up headroom, ergonomically-designed seating, a cruise altitude of 37,000 feet, large overhead bins, a spacious lavatory, increased baggage capacity, and a very important new cruise speed of 450 knots (540 mph or Mach .78) with a range of 1,300 nautical miles (1,560 statute miles).

In 1997 Embraer again decided to expand its product line by offering the ERJ-135, a 37-seat aircraft. The ERJ-135 has a 95 percent commonality with the ERJ-145. The only major difference is that the ERJ-135 is 11.6 feet shorter than its larger sibling. This important feature allows an airline commonality of flight-deck personnel, since crews trained for one aircraft are qualified to fly the other, eliminating the requirement of pilot redundancy. The combined benefits to both passengers and airlines made the *ERJ-135/ERJ-145* family an instant success.

During the Summer of 1999, Crossair of Europe announced the US $5.4 billion purchase of Embraer aircraft, the largest order ever placed for regional jet aircraft. With this giant step forward, Embraer had cemented its position as the world's leading manufacturer of regional jet aircraft.

A New Family

Recognizing the rapidly developing market segment for regional aircraft smaller than the Boeing-737, Embraer decided to develop a new family of regional jet aircraft: designated as the *ERJ-170 and ERJ-190* with seating capacities of 70 and 108, respectively.

This was an entirely new family of aircraft since the design was entirely different. The ERJ-135 and ERJ-145 both had engines mounted aft, on the fuselage, at the rear of the passenger cabin. The new *ERJ-170 and ERJ-190* twin turbofan engines were mounted under the aircraft's wing, utilizing the traditional pylon-design attachment. The flight deck and controls all incorporated state-of-the-art, fly-by-wire technology.

Firm orders were booked in 1999 for 70 aircraft in addition to options for an additional 105 units. The ERJ-170 first flight is planned for 2001 and the ERJ-190 in 2003. Deliveries to customers are planned for 2002 and 2004, respectively.

The Competition

The regional aircraft market can be divided into five segments:

1) Turboprop aircraft
2) Jets with 25–40 seats
3) Jets with 40–60 seats
4) Jets with 60–95 seats
5) Jets with more than 95

By 2000, the turboprop market had only three manufacturers: Bombardier in Canada, Embraer in Brazil and Fairchild in the United States. Both Saab and Fokker had withdrawn from this segment because of the intensity of the competition in addition to its mature product life cycle.

The regional jet market is in the middle of its growth cycle and is attracting the attention of several manufacturers, including some new ones. Five years ago both Airbus Industrie and Boeing were too busy in the major jet transport business to consider the manufacture of regional jets. However, when the Asian economic recession started in 1997 and resulted in cancellation of large aircraft orders in 1998, both revisited their decision to abstain from the regional jet business.

Both of these companies presented the "bottom-end" of their product-line to the regional jet market: the Airbus A-319 and the Boeing 717. Neither of these aircraft's initial designs were intended for the regional jet market. They both had certain disadvantages (lacking flight system compatibility with any other regional jet, among others) as well as certain advantages (nearly all of the development costs had already been written off as part of their original program).

Airbus entered the regional jet market only after Boeing announced its plans. It later became apparent that Boeing was pursuing the regional jet market primarily out of loyalty to the suppliers who had committed time and money in support of the former McDonnell-Douglas MD-90, which Boeing was now offering as a Boeing-717.

From the table below, it became apparent that

1) Manufacturers were sensitive to the product life cycle of various classes of aircraft, with Saab and Fokker withdrawing from the turboprop segment.

2) Smaller value added aircraft, in particular those with less than forty seats were of lessor interest.

3) The higher value added, more expensive aircraft were perceived to have the largest potential for growth.

4) Because of item 3), the competition in both technology and pricing of the larger aircraft would be the greatest.

Regional class	Small	Medium	Large	Very large
Seating Capacity	< 40	40–60	60–95	> 95
Competitors	Fairchild[f]	Bombardier[b]	Bombardier[b]	Airbus[e]
	Embraer[a]	Embraer[a]	Embraer[c]	Boeing[d]
		Fairchild[f]	Fairchild[f]	Bombardier[b]
				Embraer[c]
				Fairchild[f]

[a]Flight system compatibility
[b]Flight system compatibility
[c]Flight system compatibility
[d]Flight system incompatible. This is an MD-90, a rear-engine mounted upgrade of the McDonnell-Douglas MD-80, which Boeing received during its acquisition of McDonnell-Douglas in 1997.
[e]This is a shortened version of the Airbus-320, single aisle, twin-engine and is compatible with the other aircraft in the A-320 series.
[f]Flight system compatibility not yet determined.

The Organization

Founded in 1969 as a Brazilian State Company, Embraer developed high-performance, high technology aircraft, primarily in support of Brazil's national defense requirements. The TBA-123 turboprop aircraft was the best plane in its class, but it cost 50 percent more than its closest competitor. As a result, Embraer struggled as an economic entity, losing money in virtually every year of its existence. As the company was successful in the development of both the EMB-110 *Bandeirante* and the *EMB-120 Brasilia* it appeared the company might break-through the "profit-barrier."

However, in 1995, Brazil's president decided to privatize several state-owned companies in a clear direction for a more transparent, free-market economy in Brazil. Accordingly, during the transition to privatization (1995–1997), Embraer was steadily increasing its revenue with aircraft that achieved high market acceptance, but not profitability: albeit the losses were reduced in each of the three transition years.

Finally, in 1998, the "profit-barrier" (nearly as exciting as the sound-barrier) was broken as Embraer achieved a gross profit before tax of US $ 119 million. The trend continued into 1999 and is expected to continue further beyond 2000. (see Exhibits 1 through 5.)

The privatization was accomplished by the sale of Embraer to six investor groups (see Exhibit 6). The controlling shareholders, representing 55.3 percent of the voting stock, comprise the Bozano, Simonsen Group and two pension funds; Sistel and Previ. The Brazil Investment Bank and smaller investors purchased the balance of the stock. The government continued to hold 6.8 percent along with one "golden share;" allowing the government to block any policy or investment change that would be detrimental to Brazil's national defense policy. Thus, the government effectively privatized the company, but through the golden share, maintained its capability to preclude private interest conflicts with National Defense policy.

Several reasons contributed to Embraer's profit-breakthrough. Continued success in the marketplace

Exhibit 1   Selected Financial Data Years Ending December 31

Stated in 1,000's of Brazilian reals

Income statement highlights

	9 months 1999	1998	1997
Gross sales	2,416,477	1,580,960	832,989
Operating income	469,246	247,081	93,060
Net income (Loss)	185,810	132,046	(33,040)

Balance sheet highlights

Total assets	3,046,304	2,055,991	1,424,516
Total liabilities	2,488,957	1,638,117	1,083,435
Shareholders' equity	557,347	417,874	341,081

Other Data

Earnings (loss per 1,000 shares (R$)		2.72	(0.68)
Number of shares (000,000)		48,449	48,449
Market price per common		10.40	13.00
1,000 shares (R$) preferred		15.00	17.00

resulted in a steady increase of revenue. In addition, without the political pressures of a state-owned enterprise, Embraer management could now control their employment levels, resulting in exciting productivity improvements (see Exhibit 7). The increase in revenues gave management the opportunity to achieve profitability and management's controlling of employment levels took advantage of the opportunity.

Following privatization, the company was structurally reorganized along more effective functional lines. This new structure created separate executive vice-presidents for both the defense markets and the airline markets. Most other functional departments such as engineering, manufacturing, materials and staff/support functions served both airline and defense products (see Exhibit 8).

During the 1990's all of Embraer's growth resulted from the airline market vis-a-vis its ERJ aircraft, causing a shift in the balance of revenue between airline and defense sales as follows:

	Defense	Airlines
1970–1990	37 percent	63 percent
1990's	10 percent	90 percent

As an important activity of the airline marketing department, Embraer organized an advisory board, consisting of customers from 20 regional airlines in addition to supplier/partners. This group would meet periodically to review design and performance criteria for the new ERJ-170 and ERJ-190 aircraft which was under the direction of Luis Carol Affonso, program director for the new aircraft.

Speaking about the advisory board, one of Embraer's customers, Mr. Richard Heideker, Vice President of Marketing for Crossair (Switzerland) commented about the advisory board program, "We will collaborate substantially in the discussions to ensure maximum comfort for our passengers, as well as the best operational performance for our airline in compliance with modern environmental standards. We are very happy that the airplane we have selected also meets the requirements of many other airlines."

The Risk Sharing Partner Concept

The development costs for a new design regional jet are huge. In fact, they are so large that the risk must be shared by all those who share the potential for profitability from a successful program. The concept of risk sharing partners goes beyond simply financial support from a supplier: it also includes mutually-supportive relationships between Embraer and its key suppliers.

The ERJ-170/190 partners are shown on Exhibit 9. There is a major financial commitment by these suppliers of US $ 850 million towards the development costs for the program.

| Exhibit 2 | Consolidated Statements of Income |

	1998	1997
Gross sales	1,580,960	832,989
Domestic	169,057	124,980
Foreign	1,411,903	708,009
Sales taxes	(10,924)	(8,919)
Net sales	1,570,036	824,070
Cost of sales	1,125,965	603,789
Gross profit	444,071	220,281
Operating expenses		
Administrative	53,141	40,007
Selling	119,470	64,648
Other, net	24,379	22,566
Income from operations before financial expenses	247,081	93,060
Financial expenses		
Expenses	72,934	90,942
Income	45,725	5,925
Net monetary and exchange variations	52,731	60,413
Income (loss) from operations	167,141	(52,370)
Non-operating expenses	6,805	7,471
Provision for income tax	11,714	186
Employee profit sharing	16,576	1,196
Deferred charges	–	84,000
Tax loss carryforwards		112,183
Net income (loss)	132,046	(33,040)

US$ Millions	
300	Direct support from supplier/partners
350	Indirect design support from supplier/partners
250	Design costs absorbed by Embraer
850	Total development costs

Such a level of financial support from suppliers requires a genuinely mutual supportive commitment.

A Strategic Partner

Following extensive discussions Embraer announced, on October 25, 1999 the planned formation of a strategic partnership with a group of French aerospace and defense companies. These firms were Aerospatiale Matra, Dassault Aviation, SNECMA and Thomson-CSF, and they would acquire 20 percent of Embraer's common stock.

The French companies' decision to invest in Embraer was forthcoming following Embraer's successful growing role in the world's aerospace and defense markets. It was not based upon the implementation of any specific program or project. This French aerospace group will work closely with Embraer to transfer product technology and market development. Although the group will have no controlling interest, it will act as a strategic shareholder; however, it remains subject to both Embraer's corporate criteria and also to Brazil's military and defense programs as controlled by the golden share.

Each of the companies in the French Group offers a technology potential to Embraer which the company now lacks:

Exhibit 3 Consolidated Balance Sheet

In 1,000's Brazilian Reals

Assets

	1998	1997
Current assets		
Cash and cash equivalents	313,888	104,442
Trade accounts eeceivable	152,087	74,703
Allowance for nonpayment	(2,351)	(225)
Recoverable taxes	24,615	13,613
Other receivables	24,232	12,322
Inventories	682,274	367,376
Prepaid expenses	8,324	8,294
Total current assets	1,203,069	508,525
Noncurrent assets		
Accounts receivable	23,755	21,514
Compulsory loans	7,194	7,173
Other receivables	38,775	12,113
Tax loss carryforward	103,837	112,183
Total noncurrent assets	173,561	152,983
Permanent assets		
Investments	4,315	148
Property, plant, and equipment	302,592	300,901
Deferred charges	372,454	389,959
Total permanent assets	679,361	691,008
Total assets	2,055,991	1,424,516

1) **Aerospatiale Matra:** A major partner in the Airbus Industrie consortium.
2) **Dassault Aviation:** High technology in military applications, including design and manufacture of the highly successful French Mirage fighter plane.
3) **SNECMA:** High technology jet engine design and manufacture under license from General Electric of USA.
4) **Thomson-CSF:** High technology electronics and avionics equipment.

Embraer, on the other hand, offers to the French group the successful technology, manufacture and marketing of regional jet aircraft since the French Group only has turbo-prop technology.

Looking to the Future

As Embraer top management considered the present and near-future of the regional jet market they concluded the company:

1) Successfully privatized
2) Successfully designed and profitably manufactured the ERJ-135 and ERJ-145 family.
3) Successfully developed a profitable order backlog (Exhibit 10).
4) Successfully designed the new ERJ-170 and ERJ-190 family
5) Successfully aligned with a strategic European partner.

Exhibit 4 Consolidated Balance Sheet

In 1,000's Brazilian Reals

Liabilities and shareholders' equity

	1998	1997
Current liabilities	665,654	251,818
Suppliers loans	248,981	190,063
Customers' advances	174,857	173,700
Taxes & social charges	27,226	30,661
Dealers & sales agents	2,808	3,867
Accrued liabilities	60,222	29,544
Accounts payable	35,766	22,191
Dividends	33,953	—
Total current liabilities	1,249,467	701,844
Long-term liabilities		
Loans	149,887	130,745
Accounts payable	13,723	14,211
Customers' advances	117,691	76,408
Taxes & social charges	53,716	78,399
Accrued liabilities	47,675	72,842
Suppliers	4,509	7,850
Deferred income tax	757	222
Total long-term liabilities	387,958	380,677
Deferred income	692	914
Shareholder's equity		
Capital	354,619	354,619
Capital reserves	7,140	—
Retained earnings (deficit)	56,115	(13,538)
Total shareholder's equity	417,874	341,081
Total	2,055,991	1,424,516

6) Successfully developed three strategic core businesses:
   a) Regional jet airliners
   b) Defense aircraft
   c) Sales and aftermarket support

The top management was now considering Embraer's strategic direction for the period 2005–2015: both products and markets.

Stated in 1,000's Brazilian Reals

	1998	1997
Sources of funds		
Provided by operations	272,851	85,997
Provided from shareholders		
Capital increase	–	6,020
Subtotal	272,851	92,017
Provided from third parties increase in long-term liabilities		
Customer's advances	150,325	92,537
Loans	26,220	41,892
Suppliers & other	12,936	15,053
Deferred income	–	151
Transfer from non-current assets	24,291	17,160
Subtotal	213,772	166,793
Total sources	486,623	258,810
Application of funds		
Increase in non-current assets	49,676	37,602
Increase in permanent assets		
Investments	4,151	9
Property, plant, & equipment	34,675	30,023
Deferred charges	52,819	52,916
Transfer to current liabilities	215,128	112,206
Dividends	55,253	–
Total application of funds	411,702	232,756
Increase in working capital	74,921	26,054
Working capital end of year		
Current assets	1,203,069	580,525
Current liabilities	1,249,467	701,844
	(46,398)	(121,319)
Working capital beginning of year	(121,319)	(147,373)
Increase in working capital	74,921	26,054

Exhibit 6   Privatized Ownership Pie Chart

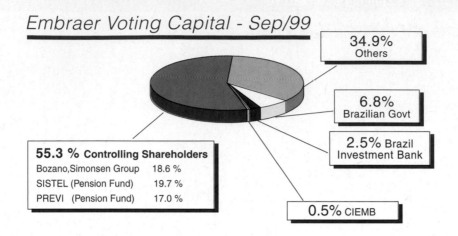

Embraer Voting Capital - Sep/99

34.9%
Others

6.8%
Brazilian Govt

2.5% Brazil
Investment Bank

0.5% CIEMB

55.3 % Controlling Shareholders

Bozano,Simonsen Group	18.6 %
SISTEL (Pension Fund)	19.7 %
PREVI (Pension Fund)	17.0 %

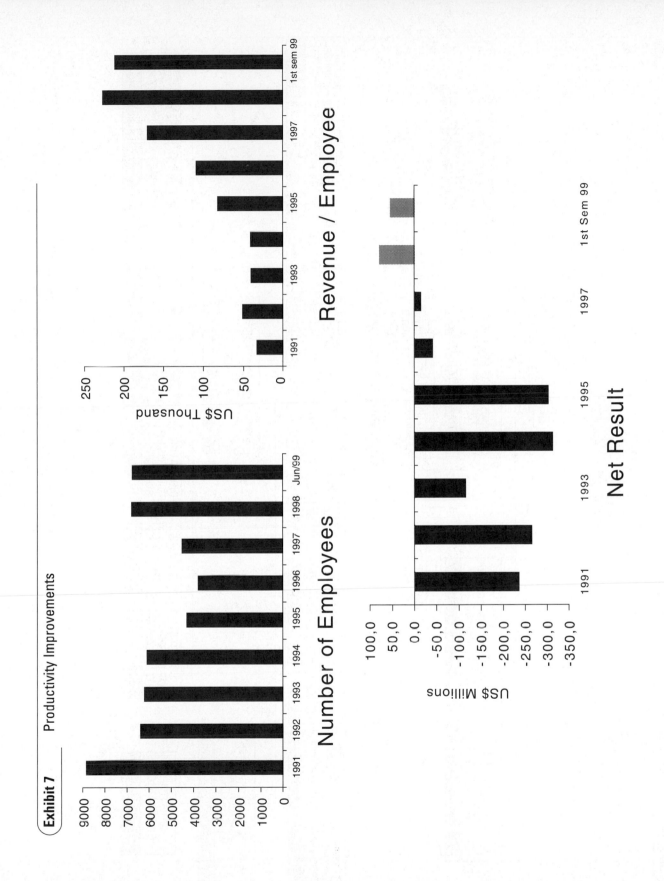

Exhibit 7 Productivity Improvements

Revenue / Employee

Number of Employees

Net Result

Exhibit 8 Organization Chart

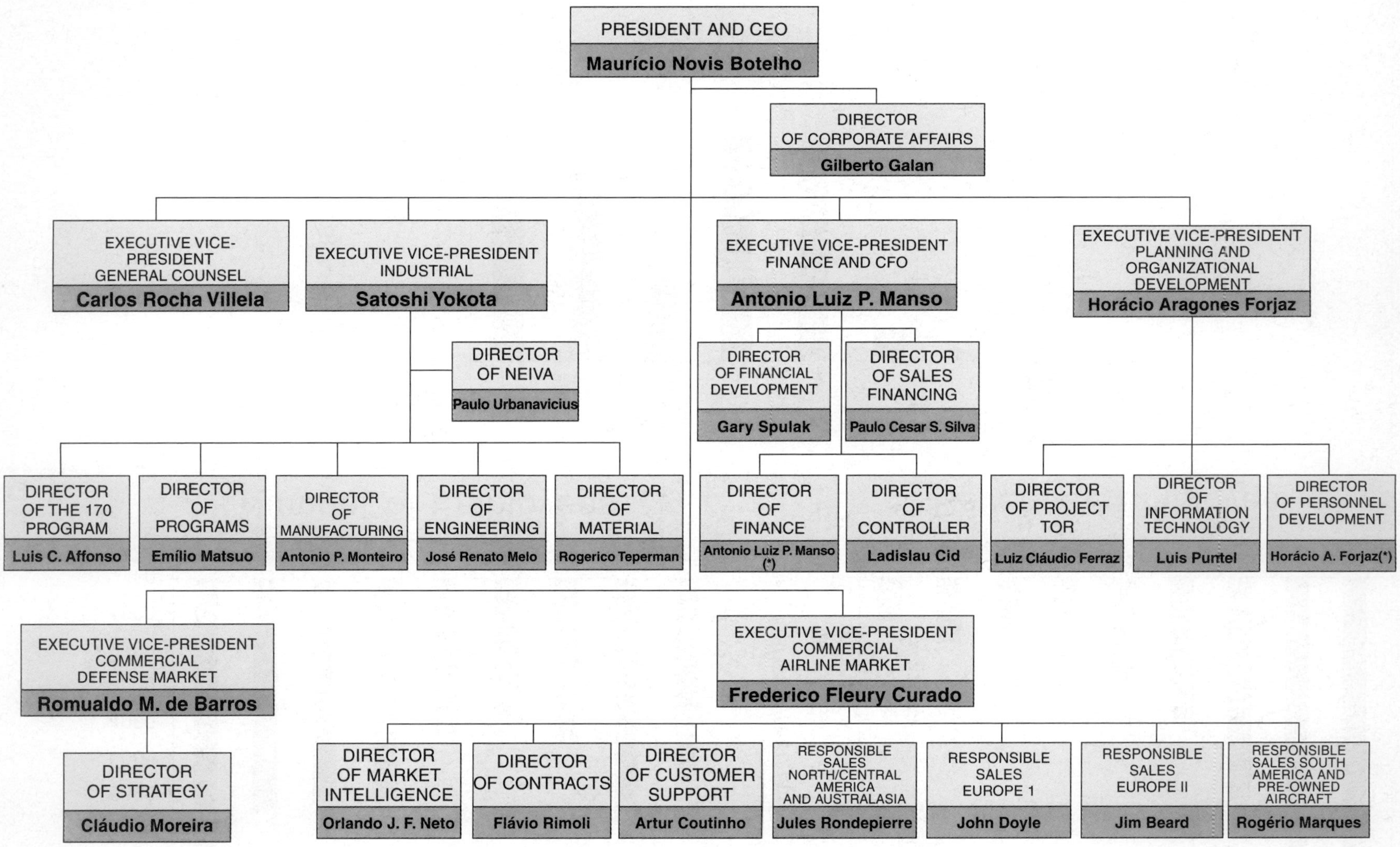

Organization chart for Embraer showing reporting structure.

PRESIDENT AND CEO
Maurício Novis Botelho

DIRECTOR OF CORPORATE AFFAIRS — Gilberto Galan

EXECUTIVE VICE-PRESIDENT PLANNING AND ORGANIZATIONAL DEVELOPMENT — Horácio Aragones Forjaz
- DIRECTOR OF PERSONNEL DEVELOPMENT — Horácio A. Forjaz(*)
- DIRECTOR OF INFORMATION TECHNOLOGY — Luis Purtel
- DIRECTOR OF PROJECT TOR — Luiz Cláudio Ferraz

EXECUTIVE VICE-PRESIDENT FINANCE AND CFO — Antonio Luiz P. Manso
- DIRECTOR OF SALES FINANCING — Paulo Cesar S. Silva
- DIRECTOR OF FINANCIAL DEVELOPMENT — Gary Spulak
- DIRECTOR OF CONTROLLER — Ladislau Cid
- DIRECTOR OF FINANCE — Antonio Luiz P. Manso (*)

EXECUTIVE VICE-PRESIDENT GENERAL COUNSEL — Carlos Rocha Villela

EXECUTIVE VICE-PRESIDENT INDUSTRIAL — Satoshi Yokota
- DIRECTOR OF NEIVA — Paulo Urbanavicius
- DIRECTOR OF MATERIAL — Rogerico Teperman
- DIRECTOR OF ENGINEERING — José Renato Melo
- DIRECTOR OF MANUFACTURING — Antonio P. Monteiro
- DIRECTOR OF PROGRAMS — Emilio Matsuo
- DIRECTOR OF THE 170 PROGRAM — Luis C. Affonso

EXECUTIVE VICE-PRESIDENT COMMERCIAL AIRLINE MARKET — Frederico Fleury Curado
- DIRECTOR OF CUSTOMER SUPPORT — Artur Coutinho
- DIRECTOR OF CONTRACTS — Flávio Rimoli
- DIRECTOR OF MARKET INTELLIGENCE — Orlando J. F. Neto
- RESPONSIBLE SALES NORTH/CENTRAL AMERICA AND AUSTRALASIA — Jules Rondepierre
- RESPONSIBLE SALES EUROPE 1 — John Doyle
- RESPONSIBLE SALES EUROPE II — Jim Beard
- RESPONSIBLE SALES SOUTH AMERICA AND PRE-OWNED AIRCRAFT — Rogério Marques

EXECUTIVE VICE-PRESIDENT COMMERCIAL DEFENSE MARKET — Romualdo M. de Barros
- DIRECTOR OF STRATEGY — Cláudio Moreira

Exhibit 9   Risk Sharing Partners, ERJ-170/190

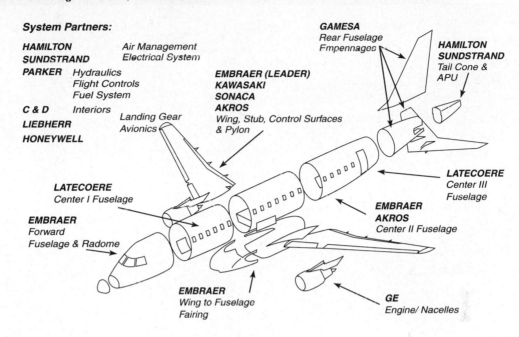

System Partners:

**HAMILTON
SUNDSTRAND**

Air Management
Electrical System

PARKER Hydraulics
Flight Controls
Fuel System

C & D Interiors

LIEBHERR

HONEYWELL

Landing Gear
Avionics

**EMBRAER (LEADER)
KAWASAKI
SONACA
AKROS**

Wing, Stub, Control Surfaces
& Pylon

GAMESA
Rear Fuselage
Fmpennages

**HAMILTON
SUNDSTRAND**
Tail Cone &
APU

LATECOERE
Center I Fuselage

EMBRAER
Forward
Fuselage & Radome

LATECOERE
Center III
Fuselage

**EMBRAER
AKROS**
Center II Fuselage

EMBRAER
Wing to Fuselage
Fairing

GE
Engine/ Nacelles

Exhibit 10   Embraer Regional Jet Order Book As of September 30, 1999

Client	Country	Firm Orders	Options	Delivered	Backlog
ERJ-135					
American Eagle	US	95	115	5	90
City Airline AB	Sweden	1	2	0	1
Continental Express	US	25	50	3	22
Flandre Air	France	9	10	0	9
Proteus	France	5	5	0	5
Regional Airlines	France	5	0	0	5
Totals		140	182	8	132
ERJ-145					
Alitala Express	Italy	6	15	0	6
American Eagle	US	50	17	39	11
British Midland	UK	10	10	3	7
British Regional	UK	20	5	12	8
Brymon Airways	UK	7	14	0	7
Cirrus	Germany	1	0	0	1
Continental Express	US	75	125	52	23
Crossair	Switzerland	15	25	0	15
ERA	Spain	2	3	2	0
Flandre Air	France	1	0	0	1
InterCanadian	Canada	6	6	0	6
KLM Excel	Holland	3	2	0	3
LOT	Poland	6	6	2	4
Luxair	Luxemburg	9	2	5	4
Portugalia	Portugal	6	0	6	0
Proteus Airlines	France	8	0	0	8
Regional Airlines	France	15	0	9	6
Rheintaflug	Austria	2	6	0	2
Rio-Sul	Brazil	15	15	12	3
Skyways	Sweden	4	11	3	1
TansStates	US	15	12	8	7
Wexford	US	10	20	3	7
Undisclosed		38	66	0	38
Totals		324	360	156	168

FedEx Corp.: Structural Transformation Through e-Business

Pauling Ng and Ali F. Farhoomand

The University of Hong Kong

> *[FedEx] has built superior physical, virtual, and people networks not just to prepare for change, but to shape change on a global scale: to change the way we all connect with each other in the new Network Economy.[1]*
>
> *[FedEx] is not only reorganizing its internal operations around a more flexible network computing architecture, but it's also pulling-in and in many cases locking-in customers with an unprecedented level of technological integration.[2]*

Since its inception in 1973, Federal Express Corporation ("FedEx"[3]) had transformed itself from an express delivery company to a global logistics and supply-chain management company. Over the years, the Company had invested heavily in IT systems, and with the launch of the Internet in 1994, the potential for further integration of systems to provide services throughout its customers' supply-chains became enormous. With all the investment in the systems infrastructure over the years and the US$88 million acquisition of Caliber Systems, Inc., in 1998, the Company had built a powerful technical architecture that had the potential to pioneer in Internet commerce. However, despite having all the ingredients for the makings of a successful e-business, the Company's logistics and supply-chain operations were struggling to shine through the historical image of the Company as simply an express delivery business. Furthermore, competition in the transportation/express delivery industry was intense and there were reports that FedEx's transportation volume growth was slowing down, even though they were poised to take advantage of the surge in traffic that e-tailing and electronic commerce (EC) were supposed to generate. Hence, on 19 January, 2000, FedEx announced major reorganisations in the Group's operations in the hope of making it easier to do business with the entire FedEx family. The mode of operation for the five subsidiary companies was to function independently but to compete collectively. In addition to streamlining many functions, the Group announced that it would pool its sales, marketing and customer services functions, such that customers would have a single point of access to the whole Group. The reorganisation was expected to cost US$100 million over three years. Was this simply a new branding strategy or did FedEx have the right solution to leverage its cross-company synergies and its information and logistics infrastructure to create e-business solutions for its customers?

The Express Transportation and Logistics Industry

FedEx invented the air/ground express industry in 1973. Although UPS was founded in 1907 and became America's largest transportation company, it did not compete with FedEx directly in the overnight delivery market until 1982. Competition began with a focus on customer segmentation, pricing and quality of service. For most businesses, physical distribution costs often accounted for 10–30 percent of sales or more. As competition put pressure on pricing businesses began to look at ways to cut costs yet improve customer service.

The solution was to have a well-managed logistics operation to reduce the length of the order cycle and thus generate a positive effect on cash flow.

The growth of the express transportation and logistics industry was brought about by three main trends: the globalisation of businesses, advances in information technology (IT) and the application of new technology to generate process efficiencies, and the changing market demand for more value-added services. As businesses expanded beyond national boundaries and extended their global reach to take advantage of new markets and cheaper resources, so the movement of goods created new demands for the transportation and logistics industry. With this, the competitiveness of transportation companies depended upon their global network of distribution centres and their ability to deliver to wherever their customers conducted business. Speed became of significance to achieve competitiveness, not only for the transportation companies but also for their customers. The ability to deliver goods quickly shortened the order-to-payment cycle, improved cash flow and created customer satisfaction.

Advances in IT promoted the globalisation of commerce. The ability to share information between operations/departments within a company and between organisations to generate operational efficiencies, reduce costs and improve customer services was a major breakthrough for the express transportation industry. However, of even greater significance was the way in which new technology redefined logistics. At a time when competition within the transportation industry was tough and transportation companies were seeking to achieve competitive advantages through value-added services, many of these companies expanded into logistics management services. Up until the 1980s, logistics was merely the handling, warehousing and transportation of goods. By combining the functions of materials management and physical distribution, logistics took on a new and broader meaning. It was concerned with inbound as well as outbound material flow, within companies as well as the movement of finished goods from dock-to-dock. With this, the transportation industry responded by placing emphasis not only on the physical transportation, but also on the coordination and control of storage and movement of parts and finished goods. Logistics came to include value-added activities such as order processing, distribution centre operations, inventory control, purchasing, production and customer and sales services. Interconnectivity through the Internet and Intranets and the integration of systems enabled businesses to redefine themselves and re-engineer their selling and supply-chains. Information came to replace inventory. Just-in-time inventory management helped to reduce costs and improve efficiency. With the advent of IT, express transportation became an aggregation of two main functions: the physical delivery of parcels, and the management and utilisation of the flow of information pertaining to the physical delivery (i.e., control over the movement of goods).

FedEx Corp.

FedEx was the pioneer of the express transportation and logistics industry. Throughout the 27 years of its operation, FedEx's investment in IT had earned the Company a myriad of accolades. Since 1973 FedEx had won over 194 awards for operational excellence. Fundamental to the success of the FedEx business was the vision of its founder.

The Visionary behind the Business

"If we're all operating in a day-to-day environment, we're thinking one to two years out. Fred's thinking five, ten, fifteen years out."

—William Conley, VP, FedEx Logistics, Managing Director Europe

Fred Smith, Chairman, President and Chief Executive Officer of FedEx Corporation, invented the express distribution industry in March 1973. By capitalising on the needs of businesses for speed and reliability of deliveries, FedEx shortened lead-times for companies. Its next-day delivery service revolutionised the distribution industry. The success of FedEx's distribution business in those early days rested on Smith's commitment to his belief that the opportunities open to a company that could provide reliable overnight delivery of time-sensitive documents and packages were excellent. Despite losses in the first three years of operation due to high capital investments in the physical transportation infrastructure of the business, FedEx began to see profits from 1975 onwards. To compete on a global basis, the key components of the physical infrastructure had to be in place to connect the world's GDP. The underlying philosophy was that wherever business was conducted, there was going to have to be the movement of physical goods.

Under Smith's leadership, the Company had set a few records with breakthrough technology. In the 1980s, FedEx gave away more than 100,000 sets of PCs loaded with FedEx software, designed to link and log customers into FedEx's ordering and tracking systems. FedEx was also the first to issue hand-held scanners to its drivers that alerted customers of when packages were picked up or delivered. Then in 1994, FedEx became the first big transportation company to launch a website that included tracking and tracing capabilities. Very early on, Smith could foresee that the Internet was going to change the way businesses would operate and the way people would interact. By applying IT to the business, FedEx leapfrogged the rest of the industry. Smith was the visionary who forced his company and other companies to think outside of the proverbial box. The core of FedEx's corporate strategy was to "use IT to help customers take advantage of international markets."[4] By 1998, FedEx was a US$10 billion company spending US$1 billion annually on IT developments plus millions more on capital expenditure. It had an IT workforce of 5,000 people.

Building the Transportation and Logistics Infrastructure

In the early years of the FedEx transportation business, Smith insisted that the Company should acquire its own transportation fleet, while competitors were buying space on commercial airlines and sub-contracting their shipments to third parties. The strategy of expanding through acquiring more trucks and planes continued. By the tenth year of operation FedEx earned the accolade of being the first US company to achieve the US$1 billion revenues mark within a decade without corporate acquisitions and mergers.

FedEx was quoted as being the inventor of customer logistics management.[5] As early as 1974, FedEx started logistics operations with the Parts Bank. In those days, a few small set-ups approached FedEx with their warehousing problems and decided on the idea of overnight distribution of parts. With those propositions, FedEx built a small warehouse on the end of its sorting facilities at Memphis. This was FedEx's first attempt at multiple-client warehousing. Customers would call up and order the dispatch of parts and the order would be picked up on the same day. That was also FedEx's first value-added service beyond basic transportation. From there, the logistics side of the business snowballed.

Throughout the next three decades, FedEx's transportation business growth was attributable to a number of external factors that FedEx was quick to capitalise on. These included:

- Government deregulation of the airline industry, which permitted the landing of larger freight planes, thus reducing operating costs for FedEx.
- Deregulation of the trucking industry, which allowed FedEx to establish a regional trucking system to lower costs further on short-haul trips.

- Trade deregulation in Asia Pacific, which opened new markets for FedEx. Expanding globally became a priority for FedEx.
- Technological breakthroughs and applications innovations promoted significant advances for customer ordering, package tracking and process monitoring.
- Rising inflation and global competition gave rise to greater pressures on businesses to minimise the costs of operation, including implementation of just-in-time inventory management systems, etc. This also created demands for speed and accuracy in all aspects of business.

As of January 2000, FedEx served 210 countries (making up more than 90 percent of the world's GDP), operated 34,000 drop-off locations and managed over 10 million square feet of warehouse space worldwide. It had a fleet of 648 aircraft and more than 60,000 vehicles, with a staff of nearly 200,000. It was the world's largest overnight package carrier, with about 30 percent of the market share.

Building the Virtual Information Infrastructure

"We are really becoming a technology company enabled by transportation."

—David Edmonds, VP, Worldwide Services Group, FedEx[6]

Even as early as 1979, a centralised computer system—Customer, Operations, Service, Master On-line System (COSMOS)—kept track of all packages handled by the Company. This computer network relayed data on package movement, pickup, invoicing and delivery to a central database at Memphis headquarters. This was made possible by placing a bar code on each parcel at the point of pickup and scanning the bar code at each stage of the delivery cycle.

In 1984, FedEx started to launch a series of technological systems, the PowerShip programme, aimed at improving efficiency and control, which provided the most active customers (over 100,000) with proprietary on-line services (see Exhibit 1 for a chronological list of FedEx systems). In summary, these PowerShip systems provided additional services to the customer, including storing of frequently used addresses, label printing, on-line package pick-up requests, package tracking, and much more.

The emergence of electronic data interchange (EDI) and the Internet allowed companies to build one-to-one relationships with their customers. This was the perfect scenario for many manufacturers: the ability to match supply to demand without wastage. FedEx took advantage of such new technologies and started to track back

Exhibit 1 | FedEx's Record of Systems Innovations

1979 COSMOS (Customer Oriented Services and Management Operating System), a global shipment tracking network based on a centralised computer system to manage vehicles, people, packages, routes and weather scenarios on a real-time basis. COSMOS integrated two essential information systems: information about goods being shipped and information about the mode of transportation.

1980 DADS (Digitally Assisted Dispatch System) co-ordinated on-call pickups for customers. It allowed couriers to manage their time and routes through communication via a computer in their vans.

1984 FedEx introduces the first PC-based automated shipping system, later named FedEx PowerShip; a stand alone DOS-based system for customers with five or more packages per day. The customer base was immediately transformed into a network that allowed customers to interact with the FedEx system and download software and shipping information.

1984 PowerShip Plus, a DOS-based shipping system integrated with customers' order-entry, inventory-control and accounting systems, for customers who ship more than 100 packages per day.

1985 FedEx was the first to introduce bar-code labeling to the ground transportation industry.

1986 The SuperTracker, a hand-held bar-code scanner system that captures detailed package information.

1989 FedEx launches an on-board communications system that uses satellite tracking to pinpoint vehicle location.

1991 Rite Routing demonstrates the value of a nationwide, centralised transportation management service.

1991 PowerShip PassPort, a Pentium-class PC system that combines the best of PowerShip and PowerShip Plus for customers who ship more than 100 packages a day. (1,500 users)

1993 MultiShip, the first carrier-supplied customer automation system to process packages shipped by other transportation providers.

1993 FedEx ExpressClear Electronic Customs Clearance System expedites regulatory clearance while cargo is en route.

1993 PowerShip 3, a client-server shipping system for customers who ship three or more packages per day.

1994 The FedEx website debuts at www.fedex.com, the first to offer on-line package status tracking so that customers can actually conduct business via the Internet.

1994 DirectLink, a software that lets customers receive, manage and remit payments of FedEx invoices electronically.

1995 FedEx Ship, a Windows-based shipping and tracking software allows customers to process and manage shipping from their desktop. (650,000 users) It extended the benefits of PowerShip to all FedEx's customers, providing software and toll-free dial-up to the FedEx network.

1995 FedEx launches the AsiaOne network, a transportation routing system.

1996 FedEx became the first company to allow customers to process shipments on the Internet with FedEx interNetShip, available through www.fedex.com. (65,000 users) This allowed customers to create shipping labels, request courier pick-ups and send e-mail notifications to recipients of the shipments, all from the FedEx website.

1996 FedEx VirtualOrder, a software that links Internet ordering with FedEx delivery and on-line tracking. It also puts customers' catalogues on their websites for them.

1997 FedEx introduces e-Business Tools for easier connection with FedEx shipping and tracking applications.

1998 FedEx Ship for Workgroups, a Windows-based software housed on a server that lets users share information, such as address-book information, access to shipping logs and a tracking database. The server can be connected to FedEx via either modem or the Internet.

1998 PowerShip mc, a multi-carrier electronic shipping system.

1999 The FedEx Marketplace debuts at www.fedex.com, providing easy access to on-line merchants that offer fast, reliable FedEx express shipping.

1999 The EuroOne network was launched to link 16 cities to FedEx's Paris hub by air and another 21 cities by road-air. Lake AsiaOne, this was a transportation routing system.

| Exhibit 1 | FedEx's Record of Systems Innovations *(Continued)* |

1999   FedEx MarketPlace, a convenient link to on-line shopping. Through this new portal, shoppers had one-click access to several top on-line merchants that utilised FedEx's delivery services, including value America, L. L. Bean, and HP Shopping Village (Hewlett-Packard's consumer EC Website).

1999   FedEx made a deal with Netscape to offer a suite of delivery services at its Netcenter portal. This entailed automatically integrating Netscape with the FedEx site. Although customers of Netscape could choose not to use FedEx, the use of an alternative shipper meant that they would not benefit from the efficiencies of the integrated systems. Considering the Netscape Netcenter had more than 13 million members, the deal was a winner for FedEx.

(NB. PowerShip had 850,000 on-line customers worldwide; PowerShip, PowerShip 3 and PowerShip PassPort were hardware-based products.)

along the supply chain to the point of raw materials. As they did so, they identified points along the supply chain where they could provide management services. Often, these services included transportation, order processing and related distribution centre operations, fulfilment, inventory control, purchasing, production and customer and sales services. The ability to interconnect and distribute information to all the players in a supply-chain became the focus of FedEx's attention. For many of its customers, logistics was viewed as a key means for differentiating their products or services from those of their competitors (see Exhibit 2 for examples of some customer solutions). In other words, logistics became a key part of strategy formulation. As businesses were placing more emphasis on the order cycle as the basis for evaluating customer service levels, FedEx's role in providing integrated logistics systems formed the basis of many partnership arrangements. By helping them to redefine sources and procurement strategies so as to link in with other parties in the supply-chain, such as raw materials suppliers, customers were outsourcing their supply-chain management functions to FedEx, functions that were seen as peripheral to the core of their business (see Exhibit 3 and 4 for FedEx's coverage of the supply chain through integrated systems). By improving, tightening and synchronising the various parts to the supply-chain, customers saw the benefits of squeezing time and inventory out of the system. Tighter supply-chain management was no longer viewed as a competitive advantage but a competitive imperative.

Businesses sought ways to improve their return on investment and became interested in any business process that could be integrated and automatically triggered (e.g., proof of delivery and payment) as opposed to being separately invoked. So not only was FedEx pushing its customers for integration, but its innovative

customers were also demanding greater integration. Some customers had even jumped ahead of FedEx. Cisco, for example, had developed an extranet that allowed its customers to order FedEx services without leaving the Cisco website. By integrating its services within the supply-chain of its customers, and thus generating increases in customer loyalty and in customers' switching costs. FedEx managed to effectively raise the barriers to entry for competitors.

The Internet refined the COSMOS system. Whenever new information was entered into the system by FedEx or by customers through the Internet, all related files and databases were automatically updated. For example, when a FedEx customer placed an order through fedex.com, the information would find its way to COSMOS, FedEx's global package-tracking system. The courier's Route Planner—an electronic mapping tool—would facilitate the pickup and delivery of the order from the customer. A product movement planner would schedule the order through the Company's global air and courier operations. The customer would be able to track the status of the shipment through PowerShip or FedEx Ship. The COSMOS system handled 54 million transactions per day in 1999.

In 1998, FedEx decided to overhaul its internal IT infrastructure under Project GRID (Global Resources for Information Distribution). The project involved replacing 60,000 terminals and some PCs with over 75,000 network systems. The decision to go with network computers was made to avoid the "desktop churn" found with PCs.[7] The network computers linked over a global Internet Protocol network aimed to enhance the quality and quantity of services FedEx could deliver to its customers. For example, FedEx employees at any location at any time could track a package through the various steps in the FedEx chain. Other applications planned to be

Exhibit 2	Customer Solutions

Dell Computers pioneered the direct selling model in the computer industry and succeeded because it was able to keep inventory very low. FedEx provided the system to track and monitor the assembly of each PC on order. Because the assembly line could be in any one of five manufacturing locations around the world, however, FedEx described itself as the conveyor belt for that manufacturing line. FedEx was a key partner for Dell, allowing customised, built-to-order products to be delivered within days of a customer placing an order, a huge advantage in an industry whose components become obsolete at the rate of two percent per month.

Five years ago, **National Semiconductor Corp.** decided to outsource its warehousing and distribution to FedEx. By 1999, virtually all of NatSemi's products, manufactured by six factories (three being subcontractors) were shipped directly to FedEx's distribution warehouse in Singapore. Hence, FedEx had control over the goods, the warehouse and the dispatch of orders (via FedEx transportation, of course). Having complete visibility of NatSemi's order systems allowed FedEx to reduce the average customer delivery cycle from four weeks to two days, and distribution costs from 2.9 percent of sales to 1.2 percent. FedEx could pack and fulfill orders without NatSemi having to notify them. In effect, it became the logistics department of NatSemi. Furthermore, this arrangement enabled NatSemi to dispense with seven regional warehouses in the US, Asia and Europe. NatSemi reported savings in the region of US$8 million over the five-year period (see Exhibit 4).

For **Omaha Steaks,** when orders were received, they would be relayed from Omaha Steaks' IBM AS/400 to its warehouse and simultaneously to FedEx by dedicated line. FedEx would generate the tracking and shipping labels and the orders would be delivered to one of FedEx's regional hubs for onward delivery.

Cisco Systems was a Silicon Valley Internet hardware maker that transacted 80 percent of its business over the web. At the end of 1999, FedEx had signed an agreement with Cisco to co-ordinate all of Cisco's shipping over the next two years, and to gradually eliminate Cisco's warehousing over the following three years. How could this be possible? Cisco had factories in the US, Mexico, Scotland, Taiwan and Malaysia. The finished parts were stored in warehouses near the factories awaiting completion of the whole order before it was dispatched to the customer. But Cisco did not want to build more warehouses, pay for reshipping and hold massive volumes of inventory in transit. So the solution was to merge the orders in transit. As soon as parts were manufactured, they would be shipped to customers. Once all the parts had arrived at the customer's site, assembly would take place, thus doing away with warehousing. (This was known as the "merge-in-transit" programme offered to companies such as Micron Computers.) FedEx created a unique system for Cisco that would automatically select routes and pick the most effective and economical mode of transportation, which included carriers other than FedEx's fleet of trucks and planes. Just as critical, however, was that the real-time information status of the synchronisation operation was constantly available on the Internet.

launched included COSMOS Squared, which allowed Non-Event Tracking, a feature that triggered alerts when scheduled events, such as the arrival of a package, did not occur. Through a 24-hour, seven-day operation called the Global Operations Command Centre, the central nervous system of FedEx's worldwide system in Memphis, FedEx was able to provide efficient gathering and dissemination of real-time data. The operation housed huge screens covering the walls that tracked world events, weather patterns and the real-time movement of FedEx trucks and aircraft. New systems were also introduced to predict with greater accuracy the amount of inbound traffic. This system allowed FedEx to prioritise the hundreds of variables involved in the successful pickup, processing and delivery of a parcel. Senior managers at FedEx believed that having current and accurate information helped them to reduce failure in the business.

As well as the data centre in Memphis, FedEx operated other centres in Colorado Springs, Orlando, Dallas-Fort Worth, Singapore, Brussels and Miami.

Also in 1999, FedEx signed an agreement with Netscape to adopt Netscape software as the primary technology for accessing its corporate intranet sites. FedEx's intranet included more than 60 websites, created for its end users and in some cases by its end users. Customers could build integrated websites using FedEx Applications Programming Interfaces (API) or FedEx intraNetShip (free downloads from fedex.com) and incorporate a link that would allow them to track packages directly from their own site. Over 5,000 Websites fed hundreds of thousands of tracking requests through to the fedex.com site.

"Our API solutions are designed to give global visibility and access across the supply-chain, from manufactur-

Exhibit 3   FedEx Solutions for the Entire Supply Chain

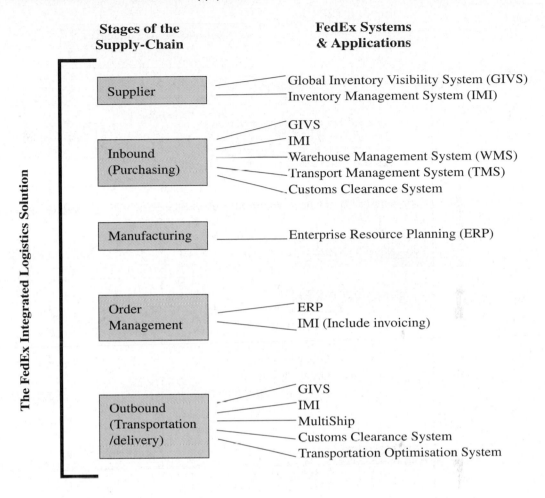

ing to customer service to invoicing. We've managed to wipe out those irritating WISMO (Where Is My Order) calls because we've seamlessly linked our customers to their customers."

—Mike Janes, former VP, Electronic Commerce & Logistics Marketing, FedEx[8]

At the beginning of 1999, FedEx launched an enhancement to its package-tracking service. Customers could query and receive package status information for up to 25 shipments simultaneously, and forward this information on to up to three e-mail recipients. Furthermore, users in France, Japan, Italy, Germany, the Netherlands and Portuguese- and Spanish-speaking countries could access this information on-line in their native languages through fedex.com.

FedEx claimed to have the largest on-line client server network in the world that operated in real-time.

Information became an extremely critical part of its business.

"We're in the express transportation business, but we've discovered how to lock up a lot of value in the information that we have."

—Mark Dickens, VP Electronic Commerce & Customer Services[9]

". . . even when on the physical side of the business, we outsource, for instance, the pick-up or the delivery or the warehousing activity for a customer, we have never outsourced the information. Protecting the brand has always been very, very critical for us."

—William Conley

The benefits of these services were not limited to FedEx's customers. For FedEx, its on-line services, which in 1999

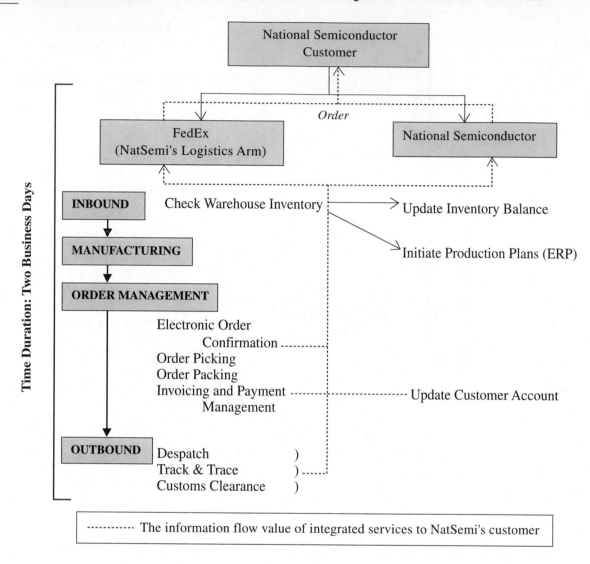

---------- The information flow value of integrated services to NatSemi's customer

handled 60 million transactions per day, saved FedEx the cost of 200,000 customer service employees. In turn, the Company reported spending 10 percent of its US$17 billion annual revenue on IT in 1999. Information had allowed FedEx to lower its costs such that the cost to customers of using FedEx in 1999 was lower than it was 25 years ago.

Going beyond delivery services, FedEx aimed to fully integrate its corporate partners every step of the way along the supply-chain. Fundamental to FedEx's strategy for establishing its e-business and logistics operations was how well it could forge technology links with customers.

"It's all about integration, whether it's inside FedEx, with our technology partners, or with our customers."
—Laurie Tucker, Senior VP, Logistics Electronic Commerce & Catalog[10]

"Integration of Internet services with our transportation offerings is not an addition to our core business; it is our core business."
—Dennis Jones, CIO[11]

"When it comes to managing synergies across businesses, we've found that seamless information integration is a critical component."[12]

Management and Operations Issues

Branding and Business Structure Up Until 19 January, 2000

In the first 21 years of business, FedEx operated under the corporate name of Federal Express Corporation. Its customers came to recognise it as "FedEx" in short and the brand took off as the Company grew and expanded its service offerings under the purple and orange flag. Hence in 1994, it seemed natural that the Company should change its brand name to "FedEx."

The Parts Bank was given official recognition when it became a division of FedEx Corp. in 1988 and became known as Business Logistics Services (BLS). It operated as a separate and independent company. In line with the express transportation side of the business, BLS developed expertise in the high-value, high-tech industries. It was involved in the express inbound, outbound and redistribution of goods. However, it focused mainly on the small parcel business. FedEx based its solutions on just-in-time logistics. As the business grew, concern was raised that the logistics business was not generating revenue for the express transportation business, but rather feeding this through to other carriers. Hence in 1994, BLS was renamed FedEx Logistics, and it became mandatory for the logistics business to include FedEx transportation as part of its solution to customers. In 1996, the division changed its name yet again, to FedEx Logistics and Electronic Commerce (FLEC). The Company started to focus its resources on doing business on the Internet, and the name change was to reflect the changes in the marketplace.

Following the acquisition of Caliber Systems, Inc., in 1998, five separate subsidiary companies were formed: Federal Express, RPS, Roberts Express, Viking Freight and FDX Logistics. The latter four were Caliber businesses. Each subsidiary was managed independently and was responsible for its own accounts (see Exhibit 5). However, Caliber and FedEx's logistics operations were fundamentally different in that they had completely distinct customer bases and service offerings. Caliber developed expertise in moving raw materials, plates of steel and steel bars and managing work-in-progress. It would manage the manufacturing of cars and forklift trucks. Caliber provided an elaborate logistics operation concentrating mainly on high-priced goods industries, and it provided a fuller supply-chain solution than FLEC did, whereas FLEC was primarily focused on finished goods, transportation logistics, and reverse logistics (i.e., handling returns). One was concentrating its business at the front-end of the supply chain (e.g., receiving, work-in-progress) while the other was more involved in the back-end operations of the supply-chain (i.e., warehousing, transportation). Hence the two operations continued to operate independently of each other. Logistics systems and applications were also developed independently. Caliber Logistics became a subsidiary company under FDX Logistics, while FLEC continued as a division within Federal Express, the express transportation arm.

The acquisition served to reinforce FedEx's commitment to becoming more than just an express delivery company. Yet commentators and customers continued to associate the FedEx brand with transportation, and FedEx fought to transform the image of the Company outside of this mould. One solution was to rename the Company. With the acquisition, the Company created a holding company, "FDX Corporation." However, FedEx did very little to promote its new FDX corporate brand. Furthermore, its transportation subsidiary continued to operate under the Federal Express name with the purple and orange FedEx brand on its trucks and vans. The FedEx brand lived on, but with no advertising or aggressive promotion of FDX, the name did not resonate in the marketplace. While the likes of UPS had the advantage of promoting just one brand—UPS—to sell the entire company and its many service offerings, FedEx was trying to promote five different subsidiary companies with completely unrelated names and business logos under the FDX banner through distinctly separate sales and customer service teams. Furthermore, with two separate logistics businesses within the Group, separate sales forces selling services offered by different parts of the Company, separate customer services staff to deal with different queries and IT resources spread across the Group, customers were confused and resources were duplicated.

Despite the confusion, by 1999 FedEx purported to offer companies "total one-stop shopping" for solutions at all levels of the supply-chain. Each subsidiary continued to operate independently, with separate accounting systems and customer service staffs while competing collectively. However, while maintaining the autonomy of each subsidiary company, the challenge for FedEx was how to bring the companies closer together to create those synergies. Providing customers with a single point of access to the whole Group was the ultimate goal. In practical terms, the task was to decide how each of the subsidiary companies should leverage its skills and services to a broader audience.

Events Leading Up to the January 2000 Reorganisation

FedEx needed to address a number of factors that would affect the prospects of the Company.

- **Federal Express** was the world leader in global express distribution, offering 24–48–hour delivery to 211 countries that comprised 90 percent of the world's GDP. In 1998, FedEx was the undisputed leader in the overnight package delivery business. It had a fleet of 44,500 ground vehicles and 648 planes that gave support to the US$14-plus billion business. It had 34,000 drop-off locations, and 67 percent of its US domestic shipping transactions were generated electronically. Goods shipped ranged from flowers to lobsters to computer components. This company was constantly running in crisis mode, seeking to move packages through all weather and conditions to fulfil shipments overnight. The underlying philosophy that ensured high service levels was that every package handled could make a difference to someone's life. The company handled nearly three million shipments per day in 1998.

- **RPS** was North America's second-largest provider of business-to-business ground small-package delivery. It was a low-cost, non-union, technology-savvy company acquired with the Caliber purchase. The company specialised in business-to-business shipments in one to three days, a service that FedEx could not attract because it was unable to offer prices low enough to attract enough volume. Being a 15-year-old company, RPS prized itself on having one of the lowest cost models in the transportation industry. It employed only owner-operators to deliver its packages. In terms of volume and revenue growth, RPS out-performed FedEx. For the future, plans were to grow RPS's business-to-consumer delivery service to take advantage of the growth of electronic commerce, thus carving a niche in the burgeoning residential delivery market. In 2000, the company owned 8,600 vehicles, achieved annual revenues of US$1.9 billion and employed 35,000 people, including independent contractors. It handled 1.5 million packages per day.

- **Viking Freight** was the first less-than-truckload freight carrier in the western United States. The company employed 5,000 people, managed a fleet of 7,660 vehicles and 64 service centres, and shipped 13,000 packages per day.

- **Roberts Express** was the world's leading surface-expedited carrier for non-stop, time-critical and special-handling shipments. The service offered by Roberts Express has been likened to a limousine service for freight. In 1999, the company handled more than 1,000 shipments per day. it was the smallest company within the FedEx Group. Urgent shipments could be loaded onto trucks within 90 minutes of a call and shipments would arrive within 15 minutes of the promised time 96 percent of the time. Once loaded, shipments could be tracked by satellite every step of the way. Goods such as works of art or critical manufacturing components often required exclusive-use truck services. Exclusivity allowed customers greater control but at a price. This service was an infrequent necessity for most customers. Roberts had exclusive use of a handful of FedEx aircrafts, but the company still had to pay for use and for crew time.

- **Caliber Logistics** was a pioneer in providing customised, integrated logistics and warehousing solutions worldwide. The acquisition of Caliber in January 1998 brought with it over-the-road transportation and warehousing capabilities. Since the acquisition, FedEx tried to move away from traditional logistics offerings to providing total supply-chain management solutions, and Caliber Logistics was renamed FDX Logistics. To the customer, this meant that FedEx could provide warehousing services, but only if this was part of a bigger deal. In September 1999, FedEx bought its first freight forwarder, Caribbean Transport Services (formerly GeoLogistics Air Services). Caribbean had a strong overseas network. FDX Logistics was the parent company of FedEx Supply-chain Services and Caribbean Transportation Services.

FedEx's Performance

In the year ending 31 May, 1999, the Company had out-performed analyst expectations, posting record earnings of 73 percent, an increase of 28 percent over the previous year.[13] Net income had risen 30 percent to US$221 million. However, results took a downturn in the following financial year. For the first quarter ended 31 August, 1999, FedEx announced that rising fuel prices had severely impacted upon the Company's net income, causing it to miss its first-quarter target. With no sign of improvements in fuel prices and with the US domestic market growth slowing down, FedEx warned that earnings for the second quarter and the full fiscal year may fall below analyst expectations. Bearing in mind that the express transportation business (mainly Federal Express and RPS) accounted for over 80 percent of the Group's revenue, and that the US market accounted for approximately US$10 billion of the Group's revenue, both trends had a significant negative impact on net income.

Sure enough, FedEx reported that for the quarter ended 30 November 1999, operating income was down by 10 percent on the previous year and net income was down by six percent. The Company was not achieving the level of US domestic growth as expected. Rising fuel prices continued to erode operating income. However, operations other than express transportation (i.e., Viking Freight, Roberts Express, FDX Logistics and Caribbean Transportation Service) achieved revenue and operating income increases of 27 percent and 12 percent respectively in the second quarter. With the adverse fuel prices alone, the Company anticipated that operating income could be down by more than US$150 million for the year ending 31 May, 2000. This called for some immediate remedial action.

Other trends within the express transportation and logistics market were also putting pressure on the Company to re-think its business strategy.

The Internet Market and e-Tailing

The Internet changed the basis for competition for most businesses. Its low cost and diversity of applications made it appealing and accessible. The Internet levelled the playing field such that, once a company was on-line, as long as it fulfilled its orders to the expectations of its customers, the size of the company was of no significance. The impact of the Internet on FedEx was twofold. Firstly, it opened up opportunities in logistics management for FedEx as businesses were using the Internet to re-engineer their supply-chains. So long as customers were satisfied, it really did not matter whether the goods were warehoused or not, whether the goods came directly from a factory in some distant location or whether the goods had been made to order. Integration with customer supply-chains was the key.

Secondly, the express transportation needs associated with the growth in e-tailing (expected to reach US$7 billion in 2000) and business-to-business EC (expected to reach US$327 billion by 2002) presented enormous opportunities for companies such as FedEx.[14,15]

FedEx was sure that it had the right business model to take advantage of these opportunities.

> "We're right at the centre of the new economy. . . . Businesses are utilising the Internet to re-engineer the supply-chain. In the new economy, the Internet is the neural system. We're the skeleton—we make the body move."
> —Fred Smith[16]

But so were its competitors.

The Competition

In January 2000, CBS MarketWatch Live reported that FedEx's express delivery business was maturing and was not growing as fast as it used to.[17] Furthermore, the industry was loaded with companies, local and global, that provided a myriad of transportation services to a wide range of businesses. Competition was fierce. All major transportation and delivery companies were betting big on technology. Although FedEx pioneered the web-based package-tracking system, such systems became the industry norm rather than a competitive advantage.

The four leading companies in the international courier business were DHL, FedEx, UPS and TNT. Between them they held more than 90 percent of the worldwide market.[18]

UPS

Since 1986, UPS had spent US$9 billion on IT and had formed five alliances in 1997 to disseminate its logistics software to EC users. However, while FedEx developed all its ITS software in-house, UPS made a point in stating that it was not a software developer and that companies taking that route were "trying to go a bridge too far."[19]

In early 1998, UPS formed a strategic alliance with Open Market, Inc., a US-based provider of Internet software, to deliver a complete Internet commerce solution providing integrated logistics and fulfilment. They were also working with IBM and Lotus to standardise formats on their website.

In 1999, UPS raised US$5.47 billion through its initial public offering, the largest in the US IPO history. The company shipped more than 55 percent of goods ordered over the Internet and offered over the full range of logistics solutions to its customers.

DHL

In 1993, DHL announced a four-year US$1.25 billion worldwide capital spending programme aimed at investing in handling systems, automation, facilities and computer technology. The company launched its website in 1995. It was 25 percent owned by Deutsche Post and 25 percent owned by Lufthansa Airlines. Plans were under way for an initial public offering in the first half of 2001. Though the company dominated the UK market, it projected an increase in worldwide turnover of 18 percent to US$5.26 billion.[20]

TNT

In 1998, TNT launched a web collection facility on the Internet. Later the same year, TNT launched the world's first global price checker service on its Website that allowed customers to calculate the price of sending a consignment from one place to another anywhere in the world. Other applications were under development that would allow customers to integrate with TNT's on-line services. Then in 1999, TNT launched Quickshipper, a one-stop on-line access to TNT's entire range of distribution services, from pricing to delivery. This new service was to be integrated with existing on-line tools such as web collection and price checker.

Also in March 1999, TNT launched the express industry's first dedicated customer extranet, Customised Services environment. This offered regular customers easy access to detailed and personalised shipment information through the use of user IDs and passwords. With this came a host of service offerings.

While FedEx had pioneered many logistics solutions that had helped it to achieve economies of scale faster than its competitors, the advantages were quickly eroding as newer technologies became even more powerful and less expensive.

The January 2000 Announcement

"All of your transportation and logistics needs can now be met by one organisation—FedEx Corporation."[21]

On 19 January, 2000, FedEx announced three major strategic initiatives:

- A new branding strategy that involved changing the Company's name to "FedEx Corporation," and extending the "FedEx" brand to four of its five sub-

sidiary companies. The subsidiary companies became:
- FedEx Express (formerly Federal Express)
- FedEx Ground (formerly RPS)
- FedEx Custom Critical (formerly Roberts Express)
- FedEx Logistics (formerly Caliber Logistics)
- Viking Freight (no change)
  (See Exhibit 6)
- Major reorganisations such that there would be one point of access to sales, customer services, billing and automation systems. With these consolidations, the Company announced intentions to form a sixth subsidiary called FedEx Corporate Services Corp. in June 2000 (see Exhibit 7 for new Group structure). The new subsidiary would pool together the marketing, sales, customer services, information technology and electronic commerce resources of the Group. The invoicing functions would also be combined for all the companies.
- Introduction of a new low-cost residential delivery service, FedEx Home Delivery, to be launched in the U.S.

Of significance was the merging of the two logistics operations (Caliber Logistics and FLEC) into FedEx Logistics. The two companies seemed to complement each other in terms of their service offerings and customer base. Both had a few of the same customers but many different ones. Furthermore, Caliber's presence was mainly in North America and Europe, while FLEC had expanded into other continents. FedEx Logistics brought together all the splintered operations of logistics in all the subsidiary companies, streamlining costs, presenting one

Exhibit 6	Before and After the Reorganisation
Before	**After**
Multiple brands under FDX umbrella	A single branding system leveraging the power of the FedEx brand so more customers can use FedEx reliability as a strategic competitive advantage.
Separate sales force with directed co-operation	A single, expanded sales force especially targeting small- and medium-sized businesses, cross-selling a wide portfolio of services and pricing schemes
Multiple invoices and account numbers	A single invoice and single account number from FedEx
Multiple automation platforms offering all FDX services	Streamlined customer automation systems to handle electronic transactions and database management needs for small and large businesses
Separate customer service, claims trace functions	Single customer service, claims and trace functions by calling 1-800-Go-FedEx® (800-463-3339) or visiting its website at www.fedex.com

Exhibit 7   Group Structure

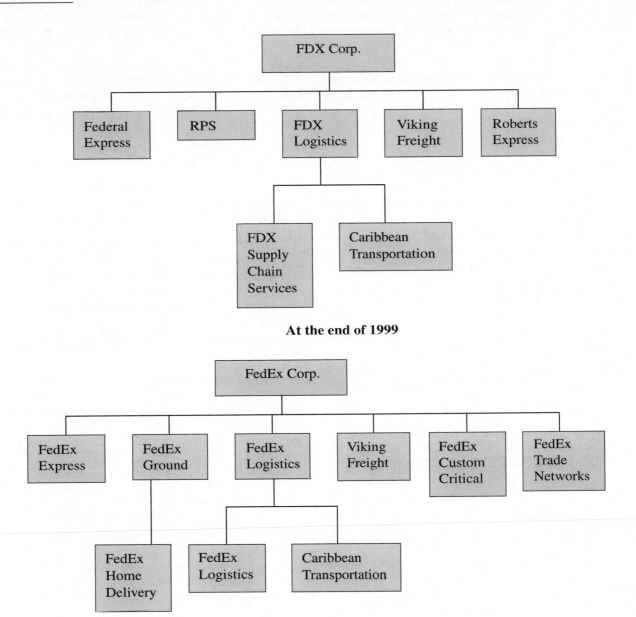

At the end of 1999

Following the January 2000 Reorganisation

menu of logistics service offerings to customers, and aligning R&D of systems upon common, agreed platforms. This reorganisation also brought about another major change in operations. It was no longer mandatory for the logistics business to use FedEx transportation as part of its solutions to customers. Being "carrier-agnostic" meant that FedEx Logistics would use FedEx transportation where it fitted, both in terms of cost and in terms of

geographic coverage. The decision would also rest on customer preference and the kind of goods being transported. For example, Caliber was transporting fork-lift trucks, cars and steel plates that FedEx did not have the physical capacity to handle.

Combining the two operations brought together the IT expertise and the know-how of the logistics business. Under one CIO, standards were set for the development of systems on a worldwide basis, including vendor selection. In the past, regions developed their own solutions and operated in isolation. However, the Internet forced the Company to consolidate its systems and solutions as customers demanded global solutions. Through the IT groups located in Memphis, Leiden (Holland) and Singapore, the Company resolved to develop global systems for worldwide implementation, with functions such as multiple currencies and multiple languages. FedEx Logistics forecast a 70 percent growth rate in the year ending 31 May, 2000. However, the business so far failed to generate any profit. The company aimed to built on its expertise in the five market segments: health care, industrial, high-tech, automotive and consumer.

The Company anticipated having to spend US$100 million on these changes over three years. The intention was to take advantage of one of its greatest assets, the FedEx brand name; the name that customers could count on for "absolutely, positively" reliable service and cutting-edge innovation. The value of the brand had been ignored, particularly when the Company decided to change its corporate name to FDX in 1998. Realising its mistake, the renaming of the Company as FedEx Corporation and the extension of the brand to its subsidiaries fell in line with its intention to provide customers with an integrated set of business solutions. Customers wanted to deal with one company to meet their transportation and logistics needs.

Each subsidiary company was to continue operating independently, but collectively the Group would provide a wide range of business solutions. It was this collective synergy of solutions that FedEx believed would form the competitive advantage of the Company in the future. For customers, the benefits included easier means of doing business with FedEx. There was to be one toll-free telephone number, one website, one invoice and account number, one sales team, one customer service team and a streamlined customer automation platform to handle electronic transactions for small and large businesses (see Exhibits 6 and 7 for details of the changes following reorganisation). The new organisation was aimed at helping businesses of all sizes to achieve their shipping, logistics, supply-chain and e-business objectives. However, analysts questioned whether the new Group structure would work, given that there would still be different teams of delivery and pickup staff for the different operations. Hence, one person could pick up one package sent by ground and another person could pick up another package sent by express from the same company. Companies such as UPS, on the other hand, would have one person pick up both types of packages.

In addition to these changes, FedEx anticipated growth in consumer EC and planned to start a new service called FedEx Home Delivery (within the FedEx Ground subsidiary company) to meet the needs of businesses specialising in business-to-consumer e-tailing. FedEx had been successful in providing services to the business-to-business EC market. Now it aimed to achieve the same leadership status in the business-to-consumer EC market. However, expanding the residential delivery business was one segment that FedEx consciously made a decision not to pursue throughout the 1990s. This gave UPS the opportunity to lead in residential delivery services.

In late 1997, Smith was quoted as saying,

> "We've made huge (investments in our networks, and now that bow wave had passed. We think we have a good chance of harvesting a lot of that investment."[22]

In the two years that followed, the results of the Company showed little signs of a harvest. Was the January restructuring going to bring in the harvest? The announcement certainly served to tell investors that they were making some major changes to address some competitive issues. However, analysts took a pragmatic view to the announcement, saying that "the proof is in the pudding."[23]

> "Our biggest challenge is to correctly manage everything that's on our plate."
>
> —Fred Smith[24]

Was the reorganisation going to leverage the power of the networks and the information and logistics infrastructures that FedEx had built? Did it provide the right ingredients to achieve the objectives of creating value for FedEx customers while at the same time improving profitability for FedEx? Given the speed at which technology and the marketplace were changing, would the new organisation structure be adaptable to the changing business environment? Were there better alternative solutions that the Company could have considered?

Endnotes

1. 1999 Annual Report.
2. Janah, M. and Wilder, C., "Special Delivery," *Information Week*, URL: http://www.FedExcorp.com/media/infowktop100.html, 1997.
3. The Company was incorporated as Federal Express Corporation" in 1971. In 1994, the Company was renamed "FedEx Corporation" and subsequently renamed "FDX Corporation" in 1998 and then "FedEx Corporation" in 2000. However, throughout the case, the Company is referred to as "FedEx" to avoid confusion.
4. Garten, 1998
5. Bruner, R. F. and Bulkley, D., "The Battle for Value: Federal Express Corporation versus United Parcel Service of America, Inc. (Abridged)," University of Virginia Darden School Foundation, 1995.
6. Krause, K., "Not UPS with a Purple Tint," *Traffic World*, URL: http://www.trafficworld.com/reg/news/special/s101899.html, October 1999.
7. "Desktop churn" refers to the rapid obsolescence of PCs as new applications eat up processing power.

Case 15 / FedEx Corp.: Structural Transformation Through e-Business

8. Gentry, C., "FedEx API's Create Cinderella Success Stories," October 1998, URL: http://www.fedex.com/us/about/api.html.

9. Janah, M. and Wiler, C., "Special Delivery," *Information Week*, URL: http://www.FedExcorp.com/media/infowktop100.html, 1997.

10. Janah, M. and Wilder, C. (1997).

11. Cone, E. and Duvall, M., "UPS Keeps Truckin'; FedEx: A Documented Success," *Inter@ctive Week*, 16 November, 1999.

12. 1999 Annual Report.

13. Gelsi, S., "FDX Posts Stronger-than-Expected Profit," CBS MarketWatch, 30 June, 1999, URL: http://cbs.marketwatch.com/archive.../current/fdx.htm?source=&dist=srch, February 2000.

14. Lappin, T., "The Airline of the Internet," *Wired*, 4 (12), December 1996, URL: http://www.wired.com/wired/4.12/features/ffedex.html.

15. Erwin, B., Modahl, M. A., and Johnson, J., "Sizing Intercompany Commerce," *Business Trade & Technology Strategies*, 1 (1), Forrester Research, Cambridge, MA, 1997.

16. Collingwood, H., 1999.

17. Adamson, D., "FDX Corp. Changes Name to FedEx," CBS MarketWatch Live, 19 January, 2000.

18. Murphy, D. and Hernly, K., "Air Couriers Soar Despite Mainland Gloom," *South China Morning Post*, 30 May, 1999.

19. Blackmon, D. A., "Ante Up! Big Gambles in the New Economy: Overnight Everything Changed for FedEx," *The Wall Street Journal Interactive Edition*, URL: http://www.djreprints.com/jitarticles/trx0001272701443.html, 4 November, 1999.

20. Exolby, J., "Interview—DHL UK Foresees Tough Market," URL: http://blz.yahoo.com/rf/000117/mq.html, 17 January, 2000.

21. Corporate Overview, FedEx Corporation, URL: http://www.fedexcorp.com/aboutfdx/corporateoverview.html, 20th January, 2000.

22. Grant, L., "Why FedEx is Flying High," 10 November, 1997, URL: http://pathfinder.com/fortune/1997-971110/fed.html.

23. Bazdarich, C., "What's in a Name?: Traders Swayed by Nominal Changes," CBS MarketWatch, 21 January, 2000, URL: http://cbs.marketwatch.com/archive...st.htx?source=htx/http2_mw&dist=na, February 2000.

24. Collingwood, H., 1999.

Halterm

Mary Brooks

Dallhousie University

Introduction

It was mid-November 1996 and Patrick Morin, President of Halterm, was making his way towards Gate 24 Terminal 3 at Heathrow airport. There was still plenty of time to make the noon flight to Halifax. He was on his way home after touring a number of European container terminals and visiting with customers. The trip had been well worthwhile in helping him develop his ideas about the business plan he would present to his Board in December.

He'd been at Halterm a half year. It was an exciting time to work in this business but the stakes were high. The day before the previous Board meeting, P&O Containers had announced its merger with Nedlloyd, creating one of the world's largest container lines. Any rationalization could result in lost business. P&O, a customer of Halterm, was a member of the Grand Alliance while Nedlloyd was a member of the Global Alliance; assuming the European Commission approved the merger, which alliance would the new company choose? That approval was expected mid-December.

However, it was more complicated than that. P&O was a participant in the Grand Alliance's Asia East Coast Express (AEX) service calling at Halterm and its Pacific Atlantic Express (PAX) service that called Ceres, Halifax's other container terminal. The alliance members had decided to consolidate terminals within ports of call.

Therefore, even if P&O remained within the Grand Alliance, it was possible that Halterm would lose its P&O business to Ceres. In addition, this proposed merger was probably only the beginning; the industry was entering a period of consolidation and restructuring, as technology challenged traditional approaches. The Board was looking for concrete plans in the face of these uncertainties.

About the Company

Halterm operates a 70-acre ship-to-shore cargo transfer and storage facility in Halifax, Nova Scotia. As Canada's largest Atlantic coast container terminal operation, it services the needs of domestic and international shipping lines that call at the Port of Halifax by providing the logistical link between the ocean-going vessels and the inland transportation system. Although specializing in handling container cargo, the facility is a full-service operation and provides stevedoring services for ro-ro and break-bulk cargo[1] as well. Halterm's other competitive advantages are its deep-water berths, its link to the Canadian National (CN) inland rail network and its ability to provide efficient, low cost container handling services to most container vessels. The terminal operates at the mouth of Halifax harbour on premises leased from the Halifax Port Corporation (HPC). (See Appendix A.)

Located within one hour of the Great Circle Route,[2] the Port of Halifax is well situated to service the needs of major international shipping lines that carry cargo between North America and Europe, the Mediterranean, and Southeast Asia and services diverse geographic locations. (See Appendix B.) Halifax is the first port-of-call inbound and the last port-of-call out for North America-Europe trade; this means that import cargo discharged in Halifax can be delivered to inland customers more quickly than from other east coast ports. Conversely,

inland shippers have more time to get export cargo ready for shipment through Halifax as compared to other east coast ports. Finally, the Port of Halifax is ice-free on a year-round basis.

The Port's principal disadvantage is its lack of a local market. Halifax depends largely (80 percent) on its ability to service inland markets that are located 1300–2500 km (800–1500 miles) from the port. This makes the cost of inland transport more expensive relative to other major east coast ports.

History

Halterm started operations in 1969 as a joint venture company owned by Clarke Transport Canada Inc. (Clarke), CN and Halifax International Containers (Halicon), itself a partnership of the Province of Nova Scotia and the City of Halifax. Halterm was initially established to service the needs of Dart Container Line, a shipping consortium that included Clarke.

In 1968, Brian Doherty, Halterm's first terminal manager and an employee of Clarke, was assigned by Clarke to set up a new container facility. National Harbours Board (NHB), the predecessor of HPC, was building a new pier (Pier C) south of Pier B for Clarke as a private facility. Dart wanted to establish a North Atlantic container service with a Canadian call and was exploring possibilities in Montreal, Saint John and Halifax. Port characteristics at the time favoured Halifax. In return for making the private terminal at Pier C a common user facility, Clarke acquired a long-term management contract. In return for a small investment, each partner (Clarke, CN and Halicon) took one-third ownership. For its part, Dart promised to make Halifax its Canadian port of call as long as it called at Canada. Halterm, the first common user container terminal in North America with on-dock rail facilities, was born.

By 1972 Halterm was in full operation with two ship-to-shore gantry cranes, two ship berths and the required support equipment. In 1974, a third ship-to-shore gantry crane was added and steady growth followed throughout the 1970s. However, the 1980s brought more than a worldwide recession. Brian Doherty describes the events that almost destroyed Halterm ten years after its founding:

By the late 1970s there was a perception that the terminal didn't have the capacity to handle future volumes. The Chairman of Halterm, lawyer Bill Mingo, was keen to expand capacity and began to look at the development of a second facility with the intention that Halterm would operate both facilities. Despite what Halterm management believed was the best proposal to operate the facility, NHB chose to seek another operator [Ceres]. What this did was encourage a price war with disastrous financial results for both terminal operators. Prices dropped by a third. Although ZIM [ZIM Israel Navigation Company] and Dart remained with Halterm, both ACL and Hapag Lloyd moved to the new terminal.

Brian Doherty continues:

Then Dart was acquired by OOCL [Orient Overseas Container Limited]. Dart was in financial difficulty. OOCL moved Dart operations to Montreal. This was Halterm's lowest point; it had gone from a financially well-off company to a loss position. A lawsuit was launched against Dart because it breached its promise to stay in Halifax. About this time, Stanley Clarke sold his business to NCC [Newfoundland Capital Corporation Limited].

In 1984, Halicon terminated its participation in Halterm as the government could not be seen as a partner in only one of two competing facilities. Halterm purchased Halicon's shares and put them in trust, hoping to find a new partner to buy them. Brian Doherty continues:

As the managing partner of the joint venture, NCC was not interested in absorbing the potential losses. We went to New York and convinced an alliance of K-Line, NOL [Neptune Orient Lines] and OOCL to relocate their Pacific service from Saint John to Halifax in return for dropping the lawsuit against Dart and giving Furness Withy Terminals, an OOCL subsidiary, the opportunity to take up Halicon's shares. This put us back on a recovery track.

Since then, the facility has undergone two significant capital expansions. In 1984 the operating system of Halterm was renewed at a cost of approximately $10 million; the yard cargo-handling system was changed from a maintenance-intensive straddle carrier system to one that employed rubber-tire yard gantries, yard tractors and chassis. In 1991, a fourth conventional ship-to-shore gantry crane and additional support equipment were added at a total cost of approximately $15 million. Brian Doherty, then President of Halterm, recalls the thinking of the day:

At the end of the 1980s we started to do studies. The first post-Panamax[3] ships were being built and we got quotes on the price of a post-Panamax crane. It didn't make sense to buy just one but one was all we needed for our existing business. We weren't prepared to make the infrastructure investment to support only one post-Panamax crane so we added a traditional one. This way we could guarantee service.

The terminal was simultaneously expanded with the addition of a new 12-acre working pier at Pier B, increasing the total area to its present size and adding a third deep-water

berth. The company needed Pier B for feeder operators and smaller vessels in order to keep the main berth at Pier C free for the larger vessels that had berth guarantees in their contracts.

Patrick Morin became President of Halterm in March of 1996. Born in Northern Ontario, he grew up in Sept Isles on the north shore of the St. Lawrence River, where his parents worked for the Quebec North Shore and Labrador Railway. In 1973, armed with a degree in electrical engineering from the University of Ottawa, he returned to Sept Isles to work for the Iron Ore Company of Canada (IOC) for the next 17 years. During that time he wore many hats, including managing the IOC's in-house consulting group that had a mandate to optimize the train system for the handling of IOC's logistical needs. In 1989 he joined St. Lawrence Stevedoring, one of the Cast group of companies; its primary business was to transfer iron ore coming in from Brazil to the smaller vessels that would take the ore into the Great Lakes system. When the company was sold in 1991, he stayed with Cast, working as Vice-President, Cast Terminal Inc. in Montreal.

In 1993 Morin moved to Zeebrugge, Belgium to take over the European end of the Cast operation as Vice-President Customer Service. By this time, Cast was one of two large container operators on the Montreal-North Europe route. However, Cast's major creditor, the Royal Bank of Canada, was keen to extricate itself from the company whose shares it had acquired in a 1983 restructuring. When CP's proposal to acquire Cast passed the scrutiny of the Competition Bureau and the National Transportation Agency in early 1995, it was clear to Morin that CP would move in its own management. He returned to North America and worked for a small company he hoped to acquire. However, the Halterm opportunity came up and, in March 1996, Morin arrived at Halterm.

Halterm was not an unknown company to Morin. On behalf of Cast, he had explored Halterm as an alternative to Montreal several years earlier. He believed the company was a good business, fairly efficient but very expensive. Morin described his early days at the company:

> On arrival, my first order of business had to be visiting customers; 80 percent of our stevedoring contracts with the lines were up. Within the first six months, we concluded contracts with Melfi (a new call), renewed our contracts with SPM, Maersk and ZIM with changes, and worked towards the setting up of the Halifax Employers' Association [to negotiate with the unions].
>
> In getting to know our customers, I found that Halterm was not viewed as the most expensive of terminals. However, it was only working at 60 percent capacity. Its labour reputation was good but not progressive. Labour [in Halifax] is quite entrenched in its thinking. They still

> insist on a lunch hour when all work stops. The current situation works best for under-performing lines but is not optimized for those who run on a tight schedule.
>
> At my first Board meeting I was asked to produce a mission and a strategic plan for the business. We had previously developed strategies but something new was needed. The next meeting, we presented the mission and were given the go-ahead to develop the strategy.

It is that strategy that Morin will present at the December board meeting.

Halterm Facilities and Operations Today

Halterm's primary business is the efficient loading and unloading of container ships that range in size from small coastal feeder vessels (having the capacity to carry 275 TEUs[4]) to large, fourth-generation container ships (capacity up to 4,000 TEUs). The overall length of the berths is 990 metres (3,250 feet.) The terminal's main berth at Pier C can accommodate ships with a maximum draft (depth of the ship beneath the water line) of 14 metres (45 feet), more than any other North American east coast port. (See Appendices A and C.)

Ships are loaded or unloaded at a rate of 22–25 containers per crane working hour. The number of container moves achieved per crane hour is the single most important measure of terminal efficiency used by the shipping lines and crane productivity is generally higher on larger container ships. As such, it is a major criterion used by shipping lines when selecting a terminal operator.

The majority of import containers discharged in Halifax are destined for the inland markets of Montreal, Toronto, and Chicago via CN's double-stack rail service to these centres. Halterm's operating system is designed to transfer containers directly from the ship to rail. Import containers destined for local markets by truck are delivered from the ship to a pre-determined terminal storage area where they are held until picked up by a local trucking firm (contracted by the shipping line).

Containers to be loaded onto a ship (export containers) arrive at Halterm either by truck or by rail, with the majority arriving by rail. CN delivers these containers directly to the on-dock rail facility, where they are off-loaded and stored awaiting the arrival of the ship. Halterm has the capacity to store 12,500 TEUs. Halterm has a total of 2,800 metres of rail track, sufficient to hold an entire unit train that can be assembled and discharged directly from the terminal to its final inland destination. In addition, a 1,525 meter loop track, following the perimeter of the terminal, provides for buffer rail storage capacity.

To facilitate the efficient movement of truck traffic to and from the terminal, Halterm and the HPC invested

$700,000 in a new, automated truck-handling facility in 1994. This increased the truck-handling capacity from an average of 130 container moves per day to 300 per day. As a result, truck turnaround times improved substantially.

Halterm also established an Electronic Data Interchange (EDI) system in partnership with CN and several of its larger customers. EDI allows Halterm to electronically receive and send cargo information on all rail movements as well as that concerning cargo to be loaded or discharged from ships. On the trucking side, hand-held computer units automatically update the yard control system in real-time and eliminate the need for multiple data entry at various stages of the operation. This technology will be extended to rail, terminal and ship operations in the near future. At its present volume, Halterm is operating at 60 percent of its capacity.

Finances

Halterm receives handling container handling revenue from its customers based on the volume of containers handled and the ancillary services provided. Container handling rates charged to Halterm's customers are established by contract and are unregulated. Contracts that continue to the end of 1998 or longer account for over 95 percent of Halterm's forecasted volume. Approximately 70 percent of Halterm's costs are variable based on throughput. The largest single cost is salaries and wages, which represent 56 percent of total costs. The next single largest expense is wharfage and berthage assessments (13 percent); these assessments are a "pass-through" expenditure collected from Halterm's customers and paid to HPC. Other costs include equipment repairs and maintenance, land and building rental, fuel, and general administration.

The single largest capital item for Halterm is a ship-to-shore gantry crane (replacement cost approximates $7 million). These cranes, given proper repair and preventive maintenance, have a useful life of 30–40 years. Halterm has an aggressive repair and maintenance program, and estimates that, for other than cranes, annual capital expenditures required to maintain throughput capacity over the next 10 years will average $850,000. Halterm's financial data are in Appendix D.

Employees and Labour Relations

The Port of Halifax has enjoyed a stable relationship between its employers and unionized workers for the past 20 years. Halterm employs a full-time staff of 30 non-unionized personnel who are responsible for the co-ordination of Halterm's operations and the adminis-

tration of Halterm's business. Many of these personnel are long-term employees. Three groups of unionized employees form a basic work force of 165. Halterm and its unions operate under the terms of a collective agreement negotiated by the Halifax Employers' Association that represents all employers of unionized labour in the Port of Halifax. Five-year collective agreements with all union locals expired on December 31, 1995, and the parties are now engaged in negotiations for a new contract. Until these negotiations are completed, the existing agreement will prevail. The last major work interruption occurred in 1976. Morin commented:

Contract negotiations have been continuing since my arrival. There are three unions and we've completed none of the labour contracts to date. If we are seriously going to attract the lines of the next century, we need to have greater flexibility in the union contracts.

Customers and Requirements

Halterm services 13 domestic and international shipping lines that call at the Port of Halifax. The terminal's three largest customers are ZIM, Maersk Canada Inc., and NOL. Combined, these three carriers account for 70 percent of Halterm's current total container volume. ZIM is Halterm's largest single customer and has been using Halterm for over 25 years. NOL began its service relationship in 1986 and Maersk in 1989. A list of customers is in Appendix E.

Customers use Halterm under service contracts that are generally reopened for rate negotiations at the end of each three-year period. The contracts set out the services to be provided and the corresponding rates of compensation. Services may include the loading or discharge of containers to and from container ships, intra-terminal movement of containers, the receipt and delivery of containers to and from rail cars and trucks, the stuffing and stripping of cargo, the provision of power and storage space for temperature-controlled containers, and so on. Each rate is calculated on the basis of the cost of labour plus an appropriate mark-up for overhead services. Contracts with major customers may contain volume rebate allowances to encourage greater use of Halterm. The typical contract with customers contains performance guarantees (in the forms of the number of lifts per hour), cranes to be made available, and so on.

Because of lines' requirements for service guarantees and their unwillingness to wait for a berth, asset utilization in the industry is mediocre. Morin is particularly concerned that Halterm is not getting the lifts per crane or lifts per hour offered by other terminals. It has become quite clear during this trip that Canadian terminals have not kept pace with their European counterparts, particularly in investing in new technology. The productivity improvements Morin had seen at European terminals were impressive. (See Table 1.)

The terminal must understand the lines' requirements more broadly that just providing a list of services. With the massive capital investment required to be a player in the container market, shipowners will avoid calling at any port where berth space is not available on demand. Berth availability is only a minimum condition for consideration as part of the carrier's network; port choice hinges on services, landside connections, door-to-door costs and transit time. The line essentially buys the port's services with an eye to selling its own. Therefore, they are looking for additional services, electronic data interchange (EDI), on-dock transfer, and distribution and warehousing facilities to make the port an integral part of the just-in-time concept. In addition, the first port-of-call status on inbound cargo and last port-of-call status on outbound is the most desirable position as it enhances a port's ability to attract time-sensitive cargoes. If shippers are buying container services on transit time, such a status will very often give a port the edge in seeking to match shippers and carriers. Once the port is chosen, there remains the choice of terminal.

Although the list of customers for any terminal tends to be short, marketing a terminal is not easy. Visiting customers is a key role for the President. Customer relations tend to become personal but, in the end, terminal choice by the shipping line is a serious commercial decision based on the terminal's operating performance and berth availability. For Morin, the relationships have been carefully tended but operations must deliver the desired service.

Morin believed that understanding the lines' requirements was insufficient; the terminal must discern the requirements of the customer's customers. Shippers tend to be port-blind. They buy the services of a carrier and pay very little attention to the route. They expect the carrier to deliver what it has promised in terms of any special equipment, services, and delivery time at an agreed time and price. It is up to the carrier to ensure that the quoted price delivers profit. Once the carrier has booked the cargo, it is a matter of ensuring that its choice of port delivers what has been promised the customer. This includes choosing a terminal that will minimize labour costs for a given standard of productivity; calls with time and a half or double time labour charges erode the profit margin on the sale. The carrier's schedule must work to attract the shipper's booking and still earn the carrier an acceptable profit.

Customers have the right to cancel their terminal contracts on 90-days written notice. (While being re-negotiated, the terms of the existing agreements prevail.) Of Halterm's volume, 72 percent is from shipping lines whose contracts expire on December 31, 1998. An additional 25 percent of volume is covered by service contracts due to expire December 31, 1996 and which are presently under re-negotiation. To win the business long-term, Halterm must at least match, if not exceed, the productivity achieved by the best terminals in the business while keeping prices to the lines low enough to allow them to offer their customers a competitively priced door-to-door package.

Business Development

As a result of internal discussions, the company developed its mission statement:

Table 1	Ports and Performance Benchmarks			
Terminal	TEU (000)	Average Lifts/hr	Annual Lifts/crane	Operation*
Cast (Montreal)	200	25	67,000	RTG
Racine (Montreal)	280	22	70,000	RTG
Halterm (Halifax)	155	22	39,000	RTG
FCT (Zeebrugge)	170	39	57,000	Straddle
ECT (Rotterdam)	580	25	72,500	Auto
Felixstowe	1,400	21	70,000	RTG
Hesitance (Antwerp)	600	35	75,000	Straddle

Note: *RTG=rubber tired yard gantries; straddle = straddle carriers; auto=robotized
SOURCE: Halterm

Halterm's mission is to become the container terminal of choice for shipping lines serving Canada and midwest US by providing superior, cost-effective performance.

To support this objective, the terminal launched a number of initiatives aimed at improving customer service and reducing terminal operating costs. Customer service initiatives focused on improved ship productivity, faster truck turnaround times, and embedding a service quality culture throughout the operation. Higher ship and terminal productivity also resulted in reduced operating costs and improved margins. With respect to new business development, Halterm maintains an active marketing program that concentrates on developing relationships with those carriers known to be considering a North Atlantic east coast port-of-call. Halterm is targeting customers with a particular interest in serving midwest US markets through Chicago, in order to maximize the potential of investments made by CN.

In 1995, CN opened its new $200 million St. Clair tunnel, linking Sarnia, Ontario to Port Huron, Michigan. Prior to the opening of the tunnel, Halifax was neither price- nor time-competitive into Chicago. The tunnel reduced the transit time from Halifax to Chicago to 54 hours, a full 24 hours less than before the tunnel opened. CN now has the capacity to carry double-stack containers from Halifax to Chicago; double-stack systems reduce unit costs and allow for more competitive inland transportation pricing. In addition, in May 1996, CN broke ground on a new 67-acre intermodal rail transfer facility in Chicago developed in conjunction with the Illinois Central. The facility has a capacity to handle up to 225,000 container or trailer units, a dramatic increase from the previous capacity of 75,000 units. The facility also permits more efficient connections with the Illinois Central. These two investments by CN have meant that Halifax is now service-competitive for traffic to Chicago and the mid-south, destinations like Memphis, Kansas City and St. Louis. Halifax's US midwest business has grown from "abysmally low," to quote Craig Littzen, Vice-President Intermodal of CN to 40,000 TEUs. The service to the US midwest via the North American east coast has a total potential market of 1.5 million TEUs (Appendix F). CN's investments and a new business plan for Halterm should ensure a larger share of midwest traffic for Halifax.

Management of Halterm

Halterm shares are owned equally by Newfoundland Capital Corporation and Canadian National, the Furness Withy shares held by OOCL having being acquired by the other two in October of 1996. The management contract is held by NCC.

Newfoundland Capital Corporation is a publicity-traded management company engaged in the transportation and communications sectors. Through the Clarke Transport Group, NCC has joint venture interests in a shipping firm and positioned itself as an integrated, full service provider of transportation services and logistical solutions. Through its communications group, NCC owns 30 newspapers and specialty magazine publications and operates 13 radio stations across Canada. NCC has managed Halterm since 1981 when it acquired Clarke.

According to Morin, Halterm's relationship with NCC is fairly autonomous; it operates as a distinct responsible entity. Roy Rideout, President and Chief Operating Officer of NCC, concurs:

The most important roles I have in relation to Halterm are the selection of the president and providing the necessary coaching. Newfoundland Capital is there to assist the president where on-site resources may be thin. I try not to get involved in the day-to-day business.

Morin believes that NCC brings financial and human resources expertise to assist the company, while Clarke has significant transport expertise of use to the company. In addition, there is a strong relationship between Clarke and CN through the Pool Car Division of Clarke However, the future of NCC is somewhat uncertain. Patrick Morin:

Right now Newfoundland Capital is under significant pressure to increase shareholder value. It has been trading at $3–4 a share over the past few years and is considerably undervalued. The communications analysts don't understand transportation and so they undervalue it. The transportation analysts don't understand communications and so they undervalue it. Both discount it because its dual focus is perceived as a lack of focus.

Canadian National is the sixth largest freight railroad in North America. It operates the larger of Canada's two principal railroads, serving the major cities, ports and natural resource regions in Canada with connections to most major United States railroads. The government-owned company was privatized in Canada's largest initial public offering on November 17, 1995.

Canadian National's interest in Halterm was one of the files Craig Littzen acquired when he arrived at CN in the summer of 1995 as CN was being readied for privatization. Early on he pushed for the removal of OOCL's interest through Furness Withy, feeling:

I was unhappy with the ownership structure. We were a passive owner, as was OOCL. Why should a company [OOCL] that gained its interest through call guarantees be entitled to a share of the profits when it no longer calls at Halifax? As a publicly owned company, we couldn't be seen to be active in the management of the terminal. Now that CN is a private company, it can take a more active role, given the strategic importance of the Halifax gateway to CN.

Both Littzen and Rideout pushed for the acquisition of OOCL's interest in the terminal. They are keen to pursue a new vision for Halterm and eager to see Morin's strategy and business plan.

The Global Container Shipping and Port Industries

The concept of containerized shipping services was first developed in 1956 for relatively high value and volume cargo that required special protection. It was not until the late 1960s, however, that containerization was adopted widely by the shipping industry. The use of containers had benefits both portside and inland. Operating efficiencies led to a dramatic growth in business. Containerization permitted shipping lines to offer their customers a fully integrated water and land-based transportation system. Container shipping is faster, less costly and offers better cargo protection. As a result, it has become the dominant means of transporting manufactured and semi-finished goods to markets around the world.

World-wide container terminal throughput has grown at an average annual rate of 9.5 percent over the past 15 years and is forecast to grow at 7.2 percent annually until 2010, according to *The Greater Halifax Multi-Modal Transportation Study* prepared by Booz-Allen & Hamilton Inc. Throughput volumes at the Port of Halifax have grown at an average annual rate of 3.8 percent over the past 15 years and an average annual rate of 5.0 percent over the past 5 years and are forecast to grow by 5 percent per year until 2005. Over the period 1980–1995, container throughput over North American ports increased from 9.9 million TEUs to 21.8 million TEUs, an annual growth rate of 5.4 percent.

Container traffic growth has been highest in East Asia where container terminal throughput increased annually by 13.6 percent over the 1980–95 period. The greatest future growth is expected to occur in Southeast Asia, particularly Thailand, Korea, and Singapore. Markets in China and India are also anticipated to provide significant growth opportunities, with China expected to be the market growth leader over the next decade. Goods shipped from Southeast Asia and India to markets such as Montreal, Toronto, and the US midwest can be cost-effectively delivered to the east coast of North America via the Suez Canal. The route has prospects for a very high growth rate. Maersk already provides a direct shipping link to these markets through its Suez services.

In addition to the increasing containerization of trade and rising trade volumes, there are a number of important structural and operational changes happening in the international container shipping industry.

First among these is the trend toward industry rationalization. Many carriers, rather than operating their own ships on select trade routes, have joined major global alliances where several lines combine ships in an operating consortium and expand their market reach. Four global alliances have been announced over the past year: (1) Maersk and SeaLand; (2) The Grand Alliance of NYK, P&O, Hapag-Lloyd and NOL; (3) The Global Alliance of APL, Mitsui O.S.K., Nedlloyd and OOCL; and (4) the alliance of Hanjin, DSR-Senator and Cho Yang. Two of these major alliances call on the Port of Halifax: the Maersk/Sea-Land alliance with its North Atlantic and Suez services, and the Grand Alliance with its AEX service calling Halterm and its PAX calling Ceres.

The second major trend is the growth in ship size. The largest containership in 1980 was 3,055 TEU; by 1996 the largest ship was rated to carry 6,250 TEU. As ships became larger, the depth advantages offered by Halifax over New York translated into more cargo as vessels sought to lighten their load before calling New York westbound or to add cargo before heading east.

Furthermore, *Containerisation International* recently noted that 60 percent of the new vessels on order were post-Panamax size. This is a dramatic change from the industry's original reticence to adopt the technology. After American President Lines' (APL) delivery of 5 in 1988; it was another four years before Hyundai Merchant Marine followed APL's lead. Since then, shipping lines have continued to order ever larger container ships in an effort to further reduce per TEU ocean cargo costs; ship-related cost savings are projected to be as high as 20 percent. (The Top 20 container shipping companies are presented in Appendix G while those ordering post-Panamax ships are noted in Appendix H.) Because of their larger size, post-Panamax ships require deeper harbour entrance channels and terminal berths. The minimum depth requirement is between 13 and 14 metres (42–45 feet). This will present a problem for many east coast North American ports as evident from Appendix C. Post-Panamax ships have been deployed on the largest, fastest growing trade routes to service the Europe/Far East, Asia/West Coast North America and intra-Asian trade routes. They are not expected to be in service on the North Atlantic for another five years as there are no facilities currently capable of servicing these vessels. The Port of Halifax is the east coast North Atlantic container port that could best handle the latest generation of post-Panamax ships on order.

With new post-Panamax vessels costing in excess of US$100 million, and many lines ordering sufficient numbers to optimize network schedules, the decision about ports served becomes more critical. How do consortia view terminal choice? A recent article in *Container Management* summed it up: apart from terminal costs, other criteria that are important in terminal choice include crane performance and turnaround time, berthing windows, port deviation times and the advantages of being able to develop a hub-and-spoke network. To compete, the article noted, many have lowered their prices and added performance guarantees (in terms of moves per crane hour). Some ports have also offered volume discounts to attract certain types of cargoes.

The *Multi-Modal Transportation Study* concluded that "international container trade is the platform of port-related economic growth." It also noted that the two container terminals in Halifax have the capacity at the berth of handling in excess of 1 million TEUs, but land storage at both terminals limits Halifax to serving only 500,000 TEUs. Furthermore, the study noted that New York, Baltimore, Hampton Roads and Montreal have all announced infrastructure investments. These range from $7 million being spent in Montreal to expand Racine Terminal by 6 acres to the $675 million allocated by New York for redesign of the terminals and deepening of the channels. (Appendix I provides more data from this study.)

The dilemma of port development is that private terminals like Halterm must often compete with heavily subsidized public facilities. (Some ports are disadvantaged by their competitors' access to public funds as local municipalities subsidize economic development with various tax concessions; it is also common for governments to allow ports to issue low-grade bonds to raise capital.) For example, the Port of New York's dredging program, once authorized, will be provided by the US Army Corps of Engineers and not reflected in New York's financial statements or its charges to its customers. The port industry is undergoing a dramatic shift worldwide as governments privatize or corporatize their facilities, and port management companies like Hutchison Ports, P&O Ports and PSA Corporation spread their operations globally.

Competitors

Halterm's competitive position must be considered in two distinct contexts. The first is the overall competitive position of the Port of Halifax compared to alternative east coast North American ports. The second is Halterm's direct competitive position with the competing container terminal in the Port of Halifax, the Ceres terminal at Fairview Cove. Morin:

Marketing a container terminal is really marketing Halifax as a port of call. If a line chooses Halifax, we have a 50 percent chance of getting the business. Capacity limits how many lines will call one terminal.

What's important to our customers, the shipping lines, is the productivity of the port call. Quick turnaround is the key. What is the point of them working hard to make gains on the water side if we waste it at the terminal? The lines also force us to compete on price. The shipper weighs the service he gets from the line against the price he is charged. If he chooses Maersk, he doesn't care if the box is loaded at New York or at Halifax. This means that the carrier's going to look to cost to make the decision and productivity is part of that cost.

The Port of Halifax is served on a direct-call basis by many of the world's larger container carriers. It has established a relatively strong position on the North Atlantic, Mediterranean and Far East trade routes that serve markets in Atlantic Canada, Quebec and Ontario. Over the past two years, the Port of Halifax has begun to make inroads into the midwest US market and participate in the growth represented by trade with Southeast Asia via the Suez Canal.

Volume growth in the Port of Halifax tends to parallel that of the North American east coast port system as a whole, which includes, in addition to the Port of Halifax, the Ports of Montreal, Hampton Roads, New York/New Jersey, Baltimore, Boston, and Philadelphia. Geographically, Halifax does not compete with Charleston, Savannah, Jacksonville or Miami.

Over the long term, the Port of Halifax is well positioned for the trend towards large ships; its water depth and ease of access make it a natural selection. One distinct future possibility is that the Port of Halifax will be used to lighten post-Panamax ships to reduce their draft to a level where they can enter shallower east coast United States ports such as New York. This would require the discharge of substantial additional cargo in Halifax to reduce ship draft from 14 metres (45 feet) to 11.6 metres (38 feet).

As for the competing terminal operation in Halifax, it is owned and operated by Ceres Terminals Inc., a US-based company that also operates container terminals in Europe and on the east coast of the United States. The two compete for customers on the basis of price, service and capacity availability. (See Appendix A for more information on the Ceres terminal at Fairview Cove.) Morin explained:

They [Ceres] are a very traditional well-run company. They've been in business a long time and they have one key advantage over us. Because they are part of a network of terminals [over 30 in Canada and the US], they can move equipment in from other locations and the best of what they learn elsewhere can be applied here. In addition, they can spread their base costs over many operations. As an independent operator we don't have that.

Halterm has maintained a dominant position in the local market since 1989–1990 and its current market share is 63 percent based on the most recent estimate of total port throughput for 1996 (Appendix B). The largest single customer calling Halifax, ACL, calls at Ceres.

The Future

Looking forward, Morin could see three issues he needed to consider in developing his business plan for the Board meeting on December 11 and the proposal for the AEX/PAX service, due on December 12: (1) the potential approval of the P&O merger with Nedlloyd by the European Commission and the uncertainty about which alliance the merged company would choose; (2) the imminent consolidation of the AEX/PAX service at one of the terminals; and (3) long term, the likelihood of investment in post-Panamax facilities by one of the Halifax terminals within the next five years.

As for the first, Morin expected that the P&O Nedlloyd merger would be approved and that the merged company would join the Grand Alliance (offering the AEX/PAX service) rather than Nedlloyd's current alliance (the Global Alliance).

Less certain and of considerable concern was the terminal choice to be made by the AEX/PAX service. The service represented a new Suez routing and accounted for close to 20 percent of Halterm's business. More important, the alliance was likely to be very successful on the route. In addition, Halterm was not able to guarantee the crane times requested as they conflicted with those already offered to existing customers; Halterm had heard that Ceres faced the same problem in developing their proposal for the service. Furthermore, relations with Hapag Lloyd, the lead negotiator for the AEX/PAX service, were strained. P&O was indifferent and support from NYK was unknown but not likely positive. The only one of the four lines in the service clearly in favour of Halterm appeared to be NOL. The SPM contract would be up the end of December and, as a feeder to Hapag Lloyd, it was likely that SPM would follow whatever decision was made by Hapag Lloyd. The odds were clearly in favour of Ceres winning the AEX/PAX business.

As for the longer-term, it was only a matter of time before Halifax needed to make a post-Panamax facility

investment decision. With an investment of $22 million or two post-Panamax cranes and yard support equipment coupled with a further investment of $4 million by the Halifax Port Corporation to change the rail gauge for the cranes on the berth, Halterm could convert its existing facility to service post-Panamax ships. However, this would only be a short-term investment because it would not increase the capacity landside to handle larger volumes through the terminal. There is not really any adjacent land available for expansion.

Although none of Halifax's competitor ports on the US east coast have made the complete investment (cranes, dredging, berth strengthening, additional rail facilities, etc.) necessary to seize this business opportunity, it was only a matter of time. Just a few days ago the Greater Halifax Partnership released its *Multi-Modal Transportation Study* (Appendix I for key details) including details on proposed investments at competing ports. With plenty of media present at its release, the high-profile report argued that Halifax needed to do something about serving post-Panamax shipping or the port would be relegated to a feeder role in the new restructured global networks. Public pressure was mounting to do something. Even taxi drivers had added the post-Panamax word to their vocabulary. Morin did not want to move sooner than might be financially advisable. If Halterm built a post-Panamax facility, would the business materialize or would it be a "field of dreams"?

As the plane prepared to land in Halifax, Morin recalled the points made by Brian Doherty in a recent conversation:

> *Today we face three problems in this port. First, there is the labour problem; labour doesn't want to change. We need the right people with the right skills and the right agreement. If we don't have a contract with labour that makes sense, the lines will leave.*
>
> *Second, we must resolve the matter of the two terminals. There are days when ships are waiting for one to become free and there is berth space available at the other. We need to maximize the utilization of Halifax's assets. No one will invest until this is resolved. We must get beyond this mistaken belief that we need [local] competition.*
>
> *Third, the rail line needs to deal with only one terminal [operator]. They are getting poor utilization of their doublestack equipment. They are ready to come to the table if this is resolved.*

The plane touched down and Morin knew he must now begin to put his ideas on paper and prepare his presentation to the Board.

	Halterm	Ceres
Ship Berths	3	2
Length	C = 600 m (1968 feet)	660 m (2165 feet)
	B = 381 m (1250 feet)	
Ship-to-shore cranes	4	3
Acreage (Open)	71.6	61.5
Rail capacity	450 TEUs	250 TEUs
Storage	12,500 TEUs	7,000 TEUs

Map of Halifax

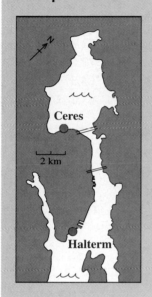

Map of Halterm

Year	Port of Halifax Total Volume (Containers)	Halterm Volume (Containers)	Halterm Percentage of Total Volume
1985	165,190	49,947	30.2
1986	174,352	65,288	37.4
1987	211,925	98,889	46.7
1988	261,925	128,310	49.0
1989	287,503	143,026	49.7
1990	278,313	135,613	48.7
1991	219,286	122,914	56.1
1992	181,391	124,183	68.5
1993	184,002	124,642	67.7
1994	187,682	135,508	72.2
1995	229,948	148,234	64.5
1996 Forecast	236,000	148,500	63.0

SOURCE: Halterm

Container Cargo Handled by the Port of Halifax by Geographic Region

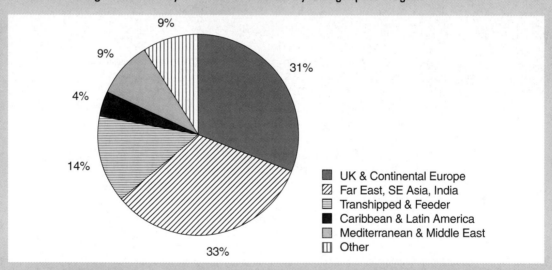

SOURCE: *Port of Halifax Directory.*

Rank	Ports	TEU (000) volumes	Labour (Lifts/hr)	Depth Restrictions (Feet)**	Terminal Utilization (percent)
1	New York/New Jersey	2,276	25	36	56
2	Hampton Roads	1,078	24	42	62
3	Charleston	1,031			
4	Jacksonville	911			
5	Montreal	726	24	36	89
6	Miami*	656			
7	Savannah*	627			
8	Baltimore	535	23	39	32
9	Halifax	383	25	45	75
10	Palm Beach	162			

Note: *The only post Panamax cranes in the Top 10 ports are at Miami and Savannah.

    **Channel or berth, whichever is shallower.

SOURCE: Port rank and volumes come from *Containerisation International Yearbook;* depth restrictions, labour productivity and terminal utilization from Greater Halifax Partnership (1996), *The Greater Halifax Multi-Modal Transportation Study* by Booz-Allen & Hamilton Inc.

	Years ended December 31 (in $000)				
	1996(F)	1995	1994	1993	1992
Revenue	36,118	35,161	31,747	28,847	28,476
Operating and administrative costs	30,393	29,610	26,515	24,111	23,869
Earnings before interest, marketing fee, depreciation and amortization	5,725	5,551	5,232	4,736	4,607
Interest	719	824	780	851	944
Marketing fee	406	657	539	394	470
Depreciation and amortization	1,736	1,798	1,958	2,049	1,947
Net income	2,864	2,272	1,955	1,442	1,246

Note: (1) Marketing fee paid to a third party, which obligation was terminated in September 1996.

Balance Sheet (as of December 31 in $000)

	1996 Forecast	1995 Actual
ASSETS		
Current Assets		
Accounts receivable	5,529	4,123
Prepaid expenses and supplies	765	971
Total current assets	6,294	5,094
Long-term Assets		
Due from related company	1,997	1,064
Property and equipment less accumulated depreciation	10,388	11,802
Deferred charges, net of accumulated amortization	2,716	–
Total Assets	21,395	17,960
LIABILITIES AND SHAREHOLDERS' EQUITY		
Bank indebtedness	1,528	1,529
Accounts payable and accrued liabilities	3,274	3,184
Due to related party	282	252
Current portion of long-term debt	1,600	1,100
Total current liabilities	6,684	6,065
Long-term debt	8,250	6,100
Shareholders' equity	6,461	5,795
	21,395	17,960

Line	Routes	Routes (incl. Halifax)	Owner (Headquarters in North America)
Hapag-Lloyd	Global	AEX and PAX Europe-N. America	Germany (New Jersey)
Maersk Canada	Global	East coast-Suez	Denmark (New Jersey)
Melfi Marine Corp.	Niche	Halifax-Cuba	Cuba
NYK Line (Canada) Inc.	Global	AEX and PAX	Japan (New Jersey)
National Shipping Co. of Saudi Arabia	Niche	N. America east coast-Med.-Gulf	Saudi Arabia (New Jersey)
Navis Shipping Inc.	Niche	Halifax-Cuba	Canada (Nova Scotia)
Neptune Orient Lines	Global	AEX and PAX	Singapore (New Jersey)
Oceanex Limited Partnership	Regional	Halifax-Newfoundland	Canada (Quebec)
P&O Containers	Global	AEX and PAX	UK (New Jersey)
Sea-Land Services Inc.	Global	Global with Maersk	US (New Jersey)
St. Pierre Ro-Ro Services and SPM Containerline	Regional	St. Pierre-Halifax-Portland/Boston	France (St. Pierre)
Transatlantic Agencies	Transatlantic	Germany-Halifax	Germany (Maryland)
ZIM Israel Navigation Company (Canada) Ltd.	Global	Asia-N. America-Med.	Israel (New York)

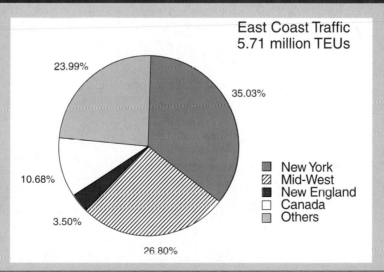

Note: Halterm's traffic is 78% to Canada and 22% to New England and the Mid-West.
SOURCE: Halterm data.

Case 16 / Halterm

Rank	Company	Vessels	Total TEU	% Vessels Over 3500 TEU
1	Sea-Land	109	196,708	12
2	Maersk	97	186,040	19
3	Evergreen/Uniglory Marine	90	181,982	10
4	Cosco	148	169,795	6
5	NYK/TSK	73	137,018	12
6	Nedlloyd	60	119,599	13
7	MOL	66	118,208	14
8	P&O	46	98,893	20
9	Hanjin	35	92,332	23
10	Mediterranean Shipping	71	88,955	0
11	APL	38	81,547	18
12	ZIM	60	79,738	0
13	K Line	43	75,528	0
14	DSR-Senator	39	75,497	0
15	Hapag-Lloyd	28	71,688	29
16	Neptune Orient Lines/PUL	35	63,469	23
17	Yangming	27	60,034	11
18	Hyundai	23	59,195	26
19	OOCL	23	55,811	4
20	CMA	26	46,026	15

SOURCE: Data are from John Fossey "TopShots," *Containerisation International* (November 1995): 55–59 at 56.

Appendix H — Leading Operators of Post-Panamax Tonnage (as of November 1, 1996)

Carrier	TEU (Ships) in Service	TEU (Ships) on Order	Projected Fleet Size
Hyundai Merchant Marine	59,772 (12)	11,102 (2)	70,874 (14)
APL	50,692 (11)		50,692 (11)
Maersk Line	24,000 (4)	48,000 (8)	72,000 (12)
OOCL	29,760 (6)	9,936 (2)	39,696 (8)
Mitsui OSK Lines	23,606 (5)		23,606 (5)
Evergreen Line	16,092 (3)	53,640 (10)	69,732 (13)
P&O Nedlloyd (if merged)	12,613 (3)	28,750 (5)	42,940 (8)
Hanjin	10,604 (2)	26,696 (4)	39,309 (7)
MISC	8,938 (2)		8,938 (2)
Cosco		31,500 (6)	31,500 (6)
Neptune Orient Lines		39,272 (8)	39,272 (8)
Yang Ming Marine Transport		23,500 (5)	23,500 (5)
Total	250,267 (51)	288,302 (53)	538,569 (104)

SOURCE: *Containerisation International Yearbook.*

Appendix I — Data from the Multi-Modal Transportation Study

Port Shares

Port	1980 Volume	1980 Share	1995 Volume	1995 Share
New York/New Jersey	1,947	55.6%	2,263	45.5%
Hampton Roads	391	11.1%	1,078	21.6%
Montreal	301	8.7%	726	14.6%
Baltimore	663	18.9%	535	10.7%
Halifax	201	5.7%	383	7.7%
Total (5 ports)	3,503	100.0%	4,985	100.0%

Cost of Planned Port Construction

Port	Investment ($M)	Acreage	$000 per Acre
Charleston	$137	65	$2,100
Hampton Roads	$548	238	$2,300
Seattle	$367	105	$3,500
Long Beach	$411	170	$2,400
Vancouver	$224	92	$3,400

SOURCE: Greater Halifax Partnership (1996), *The Greater Halifax Multi-Modal Transportation Study* by Booz-Allen & Hamilton Inc.

Endnotes

1. Ro-ro (roll on/roll off) cargo is that which moves on wheeled trailers or flatbeds and includes cars. Breakbulk cargo is packaged in some format, most commonly pallets.
2. The shortest shipping route between north Europe and the east coast of the US.
3. The classic distinction in the ship size is between Panamax ships (those that carry up to 4,000 TEUs, no more than 13 across and can pass through the Panama Canal) and post-Panamax (those that generally carry in excess of 5,000 TEUs, with 16 or 17 containers in width and are too wide to pass through the Panama Canal). The Suez Canal can handle post-Panamax vessels. Conventional cranes cannot service post-Panamax vessels efficiently because of container stack height and the limitations of crane reach. While the reach issue can be dealt with by stowing all cargo for a particular port on one side of the vessel, this may result in stability problems for the vessel, particularly during loading/unloading operations.
4. A TEU is a Twenty-foot Equivalent Unit, a standard measure for container cargoes. A container measuring $40' \times 8' \times 8'$ would be 2 TEU in size.

www.Home_Improvement.com (A)

Jonathan Lachowitz
Brian Rogers
Nirmalya Kumar
International Institute for Management Development

> *I like making order out of chaos. The idea of bringing value to a customer and creating something new is what drives me, but I know I have limitations. We need someone to help lead us to the next level.*
> —Richard Shane
> Founder, Home_Improvement.com

On February 4, 2000, Richard Shane, the founder and first CEO of Home_Improvement.com, was pacing the company's rapidly expanding office space in California's Silicon Valley, the home to dozens of other dot.com companies. He was anxiously awaiting the arrival of his replacement, Hal Smith, the newly appointed CEO, who planned to address employees for the first time later that day. Shane remarked, "In the battle for category domination, Hal is the perfect complement to our team."

Shane was excited about the arrival of Smith, as he reflected on where Home_Improvement had started and the challenges that lay ahead: Shane had spent over a year of seven-day workweeks building the company, and in February 2000, three months after opening for business, he knew that his team needed to re-focus in order to be successful in the fast-changing Internet environment.

The competition for on-line sales in the Do-It-Yourself (DIY) home improvement category was heating up quickly. Amazon.com, Hardware.com and Cornerhardware.com were just three of the many on-line merchants that had recently begun to sell competing

products over the Internet. Home Depot and Lowe's, the two largest traditional home-improvement merchandisers, had also announced plans to begin selling their products over the Internet in early 2000.

Shane felt that he did not have to beat bigger competitors like Home Depot to build his business. However, he still wondered how Home_Improvement.com could build its brand name in the midst of the millions of dollars being spent to promote on-line purchases. Shane also wondered if the company would be able to turn a profit by providing superior customer service and streamlining the supply chain.

Raising Initial Funding for Home_Improvement.com

> *In spite of all the obstacles, all the fears, I just kept pushing ahead. I was thinking there is a pot of gold at the end of the rainbow. I can get there.*
> —Richard Shane

In October 1998, Richard Shane was working at Intel Corporation and formulating plans for his latest business venture. Shane was no stranger to generating ideas for start-up companies. He had previously made attempts at commercializing on-line tutoring, on-line games with advertising revenue, and content-based advice centered on fun activities. Intel had turned down his latest idea, the creation of a free e-mail service to leverage Intel Corporation's vast network. Prior to Intel's rejection, however, Shane had secured a meeting with angel investor Mike Santullo to discuss the e-mail idea. Despite the rejection at Intel, Shane did not cancel his meeting with Santullo. He acknowledged:

> *I kept the meeting with him [Mike Santullo] because it took me a long time to get it. I figured I would have*

something to talk about. Then I got this idea for Home_Improvement.com and selling home improvement products on-line. At the meeting, Mike Santullo said, 'If you do these five things by the time I return from vacation, I will consider financing you.'

By the time Santullo had returned from vacation in January 1999, Shane had compiled extensive data on the United States DIY market. He was familiar with the major competitors, the current supply chain, and opportunities to better serve the customers where traditional retailers were falling short. He compiled a comprehensive business plan and prepared for his second meeting with Santullo. Shane recalled:

> Santullo dangled a carrot in front of me. He said he would fund me out of his own pocket, and he reassured me that if this idea did not work, we would try something else. It gave me the freedom to get going. At the time I had two children. Santullo's offer enabled me to leave Intel and channel my energies into launching Home_Improvement.com.

Shane quit his job at Intel in February 1999 and set out to build the company. His challenge was to sell his idea of "providing a customer experience second to none" in the on-line DIY category to both potential investors and potential employees. During the spring of 1999, Shane visited no less than 30 different venture capitalists (VCs) in his attempt to get financing. He considered himself lucky to get in the door in many places because each firm usually received dozens of business plans each week, and would only review those with high-growth potential. Shane's persistence resulted in strong interest from several well-known firms. He recalled, "Once you have multiple suitors, you start thinking about the pedigree of the money. I decided to go with Sequoia and Accel because I thought they were the best brands."

In June 1999, Shane had secured $9 million in initial venture capital money, though he was still dealing with the challenge of hiring and retaining good people. He added:

> In the beginning, if you were starting an Internet company and were setting up a website, people were impressed. Now everyone has an Internet company, and there is so much money chasing deals. You tell a potential employee that you have pre-IPO equity, that you are backed by top venture capitalists, and they say, 'Tell me a story I haven't heard.' They probably have three other offers from companies with similar profiles.

Shane continued hiring throughout the summer. He began the company's march towards launching a DIY e-commerce website in a race to be on-line before the Christmas holiday buying season, and before the market was too crowded.

The DIY Home Improvement Market

The 1999 DIY home improvement market was $172 billion, compared to $160 billion in 1998. Annual growth rates were 5 percent to 10 percent during the 1990s. As the baby boom generation aged, demand for DIY projects had increased in the home improvement category. Home centers, which were warehouse-sized retail stores that sold home improvement products, represented the largest growing distribution segment. In 1999, home centers accounted for 40 percent of the market, and were continuing to cannibalize sales from smaller stores. Home Depot and Lowe's, the two key national home centers, accounted for 23 percent and 10 percent of market share respectively. Even though the market place had seen considerable consolidation over the past two decades, there were still over 43,000 retail outlets in the United States at the end of 1999.

Home Depot

> Our vision of providing total solutions for our customers [is] offering the right products and services at the right price—when they want them, how they want them, and where they want them. We believe that, by doing business on the customers' terms, we will continue to enhance our leadership position in the industry.
> —Arthur Blank
> President, CEO and co-founder of Home Depot

Home Depot's model for success had been to provide the service and convenience of a local hardware store in a warehouse that averaged 130,000 square feet, including the outdoor garden center. Home Depot offered "low day-in, day-out pricing," and kept gross margin high by becoming experts in merchandising, continuously improving its in-store services, and relentlessly putting price pressures on suppliers. Home Depot had over 900 retail outlets, though it was estimated that a new store opened every 53 hours. The average transaction was $60. Revenues were approximately $850,000 per store per week, and sales for the year ended January 31, 2000 exceeded $38 billion. (*Refer to Exhibit 1 to view comparative income statements.*)

Home Depot had aggressive plans for the future, which included adding home appliances to its assortment and selling products over the Internet. According to *Fortune* magazine, Home Depot was one of the 10 most admired American companies, and was ranked second in long-term investment value.

Fiscal Year Ended	January 31, 2000 (52 Weeks)	January 31, 1999 (52 Weeks)	February 1, 1998 (52 Weeks)	February 2, 1997 (53 Weeks)
NET SALES	$38,434	$30,219	$24,156	$19,535
Cost of Merchandise Sold	27,023	21,614	17,375	14,101
Gross Profit	11,411	8,605	6,781	5,434
OPERATING EXPENSES:				
Selling and Store Operating	6,832	5,341	4,303	3,529
Pre-Opening	113	88	65	55
General and Administrative	671	515	413	324
Charge	–	–	104	–
Total Operating Expenses	7,616	5,944	4,885	3,908
OPERATING INCOME	3,795	2,661	1,896	1,526
Interest & Taxes	1,475	1,026	742	615
NET EARNINGS	$2,320	$1,614	$1,160	$938
BASIC EARNINGS PER SHARE	$1.03	$1.10	$0.80	$0.65

Lowe's

Lowe's was considered the only credible threat to Home Depot. However, the management of Lowe's took a different approach to the market than Home Depot, since the company's research indicated that women drove the majority of home improvement decisions. Therefore, Lowe's stores tended to have better lighting, a cleaner and more organized look, and products aimed at the home décor segment. In addition to being more female friendly, newer Lowe's stores were slightly larger than Home Depot's at 121,000 square feet, excluding the garden center. Its newer stores also had larger garden centers and bigger parking lots. Lowe's aggressive focus on home appliances had made them the number three retailer in this segment. In early 2000, Lowe's had over 500 stores, and average weekly revenue per store was $615,000. Sales for the year ended January 31, 2000 were $16 billion, while earnings reached $700 million.

Lowe's had traditionally opened stores in small- to mid-size metropolitan areas, and saw its competition coming more from local neighborhood stores, sometimes referred to as "mom and pop" stores, and lumberyards—not Home Depot. The company's aggressive expansion plans called for opening 95 stores in 2000 and an additional 125 stores in 2001.

Other Competitors

There were several other regional home centers, like Payless, but none accounted for over 3 percent of the market. In addition to these large home centers, Ace Hardware had a nationwide franchise of over 5,000 stores. Ace Hardware stores were often located in suburban shopping areas, and averaged 10,000 square feet. Individual owners had flexibility in product and service offerings, and benefited from nationally coordinated purchasing and marketing campaigns. Stores were generally advertised as providing friendly and helpful customer service.

E-Commerce at the Turn of the 21st Century

In 1999, the 32 biggest publicly held e-commerce companies had revenues of $4 billion. The top five companies—Amazon.com, Priceline.com, Egghead.com, ValueAmerica and Ebay—accounted for 75 percent of this sales volume. Though Internet companies tended to have high market capitalization compared to their sales or earnings, it was believed that investors had become more cautious about Internet stocks. Only 9 of the 32 biggest Internet companies were trading above their first-day closing prices as of February 2000. (*Refer to Exhibit 2 for additional data.*) Yet, it was estimated that 100 Internet start-ups considered going public in early 2000. While business-to-consumer (B2C) products were the drivers of the first wave of Internet companies, experts speculated heavily about the more promising potential of business-to-business (B2B) e-commerce.

Most e-commerce companies invested heavily in marketing. Acquisition costs per customer were often several hundred dollars or more. Customers had the ability to compare prices and services quickly on-line; therefore, switching costs for consumers were low. In addition to traditional retailing challenges, such as retaining customers and competent employees, e-commerce companies also faced many of the following issues:

- Which products and services are best suited to e-commerce?
- Why are the market valuations of Internet stocks so different from traditional equity pricing models, and when will investors start demanding profits?
- Which Internet business models will be profitable?
- How can companies produce "sticky"[1] content to build a solid repeat consumer base?
- Will the supply chain evolve to include more, less or different intermediaries in on-line transactions, and which types of intermediaries are best situated to make profits?

Developing the Home_Improvement.com Business Model

Home_Improvement.com empowers consumers by bringing home improvement solutions to one exciting, helpful, and easy-to-use Internet destination. [The company] enhances the value of its site for consumers by fully integrating four distinctive elements: a comprehensive catalog, rich information on projects and products, helpful community resources, and superior customer service.
—Richard Shane

The consumer market for home improvement DIY was segmented based on attitude towards home improvement projects—reluctant or enthusiast—and the number of projects undertaken in a year. (*Refer to Exhibit 3 for a more detailed description.*) Home_Improvement.com targeted the heavy and moderate enthusiasts as well as the slightly reluctant consumer. Managers at Home_Improvement.

com identified opportunities aimed at improving the shopping experience for these segments, so that they would make their purchases on-line, instead of in traditional brick and mortar stores. (*Refer to Exhibit 4 for additional details.*)

Home_Improvement.com also decided at an early stage to build its website in-house. Neil Day, a vice president in engineering, (*refer to Exhibit 5 to view an organization chart*) commented:

> *Our biggest challenge in building the website has always been product definition—what features we are going to include. The next challenge is scalability. By designing the whole site in-house, we continue to have maximum flexibility. We can add a new feature in days, not weeks or months like the off-the-shelf solutions. We did the whole thing for an initial cost of about $1 million, much cheaper than outsourcing. The technology is not any concern at all. It keeps coming back to product definition, and that's where we need the team to be focused on creating advantages that are hard to duplicate.*

Home_Improvement.com positioned itself as the premier home improvement partner on the Internet for DIY customers of all levels. The website aimed to offer a "superior selection of hand and power tools, plumbing and electrical supplies, lawn and gardening equipment, housewares and hardware products." The company's product mix was somewhat different from traditional home centers (*refer to Figure 1 below*). The primary difference on-line was that Home_Improvement could offer more SKUs without taking up more floor space. However, some popular home improvement items, like lumber and cement, which had low unit value but high shipping costs, were not offered.

In addition to selling products, Home_Improvement. com provided product information, project expertise,

Figure 1	Home_Improvement.com Product Assortment Breakdown	
Department	SKUs	SKU %
Hardware	9,107	26.02
Hand Tools	4,935	14.10
Power Tools	4,879	13.94
Electrical	4,785	13.67
Paint Adhesives	3,955	11.30
Plumbing	3,094	8.84
Lawn Garden	2,716	7.76
Housewares	1,526	4.36
Total	35,000	100.00

Exhibit 2 Stock Price Data on Internet Companies

Company	Date of IPO	First Day Closing Price	February 11, 2000 Closing Price	Market Capitalization ($ Million)	September 1999 YTD Revenue ($000)	September 1999 YTD Net Income ($000)
Amazon.com	May 1997	$1.96	$76.19	$25,964	$963,797	$(396,755)
Ebay	September 1998	$15.79	$162.38	$20,963	$147,827	$5,933
Bluefly	May 1997	$2.88	$10.50	$52	$1,909	$(7,505)
Preview Travel	November 1997	$11.00	$38.75	$540	$21,901	$(24,312)
Egghead.com	April 1997	$5.88	$12.88	$478	$83,959	$(18,199)
Shopnow.com	NA	$11.69	$16.94	$595	$23,537	$(13,131)
Streamline.com	June 1999	$7.63	$8.00	$147	$3,600	$(5,300)
Fatbrain.com	November 1998	$19.94	$20.75	$237	$23,484	$(20,283)
PCorder.com	February 1999	$47.13	$44.50	$712	$13,100	$(700)
Value America	April 1999	$55.19	$5.38	$241	$121,438	$(97,817)
Iturf	April 1999	$57.44	$12.00	$227	$4,602	$(6,354)
Musicmaker.com	July 1999	$23.94	$5.25	$173	$256,921	$(14,324)
Etoys	May 1999	$76.56	$15.19	$1,819	$21,281	$(65,727)
Fashionmall.com	May 1999	$13.00	$4.22	$32	$2,609	$(4,108)
Cyberian Outpost	July 1998	$20.50	$11.69	$205	$112,536	$(25,789)
Garden.com	NA	$19.06	$6.94	$121	$1,400	$(5,600)
Beyond.com	June 1998	$13.25	$5.19	$188	$82,020	$(90,756)
Smarterkids.com	NA	$14.00	$6.06	$117	$300	$(470)
Cdnow	February 1998	$22.00	$9.84	$296	$36,600	$(34,100)

Notes: Egghead Revenue and Earnings are the 6-month period ending Oct 1999.
Fatbrain Revenue and Earnings are 9 months encing Oct 1599.
Etoys Revenue and Earnings are 6 months fiscal YTD ending Sep 1999
Iturf Revenue and Earnings are 13 weeks ending Oct 1999 as per latest IOQ.
Cyberian Outpost Revenue and Earnings are 9 months ending Nov 1999.
SOURCE: Data as of February 11, 2000 Compiled from http://www.Quicken.com, http://www.Hoovers.com and Hardy, Quentin. "The last e-tail." *Forbes Global*, 7 February 2000:43

Exhibit 3   DIY Market Segmentation

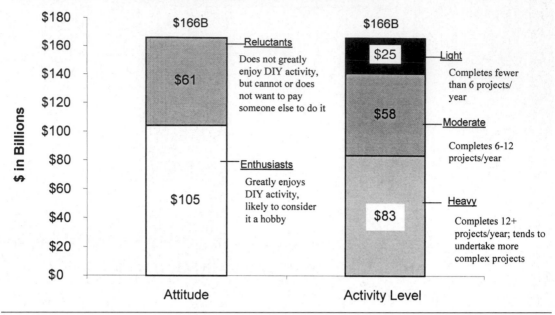

Attitude and Activity Level Can Segment Customers in the $166B DIY Market[3]

[3]DIY Retailing Market Measure 2000; Stanley Corporation Research; Home_Improvement.com Analysis

home improvement ideas and even answers to consumers' home improvement questions. In order to enhance sales volume, the company also actively promoted projects. Home improvement projects included multiple products with a wide range of accessories and add-ons. The website provided an extensive product assortment for cross-selling and up-selling opportunities.

The website also featured "home pros," who were Home_Improvement.com's resident home-improvement experts. They responded to customers' phone and e-mail inquiries. They also added to the site's wealth of home improvement tips, how-to information and community features. Home_Improvement.com started with a staff of a dozen home pros, many of whom were retired or injured tradesman with decades of professional home improvement experience. In addition to working closely with customers, the home pros were also an integral part of content production for the company's website. In conjunction with the editing staff and a technical crew, the home pros performed home improvement projects. These projects would, in turn, be documented using video, flash animation and written explanations in order to create the "how-to projects" section of the Home_Improvement.com website.

Home_Improvement decided to adopt a "Good, Better, Best" merchandising strategy for the on-line pre-

sentation of its products. This philosophy intended to bring the customer through the trade-up process, while simultaneously highlighting the desired product line and increasing gross sales and margin. When a customer inquired about a product in a certain category, the website would list the available SKUs in order and by price, showing the least expensive item first. Home_Improvement.com's pricing policy was to match Home Depot on the top 250 to 500 SKUs, and to be no more than 10 percent more expensive than Home Depot on the remaining SKUs.

As for all on-line retailers, developing a customer-friendly but cost-efficient fulfillment model was a significant challenge. Initially, it was decided that orders would be fulfilled through a single distributor. Once on-line orders were received, they were then forwarded electronically to the distributor, who shipped the products to the customer. The customer received an e-mail to confirm that an order had been received; another e-mail was sent once the order had been shipped.

Based on its target market and revenue assumptions, the company believed that under a high-growth scenario, its sales volumes would surpass $20 million by the end of the first full calendar year. (*Refer to Exhibits 6 and 7 for additional data.*)

Exhibit 4 — Opportunities for Home_Improvement.com to Add Value

Segment	Primary Channels	Needs/Desires	Areas Underserved	Opportunity?
Moderate Enthusiast	• Home Depot/Lowe's • Orchard Supply Hardware/Eagle	• Information and assistance • Recognized brands • Browsing for ideas • Liberal store policies • Ability to show accomplishments	• Finding help with products or projects is currently inconsistent across shopping trips and stores	Yes
			• Little product information available beyond salespeople, so uses name brands as a proxy for product quality	Yes
			• Shops OSH-type stores to avoid long lines and overwhelming selection/presentation of big boxes	Yes
			• Goes up and down aisles for ideas and inspiration but is often overwhelmed and unsure how to take the next step	Yes
			• Makes frequent trips to the store to return incorrect items and pick up correct or overlooked items	Yes
			• No organized way to show off accomplishments to fellow DIYers	Yes

Heavy Enthusiast	• Home Depot/Lowe's
	• Specialty Retailers for
	  – Plumbing Fixtures
	  – Electrical Fixtures
	  – Specialty Tools
		• Everyday competitive pricing
		• Browsing for enjoyment
		• Broad, in-stock selection
		• Community interaction
			• Get everyday competitive pricing at big box stores	No

			• Enjoys making trips up and down each aisle at the big box to see what's new, touch the product, and to get project ideas and inspiration	Maybe
			• Most of product needs served at big box; however, often frustrated by out-of-stocks and expects to shop specialty retailers to get depth required in some areas such as fixtures or specialty tools	Yes
			• Has a circle of friends and neighbors who help with projects but who can also appreciate accomplishments	Maybe
			• High knowledge level means need for assistance from stores is minimal because they use circle as primary source of information	No
Light DIYer	• Orchard Supply Hardware/Eagle • Ace/True Value • Restoration Hardware	• Convenience • Information and assistance • Recognized brands	• The most time-pressed group, this segment does not always have a good solution for both good assortment and fast in-and-out	Yes
			• Finding help with products or projects currently inconsistent across shopping trips and stores	Yes
			• Little product information available beyond salespeople, so uses name brands as a proxy for product quality	Yes

Exhibit 5   Home_Improvement.com Organization Chart (February 2000)

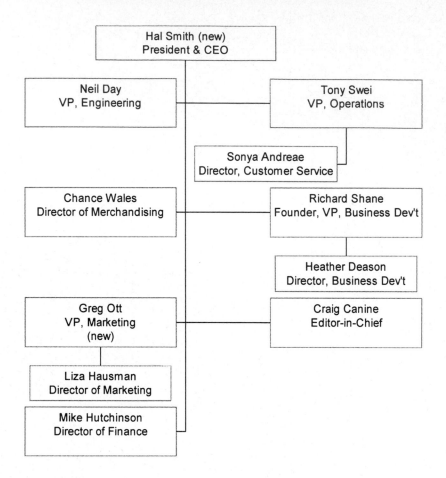

Initial Launch and Market Response

I ordered four items Tuesday of this week and they arrived today! Your site was easy to use, prices good and the free gift-wrapping a real plus. Thank you! Ruth, Utah

On October 29, 1999, Home_Improvement.com launched its e-commerce site. The company cruised through the holiday season and delivered on its objectives of providing a positive on-line shopping and customer service experience. After seven weeks, the company reported the following positive feedback from its customer services group:

- Average time for customer service representatives to answer calls: 22 seconds
- Average telephone waiting time to speak to a home pro: 8 seconds
- Average time for resolving all e-mail queries: 9 hours
- Up-time for website: 99.91 percent
- 98.7 percent order fulfillment rate in the holiday season.

As part of its overall customer acquisition plan, Home_Improvement.com actively sought on-line partnerships with Internet companies that would provide links to their websites. In exchange for this service, Home_Improvement.com paid for on-line customer traffic generated through these companies. By February 2000, Home_Improvement.com had established over 20 agreements, which were mostly valid for one year. These agreements fell into three major categories:

- Pay the affiliated site a *percentage of the sales revenue*—normally about 10 percent—that was generated by traffic from its site. Home_Improvement had established an affiliate program, which allowed any person or organization who operated a website to sign up as an affiliate and establish a link to the Home_Improvement.com website. *(Refer to Exhibit 8 for the top referral sites.)*
- Pay a fee for each user who *clicked through* to the Home_Improvement.com site; or,

- Pay on a *CPM* basis, or cost per thousand impressions, a fee based on the number of eyeballs that were exposed to the Home_Improvement.com banner advertisement on an affiliate's website. The company estimated that the cost per thousand impressions was $30. In the first two months of operation, Home_Improvement.com observed a 0.5 percent click rate on its banner advertising. Of those who clicked through to the Home_Improvement.com site, 2 percent made a purchase.

> *Our click-through rate has been good, but the buying rate is not great. I think the site experience is not what it needs to be. You need to know what you want before you get there. We need to improve this before the crucial March-to-June buying season.*
>
> —Heather Deason
> Director of Business Development

Home_Improvement.com was also aggressive in other media. During the holiday season, ads were placed in 21 newspapers in 12 major markets. Additional print advertising was purchased in *Time, Newsweek* and *US News and World Report*.

A survey of 15,000 Yahoo visitors was part of an on-line promotion that combined advertising and market research. Findings indicated that home improvement enthusiasts were the segment that was most likely to buy on-line, and that power tools were the most popular on-line purchase. Power tools were a popular gift item, and Home_Improvement.com generated significant volume with aggressive pricing during the holiday season.

Home_Improvement.com also launched a shipping promotion in December to encourage sales. Orders over $50 received free second-day air shipping. This promotion was very popular, but freight charges had proven to be costly, amounting to 32 percent of revenues. The company hoped to streamline the supply chain by opening its own distribution center. In addition, the company wanted to increase the use of manufacturers who would drop ship orders directly to consumers.

> *The big operations question is when we will open our own distribution center. It looks like the south will be the best location. We should get this up and running as soon as possible. This will give us more control, a scaleable infrastructure, and it will get rid of that margin hit we are taking by outsourcing. Even if we assume our medium growth model of $12, $42, and $78 million in revenues over the next three years, we will save substantially by having our own distribution center.*
>
> —Tony Swei
> Vice President of Operations

As for all on-line retailers, finding a profitable business model was a challenge. After a couple of months on-line, Home_Improvement.com's management was continuing

---

Figure 2   Home_Improvement.com Revenue by Category November and December 1999 (Figures have been disguised to protect confidentiality.)

HomeWarehouse.com
Revenue by Category
December 1999

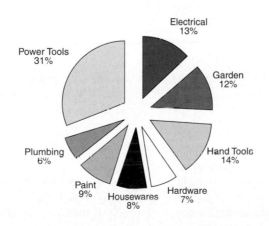

Exhibit 6 — Home_Improvement.com Income Statement CY 2000–2002 ($000)

	2000		2001		2002	
Revenue						
Merchandise Sales	$23,353.5	100.1%	$88,099.7	89.8%	$213,765.4	86.0%
Shipping Charges Collected	1,250.0	5.4%	13,955.9	14.2%	44,264.8	17.8%
Gift Wrap Sales	18.4	0.1%	67.3	0.1%	160.0	0.1%
Merchandise Returns	(817.4)	−3.5%	(3,083.5)	−3.1%	(7,481.8)	−3.0%
MDF Funds	-	0.0%	-	0.0%	-	0.0%
Promotional Discounts	(467.1)	−2.0%	(881.0)	−0.9%	(2,137.7)	−0.9%
Total Revenue	$23,337.5	100.0%	$98,158.4	100.0%	$248,570.9	100.0%
Revenue per Day	$63.9		$268.9		$681.0	
COGS						
Merchandise COGS	19,445.0	83.3%	67,690.8	69.0%	151,390.5	60.9%
Shipping Expense	5,102.6	21.9%	18,607.9	19.0%	44,264.8	17.8%
Gift Wrap Expense	13.2	0.1%	48.1	0.0%	114.3	0.0%
Merchandise Returns	(680.6)	−2.9%	(2,369.2)	−2.4%	(5,298.7)	−2.1%
Total Cost of Goods Sold	23,880.2	102.3%	83,977.6	85.6%	190,471.0	76.6%
Gross Margin	(542.78)	−2.3%	14,180.84	14.4%	58,099.87	23.4%
	−2.3%		14.4%		23.4%	
Transaction Related Expenses	1,483.0	6.3%	5,794.1	5.9%	14,612.0	5.9%
Subtotal	(2,005.7)	−8.6%	8,386.7	8.5%	43,487.8	17.5%
Department Operating Expenses						
Product Development	12,685.7	54.4%	13,954.3	14.2%	15,349.7	6.2%
Customer Acquisition Discount	2,335.5	10.0%	-	0.0%	-	0.0%
Marketing Programs	60,298.9	258.4%	75,000.0	76.4%	75,000.0	30.2%
Other Marketing Expenses	6,223.2	26.7%	7,779.0	7.9%	8,556.9	3.4%
Administrative	2,720.6	11.7%	3,400.7	3.5%	3,740.8	1.5%
Capital Lease Payments	599.1	2.6%	659.0	0.7%	724.9	0.3%
Total Operating Expenses	84,862.9	363.6%	100,793.0	102.7%	103,372.3	41.6%
Operating Income before Interest	(86,868.7)	−372.2%	(92,406.3)	−94.1%	(59,884.4)	−24.1%
Interest Payments	538.1	2.3%	0.0	0.0%	0.0	0.0%
Operating Income before Taxes	−$87,406.8	−374.5%	−$92,406.3	−94.1%	−$59,884.4	−24.1%

to assess its business model and revenue assumptions based on initial financial results and future forecasts. (*Refer to Exhibit 9 for more information.*)

We have some aspects of our business model that require some refinement. For example, our current customer acquisition cost is around $800. The lifetime value of the customer doesn't support that cost. Also, subsidizing shipping costs at an average of $15 per order will require us to be more efficient in other operating costs than tradi-tional brick-and-mortar hardware stores. However, this market is so large and fragmented. I'm confident we can find a business model that can generate a reasonable return on sales in the future.

—Michael Hutchinson
Director of Finance

There are so many challenges—customer acquisition, dealing with people's fears of buying on-line and then building the Home_Improvement.com brand name. But I

Exhibit 7 Home_Improvement.com Revenue Assumptions CY 2000–2002 ($000)

	Year 2000	Year 2001	Year 2002
Revenue			
Merchandise Sales	$23,353.5	$88,099.70	$213,765.40
Shipping Charges Collected	1,250.0	13,955.9	44,264.8
Gift Wrap Sales	18.4	67.3	160.0
Merchandise Returns	(817.4)	(3,083.5)	(7,481.8)
MDF Funds			
Promotional Discounts	(467.1)		(2,137.7)
Total Revenue	$23,337.5	$98,158.4	$248,570.9
Revenue Related Assumptions			
Visitors to Site (000)	9,684.8	20,000.0	33,333.3
Conversion Ratio	2.2%	2.5%	3.0%
New Customers (000)	216.0	500.0	1,000.0
Repeat Customers at beg of Period (000)	4.0	154.9	418.7
Customer Churn (000)	(65.0)	(236.3)	(496.3)
Total Customers at end of Period (000)	154.9	418.7	922.3
Marketing Programs Budget	$60,299.00	$75,000.00	$75,000.00
Acquisition Cost per New Customer	$279.00	$150.00	$75.00
Transactions by New Customers (000)	216.0	500.0	1,000.0
Transactions by Repeat Customers (000)	39.2	430.4	1,213.2
Total Transactions (000)	255.1	930.4	2,213.2
Total of Transactions by Repeat Customers	15%	46%	55%
Return Transactions (000)	8.9	32.6	77.5
Return Rate	3.5%	3.5%	3.5%
Average Transactions per Customer per Year	1.61	1.62	1.65
Average Merchandise Transaction Size	$92.00	$95.00	$97.00
New Customers	$90.00	$90.00	$90.00
Repeat Customers	$100.00	$100.00	$102.00
Average Merchandise Sales per Day ($000)	$64.00	$241.40	$585.70
Shipping Charge per Transaction	$4.90	$15.00	$20.00
Gift Wrap—% of Transaction	2.1%	2.1%	2.1%
Gift Wrap—Revenue per Transaction	$3.50	3.50	3.50
Promotional Discounts—% of Revenue	2.0%	1.0%	1.0%
Avg. Gross Margin % on Merchandise	16.7%	23.2%	29.2%
Avg. Gross Margin % on Shipping	−308.2%	−33.3%	0.0%
Avg. Gross Margin % on Gift Wrap	28.6%	28.6%	28.6%

think our biggest marketing challenge is that we have this tug of war between customer acquisition and profitability.

—Liza Hausman
Director of Marketing

Facing the March-to-June 2000 Sales Window

The March-to-June period was when new home improvements projects tended to occur. Thirty-five percent of all

Source of Customer	Type
AOL	CPM
CouponSurfer.com	% of Revenue
dash.com	% of Revenue
Dealcatcher.com	% of Revenue
Excite	Click
Flamingo World	% of Revenue
iGive.com	% of Revenue
Inktomi	% of Revenue
Learn2	CPM
LifeMinders	–
MyPoints	% of Revenue
Other	–
piiq.com	% of Revenue
Santa.com	% of Revenue
Women.com	CPM
Yahoo! Contest	–
Yahoo!	CPM
Totals	

Type of Contractual Agreements:

- **Percentage of sales revenue** generated by traffic from the source website—normally 10%.
- Payment of a fee for each user who **clicked through** to the web site.
- **CPM** is a fee paid per thousand impressions, or how many people view a banner advertisement.

yearly home improvement sales fell in this period, and the competition for these sales was strong. Since the launch of Home_Improvement.com, new on-line retailers were targeting the DIY home improvement category, while traditional brick and mortar retailers were also threatening to make significant on-line moves.

Internet Competitors

Ourhouse.com, Hardware.com and CornerHardware. com started selling home improvement products in early 2000. Their websites were content-rich on product information, how-to projects, and touted tens of thousands of available SKUs. These on-line DIY companies planned to offer a valuable service to consumers, and provide advice and information they hoped would win over loyal customers. Marketing budgets were significant:

Ourhouse.com had a $100 million budget to launch its marketing efforts, while Cornerhardware.com raised $50 million.

In addition to the above players, Amazon.com also entered the home improvement category as part of its strategy to constantly add categories, and hoped to leverage its existing customer database. In late 1999, Amazon purchased the catalog retailer Tool Crib of the North to gain momentum in the sales of home improvement products.

Brick and Mortar Retailers on the Internet

In May 1999, Home Depot sent a letter to over 1,000 of its suppliers threatening to drop them if they began to sell their products on the Internet. At the same time, Home Depot management announced that they intended to

Sales	
Merchandise	99.3%
Gift Wrap	0.0%
Shipping	2.4%
Gross Sales	101.7%
Less Returns	−1.7%
Net Sales	100.0%
COGS	
Merchandise	82.0%
Gift Wrap	3342.9%
Shipping	1271.1%
Distribution Fulfillment	
Less: Returns	
Total COGS	120.1%
Gross Margin	−20.1%
Promotion Discount	18.7%
Margin after Promotion Discount	−38.8%
Payroll	465.0%
Professional Services	68.2%
Office Expenses	38.1%
Equipment & Related	20.7%
Travel & Entertainment	22.8%
Facilities	35.1%
Marketing Communications	1187.8%
Engineering	4.1%
Depreciation	32.9%
Total Expenses	1874.7%
EBIT	−1913.5%
Net Interest Income/Expense	4.6%
Net Operating Income	−1908.8%

rollout Internet sales from the company's website in the third quarter of 1999. Home Depot missed this target, but in the third quarter of 1999, it re-designed its website to focus on offering how-to advice to the customer. According to Ron Griffin, Home Depot's senior vice president of information services, "We hope to stimulate demand [with our website content] [. . .] How-to tips are what they [customers] want most [. . .] selling on-line is not the end game [. . .] we are going to dominate the market using this technology."[2]

At the end of 1999, Home Depot had announced that it would pursue a limited e-commerce rollout later in 2000 with a regional pricing approach. It was anticipated that customers would be given a choice between home delivery and picking up their merchandise from a nearby Home Depot store.

Lowe's also hoped to start selling over the Internet in 2000, but the company planned to begin with business-to-business customers first. Contractors would be able to order on the Lowe's website and arrange delivery to job sites. Regarding Internet sales to customers, Lowe's preferred to take a wait-and-see approach, and planned to sell products on-line that "made sense."

Ace Hardware established its own content-rich website, though it also had a strong affiliation with on-line retailer Ourhouse.com. Ourhouse planned to make the Ace Hardware store network a key competitive advantage in its attempt to win the battle for customers and sales in the on-line home improvement market.

While the battle for on-line customers for home improvement products had begun, the potential size of the on-line market was unclear. In 2000, estimates ranged from $100 to $200 million. Growth projections for 2004 were as high as $7 billion, which represented about 5 percent of the total DIY market. A more conservative estimate had on-line home improvement sales reaching $700 million by 2003.

The Arrival of Hal Smith

We have a great team of people here; we have all been working hard towards getting the Internet site launched.

Now we need someone else to lead, someone to carry the torch, someone who has had IPO experience.

—Richard Shane

Hal Smith, formerly the president of Bass Pro Companies, the world's largest supplier of outdoor recreational products, joined Home_Improvement.com as the company's new president and CEO in early 2000. During his tenure as president at Bass Pro from 1998 to 2000, the company had doubled in size due to an aggressive increase in presence in both the retail and Internet channels. In the 17 years prior to joining Bass Pro, Smith had also been the president and CEO of Builders Emporium, Ernst Home and Nursery and Homeowners Do-It-Yourself Centers. As a consultant, he had helped Home Depot establish its Northwest region strategy.

Smith was expected to provide leadership and direction to the young Home_Improvement.com team. Direct competition in the on-line home improvement market and indirect competition for funds in the financial markets had propelled the young company into an uncertain environment. Smith was expected to announce an aggressive growth strategy for Home_Improvement.com, but only the future would reveal whether the company would be one of the survivors of the next generation of e-commerce companies.

Endnotes

1. "Sticky" content is an Internet industry term for the on-line information or experience that keeps or is intended to keep an Internet user on a website for a longer period of time—the idea being that the longer users are connected, the more likely they are to purchase goods or services.
2. "Depot Takes Next Step Towards Online Selling," *National Home Center News*, Vol. 25, No. 14, July 1999: 8.

Hopewell Holdings Limited

Rudy Law, John Luk, and Geoffrey Lieu

Hong Kong Polytechnic University

Richard L. Priem

University of Wisconsin—Milwaukee

Scott Scarborough

University of Texas at Arlington

Sir Gordon Wu, founder and chairman of Hopewell Holdings Limited (HHL), insisted in the fall of 1997 that he had not received any official cancellation notice of his firm's infrastructure project from the Thai government. Wu stated that if he were to receive such a notice, HHL would continue to seek, and ultimately would obtain, a successful contract resolution with the Thai authorities, anyway. He argued that HHL had no intention of quitting and was firmly committed to completing the project.

The Bangkok Elevated Road and Train System (BERTS), a planned 60-kilometre dual three-lane highway and community train system, was expected to provide some relief for Bangkok's traffic chaos. The BERTS concession had been awarded to HHL in November 1990 by the Thai Ministry of Transport and Communications and the State Railway of Thailand, following a public bidding process. The project was bid by HHL on a build-operate-transfer (BOT) basis. This meant that Hopewell would finance and build the system, and would be "paid" through the usage fees generated by the completed system over a specified period of years. After the concession period, the system and its operation would be turned over to the Thai government. The term of the concession for the BERTS project was 38

years, allowing for an 8-year construction period and 30 years for HHL to recoup its investment and make a reasonable profit.

The first phase of this HK$24 billion construction project was scheduled to be completed by mid-1998. However, the financial crisis in Asia devasted the baht and HHL's project, making it unlikely that the planned fares would be enough for profitable system operation. After hearing HHL's request for a rate increase, officials from Thailand's Ministries of Railway and Finance said they would cancel the project rather than raise fares. Several Hong Kong newspapers reported that the Thai government soon would give HHL an official ultimatum: either complete the BERTS project in accordance with existing contract terms, or face aggressive legal action and restitution claims of up to HK$12.4 billion.

Could Sir Gordon Wu take steps to complete BERTS at a profit? Even if the project was ultimately successful, did the near-debacle with BERTS indicate that large BOT projects in developing countries were simply too risky for firms like HHL? When questioned about HHL's focus for the future, Wu noted that HHL could easily return to its earlier emphasis on property development if large-scale infrastructure projects became infeasible.

Sir Gordon Wu: A Man of Vision

Gordon Wu, chairman and managing director of HHL, was a Princeton-educated engineer known throughout Hong Kong as a local boy who made good internationally. After studies in civil engineering, Wu rejoined his father in Hong Kong in 1962 to help build a family real

This case was prepared by Dr. Rudy Law, John Luk and Geoffrey Lieu of the Hong Kong Polytechnic University and Dr. Richard L. Priem and Scott Scarborough of the University of Texas at Arlington as a basis for class discussion rather than to illustrate either effective or ineffective handling of an administrative or business situation.

This case was presented at a working session of the Western Casewriters meeting in March, 1999 at Redondo Beach, California, USA. At the meeting, the Hopewell case was awarded first prize in the 1999 East Asian Case Competition sponsored by the Center for Asian Business at Loyola Marymount University.

estate development company. When his father retired in 1969, Wu began his own business with a HK$2.5 million bank loan guaranteed by his father.

Born in 1935, Wu was knighted as Sir Gordon Wu in 1997 as part of the last Hong Kong birthday "list" of Britain's Queen Elizabeth II. Over the past three decades Wu had turned HHL, once just another property development company in Hong Kong, into a truly international infrastructure and power supply developer. In 1972, he built his corporate headquarters—the 66-story, cylinder-shaped Hopewell Centre—in Wanchai, Hong Kong. It was Hong Kong's tallest structure, and it gave a clear signal that Wu, little known outside Hong Kong, wanted to make his mark in the Asia Pacific arena.

HHL was listed on the Hong Kong Stock Exchange in 1972. As a property company, HHL developed a portfolio that featured the 1,026-room Kowloon Panda hotel and included many office developments and shopping centres in Hong Kong. Another showcase in the property portfolio was the Hong Kong International Trade and Exhibition Centre (HITEC) in Kowloon Bay. HITEC offered over 13,000 square metres of exhibition space and 22,000 square metres of showroom floors, all devoted to promoting trade and industry in Hong Kong.

In the early 1980s, Wu saw great potential in the infrastructure development markets of the Asia-Pacific Region's developing economies. He decided to leave the highly profitable property development market in Hong Kong and began his first undertaking in China: the Guangzhou-Shenzhen-Zhuhai Superhighway. For the next twelve years, Wu led HHL to undertake other highway and electricity generation infrastructure projects throughout the Asia-Pacific region. Most prominent among these projects were the power plants of Consolidated Electric Power Asia (CEPA), the Bangkok Elevated Road and Train System (BERTS), and the Luzon Toll Road in the Philippines. HHL undertook these projects on a Build-Operate-Transfer (BOT) basis. This meant that HHL: 1) obtained financing and built the projects, 2) operated the completed project for a specified number of years (the "concession") to recoup costs and earn profits, and 3) then turned the project over to the sponsoring government.

Wu was recognized by many as a man of vision and courage. Other property developers in Hong Kong prospered enormously, however, and were listed among the world's richest business people. Despite Wu's foresight, and despite the contributions of HHL's infrastructure projects to the economic development of the Pearl River Delta area, many impatient shareholders and financial analysts were critical of the slow return on investment for these projects. In late November 1997, HHL's stock was trading at HK$2.10 per share while the face value

was booked at HK$6 to $7 per share (see Exhibit 1). HHL had no new residential or commercial property investments underway locally, although Wu had stated his intention of building a 93-story Mega Tower Hotel, another potential Hong Kong landmark.

The bulk of HHL's 1997 activities was concentrated in the Asia-Pacific region rather than in Hong Kong. HHL was the one local construction company that had succeeded in exporting its services outside the territory; HHL had made a name for itself as an international builder of highways and power generation stations. The question is whether this "export success" was worth the cost to HHL's shareholders.

The Build-Operate-Transfer Method of Financing

BOT was one way of financing and implementing *very* large projects that were usually infrastructure related. It was promoted by many developing countries and the World Bank to facilitate funding, efficient construction, and transfer of technology between countries when planning and carrying out infrastructure projects. BOT first involved a contractor obtaining financing for and building a mega project. Costs were recouped and profits realized through a "concession" period, during which the constructor operated the project and received its profits. After the concession period, the project was turned over to the sponsoring government. A key to HHL's success in attracting infrastructure development projects was its willingness to employ the BOT method of financing. Many developing countries facing high industrial growth favored this form of privatization and commercialization of their infrastructure projects. This approach attracted private capital from foreign markets and "freed up" large amounts of public capital, which then could be used for social programs instead of for building infrastructure.

Asia needed large amounts of infrastructure capital in 1997. The World Bank had estimated that, between 1995 and 2004, East Asia would need to spend US$1.5 trillion on energy, transportation and communications projects. Of this amount Indonesia, Thailand, the Philippines and Malaysia would need to spend nearly US$440 billion. But China by itself had an estimated infrastructure bill of US$750 billion. To win a slice of the large China pie, many Hong Kong companies had set up infrastructure arms and rushed across the border. Most were offering to undertake projects on a BOT basis.

The economic and financial instability in Asia from overheated property and stock markets in 1997 raised questions about the near-term viability of many of the region's mega projects. This was especially true for those

Exhibit 1 HHL Stock Price (US$)

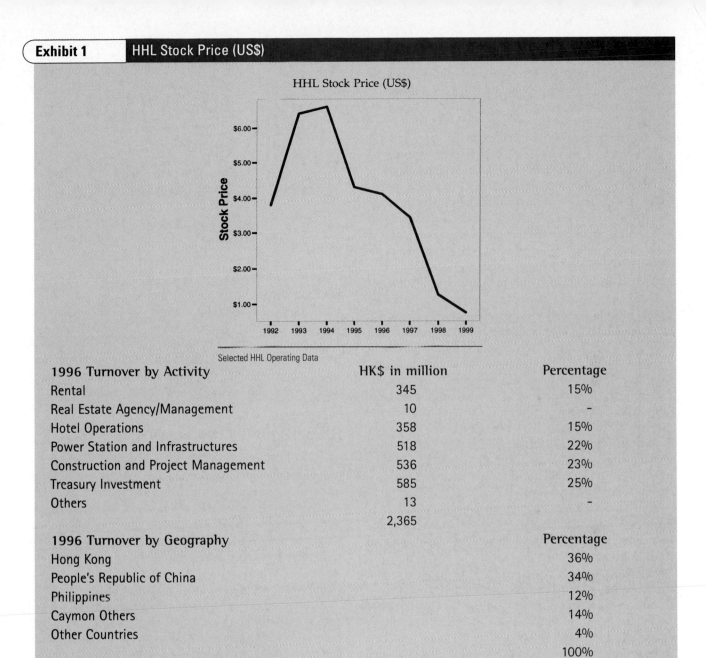

HHL Stock Price (US$)

Selected HHL Operating Data

1996 Turnover by Activity	HK$ in million	Percentage
Rental	345	15%
Real Estate Agency/Management	10	–
Hotel Operations	358	15%
Power Station and Infrastructures	518	22%
Construction and Project Management	536	23%
Treasury Investment	585	25%
Others	13	–
	2,365	

1996 Turnover by Geography		Percentage
Hong Kong		36%
People's Republic of China		34%
Philippines		12%
Caymon Others		14%
Other Countries		4%
		100%

projects where revenues were denominated in unstable foreign currencies. The potential rewards of the mega projects were high, but these ventures were also fraught with risks. Bureaucrats might be obstructive and local partners unreliable. It could therefore be difficult for an outside contractor to keep a project on schedule and on budget. Politicians might try to curry local favor by demanding that agreed-upon tolls or tariffs be lowered. Currency volatility could savage profits. And there was always the "doomsday" scenario: whenever a government cabinet was re-shuffled or toppled, a project might be nationalized or put on hold, with little or no com-

pensation for investors. A review of HHL's recent infrastructure projects in power generation and highway construction highlights the risks associated with large-scale BOT infrastructure projects in developing countries.

HHL's Consolidated Electric Power Asia (CEPA) Limited

In 1979, Wu had predicted that China reform and the new open-door policy would be successful. Constant power blackouts, however, threatened construction of one of his company's prized property development projects: the 1,200-room, five-star China Hotel in Guangzhou. It was to be the first major venture in that city, and would produce one of the largest hotels in Guangdong Province.

The power blackouts were annoying but, true to his engineering training, Wu saw the problem as an opportunity. People in China needed a dependable power supply to support growth. The hotel Wu was building also needed dependable power; candlelight dining is not very romantic in south China without air conditioning! Therefore, rather than just continuing with property development, Wu decided to start building power generation plants as well. HHL built an award-winning, coal-fired power station in Guangdong—the Shajiao C project. Its great capacity and ability to fluctuate power output from 250 to 660 MW per unit ensured it would contribute to increasing supply reliability, especially during peak demand.

China continued the rush to build new power plants, prompted by the unprecedented surge in electricity demand. Shajiao C, the leading power station in China, conforms to the Guangdong Provincial Government's requirement of "high standard, high quality, high reliability, and high efficiency." The plant took four years to construct. According to the Ministry of Power Industry, China would need to add 15 million kilowatts generating capacity by 1997 and another 20 million kilowatts by the year 2000. Total generating capacity would then reach 210 million kilowatts.

HHL's 60.3 percent-owned subsidiary, Consolidated Electric Power Asia (CEPA) Limited, was Asia's largest independent power production company, with projects in the People's Republic of China, the Philippines and Indonesia. It was set up in April, 1993 to hold the majority of the power projects developed by HHL. CEPA was listed on the Stock Exchange of Hong Kong in December, 1993. It was one of the largest new public companies ever listed in Hong Kong.

Power generation would likely be a future growth area in many parts of Southeast Asia. Maintaining industrial growth would produce increased demand for power. CEPA had completed two power plant projects in Shenzhen, China and four in the Philippines, with a total combined installed capacity of 3,995 megawatts. CEPA pioneered the use of the BOT method of financing for power generation with its participation in emerging Asian markets like China and the Philippines.

HHL claimed that CEPA was one of Asia's largest independent power producers, with coal fired power stations in the following countries:

Already in operation: People's Republic of China (Shajiao)—2,680 mw

(estimated project cost US$1.4 billion) The Philippines (Pagbilao)—1,315 mw
(estimated project cost US$888 million)

Under construction: The Philippines (Sual)—1,200 mw (estimated project cost US$1.3 billion)
Indonesia (Tanjung)—1,320 mw (estimated project cost US$1.8 billion)
Pakistan (Keti Bandar)—1,320 mw (estimated project cost US$1.6 billion)

CEPA was often seen as a prized possession. Even HHL's critics said that power generation was one of the businesses in which HHL had so far excelled. Should HHL urgently need to raise funds at some future time, CEPA would probably be involved because it generated impressive income. As a result of CEPA's success, Wu was confident that HHL could pursue other infrastructure development projects, such as highway construction.

HHL's Highway Projects

Sir Gordon Wu's strengths included creativity, engineering acumen and long-term view of business. He was full of ideas, in part because of all he had seen while a student in the United States. He first saw the New Jersey Turnpike, for example, as a college freshman in 1954. It was clear to him that major highways such as this were reshaping transport and creating huge opportunities, just as canals had in the 18th century and railroads had in the 19th century.

As an engineer, Wu was trained to identify problems and to propose solutions that were feasible and pragmatic. A second example of his problem-solving acumen occurred when he was developing the China Hotel in Guangzhou. Wu made numerous trips between Hong Kong and Guangzhou, with each trip taking five or six hours, one way, by train. Wu deemed this arduous journey a problem that was holding back area development and that definitely needed solving.

On one such trip, while he stopped in Shenzhen for lunch, Wu thought to himself that Guangzhou was really not very far away. He wondered about the possibility of building a toll highway between Hong Kong and Guangzhou, just like the ones he had seen in the United States. When he went public with his idea, some people in Hong Kong thought he was crazy. How could people in China *ever* afford to own private cars? Plus, those in authority in China still believed that railroads were the best means to transport people. But Wu believed that traffic would always increase over time. When he first saw the New Jersey turnpike, it was only four lanes; later it became 12, and of course people still complained about traffic. The number of private cars per 100 people in China was far less than one. With a population of 1.2 billion, however, the inevitable growth in the number of commercial vehicles would be phenomenal.

Sir Gordon's idea ultimately became reality as the Guangzhou-Shenzhen-Zhuhai Superhighway project. Completion of the first leg of the project in 1994 cut the travel time between Guangzhou and Hong Kong from five hours to 75 minutes. This created a springboard effect on the wealth of the communities surrounding the superhighway. As accessibility to southern China became easier, property development and other infrastructure projects were quick to follow.

Transportation was another pressing need if the Chinese were to continue with the high rates of economic development they had sustained over the past several years. HHL was first to enter China to develop transportation infrastructure using the BOT method of financing. In June 1996, HHL completed the 123 kilometre Guangzhou-Shenzhen-Zhuhai East Superhighway (Phase One). Work was continuing on the GSZ-West Superhighway (Phase Two, cost estimated at RMB 4.7 billion) project, which was to provide an additional 58-kilometre link to Nanhai, Zhongshan, and to State Road 105, which would stretch from Zhuhai to the Macao border. The concession period was for 30 years. The GSZ East section recorded an average of 61,700 vehicles per day in August 1996.

Transportation development involved not only building and operating toll roads, but also property development at the interchanges. HHL acquired land parcels at many of the GSZ East Superhighway's 16 interchanges to develop shopping spaces and commercial centres. The ultimate plan called for extending the highway from Guangzhou to the Yangtze River in central China, thereby creating a 960-kilometre toll road.

HHL also invested in two other projects in Guangdong that would connect traffic to and from the Superhighway. The 102-kilometre, dual three-lane Shunde Toll Road in the Shunde municipality was completed in August 1996. It recorded an average traffic flow of 72,240 vehicles per day. The Guangzhou (East-South/West-South) Ring Road would provide a total of 39 kilometres of dual three-lane toll road when it opened in late 1998. The value of HHL's BOT transportation portfolio is shown in Exhibit 2.

HHL was driving into the highway development business again with a US$412.2 million expressway upgrading and construction joint venture with the Philippine National Construction Corporation (PNCC): the Luzon Tollroad Project. The agreement was signed in June 1996. Under the joint venture, 27 kilometres of toll roads would be upgraded and 84 kilometres of new roads built in the northern Philippines province of Luzon. Then Philippine President Fidel Ramos said at the joint-venture signing that the road development would accelerate and sustain economic growth in the Philippines. Work on the highway began in February 1997 with a projected completion date in 2000.

Exhibit 2	HHL's BOT Transportation Portfolio in Asia

Net Asset Value Analysis of HHL Transportation Infrastructure Projects

GSZ East Superhighway	HK$15,776 Million
Shunde Highway	HK$ 1,079 Million
Guangzhaou Ring Road	HK$ 1,718 Million
BERTS, Thailand	HK$ 5,100 Million

[from *ABN AmRO Hoare Govett Asia, 1997*]

Lessons from China Highway Construction

Some investors believed that HHL failed to do its homework before charging ahead with the GSZ Superhighway. "Hopewell misjudged the speed of major civil engineering construction in China, the complexities of land acquisition and budgeting," according to Michael Green of Nomura Research Institute. HHL's Guangzhou-Shenzhen Superhighway did provide a snapshot of some of the risks associated with infrastructure development in a foreign country. The company took six years to acquire all the land along the highway's 123-kilometre route, in part because it could not secure the full backing of its Chinese partner after a disagreement over the highway's design. After HHL snipped the ceremonial ribbons in July 1994, traffic flows (and thus toll revenues) turned out to be lower than originally projected. The toll road traffic had not yet reached an average of 100,000 vehicles per day.

HHL investors had since been on a dizzying journey. In mid-1995, news emerged of a US$718 million cost overrun on the GSZ highway and the company's stock price tumbled. The situation turned around in 1996. HHL sold 2.5 percent of its share in the GSZ Superhighway in China to the Japanese trading firm Kanematsu. The stake went for US$125.2 million, putting a face value of US$6 billion on the whole road—

nearly three times higher than most estimates. Early traffic was said to be below expectations, but nearly everyone believed that the 123-km toll road would eventually make money—some day.

The problems of the GSZ Superhighway were caused by several factors:

- Continuous design changes.
- Vastly under-estimated relocation expenses.
- HHL did not always have the financial resources to go at it alone, whereas previously the company had refused to take on financial partners.
- Wu formed solid relationship with top Chinese VIPs. However, Wu's relationships with some working level officials who were responsible for many daily operations were much less harmonious.

HHL was also criticised for breaking the cardinal rule of mega-projects: "keep the costs off your own books." A project banker said: "The good thing about Hopewell from a banker's viewpoint is that it is quite happy to use its balance sheet to get projects done quickly. But in terms of shareholders, the company ended up with a much larger liability." That was also true of Wu's other mega-deals. To meet the huge costs of infrastructure projects, private developers typically put in about 25 percent of the capital—on their own or with other equity partners—and raised the remainder through bank loans. The debt was secured against the project itself. The price: the developer did not get back the bulk of his money until all the loans were paid, and in the meantime might suffer a negative cash flow.

The Bangkok Elevated Road and Train System (BERTS)

Sir Gordon Wu envisioned BERTS in 1989, while he and four HHL engineers were stuck in a Bangkok traffic jam for two hours. "If I was stuck in a car with four pretty girls, this probably would not have happened, and I would have had some other ideas on my mind," Wu joked. To ease the chronic traffic congestion in Bangkok, Wu decided that HHL should construct and operate a six-lane expressway atop elevated railway and commuter train tracks. BERTS would solve the traffic problem and also create a lifetime of work for many people. The completed project would include the transit system, car parks, and office, retail, commercial and residential developments to be built along the route. Revenues would come from tolls and train fares, as well as rents from retail spaces in train stations and property developments. Wu was so confident of the project's viability that HHL had already committed HK$3.2 billion so far for the development.

BERTS was designed to offer a 60-kilometre, dual three-lane highway and community train service to relieve Bangkok's traffic chaos. Pursuant to public bidding in November 1990, the Thai Ministry of Transport and Communications awarded the concession for BERTS to Hopewell Thailand Limited (HTL), HHL's wholly-owned subsidiary. The project used the BOT method of financing and the term of the concession was for 38 years, allowing for an 8-year construction period. There were provisions in the agreement for two renewals of 10 years each. Although the project was to be completed in eight years, there was a provision in the contract for an extension of eight years if the project was not completed on time. The contract did not stipulate a fine in case the company was unable to finish the project within the prescribed period.

HTL started BERTS in 1990, with an estimated total development cost of HK$25 billion. The first of the two phases was expected to be finished in time for the Asian Games in 1998. The BERTS project included the construction of an elevated toll road and railway system, and procurement of the trains themselves. HTL signed three major contracts with the Thai government, subject to various conditions such as HTL obtaining the necessary financing.

The Thai government of Chatichai Choonhavan approved the concession, but the rapid progress HTL anticipated never happened. "There were numerous disputes over approvals, design changes as well as [the option] of going underground," HHL reported. Thailand also went through a very turbulent time: Chatichai Choonhavan was toppled in a military coup in 1991, bloody pro-democracy protests erupted in 1992 and four governments came and went before the ruling coalition led by Prime Minister Banharn Silapaarcha took the reins last year. Meanwhile, HTL had sunk US$480 million into piling and substructure work.

In the past, foreign firms had a bumpy time trying to do infrastructure projects in Thailand. In 1992, a change of government cost Canada's SNC-Lavalin its contract for a Skytrain project. Two years later, Japanese construction giant Kumagai Gumi sold its 65 percent stake in the $80 million second stage of a Bangkok expressway to a local party in a deal partly brokered by Bangkok Bank. The Japanese gave up after a wrangle with government agencies over toll sharing and land rights.

The State Railway of Thailand and HTL issued a joint press release in May 1996, confirming the Thai authorities' support for BERTS and for HTL's implementation of the project under its concession agreement. The release also supported an extension of time for the project's completion. HTL continued to state its commitment, however, to completing the project's first phase before the Asian Games started in Bangkok in December 1998.

In July 1996, HTL signed additional piling contracts and a main civil engineering contract. Discussions with railway contractors had been concluded in October 1996.

BERTS was one of three major metropolitan mass transport programs in Thailand. Although HHL and HTL had already expended HK$5.3 billion in the project and completed 20 percent of Phase 1 by January 1997, they were still working closely with financial advisers to structure the financing package. They had yet to put together the complete financing for the project. The limited recourse financing was to be comprised of export credits from Europe and loans from international commercial banks. Additional financial information is shown in Exhibits 4 and 5.

In September 1997, after the depreciation of the Thai baht (see Exhibit 5), HTL requested that the Thai government adjust the tolls and tram fares for BERTS. HHL disclosed in October 1997 that its investment in BERTS could have secured a return of 18 percent with the previous fare structure *before* the depreciation of the Thai currency, and 15 percent assuming no earnings from property. In its FY 97 financial results analyst meeting in late October 1997, HHL announced an exceptional loss of HK$5.133 million from provisions (not write off) made for the company's Thailand investment. No additional capital was to be committed. In light of the fact that HHL's investment in Thailand was now being provided for, and given the country's economic and political turmoil, some speculated that HHL might be looking for an exit with some compensation from the Thai government.

Investors were not going to put more money into the Thai project until they were sure that the BERTS contract would be a water-tight agreement. If HTL could not prove its capability to complete the Phase One expressways that were scheduled for mid-1998, the Thai government might terminate BERTS and seek restitution. Given the complications from the depreciation of the baht and the reluctance of the Thai government to amend the concession agreement, some analysts suggested that HHL would be better off quitting the Thai project and focusing on its China investments.

Wu was adamant that HHL had no intention of quitting, and indeed would fight in the courts if the Thai government cancelled BERTS. "Hopewell could be entangled in a legal dispute for months, possibly years," noted Alex Tang of Yamaichi Securities in Hong Kong. The fight obviously would not be easy for Wu. "When you add the complexity of politics in Thailand, an acute traffic problem and a private-sector developer with contentious government backing, you have a cocktail for immense complications for Hopewell," says Nomura's Green. Yamaichi's Tang, however, was more optimistic:

"Gordon is a very good negotiator. Hopefully at the end of the day, he will win." But if BERTS failed, both Wu and the Thai authorities would be scrambling to salvage more than their reputations.

HHL's Financial Status

As its stock price fell from HK$5.45 per share in October 1996 to below HK$2.10 per share in November 1997, HHL took more blows to its already dwindling fortunes. Critics said Wu's infrastructure-to-power empire was stretched too thin. Most of the debt required to fund the capital-intensive projects was in Hong Kong or US dollars, secured against individual projects. Wu was considering raising funds by selling stakes in the Guangzhou-Shenzhen-Zhuhai Superhighway, in hopes of replicating the return from the 1995 sales of 2.5 percent interest in the toll operations. The shopping centres and commercial areas of Phase One of the GSZ East Superhighway also could be sold to the Japanese trading firm—Kanematsu—at HK$964 million. This would put the face value of the whole road at HK$38.56 billion. This money would strengthen HHL's balance sheet (see Appendix 1), which had been hit hard by cost overruns and RMB 6 billion additional investment in the completed GSZ East Superhighway alone. Without such funds, Wu could face a cash crunch that could endanger projects in China, Indonesia, the Philippines and India.

Wu had met his stockholders in November 1996, as usual in the Hopewell Centre. This time he had a difficult agenda; Wu had to convince investors that a 21 percent drop in operating profits (to HK$769 million) and a 70 percent cut in dividend payments (to 6 cents per share) were in the shareholders' long-term interest (see Appendix 2). The Hong Kong stock market was not impressed by Wu's argument. HHL shares continued the slide that began before the annual meeting. From the high of HK$5.5 per share in July, 1996, the price dropped to less than HK$3 per share in October. According to a security analyst at brokerage James Capel in Hong Kong, there was a market expectation that HHL needed to take action in the next six to nine months to straighten out its cash flow situation.

Industry watchers said HHL simply had too much debt—and that the debt would affect its cash flow. Aside from the surprise profit and dividend cuts, HHL also reported a debt-to-equity ratio of 92 percent, up from 62 percent the previous year because of new loans. However, HHL said much of that was for project financing and that the debt was arranged on a limited recourse basis which, secured by revenue from the projects undertaken, would not require HHL to incur any material liability.

There were also complaints that HHL was liquidating assets too soon, when they were still capable of generating high-quality, recurring income. HHL sold its 51 percent interest in a Happy Valley (Hong Kong) residential development for HK$1.5 billion, for example, at a time when the 1994 property market remained sluggish. HHL may have had little choice of timing, however, given its heavy debt.

Wu insisted that HHL was on track. Bankruptcy looked unlikely, even to his critics. HHL's bankers, among them Hongkong Bank and Hang Seng Bank, had granted much to HHL already, and would help Wu prevent HHL from going under. "They're informed of my plans," said the tycoon. "That's why they're comfortable.

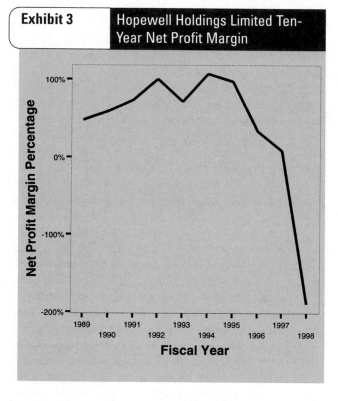

Exhibit 3 — Hopewell Holdings Limited Ten-Year Net Profit Margin

No one was ruling out the possibility of Wu turning the situation around, and selling big stakes in the GSZ East Superhighway could be the way to do it. Wu had piled up a personal fortune estimated at HK$1.7 billion through risk-taking. He was the first to build privately financed hotels in China. He sealed his reputation as a can-do builder with fast work on the Shajiao B power plant in China. "Wu's a visionary but his approach is very practical," said long-time friend Simon Murray, head of Asian operations of Deutsche Bank. Wu's track record still counted for something. "If you look at other project developers in Asia, HHL is among the few that have delivered," said Bob Dewing, head of project

finance at Citicorp. Comparisons to HHL to other property developers are shown in Appendix 3. The GSZ superhighway would turn out to be a key link in one of China's fastest-growing economic corridors. Wu said GSZ superhighway project had made HK$2 billion from the last three years.

Wu argued that once the infrastructure projects were built and the debt was repaid, they would produce stable cash return. However, Wu needed to convince investors and creditors that he could keep things going until then, and that he could minimize surprises along the way. The September 1996 issue of *Asian Business* touted HHL as one of the few large Hong Kong-based companies that had been successful in raising capital in international capital markets to finance infrastructure projects. In 1996, HHL was granted bank loan facilities of about HK$7 billion for long term project finances. "Infrastructure projects cost megabucks, but it's easy to get banks to invest," Wu contended, noting that managers must show a need for the project, demonstrate an income stream, hit the deadline for completion and control costs. "Asians play for the long-term," said Wu, "in fact, negotiations can take from one to 10 years."

The Asian Currency Crisis

The currency crisis that swept across Asia in mid-1997 raised many concerns and prompted speculation about future economic performance in the Asia-Pacific region.

Professors Radelet and Sachs of Harvard University, however, offered the following comments in the November/December 1997 issue of *Foreign Affairs*:

> *Asia, with 66 percent of the world's population, had a meager 19 percent of world income . . . in 1920. In 1950 . . . one of the great changes of modern history began, with the rapid growth of many Asian economies. By 1992, fueled by high growth rates, Asia's share of world income had risen to 33 percent.*
>
> *Asia's sudden ascent has become something of a Rorschach test for the economics profession and the foreign policy community. For some, Asia's rapid growth is an economic miracle that calls for a reevaluation of Western economic strategies. For others, such as the MIT economist Paul Krugman, . . . the rapid growth has looked hollow. Not only has there been no miracle, but there was reason to believe that Asian growth might display weaknesses similar to those of the period of rapid Soviet growth in the 1950s and 1960s. These doubts seemed to find support in the sudden, sharp currency crises that gripped several high-flying Southeast Asian economies (especially Indonesia, Malaysia, the Philippines, and Thailand) in*

Exhibit 4 Ten-Year Revenue, Net Income, and Profit Margin: HHL

Year	Revenue (US$mil.)	Net Income (US$mil.)	Net Profit Margin
1998	190.5	(362.8)	(190.4%)
1997	367.9	27.6	7.5%
1996	305.6	99.4	32.5%
1995	281.3	271.5	96.5%
1994	298.2	315.4	105.8%
1993	373.2	261.9	70.2%
1992	209.9	209.9	100.0%
1991	126.8	92.9	73.2%
1990	137.7	80.4	58.4%
1989	140.3	66.3	47.3%

The unusual relationship between turnover and group profit is attributable to four items:
(1) extraordinary gains and losses, (2) share of net income or losses in associated companies, (3) taxes owed or tax refunds due, and (4) net income or losses attributable to minority interests.

mid-1997. Even money managers formerly enamored of the region decried underlying institutional weaknesses, including corruption, nepotism, populist policies, and insufficient banking regulation.

"The Southeast Asian currency crises of 1997 are not a sign of the end of Asian growth but rather a recurring—if difficult to predict—pattern of financial instability that often accompanies rapid economic growth. Just as Indonesia, Malaysia, and Korea rapidly recovered from financial crises in the 1970s and 1980s, so the Asian economies are likely to resume rapid growth within two to three years."

Meanwhile, the Hong Kong property market was seeing a downturn in residential sales. The Special Administrative Region Government declared, immediately after the July 1 return of sovereignty to China, that one of its key policy interests was to make home purchases more affordable to Hong Kong residents. Prices in the property market previously had escalated beyond the financial reach of many residents. In the coming years, more land parcels were to be made available for public auction, and home ownership schemes of various types were to be introduced. One promise was to build and make available to the market each year 50,000 subsidized housing units and 35,000 private property homes.

Hong Kong property prices had dropped by about twenty to thirty percent in just a few months. Although few individuals in Hong Kong felt that property prices would continue to drop, there was a general feeling that the rapid increases of the past would not be likely to happen again soon. The overall economy was not encouraging either. Financial and currency crises had many residents concerned about Hong Kong's economic future. Tourism, a booming economic activity before the return of Hong Kong's sovereignty to China, dropped markedly. Retail sales also fell. Yaohan, a major Japanese company with a number of department stores throughout Hong Kong, closed in the SAR because of

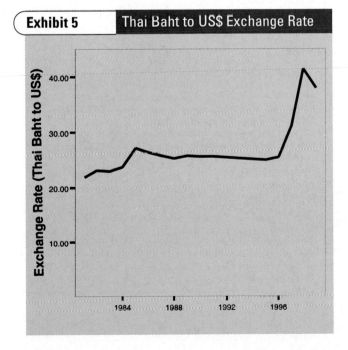

Exhibit 5 Thai Baht to US$ Exchange Rate

financial problems. The Hong Kong stock market experienced a sharp drop when the Asian currency crisis began. Although the market had crept back up again, the Hang Seng Index still had a long way to go to regain the heights it had reached just before the sovereignty transfer.

Nonetheless, major infrastructure projects and government subsidized housing projects were forging ahead. The SAR Government and local economists projected that Hong Kong's economic condition would stay strong and continue to experience growth, albeit less rapid than in past years. Close business and trade relationships with China would continue to support and stimulate Hong Kong's economy. Hong Kong's future, many people asserted, should continue to be positive.

The Strategic Choice

Sir Gordon Wu had been the key figure directing HHL's growth and development strategy for the past 25 years. Wu had realized many of his skyscraper-sized ambitions. He had built towers in Hong Kong, superhighways in China, and power plants in the Philippines, and had been a major regional player. He was well respected for his strong commitment and achievements in the power generation industry and other infrastructure sectors across Asia. By November of 1997, however, Wu's 66-story, cylindrical Hopewell Centre had been dwarfed by many taller buildings in Hong Kong.

The stalling of the BERTS project was a great disappointment. HHL had already poured HK$5.3 billion into BERTS, and had completed more than 20 percent of Phase 1. Hopewell wanted to re-open negotiations with the Thai government, but the new cabinet had only been in place for a few weeks. It seemed unlikely that the BERTS issue could be resolved, one way or the other, anytime soon.

At age 62, Wu still had a number of unfinished mega projects on hand or on the drawing board, including: the Tanjung Jati B Power Station in Indonesia, the Guangzhou-Shenzhen-Zhuhai West Superhighway, and the 93-story Mega Tower Hotel in Hong Kong. When asked who would succeed him should he retire, Wu claimed that HHL currently had very capable executives and the question of a successor did not need to be addressed right away. Wu's son was 24 years of age and still in school studying business administration; it would be quite a while before he would be able to help his father direct HHL.

Most pressing, however, was the question of how aggressively HHL should continue to pursue infrastructure development. HHL's successes and failures had long been tied to the region's economic success. On October 20, 1997, officials in Macao announced a 27 kilometre "superbridge" project linking the Portuguese enclave, Zuhai (PRC), and Hong Kong's Lantau Island. Dr. Leonel Miranda, Government Planning and Co-operation director for Macao, noted that "The main idea is to connect the east and west sides of the Pearl River Delta. It is possible for the Pearl River Delta to become the biggest economic zone in the world." Dr. Miranda also revealed that the project was backed by a group of Hong Kong and mainland investors, led by HHL. Thus, it appears that Sir Gordon Wu intends to continue HHL's infrastructure development business. Is this the right decision for HHL's shareholders? Can HHL take steps to minimize the risks associated with future infrastructure development projects? Alternately, would an entirely new corporate strategy—perhaps one that concentrates on its property development business—be better for shareholders?

References

1. Charlie Pahlman, *Source Watershed*, Vol. 2 No. I, published by Towards Ecological Recovery and Regional Alliance (TERRA), Bangkok. Publication, July–October 1996.
2. Matthew Flecter, "Hanging on at Hopewell, Asia Watches as Wu Acts to Shore Up His Infrastructure Empire", *Asiaweek*, July 1997.
3. Stewart Oldfield, "Hopewell has watertight deal with Thai agencies," September 20, 1997.
4. Leonor A. Briscoe, "Philippines Hopewell Power Project to Receive $110 Million Financing from IFC", February 5, 1993.
5. Southern Company Press Release "SEI Holdings acquires outstanding CEPA shares from Hopewell", July 15, 1997.
6. Gordon Wu, "Slowly does it as systems move to full integration", *South China Morning Post,* May 26, 1997.
7. Dr. J. Michael Cobb, "Implications of the Current Regional Financial Crisis and the Hopewell BERTS Project Announcement", October 1997.
8. BIZ Report, Blue Bridge Enterprises, "The New Guangzhou Beltway Setback of a Major Construction Company", September 16, 1996.
9. *Financial Day News,* "Hopewell Future", April 9, 1996.
10. Simon Pitman, TDC, Hong Kong Construction & Architecture "a regional power".
11. TDC, Hong Kong Construction & Architecture "Power Project Completed".
12. Dahid Hussain, "Highway to Nowhere", *Information Times,* July 1997.
13. Allen T. Cheng, "A $1.5 Trillion Market", Asian Inc., March 1997.
14. TDC, "Hopewell Helps 'Road to Development' ".
15. "No Relief in the Philippines", *Asiaweek*, November 16 1996.
16. Amornrat Mahitirook, "Suwat wants guarantee from Hopewell", *Bangkok Post* January 5, 1997.
17. Matthew Fletcher and Steven K.C. Poh, "POWER TYCOON", *Asiaweek.*
18. *Financial Day News,* "Wu's Promise", April 10, 1996.
19. Matthew Fletcher, "TRAIN TO BANGKOK, Can Gordon Wu hang on to his Thai project—and Hopewell?", *Asiaweek.*
20. Success in Asia: Goodwill, Business Acumen and a Long-term View, October 4, 1996.
21. Kevin Rushton, Coopers & Lybrand Consulting "The new power triangle in Asia".
22. Joseph Kahn, Erik Guyot, Paul Sherer, "Hopewell's cancelled deal in Thailand reflects tough infrastructure climate", AWSJ October 1, 1997, p.1.
23. John Liden, Rexie Reyes, and Erik Guyot, "Delay befalls potential Hopewell project in Philippines", AWSJ October 1, 1997, p.3.
24. Erik Guyot, "Hopewell takes provision on investment in Thailand", AWSJ Oct. 29, 1997, p.3.
25. "Wu's Big, Big Woes", Asia, Inc., September 1996.
26. "Week in Quotes," *South China Morning Post,* Sunday, October 13, 1996.
27. Pete Engardio, "Is Gordon Wu Stretched too Thin?", *Business Week,* October 9, 1996.

28. Niall Fraser, "Massive Bridge Project Revealed", *South China Morning Post,* October 20, 1997.

29. Photographs courtesy of R. Priem, www.photodisc.com, John Butler, and the US National Aeronautics & Space Administration.

Appendix 1 — Condensed Balance Sheet and Income Statement: HHL

	1998 (US$ mil.)	1997 (US$ mil.)
Cash	45.5	78.8
Net Receivables	130.4	103.7
Inventories	2.3	2.2
Other Current Assets	209.4	116.7
Total Current Assets	387.6	301.4
Property, Plant, & Equipment	3,619.7	4,289.6
Total Assets	4,007.3	4,591.0
Short-Term Debt	257.3	551.0
Other Short-Term Liabilities	355.1	397.3
Total Current Liabilities	612.4	948.3
Long-Term Debt	1,328.1	811.1
Total Liabilities	1,940.5	1,759.4
Equity	2,066.8	2,831.6
Total Liabilities & Equity	4,007.3	4,591.0
Revenue	190.5	367.9
Expenses	92.8	151.5
Operating Income	97.7	216.4
Taxes and Other Provisions	460.5	188.8
Net Income	(362.8)	27.6

Appendix 2 — Five Year Financial Summary: HHL (in HK$ Million)

	1992	1993	1994	1995	1996
Turnover[1]	1,622	2,889	2,305	2,175	2,365
Group Profit[1]	1,623	2,028	2,438	2,100	769

Five Year Assets and Liabilities in HK$ Million

	1992	1993	1994	1995	1996
Fixed Asset	9,256	8,546	12,889	22,113	22,431
Properties	443	635	672	647	694
Associated Co.	718	829	672	647	694
JV/Concession	2,831	6,788	19,340	26,255	26,532
Other Investment	35	78	480	209	226
LT Loans Collect	–	–	–	221	367
Deffered Charge	–	–	–	–	49
Net Current Asset	5,696	3,799	3,031	1,996	820
LT Liabilities	(1,237)	(3,913)	(11,736)	(20,476)	(22,174)
Minority Interest	(804)	(74)	(5,233)	(5,449)	(6,017)
Net Assets	16,940	16,690	20,262	24,914	23,478

[1]The unusual relationship between turnover and group profit is attributable to four items:
(1) extraordinary gains and losses, (2) share of net income or losses in associated companies, (3) taxes owed or tax refunds due, and (4) net income or losses attributable to minority interests.

Appendix 3 — Comparison of HHL to Other Hong Kong Property Developers

Average Net Profit Margins Percentages for the Past Ten Years

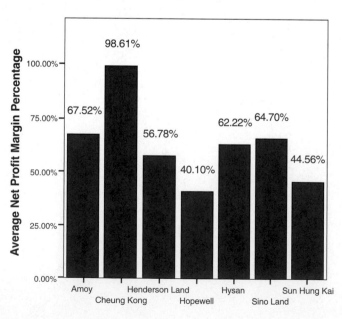

Net Income Trends

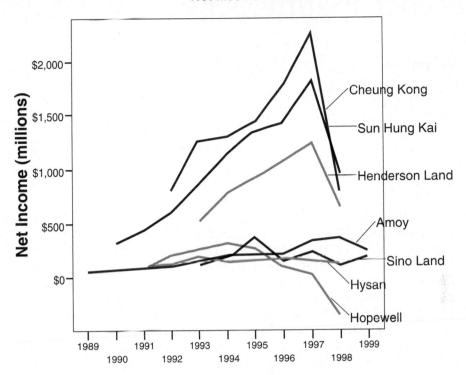

InterPost Prague, s.r.o.

Joan Winn

University of Denver

"The people in Holland didn't really know what to do with me," explained Heidi. "Now I'm not sure I know what to do with this company." Heidi Stone had come to Prague in 1994 to start a central-European distribution center for Royal Dutch Post PTT International, the Dutch Post Office. By 1998, Heidi had repositioned the Prague business as a direct-marketing and magazine-subscription service. When PTT Post arranged the sale of her company to Wegener Arcade, a Dutch conglomerate consisting of information, communication and entertainment enterprises, Heidi felt like she was in the case studies she had read about as an MBA student. "I want this company to have a regional presence, and Wegener does too, but I'm not sure where to start. I learned every strategic analysis model in the books, but now I'm being challenged to apply them."

The beginning of March had been particularly stressful. "I feel like I'm drowning right now. I'm looking for new office space, working with the Ernst & Young audit team, coaching my sales team, trying to keep some people in line and motivate others, giving feedback to customer service. And I've got to prepare for my meeting next week with Wegener. They're expecting me to present a proposal, but I'm not sure what I can tell them at this point."

In Early 1998, her operation had eight employees and their present office space would not be big enough to handle additional activities. Heidi believed that she had the organization skills the company needed during its development phase, but wondered if she was the right person to manage the growth and expansion. Heidi liked starting things, so she contemplated the possibility of starting satellite offices to give the company a regional, rather than a local presence. The International Director at Wegener had suggested she think about assuming a role of New Venture Director, or something like that, to spearhead new projects and expand Wegener's presence in central Europe. Wegener's interest in this venture really reflected their interest in her, not just what her Prague company had to offer. On the other hand, Heidi had built this organization and was interested in exploring other product arenas and attaining profitability. She liked Prague, understood the market, and now spoke Czech well. At this stage, she wasn't sure that the Prague operation would be successful without her. She was torn between looking for new product opportunities for the Prague office or moving on to launch something new. "I'm not sure I know what to do with this company," she confessed, "and I don't know what to do for myself."

Heidi Stone's Background

Having spent a year in Stockholm as an exchange student in high school, Heidi Stone knew she preferred living in Europe to the United States. In 1981, she moved from her hometown in Indiana to Washington, D.C. to go to Georgetown University. She spent her junior year of college at Science Politique de Grenoble in France and graduated from Georgetown's School of Foreign Service with a major in Humanities in International Affairs in 1985. She had worked her way through college as a photographer and after graduation got a job as circulation director for *New Dominion Magazine* where she learned about distribution and subscription marketing.

In 1991 she enrolled in Katholieke Universiteit Leuven in Belgium and received an MBA in 1993. She spent six months in Lyon, France, doing free-lance translation work, trying to get a permanent job. She finally got an offer from the Paris office of *Communications Week International* to work in the marketing department of their New York office. Serendipitously, she learned about the publishing industry from multiple points of view.

> *I was the only smoker in the marketing group, but the distribution department had lots of smokers and I'd chat with them outside in the "smoker's corner." I naturally decided to capitalize on the situation and began to bring reports downstairs to see how distribution would impact my project going to Paris. All the departments were involved in this project, so I learned a lot about international distribution, and gained a lot of valuable information which helped me in my next position.*

Working in New York, despite its focus on international markets did not fit Heidi's desire to move out of publishing and into management, nor did it fit with her desired lifestyle. She was continually on the lookout for opportunities abroad and used her networking abilities to scout out positions that would allow her to live and work in Europe.

> *I had met the president of InterPost North America at a conference. He was a Dutchman. He had said, "If you ever want to do anything, give us a call because you speak Dutch and you're in our target audience, publications." So when I was looking for work I did give him a call. I was in Belgium at the time and he was on holiday, but he forwarded my c.v. to his boss, who was the managing director for PTT Post International. He gave me a call, and we set up an interview.*

PTT Post and InterPost Prague

Royal Dutch PTT Post Telecom and Telecommunications (PTT Post) was the largest employer in the Netherlands. PTT Post, formed in 1989 as a joint venture between the newly-privatized Dutch Post Office and KLM Royal Dutch Airlines, was an international network which collected, sorted and delivered mail throughout the world. PTT Post was one of the first postal operations in the world to privatize. As a result, they were able to look for opportunities outside their home market, and were able to be sales and market driven. They reduced the number of employees through natural attrition, and further increased efficiency through technological innovations and volume. Since they were a large institution, they could set up subsidiary operations in foreign countries and open up bank accounts in those locations. A PTT Post innovation was setting up accounts so that customers could pay in their local currency, rather than by

sending a US-dollar-cheque, the standard convertible currency. In 1994, PTT Post was listed on the Amsterdam stock exchange. By 1995, most European mail from Canada and China and up to a quarter of Europe's foreign magazines were estimated to have passed through the Netherlands via PTT Post.

In 1994, Interdisc, a Netherlands-based distributor of erotica products and publications (so-called "marital aids"), decided to expand its operations into the Czech Republic. PTT Post contracted with a local Czech company, TCPS, to provide marketing, translation, logistics, customs clearance and delivery services for Interdisc. When Interdisc began to question the value of PTT's involvement the project and proposed to work directly with TCPS, PTT Post looked for someone to act as its regional representative, to set up a Prague office to take over the role of TCPS.

Heidi was hired by the international division of PTT Post in August 1994, and spent a month in Holland as a management trainee. She was offered positions in London and Prague. Seeing the current emergence from Communism in the Czech Republic as an opportunity for market innovation, she chose the Czech assignment. She arrived in Prague for the first time in October 1994.

Developing the Business

Heidi's move to Prague in 1994 was during a period of growth and expansion for PTT Post. At that time, PTT Post was investigating "value-adding service" products to create a portfolio of offerings to bind clients to the Post's distribution services. Heidi arrived in Prague in October 1994 with a mandate from PTT Post "to develop and implement new and existing products in the field of direct marketing, including but not limited to, warehousing [storage] and fulfillment [packaging and delivery]." To carry out this mandate required the establishment of a legal entity within the Czech Republic. Through the Dutch Chamber of Commerce in Prague, Heidi met Andrea, then 19, who spoke English and Dutch and who could provide translation services into Czech. To minimize the time and paperwork involved in setting up a subsidiary of PTT Post, InterPost Prague was incorporated in November 1994 as an independent business with Heidi and Andrea[1] as joint owners. PTT Post would provide expertise and financial support. Legal liability, however, was borne by Heidi and Andrea, a fact that was difficult for Andrea to deal with psychologically. Heidi "bought out" Andrea's share in January, thus putting InterPost Prague solely in Heidi's name.

Heidi set to work doing what she did best: building an organization and assembling a team of well-trained and dedicated staff. She put together flow-charts and job descriptions. She trained people in politeness, promptness, and customer service. She held regular meetings to make sure that everyone in her office understood everyone else's duties so that they could work together. She wanted to guard against information hoarding and inefficiency that plagued so many Czech companies. While she didn't want her employees to be able to conceal any company-related missteps, she also wanted them to feel secure enough to expose their own deficiencies, help each other, and communicate problems and suggestions to her and to each other.

Heidi was determined to keep the Interdisc project going and, in addition, develop a strategy to target other mail order companies and the publications market which had proved so lucrative to PTT Post in Holland. She wanted to make the Prague office a model for expansion to other developing countries, such as Poland, Hungary and Slovakia. She began investigating alternative markets and customers, including direct-mail, custom catalogue advertising and fulfillment services, and subscriptions services.

Heidi's research showed that direct-mail services such as consultancy, "list broking" (compiling and selling mailing lists), and magazine subscription services would yield the highest gross margins and had the best chances of success in the current competitive arena. She was confident that her marketing experience and organizational abilities would put her in a good position to build a successful subscription service and direct-mail business.

Advertising and Direct-Mail Services in the Czech Republic

In November 1989, Czechoslovakia emerged from forty years of Soviet rule, planned economic system and state-controlled businesses. The new government moved quickly to develop a macroeconomic strategy for the transition to a market economy. On the microeconomic level, government policy was concentrated on massive privatization schemes and liberal pricing policies. At the end of 1992, the Czech and Slovak Republics divided along ethnic borders, but the principles of democracy and capitalism remained as a strong foundation for the constitutions, legal systems, and economic structure of both countries. By 1994, the Czech Republic was heralded as the most stable of the post-communist transition countries, with a low unemployment rate, a positive growth rate, and a stable currency linked to the US dollar and the German mark.

By 1996, with the increasing internalization and modernization of products and services, Czechs had become familiar and at ease with western media, advertising, and purchasing opportunities. Companies were quickly recognizing the need for more cost-efficient and effective channels of reaching their customers. Advertising in magazines and television had become increasingly expensive and advertising budgets were typically lean. While the 1997 summer devaluation of the Czech Koruna ("crown", the local currency) put pressure on local branches of international and domestic advertising agencies, flows of foreign capital and foreign entrepreneurs were transforming the capital city of Prague into an advertising mecca.

In general, the Czech market was beginning to resemble a Western-style marketplace with its proliferation of goods and services. The primary difference between this transitional market and a market such as the American, British or Dutch markets, was the lack of a customer-service orientation. Companies which had started to offer a good service level were already commanding more of the market. Few companies understood how to deliver this service; fewer still understood how to effectively reach potential customers.

According to *The Economist*[2], "The low costs of direct marketing was creating a huge and fast-growing industry—made up of direct mail, telemarketing, database marketing, the Internet and free-phone TV, radio and print advertisements." According to Robert Wientzen, president of America's Direct Marketing Association, "in Russia and the Czech Republic most junk mail is opened and read—indeed the average piece is pored over by more than one person. Even in China, despite an unreliable postal service and few credit cards, the government is encouraging direct marketing, partly to stop people migrating to cities in search of things to buy."

Despite the lack of a sophisticated data base, direct-mail advertising and telemarketing were becoming more acceptable means of communication between client and consumers, with hotels and financial services leading the way. All direct marketing companies had access to the Czech Register of Companies. Many companies had developed CD-ROM products which used a variation of the Czech Register. Of the business-to-business lists that Heidi had used or seen, most were not updated frequently enough to include staff changes or address changes. The Czech Post Office did not have a Change of Address System which would allow list managers to easily update their files. Most companies and individuals did not register their new address with the post office, and the Czech Post had many outdated entries on its list. Among obsolete records was a 3-year-old address for PTT Telecom, the Czech telephone company, which provided the single largest investment in the Czech Republic since 1991.

A database of accurate addresses and phone numbers, while currently difficult to find and update, would be too valuable for companies that perceived direct-mail brochures and telephone solicitations as an effective marketing strategy. Because most businesses believed it would be too much work to maintain or merge databases, list broking—selling mailing lists to other businesses—had been slow to develop. Some companies were afraid that their competitors would benefit from sharing customer lists.

In 1995, the Czech Association of Direct Marketing and Mail Order (ADMAZ) was founded, with InterPost Prague as one of its original members. At that time there were 50 companies offering direct marketing services, but only five appeared to be developing operations on a serious scale. By 1998, ADMAZ reported thirty members (including InterPost Prague) but had not developed a pro-active stance in developing the direct marketing business. The Czech Republic, like its neighboring countries, was slow to develop business-to-business mailing-list rental to facilitate direct-mail services.

Heidi had identified 73 mail-order businesses in Prague in 1996, but found no more than ten which had achieved substantial growth. Up to 40 percent of the packages delivered by the Czech Post Office were returned unaccepted, having been delivered to an incorrect address. Mail-order in general had a bad reputation due to sub-standard goods and poor customer service.

Subscription Services

Most magazines and newspapers in the Czech Republic were purchased at news kiosks. The Czech Post Office had been the sole vehicle for subscription magazine and newspaper distribution prior to 1991. Regular subscribers could reserve copies through the state-owned subscription agent who merely removed the copies from the kiosks and placed them at the post office for consumer pick-up. By 1994, publishers had started to move into subscriptions and away from standard newsstand sales for their primary readership. Early consumer-response indicated that working in a more Western-oriented society placed greater demands on their time, which meant less time to browse at the local newsstand.

According to the UVDT (Daily Newspaper Publishers Association) 1995 statistics, 170 different magazines sold 217.8 million copies in the Czech Republic that year. There were approximately 3000 different newspaper and magazine titles on the market. Of these, approximately 1,000 were popular in terms of advertising and circulation sales. Of the 3000 different titles, approxi-

mately 800 of them had different frequencies, other than daily, weekly or monthly.

According to the UVDT, 38 percent of all newspapers and magazines were sold by subscription in 1995. Magazines accounted for a much smaller percentage of subscription sales than daily newspapers. Despite the predominant pattern of single-copy sales purchased at news-stands, a total of 35 million magazines were delivered by subscription in 1995, with approximately one million people/companies considered as subscribers. Estimates for 1996 predicted an increase of 15 percent.

Roughly 25 percent of the print circulation market in the Czech Republic was sold by subscription agents, with the former monopolist agency PNS commanding roughly two-thirds of the subscription market. Prior to 1995, PNS neither gave publishers the full subscription fee in advance, nor the name and address of the subscriber. PNS had recently started to make their subscription lists available to publishers and to make subscription ordering easier. Subscription sales were expected to grow by an average of 5 percent a year over the next five years and several companies were preparing to enter the market.

Launching the Business

Heidi saw a narrow window of opportunity for subscriptions services, as the market was ripe for the right company to come in and establish itself as a competitive, service-oriented alternative to PNS. Capitalizing on PTT Post's expertise in magazine subscription deliveries, Heidi's first project was a Subscriptions Catalogue. She envisioned that a catalogue offering a variety of magazine titles which promoted direct-delivery of these subscriptions would be a low-risk, cost-effective vehicle to attract publishing business, and would help establish InterPost Prague's expertise and level of commitment with local suppliers and consumers. In addition, the catalogue would provide InterPost Prague with a prospecting tool; its goal was to lead to spin-off project work in areas such as marketing consultancy and direct-mail list management. Heidi explained,

> We decided to produce a catalogue which would convey high-quality, long-term commitment to both publishers and readers. Our definition of quality included heavy weight paper, laminated perfect bound cover, and easy perforated pull-out forms. We wanted to be seen as a serious "reference book plus." We selected 100,000 business addresses from two local suppliers. We chose business addresses over consumer addresses thinking that not

only would we be targeting people with money to spend *(middle and upper management) but that with six order forms, the catalogue would be passed around and used within one office environment.*

Exhibit 1 outlines Heidi's plan for differentiating InterPost Prague's subscription services from the current method of purchasing magazine subscriptions. Heidi expected that InterPost Prague could obtain 11,000 subscription orders from its first catalogue mailing. The expected profit margin from subscription services was 36 percent. Her initial projections estimated 15,000 publication orders (at 1,800 Kc each) for a gross return of over 800,000USD at the current exchange rate. However, despite careful market research, she was not prepared for the "wait and see" attitude that the Czechs had to new products or new ways of doing business.

The first Subscriptions Catalogue was published in May 1996. Total returns from the first edition of the catalogue were 1273 orders, with the average spend per order of 682.92 Kc, and the average number of publications per order 1.23. Despite these discouraging returns, she believed that the catalogue held promise, both for eventual profitability and for name recognition in attracting both international and local publishers for distribution and consulting services. Heidi reflected, "We took a 4 million Kc loss (about $12,000USD) on that first edition, but we're looking ahead. We've on the steep part of the learning curve now."

Building a Self-Sustaining Operation

Despite Heidi's conscientiousness in marketing Interdisc's products in Prague, toward the end of 1996 Interdisc's owner decided to sell to his largest competitor, whose expansion plans excluded Central and Eastern Europe. Their only profitable client gone, PTT Post had no compelling reason to stay in the Czech Republic. Heidi's subscriptions services did not yield sufficient returns to convince PTT Post to continue their investment in maintaining an office in Prague.

Heidi knew that PTT Post intended to close the Prague office and transfer her to another location. Despite the fact that Heidi was the legal owner of InterPost Prague, she did not have the financial capital to continue operations on her own. She knew that she would need to quickly make her office self-sustaining if she were to stay in Prague. In addition to Prague as an attractive place to live, Heidi viewed the InterPost Prague project as the challenge that she had been looking for and she was determined to make this venture work.

The Subscriptions Catalogue had fulfilled one of its objectives: provided hassle-free subscription marketing to international and local publishers. It had not, however, succeeded in generating a large volume of subscription sales. Heidi was not sure whether this was due to improper targeting of the catalogue, insufficient catalogue offerings, lack of reputation in the market, unexciting product, or market resistance to subscriptions in general. She had received several customer comments indicating their satisfaction with the ease of subscription, and suggesting a wider selection of subscription offerings and a desire for a larger and more pleasing format.

The Subscriptions Catalogue had also fulfilled a secondary objective: to increase publisher awareness of InterPost Prague's agency services. As a result of articles in the Publisher Multinational Direct newsletter and DM News, InterPost Prague had received inquiries for mailing quotes. Most of these, however, had indicated an interest in region-wide activities (Poland, Hungary, Slovakia). Despite the disappointing financial returns, Heidi believed that the catalogue was an important vehicle to attract both international and local publishers' interest in consulting services.

Heidi worked with her staff to expand and improve the subscription catalogue and increase their direct-mail services. At the same time, she began to explore the possibility of launching an information and list broking service. Several companies had already entered the list broking market, but few understood how to properly promote the lists they managed. No attempts had been made to explain to list owners the benefits of releasing their list for rental. A few companies had already approached Heidi for help in promoting their lists. Her personal connections and InterPost Prague's reputation had helped build a good image and establish trust in the market. Computer software was available to collect information on current and potential customers, compile this information into a database, and sort by any of a number of categories to appeal to businesses who wanted to target their advertising brochures. By 1997, InterPost Prague already had compiled 90,000 addresses on their in-house list from their subscriptions and current direct-mail customers. InterPost Prague had signed contracts with its mail order clients until the end of 1998.

By the end of its second year, the subscription catalogue was starting to show signs of profitability [see Exhibit 2]. Starting with 26 publications in the first edition, the fourth edition of the Subscriptions Catalogue listed 61 publications and included directories, updates and CD-ROMs on its order form. Pricing for inclusion for the catalogue had evolved from a single inclusion fee to different levels of inclusion. The latest edition would include publishers who paid a nominal fee for a thumbnail inclusion to those purchasing a larger 1/6-page ad.

Case 19 / InterPost Prague, s.r.o.

Exhibit 1   The Publications Market

Number of Titles

Local publications: 1,367 titles, Total circulation 287.5 million.

Foreign publications: 273 foreign titles handled by largest foreign press distributor, of which 39 percent of titles sold are German or Swiss, 16 percent of titles sold are from the UK, 26 percent of titles sold, including the *International Herald Tribune,* are American

Methods of sales:

Current Czech method	Proposed methods
Advertising (image)	**Advertising (Direct response)**
• Billboards • House and other newspaper ads • Television ads • Radio • Kiosks Advertising aimed at encouraging consumers to either pick up a copy at the newsstand or buy a subscription via the post office	• House ads • Local newspapers • Television ads • Radio • Trams • Telephone cards Advertising aimed at encouraging consumer to buy directly from the publisher
Order method	**Order method**
• Potential subscriber goes to local post office and gives the post office his name, address, and desired choice of publication	• Subscriber is invited to fax, phone, or write in subscription order
Print order information	**Print order information**
• The post office informs the publisher the number of copies required for its subscription delivery service.	• InterPost Prague s.r.o. provides the publisher with the number of copies required per print run
Data base management	**Data base management**
• The post office retains all names and addresses at the local level • Some publishers have negotiated access to their subscriber names, but typically, the post office is considered the "list owner" • Names are not kept in a central location but are written in the postman's delivery book • Names are not kept on computer media	• InterPost captures the names and addresses of subscribers • InterPost "shares" the names with the publisher, who is the list owner • Names are kept at InterPost • Names are maintained on a computer database
Billing options	**Billing options**
• Subscribers are typically billed after receipt of the product • Subscribers most frequently are invoiced and pay on a monthly basis (cash flow management) but can pay for a year's subscription in advance • The only incentive to pay in advance is to avoid a visit to the post office or to have to have the money on hand when the postman comes to visit	• Subscribers have payment upfront and "Bill Me" options • Payment instruments are credit card, wire transfer, and local payment form • If paying by credit card, payment can be handled via fax • If payment is through local post office or bank transfer, subscriber uses the enclosed pre-printed payment form
Publisher receipts	**Publisher receipts**
• Publisher receives payment from the post office on average two (2) months after invoice is paid	• Publisher receives a wire transfer from InterPost in the currency of his choice

Exhibit 2   InterPost Prague s.r.o. Revenue Summary

Income Statements divided to activities (in Czk 000)*	Consolidated			The Subscriptions Catalogue					Consultancy			
	1995	1996	1997 Est.	Ed 1	Ed 2	Ed 3	Ed4	Total Cat	1995	1996	1997	Total Cons
Revenues												
Advertising in catalogue (a)	0	1,142	1,952	347	812	657	1,295	3,111	0	0	0	0
Subscriptions sold (b)	0	1,940	3,638	948	992	1,138	2,500	5,578	0	0	0	0
Fixed fees (c)	0	105	670	0	105	0	670	775	0	0	0	0
Consultancy (1)	4,779	7,865	9,687	0	0	0	0	0	4,779	7,865	9,387	22,031
Other sales	12	131	0	0	0	0	0	0	12	131	0	143
Total Revenue	4,791	11,183	15,947	1,295	1,909	1,795	4,465	9,464	4,791	7,996	9,387	22,174
Direct costs												
Graphic design (2a)	205	224	227	70	0	75	100	245	205	154	52	411
Printing services (2b)	0	2,857	1,672	2,187	256	329	972	3,744	0	414	0	414
Prepress materials: films & chromalins (2c)	142	87	89	12	6	84	65	167	142	69	0	211
Bulk subscriptions (3)	0	1,556	2,692	759	797	842	1,850	4,248	0	0	0	0
Lettershop & distribution & fulfilment (4)	398	2,462	1,382	1,256	660	468	1,063	3,447	398	546	0	944
Total Direct Costs (d)	745	7,186	6,062	4,284	1,719	1,798	4,050	11,851	745	1,183	52	1,980
Gross margin InterPost (a+b+c+1–d)	4,046	3,997	9,885									
Gross margin subscription catalogue (a+b+c–d)				–2,989	190	–3	415	–2,387				
Gross margin consultancy (1–d)				NA	NA	NA	NA	NA	NA	NA	NA	NA
Wages and salaries	357	1,070	1,329	274	122	240	324	960	357	674	765	1,796
Business services												
Advertising	1,481	470	5,343	75	30	152	218	475	1,481	365	4,973	6,819
Postage & delivery	9	75	352	0	0	0	0	0	9	75	352	436
Travel expense	130	377	232	0	0	0	0	0	130	377	232	739
Office rent	398	1,657	802	414	414	201	201	1,229	398	829	401	1,628
Telephone	156	277	256	55	62	30	30	177	156	160	196	512
Other	0	57	50	0	0	0	0	0	0	57	50	107
Total business services	2,174	2,913	7,035	544	506	152	449	1,651	2,174	1,863	6,435	10,472
Office equipment	209	430	60	107	107	15	15	244	209	216	30	455
Office supplies	709	222	218	56	56	55	55	221	709	111	109	928
Professional services	402	939	1,021	75	103	45	25	248	402	761	951	2,114
Financial expenses	664	146	67	11	11	14	18	54	664	124	35	823
Net result before management fee	–469	–1,723	155	–4,056	–715	–524	–470	–5,764	–469	3,065	1,011	3,607
Management fee	1,537	1,537	1,537	384	384	384	384	1,536	1,537	768	768	3,073
Net result after management fee	–2,006	–3,260	–1,382	–4,440	–1,099	–908	–854	–7,300	–2,006	2,297	243	534

*exchange rate for Czk/USD=1000Czk/$30 approx.

She hoped that the more standardized format and larger, more legible graphic would perform better in attracting new subscribers and justify the additional cost for them to participate.

New Parent: Wegener Arcade

In November 1997, PTT Post embarked on an acquisitions and divestiture program to restructure the corporation around their central core of distribution and fulfillment services. InterPost Prague's emphasis on direct-mail and subscription services did not fit these core competencies. Although InterPost Prague was, legally, an independent company, Heidi knew that unless PTT Post could sell her operation to another company, she would have to take her operation afloat on her own capital. While Heidi enjoyed the autonomy that PTT Post had given her, she also enjoyed the comfortable funding situation that she was in.

> I had the option of taking over the company because I had all the shares in my name, but I liked having the money, stability, and know-how that a large company provides. It's not easy getting bridge loans when you're small. PTT Post had been good to me. They also gave me the option to move with them, but I didn't want to move. We didn't fit their core business. They don't do direct marketing, they do distribution. From day one they never intended to set this up to do distribution and they didn't really want to do fulfillment. They told me to do direct marketing, so that's what I did. Then their shareholders told them to stick to their knitting. We're not their knitting, we're not even their ball of wax. And it's time for them to go back, get rid of us and stick to their core business.

In February 1998, PTT Post received an offer to purchase Heidi's Prague business from Wegener Arcade NV, a Dutch holding company for more than 40 enterprises in the information, communication and entertainment industries, operating widely in Western Europe. Wegener's involvement in direct marketing fit nicely with Heidi's current projects and their desire to expand into Central Europe made InterPost Prague an attractive investment. In addition, Wegener's current expansion strategy fit with Heidi's desire to build a regional office and expand her current direct-mail activities into neighboring countries. However, Heidi knew that, unlike PTT Post, Wegener was a conservative company and would need to see market data and profitability projections before she would be allowed to pursue new projects.

> We fit Wegener's core business, we're a very good match. But they had never considered doing business in this part of the world. They normally go after the number one or number two position companies, that is their strategy. They buy, they do not make. However, Wegener was looking to expand and the man who sold the information service in Holland to Wegener was a very good friend of both Wegener and my previous boss, and he knew me also. It was very much a timing issue and a trust issue and we weren't a big investment risk.

At the time of Wegener's purchase of InterPost Prague, the majority of the Prague office's overhead and costs were being spent on mail order consultancy, however Heidi believed that direct-mail activities had the most potential for profitability and growth. She believed that InterPost Prague's position was excellent, given its local presence and experience. So far, InterPost Prague did not have any competitors such as subscription marketing agents in the area of marketing ideas and circulation know-how. However, PNS, the former state subscription and newsstand distribution monopoly, had recently received investment from foreign sources and was expected to consolidate their large database and begin to produce mailings to their client base. She saw this integration of data as an opportunity for list rental in the near future. Competitors in the area of direct marketing fulfillment, list broking and mail bags were still in their early phase of development and did not pose an immediate threat.

As Heidi prepared for her first meeting with her new boss at Wegener, she debated about what role she wanted to take with this new parent company. There was an obvious window of opportunity to launch direct response products. For InterPost Prague to capitalize on this opportunity it would have to impact the market by hitting aggressively with a unified sales campaign. This would require an infusion of capital from Wegener. The Subscriptions Catalogue still needed to be re-worked into a formula-product to become profitable in a publishing market increasingly threatened by tight margins and heretofore uneducated about subscription marketing. Heidi believed that synergies between an information service and the subscription catalogue would help in the transitional period to product launch. Consulting services could serve as a bridge for mail order and direct mail activities. Heidi began compiling ideas for expanding InterPost Prague's current business offerings to other countries [Exhibit 3].

Integration into the Wegener Direct Marketing Groep would be an important transition for the company. Clearly this would be a period of changes for InterPost Prague employees. They would need to be informed and trained on any new products and services as well as learn about this new mother company. Contacts would need

Exhibit 3   Heidi's Expansion Ideas

Regional Publication Agent Via the Subscriptions Catalogue

To set up a region-wide bi-lingual Subscriptions Catalogue would require:
- Translation services (can be outsourced)
- Banking Services (can be outsourced)
- Invoicing services (can be outsourced)
- Local address and customer service (can be outsourced)
- Local sales force to sell local publications to round out the product (harder to outsource)

Outsourcing always entails middleman margins and travel costs, and would in effect increase the variable cost of the product. On the other hand, establishment of branch offices would necessitate fixed overheads, making outsourcing a more attractive option in the short run.

Possible countries for this service: Poland, Hungary, Slovakia, Russia, Romania

Central Europe

InterPost Prague has a minor network in Poland and Hungary. No business contacts have been set up in Slovakia, but it should not prove too difficult. Furthermore, Slovakia has the added advantage of a having a shared history with the Czechs, a similar language, and a parity with the Czech crown.

Russia

It would be possible to develop a product for the Russian market in conjunction with Independent Media. InterPost Prague could assist in the set-up of a professional subscription customer service and database. The only problem might come from Independent's not wanting to help promote competitors.

Romania

InterPost Prague has solid contacts in Romania, and can help countries exploit this market of 24 million inhabitants. However, outsourcing would also be required as KPN does not have an established legal entity in the country.

Reader Service

Publishers in other countries often include data cards to be returned to the Publisher or supplier which then prints labels and disseminates the products. This would allow InterPost Prague to build a sizeable database, achieve cost efficiencies with its printing of labels and addresses, and perform a publisher and advertiser service. This service would also generate leads from non-publishing clients.

Co-Operative Mailings

Through InterPost's Subscriptions Catalogue, we have been approached by various businesses in the Czech Republic to assist them in achieving their marketing aims. One problem which faces all companies, large or small, are insufficient budgets to handle the high cost of direct mail production. InterPost Prague proposes to design and develop a co-op mailing program which would bring together a variety of services and products in one catalogue or package. The synergies would be in handling the pre-press and handling as well as the customer service and address generation for the clients. All responses would come to InterPost Prague who would then disseminate the information to the various companies concerned.

to be established and additional employees recruited to meet new sales and organizational goals. Close monitoring of profitability targets and projections would need to be sent to the head office on a regular basis.

The current office space could accommodate a total of 9 employees comfortably. Heidi was already looking for a larger space to facilitate growth plans. She knew that the move would cause some upheaval in the day-to-day operations, but believed that she could minimize the disruption with advance planning regarding customer notification and logistics outlines. The good news was that a lot of renovated and new office space had recently become available on the market, driving down the rental prices.

As Heidi prepared her presentation to her new boss, she considered her options. She was excited about the possibility of leading InterPost Prague in new directions: building the mail-order and consultancy business, launching an information service, and refining the subscriptions catalogue. On the other hand, this was the perfect time for someone new to come in and manage the growth of the organization she had built. An experienced sales manager would be able to put together a bid package to select an advertising agency partner to assist in launching the information service. Additional clients would need to be courted in order to achieve the image and economies of scale that such an endeavor required.

A further concern was the role that Wegener sought to take in this venture. Up until now, Heidi had had virtual autonomy. PTT Post had not been concerned about profitability; they wanted visibility in central Europe to further their world-wide agenda. When InterDisc had pulled out, Heidi had had to defend her operation's existence, but, again, PTT Post was not concerned as long as InterPost Prague was not a significant drain on corporate resources. Wegener, on the other hand, wanted a profitable operation. Heidi would be asked about income projections and market share. She would need to justify any new products that she intended to launch. She would have to defend her choices on the basis of Wegener's corporate objectives. With InterPost Prague entering its fifth year, Wegener expected this new acquisition to generate profits. Heidi would have to explain why her team was not already on a steep sales growth trajectory and why her company had not yet achieved higher returns.

Heidi saw herself more as an organization builder than an office manager. She loved designing systems and doing market research. She derived satisfaction from training and developing people and stretching them in new directions, but day-to-day complaints and the Czech resistance to change were wearing her down.

I love to start, I hate to finish. I'll get you 85 percent of the way and I'm bored by that time. I say 85 percent because I'll take it beyond just a start-up. I'll put in structures and point the way, set up filing systems, build your personnel section, but I will get ultimately bored, so I'm looking for the finishers. That's what I'm always looking for when I hire somebody. Somebody who can improve what I'm doing. Somebody who says, "I can do better than that, this isn't so great. I can make it look better."

The prospect of starting something new excited her. But she did not look forward to leaving the team that she had worked so closely with and had brought so far. The thought of starting all over was daunting, if not frightening. At one time she had wanted to get out of the publications industry and try her hand at something different. At one time she envisioned herself living in Belgium or The Netherlands, working on the cutting edge of technology and innovation. But now that she finally understood the Czech language and culture, she was not so eager to move west. She understood the pace of business in Prague and had already roughed out a plan to launch new products that would fit Wegener's portfolio nicely [see Exhibit 4].

Wegener wanted to expand regionally and Heidi knew that she had the ability to lead the process. She

---

Exhibit 4   Proposed Business Activities for InterPost Prague

Publications Business

Subscriptions Catalogue Division	Publications Projects Division	Training & Information Division	Consulting Division	Newsletter Division
Coop mailings, one product & many publishers	Campaigns focused on single publisher needs Primarily focused on international publishers	Local market seminars and training of circulation managers	International M&A, Market entry Local positioning	Newsletter targeting international publishers Newsletter targeting circulation managers

(continued)

Exhibit 4   Proposed Business Activities for InterPost Prague *(continued)*

Mail Order Business

Consumer Catalgue Division Coop mailings, one product & many publishers	Mail Order Project Management Media Buying Order Receipt and Reporting	Mail Order Consultancy International mail order companies market entry consultancy	Newsletter Division Newsletter targeting international mail order companies

could use the procedures and training manuals that she had already crafted to launch a new enterprise, in a new location. With Wegener's backing, Heidi could start by acting as a broker for local Czech companies desiring to promote their lists abroad. This might be the right time to start the regional expansion. Heidi had already been given Wegener's blessing to investigate new markets. But while she might be given more freedom to test new waters, other cities in central Europe were less advanced than the Czech Republic's capital city of Prague, and the market potential was less certain.

She believed that she could play a pivotal role in establishing Wegener's presence in central Europe and leading the way for change. But she was not yet sure what that role should be.

Endnotes

1. While there were no legal restrictions preventing Heidi from registering as sole owner of this new company, it was much easier to negotiate with authorities as an owner if you spoke Czech, rather than work through an interpreter. In 1996 the Czech law was changed to require all new company registrations have at least 50% ownership by a Czech citizen. "s.r.o." is the Czech equivalent of "Inc."
2. "Direct Hit," *The Economist*, January 9, 1999, 55–57.

Kacey Fine Furniture: Human Resources Management in the Face of Change

Joan Winn

University of Denver

Leslie Fishbein, president of Kacey Fine Furniture in Denver, Colorado, was not pleased with the recent city council approval of a new basketball stadium in the area bordering her flagship store. In 1992, when she had renewed the lease for the seven-story brick building in Denver's lower downtown (LoDo), she had been confident that this location put her company in a prime position to take advantage of the redevelopment planned for the neighborhood.

By 1995, though, events had changed her outlook. During a quarterly meeting with her employees, Leslie spoke candidly about the problems and challenges that lay before them:

> We're at a major decision point for our company. We need to decide where we want to be and what we want to look like. We have six more years on the downtown store lease. Can we keep our energy high and make these six years pay off? Or will we faint and die on the vine? If we can keep the momentum up, we can look at these six years as planning years. But we have to share the same vision and work to achieve the same goals. We have a shared responsibility here. One hundred sixty families depend on you. If we work together, we can accomplish anything. But we can only succeed if we all play the game.

Conditions had not improved by the spring of 1996, and Kacey Fine Furniture faced six more years on an inflexible lease. Leslie was unsure how to keep her employees motivated, knowing that sales levels (and therefore their sales commissions and bonuses) would be increasingly difficult to maintain. Her plans for the company's growth were being threatened as she was diverted to a plan for its survival. Leslie lamented,

> Our downtown store is our biggest concern right now. We are the front yard of the largest entertainment complex in a five-state area. Selling furniture is harder than it used to be, especially because downtown is no longer the furniture district that it used to be. When sales decline, employees become non-motivated and are reluctant to initiate changes or take on new responsibilities. We need to keep the energy level high and make sure that all our employees share the same vision so that we're all contributing to the same goals.

The Denver Furniture Market

There were over 250 retail furniture stores in the greater Denver metropolitan area in 1995 serving a population of about two million people. Also in competition with Kacey were the more than 50 establishments that sold used furniture, as well as the many stores that competed in specialty or accessory goods, such as electronics, carpet & floor coverings, artwork and knickknacks. The ten largest furniture retailers in the Denver metropolitan area are listed in Exhibit 1.

Denver, described by Tom Edmonds of *Furniture/ Today* as a "boom-or-bust town,"[1] was the fastest-growing furniture market in the U.S. in 1993, and new housing starts promised continued increases over the next several years. In 1993, the six-county Denver metropolitan area furniture sales hit $514 million, with the top four independent furniture retailers commanding 74 percent or about $380 million.[2] In 1994, Denver area furniture sales reached $639 million, a 27.3 percent increase over 1993.[3] Pre-tax profit margins for full-service retailers typically hovered below 4.5 percent, as companies increasingly competed on price. Edmonds remarked, "The action here is fast and furious, to the point that abandoned service stations are finding second lives as sleep

Exhibit 1   Top Denver Area Full-Service Furniture Stores

The Largest Furniture Retailers in the Denver Metropolitan Area 1993–94

Store	Sales ($millions) *1993/1994	1994 Sales* Metro Denver Only	Number of Stores[1]	Sq Feet (000)	Sales per sq foot	Employees
American Furniture Warehouse	$85.0/$104.0	$94.0	4/8	412	$253	350
Weberg Enterprise	$132.1/$138.5	$60.0	4/32	980	$150	
Homestead House	$101.0/$119.0	$22.0	4/21	190		425
Kacey Fine Furniture	$24.0/$28.0	$26.5	3/4	115	$233	160
Montgomery Ward**	$770.0/NA		7/347			
Levitz**	$985.6/$1036.3		3/135	6,570	$165	6500
Ethan Allen**	$87.0/$123.5		3/54[2]			5880
La-Z-Boy Furniture Gallery**	$372.4/$412.2		4/263	42 (average)	$171	
Sears HomeLife**	$900.0/$600.0		2/NA	12		
Thomasville**	$202.1/$228.0		2/86	120		8000
Foley's Home Store**	$52.0/$53.0		1/40	6		
Industry Total	$42,500/$45,300	$639			$120	

*Sales in millions. Figures are for calendar year or most current fiscal year. [1]Denver metropolitan area/Total US [2]Company owned stores only; there are also 233 dealer-owned stores.
**National chains; sales totals reflect nation-wide operations.
SOURCE: *Furniture Today*, May 23, 1994, March 6, 1995, May 29, 1995, July 31, 1995, August 21, 1995.

Case 20 / Kacey Fine Furniture: Human Resources Management in the Face of Change shops and futon stores."[4] Contributing to Denver's growth was a population boom fueled by the construction of a new airport and a new baseball stadium. However, most of the population growth was in the outlying suburban areas, as far as 20 miles away from downtown through increasingly heavy traffic. While economists predicted a slowdown, Rick Pederson, of real estate development firm Frederick Ross, had expected Denver's furniture market to remain strong. "1995 is still going to be a very good year. There's a good deal of furniture to be bought for those homes that were bought and were built in 1994."[5] Despite this optimism, 1995 returns indicated a sooner-than-predicted slowdown in sales.

The Denver furniture market was dominated by four full-line independent merchandisers, three national department store chains, and several gallery showrooms and smaller independents which primarily targeted upscale clientele. Competition was fierce between the four largest stores: American Furniture Warehouse, Weberg Furniture, Homestead House, and Kacey Fine Furniture. Each store carried a broad range of products. Homestead House and Kacey offered name-brand merchandise and positioned themselves toward a middle- to upper-middle quality range, and competed primarily on fashion and service. American and Weberg attracted people who tended to be more price-sensitive and less knowledgeable about quality and durability. In many cases, customer groups overlapped significantly, largely because of the subjectivity of furniture style and quality and partly because of the difficulty in differentiating store merchandise in out-of-store advertising. Inside the stores, the layout, sales staff, and merchandise gave clear signals of quality and price range. The department stores, specialty shops, sofa houses, and electronics chains competed in both areas. All major competitors had multiple store locations, including smaller stores in outlying areas. Kacey was the only major full-line retailer with its main store in the downtown area.

While each furniture retailer believed that it was targeting a particular market niche, there was little visible difference in advertising copy or media. There appeared to be little discernible store or brand loyalty, and most customers shopped around. As competition for consumer dollars increased, specialty and department stores positioned themselves against the low prices of the discounters and touted the service of the showroom and design centers. Corrine Brown, owner of the upscale Roche Bobois franchise in Denver, believed that customer service was the key to success. She explained:

> I still make house calls on weekends and evenings. I do a lot of the sales training too. There's always [employee] turnover in this business. If people aren't making money with us they're in the wrong business. This is the easiest hard business in town that I know of. Design is not a factor—being a good [interior] designer has nothing to do with being successful in our store. We can cover for that. But being a people person—understanding the psychology of selling—is so much more important. The sales training, teaching people how to open, to qualify, to expand the sale, to service, to make sure a customer will come back to you instead of someone else. We cover people on salary during training but then they're paid straight commission. We pay the highest commission in the city but they have to work for it. Most of our sales are pretty large. We have a very sophisticated clientele so it takes a pro to close a sale. Even the dollar amount, the more demanding they are, the more willing they are to trust you. Why do you hire a financial counselor when you have a huge amount of money to invest? You'd never think of doing it on your own. You want expert advice as to what stocks are good. So that's why there's room at the top. That's why the good designers make good money. Because good customers trust that their image will be maintained intact.

Leslie observed,

> There are three very big players in Denver. We're number four. We're the littlest of the big guys. All things being equal, there's a fairly equivalent playing field—not necessarily in terms of customer perception but in terms of reality. What I mean is, a sofa is a sofa. It's a prosthetic device. We have designed it for our health, welfare, safety and comfort but once you get that accomplished the real difference is in customer service. We can't compete head-to-head with the big guys because we're one-fourth their size. So we elected to take a different road.
>
> Our modus operandi is to make sure we're sleek and flexible and can move around them. Now I believe the key to that is people. They believe the key to that is made with bricks and mortar or other resources such as inventory or price or selection and I don't think that. There are a lot of alternative distribution outlets now for our products. A lot of customers don't have the brand or store loyalty that they might have had in the '50s or '60s. So what we're hoping is that we can give a fashion-focused, value-oriented reason for coming in.
>
> Hopefully they'll come in because we have a specific appeal in terms of financial transaction or greater service after the sale. We're one of the only ones that offers a full range of products. We carry everything for your home, including window coverings, floor coverings, electronics, furniture. We're trying to make ourselves into a one-stop shop.

Sam Fishbein, who was responsible for all of Kacey's marketing, believed that Kacey's edge over the larger chains lay in its customer orientation. Kacey tracked buyer purchases by style, color, and price range. All order information, including inventory, purchases, and customer accounts, were tracked and analyzed. Sales people were trained and evaluated on customer satisfaction and service after every sale. Sam Fishbein believed that "everyone's looking for a good deal, but if the service isn't there, the price doesn't matter."

Company History

Kacey Fine Furniture began as Kacey the Linoleum King in 1950. "I didn't want my name on it," explained founder Jack Barton, "because I didn't want the store to be a reflection of me; I wanted the store to focus on delivering the best products and services to our customers." Jack chose a name that he thought would be easy for people to pronounce and remember. In 1965 he changed the name to reflect his new product line: fine furniture. His wife, Shirley, joined the store in 1966 when the store employed only two sales people and a driver who used his own truck for furniture deliveries. Jack mused: "We were overwhelmed with customers, sometimes 5 or 6 in one day."

Jack and Shirley's oldest daughter Leslie started working at Kacey Fine Furniture in 1974 after graduating from the University of Colorado with a degree in Fine Arts. She married Sam Fishbein in December 1976. Sam had recently completed a degree in marketing at the University of Colorado and was working as a building materials salesman. Knowing nothing about the furniture business, Sam eased into the business by helping with Kacey's promotions and advertising. Within five years, Sam's marketing skills and Leslie's managerial and design skills transformed Kacey from a small family business to a major player in Denver's growing furniture market. By 1984, Sam and Leslie were running the show.

Kacey moved into its current location on December 23, 1982, having been given notice in September 1982, to move by the end of that year. The building they had occupied for 15 years was sold quickly because the owner had died. The new owner planned to raze the building to build a more modern structure. Kacey was able to secure a 10-year lease on a seven-story, 65,000-square-foot brick building in lower downtown, only a few blocks away from the previous location. In addition to its larger showroom space, this new location had ample room for parking behind the building. The move was difficult, however, for the employees whose schedules and duties were interrupted and whose sales commissions suffered during the transition. Some employees left, fearing the vulnerability of the company—and their jobs.

The early '80s were expansion years. In 1981, Leslie and Sam opened a small (6,500 square feet) store in the mountain town of Frisco. In 1983, a 30,000-square-foot store was opened in the northwest suburb of Lakewood. Later that year, they leased 126,000 square feet of warehouse space in a former Gates Rubber Company facility. By 1984, sales reached $4 million.

Sales grew over the next three years, but the late 1980s brought an economic downturn which made the furniture industry a difficult business. By 1988 Kacey was barely breaking even and morale was low. In 1990 Leslie and Sam sold their house and worked without a paycheck to avoid laying off any of their employees. Leslie and Sam, while role models of hard work, found it increasingly difficult to get their employees to take initiative. Employees were paid on a commission basis, which directed their behavior toward making a sale, with little thought about operational efficiencies, vendor relations, or customer service that might bring in repeat business.

Leslie explained:

> In 1987 we were at $14 million and in 1989 were at $12 million. We went backward which was not a fun thing to do. We really were frustrated because I wanted people [employees] to take it upon themselves to handle problem situations and satisfy customers without coming to me or a manager for help all the time. I couldn't figure out why they weren't capable or comfortable making decisions. As it was, I was working 10–14-hour days and I didn't want to make all the decisions in my company. I was tired of that.
>
> We're not a high-tech industry. Our concerns center around people as our major resource: we're labor intensive as are most small businesses, especially if you're in the retail business. We're driven by sales and the quality of sales people drives our business to a large degree. As an owner I was very interested in trying to get people to act like owners—to take greater ownership. Because we're a small business, we each wear lots of hats. I wanted people to have greater accountability and responsibility. But they kept coming to me as if I had all the answers.

Employee Involvement to the Rescue

Leslie discovered a vehicle for increasing her employees' accountability and responsibility in a 1992 seminar run by Jack Stack, CEO of the Springfield Remanufacturing Corporation. Springfield Remanufacturing Corporation had emerged from an employee-buyout of one division of International Harvester's bankruptcy reorganization in 1979. Stack's book, *The Great Game of Business*,[6] is a managers' guide to profitability through employee involvement and open-book management. Leslie and Sam Fishbein found that Stack's managerial philosophy squared with their own orientation toward employee involvement, and in October, 1992, began its implementation.

> The Great Game of Business is a company-wide open-book management system. It's become part of our corporate culture so that everyone shares the same mission and buys into the plan. We teach all of our employees cash flow analysis, income statement, balance sheet—based on their level of education or understanding. They are involved in decision making at all levels of the organization. We have a gain-sharing program based upon what everybody achieves according to preset profit goals. We paid out $750,000 in bonus checks in 1994. All employees received at least 11 percent in bonuses. The managers get 45 percent of their salaries as bonuses. It's very lucrative. I believe in the "what's in it for me" aspect.
>
> When we started the Great Game of Business I was worried about certain parts of the company. I went to people in the warehouse and shop who are very important to our business and I said to them, "If you can understand arcane baseball statistics, which make no sense to me, you can understand business." And they looked at me wide-eyed because most people don't get any economics, any information about how a business runs, what impacts it, what expenditures are, how to balance it to make a profit or not. They don't learn that in school. Our education system is totally deficient in this.
>
> We tell our employees, "this is the company you work in, this is what it does, this is how you impact everybody, this is what your decision will do, we're going to let you make that decision but you'll have more information to make it." That opens up a whole new world to somebody. Sometimes they'll come to me [for advice] and I'll say, "you can make as good a decision as I can. I've never done this before either," and it's interesting to see how that works. They often know what they need to do better than I do. Certainly I've made a lot of mistakes and mine are usually pretty costly.
>
> We spend a lot of time, energy and resources teaching our employees things that most people don't have access to. The reason I think this is so critical is because you can stop me but you can't stop 160 people. We are in a fairly competitive environment. Denver is considered one of the most competitive retail furniture environments in the country. We are the littlest of the big guys here and so we look to have a strategic advantage through our people.

Tom O'Donnell, Operations Manager, believed that Kacey's company-wide gain-sharing bonus plan gave delivery drivers

> . . . a chance to keep up with the rest of the world. These people typically live month-to-month and something unexpected—like a car repair—can put them under. Bonuses can add 10 percent to their base salary and allow them to get ahead.
>
> This system gives them the rules of the game. They see how they can make a difference. Last month we had a bad snow storm. Everyone was here at 6 am. We had no delays. No tow bills. We had seven trucks instead of six on Saturday because one of our drivers volunteered for extra duty. We delivered $208,000 worth of furniture on Saturday [which was a record for a single day's deliveries].

Mike Bradford, Kacey Chief Financial Officer, was responsible for making sure that every manager's sales and profitability targets were recorded and monitored. At bi-weekly staff meetings, all financial information was displayed interactively on a computer-drive 60" color television. [See Exhibits 2 and 3 for Kacey Financial performance summaries.]

Leslie explained,

> Everybody has certain expense categories that they're responsible for, so if they're over budget they have stand up in the meeting and explain why. For example, I went over on our cleaning budget because I felt that the stores had to be cleaner than they were, so I authorized increasing our cleaning schedule—we have a contract with an outside cleaning company—without going to the committee. So I had to stand up at a Great Game of Business meeting and say, "this is my rationale for doing this. If you all disagree, I'll cut it back," but everyone agreed. If anyone is over budget in any area, including wages, then they have to stand up and defend their position. It may be justified, but we don't want expenses to become runaway. We need to understand where they come from. It's easy to see retained earnings. They can see that I haven't taken much out.

All employees understood the cost of repairs and maintenance, display supplies, utilities, promotions, returns, sales tags, and light bulbs. Employees took the lead in cost-cutting. Leslie recalled,

> One of the managers decided that we weren't dealing with our freight problem very well. Everything has to come in from somewhere and freight is a very significant factor in our company's profit picture. So he went to school and learned everything he could about freight. Now, if you know anything about freight, you know that it's very arcane. But as a result of his ideas we now have one of the lowest incoming freight rates of anybody in the country. We were delighted to reward him for it and participate in that.

Exhibit 2   Kacey Income Statements

Year ending May 31	1995	1994	1993	1992	1991
Revenues					
SO1: Downtown	$15,033,979	$12,320,080	$10,020,263	$9,482,092	$7,753,878
SO2: Frisco	$1,732,679	$1,468,804	$1,367,449	$1,079,747	$1,004,290
SO3: Lakewood	$9,076,013	$7,947,617	$6,930,604	$6,143,633	$4,236,460
SO6: Clearance Center	$1,613,965	$1,015,733	$859,796	$753,378	$336,130
Total store sales	$27,456,636	$22,752,234	$19,178,112	$17,458,850	$13,330,758
Sales to employees	$136,056	$81,345	$29,757	$38,761	$19,822
Gross sales	$27,592,692	$22,833,579	$19,207,869	$17,497,611	$13,350,580
Cost of goods sold					
SO1: Downtown	$8,290,229	$6,596,012	$5,304,338	$5,243,989	$4,182,463
SO2: Frisco	$930,948	$781,933	$735,892	$603,851	$563,568
SO3: Lakewood	$4,991,667	$4,268,936	$3,670,655	$3,407,935	$2,405,011
SO6: Clearance Center	$1,106,015	$829,448	$645,986	$710,304	$338,566
Total CGS	$15,318,859	$12,476,329	$10,356,871	$9,966,079	$7,489,608
Operating expenses					
GSA	$3,584,175	$2,770,602	$2,932,294	$2,252,403	$1,836,821
Advertising/promotions	$2,017,409	$1,787,992	$1,736,428	$2,003,507	$1,367,629
Misc delivery/handling	$1,332,509	$1,168,338	$871,999	$730,076	$543,265
Operating expenses					
SO1:	$1,935,630	$1,646,453	$1,535,856	$1,378,142	$1,202,442
SO2:	$383,060	$351,600	$312,963	$233,868	$214,542
SO3:	$1,153,459	$1,054,519	$884,150	$691,905	$569,044
SO6:	$440,267	$220,057	$208,291	$123,318	$105,010
Total operating expenses	$10,846,509	$8,999,561	$8,481,981	$7,413,219	$5,838,753
Other (vendor fees)	($37,292)	($54,838)	($19,487)	($4,953)	$41,165
Net profit before bonus/tax	$1,464,616	$1,412,527	$388,504	$123,266	($18,946)
Bonus paid	$853,035	$709,658			
Net profit before taxes	$611,581	$702,869	$388,504	$123,266	($18,946)
Taxes	$224,544	$258,115	$151,283	$15,799	$5,344
Net profit	$387,037	$444,754	$237,221	$107,467	($24,290)

The Emerging Company Culture

Kacey Fine Furniture had had a "family focus" since its inception. "Kacey's been in my family since I was a little kid," remarked Leslie. "It was part of our life." In 1995,

Kacey was still oriented toward families and community involvement.

Because we're a family corporation we have lots of families who work for our company. We have brother–

| Exhibit 3 | Kacey Building Sheets |

Year ending May 31:	1995	1994	1993	1992	1991
Cash on hand	$187,324	$707,593	$122,192	$63,231	$416
Accounts receivable	$260,976	$96,321	$197,556	$126,364	$111,810
Inventory at landed vost	$4,074,981	$3,559,222	$3,136,816	$2,708,124	$2,723,128
Income tax refundable	$18,409				$22,064
Prepaid expenses	$123,864	$42,901	$40,610	$60,613	$84,302
Deposit—current					$20,500
Deferred tax asset	$147,431	$126,486	$120,420	$94,392	$90,810
Property/plant/equipment (PPE)	$2,245,904	$2,156,540	$1,679,323	$1,575,045	$1,648,284
Less: accumulated depreciation	($1,373,182)	($1,379,567)	($1,240,236)	($1,138,400)	($1,223,772)
PP&E Net	$872,722	$776,973	$439,087	$436,645	$424,512
Other	$269,780	$301,628	$309,291	$240,403	$162,872
TOTAL ASSETS	$5,955,487	$5,611,124	$4,365,972	$3,729,772	$3,640,414
Line of credit	$0	$0	$65,000	$0	$180,000
Current portion/due on account	$68,516	$59,348	$5,982	$14,761	$22,850
Accounts payable	$1,128,497	$1,254,240	$978,993	$860,185	$953,219
Accrued liabilities	$701,471	$604,636	$459,096	$252,388	$226,067
Customer deposits	$1,798,175	$1,648,861	$1,501,211	$1,622,601	$1,382,851
Income tax payable		$110,134	$157,192	$12,578	
Total current liabilities	$3,696,659	$3,677,219	$3,167,474	$2,762,513	$2,764,987
Long-term debt	$228,538	$290,652		$5,982	$21,617
Equity	$2,030,290	$1,643,253	$1,198,498	$961,277	$853,810
TOTAL LIABILITIES & EQUITY	$5,955,487	$5,611,124	$4,365,972	$3,729,772	$3,640,414

sister, husband–wife, nieces, nephews, cousins, lots of people who work together. We not only allow nepotism, we promote it. We make sure that one family member does not supervise another family member but they can work side by side. It gives us a chance to have a more coherent team to start with. We make sure everyone knows they stand alone so a brother or cousin or spouse doesn't affect their performance.

Several employees expressed the difference in attitude at Kacey's compared to other stores where they had worked. Brenda, a sales associate who had worked at Kacey for several years, expressed a typical sentiment:

There's a real difference here in how they take an interest in what we have to say. They take our suggestions to heart. They listen to what we have to say and they care about what we say and they're not just thinking of themselves . . . it's a group effort. We actually get paid for ideas that they put into effect, or just suggestions—we have a place to voice our opinions.

Leslie's interpretation of Stack's Great Game of Business involved more than opening the books to her employees. In preparation for changing employees' behavior, she hired a management consultant and conducted employee satisfaction surveys. She tried to understand why some employees worked well together and why others remained isolated. She examined her own behavior as well, and decided that poor performance was better dealt with through training and coaching than through reprimands and firing. An inspirational motivator herself, she didn't want to be too tough on employees, while at the same time she knew that she needed a better control system that didn't require top-down management authority and control.

Leslie acknowledged,

> We're not an easy company to work with or for. Because we're retail we're open 9 to 9. The only time we can have our company-wide meetings is at 7:30 in the morning. We're not a democracy, but we require a great degree of participation, involvement, and continuing education and that's not really easy. We have a lot of meetings at our company and we expect a lot of people to participate at odd times. For example, our quarterly meetings are mandatory for everybody and they also need to participate in one major huddle [department] meeting a month. We don't do company picnics or parties, because we have enough meetings and we believe your private time is your private time and we don't want to impinge upon that. But we do try to find ways to have fun. We do skits and songs at our quarterly meetings and have games where we give out goofy prizes.

Quarterly meetings began to take on a different tone. Some of the early meetings were orchestrated by Leslie and her father. They performed skits, conducted sing-a-longs and role-plays, and gave out prizes for cost-reduction ideas such as delivery routings and scheduling, and revenue-generation ideas such as billboard-type logos on their delivery trucks earned cash bonuses. As employee suggestions and involvement increased, the nature and format of the meetings changed.

Mike Bradford's job changed from compiling information and tracking revenues and expenses to conducting accounting and training seminars. Everyone was required to understand basic accounting principles, and short-courses were designed to accommodate employees' work and family schedules and preferences. A tuition-reimbursement program was instituted so that employees could take courses at nearby universities, in subjects ranging from finance and accounting to graphic design.

By 1995, department managers had created their own awards. A monthly newsletter became a forum for idea exchange and information sharing. Employee birthdays, marriages and anniversaries, births and transitions were celebrated. Illnesses and tragedies brought compassion and assistance. Different people took turns making presentations or announcements at the company-wide gatherings. New employees were introduced, promotions and accomplishments acknowledged, teamwork and departmental productivity publicized. Customer-appreciation letters as well as customer-complaint letters were read and publicized in company newsletters.

Increasingly, managers took on the role of coaches and trainers instead of schedulers and disciplinarians. Employees often formed study groups and shared information and ideas. The lines separating owners and managers and staff and customers became less distinct as titles and job descriptions took a back seat to camaraderie and strategic planning. Each department had control of its own operations, with profit sharing based on store-wide and company-wide profitability. Approval for new ideas or programs was based on cost-revenue projections and employee participation, not management preference. Employees at one store decided to change their hours of operation to allow more evening shopping opportunities. ("Can you imagine me suggesting such a thing?" Leslie remarked.)

> I think that education is one of the most critical things we can do as a business. The more education my workforce has and the more involved that they are in understanding issues—even contemporary issues—the more responsible they will be. I think of my employees as citizens and they must relate to the world as a whole. We also have a "great voter turnout" program. Now that may not seem very important to you but it is to me. I don't care who you vote for but I want to make sure they participate. As a consequence of understanding more about business and what they can do to affect their businesses, they've actually had more outreach into the community and I'm absolutely delighted about that. It's something that I kind of predicted but didn't think would happen as quickly as it did.

The Changing LoDo Neighborhood

The South Platte River, the major waterway between the Rocky Mountains and the Great Plains, divided the western third from the eastern two-thirds of the city of Denver. Until the early 1970s, Denver dominated the six-county metropolitan area. In 1973, 45 acres bordering the west bank of the Platte River were cleared and sold for commercial and industrial redevelopment. In 1976, 169 acres of land east of the Platte River were developed into the Auraria Higher Education Center, which housed

Metropolitan State College of Denver, the University of Colorado at Denver, and the Community College of Denver. The national economic downturn, fueled by heavier dependence on foreign oil, took its toll on Denver, creating high unemployment and a deteriorating downtown area, as the population shifted to outlying suburban areas. By the late 1980s, only one-third of the metropolitan area population remained within the Denver city limits.

In 1986, the 45 acres on the west bank of the Platte River, known as "lower downtown" or LoDo, was a run-down commercial and industrial center adjacent to the largest tract of undeveloped land in the metro area. While much of the land was still owned by the Southern Pacific Railroad, the mayor commissioned a steering committee, composed of "community, business, railroad and property owner representatives from neighborhoods within and adjacent to the Central Platte Valley"[7] to develop a comprehensive plan for the area. Following the recommendations of the committee's 1991 comprehensive plan amendment, LoDo underwent urban redevelopment. Art galleries and retail establishments cropped up between the railyards and the warehouses, taking advantage of low rent and ample parking. Following the rehabilitation of some of LoDo's historic buildings, the granting of a major league baseball franchise in 1993, the relocation of Elitch gardens (a $95 million, 67-acre Amusement Park) to LoDo in 1995, the Gates Foundation pledge in December 1994 of $1.2 million toward a $64 million public aquarium to begin construction in 1996, "the development of hundreds of units of new housing, the opening of 16 new restaurants and bars in [1994 and 1995], plans to create a new historic district and revise the area's zoning"[8] and the proposed construction of additional sports and entertainment complexes, the face of LoDo began to change visibly.

On March 31, 1995, the first Colorado Rockie's exhibition game was played at Coors Field, one mile north of Kacey's downtown store. The baseball season officially opened on April 26, 1995, to a capacity of 50,200; attendance averaged 45,000 throughout the summer and fall of 1995. The Rockies played in the National League Championship Series in 1995, ensuring their popularity with the home crowd for the 1996 season.

As lease rates increased from $8–$10 to $18–$20 per square foot, many art galleries moved away from LoDo and restaurants, brew-pubs and housing units moved in. By 1996 there were 60 restaurants in LoDo—up from 35 in 1993—all sustaining year-round traffic. "One of the things Coors Field has done has been to demystify lower downtown for people who didn't know what it meant," observed Richard Holcomb, executive director of the Lower Downtown District Inc.[9] Townhouses and loft apartments increased from 270 in 1993 to 340 in 1996, with more than 370 new units planned by 1999. The number of LoDo residents was expected to double, from 1,500 to 3,000.

On April 26, 1995, Entertainment Development Group announced an agreement with United Artists Theater Circuit, Inc., to construct an 80,000-square foot theater and entertainment complex on the 16th street mall, at the southeast edge of LoDo.[10] The following month, Ascent Entertainment Group (owner of the Denver Nuggets basketball team) acquired a National Hockey League franchise by purchasing the financially distressed Quebec Nordiques, renamed the Colorado Avalanche. The Avalanche's first season success in the Stanley Cup playoffs overlapped the 1996 baseball season with sell-out crowds for both teams' games throughout April and May.

LoDo was changing from a low-rent commercial district to a high-rent entertainment area, with increased activity in the area east of Cherry Creek. The buildings between Auraria Parkway and the railroad tracks, however, that once housed the furniture district, were soon vacant and Kacey's seven-story building was a drive-by landmark, a destination place only for those who went out of their way to stop.

Although the number of housing units increased, furniture sales in LoDo suffered. On April 10, 1995, Franklin Furniture, located two blocks from Coors Field, announced that it planned to move to the suburbs by spring of 1996. "Business has been getting worse in the last two years because there is no parking," and sales have dropped 20 percent, owner Jerry Kozatch explained.[11] While Franklin Furniture owned its building, it had to buy parking permits for trucks at its loading dock.

Despite public criticism of both the building of a new basketball stadium (the current Nuggets stadium was only 18 years old) and the revenue consequences of public subsidies, the City Council approved a contract for the new stadium. PepsiCo had agreed to pay $68 million (of the $132 million estimated costs) for its name on the stadium and exclusive advertising and "pouring" rights. After heated negotiations between Phil Anschutz, majority owner of the Southern Pacific Railroad's 43-acre Platte Valley site, and Ascent Entertainment, construction of the "Pepsi Center" stadium was expected to begin by the end of the summer of 1996. Construction was expected to take two years. Leslie explained how the changes affected her store:

> The Nuggets [basketball] stadium is going directly behind my store. That is an absolute, unqualified disaster. We are beside ourselves right now because between the

baseball and ice hockey here now, this is becoming a sports and entertainment area. Frankly, the consequence for a retail store is that nobody's going to get in or out of here. The city council members don't seem to understand that if you add 20,000 people coming for a Nuggets game to the Auraria Higher Education [college campus] night student traffic, same-time use with Elitch's [amusement park], the Aquarium and the [proposed 12-screen movie] theaters, you could have the potential of anywhere from 50,000 to 75,000 to 150,000 people trying to get into an area. Now the parking spaces that they have for all of us is 44,000, with the Rockies [new baseball stadium] it's 88,000. We're already seeing a decline in customer traffic during Rockies games. Now they want to move the Nuggets closer to us also. (sarcastically) I can hardly wait.

Weathering the Storm: Bracing for a Downturn in 1996

Both the extent of the changes in LoDo and the evolving nature of those changes troubled Leslie when she contemplated the future of her downtown store. What had once seemed promising now appeared threatening to Kacey. Leslie explained,

> *The original plan for the Platte Valley included mixed use, which was retail, residential and commercial. That would have been a whole different idea. People who come downtown for sports events are not the people who come downtown to buy furniture. We looked at our lease to try to figure out if we could get out of the situation that we're going to be in, but the owner won't budge. With all the changes taking place in this area, I think there are better uses for this building than us, but it doesn't appear that the principal agrees with us. He has refused to let us sublet the building or buy it from him. If customers can't get here, our sales people may have to be more adept at housecalls and getting into the customer's home and taking things to them versus having the customer come to us. And that's not entirely unfeasible. It's possible, but that would require a lot of training and orientation.*

Not everyone believed that the downtown location was a liability. Operations Manager Tom O'Donnell believed that "as we become more of a dominant regional player, the visibility of our downtown store will be more of an asset." He explained,

> *Each of our stores is different, yet the downtown focal point draws customers from all of our outlying stores. We may need to reorient our sales staff and change our service options, but this might not be a bad thing. There's lots of money to be made on in-home sales and that market is*

wide open. There's a lot of potential for creativity. We could drop down to four—even three—floors at this location and still keep our image while we're in the process of relocating to a better location. We have six more years on this lease, but even if we started today, it would take us at least two years to get a big, full-size formal showroom up and running in another location.

> *We're not the upper-end designer market, nor are we the lower-end American or Weberg market. Our most serious competition in this area is probably Ethan Allen. Our market niche is an educated, serious furniture buyer. You're talking about a consumer who's going to spend $10,000–$20,000 on a dining room or bedroom suite, or get into a specific design group and over a period of three or four years spend maybe $25,000. That's a major lifetime commitment. When you're going to spend $25,000, you'll spend the day and go where you can get the best price. We can't build seven or eight complete stores. Nor is it necessary. You'd end up with seven or eight times the amount of shop-worn furniture in the process anyway. But we need one key dominant store where we can refer people to, where an entire group can be shown. And that's the kind of store we have downtown today. Is it the right building, the right facility? It really doesn't matter if it's a different building, different numbers of floors, a little smaller, a little larger. It allows us to have a central theme and I think that's important. To be a leader in this market, we need to have a dominant regional presence. I think a flagship store is a good idea, but only if we can offer the personalized service people want.*

Leslie was sure that accessible, attractive showrooms were essential. People needed to see and touch furniture before they would buy it. Bringing fabric samples to someone's home would not be enough. Whether or not they moved away from downtown, the next six years would place a strain on all Kacey employees. Leslie believed that employee confidence and sustained profitability would be essential for the company to position itself for a big move.

> *Even if we decide to move away from downtown eventually, we need to stay put and deal with what we have now. The suburban area rents are priced at the top of the market right now. Denver is a competitive market; our margins are low. If we can hang on until the shakeout, we'll have some options.*

Leslie knew that the human resources systems that she had worked so hard to establish would be severely tested. She hoped that the Great Game of Business would be enough to maintain the commitment and enthusiasm that would be needed to keep the downtown store profitable until feasible relocation options could be explored. But already, the spring 1996 sales figures did not look promising. If sales continued to dip below projections, employees would not get fiscal-year-end bonus checks in June. Would her "Great Game" strike out? Leslie was not sure how to rally her employees for the challenging times that lay ahead.

References

1. Edmonds, T. (March 6, 1995) Boom-or-bust market keeps riding the tide, *Furniture/Today*, 24.
2. Ibid.
3. Conklin, M. (May 1, 1995). Interior designs, *Rocky Mountain News*, 34A.
4. Edmonds, T. (March 6, 1995) Boom-or-bust market keeps riding the tide, *Furniture/Today*, 24.
5. Edmonds, T. (March 6, 1995) Denver. A mile higher. *Furniture/Today*, 22.
6. Stack, J. (1992) *The Great Game of Business,* Currency Books.
7. *Central Platte Valley Comprehensive Plan Amendment* (June 1, 1991). Planning and Community Development Office, City and County of Denver, p 1.
8. Steers, S. (May 19–25, 1995) Builders hit homers in ballpark district, *The Denver Business Journal,* p 4A.
9. Parker, P. (April 7, 1996) "Eateries survive pennant loss, dire predictions," *The Denver Post,* 1G, 6G.
10. Rebchook, J. (April 26, 1995). UA complex big draw for tenants, *Rocky Mountain News,* 41A
11. Conklin, M. (April 10, 1995). Furniture store may strike out, *Rocky Mountain News,* 41–42A.

Kentucky Fried Chicken and the Global Fast-Food Industry

Jeffrey A. Krug

University of Illinois at Urbana-Champaign

Kentucky Fried Chicken Corporation (KFC) was the world's largest chicken restaurant chain and third largest fast-food chain in 2001. KFC held more than 55 percent of the US market in terms of sales and operated more than 10,800 restaurants in 85 countries. KFC was one of the first fast-food chains to go international in the late 1950s and was one of the world's most recognizable brands. KFC's early international strategy was to grow its company and franchise restaurant base throughout the world. By early 2000, however, KFC had refocused its international strategy on several high growth markets, including Canada, Australia, the United Kingdom, China, Korea, Thailand, Puerto Rico, and Mexico. KFC planned to base much of its growth in these markets on company-owned restaurants, which gave KFC greater control over product quality, service, and restaurant cleanliness. In other international markets, KFC planned to grow primarily through franchises, which were operated by local business people who understood the local market better than KFC. Franchises enabled KFC to more rapidly expand into smaller countries that could only support a small number of restaurants. KFC planned to more aggressively expand its company-owned restaurants into other major international markets in Europe and Latin America in the future. Latin America was an appealing area for investment because of the size of its markets, its common language and culture, and its geographical proximity to the United States. Mexico was of particular interest because of the North American Free Trade Agreement (NAFTA), a free trade zone between Canada, the United States, and Mexico that went into effect in 1994. However, other fast-food chains such as McDonald's, Burger King, and Wendy's were rapidly

expanding into other countries in Latin America such as Venezuela, Brazil, Argentina, and Chile. KFC's task in Latin America was to select the proper countries for future investment and to devise an appropriate strategy for penetrating the Latin American market.

Company History

In 1952, fast-food franchising was still in its infancy when Harland Sanders began his travels across the United States to speak with prospective franchisees about his "Colonel Sanders Recipe Kentucky Fried Chicken." By 1960, "Colonel" Sanders had granted KFC franchises to more than 200 take-home retail outlets and restaurants across the United States. He had also established a number of franchises in Canada. By 1963, the number of KFC franchises had risen to more than 300 and revenues topped $500 million. The Colonel celebrated his 74th birthday the following year and was eager to lessen the load of running the day-to-day operations of his business. Thus, he looked for potential buyers and sold his business to two Louisville businessmen—Jack Massey and John Young Brown Jr. —for $2 Million. The Colonel stayed on as a public relations man and goodwill ambassador for the company. During the next five years, Massey and Brown concentrated on growing KFC's franchise system across the United States. In 1966, they took KFC public and the company was listed on the New York Stock Exchange. By the late 1960s, a strong foothold had been established in the United States, and Massey and Brown turned their attention to international markets. In 1969, a joint venture was signed with Mitsuoishi Shoji Kaisha, Ltd. in Japan and the rights to operate franchises in England were acquired. Subsidiaries were later established in Hong Kong, South Africa, Australia, New Zealand, and Mexico. By 1971,

KFC had established 2,450 franchises and 600 company-owned restaurants in 48 countries.

Heublein, Inc.

In 1971, KFC entered into negotiations with Heublein, Inc. to discuss a possible merger. The decision to pursue a merger was partially driven by Brown's desire to pursue other interests that included a political career (Brown was elected Governor of Kentucky in 1977). Several months later, Heublein acquired KFC. Heublein was in the business of producing vodka, mixed cocktails, dry gin, cordials, beer, and other alcoholic beverages; however, it had little experience in the restaurant business. Conflicts quickly erupted between Colonel Sanders and Heublein management. In particular, Colonel Sanders became increasingly distraught over quality control issues and restaurant cleanliness. By 1977, new restaurant openings had slowed to only twenty a year, few restaurants were being remodeled, and service quality had declined. To combat these problems, Heublein sent in a new management team to redirect KFC's strategy. A "back-to-the-basics" strategy was implemented and new restaurant construction was halted until existing restaurants could be upgraded and operating problems eliminated. A program for remodeling existing restaurants was implemented, an emphasis was placed on cleanliness and service, marginal products were eliminated, and product consistency was reestablished. This strategy enabled KFC to gain better control of its operations and it was soon again aggressively building new restaurants.

R.J. Reynolds Industries, Inc.

In 1982, R.J. Reynolds Industries, Inc. (RJR) acquired Heublein and merged it into a wholly owned subsidiary. The acquisition of Heublein was part of RJR's corporate strategy of diversifying into unrelated businesses such as energy, transportation, food, and restaurants to reduce its dependence on the tobacco industry. Tobacco had driven RJR's sales since its founding in North Carolina in 1875; however, sales of cigarettes and tobacco products, while profitable, were declining because of reduced consumption in the United States. Reduced consumption was primarily the result of an increased awareness among Americans of the negative health consequences of smoking.

RJR, however, had little more experience in the restaurant business than did Heublein when it acquired KFC eleven years earlier. In contrast to Heublein, which tried to actively manage KFC using its own managers, RJR allowed KFC to operate autonomously. RJR believed that KFC's executives were better qualified to operate the business than its own managers; therefore, KFC's top management team was left largely intact. By doing so, RJR avoided many of the operating problems that plagued Heublein during its ownership of KFC.

In 1985, RJR acquired Nabisco Corporation for $4.9 billion. The acquisition of Nabisco was an attempt to redefine RJR as a world leader in the consumer foods industry. Nabisco sold a variety of well-known cookies, crackers, and other grocery products, including Oreo cookies, Ritz crackers, Planters peanuts, Lifesavers, and Milk-Bone dog biscuits. RJR subsequently divested many of its non-consumer food businesses. It sold KFC to PepsiCo, Inc. one year later.

PepsiCo, INC.

Corporate Strategy

PepsiCo, Inc. was formed in 1965 with the merger of the Pepsi-Cola Co. and Frito-Lay Inc. The merger created one of the largest consumer products companies in the United States. Pepsi-Cola's traditional business was the sale of soft drink concentrates to licensed independent and company-owned bottlers that manufactured, sold, and distributed Pepsi-Cola soft drinks. Pepsi-Cola's best known trademarks were Pepsi-Cola, Diet Pepsi, and Mountain Dew. Frito-Lay manufactured and sold a variety of leading snack foods that included Lay's Potato Chips, Doritos Tortilla Chips, Tostitos Tortilla Chips, and Ruffles Potato Chips. Soon after the merger, PepsiCo initiated an aggressive acquisition program, buying a number of companies in areas unrelated to its major businesses such as North American Van Lines, Wilson Sporting Goods, and Lee Way Motor Freight. However, PepsiCo lacked the management skills required to operate these businesses and performance failed to live up to expectations. In 1984, chairman and chief executive officer Don Kendall restructured PepsiCo's operations. Businesses that did not support PepsiCo's consumer product orientation (including North American Van Lines, Wilson Sporting Goods, and Lee Way Motor Freight) were divested. PepsiCo's foreign bottling operations were then sold to local business people who better understood their country's culture and business practices. Last, PepsiCo was organized into three divisions: soft drinks, snack foods, and restaurants.

Restaurant Business and Acquisition of KFC

PepsiCo believed that the restaurant business complemented its consumer product orientation. The marketing of fast-food followed many of the same patterns as the marketing of soft drinks and snack foods. Pepsi-Cola soft drinks and fast-food products could be marketed together in the same television and radio segments, thereby providing higher returns for each advertising dollar. Restaurant chains also provided an additional outlet for the sale of Pepsi soft drinks. Thus, PepsiCo believed it could take advantage of numerous synergies by operating the three businesses under the same corporate umbrella. PepsiCo also believed that its management skills could be transferred among the three businesses. This practice was compatible with PepsiCo's policy of frequently moving managers among its business units as a means of developing future executives. PepsiCo first entered the restaurant business in 1977 when it acquired Pizza Hut. Taco Bell was acquired one year later. To complete its diversification into the restaurant industry, PepsiCo acquired KFC in 1986. The acquisition of KFC gave PepsiCo the leading market share in the chicken (KFC), pizza (Pizza Hut), and Mexican food (Taco Bell) segments of the fast-food industry.

Management

Following its acquisition of KFC, PepsiCo initiated sweeping changes. It announced that the franchise contract would be changed to give PepsiCo greater control over KFC franchisees and to make it easier to close poorly performing restaurants. Staff at KFC was reduced in order to cut costs and many KFC managers were replaced with PepsiCo managers. Soon after the acquisition, KFC's new personnel manager, who had just relocated from PepsiCo's New York headquarters, was overheard in the KFC cafeteria saying "There will be no more home grown tomatoes in this organization."

Rumors spread quickly among KFC employees about their opportunities for advancement within KFC and PepsiCo. Harsh comments by PepsiCo managers about KFC, its people, and its traditions, several restructurings that led to layoffs throughout KFC, the replacement of KFC managers with PepsiCo managers, and conflicts between KFC and PepsiCo's corporate cultures created a morale problem within KFC. KFC's culture was built largely on Colonel Sanders' laid-back approach to management. Employees enjoyed good job security and stability. A strong loyalty had been created among KFC employees over the years as a result of the Colonel's efforts to provide for his employees' benefits, pension, and other non-income needs. In addition, the Southern environment in Louisville resulted in a friendly, relaxed atmosphere at KFC's corporate offices. This corporate culture was left essentially unchanged during the Heublein and RJR years.

In contrast to KFC, PepsiCo's culture was characterized by a much stronger emphasis on performance. Top performers expected to move up through the ranks quickly. PepsiCo used its KFC, Pizza Hut, Taco Bell, Frito Lay, and Pepsi-Cola divisions as training grounds for its executives, rotating its best managers through the five divisions on average every two years. This practice created immense pressure on managers to demonstrate their management skills within short periods in order to maximize their potential for promotion. This practice also reinforced the feelings of KFC managers that they had few opportunities for promotion within the new company. One PepsiCo manager commented that "You may have performed well last year, but if you don't perform well this year, you're gone, and there are 100 ambitious guys with Ivy League MBAs at PepsiCo's headquarters in New York who would love to have your job." An unwanted effect of this performance driven culture was that employee loyalty was often lost and turnover was higher than in other companies.

Kyle Craig, president of KFC's US operations, commented on KFC's relationship with its corporate parent:

> The KFC culture is an interesting one because it was dominated by a lot of KFC folks, many of whom have been around since the days of the Colonel. Many of those people were very intimidated by the PepsiCo culture, which is a very high performance, high accountability, highly driven culture. People were concerned about whether they would succeed in the new culture. Like many companies, we have had a couple of downsizings which further made people nervous. Today, there are fewer old KFC people around and I think to some degree people have seen that the PepsiCo culture can drive some pretty positive results. I also think the PepsiCo people who have worked with KFC have modified their cultural values somewhat and they can see that there were a lot of benefits in the old KFC culture.
>
> PepsiCo pushes their companies to perform strongly, but whenever there is a slip in performance, it increases the culture gap between PepsiCo and KFC. I have been involved in two downsizings over which I have been the chief architect. They have been probably the two most gut-wrenching experiences of my career. Because you know you're dealing with peoples' lives and their families, these changes can be emotional if you care about the people in your organization. However, I do fundamentally believe that your first obligation is to the entire organization.

A second problem for PepsiCo was its poor relationship with KFC franchisees. A month after becoming president and chief executive officer in 1989, John Cranor addressed KFC's franchisees in Louisville in order to explain the details of the new franchise contract. This was the first contract change in thirteen years. It gave PepsiCo greater power to take over weak franchises, relocate restaurants, and make changes in existing restaurants. In addition, restaurants would no longer be protected from competition from new KFC units and PepsiCo would have the right to raise royalty fees on existing restaurants as contracts came up for renewal. After Cranor finished his address, there was an uproar among the attending franchisees who jumped to their feet to protest the changes. KFC's franchise association later sued PepsiCo over the new contract. The contract remained unresolved until 1996, when the most objectionable parts of the contract were removed by KFC's new president and CEO, David Novak. A new contract was ratified by KFC's franchisees in 1997.

PepsiCo's Divestiture of KFC, Pizza Hut, and Taco Bell

PepsiCo's strategy of diversifying into three distinct but related markets—soft drinks, snack foods, and fast-food restaurants—created one of the world's largest consumer product companies and a portfolio of some of the world's most recognizable brands. Between 1990 and 1996, PepsiCo's sales grew at an annual rate of more than 10 percent, surpassing $31 billion in 1996. PepsiCo's growth, however, masked troubles in its fast-food businesses. Operating margins (profit after tax as a percent of sales) at Pepsi-Cola and Frito Lay averaged 12 and 17 percent between 1990 and 1996, respectively. During the same period, margins at KFC, Pizza Hut, and Taco Bell fell from an average of more than 8 percent in 1990 to a little more than 4 percent in 1996. Declining margins in the fast food chains reflected increasing maturity in the US fast-food industry, more intense competition, and the aging of KFC and Pizza Hut's restaurant bases. As a result, PepsiCo's restaurant chains absorbed nearly one-half of PepsiCo's annual capital spending during the 1990s, but they generated less than one-third of PepsiCo's cash flows. This meant that cash had to be diverted from PepsiCo's soft drink and snack food businesses to its restaurant businesses. This reduced PepsiCo's corporate return on assets, made it more difficult to compete effectively with Coca-Cola, and hurt its stock price. In 1997, PepsiCo decided to spin off its restaurant businesses into a new company called Tricon Global Restaurants, Inc. The new company would be based in KFC's headquarters in Louisville, Kentucky (See Exhibit 1).

Exhibit 1   Tricon Global Restaurants, Inc. - Organizational Chart (2001)

Tricon Global Restaurants, Inc.
Corporate Offices
Louisville, Kentucky
Andrall E. Pearson, Chairman of the Board
David C. Novak, Chief Executive Officer

KFC USA
Louisville, Kentucky
Terry D. Davenport, Chief Concept Officer
Charles E. Rawley, Chief Operating Officer

Pizza Hut USA
Dallas, Texas
Michael S. Rawlings, President & CCO
Michael A. Miles, Chief Operating Officer

Taco Bell USA
Irvine, California
Peter C. Waller, President & CCO
Robert T. Nilsen, Chief Operating Officer

Tricon Restaurants International
Dallas, Texas
Peter Bassi, President

PepsiCo's objective was to reposition itself as a beverage and snack food company, strengthen its balance sheet, and create more consistent earning growth. PepsiCo received a one-time distribution from Tricon of $4.7 billion, $3.7 billion of which was used to pay off short-term debt. The balance was earmarked for stock repurchases. In 1998, PepsiCo acquired Tropicana Products, which controlled more than 40 percent of the US chilled orange juice market. Because of the divestiture of KFC, Pizza Hut, and Taco Bell, PepsiCo sales fell by $11.3 billion and assets fell by $7.0 billion between 1997 and 1999. Profitability, however, soared. Operating margins rose from 11 percent in 1997 to 14 percent in 1999 and ROA rose from 11 percent in 1997 to 16 percent in 1999. By focusing on high cash flow market leaders, PepsiCo raised profitability while decreasing its asset base.

Fast-Food Industry

According to the National Restaurant Association (NRA), food service sales increased by 5.4 percent to $358 billion in 1999. More than 800,000 restaurants and food outlets made up the US restaurant industry, which employed 11 million people. Sales were highest in the full-service, sit-down sector, which grew 7 percent to $121 billion. Fast-food sales grew at a slower rate, rising about 5 percent to $110 billion. Fast-food sales surpassed the full-service sector during the mid-1990s; however, maturation of the fast-food sector and rising incomes among many Americans helped full-service restaurants again overtake fast-food as the largest sector in the restaurant industry.

Major Fast-Food Segments

Eight major segments made up the fast-food segment of the restaurant industry: sandwich chains, pizza chains, family restaurants, grill buffet chains, dinner houses, chicken chains, non-dinner concepts, and other chains. Sales data for the leading restaurant chains in each segment are shown in Exhibit 2. Most striking is the dominance of McDonald's, which had sales of more than $19 billion in 1999. McDonald's accounted for 15 percent of the sales of the nation's top 100 restaurant chains. To put McDonald's dominance into perspective, the second largest chain—Burger King—held less than 7 percent of the market. The full-service and fast-food segments were expected to make up about 65 percent of total food service industry sales in 2000.

Sandwich chains made up the largest segment of the fast-food market. McDonald's controlled 35 percent of the sandwich segment, while Burger King ran a distant second with a 16 percent market share. Despite continued success by some chains like McDonald's, Carl's Jr., Jack in the Box, Wendy's, and White Castle, other chains like Hardee's, Burger King, Taco Bell, and Checker's were struggling. McDonald's generated the greatest per store sales of about $1.5 million per year. The average US chain generated $800,000 in sales per store. Per store sales at Burger King remained flat and Hardee's per store sales declined by 10 percent. Franchisees at Burger King complained of leadership problems within the corporate parent (London-based Diageo PLC), an impending increase in royalties and franchise fees, and poor advertising. Hardee's corporate parent (CKE Enterprises), which also owned Carl's Jr. and Taco Bueno, planned to franchise many of its company-owned Hardee's restaurants and to allow the system to shrink as low performing units were closed. It also planned to refocus Hardee's strategy in the southeastern part of the United States, where brand loyalty remained strong.

Dinner houses made up the second largest and fastest growing fast-food segment. Sales of dinner houses increased by more than 13 percent during the year, surpassing the average increase of six percent among all fast-food chains. Much of the growth in dinner houses came from new unit construction, a marked contrast with other fast-food chains, which had already slowed US construction because of market saturation. Much of the new unit construction took place in new suburban markets and small towns. Applebee's and Red Lobster dominated the dinner house segment. Each chain generated more than $2 billion in sales in 1999. The fastest growing dinner houses, however, were chains generating less than $500 million in sales such as On The Border, The Cheesecake Factory, O'Charley's, Romano's Macaroni Grill, and Hooters. Each of these chains increased sales by more than 20 percent.

Increased growth among dinner houses came at the expense of slower growth among sandwich chains, pizza chains, grilled buffet chains, and family restaurants. "Too many restaurants chasing the same customers" was responsible for much of the slower growth in these other fast-food categories. However, sales growth within each segment differed from one chain to another. In the family segment, for example, Friendly's and Shoney's were forced to shut down restaurants because of declining profits, but Steak 'n Shake and Cracker Barrel expanded their restaurant base by more than 10 percent. Within the pizza segment, Pizza Hut and Little Caesars closed underperforming restaurants, but Papa John's and Chuck E. Cheese's continued to aggressively grow their US restaurant bases. The hardest hit segment was grilled buffet chains, which generated the lowest increase in sales of less than 4 percent. Dinner houses, because of

Exhibit 2   Top 50 US Fast-Food Restaurants (Ranked by 1999 Sales, $ 000s)

Rank	Sandwich chains	Sales	Share	Rank	Dinner houses	Sales	Share
1	McDonald's	19,006	35.0%	9	Applebee's	2,305	14.9%
2	Burger King	8,659	16.0	15	Red Lobster	2,005	13.0
3	Wendy's	5,250	9.7	16	Outback Steakhouse	1,729	11.2
4	Taco Bell	5,200	9.6	17	Olive Garden	1,610	10.4
7	Subway	3,200	5.9	19	Chili's Grill & Bar	1,555	10.1
10	Arby's	2,260	4.2	22	T.G.I. Friday's	1,364	8.8
11	Dairy Queen	2,145	4.0	30	Ruby Tuesday	920	5.9
12	Hardee's	2,139	3.9	49	Lone Star Steakhouse	468	3.0
18	Sonic Drive-In	1,589	2.9		Other chains	3,520	22.7
20	Jack in the Box	1,510	2.8		Total segment	15,476	100.0%
32	Carl's Jr.	887	1.6				
46	Whataburger	503	0.9				
	Other chains	1,890	3.5				
	Total segment	54,238	100.0%				

Rank	Pizza chains	Sales	Share	Rank	Chicken chains	Sales	Share
5	Pizza Hut	5,000	44.0%	6	KFC	4,378	55.2%
8	Domino's	2,560	22.5	28	Popeyes	986	12.7
21	Papa John's	1,426	12.6	29	Chick-fil-A	946	12.1
23	Little Caesars	1,200	10.6	34	Boston Market	855	11.0
50	Sbarro	466	4.1	38	Church's	705	9.0
	Other chains	703	6.2		Total segment	7,870	100.0%
	Total segment	11,355	100.0%				

Rank	Family restaurants	Sales	Share	Rank	Other dinner chains	Sales	Share
13	Denny's	2,079	22.7%	37	Long John Silver's	716	15.7%
24	Cracker Barrel	1,163	12.7	41	Walt Disney Co.	666	14.7
26	IHOP	1,077	11.8	43	Old Country Buffet	589	13.0
33	Shoney's	869	9.5	47	Luby's Cafeteria	502	11.0
35	Perkins	790	8.6	48	Captain D's Seafood	499	11.0
36	Bob Evans	727	8.0		Other chains	1,574	34.6
40	Friendly's	671	7.3		Total segment	4,546	100.0%
42	Waffle House	620	6.8				
	Other chains	1,144	12.6				
	Total segment	9,140	100.0%				

Rank	Grill buffet chains	Sales	Share	Rank	Non-dinner concepts	Sales	Share
31	Golden Corral	899	32.3%	14	Dunkin' Donuts	2,007	42.9%
39	Ryan's	704	25.3	25	7-Eleven	1,117	23.8
45	Ponderosa	560	20.1	27	Starbucks	987	21.1
	Other chains	621	22.3	44	Baskin-Robbins	573	12.2
	Total segment	2,784	100.0%		Total segment	4,684	100.0%

SOURCE: *Nation's Restaurant News.*

their more upscale atmosphere and higher ticket items, were better positioned to take advantage of the aging and wealthier US population, which increasingly demanded higher quality food in more upscale settings. Even dinner houses, however, faced the prospect of market saturation and increased competition in the near future.

Chicken Segment

KFC continued to dominate the chicken segment with sales of $4.4 billion in 1999 (see Exhibit 3). Its nearest competitor, Popeyes, ran a distant second with sales of $1.0 billion. KFC's leadership in the US market was so extensive that it had fewer opportunities to expand its US restaurant base, which was only growing at about 1 percent per year. Despite its dominance, KFC was slowly losing market share as other chicken chains increased sales at a faster rate. KFC's share of chicken segment sales fell from 71 percent in 1989 to less than 56 percent in 1999, a ten-year drop of 15 percent. During the same period, Chick-fil-A and Boston Market increased their combined market share by 17 percent (see Exhibit 4). In the early 1990s, many industry analysts predicted that Boston Market would challenge KFC for market leadership. Boston Market was a new restaurant chain that emphasized roasted rather than fried chicken. It successfully created the image of an upscale deli offering healthy, "home-style" alternatives to fried chicken and other fast food. In order to distinguish itself from more traditional fast-food concepts, it refused to construct drive-thrus and it established most of its units outside of shopping malls rather than at major city intersections.

Exhibit 3	Top US Chicken Chains						
	1994	1995	1996	1997	1998	1999	Growth Rate
Sales ($Millions)							
KFC	3,587	3,740	3,935	4,002	4,171	4,378	4%
Popeyes	614	660	677	720	843	986	10%
Chick-fil-A	451	502	570	643	767	946	16%
Boston Market	371	754	1,100	1,197	929	855	18%
Church's	465	501	526	574	620	705	9%
Total	5,488	6,157	6,808	7,136	7,330	7,870	7%
US restaurants							
KFC	5,081	5,103	5,078	5,092	5,105	5,231	1%
Popeyes	853	889	894	945	1,066	1,165	6%
Chick-fil-A	534	825	717	749	812	897	11%
Boston Market	534	829	1,087	1,166	889	858	10%
Church's	937	953	989	1,070	1,105	1,178	5%
Total	7,939	8,599	8,765	9,022	8,977	9,329	3%
Sales per unit ($ 000s)							
KFC	706	733	775	786	817	837	3%
Popeyes	720	742	757	762	790	847	3%
Chick-fil-A	845	608	795	859	945	1,055	5%
Boston Market	695	910	1,012	1,027	1,045	997	7%
Church's	496	526	532	536	561	598	4%
Total	691	716	777	791	816	844	4%

SOURCE: Tricon Global Restaurants, Inc., *1999 Annual Report;* Chick-fil-A, corporate headquarters, Atlanta; Boston Chicken, Inc., *1999 Annual Report;* Nation's Restaurant News, 2000.

Case 21 / Kentucky Fried Chicken and the Global Fast-Food Industry

Exhibit 4 — Top US Chicken Chains—Market Share (%, based on annual sales)

	KFC	Popeyes	Chick-fil-A	Boston Market	Church's	Total
1989	70.8	12.0	6.2	0.0	11.0	100.0
1990	71.3	12.3	6.6	0.0	9.8	100.0
1991	72.7	11.4	7.0	0.0	8.9	100.0
1992	71.5	11.4	7.5	0.9	8.7	100.0
1993	68.7	11.4	8.0	3.0	8.9	100.0
1994	65.4	11.2	8.2	6.7	8.5	100.0
1995	60.7	10.7	8.2	12.3	8.1	100.0
1996	57.8	9.9	8.4	16.2	7.7	100.0
1997	56.1	10.1	9.0	16.8	8.0	100.0
1998	56.9	11.5	10.5	12.7	8.4	100.0
1999	55.6	12.5	12.0	10.9	9.0	100.0
5-Year Change (%)	−9.8	1.3	3.8	4.2	0.5	0.0
10-Year Change (%)	−15.2	0.5	5.8	10.9	−2.0	0.0

On the surface, it appeared that Boston Market and Chick-fil-A's market share gains were achieved primarily by taking customers away from KFC. Another look at the data, however, reveals that KFC's sales grew at a stable rate over the last ten years. Boston Market, rather than drawing customers away from KFC, appealed primarily to consumers who did not regularly frequent KFC and wanted healthy, non-fried chicken alternatives. Boston Market was able to expand the chicken segment beyond its traditional emphasis on fried chicken by offering non-fried chicken products that appealed to this new consumer group. After aggressively growing its restaurant base through 1997, however, Boston Market fell on hard times as it was unable to handle mounting debt problems. It soon entered bankruptcy proceedings. McDonald's acquired Boston Market in 2000. It had acquired Denver-based Chipotle Mexican Grill in 1998 and Columbus, Ohio-based Donatos Pizza in 1999. McDonald's hoped the acquisitions would help it expand its US restaurant base, since fewer opportunities existed to expand the McDonald's concept. Chick-fil-A's success came primarily from its aggressive shopping mall strategy that leveraged the trend toward large food courts in shopping malls. Despite gains by Boston Market and Chick-fil-A, KFC's customer base remained loyal to the KFC brand because of its unique taste. KFC also continued to dominate the dinner and takeout segments of the industry.

Popeyes replaced Boston Market as the second largest chicken chain in 1999. Popeyes and Church's had traditionally followed similar strategies—to compete head-on with other "fried chicken" chains. Popeyes, however, was in the process of shifting its focus to Cajun fast-food, after it successfully launched its Louisiana Legends One-Pot Cajun Meals of jambalaya, gumbo, shrimp, and crawfish étoufée. Church's was determined to distinguish itself by placing a heavier emphasis on its "made-from-scratch," Southern image. In 1999, it broadened its menu to include buffalo chicken wings, macaroni and cheese, beans and rice, and collard greens. Chick-fil-A focused on pressure-cooked and char-grilled skinless chicken breast sandwiches, which it had traditionally sold to customers in sit-down restaurants in shopping malls. As more malls added food courts, however, malls became less enthusiastic about allocating separate store space to restaurants. Therefore, Chick-fil-A began to open smaller units in shopping mall food courts, hospitals, and colleges as a way of complementing its existing sit-down restaurants.

Demographic Trends

A number of demographic and societal trends influenced the demand for food eaten outside of the home. During the last two decades, rising incomes, greater affluence among a greater percentage of American households, higher divorce rates, and the fact that people married later in life contributed to the rising number of single households and the demand for fast-food. More than 50 percent of women worked outside of the home, a dramatic increase since 1970. This number was expected to rise to 65 percent by 2010. Double-income households contributed to rising household incomes and increased the number of times families eat out. Less time to prepare meals inside the home added to this trend. Countering these trends, however, was a slower growth rate of the US population and an overpopulation of fast-food chains that increased consumer alternatives and intensified competition.

Baby Boomers aged 35 to 50 years of age constituted the largest consumer group for fast-food restaurants. Generation X'ers (ages 25 to 34) and the "Mature" category (ages 51 to 64) made up the second and third largest groups. As consumers aged, they became less enamored with fast-food and were more likely to trade up to more expensive restaurants such as dinner houses and full-service restaurants. Sales of many Mexican restaurants, which were extremely popular during the 1980s, began to slow as Japanese, Indian, and Vietnamese restaurants became more fashionable. Ethnic foods in general were rising in popularity as US immigrants which constituted 10 percent of the US population in 2000, looked for establishments that sold their native foods.

The greatest concern for fast-food operators was the shortage of employees in the 16 to 24 age category. Most Americans in this age category had never experienced a recession or economic downturn. During the 1970s, Americans experienced double-digit inflation, high interest rates, and high unemployment, as well as two major oil crises that resulted in gas shortages. The US economy began to expand again during the early 1980s and continued to expand almost unabated through 2000. Unemployment was at its lowest point in more than two decades and many high school and college graduates, especially those in business and engineering, enjoyed a robust job market that made it more difficult for fast-food operators to find capable employees.

Labor costs made up about 30 percent of the fast-food chain's total costs, second only to food and beverage costs. Intense competition, however, made it difficult for restaurants to increase prices sufficiently to cover the increased cost of labor. Consumers made decisions about where to eat partially based on price. Therefore, profit margins were squeezed. In order to reduce costs, restaurants eliminated low-margin food items, increased portion sizes, and improved product value to offset price increases. Restaurants also attempted to increase consumer traffic through discounting, by accepting coupons

from competitors, by offering two-for-one specials, and by making limited-time offerings.

Costs could also be lowered and operations made more efficient by increasing the use of technology. According to the National Restaurant Association, most restaurant operators viewed computers as their number one tool for improving efficiencies. Computers could be used to improve labor scheduling, accounting, payroll, sales analysis, and inventory control. Most restaurant chains were also using point-of-sale systems that recorded the selected menu items and gave the cashier a breakdown of food items and the ticket price. These systems increased serving times and cashier accuracy. Other chains like McDonald's and Carl's Jr. converted to new food preparation systems that allowed them to prepare food more accurately and to prepare a great variety of sandwiches using the same process.

Higher costs and poor availability of prime real estate was another trend that negatively affected profitability. A plot of land suitable for a normal sized freestanding restaurant cost between $1.5 and $2.5 million. Leasing was a less costly alternative to buying. Nevertheless, market saturation decreased per store sales as newer units cannibalized sales from existing units. As a result, most food chains began to expand their US restaurant bases into alternative distribution channels in hospitals, airports, colleges, highway rest areas, gas stations, shopping mall food courts, and large retail stores or by dual branding with other fast-food concepts.

While the news media touted the benefits of low-fat diets during the 1970s and 1980s, consumer demand for beef began to increase again during the 1990s. The US Department of Agriculture estimated that Americans ate an average of 64 pounds of red meat each year. The growing demand for steak and prime rib helped fuel the growth in dinner houses that continued into 2000. According to the NRA, other food items that were growing in popularity included chicken, hot and spicy foods, smoothies, wraps and pitas, salads, and espresso and specialty coffees. Starbucks, the Seattle-based coffee retailer, capitalized on the popularity of specialty coffees by aggressively expanding its coffee shop concept into shopping malls, commercial buildings, and bookstores such as Barnes & Noble. Starbucks increased its store base by 28 percent in 1999, the greatest increase of any major restaurant chain.

International Fast-Food Market

As the US market matured, many restaurants expanded into international markets as a strategy for growing sales. Foreign markets were attractive because of their large customer bases and comparatively little competition. McDonald's, for example, operated 46 restaurants for every one million US residents. Outside of the United States, it operated only one restaurant for every three million residents. McDonald's, KFC, Burger King, and Pizza Hut were the earliest and most aggressive chains to expand abroad beginning in the late 1950s. By 2001, at least 35 chains had expanded into at least one foreign country. McDonald's operated the largest number of restaurants (more than 12,000 US units and 14,000 foreign units) in the most countries (119). In comparison, Tricon Global Restaurants operated more than 20,000 US and close to 30,000 non-US KFC, Pizza Hut, and Taco Bell restaurants in 85 countries. Because of their early expansion abroad, McDonald's, KFC, Burger King, and Pizza Hut had all developed strong brand names and managerial expertise operating in international markets. This made them formidable competitors for fast-food chains investing abroad for the first time.

Exhibit 5 lists the world's thirty-five largest restaurant chains in 2000. The global fast-food industry had a distinctly American flavor. Twenty-eight chains (80 percent of the total) were headquartered in the United States. US chains had the advantage of a large domestic market and ready acceptance by the American consumer. European firms had less success developing the fast-food concept, because Europeans were more inclined to frequent more mid-scale restaurants, where they spent several hours enjoying multi-course meals in a formal setting. KFC had trouble breaking into the German market during the 1970s and 1980s, because Germans were not accustomed to buying take-out or ordering food over the counter. McDonald's had greater success penetrating the German market, because it made a number of changes to its menu and operating procedures to appeal to German tastes. German beer, for example, was served in all of McDonald's restaurants in Germany. In France, McDonald's used a different sauce on its Big Mac sandwich that appealed to the French palate. KFC had more success in Asia and Latin America, where chicken was a traditional dish.

Aside from cultural factors, international business carried risks not present in the domestic market. Long distances between headquarters and foreign franchises made it more difficult to control the quality of individual restaurants. Large distances also caused servicing and support problems. Transportation and other resource costs were higher than in the domestic market. In addition, time, cultural, and language differences increased communication and operational problems. As a result, most restaurant chains limited expansion to their domestic market as long as they were able to achieve cor-

porate profit and growth objectives. As companies gained greater expertise abroad, they turned to profitable international markets as a means of expanding restaurant bases and increasing sales, profits, and market share. Worldwide demand for fast-food was expected to grow rapidly during the next two decades, because rising per capita incomes worldwide made eating out more affordable for greater numbers of consumers. In addition, the development of the Internet was quickly breaking down communication and language barriers. Greater numbers of children were growing up with computers in their homes and schools. As a result, teenagers in Germany, Brazil, Japan, and the United States were equally likely to be able to converse about the Internet. The Internet also exposed more teenagers to the same companies and products, which enabled firms to more quickly develop global brands and a worldwide consumer base.

Kentucky Fried Chicken Corporation
Marketing Strategy

Many of KFC's problems during the 1980s and 1990s surrounded its limited menu and inability to quickly bring new products to market. The popularity of its Original Recipe Chicken allowed KFC to expand through the 1980s without significant competition from other chicken chains. As a result, new product introductions were not a critical part of KFC's overall business strategy. KFC suffered one of its most serious setbacks in 1989 as it prepared to introduce a chicken sandwich to its menu. KFC still experimented with the chicken sandwich concept when McDonald's test-marketed its McChicken sandwich in the Louisville market. Shortly after, McDonald's rolled out the McChicken sandwich nationally. By beating KFC to the market, McDonald's developed strong consumer awareness for its sandwich. This significantly increased KFC's cost of developing awareness for its own sandwich, which KFC introduced several months later. KFC eventually withdrew the sandwich because of low sales. Today, about 95 percent of chicken sandwiches are sold through traditional hamburger chains.

By the late 1990s, KFC had refocused its strategy. The cornerstone of its new strategy was to increase sales in individual KFC restaurants by introducing a variety of new products and menu items that appealed to a greater number of customers. After extensive testing, KFC settled on three types of chicken: Original Recipe (pressure cooked), Extra Crispy (fried), and Tender Roast (roasted). It also rolled out a buffet that included some 30 dinner, salad, and dessert items. The buffet was particularly successful in rural locations and suburbs. It was

Exhibit 5 The World's 35 Largest Fast-Food Chains (2000)[a]

	Franchise	Operational Headquarters	Parent Country	Countries
1.	McDonald's	Oakbrook, Illinois	U.S.A.	119
2.	Pizza Hut	Dallas, Texas	U.S.A.	88
3.	KFC	Louisville, Kentucky	U.S.A.	85
4.	Subway Sandwiches	Milford, Connecticut	U.S.A.	73
5.	TCBY	Little Rock, Arkansas	U.S.A.	68
6.	Domino's Pizza	Ann Arbor, Michigan	U.S.A.	64
7.	Burger King	Miami, Florida	U.K.	58
8.	T.G.I. Friday's	Dallas, Texas	U.S.A.	53
9.	Baskin Robbins	Glendale, California	U.S.A.	52
10.	Dunkin' Donuts	Randolph, Massachusetts	U.S.A.	41
11.	Wendy's	Dublin, Ohio	U.S.A.	29
12.	Sizzler	Los Angeles, California	U.S.A.	22
13.	A&W Restaurants	Livonia, Michigan	U.S.A.	21
14.	Popeyes	Atlanta, Georgia	U.S.A.	21
15.	Chili's Grill & Bar	Dallas, Texas	U.S.A.	20
16.	Little Caesar's Pizza	Detroit, Michigan	U.S.A.	19
17.	Dairy Queen	Edina, Minnesota	U.S.A.	18
18.	Taco Bell	Irvine, California	U.S.A.	15
19.	Carl's Jr.	Anaheim, California	U.S.A.	15
20.	Outback Steakhouse	Tampa, Florida	U.S.A.	13
21.	Hardee's	Rocky Mt., North Carolina	U.S.A.	11
22.	Applebee's	Overland Park, Kansas	U.S.A.	10
23.	Arby's	Ft. Lauderdale, Florida	U.S.A.	10
24.	Church's Chicken	Atlanta, Georgia	U.S.A.	9
25.	PizzaExpress	London, England	U.K.	9
26.	Denny's	Spartanburg, South Carolina	U.S.A.	6
27.	Mos Burger	Tokyo	Japan	5
28.	Taco Time	Eugene, Oregon	U.S.A.	5
29.	Yoshinoya	Tokyo	Japan	5
30.	Loterria	Tokyo	Japan	4
31.	Orange Julius	Edina, Minnesota	U.S.A.	4
32.	Quick Restaurants	Brussels	Belgium	4
33.	Skylark	Tokyo	Japan	4
34.	IHOP	Glendale, California	U.S.A.	3
35.	Red Lobster	Orlando, Florida	U.S.A.	3

[a]Case writer research.

less successful in urban locations because of space considerations. KFC then introduced its Colonel's Crispy Strips and five new chicken sandwiches to appeal to customers who preferred non chicken-on-the-bone products. KFC estimated that its Crispy Strips and chicken sandwiches accounted for $250,000 (30 percent) of KFC per restaurant sales, which averaged $837,000 per year. One of the problems with these items, however, was that they cannibalized sales of its chicken items; they were less expensive and easier to handle. The latter was especially appealing to drive-thru customers.

Overcapacity in the US market made it more difficult to justify the construction of new free-standing restaurants. Fewer sites were available for new construction and those sites, because of their increased cost, drove profit margins down. KFC initiated a three pronged distribution strategy that helped beef up sales. First, it focused on building smaller restaurants in non-traditional outlets such as airports, shopping malls, universities, and hospitals. It also experimented with units that offered drive-thru and carry-out service only, snack shops in cafeterias, scaled-down outlets for supermarkets, and mobile units that could be transported to outdoor concerts and fairs. Second, KFC continued to experiment with home delivery, which was already firmly established in the Louisville, Las Vegas, and Los Angeles markets. Third, KFC established "2-n-1" units that sold both KFC and Taco Bell (KFC/Taco Bell Express) or KFC and Pizza Hut (KFC/Pizza Hut Express) products. By early 2000, Tricon Global Restaurants was operating 700 multi-branded restaurants that simultaneously sold products from two of the three chains. It was also testing "3-n-1" units that sold all three brands.

Refranchising Strategy

When Colonel Sanders began to expand the Kentucky Fried Chicken system in the late 1950s, he established KFC as a system of independent franchisees. This strategy helped the Colonel minimize his involvement in the operations of individual restaurants and to concentrate on the things he enjoyed the most—cooking, product development, and public relations. The franchise system resulted in a fiercely loyal and independent group of KFC franchises. When PepsiCo acquired KFC in 1986, a primary objective was to integrate KFC's operations into the PepsiCo system to take advantage of operational, financial, and marketing synergies. This strategy, however, led to greater interference by PepsiCo management in franchise menu offerings, financing, marketing, and operations. This interference was met by resistance by KFC franchises. PepsiCo attempted to decrease these problems by expanding KFC's restaurant base through company-owned restaurants rather than through franchising. It also used its strong cash flows to buy back unprofitable franchises. Many of these restaurants were converted into company-owned restaurants. By 1993, company-owned restaurants accounted for 40 percent of KFC's worldwide system. When PepsiCo spun off its restaurants into Tricon Global Restaurants in 1994, Tricon's new top management team began to sell company-owned restaurants back to franchises they believed knew the business better than they. By 2000, company-owned restaurants had fallen to about 27 percent of the total KFC system.

International Operations

KFC's early experiences operating abroad put it in a strong position to take advantage of the growing trend toward international expansion. By 2001, more than 50 percent of KFC's restaurants were located outside of the United States. Historically, franchises made up a large portion of KFC's international restaurant base, because franchises were owned and operated by local entrepreneurs who had a deeper understanding of local language, culture, customs, law, financial markets, and marketing characteristics. Franchising was also a good strategy for establishing a presence in smaller countries like Grenada, Bermuda, and Suriname, which could only support a single restaurant. The costs of operating company-owned restaurants were prohibitively high in these smaller markets. Of the 5,595 KFC restaurants located outside of the United States in 1999, 69 percent were franchised, while 21 percent were company-owned and 10 percent were licensed restaurants or joint ventures. In larger markets such as Mexico, China, Canada, Australia, Puerto Rico, Korea, Thailand, and the United Kingdom, there was a stronger emphasis on building company-owned restaurants. By coordinating purchasing, recruiting and training, financing, and advertising, fixed costs could be spread over a larger number of restaurants. Increased bargaining power also enabled KFC to negotiate lower prices from suppliers. KFC was also better able to control product and service quality.

Latin American Strategy

KFC operated 438 restaurants in Latin America in 2000 (Exhibit 6). Its primary presence was in Mexico, Puerto Rico, and the Caribbean. KFC established subsidiaries in Mexico and Puerto Rico beginning in the late 1960s and expanded through company-owned restaurants. Franchises were used to penetrate other countries in the Caribbean whose market size prevented KFC from profitably operating company-owned restaurants. Subsidiaries were later established in the Virgin Islands, Venezuela, and Brazil. KFC had planned to expand into these regions using company-owned restaurants. The Venezuelan subsidiary, however, was later closed because of the high costs of operating the small subsidiary. KFC had opened eight restaurants in Brazil but decided to close them in 1999 because it lacked the cash flow needed to support an expansion program in that market. Franchises were opened in other markets that had good growth potential such as Chile, Ecuador, Peru, and Colombia.

	McDonald's	Burger King	KFC	Wendy's
Mexico	170	108	157	7
Puerto Rico	121	148	67	30
Caribbean Islands	59	57	91	23
Central America	80	85	26	26
Subtotal	430	398	341	86
% Total	24%	80%	78%	60%
Colombia	21	0	19	3
Ecuador	7	12	18	0
Peru	10	10	17	0
Venezuela	83	13	6	33
Other Andean	6	7	0	0
Andean Region	127	42	60	36
% Total	7%	9%	14%	25%
Argentina	205	25	0	21
Brazil	921	0	8	0
Chile	61	25	29	0
Paraguay + Uruguay	32	5	0	0
Southern Cone	1,219	55	37	21
% Total	69%	11%	8%	15%
Latin America	1,776	495	438	143
% Total	100%	100%	100%	100%

Note: Restaurant data obtained from corporate offices at McDonald's Corp. (as of 12/99), Burger King Corp. (as of 6/30/00), Tricon Global Restaurants, Inc. (as of 6/30/00), and Wendy's International (as of 5/15/00).

KFC's early entry into Latin America gave it a leadership position over McDonald's in Mexico and the Caribbean. It also had an edge in Ecuador and Peru. KFC's Latin America strategy represented a classic internationalization strategy. It first expanded into Mexico and Puerto Rico because of their geographic proximity, as well as political and economic ties, to the United States. From these regions, KFC expanded its franchise system throughout the Caribbean, gradually moving away from its US base as its experience in Latin America grew. Only after it had established a leadership position in Mexico and the Caribbean did it venture into South America. McDonald's pursued a different strategy. It was late to expand into the region. Despite a rapid restaurant construction program in Mexico during the 1990s,

McDonald's still lagged behind KFC. Therefore, McDonald's initiated a first mover strategy in Brazil and Argentina, large markets where KFC had no presence. By early 2000, more than 63 percent of McDonald's restaurants in Latin America were located in the two countries. Wendy's pursued a slightly different strategy. It first expanded into Puerto Rico, the Caribbean Islands, and Central America because of their geographical proximity to the United States. The shorter distance to the United States made these restaurants easier to manage. Wendy's late entry into Latin America, however, made it more difficult to penetrate the Mexican market, where KFC, McDonald's, and Burger King had already established a strong presence. Wendy's announced plans to build 100 Wendy's restaurants in Mexico by 2010; however, its primary objective was to establish strong positions in Venezuela and Argentina, where most US fast-food chains had not yet been established.

Country Risk Assessment in Latin America

Latin America comprised some 50 countries, island nations, and principalities that were settled primarily by the Spanish, Portuguese, French, Dutch, and British during the 1500s and 1600s. Spanish was spoken in most countries, the most notable exception being Brazil, whose official language was Portuguese. Catholicism was the major religion, though Methodist missionaries successfully exported Protestantism into many regions of Latin America in the 1800s, most notably on the coast of Brazil. Despite commonalities in language, religion, and history, however, political and economic policies often differed significantly from one country to another. Historically, frequent changes in governments and economic instability increased the uncertainty of doing business in the region.

Most US and Canadian companies were beginning to realize, however, that they could not overlook the region. Geographic proximity made communications and travel easier and quicker between countries and the North American Trade Agreement (NAFTA) had eliminated tariffs on goods shipped between Canada, Mexico, and the United States. A customs union agreement signed in 1991 (Mercosur) between Argentina, Paraguay, Uruguay, and Brazil eliminated tariffs on trade among those four countries. Many countries such as Chile and Argentina had also established free trade policies that were beginning to stimulate growth. These factors made Latin America an attractive location for investment. The primary task for companies investing in the region was to accurately assess the different risks of doing business in Latin America and to select the proper countries for investment.

Miller (1992) developed a framework for analyzing country risk that was a useful tool for analyzing the attractiveness of a country for future investment. He argued that firms must examine country, industry, and firm factors in order to fully assess country risk. *Country factors* addressed the risks associated with changes in the country's political and economic environment that potentially affected the firm's ability to conduct business. They included the following:

(1) Political risk (e.g., war, revolution, changes in government, price controls, tariffs and other trade restrictions, appropriations of assets, government regulations, and restrictions on the repatriation of profits).

(2) Economic risk (e.g., inflation, high interest rates, foreign exchange rate volatility, balance of trade movements, social unrest, riots, and terrorism).

(3) Natural risk (e.g., rainfall, hurricanes, earthquakes, and volcanic activity).

Industry factors addressed changes in the structure of the industry that inhibited the firm's ability to successfully compete in its industry. They included the following:

(1) Supplier risk (e.g., changes in quality, shifts in supply, and changes in supplier power).

(2) Product market risk (e.g., changes in consumer tastes and availability of substitute products).

(3) Competitive risk (e.g., rivalry among competitors, new market entrants, and new product innovations).

Firm factors examined the firm's ability to control its internal operations. They included the following:

(1) Labor risk (e.g., labor unrest, absenteeism, employee turnover, and labor strikes).

(2) Supplier risk (e.g. raw material shortages and unpredictable price changes).

(3) Trade secret risk (e.g., protection of trade secrets and intangible assets).

(4) Credit risk (e.g., problems collecting receivables).

(5) Behavioral risk (e.g., control over franchise operations, product quality and consistency, service quality, and restaurant cleanliness).

Many US companies believed that Mexico was an attractive country for investment. Its population of 103 million was more than one-third as large as the US population and represented a large market for US goods and services. In comparison, Canada's population of 31 million was only one-third as large as Mexico's. Mexico's close proximity to the United States meant that transportation costs between the United States and Mexico were significantly lower than to Europe or Asia. This increased the competitiveness of US goods in comparison with European and Asian goods, which had to be transported to Mexico across the Atlantic or Pacific Ocean at significantly greater cost. The United States was in fact Mexico's largest trading partner. More than 80 percent of Mexico's total trade was with the United States. Many US firms also invested in Mexico to take advantage of lower wage rates. By producing goods in Mexico, US goods could be shipped back to the United States for sale or shipped to third markets at lower cost.

Despite the advantages of doing business in Mexico, Mexico only accounted for about 20 percent of the United States' total trade. Beginning in the early 1900s, the percentage of total US exports going to Latin America has declined as exports to other regions of the world such as Canada and Asia have increased. The growth in economic wealth and consumer demand in Canada and Asia has generally outpaced Mexico for most of the last century. However, the volume of trade between the United States and Mexico has increased significantly since the North American Trade Agreement went into effect in 1994.

A commonly held perception among many Americans was that Japan was the United States' largest trading partner. In reality, Canada was the United States' largest trading partner by a wide margin. Canada bought more than 22 percent ($154 million) of all US exports in 1998; Japan bought less than 9 percent ($58 billion). Canada accounted for about 19 percent of all goods imported into the United States ($178 billion); Japan accounted for 13 percent ($125 billion). The perception that Japan was the largest US trading partner resulted primarily from extensive media coverage of the long-running US trade deficit with Japan. Less known to many Americans was the fact that the United States was running a balance of trade deficit with China that almost equaled the deficit with Japan. China was positioned to become the United States' largest trading partner in Asia within the next few years.

The lack of US investment in and trade with Mexico during the 20th century was mainly the result of Mexico's long history of restricting foreign trade and investment. The Institutional Revolutionary Party (PRI), which came to power in Mexico during the 1920s, had a history of promoting protectionist economic policies to shield Mexico's economy from foreign competition. Many industries were government owned or controlled and many Mexican companies focused on producing goods for the domestic market without much attention to building exports. High tariffs and other trade barriers restricted imports into Mexico and foreign ownership of assets in Mexico was largely prohibited or heavily restricted.

A dictatorial and entrenched government bureaucracy, corrupt labor unions, and a long tradition of anti-Americanism among government officials and intellectuals also reduced the motivation of US firms to invest in Mexico. The nationalization of Mexico's banks in 1982 led to higher real interest rates and lower investor confidence. This forced the Mexican government to battle high inflation, high interest rates, labor unrest, and lower consumer purchasing power during the early to mid-1980s. Investor confidence in Mexico, however, improved after 1988, when Carlos Salinas de Gortari was elected president. Salinas embarked on an ambitious restructuring of the Mexican economy. He initiated policies to strengthen the free market components of the economy, lowered top marginal tax rates and eliminated many restrictions on foreign investment.

The privatization of government owned companies came to symbolize the restructuring of Mexico's economy. In 1990, legislation was passed to privatize all government run banks. By the end of 1992, more than 800 of 1,200 government-owned companies had been sold, including Mexicana and AeroMexico, the two largest airline companies in Mexico, and Mexico's 18 major banks. More than 350 companies, however, remained under government ownership. These represented a significant portion of the assets owned by the state at the start of 1988. Therefore, the sale of government-owned companies in terms of asset value was still modest. A large portion of the remaining government-owned assets was controlled by government-run companies in certain strategic industries such as steel, electricity, and petroleum. These industries had long been protected by government ownership. However, President Salinas opened up the electricity sector to independent power producers in 1993 and Petroleos Mexicanos (Pemex), the state-run petrochemical monopoly, initiated a program to sell off many of its non-strategic assets to private and foreign buyers.

North American Free Trade Agreement (NAFTA)

Prior to 1989, Mexico levied high tariffs on most imported goods. In addition, many other goods were subjected to quotas, licensing requirements, and other non-tariff trade barriers. In 1986, Mexico joined the General Agreement on Tariffs and Trade (GATT), a world trade organization designed to eliminate barriers to trade among member nations. As a member of GATT, Mexico was required to apply its system of tariffs to all member nations equally. Mexico subsequently dropped tariff rates on a variety of imported goods. In addition, import license requirements were dropped for all but 300 imported items. During President Salinas's administration, tariffs were reduced from an average of 100 percent on most items to an average of 11 percent.

On January 1, 1994, the North American Free Trade Agreement (NAFTA) went into effect. The passage of NAFTA created a trading bloc with a larger population and gross domestic product than the European Union. All tariffs on goods traded between the United States, Canada, and Mexico were eventually phased out. NAFTA was expected to benefit Mexican exporters, since reduced tariffs made their goods more competitive compared to goods exported to the United States from other countries. In 1995, one year after NAFTA went into effect, Mexico posted its first balance of trade surplus in six years. A large part of this surplus was attributed to greater exports to the United States.

Despite its supporters, NAFTA was strongly opposed by farmers and unskilled workers. The day after NAFTA went into effect, rebels rioted in the southern Mexican province of Chiapas on the Guatemalan border. After four days of fighting, Mexican troops drove the rebels out of several towns the rebels had earlier seized. Around 150 people—mostly rebels—were killed. Later in the year, 30 to 40 masked men attacked a McDonald's restaurant in the tourist section of Mexico City. The men threw cash registers to the floor, smashed windows, overturned tables, and spray-painted "No to Fascism" and "Yankee Go Home" on the walls. Such protests continued through 2000, when Mexican farmers dumped gallons of spoiled milk in the streets to protest low tariffs on imported farm products. Farmers also protested the Mexican's government's practice of allowing imports of milk powder, corn, and wheat from the United States and Canada above the quotas established as part of the NAFTA agreement. The continued opposition of Mexican farmers, unskilled workers, and nationalists posed a constant threat to the stability of the NAFTA agreement.

Another problem was Mexico's failure to reduce restrictions on US and Canadian investment in a timely fashion. Many US firms experienced problems getting required approvals for new ventures from the Mexican government. A good example was United Parcel Service (UPS), which sought government approval to use large trucks for deliveries in Mexico. Approvals were delayed, forcing UPS to use smaller trucks. This gave UPS a competitive disadvantage vis-a-vis Mexican companies. In many cases, UPS was forced to subcontract delivery work to Mexican companies that were allowed to use larger, more cost-efficient trucks. Other US companies such as Bell Atlantic and TRW faced similar problems. TRW, which signed a joint venture agreement with a Mexican partner, had to wait 15 months longer than expected before the Mexican government released rules on how it could receive credit data from banks. TRW claimed that the Mexican government had slowed the approval process to placate several large Mexican banks.

Foreign Exchange and the Mexican Peso Crisis of 1995

Between 1982 and 1991, a two-tiered exchange rate system was in force in Mexico. The system consisted of a controlled rate and a free market rate. A controlled rate was used for imports, foreign debt payments, and conversion of export proceeds. An estimated 70 percent of all foreign transactions were covered by the controlled rate. A free market rate was used for other transactions. In 1989, President Salinas instituted a policy of allowing the peso to depreciate by one peso per day against the dollar. In 1991, the controlled rate was abolished and replaced with an official free rate. The peso was thereafter allowed to depreciate by 0.20 pesos per day against the dollar. When Ernesto Zedillo became Mexico's president in December 1994, one of his objectives was to continue the stability of prices, wages, and exchange rates achieved by ex-president Carlos Salinas during his tenure as president. This stability, however, was achieved primarily on the basis of price, wage, and foreign exchange controls. While giving the appearance of stability, an over-valued peso continued to encourage imports that exacerbated Mexico's balance of trade deficit. At the same time, Mexican exports became less competitive on world markets.

Anticipating a devaluation of the peso, investors began to move capital into US dollar investments. On December 19, 1994, Zedillo announced that the peso would be allowed to depreciate by an additional 15 percent per year against the dollar. The maximum allowable depreciation at the time was 4 percent per year. Within two days, continued pressure on the peso forced Zedillo to allow the peso to float freely against the dollar. By mid-January 1995, the peso had lost 35 percent of its value against the dollar and the Mexican stock market plunged 20 percent. By the end of the year, the peso had depreciated from 3.1 pesos per dollar to 7.6 pesos per dollar. In order to thwart a possible default by Mexico, the US government, International Monetary Fund, and World Bank pledged $25 billion in emergency loans. Shortly thereafter, Zedillo announced an emergency economic package called the "pacto" that included reduced government spending, increased sales of government-run businesses, and a freeze on wage increases.

By 2000, there were signs that Mexico's economy had stabilized. Gross domestic product was increasing at an average annual rate of 24 percent and unemployment was low at slightly more than 2 percent (see Exhibit 7). Interest rates and inflation were also low by historical standards (24 and 17 percent in 1999), far below their highs of 61 and 35 percent in 1995. Interest rates and inflation were, however, still considerably higher than in the United States. Higher relative interest rates and inflation put continued pressure on the peso to depreciate against the dollar. This led to higher import prices and contributed to inflation.

A number of social concerns also plagued President Zedillo's government. These included a lack of success in controlling organized crime surrounding the drug trade, high profile political murders (e.g., the murder of a Roman Catholic Cardinal at the Guadalajara airport in 1993), and a high poverty rate, particularly in southern Mexico. These social problems, and voters' disenchantment over allegations of continued political corruption, led to strong opposition to the ruling PRI. In 2000, the PRI lost its first presidential election in five decades when Vicente Fox, leader of the opposition National

| Exhibit 7 | Mexico—Selected Economic Data (Annual Growth Rates) |

	1994	1995	1996	1997	1998	1999	Annual Growth Rate
Population (millions)	93	91	97	96	100	102	2%
Gross domestic product	13%	29%	36%	27%	19%	21%	24%
Money supply (M1)	4%	5%	43%	33%	19%	26%	22%
Inflation (CPI)	7%	35%	34%	21%	16%	17%	22%
Money market rate	17%	61%	34%	22%	27%	24%	31%
Peso devaluation against $US	71%	44%	3%	3%	22%	−4%	23%
Unemployment rate	3.6%	4.7%	3.7%	2.6%	2.3%	n/a	

SOURCE: International Monetary Fund, *International Financial Statistics*, 2000.

Action Party, was elected president. Fox took office on December 1, 2000.

Risks and Opportunities

KFC faced a variety of risks and opportunities in Mexico. It had eliminated all of its franchises in Mexico and operated only company-owned restaurants that enabled it to better control quality, service, and restaurant cleanliness. Company-owned restaurants, however, required more capital than franchises. This meant that KFC would not be able to expand as quickly as it could using a franchised restaurant base. KFC still had the largest number of restaurants in Mexico of any fast-food chain. However, McDonald's was growing its restaurant base rapidly and was beating KFC in terms of sales. KFC's other major competitors included Burger King and El Pollo Loco ("The Crazy Chicken"). Wendy's had also announced plans to open 100 restaurants in Mexico by 2010, though Wendy's emphasis in Latin America continued to be in Venezuela and Argentina. Another threat came from Habib's, Brazil's second largest fast-food chain, which opened its first restaurant in Mexico in 2000. Habib's served traditional Middle Eastern dishes such as falafel, hummus, kafka, and tabbouleh at prices below KFC or McDonald's. It planned to open 400 units in Mexico between 2000 and 2005.

Another concern was the long-term value of the peso, which had depreciated at an average annual rate of 23 percent against the US dollar since NAFTA went into effect. This translation risk lowered Tricon Global's reported profits when peso profits were translated into dollars. It also damaged Tricon Global's stock price. From an operational point of view, however, KFC's Mexico operations were largely insulated from currency fluctuations, because it supplied most of its needs using Mexican sources. KFC purchased chicken primarily from Tyson Foods, which operated two chicken processing plants in Mexico. Tyson was also the primary supplier of chicken to McDonald's, Burger King, Applebee's, and Wal-Mart in Mexico.

KFC faced difficult decisions surrounding the design and implementation of an effective Latin American strategy over the next twenty years. It wanted to sustain its leadership position in Mexico and the Caribbean, but it also hoped to strengthen its position in other regions in South America. Limited resources and cash flow, however, limited KFC's ability to aggressively expand in all countries simultaneously. What should KFC's Latin American strategy be? KFC's strategy in 2001 focused on sustaining its position in Mexico and the Caribbean, but postponed plans to expand into other large markets like Venezuela, Brazil, and Argentina. This strategy carried significant risk, since McDonald's and Wendy's were already building first mover advantages there. A second strategy was to invest more capital in these large markets to challenge existing competitors, but such a strategy might risk KFC's leadership position in Mexico and the Caribbean. Another strategy was to focus on building a franchise base throughout Latin America, in order to build KFC's brand image and prevent competitors from establishing first mover advantages. This strategy, however, was less effective in building a significant market share in individual countries, since market leadership often required a country subsidiary that actively managed both franchised and company owned restaurants and took advantage of synergies in purchasing, operations, and advertising. A country subsidiary could only be justified if KFC had a large restaurant base in the targeted country. KFC's Latin

American strategy required considerable analysis and thought about how to most efficiently use its resources. It also required an in-depth analysis of country risk and selection of the right country portfolio.

References

General References

Direction of Trade Statistics, International Monetary Fund, Washington, DC.

International Financial Statistics, International Monetary Fund, Washington, DC.

Miller, Kent D., "A Framework for Integrated Risk Management in International Business," *Journal of International Business Studies*, vol. 23, no. 2, pages 311–331, 1992.

Standard & Poor's Industry Surveys, Standard & Poor's Corporation, New York, NY.

Quickservice Restaurant Trends, National Restaurant Association, Washington, DC.

Periodicals

FIU Hospitality Review, FIU Hospitality Review, Inc., Miami, FL.

IFMA Word, International Foodservice Manufacturers Association, Chicago, IL.

Independent Restaurant, EIP, Madison, WI.

Journal of Nutrition in Recipe & Menu Development, Food Product Press, Binghamton, NY.

Nation's Restaurant News, Lebhar-Friedman, Inc., New York, NY (http://www.nrn.com).

Restaurant Business, Bill Communications Inc., New York, NY (http://www.restaurant.biz.com).

Restaurants & Institutions, Cahners Publishing Co., New York, NY (http://www.restaurantsandinstitutions.com).

Restaurants USA, National Restaurant Association, Washington, DC. (http://www.restaurant.org).

Associations

National Restaurant Association, 1200 17th St. NW, Washington, D.C. 20036-3097, (202) 331-5900, http://www.restaurant.org.

International Franchise Association, 1350 New York Ave. NW, Suite 900, Washington, DC. 20005-4709, (202) 628-8000, http://www.franchise.org.

Books

Dave's Way: A New Approach to Old-Fashioned Success, by R. David Thomas (founder of Wendy's), Berkley Publishing Group, 1992.

Golden Arches East: McDonald's in East Asia, by James L. Watson (ed.), Stanford University Press, Palo Alto, CA, 1998.

Grinding It Out: The Making of McDonald's, by Ray Kroc (founder of McDonald's) and Robert Anderson, St. Martins, 1990.

I'd Like the World to Buy a Coke: The Life and Leadership of Roberto Goizueta, by David Greising, John Wiley & Sons, 1999.

It's Easier to Succeed than to Fail, by S. Truett Cathy (founder of Chick-fil-A), Oliver-Nelson Books, Nashville, TN, 1989.

Kentucky Fried Chicken Japan Ltd.: International Competitive Benchmarks and Financial Gap Analysis, by Icon Group Ltd., 2000.

Kentucky Fried Chicken Japan Ltd.: Labor Productivity Benchmarks and International Gap Analysis, by Icon Group Ltd., 2000.

McDonaldization Revisited, by Mark Alfino, John S. Caputo, and Robin Wynyard (eds.), Greenwood Publishing Group, 1998.

McDonald's Behind the Arches, by John F. Love, Bantam Books, 1986, 1995, 1999.

Selling 'Em by the Sack: White Castle and the Creation of American Food, by David Gerard Hogan, New York University Press, 1999.

Taco Titan: The Glen Bell Story, by Debra Lee Baldwin, Summit Publishing Group, 1999.

The Globalization Reader, by Frank Lechner and John Boli (eds.), Blackwell Publishing, 2000.

The McDonald's Thesis: Explorations and Extensions, by George Ritzer, Sage Publications, 1998.

The McDonaldization of Society: An Investigation into the Changing Character of Contemporary Social Life, by George Ritzer, Pine Forge Press, 1995.

Web Pages

Boston Market Corporation (http://www.bostonmarket.com).

Burger King Corporation (http://www.burgerking.com).

Chick-fil-A (http://www.chickfila.com).

Church's Chicken (http://www.churchs.com).

McDonald's Corporation (http://www.mcdonalds.com).

Popeyes Chicken & Biscuits (http://www.popeyes.com).

Tricon Global Restaurants, Inc. (http://www.triconglobal.com).

Wendy's International Incorporated (http://www.wendys.com).

Luby's Cafeterias: Will Changing the Recipe Improve Performance?

Richard Menger

St. Mary's University

Introduction

On New Year's Day 1999, Barry Parker didn't have the luxury of spending all day watching football games. In one week, on January 9, he would be facing the shareholders of San Antonio, Texas-based Luby's Cafeterias for the second time as president/CEO. Parker thought about how he would address shareholders' and analysts' concerns regarding the firm's continuing decline in performance: net income had fallen 87 percent while revenues had increased 30 percent since 1994 and its stock price was down 37 percent from its 1996 high of $25.25, closing yesterday at $15.88. Could he continue to leave operations basically the way they were and just continue to squeeze out more costs or did the changes need to be more drastic? What could he do to improve Luby's operating performance and, at the same time, have a positive effect on its stock price? Could performance improvement be gradual or were dramatic improvements needed to increase Luby's stock price to the $20 to $25 range?

Background

Luby's was founded in 1911 in Springfield, Missouri; by 1920, the firm was operating seven locations in Missouri and Oklahoma. This number increased over the next 87 years so that, by year-end 1998, Luby's Cafeterias could be found in 223 locations in 11 states throughout the Midwestern, Southern and Southwestern US.

Luby's shares are listed on the New York Stock Exchange. Of its 11 board members, four could be considered insiders: the president/CEO, the board chairman and two other directors; in addition to Parker, the current president/CEO, each of the other three had previously served either as CEO or acting CEO of Luby's at one point in their careers. The other seven directors are outsiders and bring varied backgrounds to the board.

The 11 directors of Luby's, as a group, held slightly over 1 million shares of Luby's stock or 4.63 percent of all outstanding shares at the close of the firm's 1998 fiscal year. The largest individual shareholder is a company founder who has served on the board since 1959 and has served the company in various capacities since its founding; he holds 3.17 percent of Luby's common shares. The largest Luby's shareholder is NBD Bank (Detroit, Michigan) which holds 5.70 percent of Luby's stock. NBD Bank has sole voting and disposal power over these shares, which are held in advisory and discretionary accounts for investors. Institutional investors held approximately 42 percent of the company's stock.

Company Management

David Daviss, chairman of the board, was elected to his current position in October 1997. Daviss served as acting CEO for six months prior to his election as board chairman and has served as a Luby's director since 1984. Daviss chairs the executive committee and serves on the firm's corporate governance committee.

Barry Parker, president/CEO, joined Luby's in October 1997. He previously had served as chairman of Hoak Capital Corporation and, from 1989 until July 1996, as chairman, president and CEO of County Seat Stores, a casual clothing retailer. Parker is the first outsider to serve as president/CEO of Luby's.

Laura Bishop, senior vice president and chief financial officer since 1997, has served Luby's in various finance-related managerial capacities since 1992.

C.304

Case 22 / Luby's Cafeterias: Will Changing the Recipe Improve Performance?

Robert Burke, senior vice president for marketing, has been with Luby's since 1996. Prior to joining Luby's, Burke was vice president of sales and marketing for Pace Foods, a division of Campbell Soup Company.

Alan Davis, senor vice president for real estate development has served in that capacity since May 1998. Prior to joining Luby's, Davis served as vice president-real estate for Boston Chicken and its real estate subsidiary.

Sue Elliott, senior vice president for human resources has served in that position since May 1998. Prior to joining Luby's, Elliott was vice president of Friday's Hospitality (a national restaurant operator).

Raymond Gabrysch is senior vice president for operations. He has been a Luby's officer since 1988 and served as senior vice president and vice president of human resources, and as an area vice president of the firm prior to assuming his current position in September 1997.

Clyde Hays, senior vice president of operations has been a Luby's officer since 1985. He served as vice president of operations prior to assuming his current position in 1996.

Industry Structure and Rivalry

Luby's competes in the highly competitive and fragmented food service industry. In addition to other cafeteria operators and traditional restaurants which are its primary competitors, Luby's also competes with firms in the fast-food industry and with take-out, prepared food delis in large supermarkets. Firms in this industry also target families that cook and eat at home rather than go to a restaurant to dine or for take-out. It generally is believed that the most important factors in food service competition are the quality of food served relative to its price and the firm's reputation. Other competitive factors include location, marketing and menu variety.

Luby's competitors include not only small, locally owned and operated restaurants, but also include a broad range of national and regional restaurant and fast-food chains with a presence in its markets. A profile of leading regional and national competitors with which Luby's directly competes is presented in Table 1.

Table 1	Luby's Competitors: National and Regional Restaurant Chains
Restaurant/Chain	**Description**
Piccadilly Café	Owns and operates cafeteria-style restaurants under Morrison's and Piccadilly names.
Cooker Restaurant	Owns and operates 62 full-service "Cooker" restaurants in the Midwest and Southeastern US.
Bob Evans Farms	Operates full-service, family restaurants under the Bob Evans Restaurants, Bob Evans Restaurant & General Stores and Owens Family Restaurant names. The Restaurant & General Stores feature a combined restaurant and gift shop.
Sizzler International	Owns, operates, franchises and joint ventures Sizzler Restaurants in the US. Also owns and operates KFC in Australia.
Shoney's	Diversified food service chain that consists of three restaurant divisions: Shoney's, Captain D's and a casual dining group. It operates two casual dining restaurant concepts: Fifth Quarter (steakhouse) and Pargo's (fresh, made-from-scratch dishes).
Darden Restaurants	World's largest full service restaurant operation with 1,118 restaurants in 49 states. It operates 648 Red Lobster, 461 The Olive Garden, 6 The Olive Garden Café and 3 Bahama Breeze Restaurants.
Star Buffet	Owns and operates 16 franchised Home Town Buffet restaurants, 7 JJ North Grand Buffets and 2 Casa Bonita Mexican-themed restaurants.
Ryans Family	Develops, operates and franchises Ryans Family Restaurants featuring steaks, buffet and bakery.
Garden Fresh	Operates 58 buffet-style restaurants in the Western, Southwestern and Southern US under the Souplantation and Sweet Tomatoes names. Restaurants feature fresh salads and other complementary foods.
Furr's/Bishop's	Regional operator of family-style cafeteria restaurants in regional US markets.

SOURCE: StockSelector Industry Comparison <http://www.stockselector.com/industrycomp.asp?symbol=lub>. May 19, 1999.

Until 1991, Luby's spent less than 0.5 percent of sales on marketing, relying instead on customers' word-of-mouth advertising and community relations activities to promote its business. From 1991 through 1998, it maintained its marketing budget at 2 percent of sales. The majority of this budget—approximately $1 million in fiscal year 1998—was designated for radio and television advertising, including the promotion of product/menu-specific promotions and also supported increased local marketing activities by individual cafeterias. Beginning in fiscal year 1999, Luby's increased its marketing budget to 2.5 percent of sales.

Historically, Luby's strategy for expanding into new markets or for increasing its penetration of existing markets generally can be described as greenfield ventures. New sites were purchased or acquired under long-term leases in markets perceived as being attractive for entry or expansion and new cafeterias were built. In 1997, in a departure from its standard approach, Luby's purchased 20 Wyatt Cafeterias from Triangle Food Service Corporation for $14 million in a cash acquisition. An additional $5 million was spent to refurbish the acquired units and 15 were reopened under the Luby's Cafeteria name.

The cost to open a new Luby's Cafeteria ranges from $1.2 million to $1.4 million for leased facilities and $2.5 million to $2.7 million for free-standing cafeterias, including land cost. A typical Luby's Cafeteria seats 250 to 300 guests and contains 9,000 to 10,500 square feet of floor space.

As a means of diversifying, Luby's entered into a joint venture with Waterstreet, Inc, an operator of seafood restaurants in Corpus Christi, Fort Worth and San Antonio, Texas in 1996. The venture calls for up to five Waterstreet Seafood Company restaurants to be opened during the term of the venture. Four restaurants have been opened in San Antonio, Austin, Houston and Lewisville, Texas; the Houston restaurant was closed within 12 months.

Company Operations

At year-end 1998, Luby's operated 223 cafeterias in 11 states as shown in Exhibit 1. Of these, 133 were at loca-

---

Exhibit 1   Locations of Luby's Cafeteria

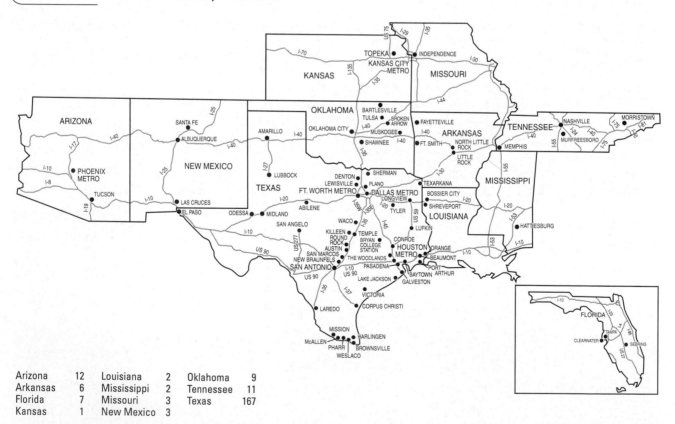

Arizona	12	Louisiana	2	Oklahoma	9
Arkansas	6	Mississippi	2	Tennessee	11
Florida	7	Missouri	3	Texas	167
Kansas	1	New Mexico	3		

SOURCE: Luby's Cafeterias, Inc. <http://www.lubys.com>.

Case 22 / Luby's Cafeterias: Will Changing the Recipe Improve Performance?

tions where the land and improvements are owned by the company; 90 occupied leased premises.

Each Luby's Cafeteria operates as a separate unit under the control of a manager who is responsible for day-to-day operations, including food purchasing, menu planning, employment and supervision. Of 223 cafeteria managers, 177 (80 percent of all cafeteria managers) have been employed by Luby's for more than 10 years. Cafeteria managers are compensated with a salary plus a share of their cafeteria's annual profits, regardless of profit changes, positive or negative.

Each Luby's Cafeteria prepares substantially all of the food served, including breads and pastries. Company policy allows each manager to buy the ingredients for his or her cafeteria from vendors of his or her choosing, even though this potentially could have a negative effect on costs, prices and product quality. Managers supervise the preparation of some 12 to 14 entrees, 12 to 14 vegetable dishes, 15 to 20 salads and 18 to 20 deserts daily and decide on each day's menu which generally differs from cafeteria to cafeteria. A standard set of recipes is used, with variations to meet local tastes. As one example of Luby's in-house food preparation tradition, 1300 employees in more than 90 percent of the cafeterias (10 percent of Luby's workforce) spend part of their day making mayonnaise from scratch.

Quality control teams are used to help maintain uniform food-preparation standards throughout the chain. These quality teams visit cafeterias periodically to check adherence to company recipes, train personnel in new techniques and evaluate new procedures for possible adoption throughout the chain.

Luby's conducts training in its San Antonio training facilities. Training represents a combination of both classroom and on-the-job training and recently has been expanded to include satellite-based training in key restaurants to make training more accessible at the local level.

Luby's has approximately 12,800 employees. This includes some 11,900 non-management cafeteria workers, 739 cafeteria managers/associate managers/assistant managers and 142 executive/administrative staff at the firm's San Antonio, Texas headquarters. Employee relations are considered excellent. Luby's never has had a strike or work stoppage and is not subject to any collective bargaining agreements.

Operating Performance

Luby's operating performance has declined significantly in the previous two fiscal years. While revenues increased 13 percent, from $450 million in 1996 to $509 million in 1998, net income declined 87 percent, from $39.2

million to $5.1 million during the same period. The average sales volume for all cafeterias open during both 1997 and 1998 increased only slightly to $2.250 million average sales per cafeteria in 1998 from $2.244 million average sales per cafeteria in 1997. Luby's 1998 sales of $509 million represented slightly less than one percent of total restaurant industry sales.

Same-store customer counts declined by one percent in fiscal year 1998, the second consecutive year that these counts had declined. However, this decline was offset by higher per customer/tray revenues and the effects of a 3.5 percent price increase instituted in 1996. During the 1996–1998 period, food costs increased by 17.3 percent; this followed a 12 percent increase during the 1994–1996 period.

The major increase in expenses for Luby's during fiscal years 1997 and 1998 was the provision for store closings, which totaled $36.9 million in 1998, up from $12.4 million in 1997 and zero in fiscal years 1994–1996. The provision included approximately $15 million to close 14 under-performing cafeterias, $11 million to relocate 16 cafeterias to improve their performance and $11 million to write down the value of properties which will continue to operate. In fiscal year 1998, Luby's closed five cafeterias and opened five; they planned to open six and close 12 cafeterias in fiscal 1999. Income statements for fiscal years 1994–1998 are provided in Table 2.

Luby's stock price appeared to reflect its deteriorating financial performance. Over the four-year period, 1995–1998, Luby's stock price generally has drifted lower. During Luby's 1996 fiscal year, its stock price ranged from a low of $19.88 to a high of $25.25; from a low of $17.63 to a high of $24.38 in fiscal year 1997; and, from a low of $15.25 to a high of $21.38 in fiscal year 1998, ending the year at $15.88.

Despite the downward trend in its stock price, Luby's appeared to have outperformed its industry peer group as illustrated in Table 3. Stock market and operating performance data for Luby's, the restaurant industry and its peer groups are presented in Exhibits 1 and 2, respectively. Luby's stock price ranges by quarter for fiscal years 1996, 1997 and 1998, and the year-end 1998 closing price are shown in Exhibit 3.

Getting Ready for the Shareholders Meeting

As Parker reflected on Luby's continued decline in performance during his 15-month tenure as president/CEO, he asked himself what more could be done to improve the firm's operating performance so that its stock price would increase.

	1994	1995	1996	1997	1998
Revenues	$390,692	$419,024	$450,128	$495,446	$508,871
Costs/expenses:					
Food	98,223	103,611	110,008	121,287	129,126
Payroll & related	104,543	113,952	124,333	146,940	155,152
Occupancy	113,546	123,907	132,595	150,638	154,501
Provision for Store Closings	–	–	–	12,432	36,852
General & Administrative	15,330	18,672	20,217	19,451	22,061
Total Operating expenses	331,642	360,142	387,153	450,748	497,692
Income from operations	59,050	58,882	62,975	44,968	11,179
Net Income	$ 39,335	$ 37,015	$39,208	$ 28,447	$ 5,081

Note: Luby's fiscal year ends August 31.
SOURCE: Luby's Cafeterias, Inc. *Form 10-K* for the fiscal years ended August 31, 1997 and August 31, 1998.

Parker wondered if it would be practical to use the activity or value chain framework—a concept he recalled from his college days—as a tool to analyze Luby's operations. He felt that this might be a useful way to disaggregate the activities performed by the firm and minimize the likelihood of overlooking any opportunities to make changes that would reduce costs or increase value.

Parker immediately recognized that there should be significant economies available from changing the way that food purchasing was structured. Should he consider reducing individual cafeteria managers' control by cen-

Table 3 | Luby's Stock Market Performance Relative to its Peer Groups

Five-year Cumulative Return[1]

Year	Luby's	1998 Peer Group[2]	1997 Peer Group[3]	S&P Small Cap 600
1993	$100	$100	$100	$100
1994	94	76	78	104
1995	82	65	66	127
1996	100	54	61	144
1997	87	55	56	193
1998	70	52	52	134

Notes: 1. Cumulative total shareholder return computations assume the investment of $100 on August 31, 1993 and the reinvestment of all dividends. Returns for each individual peer group-firm have been weighted according each firm's stock market capitalization.
2. Firms in the 1998 Peer Group are Bob Evans Farms, Inc., Buffets, Inc., Furr's/Bishop's, Inc., Piccadilly Cafeterias, Inc., Ryan's Family Steakhouses, Inc., Shoney's, Inc. and Sizzler International, Inc. Peer companies are multiunit family restaurant operators in the mid-price range with similar stock market capitalization.
3. Firms in the 1997 Peer Group are Buffets, Inc., Piccadilly Cafeterias, Inc., Ryan's Family Steakhouses, Inc., Shoney's Inc., Sizzler International, Inc. and Vicorp Restaurants, Inc. Peer companies are multiunit family restaurant operators in the mid-price range with similar stock market capitalization.
SOURCE: Luby's Cafeteria, Inc. *Schedule 14A*, December 1, 1998.

Exhibit 2 | Comparative Stock Market Performance Data, 1993–1998

Market Measure	Luby's	Industry
PE ratio	79.3	6.3
PE based on fiscal year estimate	12.8	15.9
PE based on next year's estimate	11.5	14.5
Price to book value	2.0	2.1
Dividend yield	4.6%	.3%
Institutional ownership	42.1%	35.4%
Insider ownership	5.9%	18.7%
Short interest ratio	1.5	2.0
Beta	.6	.8
One-year return	1.3%	(9.8)%
Five-year return	(7.8)%	36.9%

SOURCE: Stock Selector Industry Comparison <http://www.stockselector.com/industrycomp.asp?symbol=lub.>, May 19, 1999.

Exhibit 3 | Comparative Balance Sheet and Performance Ratios, 1997–1998

Performance Measure	Luby's	Industry
Debt-to-Equity	.5	2.5
Historical Growth Rate	(3.2)%	14.0%
Estimated Growth Rate	9.0%	19.0%
Return on Equity	2.4%	13.3%
Return on Assets	1.4%	.4%
Return on Investment	11.0%	8.6%
Profit Margin	.9%	(.3)%

SOURCE: StockSelector Industry Comparison. <http://www.stockselector.com/industrycomp.asp?symbol=lub.>, May 19, 1999.

tralizing food purchasing activities to reduce food costs? If so, what savings might be possible? In a similar vein, he wondered if costs could be reduced further by finding an outside supplier or manufacturer to eliminate the need to make mayonnaise in house without sacrificing quality or flavor (mayonnaise is a key ingredient in several salad dressings, tartar sauce and basting recipes for fish entrees).

Parker also realized that, if the firm reduced the responsibilities of individual cafeteria managers by centralizing food purchasing, they also would have to make changes to their managers' compensation scheme. Under the current scheme, all cafeteria managers were eligible for a bonus based on their individual cafeteria's profits. He wondered how the compensation system could be modified to offset any negative effects from eliminating managers' food purchasing responsibilities

and, at the same time, provide individual managers with better performance incentives. While selling such a change might meet with some resistance, Parker felt that a change could be sold based on equalizing bonus-related opportunities for all managers, especially if managers in high tax, high rent locations saw their chances of earning a bonus improve under a new system.

Although the provision for store closings was high ($36.85 million in 1998), Parker wondered if additional cafeterias should either be closed or relocated. If so, what criteria should he use to make those decisions?

The vast majority of Luby's Cafeterias were located in major metropolitan areas. Parker and others often had entertained the idea of entering some of the smaller communities in their primary marketing areas. If so, could these smaller communities support a standard-

Fiscal Quarters ended	High	Low
November 30, 1995	$22.88	$19.88
February 29, 1996	23.00	20.13
May 31, 1996	25.25	20.38
August 31, 1996	25.25	22.50
November 30, 1996	24.38	20.75
February 28, 1997	22.88	19.88
May 31, 1997	20.63	17.63
August 31, 1997	20.63	18.81
November 30, 1997	21.38	18.88
February 28, 1998	19.69	16.00
May 31, 1998	19.50	17.13
August 31, 1998	18.94	15.25
November 30, 1998	16.13	13.25
December 31, 1998[1]	15.88[2]	13.25

Notes: 1. This represents the price range for only one month of the firm's fiscal 1999 second quarter.
2. The closing price at the time of the case's decision scenario is $15.88

SOURCE: Luby's Cafeteria, Inc. *Form 10-K* for fiscal years ended August 31, 1997 and August 31, 1998; *Wall Street Journal*, 1999 (January 4).

size Luby's or should the firm consider experimenting with smaller-sized facilities to better match firm offerings with a community's population characteristics? What advantages could expansion into smaller, rural markets provide?

As he thought about how food was delivered and sold, Parker recalled that approximately 90 percent of all meals sold by fast-food restaurants were sold through drive-throughs or as take-out during the mid-1990s. He wondered if these same ideas could be used to provide additional convenience to customers and improve sales at Luby's and which cafeterias might prove to be the best prospects for adding drive-through capability. Specifically, he wondered, should Luby's experiment with drive-through sales? In addition, Parker also thought that it might be useful to expand the take-out facilities for customers who did not choose to stay and eat their meal at the cafeteria.

Parker also felt that he should have someone interpret the information available regarding Luby's performance relative to the restaurant industry and its peer group to determine how significant the impact of these changes on Luby's performance might have to be to regain the confidence of individual and institutional shareholders and analysts so that the stock price would reverse its downward trend.

After jotting down these ideas, Parker decided that, on Monday morning, he would ask a group of recently hired management trainees to look over his notes and prepare some in-depth recommendations that he could use to prepare for questions from shareholders and to write his speech for next Friday's shareholders' meeting.

Now, he could sit back and enjoy New Year's Day with a clear conscience.

References

Horovitz, B. 1999 (May 20). Food chains stake out their 'share of stomach.' *USA Today*, p. B1.

Industry Comparison for LUB, 1999 (May 17). StockSelector. <http://www.stockselector.com/industrycomp.asp?symbol=lub>.

Luby's Cafeterias, Inc. *Form 10-K* for the fiscal year ended August 31, 1997.

Luby's Cafeterias, Inc. *Form 10-K* for the fiscal year ended August 31, 1998.

Luby's Cafeterias, Inc. <http://www.lubys.com>.

Luby's Cafeterias, Inc. *Schedule 14A*, December 1, 1998.

Weil, J. 1999 (April 7). After some stale years, Luby's may have a recipe for success. *Wall Street Journal*, p. T2.

Lufthansa 2000
Maintaining the Change Momentum

Dr. Heike Bruch

University of St. Gallen (Switzerland)

Abstract

In 1991 Lufthansa was almost bankrupt. Eight years later, at the general business meeting on the 16th of June 1999 Jürgen Weber (CEO) announced record results in Lufthansa's more than 70-year history. In eight years, the company had gone from the brink of bankruptcy to becoming one of the world's leading airline companies, a founding member of the STAR ALLIANCE—the airline industry's most comprehensive network—aspiring to become the leading aviation group in the world.

Lufthansa had undergone some radical changes that reversed a record loss of DM 730 million in 1992 to a record pre-tax profit of DM 2.5 billion in 1998 (an increase of 42 percent compared to 1997 when the pre-tax profit was DM 1.75 billion). Revenues increased by 4.8 percent, from DM 21.6 billion in 1997, to DM 22.7 billion in 1998. The Seat Load Factor (SLF—proportion of seats filled) reached 73 percent, a record performance in Lufthansa's history (1.5 percentage points increased compared to 1997 and 9 percentage points increase compared to 1991).

After the first step of the turnaround it was apparent that transformation had just begun and that a much more fundamental change had to follow to assure the company's future. The Lufthansa Executive Board (Vorstand) and the Supervisory Board (Aufsichstrat) decided to follow a concept of sustaining renewal (redevelopment) at 3 levels, operational, structural, and strategic. In 1999, none of these processes were fully completed. In fact, sustaining the change process was seen as the key management challenge.

This case was written in co-operation between LBS and Lufthansa School of Business by Dr. Heike Bruch, Visiting Scholar at LBS from the University of St. Gallen (Switzerland), under the supervision of Prof. Sumantra Ghoshal. It is intended to be used as a basis of discussion rather than to illustrate either effective or ineffective handling of a business solution.
© **London Business School**
Sussex Place, Regent's Park, London NW1 4SA, United Kingdom
Lufthansa School of Business
Lufthansaring 1, 64342 Seeheim-Jugenheim, Germany
January 2001
Distributed by The European Clearing House, England and USA.
North America, phone +1 781 239 5884, fax: +1 781 239 5885, e-mail: ECCHBabson@aol.com.
Rest of the World, phone: +44 (0)1234 750903, fax: +44 (0)1234 751125, e-mail: ECCH@cranfield.ac.uk.
All rights reserved. Printed in UK and USA. Web Site: http://www.ecch.cranfield.ac.uk.

Lufthansa 2000: Maintaining the Change Momentum

In 1991 Lufthansa was almost bankrupt. It was *the* national airline carrier of the Federal Republic of Germany, state owned, monolithic, and unprofitable.

Eight years later, in 1999, it was a privately owned, profitable company, a core element of the strongest world-wide alliance in the airline industry, aspiring to become the leading aviation group in the world. During the years of 1992–1999, Lufthansa went from a record loss of DM 730 million to a record profit of DM 2.5 billion (Appendix 1). The number of passengers increased from 33.7 million in 1992 to 40.5 million in 1998, while the number of employees decreased from about 64000 in 1992 to about 55000 in 1998.

Recent History
Era before Weber

Founded in 1926, liquidated in 1945 and reborn in 1953, Lufthansa historically represented the characteristic strengths of German industry: a strong focus on reliability, order and technical excellence. Majority owned by the German state, its strategy, organization and culture represented an amalgam of a strong technical orientation, dominated by engineers, together with the bureaucratic values of public administration. It's role as an organ of the state was reflected in its values and beliefs: formal, rule-driven and inflexible, the yellow badges of Lufthansa symbolized independence, permanence and sovereign dignity.

In the second half of the 1980's, under the leadership of Heinz Ruhnau, Lufthansa pursued a policy of "growth through own strength." Based on the belief that only the largest airlines will survive in an era of global competition, Ruhnau had committed the airline to a rapid fleet expansion in order to capture market share. When Jürgen Weber was appointed as CEO in 1991, Lufthansa had enlarged its fleet by some 120 aircrafts to 275.

Gulf War and the Break Down of the Aviation Market

In the late 80s, deregulation triggered intensive price competition. This process, coupled with the steep fall in air traffic during the Gulf War and the subsequent recession, led to a serious over-capacity for the airline industry on a global basis, and severe market slump in Europe. In 1991, the Seat Load Factor (SLF—proportion of available seats filled) went down to about 57 percent in Europe, compared to a world-wide average of about 65 percent.

The problem was aggravated because of a remarkable inflexibility concerning capacities and services offered. Deregulation of the airline industry started in 1978 in the US. In Europe, in contrast, while there were some relaxation in regulations, over the 1980's most airlines continued to be owned by their respective national governments who continued to maintain strict control over both routes and landing slots at airports.

Reunification and Plans for Growth

Lufthansa noticed the crisis later than other companies. Because of the German reunification, Lufthansa enjoyed a boom at a time when the rest of the industry faced this severe market downturn.

In 1991, while overall traffic dropped by 9 percent in Europe, Lufthansa had an increase of passenger numbers by 11 percent because of the German reunification. But despite this growth, Lufthansa reported an after-tax loss of DM 444 million in 1991. This result was largely attributed to unique non-influenceable factors like the Gulf war. But results in the second half of 1991 and in the beginning of 1992 also fell below expectations. Although an awareness of a serious crisis began to spread in early 1992, Lufthansa was so programmed on growth and success that employment continued to rise during the first six months. Being a state owned company, immortality was taken for granted.

Even when the crisis became very obvious people still thought: 'We are the German Airline Company, state owned and a prestige organisation. They will never let us

die.' (Jochen Hoftmann, Senior Vice President & Executive Vice President Personnel and Labour Relations, Deutsche Lufthansa AG)

The Turnaround
Bankruptcy

Outsiders were not so sure about the survival of Lufthansa. In 1992, with only 14 days of operating cash requirements in hand, Jürgen Weber went to all the major German banks asking them for money to pay employee salaries. No private bank believed in the survival of Lufthansa: only a single state owned institution—the Kreditanstalt für Wiederaufbau—agreed to give Lufthansa the money it needed to pay its people.

Redevelopment Workshops

The starting point of the redevelopment concept was a four-week management program about change management, which at the same time was also the birthplace of a group called the "Samurai of Change". The members of this group discussed the results of the program with Jürgen Weber and convinced him of the urgency of a redevelopment process.

On a weekend in June 1992, as a result, Weber invited about 20 senior managers to the training centre at Seeheim[1] for a meeting that was originally entitled "Mental Change". It was aimed at building a network of change-minded managers who would drive the redevelopment process within the company. Shortly before the workshop Jürgen Weber got a deeper insight into the acuteness of the crisis and changed the title from "mental change" to "crisis management meeting". The turnaround began.

The process of this meeting was as important as the outcome. For some managers this Seeheim crisis management meeting was one of their first experiences with interdepartmental co-operation and non-bureaucratic problem solving. The opinions concerning the necessity of drastic actions and the directions of change did not differ much. Facts were too obvious.

"No one had an idea of the gravity and the brutality of the crisis. After a long phase of denial or 'not wanting to believe', there was a next phase of "searching for the guilty people" which was followed by an awareness that there was a massive pressure to act. After this, everything went very fast. The goals we committed ourselves to at Seeheim were very ambitious and nobody believed that we could ever meet them, but after this process we committed ourselves to them. The critical question was how to win over other managers and employees for these 'stretching'

goals and activities." (Wolfgang Mayrhuber, CEO Lufthansa Technik AG and former member of the Operations Team)

One way to involve a larger group of managers was to repeat the Seeheim workshop three times with different groups of 50 people. This was done in order to let them live through the same process, let them feel the threat and the urgency and not just inform them of the facts and the appropriate strategy which they had to implement. After the meetings the majority of senior managers within the company were convinced of the necessity for drastic change and committed to a set of extremely ambitious goals.

"In the turnaround we have consciously tried to win the commitment of people through workshops, Town Meetings etc. With everything I do, I try to demonstrate that at first we have to reach the emotional mobilisation before a rational mobilisation becomes possible at all. Briefly one could say: Hard success through soft processes." (Dr. Heiko Lange, Chief Executive Personnel, Deutsche Lufthansa AG)

"The most important decision was downsizing the fleet, which meant putting aeroplanes into the desert. This was a completely unconventional step. It was necessary for the second important decision: the reduction of staff which also demanded a complete change in mentality because it was simply the opposite of what we had planned." (Dr. Peter Hach, Senior Vice President Corporate Controlling)

The output of the Seeheim meetings was a set of 131 projects or key actions concerning drastic cuts in staff numbers (8000 positions), lower non-personnel costs including downsizing of the fleet (savings of DM 400 million), and increasing revenues (DM 700 million) in order to reduce the losses of DM 1.3 billion. To implement these actions, Lufthansa adopted the idea of Town Meetings and Jürgen Weber decided to hold as many such meetings himself as possible when visiting different Lufthansa units. By the summer of 1999 he had personally participated in over 200 Town Meetings.

Other senior managers also held Town Meetings in their departments and, in 1999, this practice still remained very prevalent all over the Lufthansa organisation.

Town Meetings

Lufthansa Town Meetings follow a certain structure: When they take place in a foreign country, Jürgen Weber first gets together with key contacts (e.g. transport ministers) and then meets key customers. After this he talks to the local Lufthansa management about their situation, problems, plans, etc. Finally the main item of the agenda is a long and intensive dialogue with the employees. Jürgen Weber explains to them the latest plans and the staff ask questions and present their perspectives on problems and potential improvements.

"It was decisive for the turnaround that we told the employees openly what the situation was. It allowed us to develop common goals between employees, management, work councils, and unions. We could even discuss issues such as staff reduction and productivity increase openly and personally." (Jürgen Weber, Chairman and CEO, Deutsche Lufthansa AG)

"Jürgen Weber wins people personally by his open and authentic communication. He tells them the unvarnished figures and explains how he feels about them. During the turnaround phase, he told them that every morning when looking into the mirror he had an overwhelming feeling of responsibility knowing that Lufthansa would again 'produce' DM 4 million of losses that day. There was a staff of 60000 and an average of 2 or 3 other people with them depending on Lufthansa, so that he was responsible for 2000000 people. That gave him the enormous urge to change the situation. . . . People are taken by his leadership emotionally and willing to go the way Jürgen Weber points them because they simply understand what he says. It is ingenious because it is so simple. However, it works!" (Ursel Reininger, Staff Manager, Chairman's Office)

"With an almost superhuman involvement Jürgen Weber was getting in contact with people in order to make clear that we were in a serious crisis. The explicit articulation of the crisis was one of the central 'events' in the turnaround. Another important aspect was the direct dialogue with the employees. There was a saying in those days: 'Schlede[2] is collecting the money, Weber is collecting the people'." (Dr. Hans Schmitz, Chief Executive of the Lufthansa Technik Logistik GmbH)

A second implementation measure was the installation of a special "redevelopment controlling" under the direction of the corporate controller Dr. Peter Hach. This program aimed at monitoring progress and results concerning personnel and non-personnel cost-cutting and the enhancement of revenues.

Last but not least, the Executive Board appointed a group of 12 senior managers representing the main departments of the company—called the San Team (Sanierungsteam = Redevelopment team). This San Team had the task of implementing the 131 projects of "Programm 93". But the team turned out to be too large and not effective enough. Therefore, Jürgen Weber decided to form a smaller and more forceful group. The so-called OPS Team (Operations Team) became an important motor in the implementation process. It consisted at first of Angelika Jakob, head of Cabin Services, Wolfgang Mayrhuber, Technical Director of Lufthansa Maintenance, Matthias Mölleney, Senior Manager Personnel, and an external consultant. Later the OPS Team was joined by Dieter Heinen, Chief of Sales in Germany, and Dr. Christoph Frank, an internal consultant with experience in various change projects. The OPS Team put in enormous effort and succeeded in driving the Programm 93 initiatives into action by defining concrete activities and by constantly monitoring, advising, and supporting the line managers who had the ultimate responsibility for implementation.

Principles of OPS procedures were: *"We made clear that we would not accept excuses. We were pitiless, persistent and unconditional concerning the implementation of the measures. Compared to consultants and the Executive Board we had an important advantage: We knew the company and therefore we had not only personal networks but we also knew what was realistic. We were credible for the people. But the most important factor was that we were sitting in the same boat as them. It was obvious that we did not want to harm them but that we were serious because we had the same personal interest to survive. We did not have a formal hierarchical empowerment—only the power to convince people of the vital necessity of fundamental change."* (Wolfgang Mayrhuber, CEO Lufthansa Technik AG and former member of the OPS Team)

Jürgen Weber showed his unconditional commitment to the OPS Team and personally supported all their needs. His demonstrated involvement with the change process was accompanied by various visible actions such as the Executive Board's waiver of 10 percent of their annual salaries in 1992.

In total, about 70 percent of the 131 Projects of Programme 93 were successfully implemented during the turnaround. The remaining 30 percent were put into action later and implementation was still going on in 1999. Jürgen Weber intentionally did not insist on immediate implementation of the remaining 30 percent in order not to risk the consensus with the unions. The absence of strikes and a high level of consensus between management and other stakeholders, in particular the labour unions, was a remarkable feature of the Lufthansa crisis management. And the same philosophy continued

to influence all the subsequent decisions and actions as the change process continued into the 1990s.

Consensus as a phenomenon of Lufthansa's Soul

"Implementation usually doesn't come easy at Lufthansa. Before you implement anything you need a consensus. More often than not our Executive Board would refuse to decide on an issue because it had not been sufficiently reconciled. 'Open cards' was the outspoken policy of Jürgen Weber. Following that policy we not only achieved a zero pay rise in 1993, but also the privatisation of Lufthansa, the restructuring of our pension scheme, the modernisation of our company structure, and —last but not least—a drastic decrease of workforce resulting in a badly needed increase in productivity. These were dramatic changes. They would never have occurred without the consent of all constituents."[3]

Implementation of staff cuts was the responsibility of line management. For the implementation of Programm 93 it was important that line managers take responsibility for the process in order to realise the unavoidable cuts, on the one hand, and to motivate the remaining employees, on the other hand.

"The most important factor during this hard phase was credibility. This is communication during the crisis. The flying personnel are not only the producing staff but also have direct customer contact. So they should be well informed and must be loyal—even in hard times. This took a lot of energy but was worthwhile." (Jürgen Raps, Senior Vice President Flight Operations and Chief Pilot)

Certainly the cuts of staff caused problems and some very talented "high potentials" left the company because of the perceived threat to their prospects and career aspirations. But, there were also many who concluded exactly the opposite; they were attracted by the challenge to widen the existing scope of thinking and action in order to redevelop Lufthansa in spite of all the difficulties and personal sacrifices needed.

"During the crisis it was a very important experience that working under pressure was also exciting. Nobody complained. On the contrary, people accepted the challenge and really gave their best." (Dr. Peter Jansen, General Manager Costmanagement, Programm 15)

In 1993 the first effects of the effort were noticeable. Numbers of passengers increased, revenues increased, and costs decreased. In November 1993, 18 months after the crisis management meeting, the first success was reported in press and television: "The crane has upwind again."

But Lufthansa was quite aware that the superficial recover could not guarantee a sustaining success and that a more fundamental change had to follow. To secure its future, the company had to deal with some broader issues including strategic cost savings, privatisation, and the organisational structure. Said Weber:

> "We have learned our lesson: don't invest in growth counting on "automatic" economies of scale. Instead, get your costs down first, then hit the market ready and able to fight a price war. We have to achieve cost leadership and are not yet there. That's why we need a second phase in this turnaround: we can't reduce personnel or salaries further or else the good people will leave. So, we have to restructure Lufthansa, to create cost consciousness, to create transparency, and to push responsibility and entrepreneurship to the lowest possible level".

At the outset of the turnaround, Lufthansa had embarked on negotiations with the German government to privatise the airline. One important stumbling block for privatisation was replacing the pension fund "VBL" (VBL—Versorgungsanstalt des Bundes undder Länder) binding Lufthansa to the German state. It was extremely difficult to untie these "golden chains".

> "There were many discussions about VBL and it was quite obvious that it was almost impossible to get out of these obligations. If someone had asked, 80 percent would have said 'You will never achieve this!' But we made it." (Jochen Hoffmann, Senior Vice President & Executive Vice President Personnel and Labour Relations, Deutsche Lufthansa AG)

In May 1994, the problem of the pension fund was resolved. The German government diluted its holdings to 36 percent and agreed to a payment of DM 1 billion into the VBL to cover disbursements to present retirees as well as to offer an allowance and guarantee for constituting a separate Lufthansa pension fund. In 1997, Lufthansa became fully privatised.

Strategic Cost Savings—Programm 15

As a private company, Lufthansa experienced increased pressure to be competitive and strategically cost effective. This pressure became even more acute because of the continuing decline of yields (averaged proceeds per ticket sold), driven by strengthening price competition within the airline industry and a threat of substitution by other transport alternatives (primarily high speed trains). As a strategic answer to these developments

Lufthansa continued its transformation process and started "Programm 15".

Programm 15

Programm 15 was a wide-ranging strategic cost management program, designed to make Lufthansa more competitive through cost management and cultural change. The program's goals included:

- Improving the competitive position through cost reduction
- Internationalisation of cost structure and
- Making staff at every level highly cost-conscious and cost-effective in their daily work.

The number 15 stood for 15 pfennig per SKO ("seat kilometers offered"; the cost target for transporting one aircraft seat one kilometre). Lufthansa intended to reduce its costs from 17.7 pfennig in 1996 to 15 pfennig in 2001. This implied an overall cost reduction of 20 percent within five years (4 percent annual reduction all over the Lufthansa Group). All Lufthansa departments and companies were affected.

Like the OPS team that monitored and maintained progress on Programm 93, a Programm 15 team was put in place and it worked with certain principles that were distinctively applied making use of the experiences of the turnaround:

The rules of the game for the Programm 15-team

- We confront contentious issues.
- We do what we say.
- We prefer facts not prejudices.
- We let ourselves be monitored whenever required.
- We inform continuously and currently— together with the responsible departments.
- We inform managers, employees and their respresentatives before the external public.
- We utilise informal networks to ensure inter-departmental and hierarchy-overlapping communication.
- We try to avoid catchphrases and self-overestimation.

Programm 15 was based on integrated responsibility: The line managers had the responsibility for cost reductions which meant that the achievement of Programm 15 was integrated within their "normal" management objectives and was part of their performance expectations. Programm 15 consciously set stretching goals which were challenging but achievable. Concerning the goals, no compromises were made, but the Programm-15 team consulted line management about the means of cost savings and tried to solve problems through open and honest discussion with those who were responsible for implementation. A tight monitoring and public sharing of results (actual performance data for each individual manager were published regularly) ensured accountability and continuous feedback.

> "Programm 15 had to take into account some issues that could be called 'typically Lufthansa'. One of the characteristic features of the 'Lufthansa style' is the specific combination of consensus orientation and persistence. Nobody tries to force certain solutions and people are willing to compromise but only in terms of the way of goal achievement not concerning the goal itself." (Dr. Peter Jansen, General Manager Costmanagement, Programm 15)

To preserve discipline and attention to strategic cost goals, Programm 15 initiated a number of both symbolic and substantive measures. Those included, for example, the location of its office next to the office of Jürgen Weber, discussions of cost reduction measures in Town Meetings, weekly reports in the "Lufthanseat" (the staff journal), and wide-spread publicity for a few well-selected impressive "success-stories".

Corporate Restructuring

At the beginning of the 90s, Lufthansa was functionally organised with five departments (finance, personnel, maintenance, sales and marketing, and flight operations) each led by a member of the Executive Board (Appendix 2).

This structural solution turned out to be inefficient showing symptoms such as high involvement of top management in operational problems, slow decision processes, lack of accountability, low transparency and, finally, an insufficient market proximity. These problems were enhanced by developments in the external environment—airlines were more and more confronted with time-based competition, price competition, and a need for transparency of products and services.

Lufthansa realised that it could not effectively respond to the emerging competitive challenges with its existing functional structure. The goals of Lufthansa's restructuring process therefore were to increase both market proximity and transparency of costs and proceeds, and to reduce the fragmentation of decision processes. The guiding idea behind the restructuring was that Lufthansa would be more successful as a federative group of independent small units than as a monolithic functional block.

Lufthansa considered various organisational alternatives, both in terms of how to break up the integrated operations into smaller, self-contained units and the specific legal and administrative structures for governance of these units. They key criteria for choosing among these alternatives included detailed assessments of the strategic scope of each business, their needs for entrepreneurial freedom, responsibility and accountability, the role of third party business, and the nature of the resulting internal customer-supplier relationships. Finally three business areas were formally separated as legally autonomous and strategically independent subsidiaries: LH Cargo AG (airfreight), LH Technik AG (technical maintenance service) and LH Systems GmbH (IT Services). These joined the existing subsidiaries CityLine (domestic flights), Condor (charter flights), and LSG Sky Chefs (catering). At the same time the tasks and responsibilities of the Executive Board were redefined by strengthening their strategic focus and giving the core business "Passenger Service" (so-called "Passage") a stronger weight (Appendix 3).

Persistence with the idea of decentralisation led Lufthansa in 1997 to further operational independence of Lufthansa Passenger Service—the original core of the former airline company "Lufthansa". With 26,000 employees, including 12,500 flight personnel in the cockpit and cabin, Lufthansa Passenger Service was restructured as a Profit Centre, to be led and directed by a six member Management Board. While tax and landing slot considerations prevented the Passenger Service business area from becoming a separate legal entity, this restructuring clearly separated the business from day-to-day influence of corporate top management.

In 1999 the Lufthansa Group Management Board directed the activities of the entire Group through three central functions: the Chairman's Office and the Finance and Human Resource Management functions.

Building a Strategic Network— STAR ALLIANCE

Apart from the focus on internal costs and structural redevelopment, Lufthansa constantly worked on its external relationships. Having experienced extreme overcapacities by following the philosophy of "growth through own strength", it decided to choose an alternative strategy: "growth through partnerships".

Lufthansa was one of the central founding members of the most comprehensive and probably the most competitive airline network in the world. Since April 1999, when Air New Zealand and Ansett Australian joined the STAR ALLIANCE, the network included 8 members operating in 720 destinations in 110 countries (Appendix 4). In October 1999, ANA (All Nippon Airways) joined the STAR ALLIANCE. This was an important step for the Asian expansion strategy of the alliance (Appendix 5).

Changing Pattern of Competition in the Airline Industry

The STAR ALLIANCE started functioning in May 1997. By 1999, three other global alliances had emerged: Oneworld, Wings and Qualiflyer (Appendix 6). With the launch of Oneworld in Feb. 1999 competition in the airline industry had taken on a new dimension. This new alliance had five founding members, a common logo and shared the STAR ALLIANCE vision of seamlessly linking the partner airlines' route networks. Lufthansa believed that the Anglo-Saxon culture binding the Oneworld partner airlines could facilitate mutual understanding and shared decision making, making the alliance a potentially cohesive and dynamic force.

Strategically, these developments were of vital importance. At the end of the 20th century, the economic structure of the airline industry was changing from competition between airlines to competition between networks. In consequence, airline networks were striving to intensify integration and common alliance strategies. In 1999, the biggest challenge for STAR ALLIANCE lay in defending its leading position and in expanding its market leadership through integrated network management in a new phase of intensifying competition among the rival networks.

Traditional Advantages of Airline Alliances

Traditionally the core of airline alliances was code-sharing, i.e. using the same flight numbers. In 1999, Lufthansa and United Airlines, for example, served not less than 130 code-share flight destinations. Lufthansa reported that in 1998 a supplement of DM 450 million of revenues was due to the alliance.

Important synergies were also realised through joint sales activities (joint advertising, common frequent flyer programs, joint travel agency contracts etc.), collective market research, shared facilities such as lounges, and staff exchange. The Landlord Concept introduced within the STAR ALLIANCE in 1997 illustrates the nature and extent of these potential benefits. Aimed at developing a common ground service (ticketing and check-in), 27 key hubs were identified world-wide to start this integration process of sharing airport facilities and services under one roof. At each station one carrier was appointed "landlord" and given the responsibility for airport services like check in and ticketing for all the other STAR ALLIANCE members. Since the other airlines did not retain any activity in these hubs, the program implied a take over of the entire staff of all the other partner airlines by the "landlord" airline. For example in November 1997 all the former Lufthansa employees at Copenhagen were transferred to SAS while Lufthansa took all the SAS employees in Frankfurt.

Emergent Challenges—STAR ALLIANCE Management and Strategy

Beyond these traditionally important operational synergies, in 1999 the STAR ALLIANCE was beginning to approach the much more demanding challenges of co-ordinating and integrating strategic activities such as establishing a common global brand, developing a shared technology platform, joint training, and personnel development. While the operating synergies could be managed through ad-hoc teams and task forces, effective co-ordination of these strategic issues required an integrated management structure for the overall alliance as well as a systematic process for co-ordinating the internal strategic activities of all the partners.

In December 1998 the STAR ALLIANCE airlines formed a focused management team to lead the alliance on a day-to-day basis. Until then the alliance activities were co-ordinated by a set of committees and project teams. The presidents of the airlines decided to bundle responsibilities for strategic issues. Jürgen Weber personally championed the need for a permanent management structure in order to give further force and dynamism to the Alliance. The newly appointed Alliance Management Board consisted of six executives who were made responsible for dealing with all the strategic issues of the network and to implement the five-year business plan approved by the airlines' presidents at their meeting in October 1998 in Rio de Janeiro.

There were four key issues of major strategic importance:

- The global network
- Marketing and sales
- Service and product development and
- Information Technology.

The Management Board was chaired by Lufthansa's Friedel Rödig with Bruce Harris of United Airlines serving as his deputy. The other core members of the

Management Board were responsible for specific areas of activity. Ross McCormack of Air Canada was in charge of the global network development, Per Stendenbakken of SAS was responsible for seamless service and product development, Dieter Grotepass of Lufthansa looked after sales strategy, marketing communications and co-ordination of frequent flyer programs, while all issues related to Information Technology and Automation were the responsibility of United's Bruce Parker.

With the new structure in place, the alliance progressed beyond the stage of a committee-based collaboration, but it was not considered sufficient for a true strategic integration. The central question was whether the success of the alliance demanded a fusion of the partners' different corporate cultures:

> "The key issues for the STAR ALLIANCE will be a common training and development of staff in order to support interorganisational learning of partner companies, to build a strong alliance glue and network culture but most of all to create a shared customer obsessed alliance spirit." (Thomas Sattelberger, Corporate Senior Vice President Executive Personnel and Human Resource Development)

Another vital question was how such closer integration within the alliance would affect the other Lufthansa companies. A common network strategy and cultural integration were inevitably connected to critical issues concerning branding and identity within the Lufthansa Group. The specialisation within the STAR ALLIANCE and particularly the planned extension of joint procurement could cause serious economic problems for some of Lufthansa's subsidiaries.

For example the search for synergies within the STAR ALLIANCE included the joint development of IT solutions. In April 1999 the Management Board of the STAR ALLIANCE signed a Memorandum of Intent concerning the formation of a central STAR ALLIANCE IT Organisation. The main task of this organisation would be to develop a common information system for all the STAR ALLIANCE partners. As a first step, a small team of about 20 people would work on this solution. They would be located in one place, thus eliminating the problems of working across different geographies and time-zones. For LH IT Services this development represented a vital threat for their main market.

> "Within the STAR ALLIANCE Management, United Airlines took responsibility for the EDP. Being a monolithic bloc, United Airline embodies its own IT department which is supposed to take charge of the entire STAR ALLIANCE IT-solution. The market is neglected in this case and Lufthansa IT Services is treated as an external

provider. 'standing outside the door' together with 'real externals' such as IBM and Debis[4]. The policy of improving synergy within the STAR ALLIANCE can cost us our main client, Lufthansa. Then we will be completely out of business because other Alliances will not let us in either." (Dr. Peter Franke, Chief Executive Lufthansa IT Services and Lufthansa Systems GmbH)

Lufthansa in 2000

Simultaneous to the STAR ALLIANCE integration process, Lufthansa aimed to evolve from an airline company into an aviation group: the explicit goal was to become the leading provider of air transport services in the world. Lufthansa was trying to achieve this change through

- Growth through partnerships, not by dominance (STAR ALLIANCE),
- Tight cost management (Programm 15),
- Strengthening the company's revenue base i.e. by expanding direct sales activities.

Lufthansa had identified seven major business areas in the Group and centrally co-ordinated their strategy development process.

Strategy Planning Process

Strategic aims of the subsidiaries and their implementation priorities were established in a systematic, ongoing planning process, in which all the companies were involved. It rested on two pillars: The shaping of business area strategies, and the region oriented planning process (Appendix 7).

Business Area Strategies

In an annual strategy process the Lufthansa Group Executive Board and the Management Board of each Group company developed a strategic plan for the next five years. At the heart of this process was a structured, intensive dialog rather than detailed financial analysis. Results of this strategy meeting were the methodical guidelines and strategies for each business area (starting with "Passenger Service") for the next five years. This applied particularly to global expansion, the approach to customer requirements, market and competitive changes, and relations with other companies in the Group.

Regional Workshops

When the strategies of each Lufthansa company were defined, regional workshops followed. These focused on major regions such as Asia, Europe etc. in order to take into account synergies between different business areas and to develop solutions for internal co-operation. As all Group companies provided either air transport services or services for airline companies, there was a lot of potential for co-ordinating activities of all the companies operating in certain markets. During these workshops core markets were identified, region specific aims were set and possible means were evaluated. The importance of regional strategies was expected to increase over time with the growing global presence of the Lufthansa Group.

The Seven LH Business Units— Strategic Positions and Growth

Lufthansa Passage (Passenger Service) was committed to the strategy of "growth through partnerships" and in 1999 already operated in a strong global network with its STAR ALLIANCE partners. Any of the other companies in the Lufthansa Group considering business ties with a competitor of Lufthansa Passage had to obtain prior approval from the Executive Board. However, alliances were not considered the appropriate growth strategy for all LH subsidiaries.

Each of the seven main companies was supposed to aim at achieving profitable, sustainable growth and a leading position in its world market segment (Appendix 8). In terms of their competitive positions, most of the business areas were already in leadership roles (Appendix 9). Nevertheless their strategies for growth and globalisation varied significantly.

Passenger Service—Lufthansa's Airline, Lufthansa CityLine and Team Lufthansa

In 1999 Lufthansa Passenger Service was by far the strongest business area within the Lufthansa Group. Consisting of *Lufthansa German Airlines* (DM 16.5 billion in revenues in 1998) and *Lufthansa CityLine* (DM 1.5 billion in 1998), "Passenger Service" contributed about 60 percent of the revenues of the Lufthansa Group (DM 18 billion in 1998).

While Lufthansa German Airlines was an operationally independent unit within the Group, Lufthansa CityLine was an autonomous fully-owned company. CityLine complemented the German and European route networks with scheduled passenger flights on aircraft of up to 80 seats. Coupled with its separate wage agreements, its cost structure allowed Lufthansa CityLine to serve routes that were not profitable for the actual airline unit (in Europe). In 1998 the number of passengers served by the overall business area increased by 14.5 percent from 3.8 million in 1997 to 4.4 million.

In addition to this, since 1996 new cooperative arrangements with selected regional carriers (Contact Air, Augsburg Airways, Cimber Air and Air Littoral) had led to all of them flying under the brand name *"Team Lufthansa"* on a franchise basis. These carriers brought passengers to the main hubs of Frankfurt and Munich so that they could use connecting flights within the STAR ALLIANCE route net.

The overall strategic focus of the business area "Passenger Service" was long-term growth linked to strategic partner firms (Appendix 10).

Lufthansa Cargo AG

Since 1995 Lufthansa Cargo AG (the freight company) has been an autonomous 100 percent Lufthansa owned subsidiary with revenues of DM 3.9 billion in 1998 (1 percent decrease from 1997 revenues). In 1999 the strategic intent of LH Cargo AG was to become the leading logistic provider in the global market (Appendix 10). It was trying to realise this intent by following a mixed growth strategy. This included international alliances with some STAR ALLIANCE members, vertical integration through networking with forwarders in order to offer customers a complete door-to-door logistic chain, and finally, acquisitions. These strategies were linked to a fundamental change within the cargo business from a traditionally unintegrated transport provider (as a low involvement standard service) to an individualised complex solution supplier. Beyond pure freight transport, Lufthansa Cargo intended to offer solutions for complex global logistics requirements. This was an answer to the increasing demand for full service (door-to-door logistics) and the fast growth of the supply chain management market.

Therefore, future requirements in the Cargo business included a strong customer focus, branch orientation and the competence to build partnerships and alliances over the whole transport chain. These developments were linked to completely new needs concerning competencies and self understanding: Cargo had never been (with the exception of a smaller cargo charter unit) an autonomous organisational unit before, but a "dependent child" of the passenger business ("Passage"). It was never used to direct customer contact and had never been a provider of complex logistics services.

"There is a need for a mental change. We have not done this sufficiently. Still there is this traditional Lufthansa 'Passage-driven' mentality while an innovative, creative and actively involved organisation is demanded. In 1996 we had a change campaign with different initiatives including an activity tent and numerous workshops that showed an effect but only for a short period. We need

a sustaining change of the role and self-image of people. Cargo cannot achieve this from its own resources. We need this human capital from outside through acquisitions or recruitment." (Michael Kraus, Vice President Global Account and Logistics Lufthansa Cargo AG)

C&N—Tourism

In 1999 Lufthansa's tourist activities were co-ordinated by a holding company named C&N Condor Neckermann Touristik AG. C&N was one of the top three providers of tourist services in Europe. C&N was the result of Condor's vertical integration strategy which led to its merger with NUR (NUR Touristic GmbH, Oberursel) in 1999. The strategic aim of C&N was to establish a high-performance travel group with a leading position in the European tourism market (Appendix 10).

Technical Services

LH Technik AG was a 100 percent owned Lufthansa subsidiary, which generated revenues of about DM 3.2 billion in 1998. With a market share of 8 percent in 1999, LH Technik was the global market leader in full-service aircraft maintenance and VIP cabin outfitting. Since its foundation in 1995, Lufthansa Technik AG had succeeded in strengthening its position in the global market. For Lufthansa Technik AG, external non-Lufthansa customers had traditionally played an important role and this importance continued to increase in the late 90s. In 1998, 47 percent of its revenues were derived from the external market.

In 1999 the strategic focus of Lufthansa Technik was on growth through co-operations with STAR ALLIANCE partners, entry into new markets (through product or service innovations and new facilities) and acquisitions (Appendix 10). For Lufthansa Technik it was difficult to build alliances because it could not develop a network independent from the STAR ALLIANCE. On the other hand it was almost impossible to build an alliance with STAR ALLIANCE partners because United still had a monolithic structure and did not consider "technical maintenance" as a business. For three years (1996–1999) several teams of the STAR ALLIANCE partners worked on potential options for co-operation, the executives of the technical department met on a regular basis (once every three months). The only outcome was the foundation of AirLiance Materials. In 1998, Lufthansa Technik, together with United Airlines and Air Canada, founded this company, which became a trade and service centre for spare parts in Chicago. It aimed at setting a counterweight against the increasing market presence of aircraft manufacturing corporations, which were trying to tie customers closer to themselves by providing maintenance and reconditioning services. They were not only becoming serious competitors for Lufthansa Technik but were also gaining an increasingly monopolistic position.

Catering

Lufthansa LSG Sky Chefs was the catering company of the Group. It generated revenues of DM 2.5 billion in 1998. Its vision was to make the leap from a catering company to a catering group. Other strategic goals included increasing its market share, developing a non-airline catering business such as services for petrol stations and service areas, and going public (Appendix 10).

Ground Services (GlobeGround)

With revenues of DM 0.9 billion in 1998 and a market share of 10 percent derived from its activities in 80 locations in 23 countries, GlobeGround was the Number One worldwide on the free accessible market for ground services. In 1999 this business was focused primarily on global expansion and strengthening of its market leadership (Appendix 10). GlobeGround had started by focusing on global branding and expanding its global presence through regional partnerships and acquisitions primarily in the US. In March 1999 GlobeGround acquired Hudson General Corp. With 5000 employees, Hudson was the leading provider of airport services in North America which accounted for 44 percent share of the ground services market worldwide.

Information Technology

Lufthansa Systems GmbH offered IT-based products and services for airlines and companies in transport, travel and tourism industries. In 1998 it generated revenues of DM 0.7 billion. Only 20 percent of its revenues came from business with external non-Lufthansa customers. In 1999 all IT-related Lufthansa companies formed the business area "Lufthansa IT Services" with Lufthansa Systems as its core. The world-wide market position of Lufthansa IT Services was considered to be expandable. The strategic focus of Lufthansa IT Services was the development of integrated IT activities in the business unit and international expansion through partnerships (Appendix 10).

Internationalisation and Branding of the Lufthansa Subsidiaries

In 1999 not only the growth strategies of the Lufthansa companies varied. Differences could also be seen in their degrees of internationalisation and in their relationships to the brand "Lufthansa": the patterns of the Passenger Service—the airline and traditional core of Lufthansa—and the new emerging decentralised cores of the aviation group varied immensely. Being a member of the STAR ALLIANCE meant that for Lufthansa Passage (Passenger Service), the development could be seen as a "renationalisation" process, especially when taking the Landlord concept into account. In contrast to this, GlobeGround and the LSG Sky Chefs had a business linked to local needs and local infrastructures of the respective regions. This not only implied the need for an international orientation and for local integration in each market, but also created a potential tension with regard to the use of the Lufthansa brand. Therefore the name "GlobeGround" was deliberately chosen as a "Lufthansa-neutral" name.

The business characteristics of Lufthansa Technik AG and Lufthansa IT Services were very different. These technically dominated services were less local and demanded a global strategy that was closely associated to the brand Lufthansa, which was meant to indicate competence, high quality and experience in the airline industry.

> *"Lufthansa stands for German values such as preciseness, technical reliability, high quality or expertise which are important positive indicators of our business. The 'Germanness' of Lufthansa is of direct use for our image while this can be the other way round for customer services, which demand more 'non-German' traits such as friendliness or modesty. The name 'Lufthansa' opens doors. We will always be 'Lufthanseats'."* (Dr. Peter Franke, Chief Executive Lufthansa IT Services and Lufthansa Systems GmbH)

What Did Lufthansa Learn from the Change?

Involvement of People

During the turnaround Lufthansa had developed a certain style of involving people in strategic business processes and networks that was maintained and later supported by the Lufthansa School of Business (founded in 1998). Furthermore, Town Meetings had become a fixed element of the Lufthansa dialogue culture.

> *"We learned to count on people and we got to know that the same people can behave very differently in different situations."* (Wolfgang Mayrhuber, CEO Lufthansa Technik AG and former member of the OPS Team)
>
> *"A crisis can split people into losers and winners. It challenges people and leads some to personal excellence because they are pushed to their limits and in that process they learn to overcome themselves."* (Ralf Teckentrup, Executive Vice President Network and Controlling, Lufthansa German Airlines)
>
> *"Since the crisis, employees are much more concerned about what happens in the company, they are more*

informed and they feel more responsible for general business processes." (Jürgen Raps, Senior Vice President Flight Operations and Chief Pilot)

Weak Signals, Fundamental Problem Solving and Strategy Process

Through the experience of being "surprised" by a crisis that the company almost did not survive, Lufthansa developed a sense for weak signals and a specific way for "deeper" problem solving:

> *"Today we handle problems in a different way. We are practising active management. This means that we go deeper, we approach problems and try to solve them instead of being satisfied with superficial façade-solutions."* (Dr. Peter Franke Chief Executive Lufthansa IT Services and Lufthansa Systems GmbH)
>
> *"We have learned in this process that there is nothing that you cannot change."* (Dr. Peter Hach, Senior Vice President Corporate Controlling)

Moreover Lufthansa had gained the competence of systematic strategy thinking and planning.

> *"Before the change process, people were just doing their jobs. Since the crisis there has been a strategic consciousness and a systematic planning of future actions on a high level."* (Dr. Peter Hach, Senior Vice President Corporate Controlling)

Lufthansa's "Changed Soul"

> *"Through this process we have improved customer orientation, service orientation, cost consciousness, and thinking in business terms. Before the restructuring you were almost not allowed to use the word 'profit'. Now there is a pronounced market-oriented thinking and acting."* (Jürgen Weber, Chairman and CEO, Deutsche Lufthansa AG)

> "Lufthansa has come a long way. We try no longer to treat our customers as petitioners, with the proverbial arrogance we were once famous for. (. . .) We no longer consider the selling of tickets as an act of state but as a skill that we will do better than our competition. (. . .) And last but not least, we have learned to set ourselves ambitious goals and to achieve them. But old habits die hard."[5]

Present and Future Challenges (in 2000)

Operational Excellence

In 1999 one of Lufthansa's most serious challenges was to achieve radical improvements in operational areas such as punctuality, luggage safety, waiting periods, technical reliability and telephone availability. In order to improve the situation for Lufthansa's customers, Jürgen Weber announced a quality offensive at the annual general meeting in June 1999. "Operational Excellence", a project with ambitious goals and significant resources was targeted to establish a basis for drastic improvements in punctuality and quality. The three-year program was expected to work with similar methods and persistence as its predecessor Programm 15.

Management of the Alliance

With the arrival of network-versus-network competition rather than the historical airline versus airline battles, the key challenge was to manage the STAR ALLIANCE as a whole. This raised questions such as how to establish the network in the market, how to form a "STAR ALLIANCE" brand, how to create a network identity, and how to handle network borders. A problem linked to this was the inner structure of STAR ALLIANCE which had to cope with the challenges of managing the mental change, getting used to the mechanism of "competition", and shaping the different relationships within the ALLIANCE.

> "STAR ALLIANCE is an organisational innovation. A global network of such flexibility and fluidity coupled with a good balance between integration and differentiation, but also between profit-sharing and trust did not exist in that large scale dimension before. One optional scenario of the inner structure of the STAR ALLIANCE is a further exploitation of the various relationship intensities between different partner companies. For example it is possible that Lufthansa, SAS and Singapore Airlines use their very intense relation for developing a global cargo integrator. The emergence of specialised sub-networks and corresponding services within the STAR ALLIANCE and a potential differentiation between core members and associates would imply productive tension as well as a lot of business opportunities." (Thomas Sattelberger, Corporate Senior Vice President Executive Personnel and Human Resource Development)

Preserving Identity

One vital issue connected to the alliance strategy on the one hand and to the development to an aviation group on the other hand was the preservation of the "Lufthansa" identity. The question was how Lufthansa could become an integrated part of a strong global airline network and at the same time form an integrated aviation group in which the Passenger Service was only one part among others?

> "It is important to preserve the Lufthansa brand under the roof of the STAR ALLIANCE." (Jürgen Weber, Chairman and CEO, Deutsche Lufthansa (AG)
>
> "We have to define what the label 'Lufthansa' means—to us and to others." (Dr. Michael Heuser, Head Lufthansa School of Business)
>
> "There often is a misunderstanding that Lufthansa Group equals Lufthansa which equals Passage (Passenger Service). Everybody learned this for years and this is the old shared identity." (Dr. Hans Schmitz, Chief Executive of the Lufthansa Technik Logistik GmbH)

Developing a "new" identity demanded defining or developing internal relationships. A core element of the aviation group strategy was a system of clear customer-supplier-relationships between the companies within the Group. These agreements were supposed to be based on market conditions with the stipulation that the Group companies be conceded a "last call".

> "One of the problems of increasing importance throughout the Lufthansa Group is the lack of relations management. We have not yet developed the customer-provider relationships that are necessary for a market-based internal coordination. Internal customers do not behave like normal customers yet. They demand conditions they would never dare to ask for in the external market." (Dr. Peter Franke, Chief Executive Lufthansa IT Services and Lufthansa Systems GmbH)

Preserving Consciousness of the Crisis and Openness for Change

Lufthansa's sharpened consciousness for weak signals, costs etc. and the openness for change caused by the crisis were clearly very important for the record performance in 1998 and 1999. One challenge was how to preserve these attitudes in good times.

> "Lufthansa has to continue in its success path and not become arrogant or practice cost cutting indiscriminately. The most difficult part is to keep people motivated now when the pressure has eased off." (Jürgen Weber, Chairman and CEO, Deutsche Lufthansa AG)
>
> "Besides its inner desire to achieve something outstanding, Lufthansa seems to need a real or possible crisis or enemy to achieve quantum-leap change. People need a 'push' to believe in their ability to do so. It seems that from

the three drivers of change—joint vision, joint enemy and joint necessity—the last two are the dominant ones." (Thomas Sattelberger, Corporate Senior Vice President Executive Personnel and Human Resource Development)

"There is a need to keep the consciousness alive how to handle a crisis—even in good times. Another challenge is to preserve the openness for change that we had during the crisis. During the turnaround, there was an immense openness for change. It is unbelievable what dimensions of change we managed during the turnaround. And today? It takes ages to implement mini-innovations, which we would not even have discussed those days. We do not dare again to do things that help us to learn because we are afraid of making mistakes." (Jochen Hoffmann, Senior Vice President & Executive Vice President Personnel and Labour Relations, Deutsche Lufthansa AG)

Shaping the Future— Lufthansa School of Business

To keep the "sense of urgency" for change and transformation alive, to form a cultural and knowledge platform for the Lufthansa Group and to drive learning and experience along the strategic core processes, Lufthansa established the Lufthansa School of Business at a corporate level in April 1998.

The school's philosophy and activities extended far beyond traditional approaches of training and development. Its task was to tighten and links between strategy, organisational and individual development in order to support the company's key priorities for transformation and future performance.

Thomas Sattelberger, since July 1999 Executive Vice President Product and Service, who was credited as the conceptual architect of the Lufthansa School of Business, explains the particular advantage for Lufthansa as follows:

"In flexible organisations like Lufthansa and even more in a fluid alliance and network organisation like the STAR ALLIANCE, a mental cultural core is necessary. When there is almost no formal system of procedures and regulations there is a need for a mental integration. Like the rock in the river shaping the water, this is one of the central tasks of the Lufthansa School of Business."

Lufthansa School of Business Explicitly Follows Five Goals:

- Effectively and efficiently supporting key strategic issues of the Lufthansa Group
- Building and tying intellectual capital to the company

- Linking academic expertise and experiences of partner companies to Lufthansa business practice and its needs
- Fostering and developing a corporate leadership and performance culture
- Creating options for personal development and challenges

Within a demanding range of programs the Lufthansa School of Business entered into close world-wide "learning partnerships". Almost all programs—from Masters degree programs to non-degree top management programs—were designed, run and evaluated with global companies to learn with and from the best ("Benchlearning"). By building close relationships with some well selected academic institutions, the Lufthansa School of Business deliberately avoided concentrating its academic relationships, preferring instead to build a network of leading business schools and universities (among them the London Business School, INSEAD, McGill in Montreal, Indian Institute of Management in Bangalore and Hitotshubashi University in Tokyo).

Initiatives launched by the Lufthansa School of Business included shaping of the so-called "transformation and change networks" of several hundred young potentials or experienced managers. These programs usually lasted 12 months in total. What was characteristic and remarkable about them was their specific composition and setting: Processes of individual learning were directly linked to strategic development and changes in business practices.

"Lufthansa School of Business creates value by the change it initiates for both the individual and the organisation 'Lufthansa'. Our action learning networks contribute not only to the required mental change, they also show visible innovation results." (Dr. Michael Heuser, Head Lufthansa School of Business).

Networks "Explorer 21" and the "Climb Program"

"Explorers 21" challenges well-selected young professionals to become change leaders early in their careers. Each session consists of 210 Explorers. The *"Climb Program"* is an action learning network of 160 managers world-wide.

The overall goals of these programs include:

- Initiating and fostering mental change
- Creating transformation platforms in critical scale and range

(continued)

- Delivering significant contribution for putting leadership into action
- Producing visible results and transfers
- Offering self-assessment and benchmarks and
- Forming knowledge and change networks across and within Lufthansa businesses.

Both programs start with a self-assessment based on Lufthansa's leadership tools such as the Lufthansa Leadership Compass (Appendix 11) and the Lufthansa Leadership Feedback (Lufthansa's 360° feedback). During the programs, participants visit excellent companies all over the world to analyse their areas of excellence and to work out business recommendations for Lufthansa. At various times, all network members come together in congresses to discuss findings and recommendations with the Lufthansa management and to make concrete goal agreements.

Sponsors at management levels and peer support are considered vital components of the learning processes. The participants are encouraged to negotiate changes in their job assignments so that they can follow through with implementing the changes they propose.

"Making recommendations and agreements reality becomes part of the line responsibility again. The participants are supposed to become the change agents for the initiatives including the implementation of their recommendations in their divisions. The specific advantage of these projects is that there is not just a single person in charge of the charge process but also a large action network of supportive individuals with the same experience, desire involvement and commitment to innovation." (Dr. Michael Heuser, Head Lufthansa School of Business)

Jürgen Weber put the value of the Lufthansa School of Business for the entire Lufthansa Group in these words:

"Our business requires a global mindset and networking capabilities across borders. These capabilities can't be developed with quick-fix solutions. Our Lufthansa School of Business supports our business and strategic objectives. It creates value by building intellectual capital that is difficult to imitate by others." (Jürgen Weber, Chairman and CEO, Deutsche Lufthansa AG)

Operational ratios		1998	1997
Profit-revenue ratio			
(profit from ordinary activities/revenue)[3]	per cent	11.0	8.1
Total return on investment			
(profit from ordinary activities)			
plus interest on debt/total assets[3]	per cent	13.0	10.9
Return on equity			
(net profit/loss for the period/capital and reserves[5]	[8]per cent	22.1	20.5
Return on equity			
(Profit from ordinary activities[3] capital and reserves[5]		38.4	33.2
Equity ratio			
(capital and reserves [5] total assets)	[8]per cent	26.9	23.1
Net indebtedness—total assets ratio		6.0	10.2
Internal financing ratio[8]	per cent		
(cash flow[7] capital expenditure)	[8]per cent	91.2	165.2
Net indebtedness—cash flow ratio[7]	per cent	39.6	59.3
Revenue efficiency	per cent	16.1	18.1
(cash flow[7]/revenue)			
Net working capital			
(current assets less short-term debt)	DM billion	-0.3	0.3
Personnel ratios			
Annualised average employee total		54,867	55,520
Revenue employee	DM	412,886	389,226
Staff costs/revenue	per cent	24.8	25.6
Output data Lufthansa Group[3]			
Total available tonne-kilometres	millions	20,133.6	19,324.6
Total revenue tonne-kilometres	millions	14,170.4	13,620.9
Overall load factor	per cent	70.4	70.5
Available seat kilometres	millions	102,354.4	98,750.0
Revenue passenger-kilometres	millions	74,668.4	70,581.4
Passenger load factor	per cent	73.0 40.5	71.5
Passengers carried			
Paid passenger tonne-kilometres	millions	7,474.1	37.2
Freight/mail	millions	1,702,733	7,071.1
Freight/mail tonne-kilometres		6,696.3	703,657
Number of flights	millions	618,615	6,548.0
Flight kilometres		636.4	596,456
Aircraft utilisation	millions	1,010,897	614.6
Aircraft in service		339	963,675
			326

[1]As from the 1997 financial year, the financial statements are prepared according to the International Accounting Standards. Thus, previous years' figures are not comparable
[2]Up to 1996 profit from operating activities
[3]Up to 1995 before net changes in special items with an equity portion
[4]Up to 1996 before withdrawal from transfer to retained earnings and before minority interest
[5]Up to 1995 including the equity portion of special items and up to 1996 including minority interest
[6]Up to 1995 including the debt portion of special items
[7]Calculated as net cash from operating activities as per cash flow statement, up to 1996 financial cash flow
[8]As from the 1995 financial year, the special items with an equity portion set up in individual company financial statements for tax purposes are not included in the consolidated financial statements according to the HGB. The special items brought forward from the 1994 financial year were released in 1995 as extraordinary income amounting to DM 879 million. This additional income was allocated to retained earnings. As a result of this reclassification, earnings before taxes, the net profit for the year, retained earnings and equity (including the equity portion of special items) were all shown with correspondingly higher totals

(continued)

1996	1995	1994	1993	1992	1991	1990	1989
3.3	3.8	3.9	0.4	-4.3	3.5	0.2	4.3
4.9	5.7	6.3	3.4	-1.1	-0.7	2.2	5.9
10.4	21.1[12]	7.4	-3.1	-13.0	-11.7	0.4	2.5
12.8	15.3	17.9	2.6	-24.3	-15.4	0.9	12.8
28.6	26.8	22.5	16.7	17.9	22.8	29.0	35.8
7.7	10.8	19.8	33.6	36.2	33.5	27.5	17.4
122.8	181.8	121.3	110.9	59.8	58.1	43.1	80.2
58.7	79.6	141.9	303.1	383.2	302.1		
11.7	2.5	13.4	10.9	9.3	11.0	0.9	14.1
3.3	2.4	2.5	2.6	1.5	1.7	1.6	1.6
57,999	57,586	58,044	60,514	63,645	61,791	57,567	51,942
359,708	345,577	324,507	293,002	270,862	260,565	250,960	251,344
27.6	27.1	27.9	30.6	33.8	32.4	33.0	33.1
20,697.5	19,983.2	18,209.8	17,123.4	16,369.8	14,292.2	13,679.6	12,462.3
14,532.8	14,063.1	12,890.0	11,768.4	10,724.8	9,376.2	9,118.5	8,580.8
70.2	70.4	70.8	68.7	65.5	65.6	66.7	68.9
116,183.1	112,147.2	03,876.9	98,295.3	94,138.1	81,661.8	75,504.6	65,058.5
81,716.3	79,085.3	72,750.9	67,017.5	61,273.8	52,344.2	50,685.1	44,669.4
70.3	70.5	70.0	68.2	65.1	64.1	67.1	68.7
41.4	40.7	37.7	35.6	33.7	29.5	26.6	23.4
8,084.8	7,828.4	7,202.4	6,636.6	5,882.3	5,026.6	4,874.8	4,296.3
1,684,729	1,576,210	435,636	1,263,698	1,197.87	125,168	1,056,526	1,004,600
6,448.0	6,234.7	5,687.6	5,131.8	04,842.5	4,349.6	4,243.7	4,284.3
595,120	580,108	536,687	501,139	492,606	431,102	358,522	310,882
720.5	659.0	620.9	561.1	598.7	516.0	470.0	412.7
1,000,723	1,070,238	992,45214	973,504	964,776	835,000	817,604	660,431
314	314	308	301	302	275	220	197

[9]In 1996 the face value of the shares was diluted to DM 5; previous years figures were adjusted
[10]DM 1.15 on preference shares
[11]Only guaranteed dividend on preference shares
[12]Net profit less extraordinary result
[13]As from the 1997 financial year, Condor is no longer included
[14]Method of calculation changed

```
                        ┌──────────────────────┐
                        │   Chief Executive    │
                        │       Officer        │
                        └──────────────────────┘
```

| Chief Executive Finance | Chief Executive Personnel | Chief Executive Marketing and Sales | Chief Executive Technical | Chief Executive Flight Operations |

Appendix 3:   The Lufthansa Group in 1999

Business Areas of the Lufthansa Group

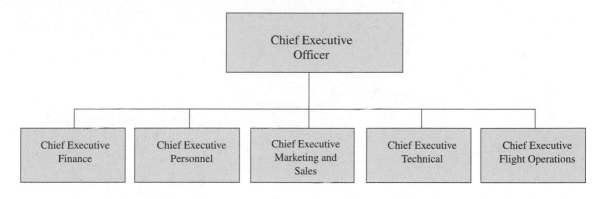

CEO, Chief Executive Finance, Chief Executive Personnel

Passage
Lufthansa Passage Airline | Lufthansa CityLine GmbH

Logistik
Lufthansa Cargo AG | DHL

Technik
Lufthansa Technik AG AMECO

Catering
LSG Sky Chefs

IT
Lufthansa Systems GmbH Amadeus Start

Ground Services
GlobeGround GmbH

Touristik
C&N Touristic AG (50%0

Appendix 4:   Quantitative Profiles of the Star Alliance Members in 1998, Focus 5/1999

Airline	Revenues in billion DM	Employees	Aircraft	Destinations	Passengers in millions
United Airlines	29.2	92.000	576	257	84
Lufthansa	22.8	58.000	326	271	44.5
All Nippon Airways	14.3	15.000	143	64	40
SAS	8.6	22.000	178	100	21
Varig	5.7	18.000	87	122	10
Thai Airways	5.2	25.000	74	73	15
Air Canada	4.3	24.000	243	124	17.5
Ansett Australia	3.5	17.000	72	95	13.5
Air New Zealand	2.8	10.000	73	69	3

1959	SAS and Thai Airways found Thai Airways International
October 1992	Air Canada and United Airlines sign a co-operation letter of intent
October 1993	Lufthansa and United Airlines build a strategic alliance including code-share-flights
June 1994	Lufthansa and United Airline operate first code-share-flights
May 1995	Lufthansa and SAS agree upon an extensive strategic alliance, including code-share-flights. In the same time United Airlines and Air Canada extend their offer
June 1995	Lufthansa and Thai sign a code-share-agreement
September 1995	United Airlines and SAS sign a co-operation letter of intent starting in April 1996
October 1995	Lufthansa and Thai offer first code-share flights
February 1996	Lufthansa and SAS start joint flights between Germany and Scandinavia
March 1996	Lufthansa and Air Canada become strategic partners
May 1996	The US-Department of Transport (DOT) frees Lufthansa and United Airlines from the American competition law (Antitrust-Immunity)
June 1996	Lufthansa and Air Canada start joint flights between Germany and Canada
October 1996	SAS and Air Canada announce the signature of a strategic alliance
November 1996	Lufthansa, SAS and United Airlines receive the trilateral Antitrust-Immunity from the DOT
May 1997	Foundation of the STAR ALLIANCE in Frankfurt with the members, Air Canada, Lufthansa, SAS, United Airlines and Thai Airways
October 1997	Varig becomes sixth member of the STAR ALLIANCE
April 1999	Air New Zealand and Ansett Australia join the STAR ALLIANCE
September 1999	All Nippon Airways becomes member of the STAR ALLIANCE

Appendix 6: The Big Four—Dates and Figures of the Major Airline Alliances 1998 or 1997, Wirtschaftswoche, No. 4, 1.4.1999, pp. 122ff.

Alliance	Members	Type of co-operation	Management	Revenues in billion US$	Destinations/Countries	Aircrafts	Employees in 1000	Passengers in mio
Star Alliance	Lufthansa, Air Canada, Air New Zealand, Ansett Australia, SAS, Thai Airways, United Airlines, Varig, All Nippon Airways,* Singapore Airlines*	Mostly joint-sale, LH/SAS joint ventures	Management Development Board (MDB) and working committees Determination of the Alliance strategy by 6 members of the MDB elected by airline presidents and responsible for specific areas of strategic importance	49.9***	720 destinations in 118 countries****	1629****	265****	212***
Oneworld	British Airways, American Airlines, Canadian Airlines, Cathay Pacific, Iberia, Qantas, Finnair, Japan Airlines,* Deutsche BA**	Planned: AA/BA revenue sharing on North Atlantic routes	1 Managing Director as Direct Report for AA/BA chairmen, plus integrated full-time well resourced management teams	44.5***	680 destinations in 143 countries	1783***	256	206**
Qualiflyer	Swissair, Austrian Airlines, Air Littoral, AOM, Crossair, Lauda Air, Sabena, Tap Air Portugal, Turkish Airlines, Tyrolean, Delta Air Lines**			27.1***	338 destinations in 100 countries	1029***	118***	153**
Wings	KLM, Alitalia, Northwest Airlines, Kenya Airways, Braathens, S.A.F.E., Eurowings, Transavia, Martinair			35.0	680 destinations in 100 countries	1200	101	182

*Membership placed/data not taken into account, **Associated society, *** 1997, ****Including new members Air New Zealand and Ansett Australia

Appendix 7: Strategic Process in 1999

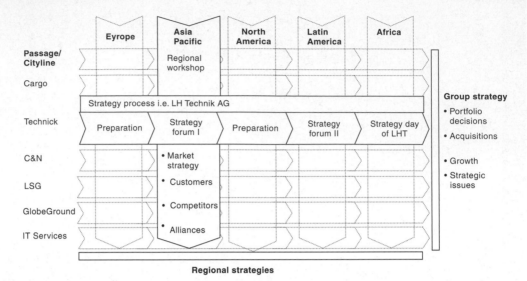

Regional strategies

Appendix 8: Lufthansa Group Strategy in 1999

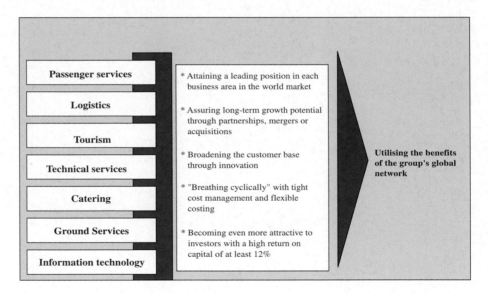

Case 23 / Lufthansa 2000 Maintaining the Change Momentum

Passenger Service	No. 7 in the world market, with Star Alliance No. 1
Logistics	With 6% market share LH Cargo is No. in international airfreight traffic
Tourism	C&N is one of the top 3 in the field of tourism in Europe
Technical services	With 8% market share LH Technik is No. 1 world-wide
Catering	LSG Sky Chefs is with a market share of 33% No. 1 in the world
Ground Services	LSGS (Globe Ground) is No. 1 with a market share of 10% of the free accessible market
Information technology	The position can be strengthened world-wide

Appendix 10: Strategic Focuses and Aims of the Business Areas of the Lufthansa Group in 1999

Business area	Strategic focus and aims
Passenger services	**Long-term growth linked to strategic partner firms** • Completion of the STAR ALLIANCE and the development of a European competence with regional partner companies • Extension of target customer management • Reduplication of direct sales until 2003 • Simplification of ground and customer processes • Ensuring capacity expansions at German airports through strategic partnerships • Strengthening quality leadership
Lufthansa Cargo AG	**Becoming the leading logistic service provider on a global market** • Completion of the global Cargo alliance • Building and expanding the business partnership program with freight forwarders • Time-definite services • Providing customer oriented integrated solutions for transport and logistics • Development of new sales channels (e.g. internet/virtual malls) • Building a global network with partners
C & N–Tourism	**A leading position in the European tourist market** • Becoming a powerful, vertical integrated tourism company • Concentrating on the most important European markets and becoming No. 1 or 2 in these markets • Market leadership in all important segments—disproportionate growth in the premium segment • Developing an integrated capacity and yield management • Entering new sales channels (e.g. internet)

(continued)

Technical services	**Growth**

- Extension of co-operations with STAR ALLIANCE partners as a counterweight to an increased market presence of aircraft technique manufacturers (such as GE)
- Entering new markets through global presence and extension of array of products
- Development of new production platforms (facilities) primarily in Asia and North America
- Ensuring growth through acquisition and investment

Catering — **Becoming a large catering group and strengthening the global market leadership**

- Increasing it's market share until 2003
- Development of non-airline catering such as services for petrol stations and service areas
- 10 percent revenue share with non-airline catering
- Going public

Ground services — **Strengthening the market leadership combined with a global expansion strategy**

- International market presence through global branding as GlobeGround and global Key Account Management
- Global expansion through regional partnerships with strong local partners
- Implementing a strategic partnership with Frankfurt airport company

Information technology — **Integration of IT activities in a business unit and international expansion through partnerships**

- LH becomes a global and integrated provider of IT with a focal point in travel and transport
- Global expansion through co-operations and acquisitions
- Bundling and organising IT activities in five business units (reservation systems, infrastructure, airline services, customer services and channel services)
- Development of the brand "LH IT Services"

Case 23 / Lufthansa 2000 Maintaining the Change Momentum

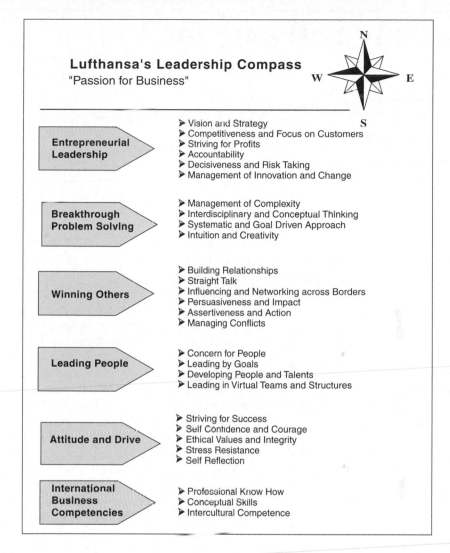

Lufthansa's Leadership Compass
"Passion for Business"

Entrepreneurial Leadership
➤ Vision and Strategy
➤ Competitiveness and Focus on Customers
➤ Striving for Profits
➤ Accountability
➤ Decisiveness and Risk Taking
➤ Management of Innovation and Change

Breakthrough Problem Solving
➤ Management of Complexity
➤ Interdisciplinary and Conceptual Thinking
➤ Systematic and Goal Driven Approach
➤ Intuition and Creativity

Winning Others
➤ Building Relationships
➤ Straight Talk
➤ Influencing and Networking across Borders
➤ Persuasiveness and Impact
➤ Assertiveness and Action
➤ Managing Conflicts

Leading People
➤ Concern for People
➤ Leading by Goals
➤ Developing People and Talents
➤ Leading in Virtual Teams and Structures

Attitude and Drive
➤ Striving for Success
➤ Self Confidence and Courage
➤ Ethical Values and Integrity
➤ Stress Resistance
➤ Self Reflection

International Business Competencies
➤ Professional Know How
➤ Conceptual Skills
➤ Intercultural Competence

1. Seeheim later became the home of the Lufthansa School of Business.
2. Dr. Klaus Schlede was the Chief Executive Finance at that time.
3. Dr. Hach, P. Senior Vice President Corporate Controlling, Speech held at the Top 100-Forum at Stockholm "An Attempt of a Phenomenological Approach to Lufthansa's Soul", 22.2.1996

4. Debis is an autonomous IT subsidiary of the Daimler Chrysler Group.
5. Dr. Hach, P. Senior Vice President Corporate Controlling, Speech held at the Top 100-Forum at Stockholm "An Attempt of a Phenomenological Approach to Lufthansa's Soul", 22.2.1996

MetaSolv Software Inc.*

Seth Mincks
Haley Malchar
Joseph Hopper
Dan Dixon

It was a Friday, early 1999, and confident Jim Janicki was making his way from his office at MetaSolv's Plano, Texas headquarters to the employee lounge. There he saw the familiar faces of his loyal employees as they were preparing to end their full workweek. Janet Benton, a software architect was quietly conversing with marketing director Dana Brown. Sid Sack, the company's COO, was discussing sales projections with some members of the sales team at a table in the corner. Jim knew them all by name, over 350 employees in total. MetaSolv's story of what seemed to be overnight success had brought them all together to create this world-class operation that was leading the industry in Operation Support Systems solutions for the telecommunication industry. The company had seen enormous growth from its humble two man beginnings in 1992. Furthermore, they were poised to experience similar growth in the years to come. Nevertheless, as Jim poured himself a glass of water, took a seat, and looked upon his fellow teammates with pride, there were many thoughts taxing his mind. "What now?" he thought. Could MetaSolv, a private company in Plano, Texas, survive as it had in the past? Could they sustain the phenomenal growth to which they had become accustomed, and if so, could they stay competitive technologically as they had in the past?

Company Background

From June 1982 to July 1992, Jim Janicki worked for Texas Instruments where he served in many capacities. He was the manager of the Texas Instruments' CASE (Computer Aided Software Engineering) consulting

practice from July 1987 to August 1990. As he developed relationships with clients and gained experience in solving their specific needs, he began to see an opportunity to create a new company focused on some of the problems he dealt with everyday at TI. The CASE consulting practice was to eventually become the lifeblood of a new company called MetaSolv Software Inc. MetaSolv Software, Inc. was originally incorporated as Omnicase, Inc. in Delaware on July 6, 1992. Jim Janicki and William Sick co-founded the company before the move to Plano, Texas. Mr. Sick, a venture capitalist, chose to remain on the Board after the business got started. Jim, on the other hand, has retained a much more active role in the company and has served as the President since April 1994.

The idea behind this new company was to develop ordering software (described in detail under **Products and Services**) for different companies and then to sell generic versions of those models to other companies in similar businesses. MetaSolv decided to build these models for their clients and retain the rights to sell the model to other companies. Jim and his partners had ideas about creating many different models for many different companies in various lines of business. This, however, would not be the ultimate direction for the company. They soon realized that the market for their ordering system for telephone companies was large enough to sustain a great amount of future growth. Specifically, these integrated ordering systems allowed telecommunications companies to order equipment and services from other vendors.

Therefore, the company decided to focus its efforts on the telecommunications industry and began to only develop ordering software for telephone companies. According to Janicki, they never once looked back. The first model was completed, installed, and sold in 1994

---

*This case is intended to be used as the basis for class discussion rather than to illustrate either effective or ineffective handling of an administrative or strategic situation. We appreciate the direction of professor Robert E. Hoskisson in the development of this case.

for Century Telephone, now Alltel. Jim and his partners spent every week from April to October in Cleveland, Ohio working on this project. With their headquarters located in Texas, it was very difficult to devote any time to administrative tasks. The COO at the time was in charge of all office tasks from picking up the mail to paying the rent. Jim and the others would fly home on the weekends to see their families.

Once this model was built Jim realized that the company had found its niche and there was no need to develop models for different kinds of companies. They had the product they needed and decided the best course of action was to concentrate all of their efforts on selling this product. As they would soon learn, there would be little time to focus on anything else.

Currently, MetaSolv leads the way in the provision of order management and service fulfillment solutions for next generation communications providers. Not only does the company provide software designed to make the process of taking, managing and fulfilling orders for service easier for emerging competitive communications service providers, but these communications service providers also offer a wide range of communications services such as local and long-distance telephone services, high-speed data services and Internet services, often as a bundled offering. The Company derives substantially all of its revenue from the sale of licenses, related professional services, and maintenance and support of the Company's Telecom Business Solution (TBS) packaged software to these communications service providers.

Company Success

The company's success is attributable to many factors including hard work, dedication among the employees, and good management skills. Perhaps the most important factor in MetaSolv's success was being in the right place at the right time. In 1996, deregulation of the telephone industry occurred. Prior to this time MetaSolv had positioned itself as the only significant provider of a comprehensive ordering software package. Deregulation caused an unprecedented jump in MetaSolv's earnings. In 1998, things were better than even the most optimistic estimates. The company estimated earnings to be about $20 million; instead, they were closer to $43 million (see Exhibit 3). This surprised the management and opened their eyes to the possibility of quick and rapid expansion.

Corporate Culture

MetaSolv's corporate structure is very flat with only a CEO, COO, CFO and 5 Vice Presidents. This structure allows the company to function as a team and not as a gauntlet of authority that an idea or sales solution must pass through in order to be accepted. Each of these positions has real responsibilities. For example, the CEO and President, Jim Janicki, has a technology background so not only is he responsible for the company's everyday business strategy but he also oversees the engineering department. He is responsible for their progress and monitors this progress through daily reports made to him.

Management describes the atmosphere of daily life as relaxed and the culture as "open." Employees are allowed to wear what they like with the exception of shorts and T-shirts. This fosters the team concept by putting everyone at ease with each other. As a result, company meetings are never dull at MetaSolv. Traditionally, each MetaSolv employee speaking at the company meeting has the opportunity to choose his or her "theme music" to be played as they step up to the podium to address the audience.

Another interesting way to foster camaraderie is what management calls "Beer Friday." At 4:00 on Friday afternoon the entire office is invited to the employee lounge so that everyone can fraternize and drink beer if they choose before they go home for the weekend. This tradition started in the early days when the newest staff person would be sent around to collect money and beer orders. This practice continued for several years until one day when Jim saw two of the newest hires coming back with two handcarts stacked with cases of beer. He knew that the company had grown so much that things would have to change. They did. Now on Fridays the new guy doesn't have to make a "beer run" because there are 2 kegs in the employee lounge waiting for everyone's enjoyment.

"Beer Friday" may foster images of sloth and inefficiency in the minds of some, but that myth is exactly what separates MetaSolv from so many other corporations. When it is time to work, Janicki believes that everyone works hard to make the company a success, thus they deserve a few hours of fun each week. This devotion to corporate camaraderie seems to foster pride and a sense of family among employees.

Industry

Recently, the powerful forces of deregulation, globalization, competition and technology evolution have combined to create a significant impact on the telecommunications industry. Incumbent local carriers are changing quickly to offer long distance, wireless and Internet services through hybrid networks. Wireless providers, particularly those in Europe, are becoming

Exhibit 3   Financial Highlights

Year end December 31 (in thousands except per share data)	1998	1997	1996	1995
Statement of operations data:				
Total revenues	$42,576	$9,299	$3,822	$2,219
Gross profit	26,475	6,717	3,185	1,953
Income (Loss) from operations	(508)	65	581	(19)
Net income (Loss)	(186)	120	648	9
Earnings (Loss) per share of common stock:				
Basic	(0.02)	0.01	0.06	0.00
Diluted	(0.02)	0.00	0.03	0.00
Weighted average shares Outstanding:				
Basic	11,472	11,404	11,409	11,400
Diluted	11,472	24,943	22,440	18,050
Balance sheet data:				
Cash and cash equivalents	$7,984	$3,639	$2,983	$334
Working capital	9,761	2,393	3,482	918
Total current liabilities	11,935	5,346	1,806	296
Redeemable convertible preferred stock	12,610	2,610	–	–
Total stockholders' equity	1,826	1,939	4,314	1,189

SOURCE: MetasSolv.com, "Financial Reports," 18 Oct. 2000 < http://www.corporate-ir.net/ireye/ir_site.zhtml?ticker=MSLV&script=700>

Internet Service Providers. Entirely new types of carriers are finding their niches in areas such as network backbone provision, Internet service provision, wireless and wirelines reselling. Meeting the needs of communications service providers in this rapidly changing environment is extremely challenging, requiring software vendors to be agile and responsive and to think and execute globally. Essentially, companies like MetaSolv exist to serve this growing telecommunications industry. Therefore, to understand more about the industry in which MetaSolv operates, one must first examine the telecommunications environment that drives growth within the telecommunications software industry.

Deregulation

According to the BBC, "at the beginning of the 1990s, only about 20 percent of the world's telecommunica-tions market was open to competition; by the start of the new millennium this figure will have risen to about 90 percent as monopolies fall to the new trend."[1]

US Telecommunications Act of 1996

The Telecommunications Act of 1996 addressed five major areas of concern in the US. First, telephone service regulations were changed to promote competition in local phone markets and regulations promoting universal access to services. Second, telecommunications equipment manufacturing was affected by regulations allowing the baby bells to manufacture telephone equipment. A third effect of the act regarded cable television. Essentially, regulations were put in place to foster competition in the cable television market. The act also affected radio and television broadcasting by introducing new miscellaneous regulations directed mainly at relaxing existing regulations on broadcasters. Finally, the Internet and online computer services were affected by new regulations related to obscenity on the Internet (commonly referred to as the Communications Decency Act or CDA). Essentially, the most important way in which this legislation impacted companies like MetaSolv was in the creation of competition in the telecommunications market. This competition and subsequent increase in competitive local exchange carriers created an overwhelming increase in business for MetaSolv who, at the time, was literally the only company offering a commercial, off-the-shelf product along with the service expertise of managing ordering, equipment and circuit design, and task management.

Convergence Trend within the Telecom Industry

In a vast part of the world and certainly within the industrialized world, almost everyone has access to a telephone. Likewise, many people have televisions, and more and more people are obtaining personal computers for their homes. These three household goods are quickly converging into one entity, and this convergence has been and will continue to be a major trend within the telecommunications industry. Convergence has been occurring for about the past ten years and has sparked a substantial increase in mergers and acquisitions in the telecom industry. Many companies are being forced to reconsider corporate boundaries and make significant investments just to stay abreast in the new markets. Some industry players believe that while this trend is important, the effects of it will not be realized for some time. "The term convergence is rather nonsensical," said Peter Blakeney of IBM's media and entertainment/ e-business group. "It will probably take another ten years for a realistic expectation of content being spread on multiple devices."[2] Nevertheless, these changes will certainly impact the future of OSS software applications for the industry. Current providers must invest in research now to be prepared for whatever the future may bring.

Globalization

Worldwide telecom revenue is forecast to rise from about $976 billion in 1996 to about $1.8 trillion in 2002.[3] At the same time as technology is making rapid progress, markets everywhere are opening up to competition. Players within the telecom industry are struggling to develop a set of global alliances, linking the newly deregulated state telephone companies to their global counterparts. One need only to look at the growing realization that liberalizing telecommunications industries is key to overall industry growth to understand this phenomenon.

The nature of international telecommunications trade is evolving from a bilateral, nation-to-nation framework to a multinational, multilateral company-to-company paradigm. Major international telecommunications alliances, such as the one between British Telecom and AT&T, have taken many forms with the potential to dominate segments of international markets.

In Europe, for example, there is a move towards deregulation in the telecommunications industry. As this occurs, the market should be flooded with independent companies. In fact, the European Union decided to open up its telecommunications markets by Jan 1, 1998. This was a dramatic change indeed, since most of the markets have been traditionally ruled by state-owned monopolies. Sweden, Finland and The United Kingdom are the forerunners in this process, with different results so far. Indeed, the European telecom scene is changing nearly as fast as the US: inefficient state monopoly carriers that have historically charged high prices are being transformed by competitive pressures. These traditional European carriers have suffered their first big setbacks in the realm of international services, where the margins are highest and the incumbents most vulnerable. The attacking companies mainly come from overseas. International simple resale and callback companies, including many US-based firms, are growing at an extraordinary rate. This new competition will offer many opportunities for potential entrants in the OSS software industry in the European market.

Latin America has also shown signs of moving towards deregulation. This region is experiencing exponential growth in the Internet market in particular. This growth is not only ushering in a new era of interactive services, but it is also pushing market liberalization and placement of modern telecom infrastructure throughout this region. In the 11 nations of South America, the number of Internet hosts grew by an average annual rate of 144 percent from 1993 to 1996. This growth resulted in a total of 157,536 hosts by July 1997. According to Pyramid Research, the average annual growth rate for the region should be a strong 50 percent throughout the year 2000.[4] Of course, this transition in Latin America will not be without complications. In many parts of the region, particularly in Central America, government bodies may not always make good on their promises of privatization and liberalization. Furthermore, incumbent operators are still at the mercy of bureaucracy that often prohibits upgrades in infrastructure.

OSS Software Industry

As the telecommunications industry grows, so does the demand for telecommunications software solutions.

Currently, the industry is rather fragmented, and no one player enjoys a majority of the market share. While MetaSolv has been able to capture more of the market than their competitors, the telecom market is so large and growing so quickly even MetaSolv does not have what would normally be considered a large portion of the market.

Customers

MetaSolv's customer list includes many of the telecommunication industry's major players (See Exhibit 1). Nevertheless, these customers include all sizes of service providers, from large incumbents to new market entrants. The company has developed a unique system allowing their diverse users to have the opportunity to share their experiences and advice with their peers through the *Telecom Business Solution™* (*TBS™*) Software User Group. The *TBS™* Software User Group:

- Provides an open forum for users and developers of MetaSolv's *TBS™* products to exchange ideas, techniques and information on how to better utilize existing products and plan for future product installations and upgrades.
- Provides an open forum between members and MetaSolv Software to share concerns and discuss pertinent product issues.
- Provides MetaSolv Software an opportunity to share current functional and technical information on MetaSolv products, as well as the direction of future product development with members.
- Supports educational conferences for the exchange of information, experience and concepts related to the use of MetaSolv's *TBS™* software.

Thus far, this program has been successful in allowing customers to learn from their peers while receiving the support they need to maintain their operations.[5]

Competition

The nature of competition for the $23 billion operational support systems software industry remained seriously fragmented even after the Telecommunications Act of 1996. While many firms claim to offer software solutions for the telecommunications industry, there are very few with OSS solution rivaling that of MetaSolv's. There are many firms trying to compete in this arena, but they are either not large enough to offer a comprehensive OSS solution or so large that their culture does not allow them to stay competitive in this dynamic industry. Essentially, MetaSolv has found themselves in a unique situation. They have no direct competition in approxi-

mately 15 percent of all of their sales efforts. In the 85 percent remaining, MetaSolv has never lost to the same competitor twice in any quarter.[6] Thus, in many regards, they have become the default solution for OSS needs in the telecommunications industry. However, there are a handful of companies that do challenge MetaSolv's authority in a limited number of instances.

Telcordia Technologies, Inc.

Telcordia Technologies, Inc., based in Morristown, New Jersey, was originally part of the research arm of AT&T. It was created as a research division for the seven Baby Bells after the breakup in 1984 and named Bellcore. The company was purchased in 1996 by the defense contractor Science Applications International and renamed Telcordia. Telcordia now operates globally and is one of the world's leading providers of telecommunications networking and operations software and consulting and training services. While about 80 percent of the public telecom networks in the US have used the company in some way, they really do not currently offer a product that competes directly on par with MetaSolv. The bulk of their annual revenue comes from consulting and license fees from applications developed for the Baby Bells over the last fifteen years. They have yet to establish a major presence in the next generation market where convergence is salient. Given the size of their other operations, they are unlikely to make a concentrated effort to dominate this arena; however, such a move would be possible.

EFTIA

EFTIA is based in Ontario with branches in Toronto, New York, California, New Jersey, Illinois, New Hampshire, and Alabama. The company offers next-generation OSS product solutions that are prepackaged and tailor-made for the telecommunications service industry. These packages include inventory control, network maintenance, network problem resolution, billing, network element management, network surveillance and service provisioning. Certainly one of MetaSolv's largest direct competitors, EFTIA challenges MetaSolv in 50 percent to 60 percent every sales transaction.[7] The breadth of their customer base includes:

- Competitive local exchange carriers (CLEC)
- Data local exchange carriers (DLEC)
- Internet service providers (ISP)
- Incumbent local exchange carriers (ILEC)
- Digital subscriber line (DSL) providers
- Interexchange carriers (IXC)
- Cable, utility and transport companies, particularly power companies expanding into the telecom market such as Williams Companies.

Exhibit 1 **Current MetaSolv Customers**

Allegiance Telecom www.allegiancetele.com
Ameritech www.ameritech.com
BC Tel (BCT.TELUS Communications)—Canada www.bctel.com
Bell Atlantic Global www.baglobal.com
Birch Telecom www.birch.com
BlueStar Communications www.bluestar.net
BTI Telecom Corporation www.btitele.com
CapRock Communications Corp. www.caprock.com
Choice One Communications www.choiceonecom.com
Conectiv www.conectiv.com
Cox Communications www.cox.com
CT Communications (CTC) www.ctc.net
Digital Teleport, Inc. www.dti-usa.com
DSL.net www.dsl.net
Electric Lightwave, Inc. (ELI) www.eli.net
e.spire www.espire.net
Fibernet Telecom Group, Inc. www.ftgx.com
GST Telecommunications, Inc. www.gstcorp.com
GTE www.gte.com
GTE Global Network Infrastructure (GNI) www.gte.com
HarvardNet www.harvardnet.com
Horry Telephone Cooperative, Inc. www.htcinc.net
Illinois Consolidated Telephone Co. www.illinoisconsolidated.com
Interpath Communications www.interpath.com
IXnet www.ixnet.com
KINI L.C. (Kansas Cellular) www.kansascellular.com
Lambda Communications www.lambda.ro
LightNetworks Communications www.lightnetworks.com
Net2000 Communications www.net2000.com
NET-tel www.net-tel.net
NorthPoint Communications www.northpoint.net
NorthwesTel (Canada) www.nwtel.ca
Ovation Communications www.ocicom.com
PaeTec Communications www.paetec.com
PageNet (Paging Network) www.pagenet.com
Pathnet www.pathnet.net
TDS www.tdstelecom.com
Telergy www.telergy.net
Time Warner Telecom www.twtelecom.com
TriVergent www.trivergent.com
US Xchange www.usxchange.com
UtiliCom www.utilicom.com
Williams Communications www.wiltel.net
WinStar Wireless www.winstar.com

SOURCE: MetaSolv.com, "Customer list," 18 Oct. 2000 <http://www.metasolv.com/metasolv/pages/our_customers/customer_list/0,1170,,00.html>

The company has yet to expand its sales beyond the US and Canada, however, it is currently forming alliances with companies such as Cap Gemini Ernst & Young to make this a possibility.

Potential Competitors

Lucent Technologies

While Lucent is not currently a threat to MetaSolv, the company does have the market presence and ability to move into this market. One of the greater concerns at MetaSolv is that industry giants such as Lucent will eventually opt to enter these markets. Although they may not have a more superior product, they certainly would have the name recognition and customer base to do significant damage. MetaSolv hopes to gather as much of the market share as they can now to insulate themselves from this likely scenario.

Backward Vertical Integration

Perhaps the largest competitors facing MetaSolv are telecommunication companies that decide to develop in-house OSS software solutions. Many firms within the industry have opted to design and implement their own software. While this seems like an attractive alternative, many of these firms are not adequately equipped to deal with problems that arise with the systems along the way. Therefore, many companies choosing this option eventually seek the assistance of specialists such as MetaSolv anyway. Nevertheless, homegrown solutions are becoming more prevalent as more competitors enter the telecommunications arena.

Products and Services

MetaSolv produces a single product, a software application called Telecom Business Solution™ (TBS™). MetaSolv derives its revenues from licensing this software (55 percent of total revenues in 1998) and from related professional services and maintenance. TBS™ is an Operations Support System designed to serve the needs of telecommunications service providers.

Operation Support Systems

An OSS is a tool used to organize all the parts of a telecommunications network, including both the physical network and the network of customers, suppliers, and partners. To put it simply, the OSS is the Enterprise Resource Planning (ERP) tool of the telecommunications industry. The OSS provides an end-to-end solution to the service delivery process for telecommunication service providers. Service providers use an OSS to manage functions from order management, network inventory management, provisioning, billing, and customer care.

Telecom Business Solution™ (TBS™)

TBS™ is a comprehensive solution to the communication service provider's needs to integrate and automate their business processes. MetaSolv uses an open and flexible architecture which allows them to add services, integrate with other critical systems, and grow with the customer. They also use a packaged software strategy (as opposed to a customized software strategy) which reduces implementation time, leverages the integration capabilities of partners, and increases margins.

The advent of deregulation in the telecom industry in 1996 resulted in the influx of new service providers. The increased competition among providers resulted in extremely complex networks. MetaSolv was able to capitalize on this reality with their TBS™ software. One of the competitive advantages that MetaSolv has with this software is its complex ordering capability. So far MetaSolv has been one of the only companies to successfully answer the call for a highly advanced OSS.

MetaSolv has a strong commitment to customer satisfaction, and thus is in a continuous improvement mode for their software. Teams in design, marketing, sales, and professional services are constantly providing ideas for enhancements to the software. This dedication to improvement has led MetaSolv to continually add new features and capabilities to the TBS™ software. MetaSolv also believes in the competence of its employees and believes they are the foundation for the success and growth of the company.

One perceived shortcoming of the software is its heavy reliance on PowerBuilder in its technical architecture. PowerBuilder is a graphic PC-based client/server application development environment that allows the user to develop front-end applications that access relational database management systems without coding in a 3rd generation language such as C or C++. It is also referred to as a rapid application development tool since it facilitates development of a working application prototype much quicker than would the same development using a 3rd generation language. Janicki believes that the software has no major weaknesses in functionality but realized that users might perceive the reliance on PowerBuilder as a limit to the performance capabilities of the software. The design team has plans to phase out the use of PowerBuilder as new versions of the software are developed.

TBS™ provides a variety of service providers with solutions, including: Competitive Local Exchange Carriers (CLECs), Incumbent Local Exchange Carriers (ILECs),

Interexchange Carriers (IXCs), Internet Service Providers (ISPs), and Enterprise Users (i.e. large corporations, universities, others). In addition, TBS™ supports a variety of technologies, including traditional voice and data transfer, fiber optics, digital subscriber line (DSL), Internet services, and fixed wireless.

TBS™ is composed of several integrated subsystems (See Exhibit 2):

- *Order Management:* enables service provider to manage external and internal resale, retail, and wholesale orders.
- *Service Provisioning:* enables service provider to design, configure, and assign network inventory. Includes customized circuit design capabilities using owned, leased, or anticipated future facilities.
- *Network Inventory and Design:* enables service provider to organize and view networks in their geographical, electrical, physical, and logical dimensions. Allows user to view past, present, and future views of network inventory (both owned and leased).
- *Customer Care:* enables service provider to track complete customer service history. All information regarding a customer is tightly integrated and flows automatically to the billing system, providing the most accurate information.
- *Trouble Management:* enables service provider to more effectively handle trouble tickets by the integration of the order management, service provisioning, and network design subsystems. The customer service representative has access to the customers past and current services, services currently being installed, technical design details, and past trouble tickets.
- *Work Management:* enables service provider to assign and manage the flow of detailed tasks needed to accomplish order management and fulfillment. Allows the provider to monitor the use of physical and human resources. Customer service representatives are able to track the exact stage that an order is in the process and can therefore provide excellent service.
- *Data Management:* central repository for data entered into the system. Data is thus entered only once and accessible from all appropriate areas of the system.
- *Application Programming Interface (API) and Gateway Management:* All of the above subsystems are supported by a set of APIs and gateways which allows for the electronic exchange of information between TBS™ and other systems (such as billing software).[8]

Functionalities that are not currently built in to the TBS software include billing, customer facing, and network facing. So far MetaSolv has chosen not to enter into the billing market because there are currently many billing software providers. The market is very fragmented and competitive. Customer facing is a functionality that would allow the orders placed by the customers of telecommunication providers to flow automatically into the OSS. The current system requires providers to manually enter the orders submitted by customers. Network

---

Exhibit 2   Graphical Representation of TBS™

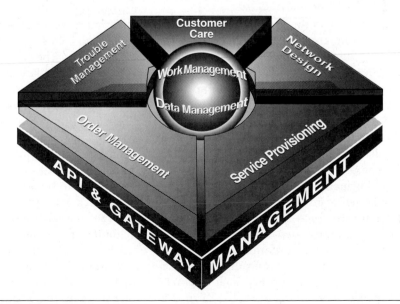

SOURCE: MetaSolv.com, "TBS Software," 18 Oct. 2000 <http://www.metasolv.com/metasolv/media/PDF/productServices/TBS_Software.pdf>

Case 24 / MetaSolv Software Inc.   C.341

facing, also known as activation, is a feature that would allow the OSS software to communicate with the separate hardware and software which controls the activation of the different components of a telecommunication circuit.

Professional Services

MetaSolv offers its customers a range of professional services including implementation support, training, and maintenance. The successful implementation of TBS™ is a challenging task that the customer must perform after licensing the software. MetaSolv provides the customer with support through the following programs:

- Framework for Success™ - set of tools and methodologies that help to provide for a smooth and successful implementation
- TBS Quickstart™ - simplified implementation program that can be installed in less than 90 days
- Rapid Results™ - customized detailed workshop training on implementation
- Data Deployment Tools - enables quick and easy transfer of data into the system
- Post Implementation Review - comprehensive review of implementation to ensure success

In addition MetaSolv conducts training courses in the actual operation of the software, and offers a maintenance and customer support plan. About 45 percent of MetaSolv's revenue came from these professional services in 1998.

Sales and Marketing

MetaSolv does not believe in the position of VP of Sales and Marketing. The company sees these two activities as completely different functions and notes that good marketing people are not necessarily good sales people and vice versa. Essentially, marketing at MetaSolv involves deciding what the product should be and how that product should be positioned within the market and how it will be distributed. The marketing team develops the strategies to efficiently price and place the product and services for the company. Currently MetaSolv employs strictly a direct selling model. They sell their product and services via a dedicated team of direct sales representatives. Indirectly, this sales force is a key source of information for the marketing department. The sales representatives relate important information regarding pricing, product features, and other concerns back to the marketers who are equipped to analyze such information and alter strategies accordingly.

Directions for Growth at MetaSolv
Funding Opportunities

In early 1999, after experiencing a 358 percent increase in revenues in 1998 over 1997, Janicki was eager to push his company to the next level. His primary concern was to provide liquidity for his investors and employee stockholders. While a private company, the stock options that his employees owned held little value. Janicki's other concerns were to continue in his vision of solving problems for telecommunications companies and to preserve the corporate culture that had evolved over the last seven years.

Janicki was in the process of considering his options. Three public companies had expressed interest in purchasing MetaSolv. The idea of selling the company was appealing in that it would provide investors and employees a liquid market for their stock (by virtue of a stock for stock exchange). Selling the company was a low-risk option. The selling price would be certain and MetaSolv's shareholders would be sure to profit. Janicki believed MetaSolv to be worth somewhere around $500 million.

Janicki met with each of the three companies to explore the possibility of agreeing to the proposed acquisition. One of the companies, a large telecommunications company, was willing to offer a price that was similar to Janicki's valuation. However, the company was just beginning its software operations. Janicki worried that the company was not clear on how MetaSolv would fit into their vision. Another company, a very large conglomerate with telecommunications operations, was also willing to offer a fair price for MetaSolv. This company was a well-established business which utilized a traditional, "old school" management style with over 40 top executives. The company did not grant stock options to its employees. Janicki was concerned that the differences in corporate cultures between their two companies might cause a mass exodus of MetaSolv employees once the acquisition was announced. The third company, another large telecommunications company, was looking to buy a software company cheap, and was only offering about 20 percent of what Janicki believed the corporation to be worth.

Another option that was available to Janicki was to take the company public. The recent trend in lucrative technology IPO's was enough to make any entrepreneur consider the option of going public. Janicki believed there would be three main benefits of going public. First, the investors/employees would have a liquid market for their stocks so that the shares they owned could actually be converted into cash easily. Second, MetaSolv would be able to build a "war chest" to insulate itself. Finally, MetaSolv would have a new currency (i.e. stock) with which to make potential acquisitions. The main drawback to taking the company public, as Janicki saw it, is the risk involved. There would be no way to predict accurately how the market will react to the offering so there would be no guaranteed return. On the other hand an IPO had the potential to be very profitable for the company and its investors.

Achieving Growth

Prior to the Telecommunications Act of 1996, MetaSolv had only 5 customers and revenues of $2.2 million. After deregulation, MetaSolv's business skyrocketed. In 1998, MetaSolv had nearly 40 customers and $42.5 million in revenue. Deregulation was key for the company's success, allowing new small telecommunication companies to enter the industry. They needed a software solution, and MetaSolv was there to provide it for them. Nevertheless, MetaSolv knew that the markets within the US and Canada would eventually not be sufficient to sustain the growth to which the company had become accustomed. Therefore, MetaSolv was seriously beginning to explore their international options. They were confident that they could locate global markets with many of the same characteristics of the US market that had brought them so much success. However, they were not quite sure how international competition would fit into their overall strategy.

Expansion with a Single Product

Compounding the problem of expansion was the reality that MetaSolv is essentially a single product company. Currently, MetaSolv's footprint, or area of presence, is in the back-office functions of telecommunications providers. Their software provides functionality in ordering, inventory, network planning, engineering, operations, and customer care. If they were to go public, MetaSolv would need to convince investors that the company has a strong growth strategy given the com-

pany's single product focus. This presented a challenge for Janicki and his top management team. What growth strategies are there for a single product company outside of international expansion? The company has considered using its talented engineering team to design complementary products. Nevertheless, they are concerned that a departure from the activity that has earned them so much success might undermine MetaSolv's overall operations rather than supplement them.

The Uncertain Future

As Janicki left the office for the day, he began to fully appreciate the challenges ahead for MetaSolv. What started out as a good idea that was in the right place at the right time had turned into a multi-million dollar corporation. Now the company was facing a defining moment, and many important decisions needed to be made to thrust MetaSolv onward down the path of continued success. While he understood the difficulty of the road ahead, he also had faith in his company, the employees, and the leadership to meet these challenges before them.

Endnotes

1. BBC Online Network, "Business: The Economy: Global telecoms revolution," 11 Oct. 1999 <http://news.bbc.co.uk/hi/english/business/the_economy/newsid_468000/468206.stm>

2. BBC Online Network, "Business: The Economy Convergence: Three Into One," 14 Oct. 1999 <http://news.bbc.co.uk/hi/english/business/the_economy/newsid_474000/474995.stm>

3. BBC Online Network, "Business: The Economy: Global telecoms revolution," 11 Oct. 1999 <http://news.bbc.co.uk/hi/english/business/the_economy/newsid_468000/468206.stm>

4. Tele Dot Com, "Emerging Economies," 18 Oct. 2000 <http://www.teledotcom.com/1197ar/tdcar97emerging.html>

5. MetaSolv Web-site, "TBS Software," 11 Oct 2000 <http://www.metasolv.com/metasolv/pages/prod_services/TBS/service_technologies/0,1201,,00.html>

6. Jim Janicki, CEO and Sid Sack, COO, MetaSolv Software Inc. Telephone Interview with authors, 4 Oct. 2000

7. Jim Janicki, CEO and Sid Sack, COO, MetaSolv Software Inc. Telephone Interview with authors, 4 Oct. 2000

8. MetaSolv Web-site, "TBS Software," 11 Oct 2000 <http://www.metasolv.com/metasolv/pages/prod_services/TBS/service_technologies/0,1201,,00.html>

Monsanto: Better Living through Genetic Engineering?[1]

Seth Brooks, Melissa Schilling, and John Scrofani

Early in the year 2000, Monsanto Company merged with Pharmacia & Upjohn, forming Pharmacia Corporation, and making Monsanto part of the third largest pharmaceutical company in the world. Later that year, Monsanto raised cash through a partial (15 percent) initial public offering. As of March, 2001, Monsanto employed 14,700 people, and at the helm was president and Chief Executive Officer Hendrik Verfaillie.

Verfaillie faced a number of interesting challenges. Monsanto was a company that had, over the last decade, dramatically reinvented itself. Throughout the twentieth century, Monsanto had acquired many companies, expanding into a diverse range of businesses. However when Bob Shapiro had stepped into the office of Chief Executive Officer in 1993, he restructured the company to be more focused on "life sciences"—or the combination of science and technology to find solutions for growing global needs. Explosive innovation in biotechnology had unleased a vast range of new potential products and offered the allure of tapping new, fast-growing markets. As of 2001, Monsanto had a new capital structure, and a new portfolio focused entirely on applying biotechnology to agriculture.

Though the company had pared down its corporate portfolio in order to have more strategic direction, Monsanto's move towards life sciences was not without its problems. One of the most successful applications of biotechnology to Monsanto's business had been *Roundup*—a popular agricultural herbicide that worked in conjunction with genetically modified crop seeds. The combination of a powerful herbicide and crop seeds that are genetically modified to resist the herbicide had been a profound innovation, and had dramatically increased crop yields. By 1996, *Roundup* accounted for 17 percent of Monsanto's total annual sales.[2] However, Monsanto's patents on *Roundup* had begun to expire in several coun-

tries in 1991, and expired in the U.S. in September 2000. To make matters worse, strong negative consumer perceptions of genetically modified (GM) foods began to surface towards the end of the decade, severely retarding the company's sales in Europe, and beginning to threaten Monsanto's American markets as well.

The Science of Life

Monsanto is an industry leader in the bioengineering of foods. "The term 'biotechnology' refers to the use of living organisms or their products to modify human health and the human environment," according to the National Health Museum's web site.[3]

> "For the thousands of years, from the time human communities began to settle in one place, cultivate crops and farm the land, humans have manipulated the genetic nature of the crops and animals they raise. Crops have been bred to improve yields, enhance taste and extend the growing season. Each of the 15 major crop plants, which provide 90 percent of the globe's food and energy intake, has been extensively manipulated, hybridized, inter-bred and modified over the millennia by countless generations of farmers intent on producing crops in the most effective and efficient ways possible."[4]

Many scientists argue that genetic engineering is simply a ". . . refinement of the kinds of genetic modification that have long been used to enhance plants . . . for food."[5] The science of genetics and the understanding of why physical traits are passed from parent to child began over a century ago. German scientist Gregor Mendel conducted the first experiments aimed at understanding the science behind genetic inheritance. Mendel used artificial hybridization, the fertilization of the flower of one species by the pollen of another species, on thousands of plants, recording the traits of the successive generations. In 1865 he published a paper about his work, Versuche über Pflanzen-Hybriden (Experiments in Plant Hybridization).[6] The idea that physical traits are passed through generations of organisms created the new field of science focused on genetics.

In 1953, James Watson, a U.S. biologist, and Francis Crick, an English biophysicist, discovered the structure of DNA (deoxyribonucleic acid).[7] DNA works like a blueprint to define all characteristics, or traits, of an organism. A DNA molecule has a double-helix shape, like a twisting stepladder. DNA strands are quite similar to a written language. The "letters" of this genetic language are formed by the DNA nucleotides, which are the "steps" in the DNA stepladder. The "words" in the genetic language are formed of codons, each codon consisting of three nucleotides. The "sentences" in the genetic language are genes, which are made up of many codons. A "book" in the genetic language is an entire string of DNA, which defines all the characteristics of an organism.

Modern understanding of the chemical properties of DNA allows scientists to "cut" the DNA strand at a certain point in the stepladder using enzymes that are produced naturally by some bacteria. With this enzyme technology, scientists can "cut" away a desirable gene from one organism, then "paste" that gene into another organism, forming what is called a recombinant DNA strand (see **Exhibit 1**). It is through this cutting and pasting of genes that scientists can give organisms traits that they previously did not have, without the use of the longer and more ambiguous process of cross-fertilization.

Genetically Engineered Crops and Herbicide

"Without efficient crop protection products, worldwide yields would fall by an average of 30 to 60 percent. They would also fluctuate wildly."[8]

Farmers across the world can either choose to spray their crops with some form of herbicide, or they can till their land on a daily basis, drastically decreasing their productivity. If they do choose herbicide, they can go the

---

Exhibit 1   Cutting and Pasting DNA

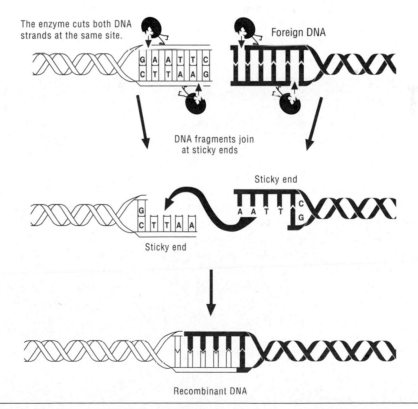

The enzyme cuts both DNA strands at the same site.

Foreign DNA

DNA fragments join at sticky ends

Sticky end

Sticky end

Recombinant DNA

SOURCE: Modified from http://esg-www.mit.edu:8001/bio/rdna/cloning.html.

path of buying very effective and expensive proprietary products such as *Roundup*, or they can buy the cheaper alternative generic brands like *Squadron, Storm* or *Post Plus*. A 1997 study indicated that *Roundup* clearly outperformed these generic brands. The results showed that *Roundup* lead to a net income per acre of $235 compared to the others, which produced $209 per acre (see Exhibit 2). *Roundup* cost about $34 per gallon compared to generic brands that cost $15–$20 per gallon[9]. In 1998, Monsanto lowered the cost of *Roundup* by $6 to $10 per gallon in 1998 in order to increase sales volume and to better compete with generic companies. Generic products were popular in developing countries where it was difficult for farmers to afford proprietary products.[10] Furthermore, competing with generic brands had become particularly important as *Roundup's* patents began to expire.

Roundup® Herbicide Technology

Roundup is a wide-spectrum herbicide, meaning that it is toxic to any plants it comes in contact with. As noted in the **Mother Jones** environmental journal," . . . its main ingredient, glyphosate, breaks down quickly in soil, so that little or no toxic byproduct accumulates in plant or animal tissue—a detail that Monsanto highlights when describing itself as an environmentally friendly company."[11] As of March, 2001, *Roundup* had been used commercially for more than 20 years and was used in over 100 countries. It was estimated that in 1998, worldwide use of glyphosphate exceeded 112,000 tons, and that 71 percent of all genetically engineered crops planted that year were designed to be resistant to herbicides such as Monsanto's *Roundup*.[12]

Roundup Ready© Crops

Monsanto genetically altered several agricultural products to be resistant to *Roundup* herbicide. These crops, including *Roundup Ready* Soybeans, *Roundup Ready* Canola, and *Roundup Ready* Cotton, are sold to farmers. *Roundup Ready* soybean, the first of Monsanto's "*Roundup Ready*" genetically altered crops, was approved for commercialization in 1995.

"Farmers using Roundup Ready *seeds can only use* Roundup, *because any other broad-spectrum herbicide will kill their crops. So, with every* Roundup Ready *seed sale, Monsanto sells a season's worth of its week killer as well. The company also keeps close tabs on the crops' progress: Farmers must sign a contract promising not to sell or give away any seeds or save them for next year's planting, and the company inspects its customers' farms for violations."*[13]

Terminal Technology

"On March 3 1998 the company Delta and Pine Land Co. (Mississippi, USA) and the U.S. Department of Agriculture (USDA) announced that they received US

Exhibit 2	**Roundup versus Generic Brands**		
Herbicide treatment	SOG	Yield BU/A	Net Income/Acre
Squadron 3 pts	PRE	33.6	$209.20
Storm 1.5 pts + Poast Plus 24 oz	21 DAP + 7 Later	33.6	$204.70
Roundup Ultra 32 oz	28 DAP	36.8	$235.80

The *Roundup* vs. best conventional herbicide alternative study was designed to evaluate the economics of the *Roundup Ready* seed/herbicide system versus conventional herbicide programs. Each herbicide program was applied at labeled rates. Net income is figured by multiplying the yield (Bu/A) by $7.00 minus herbicide costs, minus a $4.00 fee per herbicide application, and the $5.00 tech fee for *Roundup Ready* soybeans figured at a bag per acre.

In the systems study herbicide applications were made based on labeled recommendations and no other weed control was allowed. The systems studies are designed to measure the effectiveness of the herbicide management practices and input costs. Based on the 1996 trial at Marion AR the *Roundup Ready* seed/herbicide system was superior economically to the other two conventional herbicide programs. These differences can be attributed to advantages in weed control and the removal of crop stress typically associated with conventional herbicide programs.

SOURCE: http://www.asgrow.com/gknowled/CRMar96RR5.html

Case 25 /Monsanto: Better Living through Genetic Engineering?

Patent No. 5,723,765 on a new genetic technology designed to prevent unauthorized seed saving by farmers.[14]

On March 3, 1998, a company called Delta and Pine Land Company received a patent on a new genetic technology designed to prevent unauthorized seed saving. The technology enabled the environment to influence the characteristics a plant exhibits, even if the parents of the plant do not have those characteristics. With this technology it was possible to create genetic characteristics in plants that only emerge if they have the proper external stimulus. For example, two genetically altered parent plants can thrive in a moist region and exhibit characteristics of tropical plants, and their offspring can be moved to a desert region and exhibit characteristics of a desert plant, even though neither parent exhibited these desert characteristics. Monsanto hoped to capitalize on this technology by using it to prevent farmers from saving their seeds from year to year (and thus forgoing purchasing them from Monsanto). Monsanto would have utilized this technology by altering the plant's reproductive system so that unless a patented chemical was applied to the seeds at a certain time during their development, the seeds would be unable to germinate. This technology would have further strengthened Monsanto's ability to enforce its contracts with farmers, by making the farmers unable to use seeds harvested from the plants they grew using Monsanto's seeds in the next season.

Monsanto announced its intention to merge with Delta and Pine Land Co. in the spring of 1998, in hopes of acquiring this technology. However, in response to consumer and farmer outrage, Robert Shapiro wrote an open letter dated October 4, 1999, stating that Monsanto was making the public a ". . . commitment not to commercialize sterile seed technologies, such as the one dubbed 'Terminator.' We are doing this based on input from . . . a wide range of other experts and stakeholders, including our very important grower constituency."[15] Additionally, Shapiro wrote ". . . though we do not yet own any sterile seed technology, we think it is important to respond to those concerns at this time by making clear our commitment not to commercialize gene protection systems that render seed sterile."[16] Monsanto withdrew its Department of Justice filing for a merger with Delta and Pine Land Co. on Dec. 20, 1999.

History of Monsanto

Monsanto's Germination

Monsanto was founded in 1901 by John Francis Queeny, a thirty-year veteran of the Meyer Brothers Drug Company, with the goal of producing products for the food and pharmaceutical industries. The company was named after the founder's wife, whose maiden name was Olga Mendez Monsanto. In 1902 the St. Louis based company began producing saccharin. For several years after, the entire saccharin output was shipped to Georgia-based Coca-Cola Co. The company soon began producing caffeine and vanilla as well. In 1917, Monsanto entered the pharmaceuticals business when it became the first company to produce Aspirin.

As a result of financial crisis and wartime debt in the late 1920's, stock was offered to the public in 1927, one year before Edgar Queeny, the son of John Queeny, succeeded his father as president of the company. He announced his vision of an era of expansion into new businesses that would take Monsanto into the 1930's. This expansion would include immediate acquisitions that expanded the company into the rubber, chemicals, textile, paper, leather, soap and detergents industries. Monsanto also moved into the plastics and resin industries, the result of which gave it ownership of the first man-made plastic, celluloid.

During the WWII years, Monsanto became involved in uranium research for the Manhattan project. This was done in the Mound Plant in Dayton Ohio, which was used as a nuclear facility for the government for the next forty years. In the 1950's, Monsanto began to expand its chemical business. Through licensing technology from DuPont, the company began to produce acrylic fiber and nylon. Monsanto also entered into the fertilizer industry, as well as the plastic bottle industry. During this decade, Monsanto built a plant to produce ultra-pure silicone, which was used as raw material in the electronics industry.

In the 1960's, Monsanto created a new company division focused exclusively on agriculture. It introduced *Lasso* herbicide, and *Roundup* followed a few years later. In the late sixties, almost a decade after establishing the agriculture division, Monsanto moved into the seed and hybrid swine business through an acquisition. The 1972 appointment of John W. Hanley marked the beginning of an era of heavy investment in biotechnology research.

The 1980's began with a new president being named: Richard J. Mahoney. Immediately after assuming the position, Mahoney sold off the commodity chemicals portion of Monsanto's business to DuPont. Monsanto used the money for new research and development, and created new technologies including the artificial sweetener "Nutrasweet" and aspartame. In the beginning of the 1980's, Monsanto declared biotechnology as its strategic research focus. One year after this announcement, scientists at Monsanto were the first to successfully genetically modify a plant cell. This led to success in growing plants with genetically engineered traits. Two years after this success, a major restructuring of the company took place. Monsanto divested its non-strategic businesses to consolidate around its core competency, high value-added proprietary products.

The 1990's served as a decade of expanding medicine production for Monsanto. Using new techniques in bio-engineering, it was able to create new medicines at a faster pace than ever before. In the early 1990's, it sold its first *Ambien,* an insomnia treatment, and *Daypro,* an arthritis treatment. In 1993, Robert B. Shapiro was named the new CEO of Monsanto. He announced that the company would refocus its strategy and become a life sciences company. In the mid-1990's, Monsanto's first genetically altered crops were approved for commercial sale, including *Roundup Ready* glyphosate-tolerant soybeans. Monsanto formed the Solaris Unit, which produced *Ortho, Greensweep* and *Roundup* law and garden products.

As part of his effort to restyle Monsanto into an exclusively life sciences company, in 1997, Shapiro urged the company to spin off all the chemical parts of the business into a company called Solutia. Shapiro saw this as a good way for his company to increase its profitability by focusing on a key competitive advantage: Monsanto was one of very few companies to have the ability to genetically modify plants. He pondered how he could exploit this advantage and still retain a good reputation for his company. Shapiro, and later Verfaillie, would later find out that this would not be an easy task to accomplish (see Exhibit 3 for a complete corporate diversification timeline).

Monsanto's Evolved Form

On December 19, 1999, Monsanto and pharmaceutical giant Pharmacia & Upjohn, Co. announced their intention to merge. The merger was approved by shareowners on March 23, 1999, creating a new entity called Pharmacia Corporation. Monsanto's pharmaceutical business was merged with Pharmacia & Upjohn's. According to the Pharmacia website, "Monsanto Company is the wholly owned agricultural subsidiary of Pharmacia Corporation. Monsanto is committed to finding solutions to the growing global needs for food and health by sharing common forms of science and technology among agriculture, nutrition and health."[17] (please see Exhibits 4 and Exhibit 5 for Monsanto's financial information).

Monsanto's Suppliers

In its move to become a company oriented around life sciences, Monsanto had spun off its chemical businesses that made the chemicals necessary to produce *Roundup.* Though in general it was not dependent on any single supplier for a significant amount of its raw materials or fuel requirements, certain raw materials were obtained from a few major suppliers. For instance, Monsanto purchased its North American supply of elemental phosphorus, a key raw material for the production of *Roundup* herbicide, from P4 Production, L.L.C., a joint venture between Monsanto and Solutia Inc.[18]

Exhibit 3	Monsanto's Corporate Diversification Timeline

1901 Monsanto Chemical Works opens in St. Louis	**1932** Monsanto Canada Ltd. opens as a joint venture with St. Louis neighbor Mallinckrodt. Later, Monsanto buys out Mallinckrodt.
1918 Acquisition of the Commercial Acid Company of Illinois	
1919 Purchase of 50 percent of R.A. Graesser Chemical Works, Ruabon, Wales, Great Britain's leading producer of phenol.	**1935** Acquired the Swann Corp., taking Monsanto into the soap and detergents industry with phosphorus and phosphate chemistry
1929 Acquisition of Rubber Services Laboratories (rubber chemicals) based in Akron, Ohio, and Nitro, West Virginia	**1936** Thomas & Hochwalt Laboratories of Dayton, Ohio, acquired becomes the core of Monsanto Central Research.
Acquisition of Merrimac Chemical Co. of Massachusetts (chemicals for textile, paper and leather production)	**1938** Purchase of Fiberloid Corp. and 50 percent of Shawinigan Resins (100 percent in 1963), both of Springfield, Massachusetts, marks entry into plastics and resins. Fiberloid produced celluloid, the first man-made plastic and a precursor of Saflex interlayer.
1930 Monsanto purchases Southern Cross Chemical Co. Pty. Ltd., of Melbourne, Australia.	
1931 Graesser-Monsanto name changed to Monsanto Chemicals Ltd. after the acquisition of remaining Graesser stock in 1928.	

1950	Chemstrand, a joint venture with American Viscose to produce synthetic fibers, starts up.
1954	Mobay is formed as a joint venture with Bayer to work on isocyanate chemistry. (Bayer took total ownership in 1967.)
1955	Lion Oil acquired, primarily to provide petrochemical raw materials.
1957	Fifty percent of Plax Corporation is acquired, moving Monsanto into plastic bottle technology.
1957	Fome-Cor Corporation is formed as a 50/50 joint venture with St. Regis Paper Co.; Monsanto buys 100 percent in 1964.
1960	Agriculture Division created.
1969	Fisher Governor Co. acquired, becomes Fisher Controls subsidiary (sold in 1992).
1969	Monsanto Enviro-Chem Systems Inc. formed as a wholly owned subsidiary.
1969	Farmers Hybrid Companies Inc. acquired, creating small stake in seed (and hybrid swine) business (sold in 1983).
1977	Joint petrochemical venture established with Conoco at the Chocolate Bayou plant.
1980	Separations Group formed to capitalize on gas separation systems; becomes Permea, a wholly owned subsidiary, in 1985 (sold in 1991).
1981	DuPont acquisition of Conoco leads to sale of Monsanto's stake in the Conoco joint venture.
1982	Monsanto Hybritech Seed International Inc. is formed upon acquisition of DeKalb's wheat research program.
1982	Ammonium nitrate fertilizer business sold.
1983	Jacob Hartz Seed Co. (soybeans) acquired.
1985	G.D. Searle & Co. purchased, taking the company into pharmaceuticals and sweeteners.
1985–1993	Major strategic restructuring takes place, including sale of several non-strategic businesses. Monsanto consolidated businesses around high-value-added proprietary products. Emphasis was increasingly on life sciences' agriculture, pharmaceuticals and food. Divested businesses included Astro Turf stadium surface and related businesses, polyethylene film, sorbate food preservatives, Fome-Cor foam board, Fisher Controls International, and others.
1986	The NutraSweet Co. is broken out of Searle and established with a separate identity.
1988	Greensweep lawn and garden products acquired.
1991	NatureMark unit formed to sell genetically engineered insect-protected potatoes.
1993	Ortho Consumer Products business, the U.S. leader in lawn and garden products, acquired. Leads to formation of Solaris unit, built around Ortho, Greensweep, and *Roundup* lawn and garden products.
1995	Flexsys created; a 50/50 joint venture with Akzo Nobel S.A., to be the world's largest producer of rubber chemicals and instruments.
1995	Styrenics plastics business sold.
1995–1997	Major acquisitions and relationships made in life-sciences areas, including: • Kelco specialty chemicals division of Merck & Co. (1995) • Calgene Inc., a leader plant biotechnology (1995, 1997) • Asgrow Argonomics, a leader in soybean and corn seeds (1996) • Partnership with Delta & Pine Land Co., leader in cotton seed (1996) • Monsoy, for access to Brazilian soybean seed market, world's second largest (1996) • Agracetus, to strengthen technology base (1996) • Biolab Industrias Farmaceuticas S.A., to strengthen Latin American presence in cardiovascular, arthritis and women's health-care products (1996) • Syntex, strengthening Searle's long-standing market presence in women's healthcare (1996) • Holden's Foundation Seeds Inc., world's leader in "foundation" seeds, the basic genetic material for retail seeds (1997) • Major stake in DeKalb Genetics, second largest U.S. seed company (1997)
1997	Monsanto spins off chemicals businesses as Solutia Inc. in order to focus on life sciences.

SOURCE: www.monsanto.com

On the crop side of the business, Monsanto had engaged in a spree of mergers and acquisitions, expanding its business to incorporate companies that had previously supplied many of the raw materials that Monsanto used to develop *Roundup Ready* crops. Monsanto acquired or formed long-term relationships with six seed companies between 1995 and 1997 (see Exhibit 3).

Research and Development

Monsanto prided itself on being a company that develops breakthrough proprietary technology. The development of *Roundup* in the 1960's had put Monsanto's agricultural division into the forefront, and scientists in this division were working hard to develop the next generation of herbicide and seed systems. In the early 1990's, Bruce Bickner, Co-President of Monsanto's agribusiness spent $.14 per revenue dollar on R&D compared to the industry average of $.09 per revenue dollar.[19] However, some felt that Monsanto's focus on

R&D-based proprietary products might cause it to miss out on the large global market for crop protection. It was estimated that by 2001, 53 percent of the world agrochemical market would consist of generic chemicals (rather than proprietary chemicals) that developing countries could afford to buy[20]. It was already apparent that Monsanto's sales growth in international markets was far weaker than sales growth in the U.S. (see Exhibits 6 and 7).

Human Resources

Monsanto placed considerable emphasis on the value of its employees. It was often reinforced that excellent management of people was crucial to retain Monsanto's foothold in the market. HR managers were required to have a Master's degree and at least five years of HR management experience ". . . to ensure proper staffing skills, change management, coaching and counseling, project management and organizational design."[21] The senior staff at Monsanto went to great effort to place people

Exhibit 4	Monsanto Statement of Consolidated Income (loss) in millions $US[51]		
	2000	1999	1998
Net Sales	5,493	5,248	4,448
Cost of goods sold	2,770	2,556	2,149
Gross Profit	2,723	2,692	2,299
Operating Expenses:			
Selling, general and administrative expenses	1,253	1,237	1,135
Research and development expenses	588	695	536
Acquired in-process research and development			402
Amortization and adjustment of goodwill	212	128	77
Restructuring—net	103	22	94
Total operating expenses	2,156	2,082	2,244
Income from Operations	567	610	55
Interest Expense (net of interest income of $30, $26 and $27 in 2000, 1999 and 1998, respectively)	(184)	(243)	(94)
Other expense (income)—net	(49)	(104)	(21)
Income (Loss) Before Income Taxes and Cumulative Effect of Accounting Change	334	263	(60)
Income tax provision	(159)	(113)	(65)
Income (Loss) Before Cumulative Effect of Accounting Change	175	150	(125)
Cumulative effect of a change in accounting principle, net of tax benefit of $16 million	(26)		
Net Income (Loss)	149	150	(125)

[51]Data from Monsanto 2000 Annual Report.

Assets	2000	1999
Current Assets:		
Cash and cash equivalents	131	26
Trade receivables, net of allowances of $171 in 2000 and $151 in 1999	2,515	2,028
Miscellaneous receivables	283	350
Related party loan receivable	205	
Related party receivable	261	
Deferred tax assets	225	130
Inventories	1,253	1,440
Other current assets	100	53
Total Current Assets	4,973	4,027
Property, Plant and Equipment		
Land	69	82
Buildings	766	708
Machinery and equipment	2,688	2,187
Computer software	190	155
Construction in progress	746	726
Total property, plant and equipment	4,459	3,858
Less accumulated depreciation	1,800	1,639
Net Property, Plant and Equipment	2,659	2,219
Goodwill (net of accumulated amortization of $290 in 2000 and $183 in 1999)	2,827	3,081
Other Intangible Assets (net of accumulated amortization of $506 in 2000 and $362 in 1999)	779	935
Other Assets	488	839
Total Assets	11,726	11,101
Liabilities and Shareowners' Equity		
Current Liabilities:		
Short-term debt	158	
Related party short-term loan payable	635	
Short-term debt of parent attributable to Monsanto		89
Accounts payable	525	466
Related party payable	162	
Accrued compensation and benefits	172	147
Restructuring reserves	38	26
Accrued marketing programs	181	256
Miscellaneous short-term accruals	886	720
Total Current Liabilities	2,757	1,704
Long-Term Debt	962	
Long-Term Debt of Parent Attributable to Monsanto		4,278
Postretirement Liabilities	367	
Other Liabilities	299	474

(continued)

Assets	2000	1999
Shareowners' Equity		
Common stock (authorized: 1,500,000,000 shares, par value $0.01)		
Issued: 258,043,000 shares in 2000	3	
Additional contributed capital	7,853	
Parent company's net investment		4,926
Retained earnings	2	
Accumulated other comprehensive loss	(479)	(281)
Reserve for ESOP debt retirement—attributable to Monsanto	(38)	
Total Shareowners' Equity	7,341	4,645
Total Liabilities and Shareowners' Equity	11,726	11,101

[52]Data from Monsanto's 2000 Annual Report.

into the positions that fit them best, believing that a failure to properly allocate employees would result in a forfeiture of the company's competitive position.

Marketing

Monsanto targeted professional farmers by advertising *Roundup* in magazines such as *Farm & Country, Farm Journal,* and *High Plains Journal.*[22] The primary marketing message for *Roundup* was that it was a safe product to use. The productivity increase enabled by *Roundup* was already clear to farmers—at least those in the U.S. As noted in the *Economist,* "Americans in general have a positive perception of technology and are willing to accept the biological version of it. They are willing to overlook the fact that they are growing and eating genetically modified foods in return for increased yields and reduced costs."[23] Ron Thompson, a corn farmer in Illinois noted, "If there is a farm that grows corn, canola, soy, or wheat, then its farmer probably buys *Roundup*. It is in his best interest."[24]

Distribution

On July 12, 1999, Monsanto signed an agreement making Scott's Company the sole marketing and distribution agent of *Roundup* in the United States. Scott's was the most recognized agent of garden products in the United States.[25] Prior to this, Monsanto distributed *Roundup* through the Central Garden and Pet Company, which sold *Roundup* to retailers and sometimes directly to farmers. Global opportunities had also caught Monsanto's

attention. "The international potential for our existing biotechnology traits is roughly double the acreage potential within North America," noted Verfaillie. In July 1998, Monsanto purchased Cargill Seed Business, an already established worldwide seed company with operations and distribution in 51 countries in Central and South America, Europe, Asia, and Africa, in order to gain quicker access to these markets.[26]

As part of its strategy to lessen its reliance on U.S. sales and increase the acceptance of biotechnology internationally, Monsanto's near term plans included 1) working with the Brazilian government and other stakeholders to obtain approval for planting *Roundup Ready* soybeans in Brazil, 2) accelerating the commercialization of *Roundup Ready* corn by securing a license to import grain grown from *Roundup Ready* seeds into Europe, and 3) expanding its markets in Asia by securing the approval of *Bollgard* insect-protected cotton in India.[27]

Leveling the Field

Monsanto faced several large competitors. One giant in the market was American Home Products (AHP), whose agricultural subsidiary Cynamid Corporation competed directly with Monsanto through a heavy focus on R&D and marketing.[28] It had introduced alternative products that had the same chemical base as *Roundup* and thus could be used with it. DuPont Corporation and Novartis Corporation also competed with Monsanto and its parent company, Pharmacia, primarily in the areas of phar-

Case 25 /Monsanto: Better Living through Genetic Engineering?

Exhibit 6   Monsanto's Sales by Region

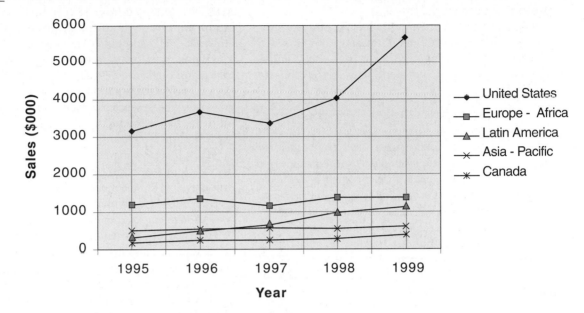

maceuticals, chemicals, and consumer home products. The patent expiration of glyphosate had further opened opportunities for companies to enter the agribusiness, an area that had long been dominated by Monsanto.

Patent Expiration

Roundup was registered for use in 1974, and by 1991 patents protecting it had expired in several countries. Patent protection for the active ingredient in the herbi-

cide expired in the U.S. in September 2000.[29] Having had a monopoly on the production and sale of Roundup herbicide for almost three decades, Monsanto now stood on the threshold of competing with other chemical firms in Roundup compatible herbicides. To protect its market share, Monsanto began selectively slashing prices on Roundup in markets where patent expiration was most likely to impact sales. Monsanto hoped to recoup in volume what it would lose in profit margins. Additionally,

Exhibit 7   Monsanto's Trade Receivables by Region

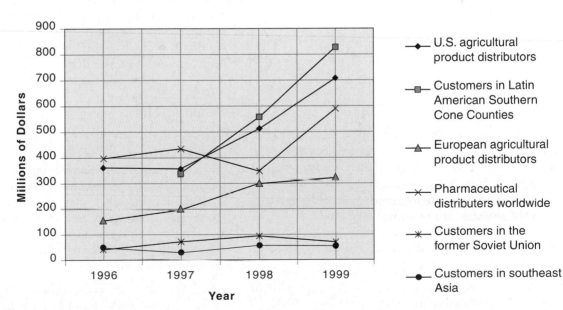

Monsanto hoped to preempt competitors from creating their own *Roundup* alternatives by entering into licensing agreements with them.

On January 19, 1999, Dow Chemical Company subsidiary AgroSciences LLC and Monsanto announced a multi-year manufacturing agreement that also licensed the rights to Monsanto's patent data for glyphosate herbicide.

> *"The agreement will allow Dow AgroSciences to register its own brand of glyphosate herbicide for sale globally. However, Dow AgroSciences will not be able to reference Monsanto data when registering its products for use in Japan. Additionally, the agreement allows Dow AgroSciences to use its own brand of glyphosate herbicide over the top of* Roundup Ready *soybeans and cotton in the year 2000 in the United States, and beginning in 2001, over the top of* Roundup Ready *corn in the United States."*[30]

Dupont

Dupont was an extremely large company with $28 billion in sales in 1999.[31] Its business was split fairly evenly between three divisions: Chemicals (which Dupont is most widely known for), pharmaceuticals, and life sciences. From 1998 to 2000 its herbicide share in the soybean market had slipped from 30 percent to 12 percent due to inroads by *Roundup*, and the company was forced to slash 800 jobs in the agricultural division.[32] However in 2000, the company began producing herbicides similar to *Roundup* under a licensing arrangement from Monsanto.

Novartis

Novartis competed in the areas of consumer health, healthcare, and agribusiness with $25 billion in sales in 1999.[33] The company was founded in 1758 under the name Ciba Geigy, and began by producing chemicals, dyes, and drugs of all kinds. At the time of Monsanto's inception in 1901, Ciba was a market leader in artificial sweeteners. Like Monsanto and AHP, it competed worldwide, offering herbicides, insecticides, plant activators, and seed treatment. While Novartis had not developed any breakthrough agricultural products in recent years, it did have the highest capital-spending budget for R&D in crop protection technologies.[34] It also licensed glyphosate from Monsanto for use in its herbicide products.

American Home Products

As mentioned previously, American Home products posed a significant threat to Monsanto. Its acquisition of Cynamid Corporation in 1994 significantly strength-ened the company on a global basis, placing AHP among the top-tier in sales of agricultural sciences.[35] AHP's sales jumped from $8.9 billion in 1994 to $13.3 billion in 1995, due to the acquisition of Cynamid.[36] However, AHP showed a net loss of $1.2 million in 1999, due to the mass restructuring of the organization to accommodate the new agricultural company. In addition, it conducted a nationwide inventory buyback program of soybean seeds in order to prepare for Cynamid's future herbicide products. This reduced 1999 net sales by $175 million.[37]

AHP's focus on market research and R&D resulted in the development of an improved alternative to *Roundup* products, EXTREME™ herbicide and PURSUIT residual. EXTREME™ used glyphosate, the same main ingredient used in *Roundup*, and combined it with a residual agent PURSUIT, which prevented new weeds from growing up to six days after application.[38] The customer could not get this benefit from using *Roundup* alone. When AHP asked customers how to improve *Roundup*, eighty-five percent of them responded, "give it residual control."[39] The two companies, Cynamid (AHP) and Monsanto, signed a multi-year agreement in July 1999 in which Cynamid (AHP) would be allowed to purchase the glyphosate for use in EXTREME™.[40] Since the product could be used in conjunction with the glyphosate-immune seeds sold by Monsanto, AHP was able to benefit by Monsanto's large installed base of existing customers (see Exhibit 8).

Growing Concerns

The genetically modified food industry had long faced opposition in Europe, and was facing increasing criticism in the U.S. In addition, Monsanto in particular was facing charges of misleading advertising, and that *Roundup's* primary active ingredient, glyphosate, had been linked to illnesses that included a form of cancer known as non-Hodgkin's lymphoma.

Patenting Life

Although in the year 2000 the controversy over bioengineered foods was only beginning in the United States, other countries had advocated against the sale of GM food for years. The use of biotechnology to create genetically modified food ". . . has set off a firestorm among European Consumers."[41] In the European Union, a legal and political battle had ensued over whether or not to allow companies to patent "life" (i.e. gene sequences which they have either discovered or engineered).

> *"In 1988, the European Commission first proposed a patent directive (law) which would have allowed such*

Case 25 /Monsanto: Better Living through Genetic Engineering?

patents. Seven years later, in 1995, the European Parliament (EP) rejected this legislative proposal because it deemed the patenting of life-forms unethical. But in 1998, the Parliament succumbed to pressure from the biotech industry and adopted the "Life Patents Directive." However, the Directive is now being challenged before the European Court of Justice and it is still not certain whether the industry will get what it wants. In addition, matters are made even more complicated by the existence of a parallel patenting system, the much older European Patent Convention (EPC), which does not allow patents on plants but is undecided on patents on animals and genes."[42]

Patents on gene sequences were first allowed in the United States. If laws banning the patenting of gene sequences were upheld, Monsanto would be unable to protect itself from other companies copying and reselling the technology in which it had invested so heavily.

The Regulation of Genetically Modified Foods

In the United States, the Food and Drug Administration is responsible for regulating the biotech industry.

"Under FDA policy developers of bioengineered foods are expected to consult with the agency before marketing, to ensure that all safety and regulatory questions have been fully addressed. FDA's policy also requires special labeling for bioengineered foods under certain circum-

stances. For example, a bioengineered food would need to be called by a different or modified name if its composition were significantly different from its conventionally grown counterpart, or if its nutritive value has been significantly altered. Special labeling would be required if consumers need to be informed about a safety issue, such as the possible presence of an allergen that would not normally be found in the conventionally-grown product."[43]

As the FDA policy existed in 2000, most products that contained genetically modified components did not need to state this fact on their labels. This raised heavy criticism from consumer advocacy groups, which lobbied to have food containing GM products labeled as such. One advocacy group, Greenpeace, released a guideline for labeling GM foods (see Exhibit 9).

Consumer advocates also criticized the FDA's policy that unless a genetically modified food is significantly different from its "natural" counterpart, the agency would not test that food product for safety. The FDA asserted that GM food is ". . . exempt from testing because it is 'generally recognized as safe' (GRAS)."[44] However, many scientists, including scientists working for the FDA, insisted that the agency should test all genetically modified products on the market.

Herbicide Risks

Many operations to the use of genetically modified food were also concerned because companies developing herbicide resistant crops had begun requesting permits

Exhibit 8	Global Herbicide Sales in US Dollars of American Home Products/Monsanto, $MM						
	1997	1998E	1999E	2000P	2001P	2002P	97–02 'CGR
Roundup	$2,188	$2,450	$2,650	$2,850	$2,850	$2,850	5%
Pursuit	540	570	600	625	650	675	5%
Prowl/Stomp	314	325	340	360	380	400	5%
Scepter	117	135	165	195	225	250	16%
Lasso/Harness	390	360	360	360	360	360	-2%
BST	160	190	210	230	250	270	11%
Squadron	68	80	95	110	125	140	16%
Other Herbicides	448	490	550	610	660	700	9%
Total Herbicides	$4,225	$4,600	$4,970	$5,340	$5,500	$5,645	6%
% Change	15%	9%	8%	7%	3%	3%	

E = Estimated, P = Predicted
SOURCE: Pharmaceutical Industry Pulse Part 6, SG Cowen Securities Corporation, October 1, 1998.

allowing higher residues of chemicals in genetically engineered food. For example, Monsanto had already received permits enabling a threefold increase in herbicide residues on genetically engineered soybeans in Europe and the U.S. (up from 6 parts per million (PPM) to 20 PPM).[45] This was particularly alarming because a study by Swedish oncologists Dr. Lennart Hardell and Dr. Mikael Eriksson published in the March 15, 1999 *Journal of American Cancer Society*, indicated a link between glyphosate and non-Hodgkin's lymphoma (NHL). The researchers maintained that exposure to glyphosate increased the risk of contracting this form of cancer.[46]

Sadhbh O'Neill, of the European organization Genetic Concern, stated that this study reinforces concerns by environmentalists and health professionals that:

". . . far from reducing herbicide use, glyphosate resistant crops may result in increased residues to which we as consumers will be exposed in our food. 'Increased residues of glyphosate and its metabolites are already on sale via genetically engineered soya, common in processed foods. However no studies of the effects of GE soya sprayed with Roundup on health have been carried out either on animals or humans to date."[47]

"The United States Department of Agriculture (USDA) statistics from 1997 show that expanded plantings of Roundup Ready soybeans (i.e. soybeans genetically engineered to be tolerant to the herbicide) resulted in a 72 percent increase in the use of glyphosate. According to the Pesticides Action Network, scientists estimate that plants genetically engineered to be herbicide resistant will actually triple the amount of herbicides used. Farmers, knowing that their crop can tolerate or resist being killed off by the herbicides, will tend to use them more liberally."[48]

Misleading Advertising

Though Monsanto marketed *Roundup* as a "biodegradable" and "environmentally" friendly, test results had shown that the main ingredient in *Roundup*, glysophate,

was the number one cause of illness among farm workers.[49] This brought them under close scrutiny by the U.S. Attorney General's office. As a result, Monsanto was forced to pay fines up to $100,000 to compensate the government for the money spent in the investigation.

To counter the European aversion to genetically modified foods, Monsanto launched a $1.6 million campaign to ease Europeans' hard feelings about genetically modified seeds and pesticides. It promised citizens that genetically modified foods were harmless to the environment and to people who eat them. It also declared that GM potatoes and tomatoes had been approved for sale in the U.K. (when in fact the U.K. had not yet approved these vegetables for sale). The European public showed a less than welcoming response to this campaign, complaining on thirteen separate occasions to the U.K. Advertising Standards Authority that these ads were false and consumers were hurt as a result.[50]

Positioning for the Future

The technological innovation embodied in *Roundup* and *Roundup Ready* seeds had given Monsanto a dominant and profitable position in the agricultural market. This product line had come to represent a significant portion of Monsanto's revenues and profits. However, with the impending patent expiration, increasing pressure from groups opposed to genetically modified foods, and other possible health concerns, the future of *Roundup*—and indeed Monsanto—had become quite murky. Verfaillie needed to position his company for the future, but to do this required addressing some very difficult questions. Could Monsanto defend its position in *Roundup*? If not, could it develop new markets that leveraged its biotechnology resources? Would genetically modified foods gain acceptance, or face increasing opposition and regulation? Was promoting genetically modified foods ethical? How could Monsanto increase its competitiveness internationally? In sum, how would Monsanto evolve to face the future?

Exhibit 9   Greenpeace's Labeling Guidelines[53]

Policy Concerning the Labelling and Declaration of Genetically Engineered Food Products

Greenpeace International, November 1997

Greenpeace is opposed to the release of genetically modified organisms (GMOs) into the environment. We also believe that stream lining of crops (sometimes referred to as segregation) is essential for the right of consumers to be provided with the choice of non-genetically manipulated food. For products that do contain or are produced by GMOs all products, seeds, animal feed, and food products and their components must be very clearly labelled.

Greenpeace has provided an example of how a label for such products could look. We are calling on the EU Commission to implement a comprehensive and immediate labelling program for its citizens that allows for the choice of non-genetically modified food for consumers.

Greenpeace Policy on Labelling in the European Union

All food products that have been produced, processed, grown or cultivated under one of the following preconditions have to be marked with a clear and easily visible label (see Annex I), to inform consumers about the production process and to allow an informed choice between genetically engineered and conventional food products.

The label has to be used as a non-removable sticker or as a direct imprint on the product itself or its packaging (whatever is displayed to the customer). The labelling policy should come into effect immediately as stickers can be used as a phase in for the interim period when direct imprints should be obligatory.

For the labelling process, the complete chain of production and all components of the final product must be taken into consideration. All ingredients and components of the final product must be listed. The technical capability to detect GMOs is not a criteria for labeling.

Additional information on the product must clearly state if the product contains proteins from plants, animals or microorganisms known to initiate allergies.

A central register of all products on the market in the European Union should be maintained. Information should be collected and results published for the public by the EU Scientific Food Committee controlling program on the short and long term effects of genetic engineering in food.

Liability for any health affects caused from food or products derived from GMOs should be the responsibility of the food processing company or company involved.

(A) Labelled "Genetically Manipulated"

Food products must be marked with the label "Genetically manipulated" if one or more of the following preconditions applies to either the finished product or one or more of its components:

1. Food products and/or their components that consist of or contain genetically modified organisms (according to the definition set out in the EU-directive 90/220/EEC). This regulation applies both for finished products and their components, regardless whether the genetical modification can be detected by currently available scientific standards or not.
2. Food products and/or their components that are produced or derived from genetically modified organisms. This regulation applies both for finished products and their components, regardless of whether the genetical modification can be detected by currently available scientific standards or not.
3. Food products, if their additives are produced or derived from genetically modified plants or animals.
4. Food products obtained or derived from animals raised and fed with genetically modified animal fodder.
5. Animal fodder must be labelled as genetically manipulated:
   if the fodder or its components consist of or contain genetically modified organisms or their parts; if the fodder or its essential components are produced or derived from genetically modified organisms.
6. Animals that are genetically engineered and sold for food or animal fodder (such as fish meal). *(continued)*

Exhibit 9 | Greenpeace's Labeling Guidelines *(continued)*

(B) Labelled "Produced with Genetic Engineering"

Food products have to be marked "Produced with genetic engineering" (without a label; in written form, placed within the list of ingredients), if one or more of the following preconditions applies to either the finished product or one or more of its components:

1. Food products that are produced with the help of production processes that operate with genetically modified organisms or their derivates.

2. Food products that contain or are produced with the help of additives (vitamins, enzymes, flavoured substances (flavour ants)) that are produced or derived from genetically modified organisms.

[53]Information taken from http://www.greenpeace.org/~geneng/.

Endnotes

1. Seth Brooks, Melissa Schilling, and John Scrofani prepared this case as the basis for class discussion rather than to illustrate either effective or ineffective handling of an administrative situation.
2. http://www.monsanto.com/Monsanto/mediacenter/background/96sep24_Herbicide.html
3. http://www.accessexcellence.org/AB/BC/what_is_biotechnology.html. The National Health Museum is a 501(c)(3) non-profit corporation, based in Washington D.C.
4. http://www.biotechknowledge.com/primer/primer.html
5. Henry Miller, M.D., Fellow at Stanford University's Hoover Institution; June 17, 1999
6. http://netspace.students.brown.edu/MendelWeb/home.html
7. http://library.thinkquest.org/10551/web1Eng/biotech2.htm
8. http://www.cp.vovartis.com/dframe.htm
9. Chemical Week; New York; Sep 9, 1998; Kerri Walsh;
10. Alice Naude; Chemical Market Reporter, New York; Mar 9, 1998; Vol. 253, Iss. 10; pg. FR8.
11. Information taken from MOJO Wire, http://www.mojones.com/mother_jones/JF97/brokaw.html
12. http://www.safe2use.com/pesticidenews/roundup.htm
13. http://www.mojones.com/mother_jones/JF97/brokaw.html
14. http://www.greenpeace.org/~geneng/highlights/pat/98_09_20.htm
15. http://www.monsanto.com/monsanto/gurt/default.htm
16. http://www.monsanto.com/monsanto/gurt/default.htm
17. http://www.pharmacia.com/facts_monsanto.html
18. Monsanto's 1999 10K
19. Anonymous; Agri Marketing, Skokie; Jun 1999; Vol. 37, Iss. 6; pg.H
20. Alice Naude; Chemical Market Reporter, New York; Mar 9, 1998; Vol. 253, Iss. 10; pg. FR8.
21. http://www.monsanto.com/monsanto/about/careers/default.htm
22. http://dir.yahoo.com/Science/Agriculture/News_and_Media/Magazines/Trade_Magazines/
23. *The Economist;* London; Jun 19, 1999; Anonymous
24. http://www.farmsource.com/Product_Info/
25. Scott's Company news release, Marysville, Ohio July 12, 1999
26. Chemical Week; New York; Jul 1, 1998; Andrew Wood
27. Letter to Shareowners, Hendrik Verfaille, CEO of Monsanto, March 1, 2001.
28. http://www.cynamid.com
29. http://www.sec.gov/Archives/edgar/data/67686/0000067686-99-000050-index.html
30. http://www.monsanto.com/monsanto/mediacenter/99/99jan19_dow.html
31. http://www.hoovers.Dupont.htm
32. Chemical Week; New York;w Jan 19, 2000; Robert Westervelt
33. http://www.hoovers.novartis.htm
34. http://www.cp.novartis.com/d_frame.htm
35. http://www.ahp.com/overview.htm
36. http://www.ahp.com/netsales.htm
37. http://www.hoovers.com
38. http://www.extremecontrol.com
39. http://www.extremecontrol.com
40. http://www.cynamid.pressrelease.com, Suzanne Thompson, Public Affairs
41. "Chefs at the Biotech Barricades", Lucette Lagnado, The Wall Street Journal, Thursday, March 9, 2000, B1
42. http://www.greenpeace.org/~geneng/
43. http://www.fda.gov/oc/biotech/default.htm
44. http://www.netlink.de/gen/Zeitung/1999/990624b.htm
45. http://www.safe2use.com/pesticidenews/roundup.htm
46. http://www.life.ca/nl/68/cancer.html
47. http://www.life.ca/nl/68/cancer.html
48. http://www.life.ca/nl/68/cancer.html
49. http://jinx.sistm.unsw.edu.au/~greenlft/1997/262/262p13c.htm
50. *The Economist;* London; Jun 19, 1999; Anonymous;

Case 26

Newell Company: The Rubbermaid Opportunity[1]

Joseph N. Fry

University of Western Ontario

In October 1998, the board of directors of the Newell Company was considering a proposed merger with Rubbermaid Incorporated to form a new company, Newell Rubbermaid Inc. The transaction would be accomplished through a tax-free exchange of shares under which Rubbermaid shareholders would receive Newell Shares valued at approximately $5.8 billion at a ratio which represented a 49 percent premium on Rubbermaid's current stock price. At the time of the transaction the annual revenues of Newell and Rubbermaid were, respectively, about $3.2 billion and $2.4 billion. If approved, the agreement would mark a quantum step in Newell's growth, but, equally, it would pose a formidable challenge to the company's demonstrated capacity to integrate and strengthen its acquisitions.

Newell: Riding the Acquisition Tiger

In 1998, the Newell Company had revenues of $3.7 billion distributed across three major product groupings: Hardware and Home Furnishings ($1.8 billion), Office Products ($1.0 billion), and Housewares ($0.9 billion). Over the past ten years the company had achieved a compound sales growth rate of 13 percent, an earnings per share growth rate of 16 percent and an average

annual return on beginning shareholder equity of 21 percent. These results were consistent with Newell's formal goals of achieving earnings per share growth of 15 percent per year and maintaining a return on beginning equity of 20 percent or above. Further financial details on Newell are given in Exhibit 1.

Acquisitions

Acquisitions were the foundation of Newell's growth strategy. Given the relatively slow growth of the product markets in which it chose to operate, Newell's corporate goal for internal growth was only three percent to five percent per annum—with internal growth being defined as the growth of businesses that Newell had owned for over two years. Actual internal growth in the past five years had averaged about five percent per annum. This put a premium on acquisitions if Newell was to meet its aggressive growth targets. Indeed, over $2 billion of its current sales were the result of over 20 acquisitions made since 1990.

Newell's approach to acquisition was both aggressive and disciplined. Its targeted acquisition candidates were generally mature businesses with 'unrealized profit potential' which further passed a number of screening criteria, including having a:

- strategic fit with existing businesses—which implied product lines that were low in technology, fashion and seasonal content and were sold through mass distribution channels.
- number one or two position in their served markets and established shelf space with major retailers.
- long product life cycle.
- potential to reach Newell's standard of profitability, which included goals for operating margins of 15 percent, and Sales, General and Administrative costs at a maximum of 15 percent.

	To End Q3/98	12/31/97	To End Q3/97	12/31/96
Net sales	$2,650,263	$3,336,233	$2,395,037	$2,972,839
Cost of products sold	1,786,640	2,259,551	1,631,253	2,020,116
Selling, general and administrative expenses	404,882	497,739	365,123	461,802
Goodwill amortization and other	40,502	31,882	22,872	23,554
Operating Income	418,239	547,061	375,789	467,367
Interest expense	43,966	76,413	54,363	58,541
Other, non-operating, net	(213,373)*	(14,686)	(12,862)	(19,474)
Profit before tax	587,546	485,334	334,288	428,300
Income taxes	250,740	192,187	132,373	169,258
Net Income	$336,806	$293,147	$201,915	$259,042
Current assets	1,767,370	1,433,694		1,148,464
Property, plant and equipment	834,486	711,325		567,880
Trade names, goodwill, other	2,001,862	1,559,594		1,342,086
Total Assets	4,603,718	4,011,314		3,058,430
Current liabilities	1,061,675	714,479		665,884
Long-term debt	912,650	786,793		685,608
Other non-current liabilities	243,862	285,241		206,916
Convertible preferred securities	500,000	500,000		
Shareholders' Equity	1,885,531	1,725,221		1,500,022
Total Liabilities and Shareholders' Equity	4,603,718	4,011,314		3,058,430
Approximate common shares outstanding (000)	173,000	163,300		162,000
Earnings per share (fully diluted)		$1.80		$1.60
Stock Price $High/Low	$54/37	$43/30		$33/25

*Primarily gain from sale of Black & Decker holdings.
SOURCE: Company Financial Reports.

The size of the acquisitions varied. In 1996, Newell made one acquisition for $46 million cash, in 1997, three material acquisitions for $762 million cash and in 1998 to date, four material acquisitions for about $413 million cash. Once acquired, the new companies were integrated into the Newell organization by means of an established process that had come to be called "newellization."

Newellization

Newellization was the profit improvement and productivity enhancement process employed to bring a newly acquired business up to Newell's high standards of productivity and profit. The Newellization process was pursued through a number of broadly applicable steps, including the:

- transfer of experienced Newell managers into the acquired company.
- simplification and focusing of the acquired business's strategy and the implementation of Newell's established manufacturing and marketing know-how and programs.
- centralization of key administrative functions including data processing, accounting, EDI, and capital expenditure approval.
- inauguration of Newell's rigorous, multi-measure, divisional operating control system.

Newell management claimed that the process of newellization was usually completed in two or three years.

Continuing Operations

A summary of Newell's product groups and major lines is outlined in Table 1. These products were, for the most part, sold through mass merchandisers. In 1997, Wal-Mart accounted for 15 percent of Newell's sales; the other top ten Newell customers (each with less than 10 percent of Newell sales) were Kmart, Home Depot, Office Depot, Target, J.C. Penney, United Stationers, Hechtinger, Office Max and Lowe's. International sales had increased from eight percent of total sales in 1992 to an expected 22 percent in 1998 as Newell followed customers and opportunities into Mexico, Europe and the Americas.

Newell's fundamental competitive strategy, which applied to all of its operations, was to differentiate on the basis of superior service to its mass merchandise customers. For Newell, superior service included industry-leading quick response and on-time, in-full delivery, the ability to implement sophisticated EDI tie-ins with its customers extending to vendor-managed inventories, and the provision of marketing and merchandising programs for product categories that encompassed good, better and best lines.

Organization

Newell centralized certain key administrative functions such as data management (including order-fulfillment-invoice activities), divisional coordination and control, and financial management. Otherwise, the presidents of the company's 18 product divisions were responsible for the full scope of manufacturing, marketing and sales activities for their product lines and for the performance of their businesses.

Divisional coordination and control were facilitated by the fundamental similarities of the Newell businesses. These similarities made it possible for corporate level management to develop a common pool of managers and know-how that could be transferred relatively easily from one division to another. The business similarities also made it possible for corporate management to apply a common set of detailed operating standards and controls across the businesses, and to play a knowledgeable role in reviewing divisional progress and plans. Corporate management held monthly reviews (called brackets meetings) with divisional presidents to track multiple operating and financial measures and to ensure that appropriate attention was given to items that were off budget. As a result, divisional management operated in a goldfish bowl under high pressure, but they were paid very well for meeting their targets.

Outlook

In Newell's view, the company's adherence to a highly focused strategy had established a sustainable competitive advantage for the corporation and this, coupled with abundant acquisition opportunities and internal growth momentum, would support the continuing achievement of its financial goals.

Rubbermaid: A Fallen Icon

Rubbermaid was a well known, and, for several decades, a renowned manufacturer of a wide range of plastic products ranging from children's toys through housewares to commercial items. From 1986 through 1995 Rubbermaid was ranked among the top 10 in *Fortune*'s list of America's most admired companies, including the

Table 1	Newell Product Lines, 1998		
Housewares	**Hardware and Home Furnishings**	**Office Products**	
Aluminum Cookware and Bakeware	Window Treatments	Markers and Writing Products	
Glassware	Home Storage	Office Storage	
Hair Accessories	Picture Frames		
	Hardware		

No. 1 spot in 1993 and 1994. But by March 1998 Rubbermaid had fallen to No. 100. After a wonderful run of growth and profitability, extending as far back as the 1960s, the company had clearly hit a rough patch.

Rubbermaid earned its early reputation by setting aggressive goals for 15 percent growth in revenues and profits and then, by and large, meeting its targets. Under the intense and very personal management of Stanley Gault, an ex-senior executive at General Electric and CEO and chairman of Rubbermaid from 1980 to 1991, the company was pressed to broaden its product line through development and acquisition and to meet demanding operating targets. From propitious beginnings Rubbermaid became an ubiquitous brand and a Wall Street darling—with sales and profits, respectively, at the end of Gault's tenure of $1.7 billion and $162 million.

Rubbermaid's earnings momentum continued into the early years of Gault's successor, Wolfgang Schmidt, but the good times were to be short-lived. In 1994 Rubbermaid was hit by a doubling of plastic resin prices.[2] The company's clumsy reactions to this shock revealed a number of accumulating problems. *Fortune* enumerated them in a 1995 article:[3]

- Customer relations: Rubbermaid angered its most important retail buyers with the heavy-handed way it has passed along its ballooning costs. Some are so angry that they have given more shelf space to competitors . . .
- Operations: Although it excels in creativity, product quality, and merchandising, Rubbermaid is showing itself to be a laggard in more mundane areas such as modernizing machinery, eliminating unnecessary jobs, and making deliveries on time . . .
- Competition: It has been slow to recognize that other housewares makers—once a bunch of no-names who peddled junk—have greatly improved over the past half dozen years. The premium prices that Rubbermaid charges over its rivals have grown too large, and customers are turning away.
- Culture: The company's extraordinary financial targets . . . seem unrealistic—and straining to reach them is proving increasingly troublesome. Some of the friction between Rubbermaid and its customers can be traced to Rubbermaid's voracious appetite for growth.

Rubbermaid's profits peaked in 1994 at $228 million. In 1995 sales were up eight percent but the company took a restructuring charge of $158 million pre-tax and net earnings fell to $60 million. The restructuring charges were taken in anticipation of a two-year program designed to reduce costs, improve operating efficiencies and accelerate growth. In 1997, Rubbermaid reported[4] that the realignment activities were substantially com-

plete and that the company "has or initiated closure of all nine locations slated for closure in the plan, completed the associated reductions, and achieved the estimated annual savings of $50 million anticipated in the 1995 program." Unfortunately, this action did not have a material effect on sales, which remained essentially flat, and operating profits, which dipped somewhat, as detailed in the financial summary given in Exhibit 2. Thus, early in 1998, Rubbermaid announced another restructuring charge, which it estimated would reach at least $200 million pretax, to fund a program that would include centralizing global procurement and consolidating manufacturing and distribution worldwide.

Rubbermaid Lines of Business

In 1998, Rubbermaid manufactured and sold over 5,000 products[5] under four key brand names:

- Rubbermaid: a wide range of household utility products encompassing five categories (Kitchen, Home Organization, Health Care, Cleaning, and Hardware/Seasonal) and 23 product lines.
- Graco: children's products in six product lines focusing on baby strollers and related items.
- Little Tikes: juvenile products, with 11 product lines focusing on toys and furniture.
- Curver: a European-based home products business with revenues of $180 million, acquired at the beginning of 1998.

Rubbermaid's international sales and operations had been growing in recent years as it followed its customers abroad. The Curver acquisition increased foreign sales, including exports from the United States, to about 25 percent of total revenues, helping the firm along the path to its goal of 30 percent by 2000.

Rubbermaid Strategy

Rubbermaid's strategy reflected an uneasy balance of not necessarily consistent ambitions. The 15 percent growth goals of the past had disappeared from public statements, but there was no question that the company remained aggressive in its goals and optimistic about its prospects. To achieve its aims Rubbermaid relied on a multi-faceted competitive strategy. It wanted, at once, to be a company with a:

- strong consumer franchise based on unique product features, quality and rapid innovation, and on brand recognition and aggressive advertising. Rubbermaid had, for example, set a goal that 10 percent of each year's sales should come from new, high value products and it had reduced new product time to market

	To End Q3/98	12/31/97	To End Q3/97	12/31/96	12/31/95
Net sales	$1,936,829	$2,399,710	$1,825,416	$2,354,980	$2,344,170
Cost of products sold	1,383,564	1,748,424	1,327,990	1,649,520	1,673,232
Selling, general and administrative expenses	353,805	416,641	314,229	432,063	402,586
Operating Income	199,460	234,645	183,197	273,397	268,352
Interest expense	27,795	35,762	28,463	24,348	10,260
Restructuring costs	73,740	16,000	16,000		158,000
Other, non-operating, net	(23,749)	(51,032)	(49,729)	4,046	4,457
Income taxes	42,586	91,370	77,717	92,614	35,863
Net Income	$79,088	$142,536	$110,746	$152,398	$59,772
Current assets	952,841	816,204		856,720	
Other assets	445,995	399,716		475,346	
Property, plant and equipment	784,228	707,974		721,914	
Total Assets	2,183,064	1,923,984		2,053,980	
Current liabilities	802,231	567,084		742,841	
Long-term debt	152,556	153,163		154,467	
Other non-current liabilities	171,302	153,385		142,992	
Shareholders' equity	1,056,885	1,050,262		1,013,700	
Total Liabilities and Shareholders' Equity	2,183,064	1,923,984		2,053,980	
Approximate common shares outstanding (000)		149,900		151,000	158,800
Earnings per share (fully diluted)		$0.95		$1.01	$0.38
Stock Price $High/Low		$30/22		$30/22	$34/25

SOURCE: Company Financial Reports.

from 20 plus months in the 1980s to six months currently, with a goal of four months by 2000.

- low-cost sourcing, production, and fulfillment base. The company was in the process, for example, of cutting product variations by 45 percent and consolidating its supplier base from 9,000 to less than 2,000 vendors.
- reliable and efficient supplier to mass merchandisers. Rubbermaid was moving, for example, to scheduling manufacturing by customer order and to just-in-time service and continuous replenishment of its best selling items.

There was a tension at work behind these aims. In its 1996 Annual Report Rubbermaid noted that its market was at a point of inflection, in which the control of information was shifting from mass marketers to individual consumers. In this context Rubbermaid claimed that it would strike a new balance in its strategies, to continue to lead in innovation while becoming a low cost producer. Similarly, in its 1997 Annual Report, the company noted that in a squeeze of higher costs and lower retail prices it was making bold moves to become the low-cost producer, while retaining world-class quality and innovation. Finally, another "point of inflection": in his 1997 Letter to Shareholders, Wolfgang Schmidt promised that, "with the initiatives of the past two years and the opportunities ahead, we are at the inflection point from which we can combine our financial strength and innovation capabilities with a more favorable cost climate to generate stronger shareholder returns."

The Outline of a Deal

Newell's appetite for all of Rubbermaid might have been whetted with its $247 million acquisition of Rubbermaid's Office Products division in 1977, adding about $160 million of annualized revenues to Newell's developing office products line of business. Whatever the stimulus, talks soon began on a total combination of the two firms.

Negotiations led to a provisional agreement under which Rubbermaid shareholders would receive 0.7883 shares of Newell common stock for each share of Rubbermaid common stock that they owned. Based on Newell's closing price of $49.07 on October 20, 1998 this represented $38.68 per Rubbermaid share or a premium on 49 percent of Rubbermaid's closing price of $25.88. Under this arrangement Newell would issue approximately 118 million shares of common stock to Rubbermaid shareholders. Rubbermaid shareholders would end up holding approximately 40 percent of the combined company. The transaction represented a tax-free exchange of shares and would be accounted for as a pooling of interests. A simple pro forma of the results, the transaction is given in Exhibit 3.

Newell management forecast[6] that, as soon as the transaction was completed, they would begin the "newellization" process and improve Rubbermaid's operating efficiencies to achieve 98 percent on-time and line-fill performance and a minimum 15 percent pretax margin. They also expected revenue and operating synergies through the leveraging of Newell Rubbermaid's brands, innovative product development, improved service performance, stronger combined presence in dealing with common customers, broader acquisition opportunities, and an increased ability to serve European markets. They forecast that by 2000 these efforts and opportunities would produce increases over anticipated 1998 results of $300 million to $350 million in operating income for the combined company.

Endnotes

1. This case has been written on the basis of published sources only. Consequently, the interpretation and perspectives presented in this case are not necessarily those of Newell Company or any of its employees.
2. Materials accounted for between 45 and 50 percent of Rubbermaid's net sales.
3. Lee Smith, "Rubbermaid Goes Thump," *Fortune*, October 2, 1995.
4. Rubbermaid Annual Report, 1997.
5. In 1997 Rubbermaid had sold its Office Product business to Newell for a $134 million pretax gain, which it promptly offset by a one-time charge of $81 million for asset impairment related to acquisitions.
6. Newell Press release, October 21, 1998.

	Newell Q3/97–Q3/98	Rubbermaid Q3/97–Q3/98	Simple Pro Forma Newell Rubbermaid Q3/97–Q3/98
Net sales	3,591,459	2,511,123	6,102,582
Cost of products sold	2,414,938	1,803,998	4,218,936
Selling, general and administrative expenses	537,498	456,217	993,715
Goodwill amortization and other	49,512		49,512
Operating Income	589,511	250,908	840,419
Interest expense	66,016	35,094	101,110
Other, non-operating, net	(215,197)*	48,688	(166,509)
Profit before tax	738,692	167,126	905,818
Income taxes	310,554	56,239	366,793
Net Income	428,138	110,887	539,025
Balance Sheet as of End Q3/98			
Current assets	1,767,370	952,841	2,720,211
Property, plant and equipment	834,486	784,228	1,618,714
Trade names, goodwill, other	2,001,862	445,995	2,447,857
Total Assets	4,603,718	2,183,064	6,786,782
Current liabilities	1,061,675	802,231	1,863,906
Long-term debt	912,650	152,556	1,065,206
Other non-current liabilities	243,862	171,302	415,164
Convertible preferred securities	500,000		500,000
Shareholders' Equity	1,885,531	1,056,885	2,942,416
Total Liabilities and Shareholders' Equity	4,603,718	2,183,064	6,786,782
Approximate common shares outstanding (000)	173,000	150,000	291,000
Earnings per share (fully diluted)	$2.47	$0.74	$1.85

*Primarily gain from sale of Black & Decker holdings.
SOURCE: Estimates based on Company Financial Reports.

Nike's Dispute with the University of Oregon[1]

Rebecca J. Morris

University of Nebraska, Omaha

Anne T. Lawrence

San Jose State University

On April 24, 2000, Philip H. Knight, CEO of athletic shoe and apparel maker Nike Inc., publicly announced that he would no longer donate money to the University of Oregon (UO). It was a dramatic and unexpected move for the high-profile executive. A former UO track and field star, Knight had founded Nike's predecessor in 1963 with his former coach and mentor, Bill Bowerman. Over the years, Knight had maintained close ties with his alma mater, giving more than $50 million of his personal fortune to the school over a quarter century. In 2000, he was in active discussion with school officials about his biggest donation yet—millions for renovating the football stadium. But, suddenly, it was all called off. Said Knight in his statement: "[F]or me personally, there will be no further donations of any kind to the University of Oregon. At this time, this is not a situation that can be resolved. The bonds of trust, which allowed me to give at a high level, have been shredded."

At issue was the University of Oregon's intention, announced April 14, 2000, to join the Worker Rights Consortium (WRC). Like many universities, UO was engaged in an internal debate over the ethical responsibilities associated with its role as a purchaser of goods manufactured overseas. Over a period of several months, UO administrators, faculty, and students had been discussing what steps they could take to ensure that products sold in the campus store, especially university-logo apparel, were not manufactured under sweatshop conditions. The University had considered joining two organizations, both of which purported to certify goods as "no sweat." The first, the Fair Labor Association (FLA), had grown out of President Clinton's Apparel Industry Partnership (AIP) initiative and was vigorously backed by Nike, as well as several other leading apparel makers. The second, the Workers Rights Consortium, was supported by student activists and several U.S.-based labor unions that had broken from the AIP after charging it did not go far enough to protect workers. Knight clearly felt that his alma mater had made the wrong choice. "[The] University [has] inserted itself into the new global economy where I make my living," he charged. "And inserted itself on the wrong side, fumbling a teachable moment."

The dispute between Phil Knight and the University of Oregon captured much of the furor swirling about the issue of the role of multinational corporations in the global economy and the effects of the far-flung operations on their many thousands of workers, communities,

[1]This is an abridged version of a full-length case, "Nike's Dispute with the University of Oregon," *Case Research Journal*, 21, No. 3, Summer, 2001. Abridged and reprinted by permission of the *Case Research Journal*. Sources incude articles appearing in the *New York Times, The Oregonian, Washington Post,* and other daily newspapers and material provided by Nike at its Web site *www.nikebiz.com*. Book sources include J. B. Strasser and L. Becklund, *Swoosh: The Unauthorized Story of Nike and the Men Who Played There* (New York: HarperCollins, 1993); D. R. Katz, *Just Do It: The Nike Spirit in the Corporate World* (Holbrook, Mass.: Adams Media Corporation, 1995); T. Vanderbilt, *The Sneaker Book* (New York: The New Press, 1998). Web sites for the Fair Labor Association and the Worker Rights Consortium may be found, respectively, at: www.fairlabor.org and www.workersrights.org. Ernst & Young's audit of Nike's subcontractor factories in Vietnam is available at: www.corpwatch.org/trac/nike/ernst. Coverage of Nike and the WRC decision in the University of Oregon student newspaper is available at: www.dailyemerald.com. A U.S. Department of Labor study of wages and benefits in the footwear industry in selected countries is available at: www.dol.gov/dol/ilab/public/media/reports/oiea/wagestudy. A full set of footnotes is available in the *Case Research Journal* version. Copyright © 2001 by the *Case Research Journal* and Rebecca J. Morris and Anne T. Lawrence. All rights reserved jointly to the authors and the North American Case Research Association (NACRA).

and other stakeholders. In part because of its high-profile brand name, Nike had become a lightening rod for activists concerned about worker rights abroad. Like many U.S.-based shoe and apparel makers, Nike had located its manufacturing operations overseas, mainly in Southeast Asia, in search of low wages. Almost all production was carried out by subcontractors, rather than by Nike directly. Nike's employees in the United States, by contrast, directed their efforts to the high-end work of research and development, marketing, and retailing. In the context of this global division of labor, what responsibility, if any, did Nike have to ensure adequate working conditions and living standards for the hundreds of thousands of workers, mostly young Asian women, who made its shoes and apparel? If this was not Nike's responsibility, then whose was it? Did organizations like the University of Oregon have any business pressuring companies through their purchasing practices? If so, how should they best do so? In short, what were the lessons of this "teachable moment?"

Nike, Inc.

In 2000, Nike, Inc., was the leading designer and marketer of athletic footwear, apparel, and equipment in the world. Based in Beaverton, Oregon, the company's "swoosh" logo, its "Just Do It!" slogan and its spokespersons Michael Jordan, Mia Hamm, and Tiger Woods were universally recognized. Nike employed around 20,000 people directly, and *half a million* indirectly in 565 contract factories in 46 countries around the world. Wholly owned subsidiaries included Bauer Nike Hockey Inc. (hockey equipment), Cole Haan (dress and casual shoes), and Nike Team Sports (licensed team products). Revenues for the 12 months ending November 1999 were almost $9 billion, and the company enjoyed a 45 percent global market share. Knight owned 34 percent of the company's stock and was believed to be the sixth-richest individual in the United States.

Knight had launched this far-flung global empire shortly after completing his MBA degree at Stanford University in the early 1960s. Drawing on his firsthand knowledge of track and field, he decided to import low-priced track shoes from Japan in partnership with his former college coach. Bowerman would provide design ideas, test the shoes in competition, and endorse the shoes with other coaches; Knight would handle all financial and day-to-day operations of the business. Neither man had much money to offer, so for $500 a piece and a handshake, the company (then called Blue Ribbon Sports) was officially founded in 1963. The company took the name Nike in 1978; two years later, with revenues topping $269 million and 2,700 employees, Nike became a publicly traded company.

From the beginning, marketing had been a critical part of Knight's vision. The founder defined Nike as a "marketing-oriented company." During the 1980s and early 1990s, Nike aggressively sought out endorsements by celebrity athletes to increase brand awareness and foster consumer loyalty. Early Nike endorsers included Olympic gold medallist Carl Lewis, Wimbledon champion Andre Agassi, and six members of the 1992 Olympic basketball "Dream Team." Later endorsers included tennis aces Pete Sampras and Monica Seles, basketball great Michael Jordan, and golf superstar Tiger Woods.

An important element in Nike's success was its ability to develop cutting-edge products that met the needs of serious athletes, as well as set fashion trends. Research specialists in Nike's Sports Research Labs conducted extensive research and testing to develop new technologies to improve the performance of Nike shoes in a variety of sports. For example, research specialists studied the causes of ankle injuries in basketball players to develop shoes that would physically prevent injuries, as well as signal information to the user to help him or her resist turning the ankle while in the air. Other specialists developed new polymer materials that would make the shoes lighter, more aerodynamic, or more resistant to the abrasions incurred during normal athletic use. Findings from the Sports Research Labs were then passed on to design teams that developed the look and styling of the shoes.

Although it was the leading athletic footwear company in the world, Nike never manufactured shoes in any significant number. Rather, from its inception, the company had outsourced production to subcontractors in Asia, with the company shifting production locations within the region when prevailing wage rates became too high. In the early years, it had imported shoes from Japan. It later shifted production to South Korea and Taiwan, then to Indonesia and Thailand, and later yet to Vietnam and China.

The reasons for locating shoe production mainly in Southeast Asia were several, but the most important was the cost of labor. Modern athletic shoes were composed of mesh, leather, and nylon uppers that were hand-assembled, sewn and glued to composite soles. Mechanization had not been considered effective for shoe manufacturing due to the fragile materials used and the short life spans of styles of athletic shoes. Therefore, shoe production was highly labor-intensive. Developing countries, primarily in Southeast Asia, offered the distinct advantage of considerably lower wage rates. For example, in the early 1990s, when Nike shifted much of its shoe production to Indonesia, daily wages there hovered around $1 a day (compared to wages in the U.S. shoe industry at that time of around $8 an hour).

Along with lower labor costs, Asia provided the additional advantage of access to raw material suppliers. Very few rubber firms in the United States, for example, produced the sophisticated composite soles demanded in modern athletic shoe designs. Satellite industries necessary for modern shoe production, plentiful in Asia, included tanneries, textiles, and plastic and ironwork moldings. A final factor in determining where to locate production was differential tariff rates. In general, canvas sneakers were assessed higher tariffs than leather molded footwear, such as basketball or running shoes. As a result, shoe companies had an incentive to outsource high-tech athletic shoes overseas, because tariffs on them were relatively low.

Many of Nike's factories in Asia were operated by a small number of Taiwanese and South Korea firms that specialized in shoe manufacturing, many owned by some of the wealthiest families in the region. When Nike moved from one location to another, often these companies followed, bringing their managerial expertise with them.

Nike's Subcontractor Factories

In 2000, Nike contracted with over 500 different footwear and apparel factories around the world to produce its shoes and apparel. Although there was no such thing as a typical Nike plant, a factory operated by the South Korean subcontractor Tae Kwang Vina (TKV) in the Bien Hoa City industrial zone near Ho Chi Minh City in Vietnam provided a glimpse into the setting in which many Nike shoes were made.

TKV employed approximately 10,000 workers in Bien Hoa City factory. The workforce consisted of 200 clerical workers, 355 supervisors, and 9,465 production workers, all making athletic shoes for Nike. Ninety percent of the workers were women between the ages of 18 to 24. Production workers were employed in one of three major areas within the factory: the chemical, stitching, and assembly sections. Production levels at the Bien Hoa City factory reached 400,000 pairs of shoes per month; Nike shoes made at this and other factories made up fully 5 percent of Vietnam's total exports.

Workers in the chemical division were responsible for producing the high-technology outsoles. Production steps involved stretching and flattening huge blobs of raw rubber on heavy duty rollers and baking chemical compounds in steel molds to form the innovative three-dimensional outsoles. The chemical composition of the soles changed constantly in response to the cutting-edge formulations developed by the U.S. design teams, requiring frequent changes in the production process. The smell of complex polymers, the hot ovens, and the clanging of the steel molds resulted in a work environment that was loud and hot and had high concentrations of chemical fumes. Chemicals used in the section were known to cause eye, skin, and throat irritations; damage to liver and kidneys; nausea; anorexia; and reproductive health hazards through inhalation or in some cause through absorption through the skin. Workers in the chemical section were thought to have high rates of respiratory illnesses, although records kept at the TKV operations did not permit the tracking of illnesses by factory section. Workers in the chemical section were issued gloves and surgical-style masks. However, they often discarded the protective gear, complaining that it was too hot and humid to wear them in the plant.

In the stitching section, row after row of sewing machines operated by young women hummed and clattered in a space the size of three football fields. One thousand stitchers worked on a single floor of the TKV factory, sewing together nylon, leather, and other fabrics to make the uppers. Other floors of the factory were filled with thousands of additional sewing machines producing different shoe models. The stitching job required precision and speed. Workers who did not meet the aggressive production goals did not receive a bonus. Failing to meet production goals three times resulted in the worker's dismissal. Workers were sometimes permitted to work additional hours without pay to meet production quotas. Supervisors were strict, chastising workers for excessive talking or spending too much time in the restrooms. Korean supervisors, often hampered by language and cultural barriers, sometimes resorted to hard-nose management tactics, hitting or slapping slower workers. Other workers in need of discipline were forced to stand outside the factory for long periods in the tropical sun. The Vietnamese term for this practice was *phoi nang*, or sun-drying.

In the assembly section, women worked side by side along a moving line to join the uppers to the outsoles through the rapid manipulation of sharp knives, skivers, routers, and glue-coated brushes. Women were thought to be better suited for the assembly jobs because their hands were smaller and more capable of the manual dexterity needed to fit the shoe components together precisely. During the assembly process, some 120 pairs of hands touched a single shoe. A strong, sweet solvent smell was prominent in the assembly area. Ceiling-mounted ventilation fans were ineffective since the heavy fumes settled to the floor. Assembly workers wore cotton surgical masks to protect themselves from the fumes; however, many workers pulled the masks below their noses, saying they were more comfortable that way. Rows and rows of shoes passed along a conveyor before the sharp eyes of the quality control inspectors. The inspectors examined each of the thousands of shoes produced daily for poor stitching or crooked connections between soles. Defective shoes were discarded. Approved shoes continued on the conveyor to stations where they were laced by assembly workers and finally put into Nike shoeboxes for shipment to the United States.

Despite the dirty, dangerous, and difficult nature of the work inside the Bien Hoa factory, there was no shortage of applicants for positions. Although entry level wages averaged only $1.50 per day (the lowest of all countries where Nike manufactured), many workers viewed factory jobs as better than their other options, such as working in the rice paddies or pedaling a pedicab along the streets of Ho Chi Minh City (formerly Saigon). With overtime pay at one and a half times the regular rate, workers could double their salaries—generating enough income to purchase a motorscooter or to send money home to impoverished rural relatives. These wages were well above national norms. An independent study by researchers from Dartmouth University showed that the average annual income for workers at two Nike subcontract factories in Vietnam was between $545 and $566, compared to the national average of between $250 and $300. Additionally, workers were provided free room and board and access to on-site health care facilities. Many Vietnamese workers viewed positions in the shoe factory as transitional jobs—a way to earn money for a dowry or to experience living in a larger city. Many returned to their homes after working for Nike for two or three years to marry and begin the next phase of their lives.

The Campaigns Against Nike

In the early 1990s, criticism of Nike's global labor practices began to gather steam. *Harper's Magazine*, for example, published the pay stub of an Indonesian worker, showing that the Nike subcontractor had paid the woman just under 14 cents per hour, and contrasted this with the high retail price of the shoes and high salaries paid to the company's celebrity endorsers. The Made in the U.S.A. Foundation, a group backed by American unions, used a million dollar ad budget to urge consumers to send their "old, dirty, smelly, worn-out Nikes" to Phil Knight in protest of Nike's Asian manufacturing practices. Human rights groups and Christian organizations joined the labor unions in targeting the labor practices of the athletic shoes firm. Many felt that Nike's anti-authority corporate image ("Just Do It!") and message of social betterment through fitness were incompatible with press photos of slight Asian women hunched over sewing machines 70 hours a week, earning just pennies an hour.

By mid-1993, Nike was being regularly pilloried in the press as an imperialist profiteer. A CBS news segment airing on July 2, 1993, opened with images of Michael Jordan and Andre Agassi, two athletes who had multi-million-dollar promotion contracts with Nike. Viewers were told to contrast the athletes' pay checks with those of the Chinese and Indonesian workers who made "pennies" so that Nike could "Just Do It."

In 1995, the *Washington Post* reported that a pair of Nike Air Pegasus shoes that retailed for $70 cost Nike only $2.75 in labor costs, or 4 percent of the price paid by consumers. Nike's operating profit on the same pair of shoes was $6.25, while the retailer pocketed $9.00 in operating profits. Also that year, shareholder activists organized by the Interfaith Center on Corporate Responsibility submitted a shareholder proposal at Nike's annual meeting, calling on the company to review labor practices by its subcontractors; the proposal gathered 3 percent of the shareholder vote.

A story in *Life* magazine documented the use of child labor in Pakistan to produce soccer balls for Nike, Adidas, and other companies. The publicity fallout was intense. The public could not ignore the photographs of small children sitting in the dirt, carefully stitching together the panels of a soccer ball that would become the plaything of some American child the same age. Nike moved quickly to work with its Pakistani subcontractor to eliminate the use of child labor, but damage to Nike's image had been done.

In October 1996, CBS News *48 Hours* broadcast a scathing report on Nike's factories in Vietnam. CBS reporter Roberta Baskin focused on low wage rates, extensive overtime, and physical abuse of workers. Several young workers told Baskin how a Korean supervisor had beaten them with a part of a shoe because of problems with production. A journalist in Vietnam told the reporter that the phrase "to Nike someone" was part of the Vietnamese vernacular. It meant to "take out one's frustration on a fellow worker." Vietnamese plant managers refused to be interviewed, covering their faces as they ran inside the factory. CBS news anchor Dan Rather concluded the damaging report by saying, "Nike now says it plans to hire outside observers to talk to employees and examine working conditions in its Vietnam factories, but the company just won't say when that might happen."

The negative publicity was having an effect. In 1996, a marketing research study authorized by Nike reported the perceptions of young people aged 13 to 25 of Nike as a company. The top three perceptions, in the order of their response frequency, were athletics, cool, and bad labor practices. Although Nike maintained that its sales were never affected, company executives were clearly concerned about the effect of criticism of its global labor practices on the reputation of the brand they had worked so hard to build.

The Evolution of Nike's Global Labor Practices

In its early years, Nike had maintained that the labor practices of its foreign subcontractors, like TKV, were simply not its responsibility. "When we started Nike," Knight later commented, ". . . it never occurred to us that we should dictate what their factor[ies] should look like." The subcontractors, not Nike, were responsible for wages and working conditions. Dave Taylor, Nike's vice president of production, explained the company's position: "We don't pay anybody at the factories and we don't set policy within the factories; it is their business to run."

When negative articles first began appearing in the early 1990s, however, Nike managers realized that they needed to take some action to avoid further bad publicity. In 1992, the company drafted its first Code of Conduct, which required every subcontractor and supplier in the Nike network to honor all applicable local government labor and environmental regulations, or Nike would terminate the relationship. The subcontractors were also required to allow plant inspections and complete all necessary paperwork. Despite the compliance reports the factories filed every six months, Nike insiders acknowledged that the code of conduct system might not catch all violations. Tony Nava, Nike's country coordinator for Indonesia, told a *Chicago Tribune* reporter, "We can't know if they're actually complying with what they put down on paper."

In 1994, Nike tried to address this problem by hiring Ernst & Young, the accounting firm, to independently monitor worker abuse allegations in Nike's Indonesian factories. Later, Ernst & Young also audited Nike's factories in Thailand and Vietnam. A copy of the Vietnam audit leaked to the press showed that workers were often unaware of the toxicity of the compounds they were using and ignorant of the need for safety precautions. In 1998, Nike implemented important changes in its Vietnamese plants to reduce exposure to toxics, substituting less harmful chemicals, installing ventilation systems, and training personnel in occupational health and safety issues.

In 1996, Nike established a new Labor Practices Department, headed by Dusty Kidd, formerly a public

relations executive for the company. Later that year, Nike hired GoodWorks International, headed by former U.S. ambassador to the United Nations Andrew Young, to investigate conditions in its overseas factories. In January 1997, GoodWorks issued a glossy report, stating that "Nike is doing a good job in the application of its Code of Conduct. But Nike can and should do better." The report was criticized by activists for its failure to look at the issue of wages. Young demurred, saying he did not have expertise in conducting wage surveys. Said one critic, "This was a public relations problem, and the world's largest sneaker company did what it does best: it purchased a celebrity endorsement."

Over the next few years, Nike continued to work to improve labor practices in its overseas subcontractor factories, as well as the public perception of them. In January 1998, Nike formed a Corporate Responsibility Division under the leadership of former Microsoft executive Maria S. Eitel. Nike subsequently doubled the staff of this division. In May of that year, Knight gave a speech at the National Press Club, at which he announced several new initiatives. At that time, he committed Nike to raise the minimum age for employment in its shoe factories to 18 and in its apparel factories to 16. He also promised to achieve OSHA standards for indoor air quality in all its factories by the end of the year, mainly by eliminating the use of the solvent toluene; to expand educational programs for workers and in its microenterprise loan program; and to fund university research on responsible business practices. Nike also continued its use of external monitors, hiring PricewaterhouseCoopers to join Ernst & Young in a comprehensive program of factory audits, checking them against Nike's code.

Apparel Industry Partnership

One of Nike's most ambitious social responsibility initiatives was its participation in the Apparel Industry Partnership. It was this involvement that would lead, eventually, to Knight's break with the University of Oregon.

In August 1996, President Clinton launched the White House Apparel Industry Partnership on Workplace Standards (AIP). The initial group was comprised of 18 organizations. Participants included several leading manufacturers, such as Nike, Reebok, and Liz Claiborne. Also in the group were several labor unions, including the Union of Needletrades, Industrial, and Textile Employees (UNITE) and the Retail, Wholesale and Department Store Union; and several human rights, consumer, and shareholder organizations, including Business for Social Responsibility, the Interfaith Center on Corporate Responsibility, and the National Consumer League. The goal of the AIP was to develop a set of standards to ensure that apparel and footwear were not made under sweatshop conditions. For companies, it held out the promise of certifying to their customers that their products were "no sweat." For labor and human rights groups, it held out the promise of improving working conditions in overseas factories.

In April 1997, after months of often-fractious meetings, the AIP announced that it had agreed on a Workplace Code of Conduct that sought to define decent and humane working conditions. Companies agreeing to the Code would have to pledge not to use forced labor, that is, prisoners or bonded or indentured workers. They could not require more than 60 hours of work a week, including overtime. They could not employ children younger than 15 years old or the age for completing compulsory schooling, whichever was older—except they could hire 14-year-olds if local law allowed. The code also called on signatory companies to treat all workers with respect and dignity; to refrain from discrimination on the basis of gender, race, religion, age, disability, sexual orientation, nationality, political opinion, or social or ethnic origin; and to provide a safe and healthy workplace. Employees' rights to organize and bargain collectively would be respected. In a key provision, the Code also required companies to pay at least the local legal minimum wage or the prevailing industry wage, whichever was higher. All standards would apply not only to a company's own facilities but also to their subcontractors or suppliers.

Knight, who prominently joined President Clinton and others at a White House ceremony announcing the code, issued the following statement:

> *Nike agreed to participate in this Partnership because it was the first credible attempt, by a diverse group of interests, to address the important issue of improving factories worldwide. It was worth the effort and hard work. The agreement will prove important for several reasons. Not only is our industry stepping up to the plate and taking a giant swing at improving factory conditions, but equally important, we are finally providing consumers some guidance to counter all of the misinformation that has surrounded this issue for far too long.*

The Fair Labor Association

But this was not the end of the AIP's work; it also had to agree on a process for monitoring compliance with the Code. Although the group hoped to complete its work in six months, over a year later it was still deeply divided on several key matters. Internal documents leaked to the

New York Times in July 1998 showed that industry representatives had opposed proposals, circulated by labor and human rights members, calling for the monitoring of 30 percent of plants annually by independent auditors. The companies also opposed proposals that would require them to support workers' rights to organize independent unions and to bargain collectively, even in countries like China where workers did not have such rights by law. Said one nonindustry member, "We're teetering on the edge of collapse."

Finally, a subgroup of nine centrist participants, including Nike, began meeting separately in an attempt to move forward. In November 1998, this subgroup announced that it had come to agreement on a monitoring system for overseas factories of U.S.-based companies. The AIP would establish a new organization, the Fair Labor Association (FLA), to oversee compliance with its Workplace Code of Conduct. Companies would be required to monitor their own factories, and those of their subcontractors, for compliance; all would have to be checked within the first two years. In addition, the FLA would select and certify independent external monitors, who would inspect 10 percent of each firm's factories each year. Most of these monitors were expected to be accounting firms, which had expertise in conducting audits. The monitors' reports would be kept private. If a company were found to be out of compliance, it would be given a chance to correct the problem. Eventually, if it did not, the company would be dropped from the FLA and its termination announced to the public. Companies would pay for most of their own monitoring. The Clinton administration quickly endorsed the plan.

Both manufacturers and institutional buyers stood to benefit from participation in the Fair Labor Association. Companies, once certified for three years, could place an FLA service mark on their brands, signaling both to individual consumers and institutional buyers that their products were "sweatshop-free." It was expected that the FLA would also serve the needs of institutional buyers, particularly universities. By joining the FLA and agreeing to contract only with certified companies, universities could warrant to their students and others that their logo apparel and athletic gear were manufactured under conditions conforming with an established code of fair labor standards. Both parties would pay for these benefits. The FLA was to be funded by dues from participating companies ($5,000 to $100,000 annually, depending on revenue) and by payments from affiliated colleges and universities (based on 1 percent of their licensing income from logo products, up to a $50,000 annual cap).

Although many welcomed the agreement—and some new companies signed on with the FLA soon after it was announced—others did not. Warnaco, a leading apparel maker that had participated in the Partnership, quit, saying that the monitoring process would require it to turn over competitive information to outsiders. The American Apparel Manufacturing Association (AAMA), an industry group representing 350 companies, scoffed at the whole idea of monitoring. "Who is going to do the monitoring?" asked a spokesperson for the AAMA, apparently sarcastically. "Accountants or Jesuit priests?" Others argued that companies simply could not be relied upon to monitor themselves objectively. Said Jay Mazur, president of UNITE, "The fox cannot watch the chickens . . . if they want the monitoring to be independent, it can't be controlled by the companies." A visit from an external monitor once every 10 years would not prevent abuses. And in any case, as a practical matter, most monitors would be drawn from the major accounting firms that did business with the companies they were monitoring and were therefore unlikely to seek out lapses. Companies would not be required to publish a list of their factories, and any problems uncovered by the monitoring process could be kept from the public under the rules governing nondisclosure of proprietary information.

One of the issues most troubling to critics was the code's position on wages. The code called on companies to pay the minimum wage or prevailing wage, whichever was higher. But in many of the countries of Southeast Asia, these wages fell well below the minimum considered necessary for a decent standard of living for an individual or family. For example, the *Economist* reported that Indonesia's average minimum wage, paid by Nike subcontractors, was only two-thirds of what a person needed for basic subsistence. An alternative view was that a code of conduct should require that companies pay a *living wage*, that is, compensation for a normal workweek adequate to provide for the basic needs of an average family, adjusted for the average number of adult wage earners per family. One problem with this approach, however, was that many countries did not systematically study the cost of living, relative to wages, so defining a living wage was difficult. The Partnership asked the U.S. Department of Labor to conduct a preliminary study of these issues; the results were published in 2000.

The code also called on companies to respect workers' rights to organize and bargain collectively. Yet a number of FLA companies outsourced production to nondemocratic countries, such as China and Vietnam, where workers had no such rights. Finally, some criticized the agreement on the grounds it provided companies, as one put it, "a piece of paper to use as a fig leaf." Commented a representative of the needle trades unions, "The problem with the partnership plan is that it tinkers at the margins of the sweatshop system but creates the impression that it is doing much more. This is potentially helpful to companies stung by public condemnation of their labor practices, but it hurts millions of workers and undermines the growing antisweatshop movement."

The Worker Rights Consortium

Some activists in the antisweatshop movement decided to chart their own course, independent of the FLA. On October 20, 1999, students from more than 100 colleges held a press conference to announce formation of the Workers Rights Consortium (WRC) and called on their schools to withdraw from or not to join the FLA. The organization would be formally launched at a founding convention in April 2000.

The Worker Rights Consortium differed radically in its approach to eliminating sweatshops. First, the WRC did not permit corporations to join; it was comprised exclusively of universities and colleges, with unions and human rights organizations playing an advisory role. In joining the WRC, universities would agree to "require decent working conditions in factories producing their licensed products." Unlike the FLA, the WRC did not endorse a single, comprehensive set of fair labor standards. Rather, it called on its affiliated universities to develop their own codes. However, it did establish minimum standards that such codes should meet—ones that were, in some respects, stricter than the FLA's. Perhaps most significantly, companies would have to pay a living wage. Companies were also required to publish the names and addresses of all of their manufacturing facilities, in contrast to FLA rules. Universities could refuse to license goods made in countries where compliance with fair labor standards was "deemed impossible," whatever efforts companies had made to enforce their own codes in factories there.

By contrast with the FLA, monitoring would be carried out by "a network of local organizations in regions where licensed goods are produced," generally nongovernmental organizations, independent human rights groups, and unions. These organizations would conduct unannounced "spot investigations," usually in response to worker complaints; WRC organizers called this the "fire alarm" method of uncovering code violations. Systematic monitoring would not be attempted. The consortium's governance structure reflected its mission of being an organization by and for colleges and universities; its 12-person board was composed of students, university administrators and human rights experts, with no seats for industry representatives. The group would be financed by 1 percent of licensing revenue from participating universities, as well as foundation grants.

Over the course of the spring semester 2000, student protests were held on a number of campuses, including the University of Oregon, to demand that their schools join the WRC. By April, around 45 schools had done so. At UO, the administration encouraged an open debate on the issue so that all sides could be heard on how to ensure that UO products were made under humane conditions. Over a period of several months, the Academic Senate, the student body, and a committee of faculty, students, administrators, and alumni appointed by the president all voted to join the Consortium. Finally, after concluding that all constituents had had an opportunity to be heard, on April 12, 2000, University of Oregon President David Frohnmayer announced that UO would join the WRC for one year. Its membership would be conditional, he said, on the consortium's agreement to give companies a voice in its operations and universities more power in governance. Shortly after the University's decision was announced in the press, Phil Knight withdrew his philanthropic contribution. In his public announcement, he stated his main disagreements with the Worker Rights Consortium:

> Frankly, we are frustrated that factory monitoring is badly misconstructed. For us one of the great hurdles and real handicaps in the dialogue has been the complexity of the issue. For real progress to be made, all key participants have to be at the table. That's why the FLA has taken so long to get going. The WRC is supported by the AFL-CIO and its affiliated apparel workers' union, UNITE. Their main aim, logically and understandably, however misguided, is to bring apparel jobs back to the U.S. Among WRC rules, no company can participate in setting standards, or monitoring. It has an unrealistic living wage provision. And its "gotcha" approach to monitoring doesn't do what monitoring should—measure conditions and make improvements.

Otis Elevator in Vietnam

Jocelyn Probert
Hellmut Schütte

INSEAD

It was summer 1995, and Mr. Vu Trong Hiep, General Director of Otis Vietnam, was reviewing progress in establishing the Otis name in Vietnam. Today he was in Ho Chi Minh City, the main hub of business activity in Vietnam, and one of three locations he spent his time shuttling between. If not there, he would be in Hanoi, the political capital of Vietnam, or in Singapore where the Otis operational headquarters for the Pacific Asia region—known as PAO—was based. In Singapore he had been (and remained for the time being) responsible for PAO market developments in Indochina, and had initially surveyed prospects for the three countries of the former French territory from there.

Like all American companies, Otis had been shut out of the Vietnamese market until the US embargo on trade and investment in Vietnam was lifted in February 1994. Meanwhile, companies from Asia countries had actively sought business opportunities and some European firms were also beginning to establish toeholds. However, Vu had taken advantage in late 1992 of outgoing President Bush's decision to relax the compete ban on American business dealings, by seeking prospective partners in Vietnam and preparing the ground for opening a representative office as soon as the embargo was lifted. During the 18 months since February 1994 he had signed two joint venture agreements, but was still waiting to receive the investment operating licence for one of them.

This case was written by Jocelyn Probert, Research Analyst at INSEAD Euro-Asia Centre, and Hellmut Schütte, Affiliate Professor of International management at INSEAD. It is intended to be used as a basis for class discussion rather than to illustrate either effective handling or ineffective handling of an administrative situation.

Vu was convinced that Otis was in a leading position among the foreign elevator companies in Vietnam. It was the only company to have a direct presence in the country. Was this first mover advantage sustainable? How could he raise the entry barriers to competitors?

The Elevator Industry

During the late 1970s and 1980s the elevator industry worldwide underwent significant restructuring. By the early 1990s the market had consolidated into the hands of a few dominant firms. These included Otis, Schindler of Switzerland and Kone of Finland, as well as Mitsubishi Electric, Toshiba and Hitachi of Japan, and Goldstar of Korea. Most companies are strongest in their domestic or regional markets. Although Otis is the market leader in the US and Europe, Mitsubishi Electric has the dominant position in Asia thanks to its strength in Japan. The fastest growing demand for elevators is in Asia, where market size in 1995 is expected to be around 80,000 units (of which 23–24,000 units will be installed in China), or roughly half of new installations worldwide.

The elevator business comprises three important elements: new equipment supply and installation; servicing and maintenance of installed units; and refurbishment of existing equipment. The first of these involves close coordination with a building's architects to establish the job's specifications, followed by negotiation and bidding for the installation contract. The maintenance element is conducted under long term contract and properly maintained elevators will operate for decades. Given the sophistication of today's elevators, it is rare for a company to service the lifts of another company. It is not unusual that elevators are sold on a cost basis, and even with loss provisions. The service and refurbishment elements of the business are where elevator companies make their money.

The Elevator Market in Vietnam

The elevator market in Vietnam in 1995 is small and undeveloped. There is also very little industry data available. An accurate picture of the market therefore requires a painstaking collection of individual pieces of information—on existing installations, new projects in the pipeline, potential projects (for example, construction projects for which financing has yet to be arranged) and new markets such as medium-height buildings requiring small, slow lifts. The chances of acquiring such proprietary information are improved if the interested party has a permanent presence in Vietnam. General estimates suggest a current market size of 200–300 unit installations per year, rising in a best case scenario over the next ten years to 1,500–2,000 units.

In 1995, Ho Chi Minh City and Hanoi were effectively the only cities in Vietnam with construction projects requiring lift installations. Even in these cities most projects are likely to be 6–10 storey office blocks and hotels, with a small number of 20–30 storey buildings. In perhaps five years' time, some of the regional cities— Danang, Nha Trang, Haiphong—will begin to take over as Vietnam's fastest-growing markets for elevators. Maybe as few as 10–20 units will be installed in the central city of Danang during the next three years, however. Given the coastal setting of many of these cities (Exhibit 1), most demand is expected to be from high class, low rise (three story) resort complexes requiring

Exhibit 1   Map of Vietnam

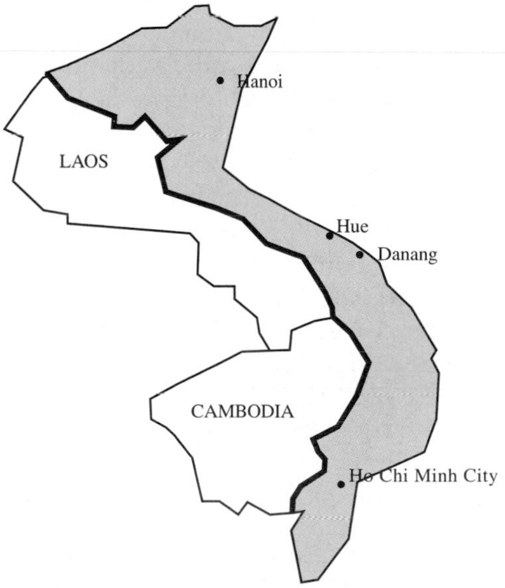

lifts operating at, and finished to, a high standard. There will be fewer high rise office buildings of the type under construction in the main cities. Later, the government may build low cost, high rise social housing projects of the type common in Hong Kong and Singapore—a highly cost-conscious market in which to compete.

In the absence of any significant local manufacturing of elevators, Vietnamese import tariffs on complete lifts are 0 percent. Although this may change over time, government policy at present is to encourage general investment by keeping construction costs relatively low. On the other hand, duties are imposed on elevator parts and components at rates of 5–15 percent according to their import category (steel components, electric switchboards, and so on). Spare parts for maintenance work, therefore, are dutiable items.

In the wake of a number of serious accidents involving elevators, the Vietnamese government has implemented an elevator safety code and established an inspectorate to check on proper installation. It has also drawn up guidelines on approved manufacturers: a building with a lift made by a company that does not figure on the list will not be penalised but may find the inspection process a tougher proposition. Moreover, in order to import its product to Vietnam, an elevator manufacturer must get authorisation from the Ministry of Labour, Invalids and Social Affairs.

At present, the distinguishing feature between the northern Vietnamese and southern Vietnamese markets for elevators is that very few of the projects in Hanoi are private sector or privately funded. Most are for government linked organisations, so political connections are important. In the south, the majority of projects are either for private domestic companies or for foreign investment-related ventures, and winning contracts for these jobs requires a real marketing approach.

Joint Venturing in Vietnam: The Regulatory Environment

The foreign investment law in Vietnam requires the domestic partner to hold a minimum 30 percent share of any joint venture. This share usually represents the value of the land, in the form of land use rights, contributed by the Vietnamese company to the joint venture. Few state-owned companies have assets—cash, technology, machinery—to contribute other than the land they have traditionally occupied. Land values are calculated on the basis of official rental prices (for example, in parts of Ho Chi Minh City, rents are US$12 per square metre per year) multiplied by the agreed duration of the joint venture. 'Goodwill' (or cash lent by the foreign partner, repayable out of the domestic partner's share of future earnings) makes up any shortfall in the local side's contribution to the venture's capital. The majority partner may have daily operational control, but Vietnamese law requires unanimity of decision-making on such issues as capital increases, business plan approvals, financing commitments, and the appointment of the General Director and the two deputy General Managers. The minority partner can, therefore, play a blocking role.

State-owned enterprises are administered either by a central government agency—such as the Ministry of Heavy Industry, the Ministry of Light Industry, the Ministry of Construction, and so on—or by a provincial or municipal People's Committee. There may be intense competition and rivalry between centrally-run and locally-run state-owned firms. The Ho Chi Minh People's Committee is particularly powerful by virtue of the amount of business activity that takes place in the city. State-owned enterprises dominate many industrial sectors. The role of private business was formally recognised only in the 1992 Constitution, and most privately-run firms are young and relatively small. Joint ventures formed by foreign investors have 98 percent state firms as their local partners.

The State Committee for Cooperation and Investment (SCCI) in Hanoi is responsible for the final decision on granting or withholding business licences for all foreign-invested firms. Only foreign firms who manufacture in Vietnam may form joint ventures or (sometimes) establish wholly owned subsidiaries; firms that wish simply to distribute their products in Vietnam may only open a representative office and do not have the right to enter into contracts with customers directly.

Despite these various constraints, Otis felt that joint venturing was its best course of action. It had experience of joint ventures in other parts of Asia, notably in China, and was confident that it could handle the cultural issues and regulatory obstacles that were bound to arise. Based on Vu's research, which revealed the fundamental differences in the markets of northern and southern Vietnam, he identified and signed joint ventures with two separate companies. By summer 1995 Otis had the investment licence from the SCCI—giving the operational green light—for its venture with Lilama in Hanoi. It was still waiting for the licence for the Ho Chi Minh City venture with CEC, with whom negotiations had begun later. Vu was confident the licence would arrive soon.

The Partners

Otis Elevator

Part of the United Technologies Group, Otis Elevators is one of the world's leading manufacturers and installers of elevators, escalators, travelators and shuttles. It has 1,700 offices in about 140 countries and its products are sold in virtually every country of the world. In its ambition to be a truly global company, Otis moved quickly into China where it already has four joint ventures, and even aims to have a presence in the smallest markets such as Cambodia and Laos.

The manufacturing of Otis products takes place in two stages. A relatively small number of factories—in the US, Japan, Spain, Berlin, and Gien (France), among others—manufacture key components which are supplied to the company's many contract factories worldwide. Key components include the machinery, controller, door mechanisms and cars. The role of a contract factory is to assemble the lifts for local installation according to job specifications, but manufacturing or buying in the non-essential components such as wall panels which are much more cost-effective to source locally. The contract factory must have a strong network of reliable suppliers from which to source its non-critical components. Each contract factory also has a list of authorised Otis factories from which to acquire key components.[1]

Lilama

The Union of Erection Companies, commonly known as Lilama, is a group of 18 state-owned companies answering to the Ministry of Construction in Hanoi. It employs 15,000 people, which makes it one of the largest companies in Vietnam. It was founded as a single unit in the 1960s to install a steel mill. Subsequently, for each new large project in a new location, a separate company was established, leaving the older ones to sink into oblivion unless they found new business. Today Lilama's companies are spread all over Vietnam and are involved in heavy industrial equipment installations ranging from cement and steel mills to hydroelectric power stations and dams. The strongest and most profitable Lilama unit is based in Ho Chi Minh City. Some Lilama companies have experience of installing lifts—and had even tried to manufacture them, despite their lack of knowledge of safety requirements, using the 'learn by doing' approach which is common in Vietnam.

The affiliation between the various units is loose. Each member company has a general director and the Union has a small management team operating a peer management system. There is no consolidation of accounts. Each company manages its own accounts, and there is no obligation for one unit to balance another's losses. This system may change in future, as the government pursues plans to form "general companies," and a more bureaucratic, formal system of management may be imposed.

Otis was interested in a partnership with Lilama, both for its importance in the industrial framework of Vietnam and for its experience in elevator-related activity.

Construction and Elevator CO. (CEC)

Before 1975, the agent for Otis in the south of Vietnam was a private company called Engenico. Through it, around 200 Otis elevators were installed, mainly in Ho Chi Minh City. Engenico was nationalised in 1975 following the defeat of the South Vietnamese regime and the unification of the country. It was then renamed CEC and placed under the administration of the Ho Chi Minh City People's Committee. Twenty years later, some of the former staff still work for the company. Although moral and sentimental values played their part, Otis's choice of CEC as a southern partner is based on its good technical knowledge of the elevator business. Compared with Lilama, CEC is very small, employing only 70 people, but the company has a good reputation in the south.

Since signing their joint venture agreement in August 1994, Otis and CEC have been waiting to receive their investment licence from the authorities.

Otis in Vietnam: Negotiating the Joint Venture Agreements

Negotiating the joint venture with Lilama raised delicate issues. Specifically, Otis insisted on signing the agreement with the overall Lilama management team, rather than with one of the constituent companies of the Union. Included in the contract is a clause of non-competition, which prevents any of the member firms from forming joint ventures with other elevator companies. (Lilama is, however, free to make agreements with firms in other businesses. Among others it has already negotiated ventures with the LG Group—which includes Goldstar—and Posco, both of South Korea, for the manufacture of steel structures.) In light of the strength of Lilama's Ho Chi Minh City-based unit, Vu was particularly keen to preempt competition from that quarter.

Vietnam is clearly divided for Otis business purposes at Danang, which falls into the southern sector. Hue and northwards are covered by the Hanoi operation. The non-competition clause also prevents the northern and southern joint ventures from competing in each other's area. Again, Lilama was deeply opposed to being closed out of the market in the south, given the strength of its Ho Chi Minh City unit. Mr. Vu was eventually able to prevail, on the grounds that competition between the two joint ventures for the same business would be self-destructive.

As the first foreign elevator company intending to establish a direct presence in Vietnam, Otis has seized the first mover advantage by forming joint ventures with two partners. It has chosen the companies it regards as the best in the country, and has removed both from the pool of potential partners for competitors. Its choice also allows Otis to address the crucial issue of competing political power structures. The backing of a company by a central government agency like the Ministry of Construction is important in Hanoi, but carries significantly less weight in Ho Chi Minh City, where the People's Committee is largely able to set the agenda. A joint venture with a company under the aegis of the local People's Committee is likely to make more rapid progress in Ho Chi Minh City than one formed with a centrally-run partner. The Ho Chi Minh City unit of Lilama lacked this local power.

Royalty Payments

A sticking point in negotiations between Otis and the Vietnamese authorities, specifically the Ministry of Science, Technology and the Environment (MOSTE), is over the issue of royalty payments by Otis Vietnam to the Otis parent company. Under the Otis internal accounting system used worldwide, factories supply elevators at cost price to the sales subsidiaries, which book the revenues and pay a technical assistance contract (TAC) fee to headquarters. The TAC covers the ongoing Otis R&D programme and permits open and continuous access by all sales offices to Otis's technological developments. Disagreements with MOSTE centre on the application base for the royalty, and on the royalty rate itself. Vietnam's laws on the transfer of technology propose a rate of 2 percent which is too low for Otis as well as most other foreign investors in Vietnam. The issue is even more serious for car manufacturing joint ventures. Some overcome the problem by charging the technology transfer fee in the import price of components. Otis does not want to resort to this arrangement and is still looking for the best solution.

Organisational Issues

The Otis share in each of its joint ventures is 70 percent. Both joint ventures are structured in exactly the same way, as shown in the organisation chart in Exhibit 2. The organisation differs from most foreign-invested joint ventures in Vietnam, in that the General Manager and two deputy General Managers out of three are expatriates. (Mr. Vu is an overseas Vietnamese who has lived for many years in France. He has a French, a South African and a Japanese as his expatriate colleagues.) The standard joint venture organisation in Vietnam has a local General

Exhibit 2   Otis Organisation in Vietnam

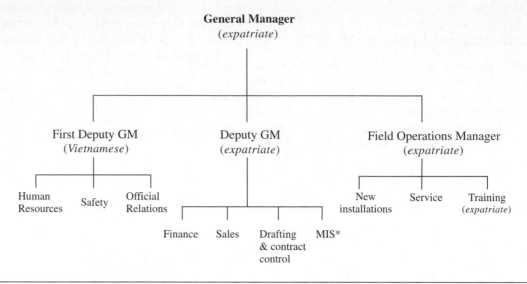

General Manager
(*expatriate*)

First Deputy GM (*Vietnamese*)
 — Human Resources
 — Safety
 — Official Relations

Deputy GM (*expatriate*)
 — Finance
 — Sales
 — Drafting & contract control
 — MIS*

Field Operations Manager (*expatriate*)
 — New installations
 — Service
 — Training (*expatriate*)

*Management Information Systems
SOURCE: Otis Vietnam

Director, supported by one Vietnamese and one expatriate deputy General Manager. Within three to five years, Otis expects to localise all except the General Manager position, and even this post should be held by a local Vietnamese as soon as Otis considers the succession capability is satisfactory.

More unusual than the organisation chart *per se*, however, is that the Otis expatriate management team of four (including the Training Manager) is responsible for both joint ventures, with members shuttling between Hanoi and Ho Chi Minh City. The two operations are also identical in terms of size and staffing, which makes it relatively easy for the expatriates to switch offices. Since each joint venture requires full time attention, the four are kept busy but are thoroughly versed in the progress at both companies. The volume of business in Vietnam is not large enough at present to justify the expense of two expatriate teams. Even though the shared team reduces the cost of operations, Vietnam will still not quickly become profitable.

By the end of 1996 each joint venture will have 50–70 staff. The Vietnamese deputy General Director of each company comes from the respective local partner. An important role for the Vietnamese deputy Director is to manage relationships with the authorities, a time-consuming but essential task which can only be fulfilled satisfactorily by a local person.

Department heads are sourced either from the partner or hired externally. Although the partners were disappointed not to supply all the department heads, personnel with the necessary skills—for example to be the Chief Accountant or the Finance Manager—did not exist within their organisations. The management information systems (MIS) person, the Sales Manager and the Estimator were all hired externally. *"We were lucky to find them,"* says Vu, reflecting on the shortage of skilled staff. Although local unemployment rates are high, rather few people have the market-oriented or technical skills sought by foreign firms. The person in charge of MIS ensures that both offices work on the same computer system. This has already involved changing all the software at the southern office (the newer venture) to assure compatibility with the Hanoi operation.

An inherent difficulty of Vietnam is the different concept of doing business. In other Otis joint ventures in Asia (with the exception of China), the local partners are simply interested in progress made and only want to be kept informed. Here, Vu feels that the partners are constantly tempted to comment on any information and interfere in the running of the business. They always want to know exactly what is happening. *"I don't need my shadow, I have a partner for that,"* he says. Vu has resisted suggestions from the local partners that, when he is away, the Vietnamese deputy should assume his responsibilities. He hopes that, if they meet the business plan, and after one or two audits by the Ministry of Finance, the partners will become less suspicious.

Approaching the Market

In the initial stages, Otis is importing elevators on a project basis from France, Malaysia, Japan, even from the United States. The local team installs the elevator system, puts it into commission, and eventually expects to maintain it over a period of many years.

The Vietnamese authorities place great emphasis on persuading foreign firms to manufacture their products locally, in the belief that the transfer of technology takes place during the manufacturing process. The Otis stance, however, is that the real technology transfer in the elevator business takes place at the maintenance stage, since an engineer may take ten or even 20 years to learn perfectly the workings of the equipment. A trained engineer is a highly skilled technician, who is not only able to troubleshoot but can also conceive the inner workings of the machinery. In contrast, any manufacturing that Otis would do in Vietnam would be simple sheetbending work, requiring relatively little skill and limited transfer of technology.

It will not be profitable for Otis to manufacture an entire elevator system in Vietnam, because the import of components that cannot be sourced locally would bear customs duties while imported complete elevators bear none. There are rumours that an Asian elevator manufacturer is preparing to establish an elevator manufacturing facility in Vietnam, but Vu cannot see how this could be cost effective. The risk is that a foreign elevator company prepared to manufacture in Vietnam will demand that the Vietnamese authorities raise import duties to give it market protection.

The Competition

Otis has won contracts for 60 elevators and escalators in the 18 months since February 1994. The majority of its jobs are in Hanoi, which Otis targeted first and where it has better market coverage. The competition is also less intense than in Ho Chi Minh City, where Mr Vu describes the contest between the world leaders in the elevator industry to win high profile projects as "cut-throat." Through Otis Lilama and CEC elevators have been installed in the guest house belonging to the Central Committee of the Vietnam Communist Party (supplied from Glen), in the Ministry of Energy and in the SCCI, as well as two escalators at the Saigon Superbowl bowling centre in Ho Chi Minh City. The Superbowl is expected to become a major venue for youth entertainment when it opens in early 1996.

Otis has not been successful in winning the largest, high profile projects in Ho Chi Minh City. The contract for the Landmark building, an office and apartment block on the waterfront, was signed (by Fujitec of Japan) before the US trade embargo was lifted, automatically barring Otis from tendering. Other contracts for office buildings and hotels have been lost to companies proposing exceptionally low prices—and therefore apparently taking on huge loss provisions—to buy their way into the market. Observation suggests that the Japanese elevator manufacturers (notably Mitsubishi and Toshiba) and Goldstar of Korea have certain advantages in winning projects invested in by firms from Japan and Korea, although this does not prevent Otis from bidding aggressively even on these contracts. In general, Otis continues to compete hard for all available projects, but is not prepared to commit itself to the extent of taking significant losses on the product installed.

Competitors present in the market include:

Mitsubishi Electric—

won the largest project to date, the Saigon Trade Centre. It will also install elevators in the Hai Thanh Kotobuki development, a joint venture between another Japanese company and the Vietnamese navy.

Toshiba—

installed the elevators in the New World Hotel, a Hong Kong–invested project creating Ho Chi Minh City's largest hotel. Toshiba was introduced by the Hong Kong company Chevalier. It also has projects in Cholon, the Chinese area of Ho Chi Minh City.

Schindler Elevator K.K. (formerly Nippon Elevator)—

Schindler's majority-owned Japanese subsidiary has been active in Vietnam since 1987, which makes it the market leader in terms of number of lifts installed. The product it has been supplying (alternative current, variable voltage elevators) uses rather outmoded technology, suggesting that its market leadership will be lost in the next couple of years to Otis, Mitsubishi, Goldstar and others unless it upgrades its offering.

Goldstar—

actively supplying Korean investors, Goldstar is very much present in the market.

Schindler—

operating in Vietnam under its own name as well as through Nippon Elevator. The company beat Otis on bids for both Saigon Centre and Hanoi Centre Towers. It proposes to send Vietnamese people to Singapore for two years for training in elevator maintenance.

present through its French subsidiary Soretec. Competitive and aggressive, the company has installed elevators in a number of the new hotels in Ho Chi Minh City.

The big companies are *"hitting hard at the upper end of the market range,"* according to Vu, offering top-of-the-range, high speed lifts for 22–30 storey buildings. At the lower end of the product spectrum several companies—Thyman of Thailand and some smaller Italian and French firms, among others—are competing. Otis's goal is to challenge both ends of the market.

Of the 200 Otis elevators installed in the south before 1975, about half are still operational despite the lack of maintenance during the last 20 years. Otis is in the process of surveying these relics and proposing a modernisation scheme. There is resistance, due to lack of money at the banks, hospitals and a few old hotels where they are installed. Nevertheless, Otis believes it is well-positioned to capture not only this specific replacement market but also contracts related to general building renovations. Many of the older buildings in Vietnam are of French design, with narrow lift shafts of the type found in many Parisian buildings. The Otis factory at Gien in France is the only facility in the world to continue to produce lifts for this size of elevator shaft for the French market. It is technically feasible for any other elevator company to make small lifts specially, but they would not be competitively priced.

Otis's largest contract to date, worth US$1 million, is to install eight escalators at a municipal wholesale trade centre in Lang Son, on the border with China. Although the escalators have been delivered and Otis has been paid in full (it was a cash agreement, good until March 1994, made under a permitted execution contract before the US trade embargo was lifted), the escalators have yet to be installed. The case highlights some of the uncertainties of construction projects in Vietnam: the municipality began construction of the trade centre before negotiating the acquisition of additional land occupied by individuals and companies. The occupants have steadily increased the compensation they require for vacating their land in line with progress on the construction site. By the time the issue is resolved, Otis will need another contract to refurbish the escalators before they can be installed.

The Otis Service Organisation

In normal market conditions, the prices and products offered by the principal elevator companies are similar. Firms differentiate themselves through their service organisations—which is also where they make their money. The Otis strategy in Vietnam is to begin to build

a service organisation immediately even though it has no service contracts yet. (Most installations are either still in progress or are still within the free one year new installation service contracts.) Otis believes this long term policy will distinguish it significantly from its rivals in the future, and contribute to its credibility and reputation in Vietnam.

To establish a credible maintenance operation to service the lifts installed will be difficult without a firm commitment to Vietnam: without a joint venture or wholly-owned subsidiary, companies will not be allowed by the Vietnamese authorities to build a service-based organisation. To bring engineers in on demand from Hong Kong or Singapore is also unsatisfactory and does not solve the problem of emergency calls.

Vu has a delicate balancing act to perform, between the need to win sufficient new installation contracts in order to build up a sufficient maintenance portfolio, and the strong wish not to burden the fledgling operation with excessive loss provisions. *"The Vietnamese market is the choice between cholera and the plague"*, he says. In his view, a company basically has two choices: 1) to accept heavy loss provisions in order to build a portfolio of an absolute minimum of 500–600 units installed. It must accept also that customers tend to be unwilling at first to spend much on maintenance and that they will be reactive, for example when breakdowns occur, rather than pro-active. In the long run it must also add the costs of establishing a proper service organisation to the pain of the heavy losses taken on installed units. 2) The second alternative is to take the initially more expensive path of establishing a direct presence and creating a service organisation at the start, while at the same time building a portfolio of installed units carrying some profit margin to offset costs incurred. It will take longer to reach critical mass, but the organisation will be more solid. Otis headquarters has already accepted that its Vietnam operations will not be profitable for many years, whereas other elevator firms may not be prepared to countenance such a situation.

According to Vu, Otis has also lost projects in Vietnam due to its unwillingness to 'play the game' or 'accommodate itself to the market'. Internal corporate rules require Otis to withdraw from any project where there is even a hint of 'under the table' money. The fact that Otis is present throughout the Asia Pacific region, including countries where bribery is certainly not unknown, suggests to Vu that the company will be able to survive in this country too. Nevertheless, its partners put pressure on Otis to win orders under all circumstances, in the interests of earning profits quickly. Vu has been able so far to resist this pressure on the grounds that good ethical behaviour eventually prevails. At the same time he is trying to educate them to recognise that service and maintenance activity is the best generator of revenue over the long term. *"We are not targeting 100 percent of the Vietnam market,"* he says. *"I tell my staff that they shouldn't panic if they lose contracts They should do their best on each negotiation, look after our existing customers well, and they will come back for more units, not just the maintenance contracts."* Both the northern and the southern partners are difficult to convince on this point.

The sophistication of the elevators Otis installs for its customers requires its engineers to undergo intensive training. *"Once someone is trained, he becomes a scarce resource,"* comments Vu. Engineers become experts in Otis products, not in—for example—Mitsubishi lifts. Because each manufacturer's lifts are technically so refined (even though the quality of offering is similar) an expert service engineer leaving to work for a competitor needs months of retraining before becoming an asset to the new employer. Nevertheless, it is difficult for Otis to avoid some staff turnover.

In addition to technical training, the staff needs education in the culture and mentality of business. Vu believes that the mass of people have become passive in reaction to long years of war and a centrally planned economy. They have become used to having all their work checked by a manager. Vu wants them to exercise initiative and become more independent in the way they work. He also sees the labour relations environment in Vietnam as potentially hazardous, based on language problems and cultural misunderstandings. Already a number of foreign-invested companies have faced protest strikes by their workforce.

Vu intends to establish a rounded compensation package with a properly organised human resource structure. As in all Otis joint ventures, he wants the Vietnamese staff to feel part of the Otis 'family'. The policy of United Technologies—and therefore of Otis—is to build a team spirit, respect the human resource environment and offer very high standards of health and safety protection. For example, Otis adds extra safety dispositions for its engineers over and above industry norms, at its own expense (in order to remain competitively priced), with the result that engineers feel safer and are more confident in their work, and fewer working hours are lost.

Issues for the Future

Otis has won first mover advantage in commercial terms through setting up its joint ventures before any of its competitors and by entering a market devoid of service industries. In other respects there has been no benefit in arriving first, neither politically from the Vietnamese authorities, nor in business access terms since latecomers are profiting from the pioneering of the early birds. Competition is significantly more fierce than Vu had anticipated: his assumption was that Vietnam would initially be a high margin market for new equipment sales, during which time Otis would have the time to get established, and that prices would trend down thereafter. Instead, contracts are already being exchanged at more than 20 percent below cost.

Having people on the spot—by virtue of its Lilama joint venture—Otis has a better understanding of the market than firms without a direct presence. Partnership with a Ministry of Construction company provides access to information held within the ministry. Otis is also better positioned generally to collect essential market data, not available from neutral sources as in other countries, on existing and future contracts for elevators.

Looking at Otis in Vietnam today, Mr Vu can see a number of threats or challenges that must be faced:

Partnership Issues

- One of the two partner companies, Lilama or CEC, may seek to form a joint venture with a strong competitor in the territory not covered by the JV with Otis.
- The partner companies, Lilama and CEC, may try to exert pressure on Otis to maximise short term profits, and to interfere in the day to day management of the joint ventures. Otis must work continually towards consensus.

Contractual Issues

- The royalty issue must be resolved. Otis cannot continue to bring in elevators from overseas on a project basis without upsetting its partners.
- Otis must find a way of persuading the authorities to issue the second investment licence (for the joint venture in the south) without further delay.

Competitive Issues

- How can Otis raise entry barriers to its competitors in Vietnam?
- How should Otis act in the cut-throat competitive environment of Vietnam to take full advantage of its knowledge and its organisation in the market?

Endnote

1. Otis Pacific Asia Operations (B): Regionalization, Harvard Business School case study N9-393-010, 1992.2. Materials accounted for between 45 and 50 percent of Rubbermaid's net sales.

Case 29

Palm Economy

Pamella Tjahyadikarta
Boston University

Melissa A. Schilling
New York University

In four short years, Palm Inc., maker of the Palm Pilot personal digital assistant (PDA), saw its revenues grow from $1 million to $564 million (Exhibit 1).[1] Palm Inc. had enjoyed immense growth and a dominating market share in the PDA market, for both its hardware and *operating system* (OS). In its brief lifetime it had launched several 'families' of PalmPilots: Palm III, Palm V, and Palm VII. Each family was differentiated in terms of aesthetics, features, upgrade capabilities, and prices, and each family also had its own range of derivative products. Though the form and functionality of PDAs shifted rapidly, one overall trend was evident: PDAs were getting thinner and faster.[2]

Palm was founded as a developer of application software—its primary product was Graffiti handwriting recognition software. Since then, however, Palm's focus has shifted twice; first, to hardware design and then to PDA operating systems. Microsoft's experience in the PC operating system market vividly demonstrated that Palm's ultimate success as a market leader depended on controlling the operating system standard. In October 1999, Alan Kessler, Palm's COO of Platform and Products, claimed that in the long run, the hardware was not where profits would be earned. He claimed that Palm's goal was to make the Palm OS the standard of the market. He also boasted that he would sacrifice revenues by losing some hardware sales to Palm's licensees to make sure that the Palm platform was used in the majority of handheld devices sold. He called this phenomenon *Palm Economy*.[3]

History of Palm

The first generation of PalmPilots was introduced by Jeff Hawkins and Donna Dubinski in 1996. At the time, Hawkins owned his own startup company, Palm Computing, which produced the Graffiti handwriting recognition software for PDAs. However, many potential customers of Graffiti were companies that had designed PDAs but had failed to launch them. Many companies appeared unwilling to tradeoff some of the potential features of PDAs, leading to products that were too large, too expensive, or both. One example was Compaq's *Concerto*, a pen-based notebook. The Concerto came with a PC card slot, a built-in handle, and a rounded look for aesthetic reasons. However, it was too heavy and too bulky in size for most consumers.[4] The reluctance of early PDA companies to make feature trade-offs was compounded by the fact that there was very little consensus about what features customers would sacrifice and what they would pay for. Most of the PDAs launched between 1989 and 1994 (e.g., Sony's *Magic Link*, Amstrad's *PenPad*, Motorola's *Envoy*, Eo's *Personal Communicators*, IBM's *Simon*) had all died quick deaths.

The many PDA failure stories inspired Hawkins to develop the *PalmPilot*. Hawkins decided to make a PDA that was "fast and simple." Additionally, he envisioned a PDA that would "exchange data easily with a desktop computer; keep [a] shirt-pocket size; and . . . cost less than $300."[5] Hawkins' design philosophy is expressed in Exhibit 2. He made working prototypes out of wooden blocks that were as big as the to-be-designed PDA, thereby helping to figure out the ease of use of the PDA. Hawkins also believed that the key to designing a successful product was to have the designers working backwards by figuring out what the consumers want from the product and use that information to design the product.[6] Hawkins accomplished his design goals, making a

Pamella Tjahyadikarta and Professor Melissa A. Schilling prepared this case for the purpose of class discussion rather than to illustrate either effective or ineffective handling of an administrative situation. The authors wish to gratefully acknowledge the help and support of Deborah Natawidjaja and Oliver Austria.

Exhibit 1   Financial Data

Palm Inc.
Income Statement ($ millions)

	May-99	May-98	May-97
Revenue	563.5	272.1	114.2
Cost of Goods Sold	315.6	157.7	77.7
Gross Profit	247.9	114.4	36.5
Gross Profit Margin (%)	44.0	42.0	31.9
Selling, General & Administrative Expenses	151.4	86.1	36.5
Operating Income	48.3	6.5	(13.5)
Operating Margin	8.6	2.4	–
Total Net Income (%)	29.6	4.2	(7.9)
Net Profit Margin (%)	5.3	1.5	–

SOURCE: Hoover's Online.

Palm Inc.
Balance Sheet ($ millions)

	May-99	May-98	May-97
Cash	0.5	0.0	
Net Receivables	95.8	81.0	
Inventories	12.2	13.8	
Total Current Assets	130.2	103.0	
Total Assets	152.2	115.4	46.0
Short Term Debt			
Total Current Liabilities	77.7	34.1	
Long Term Debt			
Total Liabilities	77.7	34.1	10.3
Total Equity	74.5	81.3	35.7
Total Liabilities and Equity	152.2	115.4	46.0

SOURCE: Hoover's Online.

number of important trade-offs. For example, he decided against incorporating a device card slot on the early Pilots and provided instead only minimal functions. Hawkins' design philosophy proved effective. PalmPilots quickly attained a dominant share of the PDA market and attracted a loyal group of users and developers.

USRobotics acquired Palm Computing for $44 million in September 1995, bringing more capital to fund development costs. USRobotics was subsequently acquired by 3Com, a network equipment manufacturer, in June 1997, in what was a $7.4 billion transaction that included Palm Computing as part of the deal. Palm Computing initially became one of 3Com's divisions, and was later spun off in an Initial Public Offering (IPO) in February 2000 to raise $368 million. Palm Computing was renamed Palm, Inc. and was traded on NASDAQ with the ticker PALM. The spin-off was expected to enable Palm Inc. to focus on the new market

| Exhibit 2 | Palm Inc.'s Design Philosophy |

Simple

There must be no complicated steps between you and your information. You don't have time to fumble with confusing menus and hourglass cursors. On a Palm™ handheld, just touch the Date Book icon and you're on today's agenda. One touch to the scroll button and you see tomorrow's.

Wearable

Handhelds need to be carried everywhere, so you can get to your information anytime. They must be light and small enough to slip into your pocket or purse without thought.

Connected

Palm™ handhelds are designed to make it easy for you to access your important information no matter where you are or where that information is—on your desktop, on the company server, at home, or on the Web. The Palm VII™ handheld was the industry's first handheld with built-in wireless connectivity to the Internet and intranets combined with easy, out-of-box account activation. Add-on wireless modems are available for other Palm handhelds.

SOURCE: Palm, Inc. Design Philosophy http://www.palm.com/about/corporate/design.html.

---

segments in PDA technology: licensing the Palm OS, targeting corporate customers, providing wireless Internet services (Palm.net), and designing PDA hardware. In addition, The IPO move was also strategic for 3Com's effort to refine its corporate strategy. 3Com believed that its management had been diverted by Palm, which consequently contributed to 3Com's poor performance relative to its competitors and the networking industry in 1999.[7] After the IPO, the independent Palm Inc. offered three products and services: the hardware, the Palm OS, and Internet services.[8]

In June 1998, Hawkins and Donna Dubinski left 3Com to start their own company, Handspring Inc. Unfortunately, for Palm, Handspring's Visor quickly became the closest rival to the newer generations of PalmPilots. Handspring's products were also designed following Hawkins' design philosophy, similar to Palm's products.

Components of the Palm Computing Platform[9]

The foundation for the Palm Computing platform was the Palm OS, which enabled various applications software to run on a PDA. All PalmPilots had the following basic functions:

- HotSync technology: Allows easy synchronization with PCs through the use of a docking cradle. HotSync synchronization was done by pushing one button, or it could be used with PalmModem to access a remote server.
- Personal Information Management (PIM) applications: Provides a range of tools, to include contact list, calculator, memo pad, appointment management, and expense records. These utilized the Graffiti script recognition technology and the pen-based user interface. The PDAs also offered email software such as Microsoft Outlook 97, Lotus cc:, and Eudora.

To leverage and maintain its market leadership position, Palm continually upgraded its operating system; launched new series of hardware or improved versions of the existing product lines; and established an Internet service to encourage the adoption of its Palm VII hardware.

Palm Operating System

The Palm OS was constantly upgraded. For Palm (and other PDA operating system competitors), predicting the direction of operating system development was crucial. One competing operating system, EPOC, was specifically designed for handheld products and was similar to Palm OS. Its development was geared towards wireless voice and data communication applications. Another competing operating system, Windows CE, was advanced in supporting color and multimedia applications (see Competitors section for details).

As of March 2000, the Palm OS had been developed to support color screens, and it had been upgraded to work with modems for wireless data applications. Similar to the typical Palm OS, this version, when embedded in the hardware, resulted in a less bulky device with a longer battery life than was typical for PDAs.[10] This version was embedded in the Palm IIIc. However, the capabilities of this version still lagged behind Windows CE in terms of supporting multimedia applications. The Palm OS, however, was still highly preferred by many customers because it was faster and required less hard disk capacity.

Hardware

Each family of PalmPilots had its own differentiating attributes and purposes. This differentiation became the selling points that would determine which particular family of PalmPilots a customer would purchase. Palm VII, for example, was embedded with Web-clipping software to access the Internet. This feature would appeal to mobile professionals who depended upon accessing real-time information. The Palm V looked sleeker and smaller in size than either the Palm III or the Palm VII, a feature that would appeal to those who relied heavily on aesthetics for their purchase decisions (See Exhibit 3 and 4 for comparison of Palm's Products).[11]

Within a family of PalmPilots, the newer generations competed against the existing generations. Due to the rapid advancement in PDAs, the older generations of products quickly became outdated. Therefore, as Palm introduced new products, it was forced to cut prices on its existing products. For example, when Palm was introducing Palm IIIc, it cut the price of Palm IIIx by $70 to $229.[12]

As of April 2000, Palm was producing a wider range of PDA models than any of its competitors. No one competitor had any product range that competed against all of the Palm families of products, thus each family of PalmPilots competed with different PDA brands. The Palm III's closest competitor was Handspring's Visor. Similarly, Palm V competed against Compaq's Aero 1530, and Palm VII competed against Psion's Revo (see Exhibit 3 and 4 for detailed comparison).

In addition to a wider range of products, another selling point of the PalmPilot platform was compatibility of hardware accessories among the different PDA families. For example, all the Palm III sub-products could share one HotSync cradle, and the accessories for the Palm III family could also be shared with the Palm VII family.

However, the compatibility feature was not extended to the Palm V, which was considered as a symbol of prestige and required different features.[13]

Internet Services

Palm's Internet services were run on Palm.net, which was a subscription service for users of Palm VII to access the Internet using their PDAs. Palm.net could also be accessed by Internet content providers and applications software developers to post new content. Some examples of content providers were Fidelity.com, E*Trade, UPS.com, ESPN.com, WSJ.com, and Travelocity, among others. As of December 1999, Palm.net was available in only 260 metropolitan areas in the United States. However, Palm expected to expand the service's geographical scope.[14] Users were required to pay monthly fees, ranging from $9.99 for 80 monthly transactions to $39.99 for 480. Excessive usage would result in additional charges.[15]

A limitation of the Palm.net service was its dependence on Bell South, which was the provider of the service. The agreement with Bell South resulted in a lack of flexibility on Palm's side because the PDAs had to be configured to work with the frequency used by Bell South. If Palm wanted to change telecommunications carriers, it would have to reconfigure all existing PDAs. Also, if Palm wanted to expand internationally, the PDAs would have to be reconfigured to work with the frequencies of the various carriers. The agreement with Bell South also increased Palm's risks, placing the service quality, reliability, and security of Palm.net in the hands of Bell South.[16]

The Personal Digital Assistant Industry

As of March 2000, the overall PDA market was growing fast, and growth was expected well into the future. The number of individuals purchasing PDAs was expected to increase quite rapidly from 4,834,000 in 1998 to 30,765,000 in 2004. However, the expected growth of *smart phones*, devices capable of both data and voice communications using cellular phone technology, was even greater. The demand for smart phones was expected to grow from 376,000 in 1998 to 94,783,000 in 2004 (See Exhibit 5).

The PDA industry could be divided into operating systems, hardware, application software, and hardware accessories. As of early 2000, there were primarily three competing operating systems: Palm OS, Microsoft's Windows CE, and Psion's EPOC. The existence of competing operating systems also directly influenced the competition among hardware makers, as hardware makers supported different standards. For example, Palm hardware supported its own operating system, the Palm OS, and competed against both Compaq's device, based on the Windows CE OS, and also Psion's PDAs, based on the EPOC OS. However, as of June 1999, the majority of hardware makers supported the Palm OS. As of December, 1999, Palm's OS held an 83.5 percent market share in the PDA industry, compared to the 9.7percent held by Windows CE.[17] EPOC's market share trailed even further behind.[18]

In the hardware market, PalmPilots also held the largest market share in both the U. S. and worldwide, with 71.9 percent and 70.4 percent respectively.[19] However, the number of competitors in the hardware market was rapidly increasing. The fiercest new rival was Handspring Inc, which also utilized the Palm OS. Other hardware vendors included Hewlett-Packard, Casio, and Sharp, among others.

Applications software was largely produced by third-party developers, and while some software applications

---

Exhibit 3   Comparison of Various Personal Digital Assistants

Palm III Family and Handspring Visor Deluxe

	Palm IIIe	Palm IIIx	Palm IIIxe	Palm IIIc	Handspring Visor Deluxe
Suggested Retail Price ($)	149	229	249	449	249
Launch Date	July 1999	February 1999	February 2000	February 2000	September 1999
Operating System	Palm OS 3.1	Palm OS 3.1	Palm OS 3.5	Palm OS 3.5	Palm OS 3.1
Weight (oz)	6	6	6	6.8	5.4
Size (inches)	4.7 x 3.2 x 0.7	4.7 x 3.2 x 0.7	4.7 x 3.2 x 0.7	5.1 x 3.2 x 0.7	4.8 x 3.0 x 0.7
Display	Backlit	Backlit	Backlit	Active Matrix Color	Backlit
Memory (MB)	2	4	8	8	8
Battery Type	AAA	AAA	AAA	Rechargeable lithium ion	AAA
Battery Life	2-3 months	2-3 months	2 months	Over 2 weeks	2 months
Input Method	Stylus	Stylus	Stylus	Stylus	Stylus
Additional Features	Designed to be easy to use, customizable, and upgradeable from Palm IIIe. This model has Infrared port connection.	Similar features with Palm IIIe, except for a larger memory size.	Similar features with Palm IIIe and Palm IIIx, except for larger memory size. This model can be customized to the needs of consumers.	Designed with a color screen application, which is the first Palm PDA with color. This model can be used with other Palm IIIs accessories. This model also has Infrared port connection.	Designed to be expandable through the use of the Springboard module. The module supports accessories, such as, digital cameras, MP3 players, pagers, modems, and microphone. This model also has Infrared port.

(continued)

Exhibit 3 | Comparison of Various Personal Digital Assistants *(continued)*

Palm V Family and Compaq Aero 1530

	Palm V	Palm Vx	Compaq Aero 1530
Suggested Retail Price ($)	329	399	299
Launch Date	February 1999	October 1999	September 1999
Operating System	Palm OS 3.0	Palm OS 3.5	Windows CE
Weight (oz)	4	4	5.2
Size (inches)	4.5 x 3.1 x 0.4	4.5 x 3.1 x 0.4	0.5 thick
Display	Backlit	Backlit	Backlit
Memory (MB)	2	8	16
Battery Type	Rechargeable lithium ion	Rechargeable lithium ion	Rechargeable lithium ion
Battery Life	1 month	1 month	14 hour
Input Method	Stylus	Stylus	Stylus
Additional Features	Designed to be a sleek and slim model to emit a sense of prestige. Its accessories cannot be used with the other Palm families accessories. Wireless modem and Internet subscription from Omnisky is available for Internet application, in addition to Infrared port connection.	Include all of the additional features of Palm V with quadruple amount of memory.	Designed to support MP3 players and other accessories. This model has Infrared port connection, and is the smallest Windows CE based PDA to date.

Palm VII and Psion Revo

	Palm VII	Psion Revo
Suggested Retail Price ($)	449	399
Launch Date	May 1999	October 1999
Operating System	Palm OS 3.2	Symbian EPOC32 v 5.0
Weight (oz)	6.7	6.4
Size (inches)	5.25 x 3.25 x 0.75	6.0 x 3.0 x 0.75
Display	Backlit	Reflective touch screen
Memory (MB)	2	8
Battery Type	AAA	700 m Ah AAA NiMH rechargeable
Battery Life	2-4 weeks	14 hours
Input Method	Stylus	Qwerty keyboard and stylus
Additional Features	Designed for wireless applications and to be used with Palm.net Internet subscription. The new feature allows software upgrades through the Internet, in addition to the Infrared port.	Designed to be used with portable modem 56K and mobile phone to access the Internet. This model is also embedded with infrared port and built-in speakers.

SOURCES: Compaq.com Handspring.com Palm.com Psion.com.

Exhibit 4 Pictures of Personal Digital Assistants

Palm IIIxe

Courtesy of Palm, Inc.

Palm IIx

Courtesy of Palm, Inc.

Palm VII

Courtesy of Palm, Inc.

Palm V and Palm Vx

Courtesy of Palm, Inc.

Handspring Visor

Courtesy of Handspring, Inc.

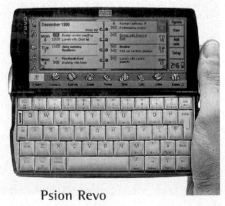

Psion Revo

Courtesy of Psion.

were developed specifically for one PDA architecture, many developers had chosen to hedge their bets by providing versions of their software for each of the competing PDA operating systems.

Target Markets

The PDA industry was composed of several market segments, with the two largest being personal users and enterprises. Palm targeted both of these markets for its hardware. Psion targeted similar markets. However, the Windows CE target market was less clear.

Palm's handheld devices were initially aimed at the individual consumers who were early adopters of new technology, commonly called *technophiles*. However, as handheld devices incorporated features such as easy synchronization with PCs, improved handwriting recognition technology, longer battery life, and smaller sizes, the PalmPilot family increasingly became a mass-market product.[20]

Palm then eyed a new market to penetrate: enterprises. In 1999, Palm charged direct sales teams with the mission to penetrate the enterprise market. New hardware accessories and applications software were also developed for the enterprise market, such as the Palm *Ethernet Cradle*, which would enable faster data transfer and synchronization of PalmPilot with the organization's server, instead of the user's PC. The latter benefit required the use of HotSync software. This enterprise configuration would enable PalmPilots to become integrated with the client-server network architecture common in larger organizations. Palm also created Palm Help Desk Training to provide technical support for enterprise clients. According to a report by Gartner Group, "As the devices [PalmPilots] became more popular among employees, large companies have wasted valuable resources by not supporting the technology in an efficient and organized manner."[21] Many analysts recommended that enterprises provide training and support for PDAs for security reasons. Synchronization between PCs and PDAs often resulted in confidential data being transferred to PDAs; thus, it was crucial for organizations to both support these technologies and exert more control over confidential data. Despite the many benefits,

Exhibit 5	Wireless Data/Portable Computing Devices Estimated Growth (U.S. & Western Europe)

Installed Base ('000)

	1998	2000	2002	2004
Portable PCs	25,379	39,085	63,660	98,171
Handheld Devices	4,834	10,212	18,734	30,765
Smartphones	376	9,618	43,059	94,783

Cellular Enabled Devices ('000)

	1998	2000	2002	2004
Portable PCs	2,235	6,408	15,692	31,965
Handheld Devices	240	1,181	3,392	7,561
Smartphones	376	9,618	43,059	94,783

% Cellular Enabled

	1998	2000	2002	2004
Portable PCs	8.8	16.4	24.7	32.6
Handheld Devices	5.0	11.6	18.1	24.6
Smartphones	100.0	100.0	100.0	100.0

SOURCE: Strategy Analytics as published in 3G Mobile, 1 (2): 5, June 2, 1999 by Baskerville Communications Corp.

supporting PDA technology could be costly. Palm platform-based PDAs could cost $2,690 per year; Windows CE-based PDAs could cost about $2,790.[22]

Competitors in the Operating Systems Market

Microsoft Corporation

Microsoft's key advantage in penetrating the PDA market was its tremendous control over several industry markets: the personal computer (PC), the network operating systems, and the applications software markets. Windows 95 and Windows 98 dominated the PC operating system market, and Windows NT was also widely used in networking environments. Microsoft was also much larger than Palm and Psion in terms of revenues and profitability (see Exhibit 6).

Microsoft launched Windows CE in 1996 as part of its "Information At Your Fingertips" campaign, which envisioned the evolution of PCs into multi-functional computer-based devices to be used in various business and personal activities.[23] As of 1999, the Palm OS was behind Windows CE in color and digital video technology, external storage, and multimedia.[24] Some analysts believed that as Windows CE was upgraded, it would become a threat to Palm, especially if the market demand shifted to PDAs offering more features. Windows CE's selling points were its functionality over simplicity and its appearance, which was similar to the Windows operating system. Microsoft hoped that its operating system customer base would prefer Windows CE for their PDAs due to familiarity in appearance and usage. However, due to its functionality, Windows CE-based devices had a shorter battery life and required larger memory capacity to run the embedded applications software when compared to Palm's PDAs.

Windows CE had strong supporters, such as Compaq, Casio, and Hewlett-Packard. However, some companies (e.g., Royal Philips Electronics) had decided to stop supporting the operating system because the sales of the CE-based PDAs were slow to take off, and because it appeared that the Palm OS had won the standards race.[25]

In 2000, Microsoft was also vigorously pushing its *Pocket PCs*, a term dubbed by the company for handhelds embedded with the improved Windows CE. Microsoft promoted Pocket PCs aggressively by going directly to the customers. Pocket PC was to be nationally launched on April 6, 2000, through its "Pocket PC Seeing is Believing Tour." The logic behind this strategy was to demonstrate the capabilities of the device to the customers, so that they would appreciate the technology embedded in the operating system.[26]

Microsoft had the capital and size to leverage its position in the handheld industry, even though the Palm held a majority market share. Some industry insiders speculated that Windows CE would be given away for free to developers in order to encourage both its adoption in hardware and the development of applications software. This strategy had paid off with the Internet Explorer browser.[27] In the long run, Microsoft was expected to be a fearsome competitor.

Psion PLC and Symbian Ltd.

Psion was formed in 1980 and became one of Britain's leaders in digital device technology. In 1982, Psion started developing handheld devices, and Psion *Organiser* was launched in 1984. Psion developed many generations of handhelds, including its well-known products such as the Series 3, Series 5, and Series 7, which were keyboard-based organizers of a slightly larger size than Palm devices.

Since its inception, Psion evolved into four separate divisions, each responsible for different product lines. Psion Computers produced handhelds and hardware accessories. Psion Dacom made PC Card modems, which were ranked as the world's third and Europe's top modems. Psion Enterprise Computing Ltd. was formed to serve the enterprise handheld market, with a distribution network in more than fifty countries in the world.

Psion also created the EPOC operating system and vigorously promoted it as a standard for handheld devices. The EPOC operating system was designed to handle wireless voice and data operations and was specifically designed for handhelds. The EPOC operating system was considered more advanced in terms of functionality, as compared to Palm OS, and not "slow and clunky" like Windows CE.[28]

To encourage the widespread use of the EPOC operating system, Psion formed a subsidiary called Symbian Ltd. to promote the standard, and later (in 1998) sold shares to some of the world's largest wireless telecommunications manufacturers, including Ericsson, Nokia, and Motorola. Matsushita joined the venture in 1999, and as of December 1999, Ericsson, Nokia, and Motorola each owned 21 percent shares in the joint venture; Matsushita owned 9 percent; and Psion owned the remaining 28 percent of the shares.[29]

Symbian was the pioneer of two categories of multifunctional handhelds: communicators and smart phones. The smart phones were primarily designed for Internet connection, fax transmission, e-mail, and PIM operations.[30] Similarly, the communicators were designed to offer voice and data communications capabilities with printer, keyboard, and Internet connection.[31] Both smart phones and communicators were built using the cellular phone technology. By having the

Exhibit 6   Financial Data of Competitors and Palm

Income Statement for FY 1998 ($ millions)*

	Palm Inc.	Psion PLC	Microsoft Corp.
Revenue	272	262	14,484
Cost of Goods Sold	158	175	1,197
Gross Profit	114	87	13,287
Gross Profit Margin (%)	42	33	92
Selling, General & Administrative Expenses	86	71	5,143
Operating Income	7	18	5,130
Operating Margin (%)	2	7	45
Total Net Income	4	31	3,454
Net Profit Margin (%)	1	12	30

SOURCE: Hoover's Online.

Balance Sheet As of FY 1998 ($ millions)*

	Palm Inc.	Psion PLC	Microsoft Corp.
Cash	0	90	3,706
Net Receivables	81	45	980
Inventories	14	21	0
Total Current Assets	103	156	10,373
Long Term Assets	12	65	4,014
Total Assets	115	221	14,387
Short Term Debt	–	1	0
Total Current Liabilities	34	63	3,610
Long Term Debt	–	1	0
Total Liabilities	34	65	3,610
Total Equity	81	156	10,777
Total Liabilities and Equity	115	221	14,387

Note: * Data were rounded to the nearest whole number.
SOURCE: Hoover's Online.

cellular phone-makers as partners in Symbian, Psion hoped to ensure the adoption of EPOC as the standard operating system for a new generation of PDAs based on integration with cellular phone technology.

In March 1999, Symbian launched the latest version of its operating system: EPOC Release 5. The newer version supported many operations, such as Internet, e-mail, text messaging, web-browsing, and contact management. Symbian was planning to upgrade its operating system in the year 2000 to support the Wireless Application Protocol (WAP) and Bluetooth platform, both standards for wireless communications.[32]

Getting PalmPilots to Market
Hardware Suppliers

Motorola supplied 100 percent of the microprocessors used in PalmPilots. Those with the backlit, black-and-white screen used Motorola's *DragonBall EZ* processor.

And those with the color screen used Motorola's *DragonBall VZ*, which has a speed of 33 MHz, twice as fast at the EZ. Motorola, on the other hand, also relied on Palm for licensing agreements for the Palm OS. Motorola planned to offer smart phones supporting the Palm OS (despite its membership in the Symbian venture), providing ample evidence to show that hardware-makers could not be relied upon to back a single OS standard.

The other components of the PalmPilots were standardized and could be purchased through multiple suppliers: DRAM memory chips from AMD, Fujitsu, and Toshiba; *liquid crystal display* (LCD) panels from Epson, Samsung, Sharp, and Philips.[33]

Outsourced Production

Production of the hardware was outsourced to *Manufacturers' Services Limited* (MSL) and Flextronics. Both companies created prototypes, sourced the parts, assembled the PDAs, controlled product quality, and shipped the finished products for Palm. MSL's production was located in Utah. The plant itself was purchased from 3Com Corp. Flextronics' production facilities were located in Mexico, California, and Malaysia. This outsourcing strategy allowed Palm to minimize both its inventory carrying costs and capital investment costs.[34]

Research and Development

In 1999, Palm spent $46 million on R&D, compared to $13.5 million and $22 million in 1997 and 1998, respectively. Palm owned four research and development centers in Washington, Illinois, California, and France. Each of the design centers developed various components of the Palm Computing platform.

In the PDA industry, technologically advanced products and continual expansion of existing product lines were considered crucial for success.[35] Palm tried to upgrade its operating system every twelve months. In hardware, its goal was to launch new products for the selling seasons: June and December (Exhibit 3 shows the launch dates of Palm's products). To achieve these two goals, Palm's R&D and marketing departments worked simultaneously in launching a new product. For example, the press releases of the Palm IIIc began when the product was in its development stage.

Application Developers and Hardware Accessory Producers

As of March 2000, there were 50,000 developers who had agreed to make applications software for the Palm OS or hardware accessories for the handhelds.[36] In March of 2000, there were at least 500 hardware accessories, and 4,500 Palm OS-compatible software applications, including games, PIM, communications, and groupware. Some of the major software applications included IBM's Lotus Organizer, Symantec's ACT!, and QUALCOMM's Eudora e-mail program.

To speed up the creation of applications software, Palm gave out Beta versions of the upgraded Palm OS to the developers in order to minimize the time lag between the launchings of the upgraded operating system and the compatible applications software.[37] Palm also gave away its operating system program code for registered applications software developers. Palm saw itself as "the leader of troops of developers and partners working in concert to create an army of users accessing Internet-based services and communicating wirelessly all on devices running on the Palm OS."[38]

Palm also created a support program for developers, called *Palm Solution Provider Program*. Any potential developer was allowed to join the program for free, and Palm provided technical and marketing support. For example, Palm provided web resources that developers could access to get the Palm OS code, technical support, and hardware discounts (See Exhibit 7 for complete list of developers' benefits).

Distribution Channels

Palm used a variety of channels in distributing its products. In the US, Palm distributed its products mainly through distributors, who in turn sold the products to national retailers or large Internet retailers (see Exhibit 8 for distributors list). Some retailers, however, did buy PDAs directly from Palm. The types of retailers that sold Palm's products included office supply stores, consumer electronics stores, and catalog/mail order retailers. These retailers in turn sold PalmPilots to individuals, small businesses, and Small Office Home Office (SOHOs). Furthermore, Palm used a direct sales force to serve the enterprise market. Palm also sold directly through its online store.

Palm's products were internationally distributed through 88 European distributors and 23 Asian distributors. The Japanese market was served through Palm's subsidiary, Palm Computing K.K. The subsidiary would manage the sales, distribution, and user and developer support in Japan. The significance of the subsidiary was emphasized by Palm's CEO, Carl Yankowski: "The formation of Palm Computing K.K. underscores our commitment to this important market and brings us even closer to our Japanese customers."

Palm also struck *original equipment manufacturer* (OEM) deals with other companies who would then sell

Exhibit 7 Benefits of Palm™ Solution Provider Program

Palm™ Solution Provider Program was intended for developers of solutions, applications software, peripherals or hardware accessories for the Palm Computing® platform.

Web Resources

* Access free development resources from Palm's web site, such as the searchable Development Support Knowledge Base, technical information, sample code, FAQs, and documentation.
* View and download information from the Development Support pages, share insights and answers on the developer forum, and even submit development questions to Development Support.
* Participate in the annual Developer Conference, which brings together thousands of developers from around the world.
* Get the on-line Marketing Communications Guidelines to help your product be successful with logo and trademark usage, product naming guidelines, and product copy samples. Also,
* increase your credibility and awareness in the marketplace by licensing the "Designed for the Palm Computing® platform" logo.

Additional Benefits

* **Development information and tools:** get pre-release tools and information for upcoming devices. Get ROM images for the Palm OS™ Emulator to test your applications against new versions of the Palm OS. Get technical diagrams and hardware development kits.
* **Marketing information and opportunities:** participate in co-marketing opportunities like exhibitions, product guides, and the ability to use the "Designed for the Palm Computing® platform" logo for your product. Feature your enterprise solutions on our Enterprise page.
* **Provider Pavilion:** access this password-protected section of our web site for Program members only. This is where you apply for special programs and access the special tools, information, and more.
* **Public Relations Action Kit:** get the on-line Public Relations Action Kit with tips to maximize press coverage and advice on writing and distributing press releases.
* **New Product Compatibility:** participate in training sessions and labs for pre-released products. Get notification of regional labs for compatibility testing. Read the monthly Palm Computing® Developer electronic newsletter for announcement of upcoming events and up-to-date product information.
* **Targeted Marketing Opportunities:** Publicize your product in InSync Online, a highly targeted email service for Palm Computing® platform product owners.
* **Enterprise Marketing:** win up to $500 for every lead that turns into an Enterprise Customer Success Story.
* **Hardware Discount Program:** purchase Palm Computing® platform devices for your development purposes at a special discount.
* **Solution Provider Newsletter:** this monthly publication is sent via e-mail to all Palm Solution Providers. It's filled with the latest news, promotions, special events, tools, marketing opportunities and much more.
* **Hardware Discounts:** purchase Palm Computing® platform devices for development purposes at a 20% discount.

Platinum Solution Provider Benefits

Platinum Solution was intended for program members whose products successfully pass compatibility testing upgrade.

* **Platinum Marketing Support:** use the "Designed for the Palm Computing® platform Platinum" logo. Access high-level marketing opportunities. Display your advertising banner on our Products and Software page. Showcase your solution on the Platinum Solutions Directory and the Platinum Solution Center from beyond.com.

(continued)

| Exhibit 7 | Benefits of Palm™ Solution Provider Program *(continued)* |

* **Platinum Development Support:** receive priority support from the Development Support group.
* **Hardware Discounts:** purchase Palm Computing® platform devices for development purposes at a 35% discount.
* **Targeted Marketing Opportunities:** Rent the Palm Computing® customer list for your promotional mailings at a discounted rate. Advertise your product in Affinity Publishing's Software and Resource Guide for the Palm Computing Platform, a quarterly catalog distributed in product packaging and at special events, also at a discounted rate for Platinum Providers.

SOURCE: Palm, Inc. Development Support http://www.palm.com/devzone/program.html.

Palm products under their own brand names. These companies were typically ones with either exceptional brand equity or better efficiency and effectiveness in managing new market penetration than Palm. For example, IBM initially aided Palm in penetrating the Japanese market by selling Palm's product as IBM WorkPad PC.[39]

Organizational Structure and Human Resources

Palm organizational structure was divided by target markets, such as personal user and enterprise, in addition to functions, such as sales, marketing, supply chain operations, licensing and developer support, product development, and platform engineering (see Exhibit 9 for a list of Palm's senior management). As of November 1999, Palm employed 632 people. Two hundred fifty-four of those were in sales and marketing, 250 in research and development, 67 in customer support and activities involved in delivering Palm's product and services, and the remainder tackled the general and administrative work.[40]

Marketing

Palm's marketing campaign emphasized the slogan "Simply Palm," and was intended to target the mass market (see Exhibit 10 for examples). Palm also encouraged its product to be featured in other firms' TV commercials (for example, Palm VII was featured in Fidelity's PowerStreet commercial). Press releases were also used to build anticipation of Palm's future products. For example, the news of Palm IIIc was released in late 1999, while the actual product was launched in February 2000. Palm also employed in-store promotions.[41] For example, in Staples, a large office supply store chain, consumers could try out Palm devices displayed in high traffic and high visibility areas of the stores. However, Palm relied mostly on word-of-mouth advertising through the existing installed base of users and developers to build greater awareness.[42]

Ongoing market research and continual feedback from customers and applications developers also helped Palm stay in touch with the market demands, as well as changing demographic and socio-economic trends.

Alliances

Palm joined forces with other major players in high technology industries to ensure the widespread use of its operating system. For instance, through an alliance with Sony, Palm would create a new version of the Palm OS to work with Sony's *Memory Stick*, a data storage device that was small in size (1.5 inches long and as thick as a chewing gum package) and had a storage capacity of 8- to 64 MB. The large capacity would allow the storage of multimedia files.[43] This alliance was anticipated to help Palm catch up with Windows CE's color imaging capabilities and would likely strengthen Palm's market leadership position.

The alliances Palm created were primarily aimed at guarding its market share from Windows CE and EPOC. However, given that alliances were rarely exclusive arrangements, it was unclear that all of Palm's alliances would really give it an advantage in winning the standards battle. For instance, Palm established an alliance with Nokia to develop smart phones using Palm's web-clipping technology and Psion's EPOC operating system. This was one of Palm's ventures to widen the use of its technology beyond its current PDA market; however, given that Nokia supported the EPOC operating system, this alliance not only failed to ensure the adoption of the Palm OS, but it also put at risk valuable information about future development directions of the Palm OS, which could be leaked to Symbian.[44]

Exhibit 8   Distribution Channels in the United States

Distributors

D & H
Douglas Stewart Company (Education only)
Ingram Micro
Merisel
MicroAge
Tech Data

Palm Online Store www.palm.com

Federal Government/GSA
CDWG
CompUSA
GE Capital IT Solutions
GTSI, Inc.
Inacom Government Systems

National Resellers

CompuCom
Inacom
GE Capital IT Solutions
MicroAge
Hartford Computer Group
Pomeroy

Mail Order Catalog Companies' Web Sites

CDW
J & R Music World and Computer World
PC Mall
MicroWarehouse
Mac Mall
PROVANTAGE
Mac Zone
PC Connection
DellWare
PC Zone
Insight

National Retailers

Best Buy
Office Depot
Circuit City
OfficeMax
CompUSA
Staples
Franklin Covey
MicroCenter
Service Merchandise
The Sharper Image

Regional Retailers

ComputerWare
Ultimate Electronics
DataVision
RCS Computer Experience
Fry's Electronics (California)
The Good Guys (West Coast)
J & R Music World and Computer World

Exhibit 9   Palm's Senior Management

Carl Yankowski	Chief Executive Officer
Alan Kessler	COO, Platform & Products
Judy Bruner	SVP & Chief Financial Officer
Satjiv Chahil	Chief Marketing Officer
Barry Cottle	Chief Operating Officer, Content and Access
William Maggs	Chief Technology Officer
Doug Solomon	Chief Strategy Officer
Mark Bercow	VP – Platform Licensing and Developer Support
Gregory S. Rhine	VP – Worlwide Sales and Service
Byron J. Connell	VP – Consumer
Chuck Yort	VP – Enterprise
Peng Lim	VP – Product Development
Dan Keller	VP – Platform Engineering
Dinesh Raghavan	VP – Global Supply Chain Operations

SOURCE: http://www.palm.com/about/corporate/executive.html.

Licensees

Palm licensed its Palm Computing platform to various companies in order to encourage the adoption of its operating system as an industry standard, both in the personal user and enterprise markets. Some of the licensees included Handspring Inc., IBM Corp., Sun Microsystems Inc., and Symbol Technologies Inc. For example, Symbol Technologies created handhelds based on Palm OS for bar scanning use, which were then sold to enterprises (thus helping Palm penetrate the enterprise market).[45]

However, these licensees could also be Palm's competitors in hardware sales. One of the biggest competitors was Handspring's Visor, which was priced lower than Palm's devices and contained more functions because of its Springboard module. The module allowed more components—digital cameras, pagers, modems, and MP3 players—and additional software to be used with the Visor, giving it great expandability.[46] As of March 2000, the sales of Visor had not yet been released by Handspring; however, there were rumors of problems in Visor's production, distribution, and technical support.[47]

The Future

Palm's alliances and relationships with third-party developers successfully strengthened its market leadership position. As of 1999, the market had demonstrated a clear preference for the Palm Computing platform. However, a lot of uncertainties still existed in the PDA market. Some analysts expected future PDAs to bear more similarity to Handspring's Visor. PDAs were expected to come with minimal functions, such as contact management and e-mail, and be expandable using some kind of module similar to Handspring's Springboard. Some analysts expected PDAs to replace PCs completely, thus, appealing to both *technophobes* and non-PC owners. Gary Meshell of Benton International, a New York City consulting company, went so far as to predict that "cell phones will ultimately become the channel of choice, even replacing palm technology."[48]

If such a prediction were to prove accurate, EPOC might emerge as the winner, as it was embedded in mobile devices with cellular phone capabilities. If PDAs replaced PCs, Windows CE could win the standards battle for its functionality. If market demand remained as it was, Palm OS could win the standards battle. Could Palm influence the future demand using its market leadership position? How could Palm ensure that its R&D efforts would pay off? Palm had also built its market leadership position through licensing and alliances. How could Palm minimize the risks imposed by its alliances or licensing strategy? Licensing was an easy way to encourage the use of Palm OS, but how would Palm be affected by increasing competition in the hardware

Case 29 / Palm Economy

market? Furthermore, many of Palm's allies were much larger in size than Palm and committed to many alliances themselves. How could Palm be sure that its allies would fully support the Palm Computing platform?

Exhibit 10   Palm Advertisement

Courtesy of Palm, Inc.

Courtesy of Palm, Inc.

Endnotes

1. Palm, Inc., 1999, SEC Filing: Form S-1 Initial Registration Statement, *EdgarOnline.com* December 13.
2. S. Miles, 1998, PalmPilot to get thinner, faster, *CNET News.com*, August 18, http://news.cnet.com/category/0-1003-200-332347.
3. Palm, Inc., 1999, SEC Filing: Form S-1 Initial Registration Statement, *EdgarOnline.com* December 13.
4. D. Silverman, 1994, Compaq's Concerto fading away; Production of notebook is halted, *The Houston Chronicle*, July 16, Business 1.
5. D. Pogue, 1999, *PalmPilot: The Ultimate Guide, Second Edition*, (California: O'Reilly & Associates), xv-xvi.
6. S. Miles, 1999, Palm cofounder shares design philosophy, *CNET News.com*, October 20, http://news.cnet.com/category/0-1006-200-921068.html.
7. Palm, Inc., 1999, 3Com announces plan to build two distinct leadership companies in networking and handheld computing, September 13, http://www.palm.com.
8. S. Miles, 2000, Is Palm using sleight of hand with its color display? *CNET News.com*, January 21, http://news.cnet.com/category/0-1006-200-1529292.html.
9. Palm, Inc., 1999, SEC Filing: Form S-1 Initial Registration Statement, *EdgarOnline.com*, December 13.
10. S. Miles, 2000, Palm slashes prices to make way for new models, *CNET News.com*, February 4, http://news.cnet.com/category/0-1006-200-1542299.html.
11. S. Miles, 1999, Palm devices with color screen coming soon, *CNET News.com* December 21, http://news.cnet.com/category/0-1006-200-1502303.html.
12. S. Miles, 2000, Palm slashes prices to make way for new models, *CNET News.com* February 4, http://news.cnet.com/category/0-1006-200-1542299.html.
13. D. Pogue, 1999, *PalmPilot: The Ultimate Guide, Second Edition* (California: O'Reilly & Associates), 15-16.
14. Palm, Inc., 1999, SEC Filing: Form S-1 Initial Registration Statement, *EdgarOnline.com*, December 13.
15. S. Miles, 1999, Palm adds new handhelds to growing market, *CNET News.com*, October 4, http://news.cnet.com/category/0-1006-200-806007.html.
16. Palm, Inc., 1999, SEC Filing: Form S-1 Initial Registration Statement, *EdgarOnline.com* December 13.
17. S. Miles, 1999, Young handheld market set to triple, report says, *CNET News.com*, December 23, http://news.cnet.com/category/0-1006-200-1529292.html.
18. Hoovers Online, April 7, 2000, http://www.hoovers.com.
19. S. Miles, 1999, Young handheld market set to triple, report says, *CNET News.com*, December 23 http://news.cnet.com/category/0-1006-200-1529292.html.
20. L. Pizzani, 1999, Banks Ponder The Power of New Internet Gadgets, *Bank Technology News*, February,1.
21. S. Miles, 1999, Palm sets sights on corporate customers, *CNET News.com*, October 18, http://news.cnet.com/category/0-1006-200-918615.html.
22. S. Miles, 1999, Hand-wringing over handheld support costs, *CNET News.com*, October 12, http://news.cnet.com/category/0-1006-200-850974.html.
23. Microsoft Corporation, March 21, 2000, http://www.microsoft.com.
24. S. Miles, 2000, Is Palm using sleight of hand with its color display? *CNET News.com*, January 21, http://news.cnet.com/category/0-1006-200-1529292.html.
25. D. Deckmyn, 1999, Palm Winning Handheld War, *PC World*, November 23, http://www.pcworld.com.
26. J. Davis and S. Miles, 2000, Microsoft to tout handheld in marketing blitz, *CNET News.com*, March 21, http://news.cnet.com/category/0-1006-200-1579503.html.
27. S. Miles, 2000, Microsoft considers giving Windows CE license to developers, *CNET News.com*, March 16, http://news.cnet.com/category/0-1006-200-1574857.html.
28. T. Mainelli, 1999, Psion Revo enters handheld fray, *PC World*, October 6, http://www.pcworld.com.

29. *Hoovers Online,* April 7, 2000, http://www.hooversonline.com.
30. Symbian Ltd., March 21, 2000, http://www.symbian.com.
31. Ibid.
32. Ibid.
33. S. Miles, 1999, Palm sets sights on corporate customers, *CNET News.com,* October 18, http://news.cnet.com/category/0-1006-200-918615.html.
34. Palm, Inc., 1999, SEC Filing: Form S-1 Initial Registration Statement, *EdgarOnline.com,* December 13.
25. Ibid.
36. Palm In., 2000, Palm Signs 50,000 Developers; Palm OS Platform Gains Momentum as Leading Handheld Computing Platform, March 22, http://www.palm.com/pr/032200.html
37. Palm, Inc., 1999, SEC Filing: Form S-1 Initial Registration Statement, *EdgarOnline.com,* December 13.
38. D. Kawamoto and S. Miles, 2000, Palm looks to raise $368 million in IPO, *CNET News.com,* January 28, http://news.cnet.com/category/0-1006-200-1535175.html.
39. Palm, Inc., 1999, SEC Filing: Form S-1 Initial Registration Statement, *EdgarOnline.com,* December 13.
40. Ibid.
41. Ibid.
42. J. Davis and S. Miles, 2000, Microsoft to tout handheld in marketing blitz, *CNET News.com,* March 21, http://news.cnet.com/category/0-1006-200-1579503.html.
43. J. Davis, 1999, Sony, Palm to team on handhelds, *CNET News.com,* November 15, http://news.cnet.com/category/0-1006-200-1438332.hmtl.
44. S. Junnarkar and S. Miles, 1999, Nokia, Palm tackle wireless Net, *CNET News.com,* October 13, http://news.cnet.com/category/0-1006-200-851179.html.
45. D. Pogue, 1999, *PalmPilot: The Ultimate Guide, Second Edition.* (California: O'Reilly & Associates), 19.
46. S. Miles 1999, Is Palm ready for the handheld challenge? *CNET News.com,* September 13, http://news.cnet.com/category/0-1006-200-117533.html.
47. C. Crouch, 2000, Can Handspring handle success, *PCWorld.com,* March 16, http://www.pcworld.com.
48. L. Pizzani, 1999, Banks ponder the power of new internet gadgets, *Bank Technology News,* February, 1.

Case 30

Paradise Farm Organics

Chris Halter
Anne Smith
Eddie Dry

University of New Mexico

Late one mild August evening, Mary Jane Butters, founder and CEO of Paradise Farm Organics, Inc. (PFO) was sitting at her kitchen table and preparing for her 2000 stockholder meeting, scheduled for just two weeks away. Spread out in front of her were financial reports, many hand written notes, and a summary of potential growth initiatives; these growth initiatives were outlined in a summer project undertaken by an undergraduate business student and sister of a PFO stockholder. This report confirmed Mary Jane's belief that many new markets existed for her delicious, organic convenience meals. Traveling, lunch at the office, and quick meals for college students were just some of the numerous occasions where fast preparation of nutritious food could be enjoyed. Her stockholders, though many of them friends, would be looking for a plan and clear direction from Mary Jane about how to position and grow her business.

Paradise Farm Organics began as a sole proprietorship in 1989, later incorporated in 1992. Her business was founded as a mail order company. In 1998, Mary Jane entered into a private label contract with an outdoor equipment company to provide organic, natural, dehydrated food; this contract continued to provide a stable source of income. By 1999, PFO had broadened its scope and was selling organic food products, on a limited basis, through the Internet. Yet Mary Jane wanted to develop PFO's brand and reduce her dependence on the private label backpacking food business. How should she grow her business?

This case was written by Chris Halter under supervision of Professor Anne Smith and Professor Eddie Dry, University of New Mexico, as the basis for class discussion rather than to illustrate either effective or ineffective handling of an administrative situation. Reprinted with permission. © Anne Smith, Chris Halter, and Eddie Dry.

Paradise Farm Organics History

Mary Jane Butters, one of five children from Ogden, Utah, grew up loving the outdoors, enhanced by numerous family camping trips and a large family garden. Mary Jane described her formative years:[1]

> As a teenager I developed a passion for the writings of Henry David Thoreau, with a desire to live even more simply. I left Utah at age eighteen, headed for a summer job in northern Idaho on a forest fire watchtower. I tried college . . . but soon left to attend trade school and become a carpenter. After another summer as a fire lookout, I became one of the first women wilderness rangers hired by the US Forest Service. I spent two summers roaming the Uinta Mountains of Utah with my home on my back.

Butters spent another two years in Idaho's Selway-Bitterroot Wilderness Area, maintaining the oldest, most remote wilderness ranger station in the continental United States. During those years of living in the back-country, Mary Jane dreamed of and designed what she described as "real food" — transportable, easily prepared, and not adulterated by chemicals or over-processing.[2]

In 1986, after completing her last assignment with the Forest Service, Mary Jane purchased Paradise Farm, eight miles from Moscow, Idaho. Her farm was located on an area referred to as the Palouse, an extremely fertile area of the United States known for its abundant production of lentils and peas. That same year, Mary Jane founded the Palouse Clearwater Environmental Institute (PCEI), an organization committed to sustainable agriculture, environmental preservation, and consumer education. Sustainable farming systems are "capable of maintaining their productivity and usefulness to society indefinitely. Such systems . . . must be resource-conserving, socially supportive, commercially competitive, and environmentally sound."[3] Some of PCEI's programs included restoring the watershed, maintaining Moscow's community garden, providing farm tours, promoting smart growth policies for the town, and educating secondary school students about the environment through such activities as planting trees and recycling.

Near the end of her tenure at PCEI, Mary Jane helped to remodel and revitalize the Moscow Food Co-op. She also began selling organic fresh produce from her own crops at this market. After establishing and directing the PCEI for five years, Mary Jane left the organization in 1991 to pursue her own business, an organic food processing and distribution company. In an effort to encourage more farmers to convert to sustainable agriculture, she created a market for their harvest. She helped local farmers by purchasing their inputs, grown in accordance with Idaho organic standards, for use in her foods. Her inspiration was not self-serving. As Mary Jane stated, "I like creating social change through the business community."[4] Mary Jane expanded her product offerings by launching a line of backpacking foods, called Backcountry Organic Food, in 1993. Nick Ogle, whose farm borders Mary Jane's, became her husband and business partner during this time.

In 1995, a *National Geographic* article about sustainable agriculture featured Mary Jane Butters and her husband Nick and their efforts to promote organic food production.[5] This article generated tremendous interest as well as investments from people who were originally from this area or had an interest in promoting their approach to farming. From this very positive response, Mary Jane and Nick created a catalogue in 1996 to expand sales of PFO food products. This catalogue contained Mary Jane's dehydrated convenience meals in addition to selected natural and environmentally friendly products that Paradise Farm distributed for other companies. In 1999, she launched a website, organic-paradise.com, to display and sell some of the catalogue items. Mary Jane never purchased mailing lists, believing that orders from this approach were too low. Rather, she developed a mailing list of people who found PFO through word of mouth or articles in publications such as *National Geographic* and *Real Life*.[6]

Mary Jane's 1996 catalogue for Paradise Farm Organics was titled "From Farmhouse to Your House." The catalogue offered several types of organic fare including dehydrated backpacking food, instant meals, and fresh farm produce. Mary Jane's backpacking foods were vegetarian and created from organically grown produce. Anyone capable of boiling water could enjoy any of her more than 30 vegetarian, quick-preparation meals, such as: Falafel, Black Bean Hummus, Lentil and Wheat Pilaf and Southwestern Couscous. These quick preparation meals were offered in small packages or in bulk under the Paradise Farm Organics label. PFO's fresh farm produce included organic vegetables, herbs, a salad greens mix and an edible flowers mix that was only available in the summer season. The salad and flower mix were combined to create "Salade à la fleur" (seen in Exhibit 1, Salade à la fleur). Her initial 1996 catalogue also included products from other organic or natural product companies that were located mainly in the Northwest. Merchandise included snacks, canned food, household items, body care, health supplements, herbal remedies, books on cooking, gardening and health, and greeting cards.

The first 500 copies of the catalogue were mailed nationwide to Mary Jane's self generated list. Mary Jane admitted that she did not track outcomes from the initial mailing and cannot state the amount of sales generated from the first mailing. However, after reviewing the orders received from this catalogue, Mary Jane described several customer profiles—traditional customers as outdoor enthusiasts; environmental activists; cancer patients; people with severe allergies; office workers; and families seeking wholesome, convenience foods. According to Mary Jane, "Many of the company's mail order customers are located in cities where backyard gardens are impractical and access to farmers' markets or other organic outlets is inadequate or nonexistent. At the other extreme are the customers who live in rural areas with no whole foods grocery stores or organic food products."[7]

One outcome of the initial catalogue was that Mountain Safety Research (MSR), maker of backcountry stoves and cookware, found Mary Jane's backpacking food. MSR decided that this food would be a perfect addition to their product line. In 1998, Mary Jane entered into a private label contract with MSR. She began supplying them with PFO's dehydrated products for distribution to Recreational Equipment Inc. (REI), Eastern Mountain Sports (EMS), and to independent outdoor stores. The brand was named Ecocuisine because the packages were environmentally friendly when compared to the packaging of other backpacking food. Her packaging was not only smaller and less bulky than competitors' products, but it also was made from aluminum-free paper that was burnable in campfires.

After subsequent catalogue mailings in 1998 and 1999, Mary Jane decided to stop publication of the catalogue. Products from other companies occupied a significant number of catalogue pages; Mary Jane had determined that handling products for other companies was not profitable. Consequently, Mary Jane also shut down the organic-paradise.com website. After making these changes, Mary Jane decided to keep the name Paradise Farm Organics to signify her corporation and to develop "MaryJanesFarm" as her new product brand name.

Exhibit 1   Fresh Farm produce

Salade à la fleur

... plucked by hand one petal at a time ...

ORGANIC WILD DARK GREENS, DOMESTIC BABY LEAVES & EDIBLE BLOSSOMS

Ingredients (Seasonal): Leaves of the Amaranthus Cruentas, Magenta Spreen, Spinacia Oleracea, Beta Vulgaris, Brassica Oleracea, Petroselinum Crispum, Arugula/Roquette, Foeniculum Vulgare var. Nigra, Foeniculum Vulgare var. Azoricum, Tetragonia, Red Orach, Green Orach, Radicchio, Daikon, Taraxacum, Ocimum Basilicum, Lambsquarter and Sunflower Sprout. Petals of the Nasturtium, Pansy, Pisum Sativum, Hollyhock, Erfurter Orangefarbige 'Calendula', Fava Bean, Borago, Sunflower, Echinacea, Tarragon, Broccoli, Radish, Tagetes and Bachelor Button.

Health Benefits:

Since Salade à la fleur is so many different green foods and since it is grown in life giving, healthy organic soil you'll be eating a vast spectrum of essential vitamins, minerals, trace minerals, antioxidants, pigments, amino acids and more.

During 2000, Mary Jane began to develop a new web presence. She predicted that the Internet would increase sales more significantly than a catalogue. Furthermore, she believed that her backpacking customers did not need a catalogue. Since MSR was responsible for 80 percent of Mary Jane's sales and they did not care to operate an Internet site, Mary Jane developed a website called backcountryfood.com for the MSR backpacking line. MSR also allowed Mary Jane to keep all proceeds from sales on this site, so she hoped that MSR customers would prefer to shop or restock online rather than in retail stores. Buoyed by this initiative, Mary Jane decided to create a new website using her new product brand name: maryjanesfarm.com. This website was developed for her long-time catalogue customers and was geared primarily toward women. Both new websites were developed in-house by an independent contractor for a total of $10,000.

Throughout 2000, Mary Jane developed new recipes and products for both MSR and MaryJanesFarm brands. Her new offerings for those brands included side dishes like Sweet Corn and Black Bean Chowder or Smoked Spuds with Roasted Garlic in addition to new recipes for breads and desserts. Her quick preparation instant meals were quite gourmet; hence the branding of her MSR products was changed to Mountain Gourmet. Mary Jane was required to dispense with her own Backcountry Organic Food brand at this time. The packaging of products offered in retail stores and on the backcountry-food.com website was that of MSR. These packages and sales materials are shown in Exhibit 2. Top Mountain Gourmet sellers included Garlic Fry Bread, Alfredo Pasta with Garlic and Basil, Vegetarian Chilimac, Curried Lentil Bisque, Spoon Drop Scones with Orange Peel and Walnuts, and Outrageous Outback Oatmeal. Most choices were offered in three sizes. From least to most

Exhibit 2   Backpacking Foods

Products/Shop

Beans | Breads | Breakfasts | Dairy | Desserts | Drinks | Energy Bars
Fruits | Grains | Herbs and Spices | Meals/Couscous | Meals/Ethnic
Meals/Pasta | Meals/Potato | Meals/Soups | Nuts | Salsas | Sampler
Sauces | Vegetables

I sell my food in 3 different types of packaging:

Download our:

PRICE LIST   PRODUCT INFO
PREPARATION INSTRUCTIONS

- EcoPouch™
- Pouch Cook
- Do-it-Yourself Bulk

 Acrobat Reader is required to view product info & pricelists

EcoPouch™

The EcoPouch™ package is a 7"x7" burnable, non-aluminum pouch that contains two standard servings of food. I use the word 'standard' to describe a portion of food standardized by our government so that consumers can easily compare foods. Let's say you want to compare the sodium content of split pea soup manufactured by three different companies. If one company calls 1 cup a serving and the other 1 ¼ cup a serving and the third company calls 2 cups a serving, it gets hard to compare and choose which one you want if you're shopping for a certain level of sodium or protein or carbohydrates. My EcoPouch™ line generally contains two 'standard' servings. A standard serving works perfect for someone like me. It is exactly the amount I eat.

Pouch Cook

The Pouch Cook package is a 7"wide x 8 5/8" tall pouch with a box bottom that allows it to stand up on its own. You can use it as your bowl for the addition of cold and even boiling water. This pouch is also technically burnable (and non-aluminum) but after you've used it as a bowl, it has wet food coating the inside. If you want to burn it, you'll have to toss it into a hot fire or dry it first. Pouch Cook is designed to feed 'one hungry camper.'

expensive were bulk, a two serving size package and single-serving pouch cook. The MaryJanesFarm brand, however, excluded the two-serving package so that her brand would be slightly differentiated from that of Mountain Gourmet and would be in compliance with the MSR contract. Mary Jane's website is shown in Exhibit 3; some products are provided in Exhibit 4. By year-end 2000, she had created over 50 items and had 500 active individual customers ordering from her websites.

Natural and Organic Food Products Industry

Paradise Farm was ahead of the curve in terms of trends toward US natural and organic food consumption. Food labeled "organic" was required to undergo rigorous inspection in order to obtain the necessary certification. On December 20, 1999, the United States Department of Agriculture issued long-awaited national standards for organic foods. These standards were, " . . . expected to boost substantially the already fast-growing $6-billion-a-year organic food industry." The definition of "organic" described food that had been produced without synthetic pesticides, chemical fertilizers or antibiotics for at least three years. Growers were not allowed to use genetically modified seeds or food ingredients, apply sewage sludge as fertilizer, or use radiation to sterilize food.[8] At the time of the announced standards, Secretary of Agriculture Dan Glickman reported that the number of organic farmers was increasing by 12 percent a year in response to consumer demand. In addition, the uniform standards should allow US farmers to export their prod-

Exhibit 3   Mary Jane's Farm Website

ucts more easily since trading partners would know exactly what were certified organic products.[9]

Organic growers hoped that the national standards would also heighten consumers' awareness of what was actually allowed in conventionally grown food. According to an article in *The New York Times Magazine,* "Pesticide residues are omnipresent in the American food supply: the F.D.A. finds them in 30 to 40 percent of food samples. Many of them are known carcinogens, neurotoxins and endocrine disrupters . . ." Conventionally grown food could also contain organophosphates, antibiotics, growth hormones, cadmium, lead, arsenic (toxic waste in fertilizers is allowed by the E.P.A), and sewage sludge. Animals were allowed to eat feed that was made from ground-up bits of other animals as well as their own manure.[10]

The changed order of government standards however, did not include many of the philosophical values of the organic movement's founders. "Organic" traditionally conjured up visions of locally grown, fresh food that had not been transported across the country. The term was normally equated with unprocessed food derived from farms that used elaborate crop rotation methods to keep the soil healthy and able to withstand diseases and pests. Ideally, organic meant a sustainable system of farming that required few purchases for inputs and returned as much to the soil as it removed. According to the new

national standards, select additives and synthetics, such as ascorbic acid and xanthan gum, were allowed. It followed that energy-intensive processing of food shipped in from many states, or even countries, would be compiled to produce a package of organic processed food! For example, a Cascadian Farm frozen entree is comprised of three-dozen ingredients that are eventually shipped to Alberta, Canada for packaging in a microwaveable bowl. These ingredients undergo various stages of processing at a number of locations prior to shipment to Canada. Processing, shipping and packaging are all energy-intensive methods that negate the original intentions of those involved in the organic movement.[11]

Advocates of organic farming had long proclaimed its methods to be environmentally sound and to produce better quality food. Until the time of the case, however, data supporting those claims had not been released. A report published in *Nature* stated that organic methods resulted in food that won in blind taste tests and improved the condition of the soil. Additionally, organic methods provided growers with greater profits for their products. The belief that organically grown crops actually tasted better had been scientifically substantiated. Organic food received higher Brix scores that measure the amount of sugars in fruits and vegetables. The reason for the higher concentration of sugar was the omission of nitrogen fertilizers that take up considerably more

Exhibit 4   MJF Products

Products/Shop

- Salade à la fleur -
Organic Fresh Hand Picked Salad Mix

Download our:

PRICE LIST
PRODUCT INFO

Get Acrobat Reader

Acrobat
Reader is required to view product
info & pricelist

what you really need is a cook, right?

How about the many times you've promised yourself you'll sit down every Sunday evening and plan the next week's menu? Your kitchen table is cluttered with cookbooks, post-its, recipe cards and pages torn from magazines. You could at least use a bookkeeper.

You list all the items you'll need for the recipes and then check your pantry. Since keeping a pantry fully stocked with fresh and rotated staples is nearly a full-time job, you've decided you'll only buy 1 cup cornmeal, 1/4 cup walnuts, 2 Tbsp. coriander, 2 cups oats, the zest of one lemon...

it's overwhelming.

Frozen dinners taste like...frozen dinners. Canned food is just too weird. Deli food and restaurants are fun until you pay the bill and get tired of restaurant noise.

Then there's the guilt. You should be able to prepare a wholesome meal from scratch at least 6 nights a week, pack a nutritious lunch, serve a breakfast that isn't a breakfast "candy" bar and keep your kitchen clean, your fridge clean, your stove and oven clean, the groceries bought, the goods in your freezer used up on time, leftovers composted (not in your fridge), your knives sharpened...

what you need is me.

I swear to you, my food is truly elegant AND easy. I promise it's easy. You'll see. You'll know exactly what you're serving for weeks in advance. You'll spend just the right amount of time in your kitchen. You'll share me with others as the solution YOU discovered.

learn to make a

Tarte Tian™

click here

water. This process diluted nutrients, sweetness and flavors from conventionally grown crops.[12] Organic soil allows moisture to move through it more freely where it can be taken up by the roots of plants. Conservationists suggested that this process is 5-7 percent more energy efficient than in conventional methods.[13] With few purchased inputs, organic compost nourishes the soil, returning to the soil as much as it removes. Profitability, on the other hand, depended on customers' willingness to pay a premium for organically grown food. The increase in consumers' willingness to pay was evident by the above mentioned industry growth, which was considerably higher (up to 40 percent growth) in Japan and countries in Europe.[14]

Not all food labeled "natural" is organic. In fact, there was no legal definition for the term "natural" as of 2000 and no Food and Drug Administration requirements for ingredients or labeling. It was assumed that ". . . natural foods are free of additives, contain no artificial ingredients or preservatives, and are minimally processed." However, products not meeting those criteria could be labeled as "natural."[15] Growing methods affecting long-term health of the soil and environmental impact were not addressed in the implicit characteristics of natural food. There has been much confusion by consumers regarding the difference between natural and organic food products. Because of the lack of clear distinction between organic and natural food for most consumers, we are treating them as one industry.

Trends in the organic segment of the food industry demonstrated that demand regularly exceeds supply. Produce led all organic product categories with 42 percent market share as a percent to the total of all organic food categories.[16] A 1999 study listed the following categories as having the highest actual and potential growth: energy bars and gels, frozen and refrigerated meat alternatives (e.g., veggie burgers), cold cereals, juices, and milk. As reported in *Progressive Grocer*,[17]

> . . . the retail market for natural foods is growing at five times the rate of the total retail food market . . . and it's not just long-time customers of natural and organic products who are contributing to growth. Fifty percent of all natural-product consumers are new shoppers to the channel . . . Sales of organic products have grown 20 percent annually for the past nine years.

More than 30 percent of natural and organic items were sold through mass-market grocers.[18] Moreover, Kraft, Kellogg, General Mills, Heinz and other mainstream food companies had begun to purchase natural or organic food companies. For example, Kraft acquired Boca Foods, maker of the frozen soy-burger brand, Boca Burger.[19] Likewise, General Mills purchased the Small Planet Food group, composed of Cascadian Farm and Muir Glen, late in 1999.[20]

The Hartman Group reported that 53 percent of American consumers purchased natural and organic products. Half of the heavy buyers of organic food were estimated to be single females with a child or another relative in the home, and a household income of $30,000 or less. Half of the light buyers were husband and wife households with incomes of $50,000 or more and tended to purchase high-end gourmet items.[21]

Consumer awareness of food production methods was rising due to the increase in negative press about mad-cow disease, genetically modified corn accidentally seeping into tacos, and other genetically modified foods. Europe's refusal of United States exports of biotech food and hormone treated beef had also highlighted this issue. Consumers worldwide were more skeptical about what they ate. The food industry had shown that it had no infallible procedures for ensuring the integrity of all ingredients. As a result, businesses that helped farmers track and certify their crops at every link in the supply chain, from farm to table, through the use of sophisticated databases had emerged. This publicity helped to intensify demand for certified organic food from companies like Paradise Farm Organics. Additionally, buyers' insistence on knowing the origins of their food was predicted to accelerate the decommoditization of a long-time commoditized industry. Not only would technology help farmers differentiate their crops, but it would also enable large retailers to set their brands apart from the competition.[22]

While there was growing consumer interest in where and how food was produced, Americans were spending less and less time preparing meals. According to the NPD Group,"44 percent of weekday meals were prepared in 30 minutes or less. Since 1995, frozen-food sales have jumped 18 percent. And every night, 10 percent fewer food items are prepared than 15 years ago."[23] Furthermore, the Bureau of Economic Analysis reported that food purchases away from home equaled 45.5 percent of total food expenditures in 1999. The increasing number of "dual-income and single-parent families tend to buy more prepared meals, which are generally more expensive than meals made from scratch," according to Standard and Poor's Industry Surveys. Complete meal solutions, which involved a small amount of preparation and cooking, were prevalent in grocery stores today. Given those trends, convenient organic and natural versions of these meals also had been rising in popularity.[24] According to the Director of Marketing at General Mills, 25 percent of the US food market was composed of "health seekers" who were interested in meal solutions. He contrasted that figure to the 10 percent of the US food market who represented the "true naturals." True naturals viewed organic processed food to be just as bad as conventional processed food. This group consisted of socially conscious consumers who were devoted to sustainable farming principles.[25]

Natural and Organic Food Products: Distribution

There were several outlets where consumers could purchase natural and organic foods. The breakdown according to where these food products were sold is shown in Exhibit 5.

Retail Grocery

At the time of the case, organic food companies (both fresh and prepared foods) used a variety of distribution channels. One ready outlet was natural foods groceries. Wild Oats Markets and Whole Foods Market dominated this retail grocery segment. Colorado-based Wild Oats Markets had become the second-largest natural foods retailer through acquisitions of small independents. Since its founding in 1987, the Wild Oats chain had grown to include over 110 stores in 22 states and Canada. In 1999 alone, 20 stores were acquired bringing total revenue to $721.1 million. The company's gross profit margin of 12.33 percent was considerably lower than the grocery industry's 28.32 percent margin, in 1999. Wild Oats net profit margins were .39 percent in 1999, as compared to a grocery industry average of 1.45 percent.[26]

The nation's largest chain of natural food stores, measured by sales volume, was Austin-based Whole Foods Market. The company began in 1980 and operated over 110 stores in more than 20 states by the year

Exhibit 5 — Total Organic Sales by Distribution Channel

Distribution Channel	% share
Grocery store/supermarket	56%
Farmer's market	14
Health food store	11
Natural food grocer	9
Co-op	3
Club store	3
Drug store	2
Mass merchandiser	1
Direct mail catalog	1

SOURCE: The Organic Consumer Profile, 1999, The Hartman Group, Bellevue, Washington

2000. Its growth had been fueled through acquisitions and by slashing prices 20 percent when moving into Wild Oats territory. Whole Foods' gross profit margin of 37.61 percent was greater than that of Wild Oats while the company's net profit margin was negative (.24 percent). Revenue for the 1999 fiscal year totaled $1.6 billion.[27]

Increased distribution into mass-market and mainstream stores by large players, however, had the most impact on this industry's growth. Companies such as Kraft and General Mills had the resources to launch sophisticated advertising campaigns, handle a variety of products, and offer more competitive prices as compared to small, independent natural and organic food producers. In fact, mass-market and mainstream stores were responsible for nearly half of all natural and organic food sales.[28]

While some small, natural and organic food producers had been successful at securing shelf space in natural grocery stores, they had found it next to impossible to obtain entry in national or regional retail grocery stores. This was mostly due to the power of the distributors and brokers that were required intermediaries between most small food manufacturers and grocery chains. A considerable amount of money paid upfront to these distributors for slotting and advertising fees was necessary before these distributors would even consider taking on a new manufacturer. In many instances, if sales at the grocery chain did not meet a predetermined goal, the food producer was obligated to repurchase all unsold product from the retail store at the higher wholesale, not distributor prices. Furthermore, the success upon which sales depended was out of the hands of the producer. The distributor handled all of the marketing activities, and the food manufacturer, many times, did not even receive a list of stores where its products were being sold.

Natural and Organic Food Products: Competitors

While the natural and organic foods manufacturing industry was very fragmented, the industry was following the larger food producer industry trends of consolidation. Through acquisition, several firms, such as Hain and Homegrown Natural Foods, have enough scale to avoid dependence on distributors. Many organic farmers and producers had limited marketing skills and tended to be producer rather than consumer oriented in their approaches. These are generally a traditional group of people and are averse to embracing mainstream business and marketing practices, seeing them as the root causes of the very problems in society that they were trying to solve. Those problems included: health problems related to chemicals in food, environmental degradation due to commercial agriculture and pollution caused by nonbiodegradable and excess packaging, and the decreasing ability to earn a living as a small, family farmer. Additionally, few organic farmers had plans to expand and only wanted to take on an amount of work that they could handle without overextending themselves.

Therefore, producers and farmers were opportunistic and local in their pursuits.

Retail Competitors

In 1999, Hain Celestial Food Group became the leading marketer of natural and organic foods with net sales of $206 million and anticipated this level to double in 2000. Since 1993, Hain had focused its activities on managing the marketing and distribution of branded natural and organic food products. To this end, Hain acquired many natural and organic companies. After acquisition, Hain management would sell the acquired firm's manufacturing facilities and outsource production. The company offered over 1,500 items from a variety of branded natural and organic product lines. According to an interview with CEO Irwin Simon conducted by *Advertising Age* in September 2000, Westsoy, Earth's Best, Health Valley and Celestial Seasonings were expected to grow at double-digit rates. Hain's offering that was most similar to PFO was a line of Near East brand and Nile Spice brand dried soups as well as Casbah brand dried vegetarian mixes. Hain's strategic alliance with Heinz, which owned nearly 20 percent of the company, had helped to fuel Hain's growth. Mr. Simon foresaw the largest growth in natural and organic foods coming from the nation's 33,000 supermarkets; he planned on launching an extensive advertising campaign to increase sales through large chain store distribution channels such as Kroger, Safeway and Albertsons.[29]

At the other end of the spectrum from Hain, as far as size and corporate image, Amy's Kitchen had somewhat of a "cult" following. Amy's Kitchen began in the home of the company founders in 1987 with the birth of their daughter, Amy, and had developed into a company selling more than 50 million frozen meals every year. The lack of convenient, organic, vegetarian meals that tasted good prompted this couple to fill in this gap in the frozen food category. Supermarkets, natural food stores and club stores contributed to this company's yearly sales of over $100 million. Amy's Kitchen did not offer catalogue or online sales at the time of this case.[30]

Another well-known natural and organic food competitor in the retail grocery channel was Annie's Homegrown. Since 1989, this company had sold a variety of organic macaroni and cheese dinners in retail stores and more recently online. During this company's early growth years, customer relations were so important to founder Annie that she spent four to five hours a day answering letters by hand. The fast-paced growth of her business, however, was too much for Annie, who allowed Homegrown Natural Foods, Inc to become majority shareholder. Like Hain, Homegrown purchased, consolidated, and grew sales of high quality, branded natural and organic food companies. Homegrown operated each newly acquired company as wholly owned subsidiaries, and they pledged to company founders to remain true to their product quality and brand heritage. Homegrown recently added Fantastic Foods, the industry leader in dried soup and meal cups, to its stable of natural brand names. The company anticipated sales of $50 million annually and had become a major player in the natural and organic foods industry.[31]

Mail Order and Internet

Catalogues of natural and organic foods had been around for decades, mostly as niche product offerings. Not surprisingly, Internet distribution channels were growing in popularity with this food segment. Organic Provisions offered the largest online selection of natural and organic food products with over 2000 healthy items on its website and in its catalogue. Its site also featured kitchenware, homecare, health and beauty, organic clothing, pet foods, and books and magazines. Those items were similar to the diverse offerings in Mary Jane's initial catalogue. Organic Provisions acted as an online distributor, featuring only selected organic food products from Homegrown and Hain. This website made a significant effort to inform consumers about its commitment to promote products that were grown, processed, manufactured and packaged in ways that minimized environmental impact and were cruelty-free. The company's $3 catalogue not only listed the items for sale, but also included educational notes about healthy living and new natural products, and recipes; it also provided descriptive information about the suppliers of natural and organic products. The cost of the catalogue was refunded with the customer's first order. Prompt accurate service was also a priority. The company's knowledgeable, experienced staff took care of web inquiries and call-in or mail order customers.[32]

Walnut Acres was America's oldest certified organic brand and former leading catalogue retailer for organic foods. However, in 1999, it sold out to new owners. Walnut Acres was the first company to vertically integrate organic farming, processing and direct marketing. It was committed to providing significant economic and social benefits to its community in Pennsylvania. Catalogue operations were recently shut down in June 2000, followed by the closure of the manufacturing plant in August 2000. The plant had been in operation since the company's founding in 1946. A series of events led to Walnut Acres' demise, beginning with a strategic partnership between the original founders and a high-tech veteran who wanted Walnut Acres to take advantage of the Internet boom. With more than $4 million in equity financing in August 1999, Walnut Acres was to be transformed into an online grocery store, handling over 1,000 products. Indeed, the e-commerce initiative was launched in September 1999, with many advanced features for a shopping website. Similar to many failed dot-com ventures in early 2000, the majority shareholder shut down operations after an analysis of manufacturing costs that revealed the operation to be unprofitable. In 2000, a new CEO and top management team took control of the Walnut Acres brand and re-launched it with only eight soups. At the time of the case, Walnut Acres distributed these soups to organic and natural food stores and a few large supermarket chains. According to the new team, soups were the company's core product, repackaged into microwaveable glass carafes replacing the former down-to-earth image of basic packaging.[33]

Outdoor Industry

There were three major brands of dried foods for backpacking: Mountain House, Backpackers's Pantry, and MSR's Mountain Gourmet. Oregon Freeze Dry's Mountain House, the industry veteran in freeze-dried backpacking food, was begun in the early 1970s.[34] Mountain House is available on the Web as well. Other Oregon Freeze Dry's offerings included military rations and advanced specialty products, such as pharmaceutical chemicals, medical devices, and sensitive biological materials. Mountain House meals were available in foil pouches with an inner plastic pouch and in 10 pound cans. The pouches required boiling water and 10 minutes to re-hydrate. Three out of Mountain House's 25 meals were vegetarian.[35] At the time of the case, MSR's Mountain Gourmet made by PFO was outgrowing this industry veteran in REI stores by 21 percent.

Leading REI store sales in backpacking food was Backpacker's Pantry, a brand that has been in existence since 1951. In addition to the main line of food, Backpacker's Pantry carried Astronaut food, non-stick cookware, and outback ovens. No-cook meals also added to the variety of assortments. The company's website contained a much more extensive list of meals than Mountain House and included 18 vegetarian entrees.[36]

The US Industry and Trade Outlook reported that the camping segment of the outdoor industry had a promising future, especially among the large baby boomer population. However, Mary Jane was bound by her contract with MSR and unable to compete against her distribu-

tor.[37] For this reason, Mary Jane had to consider other ways to build her brand and distribute her products.

Paradise Farm Organics: Strategy & Marketing

Mary Jane Butters had built Paradise Farm Organics into a strong supplier of dehydrated backpacking food—a classic cash cow for her business. In 2000, she was attempting to diversify product offerings beyond this. After shutting down her catalogue in January, she had entered into several website initiatives beyond her maryjanesfarm.com site. This section provides a discussion of several aspects of her business.

Distribution

MSR, a wholly owned division of Recreational Equipment, Inc. (REI) stores, had annual sales in excess of $36 million in 1999. It distributed MSR's Mountain Gourmet to many outdoor stores in addition to REI stores. In April of 2000, the Mountain Gourmet line won the prestigious Editors' Choice Award in widely read *Backpacker* magazine. The write-up endorsed the food as being, "Great tasting, easy prep, very filling . . . this can't be camp food."[38] As mentioned previously, Paradise Farm maintained a website, BackcountryFood.com, for Internet sales of the MSR brand. This website can be seen in Exhibit 6. Because MSR strictly dealt with brick and mortar operations, all sales generated from this BackcountryFood.com website went directly to Paradise Farm Organics for payment and fulfillment.

Private label production was a much less expensive distribution method than hiring a food brokerage company. Up-front distribution costs and special broker fees were not required under private label production. Paradise Farm was one of the very few organic food producers large enough to meet private label order volume. Conversely, large conventional producers were unlikely to dedicate equipment and facilities to organic methods in the near future.

Pricing

MSR received a distributor margin of 30 percent and retail stores add an additional 40 percent margin for Mountain Gourmet. The retail price of backpacking meals ranged from $4.95 to $7.95 for a two-serving package. Convenient single serve pouch cook prices were almost the same due to packaging costs. A thin plastic liner enabled the camper to pour boiling water into and eat from the package. Ordering in bulk was the least

Exhibit 6   Website for MSR Backpacking Products: BackcountryFood.com

expensive alternative, saving the customer two to three times the cost. Large quantities ranging from 13 to 25 pounds were specified per item.

In 2000, Mary Jane began the maryjanesfarm.com website, branding PFO's products under the MaryJanesFarm label. At the time of the case, the site was still under construction. She planned to offer a line of food with the original image of "from farmhouse to your house" that would appeal to her long time loyal customers. While Mary Jane's new website was under construction, previous catalogue customers were rerouted to the BackcountryFood.com site. Mary Jane planned for her MaryJanesFarm brand to offer different sizes and packaging to fit those customer's lifestyles. She was also considering introducing a new catalogue, however costs had increased considerably since the first one was introduced in 1996. The previous black and white version on newspaper type paper cost only .29 each to produce and $1.50 to mail. In 2000, the anticipated cost was $1 each without color, plus high mailing rates.

Other costs entered into Mary Jane's decisions concerning which channel or channels to pursue. Packaging costs for the 3-ounce single serve package of organic veg-etarian meals were nearly equivalent to costs for the 5-ounce package used by MSR. Another consideration was the cost of websites; about $10,000 was spent to develop both BackcountryFood.com and MaryJanesFarm.com websites; both sites cost $50 per month to maintain.

Promotions

Exhibit 7 provides a chronology of past promotional strategies. The first catalogue in 1996 was sent only to those who requested them and Mary Jane had no data on response rates. After the old catalogue was discontinued and before the new maryjanesfarm.com website was operational, Mary Jane hired an undergraduate business major to explore options related to promoting a brand name and expanding into new markets. However, these and her previous marketing efforts frustrated Mary Jane because they did not increase sales. She believed that the business ran better with very little traditional marketing. This attitude is similar to many traditional organic growers who disdain slick corporate approaches to business. Mary Jane's approach is that consumers have been "marketed to death." She prefers to put out her message and let interested customers find her.

Exhibit 7 | Timeline of Marketing Efforts

Trunkload of samples mailed to food cooperatives.

Participation in local and regional farmers' markets, fairs, and events by company representatives and Pay Dirt Farm School.

Media publicity in addition to the *National Geographic* article has included the *Seattle Times* and periodicals such as *Backpacker Magazine, Vegetarian Times, A Real Life, Green Money Journal* and *Environmental Magazine.*

Backpacking food brochures were included in packages shipped by Patagonia, the largest mail order business in the outdoor industry.

MSR serves samples of Mountain Gourmet at an annual trade show in Salt Lake City, Utah that is attended by international buyers from retail outdoor stores.

Outfitter guide companies, camps and nonprofit organizations were contacted and mailed free samples along with product and wholesale price information. They were encouraged to order directly from BackcountryFood.com in order to obtain wholesale prices and a free shipping introductory offer. After one or two follow up phone calls had been made, outfitter guide companies received periodic e-mails containing updated product information and an invitation to contribute to the interactive website.

Participation as a sponsor in special events ranging from volunteer trail maintenance days to outdoor enthusiast festivals and music festivals in Colorado and New Mexico was carried out. Visitors to the booths received free samples of MSR's Mountain Gourmet food, BackcountryFood.com brochures and were encouraged to sign up on mailing lists.

Athletes, such as rock climbers and mountaineers or people engaged in worthwhile physical pursuits for worthy causes were sponsored with food in hopes of receiving website contributions or other publicity for BackcountryFood.com.

E-mail introductory discounts were offered to people in return for contributions to the maryjanesfarm.com website. Articles accepted for submission included tips on creating a nontoxic home and essays written on selected special topics.

Operations

Manufacturing Process

Vegetables, herbs and flowers used in all meals were grown on either Mary Jane's farm or on farms that underwent national certification every year. Most of the other ingredients, such as grains and lentils, came from local suppliers who were certified in organic production. Only the highest quality ingredients were accepted. Even the various cheeses used were 100 percent organic cheese and contained no fillers. Many of these inputs were sent to an organic food processing company in California for dehydration. Labels and packages were purchased from another California firm. The final recipes were mixed and packaged in a small warehouse by local residents, mainly college students. Mary Jane took pride in the fact that each package was heat sealed by hand and no automation was needed. New items were added contin-uously as a result of ongoing experimentation by Mary Jane to develop proprietary new recipes and production processes. There were plentiful sources of inputs from area farmers. There were no constraints on PFO's manufacturing production, with capacity utilization at 50 percent at the time of the case.

Human Resources

Paradise Farm had nine full time and six part time employees along with various independent contractors and consultants as needed. They were passionately committed to sustainable agriculture and Mary Jane's vision of creating social change through business. In fact, most of the people involved in PFO, including some stockholders and the undergraduate business student, began as customers. They were so enamored by the product and the company that they offered their skills and/or funding to help Paradise Farm.

Customer Service

All products came with an unconditional guarantee. If the customer was not satisfied, he or she could choose to receive a refund, exchange or credit. Either Mary Jane or Nick answered the phone and were happy to aid in outdoor trip planning or discuss environmental issues. Gift-wrapping was offered, which included a card and personal note from Mary Jane. Customer relationships were also cultivated through interactive websites that she hoped would create a sense of community. Visitors to BackcountryFood.com could contribute stories, back-country tips, list job openings and exchange gear with others. The maryjanesfarm.com site concentrated on submissions for women's issues and non-toxic household tips.

Financials

Income statements and balance sheets for Paradise Farm Organics for 1997 through 1999 are located in Exhibits 8 and 9. The company was not cash flow positive but had no bank debt at the time of the case.

No public market existed for the company's stock; therefore, stockholder's investments could have been illiquid indefinitely. Return on investment was not the primary reason current shareholders became involved. Their beliefs in the "cause" and in Mary Jane were primary motivations for ownership. For example, stockholder Bobbie Cleave attended forestry classes at Utah State University with Mary Jane in 1974. They both became wilderness rangers and had kept in touch. Bobbie became a stockholder because she simply wanted to help. She admired Mary Jane for living the way she talks and for being able to "translate her core beliefs into her life's work." Shareholder Nancy Schaub, like Mary Jane, was a community activist and was encouraged by her friends to meet Mary Jane since they shared a progressive political commitment. "It is a privilege to support a female entrepreneur—and one with such a good heart. Her business is run in accord with her deepest values." Nancy's partner, shareholder Jim Sheehan, was a public defender for the nonprofit Center of Justice law firm in Spokane, Washington. The firm tackled issues from the environment, to family law to homelessness. Another stockholder, Pat Vaughan and family, returned to Moscow after retiring from the military. The urge to get back to nature prompted him to participate in Mary Jane's apprenticeship program and become an organic farmer. Pat believed that organic farming benefited the overall community by sustaining the soil, watershed, air and wildlife habitat. Finally, Brad Halter, a retired environmental scientist, had yearned to support small-scale sustainable agriculture since volunteering for VISTA in the late 1960's. While traveling between Colorado and Alaska on assignments for NOAA (National Oceanic and Atmospheric Administration), Brad searched for farmland and met Mary Jane. He spent summer vacations volunteering on her farm, prepared the food on hiking trips and at the South Pole, and then became a stockholder. "I was never interested in investing in big corporations and buying stock at Paradise Farm Organics was a good way to invest in what I believe."[39]

Strategic Alternatives

In August 2000, Mary Jane committed to building PFO beyond her private label backpacking foods. She was exploring several options.

First, she could re-launch a catalogue providing families with quick recipe ideas using her easy-to-prepare meals. This catalogue would be more limited in scope than the catalogues offered in previous years and cost around $20,000 for a mailing of 5,000. Buying names from established mailing lists was still not an option for Mary Jane. This new catalogue endeavor could or could not complement web initiatives.

Second, Mary Jane could continue to develop new websites that are directed toward the new target markets that she identified. Currently she has prototype websites and has bought the domain names related to Campus Cuisine (campuscuisine.com), Office Cuisine (Officecuisine. com) and Travel Cuisine (travelcuisine. com). She is uncertain if these should be kept as separate initiatives away from the maryjanesfarm.com branding efforts. Mary Jane is unclear how to get "eyeballs on the page" beyond her loyal customers who have purchased from the catalogue.

Third, another option would be for Mary Jane to launch a massive public relations and/or advertising campaign directed at mainstream shoppers to promote sales of her brand. She would have to retain a well-connected public relations or advertising firm in the Seattle area, which could run in excess of $50,000. Mary Jane could also decide to continue her low-cost public relations strategy, using freelance writers and article submissions to magazines and other appropriate outlets.

Fourth, Mary Jane could market her products through national/regional grocery chains by allying with a distributor. While much has been written about consumers demanding more healthy foods, the large food companies such as Kraft, Kellogg, General Mills, and Heinz along with large natural and organic foods companies such as Hain have reaped most of the rewards. Selling out to one of these large food producers was a possibil-

	1999	1998	1997
Sales	298,453	187,301	73,928
Cost of Sales			
Beginning inventory	65,062	81,102	63,846
Purchases	141,634	62,356	52,094
Labor burden	48,653	18,797	4,869
Total Cost Available For Sale	255,349	162,255	120,809
Less ending inventory	(90,036)	(65,062)	-81,102
	165,313	97,193	39,707
Gross Margin	133,140	90,108	34,221
Operating Expense			
Accounting	15,289	12,175	5,920
Advertising	6,381	5,235	3,260
Amortization	10,357	10,782	10,962
Auto	6,097	6,392	
Bad debts	3,135	168	3,600
Bank charges	2,547	2,527	1,252
Catalog	3,319	2,605	1,540
Computer costs	2,598	1,988	1,678
Demonstration/trade shows	6,448	1,583	300
Depreciation	7,850	1,447	946
Donations	1,273	768	153
Dues and subscriptions	610	343	167
Entertainment		26	108
Insurance	1,634	1,374	1,067
Insurance – life	3,484	3,484	3,484
Legal and professional	3,711	15,919	2,091
Office	3,991	3,074	2,455
Payroll tax	3,011	2,815	3,073
Product development			160
Rent	44,011	36,571	24,000
Repairs and maintenance	1,463		69
Salaries	45,181	23,595	13,815
Shipping	12,168	10,447	
Stock prospectus	11,037	2,570	9
Supplies	815	573	1,004
Taxes and licenses	1,516	1,126	941
Telephone	5,221	5,180	4,832
Travel	488	237	
Utilities	1,882	1,843	758
Total Operating Expense	205,517	154,847	87,644
Loss from operations	(72,377)	(64,739)	(53,423)

	1999	1998	1997
Other Income (Expense)			
Interest income			5
Rent and miscellaneous	5,041	5,396	156
Interest expense	(1,377)	(8,211)	(10,714)
Total Other Income (Expense)	3,664	(2,815)	(10,553)
Loss Before Income Taxes	(68,713)	(67,554)	(63,976)
Income Tax Benefit	1,673	2,044	2,013
Net Loss	$ (67,040)	(65,510)	(61,963)

Exhibit 9   Paradise Farm Organics, Inc Balance Sheet, 1997-1999

	1999	1998	1997
Assets			
Current Assets			
Cash		21,046	30
Accouns receivable	2,721	3,327	6,497
Inventory	90,036	65,062	81,102
Prepaid expenses	3,600	6,888	8,154
Total Current Assets	96,357	96,323	95,783
Fixed Assets			
Buildings, furniture and equipment	284,547	212,007	7,848
Less accumulated depreciaiton	(13,510)	(5,660)	(4,213)
Net Fixed Assets	271,037	206,347	3,635
Other Assets			
Patronage receivable	242	222	252
Nutrition analysis service	800	800	800
Goodwill	329,864	329,864	329,864
Trademarks	34,586	22,047	22,047
Organizational costs	6,497	6,497	6,497
Accumulated amortization	(73,095)	(62,738)	(51,956)
Deferred tax benefit	13,317	11,623	9,558
Net Other Expenses	312,211	308,315	317,062
Total Assets	$ 679,605	610,985	416,480
Liabilities			
Current Liabilities			
Bank overdraft	7,241		1,679
Accouns payable	25,442	9,940	5,910
Operating lines of credit	29,243		24,354
Wages payable	12,191		

	1999	1998	1997
Payroll taxes payable	3,305	659	5,588
Sales tax payable	753	239	168
Income tax payable	21	21	21
Current portion of long-term debt	30,523		17,685
Total Current Liabilities	108,719	10,859	55,405
Long-term debt, less current portion	0	0	38,996
Stockholder's Equity			
Capital stock, no par value, 10,000 shares authorized, and 415,596 shares outstanding	493,420	455,620	112,063
Additional paid in capital	515,412	515,412	515,412
Retained earnings (deficiency)	(437,946)	(370,906)	(305,396)
Total Stockholder's Equity	570,886	600,126	322,079
Total Liabilities and Stockholder's Equity	679,605	610,985	416,480

ity, but Mary Jane knew that she needed a substantial brand and customer base to attract attention as an acquisition target. She also worried about the sale of production facilities after acquisition.

Finally, Mary Jane could scale down her expectations and return to her initial focus of traditional organic-type customers using "folksy"style and low cost marketing tactics. Under this approach, she would concentrate on communicating the company's mission of supporting organic agriculture. This more incremental approach could be focused on reinitiating a small-scale catalogue and pursuing sales to co-ops and farmer's markets in the Northwest.

Facing significant external opportunities but with limited financial resources, Mary Jane had to decide what set of strategic initiatives to propose to her stockholders in two weeks.

Endnotes

1. Mary Jane Butters' Biographic Information: www.maryjanesfarm.com/About/maryjane.asp and www.backcountryfood.com/about/maryjane.asp.
2. Ibid.
3. John Ikerd, as quoted by Richard Duesterhaus in "Sustainability's Promise," *Journal of Soil and Water Conservation*, January-February, 1990, Vol. 45.
4. Verlyn Klinkenborg. "A Farming Revolution: Sustainable Agriculture," *National Geographic*, December, 1995.
5. Ibid.
6. *Real Life Magazine* informs its readers how to live healthier and happier lives through articles covering topics such as wellness, community and leisure.
7. Paradise Farm Organics, Inc. Disclosure Document, August 30, 1999.
8. Bruce Ingersoll. "US Issues Standards for Organic Foods," *Wall Street Journal*, December 21, 2000.
9. Barry Janoff. "Law of the Land," *Progressive Grocer*, September 2000.
10. Michael Pollan. "How organic became a marketing niche and a multibillion-dollar industry. Naturally," *The New York Times Magazine*, May 13, 2001.
11. Ibid.
12. Ibid.
13. It is interesting to note that, over time, the term "conventional" has come to denote crops grown using pesticides, herbicides and fertilizers!
14. Staff. "Organic Farming: Golden Apples," *The Economist*, April 21, 2001.
15. US Health and Natural Food Market Research: www.ideabeat.com.
16. Steve Meyers and Somlynn Rorie. "Facts and Stats: The Year in Review," *Organic & Natural News*, December 2000.
17. Barry Janoff. "Law of the Land," *Progressive Grocer*, September 2000.
18. Barry Janoff. "Alternative Measures," *Progressive Grocer*, October, 1999.
19. Barry Janoff. "Law of the Land," *Progressive Grocer*, September 2000.

20. Heather Granato. "Homegrown Natural Grabs Napa Valley Kitchens, Fantastic Foods," *Natural Products Industry Insider,* October 16, 2000.

21. Matthew Grimm. "Veggie Delight," *American Demographics,* August, 2000.

22. Staff. "Farming: Let Them Eat Data," *The Economist,* April 21, 2001.

23. Elizabeth Bernstein. "The Disappearing Kitchen: In Some Homes, Sinks and Stoves Give Way to Beds, Pianos; Can't Be Bothered to Cook," *Wall Street Journal,* January 13, 2001.

24. E. Bossong-Martines. 2000. *S & P Industrial Surveys, Food and Nonalcoholic Beverages.* New York: McGraw Hill and the US Department of Commerce/International Trade Administration.

25. Michael Pollan. "How organic became a marketing niche and a multibillion-dollar industry. Naturally."

26. Wild Oats Markets, Inc. Profile and Comparison Data - Hoovers Online: www.hoovers.com.

27. Whole Foods Market, Inc. - Hoover's Online: www.hoovers.com.

28. Steve Meyers and Somlynn Rorie. "Facts and Stats: The Year in Review," *Organic and Natural News,* December 2000.

29. Hoovers, Inc. *Hoover's Company Profile Database: The Hain Celestial Group, Inc.* and Stephanie Thompson, "Hain's Healthy Growth Spurt," *Advertising Age,* September 18, 2000.

30. Amy's Kitchen: www.amyskithcen.com and infoUSA Inc., *US Business Directory: Amy's Kitchen.*

31. Annie's Homegrown: www.annies.com and Business Wire, Inc. "Homegrown Natural Foods Acquires Napa Valley Kitchens and Fantastic Foods; Acquisitions Position Company As a Leader in $11 Billion Natural Food Industry," *Business Wire,* September 21, 2000.

32. Organic Provisions: www.orgfood.com.

33. Betsy McKay. "Acirca Touts Soup As Organic Version of On-the-Go Food," *Wall Street Journal,* January 22, 2001. Business Wire, Inc. "Walnut Acres Takes Organic Food Shopping Online," *Business Wire,* September 2, 1999. Food Focus/News. "Era Ends as Walnut Acres Closes Pennsylvania Plant," *Whole Foods Magazine,* August 2000.

34. Mary Jane even consumed this brand when she worked for the Forest Service!

35. Mountain House and Oregon Freeze Dry, Inc.: www.mountainhouse.com.

36. Backpacker's Pantry: www.backpackerspantry.com.

37. US Department of Commerce/International Trade Administration. (2000). US Industry Outlook 2000. New York: McGraw Hill.

38. Susan Newquist. "Editors' Choice," *Backpacker Magazine,* April 2000.

39. Stockholder Biographies: www.maryjanesfarm.com/about/stockholders/asp.

Perdue Farms Inc.: Responding to 21st Century Challenges

George C. Rubenson

Salisbury University

Frank Shipper

Salisbury University

Background/Company History

"I have a theory that you can tell the difference between those who have inherited a fortune and those who have made a fortune. Those who have made their own fortune forget not where they came from and are less likely to lose touch with the common man." (Bill Sterling, *'Just Browsin' column in* Eastern Shore News, *March 2, 1988*)

The history of Perdue Farms Inc. is dominated by seven themes: quality, growth, geographic expansion, vertical integration, innovation, branding and service. Arthur W. Perdue, a Railway Express Agent and descendent of a French Huguenot family named Perdeaux, founded the company in 1920 when he left his job with Railway Express and entered the egg business full-time near the small town of Salisbury, Maryland. Salisbury is located in a region immortalized in James Michener's *Chesapeake* that is alternately known as "the Eastern Shore" or the "Delmarva Peninsula." It includes parts of DELaware, MARyland and VirginiA. Arthur Perdue's only child, Franklin Parsons Perdue was also born in 1920.

Copyright 2001 by the authors. George C Rubenson and Frank M. Shipper, Department of Management and Marketing, Franklin P. Perdue School of Business, Salisbury University. Acknowledgments: The authors are indebted to Frank Perdue, Jim Perdue and the numerous associates at Perdue Farms, Inc., who generously shared their time and information about the company. In addition, the authors would like to thank the anonymous librarians at Blackwell Library, Salisbury State University, who routinely review area newspapers and file articles about the poultry industry—the most important industry on the DelMarVa peninsula. Without their assistance, this case would not be possible.

A quick look at Perdue Farms' mission statement (Exhibit 1) reveals the emphasis the company has always put on quality. In the 1920s, "Mr. Arthur," as he was called, bought leghorn breeding stock from Texas to improve the quality of his flock. He soon expanded his egg market and began shipments to New York. Practicing small economies such as mixing his own chicken feed and using leather from his old shoes to make hinges for his chicken coops, he stayed out of debt and prospered. He tried to add a new chicken coop every year.

By 1940, Perdue Farms was already known for quality products and fair dealing in a tough, highly competitive market. The company began offering chickens for sale when "Mr. Arthur" realized that the future lay in selling chickens, not eggs. In 1944, Mr. Arthur made his son Frank a full partner in A. W. Perdue and Son, Inc.

In 1950, Frank took over leadership of the company that employed 40 people. By 1952, revenues were $6,000,000 from the sale of 2,600,000 broilers. During this period, the company began to vertically integrate, operating its own hatchery, starting to mix its own feed formulations and operating its own feed mill. Also, in the 1950s, Perdue Farms began to contract with others to grow chickens for them. By furnishing the growers with peeps (baby chickens) and the feed, the company was better able to control quality.

In the 1960s, Perdue Farms continued to vertically integrate by building its first grain receiving and storage facilities and Maryland's first soybean processing plant. By 1967, annual sales had increased to about $35,000,000. But, it became clear to Frank that profits lay in processing chickens. Frank recalled in an interview

Exhibit 1 | Perdue Mission 2000

Stand on Tradition

Perdue was built upon a foundation of quality, a tradition described in our Quality Policy . . .

Our Quality Policy

*"We shall produce products and provide services
at all times which meet or exceed the expectations of our customers."
"We shall not be content to be of
equal quality to our competitors."
"Our commitment is to be increasingly superior."
"Contribution to quality is a responsibility shared by everyone in the Perdue organization."*

Focus on Today

Our mission reminds us of the purpose we serve . . .

Our Mission

*"Enhance the quality of life with great food and agricultural products."
While striving to fulfill our mission, we use our values to guide our decisions . . .*

Our Values

* **Quality:** We value the needs of our customers. Our high standards require us to work safely, make safe food and uphold the Perdue name.
* **Integrity:** We do the right thing and live up to our commitments. We do not cut corners or make false promises.
* **Trust:** We trust each other and treat each other with mutual respect. Each individual's skill and talent are appreciated.
* **Teamwork:** We value a strong work ethic and ability to make each other successful. We care what others think and encourage their involvement, creating a sense of pride, loyalty, ownership and family.

Look to the Future

Our vision describes what we will become and the qualities that will enable us to succeed . . .

Our Vision

"To be the leading quality food company with $20 billion in sales in 2020."

Perdue in the Year 2020

* **To our customers:** We will provide food solutions and indispensable services to meet anticipated customer needs.
* **To our consumers:** A portfolio of trusted food and agricultural products will be supported by multiple brands throughout the world.
* **To our associates:** Worldwide, our people and our workplace will reflect our quality reputation, placing Perdue among the best places to work.
* **To our communities:** We will be known in the community as a strong corporate citizen, trusted business partner and favorite employer.
* **To our shareholders:** Driven by innovation, our market leadership and our creative spirit will yield industry-leading profits.

for *Business Week* (September 15, 1972) " . . . processors were paying us 10¢ a live pound for what cost us 14¢ to produce. Suddenly, processors were making as much as 7¢ a pound."

A cautious, conservative planner, Arthur Perdue had not been eager for expansion and Frank Perdue himself was reluctant to enter poultry processing. But, economics forced his hand and, in 1968, the company bought its first processing plant, a Swift and Company operation in Salisbury.

From the first batch of chickens that it processed, Perdue's standards were higher than those of the federal government. The state grader on the first batch has often told the story of how he was worried that he had rejected too many chickens as not Grade A. As he finished his inspections for that first day, he saw Frank Perdue headed his way and he could tell that Frank was not happy. Frank started inspecting the birds and never argued over one that was rejected. Next, he saw Frank start to go through the ones that the state grader had passed and began to toss some of them over with the rejected birds. Finally, realizing that few met his standards, Frank put all of the birds in the reject pile. Soon, however, the facility was able to process 14,000 broilers per hour.

From the beginning, Frank Perdue refused to permit his broilers to be frozen for shipping, arguing that it resulted in unappetizing black bones and loss of flavor and moistness when cooked. Instead, Perdue chickens were (and some still are) shipped to market packed in ice, justifying the company's advertisements at that time that it sold only "fresh, young broilers." However, this policy also limited the company's market to those locations that could be serviced overnight from the Eastern Shore of Maryland. Thus, Perdue chose for its primary markets the densely populated towns and cities of the East Coast, particularly New York City, which consumes more Perdue chicken than all other brands combined.

Frank Perdue's drive for quality became legendary both inside and outside the poultry industry. In 1985, Frank and Perdue Farms, Inc. were featured in the book, *A Passion for Excellence*, by Tom Peters and Nancy Austin.

In 1970, Perdue established its primary breeding and genetic research programs. Through selective breeding, Perdue developed a chicken with more white breast meat than the typical chicken. Selective breeding has been so successful that Perdue Farms chickens are desired by other processors. Rumors have even suggested that Perdue chickens have been stolen on occasion in an attempt to improve competitor flocks.

In 1971, Perdue Farms began an extensive marketing campaign featuring Frank Perdue. In his early advertise-

ments, he became famous for saying things like "If you want to eat as good as my chickens, you'll just have to eat my chickens." He is often credited with being the first to brand what had been a commodity product. During the 1970s, Perdue Farms also expanded geographically to areas north of New York City such as Massachusetts, Rhode Island and Connecticut.

In 1977, "Mr. Arthur" died at the age of 91, leaving behind a company with annual sales of nearly $200,000,000, an average annual growth rate of 17 percent compared to an industry average of 1 percent a year, the potential for processing 78,000 broilers per hour, and annual production of nearly 350,000,000 pounds of poultry per year. Frank Perdue said of his father simply "I learned everything from him."

In 1981, Frank Perdue was in Boston for his induction into the Babson College Academy of Distinguished Entrepreneurs, an award established in 1978 to recognize the spirit of free enterprise and business leadership. Babson College President Ralph Z. Sorenson inducted Perdue into the academy which, at that time, numbered 18 men and women from four continents. Perdue had the following to say to the college students:

> *"There are none, nor will there ever be, easy steps for the entrepreneur. Nothing, absolutely nothing, replaces the willingness to work earnestly, intelligently towards a goal. You have to be willing to pay the price. You have to have an insatiable appetite for detail, have to be willing to accept constructive criticism, to ask questions, to be fiscally responsible, to surround yourself with good people and, most of all, to listen."* (Frank Perdue, speech at Babson College, April 28, 1981)

The early 1980s saw Perdue Farms expand southward into Virginia, North Carolina and Georgia. It also began to buy out other producers such as Carroll's Foods, Purvis Farms, Shenandoah Valley Poultry Company and Shenandoah Farms. The latter two acquisitions diversified the company's markets to include turkey. New Products included value added items such as "Perdue Done It!," a line of fully cooked fresh chicken products.

James A. (Jim) Perdue, Frank's only son, joined the company as a management trainee in 1983 and became a plant manager. The latter 1980s tested the mettle of the firm. Following a period of considerable expansion and product diversification, a consulting firm recommended that the company form several strategic business units, responsible for their own operations. In other words, the firm should decentralize. Soon after, the chicken market leveled off and then declined for a period. In 1988, the firm experienced its first year in the red. Unfortunately, the decentralization had created duplication and enormous administrative costs. The firm's rapid plunge into turkeys and other food processing, where it had little experience, contributed to the losses. Characteristically, the company refocused, concentrating on efficiency of operations, improving communications throughout the company, and paying close attention to detail.

On June 2, 1989, Frank celebrated 50 years with Perdue Farms, Inc. At a morning reception in downtown Salisbury, the Governor of Maryland proclaimed it "Frank Perdue Day." The Governors of Delaware and Virginia did the same. In 1991, Frank was named Chairman of the Executive Committee and Jim Perdue became Chairman of the Board. Quieter, gentler and more formally educated, Jim Perdue focuses on operations, infusing the company with an even stronger devotion to quality control and a bigger commitment to strategic planning. Frank Perdue continued to do advertising and public relations. As Jim Perdue matured as the company leader, he took over the role of company spokesperson and began to appear in advertisements.

Under Jim Perdue's leadership, the 1990s were dominated by market expansion into Florida and west to Michigan and Missouri. In 1992, the international business segment was formalized serving customers in Puerto Rico, South America, Europe, Japan and China. By fiscal year 1998, international sales were $180 million per year. International markets are beneficial for the firm because US customers prefer white meat while customers in most other countries prefer dark meat.

Food service sales to commercial consumers has also become a major market. New retail product lines focus on value added items, individually quick frozen items, home meal replacement items and products for the delicatessen. The "Fit 'n Easy" label continues as part of a nutrition campaign using skinless, boneless chicken and turkey products.

The 1990s also saw the increased use of technology and the building of distribution centers to better serve the customer. For example, all over-the-road trucks were equipped with satellite two-way communications and geographic positioning, allowing real-time tracking, rerouting if needed, and accurately informing customers when to expect product arrival. Currently, nearly 20,000 associates have increased revenues to more than $2.5 billion.

Management & Organization

From 1950 until 1991, Frank Perdue was the primary force behind Perdue Farms' growth and success. During Frank's years as the company leader, the industry entered its high growth period. Industry executives had typically developed professionally during the industry's infancy. Many had little formal education and started their careers in the barnyard, building chicken coops and cleaning them out. They often spent their entire careers with one company, progressing from supervisor of growout facilities to management of processing plants to corporate executive positions. Perdue Farms was not unusual in that respect. An entrepreneur through and through, Frank lived up to his marketing image of "it takes a tough man to make a tender chicken." He mostly used a centralized management style that kept decision making authority in his own hands or those of a few trusted, senior executives whom he had known for a lifetime (see Exhibit 2). Workers were expected to do their jobs.

In later years, Frank increasingly emphasized employee (or "associates" as they are currently referred to) involvement in quality issues and operational decisions. This later emphasis on employee participation undoubtedly eased the transfer of power in 1991 to his son, Jim, which appears to have been unusually smooth. Although Jim grew up in the family business, he spent almost 15 years earning an undergraduate degree in biology from Wake Forest University, a master's degree in marine biology from the University of Massachusetts at Dartmouth and a doctorate in fisheries from the University of Washington in Seattle. Returning to Perdue Farms in 1983, he earned an EMBA from Salisbury State University and was assigned positions as plant manager, divisional quality control manager and vice president of Quality Improvement Process (QIP) prior to becoming Chairman.

Jim has a people-first management style. Company goals center on the three P's: People, Products and Profitability. He believes that business success rests on satisfying customer needs with quality products. It is important to put associates first because "If [associates] come first, they will strive to assure superior product quality—and satisfied customers." This view has had a profound impact on the company culture which is based on Tom Peters view that "Nobody knows a person's 20 square feet better than the person who works there." The idea is to gather ideas and information from everyone in the organization and maximize productivity by transmitting these ideas throughout the organization.

Key to accomplishing this "employees first" policy is workforce stability, a difficult task in an industry that employs a growing number of associates working in physically demanding and sometimes stressful conditions. A significant number of associates are Hispanic immigrants who may have a poor command of the English language, are sometimes undereducated and often lack basic health care. In order to increase these associates' opportunity for advancement, Perdue Farms focuses on helping them overcome these disadvantages.

For example, the firm provides English-language

classes to help non-English speaking employees assimilate. Ultimately employees can earn the equivalent of a high-school diploma. To deal with physical stress, the company has an ergonomics committee in each plant that studies job requirements and seeks ways to redesign those jobs that put workers at the greatest risk. The company also has an impressive wellness program that currently includes clinics at 10 plants. The clinics are staffed by professional medical people working for medical practice groups under contract to Perdue Farms. Employees can visit a doctor for anything from a muscle strain to prenatal care to screening tests for a variety of diseases and have universal access to all Perdue operated clinics. Dependent care is available. While benefits to the employees are obvious, the company also benefits through a reduction in lost time for medical office visits, lower turnover and a happier, healthier, more productive and stable work force.

Marketing

In the early days, chicken was sold to butcher shops and neighborhood groceries as a commodity; that is, producers sold it in bulk and butchers cut and wrapped it. The customer had no idea what firm grew or processed the chicken. Frank Perdue was convinced that higher profits could be made if the firm's products could be sold at a premium price. But, the only reason a product can command a premium price is if customers ask for it by name —and that means the product must be differentiated and "branded." Hence, the emphasis over the years on superior quality, broader breasted chickens, and a healthy golden color (actually the result of adding marigold petals in the feed to enhance the natural yellow color that corn provided).

In 1968, Frank Perdue spent $50,000 on radio advertising. In 1969, he added $80,000 in TV advertising to his radio budget—against the advice of his advertising agency. Although his early TV ads increased sales, he decided the agency he was dealing with didn't match one of the basic Perdue tenets: "The people you deal with should be as good at what they do as you are at what you do." That decision set off a storm of activity on Frank's part. In order to select an ad agency that met his standards, Frank learned more about advertising than any poultry man before him and, in the process, catapulted Perdue Farms into the ranks of the top poultry producers in the country.

He began a ten week immersion on the theory and practice of advertising. He read books and papers on advertising. He talked to sales managers of every newspaper, radio and television station in the New York area, consulted experts, and interviewed 48 ad agencies.

During April, 1971, he selected Scali, McCabe, Sloves as his new advertising agency. As the agency tried to figure out how to successfully "brand" a chicken— something that had never been done—they realized that Frank Perdue was their greatest ally. "He looked a little like a chicken himself, and he sounded a little like one, and he squawked a lot!"

McCabe decided that Perdue should be the firm's spokesman. Initially, Frank resisted. But, in the end, he accepted the role and the campaign based on "It takes a tough man to make a tender chicken" was born. The firm's very first television commercial showed Frank on a picnic in the Salisbury City Park saying:

> "A chicken is what it eats . . . And my chickens eat better than people do . . . I store my own grain and mix my own feed . . . And give my Perdue chickens nothing but pure well water to drink . . . That's why my chickens always have that healthy golden yellow color . . . If you want to eat as good as my chickens, you'll just have to eat my chickens."

Additional ads, touting high quality and the broader breasted chicken read as follows:

> "Government standards would allow me to call this a grade A chicken . . . but my standards wouldn't. This chicken is skinny . . . It has scrapes and hairs . . . The fact is, my graders reject 30 percent of the chickens government inspectors accept as grade A . . . That's why it pays to insist on a chicken with my name on it . . . If you're not completely satisfied, write me and I'll give you your money back . . . Who do you write in Washington? . . . What do they know about chickens?"

> "The Perdue Roaster is the master race of chickens."

> "Never go into a store and just ask for a pound of chicken breasts . . . Because you could be cheating yourself out of some meat . . . Here's an ordinary one-pound chicken breast, and here's a one-pound breast of mine . . . They weigh the same. But as you can see, mine has more meat, and theirs has more bone. I breed the broadest breasted, meatiest chicken you can buy . . . So don't buy a chicken breast by the pound . . . Buy them by the name . . . and get an extra bite in every breast."

The ads paid off. In 1968, Perdue held about three percent of the New York market. By 1972, one out of every six chickens eaten in New York was a Perdue chicken. 51 percent of New Yorkers recognized the label. Scali, McCabe, Sloves credited Perdue's "believability" for the success of the program. "This was advertising in which Perdue had a personality that lent credibility to the product. If Frank Perdue didn't look and sound like a chicken, he wouldn't be in the commercials."

Frank had his own view. As he told a Rotary audience

Exhibit 2   Perdue Farms Organization Structure

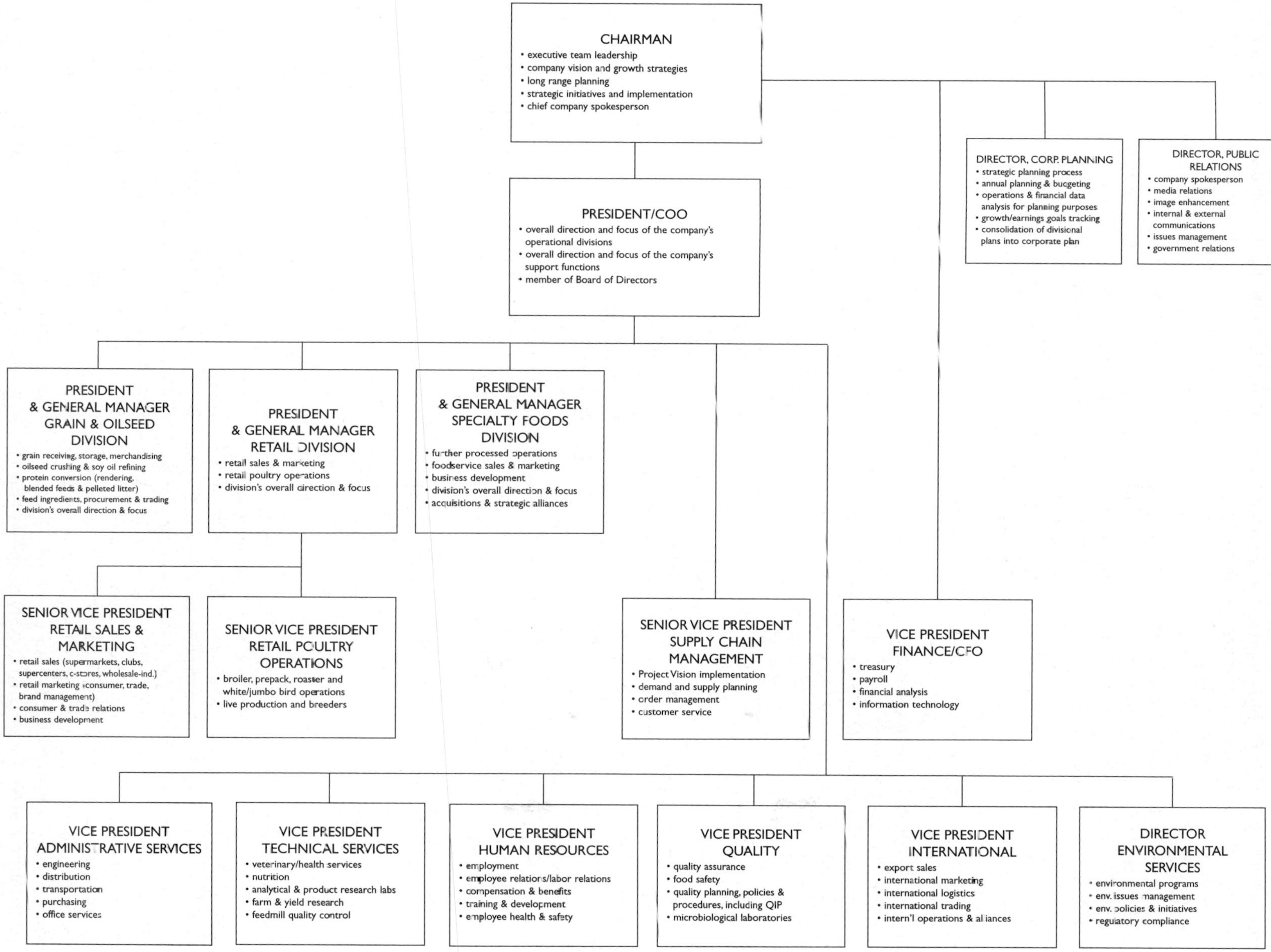

CHAIRMAN
- executive team leadership
- company vision and growth strategies
- long range planning
- strategic initiatives and implementation
- chief company spokesperson

DIRECTOR, CORP. PLANNING
- strategic planning process
- annual planning & budgeting
- operations & financial data analysis for planning purposes
- growth/earnings goals tracking
- consolidation of divisional plans into corporate plan

DIRECTOR, PUBLIC RELATIONS
- company spokesperson
- media relations
- image enhancement
- internal & external communications
- issues management
- government relations

PRESIDENT/COO
- overall direction and focus of the company's operational divisions
- overall direction and focus of the company's support functions
- member of Board of Directors

VICE PRESIDENT FINANCE/CFO
- treasury
- payroll
- financial analysis
- information technology

PRESIDENT & GENERAL MANAGER SPECIALTY FOODS DIVISION
- further processed operations
- foodservice sales & marketing
- business development
- division's overall direction & focus
- accuisitions & strategic alliances

PRESIDENT & GENERAL MANAGER RETAIL DIVISION
- retail sales & marketing
- retail poultry operations
- division's overall direction & focus

PRESIDENT & GENERAL MANAGER GRAIN & OILSEED DIVISION
- grain receiving, storage, merchandising
- oilseed crushing & soy oil refining
- protein conversion (rendering, blended feeds & pelleted litter)
- feed ingredients, procurement & trading
- division's overall direction & focus

SENIOR VICE PRESIDENT SUPPLY CHAIN MANAGEMENT
- Project Vision implementation
- demand and supply planning
- order management
- customer service

SENIOR VICE PRESIDENT RETAIL POULTRY OPERATIONS
- broiler, prepack, roaster and white/jumbo bird operations
- live production and breeders

SENIOR VICE PRESIDENT RETAIL SALES & MARKETING
- retail sales (supermarkets, clubs, supercenters, c-stores, wholesale-ind.)
- retail marketing (consumer, trade, brand management)
- consumer & trade relations
- business development

VICE PRESIDENT ADMINISTRATIVE SERVICES
- engineering
- distribution
- transportation
- purchasing
- office services

VICE PRESIDENT TECHNICAL SERVICES
- veterinary/health services
- nutrition
- analytical & product research labs
- farm & yield research
- feedmill quality control

VICE PRESIDENT HUMAN RESOURCES
- employment
- employee relations/labor relations
- compensation & benefits
- training & development
- employee health & safety

VICE PRESIDENT QUALITY
- quality assurance
- food safety
- quality planning, policies & procedures, including QIP
- microbiological laboratories

VICE PRESIDENT INTERNATIONAL
- export sales
- international marketing
- international logistics
- international trading
- intern'l operations & alliances

DIRECTOR ENVIRONMENTAL SERVICES
- environmental programs
- env. issues management
- env. policies & initiatives
- regulatory compliance

in Charlotte, North Carolina, in March, 1989, " . . . . the product met the promise of the advertising and was far superior to the competition. Two great sayings tell it all: 'nothing will destroy a poor product as quickly as good advertising,' and 'a gifted product is mightier than a gifted pen!'"

Today, branded chicken is ubiquitous. The new task for Perdue Farms is to create a unified theme to market a wide variety of products (e.g., fresh meat to fully pre-pared and frozen products) to a wide variety of cus-tomers (e.g., retail, food service and international). Industry experts believe that the market for fresh poultry has peaked while sales of value added and frozen prod-ucts continue to grow at a healthy rate. Although domes-tic retail sales accounts for about 60 percent of Perdue Farms revenues in FY2000, food service sales now account for 20 percent, international sales account for 5 percent and grain and oilseed contribute the remaining 15 percent. The company expects food service, interna-tional, and grain and oilseed sales to continue to grow as a percentage of total revenues.

Domestic Retail

Today's retail grocery customer is increasingly looking for ease and speed of preparation, i.e., value added products. The move toward value added products has significantly changed the meat department in the modern grocery. There are now five distinct meat outlets for poultry:

1. The fresh meat counter—whole chicken and parts
2. The delicatessen—processed turkey, rotisserie chicken
3. The frozen counter—individually quick frozen items such as frozen whole chickens, turkeys and Cornish hens.
4. Home meal replacement—fully prepared entrees such as Perdue brand "Short Cuts" and Deluca brand entrees (the Deluca brand was acquired and is sold under its own name) that are sold along with salads and desserts so that you can assemble your own dinner
5. Shelf stable—canned products.

Because Perdue Farms has always used the phrase "fresh young chicken" as the centerpiece of its marketing, value added products and the retail frozen counter create a possible conflict with past marketing themes. Are these products compatible with the company's marketing image and, if so, how does the company express the notion of quality in this broader product environment? To answer that question, Perdue Farms has been study-ing what the term "fresh young chicken" means to cus-tomers who consistently demand quicker and easier preparation and who admit that they freeze most of their fresh meat purchases once they get home. One view is that the importance of the term "fresh young chicken" comes from the customer's perception that "quality" and "freshness" are closely associated. Thus, the real issue may be "trust," i.e., the customer must believe that the product, whether fresh or frozen, is the freshest, highest quality possible and future marketing themes must develop that concept.

Food Service

The food service business consists of a wide variety of public and private customers including restaurant chains, governments, hospitals, schools, prisons, trans-portation facilities and the institutional contractors who supply meals to them. Historically, these customers have not been brand conscious, requiring the supplier to meet strict specifications at the lowest price, thus making this category a less than ideal fit for Perdue Farms. However, as Americans continue to eat a larger percentage of their meals away from home, traditional grocery sales have flattened while the food service sector has shown strong growth. Across the domestic poultry industry, food ser-vice accounts for approximately 50 percent of total poul-try sales while approximately 20 percent of Perdue Farms revenues come from this category. Clearly, Perdue Farms is playing catchup in this critical market.

Because Perdue Farms has neither strength nor exper-tise in the food service market, management believes that acquiring companies that already have food service expertise is the best strategy. An acquisition already com-pleted is the purchase in September 1998 of Gol-Pak Corporation based in Monterey, Tenn. A further proces-sor of products for the food service industry, Gol-Pak had about 1600 employees and revenues of about $200 million per year.

International

International markets have generally been a happy sur-prise. In the early 1990s, Perdue Farms began exporting specialty products such as chicken feet (known as "paws") to customers in China. Although not approved for sale for human consumption in the US, paws are considered a delicacy in China. By 1992, international sales, consisting principally of paws, had become a small, but profitable, business of about 30 million pounds per year. Building on this small "toehold," by 1998 Perdue Farms had quickly built an international business of more than 500 million pounds per year (see Exhibit 3) with annual revenues of more than $140 mil-lion, selling a wide variety of products to China, Japan, Russia, and the Ukraine.

In some ways, Japan is an excellent fit for Perdue Farms products because customers demand high quality.

Exhibit 3   International Volume

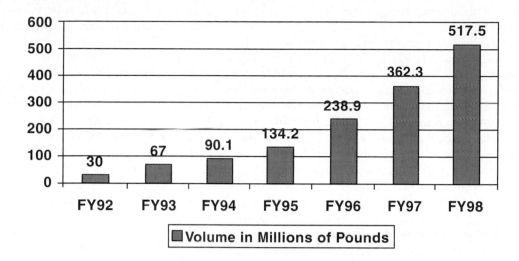

However, all Asian markets prefer dark meat, a serendipitous fit with the US preference for white breast meat because it means that excess (to America) dark meat can be sold in Asia at a premium price. On the downside, Perdue Farms gains much of its competitive advantage from branding (e.g., trademarks, processes and technological and biological know-how) which has little value internationally because most of Asia has not yet embraced the concept of branded chicken.

To better serve export markets, Perdue Farms has developed a portside freezing facility in Newport News, Virginia. This permits poultry to be shipped directly to the port, reducing processing costs and helping to balance ocean shipping costs to Asia which are in the range of 2/3 cents per pound (contracting an entire ship equal to 300-500 truckloads).

Shipping poultry to Asia is not without problems. For example, in China, delivery trucks are seldom refrigerated. Thus, the poultry can begin to thaw as it is being delivered, limiting the distance it can be transported prior to sale. One shipload of Perdue Farms chicken bound for Russia actually vanished. It had been inappropriately impounded using forged documents. Although most of its dollar value was eventually recovered, it is important for firms to be aware of the possible difficulties of ocean shipping and the use of foreign ports.

Initial demand for product in Russia, Poland and Eastern Europe was huge. By FY 1998, a significant portion of international volume was being purchased by Russia. Unfortunately, the crumbling of Russia's economy has had a devastating effect on imports, and sales are currently off significantly. Such instability of demand, coupled with rampant corruption, makes risking significant capital unacceptable.

Import duties and taxes are also a barrier. In China, according to the USDA, import duty rates for poultry are a whopping 45 percent for favored countries and 70 percent for unfavored countries. And, there is a 17 percent value added tax for all countries. Import duties and taxes in Russia have been similarly high. Hence, profits can be expected to be slim.

Perdue Farms has created a joint partnership with the Jiang Nan Feng (JNF) brand in order to develop a small processing plant in Shanghai. Brand recognition is being built through normal marketing tools. The products use the first "tray pack" wrapping available in Shanghai supermarkets. This new business shows promise because the sale in China of homegrown, fresh dark meat is a significant competitive advantage. Additionally, although government regulations do not presently permit importation to the US of foreign grown poultry, the future possibility of importing excess white meat from Shanghai to the US is attractive since Asian markets, which prefer dark meat, will have difficulty absorbing all of the white breast meat from locally grown poultry. Perdue Farms' management believes that investments in processing facilities in Asia require the company to partner with a local company. Attempting to go it alone is simply too risky due to the significant cultural differences.

Operations

Two words sum up the Perdue approach to operations—quality and efficiency—with emphasis on the first over the latter. Perdue more than most companies represents the Total Quality Management (TQM) slogan, "Quality, a journey without end." Some of the key events are listed in Exhibit 4.

Both quality and efficiency are improved through the management of details. EXHIBIT 5 depicts the structure and product flow of a generic, vertically integrated broiler company. A broiler company can choose which steps in the process it wants to accomplish in-house and which it wants suppliers to provide. For example, the broiler company could purchase all grain, oilseed, meal and other feed products. Or, it could contract with hatcheries to supply primary breeders and hatchery supply flocks.

Perdue Farms chose maximum vertical integration in order to control every detail. It breeds and hatches its own eggs (19 hatcheries), selects its contract growers, builds Perdue-engineered chicken houses, formulates and manufactures its own feed (12 poultry feedmills, one specialty feedmill, two ingredient blending opera-

tions), oversees the care and feeding of the chicks, operates its own processing plants (21 processing/further processing plants), distributes via its own trucking fleet, and markets the products—see Exhibit 5). Total process control formed the basis for Frank Perdue's early claims that Perdue Farms poultry is, indeed, higher quality than other poultry. When he stated in his early ads that "A chicken is what it eats. . . . I store my own grain and mix my own feed. . . and give my Perdue chickens nothing but well water to drink. . . . ," he knew that his claim was honest and he could back it up.

Total process control also enables Perdue Farms to ensure that nothing goes to waste. Eight measurable items—hatchability, turnover, feed conversion, livability, yield, birds per man-hour, utilization, and grade—are tracked routinely.

Perdue Farms continues to ensure that nothing artificial is fed to or injected into the birds. No shortcuts are taken. A chemical-free and steroid-free diet is fed to the

Exhibit 4	Milestones in the Quality Improvement Process at Perdue Farms

1924	-	Arthur Perdue buys leghorn roosters for $25
1950	-	Adopts the company logo of a chick under a magnifying glass
1984	-	Frank Perdue attends Philip Crosby's Quality College
1985	-	Perdue recognized for its pursuit of quality in A Passion for Excellence
		200 Perdue Managers attend Quality College
		Adopted the Quality Improvement Process (QIP)
1986	-	Establishes Corrective Action Teams (CAT's)
1987	-	Establishes Quality Training for all associates
		Implemented Error Cause Removal Process (ECR)
1988	-	Steering Committee formed
1989	-	First Annual Quality Conference held
		Implemented Team Management
1990	-	Second Annual Quality Conference held
		Codified Values and Corporate Mission
1991	-	Third Annual Quality Conference held
		Customer Satisfaction defined
1992	-	Fourth Annual Quality Conference held
	-	How to implement Customer Satisfaction explained to team leaders and Quality Improvement Teams (QIT)
	-	Created Quality Index
	-	Created Customer Satisfaction Index (CSI)
	-	Created "Farm to Fork" quality program
1999	-	Launched Raw Material Quality Index
2000	-	Initiated High Performance Team Process

Exhibit 5   Perdue Farms Integrated Operations

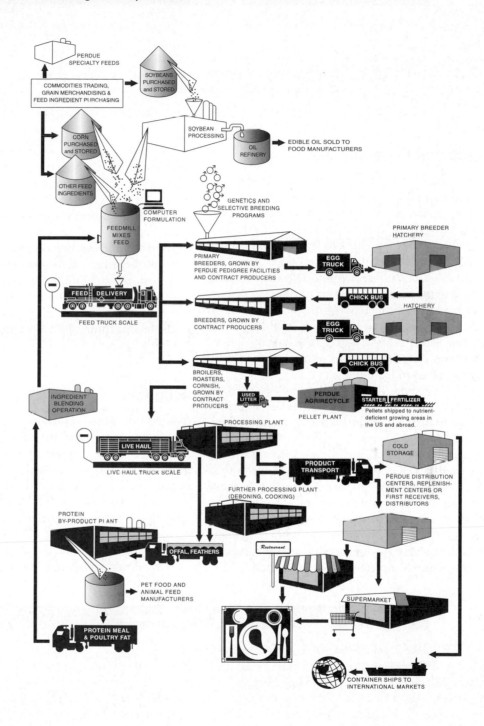

chickens. Young chickens are vaccinated against disease. Selective breeding is used to improve the quality of the chickens stock. Chickens are bred to yield more white breast meat because that is what the consumer wants.

To ensure that Perdue Farms poultry continues to lead the industry in quality, the company buys and ana-

lyzes competitors' products regularly. Inspection associates grade these products and share the information with the highest levels of management. In addition, the company's Quality Policy is displayed at all locations and taught to all associates in quality training (Exhibit 6).

Exhibit 6 — Quality Policy

- WE SHALL produce products and provide services at all times that meet or exceed the expectations of our customers.
- WE SHALL not be content to be of equal quality to our competitors.
- OUR COMMITMENT is to be increasingly superior.
- CONTRIBUTION TO QUALITY is a responsibility shared by everyone in the Perdue organization.

Research and Development

Perdue is an acknowledged industry leader in the use of research and technology to provide quality products and service to its customers. The company spends more on research as a percent of revenues than any other poultry processor. This practice goes back to Frank Perdue's focus on finding ways to differentiate his products based on quality and value. It was research into selective breeding that resulted in the broader breast, an attribute of Perdue Farms chicken that was the basis of his early advertising. Although other processors have also improved their stock, Perdue Farms believes that it still leads the industry. A list of some of Perdue Farms technological accomplishments is given in Exhibit 7.

As with every other aspect of the business, Perdue Farms tries to leave nothing to chance. The company employs specialists in avian science, microbiology, genetics, nutrition, and veterinary science. Because of its research and development capabilities, Perdue Farms is often involved in USDA field tests with pharmaceutical suppliers. Knowledge and experience gained from these tests can lead to a competitive advantage. For example, Perdue has the most extensive and expensive vaccination program in the industry. Currently, the company is working with and studying the practices of several European producers who use completely different methods.

The company has used research to significantly increase productivity. For example, in the 1950s, it took 14 weeks to grow a 3 pound chicken. Today, it takes only seven weeks to grow a 5-pound chicken. This gain in efficiency is due principally to improvements in the conversion rate of feed to chicken. The current rate of conversion is about two pounds of feed to produce one pound of chicken. Feed represents about 65 percent of the cost of growing a chicken. Thus, if additional research can further improve the conversion rate of feed to chicken by just 1 percent, it would represent estimated additional income of $2.5-3 million per week or $130-156 million per year.

Finance

Perdue Farms Inc., is privately held and considers financial information to be proprietary. Hence, available data is limited. Stock is primarily held by the family with a limited amount held by Perdue Management. Common numbers used by the media and the poultry industry peg Perdue Farms' revenues for FY2000 at about $2.5 billion and the number of associates at nearly 20,000. *Forbes* magazine has estimated FY2000 operating profits at about $160 million and net profits at about $22 million.

The firm's compound sales growth rate has been

Exhibit 7 — Perude Farms Inc. Technological Accomplishments

- Conducts more research than all competitors combined
- Breeds chickens with consistently more breast meat than any other bird in the industry
- First to use digital scales to guarantee weights to customers
- First to package fully-cooked chicken products in microwaveable trays
- First to have a box lab to define quality of boxes from different suppliers
- First to test both its chickens and competitors' chickens on 52 quality factors every week
- Improved on time deliveries 20 percent between 1987 and 1993
- Built state of the art analytical and microbiological laboratories for feed and end product analysis
- First to develop best management practices for food safety across all areas of the company
- First to develop commercially viable pelletized poultry litter

slowly decreasing during the past twenty years, mirroring the industry which has been experiencing market saturation and overproduction. However, Perdue has compensated by using manpower more efficiently through improvements such as automation. For example, 20 years ago, a 1 percent increase in associates resulted in a 1.6 percent increase in revenue. Currently, a 1 percent increase in associates results in an 8.5 percent increase in revenues (see Exhibit 8).

Poultry operations can be divided into four segments: Retail Chicken (growth rate 5 percent), Food-service Chicken and Turkey (growth rate 12 percent), International Sales (growth rate 64 percent over past six years) and Grain and Oilseed (growth rate 10 percent). The bulk of Perdue Farms sales continues to come from retail chicken—the sector with the slowest growth rate. The greatest opportunity appears to lie in food-service sales, where the company is admittedly behind, and international sales where political and economic instability in target countries make the risk to capital significant.

Perdue Farms has been profitable every year since its founding with the exception of 1988 and 1996. Company officials believe the loss in 1988 was caused by overproduction by the industry and higher administrative costs resulting from a decentralization effort begun during the mid-eighties. At that time, there was a concerted effort to push decisions down through the corporate ranks to provide more autonomy. When the new strategy resulted in significantly higher administrative costs due to duplication of effort, the company responded quickly by returning to the basics, reconsolidating and downsizing. The loss in 1996 was due to the impact of high corn prices. Currently, the goal is to constantly streamline in order to provide cost-effective business solutions.

Perdue Farms approaches financial management conservatively, using retained earnings and cash flow to finance most asset replacement projects and normal growth. When planning expansion projects or acquisitions, long-term debt is used. The target debt limit is 55 percent of equity. Such debt is normally provided by domestic and international bank and insurance companies. The debt strategy is to match asset lives with liability maturities, and have a mix of fixed rate and variable rate debt. Growth plans require about two dollars in projected incremental sales growth for each dollar in invested capital.

Environment

Environmental issues present a constant challenge to all poultry processors. Growing, slaughtering, and processing poultry are difficult and tedious processes that demand absolute efficiency in order to keep operating costs at an acceptable level. Inevitably, detractors argue that the process is dangerous to workers, inhumane to the poultry, hard on the environment and results in food that may not be safe. Thus media headlines such as "Human Cost of Poultry Business Bared," "Animal Rights Advocates Protest Chicken Coop Conditions," "Processing Plants Leave a Toxic Trail," or "EPA mandates Poultry Regulations" are routine.

Perdue Farms tries to be pro-active in managing environmental issues. In April 1993, the company created an Environmental Steering Committee. Its mission is ". . . to provide all Perdue Farms work sites with vision, direction, and leadership so that they can be good corporate citizens from an environmental perspective today and in the future." The committee is responsible for overseeing how the company is doing in such environmentally sensitive areas as waste water, storm water, hazardous waste, solid waste, recycling, bio-solids, and human health and safety.

For example, disposing of dead birds has long been an industry problem. Perdue Farms developed small composters for use on each farm. Using this approach, carcasses are reduced to an end-product that resembles soil in a matter of a few days. The disposal of hatchery waste is another environmental challenge. Historically, manure and un-hatched eggs were shipped to a landfill. However, Perdue Farms developed a way to reduce the waste by 50 percent by selling the liquid fraction to a pet food processor that cooks it for protein. The other 50

Exhibit 8	Annual Compound Growth Rate Through FY 2000		
	Revenue	Associates	Sales/Associate
Past 20 years	10.60 percent	6.48 percent	3.87 percent
Past 15 years	8.45 percent	4.48 percent	4.48 percent
Past 10 years	7.39 percent	4.75 percent	2.52 percent
Past 5 years	8.39 percent	0.99 percent	7.33 percent

percent is recycled through a rendering process. In 1990, Perdue Farms spent $4.2 million to upgrade its existing treatment facility with a state-of-the-art system at its Accomac, Virginia, and Showell, Maryland, plants. These facilities use forced hot air heated to 120 degrees to cause the microbes to digest all traces of ammonia, even during the cold winter months.

More than 10 years ago, North Carolina's Occupational Safety and Health Administration cited Perdue Farms for an unacceptable level of repetitive stress injuries at its Lewiston and Robersonville, North Carolina, processing plants. This sparked a major research program in which Perdue Farms worked with Health and Hygiene Inc. of Greensboro, North Carolina, to learn more about ergonomics, the repetitive movements required to accomplish specific jobs. Results have been dramatic. Launched in 1991 after two years of development, the program videotapes employees at all of Perdue Farms' plants as they work in order to describe and place stress values on the various tasks. Although the cost to Perdue Farms has been significant, results have been dramatic with workers' compensation claims down 44 percent, lost-time recordables just 7.7 percent of the industry average, an 80 percent decrease in serious repetitive stress cases and a 50 percent reduction in lost time or surgery back injuries (Shelley Reese, "Helping Employees get a Grip," *Business and Health,* Aug. 1998).

Despite these advances, serious problems continue to develop. In 1997, the organism Pfiesteria burst into media headlines when massive numbers of dead fish with lesions turned up along the Chesapeake Bay in Maryland. Initial findings pointed to manure runoff from the poultry industry. Political constituencies quickly called for increased regulation to insure proper manure storage and fertilizer use. The company readily admits that ". . . . the poultry process is a closed system. There is lots of nitrogen and phosphorus in the grain, it passes through the chicken and is returned to the environment as manure. Obviously, if you bring additional grain into a closed area such as the DelMarVa peninsula, you increase the amount of nitrogen and phosphorus in the soil unless you find a way to get rid of it." Nitrogen and phosphorus from manure normally make excellent fertilizer that moves slowly in the soil. However, scientists speculate that erosion speeds up runoff threatening the health of nearby streams, rivers and larger bodies of water such as the Chesapeake Bay. The problem for the industry is that proposals to control the runoff are sometimes driven more by politics and emotion than research, which is not yet complete.

Although it is not clear what role poultry related nitrogen and phosphorus runoff played in the pfiesteria

outbreak, regulators believe the microorganism feasts on the algae that grows when too much of these nutrients is present in the water. Thus, the EPA and various states are considering new regulations. Currently, contract growers are responsible for either using or disposing of the manure from their chicken houses. But, some regulators and environmentalists believe that (1) it is too complicated to police the utilization and disposal practices of thousands of individual farmers and (2) only the big poultry companies have the financial resources to properly dispose of the waste. Thus, they want to make poultry companies responsible for all waste disposal, a move that the industry strongly opposes.

Some experts have called for conservation measures that might limit the density of chicken houses in a given area or even require a percentage of existing chicken houses to be taken out of production periodically. Obviously, this would be very hard on the farm families who own existing chicken houses and could result in fewer acres devoted to agriculture. Working with AgriRecycle Inc. of Springfield, Missouri, Perdue Farms has developed a possible solution. The plan envisions the poultry companies processing excess manure into pellets for use as fertilizer. This would permit sale outside the poultry growing region, better balancing the input of grain. Spokesmen estimate that as much as 120,000 tons, nearly one third of the surplus nutrient from manure produced each year on the DelMarVa peninsula, could be sold to corn growers in other parts of the country. Prices would be market driven but could be $25-30 per ton, suggesting a potential, small profit. Still, almost any attempt to control the problem potentially raises the cost of growing chickens, forcing poultry processors to look elsewhere for locations where the chicken population is less dense.

In general, solving industry environmental problems presents at least five major challenges to the poultry processor:

- How to maintain the trust of the poultry consumer,
- How to ensure that the poultry remain healthy,
- How to protect the safety of the employees and the process,
- How to satisfy legislators who need to show their constituents that they are taking firm action when environmental problems occur, and
- How to keep costs at an acceptable level.

Jim Perdue sums up Perdue Farms' position as follows: ". . . . we must not only comply with environmental laws as they exist today, but look to the future to make sure we don't have any surprises. We must make sure our environmental policy statement (see EXHIBIT 9) is real,

Exhibit 9   Perdue Farms Environmental Policy Statement

Perdue Farms is committed to environmental stewardship and shares that commitment with its farm family partners. We're proud of the leadership we're providing our industry in addressing the full range of environmental challenges related to animal agriculture and food processing. We've invested—and continue to invest—millions of dollars in research, new technology, equipment upgrades, and awareness and education as part of our ongoing commitment to protecting the environment.

- Perdue Farms was among the first poultry companies with a dedicated Environmental Services department. Our team of environmental managers is responsible for ensuring that every Perdue facility operates within *100 percent compliance of all applicable environmental regulations and permits.*
- Through our joint venture, Perdue AgriRecycle, Perdue Farms is investing $12 million to build in Delaware a first-of-its-kind pellet plant that will convert surplus poultry litter into a starter fertilizer that will be marketed internationally to nutrient deficient regions. The facility, which will serve the entire Delmarva region, is scheduled to begin operation in April, 2001.
- We continue to explore new technologies that will reduce water usage in our processing plants without compromising food safety or quality.
- We invested thousands of man-hours in producer education to assist our family farm partners in managing their independent poultry operations in the most environmentally responsible manner possible. In addition, all our poultry producers are required to have nutrient management plans and dead-bird composters.
- Perdue Farms was one of four poultry companies operating in Delaware to sign an agreement with Delaware officials outlining our companies' voluntary commitment to help independent poultry producers dispose of surplus chicken litter.
- Our Technical Services department is conducting ongoing research into feed technology as a means of reducing the nutrients in poultry manure. We've already achieved phosphorous reductions that far exceed the industry average.
- We recognize that the environmental impact of animal agriculture is more pronounced in areas where development is decreasing the amount of farmland available to produce grain for feed and to accept nutrients. That is why we view independent grain *and* poultry producers as vital business partners and strive to preserve the economic viability of the family farm.

At Perdue Farms, we believe that it is possible to preserve the family farm; provide a safe, abundant and affordable food supply; and protect the environment. However, we believe that can best happen when there is cooperation and trust between the poultry industry, agriculture, environmental groups and state officials. We hope Delaware's effort will become a model for other states to follow.

that there's something behind it and that we do what we say we're going to do."

Logistics and Information Systems

The explosion of poultry products and increasing number of customers during recent years placed a severe strain on the existing logistic system which was developed at a time when there were far fewer products, fewer delivery points and lower volume. Hence, the company had limited ability to improve service levels, could not support further growth, and could not introduce innovative services that might provide a competitive advantage.

In the poultry industry, companies are faced with two significant problems—time and forecasting. Fresh poultry has a limited shelf life—measured in days. Thus, forecasts must be extremely accurate and deliveries timely. On one hand, estimating requirements too conservatively results in product shortages. Mega-customers such as Wal-Mart will not tolerate product shortages that lead to empty shelves and lost sales. On the other hand, if estimates are overstated, the result is outdated products that cannot be sold and losses for Perdue Farms. A common expression in the poultry industry is "you either sell it or smell it."

Forecasting has always been extremely difficult in the poultry industry because the processor needs to know approximately 18 months in advance how many broilers will be needed in order to size hatchery supply flocks and contract with growers to provide live broilers. Most customers (e.g., grocers, food service buyers) have a much shorter planning window. Additionally, there is no way for Perdue Farms to know when rival poultry processors will put a particular product on special, reducing Perdue Farms' sales, or when bad weather and other uncontrollable problems may reduce demand.

Historically, poultry companies have relied principally on extrapolation of past demand, industry networks and other contacts to make their estimates. Although product complexity has exacerbated the problem, the steady movement away from fresh product to frozen product (which has a longer shelf life) offers some relief.

In the short run, Information Technology (IT) has helped by shortening the distance between the customer and Perdue Farms. As far back as 1987, PCs were placed directly on each customer service associate's desk, allowing them to enter customer orders directly. Next, a system was developed to put dispatchers in direct contact with every truck in the system so that they would have accurate information about product inventory and truck location at all times. Now, IT is moving to further shorten the distance between the customer and the Perdue Farms service representative by putting a PC on the customer's desk. All of these steps improve communication and shorten the time from order to delivery.

In the longer run, these steps are not enough due to the rapidly expanding complexity of the industry. For example, today, poultry products fall into four unique channels of distribution:

(1) Bulk fresh—**Timeliness and frequency of delivery are critical to ensure freshness.** Distribution requirements are high volume and low cost delivery.
(2) Domestic frozen and further processed products—**Temperature integrity is critical.** Distribution requirements are frequency and timeliness of delivery. This channel lends itself to dual temperature trailer systems and load consolidation.
(3) Export—**Temperature integrity, high volume, and low cost are critical.** This channel lends itself to inventory consolidation and custom loading of vessels.
(4) Consumer packaged goods (packaged fresh, prepared and deli products)—**Differentiate via innovative products and services.** Distribution requirements are reduced lead time and low cost.

Thus, forecasting now requires the development of a sophisticated supply chain management system that can efficiently integrate all facets of operations including grain and oilseed activities, hatcheries and growing facilities, processing plants (which now produce more than 400 products at more than 20 locations), distribution

facilities and, finally, the distributors, supermarkets, food service customers and export markets (see Exhibit 5). Perdue Farms underlined the importance of the successful implementation of supply chain management by creating a new executive position, Senior Vice President for supply chain management.

A key step in overhauling the distribution infrastructure is the building of replenishment centers that will, in effect, be buffers between the processing plants and the customers. The portside facility in Norfolk, Virginia, which serves the international market, is being expanded and a new domestic freezer facility added.

Conceptually, products are directed from the processing plants to the replenishment and freezer centers based on customer forecasts that have been converted to an optimized production schedule. Perdue Farms trucks deliver these bulk products to the centers in finished or semi-finished form. At the centers, further finishing and packaging is accomplished. Finally, specific customer orders are custom palletized and loaded on trucks (either Perdue owned or contracted) for delivery to individual customers. All shipments are made up from replenishment center inventory. Thus, the need for accurate demand forecasting by the distribution centers is key.

In order to control the entire supply chain management process, Perdue Farms purchased a multi-million dollar information technology system that represents the biggest non-tangible asset expense in the company's history. This integrated, state-of-the-art information system required total process re-engineering, a project that took 18 months and required training 1,200 associates. Major goals of the system were to (1) make it easier and more desirable for the customer to do business with Perdue Farms, (2) make it easier for Perdue Farms associates to get the job done, and (3) take as much cost out of the process as possible.

Industry Trends

The poultry industry is affected by consumer, industry and governmental regulatory trends. Currently, chicken is the number one meat consumed in the United States with 40 percent market share (Exhibits 10 & 11). Typical Americans consume about 81 pounds of chicken, 69 pounds of beef and 52 pounds of pork annually (USDA data). Additionally, chicken is becoming the most popular meat in the world. In 1997, poultry set an export record of $2.5 billion. Although exports fell 6 percent in 1998, the decrease was attributed to Russia's and Asia's financial crisis and food industry experts expect this to be only a temporary setback. Hence, the world market is clearly a growth opportunity for the future.

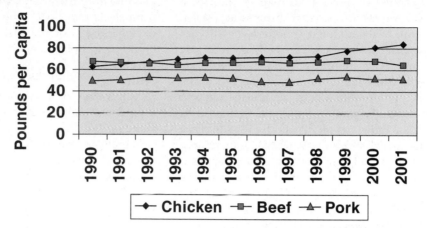

The popularity and growth of poultry products is attributed to both nutritional and economic issues. Poultry products contain significantly less fat and cholesterol than other meat products. In the United States, the demand for boneless, skinless breast meat, the leanest meat on poultry, is so great that dark meat is often sold at a discount in the United States or shipped overseas where it is preferred over white meat.

Another trend is a decrease in demand for whole birds to be used as the base dish for home meals and an increase in demand for products that have been further processed for either home or restaurant consumption. For example, turkey or chicken hot dogs, fully-cooked sliced chicken or turkey and turkey pastrami—which neither looks nor tastes like turkey—can be found in most deli cases. Many supermarkets sell either whole or parts of hot rotisserie chicken. Almost all fast food restaurants have at least one sandwich based on poultry products. Many up-scale restaurants feature poultry products that are shipped to them frozen and partially prepared in order to simplify restaurant preparation. All these products have been further processed, adding value and increasing the potential profit margin.

The industry is consolidating; that is, the larger companies in the industry are continuing to buy smaller firms. Currently, there are about 35 major poultry firms in the United States but this number is expected to drop to 20-25 within the next 10 years. There are several reasons for this. Stagnant US demand and general product oversupply create downward price pressure that makes it difficult for smaller firms to operate profitably. In addition, pressure for efficiency improvements requires huge

Exhibit 11 Chicken as a Percentage Overall Meat, Poultry and Fish Consumption, 1960-2000

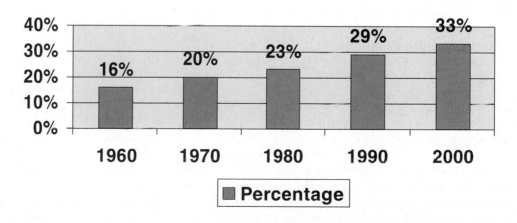

capital outlays. Finally, mega-retailers such as Sam's Club and Royal Ahold (the Dutch owner of several US supermarket chains) do not like to manage individual contracts with numerous smaller processors. Mega-retailers prefer to deal with mega-suppliers.

The industry is heavily regulated. The Food and Drug Administration (FDA) monitors product safety. The USDA inspects poultry as it arrives at the processing plant. After it is killed, each bird is again inspected by a USDA inspector for avian diseases, contamination of feces or other foreign material. All poultry that does not meet regulations is destroyed under USDA supervision. USDA inspectors also examine the plant, equipment, operating procedures and personnel for compliance with sanitary regulations. Congress has mandated that the USDA make this information available online. Additional intensive inspections of statistically selected samples of poultry products have been recommended by the National Academy of Sciences. Thus, additional FDA regulations for product quality are anticipated.

Although poultry produces less waste per pound of product than cattle or hogs, all meat industries are experiencing increased scrutiny by the Environmental Protection Agency (EPA) regarding the disposal of waste. In general, waste generated at processing plants is well controlled by regulation, monitoring, and fines. When an EPA violation occurs, the company that operates the plant can receive a substantial fine, potentially millions of dollars.

Still, the most difficult problems to deal with are those that occur as a cumulative result of numerous processors producing in a relatively limited area. For example, increasing poultry production in a given area intensifies the problem of disposal of manure. In man-made fertilizer, phosphorous and nitrogen exist in approximately a 1 to 8 ratio whereas in poultry manure the ratio can be 1 to 1. Thus, too much poultry manure can result in serious phosphorous run-off into streams and rivers, potentially resulting in aquatic disease and degradation of water quality. In 1997, an outbreak of pfiesteria, a toxic microbe, occurred in the tributaries of the Chesapeake Bay. Although the poultry industry insisted that there were many possible reasons for the problem, the media and most regulatory spokespersons attributed it primarily to phosphorous run-off from chicken manure. After much negative publicity and extensive investigation by both poultry processors and state regulatory agencies, the State of Maryland passed the Water quality Act of 1998, which required nutrient management plans. However, many environmentalists continue to believe that the EPA must create additional, stricter federal environmental regulations. Recent regulatory activity has continued to focus on Eastern Shore agriculture, especially the poultry industry. However, new studies from the US Geological Survey suggest that the vast majority of nutrients affecting the Chesapeake Bay come from rivers that do not flow through the poultry-producing regions of the eastern Shore. The studies also found that improved agricultural management practices have reduced nutrient runoff from farmlands. Jim Perdue says "While the poultry industry must accept responsibility for its share of nutrients, public policy should view the watershed as a whole and address all the factors that influence water quality."

Other government agencies whose regulations affect the industry include the Occupational Safety and Health Administration (OSHA) for employee safety and the Immigration and Naturalization Service (INS) for undocumented workers. OSHA enforces its regulations via periodic inspections, and levies fines when non-compliance is found. For example, a Hudson Foods poultry plant was fined more than a million dollars for alleged willful violations causing ergonomic injury to workers. The INS also uses periodic inspections to find undocumented workers. It estimates that undocumented aliens working in the industry vary from 3 percent to 78 percent of the workforce at individual plants. Plants that are found to use undocumented workers, especially those that are repeat offenders, can be heavily fined.

The Future

The marketplace for poultry in the 21st century will be very different from the past. Understanding the wants and needs of generation Xers and echo-boomers will be key to responding successfully to these differences.

Quality will continue to be essential. In the 1970s, quality was the cornerstone of Frank Perdue's successful marketing program to "brand" his poultry. However, in the 21st century, quality will not be enough. Today's customers expect—even demand—all products to be high quality. Thus, Perdue Farms plans to use customer service to further differentiate the company. The focus will be on learning how to become indispensable to the customer by taking cost out of the product and delivering it exactly the way the customer wants it, where and when the customer wants it. In short, as Jim Perdue says, "Perdue Farms wants to become so easy to do business with that the customer will have no reason to do business with anyone else."

In the poultry business, customer purchase decisions, as well as company profitability, hinge on mere pennies. Thus, the location of processing facilities is key. Historically, Perdue Farms has been an Eastern Shore company and has maintained major processing facilities on the Eastern Shore. However, it currently costs about

1½ cents more per pound to grow poultry on the Eastern Shore versus what poultry can be grown for in Arkansas. This difference results from the cost of labor, compliance with federal and state environmental laws, resource costs (e.g., feed grain) and other variables. Clearly, selecting favorable sites for future growing and processing facilities is key. In the future, assuming regulations will permit the importation of foreign grown poultry, producers could even use inexpensive international labor markets to further reduce costs. The opportunity for large growers to capture these savings puts increased pressure on small poultry companies. This suggests further consolidation of the industry.

Grocery companies are also consolidating in order to compete with huge food industry newcomers such as Wal-Mart and Royal Ahold. These new competitors gain efficiency by minimizing the number of their suppliers and buying huge amounts from each at the lowest possible price. In effect, both mega-companies—the supplier and the buyer—become dependent on each other. Further, mega-companies expect their suppliers to do more for them. For example, Perdue Farms considers it possible that, using sophisticated distribution information programs, they will soon be able to manage the entire meat department requirements for several supermarket chains. Providing this service would support Perdue Farms' goal of becoming indispensable to their first line retail customer, the grocer.

The 21st century consumer will demand many options. Clearly, the demand for uncooked, whole chickens purchased at the meat counter has peaked. Demand is moving toward further processed poultry. To support this trend, Perdue Farms plans to open several additional cooking plants. In addition, a criterion for future acquisitions will be whether they support value added processing. Products from these plants will fill food service requirements and grocery sales of prepared foods such as delicatessen, frozen, home meal replacement and shelf stable items. Additionally, the 21st century customer will be everywhere. Whether at work, at a sports event, in school, or traveling on the highway, customers expect to have convenient refreshment machines available with a wide selection of wholesome, ready to eat products.

Designing a distribution system that can handle all of these options is extremely difficult. For example, the system must be able to efficiently organize hundreds of customer orders that are chosen from more than 400 different products that are processed and further prepared at more than 20 facilities throughout the southeast for delivery by one truck—a massive distribution task. As executives note, the company survived up until now using distribution techniques created as many as 20 years ago when there were a handful of products and processing facilities. However, the system approached gridlock during the late 1990s. Thus, Perdue Farms invested in a state or the art information processing system—a tough decision because "we could build two new processing plants for the price of this technology package."

International markets are a conundrum. On one hand, Perdue Farms' international revenue has grown from an insignificant side business in 1994 to about $140 million in 1999, approximately 5 percent of total revenues. Further, its contribution to profits is significant. Poultry is widely accepted around the world, providing opportunities for further growth. But, trying to be global doesn't work. Different cultures value different parts of the chicken and demand different meat color, preparation and seasoning. Thus, products must be customized. Parts that are not in demand in a particular country must be sold at severely reduced prices, used as feed, or shipped frozen to a different market where demand exists. While this can be done, it is a distribution problem that significantly complicates an already difficult forecasting model.

International markets can also be very unstable, exposing Perdue Farms to significant demand instability and potential losses. For example, in 1997, about 50 percent of Perdue Farms' international revenues came from Russia. However, political and economic problems in Russia reduced 1999 revenues significantly. This high level of instability, coupled with corruption that thrives in a country experiencing severe political and economic turmoil, introduces significant risk to future investment.

Clearly, the future holds many opportunities. But, none of them comes without risk and Perdue Farms must carefully choose where it wants to direct its scarce resources.

Priceline.com

Taryn Block, Sasha Clements, Sridhar Kulasekharan, Stacey Mason Robert E. Hoskisson

The University of Oklahoma

On December 27, 2000, Priceline.com stock hit a new 52-week low, closing at $1.063, approximately one-fiftieth of its 52-week high.[1] Once a favorite pick of Wall Street analysts, investors were growing skeptical as Priceline.com alliances began collapsing. In addition, on March 16 and 26, 2001, two complaints were brought against, with others, Priceline.com and Jay Walker. These "complaints allege, among other things, that Priceline.com and the individual defendants named in the complaints violated the federal securities laws by issuing and selling Priceline.com common stock in Priceline.com's March 1999 initial public offering without disclosing to investors" that some underwriters received excessive commissions for selling Priceline.com stock.[2]

Obviously, Priceline.com faced many challenges. The Internet environment was changing rapidly and analysts were questioning the valuation of technology sector stocks. At Intel's eXCHANGE conference on October 12, 2000, Jay Walker, founder of Priceline.com, said that the market was no longer willing to wait for black ink. He further said that he believed investors had lost patience with companies that had not demonstrated profitability.[3]

In addition to its legal problems, Priceline.com was facing serious internal business issues. Walker adamantly believed that his "name your own price" system was applicable for any product. This belief led Walker to develop Priceline WebHouse Club in September 1999, a wholly owned subsidiary that allowed customers to name their own price for groceries and gasoline.[4] After sinking $195 million dollars of his own money as well as $195 million from various backers into this venture,

Priceline WebHouse Club ceased operations on October 5, 2000. Publicly, Walker stated that the venture had simply run out of cash and "that it had to stop doing business while it still had enough money to pay the parties to whom it had made legal or moral commitments."[5]

However, the Priceline.com brand was also at stake. The name "WebHouse Club" was not universally known and customers bidding for gasoline or groceries were under the impression that they were dealing directly with Priceline.com. This caused concern that dissatisfaction with the Priceline WebHouse Club service might reflect poorly on Priceline.com. Ultimately there was potential for creating bad press and affecting shareholder confidence in Priceline.com.[6]

In addition to Priceline WebHouse Club, Walker also created Priceline Perfect Yardsale in January 2000, an online operation much like eBay, which attempted to bring seller and buyer together.[7] Like Priceline WebHouse Club, Priceline Perfect Yardsale ceased operations in October 2000. While this venture never had the customer base that Priceline WebHouse Club had garnered, the failure of yet another business seemed indicative of the problems at Priceline.com.

These events, as well as a continual restructuring of Priceline.com's management, led analysts to question the viability of the business model that Walker continued to peddle.[8] A lack of confidence within the industry meant that Priceline.com needed to address critical issues if the company were to remain viable. While top executives in the company were experienced, they found it hard to overcome the overall disillusionment with Internet stocks, particularly those which had failed to show a profit. Additionally, analysts began to question Jay Walker's leadership.[9] And, there was the question of whether or not Priceline.com would survive its management crisis and emerge with a clearer vision of its business model.

This case was prepared under the direction of Professor Robert E. Hoskisson. The case is intended to be used as the basis for class discussion rather than to illustrate either effective or ineffective handling of an administrative situation.

History

In 1996, a company started by Jay Walker, Walker Digital, created Priceline.com based on the following information. Each day major airlines have more than 500,000 empty seats. Walker's team believed that if the airlines were offered a discounted price for these empty seats, they would accept, simply to cut their losses. Based on that premise, Walker Digital developed a "name your price" system that offered companies a way to sell their surplus products or services without damaging their brands, or their ability to charge full price for non-surplus items. The system was patented in late 1996 and Priceline.com was born.[10]

With a business plan in hand, Walker obtained financing for Priceline.com from the venture capital firm General Atlantic Partners and Microsoft co-founder Paul Allen's Vulcan Ventures. Initially, Walker launched the Priceline.com website with only two airlines signed on to offer seats. To create interest and generate business, Walker blitzed consumers with ads that stressed that customers could "name their own price." Priceline.com also took on a celebrity spokesperson, William Shatner, who was featured in all ads. Priceline.com attracted more than 150,000 visitors a day, totaling more than one million its first week. Ticket sales at Priceline.com have accelerated rapidly since the service was launched on April 6, 1998. In its first six weeks of operation, Priceline.com sold more than 10,000 tickets.[11]

Within the next year, Delta signed on with Priceline.com, followed by Northwest and Continental. Walker was also able to convince private investors to come on board. An IPO was offered in March, 1999 with great success. Priceline.com's IPO was the most wildly successful of 1999, during which the stock soared from $16 to $162 in one month of trading.

After its initial success in the domestic airline ticket sales market, the company initiated a growth strategy through diversification in order to utilize the full potential of the reverse auction model and to gain a strong market presence in a number of different industries. The majority of Priceline.com's new market and/or new countries were established through the use of strategic alliances and joint ventures. This strategy allowed Priceline.com to grow rapidly and with less risk than had the company entered these markets alone. Under these arrangements, Priceline.com generally received royalties for licensing its brand name and business model.

As the company expanded its services and became more widely known, revenues increased substantially. Priceline.com incurred losses in its first year (1998), but its revenues grew in 1999 to almost $500 million, while turning a gross profit of $57,831,000. Although the net loss in 1999 totaled over $1 billion, net loss in the year 2000 was much more manageable and revenues grew by more than two and a half times (see Exhibit 2 for the financial performance of Priceline.com from 1998–2000).

Priceline.com used its unique service as a marketing strategy. The "name your own price" system was used for a variety of products in seven different categories: airline reservations, car rentals, personal finances, groceries, gasoline, automobile sales, and long distance telephone. If an industry had excess capacity, such as the thousands of unused airline tickets every day, Priceline.com would sell the excess at a discounted price.

Management

Walker's successor, Richard Braddock, was named in August, 1998. He was given the titles of Chairman of the Board and CEO. Braddock was also given a 10 percent stake in the company and a free hand to change Priceline.com's business model. Most notably, Braddock's primary responsibility was to attract a management team capable of turning Priceline.com into a profitable, multi-billion-dollar company.[12] Braddock's management abilities were well known. He had spent twenty years in various positions at Citicorp and its principal subsidiary, Citibank, N.A., including as President and COO.[13]

On May 15, 2000, Braddock resigned as CEO, but remained on as Chairman of the Board. Daniel Schulman was hired to replace Braddock as President, CEO, and COO. Schulman had spent the previous eighteen years with AT&T where he worked as president of the Consumer Markets Division and was well known for his management skills.

In conjunction with these changes, Heidi Miller, Priceline.com's Senior Executive Vice President and Chief Financial Officer, assumed additional operational responsibilities and was chosen to lead Priceline.com's international and business-to-business initiatives. Miller was also responsible for Priceline.com's long-term strategy and business development operations.[14]

The top management team continued to focus on the "name your own price" system. However, they realized that the firm was too dependent upon the travel business. In 1999, 92% of Priceline.com's revenues came from the selling of airline tickets and it faced greater competition. Thus, the top management team knew that the product offerings had to be expanded.

| | Years Ended December 31, | | |
	2000	1999	1998
Travel revenues	$1,217,160	$480,979	$35,224
Other revenues	18,236	1,431	13
Total revenues	1,235,396	482,410	35,237
Cost of travel revenues	1,038,783	423,056	33,496
Cost of other revenues	2,921	–	–
Supplier warrant costs	1,523	1,523	3,029
Total costs of revenues	1,043,227	424,579	36,525
Gross profit (loss)	192,169	57,831	(1,288)
Operating (expenses)	(514,443)	(1,120,041)	(111,503)
Other income (expense)	7,129	7,120	548
Net (loss)	(315,145)	(1,055,090)	(112,243)

SOURCE: priceline.com 2000 Annual Report, p. 53.

Products

As of October 6, 2000, Priceline.com offered six different products on its website. Originally, the products included groceries and gasoline, purchased through the Priceline.com subsidiary WebHouse Club, but that venture was closed defunct on October 5, 2000. The following is a description of the remaining services offered and the way in which they operate.

Airline Tickets

At the Priceline.com website, customers were required to provide the following: the city of destination, the dates of travel, the price they were willing to pay, and the major credit card they planned to use. Priceline.com then searched the major airlines to see if any were willing to release seats within these guidelines. Airlines could select any flights departing between 6 a.m. and 10 p.m., and could require up to one connection. If seats were released, confirmed tickets were immediately issued by Priceline.com via electronic ticketing, or sent via Federal Express or USPS Express.[15]

After its success in the US market, Priceline.com entered the global arena, with access to 100 major cities. Today Priceline.com spans the globe providing services to more than 300 cities with participation of 18 major domestic and international carriers.

Hotels

Priceline.com expanded its market presence in the travel industry by adding hotel service in January 1999. The new hotel service was launched with initial market coverage in 35 US cities and resorts. Over 1,500 hotels participated in the program offering a total of 2.5 million empty rooms per month.[16] The hotel service experienced rapid growth into more than 1,100 cities and resorts in all 50 states including 4,250 brand-name hotels.[17]

Priceline.com's hotel service required travelers to provide the following: the destination city, the zone or area in the city, the dates needed, the hotel star rating, the price per night, and the major credit card used to guarantee the reservation. Travelers had to agree to stay at the first quality brand-name hotel (at the customer's star rating or above) that agreed to release a room at the traveler's price.

Priceline.com would search for a hotel willing to release a room for the specified dates and price. If Priceline.com found a room, travelers received a confirmed reservation with the hotel's name and address by e-mail, and a follow-up confirmation by regular mail. All room reservations were immediately guaranteed and charged to the customer's credit card. In order to get hotels to accept the lowest possible prices from customers, rooms reserved through Priceline.com were non-refundable and non-changeable.

Car Rentals

Priceline.com expanded its services to customers booking flights on its website by offering them car rental services. Initially, Priceline.com teamed up with National and Budget car rentals. On June 1, 2000, Hertz and Alamo announced that they would be joining Priceline.com's car rental program and would begin offering vehicle rentals on the "name-your-own-price" basis starting later that quarter.[18]

In total, National, Budget, Hertz, and Alamo accounted for 70% of all vehicle rentals at US airports. Priceline.com launched its vehicle rental program in November, 1999. In early 2000, Priceline.com reported that its rental car service had achieved positive margins after 30 days in the market. Priceline.com's rental car service also reported selling an average of over 20,000 rental car days per week toward the end of the first quarter.[19]

Automobile Sales

With Priceline.com, consumers could use the Internet to buy any new car or truck at their desired price without interacting with a salesperson. Unlike other Internet car buying services that simply have a car salesman call the customer back to provide the dealer's best price, Priceline.com let buyers name their own best price. If the buyer's price was accepted, Priceline e-mailed the customer within one business day with a commitment from a dealer who agreed, in writing, to the customer's price. Other car-buying services on the Internet signed up a limited number of dealers who paid for the right to call prospects and try to sell them a car. Instead, Priceline.com got the price from the customer and then went to all factory-authorized dealers within an area specified by the customer, without revealing the buyer's name, phone number or gender, to determine if any of them would agree to sell the car at the customer's price.

Priceline.com charged no membership costs or fees in advance. The service was free until a dealer agreed to the customer's price in writing. Once the deal was completed, the consumer was charged $25 and the dealer was charged $75.

Personal Finances

Homebuyers faced with finding a home mortgage could save money by naming their own interest rate and terms through Priceline Home Financing. Priceline.com's consumer-friendly home financing service was offered by a partnership between Priceline.com and LendingTree, Inc., an online loan originator based in Charlotte, NC.

To initiate a loan request, consumers supplied basic credit-related data and history that was used by financial institutions to evaluate their request. Priceline.com and LendingTree touted strict security procedures and technology for safeguarding personal information supplied by the consumer over the Internet. Information supplied by consumers was used only to process the loan request and participating lending institutions were bound by federal and state privacy regulations.

As part of submitting a home financing request through Priceline, consumers made a $200 "good faith" deposit with the lender, guaranteed by a major credit card. If a participating lender accepted the mortgage offer, the deposit was applied to normal lender fees associated with the loan. If the offer was not accepted, the customer's credit card was never charged.

Once a home financing request was submitted through Priceline.com Home Financing, LendingTree forwarded it to lending institutions that were most likely to be interested in the consumer's credit profile. Consumers received a response to their request within two business days. If no lender agreed to the request, the consumer could receive counter-offers with alternative terms or interest rates. If any one of those offers were satisfactory, the homebuyer could accept the counter-offer. Otherwise, the process was complete and the consumer was free to try again after a seven-day waiting period. There was no charge for additional loan requests submitted through Priceline's Home Financing.

After an offer was tentatively accepted, the homebuyer was put in touch with the lending institution to verify provided information, arrange for appraisals, complete requested documentation, and close the loan.

Long Distance Telephone

Priceline Long Distance, a wholly owned Priceline.com subsidiary, was very different from other long distance services. From the Priceline.com website, customers set the price they would be willing to pay per-minute for a block of calling time. Priceline.com Long Distance then searched its private database to determine if a customer's offer could be accepted. Once a customer's offer was accepted, Priceline Long Distance e-mailed the customer with the name of the participating provider who would supply service to the customer. The three providers with whom Priceline.com was affiliated were Net2Phone, Deltathree.com, and ZeroPlus.com.

Customers whose offers were accepted did not need a computer or an Internet Service Provider in order to place long distance telephone calls using the minutes purchased at Priceline.com Long Distance. In order to place calls using purchased minutes, customers dialed an access number from their home telephone or small business, entered a four-digit personal identification number

(PIN), and completed the call. With Priceline.com Long Distance, customers did not have to switch their current long distance providers.

Priceline.com Long Distance could make these savings possible because its Internet pricing system created new network efficiencies for telecommunications providers. For the first time, customers submitted guaranteed purchase offers for long distance calls before those calls were made. All Priceline.com Long Distance calls were routed over managed networks and not over the Internet. These networks had significantly more "fiber" to devote to incremental traffic. The use of managed networks eliminated many of the quality shortfalls customers experienced when placing IP telephone calls over the Internet. Priceline.com Long Distance's participating providers' data traffic networks could support ordinary telephone-to-telephone conversations ranging in quality from digital wireless telephones to traditional long distance service. The major competitors in this segment were other online phone card providers such as Qwest Communications.[20]

Financial Results

After expanding rapidly and announcing record second quarter profits for 2000, Priceline.com faced its first setback. On September 29, 2000 Priceline.com announced that revenue for the third quarter would fall $20-25 mil-lion short of the previous quarter. The cause was a shortfall in airline ticket sales. Earnings, too, would be one cent short of analysts' expectations.[21] Priceline's troubles were illustrated by a weak holiday season as fourth-quarter revenues were even lower than the previous quarter's (see Exhibit 2). Said Priceline.com President and CEO Daniel H. Schulman, "The 4th quarter was difficult for Priceline.com. In addition to being our seasonally weakest quarter, Priceline.com was adversely affected by the closing of WebHouse Club, [and] negative news stories about customer satisfaction. . ."[22] Overall, financial results for the year 2000 were disappointing (see Exhibits 2 and 3).

At the close of trading on December 26, 2000, Priceline.com's shares were trading at $1.125 per share. This was well off the company's 52-week high of $104.25 per share. With the stock barely over one percent of its high, revenues falling off, and the added cost of writing off the WebHouse Club warrant ($189,000,000), the financial future of Priceline.com was bleak.

Competition

Some analysts believe that Priceline.com's globalization and diversification strategy was a result of increased competition in the firm's core business of airline ticket sales.[23] On the surface Priceline.com seems to enjoy the competition—in fact, it instructs customers to obtain the

Exhibit 2	Priceline.com Incorporated Selected Quarterly Financial Data 2000			
	First Quarter	Second Quarter	Third Quarter	Fourth Quarter
Revenues:				
Travel	$311,607	$346,822	$335,699	$223,032
Other	2,191	5,273	5,635	5,137
Total revenues	313,798	352,095	341,334	228,169
Cost of revenues:				
Travel	265,051	296,767	286,134	192,354
Other	101	533	1,146	1,141
Total cost of revenues	265,152	297,300	287,280	193,495
Gross profit	48,646	54,795	54,054	34,674
Total operating expenses	64,928	62,041	248,272	139,202
Other income (expense)	2,715	2,725	2,296	(607)
Net loss	(13,567)	(4,521)	(191,922)	(105,135)

SOURCE: Priceline.com, 2000 Annual Report, p. 72.

Exhibit 3 Priceline.com Incorporated BALANCE SHEETS (In thousands)

	December 31, 2000	December 31, 1999
ASSETS		
Current assets:		
Cash and cash equivalents	$77,024	$124,383
Restricted cash	13,568	8,789
Short-term investments	10,952	38,771
Accounts receivable, net of allowance for doubtful accounts of $2,372 and $1,961 at December 31, 2000 and 1999, respectively	13,889	21,289
Prepaid expenses and other current assets	15,790	18,507
Total current assets	131,223	211,739
Property and equipment, net	37,083	28,006
Related party receivable	3,503	8,838
Warrants to purchase common stock of licensees	3,250	189,000
Other assets	20,019	4,303
Total assets	195,078	441,886
LIABILITIES AND STOCKHOLDERS' EQUITY		
Current liabilities:		
Accounts payable	$40,691	$24,302
Accrued expenses	33,172	13,695
Other current liabilities	5,434	1,253
Total current liabilities	79,297	39,250
Accrued expenses	5,108	
Total liabilities	84,405	39,250
MANDATORILY REDEEMABLE CONVERTIBLE PREFERRED STOCK	359,580	—
Stockholders' equity:		
Common stock, $0.008 par value, authorized 1,000,000,000 shares, 181,798,204 and 163,866,912 issued, respectively	1,454	1,311
Treasury stock, 5,450,236 shares	(326,633)	—
Additional paid-in capital	1,618,956	1,581,708
Deferred compensation	(13,053)	—
Accumulated other comprehensive loss	(1,156)	—
Accumulated deficit	(1,528,475)	(1,180,383)
Total stockholders' equity	(248,907)	402,636
Total liabilities and stockholders' equity	$195,078	$441,886

SOURCE: Priceline.com, 2000 Annual Report, p. 52.

lowest possible price from competitors such as Hotwire and then make a bid with Priceline.com. Priceline.com expects its competitors to increase its own revenues because they are bringing more people online. Recently, however, Priceline.com warned that third-quarter revenue wouldn't meet analysts' expectations because of weakness in selling airline tickets due to pricing competition from the airlines.[24]

Microsoft Expedia

In September 1999, Microsoft introduced a Web-based company that allows costumers to bid on a price for hotel rooms.[25] In addition, the Expedia site allows customers to choose from a list of different classes of hotels with standard rates for various cities in the United States. Expedia did not have any trouble finding hotels to accommodate its service. In fact, it has joined forces with a number of nationally recognized hotel brands.

Priceline.com felt Expedia's business model was an imitation of its reverse auction model and quickly filed a federal lawsuit against Microsoft for impinging on its patent rights.[26] (This was not the first time Priceline.com faced a battle in court. The company had actually defended itself against similar lawsuits, which claimed the Priceline.com business model replicated a model that attempted to gain a patent in the past.[27]) Undeterred by the lawsuit, the Microsoft spin-off, Expedia, launched a "name your price" feature for airline tickets later in 1999, only months after the initial lawsuit.[28]

Expedia's business model is basically the same as the reverse auction model patented by Priceline.com. However, Expedia will not only match customers with the lowest fares, but also will provide a service that answers the request in a matter of minutes.[29] If Expedia cannot find a match, it will link the customer with the lowest fares available.[30] Expedia also allows customers to make specific choices on particular airlines and departure times.[31] The added features offered by Expedia could transform the service into a formidable competitor for Priceline.com.

Travelocity.com

Priceline.com also faces strong competition from online travel agencies. Travelocity.com, a leader in online discount tickets, represents 420 airlines, more than 40,000 hotels, and over 50 car rental companies.[32] Travelocity is owned and operated by the SABRE Group, which has a proven track record for providing excellent travel-related services worldwide.[33] Travelocity.com's main feature is the range of options it offers customers. The company provides reservation capabilities for over 95% of all airline seats sold.[34] Travelocity.com's business model differs from Priceline.com's. Travelocity.com finds the best available fares and displays them on a calendar that allows customers easy access to travel arrangements.[35] Travelocity.com also adds a visual element to its website by posting hotel images for customers to view before they make hotel reservations.[36] The company offers a wide selection of packaged vacations, including cruise to ski packages. Travelocity.com also excels in customer service, offering a 24-hour customer service help desk that handles customers' disputes.[37] Travelocity.com has been honored with many awards for its excellent customer service and satisfaction.[38]

SkyAuction.com

Another new competitor, SkyAuction.com, is a Web travel auction that claims it competes directly with Priceline.com. SkyAuction.com is owned and operated by Magical Holidays, Inc, which has an established name in the airline ticket consolidation business.[39] SkyAuction uses a business model similar to eBay's. The company starts all bidding at one dollar.[40] SkyAuction.com's core business is auctioning airline tickets, although it also auctions hotel rooms, packaged vacations, and resort stays.[41] While SkyAuction offers very low and competitive prices, most items are sold close to market value. In order to bid for prices on SkyAuction, customers fill out a form and receive a free password.[42] The data obtained from the form gives SkyAuction a wealth of information on customers' preferences, allowing the company to target specific individuals with appealing auction items.[43]

Hotwire

In mid-summer of 1999, six major airlines (Priceline.com customers) developed a secret alliance to compete directly with Priceline.com.[44] The project was built in secrecy under the code name Project Purple Demon.[45] As of June 2000, the project had fifty employees and $75 million in initial funding from various investors.[46] The airlines, realizing that Priceline.com had built a competitive business by using an overlooked area of revenue, decided they wanted the revenues from the discounted business back in their hands.[47]

The airline venture was launched as Hotwire.com with major backing by Texas Pacific Group, a private investment company.[48] Other equity holders involved with Hotwire include UAL Corp.'s United Airlines, AMR Corp.'s American Airlines, Northwest Airlines, Continental Airlines, US Airways Group Inc., and American West Holdings Corp.'s America West Airlines.[49]

Hotwire does not accept bids from customers. However, it does allow customers to select a certain route and then gives the customer an actual discounted fare.[50] Hotwire does not reveal the airline, the exact time of flight, or routing until the customer has purchased the flight.[51] Hotwire believes it offers a more efficient and appealing service than Priceline.com as consumers do not have to keep re-bidding with different prices and are not forced to select starting bids, an element of Priceline.com's service that often creates confusion.

Orbitz.com

Owned by one of the largest domestic air carriers and backed by many more, Orbitz.com hopes to compete effectively against Priceline.com.[52] Using a similar business model to Hotwire's, Orbitz.com allows customers to compare fares of approximately thirty different airlines.[53] This feature gives customers the ability to search thousands of fares. Orbitz.com generates most of its revenues from sales commission. American Airlines, Continental, Delta, Northwest, and United Airlines collectively own Orbitz.com. The coalition has attracted a great deal of government scrutiny. The Justice Department fears that Orbitz.com may destroy all competition in the market and has initiated an investigation into anticompetitive behavior.

Expedia, Travelocity, SkyAuction, Hotwire and Orbitz.com are attacking Priceline.com with four different strategies. Expedia mimics Priceline.com's reverse auction business model, in that it creates an auction for customers. Travelocity.com is an online discount ticket agency that operates in the same market niche as Priceline.com. SkyAuction uses a real auction to sell tickets. Hotwire and Orbitz.com both offer discounted tickets. All of these strategies place heavy competitive pressure on Priceline.com. The diversified strategies target Priceline.com's vulnerability on several different fronts. Priceline.com overtly shows little concern, although its recent drop in airline ticket sales has negatively affected the company's revenues and financial performamce.

Challenges

Initially, the idea that the consumer could name his or her own price enthralled people, consumers and critics alike. Walker envisioned Priceline.com as the answer to the problem of the airline industry's 500,000 empty seats per day; in fact, airline tickets proved quite profitable for Priceline.com.

However, both Schulman and Braddock expressed the need for major changes and a shift in business model for Priceline.com. Their major concern dealt with customer satisfaction, and the idea of customers as "consumer freight." Additionally, both executives said that Priceline.com was in need of a new brand identity, one that was based on more than price. Their last concern was that the firm was too dependent upon the travel business. In 1999, 92% of Priceline.com's revenues came from airline ticket sales. This did not bode well for the future, which promised stiff competition from other discounters as well as the airlines themselves hoping to cut out the middleman in the distribution channel.

The announcement on October 5, 2000 that Priceline.com was closing its WebHouse Club was a major setback.[54] The Priceline WebHouse Club announced a 90-day wind-down of operations due to insufficient capital required to complete its business plan and achieve profitability. Priceline WebHouse Club said that it would refund customers for any prepaid amount, plus extra to cover for any expected savings.[55] Priceline.com had to overcome the loss of this major investment as well as the loss of confidence by investors. Priceline.com also needed to prove, despite the failure of Priceline WebHouse Club, that its core business model was economically viable.

The major question for most analysts concerned the business model's ability to increase profitability and carry Priceline.com into the future. The demise of Priceline WebHouse Club and Priceline Perfect Yardsale did not portend well for the firm's pricing system, the core competency of its business model.

Additionally, on the heels of the report of the demise of Priceline WebHouse Club, legal firms began filing class action lawsuits against Priceline.com alleging that "Priceline knew but did not disclose that its third-quarter results would not meet expectations."[56] The lawsuit also claimed that a Priceline insider sold $240 million worth of stock before Priceline.com, made public that third-quarter results would fall short of expectations.[57]

The consumer complaints did not end with the class action lawsuit. The Attorney General of Connecticut, upon the receipt of hundreds of complaints against Priceline.com, removed the firm from the Better Business Bureau. The complaints were associated with the airline as well as the gasoline business units. As a result, the state of Connecticut announced that it would investigate the possibility that Priceline.com had engaged in fraudulent business practices. The Attorney General was quoted as saying, "the model itself is not necessarily flawed, it may simply be aspects of its execution."[58]

With all Priceline.com's problems, it was not clear what the firm's future would hold. Outsiders had begun questioning Walker's business dealings and analysts were questioning the viability of the business model. In addition, the pressure for Internet companies to show a profit also led to a lack of shareholder confidence. Despite all of this, management continued to stress the need to address customer complaints and to diversify and add to its product line.

The Future

Jay Walker faces an uphill battle. He must devise a strategy to regain the confidence of the firm's shareholders and the general public. The company must also fend off increased competition in its core business in airline ticket sales. All the recent negative press about Priceline.com has tarnished the company's image. Walker must find a way to rebuild the Priceline.com brand to its former status as one of the most well known Internet companies in the world.

There is an upside to Priceline.com's current situation, however. The company is currently ranked fourth in terms of consumer mind share and is the fifth most visited site on the Internet.[59] Walker's challenge therefore revolves around transforming Priceline.com's mind share into market share. However with sliding technology stocks, Walker's depleted personal finances, the closing of Webhouse Club Inc., and Priceline.com's lack of profit, Walker's quest for profitability with little or no funding available places Priceline.com's future in doubt.

Questions that e-commerce insiders and analysts were asking include: Would Priceline.com be successful in combating complaints and legal battles concerning its business practices? Could the Priceline.com brand name be equated with more than just the lowest price, so as to capture a larger market share than simply coupon-cutters and spendthrifts? Would Priceline.com overcome the negative press that the demise of WebHouse Club and Perfect Yardsale created? Could Priceline.com compete with the steadily increasing airline reservation business? Most importantly, would the "name your own price" business model remain viable in the 21st century competitive landscape?

References

1. Yahoo! Finance, Statistics at a glance—NasdaqNM:PCLN 201, http://biz.yahoo.com/p/p/pcln.html, June 5.
2. Priceline.com Investor Relations Page, 2001, 2000 Annual Report, http://www.corporate-ir.net/ireye/ir_site.zhtml?ticker=pcln&script=700, June 4, p. 22.
3. Upside Today Newsroom, Grove: The party's over, 2000, http://www.upside.com/News/39e646860.html, October 14.
4. Market Guide Home page, Significant Developments Report for priceline.com Inc., 2000, http://yahoo.marketguide.com/mgi/signdevt.asp?nss=yahoo&rt=signdevt&rn=A1E44, October 5.
5. Loomis, C., 2000, Inside Jay Walker's House of Cards, Fortune, November 13: 127+.
6. Ibid.
7. Market Guide Home page, Significant Developments Report for priceline.com Inc.
8. Schoolman, J., 2000, Priceline on Wall Street is a Name Your Own Loser, Daily News, September 28: 44.
9. Loomis, Inside Jay Walker's House of Cards, 127+.
10. Priceline.com Investor Relations Page, For the First Time, Consumers Can Use the Power of the Internet to Name Their Own Price for Major Purchases, 2001, http://www.corporate-ir.net/ireye/ir_site.zhtml?ticker=pcln&script=410&layout=7&item_id=23938, June 5.
11. Priceline.com Investor Relations Page, Newcomer Priceline.com Sells More Than 10,000 Leisure Airline Tickets In its First Six Week, 2001, http://www.corporate-ir.net=ireye=ir_site.zhtml?ticker=pcln&script=401&layout=7&item_id=23931, June 5.
12. Priceline.com Investor Relations Page, Priceline.com Board Of Directors Announces Promotion of Daniel H. Schulman To President And Chief Executive Officer, 2000, http://www.corporate-ir.net/ireye/ir_site.zhtml?ticker=pcln&script=410&layout=7&item_id=92885, October 6.
13. Junnarkar, S., 2001, Priceline.com appoints new CEO, CNET news.com, http://news.cnet.com/news/0,10000,0-1007-200-332656,00.html, June 5.
14. Priceline.com Investor Relations Page, Priceline.com Board of Directors Announces Promotion of Daniel H. Schulman To President And Chief Executive Officer.
15. Priceline.com Investor Relations Page, Leisure Travelers Can Now Name Their Own Price for Airline Tickets, 2000, http://www.corporate-ir.net/ireye/ir_site.zhtml?ticker=pcln&script=410&layout=7&item_id=23935, October 6.
16. Priceline.com Investor Relations Page, Priceline.com Announces Plans To Add 35 More U.S. Cities To Its Hotel Service In January, 2000, http://www.corporate-ir.net/ireye/ir_site.zhtml?ticker=pcln&script=410&layout=7&item_id=23694, October 6.
17. Priceline.com Investor Relations Page, Priceline.com's New Hotel Service Now Available Over The Phone, 2000, http://www.corporate-ir.net/ireye/ir_site.zhtml?ticker|=pcln&script=410&layout=7&item_id_=23693, October 6.
18. Market Guide Home Page, Significant Developments Report for priceline.com Inc.
19. Priceline.com Investor Relations Page, Hertz And Alamo Join Budget And National In Priceline.com Car Rental Program, 2000, http://www.corporate-ir.net/ireye/ir_site.zhtml?ticker=pcln&script=410&=layout=-6&item_id=95881, October 6.
20. Priceline.com Investor Relations Page, Priceline.com To Broaden Its Cost-Saving Business Model By Offering Name-Your-Own-Price International And Domestic Long Distance Service, 2000, http://www.corporate-ir.net/ireye/ir_site.zhtml?ticker=pcln&script=410&layout=7&item_id=60064, October 6

21. Priceline.com Investor Relations Page, priceline.com Anticipates 3rd Quarter Revenue To Be Below Expectations, 2001, http://www.corporate-ir.net/ireye/ir_site.zhtml?ticker=pcln&script=410&layout=-6&item_id=119343, June 5.
22. Ibid.
23. BBC News, 2000, Priceline plunges on competition fears, June 29.
24. Rewick, J., 2000, Priceline Warns of Weak Revenue On Slow Sales of Airline Tickets, *The Wall Street Journal*, September 28.
25. Wolverton, T., 1999, Expedia to customers: name your hotel room price, CNET News.com, http://news.cnet.com/news/0-1007-200-113636.html, September 7.
26. AP, 1999, Priceline.com claims Microsoft created "copycat" service, *San Francisco Examiner*, Oct. 14.
27. Bodzewski, J., 1999, Expedia and Microsoft to Dismiss Priceline Case, Hospitality.net, http://www.hospitalitynet.org, Dec. 21.
28. Wolverton, T., 1999, Expedia price-matching tool debuts despite Priceline suit, CNET news.com, http://news.cnet.com/news/0-1007-200-1490013.html, Dec. 9.
29. AP, Priceline.com claims Microsoft created "copycat" service.
30. Ibid.
31. Wolverton, Expedia price-matching tool debuts despite Priceline suit.
32. Associatecash.com Travelocity Affilate Reviews, 1999, http://www.associatecash.com/travelocity.shtml, May 03.
33. Ibid.
34. Travelocity.com Company Overview, 2001, http://www.corportate-ir.net/ireye/ir_site.zhtml?ticker=TVLY&script=2100, June 5.
35. Ibid.
36. Ibid.
37. Ibid.
38. Ibid.
39. About.com, New Kid on the "Auction Block"—SkyAuction.com, 1999, http://www.skyauction.com/jsp/skynews.jsp#10, Feb. 17.
40. Ibid.
41. Ibid.
42. Ibid.
43. Ibid.
44. Swoboda, F., 2000, Airlines Readying a Challenger To Priceline, *The Washington Post*, June 30, p. E1.
45. Ibid.
46. Ibid.
47. Ibid.
48. Ibid.
49. Ibid.
50. Smith, J. and Ramirez, C., 2000, Multi-airline ticket site targets Priceline, detnews.com, http://detnews.com/2000/business/0006/30/b01-83686.htm, June 30.
51. Consumer Affairs.com, 2000, Major Airlines Launching Hotwire, Consumer Affairs.com, http://www.consumeraffairs.com/news/hotwire.html, June 29.
52. Schwartz, E., 2000, Airline-backed online travel agency banks on new search engine, CNN.com, http://www.cnn.com/2000/TECH/computing/10/03/airline.agency.idg/index.html, Oct. 3.
53. Ibid.
54. Market Guide Home page, Significant Developments Report for priceline.com Inc.
55. Ibid.
56. Farmer, M. and Junnarkar, S., 2000, Priceline affiliate runs out of gas, CNET News.com, http://news.cnet.com/news/0-1007-200-2936507.html, October 5.
57. Ibid.
58. Woodyard, C. and Krantz, M., 2000, Priceline Hits a Sour Chord as Connecticut Opens Fraud Investigation, *USA Today*, September 29.
59. Wolverton, Expedia price-matching tool debuts despite Priceline suit.

PricewaterhouseCoopers: Building a Global Network

Marissa McCauley
Minako Fukagata
P. Lovelock
Ali Farhoomand

University of Hong Kong

On 1 July, 1998, Price Waterhouse and Coopers & Lybrand merged to form PricewaterhouseCoopers (PwC), creating one of the world's largest full-service professional organisations. The move was an attempt to meet the increasing client needs for scale and global presence. As a result of the merger, PwC engaged in six lines of business across 24 industries in over 152 countries worldwide, with over 150,000 representatives.[1]

As service professional organisations, the companies had two major assets: their personnel, and the knowledge base of those personnel. Before the merger, both firms were already established information specialists, focused on developing efficient internal networking practices as a competitive advantage. For the new company to be successful, PwC required a system that would enable them to fully utilise their extended resources. Thus, the challenge faced by PwC in the wake of the merger was how to create a global organisation that could fully integrate and add value to the new assets it had acquired. The key to this challenge was how to successfully integrate the internal networks of the firms into one network for the new,

larger entity that would incorporate and build on the strengths of the two merging firms.

PricewaterhouseCoopers' ultimate goal was to establish a common global knowledge base: a networked information service that would be available to the PwC workforce and its clients. To achieve this, however, PwC had to consider size—about 150,000 partners and staff with a geographical coverage in 152 countries and territories—in integrating and linking them together. Prior to the merger, PW and C&L operated from different IT platforms. In addition, there were thousands of databases in different types of servers that had to be rationalised for a global knowledge database to be put into effect. How could such a knowledge-intensive firm go about creating an Intranet on a global scale? How could it create a new information product based on a global Intranet and worldwide resources of information and professional practice? What was the best means to implement the new structure such that both the PwC workforce and its clients would be able to access it?

The Industry Trend Towards Consolidation

For over 30 years since the mid-1950s, the professional services industry consisted of eight major players, known as the "Big Eight." This picture changed when the first move towards consolidation took place in the late 1980s, when Deloitte Haskins & Sells coupled with Touche Ross & Co. to create Deloitte & Touche, and Ernst & Whinney joined with Arthur Young & Co. to form Ernst & Young. In 1989, the "Big Eight" was reduced to the "Big Six."

The second wave of industry consolidation took place in September 1997, when Price Waterhouse (PW) announced its merger with Coopers & Lybrand (C&L).[2] In October 1997, Ernst & Young and KPMG Peat Marwick followed suit. The planned E&Y/KPMG merger, however, dissolved in February 1998 due to regulatory issues, client disruption and some cultural issues. On the PW/C&L side, they quietly continued to see their merger through.[3] The industry reduced to the "Big Five" when Price Waterhouse and Coopers & Lybrand confirmed the merger on July 8, 1998. All of the "Big Five"—PricewaterhouseCoopers, KPMG Peat Marwick, Ernst & Young, Anderson Worldwide, and Deloitte Touche Tomatsu—offered consulting services ranging from taxation consulting through to change management, IT, and legal consultancy.

Consolidation was considered the most effective way for companies of this nature to expand their range of services, global capabilities, market share and intellectual capital. As clients expanded their business globally, it became necessary for professional services companies to likewise expand their global presence. Clients wanted the same application to be applied simultaneously to their respective offices worldwide, which meant service professional firms were required to have a matching (and therefore global) presence in order to be able to respond to such demands.

The merger announcement made by Price Waterhouse and Coopers & Lybrand was spurred by this growing need for global scale and presence. The size of the new company as the result of the merger gave both the firm and its clients the advantages of scope and economies of scale. In the light of increasing competition, achieving global presence in terms of scale and scope was one way to gain an advantage over competitors. Achieving organisational economies of scale became important, especially as business became more technology-oriented. In a business environment where speed was one of the important elements for success, companies required new technologies that would enable them to provide better ways to conduct business. Keeping the company at the cutting edge of technology required vast capital investments, and consolidation was a solution to boost capital as well as to utilise the capital in the most efficient manner.

Scale also enabled the company to respond to requests from certain market segments (such as the growing emerging markets) that were not fully covered prior to consolidation. Expanding the scope of business was important as it enabled clients to be provided with more comprehensive services and solutions, and at the same time, it differentiated the company from its competitors. The use of technology, including Intranets, and the ability to share information fundamentally improved communication between PwC clients, its

workforce and business clients, particularly across an increasing platform (global as well as organisational). The focus of PwC on the knowledge management system would bring value to PwC clients such that it would ensure access to greater resources, with faster deployment of specialists and of new products and services through more efficient management of a larger investment pool.

PricewaterhouseCoopers: The Firm

The origins of Price Waterhouse and Coopers & Lybrand date back to the mid-1800s, when both companies started as accounting firms based in London. Each company gradually expanded its business through business partnerships, and by the late 1980-90s, they had both grown to become global companies offering professional services well beyond accounting. At the time of the merger, both companies were offering services in Assurance and Business Advisory Services (Auditing), Management Consulting, Human Resource Management, Tax and Legal Services, Financial Advisory, and Business Process Outsourcing. [Refer to Exhibit 1 for PwC industries with old company equivalents and to Exhibit 2 for PwC's chronological history before the 1998 merger.]

The two companies merged on July 1, 1998, to create one of the world's largest full-service professional organisations. As a result of the merger, the new company, PricewaterhouseCoopers (PwC), surpassed Arthur Andersen, which had previously been considered the industry giant in terms of asset size. PwC had more than 150,000 people in 152 countries and annual revenues pushing US$16 billion.[4, 5]

> "The merger brings together complementary capabilities to add value to our clients of all sizes throughout the world. Clients in the United States will benefit from Coopers & Lybrand's strengths in strategy and human resource consulting and Price Waterhouse's equally strong packaged software and global IT implementation practices. Combined, the two organisations offer clients a powerful consulting resource."
> —Cees G. van Lujik, Chairman,
>   Coopers & Lybrand Europe, and Jermyn Brooks,
>   Chairman, Price Waterhouse[6]

PwC provided unprecedented service to global, national and local companies in markets worldwide; offering a comprehensive range of business assurance, business advisory, tax, management, IT and human resource consulting services and a commitment to helping clients formulate and implement strategic solutions that drive growth and improve business performance. The two

Exhibit 1   PwC Industries with Old Company Equivalents

PricewaterhouseCoopers Industries	Price Waterhouse	Coopers & Lybrand
Financial Services Industry	**Financial Services (FSIP)**	**Financial Services**
• Banking	• Banking	• Banking
• Capital Markets	• Investment Management	• Capital Markets
• Investment Management	• Insurance	• Insurance
• Insurance	• Management Health Care	• Investment Management
• Real Estate	• Real Estate	
	• Securities	
Services Industry		**Real Estate and Hospitality Engineering & Construction**
• Government		
• Health Care		
• Education & Not-For-Profit		**Government Contracting**
• Transport		
• Hospitality		**Integrated Health Care**
• Engineering & Construction		• Health Care
• Posts		• Pharmaceutical
		• Health Information Management (HIM) related services
		Higher Education & Not-For-Profits
		State & Local Government
		Transportation
Global Energy & Mining Industry (GEM)	**World Energy Group**	**Energy, Utilities & Natural Resources**
• Oil & Gas	• Oil	• Oil & Gas
• Utilities	• Natural Gas	• Utilities
• Mining	• Chemicals	• Mining
	• Independent Power	
	• Mining	
	• Utility	**Manufacturing**
Consumer and Industrial Products (CIP)	**Products**	• Automotive
		• Consumer & Industrial
• Consumer Packaged Goods		
• Pharmaceutical		**Retail**
• Retail		
• Automotive		
• Industrial Products		
Technology, Info/Comm and Entertainment (TICE)	**Entertainment, Media & Communications (EMC)**	**High Technology**
• Technology		• Life Sciences (biotechnology & medical technology)
• Information/Communications		• New Media
• Media & Entertainment		• Computer Software, Computing and Electronic
	Technology Industry Group	• Venture Capital
	• Computers & Peripherals	
	• Life Sciences	**Information & Entertainment**
	• Networking & Communications	
	• Semiconductors & Semiconductor Equipment	**Media & Entertainment**
	• Software	

Exhibit 2　　PwC History

Year	Event
1849	Samuel Lowell Price sets up in business in London
1854	William Cooper establishes his own practice in London, which seven years later becomes Cooper Brothers
1865	Price, Holyland and Waterhouse join forces in partnership
1874	Name changes to Price, Waterhouse and Co.
1898	Robert H. Montgomery, William M. Lybrand, Adam A. Ross, Jr. and his brother T. Edward Ross form Lybrand, Ross Brothers and Montgomery
1957	Cooper Brothers & Co (UK), McDonald, Currie and Co (Canada) and Lybrand, Ross Bros & Montgomery (US) merge to form Coopers & Lybrand
1982	Price Waterhouse World Firm formed
1990	Coopers and Lybrand merges with Deloitte Haskins & Sells in a number of countries around the world
1998	Worldwide merger of Price Waterhouse and Coopers & Lybrand to create PricewaterhouseCoopers

SOURCE: URL:http://www.pwcglobal.com/gx/eng/about/press-rm/fact.html, 29 May, 2000.

firms were similar in terms of business lines and geographical coverage; however, they were not necessarily similar in terms of industry coverage. The uniting of the various practices offered by Price Waterhouse and Coopers & Lybrand was expected to bring significant benefits to clients, particularly in those industries that were rapidly converging and in which sector distinctions were becoming less pronounced and competition more intense.

For example, Coopers & Lybrand's strength in telecommunications could be combined with Price Waterhouse's global expertise in the media and entertainment sectors, creating a powerful industry specialists' group. This was also in accordance with the converging trend between these industries. Within the telecommunications industry, Coopers & Lybrand's strength was in consulting, while Price Waterhouse's strength was in auditing. Combining the two companies therefore enabled the new entity to provide clients with comprehensive and extended services. In the products sector, Price Waterhouse had significant presence in chemicals, while Coopers & Lybrand was strong in consumer products, and they were both strong in the pharmaceutical sector. In the energy sector, there were complementary strengths in oil and gas, mining and utilities. In the financial services sector, the two organisations combined offered unmatched worldwide capabilities in banking, insurance and brokerage and mutual funds. [Refer to Exhibit 3 for the specific industry strengths of PW and C&L.]

Corporate Structure

"We are global, and because we are global, we are local—there to serve you wherever you are."
—PricewaterhouseCoopers Website Home Page[7]

There was no formal headquarters for PwC, but the global leadership was based in New York, Frankfurt and London. Headquarters would be wherever services were delivered, which could be anywhere in the world.[8] PwC also split the structure into three "theatres" namely: the Americas; Europe, the Middle East and Africa; and the Asia Pacific. The Global Executive Team was composed of eight executives including the Chairman, CEO, and six Global Leaders in-charge in Industries, Geography, Service Line, Human Resources, Operations and Risk Management.

There was some overlap on the support side of business that required rationalisation as tasks performed by support staff from both companies were basically the same; downsizing was inevitable for the new organisation to function in an efficient manner. This was not an easy task and it created some tension during the consolidation process. However, overall integration was achieved relatively smoothly as PW and C&L started working together in October 1997, nine months before the merger announcement, to put the heads of the business function in place at an accelerated fashion to minimise the transition time.

| Exhibit 3 | Industry Strengths of Price Waterhouse and Coopers & Lybrand |

Price Waterhouse
- Packaged software and global IT implementation practices
- Global expertise in the media and entertainment sectors
- Auditing in the telecommunications industry

- Expertise in chemicals

Coopers & Lybrand
- Strategy and human resource consulting

- Telecommunications
- Consulting in the telecommunications industry

- Expertise in consumer products and manufacturing

- Strong in pharmaceutical sectors
- Energy sector (oil and gas, mining and utilities)
- Financial services sector (banking, insurance and brokerage and mutual funds)

As with many of the other companies in the professional services industry, both Price Waterhouse and Coopers & Lybrand were organised in a matrix structure by region, with lines of service running in one direction and industry running across in the other direction. Traditionally, both PW and C&L were very line-of-service-oriented organisations, as being more industry-focused was a relatively new phenomenon in professional services. According to David Lambert, Marketing Communications Director of PwC, "the tilt is towards line of service, but the impetus is towards industry."[9] The line of service was the historical model in which most of the PwC people were well versed. The PwC workforce was being pushed in the direction of being within the line of service, focusing on a particular industry in a certain geography. For PwC, there was the focus in the industry, but the history was with the line of service.

PwC consisted of six lines of business and 24 market sectors clustered into five groups. The seven business lines were: Audit; Assurance and Business Advisory Services; Business Process Outsourcing; Financial Advisory Services; Global Human Resource Solutions; Management Consulting Services; and Global Tax Services. The five-industry groups consisted of: Financial Services Industry; Service Industry; Global Energy & Mining Industry; Consumer & Industrial Products; and Technology, Information/Communications and Entertainment.

PwC had an annual revenue of US$17.3 billion worldwide for fiscal 30 June, 1999, a record US$2 billion increase in earnings or up 16 percent over 1998. Since announcing its merger in September 1997, global revenues at PwC increased by more than US$4.5 billion. Significant growth was seen in the Management

Consulting Services and Global Human Resource Solutions, up 27 percent and 28 percent respectively. On a geographical basis, North America and South/Central America showed the strongest growth patterns, with growth rates of 28 percent and 19 percent respectively. PwC Chairman Nicholas Moore said about PwC's robust growth in 1999: "Companies around the world clearly recognise the significant advantages of our breadth and depth of expertise. Equally important, we have already begun to capitalise on the synergies we expected our merger to produce, and have not fallen victim to the internal distractions that frequently plague organisations immediately following a merger."[10] 1999 was also a significant year for PwC as it experienced significant achievements, including the acquisition of other consulting firms and citations from various publications.

The Integration Process

Nine months before the planned announcement of the merger (in October 1997), the PW and C&L teams had already begun working to plan the structure of the new organisation. Both firms managed the transition to a global, integrated organisation and made it up and running as a global operation by 1 July, 1998. Obviously, however, full integration took some time. Overall, PwC went through the integration process in an accelerated fashion.

The planning of the corporate-wide integration was done by the headquarters-based Global Team that reviewed the overall firm and gave guidance to each local office as to how the integration should be done. GTS was the technology team responsible for the planning and implementation of the IT systems within the firm.

Overall, it took the IT team one year to completely unify, standardise and simplify both the PCs and the network infrastructure. First, the team created a bridge between the networks to facilitate communication. The next step was standardising the way LOS was connected to the network and the applications being used.

The partnership structure of PwC enabled it to give more independence to each of its offices around the globe, in terms of their respective decisions regarding the integration process. As a global entity, there were people at headquarters level who were responsible for outlining the big picture as to how the new company should look. The partnership structure, however, meant that individual offices had more flexibility in decision-making, so people could be more pragmatic about how things were done. The Global Team provided guidance, but the final decision was made at each office level at its own discretion. This allowed the GTS team at each office level to modify the original guideline and take a more realistic approach.

PwC Intranet: The Knowledge Curve

Knowledge management was to play an important role in the merger process, as the ability to share knowledge and intellectual capital across the two firms was to become the key to successfully achieving rapid integration with continued client service. The head of the PwC Global Knowledge Management Team explained why knowledge was so important in a professional services firm such as PwC:

> *"To a great extent it is all we have, and all we share and sell. It is the basis of what we do. We sell to clients the knowledge our consultants have and have access to. So managing the resources effectively and making sure we can share it across the consultancy is vital to us. It is the lifeblood of the organisation."*
> —Julia Collins,
> Head of PwC Global Knowledge Group[11]

Technical evolution has enabled cost-effective methods of capturing, updating and distributing knowledge throughout PwC by way of an Intranet. The Intranet was the entry point to capture firm-wide knowledge and make it accessible to the organisation. It was the foundation for stored knowledge, which was the core asset for a knowledge-intensive organisation such as PwC.

Knowledge Curve (KC) was the name of the Intranet introduced to PwC. Originally developed by the IT team from C&L, KC was the core of the PwC Intranet system. KC was the PwC's knowledge management system that incorporated all the assets (knowledge and people skills) of the company to be utilised by the entire firm. To achieve the scale and scope expected from the merger, such a knowledge management system was to play an important role. With careful structuring, this knowledge base could become a powerful tool that could be used as PwC's competitive advantage. Simplicity in usage was important for this knowledge base to be effective, as well as the firm's ability to capture, package and deliver the knowledge.

The KC was advanced in that it enabled extensive profiling from three dimensions: geography, industry, and line of business. As a start, KC was structured on two levels: (1) Knowledge Curve Global and, (2) Knowledge Curve at each office level. PwC's ultimate goal was to have all the knowledge base centralised under Knowledge Curve Global, which would require significant time to be fully accomplished. Thus, at the global level, priorities were given to topics that were more common firm-wide, which meant that there were limitations as to what the central global site could do. In order to complement the limitations of the global site, each office had its own KC home page that incorporated the knowledge base and the information that was important at the local level. Depending on how much a particular knowledge base could be shared firm-wide, a knowledge base at office level was incorporated into the Global knowledge base. Information that was important at the local level but did not have to be "shared," such as personal memos and reminders, was kept at the office level.

One of the GTS's main projects under the GTS Development Team was to build a Website within a local KC. The local portal was designed to complement what KC global had not been able to cover, and to customise KC Global to local needs with added features. The content page would provide the users with office-specific knowledge that would not be incorporated under the global content. As KC Global developed, some of the contents from the local page would shift to the global page. [Refer to Exhibit 5 for the Hong Kong Portal and Hong Kong KnowledgeCurve diagram as an example.]

"The Bridge" and the GTS Channel

Prior to the Knowledge Curve, PwC had a global database called "The Bridge."[12] It was a merger product and the first internal communications product. It assumed correctly that everyone had access to Lotus Notes, but that not everyone had access to the Internet or Intranet. The Bridge was very effective in that it provided a lot of information that could be accessed by everyone.

Likewise, a global database called GTS Channel, which was initially developed for the IT people (about 3,000 personnel), was put in place relatively quickly. After the merger, the GTS Channel was made available to

Case 33 / PricewaterhouseCoopers: Building a Global Network

Exhibit 4   Hong Kong Portal and KnowledgeCurve

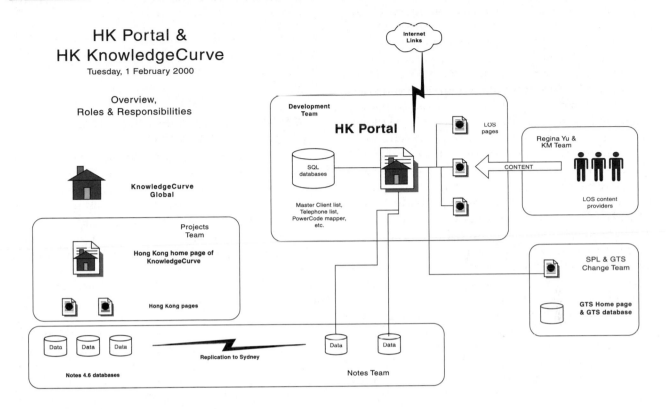

everyone. The GTS Channel had been working well: this integrated focus enabled anyone to walk into any PwC office worldwide, plug in the computer and get to work. The fundamental base-level requirement was TCP/IP, TACP servers and DNS. PwC was able to implement this project quickly, driven to a large degree by what the business was doing globally. As an organisation, PwC recognised that to capture the market space equally, all of its systems and IT had to fit together.

The Knowledge Team

As at February 2000, there were about 300 Knowledge Workers internationally. London-based Julia Collins managed the knowledge resources that served 32,000 fee-earning consultants internationally. Collins supervised 25 staff in the UK, while another 40 worked within PwC's industry and service groups. They included consultants, former consultants, information professionals, and technical experts. These intra-industry group knowledge workers had a brief that included:

- conduct research for the consultants in their teams
- "harvest" knowledge inwards by working with consultants to get knowledge from their assignments into the internal repositories kept by PwC

- help manage content in the central repositories
- ensure an open communication channel between knowledge headquarters and their industry group at the local level

PwC's focus was on making the firm a global entity, and since the merger the KC team had been moving towards global repositories rather than small databases. The industry group knowledge workers managed the content that belonged to their industry group within the global repositories. There were also central groups based in London, Dallas, and Sydney. PwC was also organised into theatres: the Americas; Europe, the Middle East and Africa; and Asia Pacific. UK was the lead for Europe, but there were also large groups in Utrecht, Frankfurt, Paris and Brussels.

One of the strengths of the function was the involvement of all the different industry and service groups; it was, however, difficult to co-ordinate it. PwC was moving quickly to an Intranet platform that would provide a greater chance to integrate everything, eventually eliminating the standard way of informing people, for example, about which database to use. The limitations of the function were mainly related to the team's ability to create awareness about KC, specifically in terms of how the team would go about educating the consultants on the available information in the KC so that they could understand its capabilities and its applications. It was a big challenge to go after the 32,000 consultants and communicate with each one of them and change over to using the global KC, a task that the KC team was still working on as of February 2000. The goal of the team was, by year 2005, to ensure that consultants understood more fully what the KC was and how they could contribute to it. PwC was still building its knowledge base and had yet to hit upon a method to capture the knowledge that existed in people's heads. Collins said that the consultants' perception of the KC varied according to how long the knowledge resources had been established in a specific country or area. A more established knowledge function was well-regarded and well-used, whilst there was more variance in those countries where it was in the process of being established.

The Manager of Communications at PwC had full-time responsibility for promoting the Knowledge Curve. This was a big task as it involved informing the 150,000 PwC workforce scattered throughout 152 different countries about what the PwC Intranet had to offer. Campaigns to increase awareness of the Knowledge Curve included visiting various offices and scheduling presentations throughout the day, spending time teaching people (one-on-one) how to use the system, and distributing literature, give-aways, boomerangs, little wallet cards, posters and flyers. There were also specific professional sessions that helped spur interest. For example, accountants were taught to use the Intranet to do research and prepare taxes for clients.[13]

Promoting the use of the KC was a massive change for PwC people, thus it was important for the staff to understand where to access help once the networks of PW and C&L were merged. Feedback from the PwC workforce was elicited through the Knowledge Point help desk. There was also a staff satisfaction survey (covering the whole of an employee's level of satisfaction with working with PwC) that contained questions related to KC. The KC tracked, year-on-year, whether the team was getting better or not.

PwC consultants could access the knowledge resources mainly through their own computers—either through Lotus Notes or on the Intranet. Once logged-on, the consultants could have access to and direct use of the following:

- all the main information repositories
- general business tools such as Dow Jones Interactive and Harvard Business School resources
- alliance databases that were more specific to the field in which people worked, such as Gartner and Forrester

Knowledge Point, the PwC global knowledge help desk, was another way for users to request searches or access resources. Knowledge Point received about 1,000 calls a month.

The Difference Between Lotus Notes and KnowledgeCurve

Lotus Notes allowed users to conduct searches across some or all of the domains. It also allowed users to search against all documents opened over a certain period. However, on Notes, information on a client was stored by industry and by the line of business, which limited its searching capability for a particular item of information. KnowledgeCurve was different in that it was possible to search for particular information by looking down the business development tree. KnowledgeCurve was introduced to facilitate the search process at a global level. However, there was another issue to be solved. KnowledgeCurve lacked an effective search engine that would allow the knowledge base to function effectively.[14] It was necessary to have a search engine that would enable people to search across databases without knowing that a particular database even existed.

According to Stephen Langley, PwC GTS Director, it would be very effective to be able to properly implement a search engine. In September 1998 the issue of implementing a search engine was discussed in a GTS global meeting in Switzerland and a task force was created to look into this. PwC went through a long process of re-evaluating it, and finally signed a global deal with Verity as the search engine. Verity was the search engine within KnowledgeCurve. As of February 2000 this was not fully implemented.

The Global Knowledge Centre

PwC opened its Global Knowledge Centre on 28 July, 1998. The Knowledge Centre was an integrated facility for knowledge sharing, training, and data warehousing project support. Based in Rosemont, Illinois, the centre was the first of a number of Knowledge Centres planned around the world. Europe was the next site.[15] Through the Global Knowledge Centre, companies would:

- receive hands-on training in many of the leading data warehousing technologies
- have access to continuous market information

- view extensive state-of-the-art product evaluations
- provide an environment where clients could work with PwC consultants to design and develop strategic knowledge-based solutions

At the global level, the Global Knowledge Group worked closely with GTS, looking into ways that could effectively leverage their knowledge assets to respond to clients' needs in a more innovative manner. At each office level, however, Knowledge Managers had been appointed only on a part-time basis by line of business. This was expected to change as knowledge management began to gain more recognition within the firm.

Issues and Challenges in Building the PwC Knowledge Base

"When we merged, we also became a global practice, as we had been country-based before. We faced big change and big challenges in getting people up to speed with how to use things, and how to use the technology which changed when our networks merged."
—Julia Collins,
Head of PwC Global Knowledge Group[16]

Integration at a global scale was not an easy task. One of the things that made the integration process complex was due to the way in which the original systems were developed by each of the firms. Prior to the merger, both PW and C&L had developed their systems around their line-of-business focus and were independent systems. The problem was that this enabled only limited access to the knowledge base by the people within the entire PwC. The new integrated system aimed to eliminate such an inefficient use of assets. Breaking up the closed structure of the original system and creating a system that would enable everyone in PwC to have access to all the knowledge base was the major goal for the new corporate IT system. This required preparation and time to be completed. Other challenges that PwC encountered included:

- Differences in IT systems and organisational structure
- E-mail networking and Intranet using Lotus Notes
- Integration of databases and servers

Pragmatism was driving the essential forward planning and business culture at PwC. The co-ordination process was streamlined and there were fewer bureaucratic procedures. According to Lambert, pragmatism seemed to be coming from a very small group of people who actually made the decisions. There was a shift at PwC because of the information technology evolution and all

of the business pressures that the firm was going through. In service organisations such as PwC, senior people (in age and experience) propelled the business, whereas people in support functions would do what they were told to. This was the case in 1995. As of year 2000, the senior people were still in control of certain parts of the business (profitability and setting high-level strategies); however, they were less involved in decision-making in the day-to-day business. Most of the decisions were down to the "younger" partners and directors, the "older" generation recognising that they were less in touch with what was going on.

Another major change was there was less corporate politics than in 1995, when there were a number of "egos" clashing. As of year 2000, the people below the hierarchy were younger and had the initiative to get things done quickly, so more work was accomplished within a shorter period of time. Although there seemed to be a flatter structure at PwC, there was still a management board that made the policy decisions and approved projects.

Differences in IT Systems and Organisational Structure

There were distinctive differences between PW and C&L in the way the companies operated. Integration was easier on the PW side of the system since its IT team had been working together on a regional basis before the merger. PW used the same software, Novell, and had worked in setting up some of the standards. Though this was rather a loose standard, PW had 70 to 80 percent of the system in common at the time of the merger, which facilitated the integration of the systems on the PW side. Having two IT Directors from each side also added some conflict in the earlier stage of the integration process, especially regarding the issue of rationalising the IT personnel.

On the other hand, C&L's IT team was more independent of the others, so there was less co-ordination among the IT teams around the world. C&L's IT team was autonomous in terms of personnel and the technology used. In addition to such a fragmented IT structure, C&L's IT level was outdated. C&L had their own Novell server version 3.0, originally set up in 1995, which they were using until the merger. This was the case with C&L's Lotus Notes; it was not the updated version. There was no TCP/IP on the network, which was a basic communication language or protocol of the Internet or in private networks such as Intranets and/or Extranets. C&L, however, was more advanced in its Audit group, where they used electronic working papers.

There were strong global IT directions at PwC that had not happened on either side before. On the scale of the merger, things happened on a global level and a strong leadership emerged and started work on planning. Two major things were achieved: (1) the Global Wide Area Network (GWAN), which was to link the wide area networks of PW and C&L, and (2) integration of the Lotus Notes Domain.[17]

E-Mail Networking and Intranet Using Lotus Notes

Linking the e-mail system was the first focus of integration. From prior merger examples, PW and C&L were aware that establishing a solid internal communications system would be a key factor for the new company to run smoothly. This part of the integration was facilitated by both firms using Lotus Notes for their e-mail and Intranet systems.[18] Still, it took the IT team one whole year of thorough planning to have the integrated e-mail system running in time with the operation of PwC in July 1999. As of February 2000, this work was still on-going.

When the Global Team announced the global e-mail networking plan, the IT officers at the office level were sceptical, as the structure and routing was so complex and impractical. In one structure, the e-mail messages between the two offices in the same geographical location were routed via distant servers, causing hours of delivery delays. For example, the global networking plan in Hong Kong required messages from PW to C&L offices to be routed via Sydney, causing two hours of delivery delay. This was addressed immediately by the IT team, who were not obligated to follow the global executives, but instead opted for the most practical solution.

The most complicated part of the e-mail integration was the restructuring of the topology of Lotus Notes Domain. The domain restructuring for PwC was said to have been one of the most complicated restructuring tasks ever done. For example, PW had 115 domains that were to be reduced to seven; while C&L had some 100 domains in Hong Kong alone, while each country had its own domain that also had to be reduced.

The Notes topology also required restructuring. As PW was one of the earliest companies to implement the system, what they had in place was a flat structure type of Notes. C&L used the latter version of Notes, which had a hierarchical structure, and PwC was to implement the hierarchical structure. There were a number of technical issues that had to be dealt with when trying to merge the two Notes versions. One of the difficulties in getting everything hierarchical had to do with the security structure of Notes. To remedy this situation required drilling down to the database level and sometimes even to the document level.

Internal and External Communication: Hong Kong and Sydney Offices as an Illustration

Before the merger, PW had a couple of mail servers, a major database server and Reuters. These all went via Sydney. On the CL side, they had a hub server, a database server, separate mail server lines of service and an audit electronic working paper, which were also routed via Sydney. The difficulty was that the link in Sydney was slow, the replication time and the Notes structure on one side was not optimal. [Refer to the Figure 1 for the old model flow of information between PW to C&L. Refer to Exhibit 4 for the Hong Kong Notes Topology effective September 1999.] As of September 1999, PwC had only one link to Sydney, which was being upgraded every other month. The number of servers, although being reduced, had yet to be rationalised as there were not that many changes done; PwC kept all the mail and audit servers.

PwC's external communication would still go through a hub. Again, the external communication systems of both PW and C&L were different prior to the merger. C&L had its own domain and its own Internet link and had to push Internet e-mail directly out from Hong Kong. PW did it through global gateways, which went through via the US. After the merger, PwC was able to quickly switch everybody onto a PwC Internet address, thus even though the two firms were internally "PW" and "C&L" to the outside world on the Internet, the Internet address was www.pwcglobal.com. This meant the hub went via the US. Only in February 1999 was PwC able to install a third Internet gateway, and was therefore hubbed into Sydney.

The remaining tasks for the Notes would be the re-certification of the Notes IDs to a global standard and getting them into a hierarchical structure, a project that would be done on a regional basis. Under the change, each Notes name would include line of service, city, and country. This would be a big process, as it would affect all of the underlying security within Lotus Notes. In addition, standardisation of the Notes templates and upgrading the entire Lotus Notes infrastructure would take place. The project started in February 2000 in Asia.

PwC had an elaborate process of setting up a dedicated, private link into the client's system, such as BAT, the purpose being to secure communication with the client. The system, however, was never fully utilised because of the complexity in its use. For example, Hong Kong set up a separate Notes domain in Asia Pacific for external clients using three gateways—Australia, New Zealand and Hong Kong—which enabled access into and out of whichever local gateway was required.

Figure 1   Information Flow Between PW and C&L

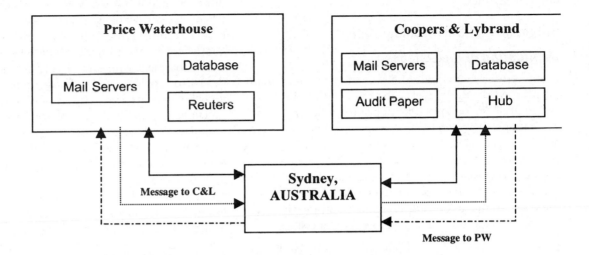

There was strong co-ordination and communication between the IT workforce in Hong Kong and in Sydney that helped in the integration and standardisation of the PwC techno-infrastructure. Langley said "Sydney had, traditionally, a competent IT team and the Hong Kong office, which was the largest office in Asia, benefited from that strong interaction."[19] For example, Sydney would run the main consolidation and re-certification of the Notes on a regional basis. Sydney also managed the Wide Area Network in Asia Pacific. Because of Sydney's

Exhibit 5   Hong Kong Notes Topology

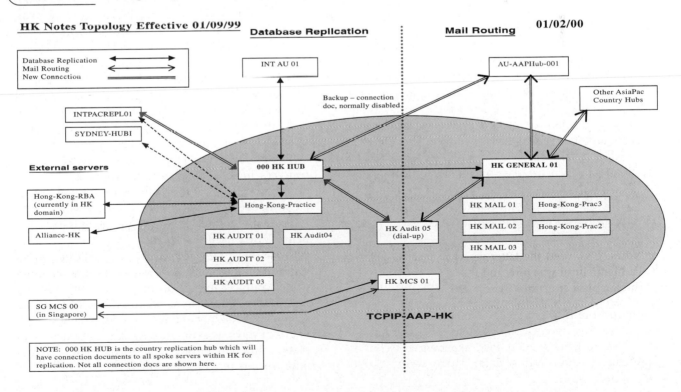

strong IT team and willingness to do work for other PwC people around the region, those who were relatively autonomous would choose to use the products produced by Sydney.

Database and Server Integration
Duplication of the Database

There were many duplications of the database that, together with the servers, required rationalisation. Rationalisation took place starting at the office level. The database problem was typified by the fact that there were hundreds of databases in one country location alone. To rationalise, the content of each database had to be checked and re-evaluated by those responsible for those databases. Such a task was beyond what the IT workforce could do, so the task was delegated to the respective line of service. The process included the following steps:

1. Identification of the data owner—a complicated and a time-consuming process, but it was completed in a relatively smooth manner
2. The identified owner was given the responsibility for updating the database on a regular basis

If the owner could not be identified, data was sent into an archive database. PwC's key to data management was to make sure that every record had an owner who could update the content on a regular basis. Preventing the data from becoming obsolete gave the data more value.

Closed Vs. Open Database

Historically, there was no one officially assigned to manage a certain database, and many of the databases were merely stored without being accessed or updated. For example, the contacts databases in the pre-merger were different. In the C&L firm, the contacts database was relatively closed—partners put their contacts in a central database and they were the only people who could view and update details on their contacts. On the PW side, there was an open database—anybody could see anybody's contacts, but only the data owners could edit it. PwC decided to have an open database as it was seen to be counterproductive to maintain a closed one.

Data Transfer

The next step in rationalising the database was to categorise it and eliminate any duplication. This, again, was a time-consuming process. However, it was a process that had to be done to create an efficient, powerful knowledge base. In January 2000, PwC experienced technical problems in transferring data. There were 25,000 records, of which about 5,000 were duplicates in the contacts database. The IT team had to go through the records and take the duplicates out; a process that was done manually. (There were instances, for example, where an old C&L partner had a PW contact in his database. In February 2000, PwC was able to develop a system where a hard copy of the data list was sent out to various partners, with every record allocated to partners. PwC had implemented a programme that facilitated updating the data: every couple of months the marketing functions prompts the data owners by sending a memo to update their contacts list.)

Generally, the type of information in PwC's Lotus Notes was in the form of documents. PW was not using SQL as it was more focused on using Notes before the merger, whereas C&L had a strong development team using SQL. This made the two systems compatible when brought together during the merger.

Plans to Improve the PwC Technical Infrastructure

At the beginning of year 2000, GTS main focus was on GTS itself: its internal policies and procedures. GTS was reviewing its administrative systems and how it could communicate better with PwC's customers.

- *Development Team* — Projects included building the local level KC, the "Executive Dimension" (a multidimensional data analysis tool that would be used for analysing Power data and many other types of data), and numerous other systems, including leave management, tax management, executive recruitment, CA Pacific and document management.
- *Network Team* — This team would continue to consolidate servers, starting with ABAS. A new application server was implemented on-line to be used firm-wide for applications and data-sharing, which facilitated the delivery of applications and systems updates across the firm. The two servers ran on NetWare 5 and were Fibre Channel servers.[20] Other concerns included network management, monitoring, security and Internet service. The Virtual Private Network (VPN) was also part of the Network team's responsibility. Notes, voicemail and (with NetWare 5) network files would be available via VPN.
- *Notes Team* — Year 2000 would be dedicated to re-certification of notes IDs. Everyone's official notes name would change to include line of service, city and country: a global standard within PwC. Other projects included: enabling notes addressing via initials for everyone, standardising the Notes mail templates, and upgrading all of the Lotus Notes infrastructure to Notes version 5.

- *Projects Team* — Maintenance and upgrade of the POWER system to the testing and implementation of the new systems and technology, such as office 2000, would be key projects. Also, the team would test and evaluate new and emerging technology such as voice recognition software.
- *Helpdesk Team* — The staffing level was at an appropriate level to be able to provide the service levels that PwC required. The major effort was focusing on how calls were answered, improving first call resolution, speedy response and utilising tools such as remote control software.

PwC had resources that other professional service organisations lack. Fully integrating all the resources at a global as well as organisational level to create a knowledge base was the main challenge. This would mean successfully integrating the internal networks and the *use* of the network. Therefore, PwC had to effectively manage and share the knowledge base across the firm. After all, knowledge was the "lifeblood" of PwC and it was all PwC had to "share and sell."

Endnotes

1. URL: http://www.pwcglobal.com, 14 January, 2000.
2. Law, G., "And Then There Were Four…", *Management* (45:1), Auckland, February, 1998. pp. 68-70.
3. "Big 6 Firm Mergers. On, Off and In Court", *Bowman's Accounting Report* (12:2), Atlanta, February, 1998, pp. 10–12.
4. US$1 = HK$8
5. Anonymous, "Top 100 People: Moore, Schiro: 'We Changed the Competitive Landscape'", *Accounting Today*, 28 September, 1998 to 11 October, 1998.
6. URL: http://www.colybrand.com/news/091897.html, 19 January, 2000.
7. URL: http://www.pwcglobal.com/gx/eng/about/main/index.html, 29 May, 2000.
8. URL: http://www.pwcglobal.com/extweb/nc…, 14 January, 2000.
9. Interview with David Lambert (Marketing Communications Director) and Stephen Langley (Global Technology Solutions Director), PwC, Hong Kong, 1 February, 2000.
10. URL: http://www.pwcglobal.com/extweb/nc…D/ CCA2BEF3DF2DCC148525686C0074296E, 11 February, 2000.
11. Thomson, S., "Focus: Keeping Pace With Knowledge", *Information Week Review* (155), Oxford, February, 2000, pp. 23-24.
12. In telecommunications networks, a bridge is a product that connects a local area network to another local area network that uses the same protocol. Bridging networks are generally always interconnected local area networks since broadcasting every message to all possible destinations would flood a larger network with unnecessary traffic. (See URL: wysiwyg://def.133/http://www.whatiscom.bridge.htm, 31 May, 2000.)
13. Leong, K.C., "Marketing Gets Innovative", *Internetweek* (763), 3 May, 1999, p. 27.
14. Larger corporate sites may use a search engine to index and retrieve the content of just their own site.
15. URL: http://www.pwcglobal.com/extweb/nc…D/ 100A24F2676A85C385256657006373E0, 30 May, 2000.
16. Thomson, S., "Focus: Keeping Pace With Knowledge", *Information Week Review* (155), Oxford, February, 2000, pp. 23-24.
17. Interview with Lambert and Langley of PwC, Hong Kong, 1 February, 2000.
18. Notes is a sophisticated groupware application from the Lotus Corporation, a subsidiary of IBM. Notes lets a corporation and its workers develop communications- and database-oriented applications so that users at different geographic locations can share files with each other, comment on them publicly or privately (to groups with special access), keeps track of development schedules, work projects, guidelines and procedures, plans, white papers, and many other documents, including multimedia files. Notes keeps track of changes and makes updates to replications of all databases in use at any site. Changes are made at the field level to minimise network traffic. (Definition of Notes from URL: wysiwyg://def.71/http://www.whatiscom.notes.htm, 30 May, 2000.)
19. Interview with Lambert and Langley, PwC Hong Kong, 1 February, 2000.
20. Fibre Channel servers use fibre optic technology between the server and the discs and have very high data transfer rates.

Sony Playstation2: Just Another Competitor?

Rita Chiu, Christopher Chou
Boston University

Melissa A. Schilling
New York University

A New Era of Game Consoles

Ken Kutaragi, president of Sony Computer Entertainment Inc., leaned back in his chair, contemplating the rapid pace of events that had been unfurling since late 1999. It was spring of 2000, and Sony had just launched its brand new 128-bit video game console, called the Playstation2, in Japan. During the opening sales weekend of March 4, 2000, Playstation2 sales reached about one million units, a figure that eclipsed by ten times the amount of original Playstation units sold during the three-day release period in 1994. Demand for the new unit was so high that on the opening day of pre-orders on Sony's website, over 100,000 hits in one minute were received, and Sony was forced to briefly shut the website down.

Such news should have made Ken Kutaragi ecstatic. Not only was he the president of the company producing the Playstation2, but he was also the inventor and genius behind both the original and new Playstation consoles. The original Playstation had been so successful that by 1998, profits from Playstation games and consoles constituted 40 percent of Sony Corporation's profit.[1] His and Sony's $2 billion gamble on the PS2 console seemed to be an assured success.

However, several issues bothered the 49-year-old former engineer. Sega had introduced its new 128-bit system, the *Dreamcast*, in late 1999. The Dreamcast, while not possessing as much power or speed as the PS2, possessed the capability of narrowband (56K) access to the Internet. It also promised players access to online gaming through its Dreamcast online network. The Playstation2 was to provide broadband, high-speed Internet access in 2001 and also contained ports for hooking up a cable TV, keyboard, mouse, digital-video camera, and modem card. The potential value was huge —however, as of spring 2000, the PS2 was not much more than a DVD and CD game player. Also, Kutaragi and his company were plagued daily by such problems as chip shortages, faulty memory cards, and underproduction. Another issue that worried Kutaragi was that of the upcoming Nintendo release of its new console, the *Dolphin*, and the unexpected announcement by Microsoft that it too would be producing a game console.

The History of Sony

Sony Corporation was founded in May of 1946, as Tokyo Tsushin Kogyo, or Tokyo Telecommunications Engineering Corporation. The founders were two young entrepreneurs named Masaru Ibuka and Akio Morita, who had become jobless after World War II. Their stated reason for forming the company was:

> *To create a stable work environment where engineers who had a deep and profound appreciation for technology could realize their societal mission and work to their heart's content.*[2]

The company officially became "Sony" after a company restructuring in 1958. Its goal was "to establish an ideal factory, free, dynamic, and pleasant, where technical personnel of sincere motivation can exercise their technological skill to the highest level."[3] Sony's focus had changed from that of communications equipment to the broader category of electronics.

Rita Chiu and Christopher Chou prepared this case under the supervision of Professor Melissa A. Schilling as the basis for class discussion rather than to illustrate either effective or ineffective handling of an administrative situation.

Exhibit 1   Sales Breakdown by Category

Year ended March 31 (Millions of yen)

	1997	1998	1999
Electronics	3,930,292 (69.4)	4,377,346 (64.8)	4,355,001 (64.1)
Audio	1,029,961 (18.2)	1,127,788 (16.7)	1,072,621 (15.8)
Video	816,582 (14.4)	870,854 (12.9)	969,129 (14.3)
Televisions	704,075 (12.4)	709,043 (10.5)	702,620 (10.3)
Information and communications	764,512 (13.5)	894,810 (13.2)	914,140 (13.5)
Electronic components and other	615,162 (10.9)	774,851 (11.5)	696,491 (10.2)
Game	408,335 (7.2)	699,574 (10.4)	760,071 (11.2)
Music	570,119 (10.1)	660,407 (9.8)	718,878 (10.6)
Pictures	438,551 (7.7)	642,714 (9.5)	540,109 (7.9)
Insurance	227,920 (4.0)	291,061 (4.3)	339,368 (5.0)
Other	87,917 (1.6)	84,388 (1.2)	81,192 (1.2)
Sales and operating revenue	5,663,134	6,755,490	6,794,619

(Figures in parentheses indicate percentage of sales and operating revenue.)
SOURCE: SEC Edgar, March 2000

During the latter half of the twentieth century, Sony Corporation was known as an industry leader in consumer electronics. Its wide range of products included audio, video, television, information and communications, and electronics components (see Exhibit 1 for sales breakdown by product category). It was the pioneer of the portable cassette player (Walkman), as well as of the compact disc (which became the de facto standard in music recording). Additionally, it had stakes in many aspects of entertainment, including music (Columbia and Epic records), video game consoles and games (Playstation), television, and movies (Columbia Pictures). Surveys found that teens considered Sony one of the "coolest" global brands, third only to Nike and Tommy Hilfiger.[4]

Sony's Organization

Sony Corporation is composed of many subsidiaries, including Aiwa Co., Sony Computer Entertainment, and Sony Life Insurance Co. (see Exhibit 2 for complete list of subsidiaries). Nobuyuki Idei took the helm of Sony in 1995 and re-structured the company so that its divisions functioned as "quasi-independent units" that "orbited" around a corporate command center.[5] In March of 1999, Sony underwent a dramatic structural change, cutting down both its workforce by ten percent and its 70 manufacturing facilities to 55.[6] Part of the reason for this change was the Japanese recession, which forced many companies to cut expenses in order to remain competitive. The restructuring also resulted in the transformation

Japan

Aiwa Co., Ltd
Sony Bonson Corporation
Sony Computer Entertainment, Inc.
Sony Components Marketing Co.
Sony Denshi Corporation
Sony Engineering Corporation
Sony Hamamatsu Corporation
Sony Inazawa Corporation
Sony Kitakanto Corporation
Sony Kokubu Corporation
Sony Life Insurance Co., Ltd.
Sony Max Corporation
Sony Minokamo Corporation
Sony Motomiya Corporation
Sony Nakaniida Corporation
Sony Oita Corporation
Sony Pictures Entertainment (Japan) Inc.
Sony Precision Technology Inc.
Sony Service Co., Ltd.
Sony Systems Service, Ltd.
Sony Shiroishi Semiconductor Inc.
Sony Tochigi Corporation
Sony Trading International Corp.

Sony Broadcast Products Corporation
Sony Chemicals Corporation
Sony Components Chiba Corporation
Sony Digital Products, Inc.
Sony Energytec Inc.
Sony Finance International, Inc.
Sony Ichinomiya Inc.
Sony Kisarazu Corporation
Sony Kohda Corporation
Sony Logistics Corporation
Sony Marketing Corporation
Sony Mizunami Inc.
Sony Music Entertainment (Japan) Inc.
Sony Nagasaki Corporation
Sony Neagari Corporation
Sony PCL Inc.
Sony Plaza Co., Ltd.
Sony Precision Magnetics Corp.
Sony Sound Tec Corporation
Sony Systems Design Corp.
Sony Senmaya Corporation
Sony Toyosato Corporation

Outside Japan

Sony Corporation of America
Sony Electronics, Inc.
Sony Pictures Entertainment Inc.
Sony of Canada Ltd.
Sony Comercio E Industria Ltda.
Sony Componentes Ltda.
Sony Europe G.m.b.H.
Sony-Wega Produktions G.m.b.H.
Sony United Kingdom Limited
Sony France S.A.
Sony Euro-Finance B.V.
Sony DADC Austria AG
Sony Espana, S.A.
Sony Electronics of Korea Corp.
Sony Video Taiwan Co., Ltd.
Sony International (Hong Kong) Limited
Sony Magnetic Products (Thailand) Co. Limited
Sony Semiconductor (Thailand) Company Limited
Sony ELECTRONICS (M) SDN.BHD
Sony MECHATRONIC PROD. (M) SDN.BHD.
Sony International (Singapore) Ltd.
Sony Precision Engin. Center (Singapore) Pte Ltd.
P.T. SONY ELECTRONICS INDONESIA
Sony New Zealand Ltd.

Sony Capital Corporation
Sony Music Entertainment Inc.
Sony Magnetic Products Inc. of America
Sony Corporation of Panama, S.A.
Sony da Amazonia Ltda.
Sony Chile Ltda.
Sony Deutschland G.m.b.H.
Sony Europe Finance PLC
Sony Overseas S.A.
Sony Europa B.V.
Sony Logistics Europe B.V.
Sony Italia S.p.A.
Sony GULF FZE
Taiwan Toyo Radio Co., Ltd.
Sony Corporation of Hong Kong Limited
Sony Electronic Devices (Hong Kong) Limited
Sony Siam Industries Company Limited
Sony Audio Penang (Malaysia) Sdn. Bhd.
Sony TV INDUSTRIES (M) SDN.BHD
Sony VIDEO (M) SDN.BHD.
Sony Marketing International (Singapore) Ltd.
Sony Display Device (Singapore) Pte Ltd.
Sony Australia Limited

of three affiliated companies—Sony Music Entertainment, Sony Chemicals Corp., and Sony Precision Technology—into subsidiaries wholly owned by Sony. It also positioned three in-house electronic manufacturers—Home Network Co., Personal IT Network Co., and Core Technology and Network Co.—as well as Sony Computer Entertainment, as the hub of its electronics division. The move symbolized Sony's serious attitude towards its vision of a fully integrated and networked future. In general, Sony gave its engineers great latitude to develop and innovate freely.

The Birth of the Playstation

In the 1980s, Ken Kutaragi of Sony began collaborating with engineers at Nintendo to produce chips that would be used in the Super NES (Nintendo Entertainment System). It was Kutaragi who proposed to Nintendo that they collaborate to develop the first CD-ROM-based console. After development was underway, Nintendo suddenly announced in 1991 that they were "realigning," and would work with Phillips to produce a new console (which, incidentally, was never introduced). Undaunted, Kutaragi and his team of engineers decided to push forward and develop their own game console based on CD-ROM technology. At first, Kutaragi was hard-pressed to find supporters for his vision. Even the corporate heads at Sony found his game console to be an "embarrassing" product idea. Finally, Norio Ohga, the CEO of Sony at the time, decided to take a chance on the product. The Playstation was launched in November of 1994 in Japan and in December of 1995 in the U.S. It took the gaming world by storm, and made executives at Nintendo and Sega, who had been the dominant players in the gaming industry, stop and take a second look at the newcomer. By spring of 2000, over 70 million Playstation units had been sold worldwide; the Playstation and its software accounted for 10 percent of Sony's revenue. In 1999, Sony controlled two-thirds of the game machine market worldwide, and one out of every four households in America possessed a unit.

Kutaragi, who directs the Sony Computer Entertainment (SCE) division which produces the Playstations, thinks of his company as a separate entity from Sony and assertively describes Sony as "a 52-year-old parent," and SCE as "the young child who will save it."[7] Kutaragi also notes that upon introducing the Playstation brand name, the Sony name was dropped from the product. While many who believe that the PS2 will become the portal for Sony's music, software, and services, Kutaragi firmly resists this view, saying that, "Synergy is 120 percent not my dream. Sony has Sony's agenda. But [I] want a very open platform, equal for every person."[7] When asked about his thoughts on Kutaragi's strong mindedness, Idei stated, "PlayStation is only 10 percent of our business. I don't understand why you're so excited by it. It's not just PS2. Almost all of Sony's products will be used on the Net."[8]

The Rapidly Changing Video Game Console Industry

In 1972, Nolan Bushnell single-handedly created the video game industry when he founded Atari and introduced Pong, a ping-pong-like game played on a user's television set with the aid of the Atari console. In its first year, Pong earned over $1 million in revenues. In 1976, Warner Communications bought Atari and turned the company's focus to making home personal computers. The next few years saw a variety of Atari computer introductions, but none would prove to be big moneymakers for Atari.

While Atari's attention was diverted towards computers, Coleco (the well-known toy maker that produced the Cabbage Patch Doll) entered the market and introduced the *Coleco Vision* video game system in 1982. (Coleco later also entered the personal computer market with a product called Adam, but this product was unsuccessful and was terminated in 1985). The Coleco Vision was very successful, and in 1983 Coleco Vision games outsold Atari games. In the mid 1980s profits for video game makers began to decline; many feared that video games had reached market saturation and that the market was declining. Compounding this, two new entrants from Japan showed up in the market: Nintendo, with its 8-bit Nintendo Entertainment System (NES), and Sega, with its 8-bit Master System.

Japan's Dominance

Sega's initial product captured very little market share, but Nintendo's NES was extremely successful and sold over one million units in the first year, apparently reviving the home video game market. The product had better graphics and more in-depth games than was seen previously in the industry. In 1987, Atari released its last 8-bit system, the *Atari XE Game System*, but the product couldn't compete with the power and graphics in the systems made by Nintendo and Sega. Furthermore, Atari only spent roughly $300,000 promoting it, while Sega and Nintendo each spent $15 million promoting their systems. Finding itself unable to compete, Atari sued Nintendo in 1988 for monopolistic practices (the court sided with Nintendo).[9] In the same year, Coleco filed Chapter 11.

Over the next few years Sega and Nintendo vied for the position of market leader. While Nintendo had a larger installed base due to its earlier entry and popularity, Sega made great strides by beating Nintendo to market in 1989 with a 16-bit system, the enormously popular Sega *Genesis.* Consumers' choice between video games systems was largely driven by the availability of video game titles; like Nintendo, Sega made little profit on the consoles and focused instead on increasing unit sales to drive software developer royalties. Sega also used less restrictive licensing arrangements than Nintendo, luring a much larger number of developers to make Sega game titles. In 1991, Nintendo introduced its 16-bit Super Nintendo Entertainment System (SNES), but it was too late to quell Sega's momentum. In 1992, Nintendo controlled 80 percent of the video game market, but in 1994 and 1995, Sega was the market leader.

Interactive Multimedia Systems

The renewed growth in the video game market began to attract new types of would-be competitors. In 1989, Philips announced its *Compact Disc Interactive (CD-i),* an interactive multimedia compact disc system that would serve as a game player, teaching tool, and music system. However, the CD-i was very complex and required a 30-minute demonstration. Furthermore, it was expensive—initially introduced at $799 and later reduced to a below-cost $500 (more than twice the cost of Nintendo or Sega systems).[10] Its role was very unclear to most consumers. While the CD-I product actually cost much more than a video-game machine, customers compared it to the popular Nintendo and Sega systems and were dismayed by its price and complexity. Making matters worse, Philips was reluctant to disclose the technical specifications of the machine, greatly limiting the software development for the system. In 1996, Philips CD-i was still being distributed but had less than a 2 percent market share, and Philips indicated that it would no longer promote the CD-i in the U.S.[11]

Other companies also introduced interactive multimedia systems, including Turbo Technologies' *Duo,* and 3DO's *Interactive Multiplayer,* but the cost of the systems ($600-$700) was prohibitive. Furthermore, the platforms failed to attract the attention of software developers, resulting in a small number of game titles being available for the systems. The Duo had all but disappeared by 1995, and 3DO exited the video game hardware market in 1996.

Increasingly Powerful Systems

In 1993, Atari made a surprising re-entrance to the video game market with the technologically advanced 64-bit *Jaguar.* At this point in time, 16-bit systems (from Nintendo and Sega) still dominated the market. (Sega would not introduce its 32-bit Sega Saturn until 1995.) However, the Jaguar was still unable to penetrate the market. It required cartridge-style games and few software developers supported the platform. Sega and Nintendo both had very large installed bases, a large number of available games, and considerable brand recognition for many of their game characters (including Super Mario and Sonic the Hedgehog). The companies had also expanded their game distribution channels to include video rental outlets. It was not until 1995 that a real threat to the video game market arrived: Sony Electronics.

Sony introduced its 32-bit Playstation in 1995, the same year that Sega introduced Sega *Saturn.* (Both the Sony and Sega platforms were based on compact discs.) Sony had access to enormous distribution channels, and its size and importance in the compact disc arena attracted the attention of software developers, ensuring that game titles were available when the hardware reached retail stores. It signed a sweetheart deal with Electronic Arts, one of the largest game software developers in the US and convinced several other developers to produce nothing but Playstation titles for the first six months after its introduction.

In 1996, Nintendo responded to the Sony Playstation by introducing a 64-bit game system called *Nintendo 64.* Nintendo adhered to the cartridge format because it enabled faster access for the graphics desired by hardcore gamers. While there were only two software titles available at the console's release (one being Super Mario), the game units were sold out within weeks of their release. From 1997 to 1999, Nintendo, Sega, and Sony fought vigorously for dominance in the video game market. In 1997, Nintendo had a 50 percent share of the worldwide market, with Sony following at 34 percent and Sega at 16 percent.[12] However, by 1999, Nintendo and Sony appeared to have edged out Sega—which clung to a scant 1 percent market share—from the game.

The Year 2000

The spring of 2000 was an exciting time to be a player in the video game industry. In 1999, sales in the industry topped $7 billion, and analysts were predicting that sales in 2000 would exceed ticket sales of movie houses.[13] The industry had evolved from one aimed primarily towards "die-hard gamers" to one possessing wide market appeal. The target market, which had been primarily nine- to 12-year-old boys, now expanded to the point where more than 59 percent of console players were over

18 years of age.[14] Sony's Playstation console had contributed much towards the growing market demand, with its wide range of games aimed towards all consumer market segments. According to *Gaming Trends*, an online collection of video game statistics, demographics, and market research, 15 percent of video game players were female in the spring of 2000, representing a large increase in the proportion of female players. (These results took into consideration video game console players, as well as PC and iMac game players).[15]

The Playstation2

With the introduction of the PS2, Sony hoped to increase the breadth of its customer base even further. In the rapidly growing age of digital technology, the PS2 was a multi-function console with the capability to play original Playstation games, as well as audio CDs and DVDs. Also, tapping the boom of the Internet age, the PS2 included broadband Internet access—consistent with President Idei's desire for Sony to be a strong contender in the new digital economy and the "first broadband entertainment company."[16] (Initial shipments of the PS2 consoles would not include this Internet access feature, but the modules enabling access were to be introduced in early 2001.) Internet access would enable the Playstation2 to become a portal for introducing online gaming and other Web functions (including downloading multimedia files) into the home as an alternative to the traditional PC connection.

At the time of its introduction, the PS2 was the most powerful game console ever introduced. Its graphics processor, called the *Emotion Engine*, increased the graphics processing capability from 360,000 polygons per second (polygons determine the level of detail in graphics) in the original Playstation to over 66 million polygons per second in the PS2.[17] Though at the time of its launch the PS2 only scratched the surface of its full potential, the system had been designed so that in the future every Sony electronics component (cameras, VCRs, Walkman's, etc.) would be able to connect to the console.

Retailers in Japan in the spring of 2000 had to deal with the huge demand for the console. On March 4, 2000, a total of 26,400 Japanese retailers (including 18,500 convenience stores and about 7,900 retail stores, current Playstation retailers, and Playstation.com) began selling the console. Many of these retailers were located in the busy "electronics" city of Akihabara, Japan. More than 600,000 units were sold at a price of $370 (~39,800 yen) through Japanese retailers during the three-day launch period, while 380,000 units were sold online. The day the units went on sale, people were crowded to stores before they even opened; within minutes of opening, the units were sold out. Retailers could not get enough units to meet the demand, in part due to a shortage of the 8MB memory cards packaged with the PS2. DVD-video software sales in Japan increased approximately two-to-four times for the retailers and constituted about 10 percent of software sales on the Playstation website.[18]

Marketing

Sony's marketing strategy to promote its games included television advertisements featuring shots of its games, plus appearances by many of the popular characters featured in its games. In 1997, Sony received an Effie award—which honors the most creative and effective television advertisements—for its commercial featuring the popular Crash Bandicoot character.[19] Sony also implemented many ads on the Web. One such advertisement, for its game "Ape Escape," won top honors for most creative online marketing strategy in the 1999 Australian Internet Advertising Awards.[20]

Suppliers for the New Console

The brains of the Playstation2 lay in its 128-bit chip, which cost $1.2 billion in development costs and which was designed through a joint venture between Sony and Toshiba. The new chip represented a significant advance in technology from the single-chip device in the original Playstation console, co-developed with LSI Logic Corporation. Sony then invested $455 million in a Toshiba plant in order to design the chips. It also built a $725 million facility to produce the chips in-house.[21] By teaming up with Toshiba and LSI Logic for the new chip, Sony was able to produce a chip that possessed both backwards compatibility and breakthrough developments in graphics processing and speed. The design of this chip also allowed the Playstation2 to play DVDs. Collaboration on the Playstation project proved to be highly beneficial for both companies. Because of its venture with Sony, Toshiba was able to design a new media-processor for networking and a 128-bit embedded processor family. Toshiba's joint venture with Sony was a coup, for many vendors in Japan vie for business from Sony's Playstation division. In March of 2000, Sony also opened a new $654 million plant in order to produce in-house high-performance semiconductors (graphics synthesizers) for its PS2 unit.[22] The console was then assembled at a Sony plant near Tokyo.

Game Developers

Sony, Sega, and Nintendo all pursued a strategy of pricing the game consoles very low and reaping profits from games developers. However, the availability and popularity

3DO	Maxis
7 Studios	Microprose
Acclaim Entertainment	Midway
Accolade	Mindscape
Activision	Namco
A.S.C.	Natsume
American Softworks	Naughty Dog
American Technos	Neversoft
ASC Games	New Kidco
Agetec	Nuby
Atlus Software	Nyko
Bandai	Oddworld Inhabitants
Blizzard	Origin
BMG (Take2)	Playmates
Bungie	Psygnosis
Capcom	Reality Quest
Cerny	Red Storm Entertainment
Crave Entertainment	Shiny Entertainment
Crystal Dynamics	Sierra
Data East	Sir Tech
Digital Anvil	Spectrum
Dreamworks Interactive	Square Electronic Arts
EIDOS	Squaresoft
Electronic Arts	Stormfront Studios
Enix	Strategic Sims
FOX Interactive	Sunsoft
GT Interactive	Surreal Software
Hasbro	Take 2 Interactive
Hot-B-USA	Technos
Humongous Entertainment	Tecmo
Incredible Technologies	TerraGlyph Interactive
Infogrames	THQ
Insomniac Games	Time Warner
Interact	Titus Software
Interplay	Ubi Soft Entertainment
Jaleco	Universal Interactive Studios
Koei Corp.	Vic Tokai
Kokopeli	Virgin
Konami	VR Sports
Lucas Arts	Westwood Studios
Mad Catz	Williams
MGM Interactive	Working Designs

from games, in turn, drove demand for the game consoles. Thus, a gaming platform gaining the initial advantage in either console sales or game titles was well positioned to dominate the market—at least until that generation of consoles was replaced by newer, more revolutionary gaming platforms. It was extremely important, therefore, to attract and retain the enthusiasm of game developers.

Game developers faced difficult choices about which platforms to support and how many games to develop. Only a small percentage of game titles were successful, encouraging companies to develop many titles in hopes that a few might be commercial successes. However, the costs of developing a game had increased dramatically over time as game developers began to incorporate increasingly complex programming and better graphics. For instance, while it had cost around $200,000 to develop a game for the Sega Genesis (a 16-bit system), it cost approximately $2 million to produce a Playstation or Nintendo64 game. PS2 games were expected to cost around $4 million to develop.[23] This meant reaching higher sales of game units in order to make a profit.

The PS2, even before launch, possessed a large amount of third-party support from content developers, publishers, and software toolmakers (see Exhibit 3 for a list of licensees). In September of 1999, long before the launch of the PS2, there were already 89 licensees in Japan. Additionally, there were also 46 North American companies and 27 European companies supporting the platform. Licensees included major players in the toys and electronics industries such as: Capcom, Dreamworks Interactive, Hasbro Interactive, and Acclaim. PS2s plethora of games was the largest available at the time, and ranged in content from role-playing games to children's games to sports games. Sony also produced its own titles in-house; *Gran Turismo*, *Gran Turismo 2*, and *Crash Bandicoot* were all top-selling games. According to *PC Data*, the top ten best-selling games for the Playstation included five titles produced by Sony (see Exhibit 4). Also, the top ten best-selling video games list included six Playstation titles, four of which were produced in-house.

Traditionally, companies like Nintendo and Sony had imposed strict regulations on their third-party game developers. During its dominance of the 8-bit video game market, Nintendo's licensing agreements stipulated that developers prepay and purchase a minimum of 50,000 game cartridges and also restricted development for other consoles for a minimum of two years. Game developers for Sony and Sega faced similar restrictions, but none were as stringent as those of Nintendo. Sony had attracted much support for its first console because it had given better terms to its developers than Nintendo, but once Sony attained a dominant market position, it too began to impose stricter regulations on its licensees. For the PS2 game titles, Sony stipulated that game developers could not discuss any details about upcoming games until after their release. This restriction came as part of Sony's directive to its developers and stated: "Publishers may not make statements regarding the launch of the PS2 system or make claims that any particular products will be available at launch."[24] Sony had also set strict requirements for any developers who wished to showcase their games at the Electronics Conference in May 2000. These restrictions included: 1) the game must have at least one level completely finished, 2) the game must be bug-free and playable, and 3) the game must show off the PS2's "next generation" hardware.[25] These restrictions were to affect the games for the US launch and were countermeasures against the bad publicity caused by the below-expected quality of the Japanese games.

Sony had provided good support for its developers since the introduction of its first Playstation. It continued this support for the PS2 developers by expanding its existing partnership with Metrowerks Inc., a leading provider of software development tools. Metrowerks was well known for its CodeWarrior programs, which enabled software programmers to write and compile programs written in computer languages such as C and C++. Metrowerks had specifically designed a new CodeWarrior program tailored to developers for the PS2. This program gave developers two advantages: more freedom to choose from among various development programs rather than from Sony alone and an easier development tool, thus reducing the time to market for new games.[26] However, Sony's relationship with Metrowerks was not exclusive— the CodeWarrior program was also available to Nintendo and Sega developers.

Competition for the Next-Generation Console

Sega's Dreamcast

By the spring of 2000, the video game industry had become a battleground between both old and new competitors to provide the standard in an all-in-one game console with access to the Internet. The new and upcoming consoles all boasted vast improvements in graphics and speed. The next generation of 128-bit consoles had begun with the 1999 launch of Sega's Dreamcast, which allowed for narrow-band (56Kbps) access to the Internet. Sales totaled 514,000 units for the first two weeks, at a price of $199 per machine. The Dreamcast was the first to offer online-gaming capability through its Dreamcast Network. However, by the spring of 2000,

Exhibit 4 — Software Titles & Rankings (www.pcdata.com)

Top-Selling Console Video Games for January 2000

	Title	Publisher	Average Price	Format
1)	Gran Turismo 2	Sony	$40	Playstation
2)	Pokemon Yellow	Nintendo	$29	GameBoy
3)	Tony Hawk's Pro Skater	Activision	$40	Playstation
4)	Donkey Kong 64	Nintendo	$56	N64
5)	Pokemon Red	Nintendo	$29	GameBoy
6)	Pokemon Blue	Nintendo	$29	GameBoy
7)	Gran Turismo	Sony	$19	Playstation
8)	Spyro the Dragon	Sony	$19	Playstation
9)	Crash Bandicoot: Warped	Sony	$19	Playstation
10)	Medal of Honor	Electronic Arts	$40	Playstation

Top-Selling *Sony Playstation* Games for January 2000

	Title	Publisher	Average Price	Format
1)	Gran Turismo 2	Sony	$40	Simulation
2)	Tony Hawk's Pro Skater	Activision	$40	Sports
3)	Gran Turismo	Sony	$19	Simulation
4)	Spyro the Dragon	Sony	$19	Adventure/RPG
5)	Crash Bandicoot: Warped	Sony	$19	Adventure/RPG
6)	Medal of Honor	Electronic Arts	$40	Action
7)	Metal Gear Solid	Konami	$20	Action
8)	NBA Live 2000	Electronic Arts	$39	Sports
9)	Museum Volume #3	Namco	$19	Arcade
10)	Crash Team Racing	Sony	$39	Simulation

users who accessed the Internet through their Internet Service Provider (ISP) could only download a few songs and movies on the Dreamcast Online site. No online games were yet available at the time for play.

Online gaming had previously been reserved for PC game players, with games such as *Quake* or *Ultima Online* attracting droves of loyal followers. With the introduction of game console online play, the industry had begun a shift away from PCs as the only access to the Internet. In anticipation of the PS2's future broadband capability, Sega announced that it too would go broadband with the introduction of an add-on Ethernet adapter, which was to debut in May of 2000 at the Electronic Entertainment Exposition convention.[27] In late March of 2000, Sega announced another marketing scheme in anticipation of the upcoming competition

with the PS2. It would offer a $200 rebate for consumers—thus making the Dreamcast free—in exchange for a two-year contract for the new high-speed SegaNet Internet service, at the cost of $21.95 per month. This offer was to be coordinated by a new company named Sega.com and was part of an effort to increase Sega's customer base. Subscribers to the service would receive a free keyboard, which reduced the problem of users having to type using the controllers.

Nintendo's Dolphin

In the spring of 2000, Nintendo's primary product was the 64-bit N64 console. Though Nintendo had traditionally released fewer software titles than Sony, it possessed the licenses to some of the most popular characters, including Pokemon, Mario, and Donkey Kong. At the time of the Playstation2 release, Nintendo had just postponed the launch of its new 128-bit system, called the Dolphin, to a release date in the first half of 2001. The Dolphin was to be a joint venture with Matsushita, one of Sony's main rivals, and IBM. The console promised a faster processor than that of the PS2, but its graphics capabilities would be similar. Unlike the PS2, however, the Dolphin would lack both backwards compatibility with N64 games and many of the features that Sony had added to its new console, such as the ability to play DVDs. Minoru Arakawa, president of Nintendo America, Inc., stated that its goal was to build a "machine with only one purpose—to play video games . . . this is what Nintendo has always known best, and what consumers have always wanted most."[28] Other reasons given for Nintendo's late launch date were to enable customers owning a N64 system to still enjoy the games that were being developed for the console and to enable ample time to build a party of strong and high-quality developers of games.

However, some questioned Nintendo's late release of its Dolphin system, as sales of N64 consoles and games were slowing. According to Acclaim Chairman Gregory Fishbach, Acclaim had responded to slow sales of its games for the N64 console by slowing down development of N64 games, thereby reducing dependence on those sales. Other developers such as THQ, Activision, and Konami were following suit due to lagging sales of the N64 games.[29] In fact, Fairfield Research's President Gary Gabelhouse stated that, "A statistically significant percentage of retailers . . . stated that N64 was a 'dead system.'"[30] Also, developer support for the Dolphin was an issue because of Nintendo's previously strict regulations and fees for developers. Many believed that in the upcoming new four-console market, developers might choose another successful console for which to develop. On a brighter side for Nintendo, sales of its Gameboy Color, a portable, hand-held game console, and its games, which included the highly popular Pokemon series, were still going strong, and Nintendo held the leading role in that market. In March of 2000, Nintendo announced that the Gameboy would soon have the capability to function as a cellular phone, a move designed to compete with the PS2. Nintendo also announced that it would begin selling an adapter for the Gameboy that would enable Internet access. To further compete against the PS2, Nintendo also announced that it would purchase a 3 percent share of Lawson, which is Japan's second-largest convenience store chain, in order to increase its distribution.[31]

Microsoft's X-Box

The introduction of game consoles that access the Internet posed a threat to home PCs. In March of 2000, software giant Microsoft suddenly announced that it too would enter the game console industry with its X-Box console. The X-Box, which was the code name for the project, was designed using standard PC architecture but was not to be positioned as a replacement for the PC.[32] The new console was expected to launch in late 2001 and would use an Intel x86 microprocessor at 600Mhz processing speed. The graphics chip to be used in the X-Box would be supplied by Nvidia Corp., which Microsoft claimed would have three times the speed of the PS2's graphics processing speed. Microsoft would pay Nvidia $200 million in advance for the development of a 3D graphics chip and multimedia subsystem for the X-Box.[33] It would also have 64MB of memory, an 8-Gigabyte hard drive, a DVD player, and an integrated Ethernet card for broadband access. By April of 2000, Sony had already begun plans for combating future competition from the X-Box by unveiling plans to launch the PS2 in the U. S. with an integrated modem and a hard drive.[34]

Microsoft was not a new player to the video game software market, as it was already the fourth largest developer of PC video games. The move by the software giant to the game console market was an indication of its belief that consumer devices could eventually replace the PC in the home. Amazingly, Japanese game software makers welcomed the introduction of a new game console by Microsoft as a possible way to lessen the power of Sony. One official at a major software company in Japan was quoted as saying, "A well-known creative company with abundant cash like Microsoft can make something very exciting, which could weaken Sony's grip."[35] Large companies such as Japan's Konami Co Ltd., Electronic Arts Inc., and Acclaim Entertainment Inc. had expressed interest in providing software for the X-Box, but whether or not games would actually be developed was still left to question. Third-party developer support for the X-Box was still questionable by the spring of 2000, and many believed that the majority of developer support for the X-Box would come mainly from PC developers. Also, the X-Box did not have many exclusive titles to claim in the spring of 2000, which would be a critical factor to its success, since much of the success of Playstation and N64 stemmed from superior game titles produced exclusively for those consoles. Microsoft's size and power, as well as its cash reserves, would give it a lot of marketing power. The services of McCann-Erickson, an advertising agency, would be used to promote the new console at a price tag of around $100 million.[36]

Playstation2 Challenges

Ken Kutaragi pushed his chair back and contemplated the recent chain of problems that had caused drops in Sony's stock and created bad publicity surrounding the PS2. In the video game industry, when a new and advanced console launch is announced, there is usually a lot of hype and gossip surrounding the news. The PS2 had been highly anticipated, and in the spring of 2000, it was yet to be released in the United States. However, upon its launch in Japan, several bugs had been revealed in the system, and news of the discovery was making headlines around the world. Users of the system reported that saving games and information to the memory card resulted in loss of information. It was also discovered that PS2's DVD capabilities could be altered to play DVD's from any country. Since makers of DVD players had agreed to universally program their players such that they could only play DVDs in a certain country, the discovery that the PS2 player could override such a function caused a scandal. Hollywood movie producers were considering a lawsuit against the PS2 for violating copyrights, but Sony had counteracted this problem by announcing that it would replace software for already-purchased game consoles to fix the programming bug that allowed it to run foreign digital video discs. The company planned to start shipping PS2 consoles with an upgraded utility software disk and memory card.

Kutaragi was also anxious about the greater than expected demand for the console. What should have been good news had become a problem, as shortages in production were anticipated around the world. Sony had sold over a million units in Japan, and stores were still experiencing large turnover rates of PS2 units. The US launch was anticipated to be even bigger, causing Kutaragi concern about shortages and a possible delay in the US launch.[37] The PS2 console was receiving 23 percent more preorders ahead of its fall 2000 launch than did the Dreamcast at a comparable time. According to a survey conducted by Fairfield Research of 200 US retailers, 78 percent of store and department managers reported that they had received advance orders for the PS2.[38]

Finally, Kutaragi also worried about the rapidly spreading perception that its Japanese PS2 game titles had been mediocre. Many players noticed that even though the graphics in the new games were improved, there were jagged edges and rough textures that ruined the effect. This was believed to be the outcome of game developers rushing to meet the deadline for the Japan launch of the PS2. The PS2 graphics chip was composed of several units, including the Emotion Engine and a *graphics synthesizer unit* (GS) that would enable developers to use that part exclusively for graphics. Most of the initial games released, however, only used the capabilities of the Emotion Engine and did not harness the potential of the GS unit. The GS unit was intended to significantly improve *anti-aliasing*, or the softening of edges. Furthermore, many game developers had not made full use of the Emotion Engine's potential.[39] However, on the bright side, future games for the PS2 console included sure-fire hits such as Final Fantasy XI, which was an extremely popular role-playing game, and which was an exclusive licensing agreement between Sony and SquareSoft. Final Fantasy XI was to be exclusively played online, which banked on the upcoming release of the PS2 broadband modules.

By May of 2000, Sony had also begun to worry about its financial status. Its profits had plummeted 32 percent in the fiscal year ending in 2000, partly due to a strong Japanese yen, which decreased the value of earnings overseas for Sony (see company financials in Exhibit 5). In addition, the costs of the PS2 development and launch sent the operating profit for its game products down 43.3 percent. Profits were also affected by poor sales of the original Playstation. Many consumers had stopped purchasing the Playstation console and games in anticipation of the PS2. Sony's poor financial statistics were also causing drops in Sony's stock price (see Exhibit 6).

Planning for the US Launch

Ken Kutaragi's thoughts wandered ahead to the launch of the PS2 in the US. Kutaragi knew that to be successful, the PS2 would have to be error-free and have high-quality games that would remove any doubt of the PS2's gaming power. Furthermore, the whole gaming industry, and indeed, the whole world, was being swept quickly into the new Internet era, and Kutaragi, like many others, envisioned a world where everyone's homes had interconnected devices that could communicate with each other and beyond via the Internet. However, the future was unclear; nobody knew whether online gaming would be a complete success or whether console players could truly adapt to accessing the Internet via a game console. In addition, the transformation of consoles to Internet accessing devices threatened to position gaming consoles more directly against PCs—and, therefore, against a huge battalion of well-established competitors. Though there was much for Sony to celebrate in

Assets	1996	1997	1998	1999
Cash On Hand:	428,518	423,286	592,210	626,064
Marketable Securities:	172,612	276,348	142,161	113,637
Receivables:	972,582	1,115,888	1,013,583	1,055,469
Inventories:	869,800	993,927	877,898	859,174
Other Current Assets:	351,951	458,028	443,541	480,296
Total Current Assets:	2,795,463	3,267,477	3,069,393	3,134,640
Prop., Plants & Equip.:	2,875,607	3,092,004	3,002,32	3,007,910
Accum. Depreciation:	1,636,696	1,744,877	1,752,571	1,752,340
Net Plants & Equip.:	1,238,911	1,347,127	1,249,751	1,255,570
Subsidiary Invest.:	786,879	850,462	980,736	1,075,594
Other Non-cur Assets:	242,727	249,066	244,537	226,387
Deferred Charges:	148,032	163,120	199,868	239,981
Intangibles:	273,920	285,308	263,160	512,273
Deposits and Other:	194,410	240,483	291,608	362,752
Total Assets:	5,680,342	6,403,043	6,299,053	6,807,197
Liabilities and Equity				
Notes Payable:	117,801	114,617	40,877	56,426
Accounts Payable:	653,826	768,152	722,690	811,031
Current Long-term Debt:	210,315	84,794	87,825	158,509
Accrued Expenses:	537,726	676,547	670,631	681,458
Income Taxes:	169,480	157,123	107,031	87,520
Other Current Liab.:	262,719	315,092	313,491	365,398
Total Current Liab.:	1,951,867	2,116,325	1,942,545	2,160,342
Deferred Charges/Inc:	173,951	147,116	120,822	184,020
Long-term Debt:	1,099,765	1,104,420	1,037,460	813,828
Other Long-term Liab.:	880,464	1,093,841	1,238,434	1,431,536
Total Liabilities:	4,106,047	4,461,702	4,339,261	4,589,726
Minority Int (Liab):	114,867	125,786	136,127	34,565
Common Stock Net:	332,037	406,196	416,373	451,550
Capital Surplus:	474,033	548,422	559,236	940,716
Retained Earnings:	767,301	965,083	1,123,591	1,223,761
Treasury Stock:	0	2,880	5,639	7,805
Other Equities:	−113,943	−101,266	−269,896	−425,316
Shareholders' Equity:	1,459,428	1,815,555	1,823,665	2,182,906
Total Liab. and Worth:	5,680,342	6,403,043	6,299,053	6,807,197

Case 34 / Sony Playstation2: Just Another Competitor?

Exhibit 6　　Sony Corp. Income Statement　　(All numbers in millions of Yen)

Fiscal Year Ended	1996	1997	1998	1999
Net Sales:	4,592,565	5,663,134	6,755,490	6,794,619
Cost of Goods:	3,439,354	4,160,563	4,889,696	4,633,787
Gross Profit:	1,153,211	1,502,571	1,865,794	2,160,832
Sales G & A:	917,887	1,132,241	1,345,584	1,500,863
Inc Bef Dep & Amort:	235,324	370,330	520,210	659,969
Non-Operating Inc:	−30,070	12,991	−3,937	−243,566
Interest Expense:	67,095	70,892	62,524	48,275
Income Before Tax:	138,159	312,429	453,749	368,128
Prov for Inc Taxes:	77,158	163,570	214,868	176,973
Minority Int (Inc):	6,749	9,399	16,813	12,151
Net Inc Bef Ex Items:	54,252	139,460	222,068	179,004
Net Income:	54,252	139,460	222,068	179,004
Outstanding Shares:	374,068	384,185	407,195	410,439

SOURCE: SEC Edgar, March 2000

the first half of the year 2000, Kutaragi knew that Sony's ability to anticipate and respond to future changes in the market would be crucial for its success.

Endnotes

1. S. Levy, 2000, Here comes the Playstation 2, *Newsweek,* March 6.
2. www.world.sony.com.
3. Ibid.
4. S. Levy, 2000, Here comes the Playstation 2, *Newsweek,* March 6.
5. T. Larimer, 2000, Sony plays for the big stakes, *Time,* March 20.
6. Sony plans job cuts in overhaul, 1999, www.expressindia.com/express/daily, March 10.
7. T. Larimer, 2000, Sony plays for the big stakes, *Time,* March 20.
8. Ibid.
9. Cheap didn't sell, 1992, *Forbes,* August 3: 52-55.
10. N. Turner, 1996, For giants of video games it an all-new competition, *Investor's Business Daily,* January 24: A6.
11. J. Trachtenberg, 1996, Short circuit: How Philips flubbed its US introduction of electronic product, *Wall Street Journal,* June 28: A1.
12. R. Scally, 1997, Next generation platforms engage in shelf-war games, *Discount Store News,* Vol 36 (7): 45.
13. S. Levy, 2000, Here comes the Playstation 2, *Newsweek,* March 6.
14. N. Croal, 2000, The art of the game, *Newsweek,* March 6.
15. www.gametrends.com

16. S. Levy, 2000, Here comes the Playstation 2, *Newsweek,* March 6.
17. T. Larimer, 2000, Sony plays for the big stakes, *Time,* March 20.
18. www.playcenter.com
19. Sony gets an Effie, http://psx.ign.com/news.
20. Sony wins top honor for Australian Internet Advertising , http://australia.internet.com/aus-news.
21. C. Dawson, 2000, Sony plays to win, *Far Eastern Economic Review,* March 2.
22. Sony opens new chip plant in Japan, 2000, *API Newswire,* 2000, http://my.aol.com/news, March 23.
23. N. Croal, 2000, The art of the game, *Newsweek,* March 6.
24. Revealed: Sony's PS2 gag order, www.dailyradar.com/features.
25. Ibid.
26. Metrowerks joins PSX2 development, 1999, www.psxnation.com/news, March 16.
27. Sega goes broadband!, www.dailyradar.com/features.
28. www.nintendo.com
29. The state of Nintendo, http://www.dailyradar.com/features.
30. PS2 preorders hotter than DC's, retailers say, http://www.mcvnow.com.
31. *Bloomberg News,* 2000, http://my.aol.com/news, March 26.
32. T. Poletti, 2000, Microsoft to unveil X-Box video game console, *Reuters,* March 9.
33. www.hooversonline.com.
34. US version of Playstation2 to have modem, hard drive, http://aol.com.cnet.com/news.
35. www.hooversonline.com.
36. X-Box advertiser determined, 2000, www.dailyradar.com/news, March 23.
37. PS2: the US launch landscape, www.dailyradar.com/features.
38. PS2 preorders hotter than DC's, retailers say,www.mcvnow.com.
39. PS2: The US Launch Landscape, http://www.dailyradar.com/features.

Stretching the Brand: A Review of the Virgin Group

Philip McCosker

Birmingham College of Food, Tourism and Creative Studies

1) Introduction

1.1) The Virgin Portfolio

The Virgin brand, which came to prominence in the mid-1970's as an independent record label and music retailer, today encompasses activities as diverse as air and rail travel, soft drinks, spirits, mobile phones, retail, cosmetics, bridal wear, financial services, ballooning and the provision of gas and electricity. The strength of the Virgin brand was illustrated by its successful expansion into the financial services market. Virgin Direct commenced business in 1995 and within 18 months had attracted almost £400 million of funds (Fox and Olins 1996 p.3). More recently, Virgin has moved into the mobile phone market. Launched in November 1999 in a joint venture with One-to-One, the business attracted 75,000 users within its first month and 500,000 users in its first year of trading. Virgin now plans to use its *'Our Price'* chain to concentrate on the sale of mobile phones and other high-tech products.

Richard Branson, the group's founder is one of the UK's best known businessmen. His reputation for innovation and challenging the establishment has won him many admirers, whilst his flair for self-publicity has

raised Virgin's profile both in the UK and overseas. When launching Virgin Brides, a one-stop wedding shop, Branson paraded down the catwalk in a white wedding dress—not the behaviour expected from a company chairman.

1.2) Poor Performance of Virgin Cola

Some critics have suggested that Virgin's continued expansion into new and highly competitive markets might be overstretching the brand. In particular, they point to Virgin's entry into the soft drinks and spirits markets, suggesting that the poor performance of vodka and cola have adversely affected the brand's reputation. At its launch in 1994 Branson brashly forecast sales of £1 billion per year and promised to shave off his beard if Virgin Cola had not overtaken Pepsi in the UK by the year 2000. Despite their efforts, by March 2000 Pepsi had a 21.5 percent share of the UK market, Virgin with UK sales of £29 million had just 1.7 percent. (Buxton 2000). Virgin Vodka, which is produced in a joint venture with William Grant, has also performed poorly and *". . . is now on sale in only a few duty-free shops and on Virgin flights."* (Anon 1998 p.83)

Other Virgin ventures have also been less than successful including its move into high street fashion. In February 2000, Virgin announced that it was withdrawing from the clothing sector less than two years after its entry. Losses of £8.6 million prompted the withdrawal (Anon. 2000). Whilst attempts to obtain the original national lottery licence and a television franchise both ended in disappointment (Fox and Olins 1996 p.3).

1.3) Virgin Rail

But it is Virgin's foray into rail transport that most concerns analysts. Although Virgin has not succeeded in all of its ventures, its failures have rarely been high profile. Rail has a higher profile than many other Virgin ventures, added to which the group has inherited the remnants of British Rail rather than starting the business from scratch. Many observers are worried that Virgin might have significantly underestimated the resources needed to improve the nation's railways, suggesting that it will take many years for Virgin Rail to show a return, and even then only after massive investment. Right from the outset management at Virgin raised customer expectations by promising to radically improve the provision of rail transport in the UK, even suggesting that Virgin Rail would become a "747 on wheels . . ." (Anon 1998 p.83). Speaking in 1997 Branson stressed that although his rail business was experiencing teething problems he was confident ". . . that by the year 2000 Virgin trains will be the best in Europe" (Honigsbaum 1997). A high profile failure will undoubtedly tarnish the Virgin brand.

1.4) Seeking to make Virgin a Global Brand

In recent years, Virgin has also tried to make its brand more global, expanding the 'Megastore' concept into the USA and Asia and announcing plans to start up a domestic airline in Australia directly in competition with the already established Quantas and Ansett airlines. Interestingly, when selling its multiplexes Virgin did not dispose of its US or Japanese cinemas and in November 1999 opened the largest cinema complex in Japan (Nakamae 1999).

1.5) Diluting the Brand

Although being engaged in such a diverse range of activities means that Virgin is not dependent upon one sector for profits, there is a danger that failure in one market will adversely affect the overall brand image. Senior Management at Virgin are aware that at some stage the brand might become overstretched and have repeatedly stated their intention to focus on the growth of its core business activities which comprise the airline, entertainment, financial services, retail and rail (Mitchell 1998). Indeed when Virgin launched its range of cosmetics and clothing, neither actually carried the Virgin brand and instead it was thought more appropriate to launch each line through Victory Corporation, a plc in which Virgin has a 50 percent shareholding. Some cynics have suggested that this was an example of Virgin ". . . stretching the brand whilst seeking to distance itself from the brand . . ." (Honigsbaum 1997).

Warning of the dangers of overstretching the Virgin brand Hamilton (1998 p.3.5) remarked that ". . . Branson has always traded on the mystique of his marketing brilliance. If that should be punctured, there may be little left."

2) Financial Resources

2.1) Group Turnover and Profits

With a turnover approaching £3 billion per annum, Virgin is one of the UK's largest private companies and if ". . . quoted on the stock market, it would be challenging for a position in the FT-SE 100 index." (Fox and Olins 1996 p.3)

In 1986 the group was floated on the stock market. However, Branson did not enjoy the restrictions that the City imposes on a public limited company (plc). He particularly disliked having to explain his actions to City analysts and institutional investors; the need to have his business decisions approved by fellow directors; and paying dividends to shareholders (Jackson 1995 p.13). It is also true that analysts and investors were not over-impressed with Virgin's performance as a plc, with profits falling well below forecasts.

Within two years Branson had bought back the shares for £248 million, and converted into a private company (Fox and Olins 1996 p.3). However, this decision resulted in massive cash flow problems that were only eased by the sale of Virgin Music in 1992 (Jackson 1995 p.13).

The Virgin Group comprises around two hundred companies, some of which are dormant. However, due to its status as a private company, the complex group structure, and the unavailability of consolidated accounts, it is very difficult to arrive at accurate figures for group turnover and profit. Analysis is made even more laborious since companies within the group do not share a common accounting year-end, and the group makes full use of offshore trusts in the Channel Islands and holding companies in the British Virgin Islands where it is not necessary to publish accounts. Branson defends the complex structure, saying that it was necessary in the early 1990's to prevent British Airways from obtaining information that could be used against Virgin, it also helps minimise the group's tax liability (Anon 1998 p83).

In recent years The Sunday Times (Fox and Olins 1996 p.3), The Economist (Anon 1998b pp.81-86) and The Mail on Sunday (Cowe and Little p.5) have each sought to review the financial position of the Virgin group. The Sunday Times analysis in 1996 estimated that the Group generated annual sales of £1.8 billion and profits of £114 million (Fox and Olins 1996 p.3). The Economist's study was based on a review of year-end accounts filed between September 1997 and January 1998. The results are summarised in appendix 1 and show that the Virgin

Company	Revenues £m	Profit / (Loss) before tax (£m)
More than 50%-owned		
Airlines	678.5	45.2
Holiday Tours	176.7	8.5
Virgin Express Holdings	101.4	2.8
Other	15.0	11.0
Sub total	971.6	67.5
less inter-company sales	85.0	-
Total Virgin Travel	886.6	67.5
Virgin Retail (UK)	28.5	(7.5)
Virgin Retail (Overseas)	300.0	n/a
Virgin Entertainment	30.6	(7.6)
Virgin Hotels	14.9	(3.8)
Other	10.0	(8.9)
Total Other Virgin Companies	384.0	(27.8)
Less than 50%-owned		
Virgin Direct	315.7	(19.7)
Virgin Cola	19.3	(2.3)
Virgin Spirits	1.9	(2.2)
Virgin Cinema	84.4	(4.7)
West Coast Trains	297.1	(11.2)
Cross Country Trains	126.4	6.9
Other	0.0	(4.3)
Total	844.8	(37.5)
Total Virgin Group	2,115.4	2.2

Summary of turnover and profits/(losses) for Virgin Group.
SOURCE: ANON., "Behind Branson" *The Economist* 21 February, 1998, pp.81–86.

Group had an annual turnover of £2.1 billion and a profit before tax of just £2.2 million (Anon 1998 p.83). Further analysis shows the group's heavy dependence upon Virgin Atlantic which contributed pre-tax profits of £45.2 million. Worryingly, two-thirds of these profits were from the increasingly competitive North Atlantic market.

More recent analysis carried out by the *Mail on Sunday* (appendix 2) shows Group turnover of £2.9 billion and a pre-tax profit of £30 million. Again, the results show the importance of Virgin Atlantic which contributed £99 million to group profits. They also indicate that large

losses are being made by Virgin Express, V2 Music, Virgin Direct and Victory.

2.2) Expansion through Joint Ventures

Often Virgin's expansion into new markets has been through a series of joint ventures whereby Virgin provides the brand and its partner the majority of capital. Although some observers have criticised Virgin for extending its brand in this way, it can be argued that joint ventures spread both the risk and cost involved in a new project,

Company	Accounts to	Sales £m	Profit/ (Loss) £m	Net (Debt)/ Cash £m
Virgin Atlantic	April 1999	1,066	99	(216)
Virgin Express	Dec 1999	181	(3)	16
Virgin Rail	Mar 1999	488	28	24
Retail	Jan 1999	500	(5)	(188)
V2 Music	Jan 1999	35	(48)	(61)
Virgin Direct	Dec 1999	577	(20)	(42)
Victory	Mar 1999	12	(21)	11
Total		2,859	30	(456)

Summary of turnover, profits/(losses) and net debt for Virgin Group.
SOURCE: CROWE, R. and LITTLE, J., "Revealed: The truth behind Virgin finances" *Mail on Sunday* 3 September 2000, Business p.5.

whilst a partner might provide Virgin with the skills and knowledge necessary to succeed in a particular industry.

For example, the £190 million purchase of the MGM cinema chain in June 1995 involved a joint venture with Texas Pacific Colony Capital and Hotel Property Group (TPG), a £750 million US leveraged buy-out fund. The agreement gave TPG a 50 percent stake in Virgin Cinemas and a minority of board seats. More important from a cash flow perspective, the deal required Virgin to initially invest just £20 million in the venture (Brasier 1995). Virgin's 50 percent stake in Virgin Direct required an initial outlay of just £15 million. Its partner, AMP, ploughed £450 million into the venture (Hamilton 1998 p.3.5). Whilst the recent move into cosmetics and clothing required an initial investment of only £1,000. Its equal partner, Victory Corporation, invested £20 million (Anon 1998 p.83).

2.3) Recurring Cash Flow Problems

Throughout its existence Virgin has experienced periods of severe cash flow difficulties. In the early 1990's Virgin had debts of £468 million and losses that exceeded £34 million (Anon 1998 p.81). To ease the group's cash flow position, in 1992 it was forced to sell Virgin Music to Thorn-EMI for £560 million (Fox and Olins 1996 p.3). As Branson said at the time, Virgin was "... *selling the past to finance its future.*" In particular the sale provided the funds necessary to develop the airline.

Rumours suggest that the group is again experiencing cash flow problems, with *The Mail on Sunday* estimating that Virgin is currently in debt to the tune of £456 mil-

lion (see appendix 2). This is caused primarily by the huge investment required by Virgin Rail. Branson himself has admitted that currently "*... his empire might look like a sprawling group of lossmakers ...*" but he insists that it is usually his partners who bare the burden of business risk (Hamilton 1998 p.3.5).

Branson also points out that Virgin is almost wholly comprised of private companies, and the running of a private company is fundamentally different from a plc. A plc must keep shareholders and City analysts happy, hence particular attention is paid to the short-term goals of high taxable profits and healthy dividends. The advantage of a private company is that its owners can ignore short-term objectives and concentrate on long-term growth, re-investing profits for this purpose. This is evidenced by Virgin Music which did not make a profit until its fifteenth year (Branson 1998 p.6). He continues to deny the existence of cash flow problems saying instead that Virgin companies have several million pounds in various bank accounts (Anon 1998 p.83).

2.4) Alliance with Singapore Airlines

During the late 1990's there were rumours that Virgin might raise cash through floating its airline on the stock exchange, however given Branson's previous experience as a plc this was always unlikely. Instead, in December 1999 it was announced that Virgin had sold 49 percent of Virgin Atlantic to Singapore Airlines for £600 million (Anon. 1999). This valued the airline at around £1.2 billion, far higher than most forecasts. The agreement suits both parties as it provides Singapore Airlines with access to North American routes (Virgin being the sixth largest carrier across the North Atlantic) whilst at the same time giving Virgin access to the Australasia market.

While some observers suggested that the sale had been forced onto Virgin due to cash flow problems, others commented that it was good business. Analysts had suggested that Virgin Atlantic's value on the open market was nearer to £800 million. Additionally with increased competition, rising fuel prices and falling profits, many thought that it was the right time to dispose of part of the airline.

However, although profits are falling, we have already seen that Virgin Atlantic is by far the most successful of Virgin's enterprises. Virgin's share of the airlines profits will now be halved possibly placing pressure on other areas of the group. In addition, Singapore Airlines will now have a major influence upon Virgin Atlantic's future strategies.

2.5) Disposal of Virgin Cinemas

The agreement with Singapore Airlines came only a few months after Virgin had disposed of its UK cinema interests to French cinema and film group UGC for £215 million. At the time Virgin was one of the UK's leading multiplex operators with over 300 screens on 34 sites (Buckingham).

Several factors are thought to have influenced the sale in October 1999. First, despite huge expenditure in new multiplex developments, Virgin identified that further massive investment would be required during the next few years, this at a time when competition between operators is intensifying causing profits to fall. In addition, although in the UK today there are almost the same number of cinema screens as in the early 1960's, admissions are less than one-third of that level (BFI 1998).

Opinion is divided over the sale. Some believe that due to falling returns it was a good time to dispose of the business. Others suggest that the sale was prompted by a decline in airline profits and the recurrence of the cash flow problems that have haunted the group. Whilst some believe that Virgin's partner in the cinema venture (TPG) forced the sale as it wished to withdraw from the industry.

There is no doubt that the sale of its cinemas enabled Virgin to considerably reduce its level of debt. In its most recent accounts, Virgin Cinemas showed losses of £11 million and almost £190 million of debt (Anon.1999). In addition, it allowed the Group to divert funds into other business areas that offer potentially higher returns. However, after entering the cinema industry in 1995 with aspirations to become the largest operator in the UK, it was a somewhat suprising withdrawal.

3) Human Resources and Company Culture

Branson has surrounded himself with individuals able to manage and develop each of his businesses and wherever possible, Virgin promotes from within. Indeed, a number of his most senior managers have worked for the group since joining from school or university (Jackson 1995 p.3). Discussing his management team, Branson said recently *"I am not a one-man band. I have a fantastic set of managers. Most of our managers who run our businesses are capable of becoming millionaires and some of them have already done so."* (Gribben 1998 p.27)

Branson tries to make himself accessible to his employees encouraging them to write to him personally with suggestions on how to improve the business. When travelling on Virgin Atlantic he is known to spend much of the flight talking to cabin crew and on landing stays in the same hotel as them. He also prefers his employees to work in small teams, and rather than locating all staff on one site, different businesses are located in separate buildings (Jackson 1995 p.3–6).

Branson suggests that his group takes an unconventional approach to business by putting the interests of its employees first. He argues that whilst most organisations see customers and shareholders as the key stakeholder groups, Virgin puts employees first. If employees are happy they will perform better and hence constantly meet and exceed customer needs and expectations, allowing the business to prosper.

Any organisation that has an annual turnover of almost £3 billion and a range of business interests as diverse as Virgin undoubtedly has a strong management team. However, the general public only sees its chairman Richard Branson, and although many of his publicity stunts have successfully promoted both himself and the Virgin brand, there is a danger that the group relies too heavily upon Richard Branson and his exploits.

Branson is acutely aware of how important he is to the Virgin brand and is trying to create a structure that can function without his presence. This could prove difficult since the public perception is that Virgin and Branson are one. Although undoubtedly the company would be able to function without him, could public perception be altered?

4) Marketing

Through its diverse range of business interests Virgin is able to cross-market its products and an advertisement for Virgin Financial Services will also promote the Virgin brand in general. Virgin Atlantic is also recognised as an important marketing tool,

". . . carrying the Virgin message (and products) to places where it would otherwise be difficult to gain a foothold. On the inaugural flight to Johannesburg . . . Branson characteristically used the wide-reaching publicity to refresh the other parts of his empire . . . moving conversation on from Virgin's cut price flights to its plans to open megastores, launch cola and vodka, and to set up a radio station . . . In the papers the following day, his face was everywhere."

—(Fox and Olins 1996 p.3)

However, it is Branson himself that is Virgin's biggest marketing tool. His record breaking transatlantic crossing in *'Virgin Challenger II'* in 1986 was good publicity for Virgin guaranteeing front-page headlines around the globe. However, his first attempt at the record almost ended in tragedy as the boat sank 255 miles from the Scilly Isles (Jackson 1995 p.134). He has also had several unsuccessful and dangerous attempts at circumnavigating the world in a hot air balloon.

Whilst Branson's exploits do keep the Virgin name in the spotlight, what would be the impact on the Virgin brand if one of his ventures were to end in tragedy? Certainly the group would be able to continue in business, but how would the loss of its figurehead affect public perception of the brand? This is an area that will become more important if at some stage in the future Branson does decide to return to the stock exchange and float part of his empire. City investors and analysts usually prefer a company chairman to keep his feet planted firmly on the ground.

5) Diversification of Business Interests

It has been suggested that Virgin operates like a Japanese keiretsu (Honigsbaum 1997). Keiretsu's like Mitsubishi, Yamaha and Toyota comprise a group of companies that use a family brand name in several unconnected areas (Dicken 1998 p.224). In this way the group is not dependent upon one market, and through diversifying is reducing exposure to business risk.

As Will Whitehorn, Corporate Affairs Director commented:

> *"In Japan nobody would be questioning Branson's strategy (of diversification). Only in Britain, where the idea has taken root that brands such as Persil and Mars must be identified with specific products is the Virgin strategy disparaged . . . there is a real opportunity for us to build Virgin as a global British brand name."*
>
> —(Honigsbaum 1997)

Whilst the diversity of Virgin's business interests has been questioned, Branson insists that the core values remain the same. *"It's about being innovative, offering value*

for money and being better than our competitors" (Honigsbaum 1997). Before entering a new market teams thoroughly research the industry and decide whether Virgin can offer something truly different. The aim being to extend the brand name into *". . . selected areas where the Virgin reputation can be used to shake up the market for a small cash outlay."* (Fox and Olins 1996 p.3)

Brad Rosser, former director of corporate development, suggests that Virgin will only put its name to a project if it meets four out of five criteria: *"The products must be innovative, challenge authority, offer value for money, be of good quality and the market must be growing."* In short, Virgin aims to provide products which offer *"First class service at business prices."* (Fox and Olins 1996 p.3)

However, as Virgin becomes larger and as Branson becomes more embroiled in the establishment, will the public believe that it continues to challenge authority, or will it be seen as just another marketing ploy by the group.

6) Summary

Virgin's biggest asset is its brand. Evidence suggests that in recent years it has been diluted by new ventures and diversification into new markets, not all of which have proved successful. Rail although profitable requires huge investment. Additionally, government subsidies will cease in the next few years and Virgin will instead start to pay the government for the privilege of running a rail business. If plans to run the *'Peoples Lottery'* come to fruition the Virgin Group will fall under even tighter public scrutiny and any adverse publicity will not only tarnish the individual business, it will also have a negative impact upon the group as a whole. The next few years could prove difficult for Virgin and will undoubtedly determine whether the Group has stretched its brand too far.

References

ANON., "Behind Branson" *The Economist* 21 February, 1998 pp.81-86

ANON., "The bartered bride" *The Economist* 25 December, 1999

ANON., "Virgin to close its West End make-up store" *Evening Standard* 1 February, 2000

BFI (downloaded 19 August, 1998) *UK Cinema admissions 1933-96* www.bfi.org.uk/right/FAQ/admissions.htm

BRANSON, R., "Branson replies: Letter to The Economist" *The Economist* 28 February, 1998, p.6

BRASIER, M., "Virgin in £200 million MGM spectacular." *Daily Telegraph* 1 July, 1995

BUCKINGHAM, L., "Branson raises the curtain on Virgin cinemas in £200 million deal with MGM." *The Guardian* 1 July, 1995

BUXTON, P., "Bitter truth Virgin is loath to swallow" *Marketing Week* 23 March, 2000

CROWE, R. and LITTLE, J., "Revealed: The truth behind Virgin finances" *Mail on Sunday* 3 September 2000, Business p. 5

DICKEN, P., (1998) *Global Shift* (3rd ed.) London: Paul Chapman Publishing

FOX, N., and OLINS, R., "Virgin Unveiled" *Sunday Times* 13 October, 1996, Business p.3

GRIBBEN, R., "Branson hits back at cash crisis claims" *Daily Telegraph* 21 February, 1998, p.27

HAMILTON, K., "Branston's pickle" *Sunday Times* 23 August, 1998, p.3.5

HONIGSBAUM, M., "Polygamous Virgin" *Independent on Sunday* 10 August, 1997

JACKSON, T., (1995) *Virgin King* London: Harper Collins

MITCHELL, A., "Virgin in FMCG u-turn: Branson culls expansion plans and concentrates on core business in wake of unsuccessful forays" *Marketing Week* 19 February, 1998

NAKAMAE, N., "Virgin Cinemas expands in Japan" *Financial Times* 20 November, 2000

Name Index

Company Index

Costco, 286
Cott Corporation, 279
Cougar Helicopters, 275, 276
Cox Communications, 18
Crate & Barrel, 87
Crum & Forster, 10
CSK Auto Inc., 283
CTV Media Ltd., 260
CUC International, 181. *See also* Cendant Corporation
Cummins Engine, 259
CVS Corp., 154–156, 157
CxNetworks, 253

D

Daewoo, 245
Daimler-Benz, 13, 217, 219, 324
DaimlerChrysler, 13, 27, 45, 48, 54, 114, 218, 219, 254, 255, 279, 281, 285, 292, 391
Dalian Rubber General Factory, 282
Dana Corporation, 307–308
Dana Undies, 291
Datatrak, 96
Days Inn, 182
Dean Witter Reynolds, Inc., 198
DEC, 322
Delahaye Medialink, 73
Dell Computer Corporation, 52–53, 76, 91, 97, 100, 112, 152, 168, 172, 191, 296, 322, 325
Delta Air Lines, 74, 371
Deutsche Bank, 139, 322, 329, 398
Deutsche Telekom, 294
DG Bank, 288
DG-Rabo International, 288
Digital Equipment Corporation, 222
Disney. *See* Walt Disney Company
Dofasco, 281
Donatos Pizza, 190
Dow Chemicals, 45
Dresdner, 329
DuPont, 74, 352
Dynergy, Inc., 224, 225, 317

E

East Asia Airlines/Helicopter Hong Kong, 275
Eastman Kodak, 61, 62, 63, 65, 73, 87, 325, 359, 360–362, 394
Eatzi's, 5
eBay, 5, 6, 8, 161, 394, 431
Ecopetrol, 281
EDS, 415
Electrolux, 373
Elektrim, 194
Elektrim Telekomunikacja, 194

Eli Lilly, 95, 96
Embraer, 276
EMC, 99
EMI, 155
Engineering Inc., 87
Enron, 43–44, 50, 197, 224, 225, 317, 318–319, 332–333, 400–402, 403
Entergy Corporation, 215
Equator, 422
ERA, 181, 289
Ericsson, 64, 99, 290
Ericsson Consumer Products, 373
Ernst & Young, 18
Ethernet alliance, 373
eToys, 9, 10
Evaluserve, 99
Excite@Home, 17, 18, 21, 28
Expedia, 193
EXPO Design Centers, 168
Exxon, 74

F

Factiva, 67
Fairfield Communities, Inc., 182
Fast Company, 48, 228
Fast Retailing, 99
Federal Express. *See* FedEx
FedEx, 76, 93–94, 147–149, 157, 167, 168, 277, 284–285
Ferrari SpA, 133–134
Fiat Group, 132, 133, 255
Firestone, 74
FISI-Madison Financial, 182
Fleetwood Boston Financial Corporation, 267
Flextronics International, 99, 248–249
Ford Motor Company, 13, 45, 74, 78, 113, 114, 139, 148, 150, 166, 191, 248, 255, 279, 281, 285, 292, 327
Fox Family Worldwide, 192, 217, 224
FPL GROUP INC., 215
France Telecom, 294
Franchise Carriers, 371
Fuji, 61, 62, 63, 65
Fuji Photo Film, 360
Fujitsu Computers (Europe), 285
Fujitsu Limited, 285
Fujitsu Siemens Computers, 285

G

Galileo International, 182, 183
Gamesa Aeronautica, 276
Gap, Inc., 9, 87, 174, 325
Gateway, 168, 172

GE Aircraft Engines, 359
GEC, 291
GE Capital, 359
GE Industrial Systems, 423
GE Medical Systems, 359
Gemplus International, 313
Genentech, 96
General Electric (GE), 43, 50, 56, 59, 73, 74, 76, 84, 114, 150, 151, 186, 197, 217, 221, 229, 230–231, 359, 392, 423
General Mills, 174, 286, 290, 422
General Motors (GM), 13, 30, 45, 81, 114, 117–118, 166, 191, 196, 248, 254, 255, 268, 278, 279, 281, 285, 291, 292, 296, 352, 422, 424, 425
Gentex Corporation, 292, 293
GE Power Systems, 359
Get Well Network Inc., 132
Gifts.com, 203
Gillette, 73, 87
GlaxoSmithKline, 220
Global Corporate Governance Research Center, 335
Global Crossing, 54, 402, 403
Global Forest Watch, 431
Global One, 294
Global Services (IBM), 384
GNG Networks, 110
Golden Arches Hotel, 288
Goodyear Tire, 138, 282
Great Plains Software Inc., 84
Green Tree Financial, 325
Greif & Company, 131
Gruner+Jahr USA Publishing, 228
Guangdong Cable TV Networks, 54

H

Halliburton Co., 356
Handspring, 90
Hansen Trust, 197
Harley-Davidson, 59, 85, 134
Harvard Business School, 396
HBO, 11, 194
Heinz, H.J., Co., 127, 129, 260
HeliJet, 275
Hennes & Mauritz, 174
Hertz, 327
Hewlett-Packard (HP), 17, 18–19, 99, 113, 152, 190–191, 213–214, 216, 217, 221, 288, 313, 321, 322, 323, 327, 386

HFS, Inc., 181. *See also* Cendant Corporation
Hilfiger, Tommy. *See* Tommy Hilfiger
Hilton International, 289
Hitachi, 63, 422
H.J. Heinz Co. *See* Heinz, H.J., Co.
Hoechst, 249
Home Depot, 76, 134, 137, 168
Home Shopping Network, 193
Honda, 45, 59, 190, 248, 255, 262, 278, 279, 281, 292
Honeywell International, 50, 59, 217, 229, 230–231
HotJobs.com, 216
Houghton Mifflin, 194
Houlihan's, 5
Howard Johnson's, 182
Huawei Technologies, 241–242
Hughes Aerospace (GM), 196
Hyundai Motor Co., 158, 160, 166–167, 245, 255

I

Iberia Airlines, 371
IBM, 8, 9, 99, 118, 130, 150, 168, 172, 190–191, 213–214, 216, 294, 295, 296, 322, 383–384, 392
IBM Global Services Inc., 130
IBP, 185
ICI Paints, 279
Ikea, 131–132
Illinois Toll Works (ITW), 399
Immunex, 217, 218
Inc., 48
Informatsionniye Biznes Sistemy (IBS), 415
Insitu Group, 288
Integrated Systems Solutions Corp., 384
Intel, 76, 150, 172, 191, 222, 294, 373, 384, 427
International Harvester, 259
International Monetary Fund (IMF), 267
Interpublic, 320
Interspar, 261
Irish Air Corps, 275
Iroquois, J.D., Enterprises Ltd., 279
ITT, 197
i2, 293

J

Jabil Circuit Inc., 99, 292
Jackson Hewitt Tax Service, 182
Jansport, 292

Subject Index

Ethical behavior
  competitor intelligence
    gathering and, 67
  governance mechanisms
    and, 331–333
  strategic leadership and,
    400–404
Ethnic mix, 47
European Union (EU), 256
  bilateral trade and, 48
Executive compensation,
  310, 323–326
  complexity of, 324
  effectiveness of, 324–326
Exit barriers, 64
Explicit collusion, 286
Exporting, international
  entry and, 258–259
External environment, 17,
  40–41. *See also* Strategic
  intent
  analysis of, 42–45, 77
  areas of, 41–43
  assessing, 45
  forecasting, 45
  monitoring, 44–45
  scanning, 44
External managerial labor
  market, 392

F

Factors of production, in
  Porter's model, 249
Fast-cycle markets
  competitive advantage
    and, 171–173
  strategic alliances and,
    281–282
Financial Accounting
  Standards Board
  (FASB), 200
Financial controls, 348–349,
  404
  in balanced scorecard
    framework, 404–406
Financial economies, 196
  internal capital market
    allocation and,
    196–197
  restructuring and,
    197–198
Financial performance, 74
Financial resources, 203
Financial slack, 228–229
Firm
  I/O model of above-
    average returns and,
    17–20
  resource-based model of
    above-average returns
    and, 20–22
  strategy in Porter's model,
    250
First mover, 161–162
Five forces model of
  competition, 17, 55, 57

Fixed costs, high, 63
Flexibility
  competitive advantage
    through, 29
  strategic, 16–17
Flexible coordination, 253
Flexible manufacturing
  systems (FMS), 58,
    137–138
Focused cost leadership
  strategy, 119, 131–132
Focused differentiation
  strategy, 119, 132,
    133–134
Focus strategies, 130–131.
  See also Focused cost
  leadership strategy;
  Focused differentiation
  strategy
  competitive risks of,
    134–135
Forecasting, environmental,
  45
Foreignness, liability of,
  254–256
Formalization, 352
Franchising, 289
  strategic networks and,
    371–373
Free cash flows, 200
  as agency problem, 313
Free trade, globalization and,
  13–14
Functional structure, 351
  business-level strategies
    and, 352–355
Future cash flows,
  diversification and, 202

G

General environment
  demographic segment of,
    41, 42, 46–48
  economic segment of, 41,
    42, 48
  global segment of, 41, 42,
    53–55
  political/legal segment of,
    41, 42, 48–49, 50
  sociocultural segment of,
    41, 42, 49–52
  technological segment of,
    41, 42, 52–53
Generic business-level
  strategies, 112
Geographic distribution, 47
Germany, corporate
  governance in, 329–330
Global brands, 13
Global corporate
  governance, 331
Global economy, 11–13
  competitiveness in, 12,
    75–76, 150–151
  cross-border acquisitions
    in, 218–219

environmental conditions
  in, 40–41
  internal analysis and,
    77–79
Globalization, 13–14. *See
  also* International
  strategies
  industry analyses and, 64
  September 11 terrorists
    attacks and, 257
  technology and, 245
Global markets. *See also*
  Globalization;
  International entry
  advantages and risks in,
    53–55
  liability of foreignness
    and, 254–256
  regionalization and,
    256–258
Global mind-set, 26
Global segment, of general
  environment, 41, 42,
    53–55
Global strategy, 252–253
  worldwide product
    divisional structure
    and, 367–368
Governance. *See* Corporate
  governance; Corporate
  governance mechanisms
Government(s)
  antitrust policies and tax
    laws of, 200–201
  policy as entry barrier, 59
  regulation by, 48–49, 50,
    217
Greenfield venture, 261–262
Gross domestic product
  (GDP), of European
  market, 11
Guanxi, 54

H

Horizontal acquisition, 214,
  216–217, 218–219, 221
Horizontal complementary
  strategic alliances, 283,
  284, 370–371
Horizontal mergers, 200
Horizontal organizational
  structures, cross-
  functional teams and,
  425
Host governments, 246
Hostile takeovers, 327–328
Human capital, 86
  in acquisitions, 222
  business-level strategy
    and, 109
  downsizing and, 234
  innovation and, 419–420
  strategic leadership and,
    386, 397–398
Hypercompetition, 11

I

Imitation, 418
Incentive
  compensation as, 324
  to diversify, 198–203
  first-mover, 161–162
Income distribution, 47–48
Independent frames of
  reference, as barrier to
  integration, 425
Induced strategic behavior,
  424
Industrial markets, basis for
  customer segmentation,
  115
Industrial organization (I/O
  model). *See* I/O model
Industry(ies)
  attractive/unattractive,
    64–65
  defined, 55
  economic recession of
    2001-2002 and, 56
  internationalization of, 13
  related and supporting
    (Porter's model), 250
  September 11 terrorism
    and, 39–40, 42
  slow growth in, 61–63
Industry environment, 42
  analysis of, 55–65
  buyer bargaining power
    and, 60
  interpreting analyses of,
    64–65
  rivalry among competitors
    and, 61–64
  supplier bargaining power,
    59–60
  threat of new entrants,
    56–59
  threat of substitute
    products, 60–61
Information
  Internet and, 52
  technology diffusion and,
    15
Information age, 15–16
Information networks, as
  strategic flexibility
  source, 138–139
Information technology (IT)
  industry, 2001-2002
  recession and, 56
Inhwa, 54
Initial public offerings
  (IPOs), 430, 431
Innovation, 21
  acquisitions and, 229,
    428–429
  cooperative strategies for,
    427–430
  and entrepreneurial
    orientation, 399
  fast-cycle markets and, 173

combination structure and implementation of, 368

Trust, in opportunity maximization management, 297

2002 Winter Olympic Games, 388, 389

U

Uncertainty
in future cash flows, diversification and, 202
managerial decisionmaking and, 81
strategy for reducing, 285

United States, globalization of firms from, 14

Universal product demand, 245

Unrelated diversification, 186, 195–198
competitive form of multidivisional structure and, 359–364
financial controls and, 349

V

Valuable resources, 21

Value. *See* Value creation

Value capabilities, 88–90

Value chain
analysis of, 92–95, 123
strategic networks and, 370

Value creation, 79, 90
diversification strategies for, 187, 188
from innovation, 426–427
strategic entrepreneurship

and, 430–432

Venture capital, innovation and, 429–430, 431

Vertical acquisition, 217

Vertical complementary strategic alliances, 283–283, 284, 370

Vertical integration, 184, 191

Virtual integration, 193

Vision, 74
strategic, 29–30

W

Wa, 54

Wholly owned subsidiary, 261–262

Wireless communication technology, 53

Women
as top-level managers, 393, 394–395
in workforce, 51

Workforce, diversity in, 47, 51

Workplace environment, 74

World Trade Organization (WTO), China and, 53–54, 241–243

Worldwide geographic area structure, multidomestic strategy implementation with, 365–367

Worldwide product divisional structure, global strategy implementation and, 367–368